The Rebeats Compilation of Leedy Drum Topics

ISBN 978-1-888408-56-0

Copyright © 2022   Rob Cook

Rebeats
P.O. Box 6, Alma, Michigan 48801
www.Rebeats.com

All rights for publication and distribution are reserved. No part of this book may be reproduced in any form or by any electronic or mechanical means including information storage and retreival systems without publisher's written consent.

Forward

Leedy's marketing did not really start until the early 1920s. They were very busy with WWI military contracts in the nineteen-teens and did virtually no advertising. U.G. Leedy realized when the military projects wound down that he now had competitors (primarily Ludwig & Ludwig) who were advertising and threatening Leedy's market share. Leedy turned to George Way to restructure Leedy's distribution from direct-to-consumer to a network of authorized retailers across the country. The other primary charge for Way was to establish an advertising plan. Way combined the tasks through the periodical he established, the Leedy Drum Topics. Through the Topics, Way established a relationship with Leedy's dealer network. It was clear that the paper was meant to support not only Leedy, but the local Leedy dealers. Dealers were encouraged to submit photos and stories featuring not only their stores, but also local drummers and percussionists. Each issue of the Topics included news of new product introductions, endorser photos and news, playing tips, and even editorials such as the effect that movies with sound would have on the theater drummer profession.

By issue #9, Leedy was printing 50,000 copies of The Leedy Drum Topics. The print run was increased to 60,000 with issue number 15. Leedy's competitors followed Leedy's lead; Ludwig published "The Ludwig Drummer", and Premier published "The Drummer".

Publication of the Topics continued into the Conn era, but on a much more limited scale; 18 issues were published in the 1920s, 10 issues were published by Conn in the 1930s, and the last issue was published in 1941.

Leedy as a division of Conn ramped up a magazine ad program in 1931 that continued through all of the 1930s and, in the 1940s, most of the war until early 1944 before it was discontinued. The ads featured product introductions and Leedy endorsers and were published in magazines such as School Musician, Piano Trade, Metronome, DownBeat, International Musician, Overture, Lyons Band News, Music Ed. Journal, Musical Merchandise, Orchestra World, Foreign Service, and Music Educator's Journal.

Thanks

Thanks to the collectors who shared their original copies of The Leedy Drum Topics to be scanned for this compilation: Dan Paul, Bob Campbell, Harry Cangany, and Dave Shinn.

Table of Contents

1	June 15, 1923	1
2	October 15, 1923	9
3	January 15, 1924	17
4	April 15, 1924	25
5	July 15, 1924	33
6	October 15, 1924	41
7	January 15, 1925	53
8	April 15, 1925	65
9	July 30, 1925	77
10	November 15, 1925	89
11	February, 1926	101
12	May, 1926	113
13	November, 1926	129
14	April, 1927	145
15	September, 1927	161
16	March, 1928	177
17	December, 1928	193
18	May, 1929	209
19	January, 1930 1st edition, Conn Era	225
20	July, 1930	241
20	July, 1930 Supplement	265
21	January, 1931	269
22	July, 1931	293
23	March, 1932	317
24	August, 1934	341
25	December, 1935	365
26	July, 1936	389
27	January, 1939	413
28	October, 1939	437
29	1941	453

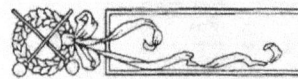 Leedy Drum Topics

Announcement

IN OFFERING THIS little journal every few months we have an object in view.

HOW DOES THE IDEA appeal to you in the following light, which is that we believe it to be a good medium for co-operation between the drummer, the dealer and the manufacturer?

TO GO STILL FARTHER, a little more get-together spirit and understanding would be well for all of us. It will give you a chance to air your views and ideas, and it will give us a chance to get the drummers' general viewpoint. If the boys will write in once in awhile, giving us their ideas and any little yarn that you think will be of interest to other drummers and friends, we will willingly publish it. Send in your stories regardless of what they concern; so long as they are of interest to drummers we will give them space and either publish or withhold your name in connection with same, as you wish.

THERE HAS NEVER BEFORE been any journal devoted exclusively to the interests of the drummer, and with your support who knows but what this little paper might grow to be something of exceptional value to you, even to the extent of locating a job?

IT IS WHOLLY up to you drummers yourselves; if you will support it and take an interest we will do the work.

THERE IS NO SUBSCRIPTION fee to DRUM TOPICS, so get your name in for your quarterly copy—it will be mailed to you free.

The Men Who Do Things for the Drummer
LEEDY MANUFACTURING COMPANY'S EXECUTIVE STAFF

U. G. LEEDY
President and General Manager

The name of U. G. Leedy is without doubt the best known of any in the drummers' world. Thirty years ago he founded the Leedy Manufacturing Company with the sole idea of better and strictly quality instruments. His career as a professional drummer ranks with the best, and the fact that his business grew from one room to the largest of its kind in the world proves that he is the leading manufacturer of instruments of percussion.

HERMAN WINTERHOFF
Vice-President

Mr. Winterhoff joined Mr. Leedy a very short time after the company was formed. He is unquestionably one of the greatest authorities on musical pitch that we have in this country, and he has invented more practical and useful ideas in bells, chimes, marimbas and xylophones than any other one person. Mr. Winterhoff has entire charge of the department covering these instruments. Mr. Winterhoff is also one of the first-rank trombone and cello players in America.

A. W. KUERST
Secretary-Treasurer

Mr. Kuerst has been with the Leedy Manufacturing Company for twelve years as one of its leading executives. He is known in the profession as one of the few musicians who is a top-notch business and financial man. It might interest many to know that Mr. Kuerst is president of the Indianapolis Shrine Band and a clarinet player of exceptional note.

GEO. H. WAY
Sales and Advertising Manager

Mr. Way's record as a professional drummer covers a period of fifteen years, nine of which were spent on the road with almost every form of theatrical organization; therefore he is in direct touch with practically all of the leading drummers in the country. In 1915 Mr. Way established his own drum manufacturing plant in Canada, joining the Leedy Manufacturing Company in 1921.

C. H. STRUPE
Superintendent and Mechanical Engineer

The working out of new ideas is left to Mr. Strupe. During the war he was one of the Government's development men in their Mechanical Department and has many valuable inventions to his credit. The perfecting of many of Leedy's later models is due to Mr. Strupe's efficiency in this line.

P. C. LAYCOCK, Correspondent

Mr. Laycock is well known over the entire country, as his signature has appeared on a great bulk of the Leedy Manufacturing Company's correspondence. He also enjoys the reputation of being one of the foremost piano players and orchestra leaders of the Middle West. One could almost consider him a drummer in addition, because his association with the Leedy Manufacturing Company for a period of ten years has given him a very thorough drummer's understanding.

For Drummers Who Care  *Leedy Equipment Leads Them All*

The Exclusive Drummers' Paper

A Well-Known Boston Tympanist

GEO. A. L. WIEHE
Loew's State Theatre, Massachusetts Avenue
Boston, Mass.

Mr. Wiehe writes us as follows:
"It is difficult for me to express in writing the great satisfaction I have derived from playing your Universal tympani during the past year. I have had absolutely no difficulty in making the quick segue changes of keys.

"Musicians who have been in the audience have remarked to me regarding the rich quality of tone that the drums produce, and as these remarks, along with other compliments, were voluntarily given, I consider them of the greatest value to both the Leedy Manufacturing Company and myself.

"I can only say that they are positively wonderful and cannot understand how we managed to get along without them for so many years past."

Drum Talk

"Broadcasting," a system of communication without wires, which preceded radio transmission by many years on the dark continent, is held largely responsible for the ever-increasing agitation among the negroes in Africa. Broadcasting, or long-distance transmission, is accomplished by means of drums, the messages being relayed over tremendous distances with great rapidity.

By "drum talk," as it is sometimes called, news of the approaching visit of American notables to Marshal Lyautey in Morocco was learned on the upper Volta about three hours after it was published in Paris. News of the death of great chiefs and warnings of approaching danger are sent in this way, and also the native propaganda which is said to be promoting unrest in eastern, western and southern Africa.

Agitation in a form resembling Bolshevism has appeared in East Africa, and sentiment favorable to the nationalist movement started by Marcus Garvey is rampant in Liberia, while the troubles in French West Africa recently required military suppression. Much of this agitation is said to be due to inflammatory reports spread among the tribes by drum talk.

NOTICE
A Prize of $10.00

There are three classes of fellows who always have a corking good story on tap. One is the traveling man, another is the actor, and, last but not least, the musician. Therefore, we believe that there is many a dandy yarn concerning the drummer that has never been given the opportunity of a hearing except in its own locality.

So, drummers, if you will send us your little stories, whether in the form of poetry, a joke or an actual happening, we will publish them and attach your name or not, as you wish.

For the best article for each issue of DRUM TOPICS we offer a prize of $10.00 in merchandise, so here is a chance to give your pet yarn a little publicity with the opportunity to also stock up on a few traps at no expense to yourself.

More Money Is Possible

It has often been said that drummers should receive more salary than other musicians (of course, excepting leaders). "Often been said" is right, but the cases of it having been done are few and far between. The "leak in the valve" is our brother musician himself. He doesn't seem to see it our way, or maybe he sees it but he doesn't lose any sleep over it. True, perhaps, he studied on his instrument longer, although it is doubtful these days, with all we have to play, but now all he has to do is put the old oboe or fiddle in the box and take his time. Last on the job and first off, with a "So long, Traps!" and there you sit buried in the "percussion pile," packing it up as the janitor puts out the lights. Ten to one you call back the next day for the stuff you couldn't carry. The rest of the bunch really know you should get more money, alright, but we will never realize it in large enough quantities to be noticed unless we make a fuss about it, and right here is where the value of the Drummers' Clubs comes in. They are the shortest road to this goal, so let's have them in every town. Lay aside all petty jealousies and let's have more good feeling among drummers. A lot more could be gained for us all if we would only do this one big thing—lay aside all personal feelings and *get together*.

Canadian Drummers

We would like to impress upon all the boys in Canada that DRUM TOPICS is for you, too. Just at present we are short of material concerning the Canadian drummers, so if you will get in touch with us we will be glad to devote a liberal amount of space under a Canadian heading. We know you have your own problems and higher prices to pay than the United States drummer and it is our desire to assist you all possible in a legitimate way.

You Can't Always Tell

There was once a girlie named Maude,
Who, they say, was a social fraude.
　In the ballroom, I'm told,
　She was haughty and cold,
But alone on the sofa—Oh, Gawd!

The "Relax" Footboard

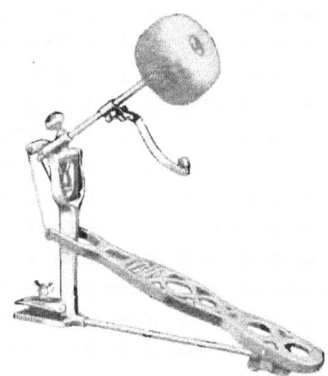

The "Relax" footboard on the Leedy-Fraser pedal means speed and comfort. Relaxation of the foot and leg below the knee is the real secret of pedal speed and comfort. It eliminates all leg fatigue.

GET LEEDY'S CATALOG

In chimes the fourth tone of the harmonic series is the predominating tone, whereas in a piano string the first tone predominates.

Personal Column

TOMMY HAWKINS, of Boston, now at the Orpheum Theatre, is considered by many one of the country's very best vaudeville drummers. However, his record in the Boston Opera and with other leading Boston musical organizations puts him in a class of the very highest order. Tommy still sticks to the overhanging pedal.

FRANK SNOW has just finished a season with Julia Sanderson in "Tangerine," closing in Chicago after almost a year on the road. It is doubtful if there is a better known drummer in the business than Frank Snow, he being one of those who made the world tour with Sousa's band and who was with that famous organization for twelve years.

E. L. BLACKBURN, a drummer of great prominence in the Middle West and who located in Lexington, Ky., last year, has opened a general music business in that city. He is doing exceptionally well with the Leedy line, receiving orders from all over the State of Kentucky.
Mr. Blackburn's success is significant of what many drummers could do in other localities if they worked along the same lines.

Another case of a drummer going into business and becoming very successful is that of CHARLES SEIBERT of the Orpheum Theatre in Peoria, Ill. He has been in business a year and kept on with his theatre work at the same time. Seibert is a hustler of the same calibre as Mr. Blackburn and there is no doubt but what these two boys will do some big things.

BOB RICE, the drummer at the Columbia Theatre on Broadway, New York, which is the country's leading burlesque house, is doing a lot of copying and arranging for leading publishers in New York. Pretty good stunt to make extra money. Mr. Rice is one of the old trouper school and used to have his own musical show on the road in Canada.

ARTHUR DEERY, of Boston, is now with the Ringling Brothers show. Some circus drummer, this boy. He plays 'em cleancut, and his Leedy drum carries through to the farthest end of a crowded circus tent. His work is a pleasure to listen to.

Send in any notes of interest to drummers. We will publish same.

CHAS. PUCHTA, of the Oriole Terrace Orchestra, is still on the road with that organization. They have made one of the real big hits on Keith's vaudeville time. Mr. Puchta is equipped completely with Leedy, including white and gold drums and Universal tympani. He is one of the real stage drummer type and commands a good part of the audience's attention.

JOE SINAI, of the Granada Theatre, San Francisco, is a hard-working, conscientious drummer. He has taken a great interest in his Universal tympani and has worked up a wonderful technique on same. His entire satisfaction with these instruments has often been expressed.

O. R. McLAIN, of the Orpheum Theatre in Seattle, is some vaudeville drummer. Ask any act on this circuit. He is also some tennis player and is just the type for the game—long and lean. To watch him swing for a crash cymbal one would know that he plays tennis by his graceful wallop.

F. L. FRASER, the drummer who invented the Leedy-Fraser pedal, has been for the past season at the Gaiety Theatre in Kansas City. Aside from this job he is secretary-treasurer of a concern that manufactures the Fold-O-Lock automobile steering wheel; therefore Floyd is some busy boy, but not too busy to have a good word for everyone, always with a smile. He is one of the friendly type of drummers whom outside men find it a great pleasure to meet.

For Drummers Who Care  Leedy Equipment Leads Them All

LEEDY DRUM TOPICS

A PAPER DEVOTED TO
THE INTERESTS OF THE DRUMMER

No subscription fee

Advertisements accepted

Published quarterly at 1033 East Palmer Street
Indianapolis, Indiana

Editor .... GEO. H. WAY
Business Manager .... A. W. KUERST

Sousa's Drum Section

August Helmecke   Geo. J. Carey   Howard N. Goulden

As a bass drummer August Helmecke is perhaps the best known in the whole United States. His record as given in the article below should be of interest to all drummers.

Geo. J. Carey, who hails from Rochester, N. Y., enjoys the reputation of an exceptionally fine xylophone player. He has been with Sousa for the past three seasons, and from all reports he is one of their permanent soloists and attractions.

Howard N. Goulden, who plays snare drum and accessories, is from Bridgeport, Conn., where he operates a full-fledged drum shop in addition to his yearly tours with Sousa.

All three of these drummers are Leedy equipped and 100 per cent satisfied that they are using the highest grade instruments that it is possible to obtain.

A New Drum Catalog

There is hardly a drummer who is not ambitious enough to want to keep posted on all things new, and prices. They all know that Leedy publishes the finest and largest book for their use. Be sure to get your name in for the new August issue.

August Helmecke

For fifteen years Sousa has considered no other bass drummer than Gus, as he is called by the boys, and this year the great band leader who considers him such an important feature of his organization is planning on giving him not only personal lithographed advertising, but a big supply of space in the newspaper columns. It is the first instance we know of where a bass drummer has been shown on the boards and in the newspapers with his instrument as shown in the opposite photograph.

Mr. Helmecke is a New Yorker; he was born in 1869, and the old-timers will recall the job on which he made a great reputation, that of being the backbone of the famous Innis Band at the Chicago World's Fair. Gus is married and has one grown boy, who is also musically inclined. His home is in New York, where his mother, who is now 80 years old, lives with him and his wife. Baseball and a friendly game of cards are Gus' favorite pastimes, and to hear one of his stories is to enjoy a real laugh.

Gus says: "My bass drum must be a Leedy."

Human Skulls for Drums

Drums made out of the tops of skulls, over which is stretched human skins, are used to make "music" in various parts of Tibet. But skulls are not the only portion of their ancestors from which these fascinating people extract melody and rhythm. Many an intriguing tune is played on a native trumpet formed from a human thigh bone drilled and holed and adapted to the production of sweet sound.—*Detroit News.*

Did You Ever Troupe?

The fellow who sleeps in the same comfortable bed every night seldom realizes the trials and hard work of the road drummer, especially the circus man. Rain, mud, hot cars and "white tops," loss of sleep, few baths and sometimes poor food are only a few of his inconveniences. To those of you who have never trouped and think it is a cinch, take a tip from an old-timer. Rest easy—it isn't half what it's cracked up to be. On the other hand, if you do go on the road, see it all. Let them call you a "tourist" if they will, but the drummer who has been through the Royal Gorge in Colorado and cannot say he saw it, because he slept all the way, has missed a big opportunity. Perhaps he will never get there again. Things like this are the bright side of a trouper's existence.

Oh, Man!

Ever have a "sweet young thing" at a dance chirp: "Oh, Mr. Drummer, I'd just love to play all those things. Does it take long to learn? How do you do it? What are those strings on the other side of your drum for?" YE GODS!

I don't mind a fellow who snores in tempo, but damn the variations.

Many a True Word Is Spoken in a Jest

We are supposed to have a forty-piece orchestra here, but this week thirty-four of our musicians left to join the various jazz bands. So, kind artist, do not expect our playing to sound as good as it did last week. Kindly bear with us in this our great misfortune in losing our fellow musicians, as there is just a shade of difference between a six-piece and forty-piece aggregation.

A word of explanation why our orchestra crabs your act: The drummer, we find, according to Webster, is a performer upon a drum—a two-headed noisy device, the two heads being made of the tanned skins of animals stretched tightly over a cylindrical shell of equal depth all around. Webster was right, but in these days we find that he is wrong according to our vaudevilistic views. The drummer earns his money too easily this way, so besides being expert enough to hammer hell out of the aforesaid noisy device, he is an artist on tympani, xylophone, bells, chimes, musette, cat-calls, duck-calls, klaxon horns, wind whistles, police rattles, imitations of babies, birds, fish, frogs, bugs, worms and other monsters. In other words, if he is called upon to render all of his fifty imitations at a first performance and misses one, the artist should think how grandly he executed the other forty-nine.

The "Utility" Tympani

Never before has it been possible for the drummer to purchase a real high-grade tympani at such a reasonable price.

Leedy's new Utility tympani have been on the market now for several months, and our statement that nothing in the way of material and quality has been sacrificed has been proven by their many satisfied users.

It will pay all drummers to investigate these instruments before purchasing elsewhere. An elaborate detailed circular will gladly be mailed you on request. They have many features that our limited space here does not permit us to comment on.

GET LEEDY'S CATALOG

It Didn't Work

"Who was that guy you were talking so nice to?"
"Aw, that's me old family druggist."
"What did he say?"
"No."

For Drummers Who Care *Leedy Equipment Leads Them All*

The Exclusive Drummers' Paper

U. G. Leedy and Paul Whiteman

There were many notables present at the opening of the Tom Brown Music Store in Chicago last February. Among them were C. J. Fairchild of Conn's, Geo. M. Bundy of Selmer's, and many others, including Mr. Paul Whiteman, the famous leader, and Mr. Leedy. These latter two gentlemen struck up an exceptional friendship. They had never met before, although Mr. Whiteman had done considerable business with the Leedy Manufacturing Company through Harold McDonald, his popular drummer. Mr. McDonald is 100 per cent Leedy equipped.

Did you know that rosewood sinks in water?

The "Stay Put" Drum Stick Holder

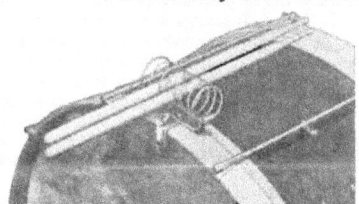

You have always wanted this one. No more shoving the sticks under your arm, sitting on them or laying them on your drum, only to have them fall on the floor at the wrong time. With the "STAYPUT" your sticks are always in place—the "right" stick comes back in the right hand. Oh, boy! Talk about speed in getting over to your bells and tympani! It has a "Bull Dog" clamp.

George W. Marsh
With Eddie Elkin's Orchestra

A popular drummer and a popular orchestra are shown above. The phonograph companies consider an Elkins record as one of their best sellers, and drummers can often pick up a tip in effects from George W. Marsh's work on these records. Mr. Marsh is a Leedy drummer in every sense of the word and prefers the Leedy make to all others.

Sound will travel farther on a damp day than on a dry one.

George Braun of the Metropolitan Grand Opera and Victor Herbert's Orchestra

George Braun, who has been for some years with the Metropolitan Grand Opera and is this summer with Victor Herbert's Orchestra, is a comparatively young man; however, he is spoken of by many leaders as one of the finest tympanists in and around New York City. His praise of the Leedy Universal Tympani is full of enthusiasm and covers about every point concerning the instruments. He writes in part:

"For over a year I have owned and played continually upon a set of Leedy Universal Tympani, and it is impossible to over-estimate their superiority over all other makes. The exacting work of the Metropolitan Orchestra demands instruments that are right "on the dot" in every respect when the "cue" comes, and the same applies to the requirements of Mr. Herbert.

"Tone simplicity, workmanship and standing up qualities are only a few of their excellent features, and the old saying goes for me that "if I couldn't get another pair, no amount of money could buy mine."

Drummers' Club Secretaries

We wish all of the secretaries of Drummers' Clubs would get in touch with us. It will be a pleasure to print your news.

Orchestra and band bells vary less in pitch than any other instrument.

Dance Men—By P. C. L.

To the musician who does a great deal of transient work arises the problem of trying to please all with respect to "time." Particularly does this condition exist in lodge work, where so often the crowds are greatly mixed. You have had it happen to you, I know. How often will one couple come up to you and tell you your music is too slow or too fast, while possibly 75 per cent of the crowd is satisfied, if not a larger percentage than this? Many times, I will gamble. Now, it is not probable that "time" suited to persons from forty to fifty years of age will come anywhere near suiting couples from seventeen to twenty-one years of age. In my opinion there is one way around. EDUCATE THE DANCERS. Educate them to the improbability of the situation as it exists. Educate them to the fact that your business is playing dances—your conception of dance time is gained from long experience and that you have but one desire and that is to please all of them.

They have come to this particular dance to have a good time. Can they have it by constantly carrying the grouch and knocking the music all evening because the time does not suit their own individual and particular tastes? Now, why cannot it be put before them in this light and make them feel THIS way about it? This orchestra plays every evening for all classes of dancers; furthermore this is the music we are going to have all evening. If it does not exactly suit me, will it not be a great deal easier for me to adjust my step to fit their time and style, as a majority of the people are doing, than continually worrying them with requests to meet the particular little step that I do? To please individual me would be very nice, but am I the only one at this dance?

How much easier would the dance musicians' life and work be if people would only follow these suggestions! There is no sensible reason why they cannot be educated to view the situation in this light.

We Want to Publish

Drummers' photographs in every issue of DRUM TOPICS, so do not hesitate to send yours in.

For Drummers Who Care  *Leedy Equipment Leads Them All*

Leedy Drum Topics

Dealers' Column

This is something new for the dealer. It will bring your store to the attention of the drummers. It will enable you to keep in touch with other dealers' doings in all parts of the country. If the dealer takes an interest in this section of Drum Topics we will give it a whole page.

Geo. J. Birkel Company, of Los Angeles, maintains one of the most complete stocks of drummers' equipment that it is possible to imagine. Their excellent service in behalf of the drummer has often been commented on, and the boys will find Mr. E. R. Stone, manager of the Small Goods Department, most agreeable and eager to please. Mr. Stone's fair and square methods of making many Leedy enthusiasts in Los Angeles would make many pages of interesting reading for other dealers. Mr. Nichol is the chief salesman in the Drum Department.

A Beautiful Window Display
By H. & A. Selmer, Inc., Boston, Mass.

There is no doubt but what Mr. Pierce, manager of the above store, fully realizes the value of an attractive display of drums for his window. The above photograph proves his artistic taste in arranging such a window, and he reports that, next to a fire, drums are the greatest "traffic blockers" he knows of.

Dealers are sometimes under the impression that the smaller towns do not offer a very wide scope for drums, but it would surprise many to know that the M. L. Price Music Company, of Tampa, Fla., operated by "Whiz-Bang" Price, is one of the largest distributors in the whole country. His method of working the mails, in addition to local sales, reaching clear to Cuba and South America, is very interesting.

The Knight-Campbell Music Company, of Denver, is another one of the firms who make a very successful effort through the mails. They have built up a fine Drum Department, both professional and amateur, throughout three of the Western States. Mr. Bohon, who is in charge of that department, seems to have gotten the "drummers' drift" thoroughly.

Charles Parker, of the Parker Band House, has lately extended his activities from the city of Waco to two other retail stores, one in Houston and one in Galveston. In the eight months he has been in Houston (which is now his headquarters) he has very cleverly corralled the bulk of the small goods business of not only that city but the surrounding territory. Charlie is indeed one of the boys, being an ex-professional musician, which in turn gives him a thorough understanding of their most detailed wants.

W. J. Dyer & Bro., of St. Paul, have always made a special effort to please the drummer, and there is absolutely nothing that a customer could call for, from a tambourine tack to a set of Universal tympani, that they could not give him immediate delivery on. Mr. Brown, who is in charge of this department, realizes that when a drummer wants it, he wants it.

The city of Portland, Ore., can well boast of other things than its Rose Festival and the Columbia Highway, for there is no more beautiful music store than that of Seiberling-Lucas. This firm has been boosting Leedy goods for a great number of years, and we cannot help but comment on the exceptionally pleasant relations that have existed between them and the Leedy Manufacturing Company. Mr. Frank Lucas makes every effort to please the drummer and counts this department as one of their most profitable.

E. F. Droop & Sons Company, of Washington, D. C., certainly took advantage of the great Shrine gathering at Washington during the week of June 4th. Their window display was somewhat similar to the one shown above in this column, and the interior of their store was especially decorated in an elaborate manner. A representative of the Leedy Manufacturing Company was on hand to demonstrate the several new models just put on the market. Mr. Philpitt is the Small Goods manager.

Space in this issue does not permit of our mentioning little items of interest about many more of our dealers. The next issue of Drum Topics will contain some notes regarding the "Frisco" Manufacturing Company of San Francisco, Bush & Lane Piano Company of Seattle, B. A. Rose of Minneapolis, Southern Conn Company of New Orleans, Atlanta Conn of Atlanta, Arnold-Edwards Piano Company of Jacksonville, Chas. McCloskey of Providence, Dean's Music Store of Springfield.

Your window full of Leedy drums artistically arranged would make the most attractive display imaginable. Be sure to get a photograph of your Leedy window—we want a dandy for the next issue of Drum Topics and herewith offer $10 for the best one.

The New Style Multi-Model

THE WORLD'S FINEST DRUM

Arthur Layfield

There are probably hundreds, yes, thousands of drummers in the country who know Arthur Layfield. His former connection with the Chicago Grand Opera and the famous original Benson Orchestra speaks for itself that he is a top-notcher. Art has recently been seriously ill with double pneumonia, and we know all old friends will be glad to learn that he is back in the harness again, playing with the Roy Bargy Orchestra. He is also an enthusiastic booster for Leedy products and was one of the first big men to recognize the superiority of the Universal tympani.

Jack Roop

JACK ROOP, who is on the road with the Giers-Dorf Symphonists in vaudeville, has made one of the biggest hits of any of the popular organized traveling orchestras in the business. His ability as a drummer and showman is away above the average, and in every town the newspapers comment on Jack's work and wonderful black and gold Leedy equipment.

Mr. Roop's wife plays trombone in the act and is one of its best features.

Troupers!

Look at the Dealers' Column in Drum Topics, and when you are in cities where one of these dealers is located do not hesitate to call on him. Very often you will find an experienced drummer connected with these stores, and of one thing we are absolutely sure and that is that you will receive courteous treatment and be quoted the proper prices.

"Slunk Calf" means the skin of an unborn calf, and they make the finest grade of heads known. The UKA brand is made only by the most skilled workmen.

In the Mail

A fellow wrote in a few days ago and asked: "What kind of an animal is the UKA that you get drum heads off of?"

Here's a Hot One

There was once a drummer who really believed that because a drum head was a product of the cow, that it would be a good idea to wash his heads with milk, because milk is also a product of the cow, and it would put life back into the heads. Here is a good suggestion for someone to sell bottled milk and call it "Drum Head Oil."

Frank Horsecroft

There are many Paul Whiteman orchestras, but the organization next in rank to the original is the Arcadia Orchestra now playing in the most beautiful dance hall in Providence, R. I. Frank Horsecroft, the drummer, believes in the highest quality of equipment obtainable, and a glance at the above photograph proves that he is a real showman. That he is a real drummer is proven by the fact that he holds one of the most important Whiteman positions. Frank swears by his Multi-Model.

For Drummers Who Care *Leedy Equipment Leads Them All*

The Exclusive Drummers' Paper

Not a Minstrel Show
Bill got a job in the Street Cleaning Department of a small town. One day his friend Jim, from the city, met him and inquired:
"Well, Bill, how do you like your new job?"
Bill—"Pretty good, except it's mighty hard work."
Jim—"What, hard work in this one-horse town?"
Bill—"You wouldn't think it was one horse if you had to clean it up."

Right-O!
When the cello player or friend "Gob-stick" makes wise cracks around the orchestra about Mr. Drummer being no musician, you can bet the price of a pair of Turk cymbals that they are only wishing they could always be as sure of their jobs.

One Remedy
Why do they always pick on the drummer? If it is an extra effect, ask the drummer. If it is another chorus to be played, ask the drummer to play it on something different. If an act wants a spoken line or two or three, ask the drummer. One local has extended a helping hand in this respect. Any act in vaudeville desiring a drummer to take part in his act by talking, even though only one word, has to pay $5.00 or more for the service. This is from Vancouver, B. C. Good stuff! Locals take note.

In Canada

The above photograph shows one of Canada's most popular hotel orchestras, who have put in a very lengthy season at the King Edward Hotel, Toronto, Ontario. George Bouchard is its efficient leader, and Harry C. Bedlington, the drummer, has an original style of working that makes him a real drawing card. He is fully Leedy equipped and high in his praise of the instruments.

"Bull Dog" Tom-Tom Holder
This holder gives service and is truly adjustable to fit any size Tom-Tom at any angle. It will stand beating upon without getting out of place.

Leo Brand

Leo Brand, tympanist with the Cincinnati Symphony ever since its organization, in a letter to Mr. Leedy states the following in part:
"It gives me genuine pleasure to play on the Leedy Universal Tympani. They are indeed a real success. The simplicity of construction, light weight for shipping, and, last but not least, their wonderful tone, make them instruments that surpass anything that has ever been produced in the way of machine tympani I have used them all."

How the New York Drummers Will Spend Their Vacations
By K. C. H.

Joe Green, when not demonstrating, will spend his leisure time receiving telegrams, cablegrams and "seagrams." Oh, boy! "Yes, we have no bananas."

Howard Kopp, after closing six Broadway productions, will try to close Central Park with Goldman. Then to Malone, which is very close to Canada.

Mike Tighe arrived home last week after a 36 weeks' trip throughout the United States and Canada with a Shubert production. His vacation plans have not been made as yet.

"Georgie" Braun, after a strenuous season at the Metropolitan, will mingle with Victor Herbert for five weeks at Willow Grove and then to the Stadium with the Philharmonic Orchestra for the balance of the season. I'd call that "some vacation."

Gus Helmcke, outside of playing the races in the afternoon, Goldman at night in Central Park, and joining Sousa on the 29th of July, will spend some Sunday morning getting acquainted with his family.

Dan Kenn will be on the "receiving end" at Jamaica, Belmont, Aqueduct and Empire, as usual. This beats working.

Jimmy Lent will be in and out all season with his "Society Orchestra."

Eddie Montray will fly them high on the roof of the Tivoli.

Jimmy Hager, when he can get away from some six different phonograph companies, will be trying out his new Packard on Long Island.

Chris Chapman will try to garner all the bullfrogs in the state, so as to have plenty of "hops" for his friends who drop in at his Freeport farm during the summer.

Billy Spedick will stick close to the Lights Club to get some new ideas for Gertie Hoffman next season. In his spare moments he will break his younger brother Harry into the business.

Harold McDonald is having the time of his life with Paul Whiteman in London. Paris to follow, and then the Ziegfeld Follies for '23 and '24.

Eddie Scherer will be busy three times a day with Vincent Lopez.

Geo. Marsh, likewise with Eddie Elkins.

Charlie Lowe will spend his vacation in vaudeville. This is his first lay-off in 26 years.

Geo. Carey, after a hard season in the Bronx, where he learned to speak Russian fluently, will get ready for the big Sousa trip. He will travel light next season—his Leedy outfit and three vacuum bottles.

Frankie Kutak, when not busy following Carl Edouarde, will study languages, so as to be prepared for his season with the All American Symphony Orchestra.

Charlie Daab has bought a canoe. He claims he'll make better time with it than by using the ferry to get to Astoria.

Xylophone and Marimba Parts for Orchestrations
Many of the leading publishers are now arranging special parts for marimba and xylophone with the popular song and dance numbers of the day. This is a great help to the average drummer, and we hope that they will express their appreciation of this additional feature to the publishers by letter, so that the practice will be continued and encourage other publishers. This is the only way the publisher has of knowing whether or not his efforts are appreciated. It is now being tried out at the request of some of the prominent drummers, xylophonists and leaders, so if all the boys will help the matter along with an expression of approval we feel sure that it will become a regular custom with all publishers to send out these parts in the future. Those making a practice of this at present are the McKinley Music Company, Walter Jacobs, Inc., Triangle Music Publishing Company, Forster Music Publishers, Inc. Some of the publishers who have made inquiries as to whether it will be a good practice are Jack Mills, Inc., and Will Rossiter. This is a great movement for the benefit of all orchestras and drummers, so let's help it along.

J. Fred Seitz
Chicago Grand Opera Company

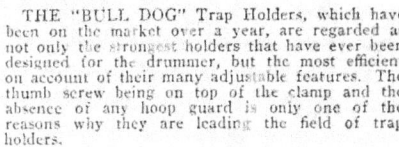

Mr. Seitz is the author of the widely known Seitz Tympani Method, published by the Leedy Manufacturing Company. This book is considered by most teachers to be the most complete work of its kind.

During the entire past season Mr. Seitz has been using the Leedy Universal Tympani and has this to say of them:
"The tone quality and ease of tuning are simply remarkable. Add to this their exquisite workmanship and design and we have truly a Leedy creation of utmost efficiency and beauty."

THE "BULL DOG" Trap Holders, which have been on the market over a year, are regarded as not only the strongest holders that have ever been designed for the drummer, but the most efficient on account of their many adjustable features. The thumb screw being on top of the clamp and the absence of any hoop guard is only one of the reasons why they are leading the field of trap holders.

Do It Well
When you make a mistake, such as a crash in the wrong place, make a good one. Let 'em know you're working; it won't sound half as bad as a little half-hearted "peck."

In Other Countries

The xylophone and marimba is known to the savages of darkest Africa. The jungle xylophone here pictured is familiar to the natives of Portuguese West Africa. In their case, however, the resonators are made of gourds.

Jimmy Lent

The New York Hippodrome has had James I. Lent as their "calf-skin pounder" for a great number of years. This is some job, and Jimmie is some drummer.

He says that his new-style Leedy Multi-Model drum is the finest instrument he has ever owned and that the "Relax" footboard on the Fraser pedal has made one of the hardest working drum jobs in the country 100 per cent easier.

Ever Hear of a Trap Tree?
All drummers should certainly be acquainted with this new accessory. A detailed and illustrated circular is yours for the asking.

DRUM TOPICS certainly trusts that all drummers will boost it along. Remember, we have had no real drummers' paper, and with your support it should amount to something big and for your benefit.

For Drummers Who Care Leedy Equipment Leads Them All

THE GREEN BROTHERS—World's Greatest Xylophone Artists

The Green Brothers' reputation as the world's leading xylophonists is in no way exaggerated. Most drummers are familiar with their record. The All-Star Trio, Sousa's Band and the principal phonograph companies are only a few of the wonderful musical connections they enjoy.

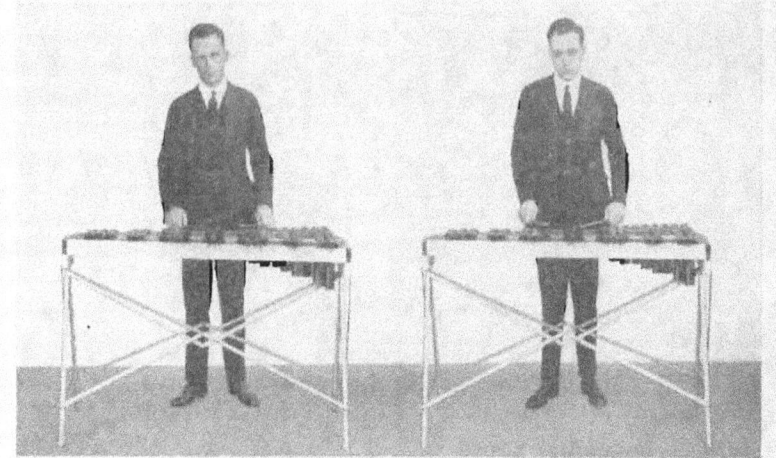

About every known wood has been tried out in xylophone construction, and real science has proven that rosewood is the one best bet for tone and wear. Rosewood in its natural state of color is not a dark red. Of course, its shade varies, but it is similar to a light chocolate color, sometimes running as light as oak. The Leedy Manufacturing Company does not kiln-dry their wood; every piece is air-dried slowly and naturally, every bar being at least four years old. No stain is used.

These instruments have many features found on no others. Wheels if desired. Note the fact that the frame and resonators break in the middle, making it easy for packing. The system of splitting the frame positively does not weaken same, and there are no thumb screws, etc., to fool with. The additional cost of these features is slight.

We guarantee no overtones in our xylophones and marimbas. The instrument shown in photograph is 3½ octaves, G to C.

THESE ARE THE LEEDY SOLO-TONE "GREEN BROS. SPECIAL" MODELS THAT THEY USE

George Hamilton Green Says:

"My many years as a professional xylophonist have naturally given me a chance not only to try different makes, but I have owned many different brands and played extensively on them all. At present I have three of the Leedy manufacture, and there is not one point on any of these instruments that is not far superior to any other make, even including the hammers and cases. I am through experimenting and shall use Leedy exclusively in the future. My brother and self fully believe that the Green Bros. Special is going to be the biggest selling xylophone the market has ever known."

Joe Green Says:

"My brother and I have been using the Green Bros. Special Xylophone, built by Leedy, for eight months, and have given it very severe usage jobbing around New York and at the phonograph studios. The instrument is making a bigger hit with me every day and I consider it far in advance of any xylophone I have ever used. The tonal qualities are exquisite, and the appearance, general make-up, workmanship and detail are wonderful, leaving absolutely nothing to be desired—the proverbial last word in xylophone construction. The Leedy Manufacturing Company is to be congratulated on their ability to manufacture an instrument that at last meets every exacting requirement."

LEEDY DRUM TOPICS

The Exclusive Drummers' Paper

POSTMASTER—Return Postage Guaranteed

LEEDY MANUFACTURING CO.
INDIANAPOLIS, INDIANA

Leedy Drum Topics Issue 2

Leedy Drum Topics

Yes, We Have No Drum Topics Left

That is, none of the first issue, because the interest shown by the drummers all over the United States and Canada far exceeded our greatest hopes, and many of the boys requested extra copies.

DRUM TOPICS did "go big," and out of the thousands of letters of comment on it there was not one that did not contain the following statement in one form or other: "It is the very thing the drummer has needed; count me in as a booster."

So here goes for the second edition. We hope you like it as well, and, remember, it is your paper—suggestions are welcome.

We think it well to repeat the ANNOUNCEMENT as given in the first issue for the benefit of the ones that might have missed same:

IN OFFERING THIS little journal every few months we have an object in view.

HOW DOES THE IDEA appeal to you in the following light, which is that we believe it to be a good medium for co-operation between the drummer, the dealer and the manufacturer?

TO GO STILL FARTHER, a little more get-together spirit and understanding would be well for all of us. It will give you a chance to air your views and ideas, and it will give us a chance to get the drummers' general viewpoint. If the boys will write in once in awhile, giving us their ideas and any little yarn that they think will be of interest to other drummers and friends, we will willingly publish it.

Send in your stories regardless of what they concern; so long as they are of interest to drummers we will give them space and either publish or withhold your name in connection with same, as you wish.

THERE HAS NEVER BEFORE been any journal devoted exclusively to the interests of the drummer, and with your support who knows but what this little paper might grow to be something of exceptional value to you, even to the extent of locating a job?

IT IS WHOLLY up to you drummers yourselves. If you will support it and take an interest, we will do the work.

THERE IS NO SUBSCRIPTION FEE to DRUM TOPICS, so get your name in for your quarterly copy; it will be mailed to you free.

Albert Ritter of the Boston Symphony Orchestra

Mr. Ritter, who is one of Germany's most proficient artists on tympani, has been in this country for over a year. He was chosen as the most able man available in a country famous for its tympanists. After thoroughly trying out the Leedy Universal Machine Tympani, Mr. Ritter adopted them and has this to say of their merits:

BOSTON, MASS., August 19, 1923.

My dear Mr. Leedy:

After having become acquainted with your instruments, I feel it my duty to say the following: The grand invention of the Leedy Pedal Tympani is a historical moment in the history of the tympani, for since the invention of the machine tympani by the famous tympanist Kundf in Leipsic, no worth-while improvements so far had been made. It ought to be the duty of all the tympanists of the world to get interested in these instruments. The first impression is almost perplexing, for in comparison with the old machine tympani the new Leedy instruments show the same high development towards perfection that we find in comparing the modern steam engines to the old ones. Special points of advantage are:

1. The ideal of each tympanist, the system of the old screw tympani, has been preserved; consequently an absolutely pure tuning has been made possible.
2. Easy response in the pp. and a wonderful soft tone.
3. Remarkable easy handling of the pedals.
4. On account of the folding mechanism the instruments can be packed into their extremely practical cases without the help of another person.

In short, the future belongs to the Leedy Tympani.

Yours sincerely,
ALBERT RITTER,
First Tympanist of the Boston Symphony Orchestra.

Geo. J. Carey of Sousa's Band

Mr. Carey's reputation as an all-around drummer is indeed famous. As tympanist and xylophonist with Sousa, he enjoys one of the country's most prominent positions. His home is in Rochester, N. Y., and his years in the higher class of theatre and concert work have placed him in a position to *know*. Read his letter to Mr. Leedy regarding the Universal Tympani:

WILLOW GROVE PARK, PA., August 12, 1923.

Dear Mr. Leedy:

I doubt if there was a tympanist in the country who was more skeptical regarding machine drums than myself. I was even prejudiced. This opinion was formed from years of experience with many other makes, but the opportunity came to try a pair of your instruments in actual work, and now I feel that I am not capable of putting into words my approval of them.

Every tympanist considers tone first, and it did not take long to know that this important item was superior to all others after using so many other makes. Then come the questions of mechanism and practicability. For anyone to be convinced on these subjects is only a matter of investigation. They have never been equaled in simplicity, workmanship and strength. The one-piece bowl has greatly reduced the chance of denting, a fear that has always heretofore troubled every tympanist. Appearance in equipment helps a lot, and even this is given full measure. The pedal action is quick, easy, and stays where it is put.

The packing features are so quick that I can get away from a concert by the time the clarinet players have cleaned and put away their instruments. Wonderful for road work.

In closing, can only say that I am more than satisfied, and if at any time I can be of benefit in convincing other tympanists, just call on me.

Your friend,
(Signed) GEO. J. CAREY,
Sousa's Band, en route.

For Drummer's Who Care Leedy Equipment Leads Them All

The Exclusive Drummers' Paper

San Francisco Tympanists
Use the Leedy Universal

1   2   3   4

1. HARRY H. CARNEY, who for the last seven years has been playing at the Imperial Theatre in Frisco, has a reputation of being a finished artist on tympani. His long and personal letter to Mr. Leedy, which is high in praise in every detail of Universal Tympani, is very interesting, but our limited space prevents us from publishing same in this issue. Harry is the inventor of the wonderful Carney Compressed Air Trap and Effect Cabinets, and his ingenuity has developed many valuable traps for the drummer.

2. JACK DOWNIE is another first-rate tympanist, and was formerly with Severi of the California Theatre and Fitzpatrick of the Strand Theatre, and has also held down many other important jobs in Frisco. At present he is playing with Rosebrook's Harmonists at the Wigwam. Downey enjoys a large class of pupils and is a man of wide experience and one who is thoroughly professional in his work and has a very pleasing personality. He says that the Universal Tympani themselves speak louder in praise than any words he could possibly offer.

3. ANDREW SETRO is not only an accomplished tympanist but a thorough musician and orchestra leader. Every musician in Frisco is familiar with his record, so it is needless to give it here; however, it is a true fact that Setro's ability is known and favorably commented on not only on the Pacific Coast but throughout a good portion of the United States. His praise of the Universal Tympani is full of enthusiasm, and the Leedy Manufacturing Company values it greatly, because he views its qualities not only from the performer's viewpoint but from that of a thoroughly talented conductor as well.

4. JOE SINAI. The famous Paul Ashe's Synco Symphonists would seem incomplete without Joe at the drums. For the past year this organization has been making quite a hit at the Granada Theatre. Sinai believes in being up to date, and has had his instruments finished in white and gold. Those who have visited the Grenada need no further details as to the ability of either the orchestra or Joe, and when he is so emphatic in his praise of the Universal Tympani it only goes to show that the instruments must be all that is claimed for them, because we know of no drummer who is more particular about his equipment.

Note to Frisco and Vicinity Drummers

In San Francisco and vicinity the drummer is always absolutely sure of a personal understanding when he calls on the Frisco Manufacturing Company, 244 Eddy Street. They carry one of the largest and most complete stocks in the whole country. Mr. Mortonson and Mr. Whittle know the drum game thoroughly, so you cannot go wrong at this drummers' headquarters.

They are both ex-professionals and are fair in price, so deserve your support to the limit. Troupers will enjoy talking to Mr. Whittle, and the rest of the boys will find Mr. Mortonson always eager to explain any question that may arise.

Phil Hacker, the man who wrote some of the first xylophone solos, has just completed a new band march called "The Booselwogg." It is *some* march!

Here are the words to another of his numbers. Music has not been written as yet, because he wants to see how the words go before putting in any time:

The Festive Boil

I once knew a fellow named Doyle,
Who had a magnificent BOIL.
Cried the DOC, " 'Twill bring health,
Which is better than wealth,"
And then he prescribed CASTOR OIL.

Now, this boil was right on a spot—
I COULD mention the spot, B U T will not.
Doyle sat down in a chair,
But went up in the air
Just as sudden as if he'd been shot.

Doyle says all this talk about health,
And BOILS being better than wealth,
May be ONE way which
Some folks can get rich,
But I prefer living by STEALTH.

A BOIL may be worth lots of "DOUGH,"
And doctors have always said so.
If you'd offer them PAY
In "DOUGH" made that way,
They'd tell you right quick WHERE TO GO.

"To what do you attribute your great age, Uncle Zeke?" asked a friend. "I can't say yet; there are several patent medicine show fellers dickerin' with me."

Get Leedy's new 1924 Catalog "M," just published. It's free. Many new novelties.

The Jazzo-Box

The Biggest Little Drum Ever—4"x14"

There is no question about the durability and pep of this little drum. It fits in places that no other will. Small orchestras, dance work, home use with the pianola or phonograph, and school orchestras. A snappy, easy-playing, little "go-getter." A real professional instrument, not a toy.

New Model Drum Sticks

After a long and careful study of the drum stick question, the Leedy Company has developed an entirely new line of models.

Opinions vary so much regarding sticks it has always been a problem to know what styles to catalog. The very stick that suits you to a "T" might be thrown aside by another very fine drummer. Therefore, the only basis to work upon was to produce a line of sticks that would meet the favor of the majority. So by taking a thousand drummers and picking out the models most used, we established what we consider the finest line of sticks yet offered.

There are four models of weight, two being sixteen inches long and two being seventeen inches long. These four models are in two different kinds of "tips" or "berries," namely the "Acorn" and the "Ball."

They are all highly polished, carefully graded, and only the first grade of white straight-grained hickory is used.

For Drummers Who Care  *Leedy Equipment Leads Them All*

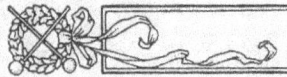

LEEDY DRUM TOPICS

A PAPER DEVOTED TO THE INTERESTS OF THE DRUMMER

No subscription fee. Advertisements accepted.

Published quarterly at 1033 East Palmer Street, Indianapolis, Ind.
Printed in U. S. A.

Editor..................................Geo. H. Way
Business Manager......................A. W. Kuerst

Chas. P. Lowe

Talk about holding a steady job! Can anyone recall how many years CHARLIE LOWE has been with the Henry Savage musical shows? We know that in twelve years Charlie has made as many trips from coast to coast and that from last reports he has signed up for life.

He was Sousa's first drummer on tour and the first man to ever make a xylophone number on the phonograph.

While in Boston a few weeks ago, Charlie gave a friend of his two passes for the show at the Colonial. The friend stuffed the passes into his pocket without examination, and when he presented them at the ticket window the treasurer burst into a loud laugh, stating that he was not accepting tips on the races.

Charlie in his haste had given the friend a small slip of paper with a memorandum of the best bets on the "fillies" at New Orleans, which read something like: "Goldfish, ten to one; Lady Dixie, five to one; Sparkplug, one hundred to one."

Get It

By the time you are reading this issue of Drum Topics the new 1924 edition of Leedy's catalog will be ready. Ask for Catalog "M."

For Your Benefit

One of the most difficult matters that confronts the drum manufacturer and the dealer is the continual changing of drummers' addresses. Many drummers do not even inform their local postoffice of a change, and mail is often returned. Do you realize that every piece of advertising for drummers' instruments is valuable to you, even though you may not need or want to purchase? It is all information, and to keep up-to-date these days it is wise to know what the other fellow is doing and using. Help us to help you. There is no obligation, so let us know if you move.

Pass Drum Topics on to your drummer friends after reading. If you want another copy let us know and it will be mailed free.

In Vaudeville

A string of "direct cues" in a difficult act is, of course, tough at times, but it's part of the drummer's business to "catch 'em" all without a "fliv." A "direct cue" is not so bad—you see the action and "catch it," but a string of "anticipation cues" is another matter. You don't see it and you "catch it," then Mr. Comic does his bit. YOU slam the cymbal, then he jumps; YOU squawk a squawker, then he looks under the carpet. Quite different from slamming the cymbal WHEN he jumps or squawking AS he looks under the carpet.

The yarn is this: One Monday morning a drummer in a leading vaudeville house received a long list of "anticipation cues" for a combination bicycle and juggling act. The ninth cue called for a short, loud wind whistle, to which Mr. Comic sticks his head from behind the tormentor—making a so-called "funny mug." The poor drummer, having no action in this spot to work on, "muffed" the cue at the first matinee. Then Mr. Comic stuck his mug around the tormentor and yelled at the drummer in loud tones: "Missed it!"

Words cannot describe how that drummer felt—his fighting blood and embarrassment raged within him. But wait—a little later in the act Mr. Comic is riding about the stage on a bicycle juggling three balls. He drops one, and up jumps Mr. Drummer, walloping his crash cymbal with all his might, and yells in loud tones: "Missed it!"

THE LAST TIME

You will have to buy a drum is when you buy a Leedy New Style Multi-Model.

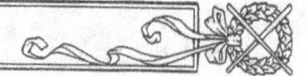

Just Like a Woman

She gazed into the music store window in which was a beautiful Leedy drum display, including a new and shiny pair of Universal Machine Tympani. After a long and interested study she turned to her friend and remarked: "Well, that's the first time I ever saw that kind of a washing machine!"

This actually happened at Hobbs' Music Store, Wichita, Kansas.

The Prize Story

"It Will Go Better Anyhow"

By H. C. K.

A foreign musician, notorious for his illiteracy, was given the contract to furnish a band at one of the city parks for a concert on the Fourth of July.

Having to make up a program, he consulted his friend the bass drummer to help him out.

"What will we play for the first number?" asked the bass drummer, pencil and paper in hand.

"Make it the '1812 Overture' by Tchaikowsky," replied the boss.

"How do you spell Tchaikowsky?" asked the bass drummer.

"Never mind; put down 'Stars and Stripes' by Sousa."

Here's One On Howard Kopp by George Carey of Sousa's Band

Howard Kopp, after a long season with the Goldman Band, of New York, has gone to Malone. This town is famous for its cider, and Howard considers it the "apple of his eye."

The Trap Problem Solved

A PRACTICAL, EFFICIENT SYSTEM OF TRAP MOUNTING

Appearance is a big factor in the orchestra of today. This addition to your outfit is wonderful in appearance and puts you in the progressive class.

Never before has the arrangement of traps been brought to such an efficient standard.

You can use more traps with less effort, enjoying more room and comfort. Nothing to kill the tone of the bass drum.

The trap trees are light yet strong, and their packing features enable a drummer to carry them about easily.

Holders for the traps are designed to be adjustable to any position on the tree. The photo tells the story of their practicability better than words.

Note that you can use the holders on any tree and in any number, arranging your own combination of traps.

Be the first in your locality to equip yourself with these progressive novelties. They will earn money for you.

Turkish and Chinese Cymbals

TURKISH AND CHINESE CYMBALS are not spun, as many drummers believe, but are cast, and hammered afterward.

For Drummers Who Care  *Leedy Equipment Leads Them All*

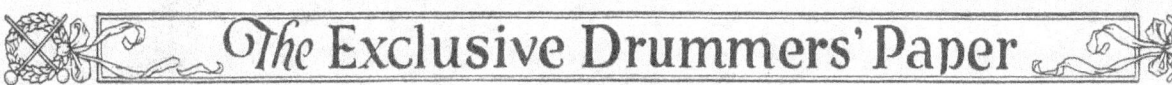
The Exclusive Drummers' Paper

Six of Los Angeles' Finest
(All Leedy Drummers)

1   2   3   4   5   6

1. FRANK KING was for a long time playing drums and tympani with the great Grauman Million-Dollar Theatre Orchestra of seventy-five men. He is now playing at the Mission Theatre here in Los Angeles and is sure a wonderful drummer.

2. E. F. MILLARD, drummer at the Morosco Theatre, is a teacher of drums in the public schools and is recognized as one of the leading drum teachers in Los Angeles. He has a very large class of pupils and is a most excellent performer himself. He has had fourteen years' experience as a teacher and says that he takes more pride in recommending Leedy goods than any other he has ever supplied his pupils with.

3. HARRY S. MOORE, who drums with the wonderful California Theatre Orchestra of seventy-five men, was recently engaged by E. R. Stone, manager of the Birkel Company's musical merchandise department, to manage the drum department. Mr. Stone says that he is now assured of drummers getting the most intelligent and practical service possible, as Mr. Moore has been a professional for some twenty years and is a very fine drummer and a courteous and affable mixer.

4. CHAS. L. WHITE is the very efficient and popular drummer of the Metropolitan Theatre Orchestra, and has used a set of Leedy Machine Tympani for many months.
His satisfaction has been expressed many times and with great enthusiasm. One of his statements is that the instruments play easily and have an excellent tone, which is equally good in the fortissimo and pianissimo passages; also that he believes every conscientious drummer who looks upon the tympani as a means of advancement would after thoroughly trying the Leedy Machine Instruments decide upon them as his choice.
Mr. White states that he will use his instruments for the coming season in "Bowl" concerts and also in the Philharmonic Orchestra.

5. H. J. WALTERS, better known among the drummers as Jim Walters, is the Philharmonic Symphony Orchestra drummer, and is at present playing at Avalon, Catalina Island, with the Catalina Marine Band. He is without question one of the best drummers in the entire country.

6. WM. LAMBERT is the drummer at one of the largest ballrooms in Venice, Cal., and is a man who can hold his own with the best of the modern jazz drummers. Leedy equipment first, last and always with him.

Note to Los Angeles and Southern California Drummers

It is a long way from the Pacific Coast to Indianapolis. In the old days you had to wait from ten days up for a new head or a pair of sticks; but now, through co-operation, the entire line of Leedy products is right on your main street. Stop in at Geo. J. Berkel Company's and ask for Mr. Stone or Mr. Moore. If it's service and right prices you are interested in, these are the gentlemen to see.

You save time and transportation charges and you have the opportunity of making a choice from many of any given model.

On special work you get detailed attention, because both Mr. Stone and Mr. Moore have made drums and drummers' wants a real study. They believe in "Drummer Correct" methods the same as the Leedy Manufacturing Company, and in addition to the above they are real fellows to meet and know.

Who Said a Drummer Wasn't a Musician?

She told a girl friend that a certain drummer "kissed divinely." Perhaps it was his "embouchere" that entranced her. Drummers can have them as well as cornet players.

What Is a Chrysoglott?

Do you know what a Chrysoglott is? It is an instrument similar to a large steel marimba and is used in the large Wurlitzer theatre organs. Leedy builds them.

J. J. Heney

Here is a young circus drummer who has had a world of practical experience for his age. Having gained his early schooling in San Francisco, he took to the road and has been with such leading organizations of the circus world as the Sells-Floto Shows and is this season with the Hagenbeck-Wallace Show. Heney is 100% Leedy equipped and is a real booster.

DRUMMERS, THIS IS YOUR PAPER

Send in your photograph and news. Ten dollars for the best story before December 1st.

Can You Answer This?

Why does a warning signal bell at a railroad crossing seem to become sharper in pitch as you approach it riding on a train, and flatter as you travel away from it?

Bass Drum Rods (Tympani Model)

Another opportunity to improve the appearance and efficiency of your outfit is offered in this new model Tympani Bass Drum Rod. They can be ordered on a new drum or purchased separately at a very reasonable price. Ease in tensioning the heads, and the superior workmanship of these rods, in addition to the better manner in which they dress up the drum, are the reasons why no drummer's equipment is complete without them.

Here Is a Chance

For the boys in the lucky towns where Sousa and the Washington Marine Band plays this fall to meet a bunch of real drummers and real fellows. They have asked LEEDY DRUM TOPICS to invite all the local drummers to step right up and say "hello." Mention DRUM TOPICS and you will receive a warm welcome from them all. They are all regulars and easy to approach. They are all Leedy drummers. Ask them why.

Signor Friscoe

Friscoe is still going big on big time vaudeville, holding down in most cases the best "spot" on the bill. He is a mighty fine drummer as well as xylophonist and there are few better showmen in the business. He uses the largest size Leedy marimba-xylophone and has often stated that he would have no other, because of its wonderful tone and wearing qualities.

For Drummers Who Care      Leedy Equipment Leads Them All

Leedy Drum Topics

PERSONAL COLUMN

Arthur Layfield has "gone and done it," so will not be seen standing on the corner at night after the job is over any longer. Therefore, LEEDY DRUM TOPICS wishes Mrs. and Mr. Layfield a long and happy married life, and we know hundreds of Art's friends who heartily join us with their good wishes.

J. H. McKnight, of the Crotona Theatre in New York, is one of the old-timers in the Big Town. "Mack," as he is called by his friends, got his early schooling at Coney Island and on Fourteenth Street. Fourteenth Street has turned out many of New York's best drummers, and McKnight is one of the top notchers.

R. L. Ugart, the snappy vaudeville drummer at the Crescent Theatre, New Orleans, has an exceptionally fine reputation throughout the entire South.

James W. Hawkes, Jr., one of Boston's leading drummers, has been for several seasons at the St. James Theatre with Hector's Orchestra. This is probably the most famous stock house orchestra in the whole country, and Hawkes is one of its chief assets. For the summer he is on a tour with D'Avino's Concert Band; however, he returned to the St. James in September. Jimmie also has a large class of pupils on all percussion instruments and is rated as one of Boston's best instructors.

Jos. L. Ross, at the Star Theatre, St. Johns, Newfoundland, is one of the most conscientious boys in the business regarding his work. He has written a very clever little story entitled "Who Is to Blame?" and we intend to publish it in the near future.

A. F. Durlauf, of Louisville, Ky., is playing at the Mary Anderson Theatre. This boy has been in the business fifteen years and has a reputation to be proud of. He was formerly with Liberita's Band, en route. He is a 100% Leedy booster.

Wilfred Gillespie, of Vancouver, B. C., is one of this city's leading drummers. He is now at the Lodge Cafe with the Arcadians, which ranks with the best of the Pacific Coast orchestras. "Will" is Leedy equipped and a thorough orchestra business manager as well as a very "peppy" drummer.

Bill Cunningham, who has been at the Allen Theatre in Cleveland, Ohio, for some time past, is another "old-time regular," having trouped for several years with many leading theatrical companies, concert bands and orchestras. He is known throughout most of the larger cities of the country, and some of the smaller places will remember Bill also, especially the towns of California, Mo., and Arnolds Park, Iowa. He also likes spaghetti, having developed this taste when on the road with a famous Italian band. As a xylophone player Cunningham has few equals. "La-Do-Si-La" is his favorite overture.

Ed Foley, formerly of Boston and Providence, is now located at Norwich, Conn., at the principal theatre. Foley was a pupil of the late Thomas Scenia, who was with the Boston Symphony Orchestra for years. He was also one of the first drummers who ever worked for Wm. Fox in New York at the old Dewey Theatre on Fourteenth Street when this manager first started in the business. Foley's ability is well known as most proficient throughout New England.

Geo. A. Smith, of Omaha, Neb., who has played for many years at the Orpheum Theatre there, is a hustler from the word "go." His drum shop, which is known to many drummers, has grown steadily, and a few months ago he was forced to take larger quarters in the downtown section of Omaha. His mail-order business covers the entire country and his activities carry great weight in the drum manufacturing world. The Leedy Manufacturing Company is proud to consider him as one of its chief distributors. Besides Mr. Smith's business ability, he ranks second to none among vaudeville drummers.

Send in any notes of interest to drummers. We will publish same. Let us know where you are.

It Is Not Always Necessary

IT IS NOT ALWAYS NECESSARY to retuck a drum head. Sometimes it is very inconvenient to do so, on account of the time required and the trouble of getting the head off the flesh hoop, especially if it is old and well tucked. Besides, there is the danger of tearing same.

Soak the whole head and flesh hoop in water—not too cold, but not warm—for five minutes, then allow it to become almost dry before putting on shell. If it is a good head it will contract. After it is about three-quarters dry you can put it on the shell and adjust same as usual. This will result in almost as good a job as retucking.

Times Have Changed

Ten years ago we never saw white, black and gold drums with beautiful pictures painted on the bass drum heads, and neither was it customary to engrave a snare drum shell, but now they are to be seen quite frequently. Of course there is a reason for this and underneath it all is good, sound business judgment. Regardless of what some drummers may think, it is true that the fellow with the fancy finished outfit is the fellow who is pulling down the big money. Of course there are many jobs where fancy outfits are not needed, but they are always an acquisition to your equipment, both from an artistic and commercial viewpoint.

A. A. Wohl—Detroit

This noted Leedy drummer and xylophone player is one of the old-timers who has been the rounds of every kind of professional experience, is a thorough vaudeville man both in the pit and on the stage.

For thirteen years he has been soloist with the City Park Band during the summer season, and for the past several winters one of the leading members of the Detroit Symphony Orchestra.

Courtesy Grinnell Brothers Music House, Detroit.

Three Drum Shows

The drummers of Chicago, Boston and New York were recently given an exceptional opportunity to come in personal contact with not only the leading dealers of the three mentioned cities, but with Mr. Leedy himself, also Mr. Way, sales manager of the Leedy Manufacturing Company. This was made possible by the putting on of three Drum Weeks, first at the Tom Brown store in Chicago, then at the Selmer stores in Boston and New York respectively. Very elaborate displays were arranged for each store and one of its pleasing features was the fact that it brought together many old acquaintances.

Joe Green, of Victor phonograph fame, was in attendance the entire time demonstrating the Leedy xylophones, and his famous brother, George Green, was an added attraction in New York. Both the drummer and dealer had many words of praise for not only the many "drummer correct" features of the Leedy line, but for the Drum Shows and the good fellowship shown by all concerned.

Union Miners Double on Drums

These union miners of Rand, South Africa, are real "Kaffirs." Music is more than a side line with them, and drums are the chief instrument.

The above photograph shows an occasion where they were used to drum up sympathy with their cause in a national coal strike which almost resulted in a race war.

Note

Reduced price on Leedy "Universal" Machine Tympani. Now $300.00.

Often the Case

Affable Clergyman (pinching a little boy's bare leg): "Who's got nice, round, chubby legs?" Little Boy: "Mamma."

Leverne Hamilton

Leverne Hamilton of Musselshell, Mont., writes: "I have been rusticating on a Montana homestead, but I feel a strong desire to get behind a couple of calfskins and a xylophone again. Have been playing country dances to keep in trim; but, unlike Chesterfields, 'they don't satisfy,' so if any of your readers know of an opening for an experienced drummer, preferably in a town of from three to five thousand, I will appreciate it if they will inform me." Box 127, Musselshell, Mont.

Ladies, Notice!

To the hundreds of lady drummers in all parts of the United States and Canada we wish to announce that DRUM TOPICS is for you as well as the men. We would like to hear from you all and will publish your photographs if you will send them in.

Improved Wood Block

Wood blocks have always been a source of worry. Here is one that overcomes all faults. Mounted on felt pad, round top, made of rock maple with exceptionally big tone. Will outlast three of any other make.

For Drummers Who Care *Leedy Equipment Leads Them All*

The Exclusive Drummers' Paper

DEALERS' COLUMN

This is something new for the dealer. It will bring your store to the attention of the drummers. It will enable you to keep in touch with other dealers' doings in all parts of the country. If the dealer takes an interest in this section of DRUM TOPICS we will give it a whole page.

Would you like a supply of Drum Topics to hand to the drummers?

We offer $10.00 for the best window display showing Leedy products.

Chas. A. McCloskey, of Providence, R. I., operates a musical instrument store that is thoroughly professional in every respect. Mr. McCloskey is a great hand to "kid" with the boys, and about his store is always an air of good fellowship. Right prices and fair dealing is McCloskey's rule. A complete stock of Leedy equipment is always on hand.

Hammann-Levin Company, Baltimore, Md., who have recently added Leedy products to their extensive line of musical instruments, is an old, well-established and reliable firm. Drummers in Baltimore cannot do better than to deal with this store. The drum department is in charge of a man thoroughly versed with this branch of business.

The Melody Music Shop, of Memphis, Tenn., was formerly an exclusive phonograph store, but several months ago it was converted into a general musical instrument merchandise house. The speed and thoroughness with which this firm has gained a solid grip on a great portion of the Memphis professional and amateur trade is phenomenal. Saul Bluenstein, its hustling manager, is to be complimented on his energetic and "go get 'em" methods. Leedy Manufacturing Company equipment is always on display.

The Southern Conn Company, of New Orleans, has broken all records for volume of sales of the great chain of Conn stores. Harry Meyers, the manager, formerly of the Rudolph Wurlitzer Company, has in the past year gained the friendship and business of a great majority of New Orleans musicians. Lately the store has been moved to larger headquarters and branches have been opened in Baton Rouge and Mobile. Mr. Meyers' pleasing personality and eagerness to really serve the musicians are only two of the reasons why he has been so wonderfully successful.

The Larkin Music House, 454 Broadway, of Albany, N. Y., is one of the rather new distributors for Leedy instruments. Their merchandising methods must be correct, for they are proving a very satisfactory connection and are doing a nice volume of business in their drum department. Mr. Francis Larkin expects to handle Leedy products exclusively in Albany, Binghamton, Troy, Utica and Schenectady.

W. J. Dyer & Bro., of St. Paul, need no introduction. This firm has always been considered one of the strongest in the Northwest, and their extensive jobbing business puts them in touch with many dealers as well as the retail trade. Their display windows always attract attention, and the illustration shown in these columns needs no explanation as to the drum line they find it most satisfactory to handle.

The J. H. Troup Music House, 15 South Market Square, Harrisburg, Pa., with branches at Lancaster and Carlisle, have found it profitable to add musical merchandise to their former line. Upon investigating it was quite natural that they should decide on Leedy for their drum department. Their advertising and business methods are making them leaders in their territory.

Bailey's, Inc., of Spokane, Wash., is operated by father and son in a manner that makes the drummer feel at home to talk over his problems, for he is bound to feel the personal service he receives. A lot has been said regarding personal service in the music store, but here is where you get it in full measure. It is one of the largest and most beautiful merchandise stores in the United States, and the new fixtures are really ahead of the times. Leedy is proud to number this company as one of its distributors. Their stock is complete and large.

More Money for the Drummer

It is not uncommon to hear a drummer complain of the fact that his outfit of instruments and their upkeep, with continued additions, etc., is too much expense considering the salary he receives.

In the majority of cases this is quite true, as his expense is considerably greater than that of most of the other musicians, excepting the leaders with their libraries, and, in rare cases, the violinist who possesses a very expensive instrument.

Of course, a piano player could not carry an instrument from job to job, but it is a wonder some managers don't want to pay him less because he has no investment.

The drummer's strongest argument is that he receives no more pay than the others, and his investment cannot be denied. The only way the boys will receive more money is to go after it. Drummers' Clubs, co-operation, cutting out knocking, and getting together in the right spirit of friendliness toward one another is the real means of accomplishing this end.

Why not apply the same methods as the business man or investor, who has something to sell based on what he has paid for it?

Take stock of your equipment the same as your grocer or druggist. What is your outfit worth? How much did you earn last year? What part of your earnings were expended for upkeep, in breakage, replacements and additions? Figure 10% per year for depreciation. Here is one way to do it:

Say your present outfit is worth $1,000.00, which would mean to include drum outfit, xylophone, tympani, bells, chimes and numerous accessories.

As an up-to-date drummer, you add possibly $100.00 worth of new creations annually.

Allowing 10% of your original outfit for depreciation would be $100.00.

Interest on your investment at 6% would be $60.00.

These are fair allowances and a business-like manner to figure them.

Summing up these expenses, which entitle you to just that much more salary than the other members of your orchestra or band, you would arrive at this summary:

Annual additions to outfit..................$100.00
10% depreciation on outfit................ 100.00
Interest on investment 60.00

Total..........................$260.00

Any musician should now agree that the drummer has a right to more money, and any fair-minded, business-like manager or leader will see it also.

Drummers, here's a tip and a legitimate one: Present your figures in the same business-like manner that any real salesman would, and your manager is bound to respect you for it. Facts and figures cannot be ignored, and this, with your ability (if you are a conscientious worker you are bound to have ability) have a value that is higher than the usual drummer's salary.

It's up to you!

Pounding the Hours Away

Wm. H. Wright, the drummer with the well-known Prof. Cox Jazz Band, a colored organization that has been playing for the past season at Jack's Cabaret and Grill, Saratoga Springs, N. Y., has kept a record of the number of hours he has played on one Leedy U K A head since December 1, 1917, until July 12, 1923, the total being 14,960 hours, and during this period he has held many prominent jobs, both permanent and on the road. The record was faithfully kept on a memorandum, itemizing every job with dates and time recorded. It makes a very interesting piece of data to look over, and we only wish we had space to publish same.

Milton L. Weber

Milton L. Weber of the Allen Theatre, Edmonton, Alberta, is one of Canada's best all-round drummers. He has had a wide experience, having played tympani at the T & D Theatre, Oakland, Cal., under Dr. De Mantle, and both tympani and xylophone in the Edmonton Symphony Orchestra, one of the few real successful symphonies in the country.

"Milt," as he is called, is a "hound" for practice, even after ten years in the business.

Xylophone and Marimbas (Improved Models)

Up to the past year no exceptional strides and improvements have been made in the construction of marimbas and xylophones. Improvements were needed and it took the Leedy progressiveness to develop them. The Solo-Tone line as it now stands embodies more real and practical improvements than have ever been offered before. If you are interested be sure to see our new 1924 Catalog "M" and note the split frame and resonator system. Also the resonator adjuster and the roller base features. The Leedy models are supplied with your choice of sharps and flats in either the elevated or level mounting.

Mexico's Famous Police Band

This very wonderful organization from Mexico City, Mexico, has been touring the United States this fall playing many of the largest fairs.

Prof. Velino Preza is its accomplished leader and the author of many standard operatic and military airs well known the world over. The band is equipped with Leedy tympani.

The New Style Multi-Model

THE WORLD'S FINEST DRUM
"BUILT LIKE A WATCH"

For Drummers Who Care *Leedy Equipment Leads Them All*

QUALITY ORCHESTRAS AND QUALITY DRUMMERS USE LEEDY QUALITY DRUMS

These are a few of the "top notchers" who know they must have the very best on earth.

The Roy Bargy Orchestra of Chicago is made up of musicians who have all had years of experience. Art Layfield, the drummer, was a full-fledged grand opera man. His versatility is wonderful.

Just ask the drummer who plays Leedy equipment.

Instruments that give perfect satisfaction to the most exacting.

This is the Paul Specht Orchestra, one of New York's most famous. Just retrned from a very successful European tour. Chancey Morehouse, the Specht drummer, ranks second to none in the East.

 Have You Seen Our New 1924 Catalog "M"? Write for it — FREE.

The famous Kentucky Serenaders is one of the most sensational hotel orchestras in the country, and John Strause is a drummer of exceptional ability.

LEEDY DRUM TOPICS
The Exclusive Drummers' Paper

POSTMASTER—Return Postage Guaranteed

LEEDY MANUFACTURING CO.
INDIANAPOLIS, INDIANA

Leedy Drum Topics Issue 3

Leedy Drum Topics

Drummers Who Did Not

See and read the first two issues of DRUM TOPICS really missed something. The second edition caused more favorable comment than the first.

Is your name in our files? If not, it should be. Why? Because this is the only magazine for drummers, so let's all support it.

All professional men have their exclusive paper and there is a good reason. They are instructive and broaden a man's knowledge of what other men in the same profession are doing in other parts of the country. Doctors, Lawyers, Dentists, Electricians, Printers and others have their own magazine, so why not the Drummer? In most all cases there is a charge for such a paper. DRUM TOPICS will be mailed to you free.

We want to thank all the readers who have written in to us and given it their support. It is certainly encouraging, as the number reaches into the thousands.

For 1924

The Leedy Manufacturing Company wishes every Drummer a job for every day of this New Year, and all the other wishes that go to make "Us Humans" Happy, Healthful, and Long-Lived.

(Signed) U. G. Leedy

ANOTHER HIGH-CLASS ORGANIZATION WHO MUST HAVE THE BEST IN DRUMMERS' EQUIPMENT.

Henry A. Buys, who is the first drummer of this band, is a man of wide experience in all branches of the profession, and has been a Leedy booster for twelve years.

The Drummer's Touch

How often we have heard discussions relative to the piano player's touch, the cornet player's embouchere, and the violinist's bowing, but how seldom do we hear any remarks relative to the drummer's touch. At first we are inclined to wonder if there is such a thing; however, a moment's thought proves that there is a great deal to the matter.

Some call it style, but that is only for the want of a better word. There is no dodging the fact that there is such a thing as "drum touch."

"System" does not cover the question, because two drummers may play with the same system and still have a different touch, so what is it all about?

Very few drummers look or sound alike in respect to the manner of playing.

"Touch" is really the kind of a blow that is applied to the drum; that is, the kind of a blow that this particular drummer uses most; not meaning the difference in a piano or forte blow, but rather in its character.

Some drummers strike a decisive straight up and down blow. This style can be divided into two kinds—one similar to a "whip-snap" and the other similar to a "lay-down" on the head, the difference being that the former technically remains in contact with the head for a less period of time than the latter.

Another drummer will describe an oval figure in the travel of his sticks during their up and down movement. This causes the sticks to strike the head at a slight glance.

Still another drummer will have a tendency to draw the sticks toward him while they are on their downward path.

Then there is the drummer who throws his sticks in almost a complete circle, sometimes to the left and sometimes to the right. There is quite a contrast between the right and left circle, because the drum is on an angle and the right circle blow pulls up against the angle of the head, while the left circle blow remains in contact with the head longer and the tip of the stick follows the head just a little more.

The crowded blow must be taken into consideration. This is the kind that hugs the drum and has very little whip or spring to it. In other words, there is a touch to the drum stick.

We do not comment here on which is the right one to use, but only hope to show that the drummer with one manner of touch could not possibly be satisfied with an instrument that would suit a drummer with a different touch.

Very often a drummer will condemn an instrument, stating that it plays too hard or that it has a "boardy" or "tinny" tone, and possibly another drummer might be perfectly suited with this same instrument.

Therefore, do not condemn a drum until you have taken your own touch into consideration. Perhaps your particular touch does not bring out the best results in a drum with thick heads, or vice versa, or perhaps you would be better suited with different snares, and again, perhaps the heads are not tensioned so as to give the best results.

For instance, the drummer with a decisive, solid blow would never be satisfied with light heads, and the drummer who uses the crowded blow would be likely to condemn a drum with thick heads, while a drummer who plays with a circular movement of his sticks very seldom approves of gut snares.

One more thing must be considered, and that is the weight of the sticks you like best. Drummers who use a fairly heavy stick prefer thick heads, and drummers who use exceptionally light sticks prefer the lighter heads.

This is very natural and correct, because they are the combinations that obtain the best results. You couldn't use a violin bow on a cello.

It is always well to consider these points before ordering a new instrument, as it will help you to choose.

Read This Photographed Letter

OFFICES OF
ORCHESTRA HALL
AND
THE CHICAGO SYMPHONY ORCHESTRA
FOUNDED BY THEODORE THOMAS
FREDERICK STOCK, CONDUCTOR

FREDERICK J. WESSELS, MANAGER
HENRY E. VOEGELI, ASSISTANT MANAGER

TELEPHONE HARRISON 0363
CABLE ADDRESS "ORCHALL"

220 SOUTH MICHIGAN AVE.
CHICAGO

Nov. 2, 1923.

The Leedy Manufacturing Co.,
1033 E. Palmer St.,
Indianapolis, Indiana.

Gentlemen:—

It is a pleasure to testify to the excellent examples of the Leedy Universal Pedal Tympani, which we are using with the Civic Orchestra of Chicago. Their tone quality is admirable, their workmanship and appearance excellent, and I commend their distinctive ease of assembly and of transportation.

Yours sincerely,

Frederick A. Stock
CONDUCTOR

For Drummers Who Care      *Leedy Equipment Leads Them All*

The Exclusive Drummers' Paper

Personal Page

Editor's Note

The "Personals" on this page are not "copy" sent in. They are truths gathered through personal acquaintance and bona fide information furnished the Editor of DRUM TOPICS, who has spent nine years on the road as a professional drummer and two years representing the Leedy Manufacturing Company.

MAURICE TUSHIN is a Boston Drummer and Tympanist, also a teacher of great prominence. Formerly with the Boston English Opera Company and now a member of the Boston Festival Orchestra and Stewart's Band. He uses Leedy Universal Tympani.

HERMAN FINK, who is now on the Orpheum Circuit with the Vincent Lopez Red Cap Orchestra, is a wonder. Has played in every branch of the business and always used Leedy Equipment. (Photo courtesy W. J. Dyer & Bro., St. Paul, Minn.)

Many drummers have sent in good material for DRUM TOPICS, but owing to our limited space we cannot use it all; however, we want to heartily thank you for your efforts, and assure you that the best material will be published in its turn as soon as it is possible to do so.

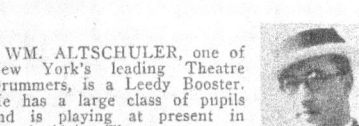

WM. ALTSCHULER, one of New York's leading Theatre Drummers, is a Leedy Booster. He has a large class of pupils and is playing at present in Loew's Alpine Theatre.

LARRY GAMERDINGER, formerly of Indianapolis, is now with Geo. White's "Scandals" as a feature of the show. His entire outfit is Leedy from "soup to nuts." As a Xylophonist he ranks A-1.

Drummers, send in your stories. Ten dollars for the best one before March 15th.

Leedy's IS the world's largest drum factory and the ONLY one that manufactures the entire line of drummers' equipment.

BILL MICHAELIAN is a well known Pacific Coast boy now playing at the Sunken Gardens, Fresno, Cal. An artist in the dance business. He states there is no snare drum like the New Style Multi-Model.

MAX FIERMAN, of the famous Hackel-Berge Orchestra, is fully Leedy equipped and is 100 per cent satisfied. Max is one of New York's best known Drummers.

WM. GLADSTONE plays Bass Drum in the world's largest theatre orchestra, The Capitol, New York City. This is some wonderful job and "Bill" is some wonderful drummer. He uses a Leedy.

W. B. STOLZ, of New Brunswick, N. J., is one of this country's most popular and efficient drummers. Here is a chap who is a business man as well as a drummer of twelve years' experience. He sells more instruments than many stores by his hustling methods.

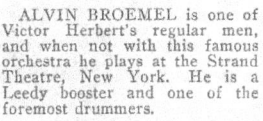

ALVIN BROEMEL is one of Victor Herbert's regular men, and when not with this famous orchestra he plays at the Strand Theatre, New York. He is a Leedy booster and one of the foremost drummers.

RUDY STARITA is a leading drummer of Providence, R. I. The broadcasting station WJAR, Outlet Company, have been featuring Rudy and his Leedy Xylophone for some time. In the summer he plays at the "Weirs."

B. N. GUSTAT has been located at El Paso, Texas, for the past four years. He is now playing at the Texas Grand Theatre and is also secretary of the local. A legitimate and schooled drummer of exceptional skill and wide experience.

GERALD SUNDE, Drummer of Minneapolis and Fargo, is in Florida again with Backman's Million Dollar Band. Sunde is one of the country's finest bass drummers, and, like G. Helmecke of Sousa's, uses no other than a Leedy solid shell bass drum.

W. H. BYRNES has been for a number of years with the Cincinnati Symphony Orchestra. This alone speaks for his ability. He has used Leedy equipment from the beginning of his career.

EARL GORE, of the Majestic Theatre, Springfield, Ill., is another "cracker-jack" in the vaudeville game. Ask any act that has played this house. He also has a large class of pupils.

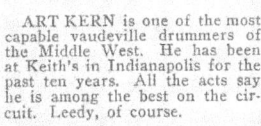

ART KERN is one of the most capable vaudeville drummers of the Middle West. He has been at Keith's in Indianapolis for the past ten years. All the acts say he is among the best on the circuit. Leedy, of course.

BILL DREW is one of Kansas City's old-timers, having held down many of the important jobs in that town. He is now at the Newman Theatre and uses Leedy Universal Tympani. He is a real artist on these instruments.

HENRY BEHRENS, of Tassillo's Orchestra, Hartford, Conn., has one of the most elaborate fancy Leedy outfits. He is an up-to-date and efficient drummer of the first order. His work is a feature of the orchestra.

P. W. LEE has been for a number of years at the Grand Opera House in Shreveport, La. He is very well known throughout the entire Southwest, and the fact that Shreveport is not one of the largest cities does not mean that this drummer is not one of the big city class. A great vaudeville man.

GEO. S. TILLINGHAST is now at Poli's Shubert Theatre in Washington, D. C. Previous to this engagement he was with the U. S. Navy Band. George hails from Providence, R. I., where he formerly operated his own drum shop. He is an all-'round efficient man on Drums, Xylophone and Tympani.

E. R. S. DAVIS, of Lynn, Mass., is the Xylophone Soloist and Drummer with the Lynn Cadet Band, also a pupil of Harry A. Bower of Boston. Twelve years a Leedy enthusiast on both drums and xylophone.

H. KINAHAN is at present in Richmond, Va., holding down one of the principal jobs. He formerly worked in one of the leading houses in Calgary, Alberta, Canada, and enjoys a well-earned reputation as a top-notch Xylophone player.

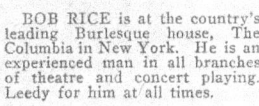

BOB RICE is at the country's leading Burlesque house, The Columbia in New York. He is an experienced man in all branches of theatre and concert playing. Leedy for him at all times.

ART HIGGS was recently married in Fort Wayne, Ind., so, we judge, will remain there for some time. Here is a man who praises his wife's first pie. Oh, boy! He is drummer at the Majestic Theatre and secretary of the local. Was formerly at Grand Rapids. The Leedy Universal Pedal Tympani is part of his equipment, and he plays them efficiently and artistically.

STANLEY PAYNE, of Milford, Conn., is a pupil of Howard Goulden of Sousa's Band. Payne is a Leedy Booster and is now located at Fort H. G. Wright, New York.

For Drummers Who Care  *Leedy Equipment Leads Them All*

 # Leedy Drum Topics

LEEDY DRUM TOPICS

A PAPER DEVOTED TO
THE INTERESTS OF THE DRUMMER

No subscription fee.

Advertisements accepted.

Published quarterly at 1033 East Palmer Street,
Indianapolis, Indiana.

Editor..........................Geo. H. Way
Business Manager................A. W. Kuerst

One of Thousands Who Like Drum Topics

October 25, 1923.

Editor Leedy Drum Topics.

Dear Sir:

Drum Topics just arrived this noon, so I was late back to the office. Couldn't help it, though, for I had to read every word before I could leave home, and then I took it with me so I could look at the pictures again. They get better each issue; keep them coming. Please enter my name on the "Super-Boosters," for I wish they were monthly instead of quarterly. Please feel free to call on me for any assistance that I may render.

Don't overlook my issue of Catalog "M," as I need it. Very truly yours,

(Signed) K. E. AMBROSE,
320 East Grand, McAlester, Okla.

Donald W. McClellan is one of the most popular dance men in Buffalo, catering especially to the more elite work.

Besides being a very clever drummer, he is assistant manager to his father at the H. B. McClellan Music House.

Nickel-plating will not go on over old work. It is absolutely necessary to remove the old nickel and start with the base metal before replating. This is a bigger job than the plating itself on a new article and is therefore the reason it often costs more to replate certain parts and traps than to buy new, xylophone and drum stands especially.

Kaffir Pianos

A big annual dance of natives of Johannesburg, South Africa. This event is one of the big shows of that region and is a tournament in which teams of natives from the inland districts compete for prizes.

The whites attend in large numbers, and the music is furnished by from fifteen to twenty native-made Marimbas, which are called Kaffir Pianos.

The "Why" of Metal Flesh Hoops

1. They are stronger.
2. They will not turn over like wooden flesh hoops.
3. They last longer.
4. They are all the same size and always fit the drum shell properly.
5. *It is possible to carry an extra head or two tucked on metal flesh hoops. To replace a broken head requires only three minutes.* This cannot be done with a wood hoop, because the head will pull it out of shape and even break it. Leedy originated the metal flesh hoop idea and a Leedy Metal Flesh Hoop will not warp or rust.
6. They greatly improve the appearance of your instrument.

Roman architects placed earthen jars in the theatre walls to increase the resonance.

Yes, More Money Is Possible

This is the third article in Drum Topics on the salary subject; however, we have a point to bring out here that was not mentioned in the foregoing numbers.

It is simply this: If drummers in one city can get more for their services, why not in other cities? It's a feeble excuse to say, "This is a poor town musically." *Make it* a good town musically. It is often done. What you should say is, "If others can do it, so can we." What's wrong? Is it your organization? Is it the lack of "get-together spirit" or is it a habit unnoticed amongst your drummers to take it the easiest way?

Surely a drummer is worth as much in one locality as in another, and if you investigate you will find that where they are getting it, there are some live-wire "heads" among them.

We cannot grasp each locality's weakness from a distance, but we do know that it can be done, for the drummers and other musicians as well.

Have you tried the new Leedy H-1, H-3 or H-5 Drum Sticks? They are nifty models and you will like them.

In Australia

Leedy drums and accessories are as well known in Australia as in the United States.

Allan & Company, one of the continent's largest distributors, have been responsible for this fact, they having many branch connections with musical instrument stores in dozens of cities.

In a future issue of Drum Topics we will show some photographs of the leading Australian drummers. It will be interesting to the States drummers to know that they are right up-to-date in their methods.

THE HEIGHT OF NERVE—A guy who borrows your drum and pokes a stick through the head, then blames it on the weather.

A Drum Head Tip

It is not heat and cold that affect a drum head, but it is the condition of the heat and cold, namely, dampness and dryness.

A damp heat will cause the head to slacken, and the same with a damp cold.

A dry heat will cause a head to tighten, and the same with a dry cold.

Therefore, watch the condition of the atmosphere rather than the thermometer and avoid head breakage. If you have tightened your head on a damp night, let it out after using to the point where you started to take it up. This will allow some slack for a "take-up" should the next day be dry.

If your drum works nicely in dry weather, leave it alone as much as possible.

Drummers who watch these points have been known to use the same heads for years.

Like an "All-Day Sucker"

Don't you hate to play through a long number with a wind whistle stuck in your "mug" just to blow a couple of "toots" for some act that needs it to help him out? Oh, well! It's all in the business.

What Next?

Joe Suchecki, of Torrington, Conn., states that drummers could save a lot of money on traps, etc., if they would follow his advice.

He owns a police dog and is training him to catch cues in the vaudeville pit. The dog is now about ready to begin work. Maybe the manager will raise Joe's salary. Anyhow, if this works out, the rosin can can be canned. In a letter to us, Joe states that this dog is of exceptional intelligence.

He also states that he has a rooster that is coming along fine, so will not have to worry about "squawks" instead of "crows" in Jolly Fellows Waltz or Comedy Acts.

However, one thing that puzzles him is the fact that these "live traps" might cost more in feed than buying new "dead ones" occasionally.

We hope that neither the dog nor the rooster "come in" at the wrong place or get to scrapping in the pit. If they do, the Leedy Manufacturing Company can always be relied upon to send on a "Dog Bark" or "Rooster Crow" that will take their place. However, we wish this new venture all kinds of success.

Electric Drum Heater

If the advantages of the Electric Drum Heater were fully understood by all, there would not be one drummer in the country without one, for no matter what kind of a drum you may own, there are times in damp weather when it would be much more snappy and "comfortable" to play on if heads and the air chamber inside were thoroughly dry.

Once a drummer has used a heater, he is never without it. Leedy originated and patented this device.

For Drummers Who Care Leedy Equipment Leads Them All

The Exclusive Drummers' Paper

Baltimore Is Noted for Oysters, Hammann-Levin and Leedy Drummers

"A Drummer's Paradise"

It is doubtful if there is a more beautifully equipped and completely stocked music store in the whole United States than the Hammann-Levin Company of Baltimore. The above photo shows a Leedy drum display in the main window. Recently this company put on a Leedy "Drum Show" with the assistance of Geo. H. Way, sales manager of the Leedy Manufacturing Company, that resulted in convincing the drummers of Baltimore that a stock of accessories and a "drummer's understanding" was at their service that had no equal in the city. Neither can it be surpassed in any other.

Mr. Levin, the president and general manager of the Hammann-Levin Company, is not one of the kind that sits in the office and tells his clerks what to do, but is a hustler who gets in amongst them and does it, showing them the fine points in the art of pleasing the musician. Any afternoon during the rush (and this is the kind of a store that has a daily rush) Mr. Levin can be found behind the counter making personal sales in the various departments. This means that the Baltimore music trade knows him well.

Speed, advertising, thoroughness and fair dealing are his creeds in business. To purchase an instrument in this store is to know that you have received full measure of all that is claimed.

Harry Woods

Is the Manager of the Musical Merchandise Department for the Hammann-Levin Company. Harry was a professional drummer of many years' trouping and vaudeville experience and is known over the entire country as one of the "regulars." He was Manager of one of Baltimore's largest Vaudeville Theatres for some time before joining Hammann-Levin. Drummers go to him when in doubt, but when they leave, the doubt is eliminated, for he makes it a point to be up on all questions. With a man of his knowledge and ability in charge, it does not take long to understand why this company enjoys the great bulk of Baltimore's drum business.

Chas. Appler

Chas. Appler's 'Garden City Orchestra is one of the leading "jobbing" outfits in Baltimore. The photograph shows his main orchestra. Appler has as many as five going in one night. Here is an example of what a hustling, business-like drummer can do. Appler is his own first and A-1 percussionist.

Joe Soistman

Writes: "I cannot conceive a better condition for the drummer than exists in our city, namely, the combination of Hammann-Levin and Leedy Manufacturing Company. We get the best obtainable in the shortest space of time, in a store where it is most agreeable to deal, both from a business and personal standpoint."

Joe Soistman is a drummer of fifteen years' experience in the professional field of playing and teaching. He is now instructor for the Boumi Temple Drum Corps, and it is due to his untiring work that the Blind War Veterans' Drum Corps at the Evergreen School (photo below) is a wonderful success.

The Leedy Manufacturing Company believes that this is a good place to point out to the drummer the real advantage of purchasing supplies from the Music Store. First—You save transportation charges. Second—You save valuable time. Third—You have your choice of several models. Fourth—You see it before you pay. Fifth—You are backed up with a guarantee and service within easy reach. Sixth—It is your duty to purchase your goods in your O. H. T. (own home town).

A Drummer's Story By Mr. Levin, Himself
"IT EVEN HAPPENS TODAY"

"In my early career, as bandmaster with a small circus which traveled principally by wagon, the musicians whom I had engaged had all arrived except the drummer, so we started rehearsals without him. During same he arrived in an intoxicated condition. I said, "Look here, my man, you can't play in this band; you're drunk." He said, "From the way it sounds to me, in order to play in it, I'd have to be drunk."

Other Baltimore "Hammann-Levin-Leedy-Ites"

Adolph Riehl, Tympanist with the Baltimore Symphony Orchestra, is one of the world's leading artists on these instruments. He endorses and uses the Leedy Universal Pedal Tympani.

Leroy Brunner is in the up-to-date class, both in ability and business methods. He believes in Hammann-Levin and Leedy, and has proven it by equipping himself with a real gold outfit with which he earns more money than the average.

Arthur Smith and his black and gold Leedy drum outfit are in demand nightly. He "sells" his nifty work and classy equipment as one. It's the drummers with his viewpoint who get the "dough." Same as Geo. Marsh with Paul Whiteman.

WORLD WAR BLIND VETERANS' DRUM CORPS
Evergreen School for Blind Soldiers

This drum corps is without doubt the most wonderful organization on record. Every man is totally blind, having given his sight for his country in the late World War. These boys have worked hard under the able direction of Joe Soistman (fourth from left).

They march and play in an efficient and rudimental manner that exceeds many of their more fortunate brothers. We take our hats off to these boys when they pass.

A Few Other Leedy Dealers

M. J. NUSBAUM, of Canton, Ohio, is in the "Big City" instrument dealer class and is one of the few who enjoy the patronage of all the professional drummers of his city. A recent Leedy "Drum Show" put on at his store was a huge success. Nusbaum believes in liberal but careful advertising.

THE EDFRED COMPANY, of Akron, Ohio, who have recently added the Leedy line, is another live-wire firm. Mr. A. L. Simmons, the manager, is a great advertiser, and their field covers a large section of the surrounding country. Drummers get real service here.

THE CLARK MUSIC COMPANY, of Syracuse, N. Y., has D. W. Greenleaf in charge of their Instrument Department, and the Leedy Manufacturing Company considers itself fortunate in counting this firm one of its chief distributors. Mr. Greenleaf's ability in this Department is far above the average.

BUSH & LANE PIANO COMPANY, of Seattle, Wash., has Mr. J. Wright in charge of the Musical Merchandise Dept. This is one of the leading firms on the Pacific Coast, and Mr. Wright knows his end of the business from A to Z. They handle Leedy exclusively.

THE ARNOLD-EDWARDS PIANO CO., of Jacksonville, Fla., with J. W. Berry in charge of the Musical Instrument Dept., have recently moved into their new home. It is one of the most beautiful music stores in the South, and their Drum Dept. is complete in every detail.

THE CONSOLIDATED MUSIC COMPANY, of Salt Lake City, Utah, is another firm that handles Leedy drums exclusively. D. R. Daynes, in charge of this department, believes in carrying a complete stock. This store is truly a drummers' "Service Station" in every sense of the word.

For Drummers Who Care  *Leedy Equipment Leads Them All*

Leedy Drum Topics

THE PRIZE STORY

By Charles F. Mutter, Jr., Paterson, N. J.

TUNED FOR THE SEASON

A local theatre, enlarging its orchestra from three to twelve men, was badly in need of a drummer.

The manager, anticipating a symphonic effect, instructed the leader that the drummer *must* have tympani.

A Knight of Percussion, with limited experience, made application for the job, and when asked whether he could play tympani, replied that he understood the execution but had little experience at tuning. However, the leader decided to give him a chance and later confronted the manager with this news:

"I have engaged a drummer."

"Can he play tympani?" demanded the manager in an enthusiastic tone.

"Somewhat," replied the leader. "You see, he can execute, but he cannot tune."

"Well," said the manager, as one having found a solution, "C. B." (a noted drummer) is in town, isn't he? Can't we get him to come around and tune them?"

About Separate Tension Rods

The slotted head, separate tension rod is fast becoming a standard for drum equipment, and the reason is practical in every respect.

If this type of head on a rod is made correctly it is not necessary to carry a key for its operation, because the slot will take any denomination of coin. (If you are broke, borrow a nickel from the leader.) However, a key is furnished for Leedy Drums and is made in a flat piece, which, of course, takes up less room in your pocket than the key that is furnished with the old style square-head rod.

The loss of the Leedy key does not in any way make it necessary to hunt up a screwdriver to tighten the drum, because of the reason mentioned above in respect to the coin. If a square-head key is lost, the inconvenience is great. Drummers invariably lose their key at night when the music stores are closed. A pair of plyers is the only solution to tighten your instrument. Try to find a pair of plyers around a dance hall or theatre pit when you want them in a hurry.

No clock key will fit the square-head type of rod most generally used. Leedy Drum Rods are equipped with slotted heads, which in technical terms are called fillister head cap screws.

Our Quarterly Arithmetic Problem

If the wear and tear on drum sticks is one-fiftieth of a mill per overture, what is the depreciation on a "Chinee" cymbal per crash?

Read How It Works

Four bass drum beats to the bar with your pedal (no cymbal) makes the tambo vibrate a short roll with each beat.

You are getting this effect without using your sticks, which leaves them free to play other traps. Great novelty—shimmy bass drum and tambo together. Just lift the tambo off the upright if not wanted for the next strain.

Will the drummer who wrote "A Neglected Phase of Modern Drumming" please write to the Editor of DRUM TOPICS again?

Emery A. Kenyon

Is now playing at the world-famous West Baden Springs Hotel, West Baden, Indiana, with the American Carlsbad Orchestra.

He is fully Leedy equipped, as the photograph shows. This being one of the highest class jobs in the whole country, it naturally calls for a drummer of Kenyon's ability.

(Photo courtesy Van De Walle Music Company, Seymour, Indiana.)

Show This to Your Manager

Why is it that a theatre manager will always throw a very pretty little note on the screen in reference to the annoyance caused by patrons talking, and never make mention that it would be more pleasant for the patrons and the orchestra if they would not pat their feet to the time of the music? It is worse than reading the titles aloud.

To Fix a Tom-Tom

Did you ever have the ring pull out of a tomtom? Doesn't it "get your goat"?

Never mind, there is a very easy way to fix it.

First, pull out the other one. Second, run a piece of steel wire straight through the old "Chinee tub" and make a couple of loops at each end to hold the rings.

If the old rings are weak or broken, get a couple of small key rings at the five-cent store. Get the drift? One end is pulling against the other when fixed in this manner, and you will have no further excuse for swearing in public.

They are made in China, so don't blame us for the way the Chinks put in these rings.

Can You Tuck a Drum Head Loose?

No, not if it is a good head, because, being a good head, it must be elastic, and if elastic to the proper degree, it will contract after tucking, no matter how "loose" you may have thought you accomplished it.

Many drummers place a saucer under a snare drum head, or a large cymbal under a bass drum head while tucking, but there is a limit to the size of the object that can be used, and a good elastic head will always take up, in drying out, more than the amount of slack caused by the "saucer tucking system."

This particularly applies to tympani heads, and when you have used an instrument a short time and the head continues to contract, pulling the flesh hoop flush with the edge of the shell, it is not because the head was tucked too tight at the factory, but because it is a good head and has elasticity; therefore, sponge it evenly and slowly, and pull it down again.

If it was good enough to contract, it will be good enough to expand.

What drummers need today is more "bank roll" in exchange for their "drum roll."

The Snare Drum Roll

From "The Gardner Modern Method for Drums," published by Carl Fischer, New York City.

The roll consists of an even reiteration of beats sufficiently rapid to prohibit rhythmic analysis. To produce an impression of sustentation, these beats must be absolutely even both in power and in sequence. Uneven beats in a roll destroy the impression of sustentation. Evenness is then the primary quality to strive for in rolling; speed is the secondary quality to strive for.

There are two possible ways of producing an absolutely even sequence: (1) hand alternation of single strokes and (2) hand alternation of double strokes. Centuries of testing as well as common sense show that these two methods of producing an *even* roll are the only ones possible; all other methods are physically impossible. Where drum sticks are allowed to bounce promiscuously, where three or more strokes are made with each stick, or where the right stick does three or four beats against two or three beats in the left hand, an even roll is obviously impossible. With these considerations in mind, we must make our ideal *evenness, not speed*. The speed ideal produces quicker results, but a superficial technic with irremediable limitations. With the even ideal in mind, speed takes care of itself, and a technic gained in this manner has no limitations up to perfection. The snare drum roll is produced by hand alternation of double strokes.

The "open roll" is produced by slow hand alternation. Two strokes in each hand alternately are produced by wrist movement and each beat should follow its predecessor in clock-like precision. When the student gains evenness and clearness of tone and when the "feel" of the sticks becomes familiar, he should gradually increase the speed up to the limit of relaxation and evenness. At this point he should stop and start anew, or he may gradually retard the speed until the starting point is reached. This process is continued as long as possible without fatigue. When the muscles tire, the student should rest; muscular fatigue is caused by the muscles becoming tense and by the unusual exercise given to muscles not commonly used. Tension of muscles must be carefully avoided and to do this the student must exercise a great amount of patience in "closing" the roll. Daily practice in the manner described above is advisable throughout a drummer's career.

White Drum Heads

White in a drum head is not natural in the hide. They have to be made white.

The "clear" or "transparent" head is the hide in its natural state.

C. C. Wiles

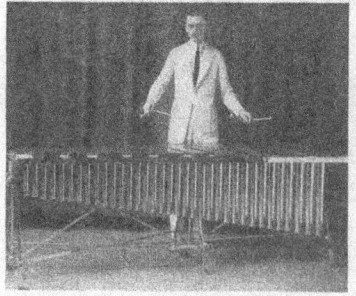

Was formerly a pupil of George Hamilton Green, and has played many of the leading vaudeville circuits as a feature.

His home is in Lincoln, Nebr., where he now resides, having given up professional playing temporarily to finish a course at the University of Nebraska. Wiles agrees with Signor Frisco and many other vaudeville artists that there is no xylophone equal to a Leedy.

For Drummers Who Care *Leedy Equipment Leads Them All*

The Exclusive Drummers' Paper

In Canada

Wilfred Gillespie and "The Arcadians" are both in a class by themselves in the cabaret and dance field. These boys hold down the best jobs to be had in Western Canada and are always busy. "Wilf" is a 100 per cent Leedy Drummer and has played in Edmonton, Calgary and Vancouver. He is highly capable in both legitimate and "jazz."

Think It Over

If a tree were to fall down and there being no one within hearing distance, would there be a noise or sound?

The answer is, theoretically, no. Why? Because noise, sound or tone is simply a sensation upon the ear.

Ted Gleason

Is now touring the Keith and Orpheum circuit with Fagan's Orchestra. The photograph shows that Ted considers no other than a complete Leedy outfit. This orchestra has been one of the biggest hits ever sent over the circuit, and Gleason is responsible for a great share of its success by his wonderful work.

By the expression of "sympathetic vibration" is meant that which we hear when the sound from one instrument causes a drum or another instrument to buzz or vibrate, which is due to the second object being either of the same vibration ratio or a multiple thereof.

It Takes Practice

A group of drummers were talking "shop" as usual. One chap during the "gab fest" sprung this one in speaking of the finest drummer he ever heard:

"I once met an old circus man that had 'em all beat. Why, do you know, that guy could double the double drag on an eiderdown pillow with a pair of feathers." Some drummer! What?

THE HEIGHT OF PESSIMISM is a guy who complains that the pit is so nice and roomy that he has to put in tympani.

Mistakes

When any other member of the orchestra makes a mistake, he gets away with it.

But when a drummer makes a mistake—Holy Moses!!

Have you got Leedy's Catalog "M"? If not, why not? It will be mailed free. Write today.

Regarding Tympani Heads

What is the difference between a clear or transparent and a white head? Some drummers prefer one and some the other, the difference in choice being one that is based mostly upon personal taste in appearance. Very few drummers offer any reason except that they have at some time owned a head of one or the other kind that pleased them in tonal quality.

Let's get down to the real facts of the difference in heads. All skins when "fleshed" and "haired," which is the first step in their manufacture, are *clear*. A clear head is in its *natural* state. The fibres are alive and the hide is elastic, therefore in the best condition to produce a resonant tone.

Now let us look at the white head. Any drummer can make a white head by soaking the clear head in luke warm water and rubbing it in his hands in the same manner as washing a handkerchief. This stretches and pulls out the fibres and when dry it will turn white. This same principle is used in the manufacture of white heads with the addition of a bleaching method to get it even. White heads are not suitable for tympani, because they are non-elastic and the fibres are pulled out; therefore it is dead and non-resonant.

It is not an easy matter to make a clear tympani head. It necessitates the highest grade of hide and the most skilled and careful workmanship to carry the hides through the many operations necessary and bring it to a finish undamaged and in its natural clear and "live-fibre" condition. It's the care and attention to little details that have made the Leedy Tympani Head famous.

THE LEADING TYMPANI PLAYERS PREFER LEEDY'S KAFETTE HEADS.

The new process LEEDY UKA WHITE snare and bass drum heads are wonderful. Try one.

Leedy Jazz Felt Sticks

(Patented Oct. 30, 1923)

These sticks are designed so that you can get more out of the various traps. They are balanced exactly like the regular drum sticks and it is possible to "roll" with them in the same manner.

Many musical effects are obtainable with these sticks. They have brought cow bells into popularity once more.

They are much easier on crash cymbals than any other stick known, and the harshness is eliminated when they are used on wood block, tom-tom, etc. An original Leedy creation.

A Real Wood Block Holder

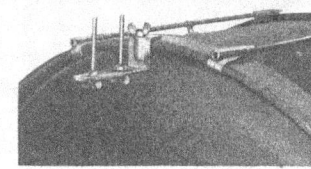

This holder enables you to place your block in an out-of-the-way and at the same time easy-playing position. The surface of the block is just above the bass drum hoop. The holder is adjustable to any size block, and it stays where you put it because it has the famous "Bull Dog" clamp.

SARAH: "I heard you were away from your work yesterday. What was wrong, your old trouble of acute indigestion?"

NORA: "No; a cute traveling drummer."

Original Kentucky Six

They are now at the Broadview Hotel, Wichita, Kansas, making a tremendous hit, and are booked for an extensive vaudeville tour. They were formerly in St. Petersburg, Fla., and Lexington, Ky. Jos. Hoffman, the drummer, has the most expensive drum equipment that it is possible to buy, and as a dance man he ranks with the best.

FOR SALE—Complete Leedy Drum Outfit, in first-class condition, at a very reasonable price. Write for full particulars. MARVIN SALLEE, Halstead, Kansas.

Geo. W. Marsh

This famous drummer has just been engaged by Paul Whiteman himself for the First Whiteman Organization, and DRUM TOPICS wishes Mr. Marsh the greatest of success.

He was formerly with the Eddie Elkins Organization, and it goes without saying that Whiteman made a very wise selection in his choice. Marsh is, of course, a great believer in Leedy products.

For Drummers Who Care Leedy Equipment Leads Them All

LEEDY DRUM TOPICS

The Exclusive Drummers' Paper
[Number Three]

POSTMASTER—Return Postage Guaranteed

LEEDY MANUFACTURING CO.
INDIANAPOLIS, INDIANA

Two of the Finest Orchestras In Chicago — Leedy Equipped

Oriole Terrace Orchestra   Al Short's Orchestra

Chas. Puchta, the drummer of this famous orchestra, hails from St. Louis. Ask anyone who has heard the orchestra, either in person or on a Brunswick record, whether his work "shines" or not. Yes, all Leedy.

This is the former Al Short Orchestra. This able leader is now conductor of the Tivoli Orchestra. Ray Ennis, one of Chicago's foremost drummers, is a member of the organization and uses complete Leedy equipment.

Leedy WORKMANSHIP IS FAMOUS

The New Style Multi-Model

From the day that U. G. Leedy made his first drum his ideals of perfect workmanship, neatness in design and quality of materials have been the ruling forces that built the World's Largest Drum Factory.

Leedy Drum Topics Issue 4

Leedy Drum Topics

A Birthday Is A Big Event

WHETHER IT BE for human beings or a magazine, so with this, the FOURTH ISSUE of DRUM TOPICS, we celebrate our first birthday and strive to make it more interesting than ever for the drummer.

WE ARE ONE year old and want our friends to know that we appreciate their loyal support, for it has made us a very large and "healthy child." If you all enjoyed the first three issues—and thousands of letters say you did—we trust you will help us continue the good work of publishing the only real drummers' paper by sending in the names of all your drummer friends to the editor. This will assure all of the boys of receiving a copy of each number free.

BE SURE to send in any news or stories that are interesting to the drummer.

DON'T FORGET THE creed of DRUM TOPICS. It is a much-used phrase, but nothing can express the drummers' greatest need any better: GET TOGETHER—know what the fellows are doing in other towns; where they are playing; what is new, and "who's who."

DRUM TOPICS is for you. Keep in touch with it and be a part of it.

LET'S GO!

Ann Pennington

Look out, boys! If girls take up drums, we will all lose out.

This famous little star of the Ziegfeld Follies is a drummer of no mean ability. She has played on many makes of outfits; however, likes her present Leedy instruments best of all. She says they have an easy playing quality found in no others.

Miss Pennington is one of the highest-salaried stars in the world.

Oh My, Yes!

Mother, may I go out with a nice young drummer?
Why, yes, my little lady;
But I'll go along as a dutiful mother
To see there's nothing shady.

Who Is the Oldest Living Drummer in the U. S.?

DRUM TOPICS would like to publish the photo and history of the oldest living drummer. If he resides in your locality, secure his picture and send it to the editor, together with your own photo.

It Can't Be Helped

Once there was a drummer who bought a fine 15-inch Turkish cymbal from a dealer. After using it a week he developed a set notion in his mind that it had a poor tone and took it back to the dealer, complaining.

Said dealer wrote the details to the Leedy Manufacturing Company, stating that this drummer was coming to Indianapolis and would bring the cymbal to the factory for exchange.

Mr. Drummer arrived, stated his case, and was taken to the stock room, where he tried out sixty different cymbals of the same type and ended up by keeping the one that he brought with him.

The point is this: No two cymbals, Turkish or otherwise, sound exactly the same pitch, owing to the fact that they are cast and vary slightly in the amount of metal contained. The pitch is a matter of personal taste.

When a drummer gets used to a certain cymbal he never likes a new one of a different pitch until he has gotten thoroughly accustomed to it, for the reason that it sounds strange to his ear, and, although the new article may be better than the old one, he invariably condemns it.

A few days ago we counted the letters sent in by drummers who praised the January issue of Leedy "Drum Topics" and asked us to "keep it coming." The count was 4,922.

If a sound were loud enough to be heard around the earth, it would take 33 hours and 31 minutes for it to travel the entire distance.

The Leader Says

If you soak a crash cymbal a little too late, you are a "dub."
If you soak it a little ahead of time, you are "too fly."
If you soak it a little too easy, you lack "pep."
If you soak it too loud, you are a "blacksmith."
And if you soak it exactly right, it is just another crash and passes unnoticed.

The invention of the drum is ascribed to Bacchus.

Rudy Starita

This popular drummer has had a world of experience and is now with the Mal Hallett Orchestra at Roseland in New York City. His careful attention to little details in playing to obtain the best results placed him in the front ranks.

He is well known in and around Boston, having held down some of the principal jobs in that locality. Completely Leedy equipped.

Don't Lay Down

It is sometimes impossible to "play the spots" and avoid hitting the triangle with the drum stick, but a drummer who forms the habit of doing so all the time is just downright lazy. It sure sounds "punk" and is very noticeable. The lazy drummer is cheating himself most of all.

How many drummers would be mute if they were forbidden to speak well of themselves and evil of others?

SPECIAL NOTICE

Mr. U. G. Leedy wishes to call special attention to malicious and false reports which are being circulated, intending to imply that outside interests now control The Leedy Manufacturing Company.

We have information that these false reports originated with one of our competitors and that same is being used as propaganda in hopes of damaging our business.

We emphatically deny such reports and want all to know that it is absolutely nothing but propaganda of the low, yellow variety.

(Signed) U. G. Leedy

LEEDY MANUFACTURING COMPANY.

For Drummers Who Care   Leedy   Leedy Equipment Leads Them All

The Exclusive Drummers' Paper

The Jazz King and His Drummer

This photo shows a combination of three that cannot be beat—Paul Whiteman, Geo. W. Marsh and a Classic Leedy Outfit. Mr. Whiteman is as loud in his praise of Leedy equipment from a musical standpoint as Mr. Marsh is from both a musical and drummer's standpoint.

The Leedy Manufacturing Company is indeed proud to have its instruments praised and used by Mr. Marsh, as it is a known fact in the musical world that he has gained the top of the ladder by way of ability.

Sick 'Em!

There are many kinds of leaders—among them violin leaders, piano leaders, baton leaders, and leaders who pick on drummers. The last-named kind should be "tarred and feathered."

A Mistaken Idea

Drummers who have never tucked a head on a metal flesh hoop often believe that it is a harder task than on the wood type of hoop. This is really not so, and, once they have tried it, there is no longer a question in their minds.

Guess and Win $1.00

DRUM TOPICS offers a prize of $1.00 to the drummer who can guess the name of the "calfskin pounder" shown below. The prize will be awarded to the one residing the greatest distance from Indianapolis who sends in the correct name. He is one of the best known drummers in the United States.

We could give a few hints, but any one of them regarding this "bird" would make it too easy to guess.

The name of the winner will be announced in the next issue.

He wrote the prize story entitled

"IT'S WISE TO DOUBLE THESE DAYS"

In a certain small town there is a picture show owned and managed by a gentleman whose Christian name is "Abe." Business was bad, so he decided to cut expenses by "canning" a few musicians from his five-piece symphony. Learning of this contemptible move, one of the local cornetists decided to "pull a nifty," so approached the Boob De Luxe, advising that he ought to have men in his orchestra who could double on one or more instruments.

The local manager, like 99 per cent of them, being entirely ignorant of things musical, was delighted with the suggestion and asked the cornetist on what other instrument he could double. The reply was, "Trumpet." Said cornetist was engaged on the spot and the regular cornetist and clarinet player discharged.

MORAL

Drummers, get a double—"Jew's Harp" preferred.

Have You Heard the Latest Joke?

A banjo player with a music rack.

By Ray E. Dearborn, Lewiston, Maine.

A Suggestion for Animal Effects

We hope that the drum game never comes to this—but who knows? They are expecting more of us all the time.

It's a Leedy Bass Drum

JOHN GOLL, of the Murat Theatre, one of the most prominent drummers of Indianapolis, owns a Fox Terrier dog that strays away from home occasionally. This "purp" is very much frightened by a thunder storm and always hides in the cellar, so when his owner desires his presence he takes his bass drum out into the yard and rolls on same as loudly as possible, imitating thunder; and, sure enough, "Bounce" comes home on all fours "pronto."

New Style Multi-Model

THE WORLD'S FINEST DRUM
"BUILT LIKE A WATCH"

Conscientious drummers, who demand the very best that is to be had in a snare drum, should make it a point to learn all about the latest improvements to the Leedy New Style Multi-Model. The shell is all one piece with a spun-over double flange, which acts as the inside reinforcing. Absolutely no solder is used in any part of this drum. The strongest hoops made. Self-aligning rods.

Very True

There is a difference in the tone of the various sized Bass Drums. However, a 28x14-inch Bass Drum will often have a better tone than a 30x16-inch when it is more scientifically tensioned. It is not always the larger size that counts, but rather the evenness with which the head is tensioned and the amount it is tensioned. This is a point many drummers overlook.

Leedy Tympani Model Bass Drum Rods make it a pleasure to devote more attention to your Bass Drum Heads and their tone. Better for the heads also, and they add to the appearance of the drum.

How to Improve Your Dog Bark

Don't hang the can on the wall and hold the end of the cord in the hand, pulling the cord from the can. Do it this way: Tie the end of the cord to a hook in the wall and hold the can in the left hand, pulling the cord from the wall toward the can. By this method you save the head of the Dog Bark, as the strain is entirely on the cord. Try it. Just as loud and better control.

Fred Sietz

The above photograph shows a very good likeness of one of the foremost tympanists in the whole world—Fred Sietz of the Chicago Grand Opera Company.

Mr. Sietz highly endorses the Leedy Universal Machine Tympani and states that they are in every way efficient according to claims made for them.

Mr. Sietz is the author of the best known Tympani Instructor that is published. It contains 188 pages, with many cuts showing the development of the Tympani from their origin by the Hindus to their present state. Published by the Leedy Mfg. Co.

In Siberia

MUSIC HATH CHARMS

The medicine man of Siberia finds this crude drum and bone drumstick invaluable in holding his power over the tribes. Their untutored ears are quick to perceive the rhythmical accentuation, and he leads and sways them in weird dances as he wills.

Eddie Mitchell's Orchestra

This orchestra is one of the most prominent in the State of Ohio and is now making a big hit in Columbus. "Spot" Hall, the drummer, has lately equipped himself completely with Leedy and is more than satisfied with the results.

"Spot" has had many years of experience with leading orchestras and bands all over the United States and is rated amongst those who know him as a "top notcher" in every respect.

It's Not So Easy

Some time when you are "faking" and playing a one-step at a dance or a 2/4 galop in the theatre, try to go through the entire number without making a roll of any length at all. You will find this hard to do, because when one is "faking" there is a natural tendency to "fall into" a roll. It becomes a habit, and many drummers do not realize that they roll too much, and there are many phases where a roll is not only incorrect from a musical standpoint, but it sounds bad and amateurish. Don't be one of the "when in doubt, roll" kind of drummers. Besides, the stunt mentioned above is very fine practice for "trueing up" the control of the sticks.

For Drummers Who Care Leedy Equipment Leads Them All

Leedy Drum Topics

Omaha Drummers Are Lucky to Have a Dealer Like Geo. A. Smith

The photo to the left is a very fine likeness of GEO. A. SMITH, the very live dealer at 314 South Nineteenth Street, Omaha, Neb.

Aside from being a competent business man and operating a very successful musical merchandise house, Smith is one of the ten best known drummers in the United States. He has been in the game since fifteen years of age, beginning his professional career under W. C. Dalbey, the bandmaster whose famous Fantasia on the "Old Kentucky Home" has been played on more musical programs than any other number written. For the past twenty-four years Mr. Smith has been in the orchestra at the Orpheum Theater in Omaha and has never missed but one day, an excusable absence, for that being his wedding day.

His reputation as a teacher is widely known, and he now maintains a competent staff of instructors in connection with his store.

Drummers the country over know the Geo. A. Smith's Omaha Pedal, of which he is the inventor, and there are many other drummers' accessories being used daily that are the result of his efforts.

A word in regard to his ability as a drummer must not be omitted, for not only other musicians and the best acts in vaudeville praise him, but audiences as well.

Geo. A. Smith's "Everything Musical," Omaha, Neb.

This interior view shows one of the show rooms of the Geo. A. Smith Store. It is complete in every detail and carries a full line for all musicians. Service, courtesy, and the all-important drummer's understanding are assured by drummers who deal here. Mrs. Smith is a very capable assistant in the management

of the store, and it is a fact that there are few small goods salesmen, even among the men, who understand the business in detail as thoroughly as does Mrs. Smith.

The local retail business of Geo. A. Smith is of great volume. However, Mr. Smith's understanding the mail-order trade has enabled him to draw orders from every State in the Union.

With the assistance of Geo. H. Way, Sales Manager of the Leedy Manufacturing Company, a "Drum Show" was recently held in this store, which resulted in 193 drummer visitors in one day, many of them coming from the surrounding towns at a great distance.

CHESTER HEYN is one of Omaha's most popular drummers, now playing in the million-dollar World Theatre, and has had many years' trouping experience with the big New York productions.

He made a tremendous hit with his own show, "Made in Germany," produced in France during the war.

Heyn has used Leedy for fifteen years and says, "There's a reason."

ERNIE ("Sticks") GORDON has held down the principal theatre jobs of Omaha for the past twenty years. For twenty-five years he has endorsed Leedy instruments and says he has yet to find their equal. "Sticks," as his friends call him, has a very fine reputation as an excellent vaudeville man and is now playing at the Empress Theatre.

JERRY CHAPOTON, formerly of the Orpheum in Lincoln, Neb., is now at the Rialto in Omaha with twenty-two men, under Harry Brader. Chapoton is an old trouper, thoroughly experienced in theatre work, and a mighty fine drummer. He is also a great Leedy enthusiast.

The Frank W. Hodek, Jr., Orchestra

WALTER MEYEN is the drummer with the above orchestra, and the word "genius" as an artist can surely be applied to this man. He has studied hard and is still at it. He now possesses a long contract with Mr. Frank W. Hodek, Jr. Meyen is one of the few dance men who make real use of Machine Tympani and Xylophones. All Leedy.

FRANK W. HODEK, JR., is the leader and manager of the above orchestra, now playing at the Roseland Gardens in Omaha. Formerly of Baltimore, and is also a thorough musician and concert pianist, having studied in Prague. Clever and novel arrangements have brought this orchestra far in advance of many, and they are now making high-class phonograph records.

Randall's Royal Orchestra

HARRY HAGEL was for four years at the Rialto Theatre. Now with the above orchestra. He is the proper man for this very elite engagement, playing at the Brandeis Store Restaurant.

Hagel's originality and effects bring much comment from professional musicians as well as patrons, and it is indeed a pleasure to listen to his work.

He states that the new Multi-Model Drum is the finest of many instruments he has owned.

CLYDE MICHAELIS is one of the busiest and most popular jobbing drummers in Omaha. He recently equipped himself with a $400.00 Leedy Gold Set of Drums and Marimba. Clyde is an able drummer in every respect and also realizes that an elaborate display of instruments has a commercial value in the profession.

In the Omaha School

Under sponsorship of the Rotary Club, fifteen drum corps of from forty to sixty students each have been formed. Geo. A. Smith is the chairman and chief director of the undertaking, which has been very successful. All the drummers shown on this page, with many more of Omaha's professional men, have been engaged to instruct these corps weekly. Leedy equipment has been adopted throughout.

For Drummers Who Care  Leedy Equipment Leads Them All

The Exclusive Drummers' Paper

Popular Personalities of Our Profession

ED. W. LOWE has been for many years the "act saver" in the principal Keith houses of New York. At present in the world's leading vaudeville house, the Palace. Enough said, as this job must have the best. Leedy always.

H. C. BEDLINGTON is now on the Orpheum Circuit with the Yerkes Flotilla Orchestra. Harry has told the Leedy Mfg. Co. that his work has been greatly improved and made easier since adopting Leedy instruments entirely. As a drummer he is exceptionally clever.

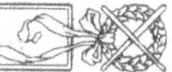
HARRY GOLDSTEIN is one of the foremost drummers and tympanists of the whole country. He plays at the Allen Theatre and with Spitallany's Orchestra of Cleveland, Ohio. He is a devoted Leedy enthusiast. In addition to this, Harry is a most likeable fellow.

ROBT. REX WARRINER, formerly of the New York Commodore Band and Loew's State Theatre, is now located at Altoona, Pa. He is one of the old-school drummers, thorough in every detail, and a real musician. He advises all drummers to equip with Leedy.

EMILE KAZELOWSKY, an "old-timer," has been in the U. S. thirty-five years. Formerly tympanist of the Royal Opera in Berlin. Now at Palace Theatre, Superior, Wis. "Casey," as he is called by his friends, is a legitimate drummer, second to none. Completely Leedy.

JOS. E. HUFFMAN is playing with and is manager of the Kentucky Kernels, now at the Hotel Adelphia in Philadelphia. Huffman uses a complete Leedy Classic Outfit. This is some high-class job and only a man of Huffman's calibre could fill it.

WALTER SHEPHERD, now at the Star Theatre, Hannibal, Mo., is a pupil of Ben Vitto of the St. Louis Symphony Orchestra.
Shepherd is a conscientious drummer who continues his studies and is bound to reach the topmost rung. He has used Leedy equipment, always.

LARRY DALY is enthusiastic over Leedy drums. He is connected with the Orvis Music House in Missoula, Mont., and plays with the Orvis Society Orchestra. Daly is a real drummer; in fact, one of the leaders in the dance field.

BILL DREW is now at the Newman Theatre, Kansas City. Bill is an "old-timer" and has played on every important job in K. C. He is rated as one of the country's leading drummers and says that the Leedy Universal Machine Tympani are wonderful.

BENJ. S. SEAMAN is one of the fastest burlesque drummers and has been ten years at the Folly Theatre, Baltimore, Md. He boosts Leedy as the only instruments for his class of work. Seaman and the Folly Orchestra are noted in the burlesque world.

O. RICH, formerly of Chicago, Ill., now has his own orchestra on the road, cleaning up in the dance game in Nebraska and Iowa. He is also an experienced theatre man and highly endorses the Leedy Machine Tympani and Marimba.

S. V. ROSENTAUB of Brighton Beach, Brooklyn, N. Y., is a very efficient dance drummer, even though he does not devote his entire time to it, being connected with the Thomas A. Edison Company. He says Leedy drums are best for dance work.

JAMES HAWKES, JR., of the Hector Orchestra at the St. James Theatre, Boston, Mass., is the chief asset of this organization. He is Leedy equipped and has an exceptionally large class of pupils, being one of Boston's best known instructors.

WM. R. STOLZ is a drummer of twelve years' experience and carries on an extensive musical instrument business in New Brunswick, N. J. He is a theatre man of the highest order, using no other than Leedy instruments throughout; also a very fine tympanist.

FRANK P. KENNEDY has just finished a tour of the U. S. with the Royal Northwest Mounted Police Band of Edmonton, Alberta, Canada. He is a very efficient drummer in all branches of work and uses none other than Leedy.

W. F. FISCHER has an outfit of Classic Leedy Drums valued at $900.00. He says he would use no other make. He is now playing with the Arcadia Orchestra in Cumberland, Md., an organization in the top-notch class. Fischer is a top-notch drummer as well.

L. L. ALLEN of Pueblo, Col., is one of that city's leading drummers. He has equipped the Shrine Drum Corps completely with Leedy field drums and is also its instructor. Allen is a very popular boy amongst the musicians of Pueblo.

NAT COOK, with the Jos. C. Smith Orchestra, Mount Royal Hotel, Montreal, Que., is a drummer of great prominence and ability. This orchestra is booked for the Grafton Galleries, London. Cook uses a Leedy Multi-Model Drum and writes that it is wonderful.

W. H. WRIGHT is one of the most prominent colored drummers in the business, now with Prof. Cox's Jazz Band at Saratoga Springs. Wright is a whole show in himself and "Speed" is his middle name. A sincere Leedy booster.

E. F. SHUE is the director and manager of the "Symphony Dancemen," Lancaster, Pa. This orchestra enjoys a wonderful reputation, due to Shue's ability as a drummer and business man. His entire outfit is Leedy and he praises their fine qualities.

AL. MORRIS and his Leighton Cafeteria Orchestra is located in San Francisco. It's the largest cafeteria in the city, and Al is both manager and drummer of the orchestra. He likes Leedy equipment best and is one of the finest drummers on the coast.

D. N. ROSENBERG states that Leedy drums are "supreme of all." Rosenberg formerly played on the Century Roof in New York. He recently toured the Orpheum Circuit with a leading dancing act. He is an all-'round, thorough, high-class drummer.

JACOB NEFF of the McNair Theatre, St. Louis, is a xylophonist of great prominence. After trying all makes of xylophones, he likes the Leedy best, especially for its tone. Neff has had years of experience in the theatre field and enjoys a fine reputation.

CLEOTUS CLOBES is an excellent drummer, full of "pep" and original ideas. He has his own orchestra, doing a good bulk of the work in Bloomington, Ill. Leedy drums are his choice, and he states that the Multi-Model is the finest drum ever built.

BOYS WHO ARE KNOWN AMONG THE FINEST

For Drummers Who Care   leedy   Leedy Equipment Leads Them All

Leedy Drum Topics

LEEDY DRUM TOPICS

A PAPER DEVOTED TO
THE INTERESTS OF THE DRUMMER

No subscription fee.

Advertisements accepted.

Published quarterly at 1033 East Palmer Street,
Indianapolis, Indiana.

Editor..................Geo. H. Way
Business Manager..........A. W. Kuerst

The Editors TOPIC TALK

A short time ago I had some business to talk over with a leading drummer in one of the Orpheum houses in the Middle West. It was necessary to go to the theatre to "catch my man," so I decided it would be well to "catch the show" at the same time.

I had a very pleasant chat with him, and just before going into the pit he apologized at great length for the way his drums sounded, saying that, owing to being busy on the outside, he had not gone over them for some time, and made it quite clear that they "just sounded rotten"; in fact, he was ashamed for me to hear them that night. I told him not to worry; that I was not there to criticize, and fully understood how certain things do happen around theatres.

Upon agreeing to meet after the show, he went to his "corner" and I to the front of the house.

Knowing my man, I felt he was conscientious in his statements, and really expected to hear some "sluggish" drums. However, such was not the case, and it was a real surprise, for in my opinion a better balanced and sounding set of drums never existed. There being a drum solo in the opening number, it was a fine opportunity to judge.

When we met after the show and the matter was discussed, it took quite a little explaining on my part to convince him that his instruments did sound "O. K." from the auditorium, because he was under the impression that I was trying to be nice.

Percussion instruments especially sound a great deal different to the listener than to the player. Many drummers forget they are playing for an audience and not for themselves, and judge the tone of their drums wholly by the way they sound to them. I have heard drummers say that their snare drum sounded just fine and to the listener at a distance it was very poor. It is a good plan, when possible, to have another drummer play on your drums, so that you can judge what they sound like from the listener's standpoint. Actors and actresses are always instructed to "make up" for the people in the last row of the house.

So, don't always judge the tone of your instruments, especially the bass and snare drum, wholly by the way they sound to you, without taking your audience into consideration.

If you are the kind of a fellow who thinks any old outfit will do, just wait until you take a job where the man before you has used the real goods.

Desire no success that is not procured by giving the highest service at your command.

Small circular skin drums are used with singing during gambling games by the Indians.

"Sleeping here is a drummer named Hugh,
Who neglected the wheel while kissing
dear Lou."

Leedy Tom-a-Phones

Many drummers are now using this very practical trap for dance work. They are not too heavy to carry around, their total weight being fourteen pounds, and as the stand folds up and the Tom-a-Phones fit neatly together, they are not bulky.

In reality they are four-tuned Baby Tympani—an exclusive Leedy achievement—called Tom-a-Phones. They have a big tone that is equal to any Chinese Tom-Tom of the same size.

If it is true novelty in flash you are looking for, this is IT—right up-to-date. Jazz effects obtainable on these instruments are impossible to describe on paper. Try a set and you will never be without them. Your leader and the dancers will compliment you on having something DIFFERENT.

They have a real big Tom-Tom tone and can be tuned to any pitch by turning the thumb-screws. NO KEY NEEDED.

A New Leedy Jazz Stick

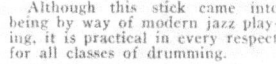

Although this stick came into being by way of modern jazz playing, it is practical in every respect for all classes of drumming.

The weight of wood that is removed from the butt end of the stick is replaced by the amount of felt attached; therefore, they are perfectly balanced. The ball is of solid medium texture of felt and not of a material that will beat flat. It is fine for quick changing to Tom-Tom, Bass Drum, Cow Bells, Wood Blocks, etc., by simply passing the sticks into the opposite hands.

You Can Often Prevent

A Chinese Wood Block from checking on the ends and chipping on the top by giving it a coat of shellac every couple months.

These blocks are seriously affected by the climate of the U. S., which is so different from that of China, where they are made.

The shellac helps to keep them from the action of the atmosphere and will preserve the block up for appearance.

FOR SALE

Genuine Mah-Jongg Sets with instructions; $2.35 complete, postpaid. MARVIN SALLIE, General Delivery, Halstead, Kansas.

Drummers, send in your stories. Ten dollars for the best one before June 15th.

In Canada—Bert Limerick

The Goodsell-Colosimo Dance Orchestra, of which Bert Limerick is the drummer, is located at Fort William, Ont., where the temperature reaches 90 degrees in the summer and 35 degrees in the winter.

Bert is Leedy equipped and claims that he has never owned a snare drum that stood up as well in these changes of temperature as his new Multi-Model.

Aside from the reputation of the orchestra, this drummer enjoys an equal popularity, owing to his efficiency.

At Times Drummers Can Keep Quiet

"Daughter, dear, who was the escort who brought you home so very late last night?"
"Why, mother, it was the drummer at the dance. Did the noise disturb you?"
"No, the silence."

"Cheek to cheek, and no movement protested;
Without the music they'd all be arrested."
—"Whiz Bang."

Be sure that you have a copy of the Leedy Catalogue "M."

Hank, the jazz drummer, says when he marries, the wife must have enough sense of rhythm to keep a strict tempo on a washboard.

Some Slap Stick!

This slap stick is louder because it has a larger striking surface and is more scientifically constructed than the old models. The popularity of the slap stick is increasing every day, as there are many effects obtained with it that can be accomplished in no other way. It is strongly built and well balanced, which enables great speed.

Serge Fockler's Ramblers

This orchestra, of which Serge Fockler is the drummer and manager, is the leading dance organization of the Lima (Ohio) district.

Fockler was a former first-rate theatre man, and the same can be said of him now that he has entered the dance business.

Special arrangements which include novel drum effects, and the businesslike way in which Fockler conducts the management of this orchestra, are the reasons for its wonderful success.

Ordinary adhesive tape is excellent for patching drum heads.

For Drummers Who Care *Leedy Equipment Leads Them All*

The Exclusive Drummers' Paper

Ask the Famous Drummers of These Famous Orchestras About Leedy

Henry Santry and His Band

This organization is now "topping the bills" of both Orpheum and Keith's Circuits, being at present on the Pacific Coast. Mr. Fail of St. Louis is the "cracker-jack" drummer of this band and is a legitimate as well as a jazz artist. It is certainly very interesting to watch this boy work, on account of his exceptional speed and skill. Both he and Mr. Santry approve of Leedy drums as a great asset to the orchestra.

Kin Brooks Symphonated Orchestra

This orchestra is located at Hull, England, and plays in the largest dance hall in the city. A. Burton Hobson, the drummer, is among the best of the dance men in England and uses Leedy products throughout his entire outfit. Hobson is very thorough in his technique and original.

It might be interesting to American drummers to know that the Rudimental School of playing originated in England.

Clyde Doerr's Orchestra

The famous Clyde Doerr Orchestra is still the big drawing card at the Congress Hotel in Chicago. Frank Worman is the very capable drummer, having many novel and original ideas that play a big part in the success of this orchestra. For many years he was one of the popular drummers on the Pacific Coast.

Mr. Worman says he has tried all makes of drums and accessories, but has obtained the desired results only from those that bear the Leedy trade mark.

Loew's Grand Vaudeville Orchestra

Atlanta, Ga., enjoys the reputation of having one of the finest vaudeville orchestras in the country, whose conductor is Floyd Bemis and whose drummer is C. E. Tatspaugh, formerly of Louisville, Ky. Tatspaugh has a reputation throughout the entire South. He is of the old school, having been in the game a good many years, and keeps his Leedy equipment right up to date. Acts who have played this house speak loud of his ability.

Zemsay's Plaza Orchestra

Edward Frank, the drummer of this orchestra, is among the best known of the profession in Philadelphia, both in a personal and artistic way. He has had many years of experience and his devoted ambition to his work has gained this prominence.

Al Zemsay, director of the orchestra, has given the Leedy Mfg. Co. a very glowing testimonial on the fact that Mr. Frank has equipped himself with Leedy instruments throughout and that the tonal qualities and blending of the music have been improved as never before.

Jonny DeDroit's Orchestra

Paul DeDroit, a drummer of several years' experience, plays with this organization at Colb's Cafe on St. Charles Street in New Orleans, La. He is one of the strongest Leedy enthusiasts amongst the Southern drummers and has used Leedy drums and tympani since he began professional playing, although he has tried out many other makes, always returning to what he terms "the most reliable."

DeDroit is progressive in every sense of the word and is looked upon by all members of the profession as a very efficient drummer.

THESE DRUMMERS INSIST ON LEEDY—THE WORLD'S BEST

For Drummers Who Care  *Leedy Equipment Leads Them All*

Leedy
DRUM TOPICS
The Exclusive Drummers' Paper
APRIL EDITION

John C. Robinson,
3158 E. Fall Creek Blvd.,
Indianapolis, Ind.

POSTMASTER—Return Postage Guaranteed

LEEDY MANUFACTURING CO.
INDIANAPOLIS, INDIANA

Listen Now To The Story Of The Drummer With The Close Roll

HOW HEEDLESS HAROLD HANDICAPPED HIMSELF

There was once a Trap Drummer who lived in the Me-trop-o-lis. This bird had learned to drum as a Business Proposition, because he had been told that Good Drummers were never Out-of-a-Job. So he worked very hard and developed a Close Roll.

In the fullness of Time he lit in a Classy Cafe where the orchestra was the Main Feature. His Work was the hottest Stuff, but he was Great at Funny Stuff. He was even prepared to drum on the cornet player's Bald Head, if necessary, to show the customers a Good Time.

"What is this?" inquired the Big Squeeze, "a Show Troupe?" "Part of my Truck," said the Fly Guy. "If I land with you I will bring over the other Two Loads."

"Your taxi bill must run into Money," said the Big Boss.

"I travel in my own little Fierce-Barrow," replied the F.G. "I am neither Proud nor Haughty. An American vehicle does very well for me."

As he had Previously Intimated, HE HAD THE OUTFIT. There were tom-toms and tam-toms and tim-toms, harpaphones, xylophones, marimbaphones and other phones. He had one bushel of jazz sticks, jazz mallets, jazz cymbals and jazz whistles. He had imitations ranging from the ravishing cry of the Bulgarian Dickcissel and the Fillyloo Bird to the raucous love note of the wild Peruvian Cat-a-swamps. Also a couple of drums to be used in case of Emergency.

* * *

We will pass over the Cat-a-clysm that accompanied the Opening Trot. Very little, if any, of what the Outsider had predicted failed to happen. Did he mop up? We'll say he did! It was a Riot.

"As soon as the Boss caught his Breath, he eased over to Nail it Down.

"How much?" he inquired with a Sigh of Resignation.

"Fifty fish," chirped Our Hero.
"Per week?"
"Don't kid me, brother," said Little Wilbur: "the Tariff is charged by the night. I need the jack to Buy Gasoline."

Heedless Harold Himself

There were a couple of Home-made Repairs on his snare head, and where his drum cord had busted he had tied it with neat Square Knots. His pedal was also Doctored with Rubber Bands. He had a Cuckoo Whistle, but it was on the Fritz.

Occasionally he saw some new Contraption in a Music Store that he wanted, but Prices-Were-So-High-Since-the-War that he Sternly Repressed his Extravagant Desires and consoled himself with the Thought that a Good Drummer with-a-Close-Roll could Get By on very little.

At that, he was Thinking of Putting in a Novelty. It was an awing to a Flock of Bottles tuned to chromatic scale, owing to a well-known Amendment he had only collected Three out of the necessary Thirteen.

About the time when he was Going Good, and Putting Away the Berries, a Fly Guy from the Outside car-a-jolt-ed himself into the Me-trop-o-lis. He claimed he was a Mean Jazz Artist, and Rough, Very Rough.

He Horned into the Classy Cafe and inquired for the Big Boss.

"I am a Jazz Drummer," he casually remarked, "from Jazzville and Points West. I crave Employment, and it is No Trouble to Show Goods."

"This is indeed Opportune," said the B. B. "My Regular Drummer, who has been with me for Years, is off tomorrow to attend a Wedding. You can substitute for him. Have you a Close Roll?"

"I always have a Roll," was the Neat Rejoinder, "but I am not Close with it. Easy Come, Easy Go with me. You have to Spend it to Make it."

"I suppose you have an Outfit?" interrogated the B. B.

"I should so inform the Flat Footed Universe," was the Come-Back. "I have Everything there is and then Some. Out in My Country the best ain't hardly Good Enough."

An hour before Time-to-go-on-watch, our Fresh Little Aspirant pulled up in front of the Palace of Terpsi-chor-can and Gas-tro-nom-ic Delight in a morose looking Petrol-Annihilator loaded with Trunks.

The Fly Guy in All His Glory

On the morrow, when the Nice boy with the Close Roll showed back, he found the alley leading to his Accustomed Place blocked by a set of Tuned Cow Bells and the Wind Machine.

"How come?" he inquired.

"My boy," said the Boss, "it now becomes my Painful Duty to present you with what is technically known as the Gate. I hate it, but it is a case of Cold Turkey with me. I needed this Rough Drummer and I grabbed him."

"But these birds from the Sticks can't drum. They never have a Close Roll," wailed the Previous Incumbent.

"As to that, Harold, I am quite uninformed. But our Customers sure think he can. And while his Roll may not be Close, it is Healthy."

* * *

Unto the drummer that hath, shall be given the swell engagement.

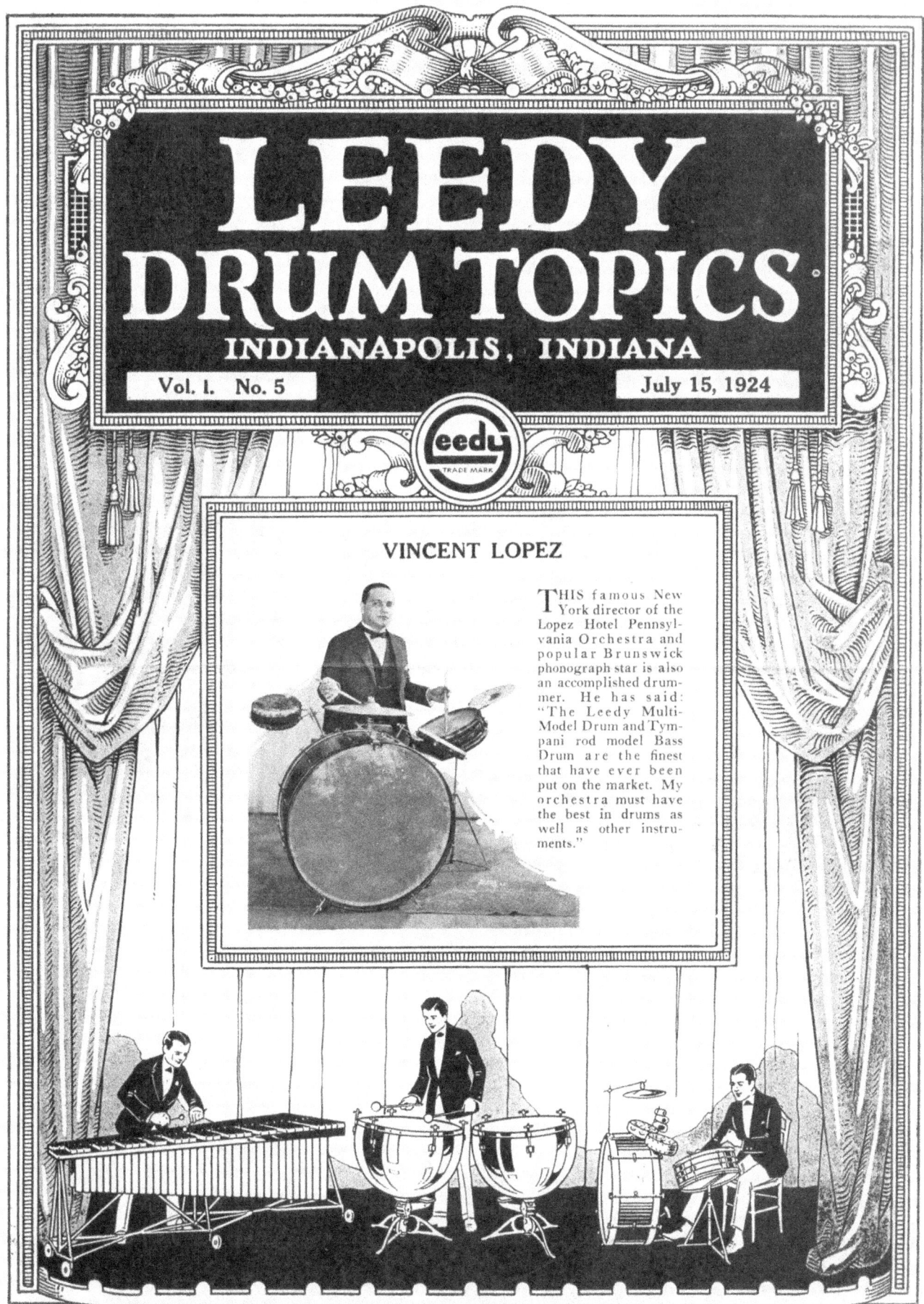

Leedy Drum Topics Issue 5

Leedy Drum Topics

Reaching for the Best

DO YOU REMEMBER, back when you were a kid, how a little boost from another boy helped when you were trying to reach the reddest, juiciest apples that always hung high in the tree where the sun hit them? There were always green apples within easy reach, but you had to climb for the rosy-cheeked fruit to satisfy youthful craving.

NOW THAT you're a man, earnestly interested in getting some place in the drumming profession, you find life a good deal the same way.

DO YOU REMEMBER when you first became interested in drums? When the whole subject seemed like an Arabian Night's mystery? When you read every catalog you could find and asked question after question, seeking information? You surely are no less interested in drums now than you were then. The only change is that you have progressed. You have moved from the green apples at the bottom to the red ones at the top. And that's where you need Leedy help and co-operation—a friendly boost!

IN ADDITION to helping produce all the important developments in the drum industry itself, Leedy helps keep you posted in your own profession through DRUM TOPICS in a manner you can't get anywhere else. (You cannot find any "tips" or "hints" regarding the care and use of your instruments in any instruction book or publication.) Every issue is filled with news items that are interesting and entertaining to all drummers—also practical information that will help you be a better drummer and make more money.

WE WANT to help you "get to the top" in every way possible, so boost DRUM TOPICS because it boosts you and your profession.

Don't Do It

Don't loosen the snares of your drum (either orchestra, band or drum corps models) after you have finished a job. Leave them at a tension—even a little more than the playing strain—and you will have an easier playing and better sounding instrument the next time you use it. Note that the best professional theatre drummers never throw off their snares after a show, nor violin and cello players let out their strings after work.

Keep your snares taught.

W. D. Kiefer

W. D. Kiefer, or just plain "Bill" as he would rather be called, has been in charge of the drum section of the Washington Marine Band under the leadership of Lieutenant Santelmann for the past ten years. "Bill" hails from Lancaster, Pa., and in addition to his long service in the "President's Own" he has had many years' theatrical and concert experience. Any drummer who has heard him play and watched his work knows that he ranks second to none as an artistic exponent of rudimental drumming.

The Leedy Mfg. Co. was more than pleased to have "Bill" spend a day at the factory during the Grotto convention week in Indianapolis, where he put in several hours examining the improved Universal Machine Tympani.

One of his frequent statements is, "My instruments must be Leedy."

"He who learns his instruments the wrong way must make his journey twice."

The New Style Multi-Model

THE WORLD'S FINEST DRUM
"BUILT LIKE A WATCH"
NOTE THE NEW "PRESTO" STRAINER

The New "Elite" Multi-Model

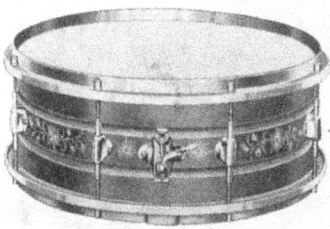

Here is a new finish of the Multi-Model Drum just added to our Full Dress Line. The shell is in gleaming black nickel, and the rods, hoops, strainer and engraving are in Nobby gold. The most beautiful drum designed at such a reasonable price.

Leedy drums are the heart-beats of music.

If many of the architects who plan theatre pits knew what drummers think of them, they would turn gray over night.

Tell your drummer friends about LEEDY DRUM TOPICS.

THEM DAYS ARE GONE FOREVER

Not long ago when on parade we used to "kick 'em"; now we "skid in Polarine."

Albert Ritter

In last October's issue of DRUM TOPICS we published a photo of Mr. Ritter of the Boston Symphony Orchestra, but it did not show his instruments. The one above shows the instruments and Mr. Ritter in a playing position.

Until he joined the Boston Symphony Orchestra Mr. Ritter was one of Germany's most prominent artists on Tympani. Shortly after coming to America he adopted the Leedy Universal Machine Tympani, and he has written the Leedy Mfg. Co. several times pointing out their superiority to all makes, both European and American.

Bass Drum Tension

Drummers will devote endless thought to the proper tension of their snare drum and their tympani, but it is surprising to note the number of very fine men who neglect to properly tension their bass drum. The reason for this is not known, unless it is because of the fact that it requires a little effort to get at the thumb-screws of the bass drum. If it is important that the snare drum and tympani are properly tensioned, it is equally so in the matter of the "bull drum." Drummers have been known to condemn a certain bass drum and try out many different kinds of beater balls and pedals when they could get the exact tone desired by treating the instrument in the same manner that they do a tympani head, which, when all is said and done, consists of evening up the head so that the tone is as near the same at all points as is possible.

One of the reasons that the Leedy Bass Drum is famous for its tone is because of the accuracy with which it is made. This makes it easier to tension more perfectly, because the counter and flesh hoops do not bind on the shell.

For Drummers Who Care *Leedy Equipment Leads Them All*

The Exclusive Drummers' Paper

In Egypt

The above picture is not one of olden times, but rather right up to date, and shows the kettle drummer of Egypt ready for full dress parade. Although the drums are really an old-time model of our present-day Tympani in the sizes of 22, 24 and 26 inches, they are noted for their volume of tone. They are used in the manner pictured above for carnivals, festivals, and in the army.

Friscoe

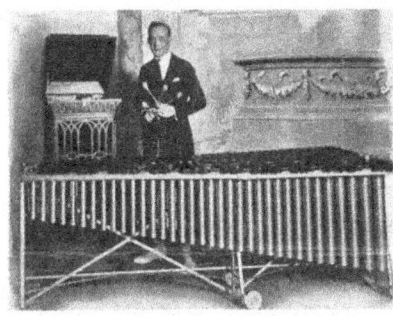

This Xylophone artist needs very little introduction, as his years of success on the Orpheum time and recording for the Edison Phonograph Company have made him one of the very best known Xylophonists of the country.

He is now preparing a gigantic act with special scenery and instruments, including eight people, to tour the Orpheum Circuit this coming fall.

The Leedy Mfg. Co. is at the present time building several special instruments for this act and is indeed proud to state that Friscoe is a sincere Leedy booster, as he has used both their Xylophones and Marimbas for the past twelve years.

Four U. S. Marine Drummers

These four Marine drummers are members of the U. S. Marine Corps stationed at Paris Island, North Carolina. A note to the editor of DRUM TOPICS states: "We are Leedy equipped and well satisfied."

The boys are, reading from left to right: Henry Gauthier, Salem, Mass.; William Hamel, Salem, Mass.; Joseph Ronlett, New York City, and Robert E. Braden, Akron, Ohio.

TOO LATE

HE: "Just one more kiss, dear."
SHE: "No. The last car passes here at 12 and it's 11 already."

There Are Others Just as Good

Did you ever notice that after you have used a crash cymbal, triangle, or tambourine for a year or more, that you get so accustomed to its particular tone no other suits you? If you have used a cymbal for a long period and break it, what a time you have finding another that seems to have as good a tone. It works on your nerves every time you use it.

Often a drummer will state that he has the best crash cymbal in his part of the country when he means that he is so accustomed to its tone that he could not be satisfied with another.

Notice

The Leedy Mfg. Co. wishes to announce that they now have a plentiful stock of 12, 13, 14, 15 and 16-inch Turkish Zildjian cymbals. These are the best grade excellent tone cymbals and are equal to any produced before the war.

No two cymbals sound exactly the same pitch, owing to their variance in weight, and they can always be exchanged providing they have not been used over five days and are in perfect condition.

Did You Ever

Reach for your strap of sleigh bells to get them ready to "come in" at a certain place in a descriptive number only to have them jingle just enough to attract the attention of the whole audience—then have them "tickle, tickle" a bit more at the end of the strain as you put them back in place? Makes a fellow feel like a fish. Get a set of Leedy sleigh bells. They can be handled without this annoyance.

See page 47, Catalog "M."

Sister thought a snare strainer was a new kind of coffee-pot attachment.

DRUM TOPICS will publish News Stories and Photographs that are of interest to drummers. Send yours in.

Watch Your Left Stick

Can you do everything with the left stick that you can do with the right one? If not, why not? Drumming is not like writing, where only one hand is used. It is similar to rowing, swimming, dancing and walking—all actions in which the right and left movements should be under control equally as well.

If you play more strokes with the right stick than you do with the left stick, practice and make the left even better than the right.

The Leedy-Sietz Tympani Method contains many cuts showing the development of the Tympani from its origin. It's the only book of its kind published.

The multiplicity of high tones in the triangle makes it possible for use in any key and eliminates the necessity of having to tune it to any one note.

May He Rest in Peace
By E. L. HENNING, San Antonio, Texas

Once upon a time there was—
You surely ought to know it—
A drummer filled with "ambish,"
Who always tried to show it.
He put stuff into every act,
Made new effects to help along.
He'd use nineteen different traps
In a "punk" little "shoofly" song.
He worried and stewed all the day,
At night he could not rest.
His nerves gave 'way, he went above—
Perhaps it's for the BEST.

Warner's Seven Aces

M. C. Park is the unusually fine drummer with Warner's Seven Aces at Atlanta, Ga. This orchestra is the premier society dance organization of Atlanta and enjoys the reputation of being one of the best sellers in the Okeh phonograph record catalog.

Park uses Leedy products, featuring chimes and tympani. After ten years of varied professional experience and having tried all makes of drummers' equipment, he recommends Leedy to all drummers.

THERE'S ONE IN EVERY ORCHESTRA

"Say, Bill, lend me two bucks till Saturday."

J. J. Heney

The Ringling Brothers and Barnum & Bailey Shows now have J. J. Heney at the head of the drum section of their band. Heney is shown above with his 12x15-inch Separate Tension Multi-Model Drum ready for the big parade. He states that he has never owned a drum in his entire circus career which had the volume and snap necessary to carry to the farthermost parts of the "big top" as satisfactorily as his present Multi-Model.

Last season Heney was with the Hagenbeck-Wallace Shows, and the season before with Sells-Floto. He is from San Francisco and enjoys the reputation of being one of the best circus drummers who ever rode ahead of the elephants.

There's many a night elevator boy who makes more hush money than his salary.

FOR SALE

Complete dance drum outfit. For particulars write EDMUND GEHRKE, Willow Lake, S. D.

FOR SALE

Fine bass drum, 12x24 inches, eight thumb-screw rods; needs one head. Price $10.00. DICK TIFFT, Ethan, S. D.

The Green Brothers Xylophone Method is now published by the Leedy Mfg. Co. at a considerable reduction of its former price.

For Drummers Who Care Leedy Equipment Leads Them All

Leedy Drum Topics

Popular Personalities of Our Profession

EARL GORE is one of the crack drummers in the vaudeville game, being located in the Majestic Theatre, Springfield, Illinois. He has a large class of pupils and recommends Leedy instruments as the best to be obtained.

WHO WILL WIN THE PRIZE for the best story in the next issue of DRUM TOPICS? It is an easy way to pick up $10.00.

Send yours in before October 1, 1924.

WILLIAM CARDGAN is the manager and drummer of the Scranton Symphonators, one of the most popular dance orchestras in Pennsylvania. Cardgan has had many years' experience and has made a wonderful success with his present orchestra.

MAX WINTRICH, who is in charge of the drum section of the Chicago Symphony Orchestra, has been with that organization for twenty-five years. He is fully Leedy equipped and recommends the Multi-Model to all drummers.

Suppose you owned a men's furnishing store and for some reason or other you moved your business to another part of town. Wouldn't you notify all your customers and firms with whom you dealt of your change of address? Right! Well, isn't drumming a form of business—your business? Let us know when you move.

JOE McKOWN is the leader of one of the best known orchestras in vaudeville. He always insists that his drummer is fully equipped with Leedy instruments. His orchestra is now on the Butterfield Circuit in Michigan.

MEYER SIBULSKY, of the Tivoli Theatre, Newark, N. J., is one of the leading drummers in that section of the country and one of the boys who takes his profession seriously. He claims that Leedy instruments are the only kind that give him entire satisfaction.

SERGE FOCKLER is at present with a very prominent orchestra at one of the leading Michigan resorts. This drummer is known throughout the Middle West States as one of the best "pig-skin fiddlers." His home is in Lima, Ohio. Fockler is all Leedy.

RALPH HENDERSHOTT has been at the leading vaudeville house in Madison, Wis., during the past winter. Everyone in the "trouping" game knows "Scrubby," as he has spent twenty years with the best and the worst and has a wonderful reputation second to none. He is a Leedy enthusiast.

A boy came sneaking in about 12:00 o'clock one night with his coupe seat under his arm. His father happened to be up and asked him what the h—— was wrong.

The boy answered: "Someone stole my Ford."

HELEN CHARNOCK, of Wheeling, W. Va., is one of the most talented lady Xylophonists in the country. After having used several makes she declares Leedy to be her choice. At present she is doing the better class of work in and around Wheeling.

JOHN McKNIGHT is one of the old-school New York drummers and is now at the Crotona Theatre in the Bronx. "Mac" is a very snappy vaudeville man, having gotten his early training at Coney Island. He says, "Leedy without exception."

DRUM TOPICS would like to have a full column devoted to the Canadian drummer in each issue, so if you boys in the North will send in photographs and material we will be glad to give you a column of your own.

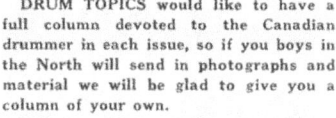
BILL WARD is the very "classy" dance drummer with the Buzz Rundio Orchestra at the Athletic Club, Columbus, O. Ward was fully equipped with Leedy drums by the Otto B. Heaton Company, Columbus, and states he is thoroughly satisfied.

WALTER KOLK is one of the youngest but most prominent of the Baltimore (Md.) drummers. He has been a Leedy enthusiast from the start and is now playing with the Folly Orchestra. Kolk is a hard worker and bound to reach the topmost rung.

R. W. FLETCHER is an old-time Leedy booster and has for years managed the famous Mounted Cow Boys' Roundup Band at Pendleton, Oregon. He also manages and plays with the Fletcher Jazz Band, a family of entertainers, who are very popular throughout the Northwest.

TOMMY HAWKINS, formerly of the Boston Opera and for many years at the Orpheum Theatre, is without doubt among the very best of the vaudeville drummers. Many of the present-day jazz beats and juggling stunts were originated by Tommy.

If you have an idea for a new drummers' accessory, send it in with full details. If the Leedy Mfg. Co. finds use for it an agreeable settlement will be made with you before it is marketed.

WILLIAM JACKSON, of the Lammer's Military Band School, Ogden, Utah, is now on tour, using a set of Leedy Machine Tympani with the "Band from the West" under the management of Hyrum Lammers, formerly with Sousa. Jackson is a very wonderful drummer.

HOWARD KOPP is back again for the summer season with the Goldman Band of New York, which is fully Leedy equipped. Kopp is as well known as any drummer in New York and is a real musician.

Many drummers have sent in good material for DRUM TOPICS, but owing to our limited space we cannot use it all. However, we want to heartily thank you for your efforts and assure you that the best material will be published in its turn as soon as it is possible to do so.

LYNN DAVIS, of St. Louis, Mo., does only the better class of work in the dance field. He is noted for original and progressive ideas and never fails to keep up to date with his Leedy equipment.

HAROLD F. SAULT is the manager of Sault's Orchestra, St. Albans, Vt., an organization which is a leader in this State. He is a legitimate as well as a jazz artist; therefore, is kept busy the year 'round. Entirely Leedy.

SINON D. COLLINS supplies bands and orchestras in and about Leavenworth, Kansas. He is an expert drummer as well as vaudeville performer and at present has his own show on the road. Collins says there is no drum like the new style Leedy Multi-Model.

For Drummers Who Care  Leedy Equipment Leads Them All

The Exclusive Drummers' Paper

LEEDY DRUM TOPICS

A PAPER DEVOTED TO
THE INTERESTS OF THE DRUMMER

No subscription fee.

Advertisements accepted.

Published quarterly at 1033 East Palmer Street, Indianapolis, Indiana.

Editor..................................GEO. H. WAY
Business Manager..................A. W. KUERST

Don't Sleep Mornings

Although drummers' working hours always come at a time when other folks are at recreation, the actual number of hours that he puts in is less than those of most any other profession that pays equally as well. Therefore there really is an opportunity for the average drummer to make some money doing other things, provided he does not sleep mornings. There are very few drummers who are not interested in making more money, and there are many ways of doing so, but the writer believes that the following suggestion is about as profitable as any, because it concerns drums, etc., and should make a desirable side line.

In the old days there were many drummers acting as agents for the various manufacturers, but since the local music stores have placed large stocks of drums in their establishments times have changed. Naturally these stores object to the drummer factory agent, because they (the stores) carry an overhead of rent, light, heat, help and advertising, whereas the agent has none of these expenses. A drummer agent is able to reach a fair share of the professional business, but nowadays, since so many new drummers have sprung up, he cannot reach all of them and new prospects, too. The stores can reach many more prospects than the professional drummer, because of window displays, location and advertising. However, there is no question of a doubt but that the store which has no one employed within its walls with a technical knowledge of drums does not do as much business as is possible. Many stores employ a professional drummer and in this way are sure of a greater volume of sales.

Now to come to the point of our little story. Suppose you had a connection with a leading music store in your city, in addition to your playing, acting in the capacity of salesman and manager of the drum department. Such a job can be made possible for a drummer who is willing to work in the mornings, not only in the large cities but the smaller ones as well. It is being done successfully in several localities. In some cases the drummer receives a stated salary and is on duty at the store a certain number of hours per day, usually from 9 until 1 o'clock, and in other cases he works both on the inside and out in the interests of the store, selling on a commission basis, not only drums but other instruments as well.

The writer is acquainted with one fellow who slips over the sale of a piano every once in a while by hustling around in the mornings. The first six months he was employed with the store he made more than his salary in the theatre.

Besides the remunerative advantages of such a position there is an opportunity for the drummer who has never had any business experience to pick up considerable education along this line, and who knows but what it might lead to a real fine job in the musical world?

Any good live music store will listen to such a proposition, and for the drummer who can do without his morning's "beauty sleep" this is one of the real opportunities awaiting him.

Painting Bass Drum Heads

Bass drums are indeed made more attractive for the dance or stage drummer when artistic paintings are put upon one of the heads. There is considerable difficulty in doing this work, for if lights are used inside the drum and the head is painted on the head in the same manner as an artist paints a picture, the brush marks will show when the lights are behind same; and if enough paint is employed so that brush marks do not show, the light throws this spot up as a meaningless object, because the light does not come through. Therefore, even though the job looks very nice when the lights are off, it looks very distorted when the lights are on.

The way to overcome this condition is to use the stipple method of painting, which is done by cutting the brush off straight or "bobbing" it. Then, instead of drawing or stroking the brush, it is used in the stipple or daub fashion. When the proper kind of paint is used, this makes a painting that is transparent and without brush marks, which is just as pleasing to the eye with or without the lights.

The above photograph shows a head finished in the new design called "The Silhouette." The figures show through perfectly clear, while the color inside the circle is a very dark blue and the color outside the circle is two shades lighter blue. This is, of course, a cheaper job than those where many colors and figures are employed, but it is very attractive and flashy and shows up in a striking manner even though viewed at a great distance.

Charles Siebert

**ASSISTANT SALES MANAGER
LEEDY MFG. CO.**

Charles Siebert, formerly drummer of the Orpheum Theatre, Peoria, Ill., where he has been for some time past, is now connected with the Leedy Mfg. Co. in the capacity of Assistant Sales Manager. Charley, as he is called, is one of the best known drummers in the Middle West and was at one time with the famous Innes Band. Many of his old friends will no doubt be pleased to meet him when he visits the various cities in the interest of the Leedy Mfg. Co.

Drummers will find him exceptionally good company, as he is one of the boys and a thorough professional high-grade orchestra and band man of many years' experience. Musical instrument dealers will find in him not only a thorough understanding of the drum line from the technical standpoint, but from a business standpoint as well, as he at one time operated his own retail store in Peoria.

The name of the "calfskin pounder" whose photo and prize story appeared in the last issue of DRUM TOPICS is Oliver Payne, now at the leading vaudeville house in South Bend, Ind.

DRUM TOPICS received dozens of letters (many of them correct as to the likeness of the photo). However, H. Vernon Gooding, of the Victory Theatre, Tampa, Fla., wins the prize.

Maurice R. Barnes

Road men who have played the old Boyd and Brandeis theatres in Omaha for years back are all well acquainted with this very fine and sociable old gentleman. He is one of the most popular figures in the Omaha Musical Union and is a welcome guest at many of the elite gatherings of Omaha society. Road show leaders have often spoken of him as one of the country's best drummers. Below is a letter he recently wrote to the editor of DRUM TOPICS, and we sincerely hope that Mr. Barnes will continue for many more years in his present health and vigor.

Omaha, Neb., June 17, 1924.
LEEDY DRUM TOPICS,
Indianapolis, Ind.
Dear Editor:

I am mailing to you under separate cover a photo of one of the oldest drummers outside of captivity. The "phiz" is that of a Civil War veteran who enlisted in 1861 at the age of 10 years and has "dispelled din" in Omaha theatres for 50 years and is still "raring to go"—only he is handicapped by excessive modesty. I am now 73 years young, and when I use a Leedy Street Drum "windows rattle and dogs bark."

Hoping you are the same, I am,
MAURICE R. BARNES.
*Courtesy of Geo. A. Smith's
"Everything Musical."*

The Prize Story

A true story by Geo. A. Robertson, Chicago, formerly of Innes' Band:

Mr. "G" was showing a copy of one of his latest compositions to several musician friends. The fact that the composition was written in 7/4 time caused many an inquiry as to the best method to conduct the number.

The composer said that it would have to be conducted in seven beats as follows: (1) down, (2) left, (3) right, (4) up, (5) down, (6) right, (7) up.

Then someone suggested beating a bar of four and a bar of three, and another suggested beating a bar of three and a bar of four. Finally a drummer, Mr. "D," voiced his opinion of conducting the number. An ambulance had to be called for Mr. "G" when Mr. "D" said:

"Aw! beat it one, two, three and a half; one, two, three and a half."

Leedy's New "Presto" Snare Strainer

The "Presto" strainer is designed on a new principle. Its action is toggle and it cannot pass a center straining point. Therefore all the past troubles of readjusting the snares after they have been thrown off are eliminated. The throw-off lever is in a new position, which enables the drummer to work faster. Snares will not cross or throw out of line. The "Presto" is made with the utmost care in its mechanical detail, and Leedy workmanship prevails.

For Drummers Who Care  *Leedy Equipment Leads Them All*

Leedy Drum Topics

Clem Bray's Orchestra

Mart Flynn, drummer with Clem Bray's Orchestra, uses a complete Leedy outfit and is especially pleased with his new style Multi-Model snare drum.

This orchestra recently finished a nine months' engagement at the Strand Theatre, Cumberland, Md., and is now on a tour over the Keith Circuit, where they have made a tremendous hit.

Flynn is a very capable drummer and is known among the boys as a good mixer.

A Cymbal Tip

A crash cymbal that hangs on a tilt is annoying and looks bad. It can in many cases be overcome by suspending it on a cord of either sash or clothes line that is as large in diameter as the hole in the cymbal. When the cord fills up the entire hole there is less chance of the cymbal hanging off balance.

Holes in crash cymbals are not always drilled in the exact center of the cup. This is because they are foreign made and in countries where hand work is mostly employed.

Another reason for their uneven hanging is that cymbals, both Turkish and Chinese, are cast and sometimes a little heavier on one side than the other. By turning the knot in the cord around to the heavier side the cymbal will often right itself to a level position. A large leather washer placed inside the cup will help also.

Sing It in 3-4

My Bonnie bent over the gas tank,
The height of its contents to see.
He lighted a match to assist him—
Oh, bring back my Bonnie to me!

The Rainbow Orchestra

Irving Sewitt, the accomplished drummer of the Rainbow Orchestra, also its leader, states that he believes in buying the best instruments that it is possible to obtain, and that is the reason he chooses Leedy drums and accessories.

This organization is one of the Loew Vaudeville Circuit headline attractions and is known as one of the snappiest in the East.

Have You Heard About the New Leedy Marvel Snare Strainer?

For many years drummers have desired a snare strainer that would keep the snares at the same tension whether muffled or in use. The new Leedy Marvel Strainer accomplishes this result by a most ingenious mechanical device. Write for illustrated circular giving full details.

Why Carry Two Drums?

The clarinet player would never go on a job without a few extra reeds, and a violinist always has extra strings. There are many drummers who would never think of going to work unless there was an extra head tucked on a Leedy metal flesh hoop close at hand. Many have two drums in case of a breakdown.

It is not satisfactory to carry a drum head tucked on a wooden hoop, because in dry weather the head will contract and bend the wooden hoop egg shape, making it impossible to put on the drum unless it is wet first. One of the great advantages of the Leedy metal flesh hoops is that they can be carried safely in a snare-drum case without buckling and are ready for immediate replacement.

If at some time you find yourself without an extra batter head, just try tucking two thin snare heads on one flesh hoop. You will find that this makes an ideal batter side combination to work on.

IT'S A FACT!
Mosquitoes shouldn't have children.

O. R. McLain

The drummer in this photo is O. R. McLain of Seattle, Wash. He has the reputation of being one of the very best men on the Orpheum Circuit.

This group shows four members of the Orpheum Orchestra who play in one of the leading hotels of Seattle for dinners and dances.

"Mac" is fully equipped with Leedy instruments both at the theatre and hotel.

Resonators as used with Xylophones and Marimbas transform the energy from duration to intensity.

The Ring in a Drum

The ring in a drum is never the fault of the kind of material used in the construction of the shell. It is always in the matching of the heads and the particular tension at which they are set.

Various drummers like a different "feel" under their sticks, and if this "feel" can only be gotten with a certain combination of heads at a certain tension (which is called the ringing combination) there is bound to be a ring in the drum, especially if struck off center.

If a drummer does not care to change the thickness or matching of the heads, or place them at a different tension, the ring can be eliminated in various ways. One method is to place a half-dollar on the head. Another is to place a large business card on the head. Either of these objects has a tendency to shorten the vibration of the batter head, slowing up its movement after being struck, which eliminates the ring.

No drum will ring if struck exactly in the center of the head.

Leedy Jingle Clogs

Here is a new effect that is growing in popularity every day. These sticks are far superior to the old type of wooden clog mallets, because the striking surface is a half-hard rubber ball; therefore, harshness is eliminated. Very effective when used on the wood block in novelty and Spanish numbers. The effect is somewhat similar to the combination of the tambourine and castanets. However, their use has a great deal wider scope.

For Drummers Who Care  Leedy Equipment Leads Them All

The Exclusive Drummers' Paper

Some Cartoon—Some Drummer

Jimmy Lent, Busiest Trap Drummer, In Action

When Jimmy Lent was one of the big features at the New York Hippodrome the above cartoon covered a whole page of a Sunday issue of the *New York Telegraph*. Jimmy has quit the theatre game and now operates one of the most popular society dance orchestras in New York City.

He conducts one of the largest studios in New York, using Leedy xylophones, marimbas and drums exclusively.

Joe Green

Joe has a world-famous reputation as a xylophonist; however, many of the boys do not know that he is the chief "house drummer" at the Victor Phonograph Recording Laboratories in New York in addition to his job of making many of their xylophone solo records.

Whenever you hear drum effects in standard Victor records you may know that it is Joe producing them with Leedy equipment.

Leedy Cow Bell Holder

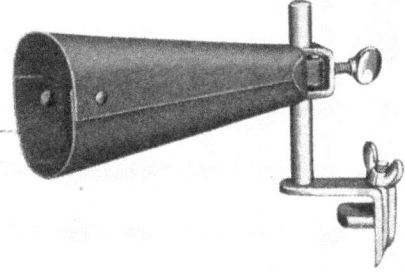

A cow bell holder that allows you to place the bells in any position. The upright is long enough to hold two bells, and the clamps can be purchased separately.

Cow bells are not passe. You will hear them on phonograph records, used with the "Two-Way" or Jazz felt sticks. Drumming on the cow bells with the drum sticks is out of date.

LEEDY DEALERS

Miss Alina Renier

The Renier Music Company, of Dubuque, Iowa, operates one of the largest music stores west of Chicago, and the musical merchandise department is in charge of Miss Alina Renier, of whom an excellent likeness is shown above. Miss Renier is an accomplished pianist and plays well on several other instruments, including drums. She is known as the most efficient woman manager of a band and orchestra department in the United States. Leedy products are one of the big features of her department.

The Musicians' Supply Company, of Erie, Pa., is operated by S. G. Anderson, a drummer of many years' experience. This firm handles Leedy exclusively and works the mails to a great advantage.

Marcellus Roper Company, of Worcester, Mass., is one of the Eastern music houses that ranks with the leaders. E. J. Delano, the manager in charge, was formerly advertising manager for the H. & A. Selmer Company, of New York, and was also a former bandmaster of the Great Lakes Naval Training Station, Chicago. Mr. Delano knows every branch of the music business and there is no better salesman in the music industry.

The Clark & Jones Company, of Knoxville, Tenn., is one of the leading music stores in this section. L. E. Miller directs the sale of brass instruments and drums and is a manager of the highest type in this business. Leedy is their exclusive drum line.

E. L. Blackburn

This well-known drummer was always interested in the selling as well as the playing game. He now operates a very fine general musical merchandise store in Lexington, Ky., and also operates branches in connection with the Russels Store Co. at Carlisle and Mt. Sterling, Ky. Blackburn was a hustling drummer and held down some of the very best jobs in various Middle West cities and he is now known as the hustling dealer in his territory.

The firm is known as the E. L. Blackburn Music Co., and the drum department is exclusively Leedy.

Harry Freiser

This well-known drummer is now on the Orpheum and Keith circuits with the Harry Stoddard Band as a headline act. Mr. Freiser is Leedy equipped throughout and high in praise of same.

Freiser's work in vaudeville is a combination of showmanship, versatility and musicianship, all of which has placed him among the leading drummers of this class.

Stoddard's Band has many popular Edison records to its credit.

Have you seen the many new circulars on new drummers' accessories that Leedy has published during the past three months? If not, write for them. They are interesting.

It Is an Easy Matter

To make a neat job of putting a new head on a tambourine. After driving home the first four tacks in the new head (which should be at opposite points on the shell) tie the head down with a length of shoe lace, making sure the lace lies flat and that the head is pulled down under same. Leave the lace tied to the shell while putting in the rest of the tacks and until the head is well dried. This will assure you a nice, smooth job when the ragged edges of the head are trimmed off with a sharp knife.

The manager of a well-known vaudeville house was asked by his orchestra leader to have the piano tuned at 4-40 and he phoned a piano tuner accordingly.

When the piano tuner came to the theatre later in the day, he met with this remark from the manager:

"Too late. My leader wanted his piano tuned at 4-40 and it's after 5 o'clock now."

Leone Williams

This very clever little lady drummer has been with Jack Fox's Clover Garden Orchestra for the past year. She is one of the outstanding features of the organization and has a reputation of being able to "put the stuff over" better than many of the boys.

This organization is now playing in what is claimed to be the largest dance hall in the world (the dancing area being one square acre) in New York. Miss Williams' entire outfit is of the Leedy make, which she recommends highly to all drummers.

For Drummers Who Care *Leedy Equipment Leads Them All*

Leedy
DRUM TOPICS
The Exclusive Drummers' Paper

JULY, 1924
FIFTH EDITION

POSTMASTER—Return Postage Guaranteed

LEEDY MANUFACTURING CO.
INDIANAPOLIS, INDIANA

!!! ANNOUNCING A TRIUMPH !!!
The Improved Leedy Universal Machine Tympani

- The Pedal Is On the Floor
- Improved Flanged Counter Hoops
- No Springs to Hold Head Tension
- Entire Scope of Pedal Only 5¾ Inches
- Pedal Never Slips Back
- Positive Action at All Times

These instruments are positively the last word in Machine Tympani development and it will pay all drummers to investigate their superior technical points. The new flanged counter hoop is a thing of beauty and strength, being so designed as to enable absolute even head tension without more than six hand screws. The pedal is on the floor and its entire scope is only 5¾ inches. There is absolutely no chance of overtuning. They work easy, the resistance being just enough to be able to judge the head strain.

WRITE FOR LARGE CIRCULAR GIVING COMPLETE DESCRIPTION

Leedy Drum Topics

Bigger Than Ever

DRUM TOPICS has been increased to twelve pages in response to the thousands of Drummers who have helped to make it a real "Drummers' Booster." ℭ We thank you all and trust you'll like it.

Better Than Ever

Much has been written and said in the music world by organizations, prominent men, manufacturers, magazines, etc., about the "getting together" of all concerned.

They have dwelt at great length upon this important subject and in most cases a great deal of real good has been accomplished for the musician. BUT where in the past has Mr. Drummer come in? Has he ever had any special attention as an important factor outside of a few items either personally or professionally?

Has he ever had his own "honest to goodness" private publication? NO! not until DRUM TOPICS came to life. DRUMMERS are realizing that DRUM TOPICS is one of the biggest things that has ever been done for them. It is not a catalog—it is not a selling medium—but IT IS the first successful "get together" program ever presented to the drummer. It's all "great stuff" to tell folks that you will show them how, and that you will do something for them; but to put up the goods and prove it, is another thing.

DRUM TOPICS HAS PROVEN that it does something for the DRUMMER. There is no "catch in it somewhere." IT'S FREE. You've often heard that musicians don't stick together. Here is the drummers' chance to at least "get together." So make use of the opportunity. Write to DRUM TOPICS — ask questions — send in photographs. What's the news? A prize is offered for the best story each issue.

SIXTH ACT—"SHOOT!"

Any drummer can play double FF. Slambanging covers up a multitude of poor execution. It's the double PP stuff that sounds good in drumming. Work for it.

We have heard that in France they call a GOOD DRUMMER a "PERCUSSIONISTE EXTRAORDINAIRE."
Oh, f'evens sake!

Here and there may be found a drummer who coughs up $300.00 for a set of Machine Tympani and then gives them less care and attention than his mother bestows upon a five-dollar carpet sweeper.

Leedy Midget Slap Sticks

Played one in each hand. Very effective and wonderful flash. Same model (12 inches long) as used by George W. Marsh of the Paul Whiteman Orchestra.

For Drummers Who Care *leedy* Leedy Equipment Leads Them All

The Exclusive Drummers' Paper

Howard Goulden

Sousa wanted a real jazz number, so Goulden put it on, and what a "clean-up" it proved to be! A special arrangement was written and Leedy built this dandy little novelty outfit in white and gold. Note how the snare drum fits on the bass drum. Howard tands up to play it.

The Best Yet

The new Green Brothers' Beginners' Method is just the book for the purpose. It starts at the very beginning and explains the very things the beginner wants to know about xylophone, marimba and bells. Many prominent teachers have adopted it exclusively.
Special retail price, $1.00.

A Good Stunt

A short time ago we saw a crack vaudeville drummer easily whip out some very fast beats on a suspended crash cymbal. On looking closer to determine in what manner the cymbal was hung, we found that the cord was not more than 2½ inches long and that the arm of the holder had several windings of felt strips wound around same at a point where the cymbal would ordinarily have hit the metal arm, making a clanky noise. Fine for theatre work where fast successive beats are necessary.

The range of steel bells could be extended higher, but our ears are not accustomed to tone of that high vibration rate, consequently they would not be practical.

Clear as Mud!!!

In an over enthusiastic effort to describe the fine orchestra she said, "The symphony orchestra was wonderful — just like a big, beautiful pipe organ."
A week later she said, "What a beautiful pipe organ! Just like a big, wonderful symphony orchestra."
She has not enlightened us in the least, but simply told her method of explanation.

Pretty?

Here is the new "Venetian Boatman Scene" for artistic bass drum heads. Painted in several colors and in a manner that shows no brush marks and looks as well with or without lights. The usual Leedy quality way.

Call a Rehearsal

Scene: A hotel in any large city.
Enter Mr. Smith and wife, who register and are shown to their room.
Next morning at breakfast Mrs. Smith says to her husband: "Do you take cream and sugar in your coffee, dear?" —*Peck*.

Who Holds the Record?

Drum Topics will publish the photo and history of the drummer who has held down the same theatre job the longest. Wonder who he is and where he works? We know of one that has sat in the same pit ten years.

The harp stop effect in the large organs is produced on rosewood bars and resonators that are of special design similar to the marimba.

Johnny Stein

Johnny Stein has played with the best in and around New York City. Eleven years of it and still going strong. His brother is also a drummer and they are both solid Leedy. Stein just purchased an entire new black and gold outfit and is playing at the Nightingale Cafe with Jimmy Durantie's Orchestra.
(Courtesy H. & A. Selmer Co., New York.)

If at some time you find yourself without an extra batter head, just try tucking two thin snare heads on one flesh hoop. You will find that this makes an ideal batter side combination to work on.

Bess Vance

Now that you are past the picture: She is Miss Bess Vance, one of the most capable lady drummers in the business. She is also a graduate of the University of Nebraska and her home is in Osceola, Neb. Now making a big hit with "Harry Waiman's Debutantes" on the Orpheum Circuit. Miss Vance states that she has tried many makes of drums, but likes Leedy best.
(Courtesy Tom Brown Music Co., Chicago.)

For Drummers Who Care Leedy Equipment Leads Them All

Leedy Drum Topics

Hugo G. Heyn

of Omaha, Neb., is truly an artist on the xylophone. For the past several months he has been a big feature on the radio, and the Leedy Mfg. Co. has received several letters from drummers all over the country stating that they have greatly enjoyed his work "through the air." Mr. Heyn kindly consented to write an article for DRUM TOPICS on request of the Leedy dealer at Omaha—Geo. A. Smith. We take great pleasure in publishing same.

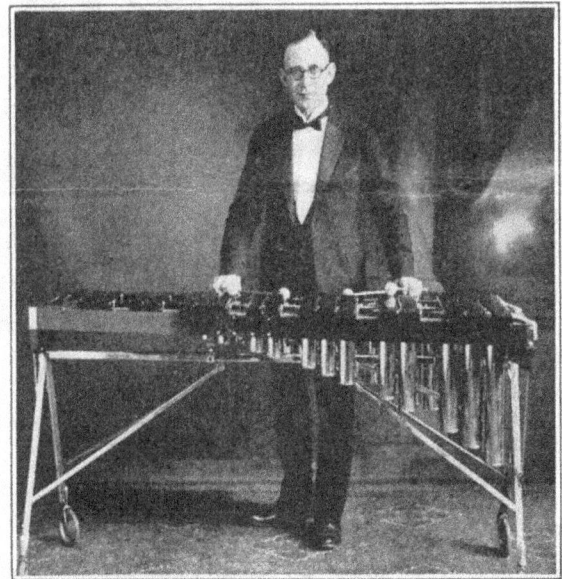

Hugo G. Heyn and His 3½-Octave Leedy Marimba-Xylophone with Improved Stand

The Possibilities of the Xylophone
By HUGO G. HEYN

Although the xylophone is one of the very oldest instruments, traced back to the heathen days when bamboo rods were strung on animal gut and pounded with crude sticks, it is peculiar that many, many years passed before it was used to any extent as an instrument of the orchestra or band, and even then it was regarded as a novelty to be used only for special effects.

A popular misconception is undoubtedly the chief reason for the apparent lack of interest in the xylophone. Ask the average person what he thinks of this instrument and nine times out of ten he will reply that it is a noisy contrivance that is all right on the stage, but becomes monotonous to listen to very long.

And why? Simply because nine out of ten so-called xylophonists are drummers, whose main idea seems to be to drum on the bars in a "clankety-clank" style with no idea of tone, touch, phrasing or interpretation—just one or two monotonous beats, rhythmic but nothing more. And in the majority of cases the drumming is done with the loud, hard mallets—even on the marimba!

Nothing could be more displeasing to the ear, and no wonder so few of this type of xylophonist ever get a great deal of work as soloists or in orchestras.

But to the schooled musician the xylophone and marimba open up a field of most wonderful musical possibilities, both as to tone, phrasing and technique. I have heard the soft strains of "The Rosary" played on the marimba with four soft felt mallets, and I doubt whether any instrument could produce a more beautiful, soothing, sweet harmony. The effect is that of a huge pipe organ in the distance. The same instrument played with hard mallets would sound terrible.

Such numbers as "Caprice Viennois," made so popular as a violin solo by Fritz Kreisler, or similar selections usually thought of only as violin solos, make the most wonderful marimba solos and offer unlimited opportunity for the display of real musical talent.

The xylophone is not a hard instrument to learn. On the contrary, it is really much easier than a violin or piano, and one can learn to play a tune on it in less time than required to draw a simple tone from violin or blow a clear note on the cornet.

Perhaps one reason that fewer people take up the xylophone is because the instrument has attracted so little attention until recently. It has always been hailed as a novelty instrument and its possibilities were not fully appreciated. It is true, however, that up until quite recently there have been limitations of tone and construction that have been a handicap to greater progress. But the new instruments are of such scientific construction that every musical longing can be readily satisfied. The new method of tuning employed by Leedy has overcome audible overtones, making it possible now to play soft passages on the extreme lower register in perfect tune, giving the sweet organ effects. The ingenious mechanical construction of these instruments permits their being folded into a small space, overcoming the objections of bulk and difficulty in transportation, heretofore a serious problem to the xylophonist.

There is a decided field in the musical world for good xylophonists. All it takes is ordinary musical ability, the same as required for any other instrument—and a lot of practice. If studied seriously, with a proper knowledge of music and harmony, there is no reason why in the near future the xylophone and marimba should not take their place beside the violin and piano on the concert stage. The possibilities are there.

Read This Photographed Letter

```
                                    Omaha, Neb.
                                    July 12, 1924.
Leedy Mfg. Co.,
Indianapolis, Ind.
                              Atten: Mr. Way, Sales Mgr.
Gentlemen:-

    The New Leedy Marimba recently ordered
from Mr. Geo. Smith, arrived promptly on schedule,
as promised, and I am so enthusiastic over it that
anything I could write would not be too much.

    For sixteen years I have been using various
makes of Marimbas and Xylophones and had about de-
cided that there was no instrument made that was
in perfect tune in the extreme lower register. All
lower bars seemed to have overtones that made them
sound sharp. You have the secret solved - my new
marimba is perfect - to the lowest "F".

    I also want to congratulate your mechanical
department, in producing such exclusive features
of design that allow folding into small space and
affording light weight with sturdy construction.
The minute details provided for every single con-
venience are certainly appreciated after using the
bulky instruments of the past.

    I also want to say a few words for Mr. Smith,
your representative here, who for several years has
been "Selling" me on Leedy and to whose conscientious
efforts I am grateful for having "Discovered" how
much better Leedy instruments are than I had ever
dreamed. Truly they are in a class by themselves.

                        Most truly yours,

                        Hugo G. Heyn
HGH.                    Director HUGO HEYN
                                 ORCHESTRA.
```

The snare drum does not record as well as some instruments on the phonograph, because of the tremendous vibration wave that is set up. A 12-inch diameter drum is mostly used. However an exceptional case took place when Bill Kieffer recorded the drum solo in "The Yorktown Centennial March" (Victor Record No. 18817) with the Washington Marine Band. A 9x15-inch Leedy Multi-Model was used and the Victor Company states it is the most realistic reproduction of drum tone ever registered. Drummers, get this record; you will certainly enjoy it.

For Drummers Who Care — **Leedy** — *Leedy Equipment Leads Them All*

The Exclusive Drummers' Paper

A Bunch of "Live Wires"

 W. C. (BILLY) BROWN, an oldtimer of New York and formerly of the 106th Infantry Concert Band, is now often called the busiest jobbing drummer in New York. He is a personal friend of the well-known Mr. Frank A. Snow. Brown has been a Leedy booster for many years.

There is usually a "pet" question in every drummer's mind to which a satisfactory answer has never been given. Why not ask DRUM TOPICS? Perhaps we can answer it and then again perhaps we can not. No obligation in asking. DRUM TOPICS will try to assist you.

 H. MURPHY, of the Royal Theatre, Perth, West Australia, plays with a theatre orchestra that is second to none in that country. Murphy has a fine reputation as being a first-class theatre man. He is entirely Leedy equipped, having purchased his outfit through the W. H. Paling Company, Ltd., of Sydney, Australia.

 CHARLES F. CAMMALL, JR., is a former pupil of the late Geo. B. Stone of Boston. Cammall is now at the Winthrop Theatre in Winthrop, Massachusetts, a leading vaudeville house, putting on xylophone solos weekly with his Leedy xylophone, which he praises highly. His solo work is making him quite popular.

 CLYDE V. BLANK, of Balboa, C. Z., has been in the Canal Zone for the past eleven years and is known as the most popular dance man of that section. He is a strong "Leedyite." For the past two years he has been connected with Curriers Orchestra.

 ARTHUR SMITH, a drummer of great prominence in Baltimore, Md., is now playing with the Frisco Five, an organization of no mean ability. "Smith," as he is called, is proud to announce that he is an exclusive Leedy recruit by way of Hammann-Levin Music Company, Baltimore.

 LEO MOSKOWITZ, of the Rainbow Novelty Orchestra, Omaha, Neb., is a very fine and modern dance drummer. Moskowitz has made great strides in the short time he has been in the business. The Geo. A. Smith Company, of Omaha, has equipped him entirely with Leedy drums.

 C. PIRMIN BURGER has written Leedy several times praising the new Machine Tympani. He is now playing at the Hamilton Theatre at Lancaster, Pa., enjoying a fine reputation as a thorough drummer. He is also connected with the Burger Music House of Lancaster.

 WALTER WHITNEY, of the Palace Theatre, Peoria, Ill., under the direction of Rud A. Born, is more than proud of his Utility Model Leedy Drum. This drummer, orchestra and leader are reputed to be among the best on the Orpheum Circuit. Whitney is a vaudeville drummer with real speed.

If the manager of your theatre is one of the kind who does not realize the drummer's importance, just let him look over DRUM TOPICS. It might change his mind.

 WILL HENDER, of London, England, has been touring the Orient for the past ten years with the Jack Waller's Enterprises. He has made some very good friends for the Leedy Company in a dozen different countries. Hender is a cracker-jack drummer and carries complete equipment that fills four trunks.

 GEORGE W. FLORES, a very prominent drummer, is playing with the Manhattan Society Orchestra at Healey's Hotel, Boston, Mass. They were formerly on the Keith Circuit. Flores recently purchased an entire new set of elaborately finished drums from the Conn Boston Company and says they are the finest he ever owned.

 PATRICK J. WARD, of Wheeling, W. Va., is a theatre drummer of fourteen years' experience, having played in several different cities on the best of jobs. Ward is also an excellent xylophone player. His entire outfit, including tympani, are of Leedy manufacture.

 L. M. BABLE, of Butte, Mont., is rated as one of the foremost drummers in the Northwest. He has had several years' experience in both theatre and dance work and is a full-fledged Leedy enthusiast, praising in particular the tone of his Leedy Standard Bass Drum.

 S. N. GRAFF is the publicity director of the Elks Club Band at Shreveport, La., and recently the Leedy Company received a letter from him stating that the entire Elks Drum Corps of Shreveport was 100% pleased with their instruments. Graff is also a very able drummer and plays in the Elks Band.

 RICHARD W. BOND is the drummer of the Sandy Creek High School Band and Orchestra of Lacona, N. Y. While he is not a veteran drummer, he does claim that he has played long enough to know the best instruments, which are at all times Leedy. Bond is working hard and will go to the top.

 GEORGE FULLER, formerly of Innes' Band and now at the Palace Theatre, Indianapolis, has the reputation of being one of the very best vaudeville men. He was one of Mr. Leedy's star pupils. Fuller believes vaudeville men should keep up-to-date as well as dance men and therefore has the latest Leedy equipment, including Machine Tympani.

You may not want to add any new equipment to your outfit right now, BUT you do want to know about everything new that comes out; so keep your latest address in Leedy files and be on the mailing list.

 LOUIS MEHLING has been using Leedy bass drums for several years with such organizations as Gilmore's Band, Victor Herbert's Orchestra, Sousa's Band, New York Philharmonic Orchestra, and the Wagnerian Opera Company. This list proves his caliber as a drummer, and the Leedy Company is indeed proud that he indorses its products.

 GEORGE W. MAULE has played in all classes of work for twelve years and has just closed two successful seasons at the Cascade Rainbow Terrace with Norval Marrs' Orchestra at New Castle, Pa. He is a wonderful dance drummer and believes in buying the best instruments procurable, therefore uses the new style Multi-Model Snare Drum.

 FRANK MacCARTHY, a former manager of the C. G. Conn drum department, is again back on the road. Part of last season he was with the Greenwich Village Follies. We doubt if there is a drummer in the business who has trouped more than Frank and he ranks among the best as an artist. He uses Leedy Machine Tympani.

 JACK SNIDERMAN, of the B. F. Keith Orchestra, Ottawa, Ont., Can., is another top-notch vaudeville man with 14 years' experience. He is also an ardent admirer of the Leedy Machine Tympani and makes real use of them in the pit. Sniderman has a considerable reputation as a composer and arranger.

 H. C. BRANCH, who plays with Coy Miller's Original Dixie Five, with headquarters in Lynchburg, Va., has just finished a long engagement at Craig Healing Springs, Va. "Barney," as he is called by the boys, is a thorough business drummer in every respect. He has used the same set of Leedy drums for seven straight years.

 JOE MAYO, with Fred Hall's Royal Dance Orchestra, which is specializing in arrangements that are West Indian in character, is making a big hit in New York with the drum effects possible in this music. They are recording for the Okeh Phonograph Company.

For Drummers Who Care Leedy Equipment Leads Them All

Leedy Drum Topics

Standard Organizations Which Engage Drummers Who Use Leedy Drums

Goldman's Band Drummers—New York

Gus Helmecke of Sousa's Band, Howard Kopp of the Victor Recording Orchestra, and Robert Kiesow of the Metropolitan Grand Opera Company are the three drummers with the Goldman Band summer concerts in New York. All Leedy.

Oscar Adler's Orchestra—Keith Circuit

"Dick" DeVaugh, the excellent drummer of this fine orchestra, is from Akron, Ohio. He was completely Leedy equipped by the Edfred Music Company of Akron and states he likes his outfit better than any he has ever owned in his ten years' experience.

Ben Bernie's Orchestra—New York

This orchestra records for Vocalion records and has played the Orpheum time as a headliner. Sam Fink, the drummer, is an exceptionally progressive boy and enjoys the reputation of being one of the best in New York. He believes that Leedy instruments are the best to be obtained.

Dave Buckley's Band—Sydney, Australia

Here is a fast dance band that has made a great hit in Sydney and vicinity. Dave Buckley is drummer, owner and manager, and it is reported that he is a very fine drummer. Fully Leedy equipped by W. A. Paling & Company, Ltd., Sydney.

Loma's Dance Band—Liverpool, England

Jack F. Pettit, the very efficient drummer of this organization, has had a career of varied experiences, having played in some of the best combinations in western England. He is a full-fledged Leedy booster and writes Leedy some very interesting letters regarding the dance game in England.

Monte Carlo Entertainers—Red Oak, Iowa

M. R. Hawkins is drummer and manager of this orchestra. Next season at Yellowstone Park. Hawkins says Leedy drums are the best of all, and we are proud to count him among our boosters, as he is indeed a clever performer.
(Courtesy Geo. A. Smith, Omaha.)

For Drummers Who Care *Leedy Equipment Leads Them All*

Leedy Drum Topics Issue 6

The Exclusive Drummers' Paper

Leedy Drum Topics

A PAPER DEVOTED TO
THE INTERESTS OF THE DRUMMER

No subscription fee

Advertisements accepted

Published quarterly at 1033 East Palmer Street
Indianapolis, Indiana

Editor .... GEO. H. WAY
Business Manager .... A. W. KUERST

"Art for Art's Sake and Art for Beefsteak"

The past has proven that musicians as a whole have not been really good business men. Many of the most famous composers and artists have died in poverty because of the one failing of lacking the necessary business sense to "sell" their wares.

Right now we know of a most wonderful drummer and xylophonist who just "gets by"—he can't sell it. And we know of a very ordinary drummer who draws an immense salary. It is not luck and it is not fate—it's simply knowing how. How about the salesman who knows hardly anything of the motor in an automobile, still he sells more than any other man in the firm. This really happens in many cities. So it is with the drummer musician. Playing as an art is one thing—selling it is another. You need both, all right, but don't let the art keep you down. Try to think of the business end of playing drums for a livelihood through the same mind as the manager of a large store or office: How can I get more customers, more work, more money? Keeping uppermost in your thoughts: It's not ALL in the playing.

How about this? Some of the most elaborate restaurants do the biggest business and serve only fair food, while an ordinary restaurant that is a restaurant only, with excellent food, just gets by. Now, we do not mean to underestimate the value of being a wonderful drummer. Be the best you can—study all you can; but it is true that the other side—the business side—needs attention as well.

Fine tools to work with are a great help. Don't worry about the investment in your equipment. You can't make money in any business unless you invest. A hat store can't sell hats unless they stock hats. Therefore have the best outfit money will buy, and plenty of it. Remember, the fellow who has is the fellow who gets.

Many drummers are lazy. We've heard them brag: "Oh, I just take along the two drums and a wood block." If you are this kind of a drummer, don't blame anyone but yourself if the trumpet or banjo player puts it over on you. You chose drums—now stay with them and do your part. The reason the drummer is interesting to the public is not because he "plays the drum," but because "How can he learn to play so many things?"

Not many people outside of the music business know a drummer when they hear one, but they will say, "He's a wonderful drummer" if you "sell" it to them with a gold outfit and plenty of traps to play on and a little showmanship in the way of letting them know you are full of pep, working and on the job. That's the way a drummer can be a business man. Hop to it!

The "Stayput" Drum Stick Holder

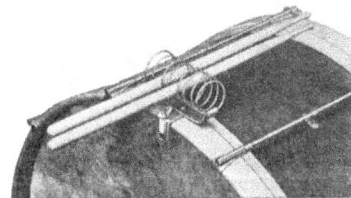

Is fast becoming a standard accessory for all drummers. It is not only handy for the dance drummers, but especially handy for the theatre drummer, as the old habit of dropping the sticks on the floor is wholly eliminated. Many of the boys are attaching the holder to the wall of the pit and using for tympani sticks and bell hammers.

In India—Ali Bux's Band

In far-away Jullundur City, India, there is a real Leedy booster and band instrument dealer—one Ali Bux. He is shown sitting directly behind the table. Note the novel "chimes and bells" at each side of the photo. Right you are; Leedy did not make them, but Leedy did send this band a new Multi-Model a few weeks ago. The first drummer of the band is Agua Fesmow.

The New Leedy "Socker" Cymbal Holder

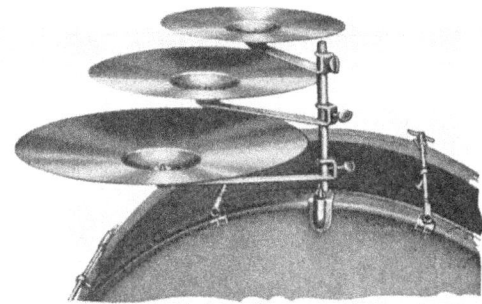

This new and handy little device is just the thing for holding from one to four cymbals. The arms will swing around on the upright to any position.

For Drummers Who Care Leedy Equipment Leads Them All

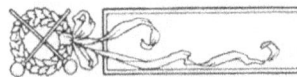 

Leedy Drum Topics

Gene Pierson

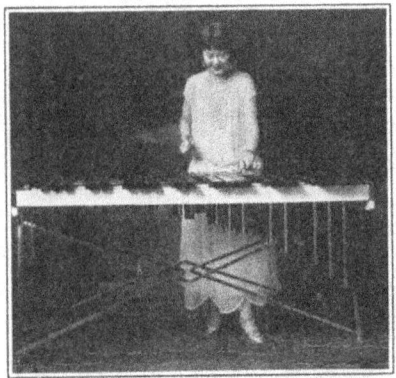

This young lady, who was formerly in vaudeville, billed as "The Musical Doll," is now making a real hit with the patrons of the Bamboo Inn, Indianapolis. She is really an exceptionally fine xylophonist and "doubles" on saxaphone equally as well. Miss Pierson uses a Leedy 3½-octave marimba-xylophone finished in white and gold. She says it is the finest she has ever seen, heard, or played upon.

The dear little sheik was so dumb that he thought the tonic note was a patent medicine.

Some Drummers Do Not

pay any attention to the BLENDING of their bass drum and cymbal, and very often allow the cymbal to "zing! zing!" a lot louder than the tone of the bass drum. In other cases the listener will hear too much bass drum and hardly any cymbal.

The best way to judge how the combination sounds is to have someone else work your pedal and you be the judge from a distance.

Do not allow the cymbal striker to hit the cymbal on the extreme edge. This causes too much vibration and excessive ring. About one inch in from the edge is best.

An evenly balanced bass drum and cymbal is truly musical, but when it's either all cymbal or all bass drum it is "killing" the whole orchestra, especially the work on a snare drum.

Watch this. A lot of fellows never think of it.

The actual pitch of bells is two octaves higher than the parts are written.

A Drummer

Rolls out of bed in the morning.
Rolls for breakfast.
Rolls a game of golf in the forenoon.
Rolls to work in his Ford.
Rolls all through work.
Rolls a "five stroke" when it should be a "seven."
Rolls "off" for "The Stars and Stripes."
Rolls a game of dice at intermission.
Rolls home in his Ford.
Rolls into bed.
Rolls over.
Rolls.

The Prize Story

"NOW I'LL TELL ONE"

By J. C. Harper, Lenoir, N. C.

A drummer traveling alone in a "flivver" was hurrying along a deserted mountain road in an effort to reach an engagement with a summer hotel dance orchestra. Darkness came on, and, to add to his troubles, a rough spot in the road left him with a broken rear spring. He determined to make a temporary support by breaking off a small sapling in a clump of trees close by, but he came back faster than he started, with a tawny mountain lioness hard at his heels. On into the car after him came the lioness and out the other side went the drummer. To his surprise the lioness curled up on the seat of the car. This gave our hero an idea; so when her measured breathing told him she was asleep, he quietly tied the end of her tail to the bass drum and gave it such a "wham" as would wake the dead. Away went the lioness full tilt and after her went the bass drum, banging from side to side and scaring the brute into wilder flight every jump.

A year passed and the drummer was again in the region hunting, when a dull, thumping sound attracted his attention and a series of moving objects attracted his eye to the skyline of a nearby hillcrest. There in plain sight was his old enemy the lioness, bass drum and all, and along behind her followed her three tawny little whelps, each with a tambourine on the end of its tail.

Ten dollars in cash for the best drummers' story not later than January 1st. You can write one. Try it.

The New Style Multi-Model

"THE SUPREME OF ALL DRUMS"

To play real PPP on your wood block with the taper part of the sticks is no easy trick; however, it sounds very much better and is more professional than "pecking" with the tips of the sticks.

Practice will enable you to snap 'em off PPP and clean, and the taper part of your sticks produces a "clock" tone instead of a "click." Much prettier.

Correction Notice

In the July 15th issue of DRUM TOPICS a mistake was made in stating the name of the phonograph company for which Vincent Lopez records. It should have read, "The Okeh Company."

Poets and advertisers often rave about the "silver-like tone" in chimes and bells. To believe that silver will assist in a superior tonal quality is purely imagination, because scientific tests have proven that it will not combine with other metals in a manner to improve tone. A set of sterling silver chime would produce a tone similar to that of lead pipes.

The Leedy chimes are made of a seamless drawn tubing of a special formula.

John Gyuka

is the man who directs the Leedy drum head department. Drummers will no doubt be interested in knowing that the brand name of "Uka" as applied to Leedy heads is taken from the last three letters of Gyuka's name. He started at the trade when only 12 years old in the part of Hungary that is now Roumania, and has been following the business for 33 years, 25 of which have been in the United States, the last 18 years with the Leedy Mfg. Co. Gyuka is responsible for the development of the world's highest class clear heads, especially the Kafette brand for tympani, which is used by almost every prominent tympanist in the grand operas, concert bands and symphony orchestras.

The best authorities declare that the "y" in xylophone should be pronounced like the "y" in "my." It's a hard job to do it after we have been saying "zi-lō-fōn" so long; however, the professors know best and we must abide.

A fellow does not become angry because another fellow tries to flirt with his girl—but he gets wild when he notices that she enjoys it.

Garnett W. Froh

is one of the leading features on the radio WBAP, Fort Worth *Star-Telegram* station, and he has also made several concert tours, covering the whole state of Texas. Froh states that he has been playing marimba for ten years and only adopted the Leedy make a little over a year ago, but that he is so thoroughly pleased with his new instrument that he will never make a change.

For Drummers Who Care *Leedy Equipment Leads Them All*

The Exclusive Drummers' Paper

Landau's Has Made Wilkes-Barre, Hazelton and Pittston, Pa., Leedy Towns

The Drum Department of Landau's
Wilkes-Barre, Pa.

Drummers in Wilkes-Barre, Hazelton and Pittston, Pa., never have to listen to "I'll order it for you," because when they drop into any of the Landau stores they know they are going to get immediate service and be able to look over a large stock to select from.

Mr. Landau (at left), the president of this firm, is a thorough retail merchant and has built the business on the foundation of service. He believes in allowing the manager of the drum department, Mr. Robert L. Knecht, a free rein in order to give the drummers the best of attention.

Mr. Harry Michlosky (below) is Mr. Landau's partner and he takes a personal interest in the drum department. He is manager of the musical instrument merchandise and is an expert violin man.

Laudau's believes in keeping in touch with all the leading musicians in their locality and does so continually by novel and interesting advertising methods. They very often use full pages in the newspapers to let the boys know what is going on in the music world.

Robert L. Knecht

Has full charge of the drum department at Landau's in Wilkes-Barre, and it is through his professional knowledge that the Wilkes-Barre drummers are enabled to receive the benefit of his personal experience in the way of advice. Mr. Knecht is drummer at the Capitol Theatre, Wilkes-Barre's first-class vaudeville house, and outside of his theatre hours devotes his entire attention to the Landau store. He also has a large class of pupils and employs the rudimentary method of teaching. Wilkes-Barre drummers are indeed fortunate to have this very able man at their service.

George Fogg

Is at present playing drums at the Savoy Theatre, Wilkes-Barre, and is also connected with the Irem Temple Shrine Band. Fogg has been using Leedy equipment for many years past and says, after having tried many styles and makes of drums, that he has never used any that could equal Leedy. His reputation throughout the East is of a very high standing.

Andrew Leach

Of the Sterling Hotel Orchestra, Wilkes-Barre, Pa., is rated as one of the best dance drummers in Pennsylvania. He was entirely equipped by Landau's and states that his Multi-Model drum is the finest instrument on the market. He emphasizes the fact that its easy playing qualities are exactly what the discriminating drummer desires.

Frank MacEnrow

Was recently engaged for the new American Theatre, Pittston, Pa., and bought an entire new outfit from Landau's of the Leedy make to open the new house. MacEnrow states that his new Multi-Model drum is the finest he has ever owned and he is equally pleased with each individual article in his outfit. As a theatre man he has more than made good and ranks with the best.

Edfred's, the Drummers' Headquarters of Akron, Ohio

Here is another live firm that looks upon their Leedy drum department as an asset. In the photo at the left is Ed. Simmons (standing), manager of the musical instrument department. Ed. is one of the boys and is a member of the Akron local. He thoroughly understands the drummers' problems, realizing the value of "having it when they want it." The gentleman sitting, holding the Multi-Model drum, is "Orrie" Smith, secretary of the Musicians' Union and drummer at the Colonial Theatre. "Orrie" is considered one of Ohio's best, and the numerous fine theatre jobs he has held for the last fifteen years carry out this conviction. Smith is an ardent admirer of Leedy products. The Edfred firm, like Landau's, is a big advertiser. DRUM TOPICS hopes soon to publish some of the photos of other prominent drummers in Akron who are personal friends of the Edfred Company, i. e., Jimmy Richards, R. E. Light, J. B. Washburn, F. R. Millinger, Ray Sillito, Clyde H. Darst, Leonard C. Krager and Geo. H. Moody.

For Drummers Who Care   Leedy Equipment Leads Them All

Leedy Drum Topics

Frank H. Snow

Is not only one of the best known drummers in the United States, but he is also one of the finest drummers, xylophonists and tympanists we have. For 12 years he was with Sousa's Band and made the famous world tour with them. For the past few years he has been traveling with the Cohan shows and other first-class musical comedies out of New York and has a host of good friends all over the country. This season Mr. Snow is with the Middle Western company of "The Thief of Bagdad." In October he visited the Leedy factory and purchased a new set of machine tympani. It goes without saying that the Leedy Company is more than pleased to have such a high-caliber man among its friends.

A Musician

Conductor—"You can't possibly have lost your ticket?"
Passenger—"I can't, eh? Why, I once lost a bass drum!"

DRUM TOPICS would like to have some real novelty photographs of drummers with their instruments. Something different would be very interesting to our readers, and there is a great opportunity to get such photos showing the fine display that a complete set of drums can make.

Ray Brothers

Is now with the Sunset Six Dance Band of Wheeling, W. Va. This boy is also a very fine minstrel show drummer and has been for the past season with the Gus Sun Honey Boy Minstrels. Brothers has a larger outfit than most drummers and uses no other than Leedy.

Facts

Funny how some tympanists dwell upon the fact that hand-hammered tympani bowls have a superior tone. Nothing could be farther from the truth. In the past the hand-hammered bowl made in two pieces was the only type that could be secured by the manufacturers in sufficient quantities to meet the market demands.

No two hand-hammered bowls are exactly alike in size or in respect to symmetrical shape or gauge. It was a physical impossibility to make them so. Therefore, no two being alike, how could "superior tone" be guaranteed?

Leedy tympani bowls are made by the drawn process by a very wonderful machine that required four years' experimenting to perfect at a cost of $20,000.00. This machine turns out one-piece bowls, exactly alike in size, shape and gauge. Therefore all parts are interchangeable and perfection in workmanship and mechanical features are assured. Accuracy is the big feature, the same as in a French horn or trumpet.

Some drummers who use the Leedy standard drum sling No. 84 make the mistake of running the neck strip under the arm. This sling is not designed for use in this manner. It should be slung around the neck as shown in the photograph on page 54 of the Leedy Catalog M. This method evenly distributes the weight of the drum on the body and is the most comfortable.

If you use the floor type of pedal (any make) you should always put your spurs on the hoop opposite the pedal. Why? Because in so doing the batter head is tilted slightly (more or less, as you desire), toward you, and this prevents the beater rod of the pedal from passing a center point. If you use the overhanging type, the spurs should be on the same side as the pedal, as they will tilt the head away from you and prevent the same occurrence.

Use Your Mornings to Make Money

Sell Milton Made-to-Measure Shirts to your friends and associates. Finest hand work, individual cutting and wide range of exclusive fabrics. Long experience in making Dress and Tuxedo Shirts for the profession. Every order pays you a liberal profit. Satisfaction guaranteed. Send for samples and measuring directions.

J. R. Milton & Company
Makers of Fine Shirts
316 E. Ohio St., Indianapolis, Ind.

We thought you would like to look at th.. picture. It is the tympanist and "drum horse" of the Fourth Royal Irish Dragoon Guard Band, a very historic regiment of England. The tympani are made of silver, being presented to the regiment. This band makes a wonderful appearance on the street in their brilliant uniforms.

It Can't Be Done

I want to be naughty, I want to be nice,
I want the fun without the price,
I want to do what other girls do—
Tease 'em, cuddle 'em, and coo.
I don't like pepper, but I do love spice,
I want to be naughty, but yet be nice;
I want the lights that brightly shine,
I want the men and I want the wine.
I want the thrill of a long dream kiss,
I want the things that good girls miss.
But what I want most is a little advice
On how to be naughty and yet be nice.

Have You Noticed

the manner in which the new Leedy tympani hoop is now being made? Below is a section showing the extra strong additional steel flange which eliminates the necessity of using more than six tension handles. Besides its being the strongest tympani hoop ever manufactured, it adds great beauty to the appearance of the instrument.

A small-town symphony orchestra was tuning up previous to rehearsal. The new cellist and the drummer engaged in conversation as follows:
Cellist: "The acoustics in this hall are not very good, are they?"
Drummer: "That so? I don't smell nothin'."

If you have any drummer friends who do not receive DRUM TOPICS, just send in their names.

For Drummers Who Care — Leedy Equipment Leads Them All

Leedy Publishes Real Testimonials Only
This is a Photographed Letter

The Leedy Universal Machine Tympani were sold to the Baltimore Symphony Orchestra by the Hammann-Levin Company of Baltimore.

> Baltimore, Md.
> March 8, 1924.
>
> Leedy Manufacturing Co.,
> Indianapolis, Ind.
>
> Gentlemen:—
>
> Permit me to express to you my great satisfaction with the splendid results Mr. Riehl, our Tympanist obtained with the Leedy Machine Tympani during last night's performance of the Baltimore Symphony particularly so since the score of Tschaikowsky Symphone Pathetique calls for four Tympani, which was so splendidly mastered by Mr. Riehl with only two of the Leedy Machine Tympani.
>
> They have now been used at many of our rehearsals and concerts and work with the clock-like precision under all conditions, and the possibilities of this instrument seem almost limitless. The simple mechanism provided for instant changes of pitch is truly marvelous.
>
> The development and perfection of the Leedy Machine Tympani reflects greatly to the credit of its inventor and truly marks a new era in the possibilities of the Tympani.
>
> Very truly yours,
>
> Gustav Strube
> CONDUCTOR
> BALTIMORE SYMPHONY ORCHESTRA

The Machine Tympani in Vaudeville
By RUD. A. BORN
Leader, Palace Theatre Orchestra, Peoria, Ill.

Arrangers and composers as well as drummers have hailed the new Leedy Machine Tympani with great enthusiasm. Composers have long dreamed of an instrument by which the bass percussion section of an orchestra could be fully exploited, and while the idea of Machine Tympani is not new, they have never before been brought to a thoroughly practical state.

With the new Leedy Machine Tympani we can now write and execute such parts as shown below. I cite this as a simple arrangement which is very effective, but it is possible to go still farther and play complete melodies and counter melodies on these instruments. The Leedy Universal Machine Tympani can be played with as much flexibility as a song whistle. The instruments are yet new in the field of music and in many cases are being looked upon skeptically; however, this condition will be overcome in the near future, as drummers are beginning to realize that they are not a burden to their pocketbooks, because they are enabling them to earn a great deal more money, and they certainly are not a burden as an instrument, as they greatly lessen the drummers' labor.

Tympani have been slighted in the vaudeville game considerably, owing to the fact that very fast manipulation was required; but with the new model instrument this is only one of the handicaps that have been overcome, and they are a great boon to the vaudeville orchestra in building up its character.

(NOTE: Mr. Walter Whitney is the drummer with Mr. Born's Palace Orchestra at Peoria, and his photo is shown on page 4 of this issue of DRUM TOPICS.)

Woody Meyers' Cincinnati Orchestra

This orchestra is rated as one of the leaders in the Midwest, playing such jobs as the Zoological Garden in Cincinnati and broadcasting from WLW station. Ernest Meyers, the drummer, is manager of the orchestra and is rated among the "top notchers." He has been a satisfied user of Leedy products for a number of years.

Why Carry Two Drums?

The clarinet player would never go on a job without a few extra reeds, and a violinist always has extra strings. There are many drummers who would never think of going to work unless there was an extra head tucked on a Leedy metal flesh hoop close at hand. Many have two drums in case of a breakdown.

It is not satisfactory to carry a drum head tucked on a wooden hoop, because in dry weather the head will contract and bend the wood hoop egg shape, making it impossible to put on the drum unless it is wet first. One of the great advantages of the Leedy metal flesh hoops is that they may be carried safely in a snare-drum case without buckling and are ready for immediate replacement.

This is a reduced photograph of an 18x13-inch poster that is being shown in the principal music stores throughout the country. As it tells its own story, hardly any explanation is necessary; however, this is certainly a fine group of very high-class drummers. Dealers who have not already received this card may have one for the asking.

A Beautiful New Finish

If you have not seen one of the new "Elite" finish Multi-Model drums you have really missed something. It is the first time that black nickel has ever been used on musical instruments of any kind. This method of electroplating, which is far superior to any form of enamel, has heretofore only been used on jewelry, as it was considered impossible to apply it to such a large surface as a drum shell. Special mechanical apparatus had to be installed for this purpose, and this most beautiful high gloss black plating is found only on Leedy drums. Have you seen the circular describing them in full? If, not send for one.

For Drummers Who Care Leedy Equipment Leads Them All

Leedy
DRUM TOPICS

The Exclusive Drummers' Paper

OCTOBER, 1924
SIXTH EDITION

```
                    r. E. Wolfington,
                        1111 Laurel St.,
                            Indianapolis, Ind.
```

POSTMASTER—Return Postage Guaranteed

LEEDY MANUFACTURING CO.
INDIANAPOLIS, INDIANA

The Improved Leedy Solo-Tone Marimba-Xylophone

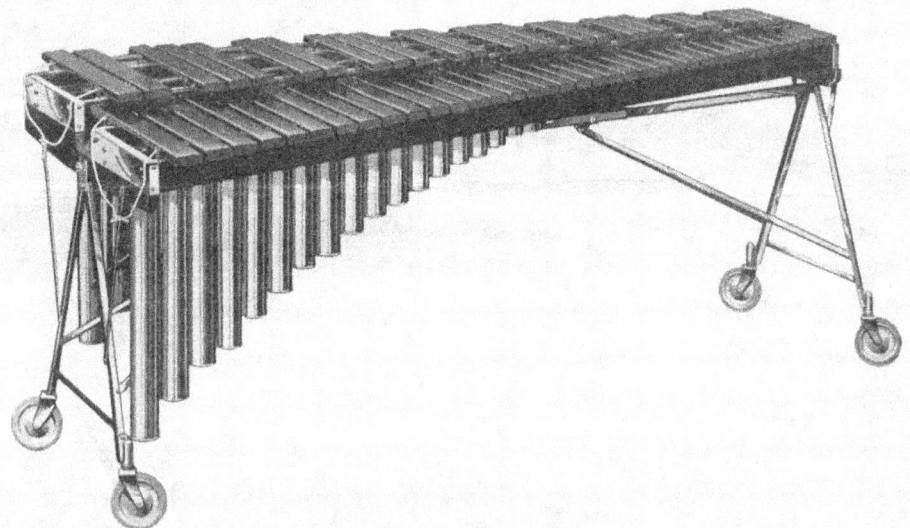

Every drummer and xylophonist who has seen this improved Leedy Solo-Tone, 5-octave Marimba-Xylophone has proclaimed it to be absolutely the finest instrument of its kind ever presented. It has three outstanding features found in no other make; i. e., the extra strong device for splitting the frames and resonators, the neat and simplified design of the take-down stand, and the late invention of tuning the bars in a manner wholly eliminating discordant overtones. This model is made in all sizes. Write for prices.

Leedy Drum Topics Issue 6

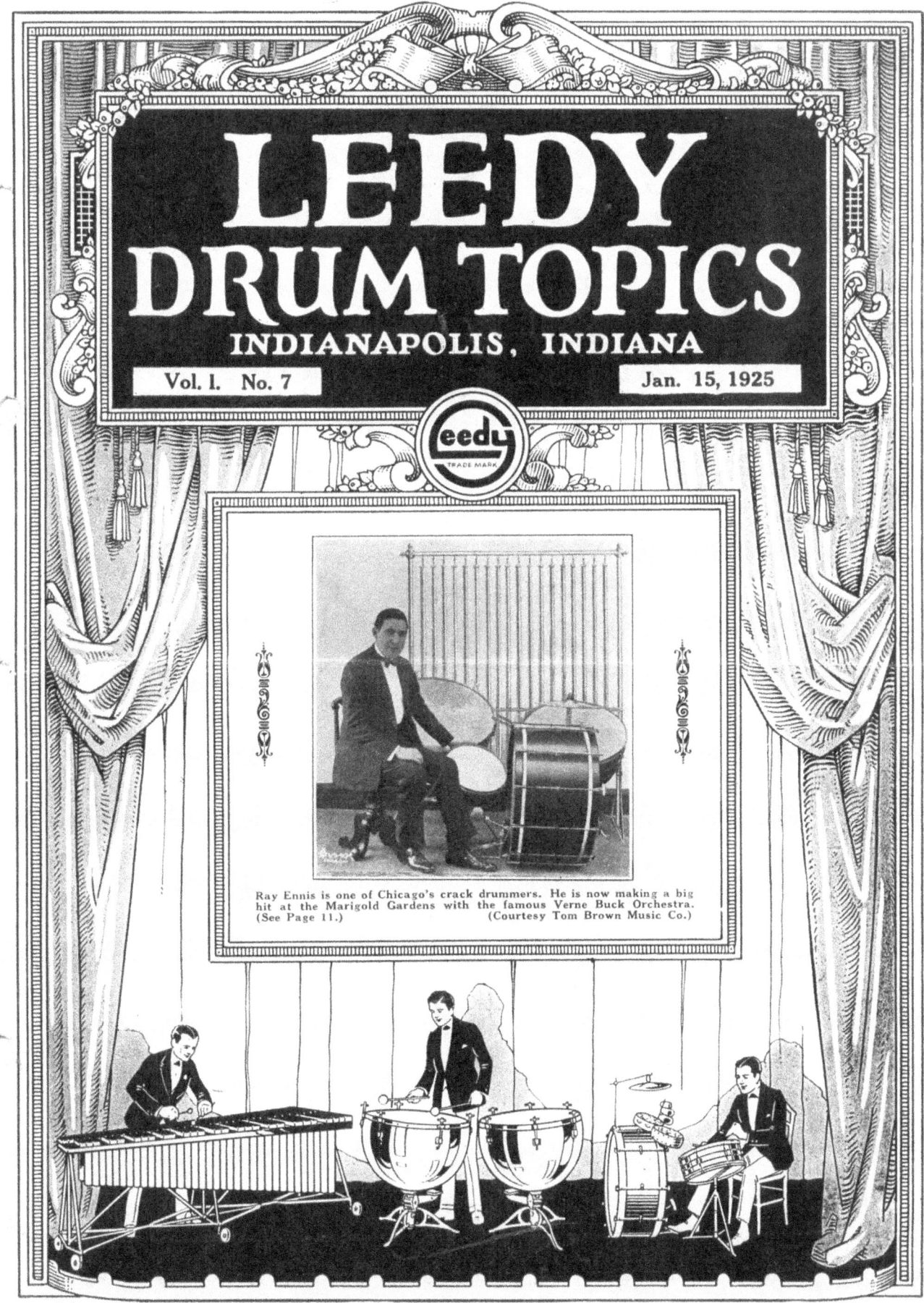

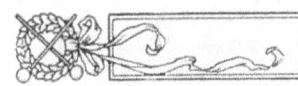 Drum Topics

Some Noise!

ABOUT Drum Topics

It's More Popular Than Ever—
Since We Enlarged It to Twelve Pages—
Now We Have to Print Ten Thousand More Copies—
Here is What Some of the Boys Write In About It—

"*Fine dope.*"—Jimmy Lent, New York City.
"*Most instructive.*"—Geo. Egner, Dallas, Texas.
"*Willing to pay for it.*"—Will Hender, London, England.
"*Keep it coming.*"—John W. Dow, Al G. Fields Minstrels.
"*Good tonic for drummers.*"—Geo. A. L. Wiehe, Boston, Mass.
"*Would feel lost without it.*"—Bill Kieffer, Washington, D. C.
"*Wish it was monthly instead of quarterly.*"—Arthur Layfield, Chicago, Ill.
"*Fine to refresh the memory of old-timers.*"—Howard N. Goulden, Sousa's Band.
"*Treats the little fellow on an equal basis with the big bugs.*"—Jack Downie, San Francisco.
"*Leedy has given the drummers just what they needed.*"—Geo. W. Marsh, Paul Whiteman Orchestra.

and this is why

The BIG questions for every drummer are:

How to earn more money—get a better job—keep in touch with the activities of the live drummers of the country, and boost yourself to a greater success.

You can do it, of course, if you will work hard enough and long enough, but you'll get a lot quicker action if you'll keep in close touch with DRUM TOPICS. This is a publication for drummers only, and it's full of news of the profession everywhere. It tells you what and how they are doing—it gives you many pointers on how you can improve your income—in fact, it's just what drummers have long needed to enable them to get together in a way that will benefit everyone. You'll find each issue filled with the kind of dope that'll do you good.

—OF COURSE IT'S FREE—all you have to do is send in your name and address and we'll see that you get it—it's LEEDY'S DONATION TO THE DRUMMING PROFESSION.

If your name's not on our list, send it in. Send in your drummer friend's name.

If it's on the list, then tell us how you like DRUM TOPICS.

Either way, send us your photograph and any news items that will be of interest and will plug for your game.

Drumming is a great profession, and if we work together we'll make it greater.

LET'S MAKE 1925 A BIG YEAR FOR DRUMMERS.

Happy New Year—Everybody

The first drum on record was the one Adam used when he "beat it" out of the garden.

The conceit rut is the deepest rut of all. It causes more failures than inefficiency or laziness.

It would sound odd to say, "That is a fine tympano head." However, it is the correct way, because "tympano" is the singular and "tympani" is the plural. The word "tympano" is derived from the Latin "tympanum," which is the membrane in the human ear.

That Guiltiest Feeling

Going down the pit stairs after missing about six cues in the last act.

Me Too

A certain drummer was asked by his leader to play a passage on bells in octaves, and, seeking a little more knowledge on the subject, asked a brother drummer:

"Say, Jake, how do you play bells in octaves?"

Jake: "Rotten."

 "WORLD'S FINEST DRUMMERS' INSTRUMENTS"

The Exclusive Drummers' Paper

It Might Be Worse

Drumming as a business isn't so bad. Stop and think of the many lines of work and trades that pay less and are much more disagreeable. Then figure out the trades that pay more. You will find that the drumming "trade" is not so far below the top of the list. In other words, there are more trades that pay less than fifty dollars a week than there are that pay over fifty.

Some drummers pronounce the "Cie" on the end of Zildjian and Cie as "See." It should be pronounced as "Cy." It is French for company.

Try This

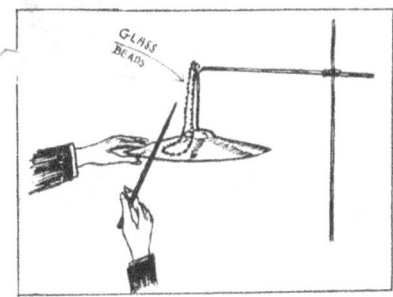

The various modern uses of cymbals are many. This one is comparatively new and is being used with great success in certain sections of the country. It consists of allowing a set of glass beads (such as found on the cheap jewelry counters) to rest on either the Chinese or Turkish crash cymbal while being beat upon with the stick, using one hand for "stops." The effect is very novel, and while the sound produced is somewhat similar to a cracked cymbal, it blends surprisingly well in up-to-date jazz.

The New Style Multi-Model

"THE SUPREME OF ALL DRUMS"

Orchestra Bells should remain in tune indefinitely unless they are continually played upon with metal hammers or allowed to rust until their original size and shape is distorted. Age itself does not in any way affect their tone.

A nice effect can be gotten by playing on the hoop of the bass drum, striking the hoop with the sticks at various lengths from the hands. There is a different tone at each point on the stick. A lot of fellows overlook the possibilities here.

Morris J. Cady

Morris J. Cady has been playing at the Blue Mouse Theatre, Seattle, Wash., with Andy Ward's Orchestra for the past sixty-seven weeks. He is now with the S. S. Leviathan Orchestra on the Orpheum Circuit, having taken the place of "Dusty" Roades, who has located in Miami, Fla. Cady is known as a "crackerjack" drummer in several western cities, and the Leedy Company is more than proud to have him as a booster. His home was formerly in Spokane. He also worked several seasons at the Majestic in San Antonio.

John M. Dow

John M. Dow, of Altoona, Pa., is this season with the Al G. Fields Minstrels, enroute. For several years he was house drummer at the Mishler Theatre in Altoona and with the Altoona City Band under Jules Neff. Dow has also held down many important jobs in Pittsburgh. His reputation as a very fine all-'round drummer is far above the average. In a recent letter to the Leedy Mfg. Co. he writes: "Drummers' equipment is put to the hardest known test in a minstrel show, and I find Leedy Drums and Machine Tympani more than meet the demand."

What is the difference between a chorus girl and a drum?
One has "tight skins" and the other has "skin tights."

Looking from the Pit

A beautiful pair of "Holeproof" in the front row is worth a dozen on the stage.

The bottom of the ocean is now fathomed by sound. Since we know the distance sound will travel per second in water, it is simply a matter of observing how long it takes the echo of a sound made just below the surface to return to its source.

Cow Bells on a Cushion

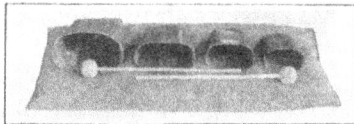

Cow bells, when placed on a real soft cushion, fairly well imbedded in same and played on with felt hammers, sound very much like the wooden Korean Temple Blocks so much in use among the drummers on the Pacific Coast. They have much more depth and volume of tone than the Temple Blocks and do not at all give the metallic tone of Cow Bells. Neither are they nearly so expensive. Stuffing cloth on the inside of Cow Bells deadens the tone.

Hickory Drum Sticks

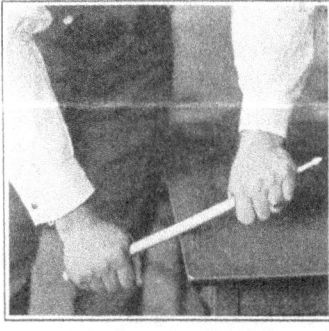

Hickory sticks will warp, some more and some less. It is not the fault of poor material or workmanship; it simply is the "nature of the beast," and no manufacturer has yet been able to overcome this action. Hickory is a light, pliable fibre wood, and the fact that it will warp is one of the reasons we see so little of it used in furniture and other articles.

Hickory drum sticks are made carefully enough and they leave the factory perfectly straight, but they will "go" even in shipment over night.

This wood varies considerably in its natural growth as to grain and some sticks will warp quicker than others. Hickory sticks will also become crooked in use, such as beating them on Cow Bells, Cymbals, Wood Blocks, etc.

Not many drummers know that the life of a hickory stick can be greatly prolonged by a simple straightening process which consists of bending the stick with the hands over a solid corner, such as a table top, as shown in the illustration above.

However, with all their faults, they are the best kind of sticks for all-around use.

"FOR DRUMMERS WHO CARE"

Leedy Drum Topics

Geo. J. Birkel Company—Los Angeles, Calif.

The above photo shows a very pretty Leedy Drum window recently shown by the Geo. J. Birkel Company, of Los Angeles, during a "Drum Show" held at their store while Mr. Chas. Seibert, the Leedy representative, was in attendance. Under the combined direction of Mr. E. R. Stone, the musical merchandise manager, and Harry S. Moore, manager of the drum department, also Mr. Seibert, the show was a complete success and resulted in all the Los Angeles and vicinity drummers paying a visit to see the special display of new model Leedy drums and traps.

The Birkel Company is very much interested in their drum department and always give it a fair share of advertising along with other instruments. Particular attention is paid to feature window displays and circularization by mail.

Mr. Stone has worked hard and long in the interests of the Los Angeles drummers, always carrying a complete stock and being ever ready to co-operate with both professional and amateur in their wants, whether large or small.

Al. B. Cruchet

In making our dealer and drummer friends acquainted with Mr. Al. B. Cruchet, manager of the Advance Drum Company, Edmonton, Alberta, Canada, LEEDY DRUM TOPICS wishes to point to an exceptional case of a drummer who has stepped far beyond the limits of the average professional.

Before Mr. Cruchet assumed the management of the Advance Drum Company, he spent twelve years as one of Canada's leading theatre men in Regina, Calgary and Edmonton. In Calgary he earned the reputation of being second to none on the Orpheum Circuit, and "between shows" he put in two years with one of the leading hardware firms of Calgary in a responsible position. For the past three years Mr. Cruchet has operated the Advance Drum Company, increasing its business each month until it now serves the majority of drummers of Western Canada by mail in a manner that has given the boys of that section a real "service station." "Lem," as he is nicknamed, is a xylophone player who can safely be termed "in the Green Brothers class."

DEALERS—Have you learned the complete details and prices regarding the New Leedy "Reliance" Bass Drums?

Publicity with Results

To "let the public know" in a way that will bring sure, profitable results is the desire of every music dealer. Many stunts have been used in addition to newspaper advertising, but here is one by the ever progressive Edfred Company, of Akron, Ohio, that proved a "knockout." Just before the Paul Whiteman Orchestra came to town this company rigged up the tramp drummer shown in the accompanying photo and had him march all over town ripping off military field beats on a 12x16-inch Standard Leedy Drum. A sign on the tramp's back told that Edfred sold the kind of drummers' equipment used by Geo. W. Marsh, the Paul Whiteman drummer. Did the public know? We'll say they did! And it brought business, too. Ted Stewart was the snappy drummer who put it over.

A Neat Transfer Sign

Hardly a day passes but what the dealer is requested to put up a sign of some sort advertising musical wares. If he put them all up, his store would look like a patchwork quilt, so it is only natural that the neatest and most artistic receive space. With this knowledge at hand the Leedy Mfg. Co. has taken special care in designing the transfer shown at the left. It is in black and gold only and has been declared the richest display yet offered. Being 5½x6 inches, it is not too large for either counter or showcase space; however, it makes a most attractive door and window sign. The words "Service Station" tell a true drummer's need. They are simple to put up and free for the asking. Write for yours today.

Southern Standard Music Company

Chattanooga, Tenn., drummers can boast of a "service station" that is a service station in every sense of the word, with stock and co-operation that would satisfy the most particular. Mr. Deering, the proprietor, has been in the music line in Chattanooga for several years. This is his new up-to-date store that is on a par with the finest big city concerns.

Leedy has recently put out a very fine display card in real photo form, 18 by 13 inches, of the U.S. (Washington, D.C.) Marine Band Drum Section. Mailed free.

"WORLD'S FINEST DRUMMERS' INSTRUMENTS"

The Exclusive Drummers' Paper

Drums of Japan

The Generic Name for Drums of All Kinds in Japan is "Taiko"

Drums came to Japan from China, but they are not of Chinese origin. It is said that they were used by the Barbarians a thousand years before the time of Confucius (550 B. C.) to accompany the worship of the gods.

The present Japanese variety was invented by the Crown Prince Umavado in the reign of Empress Suika at the beginning of the eighth century.

Japanese drummers play with great vigor, lifting the sticks as high as the head, bringing them down with a circular motion to the head of the drum.

The Uta-Daiko, the O-Tsuzumi, and the Kagura-Fuyé

The Uta-Daiko is the "song drum" and is the one most used in the theatre. It is also called the Shimé-daiko and the Geza-daiko, usually made in a 11x7-inch size, and was first introduced in Japan by Komparu Gon-no-kami, a famous Taiko player of the court band about 1540 A. D.

The O-Tsuzumi, or shoulder drum, is usually played with the hands and made up in a 9x11-inch size.

The Kagura-Fuyé is another type of shoulder drum made still smaller.

All three are often used as shown in the Japanese orchestra photo above, and, while they are tuned to about the same pitch, they are not necessarily played all at one time.

Kero is the name of a small drum used in China—according to the old records about the period of the T'ang Dynasty (618-907 A. D.) to signalize the appearance of the dawn. It is now the type used in Japan for the purpose of leading and setting rhythm of processional bands.

Johnny Auer of the U. S. Marine Band (Washington, D. C.), signs C. O. D. after his name. When asked what it meant, Johnny informed us: "Common, Ordinary Drummer."

The Prize Story

By Fred Johnson, Fort William, Ontario, Canada

EDITOR'S NOTE—We trust that our readers will accept this little bit of comedy in the spirit of fun, realizing that the most serious and artistic of professions have their human side.
Fred Johnson is a real live-wire drummer and dealer in Fort William, Ontario, where he holds down the principal theatre job and has a large class of pupils. He is an excellent xylophonist as well as being a very fine drummer.

D-R-U-M-S

The favorite American instrument, and in importance, geographically, second to none.

Drumming is a skin game.

Drummers are amphibious, ambidexterous and abstemious, but are full of the spirit of '76! Drummers are never broke or hungry; they've always got a roll.

Drummers have private opinions—of the leader and the other guys. No matter what their guise!

Drummers are generally ex-musicians that have had waivers asked on them in the Federal League, but come back as bench warmers to "strike out" in the pinches.

Some drummers play bells, others have them. Some drummers "read the spots," others improve on the composer.

Drummers are classified as musicians—when not selling dry goods.

Drummers have been known to use knives and forks intelligently and finger bowls surreptitiously, and have a pronounced predilection for flamadiddles, seven-stroke rolls, daddy-mammys, tattoos, before-and-after beats, and other edibles. In spite of these awful handicaps, the drummer is happy—blissfully so.

I know one that was operated on for appendicitis! But he was a real one and wouldn't play in a picture house factory.

A drummer must be able to speak several languages, such as soubrette, song and dance, bumps, shooting gallery, and profane. The last mentioned is very popular with vaudevillians. A vaudeville drummer must combine the qualities of a mind reader, equilibrist and juggler, otherwise his name is Mud.

A well-equipped drummer always possesses tympani, but never ask him what he cooks in "them copper kittles."

When a drummer works in grand opera he doesn't look well. No wonder. Look how many bars he loafs 'round!

I know one drummer that can count 1,678,936 bars correctly and then come in with a BANG!!!—just like that—but he is clever.

Some drummers are highly conversational. I know at least one drummer who should be called "Perpetual Motion." Talks all the time and says nothing. He put Barnum in the show business and the flicker in the cinematograph.

Drummers do not study in Europe; the correct flavor is obtained in Brazil. The teacher is almond-eyed, and the pupil is fed solely on goobers. When a drummer graduates he will never knowingly stand beneath a tree unless he is married and doesn't care.

Drummers are subject to peculiar ailments, notably pedal cramps and indigestion of the cerebrum. But this doesn't have a deleterious effect on their appetites or truthfulness, as their veracity is undoubted. I have heard several of 'em eat.

Drummers are humane and good family men, being very kind to their automobiles.

All in all, drummers are all right when you know them; but you must be well acquainted.

Non compes mentis. Get the shovel.

PASSED BY THE NATIONAL BOARD OF NON-SENSE-ER-SHIP

James E. Gilpin

Every drummer and dealer who has ever done business with the Leedy Mfg. Co. is familiar with the little blue shipping memorandum slip that accompanies the package signed "Gilp." However, few know that this is the signature of the man who is in charge of the Leedy stock room and passes on all outgoing orders. Mr. Gilpin has been a member of the Leedy firm for 21 years and is a string bass and tuba player of exceptional fame and ability. Several years ago he was well known on the road, having "trouped" with the best in that day.

Leedy   "FOR DRUMMERS WHO CARE"   **Leedy**

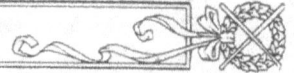

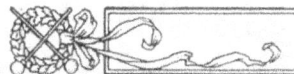

A PAPER DEVOTED TO
THE INTERESTS OF THE DRUMMER

No subscription fee

Advertisements accepted

Published quarterly at 1033 East Palmer Street
Indianapolis, Indiana

Editor..................................GEO. H. WAY
Business Manager......................A. W. KUERST

Habit

To tell a drummer that he has formed a bad habit in doing a certain thing the wrong way is indeed treading on dangerous ground if friendship is to be considered. And still it really would be an act of friendship to correct a real bad habit if the correction is truly constructive.

There are few professions where the same thing is done in so many different ways as in drumming, and neither is there another profession where opinions vary as much. Another thing that makes the "correct way" a difficult thing to agree upon is that the drummer has more to handle and more to do than any other musician. He knows he has to "be there" and no one cares how he does it, so long as he is there at the right time. Excuses don't go.

Every drummer thinks his system is the best and perhaps it is—for him. It is not the intention of DRUM TOPICS to give instructions as to how to play drums, etc. We only want to tell you what the other fellows are doing and swap hints and ideas for drummers to pick out what is best suited to their particular needs.

However, it is admitted by all drummers that there are some bad habits easy to fall into that do not exactly come under the head of the method of playing. For instance, no drummer can do his best work with his left arm resting on his knee. Lots of fellows do this where there is a handy ledge around the pit to rest his left foot on, and even dance drummers acquire the habit of putting his left foot on the rung of a nearby chair. It is very injurious to the action and flexibility of the left arm and wrist and comes under the head of downright laziness. Then there is the drummer who continually substitutes. Sometimes he will roll on the bass drum when the part calls for tympani and there is plenty of time to get over to same. Again you will see a drummer strike his triangle with the drum stick when he has had plenty of time to pick up a regular triangle beater. Tipping back in one's chair is another lazy trick. Striking the bass drum with the tips of the stick is still another, and one of the worst faults of all among drummers is the continual habit of leaving out traps when the part calls for them. Many drummers "get by with murder" in this particular stunt, as every trap is not always scored in the leader's part and therefore its omission is not noticed.

There are many more bad habits too numerous to mention here that the drummer can easily acquire.

True, there is sometimes a reason. Perhaps it's a hard job and you become tired toward the end. Perhaps it's an underpaid job and you cannot right then find a better one, and perhaps you are working for an unreasonable leader or manager and you are too discontented to do better; but these conditions can't last forever, and should some bad habits become too firmly rooted into your work they might injure you for better times that are bound to come if you keep your eyes open for opportunities. The drummer of today has more opportunity than ever before.

Check up on yourself.

Oscar M. Kapp

The Circle Theatre Orchestra, Indianapolis, Ind., for the past seven years has had Oscar M. Kapp as the drummer. He has had varied experience in the concert and theatre field, also in instructional capacities. Some of these being: Vaudeville (six years), Majestic Theatre, La Crosse, Wis.; Strand Theatre, Louisville, Ky., and instructor at Louisville Conservatory of Music, Indianapolis College of Music, and the Metropolitan School of Music.

A recent signed letter from Mr. Kapp reads in part as follows:

"I compliment you on conceiving and presenting DRUM TOPICS for drummers, and urge all to the support of it by contributing everything of interest to it. It fills a long-felt want in the profession.

"Present-day drummers must be versatile, especially so in theatre work. Based on past experience, I stress the importance of selecting proper extra cymbals. I find that, at least, these are necessary: One Italian for soft crashes, one Chinese for stop crashes, two Turkish for loud sustained crashes, and, in the same category, one very large Tam-Tam for loud sustained crashes, and, in the same category, one very large Tam-Tam and one small Tam-Tam for Oriental effects. All of these are also adapted to hard stick work.

"My Leedy equipment, including Universal Tympani, has stood the test under such capable conductors as Weil, formerly of the St. Paul Symphony; the late Natiello, of the Royal Italian Band; Schmidt, of the Boston Symphony; Kafka, of the Cincinnati Symphony; the late Kohls of the Babalan & Katz Theatre of Chicago; Altshuler, of the Russian Symphony, and the present popular Bakaleinikoff, formerly with the New York Philharmonic Orchestra. Many of these, as you know, have visited your factory, being interested in the making of the best in percussion supplies.

"The modern jazz tympani part reflects the foresight of some of the composers of the past. I cite here 'The Orgies of the Spirits, by Ilynsky. Excerpts below:

"Brother drummers know that if you can get by with a number such as this, Leedy Universal Tympani must be the last word in tonal and automatic construction."

Who Is It That—

Is not a hobo, though he beats his way through the world;
Not a drunkard, though his head is often tight;
Nor a baker, though his rolls are good.
He can patch a head, but he is not a doctor;
Sets time, but is not a jeweler;
Nor an acrobat, but can roll on his head;
Not a grocer, but he sells beats.
And though he makes breaks in the dance hall—
He's not a lowbrow, but the—POOR OLD DRUMMER!

H. C. Branch, Lynchburg, Va.

 "WORLD'S FINEST DRUMMERS' INSTRUMENTS"

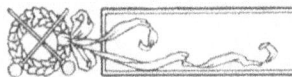 # Leedy Drum Topics

Some Prominent Leedy Drummers

 ROLAND F. FELIX, a very fine all-around drummer, of Springfield, Mass., has been using some of his Leedy equipment for ten years. He was once en route with the Central American Marimba Band and has been the past two years with Patterson's Venetian Garden Orchestra.
(Courtesy Dean's Music House)

 RALPH PULLEN, of Hutchinson, Kan., who is now on the road with a prominent western organization, has an exceptionally high rating as a real drummer. He has had twenty-two years' experience in every class of work and says there is no drum equal to the New Style Multi-Model.

Attention!
Photos of drummers make DRUM TOPICS interesting to drummers. It's a drummers' paper, so send yours in.

 DEAN RICHMOND is now one of the foremost dance drummers of Seattle, Wash. At present with Lou Jepson's Cosmopolitans. "Dean" formerly lived in Indianapolis, Ind. He is a man who uses tympani in dance work with wonderful results. Everything Leedy.

 HOWARD H. RANKIN is at present with Art Biddinger's Dance Band, of Cedar Rapids, Iowa. Rankin is in the leading class of drummers and has a long record of fine positions. He says his Leedy drums are the best he has ever owned in his many years' experience.

For You
DRUM TOPICS is printed quarterly — four times a year—January 15, April 15, July 15, and November 15. Be sure that your correct address is in our files. A copy will be mailed free.

 WALTER H. VEIL is playing at the Eastman Hotel, Hot Springs, Ark., with Chas. Fischer's Orchestra. Formerly of Kalamazoo, Mich. Veil says he likes Leedy instruments best of all. Leedy considers this a fine boost, because this drummer is one of the very best in the dance business.

 JACK MIELE, of New York City, and formerly of the Palace Theatre and Strand Roof, also Abe Small's Orchestra, is now playing with Joe Samuels at the Palais Royal in Buffalo, N. Y. One can't say too much regarding the exceptional ability of this drummer. Another confirmed Leedy-ite.

A diplomatic drummer is one who laughs at the leader's bum jokes.

Some drums are like garters — after three months there is no snap to them.

The A440 stamped on the lowest A of a 2½-octave set of bells means that the bells are at that pitch throughout. The actual bar of A440 would lie one octave lower than the lowest A found in your bells and is the A generally used when tuning an orchestra to pitch.

G. Newell Hayes

In the last issue of DRUM TOPICS there was a request for the name and photo of the drummer who has held down a theatre job for the longest period of time.
Many responded, and it was surprising to note how some of the boys stick, which proves that drummers are more steady than is generally supposed.
C. Newell Hayes, whose photo is shown above, holds the record of all replies received, having sat in the Keith Temple Vaudeville Theatre pit in Rochester, N. Y., for eighteen years. Previous to this he trouped with Al G. Fields Minstrels, Lew Dockstader Minstrels and Harry Lauder. His entire outfit is Leedy, and we are indeed proud to count this well-known and most efficient drummer as a Leedy booster.

Dutch Windmill Scene

This new painting for bass drum heads must be seen to be appreciated, because a photo cannot do justice to the beauty of the color scheme.

 JAMES C. HARPER is the fellow who wrote the prize story in the last issue of DRUM TOPICS. He is a well-known and very efficient drummer, located at Lenoir, N. C. Harper does not devote his full time to drumming at present, but claims when he does work he uses only Leedy.

 GEO. F. KATZ is one of the "old timers" of Philadelphia, having been a field drummer for the past thirty years. He was with the Second Regiment Band in 1893 and has used a Leedy in all his work since 1910. Katz enjoys a wonderful reputation.

Perhaps
You have an idea regarding drums or traps that is worth real money. Why not find out? You can consult Leedy, knowing that you will be honestly protected.

 JOHN M. SWEENEY is a very nifty drummer and entertainer of Providence, R. I., who is as good at one as the other. He has appeared at all the leading functions of Providence since 1916. Now with Jack Silva's Minstrel Six. Sweeney is strong for Leedy all through.

 L. F. GARLOW, of Adams, N. Y., plays both drums and trumpet. All his drum equipment is of the Leedy make. Now with the Hubert Melody Boys. Garlow plays all over northern New York and is kept busy every night. He is a great favorite because of his ability.

Things to Do
Get a Leedy Catalog "M" and Supplement.
See the many new circulars.
Tell your drummer friends about Drum Topics.
Send in your photo.
Send in your stories.
Be sure that we have your correct address.

 RUSSELL C. BURK has often been called "The Boy Wonder of the Drums." He is 11 years old and has studied two years with Mr. Leedy personally. At present the young man plays in his school and church orchestra. This boy is going to be in the professional class.

 ED. GRIFFITH, of Marion, Ohio, is with the Marion Steam Shovel Band. Also plays with the Prospect (Ohio) K. of P. Band and has his own ten-piece dance orchestra. He has been in the game 28 years. A real drummer in every respect. All Leedy.

Leedy "WORLD'S FINEST DRUMMERS' INSTRUMENTS"

The Exclusive Drummers' Paper

A Few More Who Are in the "Spot Light" Class

ERNIE BRUCE'S Sax Band, of Toronto, Canada, is indeed a unique and clever musical organization. Mr. Bruce is the organizer and leader as well as a Leedy drummer. It is a busy outfit, being a very popular attraction at the theatres and clubs of Toronto. Bruce's work is different and better.

AL. A. GRABS, the Majestic Theatre Orpheum Vaudeville drummer "par excellence" at Bloomington, Ill., has been on this job for five seasons. Fifteen years' experience has made this drummer one of the very best. For several seasons he was featured as a xylophone soloist on Chautauqua circuits. The picture proves Leedy.

EARL C. SIMMONS, secretary Local No. 241, Butte, Mont., formerly of Portland, Ore., is now playing at the American Theatre. He recently installed the Leedy Universal Tympani in his pit. The photo shows him with "The Columbians" of Butte. Simmons is a very thorough and capable drummer.

JULIUS MENDELSON, drummer, formerly with the Twentieth Century Jazz Boys and Chas. Lucy Serenaders, is now with the Sky Line Serenaders of Memphis. This orchestra and drummer are among the foremost in the South. Mendelson makes his headquarters at the Melody Music Shop of Memphis and is completely Leedy equipped.

HORACE BEAVER, with the Southland Orchestra, has few superiors in the dance game. At present this orchestra is going big at the leading dance hall of Columbus, Ohio, having just finished an engagement at the Orpheum Dance Palace in Terre Haute, Ind. Beaver has a most complete Leedy outfit.

FRANK BRUNIE, a favorite and excellent dance drummer of Seattle, Wash., is with the well-known "Ye Collegians Orchestra." Brunie was completely Leedy equipped by the Bush & Lane Piano Company of Seattle and is high in praise of same, especially his Multi-Model Elite Snare Drum.

   "FOR DRUMMERS WHO CARE"

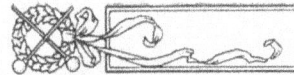
Leedy Drum Topics

Leedy Separate Tension Rods

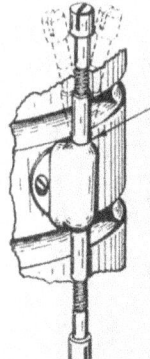

PATENTED
SELF ALIGNING UNIVERSAL
BALL JOINT.

This drawing shows the only mechanically perfect separate tension rod that was ever designed. No rod of this type can be called perfect unless it is strictly self-aligning in all directions.

The receiving tubes are of steel, not brass, and they swing universally from the strong, rigid center support. This center support is now made of four gauges heavier metal than on former models and we have never had a complaint of a binding or stripped thread.

Don Beal

After you have read this little story you will know that this gentleman of fame in the music world is not a "cake eater," but that he makes and decorates cakes fit for cake-eating kings and queens. Behold! Don Beal, who has the reputation of being as good as any minstrel show drummer who has ever "missed a parade." Four years with Al G. Fields — enough said. Don is now working with his father in the bakery biz in his home town, Terre Haute, Ind., and playing on the side. Of course he is a Leedy booster; fifteen years of it.

It is said that the best training for a dance drummer is bicycle riding.

In All Seriousness

From a letter: "Some time ago I purchased a Chinese Musette from your dealer here and am writing to inform you that there is no instructor of the Musette in this city; therefore, will you please have the Musette professor at your factory mail me instructions as to how to perform on same?"

Get Along Pretty Good

Old Man: "Do you think you can make my daughter happy?"
The Sheik: "Do I? Well, I wish you could see us in the parlor some night!"   "Ziff."

Cats Is Sheep

An erroneous idea among drummers is that gut snares (and instrument strings) are made from cat gut.

Where would we get all the cats for the millions of snares and strings used today?

No, it is not cat gut; the finest material of this kind is from the entrails of sheep.

Why is it that many good drummers will insist on buying and using the impractical 17-inch long, thin, light model drum stick? True, manufacturers make them. They have to, because of the demand and the impossibility of making a demonstration to every drummer. But any reasonable man can easily be convinced that this type of drum stick neither brings out the best tone in a drum nor is easier to play with by making a fair comparison with a model 16 inches long and slightly heavier. Some drummers believe that a long, light, thin stick is easier to drum with, especially the roll, and that it will assist in the execution. This is not true, because no drum stick, regardless of the weight or model, will go faster or better than the ability of the performer.

Foolish Question No. 6666

Leader to Drummer: "Do you want a job?"
Drummer to Leader: "Oh, no; I just called around to tell you that all the drummers in this town have had a meeting and decided that you leaders should receive a substantial increase in salary."

A Better Way

Some drummers use a spring clothespin to dampen their pedal cymbal. The "durn" thing is always falling off. Why not try a piece of adhesive tape? Just stick it on over the edge, allowing the same length on each side, like a hairpin. The more tape, the less ring. Try various lengths till the tone suits you.

Remember—too much cymbal, overpowering the tone of the bass drum, is worse than none at all.

Admission Free

Four babies have been born in the British Empire Exhibition. It is remarkable what people will do to get in without paying.

The Improved Leedy-Fraser Pedal

The Leedy-Fraser Pedal has been 100% improved at eight different points, especially the action.

You will declare this to be your choice of pedals once you have tried it.

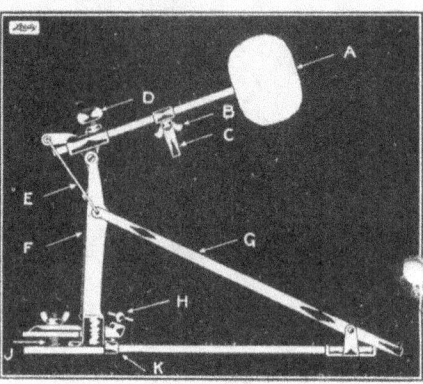

Note the improved features. They are not guesswork, but based on proven scientific principles.

A—Detachable nut and washer for quick removal of ball.
B—Jam clamp non-slip.
C—New spring device acting as a shock absorber for cymbal striker.
D—Heavier wing nut for setting beater rod.
E—Pull wire travels on new angle and arc.
F—New heavier spring, adjustable.
G—"Relax" footboard for entire foot, eliminating the necessity of lifting the weight of the foot for each beat.
H—New jam clamp to be set after hoop clamp is adjusted.
J—New spring under hoop clamp to hold upper part of clamp free while adjusting pedal to drum.
K—Jam clamp (H) acts as set screw for footboard rod. Can't pull out.

Willard W. Perry

Here is a drummer who has been using the same Leedy bass drum for 18 years and still going strong. Willard Perry is with Ray Robinson's Orchestra, of Seattle, Wash., and has a rating as high as any drummer on the Pacific Coast.

   "WORLD'S FINEST DRUMMERS' INSTRUMENTS"

Leedy Drum Topics Issue 7

The Exclusive Drummers' Paper

Signor Friscoe

One of this season's headline vaudeville attractions is Signor Friscoe and his Guatemalan Ensemble. It is also one of the most expensively staged and highest salaried acts in the business. Every drummer and xylophonist in the land knows what a wonderful artist Friscoe is. All his instruments for years have been Leedy and this latest one is entirely real gold plated, excepting the bars.

There are still a few well-known drummers and leaders left who honestly believe that a rope tension bass drum has a better tone than the rod type. Scientific tests have proven this to be far from the fact—principally because any material or construction that is placed beyond the point where the head comes in contact with the shell has no bearing on the tone.

The Double Tom-Tom

This new idea in Tom-Toms is very practical for the jobbing drummer, as it eliminates carrying the entire set of four and stand. Each one of these Tom-Toms is tunable, which is a great advantage in damp weather, and their tone is even better than the extra large size and bulky Chinese Tom-Toms, which never sound the same two nights in succession. The Double Tom-Toms are adjustable to any position on the upright of the bass drum clamp and make a very neat appearance. The large one is 14 inches in diameter, the small one is 12 inches.

The Saturday Evening Post

Every drummer should read Earl Chapin May's story called "The Reign of Reeds and Rhythm" on page 52 of the January 10, 1925, issue of *The Saturday Evening Post*. You will note that all the present-day prominent drummers mentioned in Mr. May's story are Leedy drummers and that the names of the traps, models, etc.—even to the "Maple Shell Bass Drum" used by Gus Helmecke—could be none other than Leedy.

Remember These?

WANTED

A-1 trap drummer for Bunk's Comedians. Long season south. Must have snare and bass drum and be good dresser. Boozers save stamps. No tickets. Write; don't wire.

WANTED

Trap drummer; $10.00 per and you get it. Must understand gasoline torches and behave like a gentleman when up town. Overland Dramatic Show, under canvas. Ralph Hendershott please write.

WANTED

Man and wife. Man to play drums in parade and post bills; wife to sing ballads and double in cook house. Good treatment. Buckskin Ben's Wild West Two-Car Show.

WANTED

First-class picture show in thriving Mississippi town wants drummer who has bells and can play them, also double illustrated songs. No cigarette fiends or chasers. We play Sundays. Ticket yes, if we know you. Pastime Theatre.

The Chicago Symphony Orchestra Drum Section

M. A. Wintrich, Principal of the Chicago Symphony Orchestra Drum Section, is shown here standing behind the Leedy Universal Tympani. Mr. Wintrich has been the leading drummer of this orchestra for 27 years, having been selected for this position by the famous conductor, Theodore Thomas.

A Drummer's (Coue) Cue

Day by day I "beater" better and better.

Chinese drummers are the only ones we know of who use their "sticks" to eat with.

Front Cover

Ray Ennis has been at the drums since he was 13 years of age, starting in his home town of Springfield, Ill., and later directing his own orchestra there. In 1919 he went to Chicago and has played with the best in that city—Chicago Opera Club, Tivoli Theatre and others. Ennis has no betters as a drummer. All Leedy.

```
IF YOU LIKE DRUM TOPICS
SO WILL YOUR DRUMMER
FRIENDS ~ SEND IN THEIR
NAMES
```

 "FOR DRUMMERS WHO CARE"

Leedy Drum Topics Issue 7

Leedy
DRUM TOPICS

The Exclusive Drummers' Paper

JANUARY, 1925
SEVENTH EDITION

F. E. Wolfington,
1111 Laurel St.,
Indianapolis, Ind.

POSTMASTER—Return Postage Guaranteed

Leedy MANUFACTURING CO.
INDIANAPOLIS, INDIANA

WHAT ABOUT YOU – WHEN PAY DAY COMES?

MANAGER — DRUMMER — This DRUMMER HAS NO TYMPANI SO — HE THINKS IT OVER AND — GOES TO SEE THE DEALER — AND PLACES THE ORDER — DRUMMER RECEIVES TYMPANI — DRUMMER UNPACKS TYMPANI — DRUMMER MAKES A HIT — MANAGER — DRUMMER — BECAUSE HE NOW HAS Leedy TYMPANI

Leedy Drum Topics Issue 8

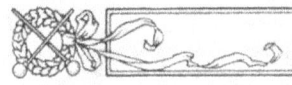 Drum Topics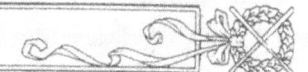

THIS ISSUE OF DRUM TOPICS IS FULL OF "INSIDE STUFF" ON HOW AND WHERE *Leedy* DRUMMERS' EQUIPMENT IS MADE

The Idea is Simply This—That You May Become Better Acquainted With Us.

We know you will enjoy these pages, because it is true that Drummers are more interested in the details of their instruments than other musicians.

The Drummer has more to do than other musicians—he has to know more about his instruments from a mechanical point of view.

(Just watch a saxophonist hurry to the repair shop when something goes wrong— how many fiddlers can rehair their own bows?) He has to be his own "fixer" in nine cases out of ten.

That's why Drummers are "originators" and, in numerous cases, real inventors—the nature of his work is original.

As with no other musical instrument, in Drums there is always something new—*Progress* is the Drummer's Creed—and so he must be always more closely associated with the makers and distributors of his "tools" than the rest of the profession.

That's the "WHY" of DRUM TOPICS—closer and personal touch between the Drummer, the Dealer and the Manufacturer.

And that's the "WHY" of this issue of "inside stuff" on—

"The World's Largest Drum Factory"

YES IT IS—
It covers 51,250 square feet of floor space. This photo does not show its real size—the "L's" of the main plant and the wood factory (a separate building) do not show.

"WORLD'S FINEST DRUMMERS' INSTRUMENTS"

The Exclusive Drummers' Paper

"Mistakes will happen in the best of regulated families." When we make one, let us know it. Don't keep quiet and harbor an unpleasant feeling over what is nothing more than a misunderstanding. We will willingly admit an error and, after all, that's all it amounts to; but if it gets by us and you say nothing, we both lose. Remember, Babe Ruth misses 'em once in a while.

Your check carefully posted.

Do You Play Canada This Season?

Four and twenty drummers,
All got very dry,
So they went across the border
And got a case of "rye."

And when the "rye" was opened
They all began to sing:
"Who the hell was Volstead?
God save the King."

Here our office staff says "Howdy." Perhaps you have met some of us, or perhaps you have had correspondence with some of our members.

1. U. G. LEEDY, President.
2. HERMAN WINTERHOFF, Vice-President.
3. A. W. KUERST, Secretary-Treasurer.
4. GEO. H. WAY, Sales and Advertising Manager.
5. C. H. STRUPE, Superintendent and Mechanical Engineer.
6. P. C. LAYCOCK, Office Manager.
7. L. W. ECHOLS, Credit Manager.
8. JAMES E. GILPIN, Purchasing Agent.
9. LEE PARADICE, Cost Accountant.
10. ROY ULREY, Stock Manager.
11. IVA E. SIMS, Chief Auditor.
12. N. SEIBERT, Stenographer.
13. MRS. DUNCAN, Stenographer.
14. E. M. WAY, Stenographer.
15. E. M. KESTNER, Order Clerk.
16. MARIE SWEET, Addressograph Clerk.
17. NOVA CARTER, Filing Clerk.

Superintendent and Cost Accountant's Office

The Superintendent's Office is where the responsibility falls for working out the new designs after it has been decided to adopt a new idea or improve an old model. Everything is handled by blueprints to instruct the various workmen, therefore it requires the entire time of a draftsman. Mr. Cecil Strupe is the Leedy Superintendent and the man who invented the Universal Tympani, also the method of manufacturing many other drummers' instruments.

The Cost Accounting Department is also incorporated in this office and it is one of the most important sections of the Leedy organization. Mr. Lee Paradice is in charge, with an assistant.

Your letter is opened at once.

Large business establishments, where many people are employed, must be run along systematic lines; however, the Leedy Mfg. Co. is not so bound by system but what your smallest want is attended to in a personal way. Our staff is large and trained to detail.

Customers or Cuss-tomers?

Many think complaints are a nuisance; others see complaints as an opportunity to cement cordial feeling with customers, for the "kick" that is handled tactfully and adjusted promptly, cheerfully and liberally will often turn a potential "knocker" into a booster for the house!

But it is the complaints that are never reported that hurt—no opportunity is given to rectify, adjust or explain. It is a queer quirk of human nature to criticize rather than commend; thus disgruntled customers become perambulators of discontent. One spoken word against a firm's methods, service or merchandise can kill more budding sales in a minute than salesmen plus advertising can create in a week. Therefore we welcome complaints and adjust them with an eye to the future.

"*By Gum.*"

And this is a partial view of the main office.

Musical instruments are a specialty and not a universal product like clothes, groceries, etc., and drummers' instruments are still more of a specialty within the musical instrument line. It takes lots of explaining regarding some things, so let us have the doubtful questions in detail and we will make every effort to help you to the correct viewpoint.

Inquiries are answered.

   "FOR DRUMMERS WHO CARE"   

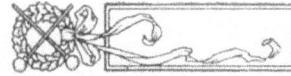 # Leedy Drum Topics

THESE ILLUSTRATIONS TELL THE STORY

A trip through the busy Leedy Plant leaves the visitor with one predominating impression—wonderful workmanship. The minute care given the minor manufacturing operations illustrates what we mean by—

"THE WORLD'S FINEST DRUMMERS' INSTRUMENTS"

The heart of manufacturing Leedy Drums is in the toolroom. It is here where all the special dies, jigs, etc., are made, and it requires a special staff of highly trained men who are far above the average machinist in skill. Drummers often ask why we don't make a certain part a little different in dimensions or shape, not realizing that their particular preference may not be that of the majority, and to change the dies that form the metal parts, even a fraction of an inch, would cost many hundreds of dollars and in some cases a thousand. For instance, Leedy spent $20,000.00 in this department in the development of the dies that form the famous one-piece copper tympani kettle. Mr. Fred Ellerkamp is in charge of this division, employing eight men.

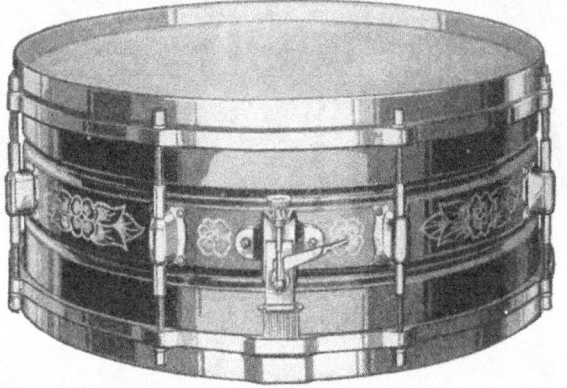

The New Leedy "Professional" Drum
FLOATING HEAD—"ELITE" MODEL

This new drum has several features long desired by drummers, but which have never before been practically accomplished. The Floating Head principle equalizes head tension and prevents the flesh hoop from touching the shell at all times, therefore eliminating all possibilities of a binding drum. Additional strength, by using four bolts instead of two, has greatly increased the efficiency of our self-aligning separate tension rod. Be sure to get full details from our new Catalog "N" regarding this wonderful drum. The photo above shows the new model in the "Elite" finish.

The Metal Shell

There is absolutely no solder used at any point in the Leedy Metal Shell. The shell is of one-piece, 22-gauge sheet brass, joined by the electric brazing process. The inside reinforcing is spun to a maximum degree of stiffness which is amply strong for any use to which a snare drum is put.

Art Department

Painting on bass drum heads, so that the work is artistic, is a "trade" all its own. All our engraved shells are high-class hand-work and not of the common machine variety. Mr. Ed. Riedwig, our artist, is permanently employed at the factory, as is also Mr. J. F. Hammond, our engraver.

   "WORLD'S FINEST DRUMMERS' INSTRUMENTS"   

The Exclusive Drummers' Paper

Orders Are Sent to the right departments.

No one likes a delay after an order is placed, and no manufacturer or dealer likes it any better than the customer. In fact, they like it far less.

You can bet that we rush your order all possible. When you think it over, you'll see that it's only natural for us to want to get it out, because it means that we receive payment that much quicker.

(Steel and Brass Storage Room)

However, we have our troubles and very often experience unavoidable delays with firms from which we buy the raw materials. For instance, in drum manufacturing many special sized steel and brass bars, rods and sheets are used. They are not carried in stock by the mills and jobbers; so, being made to order, we have to wait, especially if at the time we place the order there happens to be a big rush on in the mills for standard sizes.

Great attention is devoted to this part of our business, and we order many sizes months in advance, and Leedy service is now recognized as equal to that of any musical instrument manufacturer.

Section of Main Machine Room

Two rows 100 feet in length make up the main machine room. Power presses and many automatic screw machine lathes are assembled on this floor. It is here where all the "Bull Dog" holders, drum stands, drum rods, and other pressed steel parts are formed, some of them requiring many operations and a complete set of dies for each. Mr. Roy Jeffries, who has been with the Leedy Mfg. Co. twenty-five years, is the foreman of machine shop production. Nineteen men work under his supervision.

There is 200 pounds strain per square inch on a 14-inch diameter drum head of medium thickness when it is pulled to an average playing tension.

Another Section of the Machine Room

When you see a drummer salute a "lady friend" military fashion instead of lifting his hat, it's a cinch he is bald-headed.

Cymbals—Now and Then

This is certainly the age of cymbals for the drummer, and it's good stuff. Only a few years ago they were used principally for accented beats in concert work, "kicks," falls, etc., in theatre work, and once or twice in a dance number to be "doing something."

In these days cymbals are a necessity and are being used in an artistic and musical manner. One of the most pleasing effects from the drummer's "bag of tricks" is the modern "sock" effect obtained by the skillful use of his two or three cymbals. But don't forget—the quality of the "pans" must be good. Turkish and Italian, also Nickel Silver models, are the best to use. The Nickel Silver are fine on account of their very "stinging" tone. Leedy makes the highest grade of this model and takes especial care in selecting the imported brands.

The "node" of a bar is its point of no vibration.

A Big Press

This gigantic Toledo power press weighs 12 tons and can exert a pressure of 125 tons. Such instrument parts as the new counter hoops of the Leedy "Professional" (Floating Head) Drum and the heavy xylophone and marimba stand parts are formed on this press. It stands 10 feet high.

Bride (to salesman): "Please, sir, I'd like a little oven."
Salesman: "Er—pardon me. Not while your husband's along."

"FOR DRUMMERS WHO CARE"

Leedy Drum Topics

[The Leedy Mfg. Co.'s Plant Contains 51,250 Square Feet of Floor Space. It Is the World's Largest Drum Factory]

The Hydraulic Press

It is here that the famous One-Piece Leedy Copper Tympani Bowl is formed.

The work of developing this bowl was carried on for four years before being perfected. You will notice that the left wall of the shop is new compared with the one on the right. It was built to give the workmen strict privacy, as many of the operations are known only to a few.

It is an easy matter to form a half sphere from sheet metal, but it's a very difficult thing to extend it beyond with the 6-inch straight wall necessary on modern tympani.

Note the large disc of sheet copper and the finished bowl at the left of the photo. Leedy bowls are all perfect in shape and even throughout in gauge.

Tympani Assembly Department

All three models of Leedy Tympani are equipped with the same type one-piece bowl. In this department the instruments are assembled, and before leaving the factory they receive three rigid inspections and tests. Have you read all about the Universal Pedal model? Complete descriptive folder mailed free on request. It is the one Machine Tympani that "holds its tone."

A Nice Effect

Cut notches around the edges of your tambourine shell. Make them only one-eighth of an inch deep and one-quarter of an inch space between each one. Slightly round the edges.

When the tambourine is laid head down on your tympani and you draw a drum stick gently across the notches, it produces a hollow, low tone, with the vibration of the jingles thrown in. A nice effect, especially in real pianissimo passages.

Electric Welding

Is the most modern method of joining two pieces of metal; in fact, it makes them one. This is one of the most expensive machines in the Leedy plant, and the work turned out here is faultless. Tympani model bass drum rod handles are made an actual part of the rod on this machine. Many important articles receive treatment here.

The Polishing Room

These men prepare the work for the plating tanks. Leedy's electroplating department has the reputation of turning out work second to none in the country.

The Electro-Plating Tanks

Three thousand gallons of various plating solutions are contained in these tanks. Mr. Ralph McCracken has been foreman of electroplating for Leedy for ten years.

"WORLD'S FINEST DRUMMERS' INSTRUMENTS"

The Exclusive Drummers' Paper

Leedy SOLO-TONE XYLOPHONES, MARIMBAS, also BELLS and CHIMES are indeed the Highest Quality known in these Instruments.

They are used and indorsed by such famous artists as Geo. Hamilton Green—Joe Green—Signor Friscoe—Lamberti—El Cleve and many others.

Herman Winterhoff

Is the Vice-President of the Leedy Mfg. Co. and also acts as designer and superintendent in this department. He is unquestionably one of the greatest authorities on musical pitch in this country, and he has invented more practical and useful ideas in bells, chimes, marimbas and xylophones than any other one person. Mr. Winterhoff is responsible for the perfection of the new Vibraphone and it is he who originated tuning wooden bars in a manner that wholly eliminates discordant overtones.

Have you heard about the new Vibraphone? It is being used in Signor Friscoe's act. He has also recorded the "Gypsy Love Song" and "Aloha Oe" for the Edison Company. Get these records. The Green Brothers are using it on the radio and recording at the Brunswick and Victor laboratories. Write for particulars.

Rosewood Logs

They come from British Honduras, Central America. This wood is recognized by the leading authorities as having the best tone-producing qualities of any species. We call it exactly what it is, knowing there is nothing better to be obtained, and to give it a fictitious name would not in any way improve its quality. Only the finest logs are selected, and it may interest you to know that it is bought and sold by the pound instead of by the foot, which is customary in marketing lumber.

Resonator Making and Tuning

It requires equally as skillful and careful workmanship to make the resonators for the various instruments as it does to tune the bars. Photograph shows only a portion of this department. It is also here that the bars receive the third tuning, there being four altogether; the fourth tuning is done in soundproof rooms where several scientific devices are employed. Leedy does not use the tuning-by-ear method.

The Saw Mill

The above photograph shows where the logs are cut into approximate size bars. They are afterward put away and allowed to dry by the natural air process. We do not believe in the kiln-dry method, because this artificial and forced method is injurious to the tone.

Assembly Department

The finish is as carefully watched as the rest. The new Leedy xylophone and marimba stand is the fastest to operate ever made and a wonder for strength.

"FOR DRUMMERS WHO CARE"

Leedy Drum Topics

The Lumber Yard

The lumber used in the manufacture of Leedy wood shell drums is always inspected by Mr. Chas. Wesselhoff, the foreman of the wood shop, before it is purchased. Lumber for drums must be of a finer quality than necessary for most products, free from knots, etc., else it will not stand bending. Leedy woodwork needs little comment. Many drummers will testify to its superiority over all other makes, especially in solid wood shells. We guarantee them not to warp and there are still hundreds in use after 25 years' continual service.

Saws and Planers

The First Step of Preparing the Lumber

Shell-Bending Machine

—and this is why Leedy solid shells are heavier and superior in every respect to all others. It is the only machine of its kind in the world. Leedy built it.

For Beginners

Beginners always seek to learn—"just how tight should the heads be?" There is no set rule. After playing on a drum for a few months you soon learn a great deal about the tension of the heads. Some fellows like to play on a drum with very tight heads, while others the reverse. It's all due to the particular "feel" that suits you best. You know—just like your shoe laces. Some can't stand the feel of a tight lace. You will soon learn just how much to pull "her" up. It's sort of a sixth sense that grows with time and experience; however, most all agree on one point, and that is: the batter head should be a little more taut than the snare head. That's one reason why the separate tension system is best.

The Glue Room

This picture proves that there is a vast amount of hand work on Leedy solid wood drums. Note the many clamps holding the inside reinforcing hoops to the shells.

Hoop Turning and Shell Finishing

Leedy wood counter hoops are made of selected Rock Maple stock five-eighths of an inch thick. After bending and gluing, they are turned on this machine, which assures uniformity. Scraping and sanding must be carefully done, in order to get a fine varnish finish. The machine in the rear is for this purpose.

Hush, little New Trap,
Don't you cry;
You'll be "hokum"
Bye and bye.

"WORLD'S FINEST DRUMMERS' INSTRUMENTS"

The Exclusive Drummers' Paper

Another View of the Wood Shop

Many drummers will complain if the flesh hoops of a bass or snare drum are a little large and do not fit the shell snugly all the way around. While a loose flesh hoop (not too loose) does not look quite as nice, it is not otherwise a real bad fault, because a hoop that is free all the way around the shell will tension not only easier but with a greater degree of evenness and not be subject to binding. Evenness of tension is the secret of drum tone.

An Obstacle Overcome

It is not always convenient for the theatre drummer to erect a few chime tubes vertically in the pit. A large or small tube can be hung horizontally along under the "foots" on two pieces of cord or gut. The tone will not be impaired noticeably, provided the tube is slung in the cord at the proper distance from the end. Of course the cap end offers no problem, as there is a suspension point on the end of the same. A chime tube hung in this manner is a very handy accessory for the vaudeville man, as it can be used for numerous effects, using a chime mallet or drum sticks, for fire bells, etc.

Drum-Stick Turning

Only the finest quality second growth straight-grained white hickory is used for this most important article.

Leedy Drum Heads

Are known as the finest the market affords. A large staff of trained experts is employed and every care is taken to hold the line to the high standard of reputation it enjoys. The photograph at the right shows one of the refrigerating storage cellars where the hides are placed after arrival from the packing plants, in order to keep them fresh until they can be put in the process of manufacture. No chemicals are used in their making and a great deal of hand work is employed. The majority of symphony, grand opera and concert drummers prefer the Leedy "Kafette" tympani head. Our "Hardwhite" brand for snare drum batter heads are the finest in the world. Mr. John Gyuka is in charge of this department.

A Corner of the Beam Room

This shows the numerous tanks in which the hides are washed and rewashed many times. It is here that the flesh and hair is removed, also where the hand-skiving is done.

Hide Drying, Cutting and Sorting

When the curing is finished the hides are tacked to these large frames for drying and later cut into the various sized circles and sorted for branding. Leedy heads are carried through their entire process of manufacture without damaging the fibres of the hides.

Leedy   "FOR DRUMMERS WHO CARE"   *Leedy*

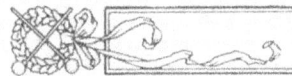 

The Paint Shop

The modern way of applying varnish and enamel finishes is with the compressed air brush. Two paint booths are kept busy every minute. A warm air drying room is a part of this department that does not show in the photograph.

Head Tucking

Great care is taken to see that all heads are tucked without any greater strain at one point than another. An evenly tucked head assures the same flexibility over its entire surface when dry.

If you receive this DRUM TOPICS, we no doubt have your correct address. However, about June 1st we will be mailing the new Leedy CATALOG "N"; so if in the meantime you should move, please be sure to send us your new address. We would also be glad to receive the names of any of your drummer friends who would like to receive both DRUM TOPICS and the new catalog.

The Eternal Red Triangle

CONSTANTINOPLE—The women of the caliph's harem left behind on his departure for Switzerland are penniless and in acute distress. A number of Y. M. C. A. secretaries visited the palace yesterday.
(From the Cleveland Plain Dealer.)

The reason some chorus men wear flowers in the coat lapel is because they can't wear them in their hair.

Tut-Ankh-Amen's tomb was opened again in Egypt recently, but it is hoped song writers will let the matter stay closed.

Get This Brunswick Record
BY THE GREEN BROTHERS

No. 2819. "Most of All I Want Your Love"—Waltz.
"Lovely Lady"—Waltz.
Castlewood Marimba Band.
LEEDY INSTRUMENTS USED

Drummers who play with the head of the drum down between their knees do not realize how much easier it would be if they would raise their drum stand to permit the head to come up to a point so that the left forearm hangs about level between the elbow and wrist; besides, it looks much more professional.

Drum Assembly Department

This photo shows just one-half of the drum assembly and drum stock department. The utmost care is taken in properly matching heads, snares, etc., and every drum is thoroughly tested by an experienced professional drummer before being shipped.

A Section of the Trunk Department

Any drummer who has trouped with a Leedy trunk will tell you that they stand up better on the road than any other make trunk used in his organization. Mr. Harry Butler is in charge of this department. All Leedy fibre and mackintosh drum cases are of the very highest quality.

   "WORLD'S FINEST DRUMMERS' INSTRUMENTS"   

The Exclusive Drummers' Paper

Part of the Stock Room

A hardware store has nothing on this. Seven men are required for its operation. James E. Gilpin, a member of the Leedy firm, oversees this division and attends to the purchasing of raw supplies as well. Did you know that just about every kind of material, in one form or other, is used in the manufacture of drummers' instruments? Try and think of something that is not needed. We can't.

Some More Stock Room

Shelves upon shelves and more shelves. Considering that the Leedy catalog lists over 1,200 numbers and that there are about 100,000 parts besides (who'd think it of drummers' "contraptions"?) it's some job to keep it all in order.

Sometimes Called a "Devil Chaser"

Once in a while you will find a Chinese Tom-Tom with a slight rattle inside. This is caused by a wire coil spring about three inches long and three-fourths inch in diameter that hangs on the inside of the instrument. Sometimes it becomes detached from the shell, which causes the rattle mentioned. Just why this spring is inserted we have never been able to discover, but there have been several theories offered by the importers. One is the spring is placed there for superstitious reasons, based on a belief that it scares away evil spirits. You will note that the spring rattles more perceptibly if the Tom-Tom is struck with great force. Another theory is that it improves the tone. We are inclined to believe this latter reason has some foundation, because after removing the spring we found a slight difference in the tone; however, this may have been caused by the removal and replacing of the head, which was necessary to get the spring out. Do not blame it on the drum factory if you hear this slight rattle, as the Tom-Toms are made in China and we have no control over the matter.

A Fable

Once upon a time there was a boy who wanted to see the world. He could have joined the navy at $30.00 a day (once a month), but he didn't think of that.

He had no money to travel, so he became a moving picture operator. This enabled him to see different cities in the Pathé News. But his eyes soon gave out and wanting to see more of the country, he got a job playing drums in a circus band. His hopes were soon shattered—the circus traveled at night.

While his journey took him from Portland, Maine, to Ditto, Oregon, he saw nothing. Eventually he lost his job with the circus band and became a tramp. One night, tired and hungry, he climbed into a freight car and fell fast asleep.

Two weeks later he awoke and crawled out of the freight car only to discover he had crossed the entire country both ways and was back in his old home town.

MORAL: Two thousand (net) years ago Aesop said: "A boy who is fond of scenery should become a theatre drummer."

The Shipping Room

And now for the final and very important touch—packing and shipping. Every dealer and drummer who has ever received shipments from Leedy knows that we can rightfully boast of this feature of our business. Chas. Kerr has been Leedy's shipping clerk for nineteen years and takes great pride in his work. He is assisted by Marshall Wilkins and six other men.

Geo. H. Way, Sales Manager for Leedy, and Chas. Seibert, Assistant Sales Manager, will be at the Geo. J. Birkel Store in Los Angeles for the big Shrine Convention, week of June 1st. We hope to meet all the visiting and local drummers. There will be a large display of drummers' instruments, with several new models and improvements, also the new Leedy "Professional" (Floating Head) Drum.

—and on its way to you.

There are no encores in a cemetery, so throw your flowers now.

The Leedy Mfg. Co. is the only firm that makes everything (excepting Chinese and Turkish instruments, also a few small metal whistles) that the drummer uses.

We wish every drummer could visit our plant. Be sure to let us know if you come to Indianapolis (the Convention City) and we will gladly show you every department of the World's Largest Drum Factory—where the World's Finest Drummers' Instruments are made.

So long for now! In the next issue of DRUM TOPICS we will revert to our regular "drummer policy." We hope you liked our Factory Number and that you feel better acquainted.

   "FOR DRUMMERS WHO CARE"   

Leedy
DRUM TOPICS

The Exclusive Drummers' Paper

APRIL, 1925
EIGHTH EDITION

POSTMASTER—Return Postage Guaranteed

Leedy MANUFACTURING CO.
INDIANAPOLIS, INDIANA

"Worlds Finest Drummers Instruments"

The above was especially drawn for the Leedy Manufacturing Company by Eldon King, a talented ... mer of Springfield, Ohio.

Ray Rohel—Don Bestor's Orchestra. (See page 10.)

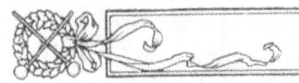 

Leedy Drum Topics

50,000 Drummers are now regular readers of "Drum Topics"

Leedy is distributing them free—and will continue to send out as many as new names come in—a real helpful and practical service for the Drummer—

THIS Indian Drummer of the Hopi Tribe in Arizona was much impressed with his first copy of DRUM TOPICS, and asked to be placed on the mailing list.

He is Joe Red Leaf, a Carlisle graduate. Joe wallops a mean tom-tom. It is a serious professional business with him. Some syncopation, too. You would certainly rave over the tone of the tom-tom shown in the photo.

GEO. W. MARSH of the famous Paul Whiteman Orchestra is a constant reader of DRUM TOPICS. It was he who originated the novel Midget Slap Sticks and willingly turned them over to DRUM TOPIC readers and others. Marsh is one of the boys who has done a great deal to raise professional standards.

Drummers in every city where the Paul Whiteman Orchestra plays are invited to introduce themselves to Geo. Marsh. They will find it worth their while, for he's a "regular fellow."

Send in the names of all of your Drummer friends and acquaintances who do not receive DRUM TOPICS. They will thank you for the favor.

Help make DRUM TOPICS more interesting by mailing in your photographs and stories. Remember, this is YOUR magazine. More ideas is what we want. You can be a part of it.

Be sure to keep DRUM TOPICS posted when you change your address.

A DRUMMERS' "CONFAB"

Some of the first raters of Los Angeles who visited the Geo. J. Birkel Music Co. Store to see the Leedy Drum Show during the Shrine Convention, week of June 1st.

HERE'S WHO

STANDING—LEFT TO RIGHT

Jack Salling—Los Angeles Country Club.
L. L. Allen—KFT Radio.
Harold McDonald—Don Clark Orchestra.
Jack Roop—Giersdorf Sisters.
Charles L. White—Los Angeles Philharmonic Orch.
E. Grimes—Highland Theatre.
Geo. H. Way—Leedy Mfg. Co.
Chas. Seibert—Leedy Mfg. Co.

KNEELING—LEFT TO RIGHT

J. K. Klein—Jobbing.
Joe Stier—Big Bear Lake.
G. M. Robinson—Melrose Theatre.
Robert Curns—Geo. J. Birkel Music Co.
C. H. Williams—Pasadena Theatre.
Chas. P. Caldwell—Geo. J. Birkel Music Co.
E. R. Stone—Geo. J. Birkel Music Co.

Leedy — "WORLD'S FINEST DRUMMERS' INSTRUMENTS" — *Leedy*

The Exclusive Drummers' Paper

Wm. H. Gilcher, San Francisco

Drummers who are anxious to increase their earnings would do well to adopt the policies of this hustling drummer. Besides playing two shows a day with the Max Dolin Orchestra at the California Theatre, he is manager of the drum department in the Conn-San Francisco Company's store.

"Gilch" is among the boys talking business from early A. M. till early A. M., visiting the various cafés, etc. The photo was taken in his salesroom. He is an "oldtimer" and one of the country's finest. Formerly several years with the St. Louis Symphony Orchestra. See "Gilch" for classy fashions as well as drums.

Mrs. Newlywed (to butcher): "I'll take that five-pound roast and a pint of gravy."

Some "Batterie"

More than half the drumming world knows these "dudes." Herbert L. Clark, conductor of the Long Beach (Cal.) Municipal Band, is justly proud of them. How they all got together in one band is a mystery to us. Left to right: C. E. Seely, O. F. Rominger, J. R. Seabrook.

Another Novel Effect

Hold your Synco Wire Brush between the pedal ball and the bass drum head—close to the head. The ball and the brush striking at the same time causes a swish effect of a deeper quality of tone than the brush on the snare drum. Very appropriate in some numbers.

There's many a drummer whose right hand knows not what his left hand is doing.

Not an Inferior Sign

Sometimes you will find a light brown or reddish brown spot in either a transparent or white drum head. This is not a sign of weakness or defect in the skin. It is simply what is called a "blood stain" in shop terms. They can be removed by the use of chemicals, but this method damages the head. Leedy believes in leaving the fibres of the hide in the natural state for the sake of even flexibility.

Sailors are said to have girls in every port, but drummers have 'em on every davenport. (Eldon King.)

Billie Mickle

The Earl Theatre of Philadelphia employs one of the best known and most capable vaudeville drummers in the East in the person of Billie Mickle. For ten years he held down the two-a-day B. F. Keith job and is using the same Leedy equipment he started with.

Sigler's Merrymakers

Carl Hancock (indicated by arrow) is the versatile and accomplished drummer with the above orchestra of Birmingham, Ala. They not only fill most of the elite engagements of that section, but are a prominent "Okeh" recording orchestra as well. Hancock is an enthusiastic Leedy booster.

One thing a vaudeville drummer hates—a wind whistle.

A Point of Progress—In Drums

Of the many improvements that have been applied in snare drum construction during the past twenty years, there are none of them more practical than the adoption of the metal flesh hoop, originated by Leedy.

There are still many drummers—in certain sections of the country—who are not thoroughly familiar with the numerous advantages of this type of hoop. They have been using the wood type so long that it has been taken for granted, and it is surprising to note how much this most important part of a good drum is overlooked.

First—The metal hoop is not nearly so apt to bind on the shell and where it is used in "floating head" construction it cannot bind. The wood hoop cannot be used in "floating head" construction. Just imagine a wood flesh hoop on a tympani.

Second—The metal flesh hoop cannot turn over or warp to cause an ugly looking drum.

Third—It is a very easy matter to tuck heads on metal flesh hoops. Some are of the opinion that it is difficult because they are smaller than the wood style, but this is not a fact. Counter hoops should NOT be applied to the drum with either wood or metal flesh hoops until the head is thoroughly dry.

Fourth—Extra heads can be carried and placed on a drum in a very few moments. Heads will not carry on wood flesh hoops safely for any length of time.

Fifth—Appearance for the better.

The metal flesh hoop is modern, efficient and a progressive improvement. Watch other drum makers follow.

"FOR DRUMMERS WHO CARE"

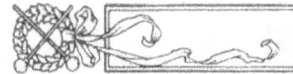

Leedy Drum Topics

The better acquainted we become with some leaders, the more we regret that birth control wasn't established years ago.

Maurice Tushin

In addition to his regular job at the Fenway Theatre in Boston, Mass., Maurice Tushin has been tympanist with the Boston Festival Orchestra and Stewart's Band for several years. He was formerly with the Boston English Opera Company. Tushin is ranked as one of the first tympanists in the country, and we are glad to announce that he is an ardent Leedy booster, using the Universal Tympani. He is also one of Boston's recognized teachers and has a large class of pupils.

The Handy Cymbal Stand

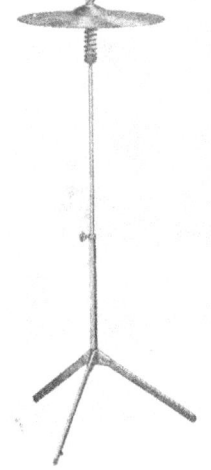

This new cymbal stand has proven to be a real labor saver inasmuch as a fellow doesn't have to reach over the bass drum. The stand can be placed so that the cymbal is close — on either the right or left side. Legs fold up — easy to carry. Many drummers using two of them. Makes a wonderful appearance.

The Same—Yet Different

A drummer's life is full of holders; even when not playing he likes to hold 'er.

The Theatre, Dance, or any other kind of Drummer who never had to earn his bread by the sweat of his brow—should realize that there are plenty of jobs a lot worse.

I Have Put Many Drummers On the Bum!

I am more powerful than the combined armies of the world.

I have destroyed more men than all the wars of nations.

I am more dreadful than bullets, and I have wrecked more homes than the mightiest of siege guns.

I steal, in the United States alone, over $300,000,000 each year.

I am everywhere — in the house, on the street, in the factory, at railroad crossings, and on the sea.

I bring sickness, degradation and death, and few seek to avoid me.

I destroy, crush and maim; I give nothing, but take all.

I am your worst enemy.

I am Carelessness.

Then and Now

We expect to get "bawled out" for publishing this photo, but we just couldn't resist the temptation of the opportunity to prove the old saying, "Start 'em young if you want 'em to become an artist." That is what happened in this case, as the photo shows, and . . . . . .

here he is today. One of the finest that ever walloped a calf-skin. Johnny Auer of the U. S. Marine Band, Washington, D. C. Johnny also plays a "mean banjo."

Here's one every vaudeville drummer will appreciate. Reprinted from a late issue of The Boston Musician. Sent in by Frank MacCarthy.

No. 1 soon as Every body take bow on Central of Stage Segel right in to No. 2.

No. 2 Segal after finish fier trick in to No ON Y V A.

ON Y VA Segal after finish of Spirit Sining right in to 3.

No. 3 Play till little Kid does about 13 time up and down by hand Stand RRRR—bum every time. Stop and he jump down of table Segal RRRR—bum & symbol Segal No. 4.

No. 4 Segel when tow boys put legs on their Heads walk back to Stage right in to No. 5.

No. 5 Play very soft and Sweet till Every body Drop Plates Pick it up fast and Louder when the Curtain Comes Down twice then stop till three men Jump Down of Shoulders please give us Cort off.

Much Oblige.

A Drummer of the Swiss Guard

The Pope of Rome has more male servants than any monarch in the world. These servants are all dressed in the most picturesque garments from the Middle Ages, the above being one of the drummers of the entourage known as the Swiss Guard. Note the position of this drummer's hands. They are absolutely correct.

The new Leedy Vibraphone has met with wonderful success in many fields of music. It is being used as a regular feature at four of the country's largest radio stations and three of the leading recording laboratories have turned out several records that are "best sellers." The Vibraphone is exclusively Leedy. Hear it on this record:

"*A Little Love, A Little Kiss*"
Played by George Hamilton Green
Edison Record No. 51550-R

Anthony Caleal

Many dance lovers in cities and towns about Fall River, Mass., know this versatile drummer by his progressive ideas and fine work. He is engaged steadily by the best orchestra leaders and plays Leedy instruments entirely.

(Hall's Music Shop, Fall River, Mass.)

 "WORLD'S FINEST DRUMMERS' INSTRUMENTS"

Page Four

The Exclusive Drummers' Paper

 Drum Topics

A PAPER DEVOTED TO
THE INTERESTS OF THE DRUMMER

No subscription fee.

Advertisements accepted.

Published quarterly at 1033 East Palmer Street, Indianapolis, Indiana.

Editor..........................Geo. H. Way
Business Manager................A. W. Kuerst

The Tone of a Snare Drum

What should it be?
Will a real standard ever be established? Why can't drummers agree upon what constitutes the best sounding snare drum?

Artists pretty well agree on what constitutes the finest tone of the various instruments in the brasses, reeds and strings, but leaders, drummers and other musicians have many opinions when it comes to the tone of a drum.

As tastes in all things vary, this is not surprising, owing to the fact that the drum can be assembled in so many different ways. The many thicknesses of heads, both snare and batter, the many kinds of snares and their sizes, and the many sizes of drums, both wood and metal shells, make it possible to produce hundreds of combinations resulting in many qualities of tone. In addition to this, any one drum will sound many different ways at various tensions of the heads, to say nothing of different weight sticks and different methods of playing or "touch."

So what pleases one drummer or his leader will not please another. If a drum "plays easy" the chances are in favor of high praise of the instrument from its owner, because there are many drummers who unconsciously think of this first.

The writer once knew a drummer who visited a dance and raved over the fine tone of a snare drum that was being played by another drummer in a large, prominent dance orchestra. A few days later the same drummer condemned the same snare drum (not knowing at the time it was the same one) when he played upon it himself, saying that it sounded "rotten," when the real reason was —it was tensioned different than he would have had it for his own particular "touch." In other words, it played differently to him than it sounded from a distance.

If all heads were the same thickness, if all snares the same size, weight and kind, if all shells one type, if all sticks the same weight, and if all drummers used the same touch—then we could establish a standard best-toned drum.

In Canada

Henry Morrison hails from Vancouver, B. C., and has held down many first-class jobs in that city, also in Winnipeg and other western Canadian towns. Now located at Edmonton, Alberta. Has also done considerable work in Seattle, Wash. Morrison never lets a new idea pass without giving it a thorough try-out. All Leedy.
(Advance Drum Co., Edmonton, Alta.)

He Had to be Shown

Not long ago a certain drummer had one "heck" of a time explaining to the sheriff at a small-town dance hall that his leaking trap case was caused by the cap coming unscrewed from his water-carrying bird whistle.

Howard Goulden

After putting in the winter with Arthur Pryor's Band at Miami, Florida, playing Tympani (Leedy Universal), Howard is now back at his regular post on drums, bells and traps with Sousa's Band—en route. George Carey and Howard are making a big hit this season doing a Xylophone Duet, using a Leedy Improved Solo-Tone Xylophone.

It is usually taken for granted that every musician knows that a chime tube should be struck on its cap or, if it has no cap, at the extreme top and never below these points. The reason for this statement is that we recently saw a whole set of chimes completely ruined by large dents in the tubes about five inches below the top. The owner complained that they were out of tune. Most certainly they were—badly—because the slightest "out of round" from any cause will alter the intended pitch of the chime and its quality.

Foolish But True

Luke—"What is the last thing a girl takes off before going to bed?"
Fluke—"I don't know; what is?"
Luke—"Her toes; off the floor."

Jim Seely

One of the country's most select jobs is the Greenbrier Hotel at White Sulphur Springs, Virginia. For two years it has been held by Jim Seely with a Meyer Davis Orchestra. Jim is from Atlantic City, where he worked in the principal vaudeville theatres and hotels for ten years. An all-'round, thorough dance, concert and theatre man. Note the novel idea he has applied to his Leedy Universal Tympani for moving them about, consisting of two wooden triangular roller bases.

Try a pair of Leedy Rubber Bell Hammers No. 370-D on your Temple Blocks. They bring out the biggest and best quality tone.

Now a Legitimate Stunt

The effect produced by syncopating on a cymbal with the right stick and letting a large metal washer or key (or like metal piece) lie on the fingers of the left hand under the cymbal so that it can be heard in contact with the cymbal, is surely holding its own in popularity.

At least 70 per cent of the drummers with leading orchestras are doing this stunt and it sure sounds fine when used with discretion.

Have you seen the dandy new Leedy Catalog "N"—the one with the red and black cover?

 "FOR DRUMMERS WHO CARE"

Leedy Drum Topics

Geo. Carstens

The Jack Rogers De Luxe Syncopators have one of the finest dance men in the Middle West at the drums.

This prominent drummer and orchestra are doing a big share of the higher class dance work in and around Davenport, Iowa. Carstens says, "My Leedy equipment is as fine as a drummer could wish for."
(Elmergreen's Music House.)

"I'll stick to you," said the hickory to the wood block.

When you turn the thumb screw of a spring type of Crash Cymbal Holder down tight it has a tendency to deaden the tone. When you leave the thumb screw loose it rattles—so here is a little tip:

Step into any drug store and buy ten cents worth of 3/16" diameter rubber tubing. Cut off a half inch length and slip it on over the threads. This prevents the cymbal from coming in contact with same. Then turn the thumb screw down tight on the rubber tube. Let the cymbal stay loose. More tone is the result.

Tod Sanborn

This "top-notch" Marimba-Xylophonist is well known throughout the United States and especially on the Pacific Coast as a wonderful artist.

Just before sailing for India and other Asiatic countries, Tod sent this photo to Mr. Leedy, writing in part as follows:

"I am on my way to India and I am taking the large Leedy Solo-Tone Marimba-Xylophone. I have had a number of Xylophones in my day, but nothing to compare with this one. Certainly is fine in every way."

Chinese Crash Cymbals

Just how the Chinese Crash Cymbals and Gongs are made, and what they are made of, has always remained more or less of a mystery to the majority of drummers.

The contents and principle of their manufacture are no secret to modern metallurgists, it being a simple matter to analyze the metal which contains certain percentages of copper, tin and zinc, heated to a molten state and cast.

However, it is not known just how the sand of the casting molds is kept apart over such a large and thin surface and just how the metal is made to flow to every part of this thin surface.

After they are cast they are hammered a few blows to break up the even, bell-like tone. Such hammering is not as much as one would think, but it causes the great multiplicity of tones which, combined with the particular combination of metals, produces the weird tone of these instruments. The reason no two of the same size have exactly the same pitch is because they all vary in weight, containing more or less metal.

They were first devised for, and are still used in, Chinese religious ceremonies. They are not made in the larger cities of China, but in the forbidden cities and towns of the far north.

Frank D. Morecock

Richmond, Va., has every reason to be proud of this popular and very fine dance orchestra. Frank D. Morecock, the drummer, is known throughout the state as one of the best in the business. He states: "My Leedy outfit suits me in every respect from snare drum to spurs."

In the Gloaming

In the gloaming, oh, my darling,
When the gas is dim and low,
That your face with powder's painted
How am I, sweetheart, to know?

Twice this month I've had to wrap up
Every coat that I possess
To the cleaners—won't you, darling,
Love me more and powder less?

Suitable hammers for Marimba can well be compared with hammers used in a piano, where you will find harder in the upper, and softer in the lower register. The reason for this lies in the fact that piano strings, like Marimba bars, have upper partials (generally spoken of as overtones) which are objectionable when heard too strong, although they are either eliminated entirely or in part, depending upon the hardness of hammers used.

What actually takes place when too soft a hammer is used in the upper register is, that being soft it does not leave the bar quickly enough to allow it to vibrate freely without subduing the tone to some extent, and when too hard a hammer is used in the lower register, the hammer being hard, leaves the bar too quickly, allowing the upper partials to predominate; therefore best results would be obtained, could one use graduated hammers such as are used in a piano. However, this is quite impossible with a hand-played Marimba, so the next best thing is to use a hard enough hammer in the upper and a soft enough hammer in the lower register; but one set of hammers will not do for the entire range in a large or modern instrument.

The Leedy 629 hammers are best for the lower register, while the 618 are best for the upper (even still harder than the 618 can be used on the upper). Either the 617 or 618 are best for the middle register.

"WORLD'S FINEST DRUMMERS' INSTRUMENTS"

The Exclusive Drummers' Paper

Lloyd Marsh—Around the World

While there have been other musical organizations that have made professional 'round-the-world trips, there are few who have done it like this orchestra—with "solid comfort" thrown in. Above is pictured a lucky bunch, the "Belgenland Collegians," who made the trip to eighteen countries and thirty-eight cities aboard the S. S. Belgenland, a 27,000-ton displacement palatial steamer that makes a yearly trip with about 500 pleasure seekers.

It's a wonderful orchestra and made a big hit playing at the leading hotels at ports of call as well as aboard ship. The drummer is Lloyd Marsh (yes, brother to George Marsh of the Paul Whiteman Orchestra) from Minneapolis, Minn., and a regular fellow as well as a regular drummer; more than that—exceptionally fine drummer.

He and the orchestra, under the leadership of H. E. Vansurdam, are going on the cruise again this winter. Some job—and there's many a drummer who wishes he had the chance.

Lloyd, like his brother, is 100% Leedy.

—and Getting Paid for It, Too

In Yokohama, Japan   *In Colombo, Ceylon*   *In Calcutta, India*

Recent Drummer Visitors to the Leedy Factory

John J. Heney—Royal Scotch Highlanders.
A. A. Wohl—Detroit.
Craig Ferguson—Bachman's Million Dollar Band.
Johnny Jackson—Johnny Jackson's Orchestra, El Paso, Texas.
Jack Lampton—Sells-Floto Circus.
Gus Edwards—Gus C. Edwards Orchestra.
Richard Mueller—Evans Melody Boys, Davenport, Iowa.
Nelson F. Bitterman—Seymour Simons Orchestra.

WE WISH YOU ALL COULD COME

A Word to the Wise

Some fellows in business say: "What's the use of doing anything extra for this firm? I won't get any more money for it anyway."

Some fellows who drum say: "I only carry two drums, a wood block and a cymbal. The job wouldn't pay any more for a truckload of stuff."

They are both alike. The point is, Mr. Drummer, that neither type of man will advance very far. He will only sit back grumbling while others go ahead and get the finest jobs and the biggest money.

A drummer is his own "firm." He is working for himself even more than the fellow in business, and the more ideas he introduces with a better outfit than the other fellow is what "brings home the bacon."

We often wonder where that lady drummer came from, but at a second look—it's only a hat box. They do look like drum cases, don't they?

Philen Cantrell

Here is an orchestra (Watson's Bell Hops) that does all classes of work—theatre, concert, dance and vaudeville—and makes a big hit wherever playing. Every man an artist, including the "snappy drummer," Philen Cantrell of Jackson, Miss. Many newspaper write-ups state that Cantrell "knows his stuff" on drums. Other drummers say the same. Leedy drums always travel with him.

Have you any questions regarding drums, etc.? If so, write to the Editor of DRUM TOPICS. Maybe he can answer them, maybe not—anyhow no harm to try. Send your picture along, too.

The Best Ever

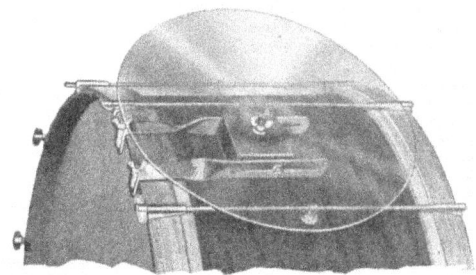

A Cymbal Holder for band use, made of pressed steel parts instead of castings, therefore will not break. The only holder that is adjustable back and forth on the bass drum shell. This feature enables the player to place the cymbal in a comfortable arm position. The cymbal rests on a large felt cushion, which assures full tone. Cannot scratch shell. A sensible, strong device.

Ebony Drum Sticks have practically been discarded by the entire profession. While they make nice-looking sticks, the wood is so short-grained and brittle that it breaks very easily.

"FOR DRUMMERS WHO CARE"

Leedy Drum Topics

The Concert Drum Stand

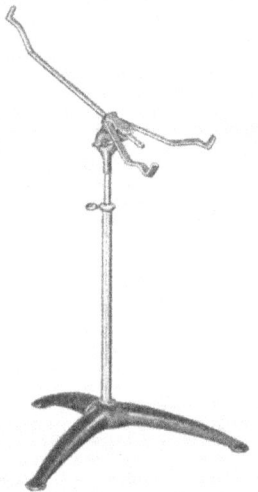

There is no chance of your drum wobbling with this stand. It is stronger and built slightly heavier than any former model. A real comfort for drummers in all classes of work. The steel base easily unscrews from the brass (nickel plated) tubing. Not too heavy for the transit drummer. Ask for Leedy Concert Stand No. 341-A.

Jack F. Pettit

One of our most interesting correspondents is the drummer shown above—Jack F. Pettit of Liverpool, England. He has written DRUM TOPICS several letters concerning the dance game in England and we only wish space permitted our publishing them all. Sometimes we hear that the English drummer is not as progressive as our own; but we want to say that if all drummers in the States took the business to heart and put forth the effort that this boy does, we would have the profession on a higher plane.

In several sections of the country, drummers are letting the tambourine "die." What is the reason?

There are many fine effects possible with this instrument. When played upon softly with tympani sticks while the tambo is in a "Bull Dog" holder or lying flat on felt (or on the tympani head) it sounds "swell." And there's plenty of opportunity for flash with it in jazz numbers. It fits in many spots. Here is a good trick: After making a roll with the thumb in the usual way, finish with an accent by snapping the head with the second finger.

The only way a drummer can make sure of a job nowadays is to marry the manager's daughter.

A New Silhouette

This sure makes a "snappy"-looking bass drum head, especially because it shows up so well from a great distance. Leedy painted heads are truly superior, because they do not show brush marks and look as well with or without interior lights.

Not Much Demand for Theatre Drummers Here

Statistics recently made public show that only 16 out of every 100 townships in Italy have theatres. In the entire country it was shown that 1,361 townships possess playhouses.

Did you know that Leedy was the first to polish and buff the bowls of copper tympani?

For Heavy Accents

Try the cross stick shot effect on your Tom-Tom as pictured above. Lay the left stick flat across the head and lift it very quickly after the right stick strikes. By lifting the left quickly, the tone of the Tom-Tom comes out full. It's different and good for heavy accents.

Miss Percy Nolan

This young lady is kept busy nightly playing with Burch's Orchestra of Kirkland, Wash., on the best class of society dance work in and around Seattle. She drives her own car and is not afraid to carry and set up a complete outfit. All Leedy. We want you all to know that Miss Nolan plays a real professional job that would give many of the boys something to think about could they hear her.

Leedy metal shells are guaranteed to contain no solder whatsoever, and to be made in one piece rolled brass.

John Lucas

Everybody in the big towns knows John. Some drummer, some boy and some bowler! His scores look like the number on a Ford engine. He has been with Ted Lewis since the band started. A great Leedy booster.

Oh, Look!

Now he's in kilts — hope he's got the "Scotch," too. Last time he had on a heavier load (uniform, we mean) with the Ringling Brothers Shows. Yep, it's J. J. Heney, drummer with the Royal Scotch Highlander's Band. "J. J." says the new Leedy "Floating Head" drum is the "Rolls-Royce" of drums.

"WORLD'S FINEST DRUMMERS' INSTRUMENTS"

The Exclusive Drummers' Paper

THE HAUSNER MUSIC COMPANY, MINNEAPOLIS AND ST. PAUL, MINN.
Two Stores That Operate Drum Departments as Drummers Would Have Them

There are music stores and music stores—big ones, little ones, good ones, better ones—some that "order a drum for you" and some that stock drummers' accessories; but here are two of the "Musician Service Stations" kind that realize the value of a real drum department, knowing that the satisfied drummer always comes back. Result: The Hausner Music Company enjoys 90 per cent of the professional drum business in the Minneapolis and St. Paul district and a big majority of the non-professional as well. Drummers well know the secret of such a success—proper treatment and "have it in stock," also a professional understanding. That's why they go to "Gus" for their wants. When a drummer buys an instrument it means worlds to him. To these stores it means as much as to the drummer, not "just a sale."

Gus A. Hausner, Pres.

Gus A. Hausner started the business with nothing, so to speak, and through his tireless and efficient methods the two stores have grown to do an enormous volume of business that few have exceeded. Hausner has introduced many ideas in the musical merchandising business that have been accepted as standard by firms in all parts of the country. But after all he is "one of the boys" and is among them all the time. He was for many years a violin leader and had orchestras in several of the Minneapolis theatres. Chas. Hausner is manager of the Minneapolis store and like his brother Gus is a professional musician (banjo) of exceptional skill. He is called by the boys "Dollar and a Half Charlie,"—the story is a good one and in no way detrimental to this "whirlwind" salesman. He is assisted by Emory White, another fine banjo player, who has been with the best orchestras. Also Roy

Adolph Vavro
Mgr. St. Paul Store

Emil T. Weflen

of the high-class Lyceum Theatre Orchestra in Minneapolis, is not satisfied to confine his ability to just so many hours per day in the theatre. He puts in many more teaching, in affiliation with the Howe School of Music. He also sells Leedy instruments through the Hausner Music Company. Weflen's rating as a fine drummer is well understood when it is known that he has, during his many years in the business, played in almost every leading theatre in the Twin Cities, also in the Minneapolis Symphony Orchestra. He was at one time on the road with Bachman's Million Dollar Band. The Weflen model drum stick is almost universally used in this section of the country.

Jack Lust

The Geo. Osborn Orchestra, of which Jack Lust is the drummer, has played for the elite hotels and cafes in St. Paul and Minneapolis for several years. At present they are at the New Nicollet Hotel in Minneapolis. The whole United States is familiar with their "wonder music" through nightly radio broadcasting.

Lust is a 100% "pep" drummer and has a world of "stuff" and cleverness to go with it. He is completely Leedy equipped and a Leedy-Hausner booster. He was also at the St. Paul Hotel for four years with the Sam Heiman Orchestra.

Herman Fink

is spending the summer at his home getting ready for another season on the Orpheum Circuit with Vincent Lopez Red Cap Orchestra. He has been with this orchestra several years. Fink is an excellent and progressive drummer in every sense of the term. He is Leedy-Hausner all through.

Alf. T. Hoover

Nowack, still another banjo player of the same class, and Meade Reynolds of the same type on saxophone. O. R. Dickhut is the company's accountant. He is a well-known and first-class violinist. The St. Paul store is managed by Adolph Vavro, who enjoys the reputation of being as fast a musical instrument salesman as ever carried an order blank. He "digs prospects out of the air." Vavro is a former pupil of Lewellyn, the famous trumpet instructor of Chicago, and when not selling he plays with the best organization in the Twin Cities, always being in demand. He is assisted by J. J. Bric, a saxophonist and salesman that comes up to the mark of all the rest of the Hausner staff.

The above photo was taken during a Leedy Drum Show that was staged in the Minneapolis store (also St. Paul) by the Leedy Mfg. Co. From left to right it shows: Emory White, Chas. Seibert of the Leedy Mfg. Co., Gus Hausner, Geo. H. Way of the Leedy Mfg. Co., and Chas. Hausner. Hundreds of drummers attended and a good time was had by all.

Dealers Notice

The new Leedy "Professional Floating Head" Drum as described on pages 8, 9 and 10 of the new Leedy Catalog "N" (the one with the red and black cover) is proving to be the biggest seller and booster that has ever been introduced in the drum business. Try a few in stock and cash in on its popularity.

For Dealers Only

Leedy has just produced a new 18"x13" window and store display card in sepia, showing Arthur Layfield of the Isham Jones Orchestra with his Leedy equipment. Mailed free on request to dealers only.

It's a real pleasure to sit through a show in the beautiful Hennepin-Orpheum Theatre at Minneapolis. Some wonderful vaudeville orchestra. Alf. T. Hoover, the drummer on this fine job, is one of the finest vaudeville men in the country—the kind that makes managers and audiences realize the drummer's importance. He is here shown among his "percussion pile." Note that it's a dandy pit. He's all Leedy-Hausner.

   "FOR DRUMMERS WHO CARE"

Leedy Drum Topics

Chord Chime Rack

There is now considerable use for a few chimes, and where a drummer cannot nail up a board to hang a few upon, this new rack comes in mighty handy.

The crown is aluminum. The rod, which telescopes to various heights, is nickel plated, and the iron base and steel upright are black japanned.

No explanation is needed to describe the wonderful appearance these chimes and rack give to any orchestra. A glance at the photo shows their beauty.

They also fill a long felt want for the theatre drummer.

Any combination of four notes can be furnished.

The complete outfit is not too heavy to be easily transported.

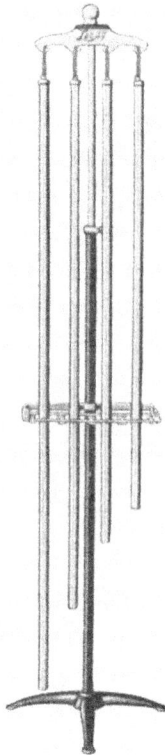

Front Cover

RAY ROHEL

This classy and clever drummer has held some of the finest engagements and is still going strong. Formerly with Frank Westphal's Orchestra at the Rainbow Gardens, Chicago, and all last season with the Arnold Johnson Orchestra at Hollywood, Florida. He is now in the East with the famous Don Bestor's Orchestra. Rohel plays a wonderful job on drums, etc., and his services are much in demand. He is from Joliet, Ill., and was a pupil of Art Layfield of Chicago, now with Isham Jones. Ray is solid Leedy.

Elsie Sperry

Elsie Sperry is not only an accomplished drummer but is directoress and manageress of the Ladies Nonpareil Orchestra of Circleville, N. Y., as well. This orchestra is much in demand throughout southern New York state, it being an A-1 musical organization. Miss Sperry is also secretary of the Musicians' Local No. 819. She is high in praise of her Leedy equipment.

We may not like some things about the business at present, but in twenty years from now we'll be talking of the "good old days."

Do you know the different gauges of gut snares? Size 15 is most used for 5" by 14" orchestra drums.

EDITOR'S NOTE

Through the courtesy of the Musical Enterprise we are glad to give our readers the following story, which we think is one of the best drummers' articles ever written.

Lazy Drummers

By J. M. GROLIMUND

He's a lazy drummer—he is contented to sit all through the concert or dance and thump away at his two drums in a careless fashion. The heads are so loose they sound like thunder miles away. If there is music in front of him the stakes are 10 to 1 he can't read it, but has it there because the other members of the orchestra have music in front of them.

He isn't going to waste his time trying to learn to read. All the successful drummers he has seen—the kind the crowd still rave about—didn't read music; they "improvised" and were the drawing card of the orchestra. He will argue that drumming is an art that is born in a man and will come out gradually.

Poor fellow. But it isn't all his fault. If the director would get after him and tell him what the modern drummers are doing and how much more he will be able to "put in" if he can read, he might be encouraged to practice. There are so many directors who continually permit their drummers to continue in the same old way. Why don't they encourage the drummer to get a set of xylophones and a good instruction book? The diversion would give him added enthusiasm.

Today, large business institutions feel the responsibility of every man who works for them. If he doesn't make a success of his work, they lose as well as he, and they feel it as much their fault as his — they should have helped him. So these firms are continually offering inducements to the man who studies and they are telling him and helping him actually do it.

Why shouldn't the director feel the same way about the men who are under him, especially the young fellow who is just starting out? This applies especially to the smaller towns, where musicians cannot be chosen, and the director is looked upon as an idol by the student.

If a drummer could only visualize what is in front of him, what he could do with his drum outfit in the way of adding tone color to the orchestra and the pleasure he would get out of playing the part as written, as well as putting in good effects that are not written, but suggested from other parts that are lacking in the smaller orchestra, he would start practicing at once with the torque of an induction motor.

Drums are the most abused instrument in the orchestra. Most anybody with a surplus of nerve can sit behind a set of drums and with a few rehearsals play dance jobs and draw as much pay as the musicians in the orchestra who have studied and practiced hard for years.

Sitting-in is the lazy drummer's long suit. When he goes to a dance it doesn't take him long to introduce himself to the drummer on duty and "offer" to "sit in." Grand-standing is second nature to this bird. Maybe he will have to arrange the tension on the pedal, tilt the drum at a sharper angle, and change things in general, which will necessitate the drummer on duty to reset his outfit. But what of that? After the demonstration a long, instructive discussion will follow, in which the visiting artist tips off the old-fashioned drummer with gut snares, on the snap of wire snares, and what he could do if he had only had his little snare. And pedals. This new bird has all the dope on the newest pedals on the market and advises a quick replacement of the antiquated one.

When I see a drummer who plays the spots, takes the xylophone solos, and if there is no part written in the drum music, plays from the violin, solo or obligato, flute, 'cello or second violin, and cues in the bells once in a while on the flute parts, I'll take my hat off to him. He is a student. I know how hard he has studied.

A drummer of this type will have separate tensioned drums of the best make that are tensioned tight enough to give a pleasing tone that gives a good foundation to the entire orchestra. If he hasn't machine tympani he has plans for getting a set, and when he has learned to play them the whole orchestra will be placed a step higher up in the musical world. Tone colorings, accented rhythms and solos are now possible with tympany, and the modern drummer is earning more money because he is out after it by working harder and investing capital. This drummer is not afraid to be caught practicing while the others may be sleeping or playing pool. He can pick up a slide whistle and play the solo from the score at sight; his trap case is full of traps. Perhaps he doesn't use each trap in each number, but he does use them where they bring novelty effects, and leaves out the freakish effect that cheapens the entire orchestra.

There is a big future ahead for the ambitious drummer, and directors should encourage the young drummer to study for his own sake. There is more pleasure in doing a thing right, and knowing that you are doing it right, than thinking you are right and being alone in the thought.

Dance Drummer wants to connect with a college orchestra making their own way through school. A desirable musician; best gold-plated Leedy "Elite" outfit; tuxedo. Is twenty-one; has sophomore rating; tenor voice. References exchanged. DRUMMER, 846 North Anderson Street, Elwood, Indiana.

So All May Hear Them

There are many phonographic records that have parts which show off drummers' work wonderfully well. Let's pass the word so they may be brought to the attention of the boys who haven't heard them. Send DRUM TOPICS the name of the record and its number along with the name of the selection and the orchestra or band. We'll be glad to publish it with your name attached. Let's gather a bunch of them.

"WORLD'S FINEST DRUMMERS' INSTRUMENTS"

The Exclusive Drummers' Paper

Drummers of High Rank Who Recommend Leedy Instruments

CHAS. WHITE tympanist of the Los Angeles Philharmonic Orchestra, is a Pacific Coast boy who has climbed to the very top of the ladder by hard work, study and experience. He now stands in a class with tympanists like Fred Sietz. The greatest leaders have proclaimed him as such. White uses Leedy Universal Tympani.

EMIL BILL is without doubt one of the very best vaudeville drummers in the business. Four years at the Strand in Lansing, Mich., three years at the Bijou in Battle Creek, and many years on the road. Originally from Fond du Lac, Wis. We are glad this boy is a Leedy booster.

ELDON KING is drummer and xylophonist of the Wittenberg-Warren Military Band (Prof. B. D. Gilliland, conductor) of Springfield, Ohio. Besides being a very fine drummer, King is also a very clever artist. He drew the pen and ink sketch of Mr. Leedy and the instruments that was used on the back of the last issue of DRUM TOPICS.

PETER ELLIOTT Nottingham, England, believes that a drummer should make the most of his opportunity in playing all jobs with a complete equipment. This idea, along with his exceptional ability, has put him in the leading class. He is now with the Mikado Orchestra of Nottingham and writes that his Leedy outfit makes his work a real pleasure.

FRANK GAYNER of the Orpheum-Grand Theatre, Calgary, Alberta, Canada, is one of the youngest chaps to hold down such an important job. Road leaders and acts say there is no better on the Orpheum time. This is the most northern theatre on the circuit. Frank is a "regular" fellow and a strong Leedy advocate.

MARTIN SNITZER of Hummel's Philadelphia Band is one of Philadelphia's best. Any drummer who plays for Hummel has to be good. Snitzer is one of the old-timers whose interest in drums has never slowed down. Years ago he was with the Victor Robbin Band of the Sells-Floto Shows.

PETE LEWIN formerly of Philadelphia, Pa., has just finished a long stay as tympanist at Gauman's Metropolitan Theatre, Los Angeles. He is now with the Venice (Cal.) Municipal Band. Pete is an old-timer—for years he has held the best jobs wherever he has been located. A Leedy booster for many years.

CHAS. E. KARL was with the Irving Berlin "Music Box Review" in '23-'24 and with "Tangerine" in '22-'23, also several seasons at Proctor's 125th Street, New York City, vaudeville house. These jobs call for the best in a drummer and Karl is always an outstanding feature. He says Leedy are the best for any drummer.

An Artist More Ways Than One

John M. Dow handed us a laugh by sending in this drawing sketched on an order. He is the wonderful minstrel drummer with the Al G. Field's Show. DRUM TOPICS happened to miss him en route.

STOP! HOW CUM, AH DON'T GET MA DRUM TOPICS?

Two things of short duration: A five-stroke roll and a permanent wave.

HAROLD McDONALD formerly of the original Paul Whiteman Orchestra, is now with Don Clark's Orchestra at the famous Santa Monica Ball Room, Cal. These jobs tell that McDonald has no betters. He made the European trip with Paul Whiteman. His entire outfit is Leedy, which he claims has no equal.

DRUM TOPICS will pay Five Dollars for the best Drum Story for the next issue.

Gus Nagel, Jr.

of New Rochelle, N.Y., plays with Emil Gisin's New Rochelle Dance Orchestra. Nagel has a fine reputation as both an old-school rudimental and popular jazz drummer. He has a knack of originating new and novel beats and writing them out for other drummers. The idea is a good one. More of the boys should do it. Nagel often writes to DRUM TOPICS and claims there is no equal to the Leedy brand for drummers.

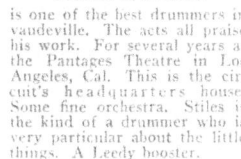

EARLE C. STILES is one of the best drummers in vaudeville. The acts all praise his work. For several years at the Pantages Theatre in Los Angeles, Cal. This is the circuit's headquarters house. Some fine orchestra. Stiles is the kind of a drummer who is very particular about the little things. A Leedy booster.

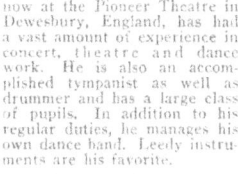

CHAS. SCOTT now at the Pioneer Theatre in Dewesbury, England, has had a vast amount of experience in concert, theatre and dance work. He is also an accomplished tympanist as well as drummer and has a large class of pupils. In addition to his regular duties, he manages his own dance band. Leedy instruments are his favorite.

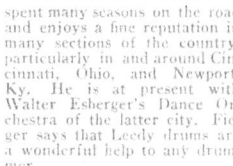

ERWIN G. FIEGER spent many seasons on the road and enjoys a fine reputation in many sections of the country, particularly in and around Cincinnati, Ohio, and Newport, Ky. He is at present with Walter Esberger's Dance Orchestra of the latter city. Fieger says that Leedy drums are a wonderful help to any drummer.

FRANK COHEN has done about every class of work from wagon shows to big time vaudeville, using Leedy all the way through. At present he is with Brown's Melody Orchestra at the Watterson Hotel in Louisville, Ky., making a big hit by his versatility on the drums.

JACK CROSTON is a Canadian drummer who served in France in the "thickest of it" with both a rifle and a Leedy drum. He was several years at the Pantages Theatre in Winnipeg. Now at the Colonial Theatre in San Diego, Cal. Jack is a real drummer and has a large class of pupils.

L. G. WALTON drummer of the Imperial Radio Orchestra, is playing for the summer at Banff Springs, Alberta, Canada. This is the official CFCN (Voice of the Plains) Calgary, Alberta, Orchestra. Walton is a "star" drummer, always up-to-date, and a hard worker. His entire outfit is Leedy.

LOU PERRY is manager and drummer of "Perry's Foot-Warmers," Madison, Indiana, a crack dance band known all over the southern Indiana district. Perry is a fine modern drummer who "sells his stuff," therefore gets the business. He states: "I use nothing in drums or traps but Leedy, for they are the world's best."

Thanks Folks!

Hope you liked this issue
Look for the next—in October

Leedy   "FOR DRUMMERS WHO CARE"   **Leedy**

Page Eleven

Leedy
DRUM TOPICS
The Exclusive Drummers' Paper
JULY, 1925
NINTH EDITION

F. E. Wolfington,
1111 Laurel St.,
Indianapolis, Ind.

POSTMASTER—Return Postage Guaranteed

Leedy Manufacturing Co.
INDIANAPOLIS, INDIANA

Supremacy

The new Leedy Professional Floating Head Drum is conceded to be the most remarkable instrument yet achieved in "Drumdom." It differs from all others in three important fundamentals—

1. The Floating Head idea is without question the superior principle. The flesh hoop does not touch the shell. This assures even head tension, like the tympani. Lessens head breakage and improves the tone and playing ease.

2. The self-aligning rod feature assures easy working rods without thread trouble. Four bolts now used instead of the former two on the center supports. The casings and tubes are two gauges heavier than on former models.

3. The metal shell contains absolutely no solder and is constructed of ONE PIECE 20-gauge brass formed by the spinning method.

BEAUTIFUL IN APPEARANCE
PRECISION IN WORKMANSHIP

A New 96-Page Catalog "N" Mailed Free on Request

Leedy Drum Topics Issue 10

Leedy Drum Topics

Progress therefore is not an accident. It is a part of human nature to build and look for things new in order to be of greater service to each other and improve our own welfare.
—Herbert Spencer

—so it is with every Drummer
—you want to know

Drum Topics— will tell you about the latest stunts—
knows where the boys are playing—
shows you their photographs—
gives you new ideas—
contains valuable tips re your instruments—
and brings us all closer together—

Every Drummer is invited to become a part of Drum Topics. It's your paper.

TE TO THE EDITOR

Drum Topics tells the world that the Drummer is the most important party in the band.

Here's a new one ———— here's another ———— and another

LEEDY CHARLESTON CUP CYMBALS

THE LEEDY CHARLESTON CYMBAL PEDAL

LEEDY REALTONE CASTANETS

Just the thing for the modern drummer. The latest device on the market. If you want a new effect to make 'em take notice—this is it. Will work with either the new Charleston Cup or any regular type Cymbal. Direct action—easy working. The metal supports are demountable for packing and Cymbals are adjustable to height.

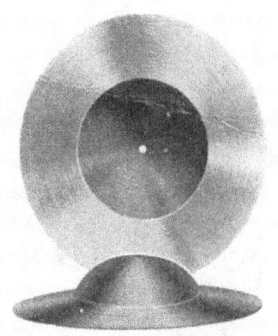

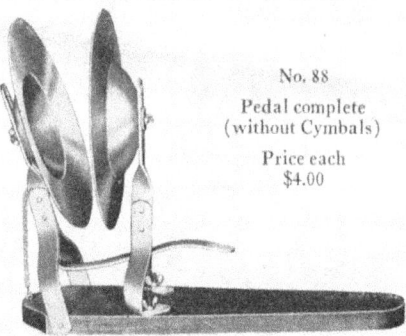

No. 88
Pedal complete
(without Cymbals)
Price each
$4.00

These new shaped 10-inch Brass Cymbals have a big hollow "squash" tone. Note the different large-size cups. They are extra wide and deep.

No. 87 Each.................$1.50

These Castanets are the best ever. The new special composition unbreakable clapper and extra thick hard rosewood anvil combined produce the most realistic tone.

No. 399 Single pair on handle...$2.00

Leedy "WORLD'S FINEST DRUMMERS' INSTRUMENTS" *Leedy*

The Exclusive Drummers' Paper

A woman's mind is as uncertain as a restaurant's hash.

Arthur Layfield

Himself in Person

Who, for the past year, has been one of the outstanding features of the Isham Jones Orchestra, has, as usual, lived up to his reputation of exceeding the limit of ability that is expected of a drummer.

There are hundreds of men who are recognized as A-1 in their particular field, be it vaudeville, concert, opera, drum corps or dance. However, Art is one of the few who has won national fame in every branch of our profession. This is because he not only has the skill of playing drums musically, but also because of his

A Reproduction of the Large Layfield Window Display Poster Seen in the Principal Music Stores

genius in creating original ideas with a style and personality plus. He was for five years with the Chicago Grand Opera, Orchestra, and for a lengthy period of time with the Chicago Symphony Orchestra under Frederick Stock. He has held down leading vaudeville engagements, leading musical shows on the road, also prominent Chicago drum corps and concert bands. He was with the original Benson Orchestra, made famous under the direction of Roy Bargy, and until joining the Isham Jones Orchestra he played with Ralph Williams at the Rainbow Gardens, Chicago.

Prominent drummers of Chicago and elsewhere have time and again agreed that Art was just a step ahead on all the jobs mentioned above. In addition to this he is a xylophonist in the Green Brothers class and a tympanist of the Sietz rank.

The Isham Jones Orchestra has recently finished a country-wide tour, "packing 'em to the sidewalks," and on Saturday, October 3rd, they sailed on the Leviathan for England, where they will play ten weeks at the elite Kit Kat Club in London. Returning to the United States, they will play three months in Florida, followed by another tour, then back to the old stand —the College Inn, Chicago—beginning September 1, 1926, for a five-year run.

The Editor of DRUM TOPICS Wishes Art Good Luck and a Good Time Across the "Pond"

Los Angeles Philharmonic Drummers

Max Wesser—Frederick Hammes—H. J. Walter—Chas. L. White

Drummers who think they have to work hard for all they earn might change their minds if they could follow these boys for a season. The Los Angeles Philharmonic Orchestra features many conductors during the summer season at the Hollywood Bowl, and it's the drummer who knows that each leader expects things different in the percussion section. They have played this summer under the batons of Fritz Reiner, Sir Henry Wood, Walter Rothwell, Stokovski, Rudolf Gans, Emil Oberhoffer and others. It is hardly necessary to comment on the calibre of these drummers; however, we cannot omit the fact that it is widely known that every famous conductor who has led them, publicly compliments their artistic work. The photo proves that they are strong supporters of the World's Finest Drummers' Instruments—LEEDY.

Anything may become popular these days. Reformers should be thankful that it's the Charleston and not St. Vitus.

A reasonably heavy drum stick is better than a real light one, because the rebound is as strong as the stroke, which eliminates a great percentage of "lifting." The less "lifting" necessary, the less motion of the hands and wrists. Extra travel of same makes drumming more difficult because of lost motion.

Another New Cymbal Effect

In addition to using a large washer or drum key and other like metal pieces in the left hand under the crash cymbal for syncopating effects in conjunction with the right drum stick, many drummers are now using a four-inch Leedy Egyptian nickel silver cymbal (No. 31-A), holding as shown in the above photo, in the usual manner under the lower surface of the Zildjian or Kiraljian crash. Have the left thumb over the top of the large cymbal so you can "slap" the small cymbal up against the under side of the former. It makes a fine "cup" or "squash" tone. The small cymbal may also be worked with a loop of braid passed through the hole and over the second finger.

"FOR DRUMMERS WHO CARE"

Leedy Drum Topics

In Italy

Speaking of "doubling," how's this? He plays six instruments at once — beating the bass drum with an elbow while the feet take care of the small drum and cymbals by wire attachments,—also playing an accordion with his hands in addition to blowing a Pan-like flute with his mouth, topping it all off with the bell accompaniment on his hat.

Be it ever so "rumble," there's no bass drum like a Leedy.

EDWARD McKAY

Of the Lyric Theatre Orchestra in Birmingham, Ala., ranks with the best vaudeville drummers in any of the big cities. He has been in the business many years and is known in many southern states. McKay is an exceptionally fine instructor and has a large class. All Leedy.

Do not loosen your snares when the drum is not in use.

It's no new idea to put a piece of rubber tubing about two inches long over the ends of your drum stand arms, but it's a good one and it's surprising how few drummers do it.

"Hap" Al Belisle

Has made himself a real feature drummer of the Neil O'Brien Minstrels. His work, particularly on the street, has won high praise over the entire route of the show. He stands with the best of all-'round drummers. "Hap" was formerly with Headley's Concert Band and Griffin's Minstrels, both on the Pacific Coast. Also several other fine positions to his credit. Ware, Mass., is his home.

Phonograph Records with Good Drum Effects

In the last issue of DRUM TOPICS we requested our readers to send in the names of records that contained good drummers' effects. Here are a few of them, and we trust that many of the boys can pick out some tips that are new to them.

We want to thank the drummers who came forward with record numbers and names. Send in some more and we will publish them as soon as possible.

COLUMBIA RECORD 406-D
  "Collegiate"
  "Stepping in Society"
  Sent in by Seth M. Damon, Wausau, Wis.

VICTOR RECORD 19662
  "Bye Bye Blues"
  Sent in by Geo. Marsh, Paul Whiteman's Orch.

BRUNSWICK RECORD 2339-A
  "You Remind Me of My Mother"
    (Note cymbal effect)
  Sent in by G. A. Rasmussen, Marshall, Minn.

VICTOR RECORD 19007-A
  "The Parade of the Wooden Soldiers"
  Sent in by Vergil Harris, Marion, Ill.

BRUNSWICK RECORD 2892-B
  "Got No Time"
    (Note wire brush effect)
  Sent in by Lynn Davis, St. Louis, Mo.

VICTOR RECORD 19693
  "The Whole World Is Waiting for Love"

BRUNSWICK RECORD 2854
  "River Boat Shuffle"
  Sent in by John P. Noonan, Bloomington, Ill.

VICTOR RECORD 19526-A
  "Washington Lee Swing"
  Sent in by Chas. B. Jones, Jr., Dallas, Texas.

Gerald Sunde

Gerald Sunde is again on the job for the third season as tympanist (Leedy Universal) with the West Palm Beach Municipal Band. This band is of exceptionally high rank, having with it some of the first chair men from several of the country's finest organizations. Sunde was formerly five years with Bachman's Million Dollar Band. He hails from Minneapolis, Minn., and enjoys a country-wide reputation as a wonderful bass drummer and tympanist.

Important

When ordering metal flesh hoops be sure to state whether they are for the former type Multi-Model or the New Floating Head Drum. They are different in size.

Something Different

Not long ago we saw a drummer use a popgun on the afterbeats of a modern arrangement of a one-step dance number. His manner of using the gun in the air made a great flash and it sounded very good.

Three Celebrities

Aldo Bortolotti, shown at the left in the above photo, received his early musical education on the French horn in Bologna, Italy. At twenty years of age he came to the United States and located in Pittsburgh, Pa. Here he played with many of the foremost bands and orchestras.

Bortolotti always liked the bass drum. When called upon quite unexpectedly to substitute during a concert, he made good to the extent that he decided to adopt this instrument in favor of the French horn. Since then he has played the bass drum almost continually and has been with Liberati, the Manhattan Opera House under Campanini and the past fifteen years with the Chicago Grand Opera Company. His skill on his favorite instrument is indeed wonderful. He has developed it to a truly fine art.

The lady in the center is Miss Bortolotti, a niece of Mr. Bortolotti, who is a well-known soprano of wide experience and high reputation in the concert field.

Mr. Chas. C. Woodruff, shown on the right, is the "par excellence" all-'round man in the percussion section of the Chicago Grand Opera Company. He has been with this company for five years. More details concerning Mr. Woodruff will be published in the next DRUM TOPICS.

They are Leedy drummers.

The New Midget Tympani Sticks

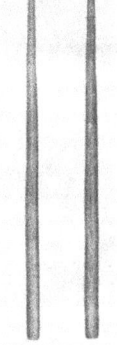

Drummers have found that it is not a large tympani stick that brings out the best tone. Today there are more professional men using smaller sticks than ever before.

This new model has a fine-grade hickory handle with the straight hand grip and a slightly tapered stock. The ball is covered with the best grade Spanish felt, sewed in such a manner that the seam is almost invisible and will not cause a different tone should it strike the head. The core of the ball is constructed of a new patented material that has great resiliency.

No. 368-E. Per pair........$1.75

"WORLD'S FINEST DRUMMERS' INSTRUMENTS"

The Exclusive Drummers' Paper

A Lot of 'Em Believe It

"I think I'll quit the restaurant and make big money. I know an 'eight-piece' orchestra that needs a saxophone player, and it won't take long to learn that many tunes."

There never was an article placed on the market that someone else couldn't make it worse and sell it for less.

Will the day ever come when all drummers take the time to carefully and EVENLY tension their bass and snare drum heads?

J. D'Andelet

Of the U. S. Marine Band is one of its most prominent and efficient members of many years' service. When in Washington, the band is often divided into various organizations to play for the many state occasions, and in these instances D'Andelet plays double drums, all Leedy. While on tour he plays bassoon; however, from his remarks, his heart is with the former. His work on both is thoroughly musical and artistic.

You All Know Him

He was the original drummer with Paul Whiteman and is now on his third season with the Don Clark Orchestra at the Santa Monica Ball Room near Los Angeles. He is here shown looking over his new Leedy Floating Head Drum. Sure it's Harold McDonald. Nuff said.

Did you know that U. G. Leedy originated the drum stand, making the first ones for the market in 1898? Drummers used chairs before that.

JAMES H. TOLLEY

One of the best in the service and formerly of New York City, has served with U. S. Marine Bands at Mare Island, Cal., San Diego, Cal., and with the "Roving Marine Band" on tour. Also trouped with Al. G. Barnes Circus. Now with the Post Band, U. S. M. C., at Quantico, Va. Always uses Leedy.

H. C. Cook

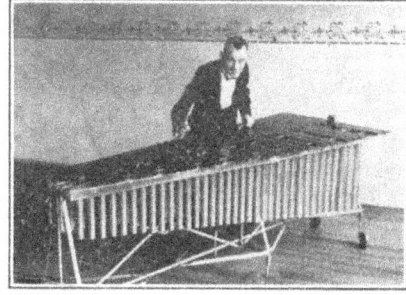

This xylophonist is now established as one of the finest in the Middle West. He has been playing for some time past with the Herb Smith Orchestra at the Dreamland Ballroom in Lincoln, Neb.

Many drummers make the mistake of hanging their crash cymbal by a too lengthy cord. Shorten it. Also shorten the cymbal holder arms. These corrections will lessen cymbal swinging.

Try Them Out

Drum Topics has received several letters of inquiry as to just what the traps are as used by Geo. W. Marsh, of the Paul Whiteman Orchestra, that sound similar to two different toned wood blocks. All write that they sound much better than blocks, being deeper and richer in tone. We are more than pleased to pass the good word along. They are simply two Cow Bells of different sizes laid on a cushion and played with Leedy rubber bell hammers No. 370-D.

A. Raymond Perkins

This chap writes us some very interesting letters from Gouldburn, New South Wales, Australia. From the contents of same we know him to be a modest and hard-working drummer who puts complete interest into his work. It is quite evident from the numerous high-class positions he has held that his ability is of a very high order. We want to call the attention of drummers in the United States to the fact that the best dance men, such as Perkins, in this far-off land, are up-to-date with the same jazz and novelty stunts as used in the States.

A True Story

There are several fine residences with spacious grounds situated near the Leedy factory. Not long ago, on Monday afternoon, the Assembly Department had just finished work on a seven-foot Giant Bass Drum. The workmen were trying it out with many hard blows, using all their strength. It sounded so much like thunder that the lady of a house a full block away was awakened from a sound sleep. She rushed to her back yard and gathered in her entire week's washing to protect it from the "rain." Shortly afterward a neighbor told her that "it was just one of Leedy's big drums," and she replied, "Darn that drum factory anyway!"

Jim McKay, of the Palace Theatre, Chicago, Visits Leedy Plant

For thirteen years Jim McKay has pleased the acts, audiences, leaders and managers at the Palace Theatre in Chicago. This is one of the country's "first five" in the high-class vaudeville field. Previous to locating in Chicago he was for six years at Keith's in Indianapolis. He held many important positions before this. We are not listing them for fear of making him seem older than he is. Always all Leedy and now he plays a Floating Head Model. The photo shows Jim and Geo. H. Way, of the Leedy Mfg. Co., looking over the new drum.

CLARENCE H. MELTZ

Appleton, Wis., is a well-known teacher of all drummers' instruments and a popular professional, with the latest ideas, who knows how to use them to the best advantage. He is now manager of his own Meltz Brothers Harmony Orchestra and also plays in the 120th Field Artillery Concert Band.

JULIUS VAN PETEGHEM

A well-known and excellent dance drummer, formerly of South Boston, is now in St. Nicholass Waas, Belgium, doing the same as when in this country — holding down the first-class dance jobs with Leedy drums and good old American ideas in playing them.

"FOR DRUMMERS WHO CARE"

Leedy Drum Topics

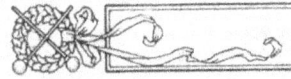

A PAPER DEVOTED TO
THE INTERESTS OF THE DRUMMER

No subscription fee.

Advertisements accepted.

Published quarterly at 1033 East Palmer Street, Indianapolis, Indiana.

Editor.........................Geo. H. Way
Business Manager.............A. W. Kuerst

Are You a Specialist?

Not so many years ago about every drummer in the professional field was expected to do fair work, should the occasion arise, on any class of engagement, including a military band on the street or even a drum corps. That he would be able to "cut it" was taken for granted.

But in this day and age there are drummers who are specialists in dance playing—specialists in vaudeville playing—specialists in band playing—specialists in symphony orchestra playing — and specialists in drum-corps playing.

They are all important in the world of drums and none of them should be underrated, but today there's many a symphony orchestra drummer who can not do an even passable dance job.

In the past years there were fewer drummers and it was only natural that they played a greater variety of jobs. Very often one would play in a parade at noon, a musical show in the evening, and a dance till 2 A. M. It was all in the day's work.

Today the dance man hardly ever plays any other class of work, and so it is in all the branches. The "closed-down" style necessary for indoor playing forms habits that are hard to dislodge in favor of the "open style" should such a drummer be called upon to turn out on the street.

Modern theatre and dance men should not belittle street work. They should "wood-shed" on the subject as often as possible. It will improve your technique, no matter what kind of a job you are on. And truly, now, what sounds worse than a drummer coming down the street playing a fine "closed" roll and "hugging" the drum on eighths and sixteenths?

In other words: Modern drummers, broaden your scope and give some thought to the kind of work the other fellows do. You might be called upon to play some other class of job at any time.

Lena E. Keeney

Lena E. Keeney, of Springfield, Mass., is busy the year 'round playing the best class of engagements. In the summer she operates her own orchestra, which is well known for many miles in all directions of Springfield. This organization is a regular feature at the Springfield Country Club. In the winter she plays with the Ladies' De Luxe Orchestra and the Ladies' Elite Concert Orchestra. Her work is of the highest calibre and her accomplishments prove that it is possible for a woman to make a genuine and profitable profession of drums.

WILLARD J. TATMAN

Has done a great deal of the better class of dance and band work in western cities, where he is well known as a "first-rater." Now located at McAlister, Okla., and plays with the 378th Infantry Band. Tatman says the best results are only obtainable with Leedy.

The man who knows it can't be done counts the risks, not the reward.
—Elbert Hubbard.

Joe Bennett's Orchestra

The above photo shows one of the South's most popular orchestras. These boys are all "top notchers." It is under the ownership and management of Joe Bennett, a progressive drummer of many years' experience in every division of the profession. This is the organization that furnished the dance music for the Tri-State Fair at Memphis this year. Leedy equipped.
(Courtesy Melody Music Shop, Memphis, Tenn.)

STERLE O. SISCO

Plays with the Skelly Orchestra of Moose Lake, Minn. They travel from Minneapolis to Duluth and their fine playing keeps them busy nightly. Sisco's snappy work is one of the reasons. He has used Leedy drums for seven years and says he will never change to any other make.

Ella—"What is a WOW?"
Fella—"Why, it is that which seldom does, but when it does it's a WOW!"

Leo Lake's Collegians

Leo Lake is a drummer who is even more than an artist on his instruments. He is a capable business man, and the orchestra bearing his name is in demand at all times.

They were at Buckeye Lake, Ohio, during the summer of 1924 and the past season at Wamplers Lake, Mich. Between seasons they do the better class of hotel, radio and vaudeville work, booking from their headquarters in Bowling Green, Ohio.

Lake is thoroughly pleased with his Leedy outfit, including the Floating Head Drum.
(Courtesy Heaton's Music Co., Columbus, Ohio.)

GEO. D. PEARSON

Formerly of Southport, Lancashire, England, served throughout the World War with the English forces. Afterward he played Leedy drums in many of the leading hotel and photo-play theatre orchestras in Southport and Liverpool. He is now located in Canton, O., and enjoys a very high rating.

When it's PP, make it so—and
When it's FF, make it so.
Don't play monotone.

ROY GRIES

Of Schenectady, N. Y., has been more than making good on all classes of engagements in central New York state. His services are much in demand, owing to his work. Formerly with Young's Band, Ruben Orchestra and the Woodbridge Hotel Orchestra. Now with Dominick's Orchestra of Saratoga, N. Y.

DONALD E. RHODES

Began playing drums at the Ann Arbor University in 1917. He has since climbed high in the profession and is now known as one of the most capable drummers in Detroit—with Finsel's Golf Club Orchestra. He has a large class of pupils and always recommends Leedy.

 "WORLD'S FINEST DRUMMERS' INSTRUMENTS"

Page Six

The Exclusive Drummers' Paper

IT'S HERE · IT'S NEW · IT'S CLASSY · IT'S WONDERFUL

The *Leedy* Trap Console

—all Leedy "Bull Dog" Holders and Trap Tree Holders are adaptable to The Trap Console

—your traps where you want them—where you need them—when you need them. The Trap Console is strong and rigid

—with a thousand adjustments

The Leedy Trap Console is for the drummer of today—the modern drummer who knows that the shortest and surest route to increase his earnings is to introduce a little showmanship into his work. It is this kind of a drummer who is a business man and who will welcome the opportunity the Trap Console offers, for it is without question the most flashy and classy device ever set up with an orchestra or band. For any class of work.

While appearance is a big factor of the Trap Console, its practicability from a "Drummer Correct" viewpoint is its principal feature. There is no end to the many ways that traps can be arranged. Higher, lower, closer or farther away, and many more, may be included than shown in the photo. The table is 3-ply wood covered with blue felt and is adaptable to height. Tom-Tom Holders are adjustable to size. Metal parts are finished in bright nickel and black enamel with some in dull nickel.

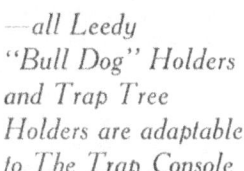

Console Trap Holders

Number		Price each
241A	Small Alum. Temple Block Clamps	$1.25
240A	Large Alum. Temple Block Clamps	1.50
985	Wood Block Holders	.60
989	Afterbeat Cymbal Holders	.60
989	Egyptian Cymbal Holders	.60
988	Small Tom-Tom Holders	.60
983	Tambourine Holders	.60
984	Cowbell Holders	.15
987	Triangle Holders	.60
86A	Large Tom-Tom Holders	4.00
85A	Trap Console, complete as shown in photo at left	$40.00

The Trap Console will be supplied without the two large circular band Tom-Tom Holders if desired. Your choice of either the goose neck or straight rod type of Crash Cymbal Holders. One of each or both the same.

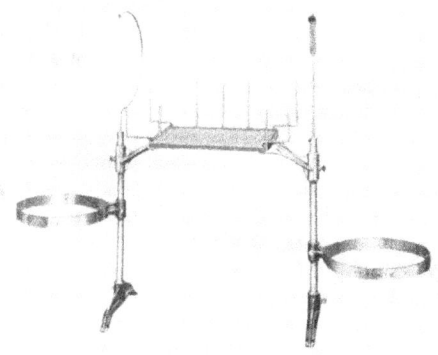

—it weighs only 50 pounds

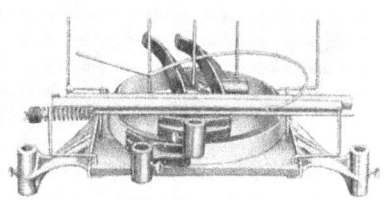

—packs into small space

"FOR DRUMMERS WHO CARE"

Leedy Drum Topics

Forty-one Drum Corps and Thirty-nine Bands Attend the American Legion National Convention at Omaha, Nebraska, October 5th to 9th.

The famous Drum and Bugle Corps of Racine, Wis., Post No. 76. They won first prize of the Drum Corps Division. Mr. Geo. Johnson is drum major and Mr. Fred Maxted is manager. Speaking of thrills—you get them plenty when this outfit "does its stuff." You just have to see them, because their drilling, playing and appearance in marching formation is indescribable. All Leedy.

It was some affair.

This is part of the Oklahoma City Band. Mike Peshek (with tuba), conductor; Paul Bennett, manager; C. D. Scribner (second from the left) first drummer. The band is only a few months old and it's a wonder. They won fourth prize.

The exact number of drummers in attendance is not known, but it is safe to state—at least nine hundred.

J. Conklin

Was the official host to the visiting Drum Corps. His untiring efforts was one of the chief reasons why so many of the boys in every city now say, "We had a wonderful time." Conklin is manager, instructor and leader of the American Legion Omaha Post Drum Corps. He is also assistant collector of internal revenue at Omaha.

All visiting musicians will long remember the fine spirit and hospitality, also the service rendered by the Omaha musicians. The Omaha bunch are sure "regular."

Geo. A. Smith

Who operates one of the country's largest drum shops, was ever on the job. His store was Official Service Headquarters, and many Legion drums were repaired by Smith and his staff.

The final Drum Corps Drill was a sight that thousands will never forget.

At times Omaha looked as though it was entertaining a Drummers' Convention.

The Monahan Post Band, of Sioux City, Iowa, is the Blue Ribbon Band of the American Legion. They have won three National First Prizes and came out winners of all three contests at Omaha. A very high-class band. Complete Leedy Drum Section.

"WORLD'S FINEST DRUMMERS' INSTRUMENTS"

The Exclusive Drummers' Paper

Harry Butler

Is the man who for the past fourteen years has superintended the Leedy Trunk Department. He is without question one of the foremost designers of special trunks and cases. Previous to coming to the Leedy plant, Mr. Butler worked in the same capacity for two of the country's largest trunk firms. Many road drummers and xylophonists are personally acquainted with him, as he has worked out for them hundreds of seemingly impossible problems of transportation.

He is assisted by Julius Schelske and three other workmen, also three women.

Leedy is indeed proud of the prestige of this department, for never has there been a single complaint on its products. It's the men on the road who know and say, "Leedy's are the finest trunks made — anywhere by anybody."

ALEX T. JOHNSON

Now of Chattanooga, Tenn., came to the United States several years ago from British Honduras. He has traveled in all the southern states and Mexico with the Southern Wanderers and De Luxe Syncopators. Johnson is known as one of the most efficient colored drummers in the business.

Drummers do not usually use large crash cymbals for phonograph recording—mostly 12-inch in the Turkish type and 15-inch in the Chinese type. These smaller sizes have a high pitch with shorter vibration waves, therefore record more clearly and true to their natural tone. The large cymbals are deeper in tone, with longer and slower "waves" that overtax the recording needle.

HARRY C. WEXLER

Is the first drummer with the famous Ringgold Prize Band. Also manager and drummer of the Wexler Dance Orchestra, of Scranton, Pa. His fine work and willingness to please have made him most popular, and Leedy is glad to count him a booster.

Improved Bass Drum Sticks

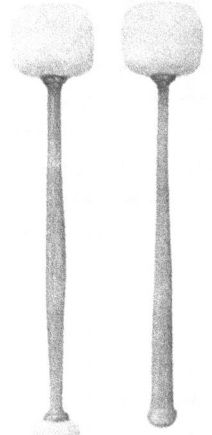

As in all other drummers' instruments and accessories, the best is none too good, but for some unknown reason many bass drummers will use any old stick. Here are two new and improved models, with strong hickory handles and a patented core covered with the highest grade felt obtainable. They have fine balance and will not beat flat.

No. 365-E Double End.....$2.00

No. 365D Single End......$1.75

The Prize Story

BY G. A. RASMUSSEN

This young drummer has made great strides in his work during the few years he has been in the business. Many have stated that he ranks with men who have been at the drums for a much longer period of time. He is now playing with the popular Stephens Novelty Band of Marshall, Minn. Drum Topics is more than pleased to award him the prize for this issue. The following story shows how well he has observed every phase of the profession.

* * *

He was a small-town drummer of three years' experience, but didn't seem to get ahead. No, he was not lazy. He knew the qualities of a lazy drummer and had tested himself on all the points and was well satisfied that he didn't belong to that class. He could read music, but didn't feel satisfied, even if he made a hit, which was not often. He was spoken of as lacking pep. He realized that, although he could read music and play the bells and marimba well, he was not a "jazz" drummer, for improvising was not born in him.

The only time he felt satisfied was when his orchestra was hired to play in a small-town theatre. The orchestra as a whole was a failure, but everybody was pleased with the drummer's playing. It was here that he realized that his previous failures lay, not in the lack of ability, but in his choosing between types of playing. He saw that his ability lay in legitimate and not in "jazz" drumming.

It was only with the greatest difficulty that he earned enough money to start lessons with a professional drummer; but, after two years of studying, the "silver lining" began to show.

His first few jobs were with small theatre orchestras, but within three more years he secured a position with one of the most noted symphony orchestras in the United States.

His friends back in the small town often wondered how the poorest drummer in town ever got past his fellow players. When asked that question, he answered: "It was my poorest move when I took up 'jazz,' and the best when I quit it. I don't mean to condemn a 'jazz' drummer, if he is best fitted for the work, but I was never meant to be one. I have seen a drummer who has worked for years and who never got ahead, yet when changing to 'jazz' he made a great success and big money, as he was a very clever improviser. A drummer, like any other musician, must put feeling and originality into his work, but he cannot do this if he dislikes the particular kind of work he is doing."

EDWARD MANN

Is one of the leading dance drummers in Buffalo, N. Y. He is playing with the Red Moon Orchestra—Frank Burkard, director. Mann has been in the game for ten years and has been connected with many prominent bands, drum corps, and dance orchestras. He always uses Leedy.

"It's a skin game," said the snare to the bass drum.

Paul Whiteman

Will, in the near future, present a new up-to-date Drummers' Correspondence Course written by Geo. W. Marsh, of the Whiteman Orchestra. The work is about completed and details will soon be announced. It will be distributed by Roy Knapp, one of Chicago's best-known drummers.

The New Leedy Floating Head Drum

The several superior mechanical features embodied in the construction of this wonderful instrument are contained in no other drum on the market. The self-aligning rods, the floating head, and the one-piece, no solder, heavy reinforced shell, also the strongest non-rusting counterhoop ever put on a drum, are exclusive Leedy accomplishments that have won first place with the majority of drummers. The floating head makes it snappier and easy playing.

Ask your music dealer to let you try one, or ask a drummer who is using one.

She—"Don't you love the Ziegfeld girls?"
He—"No, but I would if I had the chance."

Why do the great majority of stage orchestra directors place the drummer in the position of facing the audience "dead on"? Wouldn't it be good showmanship to have the drummer sit at an angle, or even sidewise, in order that his work and instruments (both of which are far the most interesting features) would show off to better advantage?

BEN ABRAHAMS

Is considered among the finest of the profession in Australia, where the dance business is flourishing and the ability of drummers is on a par with the United States. He is now at the "Ambassadors" in Sydney, N. S. W., and where Leedy instruments are the choice.

 "FOR DRUMMERS WHO CARE"

Page Nine

Leedy Drum Topics

A Diplomat

A diplomat is a gentleman who can lie in such a manner to another gentleman (who is also a diplomat) that the second gentleman is compelled to let on that he really believes the first gentleman, although he knows that *the first gentleman is a liar*, who knows that the second gentleman does not believe him.

Both let on that each believes the other, while *both know that both are damn liars*.

WILLIAM A. COOK

Has been with the "Y Boys' Orchestra," of Des Moines, Ia., for the past five years. He also plays with other well-known dance bands and is considered a most valuable asset by the various directors. Cook is one of the boys who believes in using a complete outfit (Leedy exclusively) and not being satisfied with just "getting by."

The other night, while "listening in," we caught the Frank W. Hodeck, Jr., Nightingale Orchestra, of Omaha, Neb., broadcasting from WOAW. The drummer played chimes—one note to the bar—through the greater part of a waltz number. It was certainly a beautiful effect. Hodeck has some fine orchestra.

There is only one correct way to hold drum sticks. The majority of drummers know the correct method, but have formed bad habits and gotten used to their own system. However, they overlook the fact that they could really do better work if they would just get used to the *right* way. Strange to say, the right stick is the worst offender. (See pages 12 and 13 of the Carl Gardner Drum Method, Part One.)

Al Morris

It is not uncommon on the Coast to find orchestras of the highest rank in the leading cafeterias. Al Morris, a most progressive drummer, has his own orchestra in the largest in Frisco—Leighton's. Al is not only most competent at his instruments, but a thorough business man as well.

JAMES H. SMITH

Is one of the best-known colored drummers in the business—by way of excellent work with clever and original ideas. Formerly of Fort Smith, Ark., and Tulsa, Okla. He has toured the whole United States and South America with the famous Mamie Smith Review and they are booked for Europe this season. Also two seasons with Arthur's Band in the Jimmie Cooper Review.

A new snappy drum solo with band accompaniment has recently been published by the Victor Publications, 1322 West Congress Street, Chicago. You will like this one.

The Crescent Orchestra—John Day, Drummer

If you are a radio fan you are familiar with the "wonder music" broadcasted by the Crescent Orchestra (Bernie Shultz, leader) as a regular feature over WOC—Davenport, Iowa. They are truly of the highest calibre and do the finest work in the Tri-Cities locality. John Day has been a great factor in its success, as he is a drummer of extraordinary ability. Everyone likes John—he's a real "salesman."

O. H. Elmergreen, proprietor of the Elmergreen Music Company, of Davenport, Iowa, has made a specialty of serving the professional musician and his followers. His store is headquarters for the leading orchestras and bands for miles around. His repair department and complete stock, along with his thorough understanding and pleasing methods, are the reasons for the popularity of this store. Elmergreen is a drummer of many years' experience and has played with them all in the Davenport section. He is also a fine trumpet player and can be seen fourth from the left in the Crescent Orchestra photo above.

The New Temple Block Holders

Here is a wonderful new Temple Block Holder. The Block Clamps are made of aluminum in two sizes. Ninety per cent of the drummers on the Pacific Coast are using the Korean Temple Blocks ("Tomatoes"). They procure them from the Chinese merchants. Leedy does not yet carry these blocks, as the source of supply is uncertain.

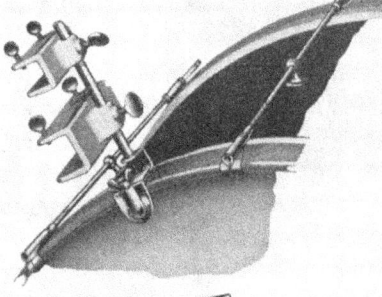

No. 240-A
Large Block Holder
$1.50

No. 241-A
Small Block Holder
$1.25

No. 242-A
Bass Drum Hoop
Clamp and Post
50c

No. 243-A
Complete Holder
$3.25

That's Different

Ted—"I had a good time last night at Helen's party."
Ned—"Did you? Who all were there?"
Ted—"Me and Helen." —Ohio Sun Dial.

"WORLD'S FINEST DRUMMERS' INSTRUMENTS"

The Exclusive Drummers' Paper

"Charley" H. C. Branch Says—

```
                                408 Roxboro Street,
                                Durham, North Carolina.

                                        September, 15, 1925.

Leedy Mfg. Co.,
Indianapolis, Ind.

Gentlemen:-

        I have recently purchased through your
local dealer, Mr. T. A. Hudson, a complete set
of Leedy Drums - the best in the catalogue, and
this is to tell you I believe them the best in
"anybody's" catalogue.

        Leedy has been my standby for years,
"piece at a time fashion" but I now realize that
one cannot fully appreciate your company's attain-
ment in the drum making business until a whole out-
fit is purchased at once. You can't buy new parts
for an old model car and expect to have a new one!
Everything is satisfactory and especially do I like
the Floating Head Drum. If I were just as good as
the drums - George Marsh would be out of work.

        Just like the little boy said: "I have
tried your drums for sometime and now find I can
not "beat" them."

        This may all be uncalled for but en-
thusiasm must have its pop-off valve.

                                Sincerely yours,

                                S. H. C. Branch
```

—and Leedy is proud of it because

"Charley" has a wonderful reputation. As he is a drummer who is classed with the very best, his word counts for much. Other drummers know he knows. That the McCoy Miller Orchestra is in the same class as its drummer, can well be judged by the above photo.

"Cursed be the rod that binds." Leedy's never do.

VALENTINE AMRHEIN, JR.

Is a young semi-professional drummer of Milwaukee, Wis. He works in the composing department of the Milwaukee Journal and plays in his spare time with a popular dance orchestra. Amrhein has worked hard and can, after the short space of two years, match up very favorably with many drummers who have been playing a great deal longer.
(Courtesy Walker's Musical Exchange.)

John Stucky

The operation of the special machine that forms the Leedy famous one-piece Tympani bowl requires a skilled mechanic of the highest order. Such is JOHN STUCKY, who is in charge of this work. He is also general factory maintenance foreman and electrician. Stucky is one of the most popular men in the plant, and we are sorry that his ever-ready smile does not show in the photo. He has been with Leedy for eleven years.

Be sure. Don't guess. Don't suppose. Find out exactly. Know. And if you don't know, ask. It's more satisfying.

Paul Carey

That Paul Carey is a hustler there is no doubt. He was busy nightly as one of Peoria's (Ill.) most prominent dance men, but this did not satisfy, and through hard and diligent effort he has become manager of the Musical Instrument Department of the large Block & Kuhl Department Store. He also plays with the "Arcadians" shown above. Paul and the store are exclusively Leedy.

A cash prize of $10.00 goes with every issue of DRUM TOPICS for the best drummers' story. Who will win next?

Bear in mind that it is to your advantage to send Leedy your new address the very day you move.

Bear in mind that DRUM TOPICS is strictly a drummers' magazine and that you are invited to be a part of it by sending in stories and photos.

Bear in mind that the greatest favor you can do for your drummer friends (and for DRUM TOPICS) is to send in the names and addresses of all drummers you know. It will be boosting your own game.

Yours, till they stop calling Tympani—
"Timfanies," "Candy Cookers,"
"Washing Machines" and "Stills"

 **"FOR DRUMMERS WHO CARE"**

DRUM TOPICS

The Exclusive Drummers' Paper

NOV. 15, 1925

TENTH EDITION

POSTMASTER—Return Postage Guaranteed

Leedy Manufacturing Co.
INDIANAPOLIS, INDIANA

A New Head That Resists Dampness—

These New Process Drum Heads give more "drum comfort" because they remain tighter in damp weather and are harder and tougher in dry weather.

They are made from fresh calf skins in the Leedy plant and with the same minute care as the famous "Uka" and "Hardwhite."

It is not claimed that "ALL-WEATHER" Heads are waterproof, but they do resist dampness to a greater degree than any head so far offered.

"All-Weather" Heavy Calf	"All-Weather" Medium Calf	"All-Weather" Light Calf
FOR BATTER SIDE	FOR BATTER SIDE	FOR SNARE SIDE
No. 438 17" for 13" shell..........$2.75	No. 438-B 17" for 13" shell........$2.75	No. 438-S 17" for 13" shell........$2.75
No. 439 18" for 14" shell........... 3.00	No. 439-B 18" for 14" shell......... 3.00	No. 439-S 18" for 14" shell......... 3.00
No. 440 19" for 15" shell........... 3.25	No. 440-B 19" for 15" shell......... 3.25	No. 440-S 19" for 15" shell......... 3.25
No. 441 20" for 16" shell........... 3.50	No. 441-B 20" for 16" shell......... 3.50	No. 441-S 20" for 16" shell......... 3.50

**AN ENTIRELY NEW PROCESS OF MANUFACTURE
NOT A TREATMENT—TRY ONE**

Chauncey E. Morehouse—Jean Goldkette's Orchestra, Detroit, Mich.—See Page 11

Leedy Drum Topics

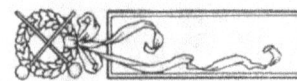
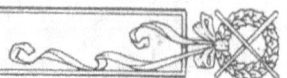

The Progressive Drummer of Today —

The Progressive Drummer

is a combination of both artist and business man—he knows more than the actual playing of his instruments—he has built up his prestige and earnings—

The Progressive Drummer of today is no longer the tail end of the band or orchestra—many are leaders, contractors and proprietors of "going concerns"—

He is an important person in the world of music, dancing and entertainment—

Let us all see that the Drummer continues to improve his position.

Drum Topics will help

This is how he began—

The lowest of the savages had no musical instruments at all, and indeed only a very limited language. For music and language always went together, and those who are studying music know that it is itself a language, understood by all civilized people, no matter what tongue they may speak.

Next above these beginners come those tribes who have percussion, or striking, instruments only. And it is with these savages that we have to deal.

We can, then, with the help of those lowest tribes, imagine a time when there was absolutely no music in the world. And then we can imagine how a savage, probably by accident, first struck two pieces of wood or stone together at regular intervals, and, judging from what we read of savages today, we can imagine how pleased and interested he would be. For, although sounds like the roaring of the wind, the rumbling of thunder, the splashing of waves, or the singing of birds, have existed as long as man has, all these sounds wanted one thing to make them of any real value as music, and that was Rhythm.

Rhythm, then, is the oldest element of music, as the drum and its kind are the oldest of musical instruments.

By striking a regular rat-a-tat-tat, two or three times, this curious ancestor of ours came to a very interesting and perfectly natural conclusion. He noticed the difference between this sound and any he had ever heard before, although he did not call that difference by its name—Rhythm. The clever man also recognized the idea of a language; and after turning it over in his mind for awhile, he came to the conclusion that the mystery and pleasure of the sound was the voice of a spirit. Having acknowledged this, the next step he took was to worship the spirit and to improve the forms in which it was to dwell. At first he simply used any sticks or stones which came to hand, and threw them away. Next he conceived the brilliant idea of hollowing out a gourd, filling it with pebbles and rattling it. Finally, after many centuries, no doubt of slow improvement, he reached the height of ingenuity from which we have scarcely departed today—he hollowed out a log, closed over the ends with skins, and beat them with sticks.

At last he made a DRUM.

The worship of the drum now became one of the forms of a strange religion which scientists call fetishism. The hollow log was dressed up with feathers, mounted on a pole and attended by priests, who carried it about among the various tribes. The pole was fixed in the ground and the people came in crowds to worship it. It was consulted as an oracle; offerings were laid at its feet.

In some tribes the religious idea was a little different; the fetish was not the spirit itself, but was possessed with magic power to drive away or mollify evil spirits. And it is a striking fact that this idea has continued all through the ages of history and among civilized nations nearly down to our times. For what is a bell but a metal drum, with the drumstick hung inside? And how many superstitions do we read of about bells and belfries in the Middle Ages—how bells were rung to insure a good harvest or fine weather. We do not stop to consider why we ring bells at weddings, funerals, or New Year's eve and other special occasions. To be sure, the only reason WE do so is that it always has been done. But our ancestors of the Middle Ages rang bells for the very same reason as our primeval ancestors rattled gourds or beat drums.

Another Drummer of Today

This is a Royal Drummer of Bunyoro, the tribal state that adjoins Upper Sudan on the south. The drum has been the popular instrument in the wilds of Africa for three thousand years.

 "WORLD'S FINEST DRUMMERS' INSTRUMENTS"

The Exclusive Drummers' Paper

The New Bass Drum "Tone-Control"

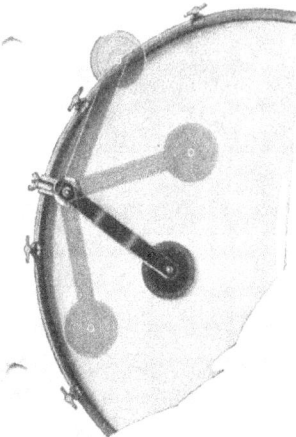

Drummers no longer consider the matter of bass drum tone in the light of "pigs is pigs." There was a time when the majority of drummers were careless about bass drum tone. If they happened to hit just the right tension the drum sounded O. K., but it was more a matter of chance rather than good judgment, and many an otherwise fine instrument gave forth ugly sounds simply on account of negligence.

Good bass drum tone depends — first, on the quality of the shell and heads; second, on the degree and evenness with which the head is tensioned, just as a clear tone on the tympani is produced only by absolutely even tension; third, on the particular pitch and degree of resonance desired for the character of the number being played.

The new Bass Drum "Tone-Control" fills a long-felt want in respect to this third point. The above photo shows that it can be adjusted to press the head at any spot over a wide arc of surface and that it can be quickly removed from the head altogether. The farther away from the hoop the felt disc is placed the less resonance is forthcoming, therefore raising the pitch of the drum, and vice versa.

No drummer can afford to be without one.

Ask for No. 668.

We take our hat off to the dumb belle in the Supper Club who asked the drummer if he could play the Parker House Roll.

Do You Think of This?

There is a right and a wrong way to place a drum on a drum stand, particularly in respect to the position of the snares.

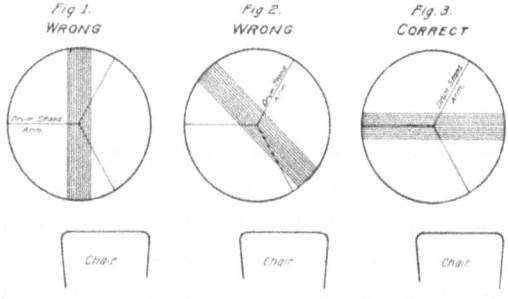

If you place your drum (the drum at an angle) as shown in Fig. 1, the snares will lay against each other and not work free and independent. The same condition exists if the drum is placed as per Fig. 2, BUT if you place it as shown in Fig. 3, the snares will vibrate individually and the P. P. P. beats and rolls will work easier. This also brings the snare strainer in a better position for faster work.

HERMAN W. SCHREIBER

One of the real old-timers of the Twin Cities, has played with "'em all"—wagon to tent shows—burlesque to grand opera. One of the country's leading all-around men. He is now playing vaudeville at the Seventh Street Theatre in Minneapolis, Minn. Herman has been using the same Leedy bass drum for twenty-two years.

(Courtesy Hausner Music Company.)

Leo Zollo

Leo Zollo (The Laughing Drummer) is at the present time delighting audiences nightly with the Meyer Davis Orchestra at the Bellevue-Stratford Hotel in Philadelphia, Pa. Zollo has had a most successful career. Formerly with the Philadelphia Concert Band and later touring the entire country in vaudeville. This was followed by a long engagement at Miami Beach, Florida, with the La Monica Dance Orchestra at the Miami Beach Casino.

He then returned to Philadelphia and filled the best class of engagements in the leading hotels.

Besides being a fine drummer and tympanist, Zollo is an exceptionally clever entertainer, and no one appreciates his versatility more than Meyer Davis himself, who takes Zollo on important society affairs after hours at the hotel. Zollo has always used Leedy equipment and states that the perfection of the Leedy instruments has helped him gain the popularity he now enjoys.

The La Monica Orchestra and Thomas Meighan, famous Paramount star. Leo Zollo second from left.

Life is more or less made up of ruts. Some of them are good for us—others bad. The trick is, not to let them wear so deep that we cannot see over the walls.

CHAS. C. WOODRUFF

Is now in the middle of his fifth season with the Chicago Grand Opera Company. Most professional drummers know that it is Fred Sietz (tympani), Chas. C. Woodruff (drums, bells, etc.) and Aldo Bortolotti (bass drum) who make up the wonderful drum section of this organization. Mr. Woodruff hails from Toledo, Ohio, where he received a complete schooling on violin and drums. He also studied under Max Wintrich in Chicago. Woodruff was for four years xylophone soloist with the Benson Orchestra, of Chicago, and also traveled out of that city with several comic opera companies as tympanist. He is a thorough artist on all drummers' instruments and one good fellow in the bargain. For the past three summers he has played with the Chicago Symphony Orchestra at Ravinia Park. He states: "The New Leedy Floating Head Drum overcomes all past faults."

Leedy designed and manufactured the first muffler snare strainer—THE IDEAL. It is still popular with many drummers who use wood counter hoop drums.

We never hear of newspapers—who are always taking slaps at jazz music through their editorial and wise-cracking columns—turning down advertisements concerning jazz phonograph records, jazz shows, jazz moving pictures, etc.

There are two ways to "work up" a crescendo roll—one being to start near the hoop of the drum and work toward the center, reaching there at the maximum power of the roll. The other way is to "work up" the roll with straight up and down beats, striking always in the same spots—one inch off the exact center of the head. Every drummer should be able to execute it both ways.

 "FOR DRUMMERS WHO CARE"

Page Three

Leedy Drum Topics

The following clever little tip was given to the Editor of DRUM TOPICS while attending the American Legion convention in Omaha last October by Ernie Gordon, the well-known drummer at the Empress Theatre in that city.

Five days later the same tip was sent in a letter from Pat Donovan, a prominent drummer of Dublin, Ireland. It is interesting to note that two drummers at almost opposite sides of the globe had the same idea at the same time and desired to pass the word along to brother drummers simultaneously via DRUM TOPICS. Here it is:

If you happen to find a small hole in your bass or snare drum head (or even tympani) burn the frayed edges with the glowing end of a cigarette. The head will then be quite safe under the usual tension for a considerable length of time.

A. F. Durlauf

There are not many drummers who begin actual playing at seven years of age. The Jasper Star Band, of Jasper, Ind., once boasted of having a young man who more than made good on the snare drum at that age, in the person of A. F. Durlauf. He is still more than making good and is now playing at the Strand Theatre in Louisville, Ky. Durlauf has specialized in theatre work, having started in this branch of the profession as leader of the Majestic Theatre Orchestra in Louisville when eighteen years old. He has since played drums in all the principal theatres of that city and has also worked on the best jobs in Lexington, Ky., and Birmingham, Ala. In addition, one season with Liberati's Band en route. Durlauf has played Leedy equipment since his first job with the Jasper Star Band.

There are snares other than those on a drum which are not foolproof.

"DUDE" BERRER

Says: "I am sure no drummer can go wrong with the Leedy trade mark." "Dude" is a very fine drummer and has been with several "big name" orchestras during his eleven years in the dance game. He recently finished a successful tour of all the Central States with his own orchestra. Henderson, Ky., is his home town.

EDWIN J. LINK

Of Columbus, Wis., has been managing a dance orchestra with considerable success for over a year. This hustling young drummer is one of the up-to-date business type and is therefore kept busy all the year 'round. He also has had considerable band concert experience. He says, "Leedy's are the only kind."

Jack Lampton and John Ballay

Here are the two boys who made the drum section of the Sells-Floto Show the talk of Circusland last season. Are they good? Ask any performer who worked with them or any musician who heard the band. Lampton, who is from Toledo, Ohio, is putting in the winter with the Little Sioux Indian Band on Keith time, while Ballay is playing in sunny Florida. They are both all Leedy.

One of the steps in the process of the manufacture of Leedy drum heads is to place the skins in a sealed room and let them hang in a dense sulphur smoke for several hours. This eliminates all possibility of the head ever throwing off any disagreeable odor whatever.

Who is the tallest drummer in the world? Send in his photo.

Giving Him Away

"John, dear, I am to be in an amateur theatrical. What would folks say if I were to wear tights?"

"They would probably say that I married you for your money."
—Jack-o'-Lantern.

"JOHNNIE" JACK BULMER

Is known as "The Popular Singing Drummer" of Gorden's Palace Dance Orchestra, Spokane, Wash. Both his playing and singing are of a high caliber, therefore his services are much in demand. "Johnnie" says, "I prefer Leedy drums because I know Leedy has a world-wide reputation for quality, and my experience has proven that they make the best toned drums of them all."

Don't strike your triangle near the opening. That's where the tone is thin and not pleasing to the ear.

Theresa Mentzer

Miss Theresa Mentzer is a most talented drummer and is one of the big factors in making the Netto Ladies' Orchestra, Rialto Theatre, Casper, Wyo. (Nelly G. Food, conductor), a favorite organization among the theatre managers of the Rocky Mountain section. Miss Mentzer has been a professional drummer for twelve years, having played on many leading theatre jobs in western cities, and has always used Leedy. She was the first lady drummer in the country to use the Leedy Machine Tympani.

 **"WORLD'S FINEST DRUMMERS' INSTRUMENTS"**

The Exclusive Drummers' Paper

In London

Warwick Barnes   Eric Little   Arthur Layfield

The last issue of DRUM TOPICS contained a lengthy story of Art Layfield, the famous Chicago drummer, who has been for the past year with the Isham Jones Orchestra. They sailed for England on October 3rd and played a very successful engagement at the "Kit Kat Club" in London, returning to the United States December 4th. On New Year's eve the Jones Orchestra opened at the Davis Island Country Club, Tampa, for an indefinite run. It will interest many to know that Layfield recently transferred his talents to the Paul Ash Orchestra at McVicker's Theatre in Chicago, where he has a long contract.

While in London, Art wrote several interesting letters to DRUM TOPICS concerning English drummers. He states they are fine fellows to know and have ability on a par with that of drummers in the United States and Canada.

The above photo was taken in London. It shows Warwick Barnes at the left and Eric Little in the center. These two boys are ranked among the best in England.

Barnes is at present with Bert Firman's Orchestra, Carlton Hotel, Pall Mall, London. They also broadcast from Station 2LO, London. He has toured all over Europe in addition to playing at the Piccadilly Hotel, the Ritz Hotel and the Criterion Roof in London. He was flight lieutenant in the Royal Air Force during the World War, having served five years.

Eric Little has been at the drums for twenty years. He also served in the Air Force during the war and was stationed at the Grafton Hotel, London, when it was an American officers' headquarters. Since then he has filled engagements at the Savoy, Claridge and Piccadilly Hotels. Little is now with Jack Hylton's Band at the "Kit Kat Club." This is a very popular Victor recording organization.

Leedy is indeed pleased to have these two very fine English drummers as boosters.

FRANK A. SNOW

Has undoubtedly as wide a circle of friends and acquaintances in the drum world as any drummer in the business. And he has trouped with more high-class organizations over a longer period of time than most drummers who have been in the game as long. The "snap" shows Frank climbing one of the "Twin Peaks" in San Francisco on one of those "no matinee today" afternoons. He is now on the road with the western "Student Prince" company. Ask any old-time drummer about him and you will hear something like this: "Do I know him— what professional drummer does not? He's the drummer who helped write the original Dodge Drum Method and was with Sousa twelve years, including the world tour— and say, he's a real gentleman and good fellow all the time."

WALLY LAGESON

Osborn's Club Orchestra, playing at Marigold Garden, Minneapolis, Minn., is often spoken of as being equal to the big-name bands in New York and Chicago. Wally Lageson, the drummer, has helped greatly to establish the reputation of this orchestra. He is one of the boys who is on the job every minute he is playing. Most drummers who visit Minneapolis manage to "listen in" on his clever work, and we are glad he is all Leedy. Lageson was a pupil of Emil T. Weflin, the Minneapolis Symphony Orchestra drummer.

(Courtesy of Hausner Music Company.)

Men do not lack strength; they lack the will to concentrate and act.
—Elbert Hubbard.

"Cotton" Clark

This southern drummer has traveled with many of the leading dance orchestras south of the Mason-Dixon line. His excellent work is spoken of highly in dance circles throughout several states. He is now with the famous Fulcher Columbia Record Orchestra, with headquarters in Augusta, Ga. "Cotton" says, "I swear by Leedy at all times."

Combination Trap Holder No. 976

This sturdy little holder with the "Bull Dog" clamp has proven to be a fine accessory for either the dance or theatre drummer. More traps in less space is its big feature. Note that they will swing around and are adjustable to height on the rod.

Never use varnish on the beating surface of xylophone bars. Thin, clear shellac is best.

If it is inconvenient to cut notches around the edge of your tambourine shell (for the stick roll effect) you can successfully use brass-head tacks driven into the shell about one-half inch apart. Be careful not to split shell—use an awl.

"FOR DRUMMERS WHO CARE"

Leedy Drum Topics

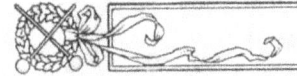

A PAPER DEVOTED TO
THE INTERESTS OF THE DRUMMER

No subscription fee.

Advertisements accepted.

Published quarterly at 1033 East Palmer Street,
Indianapolis, Indiana.

Editor..........................Geo. H. Way
Business Manager................A. W. Kuerst

Don't Stop

Handing out advice is a favorite pastime with us all—sort of a universal sport and as old as man. Every one takes a fling at it, because it is "easier to preach than to practice."

There is the good and the bad—the trick is to sift out the good points from the tons of "do this" and "do that" flung at us from all sides.

The man who succeeds is the one who has "sifted" intelligently and who has the will to put the good advice into action.

And here is our little "spiel" to certain drummers:

The greatest fault of many of the boys new in the game is that, just as soon as they become proficient enough on two drums to play with a professional orchestra and earn a fair amount of money, they consider themselves a howling success and stop studying or seeking further advice.

Many such drummers even avoid advice when they reach this stage. It is not always a case of conceit—often they are just satisfied —but when the day comes that more money is needed and it takes a better job to get it, then they begin to wish in the past tense.

The drummer in the large cities is more fortunate; he has a greater opportunity to observe others. The drummer in the smaller towns has a longer row to hoe, but either of them can cut down the hard knocks of experience if they will only study, practice, and seek advice beyond their present station.

Wise and progressive drummers do so. Meet an old-time drummer who is a real success and you will find that he is still seeking to learn and be advised.

We have heard dance drummers (the ones who fake entirely) go through a whole evening repeating over and over again only seven or eight different beats. They play them well, which proves they could learn more, but for some reason they are satisfied.

Until they change their views their earning capacity is limited. Remember, drums are easy to "get by" on, but they are not easy to succeed on.

And so this is an appeal, with advice to you who are in this class to improve.

Go to it, fellows. DON'T STOP. Work it out. George Marsh and Art Layfield didn't get there by stopping at any certain place.

Julia Goldman

When a lady drummer plays her instruments so well that "he" drummers drop in to hear her work, she certainly must be of a very high order. That's the way Miss Julia Goldman puts it over. She recently played a series of concerts at the Hotel Pennsylvania, New York, and was formerly at Scharles Inn. Miss Goldman is now with one of the finest lady orchestras in New York City, playing at Zits Central Park Casino. She is a great Leedy enthusiast.

Lloyd Marsh

Lloyd changed his mind—he didn't repeat his world tour trip on the S. S. Belgenland this winter. Instead he located with one of the country's finest—the Ernie Golden Orchestra—playing at the McAlpin Hotel, New York City. They broadcast from the grill room daily. As a drummer, Lloyd is in the same class with his brother George, of the Paul Whiteman Orchestra. And that's going some!

Frank Cork and George Carey

Like most drummers, these two can argue a question pertaining to drums so that a listener would think they were dead sore at one another. And, like most drummers, they part good friends. Frank and George always shake hands to make sure of it.

Frank Cork is recognized as one of the best in New York City. George needs no introduction to professionals, but for those new in the business we repeat—he is the wonderful xylophone soloist and tympanist with Sousa's Band.

HARRY H. MURPHY

Is not only one of the most competent and best known drummers in Kansas City, Mo., but is also chief staff photographer of the Kansas City Star. He plays now as a side line. At one time Harry studied with the famous Billy Drew.
All Leedy.

DRUM TOPICS would like to show more photos of Lady Drummers.

If you use an electric heater in either your snare or bass drum, for theatre work, run an extension wire with a switch down into the basement orchestra room. By turning it on when you come in a few moments before the overture you will have a nice snappy snare drum to start off on.

New Felt End Drum Sticks

Here's one that came out since the last issue of DRUM TOPICS. Every drummer we have shown them to wants a pair. WHY? Because the new (patented) design of the felt ends are just the thing for bass drum beats and certain effects on the cymbal. The felt is the kind that won't knock out of shape. It is not only glued to the flat end of the stick, but there is a large brass screw imbedded in the felt and passing a long way into the stick. These sticks have ball tips with a quick taper and are 15 inches long.

Ask for No. 376A.

"WORLD'S FINEST DRUMMERS' INSTRUMENTS"

The Exclusive Drummers' Paper

The Prize Story

GEO. FULLER, the well-known drummer at the Palace (Keith) Vaudeville Theatre in Indianapolis, tells this true story:

One Monday morning at rehearsal, a few weeks ago, a real sweet young thing handed out the music books for her act to each one of the boys in the pit. When she came to me she said: "Mr. Drummer, there's a long roll, all by yourself, right near the beginning. Won't you please watch for it?"

"Sure I will," I said, putting on my best (prop) smile, and, making an effort to please, added: "Do you want it piano?"

"Oh, no," she cried, "just play it on that little drum, if you don't mind."

"BUD" EBEL

Has been with the Chubb Steinberg-Gennett Recording Orchestra, of Cincinnati, Ohio, for the past three years. Previously he was with Clare Moore's Orchestra and Bill Holland's Orchestra, both of Chicago. "Bud" is a "big-time" drummer all the time and he is strong on Leedy equipment.

Some drummers chew gum while on the job—others chew the rag. One is as bad as the other.

FRED W. BROWN

Is now at the Baker Theatre, Portland, Ore. He has also traveled a great deal, having visited China, Japan, India, etc. Brown has a wonderful reputation all over the Pacific Northwest. In 1922 he was with "Paton's Sinko-Pators," a crack orchestra of Portland.

The Leedy Adjustable Bass Drum Rack

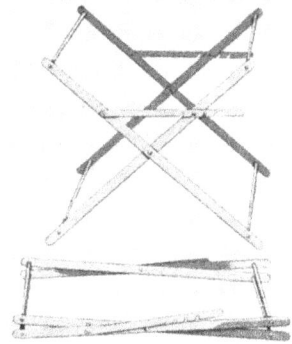

You can't beat this rack for either the located or traveling drummer. It has all the features required. The cross-braces are tubes and telescope like trombone slides, therefore the rack can be adjusted to any width drum and is also adjustable to various heights. Made in a manner that will not allow the bass drum to sway.

Weighs only 10 pounds and folds into a small space.

Ask for No. 79.

Geo. Marsh

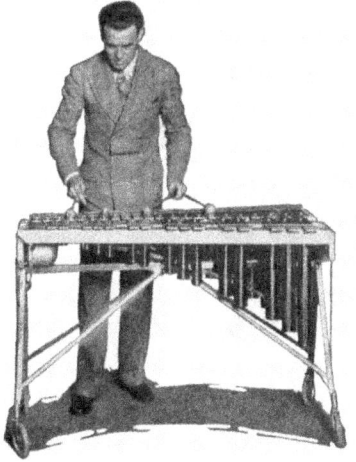

GEO. MARSH plays the new Leedy Vibraphone with the Paul Whiteman Orchestra. Have you heard this wonderful instrument? If not, drop into any phonograph store and listen to these records:

Brunswick Record No. 2677
Columbia Record No. 381-D
Edison Record No. 51401-L
Edison Record No. 51550-R

The Victor Salon Orchestra also features it. The Whiteman Orchestra goes to Coral Gables, Fla., for six weeks beginning April 15th, then they sail from New York for a four months' tour of the British Isles and Europe.

"Bob" Howard Rankin

The Wayne A. Hinkle Orchestra—touring the leading vaudeville and dance circuits—believes in advertising, rain or shine.

When it rains each member wears a slicker which tells the party's name and the instrument he plays. The photo shows their drummer, "Bob" Rankin, of Bridgeport, Ohio, formerly of Cedar Rapids, Iowa. "Bob" is a fine drummer and showman, the kind that helps to raise the standards of the profession.

Try This

Place a tambourine (inverted) on top of a Turkish cymbal that is used on a spring holder and beat on either the edge of the tambourine or the edge of the cymbal, using left hand for stops. Sounds good when one plays on the edge of the "tambo" and accents on the cymbal in "P. P." passages.
—*Vernon Johnson, Cuba, Mo.*

JIMMY McCALLUM

Is of the better class all-'round type drummers. He is well known all over the South, having trouped many seasons. For the past three years he has been a feature at the Strand Vaudeville Theatre, Salisbury, N. C. His home is in Wilmington, N. C. Leedy throughout.

PETE SNOOK

Of Winner, S. D., has had many years' experience and has played with many fine organizations in several cities. He has specialized in theatre work and says he would have none other than Leedy instruments. Pete says, "Drummers who do not keep pace with the times are out of luck."

FRED PAINE is the drummer with the Detroit News Symphony Orchestra, radio broadcasting over WWJ.

ROBT. REX WARRINER is the drummer with the Westinghouse Band at Pittsburgh, Pa., broadcasting over KDKA.

DRUM TOPICS would like to publish the names and photos of drummers who are permanently employed at radio stations. Send them in.

O. F. Rominger

"O. F." is still going strong with his fine work with Herbert Clark's Municipal Band at Long Beach, Cal.

If you expect something good, for nothing, you will get something good-for-nothing.

 **"FOR DRUMMERS WHO CARE"**

Leedy Drum Topics

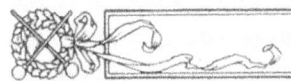

Clarence A. Stout

"THE ORIGINAL INDIANIANS," of Vincennes, Ind., are under the management of Clarence A. Stout (drummer). They have been creating a great deal of favorable comment throughout the Middle West. Mr. Stout is a noted song-writer and has quite a few hits to his credit, including the famous Bert Williams, Ziegfeld Follies and Columbia record success "O Death, Where Is Thy Sting?" He specializes in negro songs and has several new ones to be released shortly by some of the leading New York publishers. All their booking is through Vincennes, Ind. Stout uses Leedy at all times.

When you hit upon a particularly nice effect by way of a nifty beat or the use of a trap, don't overdo it; save it; make 'em listen for it.

W. P. SMYTHE

Known as "Smitty," began his professional career twelve years ago. Since then he has made a wonderful reputation for himself in several Texas cities. One year at the Liberty Theatre, Houston, and also with the Houston Municipal Band. Later "Smitty" put in three years with "Phil Baxter's Entertainers" at the Adolphus Hotel, Dallas. He is now with the Ligon Smith Country Club Orchestra and using all Leedy equipment.

Did you ever notice that the "top notchers" are not conceited?

A Practical and Handy Device

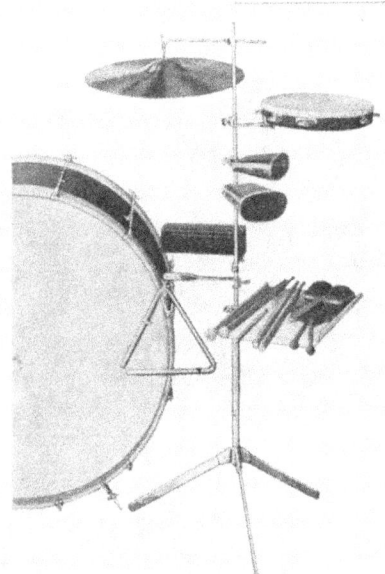

Is exactly what Leedy Trap Trees are called by hundreds of drummers. This is because they are light yet strong, and their packing features enable a drummer to carry them about easily. Holders for the traps are designed to be adjustable to any position on the tree. You can use the holders on any tree and in any number, arranging your own combination of traps. The photo tells the story of their practicability better than words. The tree alone extends to a height of 45 inches and you can use a spring cymbal holder on top of the rod if you instruct us to thread it for same. The legs fold up and rod telescopes into the base. Weighs only 3 pounds. They add wonderfully to your outfit for appearance.

Fred Ellerkamp

Holds one of the most important positions with the Leedy Mfg. Co. He is foreman in charge of the Tool Room and has been with the company for twenty-six years. Many people are under the impression that a toolmaker is an ordinary machinist. This is far from the truth. A toolmaker has to have the skill and accuracy of a handcraft jeweler. Fred is all that and more. The making of all the tools that form the hundreds of metal parts used in the manufacture of Leedy drums is under his direction. He was one of the men who helped develop one of America's first automobiles, the old Mohawk, of Indianapolis.

From close observation of chime parts we have yet to find a composer who writes them correctly in the staff. We can tell from orders placed with us that it is the impression of musicians that chimes are pitched lower than they actually sound. Some writers even use the bass clef, evidently assuming that chimes sound that low, but the lowest "C" in a regular 1½-octave set of chimes sounds actually the "C" found in the third space of the trebble clef staff. Naturally, for convenience reading, it is better to write the part one octave lower, but it should not be written in the bass clef, because it is both misleading and difficult for some drummers to read.

ARTHUR GREIG

Does not look in this photo as though he had been at the drums for thirty years. However, he assures DRUM TOPICS that it is a late picture. Greig has his own music store and is manager of a concert and dance orchestra in far-off Edinburgh, Scotland. Letters from other drummers in Edinburgh state that Greig is well rated as a first-class drummer.

John W. Cheuvront

Is not only an excellent drummer but a first-rate entertainer as well. A very clever comedian with a very fine voice who "puts his stuff over." The photo was taken when he was with Earl Fuller's first orchestra on the road. Cheuvront is now located at Marion, Ohio, doing the best class of dance work in and around that city. He writes: "I have used every make drum that is manufactured today, but not one of them can come up to my New Leedy Floating Head Model."

ALF GABRIEL

Has his own orchestra ("The Original Melody Makers") in London, England. They are a jobbing organization and are kept busy six nights a week the year 'round. When the Isham Jones Orchestra was in London, Art Layfield heard Gabriel playing on a job and wrote DRUM TOPICS that he was very fine—and an exceptionally nice chap. Gabriel now owns a new Leedy Floating Head Drum.

ANDREW DOUGHERTY

Is now with the popular Gates Metropolitan Band, of La Crosse, Wis. He hails from Indiana and has been with the "Hoosier Ramblers" and the "Madison Red Hats," also the "Genk Johnston Orchestra," of St. Louis, and the Schoenbach Orchestra, of Danville, Ill. Dougherty makes a hit on every job, because he puts his whole heart into his work. He recently purchased a complete new Leedy outfit.

"WORLD'S FINEST DRUMMERS' INSTRUMENTS"

Prominent Canadian Drummers

1. VIC LUFF is one of the best known drummers in the West. From Fort William to Vancouver the boys say, "Vic Luff in Winnipeg does it this way." He has played the Pan and Orpheum vaudeville theatres, also five years at the Walker. Now with one of Canada's greatest leaders, Earl Hill, at the Capitol Theatre, doing special stage acts in addition to the regular pit playing. Vic is a very fine tympanist and plays tympani with the Winnipeg Symphony Orchestra.

2. IRVING W. ARMSTRONG, of Toronto, Ont., is kept busy nightly with the leading dance orchestras of that city. His work is highly regarded, in as much as he is continually introducing new ideas and displaying ability full of "pep" far above the average.

3. AL. JENKINS made a wonderful reputation for himself with the Bluebird Orchestra in Winnipeg. He is considered one of the best dance men in all Canada. The orchestra is now playing a "run" engagement at the Sunnydale Pavilion at Edmonton, Alta., and Al. is making his usual hit with the local musicians and dancers.

4. HECTOR HILL is a leading theatre drummer of Edmonton, Alta. Now playing at the Rialto. Hill has been in the game six years. From the beginning he studied thoroughly on every instrument up to tympani. Leaders speak most complimentary of his work. Hill is some dandy fellow as well.

5. FRED WELLS, formerly of Moose Jaw, Sask., is now located in Vancouver, B. C. Fred is a high-grade, all 'round theatre, dance and concert man and has held many leading positions. Several years for Capitol Theatres in Brandon, Man., and Moose Jaw, Sask.; also with Mitchel's Premier Orchestra and with Art Fullford's Orchestra. Fred acted as agent for the Advance Drum Company for two years in Moose Jaw. Some hustler and regular fellow.

6. EARL W. HOWEY was formerly with the Cecil Lord Orchestra, of Edmonton, Alta. This organization played a season at Sullivan's Dancing Academy. They also did considerable stage work, including a successful engagement at the Capitol Theatre. Howey is now jobbing and his services are in constant demand, owing to his nifty work. He is a pupil of Milt Weber.

7. W. WILKINSON is the drummer with the Unity Concert Band, of Unity, Sask. This band is a prize winner, having carried off honors at the late Saskatchewan Musical Festival. Wilkinson puts up a fine job and is ever eager to do things in the right way.

8. HAROLD WISEMAN, of St. Thomas, Ont., is a most capable drummer and enjoys a wonderful reputation by way of his clever playing. He is with the Tivoli Theatre Little Symphony Orchestra, an organization very highly rated.

9. W. E. GALISTER is at the Lyric Theatre in Swift Current, Sask. He was formerly with "The Moonlight Syncopators" for two years, doing the best class of jobbing work. Galister believes in using a complete outfit and giving every new idea a thorough trial. Those who know him state that his work is excellent.

10. ERNEST GLOVER, of Roseland, B. C., plays with the Christine Lake Orchestra, also with the Elks' Band of Trail, B. C. He is rated high with all his fellow musicians.

ALL SATISFIED LEEDY-ADVANCE DRUMMERS

Quick and Easy

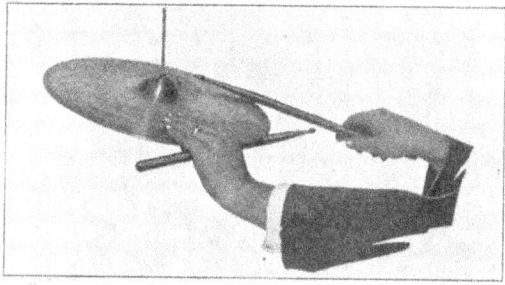

Grab the cymbal with the left hand (palm down), with the drum stick lying across the under side of the cymbal near the edge held with the thumb. Strike the cymbal four to the bar with the right stick, accenting on the afterbeat and gripping (choking) the cymbal with the left hand on the first and third beats, releasing for the accent on the second and fourth. Always allow the stick to remain in contact with the cymbal. Many other rhythmic effects are possible. Using the stick in this manner saves having to pick up another piece to get almost the same effect.

Sent in by "Dusty" Roades, the "crack" drummer with Ted Weems' Orchestra at the Muehlebach Hotel, Kansas City, Mo.

The Spider Web Girl

At one time the idea of painting scenes and figures on bass drum heads was a fad. Many drummers belittled it. Now it is a universal practice, because if the work is well done and the subject chosen with taste in keeping with music and dancing, the artistic painting attracts many more eyes to your organization. Do not choose subjects that are "dead scenes," such as straight landscapes. Pick the ones with artistic action and remember the simple ones are best. Too many colors on a too crowded scene do not show up well at a distance. Silhouettes are best. This new one is beautiful.

Dr. Ingerson

Drummers of St. Paul, Minn., have a real champion for their cause in Dr. Ingerson. The doctor is not only a drummer who can hold his own with the best of professionals, but is Grand Exalted Ruler of the Elks (and plays in their drum corps) and is a member of the Shrine Band. Therefore it's a certainty that drummers in these organizations are credited with full measure of their worth. Dr. Ingerson not only takes an interest in "his own" drummers, but always sees that the prominent traveling boys are given attention. He is a personal friend of Carey, Goulden and Helmecke, of Sousa's Band, and a wonderful time is had when the band visits St. Paul. The doctor is a full-fledged Leedy man.

A New Non-Swinging Crash Cymbal Holder

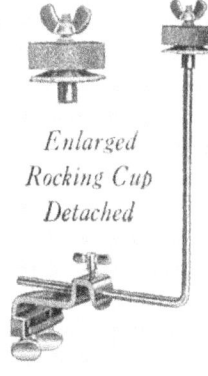

Enlarged Rocking Cup Detached

Many new effects on crash cymbals have come into being in the past few years. These call for entirely different manipulations than heretofore. This new holder is just the thing for the new and old styles of playing combined.

The cymbal rests on a "rocking cup," which rocks freely at the slightest beat or the hardest crash, insuring maximum vibration and, consequently, full cymbal tone. Free cymbal movement prevents breaking.

(This cup can be reversed if performer desires to use cymbal upside down.) Ask for No. 293.

"FOR DRUMMERS WHO CARE"

Leedy Drum Topics

In Omaha

Alton Deits   *Leo Moskowitz*

ALTON DEITS is one of the busiest jobbing drummers of Omaha, Neb. During the day he acts as salesman for the Geo. A. Smith Music Store and also assists in the drum repairing. Deits is a hustler and ever eager to please.

LEO MOSKOWITZ is with Ron's Collegians, a very popular dance orchestra with Omaha's young society set. They also broadcast from Radio Station KOIL (Council Bluffs, Iowa) regularly. Leo is one of the kind of drummers who takes a great interest in his work. He is bound to go to the top.

MADISON B. DUNCAN

Of Versailles, Ky., is a theatre and dance drummer whose fine work is known all over the state. He was five years at the Lyric Theatre in Versailles and has been for the past three years with Hawkin's Dance Orchestra. He also plays with the Versailles Optimists' Band. Duncan is a strong Leedy enthusiast.

A fresh mind keeps the body fresh. Take in the idea of today, drain off those of yesterday. —*Bulwer.*

Treat your outfit with the same care that other musicians give their instruments, and you will save money.

Speaking of Pedals

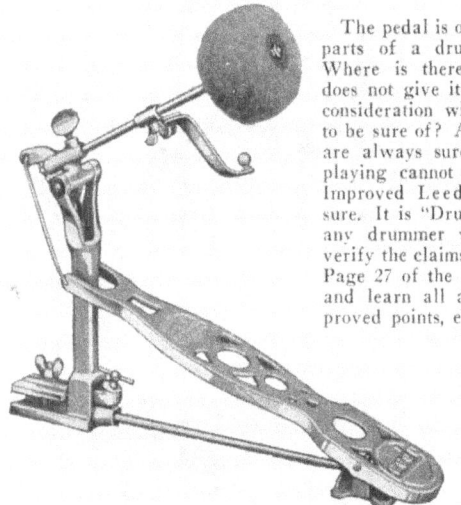

The pedal is one of the most vital parts of a drummer's equipment. Where is there a drummer who does not give it equal thought and consideration with all else he has to be sure of? And good drummers are always sure. A "miss" while playing cannot be corrected. The Improved Leedy-Fraser Pedal is sure. It is "Drummer Correct" and any drummer who uses one will verify the claims made for it. Read Page 27 of the Leedy Catalog "N" and learn all about the eight improved points, especially the action.

Some More Phonograph Records With Good Drum Effects

Drummers have written that they got some good tips from the list we published in the last issue. Send in some more.

VICTOR RECORD 19807-A
"*Nobody but Fanny*"
Sent in by Jerome Arends, San Francisco, Cal.

BANNER RECORD 1175-A
"*Parade of the Wooden Soldiers*"
COLUMBIA RECORD 416-D
"*Say, Arabella*"
"*Angry*"
Sent in by Bert Limerick, Fort William, Ont., Can.

VICTOR RECORD 17092-A
"*The Ragtime Drummer*"
COLUMBIA RECORD 265-D
"*Cross Corners*"
Sent in by Edwin L. Gerhardt, Baltimore, Md.

BRUNSWICK RECORD 2892
"*Got No Time*"
"*Isn't She the Sweetest Thing?*"
Sent in by A. F. Durlauf, Louisville, Ky. (Paul Sporledor, of the Gene Rodemich Orchestra, does some fine work on Leedy drums in this record)

VICTOR RECORD 19840-A
"*Who*"
Sent in by W. D. Kieffer, Washington, D. C.

EDISON RECORD 2325
"*Fourth of July Patrol*"
Sent in by Verne Johnson, Quinn, S. D.

HENRY R. ANDERSON

Of Detroit, Mich., has been in the game twenty-five years and always used Leedy equipment. He started with a Newsboys' Band when only thirteen. He has worked in Johnstown, Pa., Tulsa, Okla., and Texarkana, Texas, besides many seasons on the road. For the past sixteen years he has been in Detroit and has played in almost every house in that city, the last fifteen years at the Columbia Theatre on the morning and evening shifts. Other shifts have been put in at the Comique, Temple, Avenue, Cadillac, Shubert and other theatres, also with many dance orchestras.

Anderson is a true old-time legitimate drummer who enjoys a country-wide high reputation.

Introducing JUSTA WETHEAD

Justa is a wise-cracking guy and wants the world to know it. He is "*some*" drummer and has had a wide and varied experience, having played with all the leading Player Pianos and Piano Players in Hub Switch. Justa says he's good (ask him) and that all the big bands are after his services. He is an authority on everything, having studied drums a long time (four lessons) and has stood for hours watching the Drum Section of an automatic merry-go-round organ. He gets all his new beats from watching his old man beat the carpets. Justa trouped once—went ten miles to play a barn dance.

Anyway, he has consented to give the boys the benefit of his experiences. Watch for him in each issue of DRUM TOPICS.

Justa Wethead says:

"*The leader told me to choke my cymbal, but I couldn't find its neck.*"

Leedy   "WORLD'S FINEST DRUMMERS' INSTRUMENTS"   **Leedy**

The Exclusive Drummers' Paper

The metal counter hoops of the New Leedy Floating Head Drum are made of solid brass, therefore they can never rust. It requires 125 tons of pressure to form them on a 175-ton power press.

Al Pinard

Of the Guy Brothers Minstrels has been the subject of considerable favorable comment in many cities of the Eastern States and Canada where this well-known standard attraction has played. Pinard's work is very fine, both in the pit and on the street. He started on drums when only ten years old. At one time he was with Van Arman's Minstrels, also Dan Fitch's Minstrels in vaudeville, and others. His home is Springfield, Mass.

Don't Forget

DRUM TOPICS will present $10.00 CASH to the drummer who sends in the best story before April 15.

BERT LIMERICK

Of the Goodsell-Colosimo Orchestra, in Ft. William, Ont., Can., is one of the boys who sticks to his own home town and makes himself indispensable to his organization through his wide-awake efforts and efficient playing. A photo of the orchestra was in the fourth issue of DRUM TOPICS. Solid Leedy.

Procure five small sheets of polished sheet steel, $\frac{1}{8}$" thick by 4" long by $2\frac{1}{2}$" wide, with slightly curved corners. When these are tossed onto a wood or concrete floor they produce the most realistic glass crash imaginable.

B. N. GUSTAT

Now located in St. Louis, Mo., is a prominent figure among the drummers there, owing to his exceptional ability. "B. N.," as he is called, was once located in Montana. Later he put in several years at El Paso, Tex., in the leading theatre, the Texas Grand, and as secretary of the A. F. of M. in that city. He was also the Leedy agent there for some time.

The Improved Leedy Xylophone and Marimba Stand

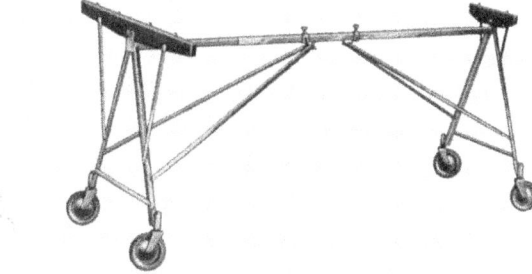

This photo gives a true idea of the finest Xylophone and Marimba Stand ever applied to these instruments. The mechanically correct lines show at a glance its wonderful strength. It can be set up or taken down at a greater speed than any former model. Comes apart in two pieces only. The long center brace telescopes. The legs are made of heavy angle steel and there are no parts that may come loose and be lost.

This cartoon was sent to DRUM TOPICS from England. It proves that the drummers, wherever located in this old world, have the same troubles, and, while it's a comedy drawing, there is the serious side of it, for here is shown one of the reasons why drummers should receive more money.

Roy Jeffries

Has been with the Leedy Mfg. Co. for twenty-six years, starting as the company's second machinist; therefore he knows every thread, nut and bolt that goes to make up Leedy Drummers' Instruments. He did some of the first work on hundreds of parts of accessories now so well known to every drummer. Roy is a hard and sincere worker, well liked by all the boys in the plant. He is now foreman of the Machine Room, where all the parts are formed, etc.

On the Cover—Chauncey E. Morehouse

The high rating enjoyed by this most progressive drummer proves that the man from the smaller town, with the right stuff in him, can climb to the top of the ladder. Morehouse hails from Chambersburg, Pa., where he began his career with Duffield, the well-known band leader. By way of always being on the job and keeping himself equipped to date, Chauncey landed with Paul Specht, remaining with him several seasons and during his rise to fame. Later he toured the United States with Ted Weems and is now with Jean Goldkette's Orchestra (Victor recording and WJR radio) in Detroit, Mich. This is one of the finest and most notable jobs for a drummer and proves his ability. Chauncey is a most likable fellow and is therefore very popular among the boys, having the reputation of always being a real gentleman. The photo shows the kind of instruments he favors.

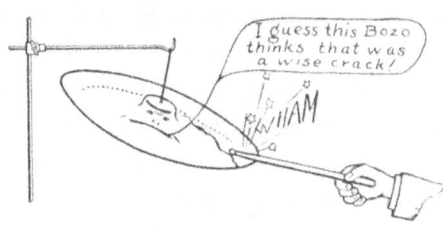

Be sure that Drum Topics has your correct address. Send in some new names. Next issue May 15th. So Long! Good Luck!

 "FOR DRUMMERS WHO CARE"

Leedy
DRUM TOPICS
The Exclusive Drummers' Paper

FEB. 15, 1926
ELEVENTH EDITION

F. E. Wolfington,
1111 Laurel St.,
Indianapolis, Ind.

POSTMASTER—Return Postage Guaranteed

Leedy Manufacturing Co.
INDIANAPOLIS, INDIANA

SPEED — here it is

The New "Speed Way" Snare Strainer

This new Snare Strainer is a real Drummer's Help. It is in no way bunglesome. The mechanism is simple and positive. The throw-off lever is designed to work with either the hand or drum stick and is adjustable to length. A wonder for speed. Put one on your drum.

The "Speed Way" Snare Strainer may be purchased separately and applied to any model Leedy Drum.
Ask for No. 27.

"Your Drum Stick Works It"

The "Speed Way" Snare Strainer is now regular equipment on all Leedy Floating Head Drums without extra charge.

Leedy Mfg. Co. INDIANAPOLIS INDIANA

Wm. H. Gilcher of Max Dolin's Orchestra, San Francisco, Cal. (See Page 15)

Leedy Drum Topics

Ask any man on earth

what he is most vitally interested in. If he tells you the truth, he will state that the greatest subject of his daily thoughts is himself. You can't get away from it—it's human nature—it's that way with Drummers, the same as other folks.

Your interest in yourself is to succeed—success is happiness—to succeed as a Drummer is to be a fine Drummer—to hold the best jobs—to increase your earnings and to be in demand. To climb higher you must go beyond your present circle of thinking and activities.

The opportunities that pass most every day must be seized and worked out—this means such things as—knowing every phase of the game—treating your profession with the same seriousness as a business man—being completely equipped—swapping ideas and "selling" yourself. DRUM TOPICS will help.

The New Leedy Trap Table

The latest device—designed especially for the jobbing and traveling Drummer. Fits any size Bass Drum. Clamps are adjustable. Will hold several traps in an efficient manner. Has fine appearance.

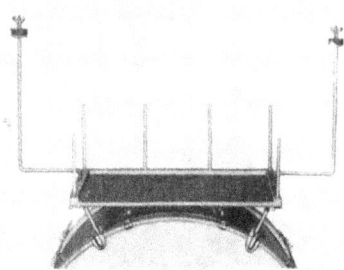

Table as Shown Above, without Holders, No. 979

Trap Holders

241A	Small Temple Block Clamps
240A	Large Temple Block Clamps
985	Wood Block Holders
989	Afterbeat Cymbal Holders
989	Egyptian Cymbal Holders
988	Tom-Tom Holders
983	Tambourine Holders
984	Cow Bell Holders
987	Triangle Holders

Showing Table Knocked Down for Traveling

Leedy   "WORLD'S FINEST DRUMMERS' INSTRUMENTS"   *Leedy*

The Exclusive Drummers' Paper

Paul Ash and Arthur Layfield

When Paul Ash posed for this photo he did not have to be told — as most leaders do — how to hold the sticks. It is only his close friends and former colleagues who know that this famous Jazz King was once a busy professional Drummer in Milwaukee, Wis. — and not just an ordinary Drummer, but one (so those who worked with him say) who was introducing original and peppy ideas in the "ragtime" days that were on a par with what many of the best Drummers are putting into the modern jazz of today. And now Paul Ash and his "Merry Mad Gang" are one of the most popular musical organizations of the United States. Columbia records have given him the same standing in many countries abroad. At McVickers Theatre in

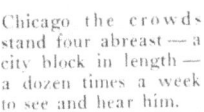

Chicago the crowds stand four abreast — a city block in length — a dozen times a week to see and hear him.

Arthur Layfield, Paul Ash's Drummer, needs no introduction to DRUM TOPICS readers. His brilliant and successful career in all branches of the business is a record few have attained. Since joining Paul Ash, Art has again set a pace with new stuff and neat work that has made him the talk of the Drum world. Only a few weeks ago he "stopped the show" with a xylophone number that was truly marvelous in speed and technique. About every Chicago Drummer goes to hear him as often as possible, and visitors should never miss the opportunity when in the city. He is now manager in charge of the musicians and is, of course, a very busy fellow; however, he always has the time to talk Drums to those who are interested and is ever willing to give the beginners constructive advice. Even with his many duties at McVickers, Art does considerable teaching. Layfield's entire outfit is Leedy and he is well satisfied with same.

Mr. Ash states, "The tone of Leedy instruments is unquestionably superior."

In Zanzibar

Zanzibar is in British East Africa. History tells us that Drums played a principal part in the lives of the people there many centuries before Biblical times. It is the same today. The above photo was taken only a few months ago. The small dot-like figures around the Drum shells are wooden pegs that can be removed for head replacement. Note the very modern metal whistle hanging from the neck of the fifth man from the left. Evidently he is the leader of this corps.

Less "inspirational stuff" and more facts is what we all need these days.

If you see a vaudeville Drummer's crash cymbal hanging within three inches of the trombone player's ear, you can bet a hat they are not roommates.

"Bill" Roberts

"Bill" Roberts has played them all—even Lufkin, Texas. He has trouped with Musical Shows, Medicine Shows, Boat Shows, Carnivals, Circuses, Wild Wests, and Grand Opera. From the Sells-Floto Show he went to the Orpheum Theatre in Peoria, Illinois, for two seasons, and is booked for Miller Bros. 101 Ranch this season. One fine all-'round Drummer and he emphatically states—"Twelve years a satisfied Leedy Booster."

Leedy   "FOR DRUMMERS WHO CARE"   *Leedy*

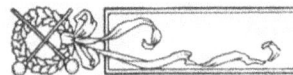 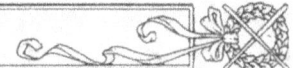

Leedy Drum Topics

When a Drummer Thinks Fast

He told his wife that he played the dance until four A. M., but her girl friend from across the hall had already reported it over at midnight.

Ronald Felix

The new Leedy Floating Head Drum made Ronald Felix, of Springfield, Mass., a 100% Leedy enthusiast. He is now in his third year with the popular "Bob" Patterson Orchestra. This orchestra is the leading feature at the famous Venetian Gardens during the summer season. They have been making a great hit at the Kimbal Hotel in Springfield the past winter and are booked to return to the Gardens in May. Felix is a firm believer in physical culture and has quite a reputation as an athlete. He claims that the Drummer who takes proper exercise can do a better job, because he feels full of "pep." There is a world of truth in this. Felix put in two seasons on the road with the Central American Marimba Band, a very fine organization that is a headline attraction. He has been at the Drums since thirteen years of age and enjoys a wonderful reputation as a very clever and artistic Drummer.

Another New Cymbal Idea

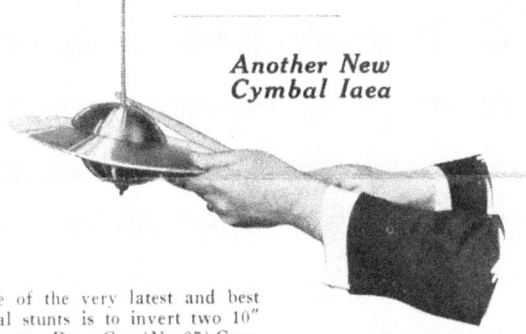

One of the very latest and best cymbal stunts is to invert two 10" Charleston Deep Cup (No. 87) Cymbals, edge to edge as shown in the above photo. A greater variety of effects can be obtained in this manner than by any method yet presented.

The idea was originally introduced by Paul Sporleder, the wizard of the Gene Rodemich-Brunswick Record Orchestra, St. Louis, Mo.

The cymbals he uses are the new shaped, extra deep cup type, Leedy No. 87. They have that hollow "squash" tone so desirable for "choking," etc.

ARTEMAS HIGGS

Besides being a thorough Drummer, Art Higgs is a well-known teacher and performer on French horn, violin, banjo, mandolin, guitar and xylophone. He was co-author of "The Newton Method for Tenor Banjo" and now has a large class of pupils in his home town, Fort Wayne, Ind. In 1910 he toured the South as xylophone soloist with Roger's Chautauqua Orchestra of Goshen, Ind. He always recommends and uses Leedy.

If at first you don't succeed there's a reason. Find it before you try again.

"Dusty" Roades

"Dusty" Roades, formerly of the Leviathan Orchestra, an Orpheum headline act, is now with the Ted Weems Orchestra, enjoying a long and successful run at the Muelbach Hotel in Kansas City, Missouri. "Dusty" is still doing his stuff in a high-class manner, and when he sings they stop dancing. Over a year ago "Dusty" took a wife—and what do you think? There is now a little "feather duster" at his house that will soon be crying for a Drum.

EMILE J. GONZALES

of New Orleans, La., has for many years been one of the most prominent Drummers of "America's Most Interesting City." He has played in many of the best cafes, hotels and cabarets, also with the leading bands. Gonzales is an excellent musician as well as an up-to-date Drummer and is an exceptionally conscientious worker. Between jobs he does repairing and selling for the Drum Department of the Conn-New Orleans Music Store.

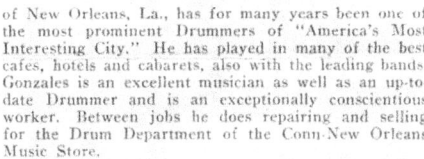

A very good effect for heavy wind- and rainstorms, on land or sea, can be obtained by placing your Snare Drum so that the snares will vibrate in sympathy with a strong roll on a Leedy Machine Tympano. Roll about three or four inches from the counter hoop and work the pedal with a slow upward and downward motion.

(Sent in by Wm. Acheson, Norwich, Conn.)

Don't forget — DRUM TOPICS wants some good summer photos for the fall issues.

Paul Janushanis

of the Sixth Infantry Band at Jefferson Barracks, Mo., is not sitting around taking things easy between turns at regular army duty. He is putting in many hours daily at practice on Drums, Xylophone and Tympani and has become an extraordinarily fine Drummer as the result. He states: "If a fellow wants to improve and is willing to study, an enlistment in the army will do the trick. We play all kinds of music indoors and out, under every condition, and I have had the opportunity to try almost all makes of Drums, etc. Now it's Leedy for mine all the time, and very often when the government issues instruments of other makes for my outfit, I have purchased the Leedy brand out of my own pocket."

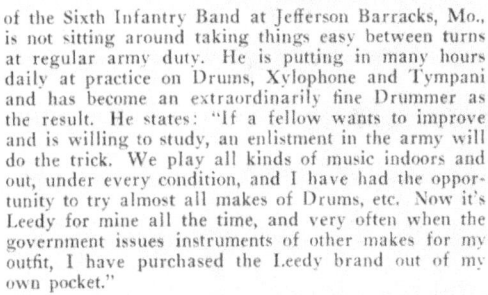

 **"WORLD'S FINEST DRUMMERS' INSTRUMENTS"**

The Exclusive Drummers' Paper

Luck means the extra hours you have put in studying; the long hours you have worked at your job; the rough spots you have not sidestepped. Luck means the word and appointments you have never failed to keep; the trains you have never failed to catch and the opportunities you have not let pass you by.

A Tambourine Stunt

Unless the head happens to be at just the right tension, you cannot always depend upon the thumb or finger for a true roll on your tambourine. Neither is there always plenty of time to wet your thumb. Besides, it is an unsanitary stunt to keep this up through a long number and the wetting process has to be repeated every few measures.

So, to make sure of the roll, try this:

Brush a light coat of clear varnish on the head around the edge of the tambourine, all except at the point where the hand grips the shell. Make the strip about two and one-half inches wide. Then wait until the varnish has dried slightly. Next rub two sheets of No. 2 sandpaper together, holding them about five inches over the head. The grains from the paper will fall into the varnish, where they will become imbedded and, when dry, form a slightly rough surface which will always act as a "triller" for the thumb.

EARL M. LOOMIS

is manager and Drummer of his own six-piece orchestra called Earl's Melodians, working out of Auburn, Neb. They travel for miles in their own autos and play all the important engagements in this district. Loomis is a thoroughly modern dance man, having had many years' experience. All Leedy.

(Courtesy Fellers Music House.)

Accommodating

Pretty Co-Ed—"I want a pair of bloomers I can wear around my gymnasium."

Clerk (absently)—"Yes, madam; what size is your gymnasium?"
—*Frivol.*

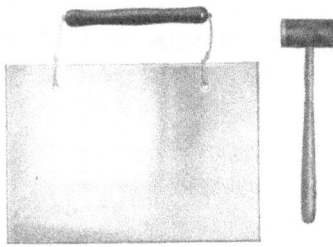

A Bell Plate

must be made of a high quality steel and be not less than one-fourth inch thick in order to have that realistic railroad bell tone. The Leedy plate is the most realistic of any on the market. It also serves as a fine fire bell when struck with hard hammers, such as the butt end of the drum sticks. It pays to have the real effect. Ask for No. 71. Costs a little more, but well worth it.

Our Drum Head Department sells the trimmings of the partly finished hides to the makers of high-grade glue. And the trimmings of the finished hides to artificial limb manufacturers.

JACK TREBELL

has evidently held some of the best jobs in London, England. He was with the "London Band" which followed Paul Whiteman at the Hippodrome when the latter first visited England. Trebell is now with Don Parker's Band playing at the Piccadilly Hotel and Kit Kat Club. All of which means that he must be among the best in London. Trebell uses the Leedy Machine Tympani and writes that "they are all that is claimed for them and a wonderful help to any Drummer."

Henry C. Ebert

Henry C. Ebert is Drummer and Business Manager of the Woodcliffe Orchestra, of Dunkirk, N. Y., shown in the above photo. This bunch of boys is known as one of the best six-piece organizations in western New York state. Ebert is a hustler and keeps them busy nightly. He is also a dance Drummer of the highest order. In a letter to DRUM TOPICS he recently stated, "I am all Leedy equipped and would use no other."

FRANK WAKELAM

of Saskatoon, Sask., Canada, has been a full-fledged Leedy Drummer for fifteen years. He has been playing Pantages vaudeville in Saskatoon and Edmonton for eight seasons. Frank hails from England, where he held some fine jobs. All his leaders declare him one of the finest of Drummers.

(Courtesy Advance Drum Co., Edmonton, Can.)

A man never realizes how weak he is until he tries to quit smoking or meets a pretty woman insurance agent.

Charles B. Jones, Jr.

Charles B. Jones, Jr., is one of the leading "live wire" Drummers of Dallas, Texas. He is now connected with the Magnolia Petroleum Band and Orchestra under the leadership of Paul E. Ashley. He was formerly with the Night Owls Dance Orchestra. "Charlie" can hold his own with many of the big boys and we predict big things for him if he sticks to the game.

"FOR DRUMMERS WHO CARE"

Leedy Drum Topics

Drummers of Rocky Mountain District Enjoy "Personal Service" Through Knight-Campbell Company, Denver

The Knight-Campbell Music Company, of Denver, Colo., ranks as one of the largest in the United States. They sell everything from pipe organs to harmonicas and maintain a staff of experts in each department. The Drum Division is regarded as important as any other. Chas. O. Bohon is manager of retail sales of Band Instruments and it is he who established the strict policy of "Personal Service" to the musician. H. J. Prada is manager of the Mail Order and Field Department. His way of doing business has made many Drummer friends for the house. Leo Childers (No. 2 below), in charge of local Drum Service, is a professional Drummer of many years' experience, who gets down to rock bottom with the boys and helps make Knight-Campbell a real Drummers' Headquarters.

1—BILLY CARLSTON, now playing with Warner Stone's Columbian's at Provo, Utah, is known throughout the West as a crack dance man—up to the minute with every new stunt. He has been with Stone several years, playing as a special theatre stage attraction and large dance-hall feature.

2—LEO CHILDERS is the kind of high-class vaudeville man of whom the particular acts at the Orpheum Theatre say, "Some Drummer and as good as any on the circuit." Leo is in charge of the Drum Department at Knight-Campbell's store and all the boys in Denver have a world of faith in his judgment.

3—ROY W. ECKBERG has covered most of the United States and all of the Orient with the Rainbow Dance Orchestra, a top-notch feature organization. They are at present doing the better class of work in and around Denver. Ray is second from the right in No. 3 photo above. He is real "peppy" and his artistic work causes complimentary comment on every job.

4—WALTER E. LIGHT has been tympanist with the Denver Symphony Orchestra for several years. He is ranked in a class with the best that the larger Eastern cities afford. He is also playing at the Rialto Theatre with a fine photoplay feature orchestra. Light is an old-timer and a real fine fellow.

5—JAKE VINCENT was for a long time manager and Drummer of the Parco Music Producers. Denver Drummers say he is one of the most clever men in the business, and this is some compliment. Jake is very popular with musicians and the ladies.

6—A. B. DeLAVERGNE, business manager of Scheuerman's Colorado Orchestra (and KOA), has no superiors in our profession. "Del" was former Drummer at the Orpheum and has for many years been secretary of the Denver Musicians' Union. One of the most popular Drummers in the country and a fine business man as well.

7—HORACE BEAVER, formerly of the Southland Orchestra of Indianapolis, is now with the Eber B. Grubb Orchestra of Denver. This is a most up-to-date bunch and Beaver is one of its chief drawing cards. He has had several years' dance experience and enjoys a wonderful reputation for originality.

8—FRED VOSS is the Drummer in charge of the Knight-Campbell Drum Department at Pueblo, Colo. He organized the Leedy Marimba Band shown in No. 8 photo. This band is a headline attraction wherever it appears. Its members are Randolph Crotty, Orman Highfell, Dan Monroe and Fred Voss.

9—CHAS. DINHAUP is with the Joe Mann Rainbow Lane Orchestra, a high-class modern dance organization that is in demand full time. They also broadcast over KLZ. Dinhaup ranks very high as a most versatile and classy Drummer. He is always looking for something new and has introduced many original ideas of his own.

"WORLD'S FINEST DRUMMERS' INSTRUMENTS"

The Exclusive Drummers' Paper

Leedy Drum Topics

A PAPER DEVOTED TO
THE INTERESTS OF THE DRUMMER

No subscription fee

Advertisements accepted

Published quarterly at 1033 East Palmer Street
Indianapolis, Indiana

Editor..................................Geo. H. Way
Business Manager......................A. W. Kuerst

Summer

Summer is here again and, as usual, many Drummers will mix a full measure of pleasure with their work at the beaches, resorts and on the road. And this brings back the thought so often expressed by DRUM TOPICS—there are a lot worse professions and trades than that of the Drummer. There are millions of men who work along in the same shop or office all through the hot weather, so you who enjoy a change of routine and can combine a good time with your work—be thankful for it.

You Can't Keep a Good Man Down

Why is it that some leaders (many of them) go through job after job "holding the Drummer down"? There seems to be a certain type who is afflicted with this peculiar disease. We do not mean, holding the Drummer down in respect to volume in playing; what we *do* mean is holding him down in scope. There are dance leaders particularly who hold the Drummer down, demanding at the same time "more forte on the Drums there." They might as well add, "but don't put in anything new."

If there is anything in the world that will break a Drummer's spirit and kill his ambition, it is the leader who jumps and makes faces at every new effect or strange sound, no matter how well introduced, that a progressive Drummer submits. True, every new idea presented by the Drummer does not fit the occasion; but if he be allowed some individuality to put in original stunts, the few "bloomers" will amount to nothing compared to the "hits." Ninety-nine per cent of the Drummers are forever trying to improve their work. They seek new ideas and have the welfare of their organization at heart equally as much as, if not more, than any member of it. Leaders who continually "bury" the Drummer would do well to put on their "specs" and look around a bit, noting some of the Big-Name Bands whose Drummers are a big part of the show. These Drummers create free advertising for the organization by way of downright hard, conscientious work and ability that required years to obtain. One can hardly think of orchestras like Paul Whiteman, Paul Ash, Abe Lyman, Ben Bernie, Max Dolin and Gene Goldkette without thinking of the Drummer. This is because these leaders realize his importance and give him encouragement instead of suppressing his originality. Not long ago a fine orchestra lost a wonderful Drummer. The leader held him down—and "you can't keep a good man down."

M. S. Winslow

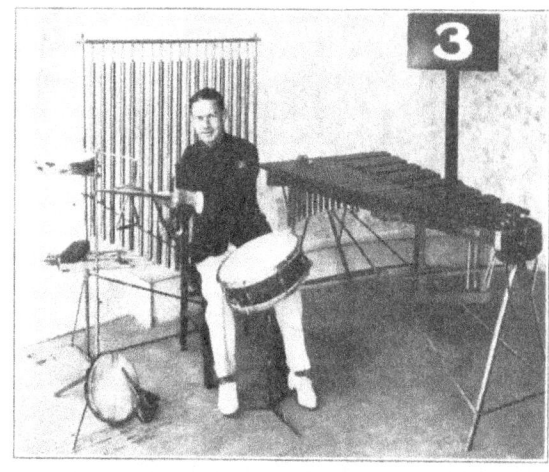

M. S. Winslow has been playing Leedy Drums and Xylophone with the Mummolo Concert Band at Miami Beach, Florida, for the past season. Many fine press notices regarding Winslow's work prove he is the kind that lets the public know that the Drummer is one of the big features of a band.

Have you ever examined the "Leedy American Method for Bells" (No. 400)? It contains one hundred pages of interesting studies and general information. The finest book ever published to assist the Drummer in becoming a sight reader. Written so you can understand it.

C. D. Scribner

says, "I'm not telling you how old I am, but I have young ideas." If you know "Scrib" you can appreciate this. He is one of the old-timers—has trouped everywhere, with everything, and is *some* Drummer in all branches of the game. For several years he has been located at Oklahoma City. This photo was taken at Fort Sill, Oklahoma, when "Scrib" had charge of the 179th Infantry Drum Corps. He now plays with the Shrine and American Legion Bands and he is noted as one of the foremost handwriting experts in the United States. He also operates the leading Commercial Art Shop of Oklahoma City. All Leedy for many years.

A New Way to Use a Triangle

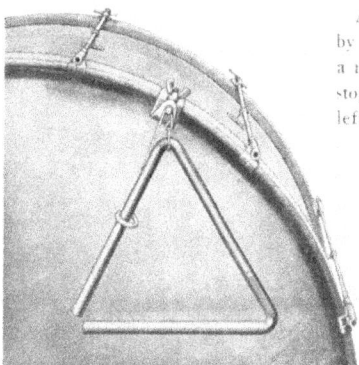

A nice effect can be obtained by playing syncopated beats with a metal hammer on a triangle—stops produced by choking with left hand. Some Drummers are using a large 10" triangle for this, with fine results. Leedy makes three nice triangles—6", 8", 10" sizes and of the finest tool steel. Note that this triangle holder (No. 666) is equipped with a non-swinging device.

"FOR DRUMMERS WHO CARE"

Leedy Drum Topics

Your Opportunity

Why not let Geo. Hamilton Green teach you to play the Marimba and Xylophone? A few months ago he introduced his new course of fifty lessons (by mail or in person) and many Drummers and other musicians have already greatly increased their earnings through same. You can do it too — it is your road to more money. The Marimba and Xylophone are not difficult to master when taught as Mr. Green teaches them. Everyone knows what a wonderful artist he is, and his many successful pupils are proof that he is also a wonderful teacher.

The Marimba and Xylophone are now standard band and orchestra instruments. They are no longer mere novelties, and the Drummer who can play them will reap a harvest from their growing popularity.

The entire course is marvelously simple. Every lesson profusely illustrated.

For further details write to Geo. Hamilton Green at his studio—
148 West 46th Street, New York City, N. Y.

Geo. Hamil[ton Green]

It has hardly been possible during the past years, for those inter[ested] in music, to think of or discuss the Xylophone and Marimba wit[hout] the association of the renowned name of Geo. Hamilton Green. [The] mallet instruments of the Xylophone family are not new (alth[ough] many real improvements have been introduced in the last few ye[ars]. In fact, the Marimba is one of the oldest of all musical instrum[ents], however, it has only been recently that they have become so pop[ular]. They are now in everything from Jazz to Symphony Orchestra[s and] their foothold in the dance field is steadily becoming more firm. [The] chief reasons for this are — better instruments and better pla[yers]. The Leedy Mfg. Co. has led the field in improvements, and Mr. G[reen] with other wonderful artists has established the Xylophone [and] Marimba as permanent and legitimate in every sense of the w[ord].

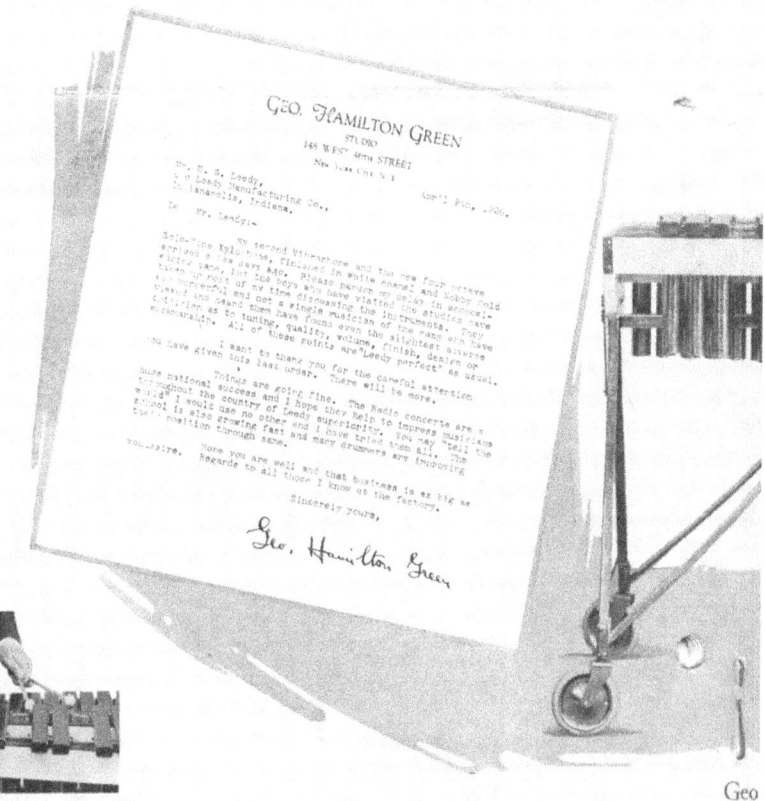

"WORLD'S FINEST DRUMMERS' INSTRUMENTS"

The Exclusive Drummers' Paper

ilton Green

"The World Famous Victor Phonograph Star"

interested
ba without
reen. The
(although
ew years).
struments;
so popul..
estras and
firm. The
er playing.
Mr. Green
phone and
the word.

A Free Treat

Hear him every Wednesday evening over Radio WEAF (New York City) and their country-wide "hook-up" with eleven broadcasting stations.

Eight to eight-thirty P. M. (Eastern standard time).

With the

"Shinola Merry-Makers"

consisting of Mr. Green's own orchestra and famous singers—all noted phonograph artists.

These most wonderful concerts are produced under Mr. Green's personal direction. They are built around him and he plays in every number on the program. Every musician will want to hear him.

These concerts are presented by the Shinola Bixby Polish Company and will continue until March, 1927.

Geo. Hamilton Green plays Leedy instruments exclusively —Xylophone, Marimba, Vibraphone, Harpaphone, Bells, Chimes, etc. Send for complete catalog. Mailed free.

You Can Hear Him On—

WEAF	New York City, N. Y.
WEEI	Boston, Mass.
WTAG	Worcester, Mass.
WCAE	Pittsburgh, Pa.
WWJ	Detroit, Mich.
WJAR	Providence, R. I.
WOO	Philadelphia, Pa.
WOC	Davenport, Iowa
KSD	St. Louis, Mo.
WCCO	Minneapolis and St. Paul, Minn.
WCAP	Washington, D. C.
WSAI	Cincinnati, Ohio

 "FOR DRUMMERS WHO CARE"

Leedy Drum Topics

Peggy Steese

whose home is in Baltimore, Md., is now in vaudeville with The Capman Boys and Fashionettes. To say that she is a real Drummer and one of the act's most entertaining features is putting it mildly. Miss Steese formerly had her own "Mayflower Orchestra" for five seasons at Great Falls Park, Va. Last season she was in New Haven, Conn., at the Far East Restaurant with Grace Simpson's Melody Girls. Miss Steese says, "I always use Leedy —they are the best."

(Courtesy Melody Music Shop, Memphis, Tenn.)

Paul Sporleder, Famous Drummer of Gene Rodemich Orchestra, Opens Exclusive Drum Shop in St. Louis

B. N. GUSTAT IS PARTNER

Paul Sporleder has recently opened the only exclusive retail Drum Shop in St. Louis. Drummers of that city have long needed that very thing and the past few weeks have brought forth hundreds of favorable remarks concerning it. Every professional Drummer in the St. Louis district knows Paul as one of the very finest artists in the business. They know he knows instruments and how to play them, therefore the success of the shop is practically assured. It is the place where the boys can get technical and authentic assistance. Paul will continue playing with the Gene Rodemich Brunswick Orchestra at the Grand Central Theatre.

B. N. Gustat has joined hands as partner in this new shop. He is another well-known Drummer of many years' experience in all branches and has held some of the best jobs in Western and Southern cities. The shop will maintain a Drum School for all instruments, with several competent teachers, who will work under the personal direction of both Sporleder and Gustat. One of these teachers is Schuyler Alward, whose photo is shown below. The Sporleder Drum Shop is located at Suite 17-18 Mid-City Building, on Grand Avenue, in the heart of the theatrical district. The Leedy line will be featured and the policy of a "Real Drummers' Service Station" will be carried out to the letter.

Leedy's is the only Drum Factory that manufactures their own trunks for Drummers' instruments.

ALEC HALLS

of Reigate, Surrey, England, has played Drums in legitimate bands and orchestras since he was eleven years old; however, as he was always a fine dancer and a natural showman, he decided to go in for vaudeville. He is now doing the better class of circuits in England, and press reports praise him as a very fine comedian, dancer and trick Drummer. He always uses Leedy.

The only race of people on earth who have never used some form of a Drum is the Eskimo.

A Fine New Gong and Cymbal Stick

Solid medium texture high-grade felt ball. Just the right weight to bring out the tone. Handle is hand turned, fine hickory. Ask for No. 631.

A Few Prominent St. Louis Drummers Who Were Leedy Equipped by Sporleder's Drum Shop

JOE MILLER

played in several of the larger cities of Illinois with well-known orchestras before locating in St. Louis. He is now one of the regulars of that city, being kept busy nightly because of his fine work. Joe is noted for his fast and original cymbal stunts, particularly the Charleston beats. A most popular boy as well.

LLOYD CLEMENT

one of the youngest professional Drummers in St. Louis, is holding down one of the most particular jobs with Maurice Barnett at the Ozark Theatre. It is predicted by all who know Clement that he will become nationally known in a few more years. He is chuck-full of natural ability and is a real student.

SCHUYLER ALWARD

formerly of Indianapolis, Ind., where he directed the Ohio Theatre Orchestra for a long period of time, is a Drummer and Xylophonist of country-wide reputation. A very high-grade man. He had his own act in vaudeville for some time. Alward now plays in one of the leading vaudeville theatres in St. Louis and is also chief instructor of the Sporleder Drum School.

DEE ORR

is now with the Frank Trumbauer Orchestra, one of the "big name" bands of St. Louis. Dee is known as "the boy with the pleasing personality" and this, with the fact that he is a real "snappy," efficient Drummer, makes him one of the big features wherever the Trumbauer Orchestra plays.

HOWARD BAIRD

has played in all of the principal theatres of St. Louis, including two years at the Missouri under the famous Joseph Littau. Howard is a high-class tympanist and xylophone soloist and is considered one of the very best all-'round men in St. Louis. He is one of the most popular boys in town. He has originated many novel ideas for Drums and effects. Now with the Allister Wylie Orchestra.

NORMAN EUBANKS

one of the busiest Drummers in St. Louis, is an instructor at the Hugo School of Music. He has a wonderful reputation in his home city and prefers to remain there in spite of many fine offers that have come from nationally known road orchestras. Eubanks is a first-class tympanist, xylophonist and drummer. He is also a hard, sincere worker at all times.

MYRON EDWARD BOONE

although only thirteen years old, is a full-fledged professional Drummer, doing regular work with well-known bands and orchestras in the vicinity of his home city, Milford, Del. All last summer he played with "Murphy's Jazz Orch." at Slaughter Beach, Del. He also plays with the Evergreen Forest Band. Master Boone not only plays Drums correctly and "reads the spots," but is a wonder on Bells and Xylophones.

Geo. W. Marsh is now in England with the Paul Whiteman Orchestra. They opened at Albert Hall in London during the week of April 5th to capacity houses and turned away thousands at each performance. They then toured a few of the larger cities and are now back in London playing afternoons at the Tivoli Theatre and at the Kit Kat Club nights. DRUM TOPICS has received over a hundred letters from the boys "over there" who have met George, and they all state that he is one fine fellow and a most wonderful Drummer.

 **"WORLD'S FINEST DRUMMERS' INSTRUMENTS"**

The Exclusive Drummers' Paper

Like Father—Like Son

George H. Lee   Irving Lee

These two very interesting Drummers live in Huddersfield, Yorkshire, England. A glance at the photos, without any further information, tells the story of their relationship.

George H. Lee began playing Drums in the British Army forty-one years ago. His description of Drums then in use is indeed interesting. Several years ago Mr. Lee retired from the service and played Drums and Tympani in the Huddersfield Theatre Royal and Opera House. Four years ago he moved to the Palace Vaudeville Theatre in the same city and has remained there ever since. He is also regular tympanist of the Huddersfield Permanent Orchestra, having been connected with same for twenty-four years. Mr. Lee states he has been using Leedy instruments with perfect satisfaction for thirteen years. These positions call for the very best in a Drummer, and we'll leave it to you—such a fine appearing gentleman certainly looks the part.

Irving Lee's career as a Drummer covers a period of twenty years and he has held about every kind of a job possible for a Drummer—active war service in the Army, Symphony Orchestra in several north of England cities, vaudeville theatres, Grand Opera, movies, and modern dance orchestras. He is now at Huddersfield Hippodrome and also teaches a large class of pupils. Mr. Lee, Jr., has been using Leedy for twelve years and states he would have no other. Like his Dad—he must be a top-notcher, else he would not have such a long list of high-class positions to his credit.

"Dusty" Roades Sends In This One

Set your empty Snare Drum case on the floor at the right side of the Bass Drum so you can strike the case and pedal cymbal at the same time, with the right stick, holding same in the middle so that one end strikes cymbal and other end the case. This gives a combination cymbal and slapstick effect and goes good for syncopated rhythm—playing four beats to the bar on the Snare Drum with left hand.

(See photo of "Dusty" Roades on page 4.)

KENNETH DRAGOO

has been at the Drums in a semi-professional way for the past seven years. He is now a sophomore at the Illinois State Normal University and plays with several local organizations in Normal, Illinois. Dragoo is a really accomplished Tympanist and Drummer of a very high order. He has had theatre, dance and concert experience. All Leedy.

Jack—"I called on Mabel last night and I wasn't any more than inside the door before her mother asked me my intentions."

John—"That must have been embarrassing."

Jack—"Yes, but that's not the worst of it. Mabel called from upstairs and said, 'That isn't the one, mother.'"   —Bison.

Road Drummers should go over their trunks with a high-grade varnish at least every three months. They will last twice as long if this is done regularly.

Triangles are made by first polishing the steel rod in the straight. They are next heated by electricity and formed on a power press, then repolished and nickel plated.

It is not the size of the snares that counts as much as it is their weight and degree of flexibility.

Cow Bells

Not so many years ago Cow Bells were one of the Drummers' strongest "stand-bys" and most used traps, but lately they seem to have fallen by the wayside and few of the boys use them to any extent.

We believe the reason for their downfall was the fact that they were too often played upon with ordinary drum sticks. The hard wood in contact with the metal produced a harsh, disagreeable tone and, at its best, was only suitable for very forte passages. Leaders and other musicians were justified in their objections and many Drummers were instructed to "cut them out."

However, with the introduction of the later model felt sticks and the improved method of mounting the bells, it is now possible to use them in a more musical way and many pleasing effects are obtainable.

By sticking adhesive tape (the amount governing the tone) on the inside of the bells near the edge, the metallic sound can be eliminated, making them sound like deep-toned wood blocks.

Another way to get this wood block effect is to lay the bells on a cushion.

For the jobbing Drummer who cannot carry Chinese Temple Blocks, Cow Bells used in either of the above manners, with felt sticks, are an equally good substitute.

EUGENE V. CLARK

of Syracuse is one of the best-known and most efficient Drummers in New York state. He is the author of "The Clark Drum Method," a very fine and complete work that is now being used by teachers all over the country. Clark also plays in the Syracuse Symphony Orchestra and the Temple Theatre.

The threads on the rods of the Leedy Floating Head Snare Drum are 10-24.

BURT MANN

has had a world of experience in the better class vaudeville houses, hotels and modern dance orchestras in many cities and on the road. Now at the Strand Theatre, Milwaukee, Wis., with Joe Lichter's Orchestra. Mann is known as "That Singing Drummer." He has a fine voice and is undoubtedly one of the snappiest and most artistic up-to-date Drummers in the business. All Leedy.

(Courtesy Walker Musical Exchange, Milwaukee.)

Jimmie Robson, Jr.

of Sanford, Florida, is not one of the boys who have gone South for the season or because of real estate. He is a real native of Sanford and has spent most of his drumming days in and around that city. However, he did troupe in 1921 with Coburn's Minstrels and in 1922 he was in an Army Band. Jimmie is solid Leedy—100% satisfied. He has played with several popular dance orchestras in his home district and is now with the "Seminole Syncopators," a very fine society orchestra. DRUM TOPICS has heard, through boys who know him, that he is a very fine Drummer.

   "FOR DRUMMERS WHO CARE"   

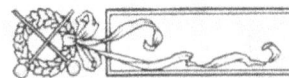 # Leedy Drum Topics

Spencer Wallace

Spencer Wallace, of Racine, Wis., is an exceptionally fine artist on the Xylophone. He has played many leading vaudeville circuits as a single act and with several big-name bands. Wallace states, "The Leedy Xylophone is my favorite, not only because I never hear discordant overtones, but also because the general workmanship makes it an instrument I am proud to own."

Here is a Good One

When playing a Charleston rhythm, use the butt end of your drum stick on the Bass Drum with a "hold beat"* and the other stick on either a "dead cymbal" or "crush" tambourine. Like this—

You can also use the felt-end sticks No. 376A or "Two-way" sticks No. 376 on the Bass Drum.

* "Hold beat" means dead Bass Drum by holding the stick on the head as long as possible to eliminate the ring.

George Carey of Sousa's Band is a Drummer Who KNOWS—Read This

Leedy Manufacturing Co.,
Indianapolis, Indiana.

Dear Mr. Leedy:

The new "Floating Head" snare drum has arrived and I really believe you have solved the problem of flexibility. It is really marvelous - plays so easily and feels so elastic under the sticks. The shell has plenty of strength for the heaviest head without sacrificing the slight humor necessary to produce the real drum quality.

I can't forsake this opportunity to say, you make the best drum in the world.

With kindest regards from

George J. Carey

About Tympani Bowls

All three models of Leedy Tympani are equipped with the wonderful one-piece copper bowl. This bowl is made in the Leedy plant by a patented process (patented January 26, 1926), the development of which required four years—at a cost of slightly over twenty thousand dollars.

It is the only one-piece copper bowl available, and the fact that it is formed up over perfect dies absolutely assures uniformity in size, shape and gauge. Nineteen-gauge Lake Superior Copper is used.

They are the only kettles manufactured that are true in shape. This is a legitimate claim. All others are hand made, therefore cannot be truly symmetrical. A perfectly true bowl is as important to Tympani tone as a perfectly round tube to brass instrument tone.

A Powerful Siren

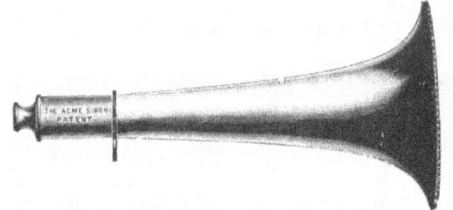

Not just a shrill whistle, but one with depth and volume of tone. Ask for No. 284A.

 **HERBERT GEHRKE**

is now with Palmer's Naval Reserve Band of Peoria, Ill. Formerly with Bat Lohman's Orchestra. Gehrke is a modern Dance Drummer of the fastest kind and makes a big hit wherever he appears. He says, "The Leedy Floating Head Drum is the only instrument I ever saw that gives absolutely no rod trouble."

(Courtesy—Block & Kuhl.)

NOTICE—If you have any Drummer friends who do not receive DRUM TOPICS send us their names and addresses on a postal. It will be mailed free.

Justa Wethead Says—

"Someone should invent a trap to imitate the 'ring' in the bath tub"

"WORLD'S FINEST DRUMMERS' INSTRUMENTS"

The Exclusive Drummers' Paper

B. P. O. E. Drum and Bugle Corps
Portland, Oregon

This photo was taken just after passing in review before the late President Harding, who remarked to Mayor Baker of Portland, "It is the finest organization of its kind I ever saw." They have taken first prize in many competitions. All Leedy.

The corps was organized six years ago by Chas. H. Starr (seated in front), an old-time professional Drummer, who has held many fine positions and is noted as a wonderful teacher. Charlie is one of the most popular boys in Portland. He still plays odd jobs and sells for the Seiberling-Lucas Music Company of Portland. Charlie plays and sells Leedy.

New Snare Drum Tone Control

If a Snare Drum rings, it is due to the improper matching of the heads and faulty tensioning; however, if you like a certain matching of heads and this is a "ringing matching," you can't get away from it without some sort of an attachment. This new mute will do it. The felt pad is pressed to the head by a spring steel arm and it can be placed in several positions on the head. Great for Tom-Tom effects and also works wonders to deep Street Drums.

Ask for No. 669.

DRUM TOPICS has received several letters asking us to introduce a Question and Answer Department. We would like to do it, boys, but space doesn't permit. It would take up a full four pages to print the questions and answers we have handled by letter since the last issue, three months ago. It is your privilege to ask all the questions you like. It is our job to try to answer them. Your letter will be answered in its turn. DRUM TOPICS is at your service and we want you all to feel that it is your paper.

It requires 18 operations to make a transparent Snare Drum Head and 27 operations to make a white Snare Drum Head.

Did you know that manufacturers of Xylophones and Marimbas are obliged to purchase Rosewood by the pound, instead of by the foot, as is customary with most forest products?

Leedy Wood Shells and Hoops are prepared for bending under what is termed dry steam pressure. Water does not touch the material. The pressure is from 20 to 25 pounds per square inch.

Phonograph Records With Good Drum Effects

The following names and numbers of records were sent in by Drummers who show the proper spirit in being willing to pass a good word along to others. DRUM TOPICS thanks them. Let's have some more—include the numbers. The boys like the idea.

John Burns, 126 Maple Street, Bristol, Conn., writes: "Drummers who want to hear extraordinary cymbal work should listen to all records by the 'Little Ramblers Orchestra' on Columbia records and the 'Goofus Five' on Okeh records."

Victor Record No. 19947-A
"Dinah"
Sent in by Arthur E. Nielsen, Harlan, Iowa.

Okeh Record
"Rose of the Nile"
Sent in by "Cotton" Clark, Asheville, N. C.

Brunswick Record No. 3082-A
"Bell Hoppin' Blues"
Brunswick Record No. 3092-B
"Sea Legs"
Sent in by Phil Peters, Ft. Dodge, Iowa.

Brunswick Record No. 3001
"Fallin' Down"
Sent in by C. V. Neff, Tulsa, Okla.

Victor Record No. 19922-B
"Flamin' Mamie"
Sent in by Roy Welch, Norman Park, Ga.

Victor Record No. 19406-B
"If I Stay Away Too Long from Carolina"
Sent in by Donald Campbell, Providence, R. I.

MARY ZOLLER

is one of the very few lady Xylophone artists in vaudeville. Her work is equal to that of the best male Xylophonists and she has played many of the leading circuits. She is also well known in the Radio field. Miss Zoller is now featuring the Leedy Vibraphone.

JACK O'GRADY

of Terre Haute, Ind., one of the foremost all-'round Drummers in the Central States, is now on the road with his own orchestra as a feature dance attraction. He formerly put in many years playing vaudeville. O'Grady is a real showman and his organization is "going over big." All Leedy.

First Artist—"The model told me that she would do three semi-nude drapes for ten dollars."

Second Artist—"How much did she say she would take off for cash?"
—*New York Medley.*

New Type Bell Hammers

These are wonderful new bell hammers. They have shelled rattan handles and rawhide balls. The balls have a threaded brass core. They won't fly off. They have less contact "click" than any hard hammers ever made. You'll like them. Ask for No. 370E.

BILL BAILEY—ST. LOUIS, MO.

has never failed to "stop the show" when playing a Xylophone Solo—with the Gene Rodemich Orchestra. He is a regular wizard for speed and technique and has introduced many stunts and beats that are now being universally used. Bill also plays saxophone and piano with the Rodemich Orchestra. He is a personal friend of Art Layfield of the Paul Ash Orchestra.

"FOR DRUMMERS WHO CARE"

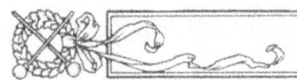
Leedy Drum Topics
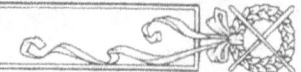

A Little About Chimes

The reason that Chimes do not always sound in tune when used in band or orchestra, is because the overtones, which are strong and discordant, conflict with the true harmony of the other instruments. This is much more noticeable to the musicians close to the Chimes than it is to the audience. It is the fourth tone of the series of tones found in Chimes that is the predominating tone. All others, though somewhat discordant, are heard in more or less degree and cannot be altered. This last statement is scientifically true, regardless of claims made by others. Furthermore, if overtones could be tuned in the same harmonical relation as they are found in other musical instruments, you would not have the Chime effect.

It is rumored that the wizard Marconi is working on a new kind of radio that will broadcast smell as well as sound. Maybe we'll soon get the aroma of garlic with our Grand Opera and the sweet fragrance of synthetic gin with our jazz. Ain't science grand? —Spice o' Life.

Raymond V. Waters

of Stoke, Coventry, Warwickshire, England, is one of the leading legitimate Drummers of that section. For the last four years he has been with the "Gaiety" Dance Band, an organization of ten men who play the best for the best and who travel many miles to fill engagements due to their popularity. Waters has also had several years' large orchestra and concert experience.

American Legion Drum Corps
Shelby, Ohio

Shelby, Ohio, has a Drum and Bugle Corps in the American Legion, O'Brien Post No. 326, of which it can well boast and be proud. It has acted as a wonderful booster for that "live wire" town, winning the Ohio state championship in 1924 and 1925 and carrying off high honors at the National Convention in Omaha, Neb., last October. A regular bunch of fellows, too. All Leedy.

The famous Abe Lyman now plays Leedy "Marine Pearl" finish Drums. We hope to show a fine photo of him in the next DRUM TOPICS.

The glued joints in Leedy solid wood shells and hoops never come apart. This is because the parts to be glued are first heated and a very high grade animal glue is used.

Ralph W. McCracken

is one of the most skilled workmen of his trade. He has been in the electro-plating business for thirty years — the past eleven with the Leedy Mfg. Co. as foreman. He is the originator of "Nobby Gold" and "Black Nickel" in the Drum manufacturing field, with many other improvements to the plater's art to his credit. Ralph is a member of the Board of Directors of the Indianapolis Platers' Society. Everyone likes him, because he strives to please and always thinks of the job first.

A Short Story

"ICE?"
"My husband is home."
"Giddap!"

The Prize Story

By A. B. CRUCHET, one of the best known Drummers in western Canada, now playing at Pantages Theatre, Edmonton, Alta. He is also manager of the Advance Drum Co. of that city — the largest Drum Shop in Canada.

He Had Everything

* * * * "The Drummer we require," ran the ad, "must be fast, very musical and have every trap made. If you are not a crackerjack, don't bother us."

One Drummer wrote that he noted their requirements and went on: "Your advertisement appeals to me strongly—stronger than prepared mustard—as I have searched Europe, Airope, Irope and Hoboken in quest of someone who could use my talents to advantage. When it comes to this drumming proposition I have never found man or woman who could get first base on me, either fancy or catch-as-catch-can. I play so fast that I have to use specially prepared sticks with platinum points and a water cooling attachment. I'm so musical that I snore the melodies of Grand Opera, and I have so many traps that they have to put another engine on the train when I travel. I run with my cutout open at all speeds and am, in fact, a guaranteed, double hydraulic welded, drop-forged and oil-tempered specimen of human lightning on a perfect frame, ground to one-thousandth of an inch.

"If you would avail yourself of the opportunity of a lifetime, wire me; but unless you are fully prepared to pay the tariff for such service don't bother me, as I am so nervous I can't stand still long enough to have my tuxedos fitted."

He got the job.

Come on, fellows, send in some more stories. Remember, TEN DOLLARS for the best one before August 1st.

Two-wheel Bass Drum Carriage

This fine carriage is light, strong and rigid. It can be taken apart quickly and packs into a small space. Rubber-tired wheels and webbing sling for Drum. A wonderful carriage for Drums up to five feet in diameter. Ask for No. 608C.

The following well-known New York City Drummers recently added the Leedy Machine Tympani to their equipment. These boys are among the best the profession affords, and it goes without saying that they were most critical in their selection. They are all 100% satisfied. The instruments were sold through the Frank Wolf Drummers' Supply House, 233 West 46th St., New York City.

Karl Glassman—Damrosch Orch
Al Broemmel—Strand Theatre
Chauncey Brown—Casino Theatre
Paul Schulze—Metropolitan Opera House
Vic. Burton—Roger Wolf Kahn Orch.
David Grupp—Ross Gorman's Orch.

DRUM TOPICS hopes to show their photographs in the next issue.

 **"WORLD'S FINEST DRUMMERS' INSTRUMENTS"**

Page Fourteen

The Exclusive Drummers' Paper

Some folks believe that electro-plating is an all-electric process. The truth is that it is only 10 per cent electricity; 90 per cent of the work comes under the head of chemistry.

George E. Gallagher

of Springfield, Mass., has been with the McEnelly Orchestra for the past nine years. He is a most progressive Drummer and is rated very high in ability all through the New England States. McEnelly has had eighteen years of exceptional success and is now playing at the Butterfly Ballroom in Springfield. They are also under a three-year contract with the Victor Phonograph Company. Gallagher is completely Leedy equipped and says, "Your Floating Head Snare Drum and Machine Tympani are far ahead of any like instruments on the market."

New Marimba Mallets

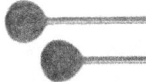

These new Marimba Mallets are made of the best grade yarn, wound with care, over a rubber core of just the proper weight to bring out the tone. Rattan handles, not stiff and not flimsy. They are fine for Vibraphone as well as Marimba. Ask for No. 630.

I am growing old — I have had much trouble — most of which never happened.

Nickel Silver Cymbals

are very popular these days. They are far superior to plain brass, having an exceptionally brilliant, stinging tone. Great for special effects, especially the smaller sizes. All sizes from 4" to 13". Leedy manufactures them.

Hugo G. Heyn, who is one of the country's finest Marimba and Xylophone artists, is still "going big" in Omaha, Neb. He is one of the leading features on WOAW Radio. The sixth issue of DRUM TOPICS contained a fine story on these instruments written by Hugo.

Where is Frank Horsecroft? DRUM TOPICS would like to hear from this good old friend.

Charles H. Wesselhoft

Leedy solid wood shells and other wood parts carry the undisputed reputation of being the highest class products of their kind in the world. Charles H. Wesselhoft, the foreman of this department (which is the second largest of the plant —occupying a complete separate building) has been the chief factor in this accomplishment. He has been a woodcraft expert for thirty-two years —twelve with Leedy—and many instruments used by Drummers of today were developed by him. Charlie is a friend to all, and all are his friends.

On the Cover—Wm. H. Gilcher

has been with the famous Max Dolin Orchestra at the California Theatre in San Francisco for the past four years. This orchestra is nationally noted as one of the best. Musicians from Chicago west need no introduction to "Gilch," for he was with the St. Louis Symphony for many years and his reputation as a most wonderful all-'round Drummer is well established in many states. His most noted characteristics, drumistically speaking, are efficient salesmanship and completeness to the last detail. Note his outfit in the photo on the cover—that's only half of it. All Leedy with a capital "L," and complete satisfaction with a capital "S." "Gilch" is the "Beau Brummel" of the Pacific Coast—it's a fact.

Another New Stunt

If you like your drum sticks padded (where the stick starts to taper) for wood block, cow bells and certain cymbal effects, just purchase a short length of rubber tubing at a rubber supply store (some drug stores have it) and after cutting it to length, soak it in luke-warm water for twenty minutes. It will then slip on over the stick nicely and wear equally as long as sewed-on felt.

Max Matson

hails from Tepsie, Ohio, where he started in the dance game. His work was recognized as "big town stuff" and Toledo soon annexed him with the well-known Walter Weller Club Orchestra. We predict big things for this fine young Drummer. Max is completely Leedy equipped and is more than pleased with same.

So to conduct one's life as to realize oneself — this seems to me the highest attainment possible to a human being. It is the task of one and all of us. —Ibsen.

Drop us a line!
See you in Sept.!
Good Luck!

"FOR DRUMMERS WHO CARE"

DRUM TOPICS

The Exclusive Drummers' Paper

MAY, 1926
TWELFTH EDITION

F. E. Wolfington,
1111 Laurel St.,
Indianapolis, Ind.

POSTMASTER—Return Postage Guaranteed

Leedy Manufacturing Co.
INDIANAPOLIS, INDIANA

The Wonderful New Marine Pearl Finish
as applied to *Leedy* Floating Head Drums

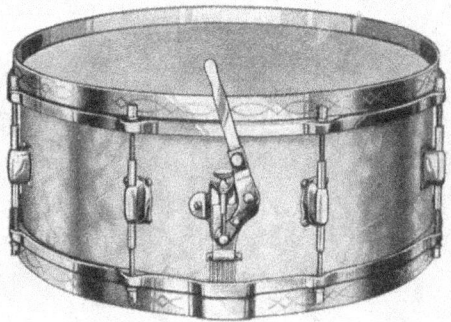

"Superb" is the only word that can even approach a description of this beautiful Drum. The Marine Pearl gives forth a thousand shafts of sparkling light, and the engraved Nobby Gold Hoops form a combination that is truly far in advance of any beauty ever conceived for a musical instrument.

Chauncey E. Morehouse

Drummer of Jean Goldkette's Orchestra, Detroit, Mich., says: "No one could possibly describe this wonderful instrument. It has got to be seen. And it's not all finish, either. The Floating Head model is the finest Drum in the world for tone and workmanship."

Marine Pearl is a Dupont Product. It is harder than most woods, and its surface is smooth as glass and sparkles like hundreds of small mirrors. It is fully guaranteed. There is a Bass Drum to match.

MAILED FREE

A large six-page folder printed in eight colors, giving complete description. Send for yours today.

KARL GLASSMAN (See Page 15)

Leedy Drum Topics

What is your Trend?

M AN—*whether he be drummer, lawyer, bank president, or laborer—does not long remain at any one level.*

It is the same in business—the stock market, the theatre, the dance hall, the orchestra, or the grocery store.

Even nature decrees that the tide, the weather and your health must travel three ways—DOWN, LEVEL and UP.

How do YOU travel in your work and your health?

It is easy to travel the downward trend and it is easy to fall into the ruts of the level grade.

The trick is to keep going on the upward trend to success and MORE MONEY.

Every drummer cannot be on the best job, BUT the drummer who is on the best job today was on the little job yesterday, so who can say but what YOU will be on a better one tomorrow?

It's up to you, isn't it? Get ready NOW—there is no standing still.

Just make sure you are on the upward trend. Spend those idle hours improving and—

Remember These Words by Two Great Men

Theodore Roosevelt

"The law of worthy life is fundamentally the law of strife. It is only through labor and painful effort, by grim energy and resolute courage, that we move on to better things."

Marshall Field
"Twelve Things to Remember"

1. The value of time.
2. The success of perseverance.
3. The pleasure of working.
4. The dignity of simplicity.
5. The worth of character.
6. The power of kindness.
7. The influence of example.
8. The obligation of duty.
9. The wisdom of economy.
10. The virtue of patience.
11. The improvement of talent.
12. The joy of originating.

EVERY DRUMMER CAN BE A BETTER DRUMMER IF HE SO DESIRES

Leedy "WORLD'S FINEST DRUMMERS' INSTRUMENTS" *Leedy*

The Exclusive Drummers' Paper

Fred S. Paine
Detroit Symphony Orchestra

Musicians of Detroit and vicinity need no introduction to Fred Paine. However, there are hundreds in other cities who have little more than just heard of this "Wizard of the Xylophone," as he is called by those who know. DRUM TOPICS wishes that he could be known all over the world and claims that he should be one of the big phonograph record stars, because his work is on a par with the very best of them. Fred was born in Windsor, Ontario, Canada, which is just across the river from Detroit. He is a full-fledged drummer and tympanist of the highest class and has played in many of the leading Detroit theatres. Several years ago he joined the Detroit Symphony and has remained active with that organization ever since. He holds the unique and distinguished record of being the only drummer who has ever played xylophone solos with a real symphony orchestra. His skill on the xylophone is truly marvelous and he has become sort of a hero with the press and music-loving public of Detroit.

fast becoming better known and it is hoped that every drummer will make an effort to hear him.

This is what Paine has to say of his Leedy instrument:

"... Now in regard to the instrument you have just built for me. I received same six weeks ago and have delayed writing in order to give it a thorough try-out. It arrived in perfect condition (how could it have been otherwise, packed in such wonderfully constructed trunks) and I want you to know that it is, without doubt, in every point the finest xylophone I ever saw, heard, or played upon. The workmanship and intonation are superb, and as for tonal quality—well, as I say, I never heard its equal. Every overtone being positively in tune with the fundamental of each bar, makes it the only perfect xylophone. In my estimation it meets and fulfills every requirement that ever has been or is likely to be demanded of such an instrument, and to say that I am more than pleased is to put it mildly. I wish I could influence every drummer and xylophonist to use a Leedy, because I know it would improve his work."

Billy Todd

has been with the Ringling Brothers, Barnum & Bailey Combined Shows Band, under the direction of Merle Evans, for the past two seasons. Billy has long been rated as one of the best circus drummers on record. However, he has also played in many other branches of the profession, having put in fifteen years "behind the drums." He hails from Albion, Neb. In a letter to the Leedy Co. he states: "I prefer Leedy equipment because all the instruments are built to last and do what is claimed for them, especially the new Floating Head Drum. It's the finest ever."

It takes a good pair of sticks to "beat" a phony pay-check.

An Effective Stunt
By J. Crofton Hall

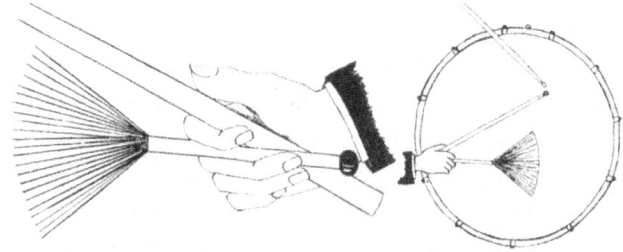

The Detroit *Evening Times* has this to say of his recent appearance as one of the orchestra's soloists:

"The other soloist was Fred Paine, the amazingly expert xylophonist of the orchestra. Effects of modulation which some artists could hardly equal on a piano, Mr. Paine gets with his little hammers on the wood blocks, while his fleet dexterity is always a source of wonderment. Yesterday he played Auber's "Masaniello" overture and aroused such a storm of approval that he was forced to add that fine old xylophone standby, the overture to "William Tell.""

And the *Free Press* reviews his work as follows:

"The appearance of Mr. Paine is always a matter of general satisfaction to his numerous followers, for a xylophone solo at his hands is not only genuine entertainment for those who enjoy this instrument, but the finish and polish of this artist's work places his performance on a very distinguished plane. Sunday he was heard in the overture to Auber's "Masaniello" with orchestral accompaniment, and the house, casting off Sunday decorum, almost shouted its approval at the close. The men of the orchestra seemed to feel the same enthusiastic lilt in his appearance that the audience demonstrated and it was a spirited performance that was provided."

Fred is also drummer and xylophone soloist with the Detroit *News* Orchestra, which broadcasts regularly from WWJ. This orchestra is made up of men from the Symphony and is rated as one of the best radio musical organizations in the country. Through this channel he is

Grasp the right-hand stick in the usual manner, then place a Synco Jazz Stick between the first and second fingers so that it crosses over the drum stick (drum stick next to the palm), holding it against the stick with the second finger. Play on the snare drum as usual, keeping the Synco stick always in contact with the head. The additional "swish" of the jazz sticks with the beats of the drum stick produces a nifty little effect that is very pleasing and new.

J. Crofton Hall is drummer and manager of his own orchestra called "Hall's Original Synco Serenaders." This is one of the most popular dance bands in British Columbia, Canada, and is located in the city of Nelson in the beautiful Canadian Rockies, not far from the Pacific Coast. Hall has had many years' experience and is a modern dance man of the highest order.

 "FOR DRUMMERS WHO CARE"

Leedy Drum Topics

Leon Knapp

Leon Knapp's Drum Shop
Grand Rapids, Mich.

Clifford Knapp

The name of Leon Knapp means much to drummers of Grand Rapids and to hundreds of others in all parts of Michigan. The fact that he has been a professional drummer of exceptionally high rating for many years, and the manner in which he carries on his business, has established him first in the minds of a vast number of followers, "drumistically" speaking. Knapp has over 200 graduated pupils to his credit who are now playing professionally. Out of forty union drummers of Local No. 56 of Grand Rapids, thirty-two were his scholars.

The photo at right shows Master Neal Maston, another pupil of the Leon Knapp Drum School. Young Neal is only eleven years old and is known as "The Boy Wonder on Drums." He is also the youngest professional in Michigan and undoubtedly of many other states. He played for some time in the Hollywood Theatre in Petoskey, Mich., and was long a feature on the xylophone at the Regent Theatre in Grand Rapids. This little fellow is a fine example of a clean-cut, ambitious American boy who has made his drums a source of fun, education and profit. His parents and the Knapp School can well be proud of his achievements, for he is a credit to the community in which he lives.

When you see a drummer handing out "two-bit" cigars to his leader—well, figure it out for yourself.

Have you seen the large Leedy drum circular printed in eight colors, entitled "Beauty in Drums"? If not, ask your dealer for one or drop us a postal. It will be mailed to you at once, free of charge.

"Everything for the Drummer—Featuring Leedy"

His Drum Shop is a mecca for the profession and is noted for its complete stock, excellent service and speedy repair department. He continues to play at the Regent Theatre and teach a large class in all drummer's instruments.

Clifford Knapp, his son, assists in the shop at selling, teaching and repairing. He is very popular amongst the boys and is a real hustler. He also plays daily at the Majestic Theatre.

Harold Gaide is another active member of the firm in the capacity of manager. He is also a professional drummer of no mean ability.

Val Wilson Ulam

There are some classy jobs for drummers in Pittsburgh. Val Wilson Ulam is taking care of two of them so well that the management of both consider him a feature and a fixture. He plays at both the Pittsburgh Athletic Association and Kaufman's Restaurant. Val is one of the most popular musicians of his home city. He is a former pupil of Joseph Sassano (of Pryor's Band for many seasons) and when only sixteen years old began playing in the Academy Theatre, holding the position for six years. Val also served all through the war. He is a staunch Leedy enthusiast.

Ruth: "Do you still run around with that little blonde?"
Ted: "She's married now."
Ruth: "Answer my question!"
—Lehigh Burr.

A Special Leedy Bass Drum Stick
Gus Helmecke (Sousa's Band) Model

When the famous South High School Band of Grand Rapids decided to own one of the world's largest bass drums they consulted Leon Knapp for advice. The discussion ended in the above drum being built by the Leedy Mfg. Co. Merle McHattie (holding drum stick), who is a pupil of Mr. Knapp's, is the young man who plays it.

Leedy is now offering this wonderful stick as a regular stock number. For many years it was made especially for the world's most famous bass drummer—Gus Helmecke of Sousa's Band. Note the extra length of the hickory handle and the oversized lamb's-wool beating head, with the smaller ball for a hand grip and rolling purposes. If you once try it you will never use any other. Ask for No. 365-F.

"WORLD'S FINEST DRUMMERS' INSTRUMENTS"

 ## The Exclusive Drummers' Paper

About Rust

Rusty metal parts about your outfit are not only eyesores but costly as well. When the base metal is brass there can be no rust, but when it is iron or steel there is no known process of plating that will make it entirely immune. If you are in doubt as to whether certain metal parts are brass or steel, you can quickly find out by placing a small magnet against the part. If it is steel or iron, the magnet will "stick"; if brass, no effect will be noticed.

You can prevent any part of your outfit from ever rusting. Just dampen a piece of cloth or an old handkerchief with a light oil, such as "3 in 1," and go over all your nickel plating at least once a week. Don't soak the cloth in oil—just dampen it—and you will find that all the nickel will retain its lustre and not show finger marks so plainly.

Jack Roop, New Assistant Sales Manager of Leedy Mfg. Co.

Many drummers from coast to coast know Jack Roop. He has trouped it back and forth time and again over a period of sixteen years with everything from tent shows to the very best of the modern bands. For the past five years he has been with the famous Giersdorf Sisters and Band on the Orpheum and Keith Circuits. His many friends amongst the drummers over the country will undoubtedly be pleased to learn that he is now on the staff of the Leedy Mfg. Co. in the capacity of Assistant Sales Manager.

Since last June he has been in Europe for Leedy and is now out on the road in the United States putting on "Drum Shows" and calling on the boys. It is the policy of the Leedy Co. to have their field men not only well versed in a commercial sense, but also that they be practical men who have had wide experience at professional playing, in order that they may be of real assistance along technical lines.

Such a man is Mr. Roop, and we know all Leedy boosters will be glad to meet him.

For Beginners

Don't place your drum at too great an angle. It is easier to let the sticks fall in a natural motion toward the head than it is to have to "steer" them in a sidewise motion.

Frederick A. Searles

is making his drums serve him well. While he is in the full-fledged professional class, having played with the Elmira (N.Y.) Symphony Orchestra and with numerous first-rate dance bands, he is also attending, for the third year, the St. John's Military Academy at Manlius, N. Y. There he plays in the band in addition to gaining an education. Fred is a former pupil of Harold H. Rochell, of the Majestic Theatre in Elmira, and also of Eugene V. Clark, author of the Clark Drum Method, of Syracuse, N. Y. His bandmaster at St. John's considers him on a par with the best of them. We are glad that Searles is a Leedy booster.

Do you own a practice pad? If not, get one and use it—it's one of the best investments you could make. Try a Leedy. Ask for No. 8.

Two-toned Tom Toms in Libreville

Libreville is an important town just fourteen miles north of the equator, in Kamerun (French West Africa). A short distance away is the first of a series of lumber camps that extend for miles up the Gabun River. They are operated by the French government for the purpose of obtaining high-grade hard woods for world trade, and thousands of natives are employed. These natives have used various forms of drums for religious ceremonies, sports, signals, etc., for centuries. However, in late years, in the more thickly populated districts, they have employed them in a commercial way. The above photo shows a set of two-toned Tom Toms at one of the river camps, acting as a relay station for messages that are transmitted back and forth. The shells are made of heavy tropical wood.

The drummer who can play louder than the whole orchestra — shouldn't.

M. C. "Shucks" Park

All ten of 'em are called "The Seven Aces" — that's because when there were only seven of them they established such a wonderful reputation that it was dangerous to drop the little name that meant such big things. "Shucks" Park has been the drummer of this fine band for four years. It has played the best in vaudeville and at hotels in all the Southern States, and it is agreed by many musicians in the South that "Shucks" is some fine drummer.

Now under a year's contract at the Peabody Hotel in Memphis, Tenn. They also record for Columbia. Park says, "I've always been all Leedy and am going to remain Leedy."

Courtesy Melody Music Shop, Memphis.

Perhaps some of your drummer friends would like to receive DRUM TOPICS. Send in their names; it will be mailed free.

   "FOR DRUMMERS WHO CARE"   

Leedy Drum Topics

Leedy Drum Topics

A PAPER DEVOTED TO
THE INTERESTS OF THE DRUMMER

No subscription fee

Advertisements accepted

Published quarterly at 1033 East Palmer Street
Indianapolis, Indiana

Editor..................................Geo. H. Way
Business Manager.....................A. W. Kuerst

Dry But True

This little flock of words could be condensed into the small number of five, but if it were put down in such an abbreviated form you would read it quickly and think: "Everybody knows that." Perfectly true—everybody does know it—that's the very reason they give it such a small amount of earnest study.

The question is, do you save a few dollars while the dollars are coming in? If not, why not? Sure there are reasons—you've been building up your outfit—you've bought a new car—you're married—there are children—you've had sickness at home—you just moved into a new house—and two hundred and sixty-four other reasons, all of which are very good ones. But, even with all the handicaps, there must be some way to build a little as one goes along toward the time when the earning capacity is lessened by old age.

It is a well-known fact that drummers and other musicians, as a class, do not give enough consideration to saving for the future. Not because they do not make fair salaries—they do—better than most trades and many professions—but because they spend it as it comes in.

After reading about this far you are most likely thinking, "There's a catch in this somewhere—let's have it." There is, but be sure you read it all. It's this: How about a little insurance? You know, the kind that comes back to you—fifteen- or twenty-year endowment stuff. You see, you place yourself under obligation for a small amount each month, which you hardly miss from your income, and after it's started you hate to give it up. First thing you know you've got a bank roll that never would have existed for you in any other way. And think of the protection you've been getting all the while.

How many musicians are there who would leave five thousand behind right now? Not many. Wouldn't you like to know that your wife, children or parents would not be financially embarrassed should you leave them suddenly? However, that's not the only idea in saving by the insurance route.

The chances are over five hundred thousand to one that you will live to be way past sixty, so if you are now thirty or thirty-five why not collect five thousand "iron men" when you are fifty or fifty-five? How many musicians are there who reach fifty years of age and who can show five thousand cash? Not many.

And now, here are the five words that could tell this whole story of facts as mentioned at the beginning: "Insurance will make you save."

Victor Berton

Every drummer aspires to the "big name" jobs. It's the "go-getter" that gets them, and in Vic Berton we have one of the fastest little "go-getters" on record. He always lands in the big-time class, not only because he is a most clever salesman but also because he plays his instruments in an artistic manner second to none in the business. He recently finished a long engagement with the Roger Wolf Kahn Orchestra at the Biltmore Hotel in New York and is now one of the very good reasons for visiting Earl Carrol's new "Vanities" on Broadway. The photo proves what Vic thinks of Leedy equipment.

Wayne "Mutt" Aylesworth

the well-known drummer with Joe Kayser and His Gang, has just finished a long engagement at The Pier, Gordon State Park, Lake St. Marys, Ohio. "Mutt," as he is called by the boys, is an exceptionally fine xylophonist and at one time was soloist with Kryl's Band. He also made an extensive tour with Zez Confrey and played the country over with his own act, "The Broadway Entertainers." He has also done considerable pit work and was on the road with "Blossom Time" and "The Birth of a Nation."

"Mutt" hails from Appleton, Wis. He says, "I've tried 'em all, but what's the use? I always stick to Leedy."

Do you lift the left stick exactly as high as the right? Do you govern its blows with exactly the same force?

Lester Grode

of Milwaukee, Wis., is an ambitious young drummer who is fast climbing to the top. For the past two years he has been playing and studying continually and is now ready to step into the best company. For seven months Grode was at the Howell Gardens and this past summer at Lake Hessus. In the winter he plays with a popular jobbing dance orchestra in Milwaukee.

Courtesy Walker Musical Exchange.

Thavin Exposition Band, Drum Section

Here they are—"The Three Twins" that make this most wonderful drum section. Left to right: Armand Le Brun of Cincinnati, Ohio, xylophone soloist, formerly with the famous Kryl's Band and marimba artist at Radio Station WLW, Cincinnati; G. Di. Nicolantonio, tympanist, who has been associated with some of the country's finest concert bands, including Creatore and Vassella; V. Nickiroff of Houston, Texas, bass drummer with Thavin for the past twelve years. All Leedy.

"WORLD'S FINEST DRUMMERS' INSTRUMENTS"

The Exclusive Drummers' Paper

Once Again We Ask—

Why is it that so many drummers, some of whom hold fine positions, insist on using the 17-inch long, skinny type of drum stick? No stick will travel faster or more skilfully than the ability of the hand that holds it. A long, thin stick does not produce as good a tone in a drum as the regular "stocky," quick-taper models, whose rebound is as strong as the stroke. Remember, you have to "lift" the thin, light stick. This is a lost motion in drumming. One never sees a real fine, artistic drummer on the big jobs using these "lead pencils." Manufacturers are forced to make them on account of the demand, but every pair that is sold is done so with the knowledge that they are not for the best results. Such a stick acts on a drum just as a violin bow would on a cello; it can't bring out the best that is in the instrument, and no drummer can execute with them as well as with the tried, true and sensible models.

How many "Rolls" does it take to make a Royce?

The Leedy Floating Head, Marine Pearl Drum

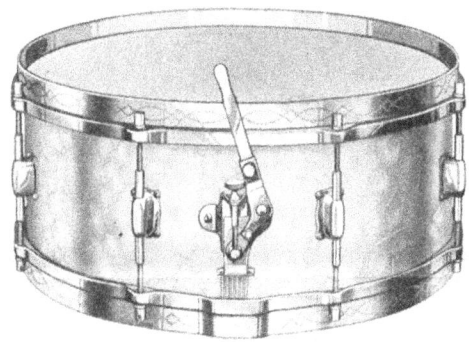

That this instrument is conceded by a great majority to be the ultimate in snare drum construction is not in the least an exaggeration. True, it is not being used by the majority, because it is new. However, we have never met a drummer who did not state that it was the most beautiful drum he had ever seen and express a desire to own one. Drop us a postal requesting a beautiful colored circular describing it in full, with prices. There is a bass drum to match. Remember, the Marine Pearl is guaranteed not to warp or crack.

Too Bad

Mrs. Brown could only buy two aisle seats, one behind the other. Wishing to have her sister beside her, she turned and cautiously surveyed the man in the next seat. She finally leaned over and timidly addressed him: "I beg your pardon, sir, but are you alone?"

The man, without turning his head the slightest, but twisting his mouth to an alarming degree and shielding it with his hand, muttered: "Cut it out, kid, cut it out—muh wife's with me."

Keith A. Reay

of Mayfield, New South Wales, Australia, has been one of the leading theatre drummers of Australia for the past ten years. He is at present at the Empress Theatre, Sydney. Reay is also a solo xylophonist of a very high order. In 1925 he worked for several months in Los Angeles and Hollywood with The Original Melody Makers. All Leedy.

Harry G. Sims

has been in the Drum Section of the U. S. Marine Band at Washington for more than twenty-nine years, with no loss of time on account of illness or other causes. Some record! Next February he retires on a pension. However, he has no intention of giving up the drums. Although he is a veteran in the sense of service, Harry is still a young man and can put over a job with the best of the youngsters. He plays a most wonderful rudimental drum and can provide any drummer with a real thrill when hitting up the old military calls, etc. Sims played for President McKinley's funeral and likewise Admiral Peary, Admiral Evans and Admiral Dewey. He has attended about every great Government and White House function for almost thirty years and has traveled all over the United States with the band many times.

W. A. Mayer

has been playing with the Magnolia Refinery Band and Orchestra at Beaumont, Texas, for the past year. Perhaps you have heard them on the radio from KFDM. Mayer is an old-timer and has a fine record as an excellent drummer to his credit. He formerly lived in Springfield, Ill., where he played with the Capital City Band, and for ten years he held some of the principal jobs in San Antonio, Texas. Mayer is all Leedy.

Did you know that U. G. Leedy designed and placed on the market the first Muffler Snare Strainer?

Jack Miller

started in the dance game in 1922 and since that time has held many fine positions in New York and New Jersey, including The Canton Rest, Utica, N. Y.; Woodlawn Park, N. J.; Trenton, N. J., Country Club and others. The past season he has been with Tommy Carey and his Sun Dodgers at the Club Seville, Shrewsbury River Hotel and Country Club, Red Bank, N. J. This is an elite social center, catering to wealthy New Yorkers. Miller is rated as a very fine drummer and is very popular with both patrons and musicians.

"I hope you behaved yourself last night, my darling daughter."
"Yes, mother, I obeyed the Golden Rule."
"How?"
"I did unto others as I wanted them to do unto me."
—Lehigh Burr.

Billy Hanson

has left a fine "rep" behind in every city he has worked in. His excellent playing, as well as his personal popularity, is the reason. From 1920 to '23, inclusive, he played with the leading orchestras of Eau Claire, Wis., and from '24 to '25 he handled the drums with Al. Levich and his Music. Last winter he went over the Keith and Loew vaudeville circuits with a headline act and this past summer he has been with Al. Gabel and his Broadway Entertainers—an M. C. A. band of ten men, doing the very best class of work. Hanson writes, "The Leedy Floating Head Drum starts in where others leave off."

"FOR DRUMMERS WHO CARE"

Leedy Drum Topics

Some Drums and Dru[mmers]

THE "broad Atlantic" is no stretch at all when it comes to drummers. [A] military unit commanded by Captain Miles Standish, and ever since the[n ...] each side. England brought to America the rudimental system tha[t] is prac[tical. ...] modern jazz methods that have proved so popular. Each has shown a grea[t ...] are always boosting their brother percussionists across the water. Surely th[e ...] drums play a part.

One can judge at a glance tha[t ...] appear on these pages are a h[ig]h-c[lass ...] Topics knows this to be true, in[a]sm[uch as ...] Jack Roop of the Leedy Mfg. Co. [spent the] past summer amongst English [d]ru[mmers in all the] principal cities with a complete dis[play of Leedy drums.] Over four thousand drummers came [to see the display] and the fine spirit of friendliness a[nd hospitality shown] by the drummers of Britain will lon[g be remembered.]

Leslie Ross, the clever drummer of "The Three Australian Boys," is now touring the high-class vaudeville circuits of the British Isles and has played with the act throughout the United States, Canada and Australia. He was one of the first six drummers to equip himself with Leedy Marine Pearl Drums. His home is in Melbourne, Australia.

These three old English field drums (15"x13½" solid shell) belonged to a battalion of Foot Guards and were used in the final battle with Napoleon at Waterloo in 1815. They are emblazoned with the monogram of King George IV, denoting that they were in service during his reign, 1820 to 1830. When discarded they were placed in the Waterloo Gallery at Windsor Castle and later presented to the Royal United Service Museum, London, by His Majesty King Edward VII.

This interesting instrume[nt is considered] by authorities to be the ol[dest English] drum in existence. It bear[s the] cypher of Queen Anne, wh[o reigned from] 1702 to 1714. The shell is [of solid con]struction, 22"x18", [a]nd is i[n good] preservation. [The co]unter[hoops] are the origina[l] ones, whil[e the] heads are not. Transferred [by] King Edward VII from W[indsor Castle to] the Royal United Service M[useum.]

These three photos were taken by Geo. H. Way of the Leedy Mfg. Co. through the c[ourtesy of ...]

This drummer crosses the ocean many times a year playing with the fine twelve-piece orchestra on the White Star liner "Olympic." He is one of its most talented members. Drum Topics apologizes for misplacing his name and hopes he will send in a nice photo with his outfit for the next issue.

Warwick Barnes (left) of the Bert Firman's Orchestra at the fashionable Carlton Hotel, London, and Geo. W. Marsh (right) of the Paul Whiteman Orchestra. These boys became fast friends during Whiteman's visit to England. Geo. says that Barnes is a "wizz" of a drummer.

H. C. Robbins has been a feature xylophonist and drummer since he was nine years of age and has held many fine positions. Now playing with Ronnie Munro and Barrie Mills, forming a most unique novelty trio at the Little Club, London, using a Leedy xylophone. Robbins has also done considerable recording for "His Master's Voice."
Courtesy
H. Hinks Martin, Ltd.

Dan Ingman, that spruce and debonair drummer, is now touring the larger cities of the British Isles with "Mercenary Mary." He played during the summer at the Midland Hotel, Manchester. Dan is one of the most completely equipped drummers in England. All Leedy.

Eric Little holds down one of the highest class jobs—with Jack Hylton at the Kit Kat Club, London. When Art Layfield was over there with Isham Jones, Eric and Art played alternately at the Kit Kat Club, and Art says: "Eric is one of the finest drummers that ever shook a tambo."

Billy Mather has [held fine] jobs on both sides of [the Atlan]tic: in New York a[nd several] English cities. Also a[board the] famous S. S. "Leviat[han." He is] now at the elite "[   ]" Restaurant in Glasgo[w. ...] A prince of good f[ellows and] a wonderful all-roun[d drummer.]

Leedy   "WORLD'S FINEST DRUMMERS' INSTRUMENTS"   **Leedy**

The Exclusive Drummers' Paper

rummers of Britain

rs. One came along on the "Mayflower" in 1620 as a member of the
there has been a continual swapping of ideas that has helped those on
practiced by thousands on this side, and America took to England the
great interest in the other, and those who have traveled back and forth
ly there is something within all men that creates understanding where

that the boys whose photos
h-class, "snappy" lot. DRUM
smuch as Geo. H. Way and
Co. spent three months of this
rummers and visited all the
display of Leedy instruments.
came to see the "Drum Shows"
ss and good fellowship shown
l long be remembered.

Wm. Parkinson of Horwich, near Bolton, Lancashire, England, has been with the world-famous Besse's O' the Barn Band of Manchester for several years. The double photo shows him both "at ease" and "in action." His skill in playing "double drums" is truly marvelous and one has to see and hear him to appreciate his work.

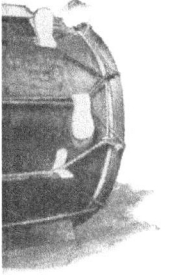

rument is considered
e oldest known bass
bears the crown and
e, who reigned from
l is of solid ash con-
in a fine state of
nter flesh hoops
while course the
rred by His Majesty
m Windsor Castle to
ice Museum.

Three Russian drums captured by the 88th Connaught Rangers at the Battle of Inkerman in the Crimea on November 5, 1854. They were presented to the Royal United Service Museum by the officers of the 1st Battalion Connaught on the understanding that if the regiment is re-raised in the British service they are to be returned to them. The shells are polished brass with a most beautifully hand-embossed emblem embodying the Russian bear.

the courtesy of the Royal United Service Museum, Whitehall, London, England

Will Hender is now touring with "Princess Charming" prior to the London opening. Will is well known in London as one of the greatest musical comedy drummers that ever sat in a pit. He is a star on drums, xylophone and tympani. A Leedy man for twelve years.

Ralph H. Ironmonger of Birmingham, England, plays with the Avon Dance Band and acts as business manager as well. This is one of the leading musical organizations of the district and they enjoy their share of the very finest work, much of which is due to the progressiveness of Ironmonger.

has held many
s of the Atlan-
rk and several
so a year on the
viathan." He is
"Grosvenor"
sgow, Scotland.
d fellows and
ound drummer.

Herbert A. Smith of Keighley, Yorkshire, England, is drummer and tympanist of "The Famous Picture House Orchestra" in that city. He is an old-timer in all branches of the business, even to having served through the war with the 2nd Yorkshires. Smith has a fine record.

Gus Green, of the La Valton Orchestra, does a big share of the fashionable society dance work in West London. He is highly rated as most clever and original. Since the above photo was taken he has equipped himself with a new Leedy outfit.
Courtesy The Saxophone Shop.

Wm. S. Hutcheon is the very high-class, all-round drummer with "The Omega Collegians," who have played many of the best engagements in England and Scotland. Now at the State Cafe, Liverpool. This is some fine band.

   "FOR DRUMMERS WHO CARE"   

Leedy Drum Topics

Ship Silhouette

This is indeed one of the most striking and beautiful scenes that has yet been applied to bass drum heads. The original came from a Paris art shop. It has grace and action, which are the very requisites of the drummer. A picture without action on a bass drum head is not in keeping with the atmosphere in which drums are used.

Ask for No. S-9.

Solder of any kind will not adhere to either Turkish or Chinese cymbals for any length of time.

"Beating" time is good business for the drummer. "Killing" it is poor business.

DRUM TOPICS is ever eager to publish good snappy drum news and photographs. Send yours in for the February issue.

L. A. Mueller

Here is a drummer who has made a name for himself in two distinct professions—Music and Chiropractic. He put in twenty-seven years at the drums and made good in almost every class of work. He has held leading theatre jobs in Chicago, Davenport, Cedar Rapids, Ottumwa, Burlington and Wichita; also spent several years on the road with everything from circus to first-rate musical shows. Mueller has invented several successful drummers' accessories that are in use daily by hundreds all over the country. He is a graduate of the Palmer School of Chiropractic at Davenport, Iowa, and now has an extensive practice in his home town—Kankakee, Illinois.

Howard H. Rankin

Howard H. Rankin (designated by arrow) is now with Billy Barber and His West Virginians. They have been touring Pennsylvania, Maryland and Delaware during the past summer and are now covering North and South Carolina, Virginia and Georgia, working their way into Florida for the winter. This is a high-class dance and theatre attraction that plays the best. Howard is one of the finest drummers in this class of business and he is a mighty fine little gentleman in the bargain. The photo was taken just before Dempsey (in center) lost the big battle.

Some drummers insist on calling the Marimba by the name of "Marimbaphone." There are very few Marimbaphones in use nowadays. It was designed so that the bars could be turned up to a vertical position. The ends of the bars were cut concaved and, by drawing a string bass bow across the ends, wonderful organ-like tones were produced. It did not prove practical, because the resin on the bow hair was very severe on the rosewood bars and they would turn sharp to a marked degree in a very short time.

Drummers of V. F. W. Post 288, Akron, Ohio

Here is the drum section that is a big factor in helping the Veterans of Foreign Wars Band, Joseph Wein Post No. 288, of Akron, Ohio, do their stuff. They carried off all honors at the V. F. W. conventions at Youngstown, Alliance and Massillon, Ohio, and have traveled all over the country, including the Eagles' conventions at Denver, Newark, St. Paul and Washington. The drummers are: Sergeant Frank Hesidance, drum major; Harley H. Long, director; Joe Washburn, first drummer; Harry Wellock, second drummer; Hugh Nickols, bass drummer. This band uses Leedy exclusively.

Courtesy The Edfred Music Company, Akron, Ohio.

To Preserve Your Wood Block

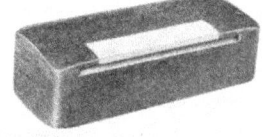

Stick a piece of ordinary adhesive tape, about ¾" wide and 3½" long, along the edge of the slot of your Chinese wood block as shown in photo. It will help to keep the block from cracking under the wear of the sticks, thereby preserving the life of the block for a much longer time. It will not hurt the tone and the tape can be renewed.

By Robert Murdock, Allenhurst, N. J.

Drums are doing their share in the good work of helping many young fellows through college.

The New CLOSED END Bass Drum Rod

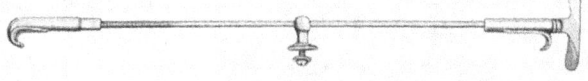

"Hooks" are what most drummers call the parts of a drum rod that go over the hoops. Mechanically speaking, they are "butts" and "collars." The "butt" is the "hook" that goes at the threaded end, and the "collar" is the "hook" that goes at the thumb-screw end. Leedy invented the pressed steel drum rod. The new closed-end "butt," as shown in the above photo, makes this rod the strongest and nicest appearing of any yet designed.

The lightning bug has better facilities for seeing where he has been than where he is going.

The old system of applying paints, varnishes, shellacs, etc., by the hand brushing method is out of date. No human hand can brush them on in as even coats as the modern compressed air gun. Leedy uses the most improved methods to insure the finest workmanship in every operation of making drummers' instruments.

 "WORLD'S FINEST DRUMMERS' INSTRUMENTS"

Page Ten

The Exclusive Drummers' Paper

A Repair Hint

If you decide to cut a crack out of a Turkish or Chinese cymbal, do not cut or file to a sharp V as drawn in Fig. 1. Rather, drill a hole at the end of the crack and cut away the metal up to the hole, leaving a round end, and file the corners as shown in Fig. 2 of drawing. This method will prevent the cymbal from cracking any further at that point.

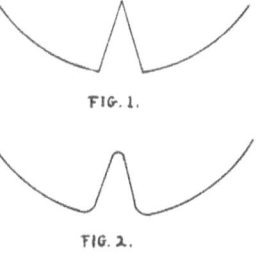

And yet people were naughty in the old days when a corset "ad" was considered daring.

Fred Johnson

has been playing for several years in both Fort William and Port Arthur, Ontario, Canada. Fred is one of the finest xylophonists in all Canada and is also a thoroughly legitimate theatre, concert and modern dance man. He is now at the Royal Theatre (of the Capitol chain) in Fort William and puts in his spare time acting as an agent for Canada's only exclusive Drum House—The Advance Drum Company of Edmonton, Alberta. He also served through the war and was overseas with a Canadian regiment.

Courtesy The Advance Drum Co., Edmonton, Alberta, Canada.

"Bill" Roberts and Col. Joe Miller

At the beginning of the "tented season" Bill Roberts, one of the best-known troupers in the business, had the Leedy Mfg. Co. make the special drum shown in this photo. It is a 10x16-inch solid maple shell, finished in gold, with twenty Nobby Gold plated separate tension rods, heavy heads and 12-gauge gut snares. The drum is said to be the first one ever used in a Wild West show that can be heard above the band in all corners of the arena and at the same time play as sensitively as a dance model. Col. Joe Miller, head of the Miller Bros. 101 Ranch Show, took such an interest in the instrument that he willingly consented to pose for a photo with Bill and the drum. Another photo of Bill with his Leedy theatre outfit was shown in No. 12 Drum Topics. He is now back on the old winter job at the Orpheum in Peoria, Illinois. Some drummer, this boy!

Bill Croft

of Luscar, Alberta, Canada, and formerly of Edmonton, Alberta, is an all-around first-rate drummer who has played theatre and dance work for many years. At present he is working with an orchestra that enjoys a big following in many towns scattered over hundreds of miles from Luscar. Alberta is longer than Texas, and Bill often travels more miles during the winter than the average trouping drummer in the U. S.

Courtesy The Advance Drum Co., Edmonton, Alberta, Canada.

A Novel Stunt—By Geo. A. Smith

"The great artists on all instruments patiently practice long tones and slow scales; drum rudiments are to the drummer what long tones and slow scales are to other instrumentalists."
By Carl Gardner in "Carl Gardner's Drum Method," published by Carl Fischer, New York City. **Sold by Leedy Mfg. Co.** Ask for No. 401-G.

Geo. A. Smith, the well-known Omaha musical instrument dealer and former professional drummer, recently scored a big triumph which was the talk of the town. A prominent dancing teacher presented her pupils at the Strand Theatre for an entire week in a skit called "The Kid-Nite Follies." The biggest hit of the production was the girls' drum corps, composed of nineteen girls ranging in age from four to seventeen. They were trained by Mr. Smith, who also furnished them with Leedy drums. Much newspaper space was devoted to the "originality of this part of the show" and "the thorough drilling the girls have received."

Traveling drummers should always make a call on Mr. Smith. They will find it well worth their while to meet him, as he is a regular fellow and knows the "drum biz" from A to Z. He recently moved his store to new and larger quarters at the corner of Nineteenth and Farnam Streets. You can't miss it, because the same old big bass drum sign swings over the sidewalk and is now nightly "lit up."

Justa Wethead says—

There's many a Drummer who has lost a good "Roll" on account of a smile.

Chas. A. Kerr

has the reputation of being one of the most efficient shipping foremen of all the factories in the country. Shipping drums and accessories is a specialty job and not like packing shoes or even china. Such commodities simply require routine knowledge, but each box and package of drummers' supplies submits a different problem, and Kerr has handled his department, including seven other men, in such a manner that our hundreds of dealers all agree that Leedy shipments are packed the neatest and safest of any they have ever seen. He has been with the company for twenty-two years.

"FOR DRUMMERS WHO CARE"

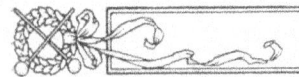 # Leedy Drum Topics

The Prize Story
By Julien Vedey, London, England

EDITOR'S NOTE — Julien Vedey holds a distinctive position among the drummers of the British Isles, inasmuch as he is not only a most capable drummer of the standard and jazz schools, but he has also taken the lead in writing exceptionally clever articles relative to drums and drummers' problems. His "Hickory, Dickory, Dock," "ƒZ" and "Drums of War," published by the Melody Maker and British Metronome, are valuable contributions to the drum world, and DRUM TOPICS is glad to have the exclusive opportunity of publishing his latest story. Vedey has been playing drums for a number of years and is now at the famous Piccadilly Hotel, alternating with the Kit Kat Club, using Leedy equipment throughout.

"The Jackdaw and the Peacocks"

Once upon a time there was a jackdaw who flew into a beautiful garden and found there some feathers discarded by a peacock. "Here's my chance," said the jackdaw to himself, "to get myself out of the jackdaw rut and become a peacock!"

So he picked up the feathers in his beak and arranged them in his plumage, bedecking himself with their multicolored hues. Trailing the long tail along the ground he practiced the peacock's stately walk and finally convinced himself so much of his own importance and picturesqueness that he looked at the other birds with disgust and treated them with haughty disdain.

Now, some of the birds stared at him with genuine admiration and envy, for they knew no better. He deceived the crows, the ravens, the sparrows and, in fact, most birds of the air, and felt quite proud of himself. All went well until, strutting about in the garden, he saw the peacocks. In his arrogance he walked right in amongst them and it was here his disillusionment took place. The peacocks were by no means deceived by his imitation. They screeched out their derision and, plucking off the gayly-colored feathers in which he had arrayed himself, they unmasked him, much to the surprise and amusement of the other birds.

And so, here in little old London, there was a drummer. He sang and juggled well. His clothes bore the stamp of Savile Row and he drove a handsome car. Many are the times I have seen him strutting up and down Archer Street, patronizing us all with a dignified nod here and there, or talking in a most authoritative manner about drums. He knew a lot about drums—he told us so—and his advice was well worth having—everybody knew that.

Now, it is an acknowledged fact in England that the best drummers come from America. This one, although an Englishman, spoke with the American accent—surely the sign of a good drummer. He also acquired the habit of chewing gum—also an American custom, I am told. But that is not all!

His instruments were of the very finest and most up-to-date that money could buy. All gold! Beautiful gold! I am not sure if he said they were plated or solid gold—anyhow, they were gold. Then again he was "hot." He was the hottest drummer in town except Perlmutter from the "Ping-Pong Club." But then Perlmutter had a bad appearance —everybody admitted that!

He convinced some people and I was almost convinced myself until I went to hear him play, and then the mischief began. He was a very good imitation indeed—but only an imitation. He did not know a five-stroke from an eleven-stroke, nor a paradiddle from a ruff. I spoke technique to him, but he colored up and had to admit his ignorance. Then the time came for the band in which he played to get a "big" job in a "big" hotel, where there was a "big" cabaret, which meant "big" manuscript for the drummer, and this is where he finished—suddenly!

That is where they all finish—all imitations. It is not sufficient to look like a drummer in these days of close competition and rapid progress. Gold-plated instruments will not play by themselves, even if they do help to get the job; neither will a ten-pound cymbal cough up a hot break unless you make it. It's one thing to be a showman and show people how well you play, but another thing entirely to play drums correctly and technically.

The men earning big money are essentially drummers in the musical sense of the word, at least it is so in England, and the imitation drummer stands no chance when it's music they want. They say, "Birds of a feather flock together," and this "bird" is alright among his own species. He is a jackdaw pure and simple. He can quite easily deceive the other jackdaws, or even the crows and the ravens—but just wait until he gets among the peacocks!

DRUM TOPICS offers a prize of $10.00 for the best story for each issue. Short stories stand an equal chance with long ones. Every drummer knows a good story—send yours in.

Korean Temple Blocks

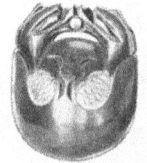 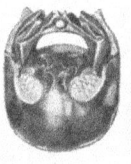 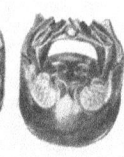 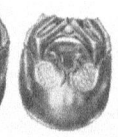 

No. 244E	No. 244D	No. 244C	No. 244B	No. 244A
6½ in.	6 in.	5½ in.	5 in.	4½ in.

The use of Temple Blocks as a drummer's effect is becoming more and more popular. They have a weird, mysterious tone much deeper and richer than the largest wood blocks. There are two kinds—one that is made in Japan, the other in Korea. The latter are far superior in tone and appearance. You can readily tell the difference, as the Korean have a glossy red finish which has given them the nickname of "Tomatoes." The Japanese make have a dull red finish and are much more crude in workmanship. Temple Blocks sound best when played upon with half-hard rubber mallets. There has been great difficulty in obtaining a source of supply that could be depended upon, but now Leedy carries them in stock in all of the above five sizes.

Order as per number.

Jean Stettler

has been "pounding the calf-skins" in and around the Twin Cities, of which Minneapolis is his O. H. T. (own home town) for fourteen years. Jean is one of the most successful drummers in the Northwest. He has played at most of the leading theatres, cafes and dance orchestras and is now with Carcio's Melody Boys of Minneapolis, a very popular bunch, who are busy nightly. Jean is fourth from the left in the above photo. Solid Leedy.

Courtesy Hausner Music Company, Minneapolis, Minn.

Maynard Kouns

Meet a thoroughbred old-timer who is as conscientious today about his drums and manner of playing them as he was when he started in the '90s. Kouns now plays in one of the leading theatres in his native town—Salina, Kan. However, he has put in many years on the road, trouping with everything from a show where the musicians "double canvas" to the finest on the road. Is he a real drummer? We'll say he is! As fine as they make 'em—tympani and all. And all Leedy!

Did you ever notice that the long front wooden strip that supports the bell bars in a Leedy bell case is slightly curved? It is made in that manner so the bars may be drilled for pegs in exactly the proper place and so the support strip will conform to the neutral node of the bars.

 **"WORLD'S FINEST DRUMMERS' INSTRUMENTS"**

The Exclusive Drummers' Paper

A Scientific Fact

It is the head of a tympano that produces the tone. The bowl acts as a "reflector" and not as a resonator. If the bowl were a resonator it would have to be made of a different size for each note the head gives forth, just as each resonator under the various marimba or xylophone bars is of a different size.

Roy Ulrey

is known to about every drummer who visits the Leedy plant, inasmuch as he is supervisor of the Snare and Bass Drum Assembly and Stock Department, which takes up almost the entire third floor of the building. This is one of the most interesting sections of the factory, and visiting professionals seem to enjoy chatting with Roy about the "whys and wherefores," on which he is an acknowledged expert. He has been with the Leedy Mfg. Co. for sixteen years and is one of their most sincere workers. Previously he was one of Cincinnati's most prominent drummers.

She (after proposal): "Oh, Jim, I can't marry you. I—I—I'm not good enough for you!"
He (dejectedly): "Aw, h-ll—just my luck!"
—Boston Beanpot.

Half-hard rubber hammers (No. 370-D) always sound better than drum sticks on a wood block; they produce a deeper and richer tone.

Lou Perry

This is the band "extraordinaire" that gets the big steamer "Cincinnati" job every season for the wonderful trip from Cincinnati to New Orleans and return, for the annual Mardi Gras. Lou Perry, on extreme right, is drummer and manager of this, his own orchestra—the famous Perry's Foot-Warmers—known throughout many Central and Southern States as "the small band that is better than many of the larger ones in the big cities." The band has headquarters at Madison, Ind. Perry is a 100% Leedy booster.

Al. Colandra

who plays with Aldini's San Carlo Orchestra, a prominent hotel, vaudeville and dance organization of Schenectady, N. Y., is more than just "putting it over." He is truly a feature drummer. Colandra has also held fine positions in Boston, New Haven and Albany. He states, "My Leedy outfit is my best friend and I would have no other make."

The "NODE" of a xylophone, marimba or bell bar is the point of no vibration across the bar. It is here that holes are drilled in the wood or steel for the cords and pegs.

New Leedy Cymbal Helps

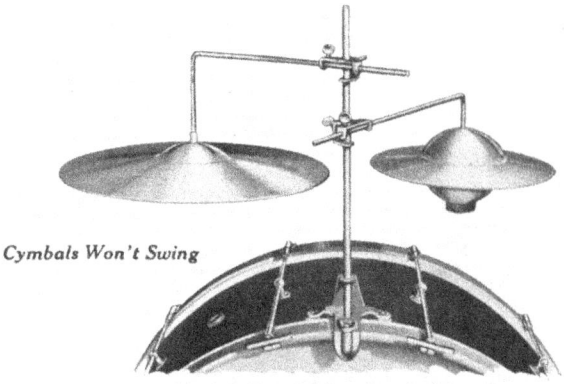

Cymbals Won't Swing

THE NEW "HEAVY DUTY" CYMBAL HOLDER

Note the new, heavier, rigid upright rod and the heavier clamp with two rubber feet that rest on bass drum shell. Also the long braced cymbal arm clamps. Cymbals are suspended on the arms themselves. No cords, no swinging. A beauty.

Holder complete (no cymbals).........No. 303
Single Arm and Clamp.................No. 303A

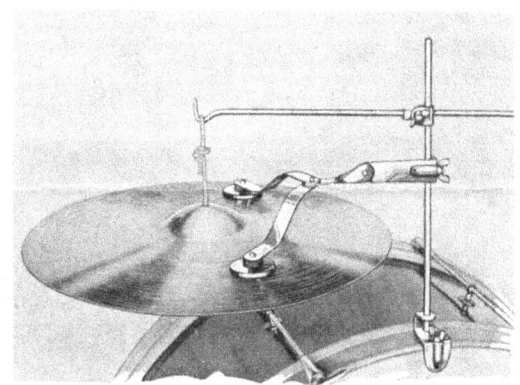

THE NEW CYMBAL SIZZLE ATTACHMENT

Can be used on any style suspended cymbal holder. The arms are adjustable to spread. Wonderful effect. The sizzlers are flexible, being mounted on felt pads.

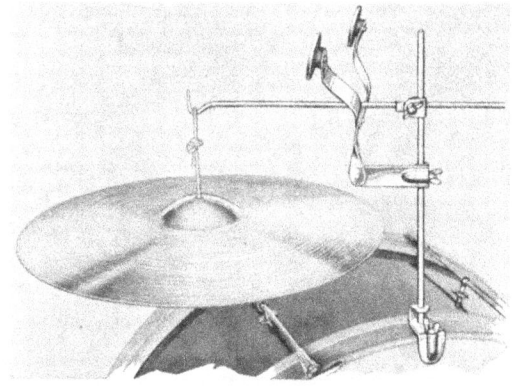

Just flip it up with your stick when not wanted.
Ask for No. 302.

"FOR DRUMMERS WHO CARE"

Leedy Drum Topics

Again—A Leedy Equipped Drum Corps Wins First Prize
American Legion Drum Corps, Post No. 130, Fort Dodge, Iowa

Pretty "snappy" looking outfit—what? Their drilling and playing are as wonderful as their appearance. This is the corps that won first prize at the American Legion convention in Philadelphia, October 11th to 15th this year. It takes some ability to win this coveted prize. About eighty corps competed. Their success is principally due to Dr. A. N. Thoms, manager; Eddie Arthur, drum instructor; Elliott Colson, drum major, and Robert Heath, drill major. The corps is equipped with twelve Leedy floating-head, separate tension, street drums.

She was a strawberry blonde, but she gave me the razzberry.

H. J. Wittman

For twenty-five years H. J. Wittman has been a "first-rater" on the drums, whatever class the job. He has specialized in theatre and concert work, but four years ago he organized his own dance band and has carried its management through to where it is considered one of the foremost of its kind. Wittman's Orchestra plays the best of work in the Erie (Pa.) section. Here is a drummer of the progressive class who is a successful business man as well. He says, "Leedy reigns supreme with me."

U. G. Leedy was the originator of spring tension snare and bass drum rods and holds a patent on same dated June 29, 1915, patent No. 1,144,452. The Leedy Mfg. Co. has been making them ever since that time and has turned out over 15,000 spring tension drums for the Wurlitzer Organ Co.

A Pedal Hint

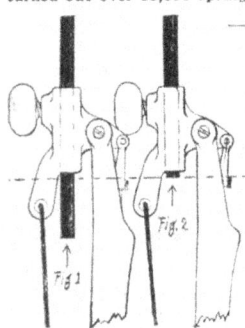

Don't adjust the beater rod (shown black in drawings at left) of your pedal so that it is long enough to allow the weight of the beater ball to over-balance the stroke, as in Fig. 2. It is better to let the rod down about an inch below the metal sleeve that holds it, as in Fig. 1; then your pedal will work easier, because the weight of the ball is better balanced.

A Recent Improvement

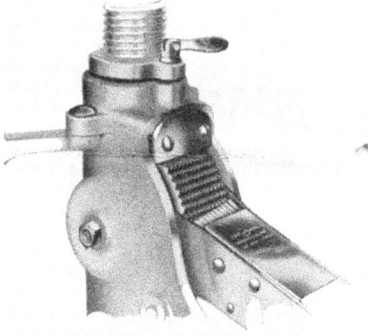

The "steps" (as shown in the close-up photo at right) of the Leedy Universal Tympani are now made of alternating layers of hardened steel and special thin sheet rubber. Therefore, when one of the pawls (locking device) engages, it does so noiselessly and there is no longer any possibility of the pawls vibrating so they can be heard.

As on former models, there are ten pawls, each one of a different length and one of which is always engaged, holding the head, no matter how slight the movement of the pedal. There can be absolutely no slipping of the pawls, therefore no dropping of the tone. There are no springs to adjust.

The Monahan Post Band of Sioux City, Iowa, is again the champion band of the American Legion, winning first prize at Philadelphia this year. This is the fourth time they have come out on top. Some record—some band. All Leedy for drums.

F. R. Brown

is the first drummer of the Percussion Section of the Ford Motor Car Band in Detroit, Mich. His original home was Washington, D. C., but for the past 25 years he has been Detroit's outstanding figure in things "drumistic." He is called "the daddy of them all" and is undoubtedly one of the most popular musicians in that section. Dozens of Detroit's best drummers were his former pupils, including that wonder xylophonist—Fred Paine. "F. R." has played in most every prominent theatre and leading musical organization of the city. He has been a Leedy enthusiast for many years.

Courtesy Bailey Bros. Music House.

 **"WORLD'S FINEST DRUMMERS' INSTRUMENTS"**

The Exclusive Drummers' Paper

On the Cover—Karl Glassman

It was Karl Glassman, tympanist of the New York Symphony Orchestra (Walter Damrosch, conductor), who was responsible for the recent success of an event in the music world which emphasizes the importance of the tympanist in such a forceful manner that it has brought in the highest score yet in recognition of our profession. Six pair of tympani (two pair of Leedy Universal Pedal Tympani and two pair of Leedy standard model) were used on the stage of the Fabian Theatre at Paterson, N. J., in a musical stage presentation entitled "The Spectacle of the Drums" as a prologue to the feature photoplay "Variety" with Emil Jannings. A Paterson newspaper comments on the event as follows:

> "The stage attraction is 'The Spectacle of the Drums,' depicting a musical march from the beginning of the time of drums and going on down through the ages. The last and final scene, in which the stage presents Karl Glassman, Edward Montray, Leo Ruffman, Joseph Sears and Irving Friedel, the five tympani players, accompanied by Miss Manilla Powers, soprano, and the Misses Theressa Kelly, Mary Gordon, Elizabeth Powers, Charleston dancers, finishes in a blaze of jazz. The enthusiasm shown when the act finished at yesterday's performance proved without a doubt that this was one of the most pleasing and entertaining stage presentations that the Fabian Theatre has ever presented."

And the Fabian Theatre program carries this announcement of the act:

McFerr Presents
"THE SPECTACLE OF THE DRUMS"
A festival of rhythm
featuring and presenting for the first time
in musical history

AN ORCHESTRA OF HARMONIC TYMPANI
Directed by Karl Glassman
Arrangements by Willy Creager

ARTISTS

KARL GLASSMAN, New York Symphony Orchestra.
EDWARD H. MONTRAY, Pittsburgh Symphony Orchestra.
LEO RUFFMAN, Vienna Symphony Orchestra.
JOSEPH SEARS, New York Philharmonic Orchestra.
IRVING FRIEDEL, Russian Symphony Orchestra.

Presented in Four Episodes.

THE DRUMS OF PRAISE:
The Witch Doctor and the Jungle Priestess pay tribute to their gods.

THE DRUMS OF ECSTASY:
In his palace the Caliph is entertained by drums and dance.

THE DRUMS OF WAR:
Against the flaming curtain of battle the Drummer Boy calls men to glory or to death.

THE GLORIFICATION OF THE DRUM:
This battery of Harmonic Tympani has a range of an octave and a half, playing the full musical scale, and is capable of harmonics equal to the violin or cello. Features of this episode: Military Overture with Tympani Solos; Vocal Solo with Tympani accompaniment; Charleston on the drums.

And here is part of Mr. Glassman's letter to Mr. Leedy regarding the event and proving what he thinks of Leedy tympani:

> I was commissioned to put on and direct the tympani part of this act, the difficult score of which was made possible of execution only by the use of two pair of Leedy Universal pedal tympani, in addition to four pair of hand-screw drums, two pair of the latter also being Leedy.
> In all my experience I have never encountered a score which could better prove the qualities of your tympani from any angle possible. Four times daily, through heat, humidity and rain, a test for any drum, your pedal tympani never faltered, answering the slightest touch on the pedal with absolute ease, rapidity of action and perfection of tone.
> I congratulate you on your achievement and I assure you that I am happy in the possession of Leedy instruments.
>
> Sincerely yours,
> *Karl Glassman*

It will undoubtedly interest progressive drummers to learn that Karl Glassman has now completed his new correspondence course, "The Art of Tympani Playing," and has opened The New York School of Tympani. Drummers who desire to improve their ability as tympanists are advised to write Mr. Glassman at 3562 Ninety-first Street, Jackson Heights, N. Y. That he is one of the finest of all tympanists is undisputed.

D. E. Bach

is cutting a niche for himself in the "Drummers' Hall of Fame." His work with the Russ Morgan Orchestra at the State Theatre, Detroit, Mich., is admittedly one of the strongest reasons why this bunch is the talk of the town. Although Bach has taken up stage band work in earnest, he also ranks very high as a hotel and dance man, to say nothing of his pit experience, having worked at the Sumit Beach Dance Hall in Akron, Ohio, and the Portage Hotel, same city, and one year at the Lyric Theatre, Hamilton, Ontario. Bach is featuring the Leedy Vibraphone, which is shown in the above photo.

A very cold night—too cold to go home. Three people—only one bed—only one blanket. How did they all keep warm?
Answer: They didn't all keep warm—one froze to death.

Send in some good photographs for the next issue of DRUM TOPICS. It comes out in February. DRUM TOPICS is a quarterly (every three months), not a monthly, as many now believe.

W. Louis Dorough

W. Louis Dorough of Birmingham, Ala., has been with Oliver Naylor's Orchestra for the past four years, playing the better class of ballroom, hotel and stage work. Louis is one of the chief reasons for this orchestra's fine reputation, he being a "top-notcher" in every respect. He was the first drummer to equip himself with the wonderful Marine Pearl drums, both bass and snare. Chauncey Morehouse of the Gene Goldkette Orchestra was the first drummer to own this model snare drum.

The Princess Patricia's Band of Winnipeg, Manitoba, Canada, composed of thirty-five members under the baton of Captain T. W. James, recently finished a twelve weeks' concert tour of the Central States. This is the organization that made such a brilliant record in the World War. Newspapers of every city in which they played in the United States have acclaimed the band one of the very finest that ever toured. L. T. C. Clifford is the snare drummer and Mr. Knight is on the bass drum. Both are A-1 drummers.

.... AND THIS, ladies and gentlemen, closes our thirteenth "broadcast." We hope you have enjoyed it and would appreciate hearing from you by letter or postal. Leedy boosters, send in your photos. Suggestions welcome. Next "concert" in February. Please stand by for Station LEEDY.

"FOR DRUMMERS WHO CARE"

Leedy
DRUM TOPICS

The Exclusive Drummers' Paper

NOVEMBER, 1926
THIRTEENTH EDITION

POSTMASTER—Return Postage Guaranteed

Leedy Manufacturing Co.
INDIANAPOLIS, INDIANA

Jess Altmiller—Fox Theatre, Philadelphia, Pa.—(See Page 13)

Leedy Drum Topics

Selling

is just as much the Drummer's job as it is the job of the man on the road who sells hardware, clothing, or foods. It used to be quite proper to term a traveling salesman a "drummer." He acquired the title from the real Drummer by making the rounds and beating the merits and prices of his wares into the heads of buyers—like the real Drummer who beats the call to action.

The modern musical Drummer has three branches of wares to sell: first, his ability as an artist—second, himself, which is called Personality—and third, the quality and appearance of his equipment. Some Drummers have all three—some have only one or two. In the old days ability was all that was needed. It still counts for the highest score, but we cannot overlook the fact that times have changed and that much is expected from the Drummer of today. He is in the spotlight more than ever.

His success will be greater if he knows the value of selling other wares besides ability alone. A man cannot develop physical personality, but he CAN develop mental personality. So can he develop appearance. It is easy these days, with the beautiful instruments that are being made.

How is your stock of ability, personality and appearance? Are they easy to "sell"? If not, put some study on them. It will pay you. They are your wares and you are the real Drummer salesman.

The New Leedy Catalog "O"—NOW READY

84 pages—285 illustrations—20 in natural colors. The most complete Drummers' Catalog ever published. From the world's largest makers of Drummers' Instruments

Many Brand New Creations
for the Progressive Drummer

Mailed Free
Send for Yours Today

Leedy Mfg. Co., INDIANAPOLIS, INDIANA

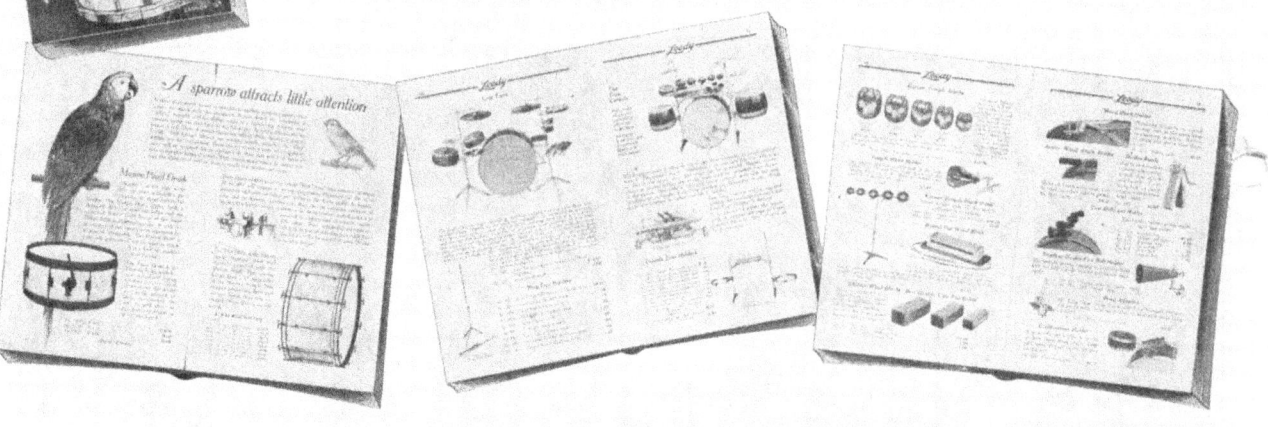

Leedy   "WORLD'S FINEST DRUMMERS' INSTRUMENTS"   **Leedy**

The Exclusive Drummers' Paper

In Indo-China

For many centuries it has been a custom of the Imperial Palace in Bangkok, capital of Siam, for the Royal Drummers to appear on the walls of the palace at sunset and "play the sun to sleep." All in the picture excepting the standard bearers are drummers. The one with the large Tom-Tom is the leader, while the two on each side play on sticks in "chop-stick" fashion. This is a rare photo of a most serious religious custom; the sun having set below the wall has thrown the figures into a beautiful silhouette effect.

A girl can be said to be afraid of her own shadow when she is careful not to stand 'twixt you and the setting sun.

Johnny Morris and Paul Specht

Among the foremost orchestras of the world is the Paul Specht organization, which recently returned from a very successful London run and is now permanently located at the Twin Oaks Cafe in New York City, also broadcasting regularly over WJZ. Among the foremost modern Drummers is Johnny Morris, who is shown above with Mr. Specht, evidently discussing a number for the Leedy Vibraphone. Morris hails from New Haven, Conn., where he was for many years a leading light amongst the Drummers of that city. There he did considerable theatre work and was a part of the well-known Cavelero's orchestra. For the past two years he has been with the No. 1 Specht Orchestra. Morris' extraordinarily fine voice is heard in the refrains of Specht's Columbia Records and it's a fine compliment to have one's leader speak of him thus: "His work on the tympani, with his clever manipulation of the drums and traps, along with his genial personality and excellent singing, makes Morris one of the outstanding features of my band." Morris uses Leedy equipment throughout.

Movie Drummers, Stay Away!

In all China, the second largest country on earth, there are only 106 moving picture theatres.

The Flam

The Flam is one of the most artistic beats of the Drummer's routine. When executed properly it has dignity, solidity and balance, combined with the character of perfection. When played poorly it has the weakness of a drunken sot.

Temple Blocks made in China, Korea or Japan often "close up" when kept in climates other than where they are made. This is due to the peculiar nature of the soft specie of pine used in their manufacture. When the edges of the "bell" touch the block becomes "dead." However, this is only a temporary difficulty and there is a quick remedy. Do not try to spring the edges apart: simply make a saw cut across the point where they come in contact with each other and you will find the tone renewed to as fine a degree as ever.

Larry Gammerdinger and the New "High Hat" Sock Cymbal Pedal

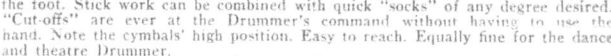

In stating that this new device will without doubt become one of the most widely used "contraptions" in the Drum World, DRUM TOPICS does not feel as though it is in the least exaggerating. The opinion is based upon the great scope it offers for cymbal effects. For single crashes it has all the utility of any other holder — even to the non-swinging feature. Sizzle effects are easily obtained by holding the two cymbals together with a light pressure of the foot. Then you can have "free" cymbals for tap work instantly by releasing the foot. Stick work can be combined with quick "socks" of any degree desired. "Cut-offs" are ever at the Drummer's command without having to use the hand. Note the cymbals' high position. Easy to reach. Equally fine for the dance and theatre Drummer.

The photo shows the well-known Larry Gammerdinger of the popular George Irish Orchestra now playing at the Indianapolis Athletic Club. Larry is one of the country's finest Drummers and Xylophone players. He is well known in New York City, where he worked for several seasons with such organizations as George White's Scandals and Charles Dornberger's Orchestra, also at the Silver Slipper Cafe.

No. 272 Pedal and Stand complete (cymbals not included)......$8.50
(Folds into space 19 inches long)

The greatest favor a Drummer can do for DRUM TOPICS is to send in new names of Drummers who would like to receive it. It's free.

No rooster would ever take a second look after hearing some Drummers blow a "hen cackle."

Miss Carmen Rovellard

That this young lady has made the most of the possibilities that drums offer to her sex is well demonstrated by her record. After putting in four years "breaking into" the dance game in her home town of Gas City, Indiana, she transferred her activities to Chicago and vicinity, holding many positions with standard orchestras playing the better class cafes and summer resorts. Miss Rovellard is now touring the Orpheum circuit with a headline dancing act, "The Kay Sisters and Band." Newspapers and managers' reports prove that her playing ability, pep and pleasing personality combine to make one of the "high spots" of the act. She uses Leedy equipment entirely and is high in her praise of same.

"FOR DRUMMERS WHO CARE"

Leedy Drum Topics

They're All the Same

Chewtherag: "Look! There goes Ann! What do you suppose she, a Christian woman, is doing out in a car with a man at this hour of the night?"

Knowsemwell: "Just about the same thing a heathen woman would, I presume."

Paul Whiteman—Geo. W. Marsh—L. Gluskin

The above photo was taken at the Cafe des Ambassadeurs in Paris during the Paul Whiteman engagement there last August. Perhaps Paul's smile means that he liked Paris and it is said that Marsh got a "kick" out of the town. To Gluskin the Boulevards and Montmartre are "old stuff"—he has been there two years playing with the famous Gasson's Orchestra at the Casino de Paris (like our Ziegfeld Follies) and doubling at all the swell affairs of the city, from European Royalty parties down to the popular ballrooms. Gluskin acted as host and guide to the Whiteman boys, especially Paul and George, and what they didn't see of Paris—"ain't." He is an old-timer of New York, where he played in many of Broadway's leading theatres, and where he is rated as one of the leaders of the profession. Gluskin also showed the "works" to Geo. H. Way and Jack Roop when they visited Paris last summer in the interests of the Leedy Mfg. Co. Mr. and Mrs. Rudy Wiedoeft were in the party, too—Oh, Boy! Was a good time had? We'll say so, and join the chorus sung by all American musicians who visit Paris . . . . "Gluskin is one helluvafine fellow."

"The Bunch" looking over a former German concrete and steel gun turret on the battlefield near Berry au Bac, France. Right to left—Jack Roop, a French ex-soldier guide, Rudy Wiedoeft, Mrs. Gluskin, Mrs. Wiedoeft, L. Gluskin.

U. G. Leedy made his first drum at Fostoria, Ohio, in 1892.

Not so long ago a photo of a Drummer with his outfit was a rarity. Times do change—every Drummer has one or two on hand these days. It's good business too: the fellow who can show himself, with a real outfit, to a leader or manager, often gets the job.

Joe Cenney

is now on the road with "Ben Hur" and its orchestra of twenty-five men. Some tymp work in this, and Joe "knocks the spots off" in regular symphony style. Cleveland, Ohio, is his headquarters, where he put in many years in the best theatres—Keith's, Hippodrome and the Allen. Cleveland musicians say he's as good as they make 'em. Joe says—"I've used Leedy for fifteen years and am going to keep right on doing so."

New Disappearing Spurs

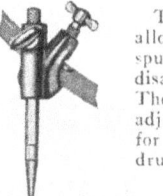

The chief reason why spurs slip on the floor and allow your bass drum to "creep" is because all former spur points hit the floor at an angle. These new Leedy disappearing spurs overcome that annoying difficulty. The spurs point straight downward. The points are adjustable and may be slipped up through the clamp for traveling. Not necessary to remove spurs from drum. The finest spur ever made.

No. 19-A. Per pair..................$1.50

The New Vise-Grip Pedal Cymbal Holder

This model cymbal holder is positively the strongest ever made. The jaws truly have a vise grip, and are formed to fit the curve of the hoop. The cymbal may be adjusted at any point on the round st rod which is flattened on one side to prevent cymbal from turning.

No. 277 ....$1.00

Many Drummers are under the impression that it is no longer possible to obtain the best grade of Turkish cymbals. Such is not the case. The Leedy Mfg. Co. maintains a source of supply and can furnish the genuine K. Zildjian & Cie models. However, shipments from Turkey are sometimes irregular and slow; therefore, it is always best to give a first and second choice of sizes. At present there is a large stock of the 12-in., 13-in., 14-in., 15-in., and 16-in. sizes available.

Benny Resh and Harry M. Cody

Harry M. Cody (standing) has been with Benny Resh and his orchestra for the past two years. These boys have held many first-rate jobs in many states, and are now at the Palais Royal in St. Petersburg, Florida—called "The Largest Ballroom in the South." Harry hails from Fall River, Mass. He has traveled with such fine organizations as Hardy's Tivoli Orchestra and Charles Fulcher's Columbia Recording Orchestra. On every job Cody's work meets with high praise, and he writes that he attributes a large share of his good fortune to his Leedy equipment, especially the Floating Head Snare Drum.

It is written in musical history that, during the reign of King Edward I of England (1272-1307) military kettle drummers mounted on horses were called "nakerers" and the King had his own private "naker," who accompanied him to give commands on the drums.

George Shutts

The name of George Shutts is as well known to the Drummers of the middle west as the name Bryan is to the folks of Nebraska. George is one of the old-time regulars, and is considered a very high-class Drummer in all branches of the work. He has played with the best of them in Milwaukee, Des Moines, Omaha, Topeka, and Chicago. At present he is taking a vacation with relatives at Centerville, Iowa, where the photo was taken at the special request of Drum Topics. Is he a Leedy Booster? We'll say he is!

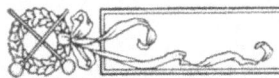 "WORLD'S FINEST DRUMMERS' INSTRUMENTS"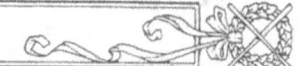

The Exclusive Drummers' Paper

Joseph Torreano

has been located with the "Shredded Wheat" Band at Niagara Falls for the past two years. He is one of the old school professionals and has "trouped it" with about every kind of a show or band that carries a bass drum in order that the leader may take it easy. Joe has been a feature Bass Drummer with such well-known outfits as The Ringling Brothers Shows, Forepaugh-Sells Shows, Barnum & Bailey's Circus, and the Sells-Floto Circus. He was for some time with Herbert L. Clark's band at Huntsville, Ont., Canada, and also made the round-the-world trip with the Kilties. On all these fine jobs, along with many others, he has always used Leedy. Twenty-three years of satisfaction. Joe says he would like to hear from his old friend, B. N. Gustat. Gustat is now a member of the firm of Sporleder's Music House, St. Louis, Mo.

In manufacturing xylophone or marimba bars a full fifty percent of the rough logs are lost by cutting and selection. Leedy uses no "sap" lengths —the kind with yellow streaks.

Earl MacLane

recently returned to his home city—"The Hub"—Boston, Mass., for a short rest after a several months' trip down the East and up the West coast of South America with a popular American orchestra. Earl is known as "Hot Mac" on account of his nifty work as a most original and clever Drummer. He has had ten years of a most varied experience, including the Brown & Dyers Shows Band, and with a headline act over the Keith and Pantages routes. He has also done considerable pit work in Eastern vaudeville and burlesque theatres. All Leedy.

Proving That Right and Wrong Are Established By Custom

Those who predict that cigarette-smoking by the women will impair the health and morals of the race will be dismayed, perhaps, to learn that both Martha Washington and the mother of Lincoln are credited with having found comfort in the society of Lady Nicotine.

Yusef Khan Grotto Drum Corps of Akron, Ohio

Here is the bunch that won first prize at the Grotto Convention in St. Louis. After hearing these twelve Drummers and eighteen buglers do their stuff behind Drum-Major Dr. V. B. Crumbaugh—"the parade is over." Dr. Crumbaugh is one of Akron's most prominent dentists. In the old days he was Drummer with such famous bands as Webber's, Bellstedt's, and the Old Ohio First Regiment. George Moody, chief Drummer (on extreme left, first row), is instructor, and a great portion of the success of this wonderful corps is due to his hard work and ability. He is a full-fledged professional in all branches of the game, having played in many of the larger cities of the country.

Vincent Lopez at Hartford, Conn.

Harry Edison   Jack E. Wills   Vincent Lopez

When Vincent Lopez and his Orchestra of fifteen men played at the State Theatre in Hartford, Conn., during the first part of February, Harry Edison, the Lopez Drummer, and Jack Wills, the State Theatre Drummer, became good friends and decided to have their photo taken together as a remembrance of their pleasant associations. When Mr. Lopez saw the boys preparing for the photo and noticed that Leedy Drums were to be included, he kindly consented to join them on account of the fact that he is a Leedy Booster as well. Harry Edison is one of New York's best known Drummers. He was formerly tympanist at the Capitol and has been with orchestras at the Knickerbocker and Rialto. These jobs, along with his position with Lopez, speak for his high rating. Jack E. Wills has been doing the better class of theatre work for twelve years in Omaha, Cleveland, Columbus (Ohio), and New York City. Jack likes Hartford and is making a big hit there at the State as a feature Drummer, Tympanist and Xylophonist. He also broadcasts from WTIC.

New Bell, Xylophone or Trap Table

Here is a new Drummer's help that can be used in various ways. It makes a dandy bell or light Xylophone stand and is also just the thing for the theatre Drummer to use as a table in the pit for traps, etc. You can easily place a board of any size desired on the cross arms. Stand is made of strip steel and has a 6-in. length adjustment. Folds compactly for traveling.

No. 265. Complete as shown in photo........$5.00

Donald L. Gaffney

started out in his home town of Frankfort, N. Y., at the age of ten as a professional dance Drummer. Even before that time he played with amateur organizations at social functions. Although now only nineteen years of age he has climbed into the spotlight with his Leedy Xylophone as one of vaudeville's headline acts. The principal circuits of the country, including Keith's, Orpheum, and Pantages, know him well. Newspaper notices from towns along these routes praise his work and consider him second to none on the vaudeville stage. Gaffney deserves a lot of credit.

Dum—"So your sweetie left town yesterday. Did the parting cause you any pain?"

Dora—"I'll say so. Every rib in my body aches."

"FOR DRUMMERS WHO CARE"

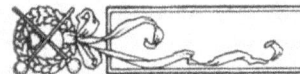 

Leedy Drum Topics

Howard Osburn

is musical director of WBBM (Stewart-Warner) Radio Station in Chicago, where he leads his own orchestra. Last summer the Stewart-Warner Co. sent Osburn across the Pacific in charge of eight men on a three months' broadcasting tour of the Philippine Islands, Japan and China. They sailed on the S. S. President Jackson early in June. Osburn is a wonderful Drummer and a real hustler—the kind that proves that the Drummer can climb if he puts his shoulder to the wheel. He is well known all over the United States, having toured the best there is with the famous Henry Santrey Band. This photo was taken in China. Osburn is in the center. All Leedy.

The markings on Chinese Cymbals that we associate with "Sam Lee's" laundry checks are not, as some believe, the name or trademark of the maker. Cymbals of exactly the same sizes and shapes as we now find them were used in China for religious ceremonies before the Christian era. Undoubtedly the "crashes" were intended to scare away "evil demons," etc. Therefore, as the cymbals represented the good spirits, they were given titles and even to this day the custom prevails to name and write upon them. The writing on each cymbal is different and, translated, means:

MOON — CLOUDS — STARS — SUN — WATER — SNOW — RAIN, Etc.

The flowers and gods are also often used.

Claude L. Burns

We wish space permitted a complete history of this "live wire," real Drummer and good fellow, who has traveled about every possible path of the profession, starting at the age of six by practicing with a pair of his mother's darning needles on the back of his father's fiddle in Hot Springs, Ark. Claude is now in his eighth year as contractor for his own "Burns' Music Masters" at the Hippodrome in Waco, Texas. Shreveport, Ft. Smith, Pine Bluff, and many other Southwestern cities, know him well by way of his snappy vaudeville work in Interstate Houses, to say nothing of years on the road with "all kinds." He is also secretary of the Waco Musicians' Union. Claude says—"Leedy's better drums put the Drummer on the map."

Red Oak (Iowa) Junior Drum and Bugle Corps

Look 'em over, oldtimers—some of 'em will be on your job some day. And that's no joke, for this bunch of ambition and youth, backed up by real ability that makes veterans applaud, is knocking 'em cold wherever they go—and they have visited almost 300 towns in the Middle West. Merrill R. Hawkins (X) is the organizer, and rightfully deserves the highest praise for his wonderful work. J. C. Meyers, manager, puts over the publicity and trips. Not only Red Oak, but all Iowa, is proud of this "gang."
Courtesy George A. Smith (Exclusive Leedy Agent),
Lyric Building, Omaha, Nebr.

Four spurs on a bass drum are better than two. If you have been using two, try out the change and note the improved quality and volume of tone.

Frank Wolf's Drum Shop, New York

The old saying, "Little, but oh, MY!" fits here as well as it ever did anywhere. The store is little, and the boss is a little "fella," but, sufferin' cats, what a business this combination produces. Frank is known well to 99% of the New York City and vicinity drummers; in fact, he was known to this extent before he went into business, on account of his professional record as without a better among thousands. He had the choice of New York's best work for many years. His list of elite jobs is too long to mention here. Frank is shown behind the counter (with glasses) holding the Hand Sock Cymbals, in the act of showing them to a brother drummer. Does Frank feature Leedy goods? Absolutely! The nifty looking gent behind the counter, holding the Leedy Floating Head drum, is none other than "Bill" Gladstone, the wizard bass drummer at the famous Capitol Theatre. Bill is some "big guy" among New York Drummers, and is rated all over the United States as not just a fine bass drummer, but really marvelous. It was he who invented the Hand Sock Cymbals, that have sold in every city like hot cakes. Bill helps Frank in the store during his spare time.

We wish people wouldn't duck their heads when the camera clicks. However, you can't fool us. It's Karl Glassman, one of the world's leading tympanists. He socks 'em with the New York Symphony Orchestra.

Harry Pierce

of the Carlson Orchestra, at the Wisconsin Roof, the "World's Largest Ballroom," atop of the Wisconsin Theatre, Milwaukee, has been on this "cream of the city's dance jobs" ever since it opened in March, 1924. Pierce's work is up to date and clever in every detail—the kind that compels dancers to realize the Drummer's importance. He also teaches drums, xylophone and tympani at the Walker Musical Exchange. Harry says —"I have a complete Leedy outfit, Marine Pearl Drums, Xylophone, Pedal Tympani and Chimes. I've tried 'em all and am now set behind Leedy equipment for keeps."
Courtesy Walker Musical Exchange.

"Digging" or "crushing" the sticks down on the drum head undoubtedly fits in some modern musical phrasing, but watch out—don't form the habit, for it certainly does not go at all in the majority of numbers. Lay on your single strokes, both PP and FF, to break yourself of too much "crushing."

Al. Wentzell

of Biloxi, Miss., is well known all along the Gulf coast as a "big timer" in both theatre and ballroom work. He has filled long engagements at the Strand and Crown Theatres, also the Buena Vista Hotel of Biloxi, and the Splendid Cafe at Gulfport. For the past two seasons Wentzell has been a feature with the popular Bertucci's Melody Boys, both in town and at the Hotel Avelez in Biloxi. All Leedy and highly satisfied.

"How many 'rolls' does it take to make a breakfast?"
Hugo Liedke, Fort Worth, Texas.

 **"WORLD'S FINEST DRUMMERS' INSTRUMENTS"**

The Exclusive Drummers' Paper

J. Reg. Kehoe

was formerly with The Musical Kehoes, a big-time act that toured the best in vaudeville, featuring Xylophone. Kehoe is from Columbia, Pa., and is now Drummer and Xylophonist with The Windsor Terrace Orchestra, a high-class road and hotel attraction—last season at the Embassy Club, Atlantic City, and the Melody Club, Philadelphia. Previous to this he made a big hit with his excellent work on the Xylophone, radio broadcasting over WGY, at Schenectady, where he was located with Miss America's Pennsylvanians, an orchestra that toured many Eastern states with Miss Ruth Malcolmson, who was Miss America (1924).

If your left leg were shorter than your right, you couldn't walk with a swing or perfect balance and your feet wouldn't strike the ground evenly. If you don't lift the left stick exactly as high as the right, your left hand is "shorter." Drumming is a *swing* from one stick to the other, *evenly balanced*. Drumming is certainly related to walking. Get it?

A circular motion of a synco wire jazz stick (held in the right hand with the wires of the stick flat against the bass drum head and the handle at a 90° angle) makes a fine effect in certain spots. Light, fast pedal beats (without cymbal) help to vary the "swishing" and also give a realistic effect of wind in trees.

By Anthony A. George, Worcester, Mass.

Dick Lucke

Dick Lucke, who was formerly in charge of the Drum Department of C. G. Conn's, Elkhart, Ind., has worked his way up the ladder of fame until he and his "Arcadians" enjoy the reputation of having no betters among like organizations anywhere in the country. Lucke is a very fine, all-round Drummer of many years' experience, and the "Arcadians" have held many of the coveted jobs in several states. They have been for several months at The Texas Hotel Ballroom, "Top O' Texas," in Fort Worth. Lucke's latest outfit is completely Leedy, furnished by the Adams Music Co. (T. Wilkins, Mgr. Band Inst. Dept.) of Fort Worth, and he states, "The Leedy Floating Head Drum is the Drummer's ideal instrument." He should know, having been so long in the manufacturing and business branch of the game.

Joseph C. Rankin

although only eighteen years of age, is a Xylophonist who holds the "high spots" on the leading vaudeville circuits. He is from Philadelphia, Pa. A newspaper critic of Chicago wrote: "It has been my privilege to listen to many Xylophonists whose chief claim to fame was a brilliant technique, but Joseph Rankin appealed because of the real musical phrasing that was as distinct and delicate as that of a fine violin artist." Rankin was a pupil of the well-known Peter Lewin of Philadelphia. Both Lewin and Rankin prefer Leedy Solo-Tone Xylophones.

The "flapper" slapped his face because she thought his remark insulting, but quickly realized her mistake. The "sheik" was honorably proposing in modern "wise cracking" style. He whispered in her ear: "Darling, let's you and I try to arrange to send our laundry out in the same bundle." It did sound like a dirty suggestion.

The New Leedy Alternating Pedal

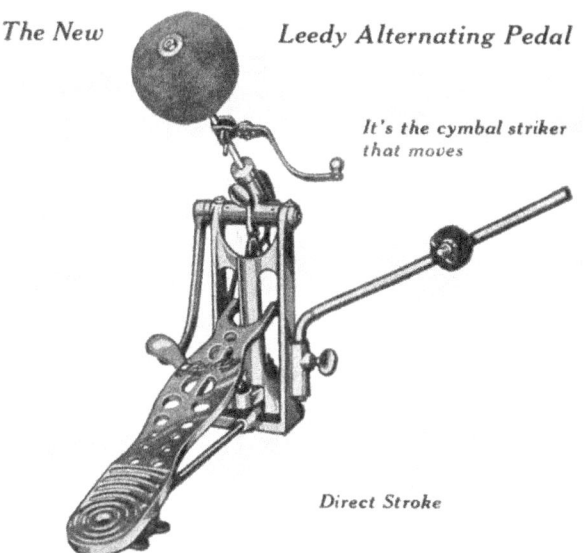

It's the cymbal striker that moves

Direct Stroke

A practical and mechanically perfect pedal that permits the drummer to change instantly from bass drum and cymbal to bass drum alone (or vice versa) for the very next note, no matter how fast the tempo, has long been the desire of the great majority of the profession. Several designs for this accomplishment have been offered from time to time, but none of them have stood the test required of such a pedal. The Leedy Alternating Pedal must be seen and tried to be appreciated, for photographs and a mile of words would not describe its efficiency. It is simplicity itself, inasmuch as the auxiliary lever works direct to the beater rod, turning the rod on the down beat, thereby throwing the cymbal striker slightly back and away from the cymbal. The mechanical action is instantaneous and direct, doing away with all lost motion of former models which contained so many parts. We guarantee no rattle in any part of this model. The pedal itself is the finest ever, one big improvement being that there is no wire link between the footboard and axle. The new connecting link is strip steel, set in bearings, which eliminates all lost motion. Positively the fastest and easiest of all pedals. Make us prove it by trying it out. Wonderful for vaudeville and dance drummers.

No. 276. Pedal complete with Disappearing Spurs........$15.00
No. 275. Pedal only.. 13.50

Albert Amolsch

This small but clever bunch—The Nightingales, of Detroit—is kept busy nightly through the efforts of Albert Amolsch, drummer, owner and manager. Their style of playing most always results in return engagements being booked on the spot. Amolsch is really in the "big time" class as a Drummer, and has had many fine offers, but being a hustler, he prefers to work for himself. He has been made a most enthusiastic Leedy booster by the Bailey Bros. Music House of Detroit, and says: "My Floating Head Drum is my best friend."

"FOR DRUMMERS WHO CARE"

Leedy Drum Topics

S. C. ROWLAND and WURLITZER
Win Favor of Los Angeles Drummers By Way of Professional Understanding and Professional Service

Rowland in action in the Wurlitzer Drum Department, putting over the Leedy line in Los Angeles.

Rowland in action with Dick Stoke's Californians, one of the Coast's popular orchestras.

That Drummers appreciate modern methods of presentation and personal service, just as the average man appreciates the high-class manner of merchandising now in vogue with most staple wares, was recently proven during a most successful Drum Week at the Los Angeles Wurlitzer Music Store, with S. C. Rowland in charge. One of the largest stocks of Drummers' instruments ever assembled, featuring the latest Marine Pearl and Sparkling Gold, with other Beauty finishes, was most artistically arranged on the main floor of the store. Between Monday, February 21st, and Saturday, February 26th, over four hundred drummers, professional and amateur, visited the "show." S. C. Rowland, manager of the Wurlitzer Drum Department, is a "wiz"—that he is responsible for putting it over there is no doubt. The Wurlitzer Co. of Los Angeles believes that "it takes a Drummer to serve a Drummer," and that is the story of the success of this Drum Department in a nutshell. Rowland is a combination of high-class Drummer and business man. He does not try to force sales, but rather lets the Drummer "sell himself" by talking facts in a professional language. Rowland hails from Crawfordsville, Ind., and has put in twelve years behind the drums in first-class vaudeville pits; two years with Fred Jewell, the famous circus bandmaster, and with the Indiana University Concert Band and Orchestra; also Steiner's Collegians, Wabash College Band, and now with Dick Stoke's "Californians," when not in the store. He has been in the merchandising field for the past two years, and his belief that "service comes first," with his original ideas and willingness to work, will carry him to the top.

Wm. H. Gilcher, S. C. Rowland, Joe Gumin

Joe Gumin (on the right) said, "That was some week at Wurlitzer's. We just had to wade through Drums and more Drums. They certainly made the boys feel as though Drums were the most important musical instruments in the world." Gumin is a nationally known feature drummer, who has been with the biggest of them — Eva Tanguay, The James Boys, Joe Howard, Plankington Hotel (Milwaukee), his own band, The Miami Ramblers (Milwaukee), and this season with Sam & Herman Timberg's Rebellion, on Orpheum time. Leedy for fifteen years.

Lang Meredith

Lang Meredith, of the famous Cocoanut Grove Orchestra, at the Ambassador Hotel, said, "If the stunt that Rowland put on at Wurlitzer's doesn't impress the populace of Los Angeles with the importance of the Drummer, I give up. It was the finest thing I ever heard of for the good of all Drummers." Lang is all Leedy equipped, and is one of the "big guns" in the game. His work is nothing short of marvelous. He has been at the drums for many years, and is one popular boy around L. A.

Wm. H. Gilcher

Bill said, "Oh, Boy! If you didn't attend that affair you ain't never attended nothin'! I was there every day. It was a regular Drummers' Convention." And Bill knows a good thing when he sees it, just as everyone west of Chicago knows Bill. "Ain't that so?" He was for many years with the St. Louis Symphony, and for four years with the famous Max Dolin of Frisco, and is, without doubt, one of the finest and most progressive Drummers that ever tickled a triangle. All Leedy, too.

Joey Starr

The Wurlitzer Co. offered a prize of a Leedy Floating Head "Colonial Gold" Drum for the letter best describing the Drum Show. Out of fifty contestants Joey Starr won. Joey is a hustler, and a very efficient drummer. He has been booking his own orchestra for some time, and is a regular feature on Radio KFI. Joey hails from Chicago, and has done several years on the road with musical comedy and modern stage bands. Leedy for ten years.

Danny Cairns

originated in Pittsburg, Kans. (many of the best come from small towns, don't forget that), and played there in the town band and local theatre. Later he went to Chicago, and on the road with musical comedies up to grand opera. He is one of the finest and best-known vaudeville men in the biz. Fifteen years in Chicago, Kansas City and Los Angeles Orpheum houses. Danny said, "I enjoyed the Wurlitzer Drum Show immensely, and am glad the theatre was so close. I spent all my spare time there. I've used Leedy for twenty years—they give service."

Among many other prominent Drummers who attended were Charles L. White, Earl C. Stiles, H. A. Winston, Jay Eslick, Warren Luce, Clarence Orlick, Harry Blanchard, W. F. Deems, E. R. Kaiser, Mack Press, Billy Markas, Waldemar Guterson, E. Owens, J. R. Winn, Ray C. Ebert, W. B. Sherman, Jerry Herdan, Ben Bordens, Eugene Hill, Sonny Clay, Jack Klein, Lloyd Williams, Floyd Burton, Joe Berggren, Leo Sadd, Milton Meyres, Chris. C. Zumberg, B. S. Johnston and H. J. Walter.

Leedy — "WORLD'S FINEST DRUMMERS' INSTRUMENTS" — **Leedy**

The Exclusive Drummers' Paper

Geo. Hamilton Green
An Artist on the Xylophone and an Artist with the Pen

Not content with being an artist on the Xylophone, George now wants to show what he can do with the pen. After looking over his drawing we'll say "the boy is there." Some years ago he was a cartoonist for an Omaha newspaper, and, although he states that he has done no art work for ten years, we believe he has sneaked a little practice now and then. George wrote a letter accompanying this drawing and stated that, "to those who desired the information, he wears a size 8-B shoe." Maybe he does, but he did not wear the 8-B's in this picture. You will note by the sketch in the upper right-hand corner that he also can tell fish stories. Well, now that we know all about his cartooning ability, we are going to put him to work on a lot more. Maybe some of his pupils will have to wait for their lessons, but we are going to get the drawings whether or no.

Geo. Hamilton Green's Instruction Course

Mr. Green's Xylophone and Marimba instruction course by mail now has over fifteen hundred enrollments. He has pupils all over the world and, without exception, every one has claimed great strides in development. In many cases true artists have been produced. The popularity of the Xylophone has only begun. It's a wonderful instrument for doubling, and is the road to greater earnings. Write a letter to his studio in New York City, No. 148 West 46th St., and you will be personally attended to by Geo. Hamilton Green himself. Have you seen his two new Xylophone Folios, No. 1 and No. 2, containing 20 standard numbers arranged for use of any accompaniment, either piano, small or full orchestra? For two and three mallets. Leedy has them in stock.

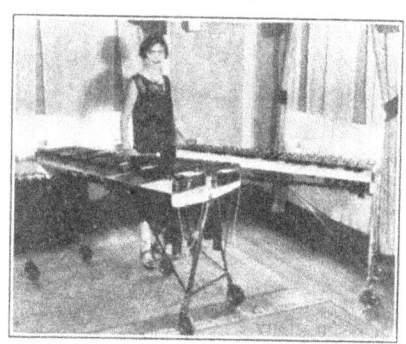

The Street Brothers (William on left, Stanley on right), of Rochester, N. Y., are both members of the Eastman Theatre Orchestra, also the Rochester Philharmonic Orchestra. They are considered among the finest soloists in the profession. Both are pupils of Mr. Green, and recommend his course highly. They also have a large class of students, and teach the Green method. Leedy instruments always used.

D. L. Moody, of Akron, Ohio, is one of the leading Drummers and Xylophonists of that section. He broadcasts regularly over WADC, Akron, and WTAM, Cleveland. Moody writes. "With Leedy instruments and Geo. Hamilton Green's course, any Drummer should be sitting pretty. I have finished the last lesson and consider my playing improved 100%."

Mrs. Henry N. Battjies, of Grand Rapids, Mich., can well be proud of her artistic work on the Xylophone and Marimba. She is a popular radio feature at Grand Rapids, also one of the social leaders of her home city. Mrs. Battjies states, "Mr. Green's course is indeed wonderful. It just makes one play, and it's what I call profitable fun. More ladies should take it up."

Geo. Hamilton Green often visits the Leedy factory and shows a keen interest in the manufacture of Xylophones and Marimbas. He has been through the entire routine as a regular workman. He is here shown with Herman Winterhoff, Vice-Pres. of the Leedy Mfg. Co. and superintendent of this department, "taking a lesson" in drilling bars at the proper angle.

   **"FOR DRUMMERS WHO CARE"**   

Leedy Drum Topics

In England and Scotland

Chas. E. Harris

of London is with one of the finest and most popular bands in England—"Alfredo's"—which has enjoyed a four-year run at the famous Princess Hotel. At present they are doubling with the hotel and "Sunny," a musical comedy hit at the London Hippodrome. Harris added a set of Leedy Pedal Tympani (through Hawkes & Son) to his already Leedyized outfit when George H. Way and Jack Roop of the Leedy Co. were in London last July. Harris is considered a "barometer" of the drum game in London. His excellent work certainly entitles him to this distinction.

Will Hender

has traveled this old world over and has looked in on about everything worth while. He is a native of Australia, where he held down the best positions of the land. Later he took his own musical act to almost every country in Asia, Africa and Europe, finally settling in London, England. Last season he was a spotlight feature on Drums, Tympani and Xylophone with "Mercenary Mary," at the Hippodrome, and this year he has repeated the stunt with "Princess Charming," both Jack Waller productions. Will is one dandy chap to know, and has no betters at the Drums in any country. Notice his gigantic outfit—all Leedy—obtained at the Saxophone Shop, London.

Matt Feggans

has been at the Drums since he was seven years of age, and has filled front rank engagements for many years. He is a true "Scot," being a native of Ayr, which, according to Robert Burns, is famous for "honest men and bonnie lassies." However, we know that Matt is one fine Drummer, 'cause we've heard him "do his stuff." He studied under Jack Humphrey, late of the Second Life Guards and the Alhambra Theatre, London. Feggans now plays at Scotland's leading hotel, the Central, at Glasgow. His entire new Leedy outfit was purchased through The Alexander Biggar Music Co. of Glasgow.

Harry Brooks

of Leeds, Yorkshire, England, is a young chap who looks upon his work as a real serious business proposition and has, therefore, developed originality and skill in his playing. His services are continually in demand amongst the leading jobbing organizations of Leeds. Brooks writes: "The Drummer who uses a Leedy kit can do a better job."

The Prize Story
Comes This Time in the Form of Poetry

Billy Mather, of Derby, England, now in Glasgow, is the "gink" who wrote it. Part of one of his letters reads: "Poetry buds forth in the spring in Scotland, as well as in other countries. Guess it's an international disease." Mather is just "Bill" to all the boys, and a fellow you would be glad to know. When the Leedy representatives were in Glasgow last summer, Bill was on the job every minute, even to lending a hand with the trunks. His assistance and friendliness will long be remembered. He is without question one of the leading Drummers of England and Scotland, and has held many of the elite jobs of London and other cities. A few years ago Bill put in several months at the "trade" with big-name bands in New York City, also eight months on the famous S. S. LEVIATHAN. He is now holding down the most prominent cafe jobs in Glasgow. We didn't want to show the same photo of "Bill" as was printed in the last issue of DRUM TOPICS, so here's one taken down the Clyde

(See next column)

on a "Sunny Sunday"—something rare in Scotland. Anyway, Drummers don't have to work there on the seventh day.

The Most Important Man in the Band
By Billy Mather

Who is the fellow who makes the show go?
Who livens things up when the act's goin' slow?
And stands to be told by a guy who don't know?
    The Drummer!

Who puts in a crash just where crashes belong?
Who hits everything from a drum to a gong?
Who smothers blue notes in a vocalist's song?
    The Drummer!

Who is the fellow who uses his wits?
Who puts in the squawks and the twiddley bits?
And frightens old women and kids into fits?
    The Drummer!

Who is the fellow who steadies the band?
Who puts in the "bump" when the acrobats land?
And never complains if he don't get a hand?
    The Drummer!

Who puts in a crash if he sees half a chance?
Who holds the tempo for the intricate dance?
And wears a dress coat over golf pants?
    The Percussionist!

Who puts in a rattle just like a Ford car?
Or a noise like a battle when heard from afar?
Who treats the boys to a souse at the bar?
    Don't You Believe It!

Who'll play for vaudeville, pictures or dance?
Who'll play any old thing at the very first glance?
If he can't read a note—then who'll take a chance?
    I'll Give You Three Guesses!

Who wears Woolworth glasses and ready-made ties?
Who sticks his music right in front of his eyes?
And if he can't read it—just grins and looks wise?
    You've Guessed It!

Bernard Miller

Beginning when only twelve years old, Bernard Miller turned out to be a "top notcher," and has worked his way up to playing in many of the leading bands of London, including Goodhearts at the Piccadilly Hotel, and Kit Kat Club. He is now with the popular Jeffries Rialto Orchestra at the Locarno Club in Glasgow. All Leedy, through the Alexander Biggar Music Company of Glasgow.

Max Abrams

Max Abrams, of Glasgow, Scotland, decided to take up Drums as a profession when he won first prize at the best Drummer in the Glasgow Battalion Boys' Brigade, at the age of sixteen. He has climbed steadily ever since, and has filled several first-class picture theatre engagements, also two years on the road with high-grade musical comedies. Max is also a fine tympanist. He was the first Drummer in Scotland to own a Leedy Floating Head Marine Pearl snare drum, purchased at the Alexander Biggar Music Co. of Glasgow.

DRUMMERS OF BRITAIN! Remember, DRUM TOPICS is as much for you as for the Drummers on this side. Send in the names of all your drummer friends. DRUM TOPICS will be mailed free every three months.

Leedy   "WORLD'S FINEST DRUMMERS' INSTRUMENTS"   **Leedy**

The Exclusive Drummers' Paper

Leedy Drum Topics

A PAPER DEVOTED TO
THE INTERESTS OF THE DRUMMER

No subscription fee

Advertisements accepted

Published quarterly at 1033 East Palmer Street
Indianapolis, Indiana

Editor .... Geo. H. Way
Business Manager .... A. W. Kuerst

Justa Wethead says—

"There are times when all Drummers have pressing engagements"

Music Store Clerk—"A head for your bass drum? Sure—what size is it?"

Drummer—"I don't know the exact size, but it's about so high."

The above is not supposed to be a joke.

There are Drummers who will not believe that just such an occurrence often happens. If you doubt it, just ask the man behind the counter in most any music store where drummers' supplies are featured.

Knowing it to be quite true, we want to make an appeal to Drummers to learn more about their instruments. The Drummer in the little story above could easily have purchased a head, either too small or too large—in the latter case losing money.

Drum Topics has stated that Drummers were more mechanically inclined than other musicians. And that is true with the majority, but there are thousands who know hardly any of the many interesting mechanical details of "how" and "why" regarding their numerous "tools," just as there are untold numbers of automobile owners who have not the least idea about the engine under the hood. The man who knows all about the engine will get more for his investment and more pleasure from driving it. So it is with the Drummer.

If he knows the exact construction and working principles of the drums and traps he has spent his good money for, he will not only make them give greater service, but he can actually play a better job, because he can make them sound more pleasing to himself and to others.

Every Drummer should know just why his bass or snare drum does not play easily or have the tone he desires. It is not at all hard to study out the true reasons. Every Drummer should make a careful study of head tension—good Tympanists know this to be true. Head tension on snare and bass drums is more important than many believe.

Have you ever noticed that the better Drummers are most often those who can intelligently discuss the many fine points of their instruments? Undoubtedly there are some very fine Drummer Musicians who are not of a mechanical turn of mind, but if they would devote some attention in this direction there is no question but what their work would improve. Their outfit, piece by piece, would be bound to sound better, because it would be in better working condition.

Ask yourself, What is the exact action of the snares? How much do I really know about the snare bed? What thickness of heads suits my style of playing best? Why do certain sticks work better on my drum than others? What takes place inside my drum when it is played upon? What makes a drum ring?

Some Drummers will say, "I know all that." BUT, DO YOU REALLY KNOW?

Hand "Sock" Cymbals

Although this trap has been in use for only a short time, it has been accepted as a "hit" by a great majority of Drummers; in fact, it has been a big problem to make them fast enough. The Hand "Sock" Cymbals were invented by Bill Gladstone, the famous Bass Drummer of the Capitol Theatre, New York. (See page 6, col. 2). They consist of two deep cup brass cymbals, operated by hand-grip aluminum "scissors." The cymbals are permanently attached and strike together flat, producing the very "sock" effect desired. A world of varied effects can be obtained. Will either "sock" or ring. Wonderful for flash work. Many Drummers use them for solo work—one in each hand.

No. 270 .... $8.00

Another Type "Handsock" Cymbals

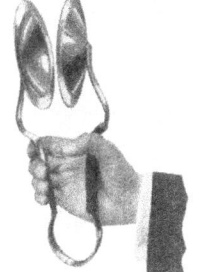 

With Bass Drum Clamp

Here is a different type of "Sock" Cymbals called "HANDSOCK." They are constructed along more simple lines than the ones above, therefore sell at a lower price. Can be used in the hand or while placed in the friction bass drum hoop clamp. A great variety of rhythm can be obtained by holding the cymbals in one hand and striking them with the drum stick, held in the other hand, in conjunction with the "sock" beats of the cymbals.

No. 269. Complete with clamp $3.50

Andy Haak

is leader and manager of his own "Andy Haak's Society Orchestra," of Paterson, N. J., a successful organization made popular by his clever, up-to-date playing and business ability. This orchestra makes extensive tours of the Eastern States, and is a hit everywhere. Haak has also been connected with other well-known New Jersey and New York dance bands, having had nine years' experience in the profession. He says: "Leedy's Drums are certainly the finest to be had."

"FOR DRUMMERS WHO CARE"

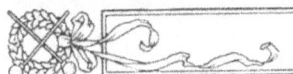 # Leedy Drum Topics

Johnnie Harrison

Johnnie Harrison is one of the boys who has made the most of the opportunities that the present era in music offers to Drummers in particular. Six years ago he organized his own "Broadlawn Orchestra" and by careful business management has brought it to an exceptionally high standing. They have been a feature at The Submarine Ballroom, Kansas City; Louvre Ballroom, Tulsa, Okla.; Sunset Plunge, Tulsa; Broadlawn Inn, Joplin, Mo.; also three seasons at the Connor Hotel, Joplin, and several other fine engagements. Harrison, besides being an efficient business man, is one of the snappiest of Drummers, with a long record of high rating. He says: "Leedy's are best in the long run. You can depend upon them."

In Memoriam

Frank McCarthy, one of the best-known road Drummers in the country, died recently in the Mayo Institute, at Rochester, Minn. He was 45 years of age and had been connected with leading Broadway and traveling musical shows for the past twenty-five years. This season, while on the road with "Rose Marie," he was forced to discontinue work on account of stomach trouble. Mr. McCarthy leaves a wife and two children in Cleveland, where he made his home. Funeral services were held there by the Elks. At one time Frank McCarthy was manager of the Drum Dept. at C. G. Conn, Ltd., Elkhart, Ind.

Reprinted from The Kokomo (Ind.) Daily Tribune. Sent in by Fred E. Albright, Laporte, Ind.

Drummer Is the Real Worker

If you wish an easy job as a musician, be a director. Energy tests recently made in Vienna show that the members of an orchestra who have the softest jobs after the director are the saxophone players and those who coax notes from other brass instruments. Pianists and players of string instruments perform even greater labor, while the Drummer in a band is the real laborer of the organization.

"Another reason why the Drummer should receive more money."

Joe W. Soistman

has been one of Baltimore's leading Drummers for many years. He now works at the Metropolitan Theatre and is also very active in both the Shrine and American Legion Drum Corps; in fact, Joe was responsible for both of these organizations being completely Leedy equipped, through the Kranz-Smith-Hammann-Levin Co., even to a big six-foot bass drum for the Boumi Temple. He is also director of the War Veterans' Drum Corps at the Evergreen School for Blind Soldiers. This is a fine Corps, and Joe deserves great credit for his excellent work.

The new Leedy "Sparkling Gold" finish, as applied to Floating Head snare drums, also bass drums, is of the same material (PYRALIN) as the wonderful Marine Pearl. It is cheaper than the Marine Pearl, however, and many Drummers prefer it. Remember, these types of finishes are positively guaranteed not to crack or chip. They are harder than wood and more durable than any other finish. See page 44 of the new Leedy Catalogue "O."

Why not have your cow bells nickel plated? It makes 'em look snappy. Costs very little. There's a nickel-plating plant near you. DRUM TOPICS has stated several times that cow bells (either "stuffed" or open), when played upon with felt sticks, produce a most pleasing effect. Many Drummers are passing this up. Try it.

Johnny Winn

started out on Drums in 1920 at Phoenix, Ariz., and in 1921 joined the Gene Dabney Orchestra at the American Dance Hall of that city. Not long afterwards Winn's aggressiveness led him to form his own combination, known as "Winn's Wandering Wops." This orchestra made a hit in Mexico City at the Sunset Inn and Hotel St. Regis, where they enjoyed a long run. Later they played the border towns of Juarez, Nogales, Mexicali and Tijuana at leading cafes. For the past two years he has been leader of "Johnny Winn's Moonlight Melody Orchestra," located at Long Beach, Cal., doing the best in jobbing, and at all prominent radio stations in that vicinity. He also plays with the Shell Oil Co. Orchestra. Winn is a top-notch Drummer and Xylophonist.

Next time you break a head on a drum that thoroughly suits you —(snare or batter, bass drum or tympani)—cut the remaining parts up into sample pieces that will fit in your pocket. Use the samples when choosing a new head. By doing this you stand a better chance of getting the drum back to where it was before in respect to tone and "feel" under the sticks.

Jock Davies
Johannesburg, British South Africa

His first name sounds like Scotland. Right—Glasgow is the town where he formerly held down the drum end of things with many leading orchestras. Jock's health forced him to move to South Africa (some jump!) and it was not long before his skillful work became known. He is now a feature Drummer and vocalist with the U. P. C. Orchestras of Johannesburg. He is also well known on the vaudeville stage. Jock was the first Drummer in South Africa to equip himself with Leedy instruments, through the Magnet Music Supply Co. of Johannesburg.

Goof—"Why is a shoulder strap such an important article?"
Goofette—"I crave information."
Goof—"It keeps an attraction from becoming a sensation."
—Mink.

Bruce M. Bristowe

of Prince Albert, Saskatchewan, Canada, is only seventeen years old, and as a pianist has passed with honors all examinations of the Toronto Conservatory of Music. Drums and the Xylophone are his greatest love, however, and there are not many of the "big timers" in the large cities who can outshine his ability. He now plays at the Strand Theatre, also in the Nighthawk Orchestra of Prince Albert. He says: "I bought my Leedy instruments through The Advance Drum Co., at Edmonton, and am thoroughly satisfied."

(Note—The Advance Drum Co. is now called The Advance Music Co., Ltd., and is located at 516 Yonge St., Toronto, Ontario. A. B. Cruchet, Mgr.)

 **"WORLD'S FINEST DRUMMERS' INSTRUMENTS"**

The Exclusive Drummers' Paper

The Perfect Way

There are few musical instruments or parts of musical instruments that cannot be manufactured, by machine methods, into far better products than by the handcraft method. Machined parts are accurate. Once the article is perfected in design, absolutely the same dimensioned parts can be reproduced by machinery, therefore assuring uniformity of quality in each instrument. Machinery is modern: no hand-made part is perfectly true—they are "tailor made," so to speak, and no two instruments can be exactly alike. So, if one tympani bowl is a *best one*, how can another hand-made bowl (when it is not true in its periphery or with the same amount of cubic inches in the air chamber) be as good? All Leedy tympani bowls are absolutely true. They are a machine-made product, drawn over a steel die. They are positively alike.

On the Cover
Jess Altmiller, Philadelphia, Pa.

Most of the "big timers" dislike flowery titles, such as "percussionist," "virtuoso," or "artist." However, to merely describe Jess Altmiller of the Fox Theatre Grand Orchestra (Adolphe S. Kornspan, conductor), at Philadelphia, Pa., as an exceptionally fine Drummer and Tympanist, would not be doing justice, so DRUM TOPICS will follow the many newspapers that have highly praised his work and introduce him to our readers as "one of the country's foremost artists of rhythm." Jess once got a whole column in a prominent Philadelphia paper on his original stunt of tearing up a window shade ("The Window Shade Rip") to the accompaniment of the orchestra. It was a riot, and he has been called upon to repeat it several times. He began playing drums when only ten years old at Hazelton, Pa., in the town band. When only fifteen he trouped with a musical show, and later filled many prominent vaudeville and musical comedy engagements in New York City, also several seasons at the Garden Pier, Atlantic City. Ten years ago he located in Philadelphia and has remained there ever since, taking over the chief position in the drum section of the renowned Fox Theatre Grand Orchestra three years ago. The public, as well as the musicians, know him, as he is ever in the spotlight with something new concocted from his ever active and creative mind. Yes, Jess is an artist *in the true sense of the word*—an artist on Drums, Tympani, Xylophone, and all the novelties. He is a great credit to the game, for his wonderful skill and good fellowship is an example that instils ambition in other Drummers and raises the plane of our profession.

NAT MAURIZIO
Fox Theatre Grand Orchestra
Philadelphia, Pa.

The photo at left shows a fine likeness of Nat Maurizio, whose excellent work on the bass drum at the Fox Theatre in Philadelphia has, like that of Jess Altmiller, brought forth several praiseworthy newspaper comments, one of which reads in part: "Most anyone can hammer the side of a giant bass drum in a bang-bang, hodge-podge fashion, but it requires the technique of a skilled musician like Nat Maurizio to pat the big drum and make it whisper like a breeze, then punish it in a most artistic manner until it roars out as the leader to a storm of instruments in a wild overture." Nat's home town is Abruzzi, Italy, where, after showing exceptional skill, he was admitted to the Maruccini Opera House. He came to America in 1910 and played for seven seasons at the Wildwood Crest Pier. Then followed several seasons with the famous Creatore's Band; then he joined the Philadelphia Municipal Band, and finally went to the Fox Theatre in 1923.

Both Altmiller and Maurizio are staunch advocates of Leedy Instruments and play them exclusively.

You may not need to play the "Rudiments" to hold your job and get the money, BUT if you learn to execute them properly your work will improve and make you a better Drummer.

Springfield, Ohio, Shrine Drum Corps
(Unit of Antioch Temple, Dayton, Ohio)

Here's a "rip snortin' bunch" that makes those on the side lines cheer as they step by. The next convention at Atlantic City in June will hear and see plenty of this snappy outfit, as it is reported they are getting better with each rehearsal. The first Drummer and instructor (first row, left) is F. B. Ridley. In the second row (extreme left) is E. Robert Hawken of the Earle K. Hawken & Sons Music Store at Springfield.

Simon Brown

is Drummer and Tympanist with the famous Charles Hector Orchestra at Loew's Orpheum Theatre, Boston, Mass. Brown's skill at the Drums has won him high recognition among those who know in Boston. He has had many years' experience and held down several of the city's leading positions. Brown is high in praise of his Leedy Pedal Tympani.

(Courtesy Conn-Boston Co.)

Jimmie Todd

This map of Jimmie Todd was taken when he was with the Sells-Floto Circus. Jimmie's home is in Albion, Nebraska, but he is now at the New Capitol Theatre in Grand Island, Nebraska. He has trouped with several of the best Western Repertoire Shows and also played in several middle-west vaudeville theatres. A thorough, all-around A-1 Drummer of ten years' experience. He writes—"I use Leedy drums because I have been convinced they are better."

Have you seen the new White Pyralin (Friscoe model) Xylophone and Bell Mallets? Balls are 1⅓ inch in diameter, made of pure white Pyralin, a material much more durable than vulcanized rubber. See page 52 of the new Leedy catalog "O", No. 370-F.

Per Pair $1.00

Joseph D. Sefchick

is well known in both Eastern and Western Massachusetts as a thorough, all-around Drummer. He has had fifteen years of varied experience in vaudeville pits, symphony orchestras, ballrooms, picture theatres, military bands and even to three seasons as a first-rate solo xylophone vaudeville act, also a season with Paul Garin in San Francisco and, while in that city, Mr. Sefchick studied under Doc Willats. He hails from Hartford, Conn., but now makes his home in Holyoke, Mass., where he has been playing for four years at the Hotel Nomatuck. He recently finished George Hamilton Green's xylophone course and highly recommends it to his large class of pupils. Joe writes—"I've tried them all and always go back to Leedy."

Leedy "FOR DRUMMERS WHO CARE" *Leedy*

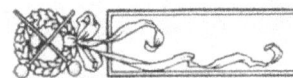
Leedy Drum Topics

Robert L. McMahan

Robert L. McMahan is now at the Liberty Theatre in Youngstown, Ohio, playing stage presentations under the direction of Ted Hall. One glance at McMahan's photo will tell more than words that he is of the class that knows how to sell his wares—appearance and style. He is also a fine xylophonist and has played on almost every job that Youngstown has to offer, including ballrooms, vaudeville, summer resorts, road shows, and band work. In all branches he is favorably known for his clever, creative ability. Note his fine outfit of Leedy equipment.

The man who carries his currency loose in his pocket will win every time in an argument over the payment of the dinner check.

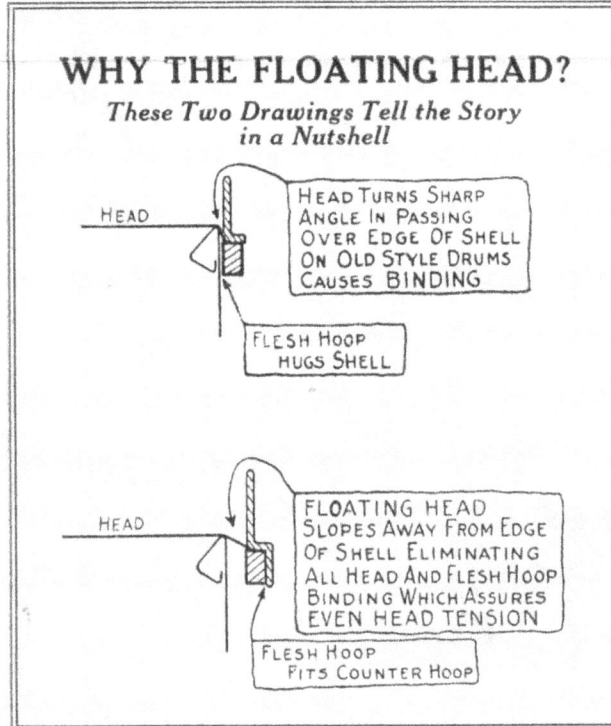

Leedy has just issued a new two-color, twelve-page Xylophone, Marimba, and Vibraphone booklet. Did your dealer give you one? If not, drop us a postal and we'll be glad to mail you one free. It's a beauty and shows photos of many prominent professionals.

Drill a small hole in the heavy end of an alto saxophone reed. Tie a piece of a good grade of cord, about eight inches long, to the reed and fasten the other end around your drum rod. Shove the reed under the snares to kill any sympathetic vibration of other instruments. You can jump from tymps to snare drum with great speed by simply pulling out the reed with a jerk at the cord with your drum stick.

By Fred S. Paine, Detroit Symphony Orchestra.

Art Layfield, the famous star Drummer with Paul Ash and his Merry Mad Gang, Oriental Theatre, Chicago, is going stronger than ever. You have to make an appointment to catch this lad. He's on the hop every minute. Not content with being manager of the Gang, also rehearsing and going home to see friend wife at least once a day, he takes on about a dozen pupils, and now he doesn't even have time to write letters.

A Drum Over One Hundred and Fifty Years Old

Knowing that most Drummers are interested in historical drums, DRUM TOPICS has been making a special effort to dig up some real old-timers. The last issue showed a group of seven real European prizes, and now we have found, after following up "clews" from all over the country, one of the most interesting instruments on record, and we believe it is the oldest drum known to be associated with the history of the good old U. S. A. Strange to say, it was located within fifteen miles of the World's Largest Drum Factory.

This drum was used to sound army calls for the Colonial troops from 1776 to 1778, and it gave the signal to charge in many a hard-fought battle of the Revolution. It was first carried by Timothy Church, a Drummer and loyal son of Connecticut, who joined his comrades of the Colonies in the revolt against King George III. He and the drum were important factors in the famous battle of Saratoga and various other engagements incident to the Colonies' invasion of Canada, where he was captured by the British and imprisoned at Nova Scotia. There he died of smallpox. The drum was recovered by his brother, John Church, who had fought by Timothy's side, and was likewise imprisoned. It was this brother who assisted Benedict Arnold from his horse after being struck by a British musket ball. John returned home to Connecticut, after being released from prison, and took the drum with him. It has been handed down in the family ever since. John passed it to his son Isaac, who was born in 1790, who in turn gave it to his son, George W. Church, born in 1814. When grown to manhood George moved from Connecticut to Erie, Pa., and in 1845 moved again to Marion County, Indiana.

In 1855 the drum passed to the present owner, Joseph W. Church, when he was one year old. The accompanying photo shows Mr. J. W. Church, who is now 73 years old, holding this historical Drum, and it was he who kindly supplied this data and gave DRUM TOPICS permission to take these photographs. The shell of the drum is 15 by 13½ inches, made of solid maple, which proves the worth of this type of construction. It has one-inch reinforcing hoops, and the shell is joined with glue and hand-made tacks (not the brass tacks that were used on drums of the 1800 period). One of the most interesting things about this old instrument is that the heads and snares are the same ones that were on it at the time of Timothy's imprisonment at Nova Scotia. The snare head is badly broken, while the batter is intact. However, both are yellow and brittle from age and would not stand much handling. A beautiful poem was written by Samuel McCoy and dedicated to this glorious old drum which played such a stirring part in the nation's history.

 "WORLD'S FINEST DRUMMERS' INSTRUMENTS"

The Exclusive Drummers' Paper

Edward Archambeault

Edward Archambeault is manager and Drummer of the Biltmore Radio Orchestra—a most popular combination doing the best class of work in and about New Bedford, Mass. Archambeault is a progressive Drummer who "sells" his ability in a manner that commands attention. He has been in the business nine years and has held several fine jobs, some of which were in Chicago and Eastern Canada. One of his letters in part reads—"You may quote me as saying that Leedy Drums have no equal."

Bill Dey

of Moose Jaw, Saskatchewan, Canada, is called "The Singing Drummer." Both his vocal work and ability at the Drums have been big factors in making Art Fulford's Orchestra one of the most popular in Western Canada. He writes—"I like Leedy drums best after trying many makes."

Courtesy The Advance Music Co., Ltd., 516 Yonge St., Toronto, Ont., Canada.

Albert Serpico

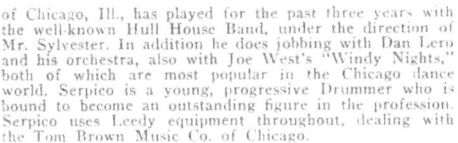

of Chicago, Ill., has played for the past three years with the well-known Hull House Band, under the direction of Mr. Sylvester. In addition he does jobbing with Dan Lero and his orchestra, also with Joe West's "Windy Nights," both of which are most popular in the Chicago dance world. Serpico is a young, progressive Drummer who is bound to become an outstanding figure in the profession. Serpico uses Leedy equipment throughout, dealing with the Tom Brown Music Co. of Chicago.

Chas. H. Dill, Jr.

of Missoula, Montana, is another college man whose clever work at the drums has not only made him a most popular boy, but brought him real money as well. He now plays with the University of Montana Band and The Nightingales Ballroom Orchestra. The latter is in big demand all over Western Montana. Dill played formerly at Hamilton, Montana, with The Harmony Four, The Footwarmers and The Daffy Dill Gang. Several reports give him big-time honors.

Did you ever notice the wonderful improvement in a Drummer's technique on a baby cry—after he has become a father?

If you have two large pieces of broken Chinese or Turkish cymbals, shove them (lying together) under your bass drum rod. Fine for stop time, afterbeat, cracked cymbal and breaks.

Another good effect is gotten by laying a Turkish cymbal (face up) on your tympani and using a medium soft stick and using the left hand for stop time, etc.
*Sent in by Bud Ebel,
Omer Hick's Orchestra, enroute.*

M. J. Romaine

formerly of Cherryvale, Kan., is now on the road with The Squashville Jazz Band, playing the principal vaudeville circuits. Romaine has been in the business twelve years, always using Leedy. He has had vaudeville, movie, road show, ballroom and stage presentation experience and is very highly rated. At one time he was located at Morgantown, W. Va., and Jefferson City, Mo.

Geo. W. Marsh, the wonder Drummer of the Paul Whiteman Orchestra, says he's glad to be back on Broadway. Whiteman's wonderful success at his new night club leads one to believe George will be there for a long time. He says his new "Sparkling Gold" drums are the admiration of many of the New York Drummers, and that several of the boys have now adopted them through the Frank Wolf Drum Shop.

Our New Addition—Business Demanded It

This new addition, now in progress, will add 20,000 square feet of floor space to the present Leedy factory. The photo shows only one-half of the building to be erected and only three of the four floors. The wooden structure (not the sheds) between the new part and the main building will be removed and another section will be constructed on this site. This will make the new addition 96 feet by 50 feet. Leedy's has been the largest Drum Factory in the world for many years. It will soon be twice as large as any other.

The Leedy Shipping Room Force

Left to right—Chas. A. Kerr (Chief Clerk), Elmer G. Servies, Marshall Wilkins, Bennie McElfresh, William Borror and John C. Sheek.

Well, that's that!
Hope you enjoyed looking this edition over—
Don't forget to send us your new address—
Keep working—you never know what's just around the corner—
See you next time—

"FOR DRUMMERS WHO CARE"

DRUM TOPICS

The Exclusive Drummers' Magazine

APRIL, 1927

FOURTEENTH EDITION

POSTMASTER—Return Postage Guaranteed

Leedy Manufacturing Co.
INDIANAPOLIS, INDIANA

Joe Green's Novelty Marimba Band is hailed as one of the most sensational hits ever presented to New York audiences. Left to right—K. Whitmer, Joe Green, Larry Abbott, K. Pitman, "Happy" Riese, Jack Shilkret, Wm. Dorn, Paul Farmer, Wm. E. Pharo—all prominent phonograph recording and radio stars. The band will soon make a tour of the country's leading movie theatres. Leedy Drums, Xylophones, Vibraphone and Marimbas.

Leedy Drum Topics

They used to take it easy

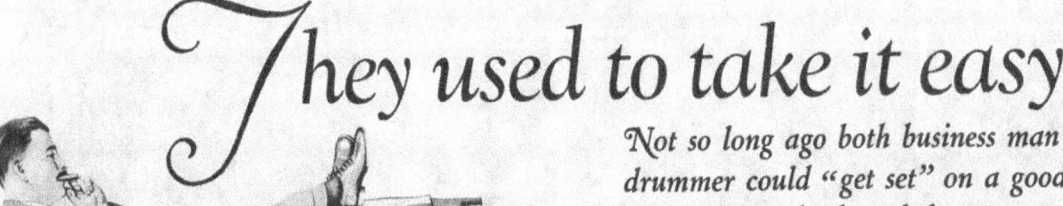

Not so long ago both business man and drummer could "get set" on a good job then lean back and do a lot of "afterbeating."

THEY can't do it today. Times have changed. Things move fast. The public is boss and demands radical changes overnight. The business man who thinks he has a good thing this week may find it dying on his hands the next. He is licked unless he is of the new-day type who can quickly scrap the old product or method and wholeheartedly adopt the new. Some stubbornly hang on to the old. Some accept the new, but with a spirit that hinders. Others grasp the public's desires and reap a harvest while popularity rules. The man who anticipates is a still greater success. Remember the automobile man who scoffed at balloon tires? Those who acted quickly and without bucking are now the leaders in that game.

Remember when the ice man was "sittin' pretty?" No one ever thought his position could be shaken. Then along came electric refrigeration. Now watch the live ones "get with it," selling and boosting the new. There are thousands of like examples.

AND so must the Drummer be of the new-day type. He can no longer "one stick" it or lean back behind an obsolete "percussion pile." Neither can he scoff at the latest effect. The public has been educated to the Drummer's worth and expects him to "do his stuff" and make a real showing. More and more music, viz.: Phonographs, Radios, and traveling bands, have let the public know, so woe be unto the Drummer who fights their ever-changing tastes or thinks it unnecessary to equip himself with the best sounding and finest appearing instruments that money can buy. Some Drummers hesitated to "put in" the wire brushes when they first came to life as an effect. Others held back on new cymbal stunts and there are still a few who can't yet see Temple Blocks. The fellow who looks upon things new as an opportunity to increase his earnings is the fellow who is working every day. How do YOU react toward the new? Do you take it easy?

THE COMING SEASON—certainly "reads" and "listens" big. If only half of the recent reports regarding planned activities of musical organizations come to life, there will be many more on the road this fall. Theatrical papers all state that there is to be a big demand for good stage bands on the various circuits. Drummers in the larger cities are all talking about new jobs. Each one seems to have something encouraging on tap. Good, let the cymbals sock.

How Do You Like Drum Topics' New Uniform?

Pretty? The little ole' "Exclusive Drummers' Paper" is growing like a weed and we were forced to print another ten thousand, so thought it would be a good idea to dress it up a bit. This issue is larger and more expensive, as you can readily see, and now we print sixty thousand. Don't forget—it's your paper. Write in. Send photos. Compete for the prize story. Be sure to let us know when you change your address. It's free, and if you don't receive it don't blame us. Published every three months.

"WORLD'S FINEST DRUMMERS' INSTRUMENTS"

Leedy   Page Two   *Leedy*

The Exclusive Drummers' Paper

Geo. W. Marsh now with Isham Jones

The Coming Season

Readers of Drum Topics are invited to become personally acquainted with these famous Drummers (names below). When they visit your city just step up and introduce yourself and mention Drum Topics. You will find them to be "regular" in every respect—no "high hat" stuff. They expect you, having agreed to this announcement so don't be backward. It's your opportunity to meet some of the "big timers" and who knows but what you might pick up some really good ideas for your work.

HAROLD MCDONALD...................PAUL WHITEMAN'S ORCHESTRA
ARTHUR LAYFIELD...........................PAUL ASH ORCHESTRA
GEO. MARSH.............................ISHAM JONES ORCHESTRA
GUS HELMECKE }
HOWARD GOULDEN } ....SOUSA'S BAND
FRANK HOLT }
BILL KESSLER.......................VINCENT LOPEZ ORCHESTRA
BILL KIEFFER }
CHAS. VINER } ....U. S. MARINE BAND
JOHNNY AUER }
CHAUNCEY MOOREHOUSE.................JENE GOLDKETT'S ORCHESTRA

Get ahead by all means, but not by any means.

It will undoubtedly interest hundreds of Drummers all over the country to learn that the congenial George, who has been with Paul Whiteman for the past five years, recently transferred his activities to the Isham Jones organization. The new Jones Band is indeed one of the country's finest, being composed of such men as Secrist, Walker, Muller, Martin, Maxim, Baker and several others. Great things are predicted for them. Already they have made a tour of the leading photo playhouses and were an outstanding hit in each city. Marsh is, without question, one of the best known Drummers in the business. He traveled almost continually while with Whiteman from coast to coast and back several times, and also made a four months tour of Europe. His pleasing personality and large measure of good fellowship has made a host of friends in every State, for George is never too busy even on one night stands to chat with all the boys who come around. In every town he has many visitors. His latest outfit consists of Leedy Sparkling Gold Drums (Leedy Catalog "O" page 44), and he claims they are the most beautiful appearing and best toned instrument he has ever owned.

Buzzzzzzzzzzzz!

Fizzle—"Say Bo! Where did you get such a fine roll?"
Sizzle—"Well, you see, kid, it's like this—I inherited it, my father was a sand paper manufacturer."

Improving Gut Snares

The fact that shellacing gut snares will improve their crispiness, etc., is an old story. Drummers have been doing it for many years with more or less good results. For those who have NOT had good results we give the following correct method: Make a mixture of two-thirds clear (not orange) shellac and one-third linseed oil. The oil prevents the shellac from drying too quickly and gives it greater penetrating qualities. Dampen a piece of cotton cloth with this solution and rub it into the gut, using even sweeps. It is best to buy the gut in the one piece twenty-foot coils for this purpose and string it up for rubbing. Let it remain there for a week, rubbing at least twice a day. More often if possible; but allow to dry one hour between times. If this method is followed out, you will have the best snares it is possible to obtain. They will be hard, smooth, and at the same time flexible, all of which insures them laying flat to the head and being extremely sensitive. If the gut is at all rough, rub it down with very fine sandpaper before applying the shellac and oil.

Frank Holt—Sousa's Band

'roof that the Drummer who lets no grass grow under his feet cannot help but progress, is most emphatically pointed out in the personage of Frank Holt of Haverhill, Mass.
He has been in the business twenty-one years on such jobs as Empire Theatre, Lawrence, Mass.; Pentucket Concert Orchestra, Haverhill; Casino, Hampton Beach, N. H.; Academy of Music, Haverhill; Chicks Concert Band, York Beach, Me.; Haverhill Masonic Band, and many others. He started with one of the country's prominent masters, Frank A. Snow, also W. T. Maloney, of the famous Stone Drum School of Boston. Exceptionally fine work has carried him to the top of the ladder—the past two seasons with Sousa. For eight years Holt has operated the Holt Drum Shop at 27 Daggett Bldg., Haverhill, and is enjoying a fine business from all over the Northeastern States. Holt says: "I use the Leedy Floating Head Drum because I am thoroughly sold on its being the best to be had."

Bill Kessler, of the Vincent Lopez Orchestra, Introduces Two Novel Effects

Bill Kessler (left) and Vincent Lopez visit the Leedy Factory.

The only reason that Drum Topics has never before published photos and data concerning Bill Kessler is simply because we haven't had the "dope." He just wouldn't come through, but when we last met up with him there was no escaping our camera. Bill offstage is one of those modest chaps, but onstage he is more than half the show. He is a born and bred New Yorker and has spent the greater part of his professional career, covering fifteen years, in that city. After playing many seasons on the leading jobs, the war broke out and Bill enlisted in the Navy and was stationed with the Navy Yard Band at Washington, D. C. After the war he played with Nathan Franko at the Claridge Hotel and later jobbed for those well known leaders, Markel and Conrad. For the last five years Kessler has been with Vincent Lopez, where his artistic work has helped toward making this orchestra a most famous organization. Kessler is noted for his originality and lightninglike speed. Below are two specially posed photos of two of his latest stunts. "Sticking the Slap-Stick" is not difficult to do, but it is most effective, inasmuch as the slap-stick itself produces one tone while the contact of the stick produces another.
Use a Leedy large size slap-stick No. 291A cut off about four inches. A midget slap-stick No. 18A is also good but it is best to substitute a plain spring in place of the hinge type now in use. These can easily be changed as all hardware stores carry these small hinges.
The photo at the bottom shows the method of producing a most wonderful effect for hot numbers. Bill calls it the "Bath Tub Sock," because it sounds exactly like pounding a large metal bath tub with a croquet mallet. Simply lay a Turkish or Italian Cymbal face down on the small Tympani tuned to approximately "D." Keep the cymbal a couple of inches away from the edge of the kettle. Play with a hard felt hammer, striking cymbal halfway between the cup and edge, using the left hand for cut-offs. Nothing as good as this for cutting through with accents in a loud red hot tune. Kessler is completely Leedy equipped, including chimes, machine Tympani, Sparkling Gold Drums, etc., and says, —"I am convinced that I can do better work on Leedy Drums. The Floating Head Snare Drum is certainly miles ahead of any other model."

Lopez speaking—

"I am fully convinced that the Leedy Mfg. Co. turns out the finest percussion instruments to be obtained."

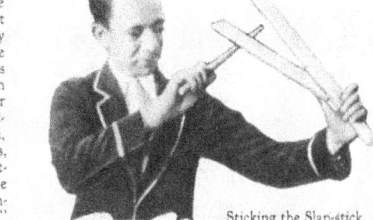

Sticking the Slap-stick

The Bath Tub Sock

"FOR DRUMMERS WHO CARE"

Leedy Drum Topics

In Detroit

Former issues of Drum Topics have contained lengthy stories concerning the three celebrities in this photo—left to right, Fred S. Paine (Detroit Symphony Orchestra and WWJ radio), Geo. Hamilton Green (Famous Victor Phonograph Star), and Chauncey E. Morehouse (Jean Goldkett's Orchestra). The photo was taken in the Statler Hotel, Detroit, last April during Mr. Green's four day demonstration of Leedy Xylophones, Marimbas and the Vibraphone. Professionals came from all over Michigan and Ohio to hear his marvelous playing, and every one of the four hundred visitors expressed great pleasure at the opportunity of meeting him personally.

(Courtesy—Bailey Bros. Music House)

Moe Spivack

Here is a hustling New York City Drummer who makes the most of the many hours outside of actual playing. Besides his duties at the Arcadia Ballroom with the well known Geo. Hall Orchestra, Moe is associated with the Karl Glassman School of Drums and Tympani—now located in the Gaiety Theatre Building. There he acts as Mr. Glassman's assistant and often teaches right up to the hour of having to report at the Arcadia. Moe is not only a wonderful dance man, but has had many years' experience in all other lines of the better class of New York jobs.

(Courtesy—Frank Wolf Drum Shop)

A Good Airplane Effect

Buy an ordinary electric door bell. A good one can be obtained for a dollar and a half. Take off the bell and hold the striker close to your bass drum head. By moving it around and placing at different distances from the head, loud and soft effects can be produced that give a realistic imitation of an airplane motor. Another method is to attach the striker to the wall and hold a snare drum (without snares) up to the bell tapper.

Rudy Starita

Almost everyone in the business knows of the wonderful success that has come to Al. Starita (brother of Rudy Starita), leader of the famous Kit Kat Club Band in London. Last February Rudy sailed to join Al. and from all reports has certainly "put it over"—over there. He was formerly with Mal Hallett at "Roseland" in New York. Rudy hails from Boston and is conceded to be one of the very best drummers in the business. He uses Leedy instruments exclusively and is equipped with the "whole works" from triangle to Vibraphone.

(Courtesy—Conn-Boston Co.)

Tympani were first used in an orchestra in 1765 by Lully of France.

Did you ever see a Drummer swing his right stick in little circles? This is a bad habit. It eliminates the decisive blow. The stick should travel straight up and down.

It's an ill wind that a Drummer can't imitate

Here lies the body of Sim Bell—
Jazz tapping hands were these,
Close rolls was his specialty,
But 'twas rolls close to their knees.

Carl Gardner

It is hard to imagine a single Drummer in any English speaking country who is not familiar with the name of Carl Gardner. Thousands owe the bulk of their professional knowledge to him, by way of the many Carl Gardner instruction books, published by Carl Fisher of New York (sold by Leedy). His record is indeed interesting. Studied music at Harvard University, thirteen years with the famous old Boston Theatre Orchestra, many seasons Drummer and Tympanist of the Boston Symphony Orchestra, President of the Boston Musicians' Protective Association, 1923-24, Xylophone soloist in Vaudeville, trouped with Comic Opera, also Grand Opera, and several leading concert bands and orchestras. Now connected with Music Department of Boston Public Schools and contributing excellent articles to many musical journals.

The "High Hat" Sock Cymbal Pedal—

This new trap will soon be a part of every Drummer's outfit. It is almost as important in modern playing as the snare drum itself. Unequaled for all manner of cymbal effects. For single crashes it has all the utility of any other holder. Sizzle effects are easily obtained by holding the two cymbals together with a light pressure of the foot, then you can have "free" cymbals for tap work instantly by releasing the foot. Stick work can be combined with quick "Socks" of any degree desired. "Cut-offs" are ever at your command without having to use the hand. Just the right height. Adjustable to length of stroke. Any make or size of cymbals can be used. Folds compactly. A great flash. (Cymbals not included.) Ask for No. 272.

It's Human Nature

He was playing in a sluggish, lazy fashion. Suddenly he burst forth socking everything within reach. Pep galore. The Leader thought he had sneaked a drink or two. Nothing of the kind. He had simply spotted another drummer in the audience.

Bernie B. Wells

has been holding down the principal jobs of Louisville, Ky., his home city, for twenty years. While he has specialized in theatre work, he is experienced in all lines and has the "rep" of being an A-1 all round Drummer on every instrument. Now at B. F. Keith's RIALTO (Vaudeville). Wells writes: "For theatre work, where one must have double forte and double pianissimo with instant succession, there is no drum to be compared with the Leedy Floating Head Model."

(Courtesy—Durlauf and Berry)

"WORLD'S FINEST DRUMMERS' INSTRUMENTS"

The Exclusive Drummers' Paper

A Point to Watch

Many beginners unconsciously make the mistake of sitting either too close to the bass drum or too far away. Those who form one or the other of these habits do not realize that they are forcing the calf of the leg and instep of the foot to do a lot of unnecessary labor in operating the pedal. Either of these positions prevents relaxation of the muscles and limits the Drummer's foot action. Perhaps you have been doing this. Take notice. You can soon tell by moving your chair backward and forward. Locate the middle distance best suited to the length of your leg. Then you'll get more out of your pedal.

Hoop Adapters

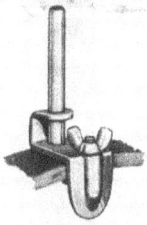

These handy little "gadgets" have many practical uses. Just the thing to slip on your Bass Drum hoop to hold that extra trap when needed on short notice. All the holders for Trap Tree, Trap Table and Trap Console will fit the Hoop Adapter. Ask for No. 250.

Charles Herstoff

Charles Herstoff of New Bedford, Mass., has been a feature Leedy Drummer with several A-1 modern Bands, viz.—Al. Stone's Melody Boys—Max Pfeilmaier's Band of Philadelphia—Aunt Jemima Band in Vaudeville—and Alex Hyde's Orchestra of New York with a year in Berlin, Germany. Herstoff is now on his second trip to Europe with the Joseph Fouch Band, the "Paul Whiteman of Germany." A real talented worker, this boy, and one that makes a hit on every job.

If you are weak on reading, better do a little "woodshedding." Jazz is improving and leaders are beginning to want those "off beats" where the composer intended them.

"Dusty" Roades and Ted Weems

When "Dusty" trouped the Keith and Orpheum Circuits with the S.S. Leviathan Orchestra, he made many staunch Drummer friends from Maine to California. Three years ago he joined the Ted Weems famous phonograph recording band and after a season at the Muehlebach Hotel in Kansas City they did the rounds of the best theatres. They are now located at the Baker Hotel in Dallas, Texas, and literally "cleaning up." "Dusty" is a high class entertainer and singer, but this does not mean that his work on the drums is lacking. Far be it—for he not only ranks with the best, but has introduced many original effects. Note his new Leedy outfit and read the following letter from the Baker Hotel Assistant Manager. Some job, this—

> **THE BAKER HOTELS OF TEXAS**
> DALLAS, TEXAS
> June 14th, 1927.
>
> Leedy Manufacturing Co., Inc.,
> Indianapolis, Indiana.
>
> Gentlemen:
>
> Ted Weems and his orchestra are now playing an engagement here at The Baker and Saturday Dusty Roades, the drummer, received a shipment of drums and a new instrument called a Vibraphone; and I am writing this letter to let you know that we are very much pleased with this outfit.
>
> We have had several orchestras in the hotel, but must say that with this equipment this orchestra stands out far above any we have had. You have certainly turned out a wonderful job and you are to be congratulated on the results.
>
> Yours very truly,
> THE BAKER HOTEL
> By H. H. Hudson
> Assistant Manager.

In Kazatshinsk

Yes, there's drummers everywhere. Get out your map and look up the Yenisei River in Northern central Siberia, Asia. Then trace the River from its mouth in the Arctic Sea down south to the Siberian Railway. There you will find the little town of Kazatshinsk near Yeniseisk. That's where the above photo was taken. The three Drummers are the local Drum Corps out to entertain the natives during a festival. The drums have no snares and are beaten on both sides with cane sticks. We'll bet they tickle a wicked "open roll."

Special Notice

Drum Topics is pleased to announce the following service for its readers. By special arrangement the Leedy Manufacturing Company have entered into an agreement with Karl Glassman (tympanist of the New York Symphony Orchestra, Walter Damrosch, Conductor) whereby Drummers may write to Mr. Glassman for advice regarding the proper technique of Drumming and Tympani playing. Mr. Glassman is one of the country's foremost artists on Drums and Tympani and we know that this rare opportunity will benefit hundreds of both professionals and amateurs, who undoubtedly have many questions in mind. There is no charge for the service. Write, enclosing a self-addressed and stamped envelope to

KARL GLASSMAN,
Gaiety Theatre Bldg.,
46th St. and Broadway,
New York City, N. Y.

FRANK WOLF (left) and KARL GLASSMAN visit the Leedy Factory—Frank Wolf is one of New York's foremost Drummers. He operates a complete Leedy Drum Shop at 233 W. 46th Street.

Problem

Q.—If a girl sits opposite you in a street car and crosses her legs, with her skirts just above her knee, what does it make you think of?
A.—Her.

"Ain't It the Truth?"

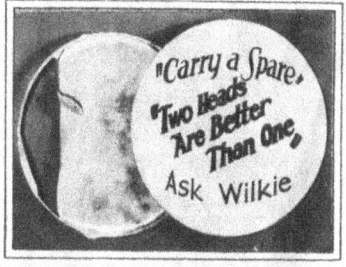

This is a photo of two drum heads that hang over the counter in the Bailey Brothers Music House, "The Drummers' Service Station" at Detroit, Michigan. The sign is painted on a Leedy "Hard white" head tucked on a Leedy metal flesh hoop. Wilkie is the popular and efficient drummer manager of Bailey Brothers.

"FOR DRUMMERS WHO CARE"

Leedy Drum Topics

About Banners

If you want one or more special banners made for your band, write to

Bradford & Co., Inc.
St. Joseph, Michigan

They do fine work and quote reasonable prices.

Anyone who tells us what is wrong and helps us make it right is a friend.

Henry Raymat, Jr.

is duly recognized as one of the leading Drummers of Havana, Cuba. His several years of active professional experience has carried him into every branch of the business. Raymat makes a specialty of teaching and has a very large class of pupils.

Miss Louise Custenborder

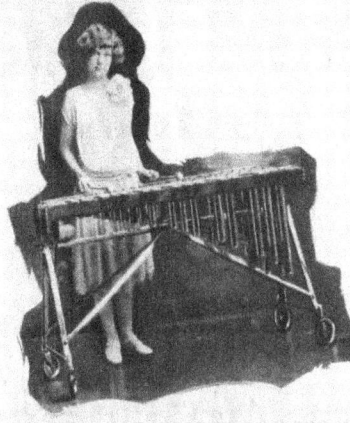

Miss Louise Custenborder, of Lima, Ohio, is a talented pianist as well as a thorough all-round drummer, even to Tympani. Recently she added a Leedy Vibraphone to her equipment, which has resulted in a constant demand for her services in the leading social circles of Lima, also in the Lima Symphony Orchestra, of which she will become a permanent member this season. Miss Custenborder is a pupil of Joseph DuPere.

Lois Moran — Norman Kerry — William Beandine

Here they are. Two famous Universal Movie Stars with their equally famous director, making a little noise on Leedy Instruments, about their latest and greatest hit, "Too Many Women."
(Courtesy S. C. Rowland, of the Rudolph Wurlitzer Co., Los Angeles, Cal.)

Double End Sticks

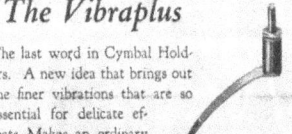

This new model eliminates several "stick worries." No matter how they are laid aside when making changes, they always "come back" in the correct position. This saves time where time is needed. Another feature is—you are never "stuck" in the middle of a number because of tip breakage. The idea was conceived by E. O. Roark of the Kansas City Symphony Orchestra. We hope to show his photo in the near future and tell our readers about this well known and clever Drummer.
Ask for No. 376B.

It should cost every dance leader from three to five dollars additional when he insists upon a Drummer taking the "whole works" out on a one night stand.

The Vibraplus

The last word in Cymbal Holders. A new idea that brings out the finer vibrations that are so essential for delicate effects. Makes an ordinary cymbal sound better and a Zildjian on the Vibraplus is a joy to any orchestra. Cymbal cannot touch metal. Adjustable to every needed position.
Ask for No. 648.

Joe Jacobs

is now at the Madison Theatre in Peoria, Illinois. This is one of the first class houses of the city, and Jacobs holds down the Drum Section with more than ordinary ability. He is considered a real artist. An "old timer" of thirty-four years' experience, covering everything from tent shows to Symphony and one "helluvafinefeller" in the bargain.

It Will Show Up

Did you ever have a small crack develop in a Turkish or Chinese Cymbal that could be "heard but not seen"? Such a crack can be quickly located by smearing a light (3 in 1) oil over one surface of the cymbal. After hitting it a few times with a stick, the oil will seep through the crack, showing its exact spot. It can then be drilled out.
(By Earnie "Sticks" Gordon, Omaha, Neb.)

Technically speaking, the "ribs" or "groves" around a metal drum shell are called Beads.

Phil. S. Sprouse

One of Chicago's hustling Leedy Drummers has more than "put it over" with several first rate bands, viz.: "The Pullman Blue Blowers," "Rodges Harmony Aces" and "Tom Brown." He is now with Bob Sweet's "Melodians" at the Niles Center "Dew Drop Inn." Sprouse got his start with the Pullman Technical High School Drum Corps and Concert Orchestra.

This Time It's Ladies Who Save the Day

Not many of the smaller cities can boast of as fine a musical organization as the thirty piece mixed band of Carson, Iowa, and we know of no other town that can claim a complete ladies' Drum Section. Miss Vera W. Cooksey (left), Drums, bells and traps, has made a specialty of Drums for the past five years. She also plays in three other local bands and orchestras and does most efficient work. Miss Georgia Caughell (center), Bass Drum and Cymbals. She, like all other good Bass Drummers, helps the leader to hold his job. Mrs. Thelma Flood (right), Snare Drum, completes this exceptionally fine trio, in regular professional style. All Leedy.

Henry D. Davis

of Boston, Massachusetts, is indeed a "top notch" xylophone artist. He has been featured in "big time" vaudeville and photoplay theatres from coast to coast. Now at the elite Symphony Cafe in Boston and broadcasting over WNAC. Davis has conducted many of the leading New England orchestras and was formerly located in Los Angeles. He states—"I always use Leedy, including the wonderful vibraphone."

"WORLD'S FINEST DRUMMERS' INSTRUMENTS"

The Exclusive Drummers' Paper

George Hamilton Green Moves to Kenosha, Wisconsin

Clarence R. Fischer

Andrew Scheuerle

Geo. Hamilton Green, the famous Victor Phonograph Star, has moved his New York studios to Kenosha, Wis. Due to the wonderful results students have obtained with his marvelous Xylophone and Marimba course by mail, hundreds more have enrolled during the past few months and it became necessary to establish himself at a more central point of the country. This will assure faster service to the great majority. Beginners and "old timers" alike should certainly become familiar with the details of this course. Address him P. O. Box 465, Kenosha, Wis. He will be heard frequently over the Chicago radios this winter, using his Leedy instruments.

Clarence R. Fischer, of Waterbury, Conn., writes in part: "Regardless of one's ability on the Xylophone or Marimba, they should 'go after' Geo. Hamilton Green's course and stick to the end. It forges the beginner ahead five years and to the professional it is Post Graduate instruction. I did not know sight reading was so easy. My time and money has been well spent and now I'm reaping a harvest of engagements. Am playing a Green model by Leedy and never heard one that could compare."

Andrew Scheuerle, whose most artistic xylophone playing has been heard many times over Radio KDKA, is one of the most sought after professional musicians of Pittsburgh and vicinity. One of his letters reads: "Using a Geo. Hamilton Green Special Leedy Xylophone. I know I have the best, for I've tried them all, and having studied Mr. Green's entire course by mail, I know I have advanced my ability to a point where only experience will improve it. What more could we ask?" Scheuerle resides at Manor, Pa.

D. L. Cruickshank

of Edmonton, Alberta, Canada, started in a family orchestra fifteen years ago. After active service in France with the Little Black Devils of Winnipeg, he toured Western Canada with both Lynch's and Sullivan's Dance Orchestras. For the past three seasons he has been at the Chateau McDonald, one of the finest hotels in Canada. Cruickshank is truly a "live wire" with extraordinary ability.
(Courtesy Advance Music Co., Toronto, Ont., Canada.)

Armand De Polis

came over from Italy and located in Philadelphia, Pa., in 1910, and has since played with many notable organizations, among them Creatore, Vassella, Ciricillo, 13th U. S. Cavalry and the Philadelphia Municipal Bands, and the Royal Palm Orchestra, Lorrain Hotel, Victor Phonograph, WOO, WJZ, WLIT Radios and the Sesqui Centennial Orchestras. De Polis is a most thorough and finished all round musician Drummer.
(Courtesy Henton Knecht Co.)

Why go through life playing on soggy drum heads? Many Drummers believe that an electric heater shortens the life of a head. This is not so unless one leaves the heater on too long. Too much of any thing is wrong. Neither do they hurt any kind of shell. Have the comfort in your work you deserve. Use a heater and use it with discretion, by turning off and on during the job. Leedy is the only firm that makes Drum Heaters.

Rick Christenson

who was born in Denmark, says he got his first drum lesson from the Indians after his father migrated to South Dakota. Then to the village band and on up through many experiences with all kinds of bands and orchestras in theatre, trouping and hotel work. Now Rick is one of the most clever and best known Drummers of the Middle West. He is now manager of the Paul Christenson Orchestra at the Fort Des Moines Hotel, Des Moines, Ia. All Leedy.

There are 762 cubic inches of air space in a 5x14 inch metal Leedy Floating Head Drum. Every time you strike it this entire amount of air is compressed for an instant.

Bob Carnahan

Here is a good likeness of a sixteen year old chap who has made them sit up and take notice in his home town of Wichita, Kansas. He studied for five years under the well known old timer, Geo. Shutts, whose photo appeared in number fourteen Drum Topics. Carnahan is not a "comer"—he has "arrived" and has been doing some real high class jobbing work in and around Wichita.

The Turkish or Italian cymbal, that has a rich and resonant tone when allowed to ring, will not produce the effect most drummers want in "cut off" or "choke" work, and the cymbal that "chokes" with that high pitch penetrating "sting" is not rich and resonant for sustained tones. The utmost to be desired in both effects cannot be combined in one cymbal. It is a physical impossibility.

S. C. Rowland (left), the hustling and result producing Drummer Manager of the Rudolph Wurlitzer Co. Drum Dept. in Los Angeles, Calif., visits the Leedy factory. The photo at right shows him standing on the office steps with A. W. Kuerst, Sec'y-Treas. of the Leedy Mfg. Co.

When it comes to "class" in both appearance and real rudimental Drum Corps work, here is an outfit that has no betters. They go to Paris for the "big doin's." Trained by that famous rudimental Drummer Jos. W. Soistman, and using Leedy equipment throughout the drum section.

American Legion Drum Corps, Baltimore, Md.
Drum Major, Chas. A. Leclick — Instructor, Jos. W. Soistman

"FOR DRUMMERS WHO CARE"

Leedy Drum Topics

On the cover—

HAROLD McDONALD
PAUL WHITEMAN
ORCHESTRA

PAUL WHITEMAN HAROLD McDONALD
U. G. LEEDY GEO. H. WAY

Photo taken on steps of Leedy Mfg. Co. May 27, 1927

Harold McDonald, "The Original Whiteman Drummer," is now back on the old job after a five years' absence. This interesting event took place during the first part of May, just too late for Drum Topics to spread the news in the drum world. By now, of course, hundreds of Drummers have heard about it; but knowing there are thousands who have not, we take great pleasure in making the announcement and publishing these exclusive photos. McDonald joined the old original Whiteman Orchestra in Los Angeles and plugged with him all through his struggle up the ladder of fame, the history of which is familiar to the majority of musicians the country over. After their great first New York success they went to England, and upon returning McDonald had the "homesick blues." He then returned to his home town, Los Angeles, and joined hands with the famous Don Clark, remaining five years. Then, like most Drummers, Mac's feet began to itch for a change, so he returned east and was playing at the

Say fellows—

We are leaving nothing undone to make Drum Topics a real Drummers' Institution. Something that every Drummer can show his friends with pride and point out the importance of his position in the musical world. Now, it's a costly undertaking, involving a vast amount of work, but we want to make it greater than ever, so won't you help by sending us the name and address of all Drummers who are not receiving it direct. This is the greatest favor you can do for Drum Topics. It will be mailed free every three months, NOT MONTHLY. Shoot in the names. Thanks.

Here is a photo of the seven Leedy trunks recently made for Harold McDonald. Yes, he carries everything. A Drummer's job with Whiteman is not a suitcase affair. Two other men of the band assist him with setting up and packing. At right, the men who built the trunks, Harry Butler, Foreman of the Leedy Trunk Dept., with his assistant, Julius Schelske.

"Arcadia," in Providence, R. I., when fate changed matters in a manner that threw him back into his old chair behind the Whiteman baton.
Drummers all over the country will have a chance to meet Harold when he takes to the road this fall with the band over the Publix Theatre circuit. All are invited through Drum Topics to step up and give him the "hello." He is a regular fellow in every respect, easy to talk to and very friendly, so don't hesitate. He will be willing to answer any questions pertaining to his work or instruments, which are all of the Leedy brand. It is hardly necessary to dwell on McDonald's ability as a Drummer. For years he has been one of the leaders in the field and, of course, he wouldn't be where he is today unless he was a most wonderful artist. However, we must add that his progressiveness and knack of originating new stunts, along with his willingness to investigate every new idea, is a chief reason for his success.

The LEEDY system of tuning Marimba and Xylophone bars (patented June 14th, 1927, No. 1632751) has certainly proved to be the salvation of these instruments. The elimination of all discordant overtones has swept away the musician's former contention that they were imperfect from a musical standpoint. And now the LEEDY brand is considered a real asset to modern arranging. This tuning system is the main reason for the growing popularity of the Marimba on the phonograph records. The various companies were quick to recognize the great improvement.

A Prize of Five Dollar

will be given to the drummer who writes the b
than two hundred words under the title of "
Means to Me." Time expires October 15,

Andy Picciano

of Cleveland, Ohio, has been for the past two years a feature with the Moran-Wahl Orchestra at Cleveland's largest dance hall, the Crystal Slipper Ball Room. He has a most complete Leedy outfit—chimes, Tympani, Marine Pearl Drums and a Vibraphone, and can everything called for with extraordinary Picciano was formerly with the Mendel Orchestra of Detroit.

Paul Whiteman said—

"I would like to drive away with all the drums in the factory. I like drums and all that go with them. Drummers' instruments are the foundation of modern jazz. Believe me, I've tried all makes in order to find the very best, and when it comes to real artistic musical effects, Leedy produces exactly what I want."

Paul Whiteman

Robert Head

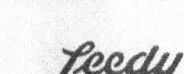

Now on tour for the M. A. C. No. 1 Circuit with Phil. Baxter and His Texas Tommies Orchestra, is a native of Omaha, Neb. He formerly played at the Brandies Theatre and Tea Room with the Gilbert Jaffy Orchestra and others. Head is a serious minded drummer, who has thrown his whole heart into the work and become a real skilled performer. This, coupled with the fact that he is a former pupil of Geo. A. Smith, is bound to carry him to the top.

(Courtesy—Geo. A. Smith, Omaha, Neb.)

THE COLORADO AMERIC
Ed. Young (Drum Major), Kenneth Campbell (Instructor). Just wait until the girls in F get a peep at this classy Leedy Corps on parade.

"WORLD'S FINEST DRUMMERS' INSTRUMENTS"

The Exclusive Drummers' Paper

LIPSTICK—"My color charms their pretty lips and keeps them more entrancing."

DRUMSTICK—"That's nothing,—my rhythm charms their pretty legs and keeps them ever dancing."

Get a few pieces of cloth and wrap your traps in them for carrying in your drum case. This will prevent them from knocking together and keep them looking nicer. Worth the effort as the more breakable ones will last much longer.

Ross Gorman and Frankie Flynn

Frankie Flynn is one of those rare "Combination Drummers"—meaning that he is both an artist on his instruments and an artist as an entertainer. Press notices make lengthy comments on his "winning smile" "remarkable personality" "excellent voice" and "clever dancing which stopped the show." Flynn was born in New York City twenty-five years ago. Seven years of jobbing on all kinds of work brought him to a season with the James Boys Orchestra in the "Little Jesse James" show. Then two years as a feature with Brook John's and the past two years with the nationally known star, Ross Gorman. Flynn says —"Leedy for me, nuff said."

On straight crashes, it is the type of blow rather than the force that breaks a cymbal. The "whip" blow is severe and dangerous, because the contact of the stick is too sudden to allow the cymbal to give. The "push" blow is less likely to cause harm, but it does not bring out the best tone. The safest is the "glance" blow. It not only brings out the best tone, but can be used with more force than any other.

DRUM AND BUGLE CORPS.

will say "Voyez, Voyez les beaux de Wild West, marchant et jouant ils font battre les ... de notres soeurs en volant." And they play as fine as they look.
(Courtesy—Knight-Campbell Music Co., Denver, Colo.)

On the Cover—Paul Ash and Art Layfield

Drum Topics would hardly seem complete without a few lines about that "wonder drummer," Art Layfield, and his leader, the man who is responsible for the present day popularity of the stage band, Paul Ash—Originator of the famous "Ash Policy." It is not always possible to show our readers new photos of this famous pair in every issue, but this time we were lucky. Art has just "stocked up" with a "flock" of new Leedy instruments including Sparkling Gold Snare and Bass Drums along with Cathedral Chimes and trunk, also several other items. That Art is a glutton for work is well known. We have never met a more conscientious drummer and progressiveness is his middle name. Drummers who visit Chicago are indeed fortunate for it presents an opportunity of hearing and seeing him work. Whether it be the latest break, gag or "hot lick," Art always has it on tap. This photo would imply that his Leader was interested in the Drum Section. True, so much so that Ash notices every little accent and is always ready to give and take in cooperating with his Drummer. He even takes an interest in every new trap or instrument that Art adds to his outfit, examining it thoroughly and they pull together like clock work. You see, Ash knows drums because he once played them in a professional way.

(Courtesy—Tom Brown Music Co., Chicago, Ill.)

A Leedy Drum Head Becomes Famous

L. GLUSKIN

Shortly after Commander Byrd, with Balchen, Noville and Acosta, made their marvelous trans-Atlantic flight to France in the "America," a most elaborate banquet was staged in their honor at the famous "Perroquet" in Paris. Gason and his Band from the Casino de Paris furnished the music, and as usual the snappy, clever work of L. Gluskin, a well known American (N. Y.) Drummer, caused great delight among the guests. Commander Byrd volunteered his signature for Gluskin's drum head, with the others following suit. It is seldom that so many world famous notables gather together, and through the courtesy of Gluskin, who presented Drum Topics with the head, we are able to show our readers its photo. Near the top, left, are the signatures of, first, Byrd, then Balchen, Noville and Acosta. Then comes Fokker, world's renowned aeronautic engineer and designer of the "America." Following is Rignot, Belloit and Doret, France's greatest flying aces. At the top, right, is Mlle. Mistinguett, of the Moulin Rouge and foremost musical comedy star of France. Next comes Florence Walton, Fanny Bryce and Norma Talmadge, whom we all know. Then Georges Carpentier, the French boxer, followed by Gasen, leader of the orchestra and also the leading French saxophonist. Next is June, the great English stage star, then Mr. Blaser, proprietor of the Perroquet. At the bottom is Fectome, notable French concert pianist. The signature in the center is that of Erica, Gluskin's most charming Hungarian wife.

A Product of Master Workmanship

The Leedy
Floating Head
Model

Fulfills every requirement of the most exacting Drummer.

Catalogue mailed Free on Request

Leedy   "FOR DRUMMERS WHO CARE"   **Leedy**

Leedy Drum Topics

The Prize Story
by Lewis Platt

Below is a photographic copy of a comedy letter composed by Lewis Platt of Salem, Ohio. It "takes the cake" for this issue of Drum Topics. Lewis Platt (photo at left) is a hustling young drummer who has "arrived" by way of earnest study at the Dana Conservatory at Warren, Ohio, where he graduated. For ten months he was with Paul West's Collegians, a touring orchestra from the Ohio University. At present he is on the road with Harry Hylan's Arcadians, a very fine eleven piece band doing stage presentations and playing the best ballrooms. Platt has also had considerable experience in theatre and military band work and, while only eighteen years of age, can do a fine job that ranks with the best. Here is the comedy letter that wins the $10.00 prize.

```
                                        Washout, Ark.
Leedy Mfg. Co.                                   1927
 Indianapolis

Gentlemens:-

 I got the drum i buy from you, but why for gods sake you doan
sen me no sticks. Whats the use a drum when she doan HAVe no sticks.

 I lose to me my job in band sure thing you doan treat me right
i rote 10 days ago and the leader he holler like hell at me at practise
becaus I no can play.

 You no we have lots of job now and i no can play the drum with
my fingers. she got no sticks so what I goan with it.

 Sean sen the sticks pretty quick i sen her bak and I goan order
some drum from a other companie.

                Goodby
                       Yours truly
                        Tony Kelsky

Since I write i fine the goddam sticks in the box. Scuse me pleese.
```

Loretta

"Just as clever as she is pretty," is what several newspaper critics have written about Loretta after seeing Jack Fines Banjo Land, one of vaudeville's feature acts. During the full year that Loretta has been with the act, she has never failed to draw an unusually "big hand" by way of excellent playing and personal charm. Loretta plays a four octave Leedy Solo-Tone Xylophone. Her former home was in Omaha, Neb.

Leon Knapp and Jack Roop

Leon Knapp (left), Proprietor of the Leon Knapp Drum Shop and Drum School at Grand Rapids, Mich., paid the Leedy factory a visit in July and as good luck would have it, Jack Roop, Assistant Sales Manager and Traveling Representative for Leedy, happened to be at the plant between trips. These two "birds" are exceptionally good friends and do a lot of chumming around together when off duty. Jack made Leon a real Leedy booster and Leon makes Jack cough up when the "White Sox" win. That guy Roop is always betting on the "Yankees."

DID YOU KNOW THAT—Geo. Carey, the noted Xylophone artist formerly of Sousa's Band, is now playing a big five octave Leedy Monarch Marimba-Xylophone with the Goldman Band in Central Park, New York City. While the band was playing a few weeks at Atlantic City, George wrote stating that both he and Goldman think it is the finest instrument of its kind they ever heard. A nice photo is promised and we hope to put it in the next issue of Drum Topics. Carey's solos have been going bigger than ever. His skill seems to get better and better. He goes back to the Cincinnati Symphony Orchestra in the fall.

Laurie Minchinton

has been with the House of David Band of Benton Harbor, Mich., ever since coming to this country from Melbourne, Australia, three years ago. That he is a "top notch" drummer is evinced by the fact that he has had offers to join several big name bands. Now touring the large photo play houses and big city ballrooms under the direction of the M. C. A. All Leedy.

Drumming with the heavy part of the sticks (where they begin to taper down) on a wood block is much more pleasing than using the tips. The execution is more difficult, but it's worth the effort.

Howard Gillaspy

began his career as a drummer at the age of nine years with the famous Press News Boys Band of Grand Rapids, Mich. Later he played two seasons at the Cushman Hotel in Petosky, Mich. Now with Floyd Eldings popular dance orchestra of Grand Rapids. Gillaspy does fine work and is often featured on the Xylophone over Radio WOOD, Grand Rapids.

(Courtesy—Leon Knapp Drum Shop)

Justa Wethead says—

"A high pitch straw makes the best hot break at the end of a soda."

A Snare Drum Music Lyre for Parade Work

by P. W. Janert, 6th C. A. Band U. S. Army, Fort Winfield Scott, California.

All you need is the Leedy tambourine holder clamp, Leedy Cat. "o," page 30, No. 667 and almost any music lyre such as used on brass instruments. The end of the Tambourine Holder that is intended to take the post takes the lyre and the clamp that is intended to hold the tambourine fastens to the counter hoop of the drum.

Arthur E. Nielsen

is located at Harlan, Iowa, and plays with the Leroy Potter Orchestra, which travels over the largest part of the State. He says: "I am sold on Leedy from spurs to chimes." Formerly with the Joe Barrier Fidelity Orchestra. Nielsen is worthy of holding down any big city job but prefers to remain at home. He is one of the outstanding examples of a "big timer" in a small town.

(Courtesy—Geo. A. Smith Drum Shop, Omaha, Neb.)

The metal hooks that pull down the metal counter hoops on Leedy Reliance and Tango Drums are called Collar Hooks.

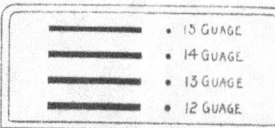

Showing exact sizes of the different gut snares—

"WORLD'S FINEST DRUMMERS' INSTRUMENTS"

The Exclusive Drummers' Paper

Notes from Back Numbers of Drum Topics

Drum Topics is now four years old. For the benefit of Drummers who have missed former issues, we have decided to reprint various back number items from time to time. Hope you like the idea.

FROM NO. ONE DRUM TOPICS—

Did You Ever Troupe?

The fellow who sleeps in the same comfortable bed every night seldom realizes the trials and hard work of the road drummer, especially the circus man. Rain, mud, hot cars and "white tops," loss of sleep, few baths and sometimes poor food are only a few of his inconveniences. To those of you who have never trouped and think it is a cinch, take a tip from an old-timer. Rest easy—it isn't half what it's cracked up to be. On the other hand, if you do go on the road, see it all. Let them call you a "tourist" if they will, but the drummer who has been through the Royal Gorge and cannot say he saw it, because he slept all the way, has missed a big opportunity. Perhaps he will never get there again. Things like this are the bright side of a trouper's existence.

Do It Well

When you make a mistake, such as a crash in the wrong place, make a good one. Let 'em know you're working; it won't sound half as bad as a little half-hearted "peck."

FROM NO. TWO DRUM TOPICS—

It Is Not Always Necessary

IT IS NOT ALWAYS NECESSARY to retuck a drum head. Sometimes it is very inconvenient to do so on account of the time required and the trouble of getting the head off the flesh hoop, especially if it is old and well tucked. Besides, there is the danger of tearing same.

Soak the whole head and flesh hoop in water—not too cold, but not warm—for five minutes, then allow it to become almost dry before putting on shell. If it is a good head it will contract. After it is dry, you can put it on the shell and adjust same as usual. This will result in as good a job as retucking.

In Vaudeville

A string of "direct cues" in a difficult act is, of course, tough at times, but it's part of the drummer's business to "catch 'em" all without a "fliv." A "direct cue" is not so bad—you see the action and "catch it," but a string of "anticipation cues" is another matter. You don't see it and you "catch it," then Mr. Comic does his bit. YOU slam the cymbal, then he jumps; YOU squawk a squawker, then he looks under the carpet. Quite different from slamming the cymbal WHEN he jumps or squawking AS he looks under the carpet.

The yarn is this: One Monday morning a drummer in a leading vaudeville house received a long list of "anticipation cues" for a combination bicycle and juggling act. The ninth cue called for a short, loud wind whistle, to which Mr. Comic sticks his head from behind the tormentor —making a so-called "funny mug." The poor drummer, having no action in this spot to work on, "muffed" the cue at the first matinee. Then Mr. Comic stuck his mug around the tormentor and yelled at the drummer in loud tones: "Missed it!"

Words cannot describe how that drummer felt—his fighting blood and embarrassment raged within him. But wait—a little later in the act Mr. Comic is riding about the stage on a bicycle juggling three balls. He drops one, and up jumps Mr. Drummer, walloping his crash cymbal with all his might, and yells in loud tones: "Missed it!"

FROM NO. THREE DRUM TOPICS—

A Drum Head Tip

It is not heat and cold that affect a drum head, but it is the condition of the heat and cold, namely, dampness and dryness.

A damp heat will cause the head to slacken, and the same with a damp cold.

A dry heat will cause a head to tighten, and the same with a dry cold.

Therefore, watch the condition of the atmosphere rather than the thermometer and avoid head breakage. If you have tightened your head on a damp night, let it out after using to the point where you started to take it up. This will allow some slack for a "take-up" should the next day be dry.

If your drum works nicely in dry weather, leave it alone.

Drummers who watch these points have been known to use the same head for years.

To Fix a Tom-Tom

Did you ever have the ring pull out of a tom-tom? Doesn't it "get your goat"?

Never mind, there is a very easy way to fix it.

First, pull out the other one. Second, run a piece of steel wire straight through the old "Chinee tub" and make a couple of loops at each end to hold the rings.

If the old rings are weak or broken, get a couple of small key rings at the ten-cent store. Get the drift? One end is pulling against the other when fixed in this manner, and you will have no further excuse for swearing in public.

They are made in China, so don't blame us for the way the Chinks put in these rings.

John B. Quick
Phoenix, Arizona

Twenty-two years ago John B. Quick broke into the business on the "piano and drum circuit" at Des Moines, Ia. Since then he has "played them all," specializing in theatre work. At one time he took his own band on a successful tour to the Pacific Coast and back. Quick has also billed several road show jobs. He is noted as being a very fine Xylophone soloist and is also well known as an arranger. For the past five years his splendid work at the Rialto (Vaudeville) Theatre of Phoenix, with a fine ten piece orchestra, has been the talk of the town. Quick says: "Experience has taught me that Leedy instruments are the quality instruments for Drummers."

Carrol P. Abrams

Is now a student at the University of South Carolina at Columbia, S. C. For the past two years he has toured with the College Glee Club doing feature work with his Leedy five octave Xylophone on the highest class jobs in the State, also broadcasting through various radio stations. His four mallet numbers always go over with a bang.

Eddie McKnight

And his Orchestra are the chief reason for the continual repeat patronage at the Silver Slipper Club at Atlantic City, N. J. Four years on the job has made this splendid band a great favorite. In conjunction they broadcast regularly over radio WPG. McKnight is a modern high speed, efficient Drummer and business man combined. The kind that sets a pace.

About Spurs on a Bass Drum

Very often Drummers will place their spurs on the same side of the bass drum as the pedal (shown in cut one). This method is wrong, because it causes the head of the drum to slant away from the pedal, making it necessary to carry the beater rod past center (denoted by the perpendicular dotted line). This requires additional force than that which has carried the beater up to center and makes a "stiff spot" in the action of the pedal. Place the spurs on the hoop opposite the pedal (shown in cut two). Then the batter head will slant toward the pedal and the beater will strike the head before it reaches the center point on the arc it is traveling.

Drummers who overlook this point often blame the pedal for working hard. It is a mechanical law that applies to any make floor pedal and when understood as explained above, the proper method of adjusting the spurs eliminates further trouble.

CUT ONE
The Wrong Way—

CUT TWO
The Right Way—

 "FOR DRUMMERS WHO CARE"

Page Eleven

Leedy Drum Topics

Tomorrow's "Big Timers"
Twelve Clever Young Leedy Enthusiasts Who Earn Real Money with Drummer's Instruments

CHARLES F. RUSS, of Wilkes-Barre, Penna., has proven what a young fellow can do when he applies himself. He is first drummer with W. B. Boys Band and also plays with The Melody Boys, a prominent dance orchestra. Besides he is a member of Camp Achahela Boys Scout Drum Corps. Young Russ is a pupil of Robert Knecht, a leading vaudeville Drummer of Wilkes-Barre.
(Courtesy Landau Bros.)

KENNETH McKINNON is a four year old wonder on the Xylophone. He gives public performances in and around St. Louis, Mo., and receives the most complimentary press notices. A pupil of Schuyler Alward of the Sporleder Music House.

FRANCIS McGUCKIN, of Omaha, Neb., is a Drum and Xylophone pupil of Geo. A. Smith, who says he is a student any teacher could be exceptionally proud of. While only eleven years old, Francis has played several professional engagements with adult orchestras. He also plays in his school orchestra.

JACK MOISE is a ten year old lad who can play most of the rudimental military beats in a most efficient style. He also plays Xylophone as well as drums in his school orchestra. Pupil of Geo. A. Smith, Omaha, Neb.

THE LEGACY BROTHERS—Thomas and Russel, two of Flint, Michigan's leading Junior artists, who are really phenomenal performers on the Xylophone. They broadcast from the Brunswick Shop Studio radio WFDF quite often and have played at WJR, Detroit. Pupils of the well known Joe McKown.

WILLIAM PREVOST, of Denver, Colorado, plays in the Morey High School Orchestra. He is completely equipped even to Machine Tympani and Marimba Xylophone. While only thirteen years of age, he can do a job that compares favorably with an experienced professional. A pupil of Leo Childers, Drummer at Orpheum Theatre, Denver.
(Courtesy Knight-Campbell Music Co.)

HOLMAN FENN, although only six years of age, is playing in professional hotel and radio work with the popular Tom Thumb Trio of Kokomo, Indiana. Several newspaper notices make strong mention of his ability and perfect rhythm.

LINDLEY A. JONES, a clever young drummer of Calipatria, California, has had considerable experience for one of his age. He is now playing in the Long Beach Summer High School Orchestra and the Rotary Club Band. Has also been with several professional dance organizations, viz.: Melody Five, Brawley Blue Boys, Red Wing Junior Five. Pupil of O. P. Rominger of The Long Beach Municipal Band.

WM. R. SEARS was a pupil of both Emil Weflen and Wallace Lageson, prominent drummers of Minneapolis, Minn. "Bill," as he is called, has been playing professionally for five years. He is now fourteen. Last year with McIntyre's Black Cats and this season with the Bryant Junior High School of Minneapolis. His leaders say that Bill does an exceptionally fine job.
(Courtesy Hausner Music Co.)

GERALD SMITH, of Elwood, Indiana, is the youngest musician that was ever admitted to the Elwood High School Band. His exceptional skill won him the position. He is just ten years of age and also plays double drums in the Christian Church Orchestra.

JOHN BLIZZARD has been playing for the past two seasons with Brown's Concert Band of Bradford, Ohio. He is a student at the Perry Studios and his teacher, Dwight L. Brown, considers him a real marvel for only ten years of age.

PAUL ANTIBUS has earned enough from his drums to pay for the complete outfit and enjoys a nice bank account in addition. Paul is a real talented thirteen year old drummer. He started in the Vincennes High School Orchestra and now plays with Dunkle's Orchestra. A pupil of Clarence A. Stout, Vincennes, Indiana.

"WORLD'S FINEST DRUMMERS' INSTRUMENTS"

The Exclusive Drummers' Paper

Leedy Drummers Who Play Where the Union Jack Flies

J. BARBER of Halifax is another English Drummer who is capable of "filling the bill" in a "top hole" manner, whether the job be Drum Corps, Theatre, Dance Band or Concert Orchestra. He has played them all since ten years of age and is an ardent student and admirer of the Harry A. Bower system. Now at the Theatre De-Luxe, Northgate, Halifax.

HARRY SCULTHORPE is one of the few modern dance men who is equally at home on any class job. He put in several years in the army as an instructor and has played leading theatres and concert work in London, Glasgow, Hastings and Yarmouth. For the past twelve months with the famous Percy Bush Band at Oxford Galleries at Newcastle-on-Tyne, one of the highest class dance bands outside of London. They broadcast frequently and Sculthorpe's Xylophone playing is one of the band's leading features.

ROY C. PEVERETT was formerly a noted 'cellist with the British National Opera Co., also the famous Scottish Orchestra. Three years ago he decided to "go after" drums and studied with that most efficient London drummer, Warwick Barnes. Peverett soon "put it over" and is now with the John Cantor Band at the Spa, Scarborough. Watch him land with one of London's finest in the future.

JACK BROOKLYN lives near the Great Crystal Palace in Anerley, a suburb of London. He is a former pupil of L. A. Lyons. Brooklyn played for some time at the Royal Albion Hotel, London, and is now doing the better class of jobbing with different first rate bands. He is reported as doing most excellent work in the modern style.
(Courtesy—Lyons and Hamilton, London)

The last issue of Drum Topics (No. 14) carried a very clever poem entitled "The Most Important Man in the Band." It was written by that most versatile chap, Billy Mather (now located in Glasgow, Scotland) and won the $10.00 prize offered for the best story selected for each issue. After receiving the prize, the boys of his band evidently "cleaned him" and he then wrote the following, which proves him to be a real sportsman:

Poet and Unpleasant
By BILLY MATHER

Your letter arrived with the tidings
 My poem had won me a prize
And Gee! when I gazed on that ten spot,
 I couldn't believe my own eyes.

You'll notice I call it a poem
 (Perhaps, I should call it a rhyme)
But I'm swelled up at getting ten dollars
 When I honestly thought I'd get "time."

The rest of the band call me "Kipling"
 ('Cause he was a poet as well),
But the old woman still calls me "Saphead,"
 Thinking my head's going to swell.

The rest of the band have all touched me
 (Drum Topics put them all wise),
And I can't get a drink on my lonesome.
 It's cost something, winning that prize.

My kid brother's borrowed my cymbal,
 Just snatched it and then ran away.
He was out throwing bricks trying to bust it.
 He'll be a drummer some day.

And just 'cause I set up a holler
 And threatened to bust him perhaps,
He told me to go and forget it
 As a poet don't need any traps.

The landlord has bumped up the house rent
 And that's the one thing makes me sore.
He says he's just heard I'm an author
 And I'll have to pay more than before.

It's cost something, winning that ten spot,
 And it's set all the hounds on my track
And all the odd dollars I've borrowed
 I've had to work extra to pay back.

But I'm glad, all the same, that I won it—
 It proves that rhyming does pay.
So good luck to Leedy's Drum Topics,
 I'll write you another some day!

Below is a copy of a letter written by that world famous artist, Charles Turner to Will Van Allen, Ltd. of London.

```
                                    4 Barcombe Avenue
                                    Streatham Hill S. W. 2.
                        COPY
Dear Mr. Van Allen:—

    The pair of Leedy Machine Tympani I bought from you several weeks ago
are still going strong at the Royal Opera House, Covent Gardens. They
tune splendidly and do all the work in a most exacting manner. We have a
hundred men here in the orchestra.

    I have recommended them to the drummer with the British Broadcasting
Co. and he has managed to persuade the Co. to buy him a pair.

    When the "Plaza" opened last year I was the Tympanist and Mr. Frank
Toms procured a pair for that show for me. Am immensely delighted with my
own set and when the opera season is over, I shall use them in all my
Festival and Concert business. Perhaps the Leedy firm would be pleased
to hear of this.

                        Yours faithfully,
                        (Signed) Charles Turner

Principal Tympanist of the London Symphony Orchestra-Royal Opera
House Orchestra and The Royal Philharmonic Orchestra.
```

ERIC LITTLE of "Kit Cat" fame has written a most excellent instructor entitled —"Rhythmical Drumming and Pedal Tympani Playing," published by Hawkes and Son (price 5 shillings net). Get it, you'll find many fine tips explained in a new and better way.

Don't forget—Drum Topics wants to go into the hands of every Drummer where the Union Jack flies, all we need is names and addresses—send them in—it will be mailed free every three months—Cherrio.

JAMES BLADES hails from Peterborough, Northants. Eight years ago he joined the City Military Band and also played with several jobbing dance combinations. Later he went in for theatre work and has held many fine positions in this line. Many cities in the north of England know him for his fine work on Drums, Tympani and as a Xylophone Soloist. Now at the leading Photo Play House in Dundee, Scotland.

WARWICK BARNES is well known to Drum Topic readers as both the eleventh and thirteenth issues carried photos of him. However, we thought the boys would like to see another of this snappy top notcher, so here he is, with an all new "Full Dress" Black and Nobby Gold Leedy Outfit. Warwick is still with the Bert Firman's Orchestra playing at the best London has to offer. Doing a lot of teaching as well.

FRANK H. SHUTTLEWORTH of Bradford started five years ago with the Savana band and is now on a par with many who have been at the game much longer. He has played with Arnold Pearson, The Brooklyn Band, The Cabaret Band and others. Shuttleworth now has his own organization called, Roddy Williams and His Golden Astorians, doing the best class of work in Bradford and vicinity.

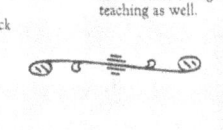

ZOE VASHTI is the owner, manager, leader and "drummeress" of the Locarno Club Orchestra, a modern ladies' organization that has played on high class jobs in London, Aberdeen, Dundee, Edinburgh and other cities of the British Isles. They have also traveled to the States and proved to be a real attraction in New York. Miss Vashti is indeed an exceptionally fine drummer of the legitimate as well as the jazz school.
(Courtesy—Alexander Bigger Co.)

"FOR DRUMMERS WHO CARE"

Leedy Drum Topics

The "Flash" Cymbal

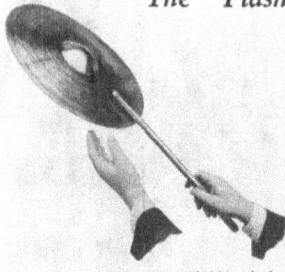

Take your Turkish or Italian Cymbal to the nearest electroplating shop and have it highly polished. It will cost about fifty cents. Then use it, without holder of any kind, in the left hand tossing it two or three inches into the air striking it with the right stick for single, double or triple strokes. When the Cymbal falls back into the left hand, the hand acts as a "cut off." The "dead beats" are played while the Cymbal is held by the hand. Hold it fairly high. The Flash of the polished Cymbal will attract additional attention to the Drummer. A lot of good stuff can be worked up with this stunt. Some Drummers are using a polished 15-inch Chinese for this effect.

Exceptionally Thin

The Leedy Mfg. Co. can now supply exceptionally thin Kiraljian (Italian) Cymbals in the 12-inch, 13-inch, 14-inch and 15-inch sizes. Negotiations have been in progress with the makers for over a year and many samples were submitted before the perfect cymbal was obtained. This cymbal has that high pitch sting which is just the right effect for modern work. There is a large supply of them now in stock. This particular brand is exclusively distributed by Leedy.

Love makes the world go round when the darn thing ought to be asleep.

Temple Block Holder

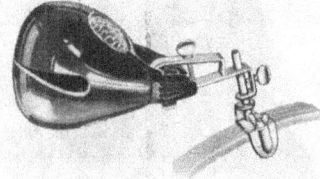

This temple block holder will fit any upright post of the Trap Table, Trap Trees or Trap Console and will accommodate any size block up to 8 inches. Made of pressed steel parts. Light in weight and very strong.

In 1892 U. G. Leedy introduced the first thumb screw rods for snare and bass drums.

Arthur W. Lee

of Auburn, Maine, began on the drums with his father (J. Frank Lee and his Orchestra) when only seven years old, playing dances in and around Auburn. Arthur has now been in business eighteen years and has taken a hand in about every phase of the game. He is considered one of New England's first and most progressive Drummers. In 1925 he was with the famous Pier Orchestra at Old Orchard, Me., in 1926 at Pleasant Pond Park and this season with Oakdale Park, Auburn. This band also broadcasts for WCSH, Portland, Me.

In Memphis, Tenn.

Drums used to be thought of as an instrument for boys and men only, but late years have proven that the girls and women find them just as interesting. Here are twenty-one young ladies who can step right along and make any boys' outfit of the same age class hustle to keep up. They do real clean cut snappy work. The city government of Memphis is the sponsor of several such ladies' organizations under the direction of Supt. of Recreation, Bob O'Brien, shown in the upper left hand corner of photo. All Leedy equipment.

(Courtesy—Melody Music Shop)

Don't forget—when you move send Drum Topics your new address.

The Sock Whisk

Get one of those extra long and extra thick whisk brooms and use it as a sock after beat with a slight swish on the big Tympani head tuned to about "C." Good effect on hot choruses with full band as it always cuts through. Also fine for light work. Has as many varied uses as the wire brush and much louder for heavy playing.

Want to hear a couple of pretty Vibraphone numbers? Get this record.

Edison 51809-L—"Andantino."
Edison 51809-R—"I'll Take You Home Again Kathleen."
Played by Signor Friscoe

Sent in by Jack Hunter, popular Drummer and entertainer at Canadian Radiophone CKCK—Regina, Sask., Canada.

Here's another good record for hot breaks on traps, etc.

Harmony Record No. 144120—(421-H) "Sensation."

Sent in by John W. Anneuheuser, Albany, New York.

Happy Gandy

has had ten years' experience in the dance game and now has his own orchestra, Gandy's Collegians, who do the better class of work in and around Cedar Rapids, Ia. He is also Assistant Director of the Rock Island Shop Band. Gandy is both a first rate conductor and Drummer.

Harold Jenkins

of Windsor, Nova Scotia, started in with a Cadet Band in 1922. He has specialized in Military Band playing on both snare and bass drum and is considered an A-1 man on these instruments. Now connected with the Windsor N. S. Concert Band.

(Courtesy—Advance Music Co., Toronto, Ont.)

Press-Lloyd Post— American Legion Drum Corps, Chisholm, Minn.

If this outfit joins the frolic in Paris this fall, the town of Chisholm will become a permanent addition to the French vocabulary. Ivar Swanson (Drum Major) is a world war veteran of considerable reputation as Drill Sergeant—C. H. Howe (Manager) and front row, left, has brought the Corps to its present high standard and Oscar Simstrem (Instructor) is widely known as a Band Leader and Drum teacher of the first rank.

"WORLD'S FINEST DRUMMERS' INSTRUMENTS"

The Exclusive Drummers' Paper

INITIATIVE

THE world bestows its big prizes, both in money and honors, for but one thing—

And that is Initiative.

What is Initiative?

I'll tell you: It is doing the right thing without being told.

But next to doing the thing without being told is to do it when you are told once. That is to say, carry the Message to Garcia; those who can carry a message get high honors, but their pay is not always in proportion. Next, there are those who never do a thing until they are told twice; such get no honors and small pay.

Next, there are those who do the right thing only when necessity kicks them from behind, and these get indifference instead of honors, and a pittance for pay. This kind spends most of its time polishing a bench with a hard luck story.

Then, still lower down in the scale than this, we have the fellow who will not do the right thing even when someone goes along to show him how and stays to see that he does it; he is always out of a job, and receives the contempt he deserves, unless he happens to have a rich Pa, in which case Destiny patiently awaits around the corner with a stuffed club.

To which class do you belong?

—ELBERT HUBBARD

J. J. Henny

J. J. thought he would quit the road so settled down some time ago in that peaceful little town of St. Augustine, Fla., at the Jefferson Theatre where he is featuring his new five octave Leedy Monarch Marimba Xylophone. You all know Henny, former Xylophone soloist with Sousa, also with the Ringling Brothers for several years, and with the Royal Scotch Highlanders Band.

Morro Castle Scene—a new bass drum head painting executed in beautiful colors by the stipple method. No brush marks to show when light is used in interior of drum.

The Difference

If Drums were handled like saxophones, trumpets, etc., the electroplating would wear just as long. The brass instruments always rest on padded stands and are either in the user's hands or in a plush lined case. They suffer no wear in transit. Drums are on the floor and sitting on unprotected metal stands to say nothing of traveling in hard fibre cases and coming in contact with the sticks and traps. Many Drummers take great care with their instruments, but there are others who are careless and wonder why the plating does not stand up. The plating is O. K.—it is the man in such cases.

Tom Glenicke

After putting in last season with Merle Evans Band at Sarasota, Florida, Glenicke moved over to Tampa to finish out with Bachman's Million Dollar Band. He then returned to Chicago, his home city, where he is well known in the Vaudeville and movie field. Now at Buckingham's Theatre. Glenicke recently equipped himself with the Leedy Machine Tympani and large Xylophone and says they are the finest instruments he has ever played. As a xylophone soloist he has 200 compositions memorized and is rated with the very best as an artist. Also has a large class of pupils.

Mrs. Iva Westfall

(Chief Accountant)

Leedy Manufacturing Co.

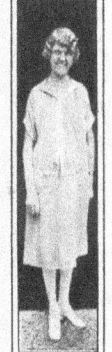

We thought our readers would like to see a photo of the lady who is more or less connected with every transaction that takes place between the Drummer and Leedy. Mrs. Westfall has the longest record of service of anyone on our office staff except Mr. Leedy himself. She has been with the company for seventeen years having started when her hair was in braids and tied with a big ribbon. Does she know the drum business—absolutely. Her middle name is "efficiency" and she is even a darn good cook.

You can tune a cow bell by forcing the edges (lips) of the opening closer together to flatten and farther apart to sharpen the tone.

Still More After This

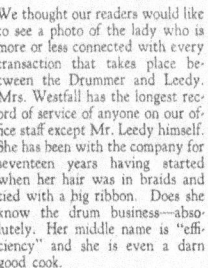

The above photo shows the new addition to the east wing of the Leedy factory almost completed. It consists of 20,000 sq. ft. Now it has been decided to add 7,200 sq. ft. to the west wing which will give much needed new space to the office, shipping room and stock room. The work started in August. This makes a grand total of 78,450 sq. ft. in the Leedy plant.

Drop us a line and tell us whether or not you liked this new style Drum Topics. Send in some new photographs and ideas. It's all for the good of the game. Suggestions welcome. Next issue in December.

Scotch Bass Drum Stick

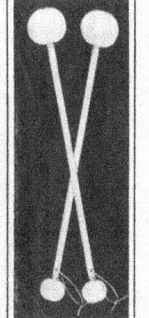

This type of stick is good for both single and double bass drum work. The handle is of the best white hickory and extra long, which gives that balanced leverage. The balls are of soft Spanish felt. Each stick over all is 16 inches. The loops of snare chord at the small end are for attaching the leather thong loops, which are furnished with every pair.

Theatre drummers can do faster work and find more comfort by using a swivel chair in the pit. Many drummers are already equipped with one.

—and for the next number on the program our Drummer will sing the vegetable song entitled "A Bunch of Beats." (*Jack Roop—Leedy popular Traveling Representative*)

Charles Bloomer

is a "red hot" drummer with a "red hot" band, Winstead's Wonders of Louisville, Ky. This band carries seven men and is in demand among a high class clientele throughout several southern states. Bloomer has been with them for the past five years and is most clever with original rhythmic beats. He has a style all his own. Recently he equipped himself with a complete Leedy Marine Pearl Outfit.

The End

"FOR DRUMMERS WHO CARE"

Leedy   Leedy

A Date Book Especially Designed for Drummers

SEND FIVE TWO-CENT STAMPS FOR YOURS TO-DAY

Bound in high grade leatherette cover—
Contains much valuable information—
Has perpetual dating system—
Good for one year starting any time—
Sent to Drummers only—
Mailed on receipt of five two-cent stamps—
Every Drummer needs this fine date book—

Leedy Manufacturing Co.
PALMER STREET AND BARTH AVE.

Indianapolis — Indiana — U. S. A.

Leedy Drum Topics
The Exclusive Drummers' Magazine
SEPTEMBER, 1927
FIFTEENTH EDITION

Joseph G. Benoit

165 Hildreth,

Lowell, Mass.

POSTMASTER—Return Postage Guaranteed

Leedy Manufacturing Co.
INDIANAPOLIS, INDIANA

Leedy Drum Topics

Remove the walls between —

Military *Concert* *Dance* *Theater* *Entertaining*

THAT there is need for more real fellowship and better understanding between the various types of Drummers, none in the game will deny. In the minds of many, walls of narrow prejudice and isolation have been slowly erected. These "walls" are built from distorted imagination—not facts. A lack of familiarity with the requisites of the other fellow's job is partly responsible. Similar conditions have existed in other professions and among business men, hence the progressive step in forming associations—Rotary, Kiwanis, Lions Clubs, etc. True, there is a vast difference in the style and knowledge required to be a skilful Drummer in each branch, but this is no reason for building walls of separation. Instead, it is the best reason in the world for encouraging Drummers to unite and boost one another. Let us all lend a hand toward acknowledging every kind of Drummer and help make the public value his worth still more. Surely there must be sound logic in such practice—the greatest business brains in the country find it worth while.

- originally, there was only one type of Drummer—the primitive who beat noisy rhythms to frighten away evil spirits.
- then came the Military Drummer to encourage men to battle and transmit signals.
- with the progress of civilization still another type was born to be the foundation of the universal language—Music.
- next came the Drummer who contributed the greatest share toward making the dance a pleasure in all lands;
- and the theatre Drummer that has helped to build one of the world's greatest institutions.
- last, but not least, the entertaining or modern Drummer with his bag o' tricks, putting new life into many forms of music.

EACH has done his individual work well. Time has not weakened his position. Each particular kind of Drummer has become such an important part of human activities that hardly any event is complete without him. And as millions the world over give Drummers due credit, so should Drummers themselves give each other credit in their respective fields. They should recognize each other's abilities and not erect walls of prejudice between the different lines of endeavor. Those on the outside know of no such walls—they exist only in Drummers' minds. They can damage the prestige of the profession. Tear them down and keep them down.

> "Every man, however obscure, is one of a group of men impressible for the good of all."
> *Charles Dickens.*

LET'S HAVE "A DRUMMERS' CLUB" IN EVERY CITY AND TOWN

Leedy "WORLD'S FINEST DRUMMERS' INSTRUMENTS" *Leedy*

 # The Exclusive Drummers' Paper

A Progressive Step by the Drummers of New York City

NOTE—The following letter came in just as this issue of Drum Topics was going to press. As it concerns a most important subject and is in keeping with our opening story on the opposite page, we managed to do some fast rearranging and are more than pleased to be able to include it in this number.

New York City.

To the Editor of Drum Topics,
Leedy Manufacturing Co.,
Indianapolis, Indiana.

Dear Sir:

Knowing that "Drum Topics" is always interested in "Drummers' doings," the officers of the newly organized Percussion Club of New York City have instructed me to give you a brief sketch of activities this far and of the ideals that are the foundation of our most enthusiastic group.

The Percussion Club is composed of several hundred Drummers of the Empire City. The membership includes men engaged in all forms of orchestral activity from symphony to dance, covering the leading theatre, hotel, recording and broadcasting ensembles. Here can be found the most prominent performers, artist tympanists, xylophone soloists and exponents of Jazz Rhythm.

The forming of this Club, however, signifies something of far greater importance than a mere array of talent. It denotes the termination of a long, dark period of petty professional strife and marks the dawn of a new era in which the principles of good-will, brotherhood and mutual aid will strive for first place.

This movement is being watched with keen interest by all other instrumentalists. Many of them are veteran performers who have spent a lifetime trying to introduce a higher code of ethics among their colleagues, but were not entirely successful because their methods were wrong. Their way called for the individual to sway the many, whereas the Percussion Club relies on its massed opinion to improve the individual.

The officers of the Club are well-known New York City drummers:

President .... AARON GEIGER
Vice-Pres .... CHARLES KRITZLER
Rec.-Sec'y .... JAMES LENT
Treasurer .... JACK ZIMBLER
Serg't-at-Arms .... DANIEL WEINSAFT

They are men who are alert to the intellectual side of their professional problems. Directing the destiny of an organization such as this requires something more than a knowledge of Cushing's Manual; it requires a knowledge of working conditions and the psychological make-up of musicians.

The members are for the most part active, and all are very enthusiastic. With their backing much can be accomplished and it is safe to say that this organization will do its utmost to raise the standard of conditions among New York and vicinity drummers and will enjoy a most brilliant future.

Fraternally yours,
AARON GEIGER,
Pres. of N. Y. Percussion Club.

Laura La Plante Congratulates Emil Farnlund—

True, fine Drummers are often congratulated by world-renowned celebrities, BUT—when one of the world's most beautiful women holds out her hand—well—that's an event to be recorded and Drum Topics is very pleased to be able to do so by showing these excellent photos. The Drummer in this case is Emil Farnlund, now playing with Rube Wolf and his twenty piece orchestra on the stage of the Metropolitan Theatre, Los Angeles. The beautiful lady is Laura La Plante, one of Universal's most famous stars. The occasion followed one of Farnlund's recent sensational outbursts of originality at the drums, tympani and xylophone. He has made one hit after another in Hollywood and Los Angeles during the past few years. He has become personally known to almost every "big name" in that section of the country—and that is where big names abide. His home is in Ogden, Utah, and in twenty years of experience Farnlund has worked on class jobs in Portland, Seattle, San Jose, Oakland, Frisco and L. A., with several seasons on the road with such shows as "No, No, Nanette," "Lady, Be Good," "Tip Toes," "Peggy Ann" and many others. After a long run at Carter De Haven's Hollywood Music Box Theatre, Farnlund joined "Pat West and his Musical Middies" at the West Coast Boulevard Theatre, also the Figueroa Theatre. Later he joined Rube Wolf, where he is now even surpassing his past record. He is also often heard over KFWB (Warner Bros. Studios) doing special xylophone and vibraphone numbers. Emil is one dandy chap, as well as a marvelous Drummer, and has hundreds of staunch friends among the professional drummers of Southern California. He uses a complete Leedy Outfit.

Miss La Plante tries out Emil's new Leedy "Sparkling Gold" drums

To Protect Tympani Heads

A circular quilted pad placed between tympani heads and the fibre discs, when the instruments are not in use, will give the heads additional protection from damage and keep out the dust and grit which otherwise pound into the pores of the vellum under the blows of the sticks. Such a pad will also prevent the rough fibre discs from rubbing on and wearing out the heads when the tympani are being transported in trunks. By sprinkling a small amount of water on the upper side of the "quilts" a slight moisture may be held in the heads, which prevents them from drying out and becoming too tight. These pads or quilts are very simple and inexpensive to make. If you have no wife, see your tailor.

A little lovin', winter and summer,
Has sure played hell with many a Drummer.

The new Leedy Jade Green Drums, with Nobby Gold rods, are beautiful. The Jade finish is Du Pont Pyralin like the Marine Pearl and Sparkling Gold. It looks like the green Sheaffer Fountain Pen. Flashy, different and neat.

The New Leedy Trap Rail

FOR TEMPLE BLOCKS—SMALL CYMBALS—WOOD BLOCKS—TRIANGLE—COW BELLS—SMALL TOM-TOMS—TAMBOURINE OR TRAP TRAY.

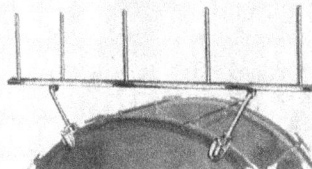

The new Leedy Trap Rail is one of the neatest and most practical trap holders yet devised. The upright posts will accommodate any of the holders that fit on the Leedy Trap Table, Trap Trees or Trap Console. The rail is 29 in. long and made of channel steel, which gives it great strength. The bass drum hoop clamps fold up under the rail. Just the thing for traveling and jobbing Drummers.

Ask for No. 278.

Of course you are alive, but—are you living?

Any type drum head that has become soiled with dirt and dust can be quickly cleaned by rubbing with ordinary art gum. It may be purchased in any stationery store. Sent in by David T. Green, Lawrence, Mass.

Ray Ennis and Verne Buck Two of Chicago's Top Notchers

Here we show two of the chief reasons why the Sheridan Theatre is one of the bright spots of Chicago—Ray Ennis (left), the Drummer, and Verne Buck, the leader of a most famous eighteen piece stage band. Ennis and Buck are the kind of fellows who have contributed the greatest "slice" in putting over the modern form of theatre entertainment. Ray is indeed one of Chicago's "regulars," both as drummer and friend. He has been in the game since thirteen years of age, starting in his home town of Springfield, Ill. At one time he directed his own orchestra there. Since locating at Chicago in 1919 Ray has been associated with the best, such as the Chicago Opera Club, Tivoli Theatre, Marigold Gardens and many others.

An Artistic Rhythmical Effect for "PP" and "PPP" Strains

By Art Layfield—Paul Ash Orchestra, Chicago

It is always a much greater problem to introduce a practical rhythm effect in the real piano strains than when the orchestra is playing forte. In searching for something new in PPP effects I discovered that the synco wire brush played on the hand-sock cymbal produces a most pleasing and, at the same time, delicate combination. The little wires of the brush lightly swishing on the top cymbal, with an occasional accent of the two cymbals coming together, make an effect that fits in the majority of piano strains. This gives the drummer a chance to "shine" where ordinarily he would be loafing and out of the picture. This effect can be played "down to a whisper."

 "FOR DRUMMERS WHO CARE"

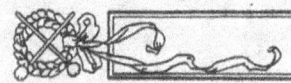

Leedy Drum Topics

The "Dead" Cymbal

The use of "dead" Chinese cymbal for "working up spots" in hot numbers seems to be increasing in popularity amongst the big-timers. Of course this one, like all other effects, will go over or flop according to the manner in which it is introduced. Those who are not using it are passing up a good opportunity for something different.

It won't be long before every drummer in the country will know Bill Gilcher's face. He is now holding down one of the "cream" jobs of the country—official studio Drummer, Tympanist, Xylophonist, etc., with the VITAPHONE at Warner Bros. in Hollywood, Calif. Everyone in the business from Chicago west knows Bill. Many years with the St. Louis Symphony, followed by several seasons with Max Dolin's orchestra in Frisco. Yes, those drums you see in the Vitaphone feature pictures are Leedy.

Karl L. King and His Drummers—

W. L. Engelbart   Phil W. Peters   Karl L. King   E. H. Holmquist

Drum Topics is certainly pleased that the above photo arrived in time for this issue. We have been trying to obtain it for some time in order to show our readers likenesses of Karl L. King and his drum section, as we have received many inquiries as to who the drummers in this famous band are.

Mr. Walter Engelbart is a native of Fort Dodge, Iowa, and officiates as Mr. King's business manager and bass drummer. He is also a cornet player of no mean ability, having had many years of professional experience in numerous theatres and dance orchestras. During the World War he served as Band Sergeant with the A. E. F. overseas.

Mr. Phil Peters, also of Fort Dodge, Iowa, has been with the band for the past five seasons, playing snare drum and tympani. Although young in the game, Peters is an accomplished student of Art Layfield of Chicago and is even yet continuing his studies. He not only "shines" as a concert band drummer, but is just as much at home in the pit and with dance orchestras, having done considerable in these branches of the business. "Pete" is known as one of the progressive type and always keeps up to the minute on new ideas.

Mr. King was born and raised in Canton, Ohio, and has been a leading composer of band music since his early teens. He has written more compositions than any other writer, living or dead. In 1917-18 Mr. King directed the Barnum & Bailey Circus Band and previous to that was with the Sells-Floto Circus Band. In 1919-20 he was director of McKinley's Own Band of Canton, Ohio. For the past six years he has directed his own band, with headquarters at Fort Dodge, where he has also established a flourishing music publishing business. This band enjoys an exceptionally fine reputation all over the Middle West.

Mr. E. H. Holmquist, known as "Hummie," also of Fort Dodge, Iowa, is a trouper of the old school, having served many years on the road, including several seasons with Merle Evans in Florida and elsewhere. He is now doing his stuff on drums and xylophone with the King Band as a regular feature. He is a most accomplished pit drummer, ranked as far above the average, and his ingenious tact for originating effects and cueing pictures always commands attention.

Did you ever hear about the Scotchman who told his wife to fry the bacon in Lux so it wouldn't shrink?

A Friendly Tip

Radio Drummers, Note—Many of the boys who are using the Leedy Vibraphone in radio work are allowing the fans in resonators to operate too fast. This sets up a too rapid pulsation of the tones and kills the true vox humano effect that the instrument is intended to produce. By raising the little speed control lever (at the upper right hand side of the instrument) the motor will run slower and enable the performer to play in a much more artistic manner. Between four and six pulsations per second is the correct speed to be truly musical.

Little Jack Horner
Played drums in a corner,
With traps piled around him sky high;
Much better than some
Did he wallop a drum
And cry, "What a fly guy am I."

The New Drum Stand Cymbal Holder

Here you have it—the neatest and most practical cymbal holder yet devised. Especially adapted to fast work, the cymbal being close to the snare drum. Cymbal can be adjusted to height and distance from the drum and will swing to any point around the drum stand. Can be set up very quickly and comes apart in three straight rods that take up very little room in a drum case. Longest rod is only 16 inches. Cymbal rocks without swinging and is responsive to the slightest vibration.
Ask for No. 279

Herbert Gottsegen

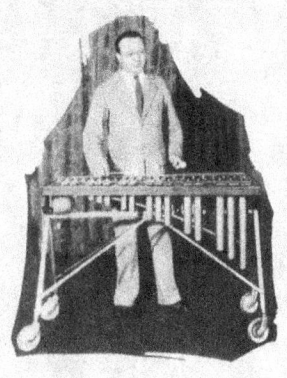

Everyone who hears the music of the Hotel Adelphia Whispering Orchestra in Philadelphia, Penna., declares it to be on a par with any hotel musical organization in the country. This orchestra is under the able management of Herbert Gottsegen, a most enterprising Drummer, whose photo with a Leedy Vibraphone is shown above. They also broadcast nightly over WFI. Gottsegen is from Schenectady, N. Y., and is well known in several Eastern cities, having worked for the Paul Whiteman, Vincent Lopez and Ray Miller offices on many elite engagements such as the Ten Eyck Hotel and Knickerbocker Grill at Albany, N. Y., Hotel Syracuse in Syracuse, N. Y., Hotel Martin in Utica, N. Y. He also had his own orchestra at Nikko Inn, Harmon-on-the-Hudson, and was later with Jerry Friedman at the exclusive 5th Ave. Club, New York. He has also done considerable first-rate vaudeville work.

Let's have just a little more from the bass drum. It's getting too feeble in some orchestras.

Gary Gillis and Arnold Johnson

The above photo shows a fine likeness of Gary Gillis, (left) drummer, and the popular orchestra leader and entertainer, Arnold Johnson. Gillis is one of the modern school boys who has established himself among the "name" drummers of the country by way of hard work and creative ability. He has been with Arnold Johnson for several years playing the highest class engagements in Florida and New York, also on the road in Keith-Albee Vaudeville, where they were a sensational hit at the Palace Theatre on Broadway. During the winter of 1926-27 at Hollywood Hills Inn, Hollywood, Fla., followed by a run at Arrowhead Inn., Saratoga Springs, N. Y. Gillis is from Anderson, Indiana. He says, "Leedy instruments have certainly helped me to do better work and I've tried them all."

The salary of the Drummers in Napoleon's army was equivalent to what is now $6.00 per month. That may seem ridiculous to us these days, but history says it was more than enough for one to enjoy life—goin' places and seein' things—during the Little Corporal's reign.

Ben Harrison—

Twenty years behind the drums in the dance and cabaret game has established Ben Harrison of Louisville, Ky., as one of the best-known "pedal pushers" in that city, also for many miles in all directions. Harrison has played with "Larry Pruett's Louisvillians," "Harry Currie's Orchestra," "Newman Spooner and his Orchestra," "Haden Reid's Orchestra," "Ray Pfaff" and others. He is now with "Art Payne's Gennett Recording Orchestra" and enjoys the reputation of having progressed with every change that has taken place in the dance business during his twenty years of active playing. He is considered an exceptionally fine modern drummer.
(Courtesy, Durlauf & Berry, Louisville, Ky.)

Henry Jacquinot

is a pupil of the well-known New York Drummer, Herman Weinberg (Loew's National Theatre). While Jacquinot is not yet playing as a full time professional, he owns a complete outfit (Leedy) and has done considerable amateur work. Mr. Weinberg states that Henry is putting in many more hours of hard practice than most students and this, coupled with his unusual sincerity and exceptional talent, will undoubtedly carry him to the top. Jacquinot is a native of Paris, France, and came to this country five years ago. One of his most interesting letters explains that he decided to take up drums shortly after the war, when he heard a few of the prominent modern American orchestras in Paris.

Leedy   "WORLD'S FINEST DRUMMERS' INSTRUMENTS"   **Leedy**

The Exclusive Drummers' Paper

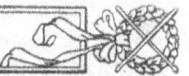

Art Barnett and Tommy Christian

When a Drummer boosts his leader and when a leader boosts his Drummer as these two do—all is well behind the bass drum. And such conditions go a long way toward making all well behind the baton, for a Drummer and Leader can make or break the "works." The "works" in this case are the fourteen men comprising Tommy Christian's orchestra, well known throughout the East from Maine to Florida and West to the Mississippi in the leading photoplay houses, dance halls, hotels and vaudeville theatres. They are always a big drawing card and often play return engagements. Barnett, the Drummer, is from Cresson, Penna., and has been with Christian many seasons. He is as clever as they come and his work always makes 'em sit up and take notice.

A New Way to Make Padded Sticks
By Walter Soderberg
Duluth, Minn.

Scrape the finish off the stick where you want the pads to go using a knife. Then brush well with LePage's glue. Next, wrap ordinary white absorbent cotton around the stick (keep turning the stick in a tight grip to work the cotton smooth) to about one-sixteenth of an inch thickness. Next wrap three-quarter inch adhesive tape around the cotton, pulling it tight. Allow the tape to overlap in the winding as shown in the photo. Trim off edges with safety razor blade and you have the best padded stick ever made. It will wear longer than any other kind. The pads DO NOT unbalance the stick. Leedy H-5 models are best for the purpose.

Edward Van Nest

of Plainfield, N. J., has been doing the better class of dance work in and around Plainfield for the past ten years; one year at "Rose Mont Lodge," three years at "Five Acres Inn" now at the "Lincoln Inn" with the Collegiate Club Orchestra. This is rated as a very fine dance organization, and Van Nest has the "rep" of being a snappy, up-to-date feature Drummer.

There Is a Vast Difference—

The TONE of a drum is one thing and the "FEEL" is quite another. A drum may sound exactly as you would have it, but due to the matching of the heads and snares (also their relative tension) it may play and "feel" terrible. On the other hand it may "feel" most wonderful under the sticks and sound very bad. Many Drummers do not define the difference between tone and "feel." It is well to have these points clearly understood in one's mind.

Did You Take Advantage Of—

the special notice in the last issue of Drum Topics in which Karl Glassman (Tympanist with the New York Symphony Orchestra, Walter Damrosch, Conductor) offered to answer any question concerning tympani playing. Several of those who did write to Mr. Glassman have since stated that they received some very valuable information in answer to their questions. Karl is a regular fellow and no one need be hesitant about approaching him by letter or in person. No "high hat" stuff required. The offer still stands—there is no charge for the service—just enclose a self-addressed and stamped envelope to—

Mr. Karl Glassman,
Gaiety Theatre Bldg., 46th St. & Broadway, New York City.

IT'S EASIER TO BELIEVE than to know—it doesn't require any research to believe

Mike L. Lake's Yankee Doodle Band with Geo. M. Cohan's "The Merry Malones"

Charlie Bessette   Mike L. Lake   Louis Mehling

Speaking of notables—such a bunch of individual "big timers" are not often found in one organization. It would require a full page of Drum Topics to give our readers the interesting story of each member of this new but already famous band. Much as we would like to do so, space forbids and we must stick to—"Drum Topics is for the Drummer first."
Charlie Bessette (No. 1) has been in the business since 1900. Frisco is his home town, but the whole country knows him from trouping with everything from the Buffalo Bill show to Grand Opera. Charlie once played at Cedar Point, Ohio, shortly after Mr. Leedy had finished there. He now makes New York City his home and is always identified with the leading bands and orchestras there. A thorough rudimental artist.
Mike L. Lake (No. 2), owner and manager of the band, is one of New York's leading composers and arrangers of music. Bessette and Mehling say—"He is one of the few who knows how to write a real drum part."
Louis Mehling (No. 3) is a native New Yorker, trained by his famous father, Michael Mehling, in the rudimental school. Mehling has been with a long list of the best, such as many seasons with the wonderful Patrick Gilmore Band—six years with the New York Philharmonic Orchestra—also Victor Herbert's Orchestra and four seasons with Sousa's Band. Such a record tells its own story of ability.
Gus Moeller, whom everyone knows as one of the world's leading exponents of rudimental drumming, is the pit drummer with this show.

The Drummer who does not receive Drum Topics can have it delivered direct to his door, absolutely free. A postal will do the trick.

"Cannon Ball" Baker and his son, Sherman Baker

Everyone interested in automobiles knows "Cannon Ball" Baker, the famous race and endurance driver who has broken over one hundred and twenty-five world records—more than any other driver on earth. He has been flirting with death for eighteen years and is still going strong. However, it is not generally known that "Cannon Ball" is quite enthusiastic about Drums. This is because his fourteen year old son, Sherman, is really a most talented drummer for his age. Sherman has been playing for three years and is now doing considerable semi-professional work. He also plays with his school orchestra of fifteen pieces and does quite a lot of church and social work in and around Indianapolis.

and he said—"How I love to see broken heads."

and she said—"Heavens, you must be a Doctor."

and he said—"No, I run a drum shop."

Leedy Triangles

While the triangle is one of the smallest items of a Drummer's kit, it is by no means unimportant. It is one of the oldest of all musical instruments and every composer considers it seriously. A good triangle is a real asset; a poor one can ruin the intended musical effect. Leedy triangles are made of the finest quality steel and have a rich, clear and distinct tone. They are obtainable in three sizes.

No. 126B—6 in. No. 126—8 in. No. 126A—10 in.

The beater is of the correct weight to bring out the tone and has a knurled non-slip handle.

Myron Coleman

had twenty years of continuous experience in England, his native country, before coming to New York. Over there he played in many of London's finest concert orchestras, movie and vaudeville theatres, also high class hotels and restaurants, including the Trocadero and Piccadilly. He was tympanist for the Provincial Cinema, Ltd. and played in many principal cities in England and Scotland, for them. Over here, Coleman has held down several leading vaudeville and photoplay theatre jobs in and around New York City.

"FOR DRUMMERS WHO CARE"

Leedy Drum Topics

Geo. Hamilton Green and Jack Roop Make Pacific Coast Tour and Visit Fifteen States in Interest of Leedy Mfg. Co.

During the past year and a half the Leedy Mfg. Co. has sponsored Geo. Hamilton Green's appearance in over one hundred cities. The last trip, in October, November and December of 1927, covered fifteen western States. More than six thousand Drummers, Xylophone and Marimba players gathered at the leading hotels to meet and hear him play. A pianist was engaged as accompanist in each city and without exception every visitor declared it was a most wonderful treat. Jack Roop, Asst. Sales Mgr. for Leedy, acts as business manager of these tours and at the same time displays the latest models of Leedy drums and accessories. Six large trunks are carried. Green and Roop report that in every city they are treated royally by the musicians and music dealers.

Geo. Hamilton Green —

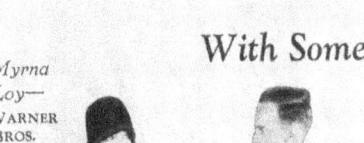

At Denver, Colo. Geo. and WALTER LIGHT, prominent Denver Drummer.

Geo. Hamilton Green's Fifty Lesson course of instruction on Xylophone and Marimba is now being offered, as a unit, at a reduced price. The finest and most thorough course ever written. Now being carried by the leading music stores. If your dealer can not supply you, write to Mr. Green, P. O. Box 465, Kenosha, Wis.

Jack Roop— Asst. Sales Mgr. for Leedy

At Los Angeles Geo. and SAM ROWLAND do a little clowning.

With Some of the Stars at Hollywood —

Myrna Loy— WARNER BROS. STAR—

Clyde Cook WARNER BROS. STAR—

Audrey Ferris— WARNER BROS. STAR—

Geo. Hamilton Green's New Creation
"THE MARIMBA SLAP"

This brand new idea, lately originated by Geo. Hamilton Green, has already proven a great "hit" by all who have given it a trial. It is especially adapted for dance work in "hot" and "blue" numbers. However, Marimba players who are looking for a real novelty will find it an attention-getter and laugh-producer in any class of work. "THE MARIMBA SLAP" is easy to play— the special hammers provided for the stunt produce a combination of three effects—a slap and sock combined with the tone of the bar. The hammers are similar to tympani sticks except that the lambs wool balls are reversed, with the leather side on the outside and the fleece on the inside. The cushion-like ball is of the correct weight to produce this peculiar and pleasing effect.

HOW TO PLAY THEM—Use at all times a SMOTHERED beat. No roll is necessary. Meaning, to strike the bars with a stiff, sharp, rigid, PRESSING blow and let the hammer lay on the bar just as a slap-stick comes together. It's a "lay down" stroke. Do not pull the hammer away until the tone is completely dead. Always accent the 2nd and 4th quarter beats in each measure (in 4/4 time) regardless of the tune.

Ex. 1—This will give the first idea of "The Marimba Slap." Note that the 2nd and 4th quarter beats are accented. Practice many times and work up to a fox trot tempo. Remember—smother ALL notes. Don't lift the hammer and let the tone ring out.

Ex. 2—gives the "Slap" in a straight scale. The dotted notes afford the best construction on which to apply the "Slap" effect. Use a rigid, stiff blow. Don't lift the hammers.

Ex. 3—shows how the "Slap" idea is used involving triplets. This is a very good form to use for all modern dance melodies—watch the accents carefully. Practice until you can play smoothly and in regular dance tempo. Press the blow.

Ex. 4—Here is a finished melody featuring the most modern style of "Marimba Slap" playing. Notice that NO FAST PROGRESSIONS ARE EMPLOYED. Never try to play fast variations with the Slap Hammers; always feature the slow drag, "blue" style. The fewer notes applied, the more Slap effect. Once the idea is grasped you will find it very easy to play any melody in this style. It is the very latest thing in modern dance rendition. Don't forget—slap down on the hammers with a stiff, rigid stroke. Let them lay.

The New Leedy Marimba Slap Hammers Ask for No. 375

"WORLD'S FINEST DRUMMERS' INSTRUMENTS"

The Exclusive Drummers' Paper

Looks Like Two Balls of Fire

Tympani bowls finished in White or Black Duco are very pretty, but many Drummers are now learning that an EXTRA BRIGHT plain copper polish on the bowls (covered with lacquer) with Nobby Gold hoops, brackets, handles and bases, will show up better from a distance than any other finish. After trying several other styles Geo. W. Marsh said—"This is the best finish of all, because the bowls look like two balls of fire from the last row in the house—it's the viewpoint of the audience that counts." This finish is the same price as the White or Black Duco with Nobby Gold trimmings.

Jack Spratt was a Drummer fat,
His wife was extra lean,
But when he started steppin' out
She socked him on the bean.

Walter Fehl and Danny Lee

Walter Fehl (standing) was formerly Drummer at the Orpheum Theatre in St. Louis, Mo. He was considered one of the finest on the circuit. After leaving the Orpheum, Walter put in several seasons with Henry Santrey and his Band. A little more than two years ago he took up the baton as leader of his own act. It is called "His Magic Wand" and consists of twelve first-class musicians and entertainers. Danny Lee is the neat and peppy little Drummer who is one of the "high lights" of this act. Is he good? He's got to be good. It's a case of a Drummer working for a Drummer and they both know their Tom Toms. The band has just concluded 104 consecutive weeks playing the major vaudeville theatres. They sailed for England on the S. S. Hamburg on January 19th, where they will tour the country in vaudeville and appear in a London revue.

The Prize Story
By Vincent L. Mott

The management of a big city, first run photoplay theatre decided to change the policy to high class vaudeville. The orchestra leader was a very fine violinist and a marvel with the legit stuff for pictures but when it came to vaudeville—get this: At the first rehearsal everything went fair enough. One of the members of an acrobatic act said, "You play that there waltz until cartwheels on stage, then make a quick segue into that there galop." "I understand," said the leader. At the first show they had the closing spot. Orchestra plays the waltz—men on stage do routine finally going into series of cartwheels. Orchestra keeps on with the waltz. "Galop" yelled an acrobat but the leader only looked blank and kept right on with the waltz. Musicians in the pit tried to tip the leader off to go into the galop—but nothing doing. Act finished. Curtain comes down—then the leader goes into the galop—too late. After the chaser the acrobats were waiting in the music room. "Say," says one of them, "why didn't you go into our galop?" "I was waiting for you to bring out the wagon wheels" replied our hero.

VINCENT L. MOTT operates an exclusive drum shop at 1032 E 25th Street, Paterson, N. J. He is also drummer and tympanist with the large symphony orchestra at the Fabian Theatre. This is a "Class" job and Vince is a "Class" drummer in every respect. Fifteen years ago he gave up the study of law to take up drums. The urge for the latter was too strong. After a lengthy course with both Harry A. Bower and Alfred Frieze he went in for theatre work and has since held many fine positions. During the war Mott was with the 31st Artillery C. A. C. Band. In 1922 he opened a general music store in Paterson but later changed it to an exclusive drum shop. This store has now become a real "Drummers Service Station" for all the boys of the district. Mrs. Mott assists in the store and knows that when a "Johnny Newcomer" asks for a pair of pegs, he means spurs.

R. G. Wyman

has been a vaudeville Drummer of extraordinary calibre for fifteen years, the past six at the Scolly Square Olympia Theatre in Boston, Mass. Born at Kennebunk, Maine, Wyman started when very young on piano and later changed to drums (a pupil of Harry A. Bower). During his professional career he has played almost every brass instrument and, being an accomplished student of harmony and composition, has written several marches, the most popular of which are "15th U. S. Cavalry Band" and "Columbia Call" (both published by Walter Jacobs, Boston). He has served with the bands of the 3rd Inf., 103rd Inf., and is now sergeant of the 182nd Inf. Band. Wyman holds three medals and rates as an expert for both rifle and pistol shooting. This is the highest honor obtainable for army marksmanship. He was also an army rifle and pistol instructor; now a member of the Boston Revolver Club.

Correct Tucking

Heads will never slip off Leedy metal flesh hoops if they are tucked correctly. Always be sure to shove the head ALL THE WAY UNDER the flesh hoop, allowing a little to go BEYOND the outside corner as shown in Fig. 1. Never tuck as shown in Fig. 2. Leedy metal flesh hoops are best because they are uniform in size and extra heads may be carried without warping.

James F. Underwood

James F. Underwood is now back in his home town, Columbus, Ohio, playing with Allen Hale and his Orchestra. This is a first-class organization doing the best class of work. For two years Underwood worked in Detroit with Gene Goldkette, Seymour & Simmons and Dick Bowen. Eight years in the business have established him as a top-notch modern Drummer in every respect.

Al Zuger

of New York City has been in the business for 19 years. He has a most remarkable record for being associated with big name organizations which certainly means extraordinary ability. A partial list follows: several seasons with Joseph Knecht at the Waldorf-Astoria Hotel—with Sam Lanin at the Roseland Ballroom—with Mike Markell and Henry Conrad, both famous society orchestra leaders—with Meyer Davis at the Pavilion Royal—with Ernie Young's Revue at Rainbo Gardens, Miami, Florida—Around the World on the S. S. President Polk—with George Olsen at Atlantic City and for the past several seasons with the noted Phil Romano's Victor Recording Orchestra. This orchestra recently finished a long engagement at the Kenmore Hotel, Albany, N. Y. Zuger says "I'm thru experimenting—Leedy gives me the best results."

Leon Knapp of Grand Rapids, Mich., Promotes Drums and Drummers By Organizing His Own Corps

Here is something for leading Drummers in every city and town to think about. Without the backing of any fraternal organization or industrial concern, Leon Knapp has organized his own personal corps under the title of "Leon Knapp's All Star Drum Corps." His sole idea is to create further interest in Drums among all classes of people in Grand Rapids and vicinity. As Leon is an old-time professional with experience in all branches and as he has operated a Drum School and shop for many years, it was no trick for him to turn out this crack corps in record time. On last Sept. 12th they made their first appearance on the street as a feature of the National G. A. R. encampment parades. They received lengthy newspaper notices and the business men now look upon the corps as a real asset to the city. Can they play? Ask any of the G. A. R. divisions who attended from all over the U. S.

Leedy — "FOR DRUMMERS WHO CARE" — **Leedy**

Leedy Drum Topics

Drummers of the Long Beach Municipal Band —
HERBERT L. CLARKE — Conductor

CHARLES E. SEELEY   O. F. ROMINGER   FRANK A. SNOW

Here are three Drummers whose individual skill and technique have built up a band Drum Section that has no betters in any city. This clean-cut team stands out in the concerts to such an extent that the audiences notice and comment on it. Being located permanently at one place, naturally many of the same people return each day and it is a well known fact in Long Beach that a big percentage of the "repeaters" go to hear and watch these Drummers work.

Charles E. Seeley (Small Drum, Bell and Xylophone Soloist) has been in the business many years doing both theatre and band work. He is what a critic would call a crackerjack, all-round man, playing Xylophone with showmanship and skill that always calls for encores.

O. F. Rominger (Tympanist) is well known in many Western cities and has done every class of work. His former home was Indianapolis, Ind. "O. F." is noted for three things — hard work, sincerity and skill.

Frank A. Snow (Bass Drum and Cymbals) is one of the best known Drummers not only in this country, but in the world. We don't know just how many years he has been in the business, but as the boys say when speaking of "old timers" — "He has been with 'em all." Frank was Tympanist with Sousa's Band for ten years and made the first world tour with them. The new drum method described below was wholly written by him and has just come from the press. It is a very fine piece of work and will undoubtedly take its place among the leading instruction books.

This band, which is under the direction of the world-renowned Cornetist and Bandmaster, Mr. Herbert L. Clarke, is the only organization of its kind in the United States. Maintained permanently and supported by the Municipality, it has been in continuous service since 1909, playing daily concerts at Long Beach, California. The band is composed of some of the best known men in the musical profession. All concerts are broadcast over KGER and KFON.

NEW — the Frank A. Snow
INSTRUCTOR OF RUDIMENTAL DRUMMING

When this new drum method, written by the celebrated Frank A. Snow, came from the press, copies were sent out to several well known teachers in various parts of the country, with a request for comments. In about every case the reply was — "I intend to adopt it in my work." Other remarks were — "It is brief" — "The rudiments are explained in a simple and impressive manner" — "The twenty martial beats and the twelve quicksteps are worth twice the price of the book" — "It's just what we teachers have been waiting for" — "Send me a dozen" — "The reading exercises are great for the serious pupil" — etc.

Every Drummer Needs A Date Book —

The jotting down of notes on past, present and future often saves time and money. This little book will help you to keep things straight in a business-like manner. It contains 24 pages of useful information, a 3-year calendar, 14 pages for cash account and a year's date space arranged in perpetual form so that you may start at any time, no matter what day, month or year. The book is bound in a high grade leatherette cover. Mailed postpaid to Drummers only on receipt of ten cents in U. S. Stamps. Owing to postal regulations we regret that we can not extend this offer to Drummers outside of the United States and Canada.

Send 10c in stamps for yours — TODAY

Crowding and Rushing —

It is as easy for a Drummer to unconsciously fall into the habit of "crowding" his work as it is to unconsciously rush the tempo. "Crowding" will stifle a Drummer's ability. "Rushing" will ruin a Drummer's reputation. Avoid them both.

Treating Old Heads —

If your heads have dried out and have lost their flexibility because of old age, try this — Put a little white vaseline on a soft cloth and rub it well over and into the heads of your snare drum, bass drum, tympani, tom tom or tambourine. The oil in the vaseline will soften them up and give them new life. Be careful not to use too much vaseline; a small amount well rubbed in is best.

Mitzi Bush —

If circumstances were such that you could not see Mitzi Bush in action, but could only hear her clever work, you would imagine that one of the first-class male drummers of the big time class was putting it over. Press notices are as a rule just press notices, but when they appear in city after city all praising an artist's efforts, then they mean something. Just such notices have been given this young lady in about every town where she has played with the Parisian Red Heads — America's greatest girl band. They have appeared in most of the largest presentation houses of the country and were the first girls' band to receive a recording contract from one of the major companies. Brunswick records exclusively Mitzi is from Elmhurst, Ill., and was formerly with Elsie Myerson's Band in Keith vaudeville. She has had several seasons' experience in modern work and is a member of the Chicago Federation of Musicians.

Chester E. Frost —

is a hustler who has proven himself to be a clever business man and orchestra director as well as an artist with the "hickories." For seven years he has piloted his own orchestra of ten men (Chet Frost and his Original Bostonians) into many of the leading jobs of the Eastern States and Canada. These include engagements at Ottawa, Ont., Montreal, Que., Portland, Me., Revere, Mass., New York City, Hampton Beach, N. H., Lakewood, N. J., Long Island, Beach Bluff, Mass., Salem, Mass., and Bermuda. His orchestra has also been a feature over WHN, WJZ, WEEI, WGY and WBZ. He is now playing at Hunt's Venetian Room, Lynn, Mass.

Speaking of atmospheric conditions: variation in the pitch of Xylophone and Marimba bars is never caused by dampness or dryness but only by heat and cold.

In Uganda

Uganda borders on the northern shore of Lake Victoria. The capital city, Mengo, is about eight hundred [ ] feet above sea level. Here we find the official Royal [ ] thirty members, who play on drums of all sizes from [ ] to 36 inches in diameter by 48 inches deep. Th[ ] gourds and stavelike shells and held taut by dozens o[ ] close together. These ropes are run thru holes cut [ ] other end to the shells. There is no tension adju[ ] main tight because damp and dry weather affect the [ ] manner. The great number of ropes and their ex[ ] siderable fluctuation caused by atmospheric conditio[ ]

The college man who used to consult his [ ] looks over his favorite jazz band.

When the Drummer in the pit watches the Drumm[ ]
..................?
When the Drummer on the stage watches the Dr[ ]
..................?
Yeah, that's the right answer.

She promised she'd play square, but all she did w[ ]

(Drawn by Gaar Williams) Reprinted by permiss[ion]

   **"WORLD'S FINEST DRUMMERS' INSTRUMENTS"**   

Page Eight

The Exclusive Drummers' Paper

(Photo by Cowling, from Ewing Galloway, N. Y.)

...ganda—
...f Lake Victoria—Nyanza, in British East Africa
...hundred miles from the Pacific Ocean and is 4000
...ficial Royal music to be an elaborate drum corps of
...l sizes from 6 inches in diameter by 15 inches deep
...deep. The heads are of ox hide stretched over
...by dozens of long, vegetable fibre ropes placed very
...u holes cut in the hide at the top and nailed at the
...nsion adjustment on these ropes. The heads re-
...r affect the ropes and heads in exactly the opposite
...d their extra length render them subject to con-
ric conditions.

nsult his tailor on the latest styles now
l.

he Drummer on the stage for more than one show

hes the Drummer in the pit after the first show

l she did was play 'round. *(Life.)*

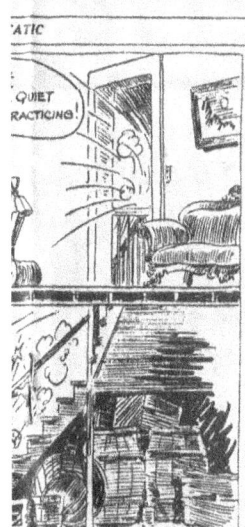

d by permission of the CHICAGO TRIBUNE

Shells Do Not Vibrate—

The shells of snare drums, bass drums and tympani do not vibrate in playing, therefore the "shell vibration" that is sometimes discussed among Drummers is imaginary, grown out of misunderstanding, and has no bearing on the quality of drum tone one way or another. If there was the least shell pulsation the tones would waver and produce what is termed "wolf tones." It is the heads only (and the snares on small drums) that do the vibrating. The shell simply acts as a means to support the heads and to encase a chamber of air. This chamber of air is compressed and expanded by the movement (vibration) of the heads. However, the shell must be stiff enough to support both an even and uneven strain to a great degree. If you are under the impression that the tympano shell does vibrate you may quickly prove the matter to your own satisfaction in the following manner. Tune the head evenly to any note. Then brace the instrument firmly against a solid wall (the counter hoop against the wall—not the shell) and have several pair of hands all around the hoop holding it firmly to the wall. Next have someone pound and roll on the head while you hold your finger tips ever so lightly to any point on the bowl. You will note that you can feel no vibration whatever from the tympano bowl or shell.

Ashley Paige—

It has been said that vaudeville audiences no longer appreciate single Xylophone acts. If there is any such tendency on the part of the public it is in no way apparent when Ashley Paige steps out to do his stuff on the Keith and Orpheum stages. The Editor of Drum Topics has caught his act four times in as many different cities and in each case he was a positive riot, being called back again and again. Paige has a rare combination to offer. He is all pep, smiles and personality and these qualities, combined with skill and clean-cut playing, make 'em demand more and more. His speed is marvelous and his six hammer numbers are exceptionally fine. No fake here—every hammer is working legitimately. Paige hails from Boston, where he is well known in every branch of the biz. He played with Bert Law on society jobbing work for three years and was several seasons with Bill Boyle at the Copley-Plaza Hotel, also Edison Light Radio WEEI. For four years he had a studio in partnership with the popular Frank Haynes, former Sousa Drummer.

Thin 10 and 11-Inch Italian Cymbals—

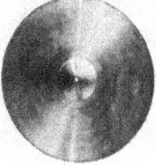

Yes, we have them in these unusually small and, at the same time, exceptionally thin models. These are dandy cymbals and of the very type that modern Drummers desire for high pitch "sting" work. Do they cut thru? We'll say they do! Especially made for Leedy by a manufacturer who was once on the staff of Zildjian in Constantinople and who moved to Italy a few years ago. We also have very thin models in the 12, 13 and 14-inch sizes.

Graeme Gardiner—

has been at the Statler Hotel, Buffalo, N. Y., with Earl Carpenter and his band (a George Olson unit) for the past year and a half. This band is now on tour playing high class ballrooms and presentation theatres. Gardiner is from Montreal, Canada, and held many prominent positions there before coming to the States. Formerly with Ray Stillwell and his band, he is indeed a clever, up-to-date Drummer who is ever on his toes introducing new ideas.

Sousa and His Drummers—

GUS HELMECKE   FRANK HOLT   HOWARD GOULDEN   JOHN PHILIP SOUSA

We could have shown this picture without any names—every Drummer in the U. S. and many in other countries are familiar with their photos and thousands know them personally because of their extensive travels. They recently finished a country-wide tour, including Western Canada and several west coast states. During the Xmas and New Year's holidays they all returned to their homes, but were soon out and going again. Gus lives in New York City and when in town between trips he visits around with the boys. Everybody likes Gus and he always has a string of great stories. Frank lives in Haverhill, Mass. (near Boston), where he operates a drum shop and school. Checking up on business during his absence takes about all of his time when at home. Howard lives at Bridgeport, Conn., and, like Frank, he also has a drum shop that gives him plenty of work when in the city. Mr. Sousa lives on Long Island just outside of New York City. We know he is as busy at home as when on the road, planning his next tour. His Drummers

"All aboard"—for another jump

all say that he is a wonderful leader to work for because he knows the possibilities in Drums and lets them do their stuff without holding them down.

Gus and Howard Meet Ronald Olfson—

When Sousa's Band played Edmonton, Alberta, Canada, last October the boys of the drum section were entertained by Ronald S. Olfson, one of the leading Drummers of that city. "Olie" plays at the Empire Theatre, a combination road show and Orpheum vaudeville house which supports a very fine orchestra. He is a skilled, all-round Drummer and is often highly complimented by traveling leaders. A finer gentleman and good fellow can not be found. "Olie" is also manager of the Edmonton branch of the Dominion Rubber Co.

DO NOT condemn and discard a new effect or any other new stunt pertaining to drums simply because you don't happen to like it at the first trial. Give it a chance to prove its worth. Who knows—it may be all the rage a short time hence.

Arthur C. Butts—

Although in the game only nine years Arthur C. Butts has made his way to the best class of theatre work in New York City—his home town. With a year at the Criterion, also a year at the Rialto to his credit, he is now at the famous Strand, one of the finest jobs on Broadway. Butts has the rep. of being one of the finest Xylophone players in New York.

(Courtesy Frank Wolf Drum Shop)

"FOR DRUMMERS WHO CARE"

Page Nine

Leedy Drum Topics

NEW — Butterfly Silhouette —

There can be no greater contrast than extreme black and white, therefore silhouettes show up more clearly at greater distances than any other type of bass drum head paintings. Here is one that is most artistic and modern in design. It is equally effective with or without lights.
Ask for No. S-12.

Sam Harris —

Fred E. Hand   Sam Harris   Prof. M. Zlatin

When a genuine Grand Opera Co. of over eighty artists tours the country, packing 'em in nightly in these days of radio, movies and jazz, it's got to be good. "The King's Henchman," a Metropolitan Opera House production, is doing that very thing. This American Opera (music by Deems Taylor) is now making a trans-continental tour of the U. S. It is hailed by the press and public as an operatic sensation. Sam Harris is the Drummer and Tympanist with this organization. He is one of the leading Drummers of New York City, being known as a wonderful routine man as well as a finished Tympanist. His wide experience on notable jobs includes many seasons with the Metro-Goldwyn-Mayer Corporation, D. W. Griffith Co., Loew's Corporation, The Fox Film Corporation and others. His exacting technique and fine musicianship always win the high favor of his conductors.

Fred E. Hand, known to all in high class theatrical circles, is the genial manager of the company. His many years' experience, both behind the footlights as a leading dramatic artist and as a keen business executive, have been a big factor in directing this organization to the success it now enjoys.

Prof. M. Zlatin, Conductor, is one of Europe's foremost Operatic Musical Directors. He also is responsible for the artistic finish of both the singers and musicians of the company. The members of the orchestra all declare it to be a pleasure to work under the baton of this most agreeable and, at the same time, painstaking director.

If you doubt the value of co-operation—try driving your car with one flat tire.

NEW — Indian Scene —

This new bass drum head painting is one of the finest we have ever seen. It is executed in the conventional poster style—meaning that four flat colors are employed. This gives decided contrasts that are most brilliant and effective. It shows up beautifully with lights, but can be used without.
Ask for No. S-11.

Justa Wethead says —

Sing a song of sixpence,
Jazz is all the rage,
Four and twenty players
Seated on the stage.
When the dance is opened
The band begins to play,
But what the Hell they're playing
Is more than I can say.

Twenty-four distinctly different kinds of felt are used in the manufacture of the various drummers' instruments and accessories of the Leedy brand.

A Rare Photograph —

(Photo by Keystone View Co.)

It is very seldom that photos of any members of the French Foreign Legion in Africa appear in public print. The Legion is composed of men from all nations and they have formed the basis of many stirring tales, both in fact and fiction, on account of their dangerous work of keeping the desert tribes of the French Colony in Africa subdued. This photo shows the Drum and Bugle Corps stationed at Algiers lined up on the barracks grounds ready to sound reveille.

Al. Nathan —

We wanted to tell our readers all about this well known New York City Drummer, but our friend, Frank Wolf (of the Frank Wolf Drum Shop) did not send in enough dope for us to do justice to this fine photograph. All we know is that Nathan has been with the Landau Recording Orchestra at the Alamac Hotel for the past two years. Don't blame Drum Topics for this punk story—blame Wolf. Now will you be good, Frank?

A Tom Tom Stunt —

If you like to use two Chinese Tom Toms of different tones for jobbing work and at the same time have to carry around the one for the purpose, here is a way out of the difficulty. Use two of the 10-inch size and cut a 5-inch diameter hole in head used on the under side of one of them. This will make the instrument produce a rather dead and much more flat tone than without the hole. The other Tom Tom with its ringing tone makes an acceptable contrast for the two effects. Use a sharp knife and cut a clean circle.

James Jerome Rosenberg —

of New York City recently finished a year's engagement with the largest theatre orchestra in the world—the Roxy, in N. Y.—and is now in the percussion section of the Cincinnati Symphony Orchestra. Rosenberg has been connected with a great many leading New York musical organizations for the past twelve years and is looked upon as one of the finest of legitimate, all 'round Drummers. He is a pupil of Karl Glassman.

(Courtesy, Frank Wolf Drum Shop)

Leo S. Johnson —

is a semi-professional Drummer who spends the winters at the University of Minnesota, playing between study periods with Sig Stregal's Orchestra. During the summers he is kept busy at the various Minnesota lake resorts. Stregal's Orchestra has the rep of being one of the best college orchestras in the country and Johnson is one of the chief reasons.

(Courtesy, Hauser Music Co., Mpls.)

"WORLD'S FINEST DRUMMERS' INSTRUMENTS"

The Exclusive Drummers' Paper

Billy Thompson —

Reliable reports state that Billy Thompson enjoys the reputation of being one of the finest rudimental Drummers in all England and Scotland. Having received a most thorough schooling while a member of the famous Black Watch Regiment band, he now applies ultra artistic rudimental work to his professional playing of modern dance work. Billy has written several technical articles for British music journals and Drum Topics regrets that there is not space to print the excellent "hot" rhythmical scores he has submitted. He also studied electrical engineering four years at Edinburgh University. For the past three years he has managed his own band, "The Broadway Five," at the Imperial Hotel, St. Andrews, Scotland.

Ernest S. Wickenden —

holds a responsible position in the British patent office at London, England. Evenings he does gig work with one of London's popular dance orchestras, filling engagements at such well known places as the Cecil Hotel, Connaught Rooms and Crystal Palace. He has also filled several cinema engagements. With nine years experience, backed by sound tuition in the rudimental school and a special course with Julian Vedey on modern dance work, Wickenden ranks high with London's best. At present he is writing an interesting series of articles for "Rhythm," that excellent English magazine for Drummers.

???????

This very nice photo from abroad reached Drum Topics without a name attached. We are unable to connect it with the many letters received and if this Drummer will write us we will be glad to publish it again in the next issue, with proper credit. Sorry.

If your drum rings, remove batter head and lay a strip of silk 2 inches wide, or a length of one-half inch elastic tape (white) across the shell. Replace head. The material touching the head will eliminate the ring. Trim off material under flesh hoop so it will not show.

By Joseph B. Boyle,
Macclesfield, Cheshire,
England

Drummers of Other Lands —

During the showing of the Famous-Players-Lasky production, "The Trumpet Call," at one of Glasgow's leading cinemas, several prominent Drummers of the city were engaged to "put over" the many effects necessary to the success of this feature photoplay. Here are shown the Drummers of the occasion with Mr. J. A. H. Biggar, proprietor of Alexander Biggar, Ltd., "The Center of Music," 102 Sauchiehall Street, who kindly furnished Leedy instruments for the event. Alexander Biggar, Ltd., are exclusive distributors for Leedy for Glasgow, Edinburgh and surrounding towns. They always carry a large stock and give both the professional and amateur the finest of service. Those shown in the photo, left to right, are:
David Butters, Ed. Wylie, Joe Mather, ?????????????????, John Findlay, Harry McKay, Bill Mather, J. A. H. Biggar, Bobbie Singleton.

Jimmie Little

Jimmie Little formerly put in several years in cinema concert orchestra playing. The St. James Cinema, Harrogate; Royal Cinema, Sheffield, and others in several cities have featured his fine work on both drums and xylophone. A few years ago he organized his own modern dance orchestra and entered the high-class ballroom field. The orchestra has played at the Cafe Dansant, Skegness; Palace Ballroom, Blackpool; Central Pier, Morecambe; Grand Hotel, Sheffield, and for the past three years at The La Scala Ballroom, Manchester.

Melville S. Hutchison —

Throughout a most active and varied career Melville S. Hutchison has kept up with his Drums. For a considerable period he successfully practiced dentistry at Montrose, Scotland, and was twice elected to the City Council. He is also well known to the legitimate dramatic stage by way of excellent work opposite Mrs. John Clyde, the famous Scottish actress, and in addition has held several important offices in Freemasonry. For the past year Hutchison has been a feature Drummer, Tympanist and Vocalist at the Tivoli Theatre, Dundee.
(Courtesy, Watt's Salons, Dundee)

Mary E. Robertson —

It is not only the male of the species who are privileged to be successful owners and managers of modern orchestras. Mary E. Robertson has operated her own band for eight years and is now at the West End Palais de Danse in Montrose, Scotland. Her versatility in playing Bells, Xylophone and novelty percussion instruments has made her most popular and the band fills numerous county engagements, frequently being called upon to play at Lord Airlie's, Cortachy Castle. She was formerly a dancing instructor at Blackpool, England.

Hector Cuevas —

Here is a Drummer well known on both sides of the Atlantic, in Mexico and Spain. Hector Cuevas was formerly with the famous Police Band of Mexico City, also the Banda del Estado in Yucatan, Mexico; Compania de Operetas, "Esperanza Iris," and del Cinema Olimpia in Mexico City. Cuevas is now playing in his native city, Zaragosa, Spain, at the Gran Cafe, "Royalty." He states that his entire outfit is Leedy excepting Zildjian Cymbals, Chinese Tom Tom and Spanish Castanets, also that the Spanish, who are world-renowned dance lovers, are most enthusiastic about modern American dance music. Several press items praise Cuevas' work highly.

Edward F. Horsman —

of Leeds, England, started out as a full-time Drummer in 1920 with Eric Arden's "Synco-Raggers," doing gig work. Since 1924 he has been with Barry Constable's Charleston Quintette at Powolny's Restaurant, Leeds. This is one of the leading jobs of the city and Horsman's neat work, combined with his ability to create novel effects, has helped to keep the orchestra on the job for such a long period.
(Courtesy, R. S. Kitchen Co., Leeds)

Do your drummer friends receive Drum Topics? If not, send us their names. It will be mailed absolutely free every three months.

Sydney M. Wall —

That the Drummers of Australia are a peppy and enthusiastic lot is evidenced by the many sincere and interesting letters Drum Topics has received from there. Sydney M. Wall is one of them. He is now playing with Ray C. Keefe's Club Royals, doing the best class of gig work in Sydney, N. S. W. This is a high-class dance orchestra. Formerly, Wall toured throughout Australia with a unit vaudeville company as a feature Drummer. His work has been highly praised in the press, principally because of originality. He writes "My New Leedy Drums have certainly put new life into my playing."
(Courtesy, W. H. Paling & Co., Sydney)

"FOR DRUMMERS WHO CARE"

Leedy Drum Topics

Twelve Large Wall Charts Make Correct Drum Corps Playing Easy—
CHARTS ARE 36"x 36"—PRINTED IN BLACK AND RED ON HEAVY YELLOW PAPER

Unity of execution is the most important factor in building a fine Drum Corps. These new Leedy Instruction Charts assure such unity because each Drummer will grasp exactly the same conception of rudimental technic.

The charts are written so you can understand them. Details are explained in a new way that makes practice a pleasure. They are practical, simple and brief. A new corps can be produced in record time and old corps will benefit greatly by studying them.

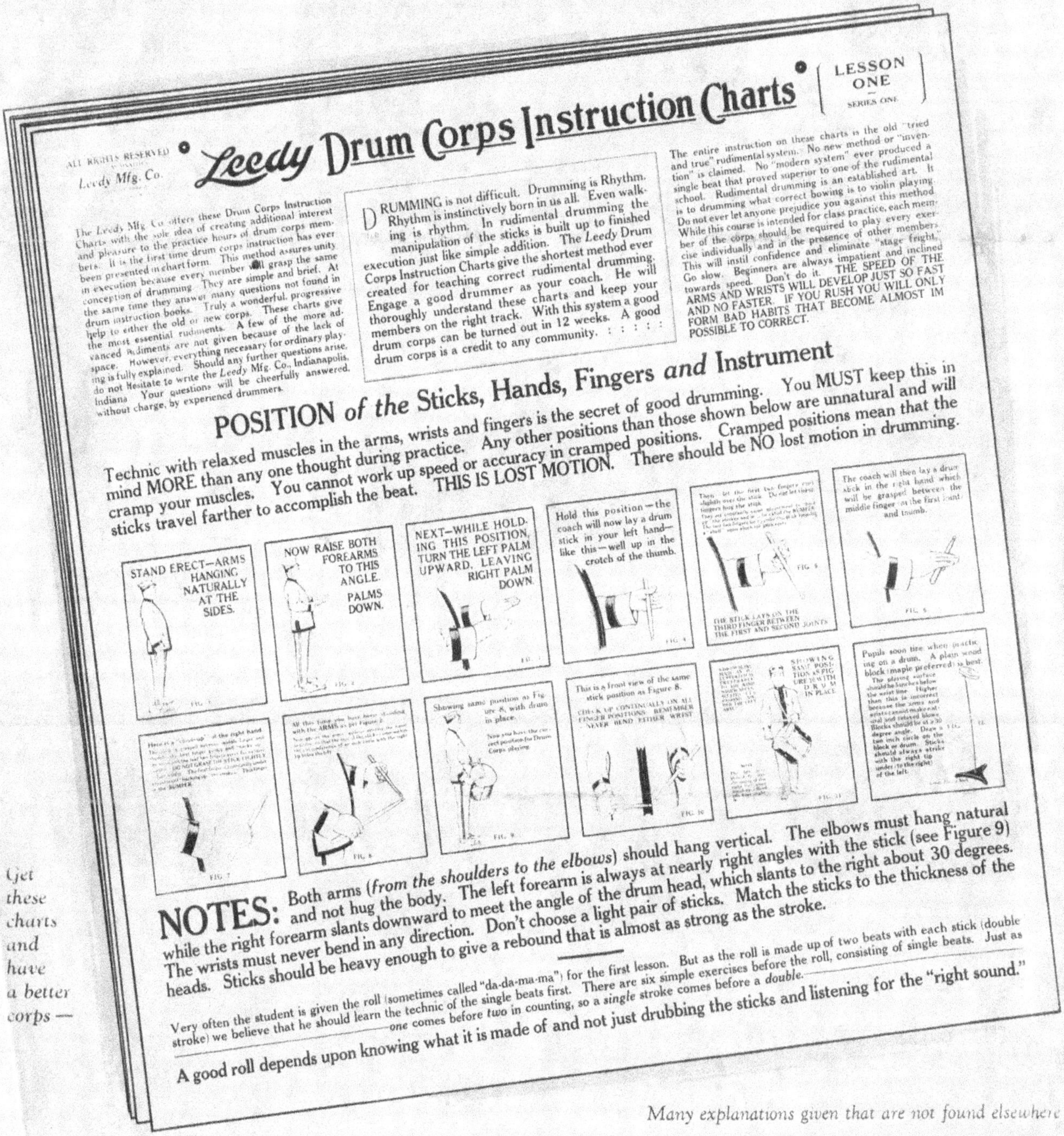

Get these charts and have a better corps—

Many explanations given that are not found elsewhere

 "WORLD'S FINEST DRUMMERS' INSTRUMENTS"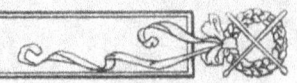

Page Twelve

The Exclusive Drummers' Paper

American Legion Drum Corps In Paris

Great Experience for Hundreds of Drummers

To tell the experiences of American Legion Drummers in Paris last September would require a whole book. Dozens of letters received from friends of Drum Topics state they had the time of their lives. Here are photos of five of the six Corps that came out on top in the drill contests which opened Tuesday, September 27th, with elimination contests, on the Champs de Mars — adjacent to Eiffel Tower.

It is regrettable that no photo was obtainable of the winner of first prize, viz: the Miami, Fla., Corps of thirty-two men. Their rating was 96.0.

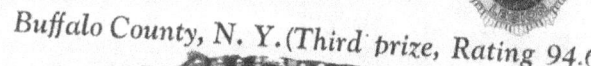

Buffalo County, N. Y. (Third prize, Rating 94.6)

Edwin B. Kenngott, President; Claub Eggleston, Vice-President; Langdon D. Drennan, Secretary; Walter D. Keller, Treasurer; John J. Murphy, Chief Musician; Harry Vogt, Drum Major. This photo shows only eighty-three men. The Corps now numbers over one hundred, one of the largest in the world and one of the finest.

Kankakee, Ill. (Second prize, Rating 95.2)

Wm. H. Maitland, Commander; Harry Thompson, Drum Major; Ray Wulff, Musical Director; A. E. Halbmaier, Bugle Sergt.; Clyde Worth, Drum Sergt. Seventy-five men comprised this fine outfit in Paris.

Fort Dodge, Ia. (Fourth prize, Rating 94.2)

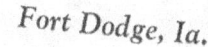

Dr. A. N. Thoms, Manager; Eddie Arthur, Drum Instructor; Elliott Colson, Drum Major; Robert Heath, Drill Major. This is the Corps that won first prize at Philadelphia in 1926 and it's a wow!

Racine, Wis. (Fifth prize, Rating 93.0)

Fred Maxted, Manager; Geo. Johnson, Drum Major. This is the Corps that won so many first prizes a few years back. They are still wonders and a tremendous force to be reckoned with next year at San Antonio.

> The American Legion Iowa State Band, Monahan Post, won first prize in the band contest for full bands at the Paris Convention. They have won this honor at every gathering for the past nine years.

Charlotte, N. C. (Sixth prize, Rating 88.0)

H. Grady Moore, Mgr. and Drum Major; Chas. E. Lambeth, Asst. Mgr.; O. F. Asbury, Jr., Asst. Drum Major and Instructor; Walter F. Stanley, Chief Bugler; C. H. Drury, Librarian; T. C. Neal, Quartermaster; B. S. Garrison, Asst. Quartermaster; V. Paul Rousseau, Treasurer; Thomas L. Alexander, Drill Master. A most wonderful Corps now numbering eighty men.

 "FOR DRUMMERS WHO CARE"

Leedy Drum Topics

The Prize Letter—

An announcement in the previous issue of Drum Topics (No. 15) offered a prize of $5.00 for the best letter written on the subject of "What Drum Topics Means To Me." Judging from the hundreds of letters received, the Exclusive Drummer's Paper means a great deal to these boys. Here is the one selected for the prize:

Oct. 5, 1927.

To The Editor of Drum Topics:—

"What Drum Topics Means To Me"

Drum Topics means to me just as much as the morning paper means to the average business man. Why does a man or woman read a newspaper? Certainly it is to get the news of the world while it is news. Through the newspaper most people keep up with the world. I can honestly say that Drum Topics keeps me up with the Drummer's World. This paper gives the latest fads and flashes while they are the latest. Helpful hints presented in an interesting way, photos of other drummers, snappy, original drummer's jokes and the latest novelties are only a part of its contents. Besides all this, Drum Topics encourages the beginner and puts new life into the old-timers of the game. "Exclusive Drummer's Paper" aptly describes this magazine published by the foremost of drum manufacturers and the first to give the drummer a paper of his own. My only disappointment is that it cannot be published more often. However, I patiently await the arrival of the postman with my copy.

(Signed) ROBERT GRANT,
19 Union Street,
Toms River, N. J.

Helen McFarland—

This young lady is now appearing as one of the true highlights of John Murray Anderson's production of "Highlights," a Publix Theatres unit attraction. Miss McFarland "stops the show" nine times out of ten with her clever showmanship and skill behind her Leedy Xylophone. Each time she is called again and again and only succeeds in getting away by giving the audience a little "chatter." Previously she toured the Orpheum and West Coast houses. For some time she was located in St. Louis and studied under the well-known Schuyler Alward. Her home is now in Los Angeles.

Notes From Back Numbers of Drum Topics—

FROM No. 3 DRUM TOPICS

What Drummers need today is more "bank roll" in exchange for their "drum roll."

White in a drum head is not natural in the hide—they have to be made white. The "clear" or "transparent" head is the hide in its natural state.

FROM No. 4 DRUM TOPICS

If a sound wave were loud enough to be heard around the earth it would take 33 hours and 31 minutes for it to travel the entire distance.

There is a difference in the tone of the various sized bass drums. However, a 28x14-inch bass drum will often have a better tone than a 30x16-inch, when it is more scientifically tensioned. It is not always the larger size that counts, but rather the evenness with which the head is tensioned and the amount it is tensioned. This is a point many drummers overlook. Leedy Tympani Model Bass Drum Rods make it a pleasure to devote more attention to your bass drum heads and their tone. Better for the heads also, and they add to the appearance of the drum.

Some time when you are "faking" and playing a one-step at a dance or a 2/4 gallop in the theatre, try to go thru the entire number without making a roll of any length at all. You will find this hard to do, because when one is "faking" there is a natural tendency to "fall into" a roll. It becomes a habit and many drummers do not realize that they roll too much. There are many phrases where a roll is not only incorrect from a musical standpoint, but it sounds bad and amateurish. Don't be one of the "when in doubt, roll" kind of drummers. Besides, the stunt mentioned above is very fine practice for "trueing up" the control of the sticks.

You can often prevent a Chinese wood block from checking on the ends and chipping on the top by giving it a coat of shellac every couple of months. These blocks are seriously affected by the climates of the U. S. and Canada, which are so different from that of China, where they are made. The shellac helps to protect them from the action of the atmosphere and will preserve them a great deal longer. It also dresses the block up for appearance. Leedy always shellacs them before they leave the factory.

FROM No. 5 DRUM TOPICS

Don't loosen the snares of your drum (either orchestra, band or drum corps models) after you have finished a job. Leave them at a tension—even a little more than the playing strain—and you will have an easier-playing and better-sounding instrument the next time you use it. Note that the best professional theatre drummers never throw off their snares after a show, nor do violin and cello players let out their strings after work. Keep your snares taut.

Did you ever notice that after you have used a crash cymbal, triangle or tambourine for a year or more you get so accustomed to its particular tone that no other suits you? If you have used a cymbal for a long period and then break it, what a time you have finding another that seems to have as good a tone—it works on your nerves every time you use it. Often a drummer will state that he has the best crash cymbal in his part of the country, when he really means that he is so accustomed to its tone that he could not be satisfied with another.

It is an easy matter to make a neat job of putting a new head on a tambourine. After driving home the first four tacks in the new head (which should be at opposite points on the shell) tie the head down with a length of shoe lace, making sure the lace lies flat and that the head is pulled down under same. Leave the lace tied to the shell while putting in the rest of the tacks and until the head is well dried. This will assure you a nice, smooth job when the ragged edges of the head are trimmed off with a sharp knife.

Can you do everything with the left stick that you can do with the right one? If not, why not? Drumming is not like writing, where only one hand is used. It is similar to rowing, swimming, dancing and walking—all actions in which the right and left movements should be under control equally. If you play more strokes with the right stick than you do with the left, practice and make the left even better than the right. WATCH YOUR LEFT STICK.

The Sizzle Cow Bell—

Suggested by—
Verne Neeley,
Irvine Theatre,
Bloomington, Illinois.

Here is a new stunt that has been tried out and proven very novel and effective. From one to four cow bells may be used. Drill a small hole in one side of the bell as shown in photo above, 1¾ inches from the edge (lip) and mount two heavy type tambourine jingles by a bolt or rivet. Be sure the jingles are loose. When the lip of the bell is played upon with felt butt or padded drum sticks a new and most pleasing effect is produced. Don't use hard sticks!

John Philip Sousa and Ted Lehr—

When John Philip Sousa visited York, Penna., as guest director of the city's first municipal opera, "The Bride Elect" (by Sousa), he became interested in the many reports concerning young Ted Lehr's extraordinary ability as a Drummer. A meeting was arranged and here we see Mr. Sousa welcoming into the realm of music the world's youngest professional percussionist. Ted is only seven years of age, but he plays with the Lehr Family Orchestra and others on first-class engagements in York and vicinity. Dozens of press notices proclaim him a marvel.

David Barkoff

of Fort William, Ont., Canada, became interested in drums thru working several seasons on the staff of the Orpheum Theatre and watching the house Drummer do his stuff. Barkoff studied and soon became a first-rate dance man. For some time he played with the "Night Hawks" of Port Arthur and is now jobbing in and around Fort William.

(Courtesy—Advance Music Co., Ltd., Toronto.)

Kitty—"I'm going to marry a wonderful Drummer and a marvelous Xylophone player."
Cat—"You can't—that's bigamy."

E. O. Roark and U. G. Leedy —

E. O. Roark (at left), well-known Drummer and Tympanist of Kansas City, Mo., is the originator of the Double End Sticks No. 376-B listed in the Leedy catalog "O" on page 36, also shown in No. 15 Drum Topics. Roark is now at the Royal Theatre in K. C., and also plays tymps in the K. C. Symphony Orchestra. In addition he teaches a large class of pupils and is connected with the Drum Dept. at the Conn-Kansas City Co. Roark is a thoroughly legitimate high-class Drummer in every respect. His painstaking methods have placed him among the leaders. This photo was taken when he visited the Leedy plant last September and spent considerable time in company with Mr. Leedy.

You can now buy Drums to match your neckties.

Jack Eggen—

Brandt's Hot-Point Orchestra is a red-hot organization playing Minnesota, North and South Dakota, Iowa and other states, traveling in their ten passenger Lincoln bus. This band carries two thousand dollars worth of scenery and equipment for a special show called the "China Town Ball." It's a riot in every town. Jack Eggen, the Drummer (marked with arrow), is a wonderful stunt and effect man. He hails from St. Paul, Minn., where he put in several years with the leading orchestras of that locality.

 "WORLD'S FINEST DRUMMERS' INSTRUMENTS"

Page Fourteen

The Exclusive Drummers' Paper

Ralph V. Lillard and Charlie Davis

The Stage Drummer of today who has a pleasing smile has a great asset, but when he has such a smile combined with unusual ability he goes over big. Ralph Lillard has both and is therefore a principal factor in the great success enjoyed by the Charlie Davis Presentation Band on the stage of the Indiana (Publix) Theatre, Indianapolis. Lillard worked with well-known orchestras in Cincinnati, Ohio, for many seasons. He has been in all branches of the business for eighteen years and is an accomplished pianist and arranger, as well as a fine Drummer. Charlie Davis is truly one of the most magnetic and popular Masters of Ceremony on the Publix Circuit. He is also the composer of "Copenhagen" and other popular numbers that have been national hits.

The "Sentinel" SILHOUETTE

Speaking of striking and original flashes for the modern Drummer, here is one that leads the ranks of bass drum head decoration. It has spirit and character and is most artistic as well. This silhouette is perfect in outline and can be plainly distinguished at a great distance. Can be used with good effect without lights. With lights it is indeed beautiful.

Ask for No. S-3

In Memoriam

Norman B. Martin of the famous "Martin Brothers" Xylophone act, passed away on December 29th, 1927, at Phoenix, Ariz. He was fifty-one years old and from 1895 to 1908 was known in this country and Europe as one of America's leading Xylophone artists and had hundreds of friends in all parts of the world. For the past few years his health was failing and he located at Phoenix, where the Arizona sunshine undoubtedly prolonged his life. He was laid to rest in the Evergreen Cemetery and many prominent Phoenix musicians attended his funeral.

Eugene S. Meserve—

That there are real opportunities for the Drummer located in the smaller towns as well as in the big cities, has again been proven by Eugene S. Meserve. In Dover, N. H., his home town, he has built up an organization of ten men, called "Meserve's Melody Boys," that is in demand in the leading vaudeville theatres, ballrooms, hotels, summer resorts and broadcasting stations throughout the New England states. Eugene is the Drummer-Manager of the orchestra and it is through his clever business ability and skill behind the Drums that they have been so successful.

SIXTY THOUSAND

Drummers are reading Drum Topics. We will send it to sixty thousand more if they will send in their names. Mailed free.

It would be interesting to know exactly the total number of Drummers in each of the different countries, also to know how many of each country are professional, semi-professional or amateurs. In other words, a Drummers census. Of course it is practically impossible to obtain such data, but such figures would be good information.

Chinese "Whang" Cymbals

Here they are—just what you've been looking for—extra small (8-inch) THIN Chinese Cymbals with a "whang" tone that cuts like a knife. The very latest effect for red-hot rhythms.

Ask for No. 31-W.

When the Leedy Mfg. Co. states that certain Drummers are using Leedy instruments you can bet it's true. Any other firm that implies by reading matter or photographs that Harold McDonald, Vic Burton, Bill Gladstone, Chas. White, Geo. Carey, Walter Meyer, Cliff Williamson and Ray Brothers are using other makes is only trying to take advantage of these nationally-known Drummers' names.

Sammy Fink—

Here is a new photo of Sammy Fink. Several seasons ago a prominent New York music critic wrote him up as—"That remarkable Drummer." The title has stuck to him like glue ever since. If you ever see and hear him work you'll agree that the critic was right. Sammy is still with Ben Bernie at the Roosevelt Hotel, doubling in big Broadway productions and going stronger than ever.

The Drummer with a family of triplets can be said to know his rudiments well.

The "Lightning" Cymbal—

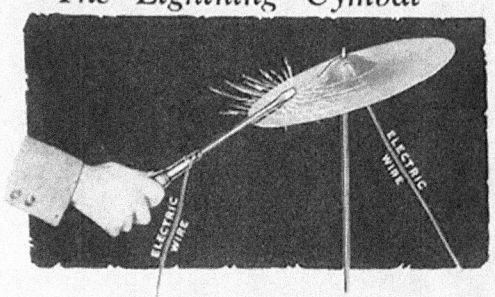

Here is a positive Knockout for stage, dance or pit work where the Drummer wants to put over something unusual. Take an old or unused Turkish type cymbal (do not use your best cymbal, as this stunt will injure it in time) and bore two small holes near the top of the cup. Run a wire through these holes from the under side and HARD solder on the top. Next, wire and tape a LARGE, cheap type WOOD handle screw-driver as shown in above photo. Be sure the electrician prepares the electric circuit with the proper resistance appliance to prevent blow-outs. When you "side swipe" the cymbal with the screw-driver you produce a BIG electric flash that is a good lightning imitation. Work it in a darkened house on climaxes and finishes. The combined cymbal tone and lightning flash make a true novelty that is new to the majority of audiences and proves another big Ad for the Drummer.

Presented by—"Chuck" Deaton,
Manchester Theatre,
Los Angeles, Calif.

She was so dumb she thought a "hot break" was part of the new Ford.

Positively—The Largest in the World—Absolutely

The last issue of Drum Topics showed a photo of the new addition to the East wing of the Leedy factory, in construction. Here is the new finished building on the West wing, which has added 7,200 square feet of floor space to the office, shipping room and stock room. The new East wing may be seen at the rear of the photo. Two new large wings added within the past year. Not bad, what? Factories only grow when business grows. Leedy continues to grow every month. It's the largest in the world, regardless of what you may read elsewhere.

If Drum Topics helps you, why not help the other fellow? The good word you spread always comes back to you with profit. Your photographs and ideas are all for the good of the game. Send them in. "Over the River" yours till the last break—

Leedy   "FOR DRUMMERS WHO CARE"   **Leedy**

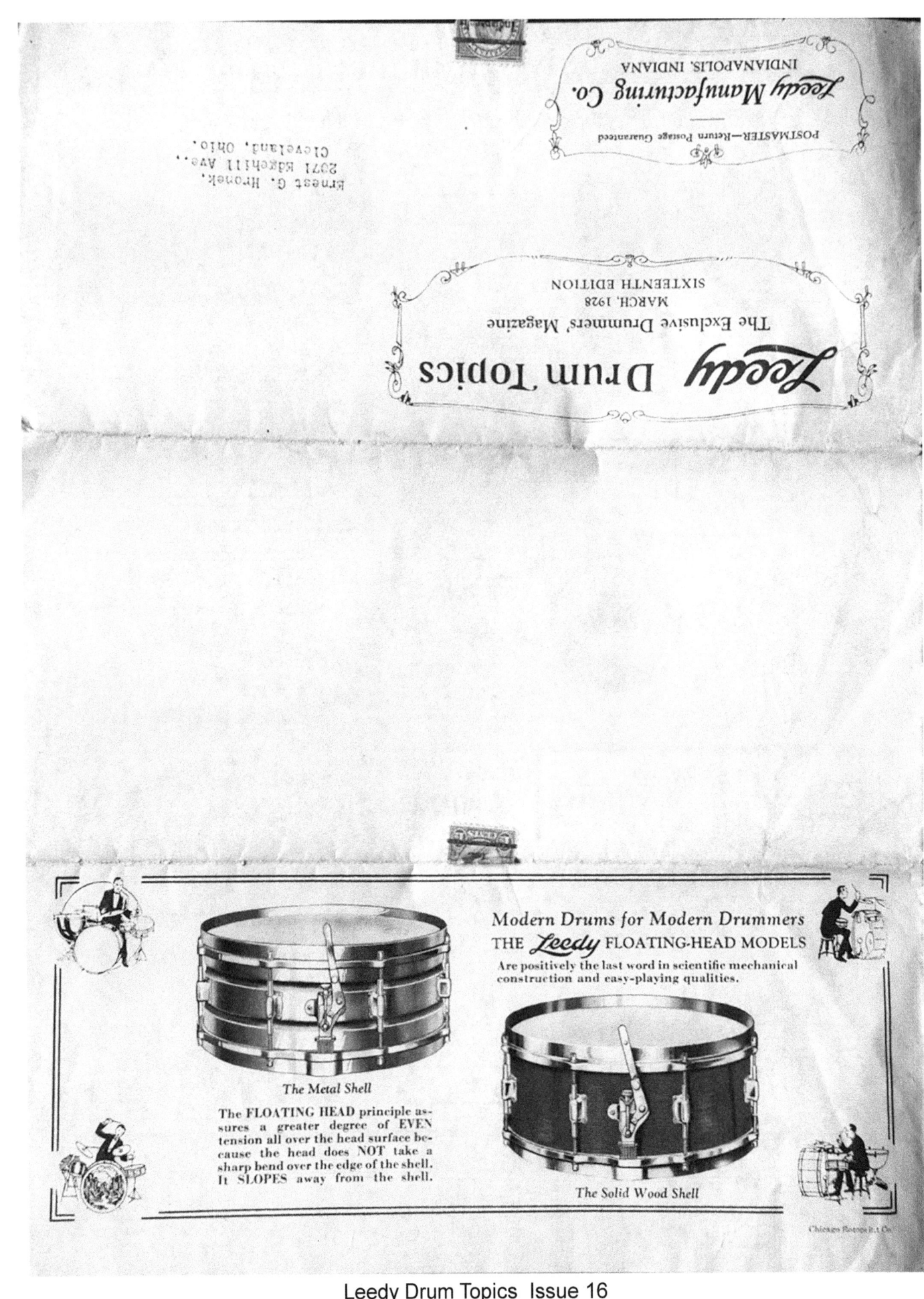

Leedy Drum Topics Issue 17

History

The new situation, viz: "canned" music and the "talkies" versus the theatre musician, is but another milestone on the march of progress. "Sound" pictures will not, in the majority of cases, permanently displace the man on the job. History has proven that every labor saving invention [and the new gag is supposed to be labor saving] has, in the end, put two men to work where there was once only one. When the linotype was introduced the type-setters threw up their hands; they took drastic steps to try and stop their use. Now there are more type-setters working than ever before. Remember the scare that went the rounds when the big theatre organs were installed? True, they did displace a few musicians; they still do, especially in the small towns and neighborhood houses, but still more and more musicians were put to work. Some thought the phonograph would put the dance musician out of business, but it proved to be without human association and altogether too mechanical.

With all scientific progress human nature remains the same. Not one invention has ever in the least dampened the desire of human beings to associate with or to see and hear other human beings. If this is not true why did not the big picture shows continue to thrive on straight pictures? Simply because the public demanded the actual presence of other human beings. That's the underlying reason why "straight pictures" needed something more to keep the crowds coming. First the managers put in big orchestras—not because they wanted to—they had to. Then they were forced to go further. Human beings in the pit were not enough; hence the presentation or the weaving of vaudeville acts around the stage band.

And now that a new invention has been born the managers think they can cast aside the human element and continue to entertain the public with a machine that cries "mechanical" in every measure. They can—for a while—just as they entertained and drew the crowds for a while with straight pictures. They are not offering "canned" music as a favor to the public—it is strictly an economy measure and one that is figured to save money in the long run by doing away with musicians, even though the cost of installation is high. They have long dreamed of such a condition—their past treatment of musicians is pretty good evidence of this.

The word "novelty" has truly been over-worked, but if there ever was a novelty, the sound pictures are it. "It won't be long now"—the public in many cities is already fed up, for as the Baltimore Sun states:

> "The said machine gun business is Vitaphoned. Close your eyes and open your ears wide and the effect is that of little brother down in the basement shooting off a damp cap pistol. Personally we're all for the trap drummer when it comes to these realistic effects."

Leedy   "WORLD'S FINEST DRUMMERS' INSTRUMENTS"   *Leedy*

The Exclusive Drummers' Paper

repeats itself~

In many other localities the theatre-goer has expressed himself, in one way or another, to the effect that this new form of entertainment is strictly a novelty and will not suffice permanently for a steady diet. Detroit and several other large cities are not in favor. The middle size and small towns have not adopted them as much as was at first predicted.

The "Talkies" and "Sounds" will stay in many instances—just as the organ stayed—but there is a catch in the whole scheme which we think the managers have overlooked, viz: that if it was necessary in the past to inaugurate, from time to time, something new to renew the public's interest and swell gate receipts, so will it be again. And it has been pretty well proven that those who attend theatres these days want something more than pictures and music, whether "canned" or otherwise. They will be satisfied for a time with the novelty of the "sound" part of it, but, as before, they will want to see human beings on the stage. And the minute an entertainer of any type steps on the stage to do his stuff, then human beings will have to be there to furnish the foundation and background with personally played music.

Joseph N. Weber, President of the American Federation of Musicians, certainly hit the nail on the head when he stated in the "Metronome"—

"The public will demand the best, and PERSONAL appearances of musical and other performers far outclass mechanical offerings."

Population is increasing—cities are growing—still more theatres will be built—and no mechanical device can curb folks' desire to see other real folks behind the footlights, which in turn means musicians on the job. Yes, history in the theatre repeats itself. They have tried to do without entertainment in the flesh many times, but so far they have not "put it over."

Leedy "FOR DRUMMERS WHO CARE" *Leedy*

 # Leedy Drum Topics

Fourteen Members of the Los Angeles Drummers' Club---

TOP ROW (left to right)—Harold Beardsley, Carlton Theatre; Ed Grimes, Orpheum Theatre; Jennie Hadderman, Enroute; Edward Gergen, Coffee Dan's Cafe; Ed. Scheidel, Hollywood Playhouse; Sherman "Shorty" Davidson ("the best-dressed man in L. A."), West Coast Boulevard Theatre. MIDDLE ROW—H. Scheidel, Commodore Hotel; Clint Williams, West Coast Theatre; William Seber (Custodian, L. A. Drummers' Club), Carmel Theatre; Len Adolph, Universal Studios; Harry Cook, Paulais Cafe; M. Hadderman, Enroute; Pete Lewin, Mason Theatre.
BOTTOM ROW—Jack Salling (Past President), Cabrillo Theatre; "Bobby" Burns (Past President), West Coast, Enroute; Geo. M. Robison (Sec'y-Treas.), Figueroa Theatre; Earl Stiles (President), Pantages Theatre; the next guy was allowed to sit in—only a visitor; L. L. "Red Hot" Allen, manager Wurlitzer's Drum Dept.

The above photo was especially posed for Drum Topics by a few members of the Los Angeles Drummers' Club at the entrance of the Municipal Stadium on the morning of June 26th, 1928. While there are only fourteen members in the photo, there are over a hundred in this progressive club. Many more expressed their willingness to join the group, but activities around the studios and rehearsals in the theatres kept the great majority away.

The club is a division of Local No. 47 A. F. of M. and was organized December 22nd, 1914, with an initial membership of fourteen. Since that time it has grown steadily until today the majority of the leading drummers of the Los Angeles local are members. Its ideals and purposes are to make better working conditions for the drummer and to state that these aims have been accomplished to a great extent is putting it mildly, for now there is a bass drum in almost every place where the transient drummer is engaged. The club wields considerable power within the general meetings of Local No. 47 and it has in many cases brought about legislation that has greatly benefited drummers in all branches, among them being a law prohibiting one man from playing bass drum and cymbals on marching engagements of bands consisting of eighteen men or more. They have also enacted many other rulings such as special prices for the playing of extra instruments, viz.: chimes, xylophone, marimba, etc., all of which have made a better working condition. Geo. M. Robison is undoubtedly a great asset to the organization, for his untiring and energetic work has put over many important issues. In a recent letter to Drum Topics he states in part:

". . . . at our regular meetings which are held monthly we generally conclude with a lunch, which is paid for out of the general fund. One of our recent meetings was held at midnight in a banquet room and we were especially pleased with the fine spirit of good fellowship that prevailed. This meeting was so successful that we have decided to hold all those in the future at midnight in a prominent cafe. I am expecting someone to suggest our getting together at Tia Juana. No doubt some of them have the old-time idea in mind, which wouldn't be so bad provided they don't go too far. We have indeed made great progress in the last few years and the club has requested that I ask Drum Topics to point out the benefit of drummers getting together, in hopes that there will be more clubs organized thruout the country, in fact there is no reason why the professional drummer should not be nationally organized and elevate himself and his profession as other professional men have done. It will take time to bring this about, but we honestly believe that the time will come when it becomes a reality. Our club has for some time been considering the importance of organizing a Drum Corps, as we believe it would stimulate interest and sociability among our members, to say nothing of the fact that it could be used for commercial purposes. Owing to our being situated in the heart of Movieland there is no doubt but what we could secure a great deal of work for such an organization from the films. There has been considerable discussion along this line and no doubt within a short time Eastern people will see the L. A. Drummers' Club on the screen, doing their stuff as an organized body in some feature picture. We are proud that the entire battery section of the Philharmonic Symphony Orchestra are members, also that of Herbert Clark's Band at Long Beach. Many of our members in the past have strayed Eastward and are now with such orchestras as the Detroit Symphony, Paul Whiteman and others."

The officers of the club for the 1928 term are: President, Earl Stiles; Sec'y-Treas., Geo. M. Robison; Vice-President, Danny Cairns; Custodian, W. H. Seber; Sergt.-at-arms, Mike Rozet; Directors, Robert Burns, Harris Harding, Chas. Roberts and Harry Rifkind.

NOTE: The Editor of Drum Topics visited Los Angeles during the International Pageant of Music last June and met many of the boys of this organization. It is truly progressive in every respect and they are a real bunch of good fellows, every member seeming to take an interest in the drummer's problems and putting their shoulders to the wheel for the betterment of all concerned. They have their own club room at the Musicians Headquarters, where an active booking office is in constant operation, placing drummers on all manner of jobs. Mr. Robison stated that he would be more than pleased to hear from drummers in other cities where there are Drummers' Clubs also from those who have not yet formed clubs but who are interested, stating that the L. A. Club will be perfectly willing to exchange ideas in hopes that drummers in all parts of the country may be benefited. Drum Topics believes that there is considerable to be gained by drummers getting together in the various cities and thinks they should go still further and link these various clubs together in a fraternal way with a close co-operative program, with a view toward establishing a national drummers organization within the A. F. of M.

Some fellows have too much—
Some fellows have too little—
The stuff they take from sheep to make snares of.

The Speed of a Drum Head---

When a drum stick strikes the head it pushes the head inward—immediately the head springs back, passing its level position to an outward position—then it regains its level position and stops. In other words there are three movements to the head with each blow of the stick, viz.: in, out and in again. Of course all this takes place with great speed and is hard to conceive. Here's what we are getting at: both the tension and the quality of a head determine its speed in action, especially the evenness of tension. If the head is faster than the stick the drum plays easy—if the head moves slower than the stick the drum plays hard—"feels" bad and "chokes." All of which points out the importance of exercising great care in tensioning your drum heads evenly all the way around.

Thirty-nine years ago—season of 1889-1890—U. G. Leedy trouped with Goodyear-Elitch and Schilling's Minstrels, playing every state west of the Mississippi.

Girl Drummers, Samoan Islands (Pago-Pago) Tutuila, South Sea

If you were to tell the lady drummers of the Samoan Islands that drumming is a comparatively new pursuit for ladies in this country they would no doubt be greatly surprised because for many centuries the female Samoan has shared honors with the males, "drumistically speaking." Many of them are considered better performers and it is the girls who have introduced the more advanced ideas. Note the modern dishpan being used with the old type instrument to give variety, also the peculiar construction of the native drum, rattan rope serving to tension the head by means of a twisting stick inserted between the strands, with the rope run thru cutouts in the cocoanut palm log. The head is dried goat skin. The island of Tutuila is situated 4500 miles southwest of San Francisco in a direct line to Australia.

It is the age of the animal that determines the thickness of drum heads. Leedy "Hardwhite" snare drum heads for batter side are from calves three to seven weeks old.

(1) Frances Lee---
(2) Ford Sterling---
(3) Nancy Carrol---

For once—too many Tom Toms. No doubt about it—everyone will agree that this interesting photo would have been still *more* interesting (and beautiful) had the clumsy old Chinese tubs been forgotten. Frances has a knowing look in her eye: we think she took advantage of them. Ford looks as though he might be in on such a plot also. And Nancy—well, had the cameraman been wise he could have coaxed her a little more to the right without her ever suspecting. Oh, well, it doesn't matter much after all, for did you ever see such naughty eyes?

—(Courtesy, Wm. Fox Corporation)

There are seventeen foremen in the mechanical departments of the Leedy Mfg. Co. Their services average eighteen and a half years each, which means that they know their business, which in turn means high quality workmanship.

   "WORLD'S FINEST DRUMMERS' INSTRUMENTS"

The Exclusive Drummers' Paper

Geo. J. Carey---

When a "trouper" settles down after many seasons with Sousa's Band and several big New York musical shows, there's a reason. No, George hasn't acquired a wife (that is, up to last reports), but he has acquired a fine job and that's reason enough for sticking in one town. This is his third year with the Cincinnati Symphony Orchestra, where his fine work on both the drums and xylophone (also in radio broadcasting) is, as usual, praised on all sides. If any of his old friends wish to get in touch with him they may do so by addressing the orchestra office in the Times-Star Bldg., Walnut St., Cincinnati, Ohio.

Cloth Over Tom Tom---

By placing a cloth (light felt, denim or flannel) over your Tom-Tom, a most peculiar tone is produced. While the ring disappears, it is not a dead thud, but rather a deep and richer tone combined with a decided "cut off" effect. Very good for certain passages, especially when Leedy No. 618 Soft Solid Felt Mallets are used. (Catalog "R," Page 63.)

George W. Ryder

In January of this year Geo. W. Ryder announced that he would take his own band into vaudeville. If he has done so we feel sure that he will meet every success inasmuch as his past activities with several high-class orchestras of Richmond, Va., including a tour of Europe and over the Keith circuit with the Virginia Military Institute's Ramblin' Keydets Orch. have placed him in the "big time" class. Last fall he was with the Majestic Club Orchestra and later joined the Chesterfield Hills Country Club Orchestra.

Johnny Robinson, the well-known radio drummer of Indianapolis, was in our office the other day and announced that he was writing a new book entitled, "The No Pressure System for Triangle Players."

Richard B. Wilson (also two good "tips")

After seven years at the Golden Gate (Orpheum Vaudeville) Theatre in San Francisco, popular "Dick" Wilson has moved over to the Granada to do his stuff with a presentation orchestra. And "some stuff" it is, he being one of the finest "triangle ticklers" on the coast. Wilson is originally from Salt Lake City, where he began behind the drums on a theatre job at only 14 years of age. He has since played in almost every branch of the business, including Hotel Utah five years, Salt Lake Symphony eight years, Held's Band, Hawkins' Orchestra, 43rd U. S. Infantry Band and many engagements thruout Idaho, Nevada and Utah, also one year at the Orpheum in Oakland, Calif. His teacher was Adelbert Beesley. Wilson is a rudimental artist and says he finds that the old school is of great assistance in jazz playing because so many of the rudiments fit properly. Here are two of his "tips" that have been tried with considerable success. (1) To fix a cracked Turkish cymbal; fill with a solder of about the same consistency as a quarter or half dollar. When brazed into the crack it will hold longer than any other metal. One fixed over a year ago by this method has withstood heavy vaudeville work without giving further trouble. (2) To take rattle out of a wind whistle; have a steel shaft put thru the fibre wheel (tightly fitted) and keep oiled. This gives a steel bearing against brass and prevents sticking.

Joe Green Visits Leedy Plant---

Last August Joe and Mrs. Green came "rolling along" in their big Packard and stopped for a day to talk about the coming season and look over the Leedy factory. We "shot" this photo while he, Mr. Leedy and Mr. Winterhoff (Vice-Pres. of the Leedy Mfg. Co.) were discussing some new ideas in the shop. Joe and his equally famous brother, George, are certainly busy guys in New York these days. They are doing feature work almost every night over the chain hook-ups of WJZ and WEAF. Wrigley's Spearmint, Philco Hour, General Motors, Klein Shoes, Royal Typewriter, Maxwell House Coffee, A & P Gypsies and Dutch Masters are just a few of the programs on which they are headliners, using Leedy Xylophones, Marimbas, Chimes, Bells and Vibraphones.

The Helen Johns' Girls---

One of the snappiest musical acts on the "big time" vaudeville circuits. Ten wonderful "lookers" comprising a modern stage band that is in constant demand by the managers. Their drum corps numbers (Leedy Mandarin Finish Street Drums) are the outstanding hit of every bill. House Drummers usually stick in the pit and we don't blame them.

To Polish Nickel Plated Parts---

Use ordinary whiting, rubbing on with dry rag. Whiting is a fine white powder that may be purchased in any drug store. It will bring the dullest nickel back to a bright polish (of course provided the nickel has not been worn off) and is also fine for polishing silverware at home. Do not wet the powder or cloth—use absolutely dry.

W. Frank Croft---

Here we have one more of the few old-timers who have entered the "modern" field and stepped to the top. W. Frank Croft is also one of the best known Drummers in the East. His home was Philadelphia, where he was extra man with the Phila. Philharmonic Orchestra for several seasons. Croft has played with Creator's Band and Leman's Symphony at Atlantic City—two years with Paul Whiteman's Arcadian Orchestra in Providence, R. I., under Al. Mitchel; on the road with "Birth of a Nation," "Intolerance" and in New York City with Earl Carroll's Vanities. Recently he put in several months with Paul Ash at the Paramount Theatre, New York, and is now signed up to make sound pictures at Camden, N. J.

 "FOR DRUMMERS WHO CARE"

Leedy Drum Topics

"Jake" and "Lee"

Just in case you want to know which is which—"Jake" on the left and "Lee" on the right. No kidding. By any old names at all these two would be just what they are—100% real fellows, real men and real drummers. A couple that the drumming fraternity can well look up to as among the leaders. Always clean-cut gentlemen and loyal to their friends. This photo was taken last May in New York when Harold left the Paul Whiteman Orchestra to join Paul Ash at the Paramount and here he is wishing good luck to George, who returned to his old job with the Whiteman organization, which is now on the road doing strictly concert work. Harold has returned to his home in Los Angeles and is doing studio work for the sound pictures, also teaching a large class of pupils.

Genius is only a superior power of seeing

Short Story—

Key lost, heads break,
  drum shot, job gone—

No job—— no pay
No pay—— no licker
No licker— no parties
No parties— no wimmen
No wimmen— ain't it hell
  and all on account of a key?

Leedy Floating Head Drums—Slotted Rods — No Key Needed—Use A Coin and Keep Smiling.

Merle A. Shower

To be a Drummer in a small town, with a small orchestra, with a big "rep," is often more desirable than being a Drummer in a big city, with a big orchestra, with a little "rep." Merle Shower says he prefers the former. He lives at Beatrice, Nebr., and plays with "Doc's" Club Novelty Orchestra. They have worked steadily for three years trouping thru Kansas, Nebraska, Iowa and Missouri. Merle is a big name as a Drummer of pep and originality, wherever they play. He also did fourteen months of stage presentation work on the southern vaudeville circuits.

Andrew V. Scott, the well known Chicago Drummer (of the Conn National School of Music), composer and writer of drum articles, was a welcome visitor to the Leedy plant a short time ago. We had a long "confab" about things "drumistic," especially the rudimental school, on which Scott is a recognized authority. One of his interesting statements was that the first instruction book ever written on rudimental drumming was the work of Samuel Potter of the Coldstream Guards of England (Regiment of King George III), in the year 1815, and that this book is the foundation of our present rudimental system.

Ray Vaughn

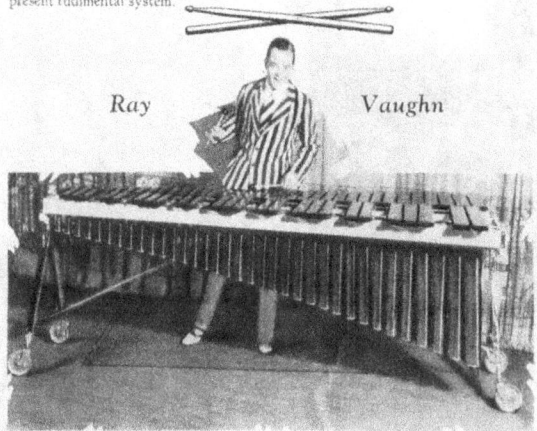

When Drummer after Drummer in the vaudeville pits spread the word that a certain Xylophone act is good—well, it's good—for there is no more severe criticism. Such are the reports we have from the boys about Ray Vaughn. Six years ago he was playing odd dance jobs in and around Los Angeles. Five years ago he was featured on the Fancho & Marco West Coast circuit of vaudeville and presentation theatres. Three years ago he received a fine contract to play the Williamson & Tait chain of vaudeville theatres in Australia and New Zealand. Two years ago this contract was renewed and one year ago Ray returned to this country and has been booked continually ever since by the Keith offices in New York. In other words, this boy has climbed to the top by way of skill, good judgment and hard work. His act is a head-line attraction on most every bill. And if you want to meet a regular fellow drop around to the stage door and say "hello" when Ray plays your town. He is now in the South playing in the larger cities.

Mexican Mahogany is used in the construction of several models of Leedy snare and bass drum shells, both solid and laminated. It has proven superior to either the African or Philippine species.

Justin Huber

For the past three years the patrons of the Strand Theatre at Cincinnati, Ohio, have been applauding the fine work of Justin Huber as Drummer, Tympanist and feature Xylophone soloist. Huber also operates a booking office, which furnishes several first-class dance orchestras with the better jobs thruout Cincinnati and vicinity. Previous to going into the Strand, Huber and his own orchestra kept busy for twelve years—society jobbing—prominent night clubs—twenty weeks Hotel Gibson—a season at Coney Island (Cinn.) Club House—three seasons Chester Park and a full season on the road in Keith vaudeville. His orchestra also recorded several numbers for the Gennett Phonograph Co. Recently Huber composed a Xylophone solo, "Tip-Toes," which is soon to be published.

The "Wash-boiler"
A Fine Effect for Forte Hot Rhythms

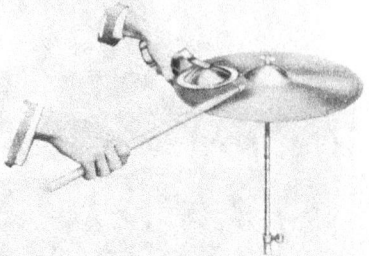

When the gang is "cutting loose" and blowing off all the steam they've got in a red-hot noisy finish, it is often difficult for the Drummer to hit on something novel that will "cut thru" and stand out. This one will. Yes, it's tin-panny and loud—that's why it's called the "Wash-boiler"—but it "goes over" when it's noise they want. Use Leedy Squash Cymbals (No. 269, page 42 Catalog "R") in left hand, sandwiched over regular Turkish or Italian cymbal. Play rhythm beats with stick on cymbal and use Squash Cymbals for "cut-off" and "sizzlers." You can get a lot out of this combination with a little practice.

Sent in by—George Hart, Coburg West, Victoria, Australia.

Fred J. Pike

has been a professional Drummer for over fifty years. Some record! He was the first to introduce drums in a dance orchestra in his home district, Cortland, N. Y. This was in 1883. For ten years he played at the Cortland Opera House under "Happy" Bill Daniels and for eleven years at the Geneva (N. Y.) Opera House under Wenzel Dousek. Most every old-time road Drummer knows Fred Pike, as both Cortland and Geneva were always on the route of the New York musical shows. He has not only worked with the road men, but has played many a big show alone and road leaders always spoke of him as being one of the best. The Editor of Drum Topics recalls having worked with Pike on Sept. 25th, 1911, at the Cortland Opera House when on the road with "Three Twins."

The New Vise Grip Tom-Tom Holder —

This new Tom Tom Holder is heavier and stronger thruout than any previous model. The hoop clamp is designed like a vise and it stays "put." Note the adjusting feature—Tom Tom will hold at all angles. Fool-proof in every way. A large fitted plate screws to shell of Tom Tom. No more pulling out of rings when you use this one. *Ask for No. 90*

Vise Grip Hoop Adapter

Every Drummer who uses the new vise grip hoop adapter clamps for holding traps, declares them to be the "last word" for strength and efficiency.

They may be purchased separately and adapted to all of the Trap Tree, Trap Console and Trap Table holders. *Ask for No. 120.*

Leedy — "WORLD'S FINEST DRUMMERS' INSTRUMENTS" — **Leedy**

The Exclusive Drummers' Paper

Easy to Imitate---

Not long ago we received a request from a prominent Drummer at one of the larger Eastern radio stations, asking for details on how to make several animal and other imitations for which standard traps are not made. Among the various animals was listed the Giraffe. We wrote back and told him the best way to imitate a Giraffe was to sit perfectly still, making no noise whatever, as the Giraffe is the only animal in the world that is not capable of uttering a sound.

Chester E. Frost of Boston, Mass., says—"After at least a hundred tests to determine the best cymbal for radio broadcasting I find that the Chinese type gives the best effect in straight playing. It should not be choked too quickly, but allowed to ring slightly—not too long, however. For 'hot' numbers it should be cut off with more speed." Frost's photo appeared in No. 16 Drum Topics. He has his own orchestra, "The Original Bostonians," and plays on class jobs throughout New England.

E. R. Kaiser and Waldemar Guterson---

Drum Topics takes pleasure in introducing Waldemar Guterson, a modern personality orchestra leader who knows and appreciates a fine drummer when he hears one. Not all leaders do so. E. R. Kaiser is the Drummer in this case, hence the reason for his four years service with "Guterson and his Orchestra," playing at the famous Solomon's Dance DeLuxe in Los Angeles. Recently Guterson moved his orchestra over to the Majestic Ballroom, the leading dance palace of Long Beach, Calif. (also broadcasting over KFON). Kaiser originally came from San Luis Obispo, Calif. He has been at the drums for eighteen years and his experience covers almost every branch—vaudeville at the Majestic Theatre in Pueblo, Colo., for two seasons—hotel and dance work throughout Colorado—musical comedy road shows for West Coast Co. and Drum Major of the 362nd Inf. Band during the war, with fifteen months overseas. He is a pupil of Harry Bower.

Drummers will always agree that there are two sides to THE question—snare and batter.

Brass is not a mineral. It is a manufactured metal composed of part copper and part zinc. For bending, forming, punching and brazing, different degrees of hardness are required. The mixture may be 75/25 or 60/40 or some other combination. The first number denotes copper and the last one zinc. Brass will not rust. Bronze is composed of copper and tin.

A Little About Bass Drum Shells

Bass Drum Shells are constructed in three ways—(1) two-ply; (2) three-ply; (3) solid wood. Technically speaking, the two- and three-ply may be called either "laminated" or "veneer." However, each manufacturer usually gives a brand name to the types he makes in order to designate them. Leedy makes all three types in order to offer a complete range of prices. The two-ply is called "Reliance." The three-ply is called "Spartan." The solid wood is called "Standard." The last named makes the finest bass drum in the world. A little more expensive, but well worth the difference.

Arthur E. Hazel

of New Orleans, La., plays with Cliff Schroy's Southern Aces, a modern band that has been more than satisfying the patrons at Monroe Park in Mobile, Ala., for the past three years. Hazel has been in the business for twelve years, having served with many fine orchestras throughout the South, some of which are—Jules Baudric's Orch.—New Orleans Rhythm Kings—Johnny Hyman's Jazzers—Half Way House Dance Orch.—Anthony Parenti's Orch.—Brownlee's Orch.—Buzzie Williams Society Syncopators and Happy Schilling's Orch. Hazel is really a very fine performer, full of pep, smiles and original stunts—the kind that lets 'em know they can't do without a Drummer.

(Courtesy—Conn-New Orleans Co.)

Earl C. Stiles and Cliff Webster---

We should call this pair "a couple of life-savers" for it's many an act that owes "the next ten weeks" to their skill. Playing at the Pantages in Los Angeles is no ordinary vaudeville job. This house is the "home office" of one of the greatest theatrical chains in the world. Cliff Webster, the leader of its crack orchestra, and Earl C. Stiles, his drummer, have been praised time and again by the management (Alex Pantages himself), the acts and the patrons. Earl is one of the best vaudeville drummers in the U. S. This is no bunk, for we've heard them all from coast to coast. He is also President of the Los Angeles Drummers' Club. The above photo shows Earl and Cliff inspecting a new Leedy Floating Head orchestra model drum recently purchased from "Red" Allen, manager of the Rudolph Wurlitzer Drum Department, and installed in the Pantages pit. We are mighty proud to have Earl playing one, especially as he states it's the finest drum he ever owned.

Howard McElroy---

Howard McElroy is well known in both New York and Chicago. For several years he played in New York City with such organizations as Harry Reser, Al Siegel and Irwin Abrams on the finest jobs in town. For the past four years he has been with the Earl Hoffman Orchestra at the Chez Pierre Club in Chicago. Previous to that he worked for the Balaban & Katz circuit, Frolics, Deauville, Town Club, Pershing Palace, 400 Club and others. McElroy enjoys an enviable reputation as a "class" performer among both musicians and patrons.

(Courtesy—Lyons Band Inst. Co.)

Woman was the last thing made by God and the product shows both His experience and His fatigue. *(Bramwords)*

Karl S. Mayers---

was a pupil of that fine "old timer," George Rambo of Reading, Pa. Mayers also hails from Reading, where he played in both the Royal and State vaudeville and picture theatres. He has also held down some big jobs with such orchestras as Al Zemsay in Philadelphia, and the Great White Fleet orchestra of Worcester, Mass., also with Harry Reiser's band at Atlantic City. For the past three years he has been going big with Roanes Pennsylvanians at the Commodore Ballroom in Lowell, Mass. Mayers is a "last word" Drummer who has the "whole works" in an outfit and the ability to play them all in a manner that makes him a real feature of any orchestra he is with.

Cow Bell Wow-Wow!

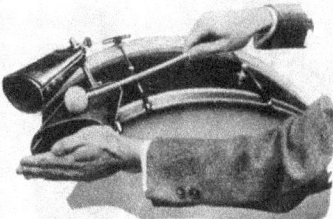

By moving the left hand (as shown in above photo) to and from the opening of a cow bell and striking the bell with a No. 617 Hard Spanish Felt xylophone mallet (Leedy catalog "R," page 63) a distinct and peculiar toned wow-wow can be produced. The hand is also used for "damping." Varied effects are possible. Try it. A little practice will bring out the many possibilities the stunt offers for the modern style of playing. This works best with the No. 638 third size and No. 639 largest size bells, and No. 379 cow bell holder with extra clamp No. 984 (Leedy catalog "R," page 53).

Frank Ferneau---

has been playing Drums in the better class dance orchestras of Columbus, Ohio, for the past ten years. Two years ago he organized his own orchestra and for the past eight months has been making a big hit at the Columbus Athletic Club. Ferneau is a modern Drummer in every respect and is bound to carry himself and his orchestra to the top as one of the most popular in the middle west.

(Courtesy—Heaton's Music Store)

 "FOR DRUMMERS WHO CARE"

Page Seven

Leedy Drum Topics

Tommy and Charlie Tibbets Calkins—

We are showing these two "show stoppers" together because they have worked side by side for several seasons on so many big jobs and are known as one of the country's fastest and most artistic teams. For many months, while at Los Angeles' most exclusive photoplay theatre—The Carthay Circle (Carli de Elinor, Conductor)—they were the talk of the town. The same was true when they were at the Million Dollar Theatre (Leo F. Forbstein, Conductor) and others. Tommy Tibbets is a thorough all-around Drummer of twenty-six years' experience covering every phase of the business. He was born in Ottumwa, Iowa, and, after breaking in, soon took to the road with a musical show, later followed by circuses and then into musical comedy road shows, traveling with some of the largest and finest out of New York. After quitting the road he located in Detroit and held down many first-class theatre jobs over a period of several years. Tommy is not only a tympani player of the symphony order, but is a xylophonist of the Geo. Green class as well. His solos are always a feature of every job he plays and, best of all, he is a genuine good fellow and 100 per cent professional all through.

Charlie Calkins hails from Fort Wayne, Indiana, and has been playing professionally for twenty-nine years. He has been with many fine organizations such as Congress Hotel, Chicago, four years; Minneapolis Symphony Orchestra, one year; Detroit Symphony Orchestra, one year; Cincinnati Symphony, one year; Million Dollar Theatre, Los Angeles, and Carthay Circle, Los Angeles. Charlie is now broadcasting regularly five hours per day with KHJ Symphony under the baton of Arthur Kay, featuring xylophone solos and making a big hit on the air. He also has a large class of pupils, teaching the Geo. Green Xylophone Course. Charlie, like Tommy, is a "regular" in every respect. His work as an all-around Drummer and Xylophonist ranks with the finest in the country and a finer fellow you'll never meet.

No, it's not Lon Chaney—

Hunting "down beats" in the great southwest.   Prospecting for "cymbal mines" in the Rocky Mts.   Victory! Ah, it's a new "goldfish" for the living room.

Funny what some Drummers do for amusement when they get a day off. Some like to shoot craps or play poker, while others like to drive at seventy miles per hour and still others like to play checkers. Once we knew one who did crocheting. With Charlie White it's the great outdoors; in the mountains and along streams with rod and gun, and judging by the evidence, he's as good with both as with a pair of tympani sticks and four kettles. As you know, Charlie is tympanist with the Los Angeles Philharmonic Orchestra and is rated as one of the country's finest artists.

AIR—when hot, is light and therefore moves or vibrates fast.

AIR—when cold, is heavy and therefore moves or vibrates slow; hence the necessity for having to move xylophone resonators closer to and farther away from wood bars (close) in warm weather and farther away in cold weather), thereby bringing the vibrations of the air column in the resonators into exact unison with the vibrations of the bar. All Leedy Xylophones and Marimbas are equipped with a unique device to efficiently take care of this condition of nature. See page 90 of Catalog "R."

Give Him Time—

Leader (at vaudeville rehearsal)—"All right boys, next number, alla breve."
Drummer (new in the game)—becomes very busy turning music.
Leader—"Whatsa matter Drummer, c'mon, let's go."
Drummer—"Sumpin wrong here, boss—no such piece in my book."

The Du Pont Pyralin (Marine Pearl—Sparkling Gold—Jade Green—Black Onyx) as used on Leedy "Full Dress" Drums, is a much THICKER and HIGHER GRADE material than found on any other make Drums. Costs a little more, but well worth the price when it comes to wear and appearance.

Horace Beaver and Zez Confrey

A "Red Hot Pair" would have been a true descriptive title for this photo, but we were afraid you might get the impression that they were "hot" only. Such is not the case. They are high-class legitimates as well. You all know Zez Confrey, one of America's foremost pianists, composers and leaders. Remember "Kitten on the Keys"? Well, he has written dozens of others just as good. As for Horace Beaver, he's just a "go gettin'" cymbal hound that knocks 'em dead with accents. He hails from Indianapolis and during the past three years he has held some fine jobs in Chicago, Denver and other cities, besides doing a lot of road work. He is now back with Confrey for a second season at the New Kenmore Hotel in Albany, N. Y., after putting in the summer at "Inn Lagola," Louisville, Ky. Horace says, "Regardless of any advertising you may read in other drum manufacturers' printed matter, I am playing Leedy instruments throughout and always will."

"Johnny" Frisco

of New Orleans, La. is now back home after a long tour of the Orpheum Circuit with "Bee" Palmer, a headline act. He is known as "The Clown Drummer" and has been a drawing card on such jobs as Max Fink's Orchestra at the Texan Theatre, Houston, for a year and a half; Brownlee's Orchestra, New Orleans; Johnny De'Droat's Orchestra, Grunewald Hotel, two years; also other "high spots" of the south. "Johnny" is an original, novelty, speed and trick Drummer if there ever was one. Now jobbing with his own orchestra.

(Courtesy, Conn-New Orleans Co.)

The Rollaway Trap Console—

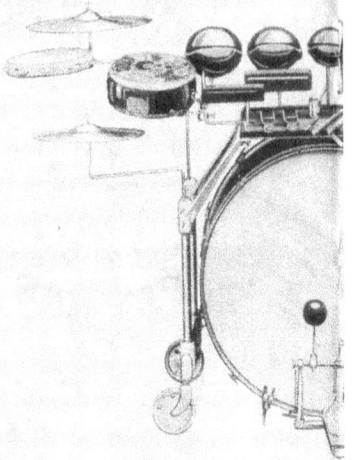

Bass Drum and all rolls away like a Xylophone slightly on pedal side and slip metal h...

The New Leedy Rollaway Trap Console is the ... model of trap holder ever invented. It is the ... nothing of its wonderful flash. The whole arran... who is often compelled to move his outfit. Just ... feet with no more effort than wheeling a Xylop... substantially braced. No wobbling or swayin... arranged that it remains in place and travels wi...

SEE LEEDY CATALOG "R"
ROLLAWAY CONSOLE AN...

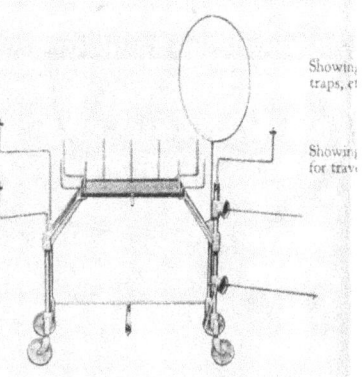

Showin... traps, ...

Showin... for trav...

The Rollaway Console is finishe... aluminum bronze. The table is co... a most pleasing appearance. On sp... in Nobby Gold at an additional c... chased without the tom tom holde...

Leedy   "WORLD'S FINEST DRUMMERS' INSTRUMENTS"   **Leedy**

Page Eight

The Exclusive Drummers' Paper

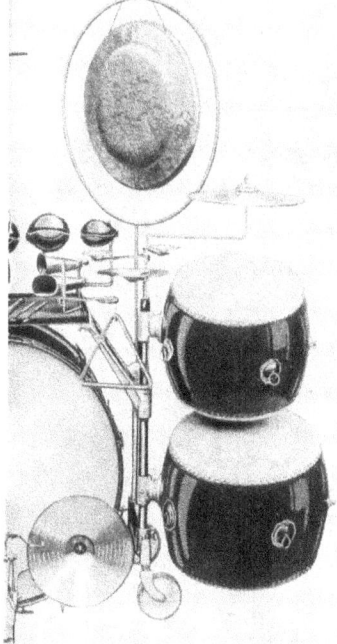

ne on wheels. Simply tip drum
holder on table over hoop.

most advanced type and also the most efficient
last word in convenience and utility, to say
ngement is especially adapted to the Drummer
push the "whole works" an inch or a hundred
phone. Every part is built for strength and
g of the traps, etc. The Bass Drum is so
ith the console wherever the latter is moved

" FOR PRICES OF THE
D ALL TRAP HOLDERS.

At Left—

g the Leedy Rollaway Trap Console stripped of all
tc. Note its graceful and sturdy lines.

Below—

g the Leedy Rollaway Trap Console knocked down
eling. Complete weight only 68 lbs.

in a combination of bright nickel and
ered with blue felt, all of which presents
ecial order all metal parts can be finished
harge. The Console may also be put-
r rods if desired.

Drummers' Dreams—

A head that will not break—
A fool-proof cuckoo—
A non-crack cymbal—
Sticks that will improve rolling—
A complete outfit that will go in a fiddle case—
A pedal that will hold the tempo—
A trunk that weighs twenty pounds and is as strong as a freight car—
Tympani that can be played without study—
A cymbal as good as the other fellow's—
To play more "hot licks" than any Drummer in town—
A new outfit every six months—
To join Paul Whiteman—
To fall heir to a million dollars—
Good Beer—
A Rolls-Royce—
Never to meet any good-looking girls—"applesauce."

Hard looks from leaders never made better Drummers.

Nickel plating (also Nobby Gold) can not be applied on top of old nickel plating. All of the old plating must be removed and the base metal must be polished smooth—even glass-like. Hence the reason for having to take every piece apart. This involves a vast amount of hand work and is very costly— more so than the price of a new article.

A Fine Locomotive Effect—
By Howard Goulden, Sousa's Band

By holding a regulation train effect wire beater-brush against the head of your tymp, with more or less pressure, and beating on head with tympani stick, a most realistic locomotive imitation is obtained. A much greater volume is possible than can be obtained with the ordinary metal-covered wood box type. A little practice to determine the right tension of the head and the correct distance between the brush and stick will soon enable you to "shade" as desired.

Tommy Thompson

When Drummers of Washington, D. C., need anything from sticks to tymps they usually call on Tommy Thompson, who, after sixteen years of active service as first Drummer with the famous Meyer Davis, is now manager of the Drum Dept. at Leonberger's Music Store, 928 New York Ave., N. W. Tommy surely knows his "double drags" when it comes to things drumistic, both in playing the job and serving the boys as a business man. He has at last established a real Leedy Drummers' Service Station in Washington. Previous to joining the Leonberger forces he played for ten years at the Willard Hotel, one season as leader on the Willard Roof Garden. He has also played in several of the largest hotels in many Eastern and Southern cities. He was born at Fredericksburg, Va., and was a pupil of Samuel Johnson, formerly of the U. S. Marine Band. Tommy now fills an occasional dance job for the David McWilliams' Orchestra of Washington.

Edwin Franko Goldman and His Drummers—

The Goldman Band is one of the foremost musical organizations of our country. To be identified with it in any capacity is a real mark of distinction. To be one of its Drummers is to hold a position which every other Drummer regards as one of the highest goals the drum world has to offer. In the photo above, from left to right, we see—KARL GLASSMAN (formerly of Indianapolis, Ind.), who ranks as an outstanding figure in things drumistic. For twenty-eight years he has been associated with the best—with Walter Damrosch, New York Symphony Orchestra, fourteen years; Victor Herbert's Orchestra, several seasons; Sousa Opera Co., Russian Symphony Orchestra, Webber & Fields Musical Comedy, Geo. White's Scandals, Roger Brothers, Ziegfeld Follies, Metropolitan Opera Orchestra, Volpe Symphony Orchestra and David Manne's Symphony Orchestra at the Metropolitan Museum, sponsored by J. D. Rockefeller, Jr. Glassman operates the largest Drum & Tympani school in New York City and is also now playing his second season with Damrosch over the National Broadcasting chain. Next is DAVID GUSIKOFF of New York City, who has been behind the drums for seventeen years. His record speaks for itself—Cleveland Symphony Orchestra, Russian Symphony Orchestra, Capitol Theatre, New York, seven years; and besides playing with Goldman he has been at the famous Roxy Theatre for the past fifteen months under the noted Erno Rappe. Gusikoff also saw service overseas in the World War. Next is EDWIN FRANKO GOLDMAN, the Bandmaster, who has made a "Symphony Orchestra" out of a Brass Band—an achievement that his indeed made him a renowned conductor. It would take a book to record his brilliant history and the numerous honors that have been bestowed upon him, but, best of all, the boys say he is "a real fellow to work for." Last but not least is R. C. ELLIS, whose home city is Philadelphia, Pa. Twenty years in the business and always with "big names," such as Grand Opera House, Philadelphia; Weaver's Military Band, Philadelphia; Philadelphia Municipal Band; Pat Conway's Band; Pryor's Band; Sousa's Band; La Scala Opera Co.; Rialto Theatre, New York City; and at present doubling between Goldman and the Earl Carroll Vanities under the baton of Vincent Lopez. With such a fine list of organizations written down in his "date book," Ellis can well be proud.

Joe K. Lloyd—

has stuck in his home town, specializing in theatre work, since starting at the game twenty-two years ago. Three years at the Academy, four years at the Crown, five years at the Victoria and ten years at the State-Congress. All of these are leading vaudeville and burlesque houses and Joe has a rep second to none as one of the finest and fastest theatre men in Chicago. His outfit is always complete, even to machine tympani, and his leaders say he never misses a cue. We've heard him do his stuff on several occasions and can say that he sure "knows his manuscripts."

Owen Fallon meets "Hoot" Gibson and Audrey Ferris
(Universal and Warner Bros. Stars)

The opportunity to meet and really know interesting celebrities of the motion picture world is one of the advantages of being a "big time" Drummer in Los Angeles. Owen Fallon's capabilities as a clever Drummer, entertainer, dancer and master of ceremonies has given him this opportunity, and he has made staunch friends among many famous stars. Owen hails from San Francisco, where he made a name for himself at the Balconades Ballroom with his own orchestra, "The Californians." Three years ago he moved his orchestra to Los Angeles, where he has been an outstanding figure in things musical ever since. The Bon Ton Ballroom at Ocean Park; the Cinderella Roof in L. A.; Redondo Beach Ballroom; Highland Park West Coast Theatre; L. A. Elks Club; KFWB, KFI and KNX Radio are a few of the prominent jobs he has held, becoming more and more popular. Even though he has become famous as an entertainer, the drums are still his "first love," and here we see him showing his new Leedy Floating Head Model to two of moviedom's leading stars.

Leedy   "FOR DRUMMERS WHO CARE"   **Leedy**

Leedy Drum Topics

Billy S. Clifford and the Late President Warren G. Harding—

Billy S. Clifford of theatrical fame has been a producer, owner, manager of and actor in New York musical road shows from coast to coast over a period of twenty-five years, and all during this time has never forgotten that he was once a professional Drummer. Off and on throughout his active career he would go back to his "first love," the drums. No wonder—he was only nine years old when he started. At one time Billy was the "Sensational Drummer" with Al. G. Fields Minstrels. He also owns and operates the Clifford Theatre in Urbana, Ohio. At every Presidential election he organizes a drum corps; the above photo shows the late President Warren G. Harding autographing Billy's Leedy street drum. President Harding wrote—"To Billy S. Clifford, a tribute to not alone the drum head but to a very wise head," and signed, "Warren G. Harding." During the recent Presidential campaign Billy worked hard with his corps for Hoover for President and Cooper for Governor of Ohio. The corps was known as the Cooper Drum Corps.

It would be interesting to know the true origin of the many names given to the various rudimental beats. The general belief seems to be that they were originated by English military drum instructors who taught by rote in the army and navy before the days of printed drum methods, and used to impress beginners as to how a group of beats should sound. It is true that some of the names do fit the groups; however, there are more of them that have no relation to each other. The word "flam" can be said to sound as the rudiment is played. The word "drag" does not fit the rudiment, as there is only one syllable to the word and three to the rudiment. "Paradiddle" fits. "Ruff" does not fit. Neither does "Flamacue." How did the names really originate? If anyone knows, DRUM TOPICS would be glad to run the story.

The woman, if willing, will find a way.

Neat Effect—Can Be Used Two Ways
By—Wm. G. Street—Eastman Theatre Rochester, N. Y.

Take a 4-inch Leedy nickel silver cymbal (No. 31A, page 39, Catalog "R") and stick a ¾-inch square piece of adhesive tape over the hole. Hold cymbal in left hand, cup out, and tap cup of cymbal lightly with vulcanized rubber xylophone mallet (No. 370C, page 63, Catalog "R"). By more or less "cupping" the palm of the hand and tapping with the mallet, a most realistic effect of either dripping water in a sink or the ticking of a big clock is produced. Very effective in quiet scenes where orchestra is playing softly. This also makes a fine novelty stunt when played with syncopated and rhythmic beats to the tune of a popular jazz number.

On the Cover—
Bob Perry and Gus Arnheim

Team work, or the lack of it, between a Drummer and Leader can make or break an orchestra, big or little. In this case the close co-operation, fine spirit and flexibility existing between Bob Perry and Gus Arnheim has been a big factor in making this orchestra not only a local favorite but close to what might be termed a "national institution." Bob says that Gus is a wonderful leader and regular fellow to work for, and Gus says that Bob's striving to please, combined with unusual cleverness, makes him the ideal drummer—the kind that every leader desires. Bob Perry is a native of Los Angeles. Even in his kid days he played drums in school bands and at the same time studied piano. During one term Bob and the now famous Harold McDonald constituted the drum section of an L. A. High School orchestra. After leaving school he took to music seriously, playing both drums and piano, later devoting all effort to the drums. And now, after many years spent in all branches of the business, he holds down one of the finest jobs in the country—with Gus Arnheim's Orchestra in the Cocoanut Grove at the Ambassador Hotel, Los Angeles, also broadcasting over KNX. Cocoanut Grove is the gathering place for elite society and the movie stars. Here is a partial list of foremost jobs Bob has held: Opened the Biltmore Hotel, L. A.—Cafe La Fayette with Ralph Fox—Vernon Country Club with Dave Snell—Toured Orpheum Circuit with Earl Burtnette—Columbus Hotel, Miami, Fla.—Castillion Royal, N. Y. with "Sleepy" Hall. He was also with the orchestra that made the first Fox "sound" picture in the N. Y. laboratories. You'll sure get a kick out of hearing and seeing the Gus Arnheim Orchestra on the Vitaphone. Like its Drummer, it's a "whiz."

Gus Arnheim started his musical career in Atlantic City, N. J. He was pianist and arranger for Abe Lyman for several seasons prior to organizing his own orchestra. His great popularity in the West and the nation-wide demand for his Okeh records have placed both him and the orchestra amongst the country's greatest names.

You Should Have Been There—

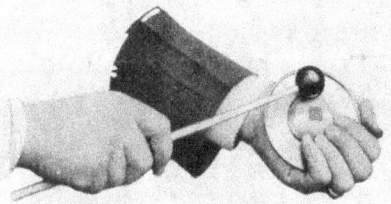

You've heard of Drummers who can dance, sing, act and even help the wife around the house, but Louis Nobile (at left of above photo) does a "double" that would make you remember him for life should you be lucky enough to be invited to a party where he officiates. He's a cook—no, that's not the word—he's a CHEF—the kind you read about. Louis is from Rome, Italy, but don't get the idea that spaghetti is his only "swell dish." He "chefs" them all from soup to nuts, AND HOW! He also plays in the percussion section of the Los Angeles Philharmonic Orchestra and the boys say he's as good a Drummer as he is culinary artist. This photo was taken after a special dinner (it was really a banquet with all the fixin's) at Jim Walter's home in Hollywood the 20th of June last; a little get-together of Drummers only in honor of Bill Spedick who was playing L. A. with the Gertrude Hoffman Girls in "A Night in Spain." Bill has been with Gertrude Hoffman since the flood. He is sixth from the left; he was so full of good eats that he couldn't hold his head up. From left to right we see—Louis Nobile, Chas. L. White (Tympanist L. A. Philharmonic Orch.—note photos and story of Charlie on page 8 of this DRUM TOPICS), Jim Walter (Drummer in the L. A. P. Orch.) who originally came from Denver, Colo., and has been "thru the mill" from coast to coast—Geo. H. Way of the Leedy Mfg. Co. (can't sit up straight because of the same trouble as Spedick)—Fred Haumes, from Chicago, where he played with all the big ones for many years and is now with the L. A. P. Orch.—Bill Spedick—and Max Wesser, who came from Odessa, Russia, and played for several years in well-known N. Y. City orchestras, now also with the L. A. P. Orch. Believe us, a mighty good time was had by everyone, all of which would have been impossible if it were not for the congenial Mrs. Walter, who let us muss up her house and dirty every dish in the place. It was she who took the photo with a little Brownie camera.

UKA—"Hold everything, I think I hear something breaking."

KAFETTE—"Don't worry, that's only my promise to mother."

George J. Cantwell—

Twenty years in the vaudeville, hotel and club field, with a long list of first-class positions to his credit, is the record of George J. Cantwell shown above with his "percussion pile" on his present job, the Keith-Albee Rialto Theatre, Amsterdam, N. Y. He was five summers at the Ft. Wm. Henry Hotel, Lake George, N. Y.—three years with the Smyth-Dunham Georgians—the Sterling Hotel, Wilkes-Barre, Pa. (a Meyer Davis unit)—Glover Theatre, Gloversville, N. Y.—Empire Theatre, Glens Falls, N. Y., and Amsterdam Theatre, Amsterdam, N. Y. Cantwell, as you can see by the photo, has every drummer's instrument an act could call for. His leader, E. W. Hutcheon, and the house manager of the Rialto say he plays them all second to none in vaudeville.

More About Banners—

Why not impress your name on the public's mind? An artistic banner is forceful and dignified advertising for any orchestra or band. Have a special one made. Write to—

Bradford & Co., Inc.,
St. Joseph, Mich.
(Atten. Mr. R. Richards)

and mention DRUM TOPICS. They will quote you prices that will surprise you and their workmanship and materials are of the very finest.

Leedy Nickel Silver and American Brass Cymbals

Here are two new sizes in Leedy own make Nickel Silver and American Brass Cymbals:

No. 31X	7-inch Nickel Silver
No. 31F	14-inch Nickel Silver
No. 30X	7-inch American Brass
No. 30F	14-inch American Brass

Strictly high quality instruments—the kind the big professionals like.

It requires 125 tons of pressure to form the Leedy Floating Head metal counter hoop.

The Best You Ever Saw— Carry-All Drum and Trap Case

Here is a winner. A new type, strong, neat appearing, black vulcanized fibre drum and trap case that will hold more traps than any other model. There are two partitions riveted in the body, which form pockets for traps up to 19 inches in length. Also a sturdy tray and two heavy leather straps that go all the way around the case. Metal (nickel plated) corners and heavy handle that will not pull out. See Leedy Catalog "R," page 74.

"WORLD'S FINEST DRUMMERS' INSTRUMENTS"

Page Ten

The Exclusive Drummers' Paper

American Legion Prize Winning Drum Corps at 1928 Convention in San Antonio, Texas

There is no describing an American Legion Convention. It is so big, so colorful and so genuinely American in character that words can never do it justice. You just have to be there to understand its spirit. And there are thrills galore. While hundreds of important things go to make up a Legion Convention, it's the Drum Corps and Bands that furnish the big punch. This year 56 Drum Corps and 27 Bands were in the four-hour parade on Tuesday, October 9th. Figuring on an average of 12 drummers to each Corps and 3 to each band, there were at least 753 drummers on the job. On Wednesday, October 10th, 40 Corps competed on the parade grounds at Ft. Sam Houston for position in the finals; 15 were chosen and on Thursday, October 11th, the "play-off" was held on an army athletic field nearby. The following photos show the five prize-winning Corps and their ratings.

Miami, Florida
Harvey Seeds Post No. 29
(First Prize—Rating 177,900)

Salem, Oregon
Capitol Post No. 9
(Second Prize—Rating 177,595)

Philadelphia, Penna.
Frankford Post No. 211
(Third Prize—Rating 176,566)

South Pasadena, Calif.
Post No. 140
(Fourth Prize—Rating 176,197)

Ogden, Utah
Herman Baker Post No. 9
(Fifth Prize—Rating 175,700)

Prize Winning Bands—

Wichita, Kansas......Thomas Hopkins Post No. 4 (First Prize, Rating 1,800)
Sioux City, Iowa........Monahan Post No. 64 (Second Prize, Rating 1,797)
Greenville, Ohio......Erk Cottrell Post No. 140 (Third Prize, Rating 1,695)
Rochester, N. Y.........Slager Post No. 941 (Fourth Prize, Rating 1,677)
Kenosha, Wis...................Post No. 21 (Fifth Prize, Rating 1,656)

Get This Book—The "Roll-off"—Free—

Everyone interested in Drums will want this wonderful 42-page book. Contains the history of the drum—scores of interesting photos and much historical data—also complete manual of Drum Major routine, with 21 photos showing positions. All organization and equipment problems answered. Send for yours today. Mailed free.

Leedy — "FOR DRUMMERS WHO CARE" — **Leedy**

Leedy Drum Topics

Dick Ulm and Ace Brigade—

Dick Ulm originally came from the small town of Delphos, Ohio, but has spent most of his time at the drums in big towns. For the past three years Dick has been with Ace Brigade and his Virginians at "Danceland" in Cleveland. This is a noted organization, having filled some of the finest engagements, with runs at—The Congress Hotel, Chicago—Swiss Gardens, Cincinnati—Monte Carlo, New York City, and others. Dick has also been with Al. Amato's Orch., Toledo, Ohio—the Seymour Simons office—the Finzel office—Goldkette's office and with The Carl Dimtsberge's Orch. He is indeed a "top notch" Drummer, with twelve years' experience on all instruments in both the legit. and jazz fields.

Chester F. Stahl—

of Boise, Idaho, is now playing with The Blue Bird Dance Orchestra. This popular bunch is ever in demand and fills engagements throughout the state. Stahl was a pupil of A. M. Bufort, proprietor of the Boise Drum and Saxophone Shop and a professional drummer of the highest order. He states that Stahl was a prize pupil and is now a real performer that is bound to go to the top. Stahl was formerly with the Melody Boys Orch.—The Black Hawk Dance Band—The Boise Boys Band and The Boise High School R.O.T.C. Band.

The Parrot—

We received so many compliments on the Parrot which was pictured with the Marine Pearl Drums in last year's Catalog "O" that we decided to use it for a new bass drum head painting. The scene is done in many brilliant colors and is effective with or without lights, although red and amber lights show it off to best advantage. For the Drummer who wants the latest (and a most attractive bass drum head) "The Parrot" will more than fill the bill. Ask for S-15.

Gilbert Holding—

We've read a lot about "boy wonder" musicians during the past few years, but here is one who fits the title 100%; in fact he is the only twelve-year-old youngster we have ever heard of who actually holds down the first chair in a drum section of a full-fledged adult band. It's the Ben Vereeckens Band of Los Angeles. He also plays in the Polytechnic High School Band of L. A. under W. J. Davis, Conductor. Gilbert is a pupil of one of L. A.'s best known professional drummers, Eddy Millard.

Ideas—

To prevent High Hat cymbal stand from "creeping away," place leg of chair through opening in heel piece. If this brings pedal too close, use a piece of cord through heel piece and around leg of chair.

By—John Thomas Graham, Lowell, Mass.

Lay eight or ten sheets of newspaper over knee. Hold sticks in the "scissor" manner so they will slap together when striking the paper. The combination gives a novel effect in syncopated rhythms.

By—King and Durlauf, Louisville, Ky.

If you use tympani sticks that have a reversed seam sewn around one side of the ball you can lessen the chances of this part striking the head by painting a narrow strip of ink along the seam. This makes it easy to see and can therefore be kept on the top side.

By—"Bink" Gustat, St. Louis, Mo.

With a little practice you can soon learn to play "hot" stuff on an all-in-one trap. The sliding tone control offers many possibilities.

By—Serge Fockler, Lima, Ohio.

I use two rubber stair treads (obtained at 5 & 10c store) under my bass drum and pedal, placed in T fashion. They prevent "creeping" of drum on polished or cement floor and are light and easy to carry in drum case.

By—Chas. A. Erath, New York City.

If you are "heavy" on cymbal crashes and experiencing too much breakage, try this—heat cymbal with blow-torch to a cherry red all the way around from edge to 3 inches in. Let it cool slowly. This slightly softens cymbal and will not sacrifice tonal qualities.

By—L. A. Mueller, Kankakee, Ill.

Attach wind whistle to apron of stage. Fix a length of proper sized rubber tubing over mouthpiece of whistle. Blowing in tube is easier on the teeth than holding whistle in mouth. Fine for fast vaudeville work in pit.

By—Joe Applegate, Chicago, Ill.

To prevent wind whistle from sticking, polish off both sides of the little fibre wheel inside with very fine emery paper. Then rub in black lead all over surface of wheel. This prevents moisture from taking effect and assures instant rotation at the slightest breath.

By—Pat Donovan, Dublin, Ireland.

Place 15 or 20 sheets of music on snare drum head. Throw off the snares. Strike a strong full length blow with drum stick. Makes great shot effect.

By—Andrew Pohl, Jr., Stillwater, N. Y.

"Hot breaks" on bells are popular in this country. We wrap thin rubber bands around the bars near the ends to kill the ring. Use thin bands. A little experimenting will enable you to get it just right.
A useful accessory for "hot" cymbal work is a pair of metal-tipped drum sticks. They are rather difficult to make, but it can be done by consulting a good machinist. He can turn the tips to suit out of a steel rod and thread hole inside. Then small metal shaft must be threaded and fit tightly into drilled hole in stick. Makes wonderful sizzle and fine for metallic beats.

By—J. V. Richmond, London, England.

Take empty Colgate's shaving stick can with screw top. Bore two small holes in center of each end. Fill with fine powdered rosin and run cord of dog bark clear through can. Run back and forth on cord once in a while to thoroughly rosin. No dirty hands when this is used. Leave can on cord.

By—L. A. Mueller, Kankakee, Ill.

Justa Wethead says—

"Hot dogs" teach me the latest "hot licks."

Talent without courage is worthless

Leedy wood shells (solid, laminated or veneer) do not, at any stage of their manufacture, ever come in contact with steam or water. They are formed on exclusive Leedy-built machines that might well be called "dry benders." The wood is literally "ironed" into a complete and true circle. When finished the shells remain in the circle without even clamping. They are guaranteed against warping. This method is two years old and a vast improvement over the old steam-bent process.

Bernard H. Sherman—

has been a "general business" Drummer in and around his home town of Boston, Mass., for the past eight years. He is a thorough all-around man and one of the type that always has a job. Three seasons with various stage bands and the past two years with Sol Farber and his Orchestra at the Revere Ballroom, Revere Beach, Mass. This is a first-class job. Sherman is very clever and has originated several trick cymbal beats that go over big.

The Marvel Drum Stand—

Here is a new drum stand with two new features that many Drummers have long desired. It holds your drum in a vise-like grip so firmly that it can not be dislodged by accident. The rubber-covered spring arms do the trick. Drum will not fall out even if turned upside down. Just as easy to set and release drum as on regular type stand. The rubber arm holders also improve tone and playing qualities of any drum. Be sure to state shell size of drum when ordering. Ask for the Marvel Drum Stand.

 "WORLD'S FINEST DRUMMERS' INSTRUMENTS"

The Exclusive Drummers' Paper

Maud May—

is a very capable Drummer now playing for her fourth consecutive year at Wellington Dance Hall, Southsea, England, with the popular "Wellington Quartette" (two ladies and two gentlemen), "all the year round" dances being featured. Previously worked several seasons with other dance bands in Portsmouth City and also met with great success at Royal Hotel and Hydro Matlock with Mr. Collicott's Orchestra. Comes of a Scottish family and is a daughter of a late naval officer who fought for his country. Was thoroughly instructed in the whole art of drumming by noted dance and cinema Drummer who was formerly in the celebrated Band of The Royal Marines. Maud May is a frequent contributor of dance news and articles on drumming to London monthly music and dance magazines.

Wm. G. Albers and Elmer Gesner—

The above Drummers have been playing side by side in the St. Louis Symphony Orchestra for twelve years. Wm. G. Albers (at left) has been in the biz for thirty years, and his experience covers every class of work, including two seasons on the road with The San Carlo Grand Opera Company. At present he is playing bass drum with the Symphony, although he has at different times filled every chair in the drum section. Elmer Gesner has been at it for eighteen years—at one time he was with Pat Conway's Band, also Victor Herbert and the Hadley Stadium Concerts. For five years he was house Drummer at the Olympic Theatre in St. Louis. All of which means that they both must be real artists in things drumistic.
(Courtesy—Sporleder Music House)

If you are interested in improving your ability on tympani, write to Karl Glassman, 1547 Broadway, New York City. He is now operating the largest percussion instrument school in New York City and is making a specialty of teaching tympani by correspondence. You'll be surprised at the wonderful help he can be. We know of several who have improved by leaps and bounds.

Giant Chee Foo Tom-Toms and Stands—

Big Tom Toms are now a standard part of the modern Drummer's equipment. The Chee Foo brand are equipped with real pig-skin heads and have a deep, rich, resonant tone, similar to that of tympani. The glossy black shells with hand wrought tacks and rings make a most pleasing appearance that gives an outfit the final professional touch. The stands are nickel plated and are adjustable to height.

*No. 94C	9" x 13"	Small Size
*No. 94D	12" x 14"	Medium Size
*No. 94E	16" x 16"	Large Size
*No. 99	Stand	

The Answer to an Old Problem—

By HERMAN E. WINTERHOFF, Vice.-Pres. Leedy Mfg. Co.

Musicians who have had considerable experience in playing open air concerts will undoubtedly recall that many times, when compositions were being played in which a soloist was stationed at quite some distance from the band (for example, "Post im Wald," "Miserere from Il Trovatore," "Musicians Astray in the Forest," etc.) there is quite a variation in pitch between the distant player and band or orchestra. Sometimes the pitch of the players seemed flat and at other times sharp. Naturally they blame each other for not being in tune, but they seldom understand the cause.

The cause is, if wind (which nearly always manifests itself) is blowing at right angles to a line between them, part of the vibrations are blown away, leaving less for either the band or distant player to hear, which somewhat lowers the pitch. Then again, when the wind is blowing from the distant player towards the band we find our distant player sharp and he hears the band as being flat, and vice versa.

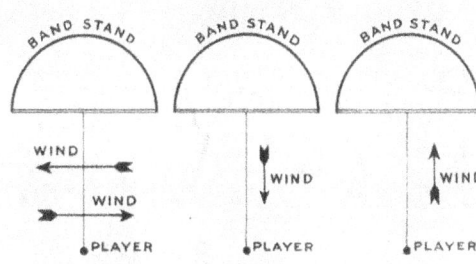

WIND BLOWING AT RIGHT ANGLE TO BAND STAND AND DISTANT PLAYER—BOTH SOUND FLAT TO EACH OTHER.

WIND BLOWING AWAY FROM BAND STAND TOWARD DISTANT PLAYER BAND SOUNDS SHARP TO PLAYER—PLAYER SOUNDS FLAT TO BAND.

WIND BLOWING TOWARD BAND STAND FROM DISTANT PLAYER—PLAYER SOUNDS SHARP TO BAND—BAND SOUNDS FLAT TO PLAYER.

To make this better understood we will cite an illustration of what occurs when one is riding on a train. You hear a bell or whistle of an approaching locomotive (traveling at a high rate of speed); at first the sound is high in pitch, but just at the instant the locomotive is at your side the pitch is somewhat lower, or normal, and after it has passed you the pitch is as much lower than normal as it was higher than normal while approaching you. This can also be easily observed while on any moving vehicle—street car, automobile, etc.

While we have cited you the cause for this occurrence, the only remedy is to play a number of this character when there is little or no wind, or in a hall.

To make this still clearer, we will say that sound travels approximately 1,100 feet per second, which is slightly more than one-fifth mile per second. To show what a wind velocity of fifteen miles per hour will do, we give the following figures:

15 miles per hour = 22 ft. per second.
Sound travels 1,100 ft. per second.
Ratio plus or minus difference $\frac{22}{1100} = .02$

Per cent of variation—2%
Difference in sound of 440 vibrations per second equals .02 x 440 = 8.8 vibrations per second, which amounts to more than one quarter semitone in pitch.

A Useful Book for Bands and Drum Corps—

This new 126-page book is the most complete work ever written on "Drill and Evolutions of the Band." It contains seven long chapters on the following subjects: (1) Organization of a Band. (2) Control of the Band by Signals. (3) The Carry Positions of Instruments. (4) The Drum Major as a Drill Master. (5) Instruction of the Individual Bandsman. (6) Drill of the Combined Band. (7) Special Evolutions. Written by Capt. R. B. Reynolds, U. S. A. (Drill Instructor of the University of Pennsylvania Band 1926-28). Single copies post paid in the U. S., $2.00 each. Twelve copies or more, F.O.B. Baltimore, $1.60 each. Write to National Service Publishing Co., Annapolis, Md.

Three Boosters Call on Mr. Leedy—

Visitors are always welcome at the Leedy plant, singly or in bunches. We like to show them through the factory. On the morning of October 26th three old friends happened to arrive at the same hour, so we "snapped" them with Mr. Leedy on the office steps. At the left is Mr. F. A. Veerkamp, the Leedy dealer of Mexico City, Mexico, one of our largest and best foreign distributors. Every year he makes a tour of the American factories and never fails to spend a day or two with us. Next is Mr. Leedy himself. Next is Fielden A. Cantrell, who is trouping this season with Shubert's "Blossom Time." Fielden is from Spartanburg, S. C.—a drummer who has made 'em sit up and take notice from coast to coast. He's been with the best on the road—"The Student Prince," "Rose Marie," "Desert Song" and many others. Does he wallop a mean calf skin? Ask his leaders. Next is that "dean of the road," Billy Spedick of Gertrude Hoffman fame. He came along with Shubert's "A Night in Spain," and we'll say that a night with Bill is to learn things a-plenty about Drums and Drummers. He knows 'em all and what he doesn't know about pushing a pedal can be put on the back of a postage stamp in letters an inch high. We take our hats off to the man who made Bert Williams step high and wide in "Bandana Land." Can you remember that one?

Ed. A. Burns—

of Adams, Mass., is house Drummer at the Empire Theatre at North Adams (Philip Lewin, leader). Burns has been in the business for five years and has had considerable experience in various bands and orchestras throughout Western Massachusetts. His work is of a high standard and he has received many compliments from those "in the know." He will undoubtedly go to the top, for even though playing professionally he keeps on with his studies. At present he is a pupil of H. D. Steel on tympani and xylophone.

A Drummer's Wife—"Luke is always complaining about his snare bed."

A Fiddler's Wife—"We think there is nothing like a Simmons."

New Leedy Gong Holder—

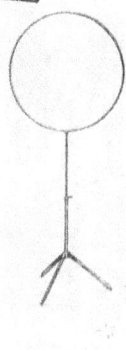

Heretofore there has been no practical gong holder that the Drummer could use for jobbing purposes. This new type has folding legs and the base may be carried in the drum case. The "loop" is light and easily moved about. There are two small holes in the top of the "loop" for suspending the gong. It has a liberal height adjustment rod and can be used in either a sitting or standing position. All nickel plated. Ask for No. 33C. State size of gong when ordering.

Leedy   "FOR DRUMMERS WHO CARE"   **Leedy**

Leedy Drum Topics

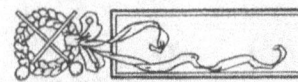 

News of the New York Percussion Club—

In the last (No. 16) issue of Drum Topics we published a letter from Aaron Geiger, President of the New York Percussion Club. It outlined the club's ideals in a most interesting manner. Since then we have often heard from the energetic recording secretary, Charles Kritzler, and, knowing how well they are progressing, we want to tell our readers something about their recent accomplishments. They now have 450 members within Local 802. This large enrollment has been the result of hard work on the part of the officers, and it goes without saying that the force of the entire group has been responsible for many new union laws that benefit the Drummer. Of special interest is the club's Employment Department, which offers service to all Drummers in good standing. Managers of orchestras, bands, theatres, etc., are relying on this service more and more each month. Another progressive step is the club's new magazine called "Rhythm." We have just looked over the first issue and find it full of announcements, news, jokes, advertisements and editorials gotten up in a most interesting style. Every Drummer in New York who is not already a member should certainly take advantage of the opportunity to join with this group of sincere officers and drummers who are plugging for the good of all concerned. They have the hearty good wishes of Drum Topics.

Mirror Assists in Playing Chimes

Drummers who use chimes in a crowded space are often compelled to place them at the rear of their chair. This means turning clear around with one's back to the leader (or at least sideways, which is just as awkward), and makes it impossible to watch the leader and the tubes at the same time. By placing a mirror—such as shown in the above illustration—to the left of the chime rack, the Drummer can adjust it so that he can watch the leader throughout the part being played. Do not attach the mirror to the chime rack as it will vibrate and not reflect clearly. Attach it to the apron of the stage or on a Leedy trap tree stand, which is adjustable to height. (See Catalog "R," page 46, No. 981.)

Victor F. Beck—

was the Drummer in the first picture show in Omaha, Nebr., twenty-eight years ago. He also played in several other Omaha theatres and concert bands conducted by Geo. Green (father of the famous George and Joel and Arthur Smith. Eleven years ago Beck moved to North Platte, Nebr., where he has been with the Keith Theatre orchestra ever since. This "old timer" certainly knows the ropes and has a most enviable reputation as a finished Drummer in all respects.

Two New Models Hickory & Rosewood Drum Sticks—

These two new model drum sticks have literally swept the country since their first appearance in the new Leedy catalog "R" (page 60) a few months ago. They are just what many Drummers have been waiting for. The H-9 model (shown on the left) is designed for general orchestra use, while the H-11 is for band or drum corps playing. Both are dandies and have that "hang" and "feel" that give a rebound as strong as the stroke. They are also furnished in rosewood.

Harry Pasternak—

Whenever you hear the Eveready Battery Radio Orchestra (Joe De Coursey, leader—Station CKNC), Toronto, Canada, on the air, you also hear Harry Pasternak playing the above array of Leedy instruments in a manner second to none in the studios. He is one of Eastern Canada's leading Drummers, having had many years' experience in most all branches of the business. Some of his past jobs have been: Bala Muskoka; leader of the Sioux City Seven at Hamilton, Canada; A Vincent Lopez unit at Lilydale, N. Y.; vaudeville tour with Vincent Carr of New York; University of Michigan Collegians, Detroit, and other modern bands too numerous to mention. Pasternak, as one can see by the photo, is most progressive, and he plays them all with finished style and neatness.

(Courtesy—Advance Music Co., Toronto)

The Prize Story—

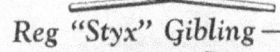

By—Frank Wolf (Prop. of Frank Wolf's Drum Shop, 233 West 46th St., New York City)

Operating an exclusive Drum Shop in New York City and serving thousands of Drummers of all schools and nationalities certainly has its humorous as well as business aspect. Here's a hot one that really happened a few weeks ago. A young dance drummer who had just broken into the business a few days before, came rushing into the store all out of breath one afternoon about 5 P. M. "Say, Frank, I just got a chance to try out with a big orchestra over in Brooklyn tonight and the leader says I must have 'tymtanies,' and if I make good the job is mine. Now I've got to have a couple of 'tymtanies' over there by eight o'clock and I want you to loan me a set. If I 'click' I'll buy them tomorrow. You arrange with transfer man and I'll pay the bill. Here's the name of the hall—and say, the leader said the big number of the evening was in G and C, so you be sure to tune them just right before they leave the store. I'll leave it to you, old kid—s'long."

Don't forget, boys—$10.00 for the best story not later than February 15th, 1929. Shoot them in and win the price of a few new traps.

Reg "Styx" Gibling—

"Styx" obtained his nickname in the Royal Navy on H. M. S. Queen Elizabeth because he always worried the rest of the bandsmen with an overdose of practice. His home town is London, where he formerly played at the Royal Surrey Theatre, a leading variety house. Some of his other jobs have been: Trocadero, London; Brighton's Corner House Orchestra, London; Hotel Metropole, Blackpool; Hotel Majestic, St. Anne's; Victor Duprez Orchestra (en tour). Gibling is now with the Provincial Cinema playing the leading houses on the north circuit, at present in Aberdeen. He also plays in the Aberdeen Symphony Orchestra. We have heard from other sources that he is one of the finest in the British Isles. "Styx" says every orchestra that suffers a crowded space because of a stubborn manager should hand him this one—"Give us the room and we'll give you the show."

Perhaps You'll Find a New Idea in a Phonograph Record—

When you hear a brother Drummer doing his stuff "in person" you may "catch" a good gag and you may not. Usually it's done so quickly that you miss the details. But when you hear a good one on a phonograph record you can play it over and over until the idea sinks in. The latest is always on the records. Listen to these—perhaps you'll find something new. Thanks to the boys who took the trouble to give us these names and numbers.

Victor Record No. 21423—All Star Orchestra playing "Oh Baby." Chauncey Morehouse is the Drummer.
Sent in by Harold McDonald, Universal Studios, Los Angeles.

Brunswick Record No. 3840—Arnold Johnson's Orchestra playing "I'm Riding to Glory." Gary Gillis is the Drummer.
Sent in by "Red" Allen, Wurlitzer's Drum Dept., Los Angeles.

Victor Record No. 52410—Green Bros'. Marimba Band playing "I Wanna Be Loved by You" and "I Can't Give You Anything but Love." George and Joe Green on the Xylophone.
Sent in by Al. Cruchet, Advance Music Co., Toronto, Canada.

Victor Record No. 20889—McEnelly's Orchestra playing "My Sunday Girl."
Sent in by Ellsworth Baker, Buffalo, N. Y.

Brunswick Record No. 3537—Palmer House Victorians playing "You Don't Like It—Not Much" and "Wild, Wild, Flowers."
Sent in by Robert Lea, Brunswick, Mo.

Victor Record No. 20829—Ted Weems' Orchestra playing "She's Got It." Dusty Roades is the Drummer.
Sent in by Jack Costello, Jr., Canandaigua, N. Y.

Perfect Record No. 12354—Playing "Under the Moon" and "Ain't That a Grand an' Glorious Feelin'."
Sent in by Russell Burke, Scranton, Penna.

Victor Record No. 20675—Goldkette's Orchestra playing "I'm Gonna Meet My Sweetie Now." Chauncey Morehouse is the Drummer.
Sent in by Roy Welch, Jacksonville, Fla.

The Finishing Department—

This department of the Leedy plant has recently been enlarged and entirely rebuilt. Considerable new equipment, such as several of the latest type spray guns and booths have been installed, along with improved methods. The department employs six men, with Ray Poland, a finisher of many years' experience, as foreman.

Did you meet the Sousa Drummers when they played your town this fall? Yes, the same "Three Musketeers" are on the job again—Gus Helmecke for the "umteenth" year, with his smile and friendly handshake; Howard Goulden for the tenth season, with his businesslike manner and willingness to talk drums; and Frank Holt for the fourth year, with his energetic and clean-cut style. Every Drummer should know this trio. To talk to them is to be inspired and refreshed.

 "WORLD'S FINEST DRUMMERS' INSTRUMENTS"

The Exclusive Drummers' Paper

Tambourine on Tympano—

Both delicate and heavy tambourine effects can be obtained by beating on the edge of shell of same, laid HEAD DOWN (this is important) on a tenor tympano tuned to D or Eb. Fine for quick changes, as it's easier to pick up the tymp. stick than the tambourine. Also fine in PPP oriental strains, beating according to rhythm. Another effect is to beat on the tympano head allowing the tambourine to vibrate in with the deep tom tom effect.

By—Keith A. Reay, Empress Theatre,
Sydney, N. S. W., Australia.

Wm. Lavin—

of Philadelphia, Pa., is a hustling young Drummer who is fast climbing into high-class company. He started five years ago in a Drum Corps, but soon went in for orchestra and band work, studying with the famous Jess Altmiller. Lavin has done considerable jobbing in dance work in and around Philadelphia with the "Phila. Sirens" Orch. During the past year he has unfortunately been quite ill and had to give up strenuous work. As a side line Lavin is selling printing and wishes Drum Topics to call attention to a special bargain in Drummer's cards he is now offering.

Drummers Business Cards—
ONE THOUSAND, ONLY $2.95
Finest Quality Material—All Hand Work.
Write for prices on other printed matter.
William Lavin,
1351 East Haines St.,
Philadelphia, Penna.

Did you see and hear Jess Altmiller, Drummer at the Fox Theatre, Philadelphia, Pa., do his stuff on the Fox Movietone News Reel the week of Nov. 5th? A five-minute "close-up" of a Drum stunt that is in a class by itself. If not you missed a treat. If so, don't you agree that he is a wonder for speed, accuracy and technique?

William L. Dowler—

This wonderful outfit sits in the Palace Theatre, Marion, Ohio—one of the finest theatres in the state. William L. Dowler (photo insert), who owns and plays these instruments, has specialized in concert, dance and theatre work for the past nine years, with several high-class jobs to his credit, a few of which have been — Grand Theatre Orch.—Murray's Dance Orch.—Lakeside Concert Orch.—Epworth Orch. and others. He enjoys a wide reputation for clean-cut, snappy work and stands high in the estimation of his leaders and managers. This photo was taken by the Master Studio, Marion, Ohio.

Bill Kieffer, Chas. Viner, Johnny Auer and Phil. Genthner, the famous Drum Section of the U. S. Marine Band, just finished a tour with the band up through the New England States. Fourteen weeks of one-night stands.

Arthur Layfield is still going strong at the Oriental in Chicago. We've heard that he goes with the lease. When Paul Ash returned to the Oriental recently after acting as guest conductor in the East, he stated that he was sure glad to get back "home" and hear Art do his stuff.

Harold McDonald has landed an A-1 job with the Universal Recording Harmonists, making sound pictures at the Universal Studios, Universal City, Calif., Joseph Cherniavsky, leader. More about this in the next issue. Mac is also operating a drum school at the Rudolph Wurlitzer Music Co. in Los Angeles.

Next to receiving a compliment from the leader, nothing pleases a Drummer more than boasting of it to other Drummers.

"Choke" Cymbals and Holders—

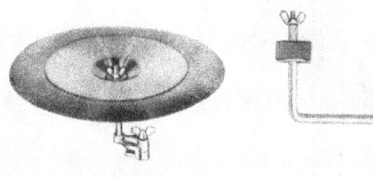

"Choke" or "dead" cymbal effects are all the rage these days. Experimenting on the part of the "big timers" has resulted in these simple combinations being chosen for the purpose. The lower cymbal is a 12-inch Chinese and the top one (turned cup down and fitting into the cup of the Chinese) is an 8-inch Leedy American Brass. The holder shown in photo at left is a new type (No. 274) designed for holding the "Choke" cymbals on the bass drum hoop, and the one shown at right (No. 275) is for holding them on a Leedy trap table—trap console or Rollaway trap console. There is an adjusting wing nut on both holders which enables the Drummer to control the tone of the cymbals as desired. Can also be adjusted for sizzle cymbal effect.

Turk McBee, Jr.—

Although young in years, Turk McBee, Jr., is a veteran when it comes to trouping and putting over a snappy xylophone act. The season of 1926 he was featured on J. A. Coburn's Minstrels, billed as "Dixie's Star Boy Xylophonist" and in 1927 he was a feature on the Publix circuit. At present young McBee is playing the Keith circuit with the Dan Fitch Minstrels (direction, Pat Casey) and many press notices sent to Drum Topics are high in praise of his artistic work. His four-mallet numbers are especially well played. This boy has everything—personality, pep and skill—and big things are predicted for his future. Turk's home is in Greenville, S. C.

A Good Shot Effect—

Take off the batter counter hoop of your drum and lay fairly heavy rubber band across head. When replacing hoop run the two rods thru the loops of the band, as shown in photo. By snapping the two strands of rubber on the head with more or less degree a realistic shot effect is produced. When not in use the band wholly prevents the batter head from excess vibration and therefore eliminates all ringing.

Sam C. Rowland—
Asst. Adv. Mgr.—Leedy Mfg. Co

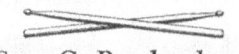

When Sam Rowland joined the Leedy staff last February it meant still more "personal service" for the Drummer who requests special assistance and information. Sam, as many of his friends know, is an ex-professional of several years experience. For three years he was located in Los Angeles, Calif., and played in many of the best cafes, clubs, hotels and theatres of that city. He also served a year and a half as manager of the Drum Dept. at the Wurlitzer Music Co., and while there worked up the largest "Drummers' Service Station" on the Pacific Coast.

LENA—"I hear that Miss Rose Wood is chasing around with that Haza Rodloose, what can she see in him?"

LOTTS—"You never can tell, dearie—maybe he shakes a mean No. 395."

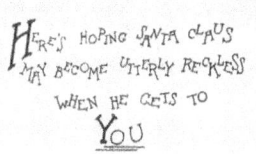

HAPPY NEW YEAR, TOO

YOURS TILL DRUM HEADS NEED HAIR CUTS

   "FOR DRUMMERS WHO CARE"   

Leedy Drum Topics

The Exclusive Drummers' Magazine

DECEMBER, 1928

SEVENTEENTH EDITION

POSTMASTER—Return Postage Guaranteed

Leedy Manufacturing Co.

INDIANAPOLIS, INDIANA

When Jack Comes to Town—

it's your opportunity to pick up the latest "dope" on Drums and Drummers. Meet a regular fellow who knows his "hickories" and has trouped with the best of them. Jack makes the rounds about once a year. He carries five big trunks full of Leedy instruments and sets them up in either the leading music store or a hotel sample room. The Drummers of each locality are notified of the time and place. Be sure to visit him and see this display; the largest and most beautiful musical instrument layout ever carried from town to town. It's for everyone interested in drums. Remember—there is no obligation when you visit him. You will not be "high powered" or even asked to buy a single thing. True, the "show" is an advertisement for Leedy, but that's all. You will benefit by meeting Jack and looking over the newest creations of the Drum World.

Five thousand years ago—and NOW Leedy Elevated Chimes

History relates that the earliest attempt to co-ordinate a series of tones more or less related was the Chinese Pien-ch'ing Chimes, in use 5000 years ago. These consisted of a series of sonorous stone slabs (usually sixteen in number) suspended by animal gut from horizontal bars, the performer striking the slabs with a root hammer. The stone slabs which gave the tones of the Chinese scale were afterwards superseded by plates of metal. These plates of metal in turn made way for a series of cast bells (without tongues) also struck with a hammer, and from these evolved our present-day bells and tubular chimes. In other countries of the Orient, a similar series of experiments preceded the casting of copper bronze and other metallic bells with tongues or clappers similar to those that have been in vogue throughout Europe for several centuries. Among the most remarkable proofs of ancient accomplishment in this field is a finely modeled Assyrian bronze bell, which was made eight or more centuries before the Christian era. The universal employment of bells of all sizes in connection with religious services, from those small bells worn on the robe of Aaron to the heavy chimes of the great cathedrals, betokens their particular spiritual and musical nature. In China, bells of enormous size hang in the towers and doubtless are still used to drive away demons. In Peking alone there are seven, each weighing 120,000 pounds. But it is in Russia that the enthusiasm for bell-building reaches its greatest height, the most remarkable, of course, being the "great bell" which was cracked during the conflagration in the Kremlin—the interior being 22 feet in diameter and over 21 feet in height.

Chimes, for centuries recognized as one of the world's standard and most beautiful instruments, today hold a higher position in things musical than ever before. However, until the perfection of the "Elevated" type they have always been considered more or less difficult to play. The old conventional, straight-in-line style mounting of the tubes was responsible for this. Progress now presents a new and more practical method. The sharps and flats are raised and set back, forming a second row above the naturals. This gives them the same note positions as the familiar piano keyboard, also the same relative bar positions as bells of the xylophone—a great assistance to the Drummer when sight-reading, playing from memory or improvising. The rack or stand of the small model (1-inch tubes) is heavier than our regulation type (Leedy Cat. "R," page 94). The new "Elevated" model is also made with the 1½-inch tubes as per our Cathedral model. All parts beautifully finished, with sharps and flats in brushed brass, and naturals and rack in bright nickel. Racks fold up for transporting. No bulky parts to bother with. A special new type ridged web separator prevents tubes from clanking together.

No. 1400—Small Elevated Chimes, 1-inch tubes, 18 notes Chromatic, F to C, without banner rack.
No. 1401—Banner Rack for Small Elevated Chimes.
No. 1402—Banner (to order) Felt Letters Sewn on Velvet.
No. 1403—Fibre hand-carrying Case for Small Elevated Chimes.

Leedy Drum Topics Issue 18

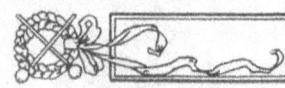 # Leedy Drum Topics

Still greater recognition is possible—

THE position that the Drummer now holds in the public's eye is one of much greater importance than ever before. The Drummer has been advertised to the public; everyone is more or less familiar with what he has to do and he is firmly fixed in the minds of the crowd, which has learned to understand and appreciate his work. He did not gain this position overnight. Ten years ago a Drummer was just a Drummer—if thought of at all—and by many he was even belittled. The steady growth of modern music has of course helped him to come to the front, but it cannot be denied that he has taken advantage of every opportunity that presented itself to create and build his own foundation, going on upward with strides that have commanded attention and admiration. His present prominence in things musical is not one of chance or mere flash. Has he reached the peak? Certainly not. There is room for him to climb higher and it is possible for him to hold his position at any height he may reach. He MUST NOT decline. In this day of fast-changing fashions, with the public ever ready to throw off the old and take on the new, nothing is impossible; therefore every Drummer should hold a tight rein and use all the ingenuity at his command to remain in the public's favor indefinitely. Still greater recognition is the Drummer's goal; it should be the most important subject in his thoughts, for it means still greater success, which in turn means more money. If the Drummers by any chance lose their present popularity they will have only themselves to blame. They must go on creating new ideas that will attract attention and keep the spotlight ever focused on the Percussion Department. Every Drummer must be "sold" on his work. If he doesn't like being a Drummer he should quit and get into work more to his liking. He must be honestly glad that he is a Drummer and have confidence in himself. He must use a little psychology and try to see himself as seen by others. Then he must continue to improve his ability by both thought and practice. Ability always develops in the one who is serious. Ability and Experience make the finished artist. There is also the personal side—Appearance, Neatness, Manner and Good Fellowship. KEEP SMILING. Cheerfulness makes Pep and Pep makes the Drummer more valuable. But think of Pep as Personality combined with a little Showmanship. Don't be an acrobat. There is a "something" about Drums that is fascinating. The public is friendly and ever ready to boost the Drummer, so don't let that "something" droop and die for want of what can well be called Enthusiasm.

Have You Thought of This?

Now that many of the large downtown photoplay houses have cut out their orchestras, acts and presentations, substituting only "sound" pictures and an organ solo, they are offering no more in the way of entertainment than the "wired" neighborhood houses. When the downtown houses were putting on real shows, with orchestras, presentations, etc., they could claim bigger and better shows than the neighborhoods, therefore the public did not mind a higher admission price. But now that the downtown show is the same as the neighborhood and the price still remains higher, is it not reasonable to expect that the public will begin to favor the outlying houses which can offer the "sounds" and "talkies" at a lesser price? The only difference is that the pictures come along two or three weeks later, but in the minds of many this is offset by the advantages of easy auto parking and the lower price. Neighborhood houses are improving; they are cozy and pretty. Many people claim that the "sounds" go over better in these houses, which are usually somewhat smaller. In other words, if there is to be so little difference in the offerings of the "downtowns" and the "neighborhoods" it will not be surprising if the former will be forced to put on more elaborate programs, and this can only mean the addition of acts and presentations, which in turn means an orchestra.

Leedy   "WORLD'S FINEST DRUMMERS' INSTRUMENTS"   *Leedy*

The Exclusive Drummers' Paper

The "Pop" Cymbal—

This new stunt has plenty of punch. The more you work with it the better you'll like it. With a little experimenting and practicing you'll discover it to be a novel and impressive effect that does not become tiresome and can be used in almost any type of rhythmic number, especially in the PP passages. The fibre "tone-hat" must be one inch smaller in diameter than the cymbal used. This is important. Larger or smaller will not give the proper results. This means that the "tone-hat" must be made to order. It should be 5 inches deep and made of .060 vulcanized fibre. It may be painted any color desired. A 5c coffee pot knob serves as a handle. A strip of felt must be sewed around the bottom edge of the "hat." Punch small holes in the fibre for this purpose as a needle will not penetrate same. Use a Leedy No. 617 hard felt xylophone mallet. Strike cymbal and hold "tone-hat" about one-fourth inch above same. It will be noticed that the tone is amplified. The "hat" acts as a reflector. When the "hat" is raised and brought down on the cymbal with considerable force while the cymbal is ringing, a decided "pop" of a new and unusual tone comes forth. It is a "cut off" cymbal effect that is better than using the hand as it gives a deep metallic "pop" embodying the tone of the cymbal as tho' it was quickly muffled in a barrel. For blue numbers it's great, and also works fine in fast syncopation. An occasional accent by striking the felt stick on the top of the fibre "tone-hat" adds to the whole scheme. The crown of a derby hat is N. G., it being too small to reflect the tone of the cymbal and not strong enough to stand the blow necessary to produce the "pop." You can have the "tone-hat" made at any trunk and bag shop. If there is not one in your locality, Leedy will be glad to quote a price.

This word "MODERN" is beginning to cover up a multitude of sins. There are too many Drummers of the younger generation doing things any old way—often the wrong way—under the guise of the "Modern School," and forming bad habits which, the further they go, the less chance they will ever have to fill a big job when it comes along. You don't see George Marsh, Art Layfield, Frank Horscroft and others of the same skill doing things wrong (especially cramped hand positions) and calling it "modern." And they are with MODERN organizations, too.

Every Drummer Needs This Date Book—

This book contains much useful information and a year's date space arranged in perpetual form. You may start any day, month or year. Bound in leatherette cover. Mailed post-paid to Drummers only on receipt of ten cents in U. S. Stamps. Postal regulations prevent our extending this offer outside the United States and Canada. Send 10c in stamps for yours TO-DAY.

If some Drummers would read the "spots" as accurately as they read the baseball scores they would make more "hits."

Bill Gladstone and David Mendoza—

Drummer and Conductor of the Capitol Theatre Grand Symphony Orchestra, N.Y., and Official Metro-Goldwyn-Mayer Sound Photo-Play Orchestra (Eastern Studios)

The name of Bill Gladstone stands for much in the Drum World. Those familiar with "Who's Who" know him to be one of the profession's outstanding examples of extraordinary ability, not only as a performer on Drums, Tympani and Xylophone, but as an authority on the technicalities of drummers' instruments and an expert on sound effects. We knew Bill 'way back in 1909 when he started in the game. There never was a young Drummer more sincere and with more "go to it." He was a night and day hound for practice and knowledge and has been like that ever since—that's why he is now at the top of the ladder. Bill has been so busy improving his ability that he has had no time to push himself in a publicity way. Whenever he has been heard of, it has been due to his associates and newspaper men who have put forth the effort, realizing that he is indeed a genius in his line. Many times have New York papers carried long and detailed feature stories lauding his skill. However, there are two points which they always overlook: first, that he is one of the most thorough and artistic rudimental Drummers on record—and second that his personality behind the drums is positively magnetic. He is the most graceful

Drummer we have ever seen—not feminine grace, but the grace of balance and ease. He never rushes, but is always there. Everyone in N. Y. knows him as everyone goes to the Capitol, and they always remember the man and his work. He has several clever trap and sound inventions to his credit, among them being the Gladstone "Handsock" Cymbal which is now in universal use. Previous to going into the Capitol several years ago Bill held some of the finest jobs in New York, including the Rialto Theatre Concert Orchestra (Dr. Hugo Reisenfeld, Conductor) and under the baton of Erno Rapee. At present Gladstone is playing the main shows at the Capitol with the Capitol Grand Orchestra under the direction of the famous David Mendoza, who is shown in the above photo trying out a Leedy Floating Head Drum. In addition to the Capitol job, Bill does the drum, xylophone and special effect work for all the Eastern M-G-M (Metro-Goldwyn-Mayer) sound photoplays, with Mendoza conducting. They also play considerably over the N. B. C. radio network, and there is where you hear Bill's fast and neat work on the Xylophone. Drummers visiting New York are missing a big bet if they fail to meet and have a chat with Bill Gladstone. No "high hat" with him—just walk up and say "Hello, Bill." And here's telling you before you meet him—he plays Leedy from soup to nuts.

DAVID MENDOZA, Conductor of the Capitol Theatre Grand Symphony Orchestra and the official Eastern studio M-G-M. Sound Photoplay Orchestra, is one of the most noted conductors in the theatre-symphony field. He is recognized as among the ablest of musical directors in scoring photoplays. Such pictures as "The Big Parade," "Ben Hur," "Merry Widow," "Greed," "Mare Nostrum," "Alias Jimmy Valentine," "The Flying Fleet," "Dancing Daughters" and "The Duke Steps Out" owe their musical success to Mendoza. During his professional career he was first violinist with the New York Symphony Orchestra and the Russian Symphony Orchestra. It is reported by Drummers who have served under his baton that he is one of those rare leaders who has a thorough knowledge of the Drum Section and, while most particular, is at the same time very congenial to work for.

George and Joe
Take Their Morning Exercise—

At least it looks that way. On the other hand, they may be demonstrating the fact that the Geo. Hamilton Green Model Xylophone is light in weight and just the thing for jobbing. They didn't offer any explanation of the "acrobatics" when they sent in the photo. As usual, they are both going as big as ever over New York's leading Radio Stations WEAF and WJZ and their networks.

We Now Have—

EXTRA THIN Genuine K. Zildjian & Cie. Turkish Cymbals in 8, 10, 11, 12 and 13 inch sizes. They are the finest quality small cymbals we have ever had in stock and are the "berries" for that very high pitch "sting" staccato stuff. Better get yours now as the source of supply is a little uncertain in regard to deliveries. We also have the genuine Zildjian in 10-inch deep cup models.

"I'm tellin' you, Jim, Mary isn't a bad girl if you get to know her real well."
"Well, what's the advantage of knowing her intimately then?" —*Green Goat*

Leon A. Nortenstraugh—

Leon A. Nortenstraugh of Roanoke, Va., is now playing with Pat Dollohan's Orchestra at the Hotel Durant, Flint, Mich. Pat Dollohan is seen in above photo at right. This Orchestra has a fine rep as a "hot-sweet" combination and Nortenstraugh is just that kind of a Drummer, with plenty of clever "neat-legit" stuff in addition. He formerly had his own Orchestras, "The Naviators," at Washington, D. C., and "Norty" and his Orchestra at Coco Solo, Canal Zone. He also played with Bob Winslow's Orchestra at the White House Cafe, Flint, Mich., and with Don Preston's Orchestra at Port Huron, Mich.

Leedy   "FOR DRUMMERS WHO CARE"   **Leedy**

Leedy Drum Topics

Percussion Section of the Metropolitan Opera House Orchestra—New York City—

STANDING (left to right) PAUL SCHULZE—ALVIN BROEMEL—GEORGE A. BRAUN. SEATED—ROBERT KIESOW.

To the best of our knowledge this is the first group photo of these four famous Drummers ever to appear in any publication. Drum Topics has been after it for some time. While the four are together daily for rehearsals and performances during the winter season, they had to do some tall "maneuvering" to get together at the photographer's. Time is valuable in New York. Now that they are here, look them over carefully, boys. The drum world can claim no more distinguished quartette, as each one of them has long standing records of association with musical organizations ranking among the finest in the world. PAUL SCHULZE has been with the Metropolitan Opera Orchestra for four years—Philharmonic Orchestra, Munich, Germany, four years—Stadt Opera House, Dusseldorf, Germany, one year—Stadt Opera House, Berlin, Germany, eleven years—Staats Opera House, Stuttgart, Germany, one year—and a tour of the U. S. with the Wagnerian Opera Co. Schulze now makes his home in Jamaica, Long Island. ALVIN BROEMEL is a native of New York and for twenty years has been rated A-1 among the best drummers there. For five years he was with the late Victor Herbert when that musical genius was in his prime. To be one of Victor Herbert's favorite Drummers is indeed an honor, for he, unlike most composers and conductors, thoroughly understood the possibilities of Drums. Broemel was also with the Mark Strand Theatre Concert Orchestra on Broadway for seven years. Besides his work at the Metropolitan he does considerable playing for the National Broadcasting Co. GEORGE A. BRAUN was also with Victor Herbert as Tympanist for eighteen summer seasons. Almost every drummer realizes that such a position called for the utmost in skilled musicianship. For twelve years he was a member of the Philharmonic Orchestra of New York City, and for the past eight years with the Metropolitan Opera, the last three of which he has been the Tympanist. Such opera conductors as Bodanzky, Serefin, Bellazza, Hasselman and Bamboschek, rank Braun among the leading Tympanists of both the United States and Europe. ROBERT KIESOW is one of New York's old-timers. We wish we had the space to set down his career of 34 years' active service behind the Drums. A few of his "high spots" are—Ballet Russe—Goldman's Band—69th Regt. Band—Franko's Orchestra—Kaltenborn Orchestra—Waldorf Astoria Hotel Orchestra—and Landen's Band. He has been with the Metropolitan Orchestra for the past nine years. Of course we are proud to announce that these "topnotchers" are "Leedyized" from triangles to tymps.

You can fake some drum parts all of the time—
You can fake all drum parts some of the time—
But—you can't fake all drum parts all of the time.

Herbert Lee—

and his Leedy Drums have been traveling in "class" company for eleven years. Lee is known as the "up-to-date boy" of every orchestra with which he has been connected. One year, California Ramblers—one year, 14 Virginians—three years, The Nebraskans—one year, Dave Bernet's Orch.—six months, Ben Bernie's Orch.—two years, Plaza Hotel, New York—three months tour of South America—also Sharp's Revue in Keith Vaudeville and with Johnny Johnson's Orch. His home town is Buffalo and he is now playing with Joe La France's Orch. at the New Asia Restaurant, Springfield, Mass.

A Drummer "Gone Turkish"—

Seated on a Turkish Rug, "hot licking" a Turkish Cymbal, he got redder than a Turkish Fez; then took a Turkish Bath, using a Turkish Towel, and called it a day by lighting a Turkish Cigarette. (We had to leave the Turkish Harem out.)

Technical Information—

Piano hammers always strike the strings in exactly the same spots. Technically speaking, marimba and xylophone mallets should always strike the bars in the same spots, but owing to the manner in which these instruments are played this is, of course, impossible. Striking the bars in different places is what produces "overtones." This would also happen if piano hammers struck in various places on the strings. Until three years ago there was no known method of controlling these overtones and more often than not they were out of tune with the fundamental note of the bar. This disagreeable "clashing" is what caused many leaders and other musicians to condemn the marimba—it almost eliminated that instrument for phonograph recording purposes. Now there is no more trouble in this respect—Leedy perfected the tuning of wood bars so that it makes no difference where they are struck. The overtones are there, but they are perfectly in tune with the fundamentals. Being in tune they automatically reinforce the tone by coupling the ever-present, tho' subdued overtones with the main notes, forming true double octaves which are always correct harmony. In other words, Leedy Xylophone and Marimba bars can not produce discordant effects in themselves as long as the fundamentals are in tune. Scientific means have harnessed the old "by-product," overtones, to the fundamental tones and thus produced a pure, rich and accurate combination. This one feature alone makes Leedy Xylophones and Marimbas the finest in the world. The method is patented.

Gwendolyn V. Sautter—

AL "RAGS" ANDERSON

This charming young lady would never have to play a musical instrument to gain popularity. However, her extraordinary skill on both the xylophone and piano has made her a social and semi-professional favorite whose presence is desired at most every function worth while in and around her home city of Delaware, Ohio. Miss Sautter is a member of the Delaware High School Orchestra, where she is now in her senior year. Although she has had several very fine offers to join high class vaudeville acts and traveling girl orchestras, she has wisely chosen to attend Wesleyan College in Delaware at the beginning of the '29 term. Miss Sautter took up the xylophone three years ago, in addition to the piano and her regular school work. She uses a 4½ octave Leedy Solo-Tone Marimba-Xylophone, and studied under the noted Al "Rags" Anderson, whose photo is shown at right. "Rags" is undoubtedly one of the foremost drummers and xylophone soloists of the day. His professional career covers fifteen years of active service with many fine organizations. Recently he finished a special engagement at the Capitol Theatre, New York City, with the "Capitolians" stage band under the direction of Walt Rosner. Besides being featured as xylophone and vibraphone soloist, "Rags" sang in the trio which was composed of "Capitolian" members. His home town is Columbus, Ohio, and he is at present enroute with O. H. Furnam's Orchestra. Last season they were at the Greystone Ballroom at Indian Lake. Besides playing with Marion McKay's Orch., Henry Lange's Orch. and the "All Ohio Six," "Rags" has done considerable vaudeville and concert work. When at home he does quite a lot of teaching and pupils travel many miles to study under his instruction.

To Obtain New Effects on Bass Drums and Tom-Toms—

Procure a piece of good grade chamois, 6 in. square—also a piece of ordinary cotton cloth of the same size. Attach the two to your bass drum head (so that the pedal ball will strike in the center of the chamois) with four strips of 1-in. adhesive tape—a strip along each side of the square. Place the cotton cloth next to the bass drum head, underneath the chamois. This little "gag" when used with a Leedy Bass Drum Tone Control No. 668 (Cat. "R," page 62) enables the dance and stage band Drummer to produce a rich and at the same time staccato tone that is most pleasing. The chamois and cloth also work keen on Tom-Toms, as it makes possible two tones from each head.
By—Hal. McClain, Durango, Colo.

"WORLD'S FINEST DRUMMERS' INSTRUMENTS"

The Exclusive Drummers' Paper

Another New Cymbal Effect —
By SERGE S. FOCKLER, Lima, Ohio

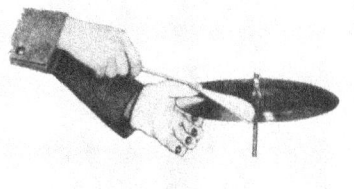 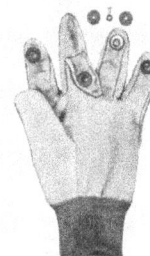

Here is one that works fine as a novelty cymbal effect, especially in piano passages where it is desirable to play a soft rhythm for a "background." Purchase a pair of plain canvas gloves at the 5 and 10 cent store. Rip the seams of the LEFT glove around the ends of the five fingers and about an inch down each side. Then attach ⅜-in. flat head rivets and ¾-in. washers (the washers give additional weight) thru the canvas, one at each point opposite the balls of the fingers. Turn the glove inside out to sew up the seams. This makes a neat job when the glove is right side out. It can be worn on the hand during the number in which it is to be used and will not seriously interfere with other work. Note that all four rivets can be sounded on the under side of the cymbal at once, making a single beat; or the fingers can play series of beats individually. The thumb acts as a "cut off." A Synco-Jazz brush or a drum stick may be used in the right hand to complete a nifty combination of light syncopated effects.

Dwayne J. Abarr —

starting in the dance game six years ago with "Buggy Mason and his Nebraskans," jobbing in and out of his home town of Columbus, Nebr. After a year's traveling thru Iowa, Kansas, South Dakota, Missouri and Nebraska with this orchestra, Abarr located for a year and a half at the Swan Theatre, a combination vaudeville and picture house in Columbus. Following this engagement he went with "The Jazz Bandits," a stage band which toured the middle west vaudeville theatres. He is now back in Columbus doing exceptionally clever stuff at the Columbus Theatre, a new vaudeville and picture house.
(Courtesy—Geo. A. Smith, Omaha, Nebr.)

Bogoba Tribe Orchestra—Philippine Islands

Black people known as Negritos appear to have been the earliest inhabitants of the Philippine Islands. They are smaller in stature than either the Igorrotes or the Filipinos and stand at the bottom of the social scale. However, they are well skilled in such arts as weaving and music of their own kind. They are divided into tribes, each having their own official orchestra. The above photo shows the Bogoba Tribe Orchestra of Negritos, whose headquarters are at Bogo, a town of twenty-three thousand population on the northeast coast of the Island of Cebu. The fine metal "knob gongs" shown in the photo are of the cast type, being of Chinese origin (Hong Kong, China, is only 750 miles east), and are tuned to a weird scale of notes. The small gongs in the rack on the ground are of the same design as the large ones played by the men. They are very heavy. Note that the man standing at left is using one hand to "cut off" the tone.

Men often complain of the badness of their memory; but never of their judgment.

The Leedy Vibraphone in Opera —

On April 23rd the Leedy Mfg. Co. received a letter from their German representatives—Jul. Heinr. Zimmermann, G. M. B. H. at Leipzig—in which they enclosed the following letter from the famous pianist and composer, Eugen d'Albert. Translated it reads:

"Messrs. Jul. Heinr. Zimmermann, G.m.b.H.
Querstrasse 26-28.
Leipzig, Germany.

Dear Mr. Zimmermann:
The Leedy Vibraphone purchased from you, and for which I have arranged special parts in my new opera "The Black Orchid," has from a musical standpoint, surpassed my fondest expectations. As you are aware, the opera was presented at the Leipzig Opera House and was received with great enthusiasm at every performance.
The Vibraphone has given me wonderful service and I hope this beautiful instrument will become more and more popular. It can well play an important part in the modern orchestra.
Yours very truly,
(SGD) Eugen d'Albert.
Ventimiglia, Italy, March 20th, 1929."

Horace "Sock" Spencer —

As you all know, Radiophone WOC, Davenport, Iowa, is a "big time" station, being noted all over North America for its high class programs. For an orchestra to receive compliments in bunches every night from far and wide over a period of two years means "filling the bill" with honors. Such is the case of the Herb Heuer's Vagabonds, house orchestra at this station—"Chief" Herb Heuer, Conductor (standing at left in photo). Horace "Sock" Spencer (center of photo) is the Drummer with this organization and the manner in which he "puts over" the percussion end of things in the great variety of music they are called upon to play stamps him as a thoroughbred in every respect. Spencer has also had considerable experience on the road throughout Iowa and Illinois with the same orchestra. Formerly he was with the S. U. I. Concert Band—The Varsity Dance Orch. of Iowa City, Iowa, and Jess Cohen's Studio Band of Madison, Wis. He also has his own band—The Hawkeye Collegians—for four seasons playing at Wisconsin summer resorts. Edgar Twamley, popular announcer and studio director is shown at the right. All three of these musical experts are high in praise of Leedy equipment.
(Courtesy—Elmergreen's Music House, Davenport, Iowa.)

Don—"That girl at the next table is trying to flirt with me."
John—"What did she do—give you the eye?"
Don—"No—crossed her legs at me."

Henry Nebrensky —

of Union City, New Jersey, has been doing some nifty work for the past year and a half with "Herman Kinas and his Ramblers," thereby attracting favorable attention. This band alternates between stage appearances, radio and jobbing dance work in Union City and vicinity, making a big hit on every engagement. Nebrensky also played for three years with the "Jersey Six" previous to joining The Ramblers. As extra work he acts as instructor for several drum corps.

 "FOR DRUMMERS WHO CARE"

Leedy Drum Topics

"Dog on Good" Drum —

"Sandy" is his name and we'd like to see anyone try to walk off with his boss' drums. Sometimes he shows his teeth and gives you the eye that says "keep off." If you can prove your worth he wags his tail and smiles. It's up to you—but no monkey business, for Sandy is quick to get your number. He is a high class pup too, his real title being Sandy O'Annan A. K. C. 431440. His boss is Robert W. Burns, an old-time Drummer of Los Angeles, Calif. Burns is known to everyone of prominence in the music biz throughout the state, having played for eighteen years in the Los Angeles Symphony Orchestra and two seasons in the Los Angeles Philharmonic Orchestra. He was also band leader of the 313th Field Artillery, A. E. F. At present Burns is jobbing in all classes of work.

She was only a trombone player's daughter —but how she kept slipping!

There are two sides to every question—yours and the foolish one.

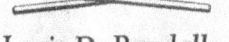

Louis D. Randall —

Louis D. Randall, of Warwick, N. Y., was with Harry Sudman and his Orchestra during 1926 and 1927. In 1927 they made a dance tour of N. Y. State, followed by ten weeks at the Red Circle Inn at Greenwood Lake, N. Y. Randall puts up a very neat job and always makes a hit in every town. He has been in the biz ten years and has several fine engagements to his credit. Formerly with Frank Holmes' Melodians, also Theron Smith's Ramblers. He writes—"From the time I was old enough to know the difference in drums I have used Leedy exclusively."

Cymbals in the Phonograph Records —

Many drummers in listening to the modern orchestras on the phonograph records have been highly impressed with the tone of the cymbal or cymbals used by certain drummers in making these records. And in many cases they have set out to procure a duplicate; the more ambitious have put forth considerable effort along these lines— after calling on their local dealers and not being able to find a cymbal that sounds the same as those in the records, they write to the various drum factories and other sources of supply, but very seldom are the results satisfactory from their point of view. There are several reasons for this. In the first place, the phonograph does not record the cymbal exactly as it sounds, due to the great multiplicity of tones which the cymbal sends forth. The phonograph usually records only a portion of the many tones and the very cymbal heard on the records and pronounced to be "just what is wanted" would, nine chances out of ten, be turned down could the listener hear the actual cymbal itself. There is no certain size or type of cymbal that records better than any other, although most drummers doing this work are using the smaller sizes. We know of one case where a drummer uses a rather thick 15-inch Zildjian that does not sound so "hot" in itself, but which records beautifully. This is due to the fact that it just happens to be set at the proper distance from the recording apparatus to pick up the most pleasing tones. Secondly, it is almost impossible to give a written description of a cymbal tone. Drummers do their best to make it understood what they want, but the subject has too much latitude. It is easy to describe something that the eye can see, but the tones of a cymbal have no association with anything else in existence. There are no two exactly alike and it is, after all, a matter of personal taste. However, Leedy is always willing to give special attention to choosing cymbals on personal orders. If we do not succeed the first time we will try again and again until a satisfactory one is selected.

Edwin E. Bacher —

His home town—Dubuque, Iowa—intimately calls him "Eddie" because he has more than made good as a spotlight xylophone soloist. He is now with the Collegians, jobbing in and around Dubuque. However, his experience covers many years as Drummer, Tympanist and Xylophonist with such organizations as three years with the Dubuque Municipal Band (C. S. Dovi, Director)—one year, East Dubuque Concert Band—four years at the head of his own orchestra, "Eddie's Entertainers"—three years with the Original Iowa Cornhuskers—two seasons with Carpenter's Dance Band en route—several seasons with the Dubuque Civic Symphony Orchestra—and two years as feature Drummer and stage Xylophonist at the Princess Theatre. His excellent work on Drums, Tympani and Xylophone has established him as a thorough all-around "big time" Drummer. "Eddie" also teaches the Geo. Hamilton Green and Harry A. Bower methods at the Renier School of Music in Dubuque.
(Courtesy—Renier Music Co., Dubuque, Iowa)

"Swish" Bass Drum Effect —

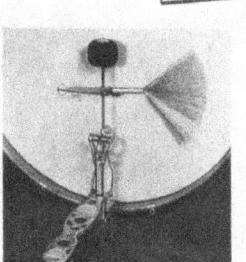

Inasmuch as the "swish" of the Synco Jazz Brush has been adopted as standard, why not allow it to come in as a subdued effect with bass drum beats? A thorough test on the part of several drummers has proven it to be most pleasing and legitimate. Simply attach the Synco Jazz Brush to the pedal ball rod as shown in photo at left, using a Leedy Cow Bell Clamp No. 984 (Page 53, Catalog R). In some cases the handle of the brush will rattle. If so, use a rubber band—one end around the loop of handle, the other end around the thumb screw of cow bell clamp.

Dorothy M. Scott —

Miss Dorothy M. Scott's success as a Drummer proves once more that drums are ladies' instruments as well as gentlemen's. Miss Scott studied under Prof. Frank Sturchio at the Syracuse Conservatory of Music in Syracuse, N. Y., her home city, and was for several months a member of the Conservatory Juvenile Orchestra. Later she joined the "Varsity Girls" and did considerable professional jobbing at the Syracuse Theatre and in Rome, Newark and Cortland, N. Y. Her style of playing is masculine and full of pep, with plenty of variety; however, one is always aware that a most attractive young lady is behind the drums. She is now with "The Florida Girls" band en route, covering several eastern states.

So Say We —

Somebody remarks that the talking movies are in their infancy. We wouldn't go that far, but they do seem to be childish.
— Baltimore Sun

Jack Kurkowski —

Sixteen years behind the drums in many leading vaudeville houses of the middle western states has built up a most excellent reputation for Jack Kurkowski. His willingness to please both the acts, leader and house employers, combined with his ability, has resulted in his always being on a prominent job. He started in the business at Rhinelander, Wis., with Danner's Band. He has also done considerable concert work in the chautauqua field and was overseas with Bandmaster Steinmetz of the 32nd Div. Kurkowski has been for several seasons and is still playing at the Murray Theatre, Richmond, Ind. He is thoroughly sold on Leedy equipment.

 "WORLD'S FINEST DRUMMERS' INSTRUMENTS" Leedy

 *The* Exclusive Drummers' Paper

That Left Stick —

When the tip (acorn) of the left stick is resting on the drum head and the middle of the stick is about one inch above the counter hoop of the drum, THE LEFT FOREARM SHOULD BE JUST SLIGHTLY BELOW A LEVEL POSITION, WITH THE STICK AT A DOWNWARD SLANT OF 45 DEGREES AND AT ALMOST A RIGHT ANGLE TO THE FOREARM. This can only be accomplished when the batter head is at a certain height from the ground or floor. Just what this height is varies with people of different statures. It is automatically arrived at when the stick is in the position described above. This applies to orchestra, band and drum corps drummers alike. It is the natural left arm, wrist and hand position as a starting point for their movements, and eliminates all possibility of contracted muscles. The fingers should also be relaxed. The stick lies well up in the crotch of the thumb. Let the first two fingers curl slightly over the stick,

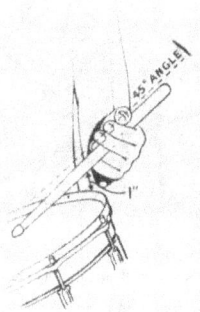

but do not let them hug the stick. These two fingers are constantly under adjustment to "back up" the strokes and may be called "bumpers." The last two fingers bend under the stick, forming a "shelf" upon which the stick rests. The stick lies on the third finger

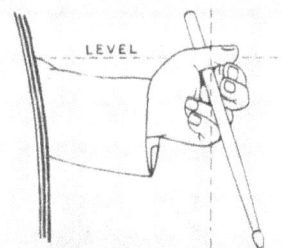

between the first and second joints. Do not bend the wrist in any direction. From the elbow to the tip of the thumb should describe an almost straight line. Every part—fingers, wrist and arm—must be relaxed. Relaxation is the secret of overcoming left stick awkwardness.

Harold Gaide —

After a long season trouping with The Earl Newton Players thru several southern states, Harold Gaide is now back in his home city, Grand Rapids, Mich. He has organized his own dance orchestra and has his boys on a job almost every night, both in and out of town. Gaide is a real up-to-the-minute hustler and an exceptionally clever boy with the "hickories." He is a graduate of the Leon Knapp Drum School of Grand Rapids and has seven years of theatre, concert and dance experience to his credit — always more than making good. For a long time he played at the Liberty Theatre in G. R., also with Clayton Lynch's Happiland Band, jobbing and WOOD Radio. (Courtesy — Leon Knapp's Drum Shop)

O. W. Clemens —

When a Drummer has been continually associated with the same leader for fourteen years it can only mean that his work is 100% satisfactory. Such is the case with O. W. Clemens who handles the "batterie" for Walter Davidson, leader of Davidson's "Louisville Loons" Orchestra. Clemens hails from Portsmouth, Ohio, and it was there that he joined Davidson in 1915. After three years at Louisville, Ky., where they literally "cleaned up," they moved on to the Swiss Gardens in Cincinnati, Ohio, for an eight months' engagement. This was followed by filling many jobs of like nature in the middle western states. They also did two years as a stage band on the Keith and Orpheum circuits. From last reports they were in their eighth month as an attraction stage band at the popular Main Street Theatre in Kansas City, Mo. Clemens is one of the fastest and niftiest Drummers of the modern school. We know — we've seen and heard him play. (Courtesy — Conn Kansas City Co.)

Drums are the heart beats of music.

Why Not? —

The modern Drummer now uses two or more Tom Toms of different sizes to produce different tones and varied effects. The same is true with his Cymbals, Temple Blocks, Wood Blocks, Cow Bells and even Tambourines and Triangles. It's the different sizes within each group that fulfill the present day demand for "color" and variety. As it works so well with the "traps," why not try it with the snare drum? Three drums of different sizes could be made to produce new combinations of effects that would "go over" big. If three cymbals give variety to a number so will three snare drums. The proper line-up of shell sizes, head thicknesses and snares could be made to produce a marked difference in tone between each one. About fifteen years ago this stunt was worked with great success on the vaudeville stage and in the pit as a novelty in descriptive numbers, but it has never been given a chance in the modern dance or stage bands. Try it out. Drum Topics will gladly assist you in choosing the combination of sizes if you are interested. Maybe you can dig up some used drums in your locality for the purpose.

Herbert F. Palmer —

Herbert F. Palmer is now doing both pit and stage presentation work with "Al's Capitol Gang" under the direction of Alexander Strauss at the Capitol Theatre, Jackson, Mich. This boy is "red hot" on the modern stuff, as well as thoroughly schooled in the legitimate. He has had eight years' experience and held several fine jobs, among them being the Orpheum Theatre in his home town of Duluth, Minn., for two seasons.

The Leedy Mfg. Co. is the only maker of Drummers' Instruments who do their own electro plating and build their own trunks.

Notice to Drum Corps Musical Directors —

Ervin H. Kleffman, 2121 Eleventh Avenue, Hibbing, Minnesota, has recently published Series No. 1 of the Kleffman Drum Corps Street Beats. This is in regular sheet music form and may be obtained thru the music store or direct from Mr. Kleffman at the above address for 25c per copy. Mr. Kleffman makes a specialty of composing and arranging special novelty Drum & Bugle Corps music to order.

And How —

Reggie—"Why is a woman like a drum?"
Algie—"Let's have it."
Reggie—"It takes a roll to play them both."

When Good Fellows Get Together —

There may and there may not have been a "stein" on the table, but in either case when Sousa played Long Beach, California, not so long ago it was an occasion for handshaking and merriment for this sextette of Drummers who have been friends for years. Left to right—Gus Helmecke, Sousa's Band—Frank A. Snow, Herbert L. Clarke's Band (formerly with Sousa and author of the Snow Drum Method)—Frank Holt, Sousa's Band—Charles E. Seeley, Clarke's Band—Howard Goulden, Sousa's Band—and O. F. Rominger, Clarke's Band.

A New Wood Block Holder —

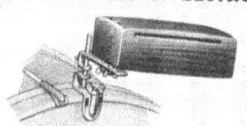

Use Leedy Hoop Adapter No. 250 (Page 52, catalog R) in conjunction with Leedy Wood Block Holder No. 985 (Page 47, catalog R). This combination makes a dandy as it permits both height and swing adjustments.

Jack W. Sanderson —

has specialized in theatre work for seventeen years, principally in vaudeville. He has been at Poli's, the leading vaudeville house at New Haven, Conn. (Frederic D. Adams, leader) with a 14-piece orchestra for eight years. He was also at the Burlesque House for four years and with the 102nd Infantry Band (Yankee Division) overseas during the World War. Sanderson is indeed one of the leading vaudeville Drummers of the country.

"FOR DRUMMERS WHO CARE"

Leedy Drum Topics

United Spanish War Veterans Drum and Bugle Corps—Detroit, Mich.—

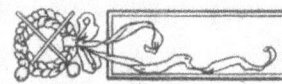

Winners of the Cuban Trophy—1st prize—at U. S. W. V. National, Havana, Cuba, Oct. 7-12, 1928. Michael E. Shaugnessy, Commander—John F. Radtke, Treas.—Joseph Hoffman, Chief Musician—Richard Hafenfeld, Principal Musician—David Wynkoop, Quartermaster Sergt.—James Daar, Color Sergt.

Thomas W. Cole Post No. 19 Campbell Corps American Legion—Sanford, Maine—

Moore Greenwood, Drum Major—H. H. Whiting, Drum and Bugle Instructor—Ernest Stanfield, Chief Drummer—Herbert Wilson, Chief Bugler. This Corps was organized in 1928 and is already considered capable of at least winning its way into the finals of any contest.

American Legion Drum Post No. 127—Glen...

H. D. Charlton, Drum Major—Dave ... Sorenson, Sergeant-Bugler—W. H. Reg... first prize at National Orange Show, ...

Leedy Drum Corps Equipment is used and endorsed by ... and by hundreds of others throughout the United State... those "in the know." Their high quality creates pri...

Fort Dodge, Iowa—American Legion Post No. 130 Drum and Bugle Corps—

Dr. A. N. Thoms, Manager—Eddie Arthur, Drum Instructor—Elliott Colson, Drum Major—Robert Heath, Drill Major. Winners of first prize at National Convention, Philadelphia, Penna., in 1926. A crack Corps.

Paul Frank Florine Post N... Drum and Bugle Corps...

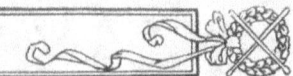

Earl Hinkle, Corps Commander—T. C. Touton, D... Stanton, Business Manager—Wm. Geldard, ...

NOTICE

The Leedy Mfg. Co. maintains a special Drum Corps Personal Service Department. All questions will be promptly answered by men of many years experience in both the professional and amateur drum corps field. We want you to feel free to write us regarding any phase of the game—there is no obligation.

Get This Book—The "Roll-Off"—Free—

Everyone interested in Drums will want this wonderful 42-page book. Contains the history of the drum—scores of interesting photos and much historical data—also complete manual of Drum Major routine, with 21 photos showing positions. All organization and equipment problems answered. Send for yours today. Mailed free.

American Legion Drum and Bugle Corps Post No. 169—One...

This wonderful Corps was formed in the spring of 1924 and has done more than its share in stimulating pride and interest in the American Legion, not only in their home state but wherever they have appeared. Drum Major, Frank Green—Instructors, Albert Timon, Ulysses S. Johnston and Ralph Durfee. Winners of first prize

Leedy — "WORLD'S FINEST DRUMMERS' INSTRUMENTS" — **Leedy**

The Exclusive Drummers' Paper

**nd Bugle Corps
, California—**

son, Sergeant-Drummer—A. U.
Manager. Winners of $1,000.00
ernardino, Calif., Feb. 24, 1929.

y Corps whose photo is shown on these pages—
eedy Instruments are made to serve and satisfy
ownership.

**166—American Legion
t. Atkinson, Wis.—**

Major—Frank Geldard, Drill Master—Clifford
ary.

**Gen. Geo. A. Custer Post No. 54
Drum and Bugle Corps American
Legion—Battle Creek, Mich.—**

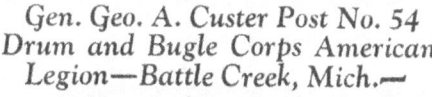

Westerman Bros., Drum Majors—C. L. Ulrich, Director.
This Corps is one of the pioneers among the American
Legion Posts. Honor winners at the National Convention held in 1920 at Cleveland; also first prize winners at
the National Convention held in Kansas City, Mo., 1921.

**Canby Ladies' Drum and Bugle
Corps—Canby, Minnesota—**

Stella Tilghman, Drum Major—Sadie Schlosser, Chief Drummer
—Thorp Barnard, Drum Instructor—Della Bailey, Chief Bugler—
John Opseth, Bugle Instructor—Don Hall, Drill Master—Thos.
Tilghman, Manager—Odelia Evensen, Secretary.

Charlotte, North Carolina—American Legion Drum and Bugle Corps—

H. Grady Moore, Mgr. and Drum Major—Chas. E. Lambeth, Asst. Mgr.—O. F. Asbury, Jr., Asst.
Drum Major and Instructor—Walter F. Stanley, Chief Bugler—C. H. Drury, Librarian—T. C. Neal,
Quartermaster—B. S. Garrison, Asst. Quartermaster—V. Paul Rousseau, Treasurer—Thomas L.
Alexander, Drill Master. A most wonderful Corps now numbering eighty men.

Leedy Drum Corps Instruction Charts—

Here is positively one of the greatest helps that has ever been presented for either the old or the
new Drum Corps—twelve large wall charts, 36 x 36 inches, printed in black and red on heavy
yellow paper. They contain more constructive drum corps information than any book ever
published. With these charts an old corps can greatly improve their playing and a new corps
can be turned out in faster time than by any other method. A wonderful help to teachers.
The charts can even be used without an experienced instructor. They contain many illustrations and every detail is fully explained. Order a set today and you will note a vast improvement in your corps work in a very short time. They make practice a pleasure and hold the
interest of your members.

, New York. Champions of Four Contests at New York State Conventions—

Alexandria Bay, N. Y., State Convention, 1924—first prize at Central Park, New York City, 1925—first prize at Niagara Falls, N. Y., 1926—first prize at Schenectady,
Y., 1928. Attended the National Convention at Philadelphia, Penna., in 1926, and the Paris, France, Convention, in 1927. For playing, drilling and appearance it
ranks among the finest Corps in the country.

 "FOR DRUMMERS WHO CARE"

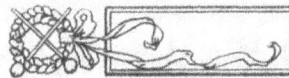

Leedy Drum Topics

Every Drummer Should Read This—

*Reprinted by special permission of the "International Musician"
Official journal of the American Federation of Musicians
Published at 37-39 Williams St., Newark, New Jersey.
As appeared in the February, 1929, issue.*

Mechanical Music in Theatres—

By President Jos. N. Weber

We hear it said quite often that in the final event it will be the theatre-going public that will determine just what place the talking movie and the so-called "sound" picture will hold in the American theatre. Undoubtedly that is true, but the statement scarcely serves to dismiss the problem of the organized musician. The public makes up its mind about what it likes or does not like in the theatre and elsewhere, but in this day and age it does not reach decisions unaided by interested influences. For illustration, if the manufacturer of a well-known food product found his market invaded by a strong rival, he would not sit back complacently and say: "The public will soon enough discover that this upstart product is inferior. I will await the result patiently." If he did adopt such a course his stockholders would complain that he was neglecting approved business practice and insist that he use advertising methods to direct and guide the public to purchase of the more meritorious product.

Hence when the great exploitation drive to sell the theatre-going public the idea that movies, synchronized with mechanical music, were in some way superior to the genuine entertainment form, the Federation President's office became active in opposing the idea and has been continuously and untiringly active since.

Musicians generally know that mechanical music, however perfect may be its reproduction, must fall short of artistic excellence. It is the opinion of Federation leadership, based upon exhaustive study, that mechanical music—with all the exploitation it may receive—will fail eventually to give satisfaction in any theatre as a substitute for the appearance of artists in person; that dehumanized entertainment, offering as it were mere photography of artistic endeavor—pale replica of the real thing—cannot win and hold public approval. With that point settled, it seemed our plain duty to oppose debasement of our art by focusing attention of the friends of music upon the purpose of sound picture proponents to accomplish a substitution. It would have been folly, I think, to sit supinely by waiting for the public to discover for itself the meretricious character of this canned substitute, while in the meantime incalculable damage was being done to the art. I feel confident that the educational work we have done has materially diminished the threat contained in the innovation.

The challenge of Vitaphone, Movietone and Photophone to the cause of music came to loom as a serious thing last summer. Your President met it with a declaration that "machines that synchronize words and music with action on the screen threaten the art of music with debasement and will be opposed by the American Federation of Musicians." This statement, which was printed in the daily newspapers throughout the country, went on to explain that one cannot mechanize an art as though it were an industrial process. I pointed out the inevitable consequences of success in selling dehumanized entertainment—displacement of musicians, the discouragement of young talent, corruption of the public taste in music and eventual restriction in the art itself, in short a cultural loss of appalling proportions.

The greatest care was exercised in this and subsequent statements to prevent giving the impression that this was another case of the worker fighting the machine, the old industrial duel in which the worker has always suffered defeat. The matter was placed squarely on a cultural basis. Publication of these views elicited widespread discussion in newspaper editorial columns, journals of opinion and by musical and dramatic critics, most of which was essentially sympathetic with our stand. By way of improving our contact with the daily press, the President undertook to send personal letters to each editor, who discussed our problem, thanking him for his interest. On the whole, I think we have been quite fairly treated by the press.

It is impractical to relate in detail all of the steps taken in our campaign of education to warn the public of an "adulterated" cultural product, but a few outstanding points may be touched upon.

In a six months' period a dozen news stories on the general topic of sound movies and our attitude toward them were released to the newspapers, most of these being carried by the Associated Press, United Press and International News Service and a few being mailed directly to the newspapers. Special articles were prepared for labor newspapers and distributed through the International Labor News Service of Washington, D. C. The co-operation of labor editors generally has been unstinted. Monthly organs of various international unions, with a large aggregate circulation, carried other specially prepared articles as did many musical journals and trade papers and business magazines.

Data was supplied to local unions to assist them in directing attention to the situation through letters to the editors of their local papers and by such other means as their ingenuity, with our advice, could devise, the general purpose being to crystallize sentiment of music lovers against the threatened damage to the art. The response of some local unions to requests for this sort of co-operation with International headquarters was splendid, but some other locals apparently did not give them the consideration the importance of the case deserved. We hope for improvement in this regard.

Direct appeals were made by letter to State Federations of Musical Clubs, to individual clubs and club leaders and to musical critics of newspapers. Responses of music club leaders to the President's letters were warmly sympathetic and I am convinced that these extremely influential groups will be of great assistance in the future.

Requests of local union leaders for information for radio speeches and similar material have been promptly complied with. We are hopeful that all locals will become active in this campaign. In many requests the sound picture crisis is a local problem and difficult to treat on an international basis as conditions very sharply differ in the various jurisdictions. In some cities employment disturbance has been of little consequence, while in others it has been quite serious. In New York City, for instance, where reaction to any theatrical innovation is apt to come rapidly, comparatively few musicians were displaced and most of these were soon absorbed by the natural increase in jobs due to growing demands for music, while in many other cities the situation has been quite distressful to some of our members.

I do not believe that the President's office has left anything undone that could have been done to relieve conditions. We might have aroused a greater uproar or taken a more belligerent attitude, but to have done so would have been unwise. Our problem has been a many-sided and delicate one, requiring finesse and diplomatic handling. There was the danger of exciting popular prejudice against us and alienating the sympathy we hoped to win if we appeared in the role of rule-or-ruin partisans ready to attack and destroy something which the public might want or at least be curious to examine.

As noted above, we have striven with some success, to prevent the controversy from drifting into the channel of the useless fight of "Man vs. Machine," stressing instead the danger of cultural debasement. There we are on firm ground and many outstanding leaders of thought have given their approval to this view. We have sought also to guard our reputation for constructiveness and veracity in making statements of fact and predictions publicly. In consequence we have never had to make a retraction or qualification of any statement, but stand today as justified in our position.

The sound picture has been on the market long enough to make clear this important point: That it doesn't draw any more people into theatres than did the silent picture, even with the advantage of novelty on its side. Larger theatres have found it impractical to use sound as a complete substitute for orchestral and organ music. In at least one city, a far-sighted manager has boldly advertised that he would not show sound pictures or talkies but would provide real musical entertainment. His experiment has been highly successful against sound competition in other houses. These and other facts in hand convince us that real music will triumph sooner or later. Ours is the job of making it sooner.

Co-operation of union members and their friends and music devotees in general in driving home this important message of warning, as pointed out in a recent circular from the President's office to all locals of the Federation, will help to hasten relief where it is most needed.

 "WORLD'S FINEST DRUMMERS' INSTRUMENTS"

The Exclusive Drummers' Paper

James M. Spencer—

has been "tapping" and "sticking" (with a few odd rolls of course) a field drum off and on for sixty-seven years. He is now eighty-one years old and turns out every once in a while to do his bit at patriotic events in his home town of Sheridan, Indiana. Mr. Spencer joined the 57th Ind. Vols. Co. H of the Union Army as a Drummer at Richmond, Indiana (his birth place), in 1861, when only fourteen years of age. He served throughout the Civil War, taking part in many of the now historical battles. He also served in the Spanish War with the 158th Regt. Ind. Vols. and in the Home Militia during the late World War.

James Whitcomb Riley, the famous "Hoosier Poet" who died in 1916, was the snare drummer in the old Adelphian Brass Band of Greenfield, Indiana, from 1868 to 1878.

Don't Be Late—

It has often been noticed in radio programs (also to the listener some distance from the player) that the beat of the Chinese Gong occurs more or less behind the intended note. This probably is not noticeable to the player and other musicians of the orchestra or band. The vibrations of the Chinese Gong are slow compared to other instruments. This is especially true when a soft mallet is employed, because a little time is required for the tone of the blow to reach the ears or microphone. This seemingly "late" tone can be overcome by slightly anticipating the beat and by using a medium hard felt mallet such as the Leedy Gong Stick No. 631—(page 62, Catalog "R").

Geo. S. Tillinghast—

Geo. S. Tillinghast, formerly of Providence, Rhode Island, joined the U. S. Navy Band at Washington, D. C., as Drummer and Xylophone Soloist, several years ago. When his enlistment expired he moved into the Loew Palace Theatre and has been located there for the past five years doing both stage and pit work under A. Harry Borjes, conductor—and Wesley Eddy, Master of Ceremonies. Being a former graduate pupil of the famous Geo. B. Stone of Boston, Mass., Tillinghast is of course a thorough artist on Drums, Tympani, Xylophone, etc. Thruout his sixteen years experience he has always been considered a feature Drummer. He also has a large class of scholars and has turned out many who are now holding fine jobs in the professional field.

Sherman "Shorty" Davidson and Lynn Cowan—

In the last issue of Drum Topics "Shorty" Davidson's photo appeared in the group of Los Angeles Drummers shown on page 4. We called him "the best dressed man in L. A." No doubt some of our readers took it to be a wise crack—nothing of the sort: he holds that rep. And other reps, too, one being an A-1 Drummer second to none in that city. A big rep, that, for L. A. has many of the country's finest. "Shorty's" home town is Chicago. He was a former pupil of Art Layfield on drums and Chas Fischer on xylophone. His experience of sixteen years continual work on the best of jobs covers a list too lengthy to set down here. For the past five years he has been with the West Coast Fox Theatres at the main office house—the "Boulevard" Theatre in L. A. A tough spot, as some one of the big bosses is always "catching the show." It is both a pit and stage presentation job. There he has played under such famous leaders and M. C.'s as Lynn Cowan—Rube Wolf—Benny Ruben—Gene Morgan—Frank Jinks—Max Bradfield—Don Wilkins and others. "Shorty" also enjoys a rep more important than drums or clothes—that of being a real friend and as fine a fellow as they make 'em.

LYNN COWAN—Master of Ceremonies at the "Boulevard" is a box office attraction with a drawing power that stands them up nightly. He is also a composer of note, having written many clever numbers, among them being "Monkey Business," "Dream House" and "Then You'll Know Why." Several feature photoplays now showing over the country owe their musical scores and arrangements to his skill in this work. Cowan was formerly a member of "Bailey and Cowan," headline Orpheum Vaudeville team.

Drum Topics is mailed to Drummers free of charge. When a Drummer does not receive it—it's only because his name is not on our mailing list.

Ralph Fox—

has been with Meyer Davis organizations for several years. He is now at the Wardman Park Hotel in Washington, D. C. (Sidney Harris, leader). Previously Fox was with Brook Johns—The Wash. Opera Co. and many seasons at the Columbia Burlesque Theatre in Washington. He is both a "legit" and "modern" Drummer of the highest order.

(Courtesy—Leonberger's Music Store.)

Geo. O. Moody—

is one of the most efficient Drummers of the Middle Western States. He is widely known as a drum corps authority and expert rudimental instructor. For the past four years he has been director and instructor of the Yusef Khan Drum & Bugle Corps at Akron, and also plays with the Shrine and Knight Templar Bands. His career covers thirty-seven years of active professional and semi-professional playing. Some of his more important engagements have been—Grand Army Band, Canton, O.—Thayer Military Band, Canton, O.—8th Regt. Band, Akron, O.—Canton Symphony Orch., Canton, O.—Norwood's Orch., Canton, O.—Great Eastern Band, New Philadelphia, O.— also in various theatres of Canton, Akron and New Philadelphia, O. Mr. Moody is at present instructing American Legion Post No. 209 Drum Corps of Akron, O.

(Courtesy—Edfred Music Co., Akron, O.)

Very often the small town steady job is the best bet in these days of "modern music" and all that that means.

Many Drummers are married because they couldn't "beat it" at the right time.

Every day you hear more about Leedy. It is not "high pressure" advertising that is doing it. It is "conversational advertising"—the most powerful kind because it comes from the satisfied user whose word is final.

Rudy Van Gelder—

Rudy Van Gelder has for seventeen years been playing in the leading vaudeville theatres in and around New York City. He was a former pupil of the renowned Karl Glassman, Tympanist of the New York Symphony Orch. for many years. At present Van Gelder is playing with his brother Leon Van Gelder (leader), at the Lincoln Theatre, Union City, N. J. This team has been featured on the Stanley-Fabian-Warner Bros. Circuit for the past two years. Rudy is considered one of the best all-around theatre and concert drummers in the East. He was born in Amsterdam, Holland.

   "FOR DRUMMERS WHO CARE"

Page Eleven

Leedy Drum Topics

New Leedy Elevated Chimes—Cathedral Model with Wheels—1½" Tubes—

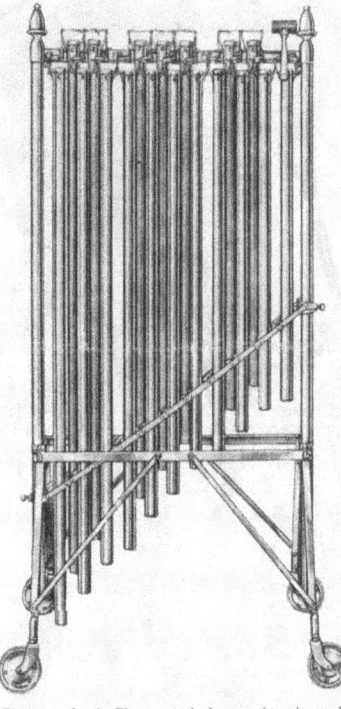

These new Leedy Chimes are the last word in advanced design for the Drummer who desires efficiency, quality and style. The new mounting of the tubes makes chime playing a pleasure instead of the "mean job" it has always been considered in the past. The sharps and flats are elevated, forming a second row back of the naturals. This places all of the notes in the same relative positions as the layout of the bars on bells, xylophones or the familiar keyboard of the piano. You can't go wrong with tricky chime parts—it's as easy as playing bells with one mallet. With wheels the Elevated Cathedral model (1½ inch tubes) measures six feet one inch in height and thirty-five inches wide. They may be obtained without wheels. Ask for No. 1411. The rack may be purchased separately—No. 1415.

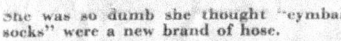

She was so dumb she thought "cymbal socks" were a new brand of hose.

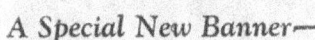

A Special New Banner—

Here's a bargain that you can't afford to pass up—a classy black velvet banner, with your name sewn on in orange felt letters at the top, combined with a few words about Leedy at the bottom. Wood hanger stick with gilt knobs and yellow cord. Cost complete to you only $4.00. Send in your order today. A banner keeps your name before the public. For other styles made to order write to Bradford & Co., St. Joseph, Mich.

The Prize Story—

"WHAT'S THE USE"

By Jack Donnelly, Drummer Keiths Theatre, Syracuse, N.Y.

I have been playing drums for twenty-one years. For twenty of those years I had been seeking a Turkish cymbal that would meet my admittedly fussy requirements. Not long ago I found one in the hands of a brother drummer and it cost me fifty-two hard-earned "bucks" to become its owner. However, what's "fifty-two," when one is fully satisfied? I was really all "hopped up" over my purchase and expected to receive a nice flock of complimentary comments from the boys in the pit and the acts on the stage. Now comes the bitter with the sweet.

At Monday's rehearsal the second act was "one of those things"—an "up-stage" woman single doing a lot of fo-de-o-do junk—the kind that requires a drummer's skill to save the "opera." During rehearsal I sort of laid low to get the drift. Nothing was said one way or another. At the matinee I decided to show my stuff and make the $52 cymbal put things over, especially in her final song. It worked great—she took many "bends"—more than she was worth. After the show, word came that said "lady" desired to converse with the drummer. So up I went and knocked on her door. When she saw it was me of the percussion pile she yelled, "Say, what the hell's the idea of trying to crab my act by beating on that cow bell?"

Every Drummer has a pet drum yarn. Send yours in to Drum Topics. If it tops the list you get $10.00 cash. Time's up August 15th.

If Someone Should Ask You—

A few simple questions about your job as a Drummer. How many can you answer CORRECTLY hot off the bat?

1—What is the real reason for the flam in drum music?
2—Why does some nickel plating rust, while some does not?
3—Why does a triangle note fit in any key the orchestra or band may be playing in?
4—What is the meaning and the origin of the word Tympani?
5—Why do chimes sometimes sound out of tune when you stand near them?
6—Why are white heads not practical on tympani?
7—How is a Turkish cymbal made?
8—Why do drum heads become tight or slack with atmospheric changes?
9—What animal furnishes the raw material for gut snares?
10—What is the best way to prevent checking in a Chinese wood block?
11—What is the real cause of some drum sticks becoming warped?
12—What is the general construction of the shell of a Chinese tom tom?
13—What is the difference between white and transparent drum heads?
14—What is the method of renewing the tone in a "dead" temple block?
15—What is the proper speed for Vibraphone fans to revolve?
16—What is the meaning and origin of the word Xylophone?
17—To what note should the bass drum be tuned?
18—Why do some drums "feel" and play easier than others?
19—Why are reasonably heavy drum sticks more practical than light ones?
20—What is the real advantage of the Floating Head principle in drum construction?

SAVE THIS ISSUE OF DRUM TOPICS—ANSWERS WILL APPEAR IN THE NEXT NUMBER

New Method of Bending Leedy Solid Wood Shells

About two years ago Leedy invented a new method for bending solid wood shells, by means of an exclusive machine that literally "irons" the wood into shape. Only dry heat is employed—absolutely no water or steam touches the wood at any stage of the process. The result is a perfectly round shell without checks, and guaranteed not to warp. Leedy solid shells have always been a high quality article—now they are better than ever.

Geo. R. Dillon—

Geo. R. Dillon, of St. Joseph, Mo., is now dividing his time between two well-known jobbing orchestras—"The Spectors' Music Makers" and "Taylor's Revelers." The result is that he is always busy filling the better class of engagements in and around St. Joe. Dillon is a clever entertainer as well as a really efficient drummer. His singing and character impersonations always go over in a big way and his work behind the drums is of the neat, speedy modern school, with plenty of originality. He has been in the game eight years, starting in his High School orch. and followed by three years with The Paramount Music Club Band.

Geo. A. LaHue—

of Waterloo, Ia., is a top-notch, all-around man with nine years theatre and dance experience in many mid-west and eastern cities. "N.Y. Entertainers," Syracuse, N.Y.—"Iowa Collegians" on the road in Wis., Ia., and Mich.—Martin Hotel, Davenport, Ia.—Blackhawks Hotel, Sioux City, Ia.—Winter Garden, La Crosse, Wis., Strand and Rialto Theatres, Waterloo, Ia. and many other fine jobs! He also has a fine voice and does considerable radio singing.

Justa Wethead says—

I always find it more difficult to play on rainy days.

 "WORLD'S FINEST DRUMMERS' INSTRUMENTS"

The Exclusive Drummers' Paper

More About Drum Sticks—

It is only natural that Drummers should want the best for their money in drum sticks the same as any other article they may purchase and we do not blame any Drummer who will turn down a pair of warped sticks. Of course the easiest way to learn whether or not a stick is warped is to roll it on a smooth surface such as the counter of a music store. This is a good stunt. As a further test we have seen some Drummers hold the sticks in their accustomed playing position and strike them alternately, listening to the tone of the contact. Oftentimes the Drummer will condemn a pair because there happens to be a decided difference between the tones. On they go thru a great number of sticks, only to find (with more or less degree) the same difference of tone between every pair they pick up.

Just where this method of testing originated and what it stands for we do not know. However, it is an erroneous idea to judge the playing qualities of a pair of sticks on the basis of their sounding qualities. Sticks should be judged by their equality of weight and their straightness. There are three reasons why no two sticks sound exactly alike when struck on a counter, practice pad, desk, drum or any other object. First, the fingers always grasp the stick below the node line and, to a certain extent, this kills the natural resonance of the tone of the stick. The left hand always grasps the stick nearer the tip than is the case with the right hand, and the left does not hold the stick as firmly as the right. These points help to make a difference between the two, but are not the only factors that decide the different tones. Second, no two drum sticks are EXACTLY alike in the density of grain. This is a condition of nature that took place when the wood was in the process of growth and no one has any control over it.

If the stick happens to be held in the hand (either the right or left) with the grain of the wood edgewise, the tone will be higher—and if the stick is held with the grain of the wood crosswise, the tone will be lower. This can easily be proven by holding the stick in the manner shown in the accompanying illustration and striking it with a half hard bell hammer, first holding the stick with the grain edgewise and then turning it until the grain runs crosswise. Striking it in this manner allows the full tone of the stick to come forth and it will be noticed that the tone varies as the grain is turned.

Third, it will also be noticed that there is a difference in the tone of either stick when it is struck on a hard surface first lightly and then with more force.

Out of 500 sticks there is only a slight chance of finding two that sound exactly alike, regardless of what test is given them, and out of this same number it is almost impossible to find two that weigh EXACTLY the same; meaning, of course, if they are weighed scientifically on a very delicate scale. The difference in weight may be so slight that human hands could not detect it, but it is there just the same, and this of course plays a part in governing the stick's tone.

Drum Sticks should be chosen to fit the drum—NOT to the SIZE of the drum, BUT TO THE THICKNESS OF THE HEADS USED. A heavy drum stick will not bring out the best tone from a light head because it overpowers the resistance of such a head. A light stick will not set up enough motion in a heavy head to bring out the best tone the instrument is capable of producing. Choose sticks of the proper weight to give them a "throw back" from the head.

The Drummer who follows these latter suggestions may be convinced that he would get better results by changing to another model, but at the same time hesitates to make the change because of being so used to those he is now using. Changing from one model to another is not serious. Any Drummer who will go on the job with the new model and leave the old model behind where they cannot be reached, will find that before the evening is over he has become thoroughly accustomed to the new and from then on it will be "smooth sailing," with improved results.

In a live cow the head is the noisy end.

Ideas—

Painted scenes or lettering on bass drum heads can be removed by using an ordinary wood scraper such as sold by all hardware stores. Have the head pulled tight and scrape with an even pressure, making sure to keep the edge of the scraper level with the head so as not to dig the corners into it. This is a better method than using a paint remover liquid. This remover does not injure the head, but often causes the paint to dissolve and work its way into the pores of the head, then nothing will get it out.
By—William R. Sears, Minneapolis, Minn.

If you carry two or more keys of a like style (trunk keys or Yale keys) you have no doubt often experienced difficulty in picking the right one in the dark. To find them quickly, file notches in the edge of the thumb grip—one notch for a certain lock—two notches for another. A drop of solder on the thumb grip, instead of the notches, also serves to tell which is which when they can't be seen.
By—Bill Kieffer, U. S. Marine Band, Washington, D. C.

Dirty Cymbals? Bon Ami does the trick. Put the powder in a cup and mix with water until a thin paste is formed. Apply paste with a soft rag and let it dry. Rub off vigorously and your cymbal will shine like new.
By—Erwin Gallery, Buffalo, N. Y.

It is always better to use a metal triangle beater rather than a drum stick. However, it is often difficult to make the switch in time. With a little practice you can learn to hold the beater between the middle and third fingers of the right hand while playing the snare drum or tympani. By doing so in numbers where the triangle beats follow the snare drum or tympani parts on the next note, without an intervening rest, you can obtain the correct triangle effect.
By—Ted Smith, London, England.

A sheet of thin tin 12 inches by 18 inches is a handy article to have in the pit for lightning crash effects. It has a different tone than any type of cymbal. Can be used alternately with cymbal. Put a strip of wood along one end of sheet to form grip and prevent cutting hands. By—Carl Govoni, Welland, Ontario, Canada

---

For airplane effect—pull small tympano to E, roll on head with drum sticks. Shading obtained by moving sticks from edge to center of head and vice versa.
By—Howard Goulden (Sousa's Band) Bridgeport, Conn.

Deaden your chimes with rubber bands or clothes line woven between the tubes. Play fox trots or "hot" numbers with two mallets. Sounds like a new type of instrument. Good over radio. By—"Red" Allen, Los Angeles, Calif.

Obtain an old wooden cheese box and remove bottom. Wet and tack an old piece of heavy bass drum head over one end. After it dries out cut ½-inch hole with clean edge in center of head. Obtain a ½-inch diameter wood stick two feet long (an old golf club handle is just the thing). Fasten very thick 1½-inch diameter leather disc on end of stick with a screw. Run stick thru hole in head with leather on inside. Rosin stick and canvas glove. A big racket can be produced and it can be used in novelty or hot rhythm dance numbers. The stick is better than a cord as it is easier to control.
By—Danny Lee, Perth Amboy, N. J.

The following cymbal stunt can be used with either the Leedy Non-Swing, Handy or Drum Stand Cymbal Holder. First, remove the wing nut from the top of the holder cup, then cup the left hand over the top cup of your cymbal. Next, beat the rhythm out with the right stick and slowly move left hand up and down directly over the cymbal and also in contact with it. With very little practice you will be producing a "wow-wow" tone which sounds similar to the effect made when you move a sea shell to and from your ear. Now take your wire brush and repeat the above method with the left hand on the cymbal, maintaining the rhythm with the brush. On soft playing this will give you a novel effect obtainable in no other way. Next, instead of moving your hand for the "wow-wow" effect, keep your left hand cupped and sock it down on the top of the cymbal cup on alternating beats with either your wire brush or drum stick. This will give you a combination of "wow-wow" and "sock" with cymbal rhythm.
By—Harold Von Linden, Central Bridge, N. Y.

Jimmie Robson Jr.—

Jimmie Robson, Jr. of Sanford, Florida, not only puts up a "knock-out" job on drums with the "Seminole Syncopators," but also does a clever and novel "big-time" vaudeville act as a xylophone soloist. He has been called upon to repeat the stunt time and again, not only at the Milane Theatre in Sanford, but in several other Florida cities. Both his wife and sister assist him. He has been playing both Drums and Xylophone steadily for twelve years and is considered one of Florida's best all-around men.

The Self Playing Tambo—

If you need a tamborine tremolo at a time when both hands are busy with bells, tymps or traps, use a Leedy Handy Cymbal Stand No. 33B. Attach tambo to holder No. 983 and place at top of stand rod. Do not tighten thumb screw of tambo holder. When tremolo is desired simply tap under side of outside edge of tambo slightly with stick or hand. The tambo will slide down the rod with an intermittent jerky motion, causing a jingle tremolo. It lasts approximately eight bars in moderate tempos. To stop, put finger or stick under tambo and it will hold until disturbed again. When playing on cymbal tighten thumb screw.
By—Bill Kessler, Vincent Lopez Orchestra, New York City

Howard T. Douglas—

After jobbing in his home town (Chicago) with Frank Barbino's Society Orch. for several years, Howard T. Douglas worked in vaudeville on the Pantages Circuit for five seasons. He then located with "Frank Soria's Whippets" at one of the West Coast houses in Santa Cruz, Calif. Later he joined the "Musical Doctors" for several months run at the famous Solomon's Dance Hall in Los Angeles. He is now at the Hollywood Roof Ballroom with the same orchestra, making his usual nightly hit with up-to-date novelty stunts and effects that have given him the "rep" of being a "red hot" dance drummer.

"FOR DRUMMERS WHO CARE"

Leedy Drum Topics

Make Your Own Tympani Stick Holder—

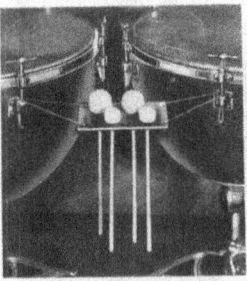

Here is a handy little "gag" that does its bit toward making things easier for the Drummer. Procure a piece of sheet metal 8 inches long by 6 inches wide. Turn down a half-inch width along both long edges to stiffen (a piece of wood board can be used instead of the metal). Bore four 1¾-inch holes in the sheet far enough apart to prevent tympani stick balls from coming together. Bore two holes in each end for cord and loop around tympani lugs as shown in above photo.

White Pyralin Bell and Xylophone Mallets—

Friscoe Models

No. 370F—1⅛-inch Balls

No. 370G—1-inch Balls

Friscoe Model Bell and Xylophone Mallets (made by Leedy) are now the most popular of all types. They are not only more durable than the vulcanized rubber style, but they really bring out better tones from these instruments. Another favorable feature is that they have LESS contact click than any other kind of hard mallet. The handles are of tough white hickory, shaped and balanced. If you have never used them you will be "sold" the instant you strike the first beat. They make a classy appearance, too.

Yarn Wound Marimba and Vibraphone Mallets—

No. 630—1½-inch Balls

No. 630A—1¼-inch Balls

Made in two weights. Wound with best grade gray yarn over rubber ball. Hickory handles, shaped and balanced.

In Answer to Many Inquiries—

"Variety is the Spice of Life"—and this means variety of opinions as well as all else. One famous Drummer says, "Do it this way"—and another says, "That's wrong; do it like this"—and so it goes. But as long as we keep plugging and try to do our best we usually make progress. So now we wrestle with another subject with a view to helping along the good work of enlightenment.

DRUM TOPICS has received several letters in which the following questions are asked in various forms. "Are the drum rudiments of any use in orchestra playing? I have been told that they are for drum corps work only." "Is a drum solo played differently in band than in orchestra?" "Should a Drummer use a different method in an orchestra than in a band or drum corps?"

Now, before diving into the whys and wherefores, let's get the basic meaning of these questions straight in our minds. They do not mean a difference between piano (PP) and forte (FF) or a difference between "open" and "closed" beating. They really mean—is there a difference in the method of execution or "sticking" between band, orchestra and drum corps playing. The answer is, positively—NO. The Drummer who does not play the rudimental system in the orchestra does not play it in the band or drum corps. And the Drummer who is thoroughly rudimental in the drum corps or band does not as a rule play otherwise in the orchestra.

We are not belittling the non-rudimental Drummer. Everyone in the profession knows that there are thousands of first-class musicians among Drummers holding down many of the country's finest positions who never even studied the rudiments. These men have done orchestra, band and corps work. We are only pointing out that if one IS a rudimental Drummer he does not play any differently on one job than another. If it is correct to play flams from hand to hand in a drum solo in band music, so should they be played in orchestra music. If it is correct to play five stroke rolls from hand to hand in Sousa's "Stars and Stripes," in band, so is it correct to use this same execution even when playing the same number double piano (PPP) in orchestra. Certainly Sousa intended the effect to be military whether played by orchestra or band. If it is correct to play paradiddles and double drags in drum corps numbers, so is it correct to use them with exactly the same "sticking" in the most delicate passages of orchestra arrangements. The trick is all in the technic. A real artist can play all the rudiments with any amount of power from double forte down to a whisper. And if one is skillful enough to play them double piano, why not employ them in orchestra work?

Does not the cornet player, the trombone player, the clarinet player (and all other musicians who play in band or orchestra) use the same method of execution on both jobs? Certainly. And remember, band instrumentalists are called upon to execute with as great a degree of proficiency as those in the orchestra. In other words, there is no difference in the method of playing any instrument on any type of job and Drummers should not harbor the impression that they must use one method in band or drum corps and another in an orchestra.

The Improved Leedy Vibraphone—

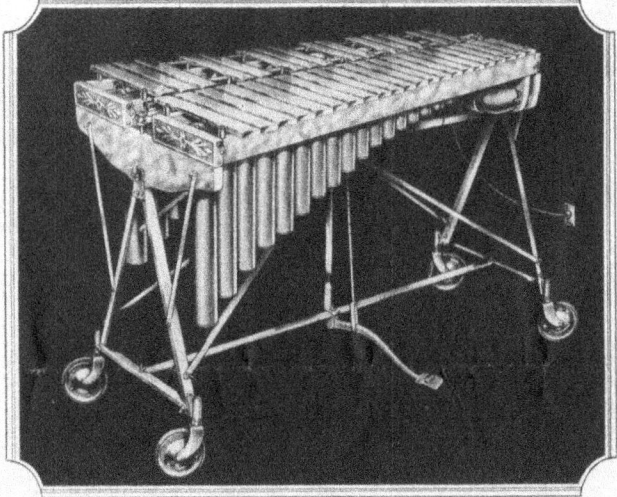

AND NOW LEEDY ANNOUNCES the most advanced design in both appearance and mechanical features ever presented in an instrument of this type. From the bars down to the wheels it is improved at every point, viz.—thick, specially-tempered aluminum bars that lift free of the frames, being mounted and strung like those on the Xylophone. No fixtures of any kind protruding above the bars to interfere with the mallets. Marine Pearl DuPont Pyralin on the front and back of the frames, also on the cross arms. New type heavy cast and embossed metal end boxes on the frames. A built-in damper with complete adjustments and which operates two ways—press down to cut off tones or press down to sustain tones. And a new system for locking the frames to the stand so that they can not be lifted off by accident.

SEND FOR OUR LARGE SIX-PAGE, FOUR-COLOR CIRCULAR WHICH GIVES FULL DETAILS—MAILED FREE.

Ralph Dickerson—

Ralph Dickerson has been with Rudolph Smith ("Doctor Jazz") and his orchestra for the past five years, both on location and trouping jobs. During the summer of 1928 they played a long engagement at Ideal Park, Binghamton, N. Y., and proved to be a phenomenal attraction. Dickerson is both a "hot" and "legit" Drummer of great skill and originality. He hails from Scranton, Penna., and was previously with Paul Viney's Harrisburg Orchestra.

The Following Lyric Appeared in the Indianapolis Star, April 12, 1929

(Reprinted by Permission)

Last Page Lyric—

By MARY E. BOSTWICK

(Dreadful howls have greeted Arthur Hammerstein's proposed plan of using canned music instead of orchestras in the theatre.)

I hope I never chance to go to
   opera or play
And find that they have taken
   all the orchestra away!
The play may be extremely dumb—
   the actors may be dumber—
But how I love to sit and watch
   the doings of the drummer!

I like it when he goes to work and
   starts the cymbals whanging—
And when he takes his drum sticks
   and upon the drum starts banging
And when he pounds the triangle
   and makes it go ding-ding!
It somehow always seems to me
   that that's a lovely thing.

Although the drummers often look
   quite delicate and fragile
When they start in to do their stuff
   they're so extremely agile!
I watch them as they go about
   their complicated stunts,
And marvel any man can do so
   many things at once!

The music may be terrible—the
   show a plot may lack—
As long as there's a drummer—I
   don't want my money back!
I love to sit and watch him—I
   think he's simply grand—
But I could never care about a
   drummer who was canned!

 "WORLD'S FINEST DRUMMERS' INSTRUMENTS"

The Exclusive Drummers' Paper

LEEDY IS ABOUT TO SPRING A BIG SURPRISE WATCH FOR IT !!

Chauncey Brown and Frank Horscroft are now at the Paramount-Famous-Lasky Studios in Hollywood, Calif. They are supervising the Percussion Dept. and sound effects for the West Coast Studios. Harold McDonald is working with them.

Geo. Carey has again signed up for another season with the Cincinnati Symphony Orchestra. He says he likes the work and the town. He will also do considerable radio broadcasting and phonograph recording with his Xylophone.

Annette Metiveir

Miss Annette Metiveir of New Bedford, Mass., has been quite prominent in junior musical circles of her home city for the past two years. She started in on drums with the Knowlton School Orchestra and later joined the Normandie High School Orchestra. She also does quite a little jobbing with professional dance organizations and is said by those she works with to be a very clever and talented young lady.

Geo. Marsh (Paul Whiteman's Drummer) goes to Hollywood with the orchestra June 1st to start work on "The King of Jazz." This is to be one of the greatest photoplays ever produced and they expect to be on the job three or four months.

You're wrong—single head snare drums are not popular in Scotland.

D. E. "Buddie" Johnson

formerly of Jacksonville, Fla., played at the Arcade Theatre and the Mason Hotel in that city. Later he played at both the Capitol City Club and Piedmont Club at Atlanta, Ga. For the past six years Johnson has been with leading orchestras in and around Los Angeles, Calif., at present with "Ralph Markey's Musical Keys" at the Egyptian Ballroom; previously at Palais de Dance and Cinderella Roof. Other L. A. Drummers have informed Drum Topics that Johnson is a top-notch artist.

David Nahinsky

For twenty-one years David Nahinsky has been playing in the leading theatres, bands and orchestras of his home city, St. Paul, Minn. Four seasons at the Capitol Theatre; seven seasons at the Metropolitan Theatre. The past two years he has been at the Park Theatre, St. Paul's finest suburban house, under the baton of Henry Schulte. In addition, Dave (as he is best known) has his own 12-piece organization, "The Gold Medal St. Paul Dance Orchestra," which plays dance programs every Wednesday night, 10:30 to 11:30, over Radio WCCO. This is a wonderful bunch. Nahinsky is indeed a thorough all-round "old-timer" who has adapted himself to modern style and is considered second to none in the twin cities.

Paul McKnight

has held many "classy" jobs during his ten years career behind the drums, among them being—Ross Reynolds' Palais Garden Orchestra—Carl Diensberger's Detroit Orchestra—Zez Confrey's Orchestra in San Francisco, and for the past three years with Jack Crawford's (The "Clown Prince of Jazz") Victor Recording Orchestra. This is a crack concert and dance M.C.A. band of a very high order. They have played at Roseland Dance Hall, New York—Arlington Hotel, Hot Springs, Ark.—Muehlebach Hotel, Kansas City—Schroeder Hotel, Milwaukee—Wm. Penn Hotel, Pittsburgh—now at Golden Pheasant Restaurant, Cleveland, Ohio. They will be at the Steel Pier, Atlantic City, after July 1st, for the third season. McKnight hails from Vincennes, Indiana, and is one of the profession's leading modern drummers.

NAN—"Dora's new sweetie is a Drummer of great versatility."
FAN—"How do you know?"
NAN—"I heard her say he played on her sympathy."

Dr. A. H. Schmidt

Here is proof of man's love for Drums. Dr. A. H. Schmidt played his way thru the University of Nebraska at Lincoln, winning his degree as a Doctor of Dentistry. He started on the drums in his home town of Elkader, Iowa, with the high school orchestra, and soon he became proficient enough to join "The Southern Rag-a-Jazz Band" which traveled thruout the west making Pacific Coast tours and later for a six months' tour of Europe, where they played before the King and Queen of England and the King and Queen of Norway. They also filled a contract at Rector's in London, which the Prince of Wales often frequents. The Prince became acquainted with Dr. Schmidt and played on his outfit on several occasions. (Most everyone knows that the Prince is an accomplished drummer. He owns two complete Leedy outfits.) The orchestra also recorded for the Edison Gramophone Co., of England. Returning to Lincoln in 1921 Dr. Schmidt entered the University as an instructor of dentistry and has remained there ever since. However, he still keeps up with his drums and is at present doing considerable professional playing on the side, jobbing and broadcasting for the Nebraska Buick Automobile Co., the home of Radio KFAB. Dr. Schmidt is in every sense of the word a real artist of percussion.

New

Send for new Leedy circular showing three new DuPont Pyralin "Full Dress" finishes for snare and bass drums. The circular is a beauty—in five colors—mailed free. The drums are the cheapest fancy finished models ever introduced.

Moe Spivack of New York is now in Hollywood directing the Percussion Dept. and sound effects for R.K.O. pictures.

Did you know that Fritz Reiner, famous conductor of the Cincinnati Symphony, was formerly a noted tympanist in the principal Symphony and Opera activities of his home city of Vienna, Austria.

On the Cover

Vic Berton—Paul Ash—Herman Fink

Almost every Drummer in the country knows Vic Berton by reputation. His marvelous and original work in "Red Nichols and His Five Pennies" phonograph records have made him famous the world over. However, thousands of his admirers do not know his history. Here it is in brief. Born in Chicago, Vic took to the drums when only six years old. He studied with such notables as Jos. Zetteman, Joe Russek and Ed. B. Straight. In Chicago he worked his way to the front thru all kinds of jobs and experiences and finally became an outstanding feature with Art Kahn's Orchestra at the Senate Theatre. A few years ago Vic moved to New York City, where his services were soon sought by many of the big leaders. He has worked with Don Voorhees in Earl Carroll's Vanities and over Radio WOR—Sam Lanin at Roseland Ballroom—substitute in Paul Whiteman's Orchestra—Roger Wolf Kahn's Orchestra at the Biltmore Hotel, and is now with Paul Ash at the Paramount Theatre in Brooklyn. Vic is not only the originator of many modern stunts such as "hot cymbal choruses" and "cymbal breaks," but is a thorough legitimate Drummer and Tympanist, having played in the Chicago Symphony Orchestra and other like "straight" engagements. He is schooled in all of the classics as well as modern works. He is a real fellow as well as a real Drummer and he has asked Drum Topics to extend an invitation to out-of-town Drummers to drop around and have a chat at the Paramount. Herman Fink, who also plays with Paul Ash at the Paramount, comes from St. Paul, Minn. His eleven years experience covers every phase of the game—Vincent Lopez, Penn. Hotel Orch., New York—Phil Spitalny's Victor Recording Orch., Cleveland, O.—Ipana Troubadours, Sam Lanin, WEAF—Walt Rosner—Capitol Theatre, N. Y., and eight months as Bass Drummer with the Capitol Theatre Grand Orch. under David Mendoza. Herman knows his stuff, as such jobs testify. He is also a dandy fellow to know.

Paul Ash, the originator of the Stage Presentation as we know it today. Being a former Drummer he knows the Percussion Department backwards, but best of all he is a gentleman and a real fellow to work with. We know that to be a fact, for Joe Stant, Art Layfield, Frank Horscroft, Harold McDonald, Chauncey Brown, Vic Berton and Herman Fink all say the same.

THAT'S ALL THERE IS
THERE ISN'T ANY MORE
Meet you here in September
Go boom! But don't faw down
CHEERIO!

"FOR DRUMMERS WHO CARE"

Leedy Drum Topics

The Exclusive Drummers' Magazine

MAY, 1929

EIGHTEENTH EDITION

POSTMASTER—Return Postage Guaranteed

INDIANAPOLIS, INDIANA

Carl Baumann,
100 Sanford St.,
Bangor, Maine.

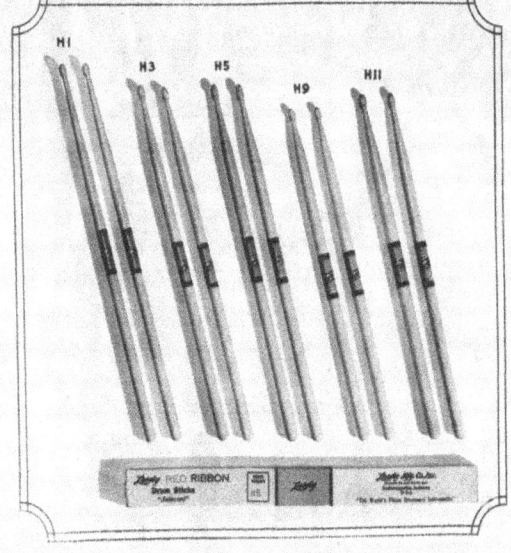

Leedy

RED RIBBON DRUM STICKS—

"It's a pleasure to play with them"

High grade workmanship and the finest material that money can buy are what make these sticks the best obtainable. The instant the Drummer picks them up he realizes that they are quality articles from end to end. Not only do they have a "classy," finished appearance, but also that professional "hang" and "feel" which is the Drummer's first consideration when choosing sticks. The hickory is second growth, straight, close-grained, white stock. The sticks are sanded, filled and sprayed with Duco clear lacquer, then hand-rubbed and sprayed again. They are polished to a high lustre and have a smooth, glassy feel in the hands. They are fine sticks for particular Drummers who want the best in order to do the best work. You will like them, too.

Palmer St. and Barth Ave.
Indianapolis, Indiana
U·S·A

Leedy Drum Topics Issue 19

Leedy Drum Topics

This Drumming Business

LET'S forget, for a moment, that the work of a Drummer is, first, last and always, creative art.

Certainly it's Art—but it's business too. And, once in a while, it is worth the time of any Drummer to step down and look it over in a hard-boiled business way.

The past year has not been particularly rosy. There has been an undeniable shortage of work in several sections of the country. But then, so has every business, trade or profession had to face these periods from time to time. Some years must be better than others—some good, and some "not so good." However, under all conditions music remains, and always will remain, a basic need of the human race. Human beings have to have it and in the long run they will pay us a fair price for producing it.

The new forms of mechanical reproduction—radio in the home and "sound" pictures in the theatres—undoubtedly caught the attention of the public and excluded the musician in person. But it is obvious that the final result of these developments can only be to increase the demand for the services of the individual performer.

The more music, of any kind, the public hears, the more they recognize their need for it—the better they come to understand it—the more clearly they come to feel the unbridgeable difference between personal performance and the distant and distorted echoes of mechanized reproduction. For the Drummer who really knows his stuff all this means the assurance of better pay, more recognition, and a higher place in the esteem of the public than ever before.

Be ready, for, as Drum Topics stated once before, no mechanical invention can eliminate the desire of human beings to see other human beings on the stage, and if it was necessary to add acts, presentations, etc., to the straight picture program, so will it be necessary to add the same to "sound" picture programs. And furthermore—the minute an entertainer of any type sets foot on the stage, human musicians will have to be near-by to assist.

Success or failure for the individual Drummer is merely a question of the spirit in which he approaches his business problems. He is in the same boat with everybody else. He can't sell 1920 performance on the 1930 market. Like the automobile makers, he has got to keep on improving his routine from year to year. Like them also, he must continually change, and improve, his sales strategy. The man who does these things is probably getting on pretty well right this minute. And certainly he has no cause whatever for anxiety about the future.

Thousands of Drummers are seeing the writing on the wall. These chaps, like the public whom they have to please, are learning new things about music, more about rhythm, more about the job of a Drummer. They are putting new sparkle, new brilliance, and a finer technique into every performance that they render. They may not be headliners today, but recognition is right around the corner. They will certainly get their share if the right spirit is there.

Our New Year's Wish for You—Happiness for 1930 to 2030 and Beyond

Happiness is the most desirable quality in life. They say that money does not mean happiness. Perhaps not, but we think it would be a hard job to convince the average musician otherwise. Therefore, we make this sincere wish for all our friends—good jobs and many of them—which in turn means money and more of it and, of course, good health. The rest is easy

Leedy — "WORLD'S FINEST DRUMMERS' INSTRUMENTS" — **Leedy**

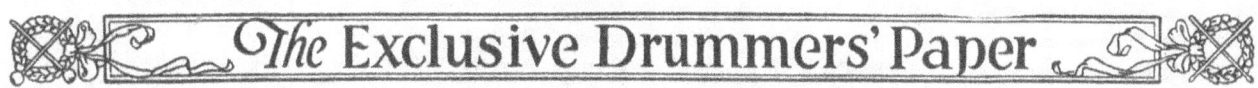

The Exclusive Drummers' Paper

To Band—Orchestra and Drum Corps Drummers of

GRAMMAR SCHOOLS — BOY SCOUTS — HIGH SCHOOLS — COLLEGES — FRATERNAL ORGANIZATIONS — AMERICAN LEGION — AMERICAN LEGION AUXILIARY — VETERANS OF FOREIGN WARS — INDUSTRIAL ORGANIZATIONS — CIVIC GROUPS and others.

Leedy has created a new department, viz.: PERSONAL SERVICE for all Drummers who play for the love of the game rather than in a strictly professional capacity. By Personal Service we mean that very thing—we want you to feel free to write us on as many subjects as desired, pertaining to Drummers' activities and instruments. Your letters will be answered in detail by men of many years experience behind the drums in both the amateur and professional fields. There will be no obligation on your part. Write us today. The service is without charge.

EACH ISSUE OF DRUM TOPICS WILL CONTAIN A SPECIAL ARTICLE FOR THE DIRECT BENEFIT OF DRUMMERS AFFILIATED WITH SUCH ORGANIZATIONS AS LISTED ABOVE AND OTHERS OF LIKE CHARACTER.

When you chose to play Drums as your favorite of all musical instruments, you chose wisely—not only because Drums are the most interesting and a pleasure to play, but also because they rank among the most important instruments of any musical organization. Yes, Drums are a pleasure to play—there's a big kick in finding yourself master of the very beats, tricks and effects you have listened to others perform. Even practice on the various Drummers' instruments is a pleasure compared to others. Of course, you who are now well into the game know all this; so let's turn to the various problems that confront you, with a view to making things still more interesting. Lack of space prevents us from taking up more than one subject at a time, but we want you to know that you are at liberty to write us at any time and on as many subjects as desired. As stated in the heading of this page, Leedy has created a new department for your benefit and there is absolutely no obligation on your part in making full use of it. We honestly feel that the "part time" Drummer deserves more consideration and this is Leedy's first step in taking that action. There are a thousand and one facts to be learned about Drumming and Drummers' Instruments. It takes years to file them in one's mind. The job is really never completed. The best of professionals learn new things daily. Until a few years ago the only sources of information were the teacher, instruction books, experience, and contact with other Drummers. Now there is a new source which is almost as powerful and constructive as all others. It consists of a vast amount of printed information gathered from every part of the world and placed in the pages of several musical and specialty publications. Drum Topics is one of them. You should read them all, because very often a tip appears here and there that otherwise might escape you for years to come. And one tip may contain a point that will actually advance your skill. As a start let us take the subject of—

Capt. O. F. Rominger, Instructor — Southern California Military Academy—Drum and Bugle Corps, Long Beach, California — Cadet Capt. Tom Welch—Leader

Instruction and the Rudiments

Paul D. Bauder, Bethlehem, Pa. High School Band

First of all, believe thoroughly that Drumming is not difficult. Drumming is simply rhythm. Rhythm is instinctively born in every human being. The up-and-down movements of a baby's arms are crude expressions of rhythm. Even walking is rhythm. When the child is learning to walk its steps are uncertain, but they soon become decisive and even. When full control is established they differ only in respect to length and force. Every one, regardless of age or station in life, is at times found unconsciously tapping his or her fingers, also the feet. All this may be classified as "natural" or "instinctive" rhythm. The more simple dances are quickly learned by all people, and what is dancing but rhythm? Drumming, like advanced dancing, may be classified as "advanced" or "educated" rhythm. Rhythm's relation to music is of the utmost importance. In fact, there can be no music without rhythm because music is really melodic or harmonic rhythm. Therefore, it is really not a relation, but a part of music itself. Some people have a more advanced sense of rhythm than others, but they also can start wrong in the first manipulation of the drum sticks. If they continue on the wrong track they form wrong "mind pictures," which in turn form bad habits. These incorrect habits continue to pile up and build an insurmountable wall not far ahead. It is then only a question of time before the student catches up with himself and is brought to an absolute halt before this "wall" of limited ability. Again we repeat—Drumming is not difficult. The only handicap is a bad start. To prove this let us cite an example of what can happen to the Drummer who begins in the wrong way. Play the old familiar "horse gallop": musically speaking, it consists of two sixteenth notes and one eighth note, repeated over and over again. Make two taps (taps are light beats) with the right stick and one stroke (strokes are heavy or accented (>) beats) with the left stick, viz.: First play it slowly and gradually increase the speed to the fastest point possible. Notice that as the speed increases the groups become uneven and "jerky." Now play the same groups with the other "sticking." This is called "hand to hand" and it balances. As the speed increases you will note that the evenness is maintained. This is Rudimental Drumming. The former is "scratching." We hope this will convince you that it is impossible to overestimate the importance of a correct start. Begin right and you will have the most complicated beats at your command before you know it. No doubt you have heard a lot about "Rudimental Drumming." Many say the rudiments are for the Military Drummer only and that they have no place in either legitimate or modern orchestral playing. Such an argument cannot be proven. True, there are non-rudimental Drummers holding down fine jobs, but this does not prove that they would not be better Drummers if they applied the rudimental school. Rudimental Drumming is an established art. It is to Drumming what correct bowing is to violin playing—correct fingering to piano playing and correct breathing to singing. The rudiments are the multiplication table of Drumming. Without them you have no "balance" between the right and left sticks. Do not ever let any one prejudice you against this method. "Scratch" Drumming means "catch as catch can," with the right stick doing the main work and the left stick coming in wherever it can find an opening. In Drumming you must be able to play equally as well with the left stick as with the right. That is why you should have a competent teacher—one who is in favor of and knows the rudimental system. Where there is no instructor available, as often happens in the smaller cities and towns, the Leedy Drum Corps Instruction Charts offer the greatest aid to all Drummers, whether in Band, Orchestra or Drum Corps activities. They have proven to be the means of improving the technique of Drummers already well into the game, and offer the shortest known road to placing the beginner on the right course of correct rudimental Drumming. These wall charts are twelve in number, 36" x 36", and are printed in large red and black letters on heavy yellow paper. They are primarily intended for class teaching, but may be used by the individual to the best advantage. No Drummer can afford to be without a set. They are now being used as official by the United States Marine Corps, also by many American Legion, Marine, Elks and other fraternal organizations. In the next issue of Drum Topics we will take up the correct position of the sticks, hands and fingers, showing eight pictures and giving complete details, following which we will explain the first six exercises of Drumming. Be sure to get your copy and send in the names of all your Drummer friends; they will be glad to get this new free service. In the meantime, write us on any drum subject you have in mind—we will be pleased to work with you. Leedy has also published a 42-page booklet called The "Roll-Off": a most valuable book to any one interested in Drums. It contains the history of the Drum, scores of fine photos and much historical data; also a complete manual of Drum Major routine, with twenty-one photos showing positions and giving full explanations. All organization and equipment problems answered. You can build a Drum Corps from nothing to a Dress Parade with the aid of this book. Get yours today. Mailed free for the asking.

Bernece Payne, American Legion Aux. Dr. Corps, Indianapolis, Ind.

   "FOR DRUMMERS WHO CARE"

Leedy Drum Topics

May We Suggest?

that every Drummer read the two-page story by George L. Stone, in the September, 1929, issue of Jacobs' Orchestra Monthly, entitled "The Buzz Roll." Boys, it's a WOW, and one of the finest educational articles relative to drumming that has ever appeared in print. You are missing twenty-five dollars — yes, more — worth of drum lessons by one of the country's leading authorities if you pass it up. We wish we could devote the space to reprinting it here. He sure tells you the difference between the "buzz" and the "scratch" roll. If you want to become a better Drummer read it at once.

An Efficiency Idea

No doubt you have often found it inconvenient to procure a new piece of rubber tubing to replace those worn out on your various cymbal holders. Next time try this . . . cut an old piece of drum head into a 3 in. square. Soak in water until soft. Place over cymbal holder stub and spread out over the regulation

Fig. 1

Fig. 2

felt washer as shown in Fig. 1. Then place cymbal over stub immediately as shown in Fig. 2. The cymbal will hold head in place while the latter is drying and conforming to the shape of the stub. Head allows full cymbal tone and will outlast a dozen pieces of rubber tubing.

The fellow who is big enough to admit he's wrong when it's so, often finds it easier to make people believe he's right when it's so.

Drum Topics Will Pay $2.00

for each drummer suggestion or hint published in the next issue (No. 20), such items to be subject to acceptance by the Editor. Authors will be given full credit. Send yours in today.

No matter how damp the day or night — you will always have a snappy Drum and more playing ease if you use a Leedy Electric Drum Heater.

Frank E. Pole

Frank E. Pole has been the "chef de tempo" at the Pantages Vaudeville Theatre in Memphis, Tenn., for the past five years. As a vaudeville specialist he has no betters . . . ask any act. He was born in Bradford, Pa., of an English family of musicians and his younger days were spent in Geneva, N. Y. His father was 1st violinist in a London Symphony Orchestra and his mother was concert pianist by appointment to Queen Victoria. Frank started in the music game 26 years ago as a violinist, but soon became interested in Drums and has remained so ever since. Fifteen seasons at the Orpheum in Memphis—four seasons of vaudeville in Knoxville, Tenn.—five seasons in band concert work at East End Park, Memphis, also Memphis Symphony Orchestra and several seasons jobbing thruout the states of New York, Pennsylvania, Ohio, Georgia and Tennessee. He is also manager and teacher of the Drum Dept. at the Melody Music Shop, 13 So. Main St., Memphis, and has been responsible for making it one of the largest and finest Leedy "Drummers' Service Stations" of the south. He also instructs and acts as Drum Major to a Memphis Public School Drum Corps of 90 pieces. Traveling Drummers who troup should be sure to drop into the Melody Music Shop and meet Frank. *(Courtesy—Melody Music Shop, Memphis, Tenn.)*

Why Bring That Up?

PROFESSIONAL—"What brand of heads do you prefer?"
AMATEUR—"Blondes."

Buddhist Priest Beating on Giant "Fish Mouth" Temple Gong—HANKOW, CHINA

Drummers, how would you like to lug around Temple Blocks of this size on one-night stands? We are told that they make them even larger in China. We have also been recently told by those who know that the orthodox Chinese resent very much the manner in which we Americans use these Temple Blocks. You see, they are held sacred by the Chinese inasmuch as they are used to drive out the bad spirits. The places where we use these gongs (blocks) over here are not Temples exactly, but all the same every professional knows that it is worth while to keep "good spirits" in the audience. Temple Blocks will help you to do it.

Gerald Sunde

is with "Moses and his Band," an organization of nation-wide reputation which has been a frequent winner in national and state band contests. They are opening in St. Petersburg, Florida, about December 22nd. Sunde is well known as a musician of outstanding ability, particularly so for his work on Tympani. He has filled a long series of engagements in association with many important outfits. Sunde hails from Minneapolis. His association with the Moses Band gives him an opportunity for southern resort work in the winter months and engagements in the north in the summer. A real set-up for a real Drummer.

There ought to be a law against revolving doors that will not take a 14 by 28.

Drum Topics is Leedy's contribution to the Drumming Fraternity in appreciation for the support of thousands of Drummers who play and boost Leedy instruments.

Drum Topics is a magazine for Drummers exclusively. Its aim is to assist by way of letting Drummers know what other Drummers are doing and how they are doing it.

Drum Topics is not strictly an advertising medium. News is its first consideration. It welcomes suggestions. We want to make it still better.

The greatest favor a Drummer can do for Drum Topics is to send in the names of other Drummers who would like to receive it. Won't you swap favors with Drum Topics? It comes to you free . . . help the good work along by sending in a few names.

Everett Conway

Everett Conway has accomplished a seemingly impossible task . . . that of becoming a Drummer under the unfortunate handicap of having only one arm. He holds both sticks in one hand, somewhat similar to the method of holding xylophone mallets for four-hammer playing. Years of diligent practice have rewarded him with skill that commands the utmost admiration. He has actually perfected most of the rudiments and can put up a job equal to many professionals. His roll is wonderful. He is also a ventriloquist of considerable reputation and combines this art with a drumming specialty. His act ("A Day at the Hospital") has played several leading vaudeville circuits. Conway has also made two trips to the principal Oriental countries at the head of his own dance and concert orchestra. Summer of '29 with the "L and Z" Circus.
(Courtesy—Conn Detroit Co.)

Art Quast

After completing a successful season with the Radio Ragadores, Art Quast is now with Glen Garrett's Dakotans. This is one of the best organizations in the middle west and Quast is to be congratulated on his hook-up. He expects to be playing in the southern states during the coming season.

"WORLD'S FINEST DRUMMERS' INSTRUMENTS"

The Exclusive Drummers' Paper

Johnny Morris
(Paul Specht's Orchestra)

says:—"Try this for a hot rhythm beat.... four pedal beats to the bar on the bass drum, at the same time charleston beat with the left foot on sock cymbal—at the same time after beats with drum stick on straight cymbal. Every one likes this when they hear it played. It takes a little 'wood-shedding' but it's worth it." Morris is now with Specht at the Gov. Clinton Hotel, New York.

When Your Snare Head Breaks

When your snare head breaks in the middle of a job—what to do? Easy . . . Place one Synco Jazz Stick No. 21 under a Leedy Snare Drum Tone Control No. 669, as shown in the above photo. This will give you enough "snare action" to get thru the evening. True, not as good as the real thing, but the stunt is a lot better than no "snares" at all.
(By—J. R. Kenney, Wallingford, Conn.)

YOU MAY NOW OBTAIN SQUARE HEAD RODS ON ANY TYPE LEEDY DRUM BY SPECIFYING SAME ON YOUR ORDER TO THE DEALER. A NEAT NEW MODEL SQUARE HEAD KEY IS SUPPLIED WITH ALL SUCH RODS.

Hot Dog!—Hot Cymbal!

"Duke" takes a few advanced lessons on "hot" cymbal playing from his master, Gary Gillis, who made the Drum Dept. of Arnold Johnson's Orchestra one of the reasons why this great band became greater. Gillis is now with the band at the Club Lido in New York City. They also do the famous Majestic Radio Hour in which Wendell Hall's contributions are a feature. Gillis hails from Anderson, Indiana.

L. Blundon Wills at WABC

Chester H. Miller   L. Blundon Wills

..."You are now listening to WABC, Key Station of the Columbia Broadcasting Co. We would like to take this opportunity to introduce to our audience L. Blundon Wills, our staff Drummer, Tympanist, Marimba and Xylophone soloist. Altho' comparatively new to radio, Wills has built a wonderful reputation for himself. His skill at improvising and his ability to convey particular musical ideas to our great unseen audiences has made him nationally known in a very short time. Wills served with the A.E.F. in France and while convalescing in various overseas hospitals (after being severely gassed) he became interested in music and decided to follow it as a vocation. After returning to the U. S. he appeared as a single Xylophone 'turn' on the 'big time' vaudeville circuits. Later he owned and directed his own music and dance presentation on the old Orpheum circuit.

Next we want to tell you about Chester H. Miller, best known to our public for his comical characterization of 'Lord Ashcart,' this role being a part of the Nit-Wit Hour as broadcast over this station each Saturday from 6:30 to 7 P.M. He has also won favorable recognition as a baritone soloist and radio playwright. In conjunction with his varied artistic efforts, Miller is also attached to the Production Department of the Columbia Broadcasting System, in charge of Studios at WABC. Mr. Miller began his radio career six years ago as manager of Station WEAN in Providence, R. I."

Sousa's Band Special Train-Wrecked

A tour with Sousa is full of adventure. These pictures show their latest. While making a "jump" between Pueblo and Trinidad, Colorado, during the week of Sept. 16th, their special played "Leaping Lena" instead of "Casey Jones," but it was not the fault of the "conductor." However, we are mighty glad to say that none of the boys were seriously hurt. Five or six did receive minor scratches and there were a couple of sprained ankles and bumped heads. The Drummers—Messrs. Goulden, Helmecke and Holt—received a few jolts, but what's a "jolt" to a Drummer? We know some Drummers who thrive on jolts. Photos by Howard Goulden. Gus Helmecke and Frank Holt are in the crowd, but we couldn't find them. Mr. Sousa is in the foreground of the top picture. And there was another adventure . . . the time Gus and Howard missed the train at Albuquerque, New Mexico, early one morning last season, (their alarm clock didn't alarm—so they say—but one of the clarinet players told us that "Drummers can't stay out till four A.M. and expect to hear that little tinkle") and had to cough up fifty bucks to hire Maj. Wardwell and his airplane to fly them to Clovis, N. M. Gus says the plane was too light a model for three such big men, and Howard says he was only raising his arms to steady his cap and there was no need for Gus to bawl him out with strong language, ordering him to sit still. They both say the "air pockets" were very severe that day. Anyway, their ride was cut short when the Major saw the train stop at a junction half way to the end of the journey and brought the plane to a landing on a flat field in time for them to make a welcome change of transportation methods.

ALOYSIUS—"What makes you think you are going to get canned?"
SUSPICIOUS—"My leader has quit asking me to get a new outfit."

You Can
put snares to "bed" but you'll never make 'em sleep.

HERE'S A WAY TO GET THAT BREAK YOU'VE BEEN CRACKING ABOUT—

Sonny Greer

They say in New York that Sonny Greer plays more syncopation than the 20th Century Limited passing over rail joints at sixty miles an hour. Be that as it may —when he swats a hot chime chorus all the customers set down their glasses to look and listen. If you want to hear him, get Victor Record No. V-38036-A, "HIGH LIFE," and pay particular attention to the last strain of same. It will not only give you a thrill, but an idea worth plenty of bucks. Sonny is indeed one of the greatest jazz Drummers in the business. He plays with Duke Ellington's Cotton Club Orch. in Harlem, New York City. This is a class cabaret. Sonny has been in the biz twelve years. His teacher was Frank Wolf, who now runs the largest drum shop in New York. He also played for five years at the Kentucky Club on Broadway and one season with Ziegfeld's "Show Girl." Ellington will soon play the R.K.O. circuit—perhaps you will hear Sonny cut loose—don't miss him if he comes to your town. His Leedy outfit includes Marine Pearl Drums and is valued at $1200.00, and he says—"They ARE the world's finest."
(Courtesy—Frank Wolf Drum Shop, N. Y.)

Don't miss single bell notes here and there in drum parts just because you haven't time to pick up a bell hammer. Use butt end of drum stick by holding perpendicularly over bell bar and dropping straight down, gripping same on the rebound. Not as good as the bell hammer, but better than leaving it out and the leader will know you're not slacking.
(By Serge Fockler, Lima, Ohio)

Leedy   "FOR DRUMMERS WHO CARE"   **Leedy**

Page Five

Leedy Drum Topics

The Left Hand Turnover

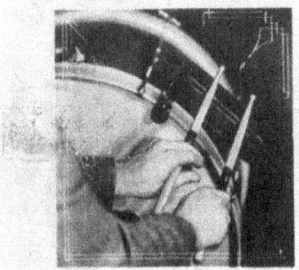

Changing from snare drum to wood block is an awkward job when the Drummer plays the latter holding the stick with the left palm upward (or approximately so). It is an easy matter to become accustomed to playing with the left palm down as shown in the above photo. When this is accomplished it is the means of the fastest possible changes. Simply turn the hand over, palm down, and it will fall into a position which allows the heavy part of the stick to strike the block. This also produces a more solid and realistic wood block tone than the tips. If you are not using this method now give it a good try-out.

Anthony Penkson

does clever and original stuff with the Penkson Melody Ramblers of Buffalo. This outfit is known as one of the most popular orchestras operating in the Buffalo territory and specializes in high grade ballroom work. They also have earned a fine reputation in the radio field.

Can you name the twenty-six drum rudiments? We will list them in the next issue of Drum Topics.

Dorothy Appleby
Pathe Feature Player

Dorothy Appleby, the Portland (Maine) beauty who made good in several New York Musical Comedies and who is now on the road to stardom as a feature Pathe player, purchased a Leedy Vibraphone for her Hollywood home from "Red" Allen, manager of the Drum Dept. at Wurlitzer's, Los Angeles.

Glances at a Few Big Timers
By Jack Roop

Billy Gladstone slapping two 22-inch Zildjian Cymbals in the N. Y. Capitol Concert Orchestra. . . . Frank Wolf's red necktie. . . . Johnny Morris singing and playing his own accompaniment with two Handsock Cymbals. . . . Vic Berton in Hollywood looking popeyed at the lady Picture Stars. . . . Arthur Layfield going in the stage door of the Oriental Theatre, Chicago. . . . Harold McDonald walking thru the lobby of the Biltmore Hotel (Los Angeles) at 4 A.M. with an armload of artificial flowers, not knowing where he got them. . . . Geo. Marsh's wonderful hair. . . . Bill Keiffer, who is always the Gentleman. . . . Billy Gilcher's turned-up collar. . . . Howard Goulden's (Sousa's Band) Derby. . . . Chauncey Morehouse's smart way of playing the "Rain or Shine" show. . . . Herman Fink on the Paramount (N. Y.) stage. . . . Bill Bitner, who weighs 215 lbs. . . . Karl Glassman's interesting conversations. . . . Joe Soistman of Baltimore and his rudiments. . . . Larry Gommerdinger (Gus Edwards Orch.) six feet two. . . . Geo. Green's "traveling man" stories. . . . Poley McClintock's (Waring's Pennsylvanians) smile.

When Practicing the Rudiments

Look at your sticks. Do not look off in the distance and depend upon your ear for the "right sound." Watch the movement of the sticks carefully. Make sure that they travel straight up and down and not in circles or half circles. In other words, you can frame a mind picture of the movements that will greatly assist toward better technic.

Johnny Robinson at WFBM

Geo. Irish   Earl B. Mounce   Johnny Robinson

When you tune in on WFBM—The Indianapolis Power & Light Co.—you will hear some real "percussion stuff." Johnny Robinson, who is the "motorman" of this department, is a wow! His Xylophone specialties are always a big hit. Twenty years ago, Johnny studied under Mr. Leedy and O. F. Rominger. Since then he has played everything from Circus to Symphony. This includes the principal theatres of Indianapolis—trouping on the road with musical comedies—and three years as a single feature xylophone act in vaudeville. WFBM supports a forty-piece high-class concert orchestra with Earl B. Mounce as conductor and program manager. Geo. Irish is asst. conductor. Johnny signs himself—"Percussionist Petite—a big shot at Deaf and Dumb picnics."

Powdered rosin rubbed into a tambourine head will give your thumb a sure grip. Great for slow afterbeats, also long and short rolls. Powdered rosin can be bought at any drug store.   (By Johnny Gruden, Lawrence, Mass.)

Moses Moreno

is with the Sanchez Novelty Mexican Orchestra of San Antonio, Texas. This outfit is well known in Texas, especially for their brilliant work in the field of fascinating Mexican music. In previous years Mr. Moreno has been associated with the Two Time Syncopators of San Antonio, and in Laredo with the National Theatre Orchestra, The Knights of Columbus Orchestra, and the Laredo Philharmonic Orchestra. Moreno is a versatile performer on the entire range of percussion instruments.

Ira W. Dalrymple

Cook's Monterey Hotel Orchestra of Trenton and Asbury Park, N. J., can boast of one of the finest Drummers and Xylophone Soloists in the hotel and dance business. Ira W. Dalrymple is his name—a name that is known in things musical for many miles in all directions from Trenton for nifty and original work. He is a former pupil of that famous artist, Geo. Hamilton Green, and is now teaching a large class of pupils in connection with his regular engagements with Cook. Mr. Cook is seen standing at the right in the above photo.
(Courtesy—Wm. Groom's Drum Shop, Trenton, N. J.)

Traveling Drummers

Do you oil the hinges and locks of your trunks? It pays to do so at least four times a year. Use a light oil such as Three-in-One—it prevents rusting and assures easy-working locks.

It is a good idea to have one of the striking surfaces of a chime mallet slightly softer than the other. Place the mallet in a vise and make several slight cross cuts with an ordinary fine tooth meat saw. This "roughs up" the surface and will eliminate that harsh contact.

Arnold W. Mock

Here is one of our good Canadian friends, Arnold W. Mock, who is now located up at Preston, Ontario. Mock is a theatre and dance Drummer, also Marimba and Xylophone soloist of considerable note. Ten years in Eastern Ontario; several seasons at the Park Theatre and with the "Joy Boys" College Orchestra of Galt. This band played for a long period at Beaumaris, one of Ontario's fashionable resorts on Lake Muskoka. Mock enjoys a large personal following of boosters, particularly on account of his excellent Marimba playing. He writes—"My Leedy Drums and Marimba never fail to help me do better work and create attention and complimentary remarks."
(Courtesy—Advance Music Co., Toronto, Ont.)

Leedy   "WORLD'S FINEST DRUMMERS' INSTRUMENTS"   **Leedy**

The Exclusive Drummers' Paper

NEW *Leedy* CREATIONS THAT HELP THE DRUMMER TO PROGRESS

The Improved Trap Rail

A WONDERFUL DANCE SET-UP
Handy for Jobbing—Light in Weight
Easy to Carry

This new Leedy creation is the most practical set-up ever presented for the dance and jobbing Drummer. A glance at the photo at the right tells the true story better than a thousand words. For utility in transportation—neat appearance—adjustable features and strength the Improved Trap Rail is in a class by itself. The Drummer who uses one of these on a one-night stand gives the impression of having brought his whole outfit. He can do better work, too. All of which builds prestige and creates a greater demand for his services.

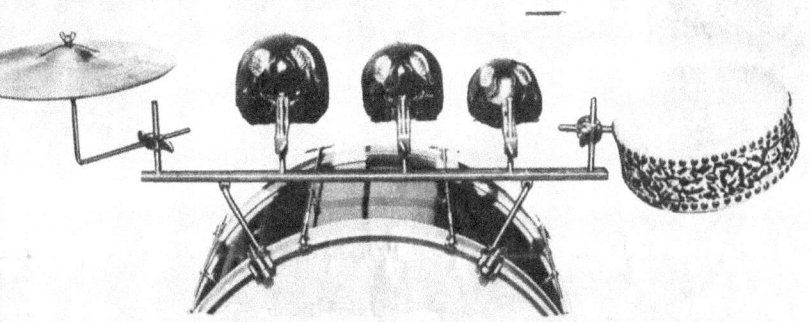

The Improved Trap Rail is designed to place on the counter hoop of the bass drum NEAREST THE PLAYER. This makes it possible to adjust the Cymbal and Tom Tom in the most practical positions for fast work. NOTE—that Vise Grip Hoop Clamps have been installed in place of the lighter Bull Dog type as used on the former Trap Rail. Also that the posts are now shorter. Clamps fold up under the rail. The "whole works" may be carried as a unit by simply removing the cymbal and folding the traps parallel with the rail.

Prices of Holders and Traps as Shown Above

No. 1501—Adjustable Post Block for Cymbal Arm		$0.75
Finished in Nobby Gold		1.25
No. 1502—Cymbal Holder Arm		.75
Finished in Nobby Gold		1.25
No. 245—Adjustable Temple Block Holder	each	.75
Finished in Nobby Gold	each	1.25
No. 1503—Universally Adjustable Tom Tom Holder		1.10
Finished in Nobby Gold		1.65
No. 330A—12" Thin Kiraljian Italian Cymbal		8.00
No. 244 B—5" Korean Temple Block		4.00
No. 244 C—5¼" Korean Temple Block		5.00
No. 244 D—6" Korean Temple Block		7.00
No. 1510—10" x 4" Leedy "Full Dress" Tom Tom (Red, Black or White Duco Shell)		7.50

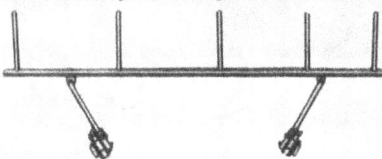

Showing the Trap Rail Without Traps or Holders
No. 1500—Finished in Bright Nickel $5.50
Finished in Nobby Gold 7.50

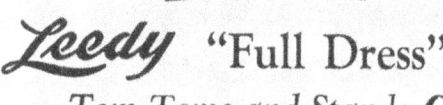

Leedy "Full Dress" Tom Toms and Stands

Tom Tom rhythms rank with Cymbals and Temple Blocks as an outstanding feature of the Drummer's outfit. A set of four Leedy "Full Dress" American-made Tom Toms presents the progressive Drummer with another opportunity to "shine." Get yours and be "out in front" with the latest idea. They are an investment that will bring returns. Leedy now offers a new type Tom Tom far superior in every detail to the ordinary Chinese models. They are instruments of beauty and durability. The shells are of laminated construction, heavily reinforced with wide inside hoops. The heads are extra heavy, close-grained steer hide, which produces a better tone and remains tighter in damp weather than the coarse Oriental pigskin. Heavy decorated tacks and strong brass rings that will not pull out are used. No more rattling or splitting of shells.

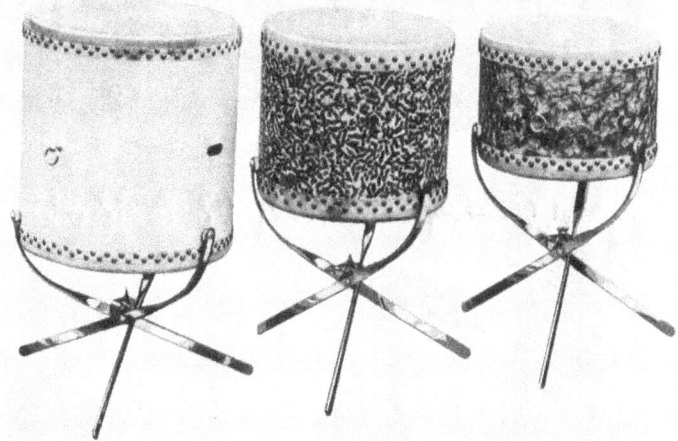

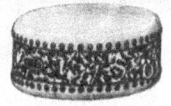

No. 1510—10" x 4"
Gold Duco	$7.50	Marine Pearl	$7.50
Black Duco	7.50	Black Onyx	10.00
Red Duco	7.50	Red Onyx	10.00
White Duco	7.50	Rainbow Pearl	10.00

No. 1513—16" x 16"		No. 1512—14" x 12"		No. 1511—13" x 9"	
Gold Duco	$27.50	Gold Duco	$22.50	Gold Duco	$15.00
Black Duco	27.50	Black Duco	22.50	Black Duco	15.00
Red Duco	27.50	Red Duco	22.50	Red Duco	15.00
White Duco	27.50	White Duco	22.50	White Duco	15.00
Marine Pearl	35.00	Marine Pearl	22.50	Marine Pearl	15.00
Black Onyx	35.00	Black Onyx	30.00	Black Onyx	20.00
Red Onyx	35.00	Red Onyx	30.00	Red Onyx	20.00
Rainbow Pearl	35.00	Rainbow Pearl	30.00	Rainbow Pearl	20.00

*No. 99—Folding Tom Tom Stand, in Bright Nickel, each $4.00
Finished in Nobby Gold, each 6.00

"FOR DRUMMERS WHO CARE"

Leedy Drum Topics

Prize Winning Drum Corps—
Drum Majors—Bands and
a few "Big Shots" at the
American Legion 11th National
Convention—Louisville, Ky.
Sept. 30th, Oct. 1st, 2nd and 3rd, 1929

Philadelphia, Penna.
FIRST PRIZE—

Henry C. Whiteling, Leader and General Instructor—Russell Murphy, I

Fort Dodge, Ia.
Post 130
SECOND PRIZE
RATING—98.00

Prize Winni
Milwaukee, Wis.,
RATIN
Columbus, Ohio,
RATIN
Kenosha, Wis., P
RATIN
Wichita, Kans.,
RATIN
Detroit, Mich., P
RATIN

O. C. Pfaff, Manager—Bob Heath, Drill Master—Elliot Collson, Drum Major—Chas. W. Eslinger, Drum Sgt.—Geo. E. Scheidel, Bugle Sgt.—Mark Taylor, Fife Sgt.

Los Angeles, Calif., Victory Post 8, FOURTH PRIZE RATING 97.45

The Men Who Put the Drum Corps Contests Over

Prize Winning Drum Majo

It's the Drum Corps, Drum Majors and other contests that provide the big show of the American Legion Convention. This year there were more entries in all divisions than ever before. 5,000 people saw the Drum Corps preliminaries and 30,000 saw the finals under bright lights at Parkway Field. However, the entire success of the greatest contest ever held was due to the untiring and clever efforts of Dr. C. C. Hawke, Robt. McDougle, of the national committee, and Capt. R. W. Norton and Heyde C. Conrad of the Louisville committee. These four gentlemen certainly deserve a vote of thanks from every member of every corps that attended. Dr. Hawke and Robt. McDougle are the men who are making these wonderful events possible year after year.

Dr. C. C. Hawke,
Winfield, Kans.
Chairman—National
Convention Contests
Supervisory Committee

Robt. McDougle,
Parkersburg, W. Va.
Chairman—National
Trophies and Awards
Committee

Capt. R. W. Norton,
Louisville, Ky.
Chairman—General
Contests Committee,
1929 National
Convention

Heyde C. Conrad,
Louisville, Ky.
Sec'y General Contests
Committee, 1929
National Convention

FIRST PRIZE
Harry C.
Thompson,
Kankakee, Ill.

SECOND PRIZE
John F. Shearer,
Wilmington, Del.

THIRD
Jame
McKeesp

 "WORLD'S FINEST DRUMMERS' INSTRUMENTS"

The Exclusive Drummers' Paper

rankfort Post 211
ING 98.53

tructor—John Swan, Asst. Drill Instructor—E. E. Widger, Sec'y.

THEY CAME, THEY SAW, THEY BROKE ALL RECORDS at LOUISVILLE

115,000 American Legionnaires, the greatest gathering that ever met at any Convention, and they formed one of the greatest crowds in history. Approximately 1,700 of them were Drummers—another record-breaker, for they undoubtedly constituted the largest number of "pig skin fiddlers" that ever came together at one time. And still another record—the longest parade. It took six hours to pass a given point. There were 121 Drum Corps, 35 Bands and scores of drill teams. But the finest record of all was the new high mark of efficiency attained by the Drum Corps. New uniforms, new instruments, new members, with new drills and stunts that would make a Ziegfeld chorus do some fast stepping to keep up. Also new musical numbers, many of which were revelations, proving the possibilities of corps music. And the ladies.... Oh, Boy! There were "gobs" of 'em in a couple of dozen or more auxiliary bands, corps and drill teams. Did they strut? Positively—AND HOW! We hope they have contests of their own next year. Why not? Well, it was a large four days, especially for Drummers, and here's hoping it will be still larger in Boston next October.

Commonwealth Edison Post 118 Chicago, Ill.
THIRD PRIZE
RATING—97.55

Bands

228, 1st Prize

, 2nd Prize

21, 3rd Prize

4, 4th Prize

59, 5th Prize

Drum Major—Ray Boegen, Director—Capt. L. J. Michels, Secretary—Thos. W. North, Quartermaster—H. R. Todd

Salem, Ore. Capitol Post 9
FIFTH PRIZE
RATING 97.10

Prize Winning Twirling Drum Majors

Prominent Drum Corps Members at Louisville

FIRST PRIZE
Lee Suttell,
Buffalo, N. Y.

SECOND PRIZE
Jerry Cannon,
St. Paul, Minn.

Henry C. Whiteling,
Frankfort, Philadelphia, Pa.

Chas. Eslinger,
Fort Dodge, Ia.

Harry Frohow,
Sioux City, Ia.

Alva C. Smith,
Elyria, Ohio

Joseph W. Soistman,
Baltimore, Maryland

   "FOR DRUMMERS WHO CARE"   

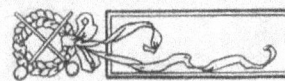 # Leedy Drum Topics

"The more I play them, the better I like them"

Wm. D. Kieffer, *Tympanist*
United States Marine Band
Washington, D. C.

—Leedy Pedal Tympani have removed seventy-five per cent of the difficulties in Tympani playing. A pressure of your foot and the note is there. Best of all, the pedal remains exactly where you set it. The more I play them, the better I like them.

Leedy UNIVERSAL PEDAL TYMPANI offer one of the most direct means of raising the Drummer's status as a musician. This, of course, paves the way to greater earnings—the goal that every Drummer strives for. They are all that is claimed. The mechanical principle has remained the same since their invention nine years ago. There have been only a few minor changes, such as strengthening of parts. They have stood the test of time and this, coupled with the "big name" Tympanists who play them, is indeed ample proof of their efficiency. They have well been named "The Tympani for Success."

and here are some other "high-ups" who say the same

H. N. Goulden, Sousa's Band | Karl Glassman, Walter Damrosch Orchestra | Chas. White, Los Angeles Philharmonic Orchestra | Fred Noak, College of Music, Cincinnati, O. | Geo. W. Marsh, Paul Whiteman's Orchestra | Bill Gilcher, Warner Bros., Hollywood, Calif. | Fred Paine, Detroit, Mich. | Art. Layfield, Oriental Theatre, Chicago, Ill. | H. McDonald, Paramount Pictures, Hollywood, Calif. | Maurice Tushin, Boston, Mass. | O. F. Rominger, Herbert Clarke's Band

and here are some of the reasons why

SIMPLICITY OF TENSIONING BELL CRANK SYSTEM

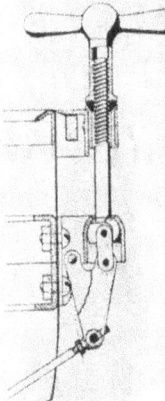

Drawing of the Bell Crank Tension System, Originated by Leedy. When you turn the handle (at the lowest note) the strain is on the brackets, not the rods.

Bear in mind that we have retained the kettle brackets as used on the hand-screw Tympani (see drawing at left) and that strain of the head at each of the six points, for the lowest note (with the pedal up as far as it will go), is applied to these brackets and not to the rods. This is a most important point, as it assures all rods pulling equally from the lowest note on up the scale. The kettles are machine formed, one-piece 19-gauge finest quality copper. The parts that are subjected to great strain are composed of steel. The stand is aluminum and designed for strength. All the steel parts are protected against rusting and the prominent fixtures are heavily nickel plated and highly polished. The copper kettles are polished and lacquered, making a combination that is very beautiful. Leedy Tympani can be set up ready to play in less than five minutes. The design has been so skilfully worked out that there are only three detached parts to each instrument. There is one simple connection to make and they are ready to tune. Nothing complicated. Complete mechanical instructions are furnished with each set.

CAN BE TILTED QUICKLY

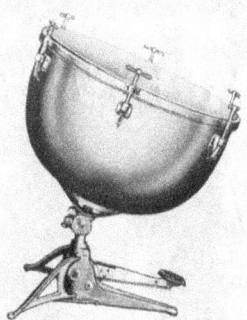

The instruments can be tilted to any angle by means of a simple thumb screw device on the back part of the stand. This feature is invaluable to the drummer who plays double drums, because they can be made to fit into close quarters of the theatre pit and played with comfort in a sitting position.

DOUBLE ANGLE COUNTER HOOP

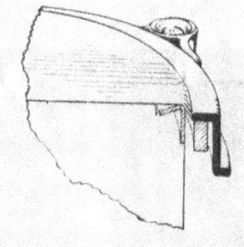

This drawing shows the extra strong double angle counter hoop. Made of heavy rolled steel, eliminating all possibility of warping. It also adds greatly to the appearance of the instrument. An exclusive Leedy creation.

No. 570—Sizes 25 in. and 28 in., per pair $350.00

Kettles in Black or White Duco or Extra Bright Lacquered Copper with Stands in Nobby Gold—$30.00 additional.

 "WORLD'S FINEST DRUMMERS' INSTRUMENTS"

The Exclusive Drummers' Paper

Justa Wethead Says

It's a sad and solemn feeling when you're out with the "ball and chain" and your "whoopee" girl appears.

An Old-Timer Comes Back

Remember the old-fashioned shot cushion such as drummers used when working effects in the piano and drum store-show days? Well, it has come back to life in a new form . . . reincarnation, so to speak. Here's how—we have seen a few drummers using them for rhythm beat stuff in modern dance numbers. It really sounds very "spiffy," especially in PP strains and when accents are snapped out in the proper spots. This is likely to spread to considerable popularity. Why not try it out? Secure a leather or imitation leather covered pad about a foot square, and use a thin, wide stick so as to produce both thuds and snappy slaps.

Billy Cleve

Here's an Ogden, Utah, boy who certainly has been hitting the high spots for the past nine years. Among his various engagements have been—Warner Stone's Pantages Stage Band, en tour, Egyptian Theatre, Berthana Ball Room, White City Gardens and Ball Room, Ogden, Utah; New Roman Gardens, La Monica Ball Room at Ocean Park, Calif.; radio work from stations KSL, KFWA, KFI, KFUR, KDYL, KSI. At present he is going stronger than ever with Warner Stone's Jantzen Beach Orchestra, playing at Portland, Oregon. This is one of the finest outfits in the Northwest; however, it always takes a good Drummer to help put any band over and Cleve is "it" in this case.

There are hundreds of different kinds of rattan and cane such as used for bell, xylophone and marimba mallets. Some makers use one kind or another for bass drum, tenor drum and even tympani sticks. It is very difficult to obtain the right quality and sizes . . . one lot comes thru good and the next bad. Owing to the peculiar formation of the grain this rattan or cane can not be turned down to a given diameter. The finest grades come from the islands of the Straits Settlements south of Siam in the Indian Ocean. Singapore is one of them.

Important Facts About Chimes

Chimes differ from most musical instruments. Generally speaking, other instruments have true harmonics or overtones, being usually spaced in fifths, fourths, thirds, etc., above the fundamental tone, and then rather feeble and hardly perceptible. In Chimes the desired tone is one of the overtones (the fourth of the series) and is the predominating tone, but instead of being accompanied by true harmonics as in most other instruments, it has three lower overtones and an endless number above this predominant tone, with none of the overtones in any true harmonic relation—there are near octaves, sixths, fifths, fourths, etc., but all too badly out of tune to sound good with the harmony of an accompanied melody unless heard from a more or less distant point, whereupon they lose the discordant effect of the overtones. This is nature and cannot be altered. In testing Chimes, octaves should not be attempted, for every Chime has a sixth partial which sounds nearly an octave with the fourth or predominating tone, yet is always sharp, and when listening to octaves for comparison (as is the usual custom with other musical instruments) we unconsciously use this sixth partial of the lowest octave Chime to judge the fourth or predominant tone of the upper octave; therefore we imagine the upper octave Chime to be flat.

Another peculiarity about Chimes which helps to explain why they are difficult to understand, is the fact that the lowest C (for example) in an ordinary set of Chimes is the C in the third space of the treble clef staff. In listening to it this does not seem possible because of the prominence of the three lower partials, which are very intense (the lowest of these three partials or overtones sound more than two octaves lower) especially when standing close; therefore they are misleading, but are hardly noticeable at a distance from the Chimes. Almost without exception Chimes are complimented by audiences on their beauty of tone, which verifies the explanations in the foregoing paragraph that overtones, partials and harmonics are noticeable and sometimes annoying near the instrument, but inaudible at a distance.

A good method of testing Chimes is to try them with a pipe organ—sounding each corresponding tone and preferably using the flute stop and advisably under a temperature of approximately 70 degrees.

The musician is first taught to tune his instrument, and it is not unusual that the finer the musician the more chance there is that he will not understand the strange characteristics of Chime tone and tuning. He treats only with the stronger fundamentals, and while the partials or harmonics are present in his own instruments, they are so weak they are hardly noticeable. Chime tones, therefore, are so widely different that it is the natural impression they are out of tune, and this will remain with him until he has familiarized himself with the singular distinctions of Chime tone construction. Consequently, his musical ability and past experience is truly a handicap rather than an aid to proper realization of Chimes, and the more prominent his position the more difficult it is to convince him. Musicians of this caliber are sincere in their belief, and the more eminent they are the more confidence is given their false opinions. This is no censure of the ability of the musician, conspicuous or otherwise; for it is possible, if he wishes to do so, to gain a thorough understanding of tone building as applied to Chimes, although unfortunately he is usually opposed to this because of his superior qualifications in things in his own musical field. He does not realize that there is something which varies from the education he has received. This musician may be particularly misled in his belief if the number played on Chimes contains intervals of fourths, fifths, or sixths, the strong overtones or partials mingling temporarily with those following give the listener a sensation of dissonance, which is not noticeable when the same intervals are heard on other instruments. It is a fact and has been proven that the human ear will easily adapt itself to these new conditions and will in time accept the multiplicity of tones which at first seemed displeasing, and the more a person hears and listens to Chimes the more enthusiastic he will become over the beauty of true Chime quality and tone.

MANAGER—"Are you sure he's a hot Drummer?"

LEADER—"He ought to be—he comes warmly recommended."

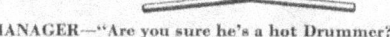

Murray Spivack Now Official Percussionist at Radio Pictures Studios—Hollywood, California

Left to right—Luther Reed, director of "Rio Rita," Radio Pictures wonderful musical extravaganza—Murray Spivack, drummer and sound effect expert, Radio Pictures—Victor Baravalle, musical director Radio Pictures—Helen Kaiser, one of the featured players of "Rio Rita." More about Murray Spivack in the next issue of Drum Topics.

Jack Roop Again Takes to the Road

Every show has its stars. The "Leedy Drum Show," which visits over a hundred cities a year, is no exception. Jack Roop (at right in photo), the Leedy Assistant Sales Manager, is just that—and more. He is the featured player, manager, juvenile man, buck dancer, warbler, property man, stage hand, electrician and transfer man of this one-man "opera." All of which means that Jack knows the drummer's angle from cuckoos to cocoanuts. For the past four years he has taken the Leedy "show" to the principal cities of the United States and even to Europe—(they say he stayed in Paris longer than necessary)—including five big trunks full of Leedy instruments, setting them up in the leading music store or hotel for the drummers entertainment. When he comes your way be sure to visit him. You will be notified. There is no charge for admission. No obligation, either. You will not be asked to buy a single thing. The ladies and children are also invited. The above photo shows Jack having a final "drumistic" chat with the Leedy Sales Manager just before rushing off to catch a "rattler" for his first "leap" on the annual fall tour.

A New Cymbal Frame-Up

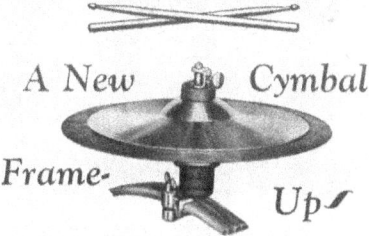

By—Frank Hussey and Irv. Wilkie, Conn-Detroit Co.

A dandy frame-up for "choke" cymbals may be made up of regular Leedy catalog items as follows: one Vise Grip Hoop Adapter No. 120 (page 52), one Cow Bell Clamp No. 984 (page 53), one 12-inch Chinese Cymbal No. 92X (page 38), one 10-inch American Brass Cymbal No. 30B (page 39) and three felt washers under the Chinese Cymbal and one on top of the brass cymbal. Different degrees of pressure in holding the cymbals together for the tone desired are obtained by adjusting the cow bell clamp up or down on the post of the hoop adapter. The cymbals are placed face to face. The best "sock" yet. Can also be used for sizzle.

He: Please, just one?
She: Nay, nay sir!
He: Please—
She: Nay! Nay!
He: For cripe's sake, was your mother scared by a horse?

(Cornell Widow)

"FOR DRUMMERS WHO CARE"

Leedy Drum Topics

The Andrew Jackson Drum

(Photo by—Coquille, New Orleans, La.)

Here we have a most interesting "find" for our readers. The drum pictured above is known as the "Andrew Jackson" Drum. It served beside this great General and Statesman at the Battle of New Orleans when the American Volunteers defeated the British troops just outside that city on January 8th, 1815. It also served with Jackson in the Seminole War and in the Mexican War. Altho' it was the personal property of "Old Hickory" himself, it was played upon for many years and thruout many sieges by Jordon B. Nobles, a mulatto drummer who acted in the triple capacity of body guard, valet and drummer to the famous soldier. Nobles later served as a captain in the 7th Louisiana Volunteers of the Union in 1863. When Jackson became President he gave the drum to Nobles. Nobles died in 1892 and later the drum became the property of Capt. Harry Allen of New Orleans, who loaned it to E. A. Palfrey, Pres. of the Louisiana Historical Assn. which then had its headquarters in the Memorial Hall. It now rests in the Cabildo Building, occupied by the Louisiana Historical Society, and which has long been one of the most interesting museums of the world. Note the bullet hole at lower left center. There is no record of when this occurred.

(Notes and photo kindly supplied by R. C. Ballard Thruston, Pres. of the Filson Club, Louisville, Kentucky.)

Roger K. Lee

Roger Lee was playing Drums, Bells and Tympani with the Pacific Grove Symphony Orch. (L. E. M. Cosmey, conductor) at Pacific Grove, Calif., when last heard from. Lee started in the business nine years ago in his home town, Salem, Mass. Since then he has had a varied and extensive experience, including vaudeville on the Keith circuit with Kenwood's Society Ramblers. At one time he headed his own band. He is a modern Drummer in every respect, has taken his work seriously and has left a fine reputation on every job.

The Prize Story

By George Claesgens,
12 Johnson Park
Utica, N. Y.

"He Knew His Horses"

One day last week my star pupil—a young chap fifteen years of age—asked me to meet him and his father the next day at our local music store to help select a new bass drum, also a pedal and a few traps. We met and decided on several numbers. During our final check-up of items the boy said to me, "Is there anything we have forgotten?" After looking everything over I said, "Yes, we forgot a pair of spurs." Up to that point the old gentleman had been satisfied to allow us to go to it and order what we liked without comment, but at the mention of spurs he looked at the bass drum, then at the boy, and growled, "What are you going to do now, ride the damn thing?"

WIN $10.00 — It will only take five or ten minutes to write up your favorite "Drummer Story." If it is published in Drum Topics you will receive a check for $10.00. Send yours in today. **WIN $10.00**

Fiji Wood Blocks

Showing two young Fijis on the Island of Tonga, South Seas, standing with native drum sticks (a little larger than our hickory models) beside two big mahogany dug-out wood blocks. While the Tonga Fijis are now practically all Christians and use these big wooden drums to call their neighborhood to out-door religious services, there was a time not so many years ago when their cannibal grandfathers used the same drums to call their tribe together for feasts, with their enemies as the main item on the menu.

Many a good drum goes wrong

because of uneven head tension. Drum Topics has "harped" on this subject before, but it's just as important now as it was then. Are your heads tensioned EVENLY all the way around? Did you make this test? Did you throw off your snares and tap the head about two inches from the hoop opposite each rod as you proceeded to tighten them, making sure that you obtained the same note at each point? It is not an easy job to do this, but it's worth the trouble because it results in not only a better sounding drum, but easier playing as well. If your ear is not sufficiently keen to tension these six or eight notes alike, ask one of the other boys in the band to help you. Unevenness in tension results in different degrees of elasticity in the head; meaning, that one or two areas of the head are "fighting" the other areas in trying to bring the whole head back to a level position. These tighter areas are unseen strains and hinder what should be a precision-like displacement of the air column confined within the shell.

CHROMIUM PLATING is now being applied to ALL Leedy Xylophone, Marimba and Vibraphone STANDS AND RESONATORS—ALSO to Chime Tubes and Stands. Leedy operates their own Chrome plant.

Frank Wolf Drum Shop Moves to New and Larger Quarters

Frank Wolf
Proprietor
Frank Wolf's
Drum Shop
232 West 48th St.
New York City

Drummers of New York City and all those who visit the "big town" are now enjoying the services of the "World's Largest Retail Drum Shop." Five floors of "Personal Service to the Drummer," located at 232 West 48th St., right in the heart of the "rialto"—the name attached to the musical and theatrical center of the country. Frank Wolf is the "big boss" and he is on the job behind the counter during every business hour of the day except to put on the "feed bag" a few minutes at noon. However, he often misses even this in order to talk Drums to some worthy. Frank is known in things "drumistic" far and near. His former shop on 46th St. was the Drum Center of N. Y. for ten years. The new store stocks everything the Drummer uses and plays from soup to nuts. There will also be a complete repair service. One entire floor will be occupied by the Karl Glassman School of Drumming and Tympani Playing. This organization is headed by Karl Glassman himself, one of the country's foremost tympanists and who for many years played under the direction of Walter Damrosch, conductor of the New York Symphony Orchestra. His school is known from coast to coast and has turned out hundreds of full-fledged Drummers who are now filling some of the highest grade jobs. Bill Gladstone (Capitol Theatre, N. Y.), Al. Broemel (Metropolitan Opera and formerly with Victor Herbert), and Arthur Butts (Pathe Sound Studio) head the various departments of instruction, with a large staff of competent and well-known teachers acting under their supervision.

Music Dealer from Manila, P. I., Visits Leedy Factory

Left to right—A. W. Kuerst, General Manager, Leedy Mfg. Co.; Manuel S. Rustia, Agent for the Government of the Philippines, New York; Gonzalo Puyat, President of Gonzalo Puyat & Sons, Inc., Manila, one of the largest musical instrument wholesale and retail establishments of the Philippine Islands.

"WORLD'S FINEST DRUMMERS' INSTRUMENTS"

The Exclusive Drummers' Paper

Thoughts of a Jobbing Drummer
By Sam Rowland

Suffrincymbals! What a bust! The sap that booked this screwey-shindig sure musta needed the lousycommish . . . . four tunes shot and still this gang hang on to their seats . . . . why don't somun start sumpin . . . . guess this music is too ultra for 'em . . . . not a ripple . . . . the dumeggs! Course this band aint like Red's—'cept me, I'm as good as Vic Berton . . . . just never got a break, 'ats all . . . . wish that sax would stop showin' off . . . . hate a guy like that . . . . an he aint even got any teckneek . . . . boy, it it wuzzin fer me this crew woulden have NO rhythm a-tall! Watch 'em open their eyes when I sock this cymbal chorus . . . . yeah, I thought so—bawled at me fer drowndin 'emall out . . . . what a band, what a band . . . . this'll be my last job with 'em . . . . no appreciation—'ats what. AWAW, here comes the liffathaparty . . . . spose he's gonna blame me cause the clams can't dance . . . . I knew it, I knew it . . . . wants us to hit up a square dance . . . . imagine me playin' this stuff—me, who's hottern hot . . . . what a come down! Jes look at these yokels—breakin their necks to dance now . . . . guess I'll play along easy—no chance to show my stuff here . . . . no 'preciation, 'ats what. Whoopee, look at that little blonde mamma! Boy, she can mend my drum covers fer life . . . . say, this dance aint gonna be HAF bad . . . . gotta meet that gal . . . . guess I'll strut my stuff . . . . "you guys lay low—let me take this next chorus" . . . . Oh, she's lookin . . . . an what a smile! Think I'll sort of saunter over her way on the intermish . . . . aint she the berries? An do I rate? Like nobody! "Say, fellers —aint this some shindig? Hope we land this crowd all winter!!"

Harry Winston

Harry Winston has held down many of the highest class theatre jobs in Los Angeles during the past six years. These include Majestic Theatre, Metropolitan Theatre with Vern Buck, Loew's State Theatre with Rube Wolfe, Gene Morgan and others. He has also done considerable work at the Hollywood Studios and at L. A. Radio Stations. After a few months absence he is now back at Loew's State making his usual daily hit with the inimitable Winston style and originality. His home is Des Moines, Iowa, where he played in the Empress and Capitol for several seasons. Harry says— "I beat the best because the best beats the rest, and that's Leedy." Others say—"Harry is one of the best beaters that beats."

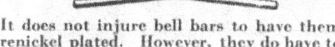

It does not injure bell bars to have them renickel plated. However, they do have to be retuned.

Emory Daugherty

heads his own orchestra playing at the Madrillon Restaurant and Arlington Hotel Roof in Washington, D. C. He is also doing splendid work at radio station WRC. His experience includes successful engagements at the Club Lido, Hamilton Hotel and Astor Restaurant.

Leon Knapp and His Drummer's Service Station at Grand Rapids, Mich.

Long before Leon Knapp opened his Drum Shop in his home city of Grand Rapids, Mich., he was one of the best known Drummers between Detroit and Chicago. His fine reputation grew both from extraordinary ability in all branches of the profession, and good fellowship. Once you meet him you never forget him, for he is six feet two, of good nature and smiles. For ten years he has operated the Leon Knapp Drum Shop, carrying a full line of Drummer's Supplies and operating a Drum School that has turned out over ninety percent of the professional Drummers of Grand Rapids and vicinity, also over a dozen top-notch Drum Corps such as Shrine, American Legion, South High School and others. For the past five years this shop has carried the Leedy line exclusively. This drum center is further strengthened by the assistance of Donald "Cowboy" Patterson, an experienced professional Drummer who has been associated with Knapp for several years in both the teaching and the service activities. "Cowboy" has trouped with some fine dance and concert organizations and has also been located on high class jobs in Louisville, Grand Rapids and other central states cities. Following we print an article by Leon Knapp which should prove interesting to every instructor.

Holding the Drum Pupil's Interest
By Leon Knapp

"Will I be able to play in the Band by next Thursday?" Is there a teacher that has not been asked this question in one form or another over and over again? Johnny buys a drum today, takes it home and turns on the radio or phonograph and if he has any sense of rhythm at all his career as a drummer is under way. Tomorrow he joins the school band and soon consults a teacher, bringing the band book with him. Then the competent teacher's problem begins, for he knows that if he tells Johnny that it will be necessary to practice the rudiments for at least three months in order to play a march with any semblance of artistry, Johnny will become discouraged and the interest in his drum is likely to end then and there. The greatest problem of the drum instructor has always been to hold the pupil's interest long enough to give him the proper foundation. Today we are experiencing a great revival of rudimental drumming, to which most of the jazz men say "bunk," and as long as leaders are in doubt as to what the rudiments are and can not express themselves properly when they desire a certain drum effect, the rudiments will never take their rightful place in music. This will continue to make it difficult for the drum teacher to get the student to realize the importance of mastering the rudiments. The shortest cut to overcoming this is to show Johnny that he can apply his drumming to a melody without much deep thinking on Johnny's part. The teacher can satisfy his desire to get started by allowing him to play a simple afterbeat to the strains of a stirring march reproduced on the player piano. From then on the pupil's interest has been awakened and it is easy to point out the importance of playing the flam from hand to hand, etc. Johnny is then eager to return next week for his next lesson, because he feels he is making progress. No amount of shouting about the importance of learning the rudiments and denouncing the untrained jazz drummer will do half as much good as to allow him to play, applying the proper foundation, to the strains of Semper Fidelis and other like numbers, which of course is possible with the player piano. The pupil is ready to forego actual playing in the band until such time as he can create a real impression. The writer has had many experiences with the type of drummer who has faked his way along for years and has suddenly discovered that he desires to play the game by rule. In one instance a pupil was so enthusiastic about his progress that he cancelled all dance engagements until such time as he could play with more satisfaction and read the music properly. The writer has trained over 600 men and boys to drum correctly and has found that the player piano is the shortest cut and the most instructive investment for this purpose. The player piano can also be used for training drum corps. If you tell the tired business man he must Daddy-Mammy for five or six weeks he will often walk out on you, but teach him a simple street beat and let him march to his own rhythm with the strains of the piano accompaniment and he will immediately become a boy again and play soldier with all his might. This places him in a receptive mood for all that is to follow and it truly proves the old adage that "the best way to lay bricks is to lay bricks." Many a boy's talent has been stifled for lack of practical application. We will have better Drummers when the band leader puts a little time and thought on the proper way to play a drum, for certainly he should have the same knowledge concerning this drum section that he has for the other sections of the Band. This enables him to express his desire to the Drummer correctly, which in turn gains the Drummer's respect, making him anxious to meet the leader's demands and play better. The teacher's position today is parallel with that of the merchant. The merchant no longer sells merchandise . . . . he sells service. The teacher must find a way for Johnny and the tired business man to apply his talents, else another faker is born.

A Modern Combination

Three progressive boys of Dayton, Ohio, have lately introduced a very novel stunt for specialty numbers with one of Dayton's prominent dance and entertaining orchestras. It consists of playing solo numbers with the following combination—Marimba, Violin and Portable Organ. This trio has created many outstanding hits at high class affairs. W. F. Kissling at his Leedy Marimba, Joe Bender on Violin, and M. R. Reichard at the Portable Organ, are the boys who are putting this new novelty over with a bang and they have generously made this known in hopes that other organizations will take advantage of the idea.

"That will be all out of you"—said the Drummer as he looked at his busted batter.

The "Washboard Tom Tom"
By "Hob" Rankin

Drive two carpet tacks in the center of the shell of your small Tom Tom at opposite sides. Cut a maple or oak yardstick off so it will extend two inches over the head on each side. Use rubber bands looped over tacks and yardstick as shown in photo above. Rubber bands can be doubled to gain the proper tension as desired. When the yardstick is struck with Leedy Jazz Felt Sticks No. 371, or Two-Way Sticks No. 376 a fine "washboard" effect is produced. Very good in hot sax or trumpet strains and can be used on alternate beats in conjunction with larger Tom Tom. Also fine for explosion and rim shot effects before or after a break in modern "race horse" style.

"Hob" Rankin is now steppin' on things in the southern states with the Jack Norman Players. Perhaps you remember "Hob" when he was with the Wayne A. Hinkle Orchestra touring the leading vaudeville and dance circuits. His home town is Bridgeport, Ohio, and he has made himself widely known because of clever work over a period of several years. "Hob" is fully Leedy equipped.

Harold Straub

Harold Straub is at present attending the Paterson N. J., State Normal School and will soon become a School Principal. He is also Xylophone Soloist with the Paterson De Molay Band and Orchestra and is considered one of the finest in N. J. on this instrument. Straub is a pupil of Vincent L. Mott, a well known Drummer and music store operator. Mott says Straub has been thru the entire Geo. Hamilton Green course and has memorized most of Green's solos. Straub is also a very fine Drummer and has done considerable professional work.

 "FOR DRUMMERS WHO CARE"

Leedy Drum Topics

Veterans of Foreign Wars—Freemond Madson Post Drum Corps—Albert Lea, Minn.
First Prize Winners—National V. F. W. Encampment—St. Paul, Minn.
—August 25th-30th, 1929

Winners of three V. F. W. Minn. State Convention Contests—'27, '28 and '29. Commander, C. N. Whealan—Sec'y-Treas., Art. Marpe—Business Mgr. and Drill Sgt., W. D. Espeland—Drum Instructor, Juel Hove—Bugle Instructor, Wm. Braaten.

United Spanish War Veterans
Detroit, Mich. Drum and Bugle Corps
First Prize Winners National
Encampment Denver, Colo., Sept. 1929

Drum Major, M. E. Shaughnessy—Chief Musician, Joseph Hoffman—Prin. Mus., Richard Hafenfeld—Sec'y., A. F. Burch—Treas., J. F. Radke—Quartermaster Sergt., David Wymkoop—SEATED, left to right—Past Com. Dr. Frank B. Broderick—Past Com., Thomas Barrett—Com.-in-chief, Fred W. Green, Governor of Michigan—Judge Advocate, Edward S. Matthias, Judge Ohio Supreme Court—Past Com., Thos. W. Payne.

Native Sons of the Golden West
Alcade Drum Corps, San Francisco, Calif.
First Prize Winners, Admission Day
Celebration—San Francisco—Sept. 9th, '29

Drum Major, Louis F. Erb—Drill Sgt., Fred Bruener—Drum Instructor, Chas. Herman—Sec'y., Harry S. Burke—Commander and Treas., F. R. Hauck.

American Legion
Arthur Cunningham Post
Drum and Bugle Corps
Hornell, N. Y.
First Prize Winners
Elks Convention
Rochester, N. Y.
June 5th, '29, also
Edison Jubilee
Buffalo, N. Y., Oct. 12th, '29

Commander and Drum Major, Mitt. Johnson—Sec'y., Geo. Litchard—Business Mgr., Glen June—Drill Sgt., James Henesee—Drum Instructors, Dan Blecker and C. Zimmerman—Bugle Instructors, James Jones and Earl Zimmerman.

 "WORLD'S FINEST DRUMMERS' INSTRUMENTS"

The Exclusive Drummers' Paper

On The Cover

MITZI BUSH

MITZI BUSH has gained a high rung on the ladder of "Drumdom." She not only enjoys the distinction of being a leading feature with "The Brick Tops"—America's Greatest Girl Band—but also that of ranking with the most skilful modern Drummers of either the masculine or feminine brand. In person Mitzi is a shy little lady with a quiet, magnetic charm all her own. Behind the Drums she retains the charm, combining it with action—AND HOW! Her outfit is one of the three largest carried on the road . . . . seven Leedy trunks full of Leedy Tympani, Chimes, Vibraphone, Large Tom Toms, Drums, and plenty of traps. She plays them as per the music, and a lot more in hot numbers. As one critic wrote—"To see Mitzi Bush in action is worth the price of admission. We marvel at how she can seemingly play so many instruments at once." Mitzi began playing eight years ago with amateur girl bands in her home town of Elmhurst, Ill. From then on she has climbed upward thru many Chicago organizations, including The All-Girls Band and Elsie Myerson's Orch. on the Keith Circuit, and for the past three and a half years has been with The Brick Tops. She is a member of the Chicago Federation of Musicians. Mitzi has often stated—"I've tried them all and like Leedy equipment the best;" also, that "If more girls knew of the opportunities they would take up drums."

BOBBIE GRICE, Conductor of The Brick Tops, started with this band six years ago as the Drummer of the organization. It was not long before her extraordinary talents and personality, both behind the Drums and in specialty numbers, became the hit of the show. The outcome was her appointment by Mr. C. E. Green, owner of the band, as Conductor. From the moment Bobbie took the stick the band went ahead by leaps and bounds. It was the critics themselves who named it "America's Greatest Girl Band" and it was Bobbie Grice who was one of the greatest factors in making this a truth . . . . her inimitable style of conducting and showmanship is the reason. She is a "Hoosier Girl" from the big Dr_m City—Indianapolis, Indiana.

CLAUDIA PECK is the smallest girl with the biggest job in the band—that of managing 14 fiery Red Heads—(any man will tell you it's a big enough job to manage one—red head or otherwise). She is also first violinist and plays both legit. and "hot" fiddle on a par with the best of them. The fact that she is an honor graduate of the Cincinnati Conservatory of Music on piano and violin tells the story of her musicianship better than words. She has been with the band for three and a half years. Her home town is Columbus, Ohio, where she played drums in several local orchestras and modern bands. The Brick Tops are booked solid for 1930—their third tour over the former Keith and Orpheum Circuit, now the R.K.O. chain of the country's highest class vaudeville theatres.

She's only a Drummer's daughter, but she's one snappy party.

Does Your Chinese Tom Tom Rattle?

If so, here is a way to stop it. Of course you know the rattle is caused by a wire "spring" tacked to the inside of the shell by the Chinese workmen. It is not advisable to remove even a portion of the tacks that hold the head, because they cannot be replaced in a manner that will regain the former head tension and tone. However, it does not damage the tone or the instrument to bore an inch and a half diameter hole in the shell. When this is done it is an easy matter to reach in with long nose pliers, or even a hook made from a piece of stiff wire, and pull the spring thru the hole. A jerk will do the rest. The hole may be left as is or patched with a wood or cork plug, then painted.

The Roll in Broadcasting

Drums are coming over the air much better these days. However, the snare drum roll is far from perfect. A long roll when played at all forte "mushes" the other instruments and destroys all "color." May we suggest that radio drummers go easy on the roll, especially in modern bands. And it sounds better when played softly in concert, band and orchestra numbers.

Answers to Questions Which Appeared in No. 18 Drum Topics Page 12

1—The flam "thickens" quarter, eighth and sixteenth notes. In other words, it gives character and balance to monotones of the drum that would otherwise sound thin.

2—Nickel rusts more readily when applied to iron and steel because of the porous nature of these metals, which absorb dampness and form a corrosion peculiar to these metals. Brass and copper are not subject to this form of corrosion.

3—The triangle note fits acceptably in any key in which the orchestra or band might be playing because of the great multiplicity of tones which are forthcoming, and also because of its extremely high pitch.

4—The word "tympani" originated from the latin "tympanum," meaning the membrane in the ear. "Tympano" is singular and "Tympani" is plural.

5—Chimes often sound out of tune when standing close to them because some one or two of the multiplicity of tones are heard more plainly by the ear, instead of the fourth tone which is the fundamental and which is heard more plainly at a distance.

6—White heads are not practical on tympani because they are not as elastic and, therefore, will not continue vibrating in order to sustain the tone as long as the transparent heads.

7—A Turkish cymbal is cast from molten metal.

8—Drum heads contract and expand with atmospheric changes because of the peculiar effect which dampness and dryness have upon the nature of the skin, which is fibrous.

9—The sheep furnishes the material from which gut snares are made—not the cat, as is commonly supposed.

10—A Chinese wood block may be prevented from checking provided it receives a coat of shellac shortly after it is imported into this country. Blocks should receive a coat of shellac every few months thereafter.

11—A drum stick warps principally because after it is turned from the dowel the core grain of the wood is no longer held in place by the greater amount of wood formerly surrounding it. In other words, when the stick was nothing more than a twig during its growth, it perhaps formed a tendency to bend one way or another. When it grew larger the center was surrounded by a great amount of wood, which overcame the natural tendency. Therefore, when this wood is released in the cutting the center of the stick again follows its original strain. The warping sometimes does not show up until several weeks after the stick is manufactured.

12—The shell of a Chinese Tom Tom is constructed of several blocks cut to form a circle. These are held in place by paper while the heads are tacked on. When the Tom Toms are transported to another climate these blocks of wood shrink and tear the paper.

13—A transparent drum head is the hide in its natural state, meaning that it has been carried thru the process of manufacture without damaging the fibres. A white head is made by stretching the skin in a scientific way during its manufacture.

14—When the tone goes "dead" in a temple block it means that the lips of the block are touching each other. Do not try to pry the lips apart, else the block will break. Simply run a saw cut between the lips to separate them and the tone will wholly be renewed.

15—Vibraphone fans should revolve to produce from four to six pulsations per second—no faster.

16—The word "xylophone" originated from the Greek "xylo" (meaning wood) and "phone" (meaning sound).

17—It is commonly accepted that a bass drum should be tuned to G for both concert, orchestra and band playing.

18—Some drums "feel" easier than others (meaning that they play easier) simply because of an even texture in the heads and particularly so because the head is tensioned evenly all the way around.

19—The reason a heavy drum stick is more practical than a light one is because the rebound is greater, caused by the weight of the stick, and a fair amount of rebound eliminates the necessity of lifting the stick.

20—The real advantage of the Floating Head principle in drum construction is that there is no sharp bend in the head where it passes over the edge of the shell. The Leedy Floating Head slopes away from the shell on a slant, therefore tensions not only easier, but makes it possible to tension the head more evenly.

Chauncey Brown and Harold McDonald

Chauncey Brown Harold McDonald

If Drummers who have never visited the studios where sound pictures are made, could do so, they would be greatly surprised at the vast amount of special instruments and paraphernalia which are used in this branch of the business. At the Paramount Studios in Hollywood there is a large room with bins, shelves, drawers and pegs which house over two thousand "effects." These are in charge of Chauncey Brown, a former New York Drummer of national reputation. His work as sound effect expert and supervisor of Paramount Sound Pictures is a big job. He has a private office with a stenographer, and two men to assist in directing same. When you hear a West Coast Paramount sound picture it is Chauncey Brown who doped out the effects and executed them.

HAROLD McDONALD is official Drummer, Tympanist and Xylophone Soloist at this same studio. Every one in the biz either knows of or has met Mac because of his long association with Paul Whiteman. However, not many know that playing for sound pictures is quite a different job than either concert, dance or theatre work. It's a knack of its own and requires considerable skill in order to cut down "play-overs" to a minimum. Mac has been "woodshedding" for the past three years and is now one of the best of Xylophonists. Listen for these two wizards when you view a Paramount Photoplay.

The "Hollow Sizzle"

By Lee S. Herr, Ashland, Ky.

Obtain a large cocoanut—cut off one-third and remove contents. Hold under edge of cymbal and move to and fro while playing syncopated stick beats. The edge of cymbal "sizzling" on the edge of the hollow cocoanut produces a fine effect in forte hot numbers. The cocoanut amplifies the tone of the cymbal. A fibre cylinder 5" x 10" may be used in place of the cocoanut.

Well, that's that! Hope you liked this issue. Write us whenever you feel inclined or have any Drum subjects in mind. We are ever at your service.

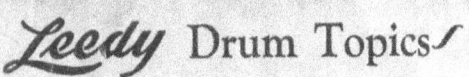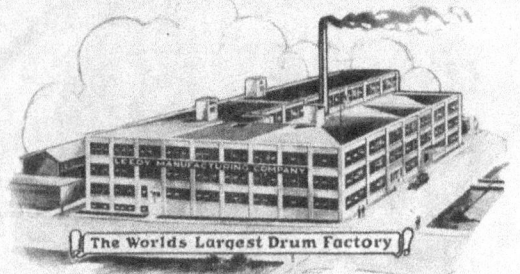

Leedy Drum Topics Issue 20

Brilliant as the Street They're Named for

Drummers have long known just what they desired in snare drum performance. They have had definite ideals. Many could describe the several requisites in detail, but science and invention had a difficult time placing them all together in one Drum. Progress has won at last and now Leedy has produced an instrument that actually meets every demand that both "old timers" and "modern" players have been requesting and hoping for. This achievement has been accomplished by new and practical construction—construction that is revolutionary in design, yet based on scientific facts, not theories. There is sound reasoning embodied in each unit of this new Drum. We know that once the discriminating Drummer has investigated he will be convinced that he has found the one Drum that has not only the tone he has dreamed of, but also one that really makes his work a pleasure because of its easy playing and sensitive qualities. You can expect the "Broadway" to out-perform all past models in every requirement. It is all we claim. A genuine revelation in the Drum World.

The Leedy "Broadway" is more than a New Drum. It is a means by which the Drummer can play a better job with much grater ease. His leader and the other musicians of the band or orchestra will quickly recognize the very tone they have wanted to come from the Drum section. The public will also take notice, for even those untrained in music will hear that clear, penetrating snap that fits whether the tune be "standard" or "modern."

The New "Broadway" is shown above in all metal shell with the three different snare assemblies. It is also available in Leedy "Full Dress" finishes and with solid mahogany shell. For prices and full details see the new Leedy catalog "S".

Leedy — World's Finest Drummers' Instruments — Leedy

COPYRIGHT 1930, LEEDY MFG. CO., ELKHART, IND.

 *The Exclusive Drummers' Paper*

EDWIN FRANKO GOLDMAN
Makes an Important Statement on Cymbals
Addressed to School and Professional Band Leaders

Every drummer knows that there are band leaders who understand and realize the importance of the drum section; also that there are others who look upon the percussion department as a necessary evil and place it in the back of their minds, musically speaking—just as they place it at the back of the band, "geographically" speaking. Edwin Franko Goldman, Sousa, the late Victor Herbert, Capt. Taylor Branson, of the U. S. Marine Band, Paul Whiteman, Capt. Charles O'Neill, Director of Music, Band of the Royal 22nd Regiment, Quebec, Canada; Harold Bachman of the Million Dollar Band, Arthur Pryor and other famous leaders are NOT in the latter class; in fact they are very much the opposite and all of them look upon drummers and drummers' instruments with equal importance as any other section of their organization. From time to time we have heard from these great musicians high praise of individual drummers and their constructive criticism has been one of the chief reasons for the progress and high place the drummer now holds in all things musical.

Sousa has on many occasions made strong public utterances in praise of Gus Helmecke, Howard Goulden, Frank Holt, Frank Snow, Joe Green and others who have made up his percussion division.

And now comes a most interesting and constructive statement from one of the most interesting and wonderful of band leaders the world over—Edwin Franko Goldman, conductor of the famous Goldman Band, New York City, whom—if you have not seen wielding the baton in person—you have at least heard with his famous organization over the radio during recent years. Mr. Goldman is not only a great musician, a great showman, a great composer and a great conductor, but also is recognized as one of the foremost critics of instruments, compositions, and musicians themselves; therefore his remarks concerning cymbals in the band should be taken seriously by every musician.

During a recent personal talk with Geo. H. Way, of the Leedy Mfg. Co., Mr. Goldman laid great stress on the question of cymbals. He, with John Philip Sousa, Capt. Charles O'Neill, Harold Bachman, Victor Grabel, Jay W. Fay, Capt. Taylor Branson and A. Austin Harding, had just finished judging the forty-two high school bands in the National High School Band Contest held at Flint, Mich., May 22nd, 23rd and 24th of this year. Mr. Goldman stated in part as follows:

"... I certainly wish there was some way of impressing both the school and professional band leaders, also the school and professional musicians, drummers and otherwise, with the great importance of cymbals. They can actually make or break a composition. No matter how well a beautiful composition may be rendered by the skillful playing of the clarinets, cornets, trombones, horns and other instruments, the entire musical effect can be murdered with one beat of a pair of inferior cymbals. I am going to recommend in my report to the executives of the National High School Band Association that they plead in all seriousness with the leaders of all bands to study the cymbal question and equip themselves with the best it is possible to obtain. And I hope that the manufacturers will get behind this movement and give it the consideration it deserves, not from a selling standpoint, but from a musical one."

The above is an important statement and should be accepted and written into the annals of musical history as official. No one is better qualified to voice an opinion on such a subject than Mr. Goldman, and there can be no denials or arguments as to its truth. Drummers and cymbal players who own their instruments should realize that they are boosting their own game by owning the best. Organizations that purchase through one individual, or even a committee, should realize that cymbals are just as important to their band as first-class cornets, bassoons or tubas; and should always remember Mr. Goldman's statement that the finest band music may be ruined with poor quality cymbals.

What constitutes the proper cymbal effect in bands? Many things. Of course a fourteen-year-old boy or girl cannot swing a 16 or 18-inch pair of heavy Turkish type cymbals. But it is not the size or even the thickness of cymbals that always determines their tone . . . it is the quality of the model. We will not go into all the whys and wherefores of the cymbal question in this article, but we would like to state that the Leedy Mfg. Co. is ever willing and ready to advise and help in selecting special pairs for either the school or professional band. Write us on the question—state the age of your player and the number of pieces in the organization—and we will go into detail and work with you in a manner which we feel sure will bring results and please such judges as Edwin Franko Goldman, which, in turn, will not only bring you higher marks in contests, but raise the standard of your band wherever it may be playing.

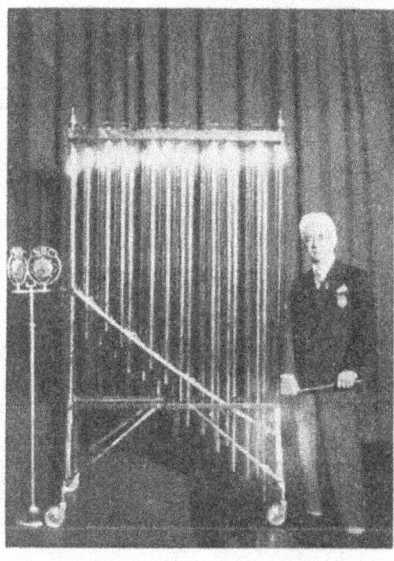

Edwin Franko Goldman

The famous leader of Goldman's Band says, here, a few words about cymbals in particular and percussion sections in general.

For Drummers Who Care

Leedy Drum Topics

If you can control the open beats you can control the closed ones.

Rogers O. Dalton

"I consider Leedy Drum Topics one of the most interesting things of the day for the modern drummer, and I anxiously await each issue." That's the fine compliment we had recently from Rogers O. Dalton, and we will return the compliment by letting you in on the fact that Dalton is one of the finest drummers in his section of the country. He has played Loew's State Theatre, Nashville, Tenn., for the last ten years.
—*Photo Courtesy Melody Music Shop, Memphis, Tenn.*

Reuben Lawson (right) conductor of the Cincinnati "Zoo" Symphony Orchestra talking things over with George J. Carey after a recent concert at the Cincinnati Zoo at which George was the guest soloist with his Leedy xylophone. Conductor Lawson is a sincere endorser of Leedy percussion equipment and George Carey, of course, is a Leedy user and booster from "way back."

A Fine Sizzle Effect

A fine sizzle effect can be produced by using a pair of No. 30E Leedy Finger Cymbals. Hold one loosely on each side of Turkish cymbal and alternate with clashing the cymbals together away from the Turkish, or socking them with the Turkish cymbal between. A great variety of effects are possible with this combination.

$2.00 award to
Richard Jacobsen,
Plentywood, Montana.

"Why didn't you walk home from that auto ride last night, daughter?"
"We went too far, mamma."

Here's a Saving Stunt

Do you need a new Bass Drum, Snare Drum, pair of Tympani or a fine up-to-date xylophone? Are you hesitating to complete your outfit or replace some out-of-date instrument because of the cost? Perhaps you can't spare the cash just now. Well, here's a way to get a start. Procure a little tin box or similar container. Place it in your dresser drawer and every night when retiring place all your loose pennies, nickels, dimes and quarters in the box. You'll be surprised at the short time it will take to save enough for the first payment on that new instrument you need. It piles up fast this way and you never miss it. Start tonight.

John T. Blizzard

Although John Thomas Blizzard, of Bradford, Ohio, is only 13 years old, he already has a long record as an accomplished xylophonist. Here's just a part of it: five years with the Greenville, Ohio, City Concert Band; five years with the Bradford High School Band and Orchestra; three years with Brubaker's Dance Band; one summer with the J. W. Wainwright Band at Oliver Lake, Ind. He has played under such famous directors as Prof. Sutphen, of Toledo, Ohio, John Philip Sousa, and Bachman of "The Million Dollar Band." Besides all of his other accomplishments, John has earned a scholarship at the New York Academy, Cornwall-On-The-Hudson, for his service in the Cadet Band. We offer him as the prize 13-year-old xylophonist of the country. Any contenders?

Dick Ulm

"Ace and I are all for Leedy equipment. At present I am using Leedy drums, chimes, song bells, tympani and vibraphone." That's the statement of Dick Ulm, famous drummer with Ace Brigode and His Virginians. Dick is one of the snappiest boys in the business. He has held his berth with Ace Brigode for nearly four years, and you've got to be right up and at 'em all the time to do that.

Leedy — World's Finest Drummers' Instruments — **Leedy**

The Exclusive Drummers' Paper

There are two kinds of success. One is of the very rare kind that comes to the man who has the power to do what no one else has the power to do. That is genius. Only a very limited amount of the success of life comes to persons possessing genius. The average man who wins what we call a great success is not a genius. He is a man who has merely ordinary qualities, but who has developed them to a more than ordinary degree.
—*Theodore Roosevelt.*

Pete Sawkins

(L. to R.) Hyman Charnisky, division musical supervisor for Publix, Pete Sawkins, drummer, and Jimmie Allard, conductor, as they appeared recently on the stage of the Palace Theatre, Dallas, Texas. Pete has played four years with Publix and has enjoyed great popularity especially with his Vibraphone which he uses with special arrangements of his own. He writes, "I have the three octave set and I find it more practical in playing solos than the two and a half octave, as you can get a beautiful organ effect on the lower octave by using fast vibrato."

J. D. Powell, Jr.

J. D. Powell, Jr., has been drummer with Eddie Miles Orchestra, of Birmingham, Ala., for the past two years. Study the wire brush effect, shown below, of which Powell is the author, and you will realize that J. D. is one drummer who is right on his toes striving to improve himself all of the time. He says that he has been using Leedy drums for the past five years and is completely satisfied.

The Tea Tray Tone

An ordinary large size tin tea tray (such as are sold at the five and ten cent stores) turned upside down on the large tympani head tuned to F or G gives an entirely different quality of tone to the instrument. Roll and accent on the head in the usual manner. Experiment by placing different weights on the tray and placing tray at different distances from the point of contact of the sticks. Also good effect for battle scenes and explosions.

Keeping Up With the Railroads

The Real Dope On Crossing Whistles.

Notice: organists, drummers and vitamen artists! How many of the foregoing know how to correctly reproduce the whistle of a locomotive approaching a crossing? If you have a locomotive whistle on organ or in drummer's traps and have a scene of a train about to cross an intersection and blowing its whistle, how would you imitate it? You say by giving two long and two short blasts like this —— —— — —; wrong, the railroads have changed in the last year and it is now one long, two short and a long, like this —— — — ——. If you do not believe me, drive out in the country where you find a railroad and wait for a train to come along (not on the track, but near it). You, not the train.

I cannot say I like the new signals, as being used to the two long and two short all my life I cannot feature the change.—*Overture.*

A Wire Brush Effect

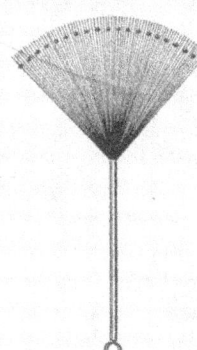

Take a pair of wire brushes and forty (40) small brass beads, not quite as big as green peas, obtainable at any 10c store. Put twenty (20) to the brush, evenly separated by putting wire through hole and bending. Some nice effects can be gotten on drum, tom tom or cymbal. See sketch at left.

$2.00 award to J. D. Powell, Jr., 7317 First Ave. Birmingham, Ala.

More Truth Than Poetry

My sweetheart told me that as soon as we were married, I could have a brand new set of vibraphones, xylophones, pedal tympani and chimes.

Well, we have been married two years, and all I've got so far is the catalogue.
—*Percussionist.*

Leedy — For Drummers Who Care — *Leedy*

Page Five

Leedy Drum Topics

Rudy Van Gelder

Drum and Xylophone Teachers, Attention

If the names and addresses of every one of your pupils are not on our mailing list to receive DRUM TOPICS, we earnestly request you to send them to us at once. Successful teachers know that a pupil who lacks interest is a hard one to teach and one who is not likely to become a great success as a percussionist. Those same teachers have also told us that DRUM TOPICS does a lot to keep their pupils interested. DRUM TOPICS will keep your pupils posted on all the latest tricks of the trade. It will keep them informed about facts and fancies, things and people in the world of drums and drummers. This is just what the doctor ordered to keep pupils up on their toes and striving to do their best all of the time.

Better sit right down now and make a list of the names and addresses of all of your pupils and send the list in to us. We'll see that every single one of the names that you send us is put on the mailing list to receive a copy of DRUM TOPICS regularly.

Somebody has said that Jersey City, N. J., isn't a place at all, that it's just a vaudeville gag! Be that as it may, the folks down in Jersey City have at least one good thing to be proud of, and that is Rudy Van Gelder, percussionist at the Stanley Theatre. He is one of the finest percussion artists in the East; always right up-to-the-minute in his playing and sometimes a jump or two ahead of most of the boys. He has a complete Leedy outfit including the "Rollaway Trap Console."

It must be fun to be a breeze
And blow about the silk-clad knees;
But still, on second thought, no, no—
A breeze can't say where it shall blow
And many knees, without a doubt,
Are nothing much to blow about.
—*Life.*

The drummer who "blends into the picture" and meets the ideas of his leader will profit to a far greater extent than the drummer who tries to force the whole band to his style.

Mrs. Catherine Fry

Harry A. Fifield
(Pictured at Right)

Get that "action" pose Harry A. Fifield, of Bradenton, Fla., always has his eye right on the leader. That fact coupled with his complete Leedy outfit makes him an A-No. 1 drummer. He is percussionist of the Bradenton High School Philharmonic Orchestra which won recognition all through the East and South for its rendition of "Second Hungarian Rhapsody," at the Florida State Music Contest, Tampa, 1928. Besides his orchestra work, Harry plays with the Elk's Drum and Bugle Corps. He at one time was a student of Tom Glenicke, of Chicago, who is well-known to the readers of *Topics*.

Mrs. Catherine Fry, of Girard, O., has a record of which anyone might well be proud. She is now 63 years old and did not start to learn drums until she was 62. Now, after a little more than a year's instruction under Ralph Perkins, drummer at the Keith Theatre, Youngstown, O., she is an accomplished drummer. Mrs. Fry says that she has had a lifelong desire to learn music, but found no opportunity to do so until she was 56 years old. Even with this late start she has accomplished much and learned to play a number of other instruments besides drums. She has received many compliments on the manner in which she performs on her Leedy outfit.

Leedy World's Finest Drummers' Instruments **Leedy**

The Exclusive Drummers' Paper

"The Vibraphone Step"

Here's the famous Eddie Peabody doing what he calls the "Vibraphone Step," while Harry Blanchard plays the first Vibraphone ever to be heard in the West. This is a feature of Peabody's act at the Metropolitan Theatre, Los Angeles. Harry Blanchard is one of the finest drummers on the Pacific Coast. Besides, playing with Peabody's act, he drums at the "Pig-N-Whistle Cafe," Hollywood. Blanchard's 18 years of drumming show a specialization of popular orchestra work, yet he has a thorough foundation of legitimate work. In other words he is a dance drummer, well-schooled and able to play anything from symphony to jazz.

The New Leedy "Two-Way" Practice Pad

Improve Your Playing With This New Idea in Practice Pads

A new idea in Practice Pads. Has two playing surfaces, one for loud and one for soft playing. Both are inclined to the proper angle. Pad is heavy and will not creep under strong beating. The soft playing side has a large piece of ¼" thick pure gum rubber cemented and tacked to the block, on which the lightest taps are audible and yet the heaviest blows will not disturb others close by. This rubber is of just the right thickness and resiliency to give true drum action to the sticks. The loud playing side consists of thick sheet fibre cemented to the block, a 2½" hole cut in the center of the block, the fibre covering same. This gives the sticks a natural rebound and produces a very loud staccato tone. Simply turn block over for either playing surface. A wonderful pad for developing technique. Every drummer should own one—fine for Drum Corps class practice.

Ella: "My goodness, Sue—you're all black and blue. Does your husband beat you?"

Sue: "Well, not exactly, dearie, but he does play 'hot breaks' on me in his sleep."

Famous Fairy Stories

"Yessir, same heads for over ten years."

"Now Benson says to me: You're the greatest drummer I ever had."

"Oh, pay me when you get the dough."

"This cymbal set me back seventy-five bucks."

"Say, I've got more work than I can handle."

"No, my drum never gets loose in damp weather."

"Never took a lesson in my life—and don't need any."

"Midnight Drummers' Club Meeting, but I'll hurry home."

"I'm the guy that invented the 'lectric drum heater."

"Boy, this band can't get along without me."

"Won a hundred smackers at craps last night."

"Take this tip—you can't lose."

"This is my last year in the business."

"Sure, all of Whiteman's boys smoke 'Old Golds'."

Pep and plenty of it—that's the secret of the success of Ned Hockensmith, of Parkersburg, W. Va. Ned is now playing with the Stewart-Warner Radio Band and getting a big hand from the dial fans. Before getting into radio work he had a dance band of his own for two years and has a long drumistic record before that. Ned plans to buy a new Leedy Vibraphone in the near future.

Rolling, rolling, with all your might and main;
It's dozens of tunes you'll have to go
'Fore dawn comes up again.
Jazzing, jazzing, through many a "hot lick" strain;
It's dozens of tunes you'll have to go
Ere the "jack" is paid again.

Leedy   **For Drummers Who Care**   *Leedy*

Leedy Drum Topics

Do You Deserve It?

IS THERE any reason why your services should be in continual demand?

Do you play better than other Drummers? Do you introduce any outstanding novelties? Have you originality? How do you hold your present position?

If you have convincing answers to these questions you need never fear of being out of a job.

Only by looking upon your job through the eyes of a business man can you hope to climb to or remain on the top.

Jerry Bodganoff

"I'm sure a Leedy booster and user from spur to cymbal holder." That's the big hand we received recently from Jerry Bogdanoff, now playing at Euclid Beach Park, Cleveland. We certainly are proud to receive such a wonderful endorsement from Jerry because he is one of the finst drummers in the business today. A list of engagements he has filled sounds like a directory of what's what in the high-class amusement world. Here are just a few of them: Miami, (Fla.) Jockey Club; Sea Food House, Miami Beach Fla.; Wafford Hotel, Miami, Fla.; Rendezvous Cafe, Chicago; Hotel Statler, Cleveland, Cinderella Ball, N. Y. C. Jerry has a complete Leedy Marine Pearl outfit including snare drum, bass drum, pedal tymps, Vibraphone and chimes.

Hubert B. Williams

Tune in on WENR, Chicago, sometime, folks, and get a load of Hubert B. Williams, drummer with the Frank Westphal orchestra. Williams is a tympani pupil of the famous Art Layfield and he has developed some clever effects of his own which are all to the good. This boy has traveled in "Big Time."

Jeannette Loff

Jeannette Loff of movie fame isn't a drummer and therefore, hasn't any right in The Exclusive Drummers' Paper, but we're taking a chance that none of our drummer readers will object. If you will examine the picture closely, you will see that the young lady is playing a Leedy Vibraphone. Yes, that's it right in front of her. Oooh! them eyes.

John L. Clem, now seventy-eight years old, was a heroic Drummer in the Union forces at the Battle of Chickamauga.

Yes, there is art in everything, even to drinking liquor. In this case the "art" is in knowing when to quit.

Leedy — World's Finest Drummers' Instruments — **Leedy**

The Exclusive Drummers' Paper

Do Not Overlook the Advantages of These Fine Spurs

Leedy Disappearing Spurs. Note that "spikes" point straight downward, passing through strong steel casting. This principle prevents creeping of drum. Spikes are adjustable for length without disturbing hoop clamp and may be left on hoop when in transit.

Leedy Catalog "S"
Page 55, No. 7100
Per Pair — $1.50

Bass Drum Beats for Eighth and Quarter Notes

A Drummer writes—"Please explain how you would play the two following measures and make them sound any different on a bass drum":

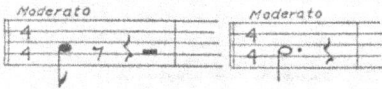

"I cannot see what difference it makes whether a note is a dotted half or an eighth, so long as it is followed by a rest."

To which we replied in part as follows:

"We believe there is some distinction that can be made in executing eighth and half notes, yet we have no concrete authority to offer. We do not think the subject has been discussed in any instruction book for drums, possibly because the majority of instructors specialize more in the rudiments for snare drumming—and possibly because they do not place much importance on bass drum playing. Our opinion is that a good bass drummer is every bit as important as a good snare drummer, and some band directors consider the bass drummer the feature of the entire band.

"We have talked to two or three of the leading bass drummers and find that they do make a distinction on those small points about which you are anxious to learn. As you know, bass drums are never struck on dead center except for special effects. If all beats were played on dead center, the resultant notes would be of the same duration, each note being a dull thud with no ringing boom. Because a bass drummer's main idea in the majority of cases is to produce a resonant tone, he uses glancing blows and strikes off the dead center. These notes are all more or less sustained, and their volume is controlled by the weight of the beat.

"Most drummers, in order to produce one-eighth notes, will immediately after striking the drum cut off the tone and vibration by placing their hands on the head. These cut-off notes make a great difference in bass drumming. Cutting off these notes and giving them their proper duration is just as important as expression and phrasing in the brass instruments. A quarter or an eighth note at the end of a piece when cut off provides the entire band with a staccato ending that was intended by the composer. Sousa's bass drummer does this; also Frank Snow, with Herbert Clark's Municipal Band of Long Beach, Calif. Mr. Snow does a great deal of this type of muffling, and in the opinion of the writer, it makes his playing stand out much better than it would if he played the notes the same.

"You might try this idea of muffling quick cut-off beats with your hand or the ball of the bass drum stick—we are sure you will like the effect."

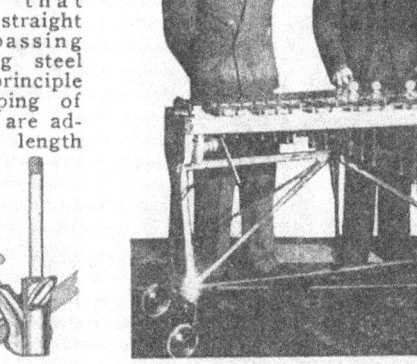

Henry J. Hammond

A well-known, Memphis, Tenn., pair, Dave Harmon, (left) director Dave Harmon's Orchestra, and his drummer, Henry J. Hammond—Henry J. has had his Vibraphone for about a year now and he wrote the other day to tell us that he's tickled to death with it, and believe us, we're certainly tickled that he's tickled, making it a rather ticklish proposition all around. Hammond has played with such great outfits as Benny Meroff's Orchestra and Lloyd I. Bach Entertainers.

IF—An Ode to Drummers

(Reprinted from RHYTHM—Popular English Musical Journal)
With most fervent apologies to Rudyard Kipling.

If you can keep your beat whilst all about you
Are losing theirs and blaming it on you,
If you can put a cymbal break in when the saxes
Miss their "pick-up" and the chords are "blue",
If the brass's intonation isn't all it might be,
And you clap them on the back and swear it's true,
If when the banjo player says you're gaining tempo
You agree with him and murmur, "Yes, how true,"
You'll be a (popular) man, my son.

If your clothes fit you like they do a tailor's dummy,
And your shirts and collars are white as driven snow,
If your patent shoes ne'er show the lack of polish
And your tie is neatly tied into a bow,
If your trousers have a crease that you could cut with,
And your hair is smooth and neat like Catesby's lino,
If you can keep your drums like showroom models,
With Elbow Grease and Vim and lots of Brasso,
You'll be worth looking at, my son.

If you know all your flams and paradiddles,
And drags and roughs and rolls and "daddy-mummy,"
If you can write a chorus for the xylo,
With harmonies not altogether rummy,
If you can coax your cymbal into rhythm,
And make your breaks staccato, clean, not gummy,
If your technique on the tymps is all it should be,
And your tuning not give rise to pains inside the tummy,
You'll be worth listening to, my son.

Photos, etc., for Drum Topics are coming in faster than we can use them. The only fair procedure on our part is to use this material in turn of its arrival, so if yours does not appear as quickly as you think it should please understand the reason. All photos, etc., will be published in their turn.

—*Editor—Drum Topics.*

The trouble with some saxophone players is that they memorize the part, then lose their heads.

For Drummers Who Care

Leedy Drum Topics

Fred E. Cooley, Jr.

Fred E. Cooley, Jr., (at the xylophone) and his instructor, John B. Quick, of Phoenix, Arizona. When it comes to drums, xylophones and tymps, Cooley is what is known as a "natural." He just eats 'em up. Here's what instructor Quick has to say about his pupil: "I have put this lad through the Gardner Method of drums and tympani, also the Green Method of xylophone. At the present time he is studying xylo and harmony with me. He has been my pupil for the past four and a half years, and he has been a real student. He always comes with a perfect lesson. Fred is one of those rare students that a teacher likes to find but seldom does. Teaching a lad of his calibre is not an effort. It's a pleasure. Fred has recently accepted the drummer's position at the Columbia Theatre, here, and his splendid work put him across with a BANG from the start!"

Talkies Need Backing of Flesh and Blood Performers

Strong Indications That Sound Houses Will Welcome Back Orchestras and Acts are in the Air

A recent issue of *Variety* says, "Show business is hearing a distinct call from its variety stages for 'flash' entertainment in support of the large majority of its talkers for next season.

"This call has reached the largest circuits general operators and they are listening."

The article goes on to say, "A previous estimate of 1,500 theatres playing acts by November 1, is now claimed to be the most conservative of many variety showmen."

In an effort to find out just how the big outfits in talkie business feel about the situation *Drum Topics* communicated with Publix Paramount Corporation. Although they would make no official statement as to what they believe the future of the sound houses in regard to live performers to be, they did say that they have installed orchestras in nine of their sound houses in various parts of the country

This does not indicate any immediate tremendous swing back to the pre-talkie basis, it does show, however, that the talkie houses are finding out that it is impossible to do without the help of living muscans and other performers. It shows that the situation will adjust itself as soon as the public taste in the matter of talkies and performers has reached a definite level.

Ralph L. Smith, Jr.

Ralph L. Smith, Jr., is a youngster who should be a world-beater some day. He is only eight years old and has studied drums for less than two years, but already knows all the rudiments from single drag to paradiddle and plays them like a master. His home is in Council Bluffs, Iowa, and one of his proudest achievements is the fact that he has played under Novak, of the Council Bluffs "Little Symphony." He is now studying xylophone and his teacher, George A. Smith, says Ralph shows amazing musical talent and executive ability.

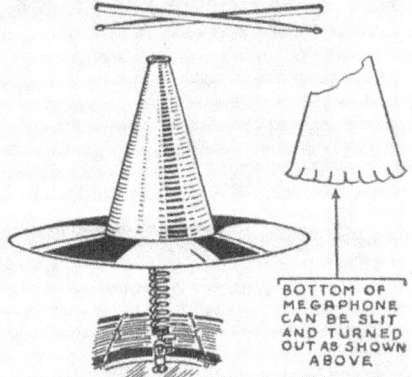

Meg-Cymbal Effect

A novel effect may be obtained by placing an inverted megaphone on top of your cymbal as shown above. This gives a decidedly different tone that is almost Oriental. It is a tone that you will never suspect was in your cymbal.

In the first place you must have either a spring or rod holder. Next, the edge of the meg which rests on the cymbal must be soft in order to eliminate vibration and rattle. The edge may be softened sufficiently simply by bending to and fro. If this is not sufficient, however, make splits about an inch or so high (as shown above) all around the edge of the megaphone. The split sections may then be bent out. If this is done, the megaphone will rest on the top of the cymbal without difficulty providing the cymbal is held fairly steady. Use either a hard felt stick or a regular hickory stick.

$2.00 award to
C. O. Palmer,
Moorhead, Minn.

George F. Cook

"I am Leedy SOLD as is also my teacher," says George F. Cook with Lockman's Dance Orchestra, Columbus, Ind. Earl Davis is George's teacher, and Earl certainly has a pupil of whom he may well be proud. Besides his work with Lockman's, George also drums for the following organizations: Post No. 24, American Legion Band; Columbus Symphony Orchestra and Tabernacle Sunday School Orchestra. He sure takes in a lot of territory.

Leedy — World's Finest Drummers' Instruments — **Leedy**

"The King of Jazz" Features the King of Drums

THE scene above is the "Happy Feet" Number from Universal's newest production, featuring Paul Whiteman and his band. This famous band uses Leedy Drums and Drummer's equipment which you see here holding the center of the stage.

"The King of Jazz" is now being shown in many of America's finest theaters. If you attend you will not only *see* Leedy equipment but you will also *hear* the lively, vibrant tones which stamp Leedy—the "King of Drums."

George W. Marsh, the versatile and talented drummer with Whiteman's Band, recognizes the importance of selecting the best rhythm instruments obtainable. He is an enthusiastic Leedy user. Outstanding professionals have, for years, chosen Leedy Drums, and discriminating amateurs are following their lead.

Every director as well as every drummer will find it decidedly worth while to inspect the Leedy line. The snappy performance and modest prices of the newest models will surprise you. See them at your dealers.

Arrange for a free trial "on the job." Or write us for catalog and details of liberal easy payment plan.

How to Organize a Drum Corps

The school drum corps is gaining in popularity rapidly. Unexcelled for musical training, discipline and improving school spirit. You can easily organize a successful drum corps for your school. Interesting 42-page book, "The Roll-Off," shows how and gives hundreds of practical hints on all phases of drum corps work. We will gladly send you a copy Free, without obligation. Just mail the coupon.

LEEDY MANUFACTURING CO., 503 LEEDY BUILDING
Elkhart, Indiana.

☐ Check here for catalog and full information on Leedy Drums.
☐ Check here for free copy of "The Roll-Off."

Name _____
Address _____
Town _____
State _____

I am ☐ *teacher*, ☐ *student*, ☐ *manager*.
(Please check which.)

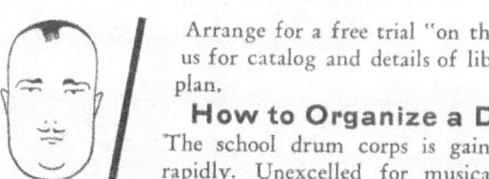

For Drummers Who Care

Leedy Drum Topics

WHEREVER THEY GO LEEDY-EQUIPPED

The Memphis, Tenn., Federation of the Parent-Teachers' Association decided to have a drum corps to represent them and this organization of Leedy equipped youngsters is the great result. There are more than 100 boys in the corps and under the leadership of instructor Frank E. Pole they have been received with enthusiastic applause at every appearance.

Equipped throughout with Leedy Marin bugle corps of the Burt Foster Post No. one of the finest outfits in the East. The has won more prizes than you could easi "civvies" and 40 and 8 cap, is Dr. Joseph in the front row at the extreme left is Jo is James E. Fry, the drum major. The
Joseph B

Quite an imposing looking outfit as you see it here, this corps of Baty Tucker Post, No. 168, of Knoxville, Ia., has added a baker's dozen of new members since this picture was taken and is now bigger and better than ever. These boys expect to furnish tough competition in the American Legion State Contest at Sioux City, and they also promise to be right in the forefront of things at the big Boston Convention. H. E. White is business manager of the outfit and also corps commander. The fellow with the big white shako is L. D. Tucker, the drum major. M. F. Langebartels is secretary-treasurer. H. L. McGraw is drill sergeant. C. F. Like instructs on drums and H. E. White takes care of the bugles in addition to his other duties. C. M. Belknap is also an officer of the corps.

This fine Drum and Bugle corps is the pride of the Southern California Military Academy, Long Beach, California. Capt. O. F. Rominger is instructor of the outfit, and the fine looking lad at the extreme right of the picture is Cadet Captain Tom Welch, the leader of the corps. When the boys of the military academy are "marching as to war" the drum corps furnishes stirring music with its Leedy drums.

Leedy — World's Finest Drummers' Instruments — Leedy

The Exclusive Drummers' Paper

...RUM CORPS WIN FAME AND APPLAUSE

The local contest committee of the 1929 National American Legion Convention at Louisville accorded honorable mention as one of the best marching, playing and uniformed auxiliary corps in attendance to the fine organization pictured below. These young ladies represent the Seventh District Legion Auxiliary. They hail from Indianapolis, Ind., home of the Leedy drum factory, and they are instructed in drumming by Sam C. Rowland, a member of the Leedy organization. All musical selections played by the corps are specially arranged to suit the instrumental sections. The corps play strictly modern music, employing a rank of tenor drums in addition to the usual line-up. Two Scotch bass drums are used. One plays fast snare drum beats and the other uses flash two-stick execution, Scotch style. Officers of the corps are: Mrs. Grace Hinkle, captain; Mrs. Blanch Breedlove, adjutant; Mrs. Mary Ann Long, 1st lieutenant; Mrs. Bernece Payne, drum major; and Mrs. Vivian Hague, Mrs. Tillie Hackney, Mrs. Eddie Munchoff, sergeants; Mrs. Ruth Gilmour, 2nd lieutenant.

...shed Floating Head Street Drums, this drum and ...American Legion, located at McKeesport, Pa., is ...ken part in all civic activities of McKeesport and ...ick at. The modest gentleman in the back row, in ...nager of the corps. The stern looking individual ...n, captain and drillmaster. Directly opposite him ...uy in the second row, center, is none other than ...in—official mascot.

From sunny California comes this great bunch of brass-hatted Legionnaires. If your eyes are good, you can read on the bass drums the fact that they represent Arthur L. Peterson Post, No. 27, of Long Beach. Each year these boys get a little better. The first year that the corps was organized the best they could do was third place in the state championship. The second year out the gang was just two beats behind the winner to grab second honors in the big state event, and in 1929, the third start in the state contest, the boys romped home ahead of 22 other entries to win the California state title. That, we believe, is as steady a record of improvement as has ever come to our attention. Officers of the corps are: Karl B. Morgan, manager; Edward L. Couron, drum major; Walter E. Geisler, drill sergeant; Al Dalot and Larry Hewitt, drum instructors; Maurice Astley, bugle instructor.

The drum corps of Lieut. Lansdale Post, No. 67, Veterans of Foreign Wars of Sacramento, Cal., has a record of which any corps might well be proud. The corps has been organized about five years and takes part in all civic and patriotic doings of the city. They have attended every encampment of the V. F. W. that has been held in California and Nevada and the boys are so enthusiastic about the corps that each one of them gladly pays his own expenses while on these trips. At a recent encampment of the V. F. W., held in San Diego, Lieut. Lansdale Post drum corps carried off a big silver loving cup as second prize in the Drum Corps Contest. James Tharpe is manager of the corps. Other officers are Andrew Chessie, drum major; Sam Bennet, sgt. drummer; and Chas. Borba, leader.

Leedy — For Drummers Who Care — *Leedy*

Page Thirteen

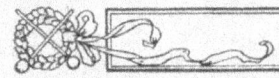 Drum Topics

Improved Floating Head Street Drum

NEW TYPE LAMINATED SHELL MAKES THIS DRUM LIGHTER WEIGHT THAN FORMER MODELS

SEPARATE TENSION

THIS DRUM IS NOW FURNISHED IN 16-INCH HEAD DIAMETER

STICKS AND SLING INCLUDED

Just as the Leedy "Broadway" Model is the Peer of all Band and Orchestra Drums, so this improved street model is the Peer of all Outdoor Drums. It is of the same high grade materials and construction throughout. All parts are carefully assembled to give the finest service demanded by Military Drummers. A wonderful instrument for volume and easy playing qualities. Note the new stronger and finer appearing center supports on the rods—also the new type snare strainer. Square head rods, Hardwhite batter heads, Uka snare heads, silk wire wound snares (gut if desired at no extra charge) and the famous Leedy Floating Head with our 3-ply Spartan shell. It is truly a life-time instrument.

9" x 15" .... No. 3135
12" x 15" .... No. 3136   } **$35**
12" x 16" .... No. 3137

EQUIPPED WITH SILK WIRE WOUND SNARES—GUT IF DESIRED

"Full-Dress" Finishes on Leedy Floating Head Street Drums

MARINE PEARL Shell SPARKLING GOLD Shell BLACK PEARL Shell GREEN PEARL Shell BLACK ONYX Shell RAINBOW PEARL Shell	WITH NOBBY GOLD METAL PARTS	WITH CHROMIUM PLATED METAL PARTS	WITH NICKEL PLATED METAL PARTS
	$25.00 EXTRA	$25.00 EXTRA	$15.00 EXTRA

Black—White—Red—Blue—Yellow—Orange and other DUCO colors on Shell and Wood Hoops—NO EXTRA CHARGE.
SEND SAMPLES OF COLORS TO ASSURE PERFECT MATCH.

Nobby Gold Metal Parts .... $10.00 EXTRA
Chromium Plated Metal Parts .... 10.00 EXTRA

Leedy **World's Finest Drummers' Instruments** *Leedy*

The Exclusive Drummers' Paper

The 26 Rudiments

Very often Drum Topics is asked, "Exactly how many rudiments are there?" Some authorities claim one number and some another. However, 26 seems to be most commonly accepted. So far as we can learn, the rather ambiguous term of "26 Rudiments" grew into prominence by way of the famous old Struble Drum Method which is considered by many to be the standard of all drum instruction. In the Struble book there are 25 preliminary lessons, each taking up one drum rudiment. In addition there is a foot note treating on the single stroke roll, which certainly is important enough to be included with the others, although for some reason Struble did not see fit to definitely include it as a lesson number. Counting the single stroke roll, we arrive at 26 as the number. The following list will acquaint the reader with Struble's 25 regular and one extra rudiment.

1. Long Roll
2. Five Stroke Roll
3. Seven Stroke Roll
4. Nine Stroke Roll
5. Ten Stroke Roll
6. Eleven Stroke Roll
7. Thirteen Stroke Roll
8. Fifteen Stroke Roll.
9. Flam
10. Ruff
11. Single Drag
12. Double Drag
13. Single Ratamacue
14. Double Ratamacue
15. Triple Ratamacue
16. The Flam Accent
17. The Flamacue
18. The Flam Tap
19. Single Paradiddle
20. Double Paradiddle
21. Flam Paradiddle
22. Flam Paradiddle-Diddle
23. Drag Paradiddle No. 1
24. Drag Paradiddle No. 2
25. The nameless strokes given as a lesson and which are used in the Quick Scotch and other quicksteps—consisting of a drag and two eighth notes, sticking L L R L R
26. The single stroke roll mentioned by Struble under lesson No. 1. Bruce & Emmet's Book, another old-time standard work, varies very little on the above, only adding a few flourishes to the fundamental rudiments. Whether we accept Struble or Bruce & Emmet, it is pretty safe to say that any one who can play the above 26 Rudiments is one mighty fine drummer. Can YOU do it?

Editor's Note—Notes kindly supplied by Geo. L. Stone, of Boston, Mass.

Beat the best, because the best beats the rest.—*Leedy.*

Drummers' Paradise

Folks, here's an inside view of drummer's paradise! But that fellow in the glasses is not St. Peter. No, sir, you're wrong again, it's Frank Wolf and he's standing behind the counter of his new, bigger and better drum shop now located at 232 West 48th St., N. Y. C. When you are in New York, don't miss Frank Wolf's Drum Shop. It's "The World's Largest Retail Drum Shop," and comprises five floors all devoted to drumming and the drummer. One floor is occupied by the Karl Glassman School of Drumming and Tympani Playing. This organization is headed by Karl Glassman, himself, one of the country's foremost tympanists and who for many years played under the direction of Walter Damrosch, conductor of the New York Symphony Orchestra.

On the Cover

Fred Grant Lower, Jr., who is pictured together with his director, Henry Theis, on this issue of *Drum Topics*, is one of the biggest men in the business today. In spite of the fact that he has only been in drumming business for about eight years and is still a very young man Lower has already climbed to the top of the profession and bids fair to go even farther. In other words, we predict that Lower will go higher. He is now playing with Henry Theis Orchestra over radio station WLW and participates in some of the biggest radio programs now on the air. Among them are: The Studebaker Champions, Cities Service Hour, Duro Automatics and the Crosley Saturday Knights.

Mr. Lower is shown on the cover with his complete outfit of Leedy equipment which he uses in all of his famous broadcasts. These are the instruments that you are listening to when you hear the percussion parts in the popular radio programs named above.

Drummer Lower is high in his praise of every instrument which is included in his complete Leedy outfit. Director Theis, too, is a strong booster for Leedy.

In addition to playing over the radio, Lower has several times made Victor recordings.

"Sez You!"

Jack Roop, Assistant Sales Manager Leedy Mfg. Co., explains the advantages of the new Leedy Broadway with Dual Snares, to John Bauman, U. S. Army Band (left) and William Keiffer, U. S. Marine Band, while Fred J. Leonberger, president, Leonberger Music Co., Inc., Washington, D. C., looks on with interest.

"Discovery of something old is easier than discovery of something new."—*Harry Emerson Fosdick.*

For Drummers Who Care

Page Fifteen

Leedy Drum Topics

Craig Ferguson
Drummer,
Ringling Bros.
Circus, 1930.

20,410 Beats per Show

Craig Ferguson, circus drummer, has figured his drum mileage per show and he gives you an interesting account of it in the article below.

"Often during my ten years as a concert and circus bass drummer I have wondered just how many times I walloped the old hide during a session. This season I determined to add them up, act by act, including the concert in the ring before the show. The number of beats for each act and number for one complete Big Show grind is listed below. No blacksmith or carpenter can equal that record for two hours and 15 minutes work, and as I have learned to change over to my left hand the result is a well developed pair of arms and muscles. No, I'm not a scrapper—just an endurance Bass Drummer who knows there is no drum equal to a Leedy."

Ring Concert

March	258
Selection	402
Fox Trot	178
Fox Trot	158

Program

March	230
Gallop	436
Elephants	756
Aerial Acts	1724
Sea Lions	252
Wire Acts	406
Riding Act	802
Leitzel	361
Menage	622
Tumbling	541
Seals	1318
High Perch	646
Wire Act	611
Poses	478
Wild West	1605
Aerial Trap	932
Liberty Horse	1166
Clown Horse	220
High Wire	208
Riding Act	1086
Clown Gallop	126
Clown Gallop	304
Acrobat Tumbling	2356
Clown Walk Around	342
Aeriel Act	242
Fox Trot	188
Jumps	472
Liberty	114
Ponies	120
Dogs, Gallops	112
Roman	192
Chariot	216
March	178
Finale	52
	20,410

To be set on a big job does not mean that you no longer need to study and improve. The Doctor or Lawyer can not quit learning simply because he holds a diploma and enjoys a good practice.

"Did you hear about the Scotch drummer on the Fourth of July?"
"I'll bet it's a hot one."
"Yeah—he loaned his pop-gun to his children."

"Hob" Rankin

"I have been bawled out, balled up, held up, held down, hung up, bulldozed, black-jacked, walked on, cheated, squeezed and mooched," says "Hob" Rankin, now enroute with the Bert Melville Co. Well, "Hob" seems to have come up smiling in spite of all the bad treatment he has received, and just between us, he can really do things with his complete Leedy outfit.

Joe Lindenbaum

Joe Lindenbaum and his Orchestra are now playing at the famous Cocoanut Grove of the Breaker's Hotel, Long Beach, Calif. You've got to be good to fill a job like that and Joe and his boys are putting things over in great shape. Joe hails from Danville, Ill., where he learned drums from Al Grabs about 16 years back.

Leedy — **World's Finest Drummers' Instruments** — **Leedy**

The Exclusive Drummers' Paper

The Night Club Murder

In No. 19 Drum Topics a Prize of $10 Was Offered for "Favorite Drummer Stories." Here's the $10 Prize Winning Effort, and it's a Cockeyed Mystery that is Guaranteed to Keep You Guessing and Gasping to the Final Period.

By CLARENCE A. STOUT
Vincennes, Ind.

A curious but ambitious Policeman while scouting for trouble and praying for a "break" that might elevate him from the ranks, came unexpectedly upon two young men. They were standing in front of one of the leading Chicago Loop theatres, discussing something that seemed to be of a sensational nature.

He was startled when he overheard the tall bird with a Menjou moustache telling the little guy in the check cap something that seemed to reveal an undiscovered crime.

After listening to a few sentences, the ambitious Bull became very excited and realized his big break had arrived and he was on the verge of an important arrest which would warrant screaming headlines in the papers. He was anticipating the smile and the slap on the back the Chief would give him when he heard about it—elevated from the ranks—a raise in salary. But this was no time for day dreams. He must act and act quickly. He hid himself behind one of the exit doors and then crept noiselessly behind the box-office until he was only a few feet away from the two conspirators. Using his ears as a dictaphone, he listened breathlessly to the following conversation:

"I've got me a swell looking pippin, now! I got tired beating that other old relic of mine, so I threw her in the basement. This new one of mine has class and looks like a million dollars. I had her at the Night Club last evening for the first time and you should have seen the suckers look her over when the spot was thrown on. Boy, when I got her tight, she sure got snappy. When I started beating on her, you could hear her all over the joint—When intermission came, a fellow wanted to look her over—As I had only a few minutes, I jerked her off the stand and was carrying her to the rest room. I had her under my left arm and in my right hand I was carrying an open pocket knife. She finally worked loose from under my arm and started to fall—I made a grab for her, stumbled and fell on top and plunged the knife through the head. Boy, I was in a jamb, believe me, with only a few minutes to go. But I always prepare for such an emergency—I quickly JERKED THE HEAD OFF—"

The cop had heard enough. He could restrain himself no longer. "Stick 'em up, you're under arrest," he yelled. "My God, man, what did you do with the body?"

The tall bird looked up in amazement—"The body? What are you talking about?"

"Why, the woman you bumped off", the cop shot back. "Wasn't you giving this bozo the low down on murdering a woman last night?"

"MURDERING A WOMAN? Hell No! I was telling Pete about my new 'Broadway' drum."

A Good Tom Tom Stunt

Cut a hole 2½ inches in diameter in one head of 10-inch Chinese Tom Tom. Beating on opposite head makes peculiar tone and eliminates ring. The hole permits removal of spring on inside that causes rattling.

$2.00 award to
Leo McCarty,
Los Angeles, Calif.

Freddie Sanborn

Recently featured on Broadway with Schubert's "A Night In Venice," Freddie Sanborn is one of the finest and most famous drummers in the country. He is one of the pioneers of xylophone ensemble playing in the style now employed by most radio artists. Strange to say, however, Freddie has never done any broadcasting, having always been too busy with the show business and vaudeville engagements. He considers xylophone the coming instrument and thinks it will never lose popularity either as a solo instrument or in ensemble playing.

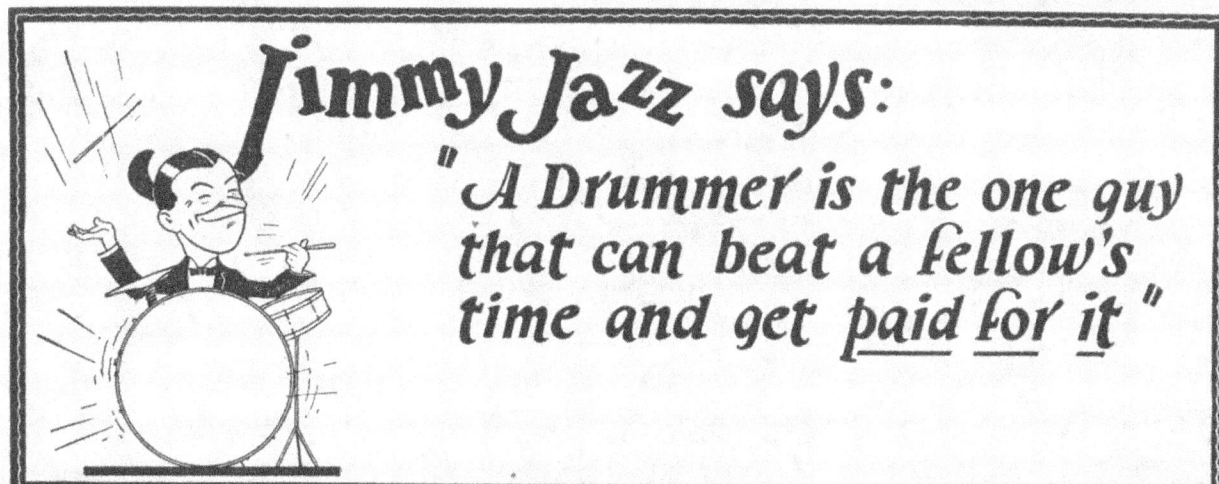

For Drummers Who Care

Leedy Drum Topics

Ashley Paige

Ashley Paige, the celebrated vaudeville xylophonist, is seen above, cooling down at his home, Onset, Mass., after a hot season on the stage. If our readers have ever heard Ashley do his stuff, they will not wonder that he finds swimming suits in season both in "The good old summer time" and "The good old winter time." Paige is one of the hottest solo performers on xylophone that has been seen in these parts for some time back. His six-hammer stuff is guaranteed to get a rise out of the toughest audience, and in spite of the rumored unpopularity of xylophone singles, they never fail to yell for more when young Mr. Paige does his stuff.

Drawn by Herbert F. Palmer, Drummer with "Al's Capitol Gang" at the Capitol Theatre, Jackson, Mich. Photo of Palmer appeared in No. 18 Drum Topics.

Dance drummers are often judged by the last eight bars.

Some Notes About Resonators

Xylophone and Marimba players often ask, "Why don't you make resonators larger and longer—wouldn't they give more tone?" The answer is, "No." Because the air column encased by the tube must be of an exact size according to the pitch of the bar. The tone is wholly in the bar when energised—there is no tone in the resonator. When struck, the bar gives forth a certain note. This note sends out a definite wave length. The resonator, being of the proper diameter and length to be in sympathy with the bar's vibration rate, simply acts as a booster for this vibration wave. In other words, the resonator harnesses the wave. The rules of cubical contents do not in any way govern the pitch of a resonator. It is the area and length in proper proportion. As an illustration, if a resonator 1" in diameter by 6" long is responsive to a certain tone, another tube 2" in diameter by about 5¾" long will be in unison with the same tone; yet it contains nearly four times as much air as the 1" x 6" size. Dummy resonators can be made in almost any size and shape for appearance sake, but the actual air column must be designed with the diameter and lengths in the correct proportions.

A More Realistic Horse Neigh

Secure a piece of brass tubing 12" long. Bore three holes at equal distances apart around one end, ¼" from edge. Screw to wooden tube of Allen Duck Quack. Makes deep, hollow and much louder sound when hands are cupped over end in usual manner. Size of tube should be just right to allow it to slip half way up on tapered end of duck quack.

Jazz serves primitive rhythm on a civilized platter.

Leedy — World's Finest Drummers' Instruments — **Leedy**

The Exclusive Drummers' Paper

A Handy Arrangement for Cymbals

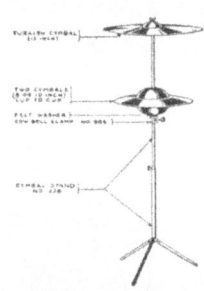

"I have always preferred to have as many of my cymbal effects as possible on the left side of my snare drum. The arrangement that I now use may be made up of Leedy parts, as follows: one Leedy cymbal stand, No. 33B; one cow bell clamp, No. 984; one Turkish crash cymbal; and two American brass cymbals of equal size. The cow bell clamp is used as a stop for the two brass cymbals, which are placed cup to cup. The Turkish cymbal is used in the regular way. The height desired for the cup to cup cymbals may be had by raising and lowering the cow bell clamp. A felt washer may be used between the cymbals and clamp if desired. By substituting another cow bell clamp for the hoop adapter, the "frame up" submitted by Frank Hussey and Irv. Wilkie (page 11, L.D.T. No. 19) may be used instead of the cup to cup cymbals. Your drum stand cymbal holder No. 279 might be used instead of No. 33B, but I am afraid that it would lack both strength and height."

$2.00 award to Raymond P. Huffman.

An old-fashioned girl is one who takes her cigarette from her mouth before putting on her nightgown.

Betty Mae Reed

Seventeen-year-old Betty Mae Reed, of Boulder, Colo., is a drummer from a drumming family. She plays with The Lady Crusaders, a Denver organization playing dances and hotels. Betty Mae's brother is a drummer and her father, also, was a drummer. She says, "I guess I'm just naturally a drummer and couldn't help it." Well, you have us convinced, Betty.

The Drummer Boy of Hollywood

Charles "Buddy" Rogers, takes time off from "Illusion", one of his latest talking pictures, to juggle the drumsticks. Rogers' favorite diversion is jazz music. He plays seven different instruments.

Johnny Gruden

"I was under the impression that Leedy drums were like other makes until I tried a Leedy Floating Head two years ago. We cannot be separated now. Leedy instruments are superior to any I've ever used." That's the statement of Johnny Gruden, percussionist with the Metro Theatre Concert Orchestra, N. Y. C. Coming from a drummer like Johnny, we consider that quite a boost because John has been "hittin' the leather" for about ten years now and he knows his way around. Besides his theatre work, Gruden has played on ocean liners, in dance bands and over the air. He has worked under such prominent directors as Alfred Forster, Frank Smith, and George Buehl.

A Window Shade Rhythm

Several (one for each phrase of "beats") scissor cuts about one inch long are made along the top edge of cloth about two inches apart. Cloth should be at least 4 ft. long by 2 ft. wide, held by left hand in upper left-hand corner. Short and long jerks with right hand (according to the rhythm) ripping each strip for a phase of the tune. Fine effect in soft passages of fast rhythmic numbers. Window shade cloth can be bought in any department store.

Miss Bertha Klawuhn

Miss Bertha Klawuhn, of St. Joseph, Mo., is an amateur Vibraphone artist, who has been enthusiastically received by the radio public. She has played Vibraphone solos over a number of prominent radio stations and always received plenty of applause from the fans. Miss Klawuhn has also played Vibraphone at a great many church services and both ministers and parishioners have agreed that the Vibraphone music as played by Miss Klawuhn is the most inspiring church music they have ever heard.

Leedy **For Drummers Who Care** *Leedy*

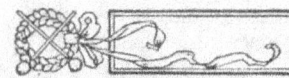 Drum Topics

The opportunity of a lifetime seldom comes heralded by a jazz band!

Endurance Drumming As An Outdoor Sport

It is not commonly known in this country that contests of endurance drumming while on the march is an outdoor sport indulged in to a considerable extent in Belgium, France and some parts of Germany. The two newspaper extracts printed below will give the reader a slight idea of these events.

(Reprinted from the New York Evening Telegram, May 12, 1928)

World's Champion Drummer Drums 800 Miles At 60 Now He's Rollin' Through Belgium

Brussels, Belgium, May 11, '28—Keeping the promise that he made last year when he established the world's record for long-distance drum playing, J. B. Mairy, of Corbai, Province of Brabant, Belgium, has begun a drumming tour through Belgium, during which he is to go through all nine provinces walking and playing his drum without respite except for his meals and sleeping hours. Mairy wants to celebrate his sixtieth birthday, which is this year, in visiting all the chief towns and centers of Belgum, giving a concert in each community through which he is to pass. He started his tour early in May and is confident he will be back by the middle of June, having covered some 800 or 900 miles. Groups of local drummers are to accompany the record drummer of Belgium along certain stretches and each town which he is to visit prepares to receive him properly. His drum, a family instrument which he inherited from his forefathers, is 150 years old.

Beating The Drum Record is an Old Form of Endurance Contest

(Reprinted from the London Daily Express, May 22, 1927)

Brussels, Belgium, May 22, 1927—A world's championship for long-distance drummers appears to be a possibility of the near future. A drummer, named Poulet, in the Walloon district of Fosses, recently made a bet that he would march from Fosses to Namur and back (a total distance of twenty-five miles) without stopping and without ceasing to beat his drum, except for one hour to be allowed him for luncheon. Poulet, who is fifty years of age, won his bet.

The record he thus established was promptly challenged by a Nimy drummer, named Robillard, aged fifty-nine, who undertook to march from Mons to Ath and back (a distance of thirty-four miles), under the same conditions. He did so, covering the distance in eleven hours.

A drummer of Maurages has now announced he will march from Maurages to Brussels and back (a distance of forty miles), to the beat of his drum. This sport is popular among the working classes of the district—mostly miners—and local competitors excite great enthusiasm.

A Note About Field Music to School Bandmasters and Music Supervisors

Field Music—what is it? And what part does it play in band activities? The United States Army considers field music very important. Most of you know that it consists of either a large or small Drum and Bugle Corps attached to and marching behind the regular military band. Its main purpose in things military is to supply continual music by playing during the intervals between band numbers, and it is almost indispensable to R.O.T.C. Bands during Parades, Reviews and other military ceremonies by effectively rendering honors, flourishes, ruffles and appropriate bugle calls.

A Band can not play continuously during parades—yet the spectators along the side lines hate, most of all, to witness a band marching by and not playing—Field Music will overcome this by performing independently of the band. There are many good drum and bugle marches published that your field music can use to good advantage. Besides playing independently and giving the bandsmen a chance to rest, nothing sounds so inspiring as field music playing with the band, featuring such numbers as "The Thunderer", "Lancaster", "Semper Fidelis" and "Religioso". Many numbers can be adapted to field music in unison or solo by rearrangement.

Field Music is a real asset to the Band. It increases the instrumentation, the volume, the flash, and opportunities for better musical repertoire.

Here is another big advantage. The bandmaster of today is ever faced with the problem of securing new members each year to fill the vacancies left by those who graduated the previous term. True, there is always a sufficient number eager to join the the band, but would not greatly lessen the task of the bandmaster and teacher could he take on boys and girls who have already received some preliminary training? If he has had field music in the form of a drum and bugle corps attached to his band the year previous, he can look to these members for his new material. They will have received not only a considerable amount of military training as to marching, bearing discipline, etc., but will also have received a whole year's experience in rhythm on drums, and both rhythm and a limited amount of melody on the bugles. This is truly a great foundation on which to build future musicians for the band; for with this experience they can go from either the bugles or the drums on to any band instrument with a greater amount of ease than if they were started in raw.

 World's Finest Drummers' Instruments

The Exclusive Drummers' Paper

Loud Speaker Drum in Siam
Photo by Ewing Galloway, N. Y.

Drums and gongs play an important part in the lives of the Siamese and they have great religious significance. Photo was taken in Miang Ku Hai, a city in northern Siam, straight north of Bangkok, the capitol. This drum is 6 feet long, the head end is wood and the horn end is pottery. Note flanged gongs at right, also ancient temple in background in contrast with modern building in foreground and the up-to-date hats on the men.

Jack Hylton Offends Mussolini

Jack Hylton, back after a tour of 7,000 miles in 62 days, where he played in 42 towns in eight countries, had a strange adventure in Italy.

A few weeks back, when conducting his band in London, he said something about "Mussolini's boys will now play." When he arrived in Milan, he was sent for by the Fascisti chief of police, and cross-examined for two and a half hours as to how dare he make fun of Mussolini like that!

"We make fun of politicians in England," said Jack.

"We don't do it here," replied the police.

The British Consul had to be sent for, and Jack had to swear he would not do anything like that in Italy. Then he was allowed to perform.

Now, you get some idea of what Fascism means.

I must be careful I don't say anything about Al Capone.
—*Variety*.

Patron: "Do you have music in this theatre?"
Ticket Seller: "Oh, yes, the best in town."
Patron: "Campbell's or Van Camp's?"

The Tympani Head Collar

Not long ago we heard a very fine High School Band of 80 pieces render an excellent concert. At the finish the young tympanist (who had done a really wonderful job for his age) proceeded to pack up. He first loosened both heads until they became "flabby", then "spun" each tuning handle down until it came to a stop of its own accord. The atmosphere, being dry at the time, brought the counter hoop flush with the edge of the bowl. This is a wrong procedure, because should the atmosphere remain dry until the next time the instruments are used there would be no "collar" (meaning the amount of head pulled down over the edge of the bowl) on the head, therefore it would not be possible to obtain less tension for low notes when needed in the next concert. In addition, there is danger of the tension handles backing off threaded lugs while the tympani are in transit. Evidently this tympanist had not been instructed that tympani heads should be left tight when not in use. Noted symphony and opera tympanists stretch their tympani heads enough to provide at least a half-inch collar over the edge of the bowls when the instruments are not in use. Carefully wiping the heads with a damp (not soaking wet) cloth to obtain this collar is a common practice in dry atmospheres. This is called "sponging" and great care must be taken in the process in order not to kill the tone of the heads and to keep them from tearing. No water must get in under the counter hoop. Sponging on both sides of the head is advisable.

Tiger or Lion Roar

Pick up snare drum and howl against the snares. Don't have snares too tight. Good for dance drummers who need this effect, but cannot carry the usual large sized trap necessary.

$2.00 award to
Ted Howes,
18 Morris St.,
Danbury, Conn.
Drummer-Manager of Ted Howes' Variety Collegians.

A Use for Ear Muffs

Ordinary old-fashioned ear muffs with ribbon steel spring clamps on both heads of 10" x 14" Chinese or Leedy "Full Dress" Tom Tom. Muff can be bought in the smaller type general stores. Takes ring out of Tom Tom and makes possible "thud" tone for rhythm beats.

Herbert R. Lee

"Lee for Leedy," says Herbert R. Lee of the Commodore Ballroom, Lowell, Mass. Herb is a New Yorker by birth and has played under such well-known leaders as Dave and Ben Bernie, Leo S. Dreyer, and Bert Lown. He's a hard worker and that's one of the reasons why he has gone so far as a percussionist. The other is that he has a whale of a personality and real musical talent.

Leedy — For Drummers Who Care — **Leedy**

Leedy Drum Topics

A fellow writes that a certain girls' band is so "hot" that at intermission the chairs follow them off the bandstand.

Earl Morin

Everyone remembers, with pleasure, Earl Morin's "Cotton Pickers." Earl is now the mainstay of the "R. K. Olians," prominent vaudeville orchestra under the direction of Hal Sanders. Earl has been smacking drum heads for about 25 years, more or less. He has played symphony orchestras, dance orchestras, and theatre jobs and for all kinds of work he has found Leedy best.

(Courtesy Melody Music Shop, Memphis, Tenn.)

The Secret of Baton Twirling Revealed!

A Novel Drummer Number

Will Rossiter, "The Chicago Publisher", 173 West Madison Street, Chicago, Ill., has a band number called, "Oh You Drummer", which should be of interest to drummers.

"Oh You Drummer" is written by J. Leubrie Hill, and arranged by Harry L. Alford. The drummer has several solos in this piece.

JOSEPH H. MATSON

Australia lost one of her best, and most popular drummers with the passing of Joseph H. Matson, of Melbourne, last year.

Mr. Matson, who at the time of his death was in the employ of W. H. Glen & Co., Pty., Ltd., had won many friends while playing. He had played at the Academy Theater with Ted Russells Review Co., with the Launceston Symphony Orchestra, the National Theater, the Claude Dampier Co., the Majestic Theater, the Masonic Danse Palais, and the Westgarth Theater.

Here's a book that every drum major has been waiting for and it's a book that every regular fellow will get a great kick out of besides. It explains in easy-to-understand fashion all the tricks of the drum major's art—the new ones and the old ones, too. Contains 17 pictures and 28 detailed pen sketches which exactly illustrate every movement.

With the help of this new Leedy book, you can learn the fascinating art of baton twirling in a few hours. All the mysteries are revealed in this great book and with a little practice you'll be twirling the baton around your hand, flashing it high up into the air, whirling it around your shoulders, under your legs, everywhere, anywhere. This book teaches you all the tricks, all the positions—and imagine the fun you'll have when you show them to your friends, even though you never intend to lead a drum corps.

But if you do intend to lead a drum corps or a band, by all means send for this remarkable book right away. Learn baton twirling by this easy, illustrated method and you'll be the hit of every parade_____Price, $1.50

The Leedy Twirling Baton, No. 1923, is especially designed for this purpose. Has thick aluminum ball that will not dent except by extreme contact. Staff is of "twisted" non-tapering brass tubing with plugged ferrule. Has just the right balance and will not creep in the hand when in motion. Brightly chromium plated and makes a wonderful flash. Length 36 inches, weight 21 ounces. Price _____$12.00

Great bunch of boys, these lads of the drum section of the Iowa State College Band. Each one of them has a black and gold Leedy Floating Head Drum for concert work, besides, the Leedy street drums which you see in the picture. Under the capable direction of Oscar Hatch Hawley, the Iowa State Band won first place at the Drake Relays last spring. Oh yes, we almost forgot to tell you these drummers' names. Reading from left to right they are: R. T. Quick, Sioux City, Iowa; G. P. Happ, Davenport, Iowa; C. H. Anderson, West Union, Iowa; A. G. Thomson, Omaha, Neb.; C. A. Bluedorn, Welcott, Iowa.
Courtesy Geo. A. Smith Music House, Omaha, Neb.

Drumming gentlemen prefer white heads.

 World's Finest Drummers' Instruments

The Exclusive Drummers' Paper

"Phooey"

—or words to that effect, is the comment of Murray Spivack, RKO sound effects expert, as he stops his ears while Mitchell Lewis, Radio Pictures star, makes merry on the Vibraphone. The fault, however, is not with the Vibraphone as thousands, who have heard the sparkling performances of Mr. Spivack on his Leedy instrument, will testify. In making the recent Radio Pictures musical extravaganza, "Rio Rita", Mr. Spivack used a full equipment of Leedy instruments including tymps, xylophone, chimes and Vibraphone.

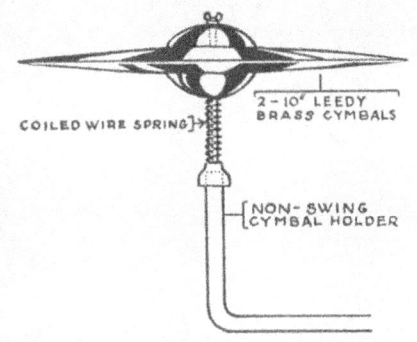

A Good Cymbal Set-Up

Cymbals arranged in the above manner good for numerous effects: sizzle, choke, etc. Coiled spring obtainable at hardware stores.
$2.00 award to
F. Hussey and Irv. Wilkie,
C. G. Conn Co., Detroit.

A bunch of guys were disussion—
Pros and cons of percussion—
When one wise cracker fair gushion—
Cried, what we need is more concussion—

Ned Albright

There are two editions of this same drummer. That is, Ned Albright of Kokomo, Ind., has a twin brother who looks just like him and is also a drummer. Albright has played in many theatre orchestras in Pennsylvania, Michigan, Ohio and Indiana. He is always there with the newest stuff and enjoys a considerable reputation. During the Big Show he was first drummer in the Headquarters Company 67th Field Artillery Band. Ned's twin brother is in New York City.

Some Interesting Dope on Castanets

How many drummers know that castanets are one of the oldest of musical instruments and have a serious meaning in the hearts of the Spanish people, in whose country they originated? They are to the finest Spanish dancers what the baton is to the greatest leaders. To the lively imagination of the Spaniard these little shell-like concavities represent voices endowed with sex—the deep, raucous click of the larger ones typifying the male, and the more acute vibrations of the smaller, the female; and woe betide the dancer who inadvertently appears with a pair of the same sex. She would be hooted and hissed into immediate retirement. Castanets received their name centuries ago from their shape, which is that of a chestnut or "castana", when the two parts are united. They are so much a part of Spanish nationality as to enter into colloquial speech of the people. "Estar uno como unas castanuelas" (to be like a pair of castanets), is, in other words, to be happy.

Bass Drum Tones

There are three kinds of bass drum tones—the "Long Boom", the "Short Boom" and the "Thud Boom". They are all important and no one of them can be accepted as the "one and only" correct tone for the bass drum. "Long Boom" tones would wreck the all-important rhythm which is the foundation of the dance orchestra. "Short Boom" tones would never be tolerated (except where notated in the music for certain effects) by the concert conductor. "Thud Boom" tones are only desirable to produce effects and in "hot" numbers. Strictly speaking, the Drummer should change from one to the other according to the character of the number being played. Of course it is not possible to do this by way of retensioning the drum—time would not permit. However, it is possible to change pedal balls between numbers with very little effort. Leedy makes three different styles of pedal balls as shown above—Lamb's Wool, soft for "Long Boom" tones—Red Piano Felt, medium for "Short Boom" tones—and Solid Spanish Felt, hard for "Thud Boom" tones. They produce tones of marked difference from each other. Of course head tensioning plays an important part in producing bass drum tones and should be given all the attention possible. The changing of the balls will, as stated before, make a noticeable difference; but where time permits retensioning of the head should be effected.

ADIOS—And Wishing You the Best of Good Breaks

For Drummers Who Care

JUST OUT!

The New *Leedy* Catalog "S"

Write for your copy today. It's free. The most beautiful drum catalog that has ever been produced. Packed with information of absorbing interest to everyone who wants to know "what's what" in the drum world. Many new models. Remarkable values. A post card request will bring it, without obligation.

LEEDY MFG. CO.
Leedy Building   *Elkhart, Ind.*

THE WORLD'S FINEST DRUMMERS' INSTRUMENTS

Leedy DRUM TOPICS
The Exclusive Drummers' Paper

July 1930
Twentieth Edition

Sec. 435½ P. L. & R.
U. S. POSTAGE
PAID
ELKHART, IND.
Permit No. 6

POSTMASTER—Return Postage Guaranteed

LEEDY MANUFACTURING CO.
Elkhart, Indiana

Joseph G. Benoit,
165 Hildreth,
Lowell, Mass.

Leedy Drum Topics Issue 20

WELL, HERE WE ARE!

FOR several weeks we have been busy moving our big plant to our new home in Elkhart, Indiana, "Band Instrument City of the World." We are now all "squared away" and are running full blast making "the world's finest drummers' instruments."

We surely like it here in Elkhart. We have now the most modern and most efficient factory in Leedy's history. Every square foot has been scientifically planned for high-grade production and low cost. We are a happy family with greater prospects than ever ahead of us and we believe that this joy in our work will be reflected in the musical instruments we produce.

MEET THE GANG!

A BETTER PRODUCT THAN EVER

LEEDY has always produced an outstanding product but we believe we are going to be able to show you an even finer product. We have the physical equipment, the rich background of experience, some of the best brains in the drum business, skillful craftsmen and artisans and an unbounded enthusiasm for our product and its improvement. The users of Leedy percussion instruments have always expected big things of us and we are just "rarin' to go" to excel our past record.

Leedy Drum Topics Issue 20 Supplement

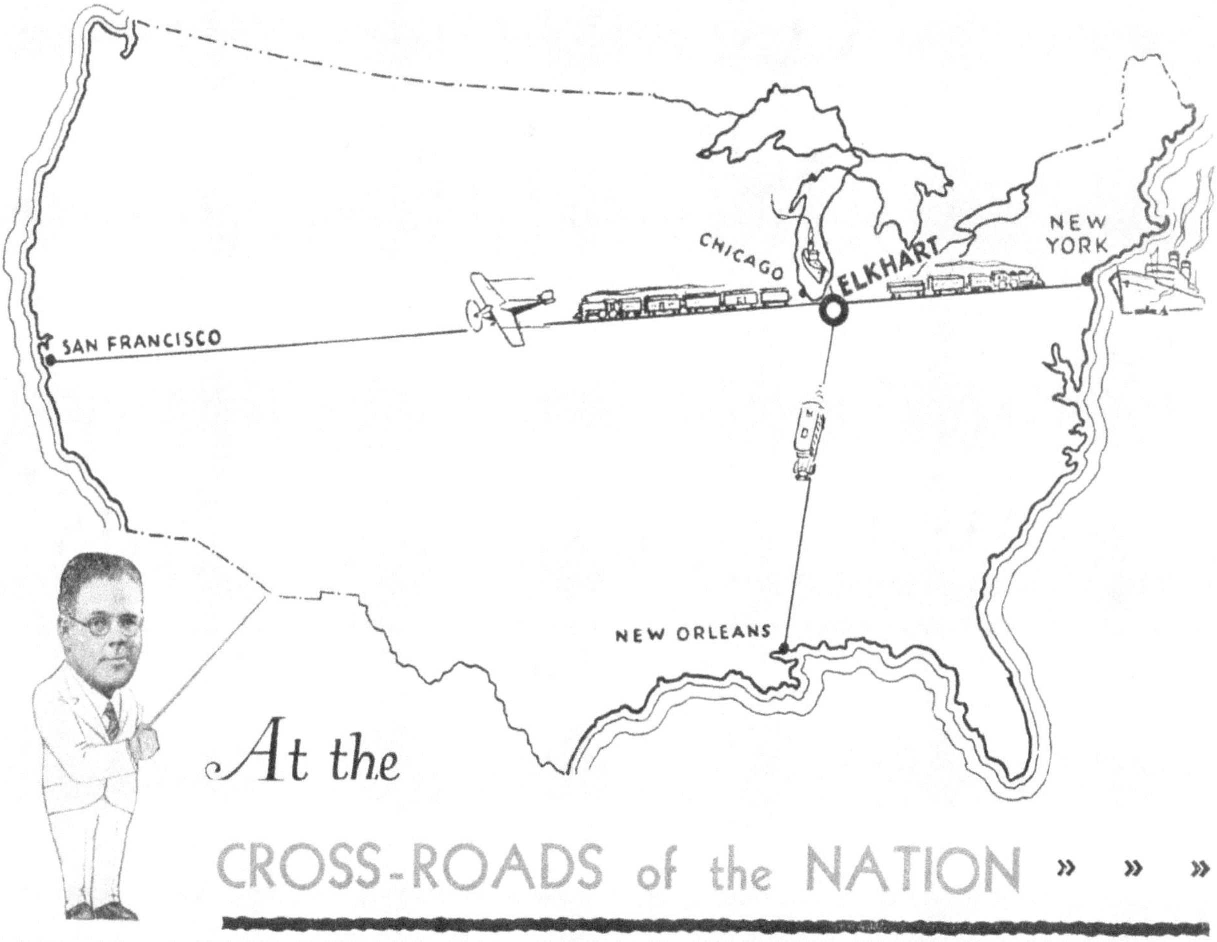

At the CROSS-ROADS of the NATION » » »

WE SURELY are "sitting pretty" now for giving rapid, efficient service to the users of Leedy products and to the dealers who sell them. Elkhart is a terminal of the New York Central trunk lines. Transcontinental air lines, transcontinental bus lines, transcontinental trails pass through Elkhart both east and west and north and south. For heavy shipping we have access to the steamers of the Great Lakes, the river boats of the Mississippi and its tributaries.

As a geographical location, we cannot conceive of one more advantageous. Not only does it facilitate securing raw products, but it also makes shipping the finished product prompt and swift. Also big time vaudeville and musical organizations that visit Chicago can step out of their back door into the Leedy factory.

Speed is the keynote of modern business. Leedy is utilizing every facility to be abreast or ahead in this type of service.

Trunks of Harold McDonald, of Paul Whiteman's Orchestra, containing complete Leedy equipment. Big time artists will greatly appreciate Leedy's new location just outside Chicago.

CLOSE TO SUPPLIES

Steel

Chicago and the Calumet District have become one of the greatest steel producing centers in the world. Leedy uses a lot of steel in the fine construction of percussion instruments. In our present location, our sources for steel are right at our elbow. The transportation of steel is an important factor in its price.

Brass

Cymbals, bugles, traps, require tons of brass. Since the American Brass Company is at Kenosha, we are close to the source of supply, eliminating heavy transportation charges. This saving can be passed on to the customer in the form of higher quality.

Lumber

Shells, hoops, sticks, tone bars, require tons of highly selected wood of various kinds. Chicago is the lumber yard for the whole Middle West, not only for domestic wood such as maple and hickory, but for imported wood such as mahogany and Honduras rosewood.

Raw Hides

One of the most important raw materials used in the manufacture of percussion instruments is raw hides. The stock yards of Chicago are the largest in the world, allowing unsurpassed opportunity for selection and price. It is very important in the curing and finishing of heads that we secure the hides fresh. We are now in the best position that we have ever been to turn out heads of unsurpassed quality.

FOR THESE AND OTHER REASONS

THERE are many other things that make us happy about our move to the new location in Elkhart, "Band Instrument City of the World." In this little message we have just hit a few of the high places. We wish you could catch a little bit of the contagious enthusiasm throughout the complete Leedy organization for our new set-up. We feel we are on the threshold of a new expansion program. We invite our old and loyal friends to rejoice with us and we are anxious to make the acquaintance of new customers and friends so we can prove to them also that we are, in every respect, Manufacturers of the World's Finest Drummers' Instruments.

Leedy Drum Topics Issue 21

Leedy Drum Topics

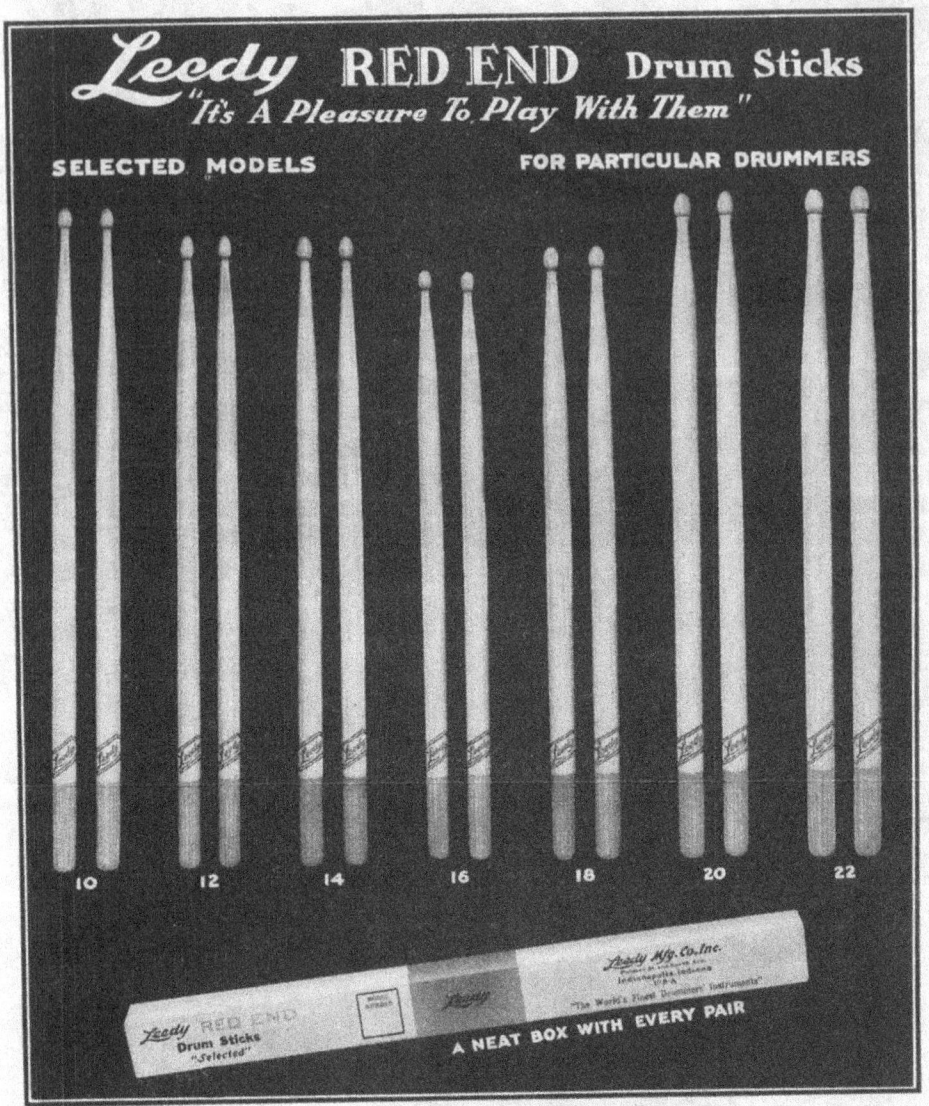

Try Red Ends — Be Convinced

The red end on Leedy Red End Drum Sticks is a means of identification of a higher quality stick. It is the stick itself that is better—a combination of the finest selected, straight-grained, second growth hickory and the most careful workmanship that money can buy. The instant you pick up Red Ends, you will have a new "feel" of confidence and you will know that you have a stick superior to all others. Red Ends have a smooth, hard, glass-like, high lustre finish from end to end. This finish gives the sticks a "classy" appearance, and makes them more durable as well. Every stick is sanded, grain-filled, sprayed with clear Duco lacquer and then hand-rubbed and sprayed again. Red Ends are matched for even weight and balance, and packed in a neat cardboard box. *Insist on Leedy Red End sticks.* They are for particular Drummers, and you will find them well worth the slight extra cost.

No. 10—For orchestra, extra light, 17" long
No. 12—For orchestra, light, 16" long
No. 14—For orchestra, light, 16" long
No. 16—For orchestra and small band, medium light 15" long
No. 18—For large orchestra and band, medium heavy 15½" long
No. 20—For Drum Corps and large band, heavy, 17" long
No. 22—For Drum Corps, heavy, 17" long

75c Per Pair

World's Finest Drummers' Instruments

Page Two

 **The Exclusive Drummers' Paper**

Are You Hiding A Million Dollars?

Many a drummer with a million dollars worth of talent and personality is hiding it beneath a shabby outfit. Read the interesting experiment described in the newspaper clipping at the right. It is proof that no musician—drummer or otherwise—can afford to hide his talent in the trappings of a beggar. Then read the story below—it "tells you why."

IN beggar's clothes an internationally known violinist fiddled a $40,000 "Strad" on the streets of Chicago for a whole day and got $5.71 for his trouble. As beggar-musicians go, this was probably a fair day's take, but for the Violinist-Prince in disguise it was chicken feed—almost an insult.

Great story, but what, you may ask, does it prove? It proves a thing that is of the greatest importance to you and every other Drummer in the business, and, as Chic Sales says, "I'll tell you why."

It proves that no drummer, no matter how talented, can afford to neglect his own appearance or that of his outfit. Whether we like it or not appearances count for a great deal in this world of ours. Old Polonius, in Shakespeare's play "Hamlet", knew what he was talking about when he advised his son, "— costly thy habit as thy purse can buy for apparel oft proclaims the man."

The fellow with the shabby looking outfit may be just as good a drummer as the fellow with the new, modern equipment, but who will believe it?

The Drummer with the out-of-date, shabby looking outfit may be just as good or better, so far as drumming ability is concerned, as the fellow with the flashy, new Marine Pearl equipment, but who will believe it? If you were the leader of an orchestra making a choice between two drummers, one with a dilapidated outfit and the other with a brand new drum set, which would you choose? You don't have to think twice to answer that one, and neither does the leader. The man who looks the part gets the job every time.

You may be the world's best Drummer but if your drums look as though they ought to belong to the world's worst drummer, that is what nine people out of ten will take you for. Of course, by all this we don't mean to say that all you need for success is a brand new set of drums. Far from it. But we do mean, and we know it's a fact, that ability combined with new, good-looking Drums gets a lot further and has a better time doing it, than ability handicapped with stuff that looks like it had recently been kicked out the back door of some pawnshop.

And there is many a drummer who proceeds something like the following when he gets ready to play a job. He blows himself to maybe five bucks worth of tonsorial traps in the form of haircut, shampoo, manicure, shoe shine, facial and what have you. He sets himself up in an equipment of clothing that checks off something like this: tuxedo $100, stiff shirt with studs, links, etcetera, $35, patent leather shoes $10, derby $10, and overcoat $75.

By the time Mr. Drummer is ready to step out, he has nicked the old bank roll for a pretty penny—as we estimate it $235. This is a lot of dough in any man's country and it has all been spent for just one thing —appearance.

Then what happens? More times than we like to think about, just this: Mr. Drummer, with his 235 bucks worth of clothes and haircuts, tucks an 1892 stem-winding model drum outfit (worth at a liberal guess $11.63) under his arm and starts out to make his living.

Funny, isn't it? Yet it's true. You know for all the jokes that you hear about plumbers if you'll take a squint at the average pipe jockey's tool kit, you'll find it right up to snuff. The plumber, the carpenter, the mechanic, the dentist—all of them know that they have got to have the latest and best tools that money can buy in order to do their work properly. But the drummer, he's different.

He can make an old wash boiler lid sound like a Turkish cymbal. He can play modern stuff on the drum his grandpa used back in the days when "Turkey In The Straw" was bringing the house down. You bet he can—just like the Eskimos can speak French. Are we right or are we wrong? Think it over and it won't take you long to decide that we are right. You need new, good looking equipment to get by these days.

An investment in the newest and best equipment is one that will pay every Drummer handsome dividends. Think it over and you'll agree.

 **World's Finest Drummers' Instruments**

Leedy Drum Topics

Freddie Weper and Charles Wilcoxon

Vaudeville acts have paid Charles Wilcoxon (at right in the photo) the finest compliment that it is possible to pay a vaudeville drummer. They say he never varies a tempo and never misses a cue! Those of you who have played in vaudeville pits know just what that means, but for the benefit of those who have never had this experience we will do a little explaining. Vaudeville leaders depend on their drummers for almost everything —tempos, shading, attacks, cues and what have you. In fact a vaudeville leader and a drummer must be a perfect team to make the show a success.

Wilcoxon is now playing the R.K.O. Keith's Palace Theatre, Cleveland, O., under the direction of Freddie Weper, who is shown at the left above. The fact that Wilcoxon has held this same position under the same leader for eight years is 'nuff said about his ability as a drummer. He is one of the country's aces in his line.

Just a word about Director Freddie Weper, the record of whose achievements in the musical world would fill a good sized book. He has been with the Keith interests for 23 years conducting only in their finest theatres. During the past year he was promoted to Assistant Music Supervisor of the entire R. K. O. circuit. He has been at the Palace, Cleveland, for the past seven years and during that time has developed the orchestra to one with a nationwide reputation.

$10.00 Reward

Drum Topics pays a reward of $10.00 each issue for a favorite drummer story. Send yours in. It may be the winning story and if so the sawbuck will be yours. The story need not be long and it need not be true—but it must be good. Don't pass up this chance to make 10 bucks easy.

Pauline: "Don't you love an evening like this?"

Paul: "You bet, but I generally wait until we get a little further out in the country."

We know a lot of leaders who ought to make good aviators—they go up in the air so easily.

Bamboo Brush for Rhythm Beats

A drummer from sunny California sends along this idea, and it's a great one as you'll agree once you've tried it. Procure a piece of bamboo about 15 inches long and two inches in diameter. There is a piece of bamboo answering this description which comes on an ordinary sink broom and is obtainable in any household furnishing department for about 50c.

Split the bamboo stick into a number of sections as is shown in the accompanying drawing. In doing this be sure to use a sharp knife and take care to keep the sections as nearly even as possible.

This trap can be used for various purposes, and is especially good for after beats on the cymbals and tomtoms. You'll be surprised at the "sock" and rhythm you can get with this stunt.

$2.00 award to Harold E. Sloat, 842 Dolores St., San Francisco, Calif.

Bill Robertson

Bill Robertson is now a member of the Texas State Highway Police but drummers will remember him as one of the big shots of the circus game. He formerly played with Miller Brothers 101 Ranch and other big circus outfits. Bill still does a job of drumming every now and then.

At right is the plaque presented to The Seven Aces as the winner of the Radio Digest orchestra popularity contest conducted over WBAP, Ft. Worth, Texas, last Winter. The Seven Aces received 220,000 votes from all over the U. S. A. and Canada. "Shucks" Parks, who is well known to the drumming fraternity, plays drums for the outfit. He is all Leedy equipped.

Leedy World's Finest Drummers' Instruments Leedy

The Exclusive Drummers' Paper

Mammoth Indian Temple Drum

Organizations laying claim to the ownership of the world's largest drum had better investigate this mammoth temple drum from mystic India before going further with their boasts. Even reclining half on its side as it is, the drum is taller than the unusually large gentleman with the skyscraper head-dress who appears in the picture just to the right of the huge affair.

The drum is used for calling the faithful to worship and perhaps is a presage of terrible doom for those who fail to obey its summons. The drummer in the picture is none other than the High Priest of the temple who alone is privileged to give performances on this gigantic tom-tom.

The drum sticks, as may be seen, are held much in the manner of tympani sticks, and the style of playing used is, indeed, somewhat similar to that used by tympanists. Rumor has it that the head of this drum is made from the hide of one of the sacred humped cows of India. These cows are highly revered by the natives as they are supposed to be the temporary resting places of departed souls. The butchering of one of them, therefore, to provide a head for the sacred temple drum is a ceremony which can only be performed by the highest of High Priests.

$2.00 Apiece for "Ideas"

Drum Topics will pay $2.00 apiece for each drummer suggestion or "Idea" that is published in the next issue No. 22. If you have a new trap of your own invention or a new way to use a standard trap or collection of traps, send a description of your "Idea" to the Editor of Drum Topics. If your suggestion is published, you will receive a $2.00 cash award and full credit when the article concerning your suggestion appears. No "Idea" or stunt is too large or too small, too important or too insignificant to find a place in this magazine so long as it has to do with drums and drummers. Think it over; haven't you some pet trick or stunt of your own that other drummers would like to know about? If so, send it along and earn yourself two bucks.

Virginia Selman

Pretty Miss Virginia Selman won second place on xylophone at the 1930 Florida State Musical Festival. She is a senior in the Bradenton High School and plays xylophone with the high school orchestra and with the Bradenton Rotary Club Orchestra. In fact, Virginia plays selections on her xylophone at almost every kind of a function in and around her home town. Her winning smile and her really high class performance on the xylo have made her popular wherever she goes.

Miss Selman got her instruction in xylophone playing from "Green Brother's Beginners' Method," the instruction book which is furnished free with every Leedy xylophone.

Sponge Bass Drum Tone Control

If you are in quick need of a bass drum tone control and happen to have an extra bass drum cymbal holder laying about, you can attach same to any point on your hoop and squeeze an ordinary 5c & 10c store rubber sponge between the end of the holder and the bass drum head.

$2.00 award to Fred Sauer, 708 Frost Ave., Rochester, N. Y.

Hick—"I know a Drummer who has been married and divorced three times."

Orie—"Well, maybe that comes from playing too much triangle."

Al Zuker

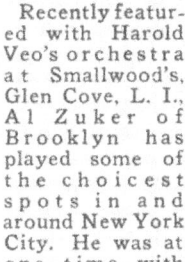

Recently featured with Harold Veo's orchestra at Smallwood's, Glen Cove, L. I., Al Zuker of Brooklyn has played some of the choicest spots in and around New York City. He was at one time with Joe Kneckt in the old Waldorf-Astoria and has also played the Club Lido both at New York and Miami Beach. His experience also includes a trip around the world with his own orchestra aboard *The President Polk*. He is a thorough drummer and a good showman.

Leedy World's Finest Drummers' Instruments **Leedy**

Leedy Drum Topics

BOSTON THRILLS TO LEGION DRUMS

Miami Post Cops Drum Corps Event

Resplendent in white uniforms the Drum and Bugle Corps of Harvey W. Seeds Post, Miami, Fla., marched off the rain-soaked field at the park of the Boston Braves winners for the third time of the American Legion Convention Drum and Bugle Corps competition. Racine, Wis., copped second honors and Frankford, Pa., last year's winners, finished in the show position. In spite of the inclement weather nearly 20,000 people witnessed the spectacle and gave a tremendous ovation to the winning Corps.

Gerlach 1st Again!

'29 Winner Repeats in Rudimental Race

For the second time in as many years Malcolm M. "Hienie" Gerlach, Pennsylvania post No. 81, beat off all competition to carry home the bacon from the Rudimental Drummers' Contest of the 12th Annual American Legion Convention. "Hienie" also was accounted best in the competition for individual strutters.

Streets Jammed As Legionnaires Stage 9 Hour Parade

Bean City Crowds Throng Curbs and Crane From Windows and Rooftops To Watch American Legion Boys On Parade In Big Event Of Convention; Music of Drum and Bugle Corps Thrills.

Staid Bostonians stood on tip-toes and held their breath, craned undignified necks from neighboring windows, peered incautiously over the edges of roof-tops and in some way held on to every other conceivable point of vantage to watch while the men of the American Legion staged the gigantic parade which marked the second day of their annual convention. The sun was high over Boston Common when the call of the bugles and the roll-off announced the beginning of the tremendous event and the moon had already begun to silver the waters of Back Bay by the time the stirring sounds of the last Drum and Bugle Corps had been lost in the distances beyond the Charles.

Two hundred and sixty musical organizations including bands and Drum Corps participated in the parade which lasted eight hours and fifty minutes starting at 10:20 A. M. and lasting continuously until 7:10 P. M. Crowds estimated variously at from 1,500,000 to 2,500,000 lined every available foot of space along both sides of the line of march forming a veritable human wall for the marchers to pass between. In its 300 years of existence Boston has never witnessed a spectacle comparable to this one.

It is an event which will live forever in the memories of those who were fortunate enough to behold it, and perhaps the most thrilling part of the whole performance was the stirring music and flashy uniforms of the 177 Drum and Bugle Corps participating.

INDIVIDUAL PRIZE WINNERS

Here, left to right, are the Legionnaires who copped the prizes in the individual contests at the Boston Convention: Lee Suttell, Buffalo, N. Y., best of twirling Drum Majors; "Bill" Hruby, Elyria, O., best of strutting Drum Majors; Howard K. Knobel, Frankford, Pa., champ Bugler; Malcolm M. Gerlach, Pittsburgh, Pa., champ Rudimental Drummer.

Flashy Beats Coming Stunt Predicts George L. Stone

Writing of the Legion Convention parade in *Jacob's Band Monthly*, George L. Stone, drum authority had the following to say about Drum Corps using flashy beats and unusual equipment:

"Many corps made use of unique drum beats, wherein the sticks were raised, alternately, high above the head. This flashing style looked good and in the contests helped pile up points under 'originality and flash.' Especially did this flashing style show up to advantage in the corps that had tenor drums and Scotch-type bass drums in addition to the regulation snare and bass drums. And about every corps that competed had all these different types of drums. The prize-winning Frankford Post of Pa., used all the different sizes, playing first eight measures soft with sticks low, then eight measures loud with snare drum sticks raised high, while tenor, Scotch and bass drum sticks were whirled over the heads. This made a handsome effect and I predict a more general use of the different types of drums, also of the baritone and bass bugles which produce a welcome variation in pitch to the 'sol-do-mi' of the regulation bugle.

Judges Agree

"As one judge remarked after the contests were over, 'They all (the Drum Corps) were wonderful, but the best ones put it over with originality and flash', which musically speaking seems to consist of nothing more than those extra types of drums and bugles, coupled with a showy way of playing them."

"Parading units would do well to place their bugles ahead of the drums. First impressions (of judges or audience) are formed as the corps approaches. The volume of drum tone blends better with that of the bugles in the ears of the listeners ahead, when the bugles precede the drums."

Leedy World's Finest Drummers' Instruments **Leedy**

The Exclusive Drummers' Paper

Slightly Spanish

This picture is slightly Spanish, that is, the little fellow perched aloft in the middle is a 14 year old drummer boy of the Spanish army. The rest of the picture is good old United States in the form of two drummers of the United States Army Band, Mr. Toromick on the left and Mr. Verhay on the right. The picture was taken during the visit of the United States Army Band to Spain and other European countries.

Harry Goldstein

Now playing at the Club St. Marks, Washington, D. C., with Meyer Goldman's and Irving Boerenstein's Music, Harry Goldstein is making a reputation for himself as one of the high class drummers of the East. His work on the xylophone is especially pleasing and has caused a great deal of favorable comment.

He has been playing drums for more than 10 years and has studied under such fine teachers as Bill Keiffer of the U. S. Marine Band, Sam Johnson and Sam Rosey.

Photo courtesy Leonberger Music Co., Washington, D. C.

Little Jack Horner
Sat in a corner,
Playing on snare drum and tymp,
He made a big hash
Of an important crash—
He's now out of work, the poor simp!

A Simple Airplane Effect

In these days when everything and everyone is going air minded, a real airplane effect should be part of every drummer's equipment. Here is one suggested by a Philadelphia drummer that is simple but very realistic.

As may be seen in the photograph, the effect is obtained by means of a cheap massage machine such as may be procured in any drug store. Some models can be purchased for as low as $2 or $3. The vacuum cup rubber attachment which is standard equipment with all such machines is the one to use.

The effect can be obtained on either tympano. The tone is determined by the tension of the head and a little experimenting will soon reveal just which is the best tone to use. Near and long distance effects are obtained by moving the vibrator from the edge of the kettle to the center of the head and applying more or less pressure according to the effect desired. This is an unusually fine "Idea".

$2.00 award to George Burnwood, 992 Wakeling St., Philadelphia, Pa.

George Burnwood

George B. Burnwood, author of the airplane effect explained above, is a theatre drummer of some 12 years experience. His home is the City of Brotherly Love, old Philadelphia, and his drumistic reputation in those parts is one of which he may well be proud. He has studied drums under Nelson Ward, xylophone under Joe Huttlin, and tympani with Oscar Schwar.

Miss Drury and Bob Loder

The interesting snapshot above shows Bob Loder, drum salesman of the C. G. Conn, Ltd., Cincinnati branch, in interested conversation with Miss Drury, drummer and one of the few lady members of the University of Kentucky Band. Miss Drury is a drummer of unusual ability and her appearance with the band always makes a big hit.

Tonic

A young bride walked into a drug store and approached a clerk timidly.

"That baby tonic you advertise—" she began—"does it really make babies bigger and stronger?"

"We sell lots of it," replied the druggist, "and we've never had a complaint."

"Well, I'll take a bottle," said the bride after a moment, and went out.

In five minutes she was back. She got the druggist into a corner and whispered into his ear:

"I forgot to ask about this baby tonic," she said under her breath. "Who takes it—me or my husband?"

J. A. Theobald

J. A. Theobald of Honesdale, Pa., started drumming with a boys band in his home town back in 1911 and one way or another he has been manipulating the sticks ever since. At the present time he is managing "The Roamers," his own band. He is also in charge of the drum section of the David McKelvy Peterson American Legion Post Fife, Drum and Bugle Corps.

He plays the legitimate stuff as well as jazz.

Leedy World's Finest Drummers' Instruments **Leedy**

Leedy Drum Topics

Some Internationally Famous Drummers

The photograph above was taken at Washington's home, Mount Vernon, during the recent visit to the U. S. of The Belgian Royal Guards Band.

When The Belgian Royal Guards Band played their recent concerts in Washington, D. C., the members of the U. S. Marine Band entertained them at George Washington's home, Mount Vernon. The photo above shows the drum sections of the two bands grouped around the leaders of the outfits on that occasion. Seated on your left is Capt. Prevost, conductor of the Belgian Band, and on the right is Capt. Taylor Branson, conductor of the Marine Band. Standing left to right: Rene Kips, Belgian Band; Charles Viner, U. S. Band; Marcel Stuble, Belgian Band; Bill Keiffer, U. S. Band; Robert Lombart, Belgian Band; Phil Genther, U. S. Band; Basile Temmerman, Belgian Band.

The boys of the U. S. Marine Band were high in their praises of these Belgian Band drummers, stating that their musicianship and execution was of a very high order. The Leatherneck drummers also stated that these Belgians were the very best of fellows.

The Belgian drummers spoke only a smattering of English, but it was enough so that the boys could make themselves understood—especially on things drumistic. Leave it to the drummers to get things across even though they speak in different languages.

Hard—Smooth—Glossy—Tight Grained

A newly discovered process involving several additional operations to the present method of making whiteheads now enables us to present a truly Superior Hard-white Batter Head. It is still whiter than former types—still harder, with still tighter fibres, which automatically make it still more damp-resisting. Try one and note the new life, new crispness and new "feel" of your drum. They are "speed heads".

For Snare Drums

Batter Side Only

No. 5717—17" for 13" shell		$3.25
No. 5718—18" for 14" shell		3.50
No. 5719—19" for 15" shell		3.75
No. 5720—20" for 16" shell		4.00
No. 5721—21" for 17" shell		4.25
No. 5722—22" for 18" shell		4.50

They throw away their money
When she casts her baby stares,
For she's a Drummer's daughter
And certainly knows her snares.

Photo by Ewing Galloway.

Drums Made While You Wait

Here's an Egyptian drum factory. Wood is scarce and metal is very expensive in Egypt so they make the shells out of clay, turned and shaped by hand on a potter's wheel and later baked in the sun. The drum heads are made of pig or goatskin and laced to the shell with animal gut. The shape of the shells with tube on one end is supposed to affect their tone. In reality it does not do so to any noticeable extent. The drums are very heavy and, of course, breakable. Luckily they are cheap, about 50c in our money.

Flossie Tulk

Miss Flossie Tulk hails originally from Melbourne, Australia, and is now playing drums with the House of David Ladies Orchestra of Benton Harbor, Mich. Under the leadership of Robert Dewhirst, this orchestra has attained wide popularity throughout the state of Michigan.

Leedy — World's Finest Drummers' Instruments — Leedy

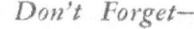

The Exclusive Drummers' Paper

Should Have Held It Until Later

Charming but Opinionated Damsel: "Now before we start for this ride, Mr. Jenks, I want to tell you that I don't drink, smoke, flirt or pet, I object to roadside parking, I visit no wayside inns, and I fully expect to be home by ten o'clock."

Jenks: "You're mistaken."

Charming Damsel (indignantly): "You mean about my not doing these things?"

Jenks: "No—about starting for this ride."

Don't Forget—

banners, especially the quality kind with deep yellow felt letters sewed on black or blue velvet such as made by the Bradford Company of St. Joseph, Michigan, are still the cat's whiskers when it comes to dressing up your audience and giving your orchestra some dignified advertising.

You'll get real personal attention if you will write to the Bedford Company and address your letter to Mr. R. Richards, St. Joseph, Mich.

Dave D. Morrison

Percy E. Johnston

Known to his friends in the profession as "The King of Rhythm," Percy E. Johnston is one of the top notch men of the country today. He is now playing with Cliff Jackson and his Krazy Kittens at the Lenox Ave. Club, a high spot in Harlem's night life.

His career is a long and varied one and includes some of the outstanding jobs of the United States, Europe and South America. His engagements in Europe have included such internationally famous spots as the Theatre de l'Etoile, Paris, Nelson's Theatre Charlottenburg, Berlin, Hotel Negresco, Nice, and the Empire, London. And in The Casino at Buenos Aires, too, crowds have kept time to the irresistible playing of "The King of Rhythm."

Johnston is the proud owner of one of the finest and most complete sets of Leedy instruments including the new improved Vibraphone. These plus the 26 rudiments, he claims, have been the foundation of his successful interpretation of modern rhythm, including his own originations The Congo and The Jungle rhythms.

(Photo courtesy Leonberger Music Co., Washington, D. C.)

John D'andelet

Dave Morrison of Winona, Minn., has been leading his own dance band, Dave Morrison's Ramblers, for more than eight years now and the outfit has enjoyed great popularity throughout Minnesota and Wisconsin resorts for the entire period.

Dave says, "I cannot speak highly enough of my Leedy Drums. Their easy playing qualities are superior to any I have ever owned or played on, and their flashy good looks are an asset to any band."

John D'andelet

John D'Andelet is a bassoon player with the U. S. Marine Band by profession, but he also doubles on drums whenever extra drummers are needed in the band's concerts. Besides this he plays drums in the various string orchestras which are made up of members of the band and which play at the many White House and other state functions.

Just because John plays bassoon does not mean that he is not a very accomplished drummer. He is a whiz, and red hot on dance stuff as anyone who has ever heard him will testify.

John's main hobby is collecting cigarette lighters. He says he has 23 different varieties of the critters in captivity at the present time and claims that they all work!

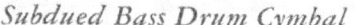

Subdued Bass Drum Cymbal

By using a 4" nickel silver cymbal (Leedy catalog "S" No. 7424, page 62) cup within the cup of an 8" American brass cymbal (Leedy catalog "S" No. 7438, page 62) on an ordinary bass drum cymbal holder—both cymbals clamped together fairly tight—a soft cymbal effect may be obtained by way of the pedal cymbal striker.

$2.00 award to Leonard Sykes, 508 Prairie Ave., Janesville, Wis.

Special Notice To Teachers

Leedy has thousands of drummer names on the mailing list but we do not know which of these drummers is making a specialty of teaching.

We would like to compile a separate list classifying all those who come under the head of instructors. Drop us a postal giving name and latest address and telling us how many pupils you have at present. We will then place you in the teacher classification. Who knows but what we might be able to assist you in one way or another some time in the future? We have a couple of good ideas on this subject if you will cooperate.

Sure Cure

"Rastus, what make dis bump on yo' haid?"

"I tell you, Liza, I'se got dandruff an' dey tol' me to put toilet water on my haid, an' de fust t'ing you know dat ol' seat flap right down on me, yes sah!"

(Bramwords)

 World's Finest Drummers' Instruments

Leedy Drum Topics

All in the Bean

No man's world is any bigger than the man himself. That which his eye can see, his ear can hear, his heart can feel, make up for him the universe. For no man has anything he can't use. What good is money to a Hottentot, or a magnificent picture to an idiot? The whole world for you lies under your own hat, and it is just as large and just as varied as your own mind will let it become.

Some Drummers

—that's what these gals are, and you'll agree when you see them in RKO Radio Pictures wartime comedy with music "Half Shot at Sunrise." They are the celebrated "Tiller Sunshine Girls," England's most famous bevy of chorines, and they are reputed to be able to play more drum tunes with their tootsies than an ordinary drummer can with a pair of sticks. Be that as it may, they are certainly easy to look at.

The drums are Leedy "Doughboy" models especially decorated and furnished with wooden batter heads so that the Tiller girls can do their tap dance on them.

The Gay Gordons

Since coming to the United States about 10 years ago, "The Gay Gordons" have always used Leedy drums in their very famous and versatile vaudeville act. The photo above shows one of their acrobatic stunts in which the drums play an important part. They do not, however, use the instruments simply for "flash," but are really first class drummers.

Those interested in Scotch drumming could get a lot of fine points from Murray Lee who is shown doing a handstand on the bass drum. He does some unusually clever two stick work.

The "Gay Gordons," play only the best of the big time vaudeville circuits. At present they are on the RKO circuit. Their drums are the Leedy "Sparkling Gold," models.

Clothes Pins Suspended for Choking Cymbals

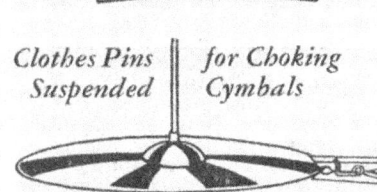

Sometimes in playing "hot rhythms" the drummer does not have time to choke the suspended cymbal and the resultant loud crash proves very discordant. In cases of this kind the idea explained here will prove very effective.

In order to choke the cymbal in a number of this kind, snap an ordinary spring clothes-pin to the edge of the cymbal before starting to play. More than one pin may be used if desired and the more pins used, the lower the resulting cymbal tone will be.

By striking the cymbal alternately with the tip and side of the drum stick, different effects can be obtained which are peculiar and effective. With a 14 inch Zenjian cymbal, the results are remarkable.

$2.00 award to Ollie Edw. Butler, 1209 16th St., N. E., Washington.

Long skirts are tough on the poor guy with a rotten memory and no imagination.

Send Us Your Picture

If your picture has not yet appeared in Drum Topics send it along and we'll get it in just as soon as possible.

Prize Inhaler

Muriel had been to the zoo for the first time, and was giving her grandmother a long account of what she had seen.

"And which animal did you like best, dear?" asked her grandmother when Muriel had finished.

"Oh, the elephant," was the reply. "It was wonderful to see him pick up buns with his vacuum-cleaner."

Sidney Dickler

"Sid" Dickler is in charge of the small goods of the Rudolph Wurlitzer branch at Niagara Falls, N. Y. Until recently, however he was with the Buffalo branch of that company. While in Buffalo he personally directed and produced the Wurlitzer radio presentations over station WEBR.

"Sid" is a drummer of long standing and is well liked wherever he goes. He has been managing and directing his own orchestra for the past six years.

They Get That Way

Lizzie—"How do you know she loves him?"

Beth—"Well, she's quit smoking, drinking and swearing."

Leedy World's Finest Drummers' Instruments **Leedy**

The Exclusive Drummers' Paper

Vise Grip Tom-Tom Holder

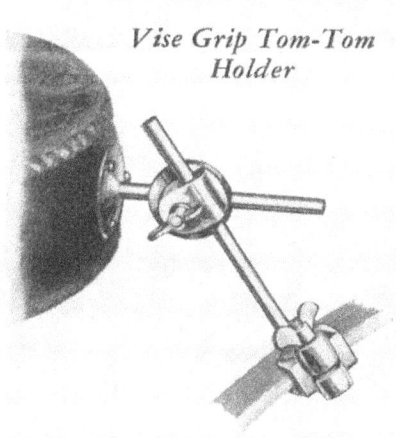

Here we present the strongest and most efficient Tom-Tom Holder ever devised. The hoop clamp and the adjusting feature for height and angle are fool-proof in every respect. A large fitted plate screws to shell of Tom-Tom. No more pulling out of rings.

No. 7720—In Nickel Plate $2.00
No. 7721—In Nobby Gold 3.00
No. 7722—In Chromium Plate 3.00

If You Don't Get Drum Topics

If Drum Topics is not sent to you, it's because your name is not on our list. Send your name along and we'll put it on the list, pronto!

Keep Your Eye on the Drum

—that is if you can. Otherwise you may take a good look at the girls of the "Follow Thru" Co., a musical comedy which has recently enjoyed great success in the East. In the photograph, Carl Shaw, drummer with the company's orchestra, is pointing out the merits of Leedy bass drums to the "Follow Thru" girls. Their smiles would indicate that they are quite pleased with what drummer Shaw is telling them.

Shaw is one of the finest drummers appearing in musical comedy today. He has been drumming for 10 years and has appeared with Schwab & Mandell shows (of which "Follow Thru" is one) for the last five years. He was the drummer with George Olsen's now famous "Good News" band, which in itself is ample proof of Shaw's ability as a drummer.

(Photo courtesy Conn Boston Co.)

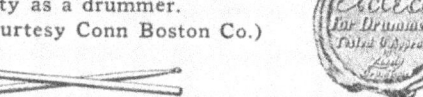

Don't Be That Way

A mother observing that her little son Willie never took his eyes away from the drummer while at a matinee, concluded that a toy drum outfit would be just what the boy would want for Christmas, so on Christmas morning she handed the various articles to little Willie by saying:

"Here is your little strapee,
Here are your little stickees,
Here is your little drumee.
Here is your little—this is bells."

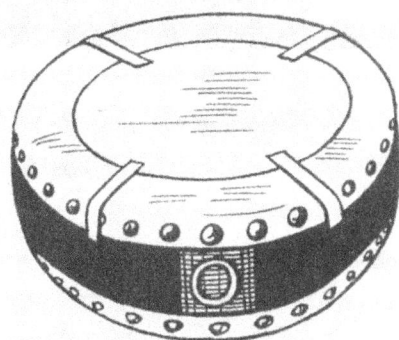

Subdued Tom-Tom

A Cleveland, O., drummer passes along this idea for subduing and mellowing the tone of a tom-tom. It is simple, practical and gives pleasing results.

Procure a circular piece of chamois skin about 6 inches in diameter and stretch it over the tom-tom head using adhesive tape to hold the chamois in place in the manner shown in the illustration. Play with felt sticks such as No. 1720 or No. 1722, page 92, Leedy Catalog "S". If desired, both heads of the tom-tom may be treated in the manner described above, the result being, of course, to subdue the tone still further.

$2.00 award to Leonard Krueger, 1224 E. 8th St., Cleveland, O.

 World's Finest Drummers' Instruments

Leedy Drum Topics

Iowa State Champs, that's the title held by the great organization shown above. They represent Baty-Tucker Post, No. 168, Knoxville, Ia.

The city of Bermingham and Post No. 1 of the A... well they may be. Although little more than a ye... last two American Legion National C...

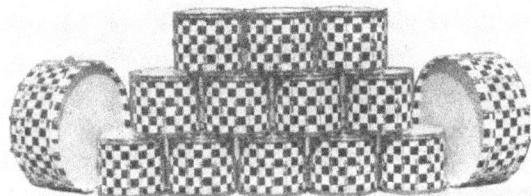

The uniquely painted drums above are the property of the Drum and Bugle Corps of Post No. 701, Amsterdam, New York. The drums were especially painted by Leedy to match the uniforms of the corps. They have two sets of drums, these for parade use and another set for rehearsal and other ordinary purposes.

Representatives of the world's smallest American Legion Post with a Drum and Bugle Corps, that's the title these fellows hold. There are 15 members in the post and 14 of them belong to the corps! Name? Fred Heath Post No. 199, Garden City, S. D.

This organization which draws its membership from the posts of Greenville and Celina, O., is what is known as a French Band. It is a combination band and Drum Corps. The Drum Corps section is furnished by the Celina post.

Down the street th... rop Post, No. 146... veteran Drum and B...

World's Finest Drummers' Instruments

The Exclusive Drummers' Paper

Wadsworth, Ohio, is the home town of the smartly uniformed corps pictured above. It is a splendid and extremely active organization.

...re proud of this fine Drum and Bugle Corps and ... already the class of its state and has attended the ... ng a fine showing on both occasions.

Within five weeks after the delivery of their equipment this fine Drum and Bugle Corps of Post No. 34, Chelsea, Mass., made its first appearance in parade. The corps has been growing stronger and more accomplished ever since and is well received whenever it turns out for an event of any kind.

It makes you an Elk if you belong to this corps for the fellows above represent B. P. O. E. Lodge, No. 111, Columbus, Ga. There are twenty-eight members in the corps and all of them are enthusiastic about their Leedy equipment. The outfit is well known all over its state

...orps of the Winth- ... This is the first all- ...rganized in greater

This is the Corps of Post No. 43, Faribault, Minn. They copped first place in the 1929 competition for Minnesota corps and were one of the first ten at the Louisville convention in the same year.

Leedy — World's Finest Drummers' Instruments — Leedy

Leedy Drum Topics

Drum Corps Helps
Complete, Authentic Information on Every Subject of Interest to Drum Corps

The Complete Drum Corps Guide FREE!

"The Roll-Off", 42 pages profusely illustrated and packed full of information and advice for Drum Corps, is offered free for the asking to you and every member of your Corps. Sit down now and address a postcard to the Leedy Mfg. Co., Elkhart, Ind. Just say, "Send me a free copy of 'The Roll-Off.'" Sign your name, put down your address and drop the card in the nearest mailbox.

You'll be rewarded for your trouble by the most valuable book of drum corps information that has ever been published. Here are just a few of the subjects discussed by experts in this completed Drum Corps guide: The Story of The Drum, Rules and Regulations for Drum Corps, Proper Instrumentation, Types of Drums, and Drum Major's Signals.

Every member of every Drum Corps should have one of these very valuable and very interesting booklets. Your copy is waiting for you now. It will be sent free, postpaid, just as soon as that postcard is received from you. Send it now while you're thinking about it.

Special Offer: Instruction Charts at Reduced Prices!

The famous Leedy Drum Corps Instruction Charts are now offered at the reduced price of $7.50 while they last. The regular price of these remarkable charts is $10.00 but we only have a few sets left and they are being closed out now at this remarkable bargain price. If you belong to a Drum Corps or are thinking of joining one, better get your order in at once before the supply is exhausted.

These charts are famous as the most complete and simple method of teaching military drumming that has ever been invented. The complete set consists of 12 wall charts. Each one is 36" x 36", a square yard of rudimental drumming instruction printed in red and black on heavy yellow paper stock.

The Leedy Mfg. Co., offers these Drum Corps Instruction charts with the sole idea of creating additional interest and pleasure for the practice hours of every Drum Corps member. The price charged represents only a part of the cost of producing these charts. They are not sold at a profit to us.

Remember, there are only a few sets of these valuable charts left. Therefore if you want a set, you should order them right now while they are still available at the bargain price of $7.50. Send cash or check with order.

Up-To-Date—Complete

The New Leedy Drum and Bugle March Book containing 15 different march pieces for Drum and Bugle Corps is offered at the extremely low price of 50 cents. Side drum, bass drum, cymbal and bugle parts are included in each of the pieces. Here's a chance to equip your corps with a complete repertoire of snappy, military marches at a low price.

Handy size book, 6½ x 10 inches printed on good grade paper with durable, heavy paper cover. Send for your copy—50 cents postpaid.

Free to Drum Corps

The two pamphlets of Drum Corps information described in the following paragraphs have been compiled especially by the Leedy Company and are available through no other source. They are offered without charge to Drum Corps. A request will bring them to you free of cost or obligation.

Officers, Rules of Order and Constitution

This is a revised, 1930 edition for Drum and Bugle Corps containing titles and duties of all officers, rules for conducting meetings, and constitution and by-laws. Complete, authentic.

Judging System for Drum—Fife and Bugle Corps Contests

A complete judging system for scoring such contests containing sample judging sheets and explanation of military and contest terms, together with hints to local contest committees. Indispensable for corps competing in contests.

World's Finest Drummers' Instruments

Page Fourteen

The Exclusive Drummers' Paper

Billy Todd

Billy Todd, a strong Leedy booster, is now playing drums with the Lasses White All Star Minstrels. He is a drummer of many years experience and a regular fellow from the word go. He is shown above holding his Leedy street drum which he prizes highly.

Believe It Or Not

The other day we heard of a trouping Drummer who, in twenty-five years on the road, had never chewed, smoked, drank, flirted, gambled or cussed. Guess he hemstitched his own nighties too.

Extra! Extra!

This is Murry Spivack, sound effects manager of the RKO Studios, holding a device of his own creation which imitates exactly the many sounds of a huge modern newspaper press.

The "spokes" of the machine are of various lengths and made of different metals. They strike at perfectly timed intervals, producing every whirring and accented noise which is heard when a big newspaper press is running at high speed. The next time you hear a huge press running in the "Talkies", think of this machine. It will, no doubt, be producing the sound which you are hearing.

Murry Spivack is a master drummer, tympanist and xylophonist. Previous to his present connection he was an associate teacher of the famous Glassman Tympani School and held many other high class positions in New York City. Many write-ups of this famous drummer have appeared in previous issues of Drum Topics.

Oren Polly

Oren Polly is connected with the Union Pacific R. R. at Omaha, Neb. He plays drums only as a side line but has mastered all of the rudimental beats and is a competent dance drummer.

(Photo courtesy George A. Smith Music House, Omaha, Neb.)

On the Cover

On the cover of this issue of Drum Topics is a photograph of "Tom" Richley, drummer extraordinary and xylophonist of distinction. "Tom" (his real name by the way is Edward Charles Richley) is staff drummer and xylophone soloist of the Crosley Radio Station, WLW, Cincinnati, O. This type of work, of course, calls for every trick in the drummer's bag. He must be hotter than Tabasco sauce on the modern jazz stuff. He must be able to handle classical compositions with the ease and artistry that only comes through a perfect familiarity with the rudimentals of drumming, and his work on the "xylo" and the Vibraphone must bring forth the absolute best that is in these instruments.

All of this "Tom" accomplishes and to the queen's taste or rather to the taste of the vast American radio audience which is somewhat more difficult to satisfy. Those of our readers who have never heard "Tom" Richley play may think this mere flattery. To them we make this earnest request, tune in on WLW whenever the studio orchestra is broadcasting. Listen for the drummer and if you don't agree with all we've said, let us know and we'll print the next issue of Drum Topics on horse feathers.

"Tom" was born and still makes his permanent address in Middletown, O. He gives his age as 28 years and admits that 16 of them have been more or less devoted to things drumistic. He studied drums under Clyde Shildneck and in addition to a lot of dance work has played with such fine musical organizations as the Armco Concert Band and the Ohio State University Glee Club.

"Tom" says, "My hobby must be handling sticks for my preference for xylophone and tympani are followed closely by a preference for golf."

And an important thing we forgot to mention, William C. Stoess is the musical director at station WLW under whom "Tom" is now playing.

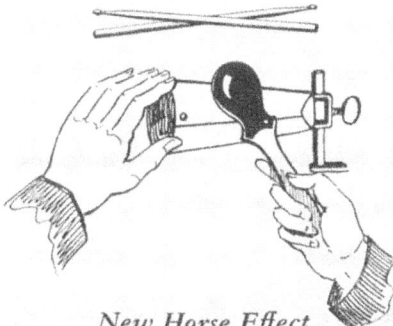

New Horse Effect

Here's a simple but very realistic effect for numbers requiring horse gallops and trots. As may be seen in the illustration, the only equipment necessary is a pair of castanets (No. 7771, P. 74, Leedy catalog "S") and a good quality cow bell (No. 7797, P. 75, catalog "S"). Hold the palm of the hand over the end of the cow bell opening and closing at intervals. At the same time tap the cow bell lightly with the castanets using a double or triple lick according to the speed with which you are playing. Try this idea, it's a good one.

$2.00 award to N. E. Reynolds, Hickory, N. C.

Police Chief—"What! You mean to say this fellow choked a woman to death in a cabaret in front of two hundred people and nobody interfered?"

Cop—"Yes, Cap, everybody thought they were dancin'."—*Fetter Clippings.*

Leedy — World's Finest Drummers' Instruments — Leedy

Leedy Drum Topics

Wop Cymbals on Tom-Tom

A peculiar sock tone, that is especially fitting for "hot" choruses where a loud rhythm beat is necessary, may be obtained in the manner illustrated above and described as follows. Lay a large piece of thin felt over either a Leedy 16" x 16" tom-tom (P. 72, Catalog "S") or a large size Chinese tom-tom. Grasp two Leedy Wop cymbals (No. 7476, P. 63, Catalog "S") in the regular manner. Beat the cymbals on the felt. Be sure to have one head of the tom-tom flat on the floor.

Idea originated by Drum Topics.

The way some guys hold their drum sticks you'd think they were afraid of getting splinters in their fingers.

Stars of the Capitol

There is probably not a finer group of drummers in the country today than the one pictured above. It is the drum section of the Capitol Theatre orchestra, New York City.

Left to right in the picture are: Conductor Bunchik, Ray Becraft, stage drummer, Bill Bitner, extra pit drummer, Bill Gladstone, pit drummer and Rechard Becher, tympanist. Each one of these drummers is an artist in the particular position which he fills and we do not believe that there are any better drummers in the country today than this all star outfit.

Bill Gladstone, the pit drummer, is a particularly talented performer and probably without peer in the United States or anywhere else in the world today. Those who are familiar with Bill's work know him to be one of the profession's outstanding examples of extraordinary ability, not only as a performer on Drum, Tympani and Xylophone, but also as an authority on the technicalities of drummers' instruments and an expert on sound effects. Numerous write-ups of this famous drummer have appeared in previous issues of Drum Topics.

(Photo courtesy Frank Wolf's Drum Shop, N. Y. C.)

A Correction

In the last issue of Drum Topics, No. 20, the article on page 15 entitled "The 26 Rudiments" gave the wrong spelling for the name of Strube, author of the famous "Strube Drum and Fife Instructor" written about 1865 and often mentioned among the best drummers today.

Oh! Oh!

Imagine the embarrassment of the St. Paul newsboy who opened the wrong door in the depot waiting room and yelled, "Extra Paper".
(Fritz-Cross Service)

Flattery is praise you know you don't deserve.

In Memoriam

On November 8th, 1929, William E. Owen, 40 Pleasant St., Haverhill, Mass., died at the New England Baptist Hospital in Boston following two serious operations for hernia.

Mr. Owen was a member of all the Masonic bodies including the Aleppo Temple Drum Corps of Boston. He was also a member of the Knights of Pythias, Burton Lodge, A. O. U. W., and of both Haverhill and Lawrence locals of Musicians' Union. He was formerly president of the Haverhill local.

The last few years he had been a member of the Haverhill Fire Dept. but was pensioned in June, 1929.

He studied drums many, many years ago with the famous Geo. B. Stone who passed on about twelve years ago.

Owen was considered one of the finest vaudeville drummers in New England. I used to watch him do his stuff when sitting in the third balcony as a kid long before I ever thought of taking up drums seriously.

He was one of the organizers of the Haverhill Masonic Band which is now well-known as a leading organization. There are eight Sousa men in this band.

Drummers throughout this district feel as though they had lost a real friend and marvelous performer who was a credit to the profession. May he rest in peace.

By Frank Holt,
Drummer with Sousa's Band.

World's Finest Drummers' Instruments

The Exclusive Drummers' Paper

Efficient Two-way Drum Sticks

Procure a pair of ladies' rubber heels from a shoe repair shop. They come about ¼" thick and 1¼" in diameter. Trim with a sharp knife to a perfect circle, smoothing up the edges and flat surfaces with coarse sand paper. Then drill a hole in the center of the rubber heel the size of the butt end of your drum stick. Scrape the finish off the drum stick and attach the rubber heel with LePage's glue. Be sure that the stick is a tight fit. These rubber discs on the ends of a pair of drum sticks provide a real utility in modern playing, especially in fast passages where it is not always possible to pick up a pair of felt or rubber sticks for use on temple blocks, tom-toms, etc.

$2.00 award to G. H. Lyon, 7 Primrose Hill, Skipton, Yorks, England.

Harry Crane

Harry Crane, a native of Cleveland, O., is now playing drums with the 7th Coast Artillery Band at Ft. Handcock, N. J. He is a thorough drummer having been in the biz for more than 22 years. Previous to his present work he has played all kinds of engagements including high class vaudeville bands and pit work. He was at one time with the celebrated Al G. Fields Minstrels.

Dale E. Watts

Dale Watts, originally of Nappanee, Ind., is now playing drums on dance jobs in and around Elkhart, Ind. He is a good modern drummer and always on the lookout for new "tips" and suggestions that will help him to improve his stuff as is witnessed by the fact that he is a constant and enthusiastic reader of Drum Topics.

James Jerome Rosenberg

James Jerome Rosenberg is now entering his fifth season as drummer and xylophonist with the Cincinnati, O., Symphony Orchestra. This is a position which, of course, calls for the highest type of work and could only have been held so successfully for such a long period of time by a really first class artist. This, Mr. Rosenberg is.

He has also played with various radio stations and at the Roxy Theatre, New York City. At one time he was xylophone soloist with the justly celebrated "Roxy's Gang." He is a graduate of the Faelton School of Music, Boston, Mass.

Joseph King

Now playing under Jack Rosello at Loews Willard Theatre, Jamaica, L. I. Joseph King has had a wealth of experience in his 12 years of drumming. He has held his present job in the pit at the Willard for three and one-half years which speaks well for his ability in these days of keen competition. Previous to his present job King was in vaudeville for five years.

Lettering Bass Drum Heads

Bass drums carried in drum corps or military bands should have the name of the organization to which it belongs lettered on BOTH heads of the drum.

The reason is simple. Unless both heads are lettered it is almost always impossible to determine the name of the organization coming down the street unless the one interested happens to be on the side of the street that has the lettered head facing it.

It was particularly annoying during the big parade of the National American Legion Convention in Boston, Mass., last October not to be able to tell who was who. And of course we on the wrong side of the street could not keep running to the opposite side in order to become enlightened.

If you really want the folks to know who you are, letter BOTH heads.

Carl Edwards

Carl Edwards is the drummer and leader of Carl Edwards and His Royal Vagabonds, a high class radio and dance combination. They have lately been well-received at the Everglades Restaurant, New York City. In the summer months the outfit plays engagements in Connecticut and other parts of New England. Throughout the Fall and Winter, however, they devote themselves exclusively to club and radio engagements.

A. G. Godley

A. G. Godley has been playing drums with Alphonso Trent's Orchestra out of Cleveland, O., for the last seven years, which, say we, is a pretty good record for any man, drummer or otherwise.

Godley is not only an exceptionally fine modern type of drummer, but he is a veritable whirlwind when it comes to nifty cymbal work. Very fast, very neat and very original ... especially with his left stick under the cymbal in combination with his right stick on top of the cymbal. He does this stunt in a different manner than any drummer we have ever seen.

 World's Finest Drummers' Instruments

Page Seventeen

Leedy Drum Topics

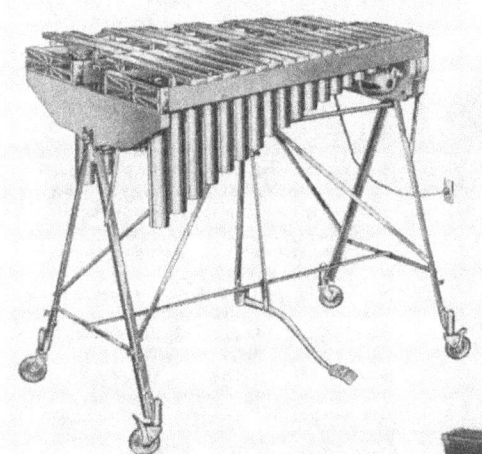

The New Leedy Light Weight Vibraphone

Here is the Vibraphone made practical for jobbing in 2½ and 3 octave models—easy to pack and carry.

In response to the increasing demand for a portable Vibraphone suitable for use by jobbing drummers, Leedy has built this new light weight instrument which can be easily carried in automobiles or street cars. Here is an instrument which will enable any drummer to increase his or her value to a musical organization and consequently will be the means of increased earning power for the drummer.

These new Vibraphones are made in two sizes—2½ and 3 octaves. They have practically all the features of the large Concert model, even to the same beautiful sweetness of tone. The bars and resonators are, of course, smaller, but the volume is almost equal.

They are equipped with tilting bars, damper locking device, tempered aluminum resonators, and chromium plated stand. The bars are of aluminum alloy and are suspended in mid-air using the same suspension principle as is found in Leedy Marimbas.

A section of each leg of the stand may be quickly detached in order to lower the instrument for playing from a sitting position. The motor is of the 110 volt Universal type with a speed regulator for the pulsating resonator fans. A most efficient damper with locking device is included.

You can now take a Vibraphone on every job. Fast to set up and take down.

The Vibraphone is the sweetest of all the mallet-played instruments and at the same time far exceeds all the other members of this family of instruments in "flash." It is easy to play, too, since the nature of the instrument makes it most adapted to slow, dreamy tempos. Here is an instrument which will add "class" and character to any drummer's outfit. If you do not already own one of these beautiful instruments, it will pay you to investigate its possibilities.

No. 5655—3 Octaves, C to C, 37 Bars, 1½" to 1¼" Wide, by ½" Thick. Level Mounting Only. Weight 67 Lbs. Length 44", Height With Wheels for Standing Position 35", Without Wheels for Sitting Position, 27" $260.00

No. 5656—2½ Octaves, C to F, 30 Bars, 1½" to 1¼" Wide, by ½" Thick. Level Mounting Only. Weight 62 Lbs. Length 38", Height With Wheels for Standing Position 35", Without Wheels for Sitting Position, 27" $240.00

Finish of Both Sizes—Silver DUCO Wood Parts—Chromium Plated Stand Polished Aluminum Bars and Resonators.

Four Pair Suitable Mallets Furnished With Each Instrument.

Hand Carrying Cases
(Illustrated Above)

For 3 Octave—Large Case Weighs, Packed—56 Lbs.
For 3 Octave—Small Case Weighs, Packed—47 Lbs.
For 2½ Octave—Large Case Weighs, Packed—49 Lbs.
For 2½ Octave—Small Case Weighs, Packed—38 Lbs.

The cases are the same as the regular Geo. Hamilton Green Xylophone type except for the different inside fittings. Every part fully protected by felt covered blocks and strong leather straps. Body of case made of heavy black vulcanized fibre with leather carrying straps all the way around.

†No. 6925—2 Cases for 3 Oct. Light Weight Vibraphone $45.00
†No. 6926—2 Cases for 2½ Oct. Light Weight Vibraphone 40.00

Indentify Leedy Leedy Bass Drum Shells By These Shields

 Marks Leedy Solid Shells

 Marks Leedy Three-Ply Laminated Shells

 Marks Leedy Two-Ply Laminated Shells

World's Finest Drummers' Instruments

The Exclusive Drummers' Paper

Behind the Scenes in the Talkies

A corner of one of the sound stages at the Paramount Studios, Hollywood, Calif. A complete description of the picture appears below.

We have called the picture above, "Behind the scenes in the Talkies," perhaps, however, it might be more to the point to call it "Behind the sounds in the Talkies," for that's what it really is. The picture was sent to us from Hollywood bearing the caption, "A corner of one of the sound stages at Paramount Studios, showing *portion* of mechanical effects used for recording purposes."

George Way, sales manager of the Leedy Co., who has been on the movie lots many times, vouches for the fact that this is correct. He says, "They just could not get all the effects in one picture and have them large enough to be discernible."

Note the large screen in the upper left hand corner, only the edge of which shows. This is the screen upon which the movies are projected while the orchestra fits the music to them.

Also note the large, square thunder sheet very near the right edge of the picture. This six foot hide was supplied by Leedy and mounted on a very large reinforced oak frame. In the rear there are gigantic electric heater cords to keep the sheet tight on damp days. The long narrow metal sheet, almost in the center of the picture, is, of course, another form of thunder sheet. Note the extra long train effect and the air whistle in the center foreground.

Chauncey Brown, formerly in charge of all such effects at the Paramount studio, has recently been transferred to New York City where he will soon take charge of effects in the Long Island studios. In the meantime he is playing in stage presentations with big name leaders in the Paramount Theatre in Brooklyn.

Harold McDonald, former assistant sound effect director in Hollywood, is now in charge of this department and also plays drums, tympani and xylophone solos in the concert orchestra.

I am going mad. I met her again today but could not speak to her. She is the most beautiful thing I have ever seen. But she is not for me I know. It is the irony of fate that keeps us apart. What would I give for just one night with her on a lonely road with the silvery moon above us! She must know how my heart yearns for her. She must feel as I do, that we were made for each other. But it can never be done, for she is a Stutz roadster and I am broke.
—*White Mule*

Quick Cymbal Sizzle Effect

Where a few bars of sizzle cymbal effect are needed the wire handle with loop end, on the end of a Synco-Jazz Brush (No. 1645 on page 67 of Leedy Catalog "S") may be used by holding lightly on either top or bottom side of cymbal while same is being played upon with the right stick.

$2.00 award to Allen E. Lilley, 75 Thomas St., New Bedford, Mass.

Here's a Laugh

Published some time ago in the Musical Enterprise—one of America's foremost musical journals.

By Heinie

Bullhide, Idaho
July 4, 1776

The Slap Stick Drum Company,
Softmarsh,
New Jersey.
Dear Sirs:

The beautiful solo bass drum stick that you made for me some months ago has been in constant use ever since. (I enclose cabinet photo of myself and stick for publication in the next number of the "Windjammers' Monthly Symposium".) As you are well aware, I have been prejudiced against American made sticks and have always used the best foreign makes, but now can truthfully say that in your new proportion smooth bore, long model drum stick you have them all beaten. The chamois cover seems to be of excellent quality and even in temperament, the stuffing seems true and perfectly in tune in all keys, while the action of the wooden handle could not possibly be improved. It shows no signs of splitting, although it has been in constant use, both in band, orchestra and solo use on the vaudeville stage. It took me a little time to get accustomed to the different bore, as heretofore I have used invariably, the medium or small bore drumstick exclusively, but now I say that for all around use the large bore stick is the goods and no mistake. Please make me up a leather, velvet lined, case for this stick and send to me by express. It is too good an instrument to run any risk of damage.

Very sincerely yours,
Bert Plugger
1st drummer Plugger's Band, also 19 years solo drummer Plugger's Drum Corps.

Fuller D. Jackson

Although only 25 years of age Fuller D. Jackson has been playing drums for 15 years. He started his drumming career with a boys band in Warren, Mass., and has been at it ever since. Jackson is now playing with Bernie McCulloch and His Aristocrats at the Hotel Three Fields, Boston. This is one of the really high class jobs in that city and speaks well for Jackson's ability as a drummer. He has also played a number of other high class jobs in and around Boston. Drummer Jackson's oufit is, of course, exclusively Leedy.

 **World's Finest Drummers' Instruments**

Leedy Drum Topics

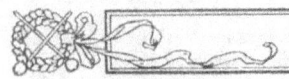

Eleanor D. Krannich

Miss Krannich is manager and booker of the Co-ed Entertainers of Akron, Ohio, which is one of the most popular girl outfits in that section of the country. She has built the outfit up from a five-piece combination to one of the best, if not the best, 11-piece girl orchestra in Ohio and Pennsylvania. Most of their engagements are in Akron, Cleveland, Columbus and Pittsburgh.

Miss Krannich is an artist in the true sense of the word. She is not only a high class drummer, but also paints and sings.

A Trio from Portland, Ore.

Above are pictured three of Portland's best. Everybody in that neck of the woods knows these boys. They are from left to right: Fred Trembly, Joe Amato, and Frank Brickell. These boys are fine musicians, dandy good fellows and all Leedy boosters. They are all fine xylophonists as well as first class drummers. On xylophone they are all graduate pupils of George Hamilton Green. Fred Trembly is teaching drums and xylophone at the Portland Conservatory of Music. Joe Amato and Frank Brickell are the mainstays on percussion of Portland Symphony Orchestra.

IN MEMORIAM
A. W. KUERST

Alfred W. Kuerst, age forty-six, for eighteen years secretary-treasurer of the Leedy Manufacturing Co., and one of the founders of the Indianapolis Symphony Orchestra, died Thursday, Nov. 6, 1930, at his home 84 North Audubon Road, Indianapolis.

In addition to being one of the founders of the Indianapolis Symphony, Mr. Kuerst was also a member of the Indianapolis Military Band. He became a member of this organization at the age of eighteen, and played in it continuously until a few years before his death.

Thousands of drummers all over the country counted "Al" as one of their friends. They knew and admired him as a loyal, lovable man and a fine musician. He was well acquainted with such prominent members of the Drummer fraternity as Karl Glassman, prominent New York tympanist, Frank Wolf, proprietor Frank Wolf Drum Shop, New York, Bill Gladstone, Capitol Theatre, New York, George Marsh, drummer with Paul Whiteman and many others.

Emergency Home Made Locomotive Effect

Four coffee cans and an ordinary spring are the principal parts of this fine home-made locomotive effect. The cans should be 4½ or 5 inches in diameter and the spring about 15 inches long and approximately 1 inch in diameter. The cans should be of the type with removable lids.

Remove the lids from the cans and fasten them with short nails or screws—preferably two to a lid—to a wooden base about 4 inches wide and long enough to extend an inch or two beyond the end cans. Space the lids about one-half inch apart. Next punch holes in the bottoms of two of the cans and place two bolts about 4 inches long in these holes securing them with two bolts and two washers in the manner illustrated above. Then, using a modern type can opener in order to avoid leaving any rough edges, cut the bottoms out of the two remaining cans. After this is done, simply place the cans in the lids, stretch the spring across them in the manner shown, and the trap is ready for use.

Use the contraption by brushing across the spring either with a drum stick or the triangle beater. This device is not only good for locomotive effects, but is also very effective for rhythm beats in jazz numbers.

$2.00 award to Martin Snitzer, 944 Granite St., Philadelphia, Pa. Courtesy Henton-Knecht Co., Philadelphia.

Leedy — World's Finest Drummers' Instruments — Leedy

Page Twenty

The Exclusive Drummers' Paper

Universal Pedal Tympani
(Patented)

Easy, Positive Action—Pedal Holds Fast in Any Position

1-Piece Perfect Symmetrical Bowls—Double Flanged Counter Hoops

Leedy Universal Pedal Tympani are used by more professional Drummers and Tympanists than any other make. They are recognized by the great majority as the finest machine type tympani ever invented. We earnestly invite comparison, point by point, and ask all interested Drummers to consult Tympanists who have had experience with various models. Pedal Tympani are now practical—practical in the sense that the motor car of today may be called practical. The pedal action is so light, positive and speedy, and the compass so liberal, that chromatic scales and melody execution are easily acquired. For "special effects" they have no equal. Modern arrangements demand Pedal Tympani and most Drummers of the leading musical organizations are using them. Leedy Universal Tympani will help you to greater success. You now have at your command instruments from which all mechanical limitations have been removed. They also help toward greater financial success, because your ability is given full sway. This will increase your value to any organization. This model makes it easy for you to master the highest type of percussion instruments with ease. Their mechanical simplicity assures success.

Read This—It's From A Man Who Knows

Chicago, Ill.
Nov. 7th, 1930

Mr. Geo. H. Way
The Leedy Manufacturing Co.
Elkhart, Ind.

Dear Mr. Way:

Thanks very much for sending on the 24" machine tympani. Used it with my other Leedy 25" x 28" and 38" in two rehearsals and in concert today. The workmanship is fine.

I get the results I want. I now have a good range from low E flat to high A natural over all four drums. Last week I ran into a composition demanding high B natural. This is in the futuristic class but we must produce it and I have it in the small kettle.

As I mentioned to you some time ago, I discarded the German pedal drums and I want to say here that I made a change for the best. Some of our wiseacres thought I was getting sacrilegious by disturbing the 40 year custom of using foreign drums. I am pleased to state the splendid tone quality of the Leedy drums brought forward comments from some of our best musicians who attend our concerts. Here are some of them—"Tone is pure." "Pianissimo roll sounds like a sustained organ tone—they penetrate in the softest passages." "Perfect intonation possible by their accuracy of construction." "Power galore." I am very thankful for all these comments and pleased to know that my judgment in changing to the Leedy kettles found favor with my listeners.

Enclosed please find check to cover invoice, and again permit me to thank you for your friendly service.

Sincerely,
(Signed) Max A. Wintrich
Tympanist—Chicago Symphony Orchestra

Effect for "Sock" Choruses

Here's a brand new effect for "sock" choruses that is very pleasing and original. Use either High-Hat or Low-Sock cymbal pedal at left side of bass drum as you operate with left foot. Use bass drum tone control on head of bass drum—preferably with any one of the pairs of special Leedy drum sticks shown on the bottom of page 66 of Leedy Catalog "S". Accent second and fourth beats of the measure and play four beats to the measure with the pedal and at the same time after beats (second and fourth cymbal beats of the measure) with the sock cymbal.

$2.00 award to Al Bennett, R. R. No. 1, Box No. 4, Kokomo, Ind.

Sizes and Prices

*No. 5500—Standard Size, 25" and 28", Per Pair (Bright Copper Bowls, other Metal Parts Nickel Plated and Polished Aluminum) $350.00

*No. 5501—Symphony Size, 26" and 29", Per Pair (Bright Copper Bowls, other Metal Parts Nickel Plated and Polished Aluminum) 385.00

Bowls in Glossy Black or White Duco—No Extra Charge

*Hoops, Handles, Stands, etc., in Nobby Gold, Extra 30.00
*Hoops, Handles, Stands, etc., in Chromium Plate, Extra 30.00

OTHER SIZES TO ORDER

Sticks and Fibre Head Protectors Furnished With Every Pair.

Leedy World's Finest Drummers' Instruments **Leedy**

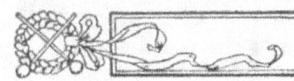 

Leedy Drum Topics

Do You Like It or Not?

If you like Drum Topics, give the editor a little hand by telling him about it in a little letter. If you don't like it, you've got a kick coming so don't hesitate to tell us just where we head in. This is your paper and we want to make it just as you like it. Oke?

Mitzi and Bobbie Grice

David Yudkin

David Yudkin of New Haven, Conn., has been on the road for several years with the famous Frank and Milt Britton and their original "Brown Derby Band." Dave got his drumistic schooling under the great Johnny Morris, drummer with Paul Specht. He has played in many New York theatres and done a great deal of jobbing around New York with stage orchestras as well. Dave is just a little bit older than "old enough to vote", but twelve of his twenty-one odd years have been devoted to drums and drumming.

The cartoon below depicts the aforementioned famous Frank and Milt Britton, in, as the saying goes, a characteristic mood. These boys are wonderful xylophone players as well as fine fellows and clever entertainers. They use Leedy xylophones throughout their act.

Here they are again, Mitzi, the drummer, and Bobbie Grice, the leader of "The Bricktops," internationally celebrated as "The World's Greatest Girl Band." Girl bands come and go but "The Bricktops" seem to keep on climbing higher and higher in public favor as the seasons roll by. They have held their place in the spotlight of fame for a good many seasons now and are likely to keep right on doing so with the ever dependable Mitzi at the drums.

Do You Know The Difference

between cast iron, malleable iron, case hardening and drop forging? You have heard these terms many times. With the exception of drop forgings, the other mentioned methods of producing metal parts are often used in the various items that go to make up drummers' equipment.

CAST IRON is technically known as gray iron. Molten metal is cast in sand molds to the required shape. Usually this makes the finished article with the exception of threading, smoothing up and plating. Gray iron is not suitable for parts subject to shocks or bending strains.

MALLEABLE IRON: While malleable iron looks very similar to gray iron it is really quite different. It is suitable for parts subject to vibration and shocks as it contains iron of the proper chemical content. It is cast in sand molds to the required shape and becomes very hard. In this state it is called white iron. The castings are then packed in annealing furnaces for a period of eight days. They then become malleable, which means they are capable of being bent cold without breaking.

CASE HARDENING: This is a term applied to a process of heat treating cast steel by adding a thin skin of carbon over the entire surface of the article and quenching it in hot water while it is red hot and thus forming a case over the surface a few thousandths of an inch thick. The length of time of the treatment determines the depth of the hardened case.

DROP FORGINGS: These are made by cutting the exact shape desired in large blocks of steel, half of the shape in one die and half in the other. These dies are placed in a large machine called a drop hammer. One-half of the die is raised three or four feet in the air and a piece of white hot iron or steel is placed on the lower die. The hammer when tripped falls with sufficient weight and force to smash the steel into the recesses of the die thus forming the correct shape. The surplus material around the outside of the form is then removed in a trimming die.

Tell Us About It

Drum Topics is not an advertisement. It is a newspaper for drummers and news is its first consideration. If you know of some news that will be interesting to drummers, send it along. We'll be glad to publish it.

World's Finest Drummers' Instruments

The Exclusive Drummers' Paper

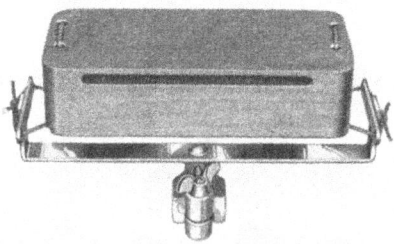

New Suspension Wood Block Holder

A new Wood Block Holder—the best ever. The block is suspended in mid air on heavy cords, which permits full tone without the usual disturbing metallic or bass drum "sub-sounds."

No. 7690—Nickel Plate		$1.75
No. 7691—Nobby Gold		2.50
No. 7692—Chromium Plate		2.50

C. W. Christian

C. W. Christian is a first class modern drummer who has played with a number of Illinois and Indiana dance bands. When last heard from Christian was playing drums with Joe Maes' Studio Orchestra at Madison, Wis. We do not know whether or not he is still connected with this outfit, but we do know that wherever he is Christian is on his toes doing a good job of modern drumming.

Justa Wethead says: Bein' married wasn't so bad in the old days, but now that the "talkies" are here, it's darn near impossible for a guy with a wife to find a place where he can spend a quiet evening.

This is the Seal of a Good Idea for Drummers

From now on when you see this seal on a Drummer suggestion you know that it is a good idea and a new one. All suggestions which appear in Drum Topics are tested and approved by a drummer of many years' experience before they are passed on to you. That's why you can bank on all the "Ideas" which you get from Drum Topics being good ones. Look for the seal, it's the mark of a good idea for drummers.

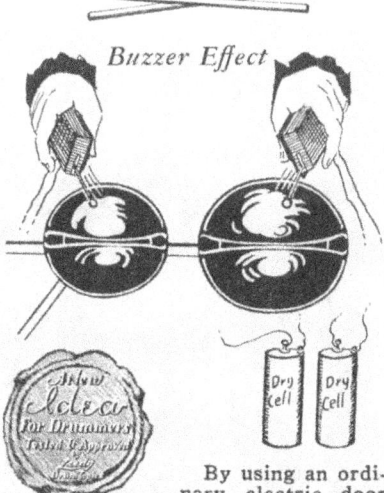

Buzzer Effect

By using an ordinary electric door bell of the cheaper variety and removing the bell, many effects can be obtained by holding the electric buzzer on various traps such as cymbals, temple blocks, tom-toms and even triangle. Two of the electric beaters can be used, one held in each hand. Two dry cells are all that is necessary to operate same and they will last a long time. A little experimenting will produce amazing results as the effect fits nicely in many modern numbers.

$2.00 award to Lee S. Herr, 315 S. 4th St., Nashville, Tenn.

"Bob" Lavigne

When the chamber of commerce secretary takes the trouble to write a letter of appreciation to a dance orchestra, they must be good, and "Bob" Lavigne and His Eagle Dance Orchestra have such a letter from the secretary at Pawtucket, R. I. "Bob" himself is the proud possessor of the letter and it is his drumming as much, if not more, than anything else that puts this peppy bunch across.

Harold G. Von Linden

Although he has only been playing drums for about two years, Harold G. (Lindy) von Linden is already an enthusiastic and accomplished drummer. He is now playing with the Yo-Sko-Haros, a dance outfit of Central Bridge, New York, under the leadership of Everett C. (Duke) Ruland.

He knows the legitimate stuff as well as dance drumming and has played with the Schoharie County Concert Orchestra of Middleburgh, New York. "Lindy" is 100 per cent Leedy equipped and says that he has received many compliments both on the tone and appearance of his outfit.

When better Drummers are made, Practice will make them.

(Apologies to Buick)

For 1931 the worst we wish you is the best of everything.

World's Finest Drummers' Instruments

Leedy DRUM TOPICS
The Exclusive Drummers' Paper

January 1931
Twenty-First Edition

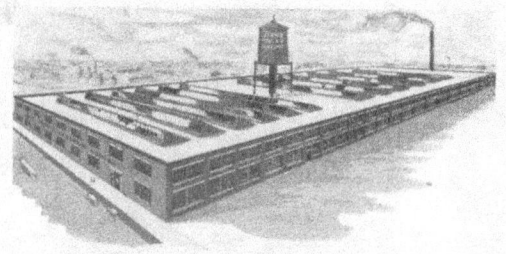

The Great New Leedy Plant
Elkhart, Ind.

POSTMASTER—Return Postage Guaranteed

LEEDY MANUFACTURING CO.
Elkhart, Indiana

Sec. 435½ P. L. & R.
U. S. POSTAGE
PAID
ELKHART, IND.
Permit No. 6

Joseph G. Benoit,
165 Hildreth,
Lowell, Mass.

This Is The "Leedy Bunch" That Is Always At Your Service

Here they are, reading from left to right: Geo. H. Way, Sales Mgr.; Jack Roop, Assistant Sales Mgr.; C. Schaefer, Advertising; C. C. Barker, Manager Drum Corps Dept.; Palmer Laycock, Service Manager; Clyde Sanders, Orders; Mrs. E. M. Way, Stenographer; Miss Dorothy Cripe, Stenographer; Miss Elaine Foster, Accountant; Mrs. Mallie Larson, Stenographer; Miss Mary Sanford, Mailing Dept.; Miss Anita Sutter, Stenographer.

Leedy Drum Topics Issue 22

Leedy Drum Topics

These New Leedy Tom-Toms Are Tunable!

Now it's your turn to laugh at Old Man Weather! For years he's been playing tricks on you—tightening and loosening the heads of your tom-toms just about as he pleased while you sat by helpless. But with these new Leedy Full-Dress Tom-Toms, you can beat the old fellow at his own game—*they're tunable!* A few simple twists of the wrist and the heads are tensioned exactly as you wish them. With the New Leedy Full-Dress *Tunable* Tom-Toms, you can always get the right tom-tom tone—full, deep, heavy, free from ring.

You've seen tunable tom-toms before, but none like these. They're beauties in appearance, the tuning rods are sturdy, simple and positive in action. In other words, they're the kind of tunable tom-toms you've always wanted—perfected by Leedy and ready for you now at no increase in price.

Folding Tom-Tom Stands

(Shown in illustration above)

Fits all "Full-Dress" Tom-Toms except the smallest size. Simply turn thumb screw for height adjustment. Stands fold into small space.

No. 7750	Nickel Plate	$4.00
No. 7751	Nobby Gold	6.00
No. 7752	Chromium Plate	6.00

Made to Match All "Full Dress" Drum Finishes

	16"x16"		14"x12"		13"x9"	
Marine Pearl	No. 8000		No. 8020		No. 8040	
Sparkling Gold	No. 8001		No. 8021		No. 8041	
Green Pearl	No. 8002	$35.00 EACH	No. 8022	$30.00 EACH	No. 8042	$20.00 EACH
Black Pearl	No. 8003		No. 8023		No. 8043	
Rainbow Pearl	No. 8005		No. 8025		No. 8045	
Black Enamel	No. 8010		No. 8030		No. 8050	
White Enamel	No. 8011	$27.50 EACH	No. 8031	$22.50 EACH	No. 8051	$15.00 EACH
Gold Enamel	No. 8012		No. 8032		No. 8052	

Other Standard Enamel Colors At Same Prices.

Leedy — World's Finest Drummers' Instruments — Leedy

The Exclusive Drummers' Paper

In Egypt a drummer mounted on a camel with these odd looking tymps is an important part of every wedding procession.

Drums Heard 'Round the World

Tom Walton, a drummer, recently made a trip around the world on a Canadian Pacific cruise aboard the S. S. Empress. In this interesting yarn he tells you about some of the drummers he met on his voyage. The pen illustrations are by John Myers, a member of the party.

Everyone knows how carpets, wives and records are beaten, but few are aware of the methods employed in providing the East with its mysterious rhythms and its many mystic and wierd throbs.

The charm of an Indian summer night with the sound of the drum coming from away over the "khuds" in a steady, even tempo can never be forgotten. And who could maintain normal blood pressure while witnessing an Egyptian Devil Dance? Strange dancers tread unholy measures to the music of a 10-piece orchestra—nine drummers and one piper.

"In Manila... a half-naked musician played a set of gongs and a tom-tom."

The drums are heated over a charcoal fire to keep up the tension.

Jingle bells are used by the mail carrier in the hilly districts of India to scare away jackals and hyenas. His steady trot and the tinkling of the jingles is a lasting memory.

In Morocco, an earthenware tom-tom serves a double purpose. Besides serving in its intended capacity, the tom-tom is used as a table decoration and vase for dried foliage.

India boasts of the smallest drums if we can exclude kiddies' toys. These are used by the snake charmers to attract an audience and are manipulated by rapidly twisting the wrist and

"In Japan the profession is graced with feminine beauty."

causing the striker, a small wooden ball on a string, to hit each head of the drum.

We were given a special treat at Manila in the form of an exhibition of native dances. These were performed to a peculiar rhythm furnished by a huge, half-naked native musician who played upon a set of gongs and a large tom-tom. That fellow was *some* wielder of the sticks.

In Japan the profession is graced with feminine beauty. There we saw three dainty feminine artists playing for the "Geisha" dance, a story in motion. One beat a peculiar, snareless drum with legs attached to it. Another manipulated a light tambourine sort of affair, and a third strummed a sort of cigar-box guitar with a heavy ivory plectrum.

What drummer wouldn't be heartbroken to find that his best pair of sticks had been exchanged during the

"India boasts of the smallest drums, if we can exclude kiddies' toys."

night for those of Loki Toshi, the Japanese drummer girl? Her sticks are simply round pieces of wood without tips or other improvements.

The East is full of strange drums and stranger rhythms. The memory of them remains with me, still vivid many months after my travels through the Orient have been concluded.

"In Egypt the drums are heated over a charcoal fire to keep up the tension."

The practical thing to do is to face the conditions as they are and see if we cannot get the best there is in them out of them—*Theodore Roosevelt.*

Leedy World's Finest Drummers' Instruments **Leedy**

Leedy Drum Topics

"Break The News To Mother"

Here's Frank Holt, famous drummer with the Sousa Band, posed on a memorial of the times when that heart rending ditty was billed as a hot number. Do you remember the Maine? If you do you're not as young as you used to be, but anyway Frank, who is known to everyone that's anyone in the drum business, is shown sitting on the capstan of that famous old battleship which was blown up in the harbor at Havana. The capstan now serves as a memorial to the event at Charleston, S. C.

"Star" Keller

C. E. "Star" Keller is drum major of the Kemper Military Academy Band, and a fine dance drummer in his own right to boot. In addition to his duties as a student and drum major at the academy, which is located at Boonville, Mo., Keller finds time to lead a dance orchestra which plays at all of the school's entertainments and dances. "Star" reports that the drum section of the Kemper band is all Leedy.

U. G. Leedy

Nov. 16, 1867—Jan. 7, 1931

On January 7, of this year, U. G. Leedy, president and founder of the Leedy Mfg. Co., passed away at his home, Indianapolis, Ind. His death takes away a man who has done more for modern drums and the modern drummer than any other single person. He was well-known to the drum fraternity and thousands of drummers counted him as one of their best friends.

Mr. Leedy started to experiment with drums while working as a drummer at the Empire Theatre, Indianapolis. Working almost single-handed, he built the Leedy business from a tiny shop to its present great size. He is responsible for most of the improvements which make Leedy Drums, the world's finest drummers' instruments.

Tony Lombardo

Here's the Tony of Pittsburgh's famous Jack and Tony team. If you have never heard these two clever boys tune in on radio station KQV some morning between 10 and 11, you'll like their stuff. In addition to being a radio performer, Lombardo has his own orchestra known as Tony Lombardo and His Blues Chasers. Tony is no relation to the famous Guy Lombardo, but it is reported that in Pittsburgh they think he is just as popular.

To Improve Your Stick Work

Rocco E. Laricha, well known drummer of East Orange, New Jersey, writes "If you really wish to become skillful with your sticks you should put in a few hours every week practicing the various rudimental beats on a SOFT SURFACE. To practice on a drum or a practice pad that gives a strong rebound of the sticks is easy, but if you will practice on something soft, while it may be harder work, you will in a short time notice a great difference in your roll and all other beats when you actually play on the drum head. I use a pillow, placing it on a table high enough to permit a standing position, with sticks of fairly heavy weight, such as Leedy H-20 or H-22. I put in several hours a week and the result has been continual and very noticeable improvement."

$2.00 Award to Rocco E. Laricha, 181 North Park St., East Orange, N.J.

"Have you a date tomorrow night?"
"It depends on the weather."
"Why the weather?"
"Yeh, whether she'll go or not."—*Wisconsin Octopus.*

Cheerleader: Now, boys, we'll give three cheers for the coach.
Scotch Player: How would two do?
—*Carolina Buccaneer.*

World's Finest Drummers' Instruments

The Exclusive Drummers' Paper

Most people's idea of happiness is to be somewhere else than where they are, or to have something they haven't now.—*The Mailbag.*

The best drummers use Leedy equipment exclusively.

Walter Mayfield

Mr. Mayfield is a resident of Quincy, Ill., and although he has only been studying drums and mallet-played instruments for about a year, he is already an accomplished performer on both types of instruments. He has a complete Leedy outfit including, Vibraphone, marimba and xylophone. Joseph K. Williams is his teacher.

A Drummer from "Down Under"

Ray Perkins is one of the really "big shot" drummers of Australia. He is now playing with the Linn Smith orchestra at the Trocadero, Melbourne. This is one of the dozen or so important jobs in the Anzac country. Drummer Perkins and the orchestra also broadcast over one of the big Australian networks. His equipment is all Leedy.

Fred Noak

Fred Noak, tympanist of the Cincinnati Symphony Orchestra and professor in the College of Music of Cincinnati, is in the top flight of the World's best tympani artists. His position as a professor of music and his standing as a tympanist both demand that he exercise the greatest care in endorsing an instrument. He cannot afford to give his approval to anything but the best. It is, therefore, with extreme pride that the Leedy Co., presents to readers of Drum Topics the following endorsement from Mr. Noak:

"I have had the pleasure of examining and playing upon the new Leedy tympani and find the instrument exceedingly satisfactory. The tone is exceptionally fine and the mechanism is dependable for rapid tuning. After many years experience with the Vienna Opera and with the Philharmonic Orchestra in Vienna, Austria, I can conscientiously say that the tympanist need worry no longer about securing good instruments. I believe that you have solved every problem that the tympanist has had.

"I am delighted to possess such instruments.

Very truly yours, *Fred Noak.*
Tympanist, Cincinnati Symphony Orchestra,
Professor, College of Music of Cincinnati."

Adolph Hahn, director of the College of Music of Cincinnati, has also given an enthusiastic endorsement of the new Leedy tympani recently purchased by the college. Here is what he has to say:

"The new Leedy tympani which you have sent to us are indeed very satisfactory, and we do not hesitate to recommend the instrument to any orchestral musician who desires to experience the convenience of rapid and accurate tuning, the delight of a true, beautiful tone and a resonance seldom encountered in the old-fashioned tympani.

"We believe that you have produced an instrument finer than any heretofore on the market. We are proud to own such instruments, to use them in our teaching and concerts, and to tell others of their superiority."

Tambourine Sock Effect

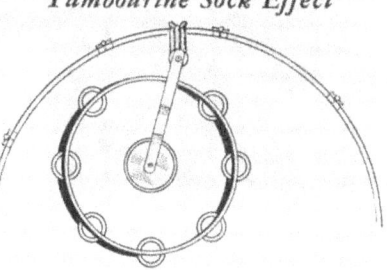

In working this effect you need a Leedy 8" or 10" tambourine, No. 7762 or No. 7761 P. 74 catalog "S", and bass drum tone control No. 7630 P. 68. The tambourine is held against the bass drum by placing it underneath the tone control, as shown in the drawing.

Different effects can be had by placing the tambourine in different spots on the drum head. The tambourine acts as a muffler while the vibration of the bass drum head causes the jingles on the tambourine to move, producing a novel bass drum tone.

The most effective beats to use are four to the bar, accenting either one and three, or two and four.

$2.00 award to Serge S. Fockler, 521 W. Wayne St., Lima, Ohio.

Len Wright

California dial fans are enthusiastic about the playing of Len Wright who has often been heard over station KEJK, Beverly Hills, in Vibraphone solos and doing his stuff with the studio orchestra. Len hails originally from Rockford, Ill., where he started his career in the pit of the Orpheum Theatre.

 World's Finest Drummers' Instruments

Leedy Drum Topics

"Smile Please"

—that was evidently the command given by the photographer when this picture was taken, and my how these boys are obeying orders! The xylophone is in the picture merely by way of a kind of symbolism, representing sound effects, for these gentlemen are some of the big pow-wow men from the "Talkies." They are (L. to R.) Murray Roth, Vitaphone writer, Bryan Foy, Vitaphone supervisor and director, and Hugh Herbert, Vitaphone writer.

(Photo courtesy Warner Bros.)

$2.00 Apiece for "Ideas"

Drum Topics will pay $2.00 apiece for each drummer suggestion or "Idea" that is published in the next issue No. 22. If you have a new trap of your own invention or a new way to use a standard trap or collection of traps, send a description of your "Idea" to the Editor of Drum Topics. If your suggestion is published, you will receive a $2.00 cash award and full credit when the article concerning your suggestion appears. No "Idea" or stunt is too large or too small, too important or too insignificant to find a place in this magazine so long as it has to do with drums and drummers. Think it over; haven't you some pet trick or stunt of your own that other drummers would like to know about? If so, send it along and earn yourself two bucks.

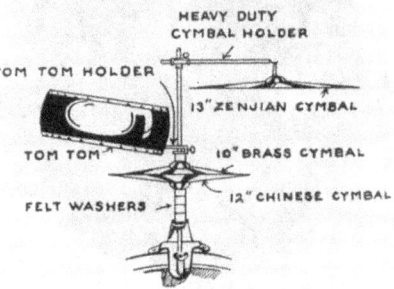

Assembled Parts Make Handy Cymbal and Tom-Tom Set-up

Here is a fine idea for drummers who like to have as many traps as possible on one holder. The parts included in the set-up are all listed in Leedy Catalog "S" and their proper arrangement is clearly explained by the accompanying illustration. A list of the names of the parts and the pages in the Leedy catalog where they will be found, follows:

1 Chinese Tom-Tom, No. 7715 ... P. 73
1 Bull Dog Tom-Tom Holder, No. 7725 ... P. 73
1 Bull Dog Heavy Duty Cymbal Holder, No. 7585 ... P. 65
1 10" Brass Cymbal No. 7440 ... P. 62
1 12" Chinese Cymbal, No. 7352 ... P. 61
1 13" Zenjian Cymbal, No. 7313 ... P. 61

Four felt washers are also included in the set-up. Three of them are used, as shown, underneath the Chinese cymbal and one is used between the brass cymbal and the tom-tom holder. The cymbal tones are determined by the pressure with which they are held together and this may be regulated by moving the tom-tom holder up or down on the stand.

$2.00 award to William Gilb, 423 W. 12th St., Newport, Ky.

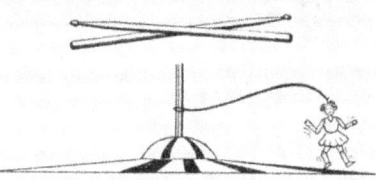

The Dancing Cymbal Doll

The accompanying drawing shows the idea of this stunt better than words can describe it. Little loose jointed dolls are obtainable at toy stores. Sidney E. V. Rowe, a well known drummer in England who sends this in, writes as follows— "Here is a little novelty I put over sometime ago that caused a great deal of amusement among the dancers. Get a little wooden doll with loose joints (if you cannot buy one they are quite easy to make), attach a flat wire spring to the waist of the doll at one end and between the top of your cymbal and under the thumb screw at the other end. After very little experimenting you can adjust the doll so that its feet will just touch the cymbal. It can readily be seen that the legs of the doll will dance when the cymbal is played upon. I have seen dancers stand and watch this for many minutes."

$2.00 award to Sidney E. V. Rowe, 31 Oakfield Street, Lincoln, England.

Explanation

A patient who complained of digestive troubles was told by a specialist that he was drinking too much and would have to knock it off.

"Well," said the patient, "what am I to tell the wife?"

The doctor thought for a few minutes and then said, "Tell her you are suffering from syncopation. That will satisfy her."

The patient did as he was told.

"What is syncopation?" asked the wife.

"I don't know," said the husband, "but that is what he said."

When her husband had gone out, the wife looked up the word in the dictionary and found it meant "irregular movement from bar to bar!"

Freddie Etzel

An old timer in the business is Freddie Etzel. He has been playing drums for more than 15 years and is now doing his stuff with Babe Fuller's Iceland Band at the Iceland Ballroom, New York. Freddie is 100 per cent Leedy and says he never hopes to play on a better set of drums than his Marine Pearl outfit.

(Photo courtesy Selmer-Conn, N. Y.)

Leedy World's Finest Drummers' Instruments **Leedy**

The Exclusive Drummers' Paper

The RUMBA
A Great New Chance for Drummers

George Marsh, Paul Whiteman's drummer, using a set of Leedy Maracas in a Rumba number. The King of Jazz and his drummer both endorse Leedy Maracas

Leedy Maracas

No. 7777
$4.00 per pair

THE RIGHT SOUND

The right sound is all-important in Maracas. They must have a "sting" to them or the effect is lost. Leedy Maracas are designed to give exactly the correct tone. They sound *right*, and they have plenty of volume.

The ball of the Leedy Maraca is four inches in diameter and weighted with shot. The handles are finished in red lacquer. The instrument has a fine "feel" and wonderful balance. It is strong and durable, will not crack or check.

Leedy Maracas should be part of the kit of every drummer. Big name bands are using them with marvelous effect on such numbers as: "The Peanut Vendor," "Lonesome Lover," "Mama Inez," and many other Rumbas and Fox-trots.

If your local dealer cannot supply you, write the factory direct.

"I want to do the Rumba." All over the country folks who dance and folks who only wish they could are shouting about their desire to waddle their hips and slither their feet in this cannabalistic new dance. They all want to do the Rumba. It's the stormiest dance-craze since the Toddle, and for drummers, the Rumba is just what the doctor ordered.

You can do a waltz, a foxtrot, even a black bottom without benefit of drums or a drummer, but not the Rumba. When they play that newest and wierdest bit of rhythm the fellow with the sticks has got to be right on hand. He's the head man.

Rumba numbers place the drummer in the spotlight. They call for new effects with plenty of flash, and drummers with good looking, up-to-date outfits are now cashing in heavy. In pieces like "The Peanut Vendor," which is, of course, the original Rumba hit, big name bands like Paul Whiteman are featuring the drummer using Leedy Maracas.

Maracas are the essence of the Rumba. Their peculiar swishing rattle furnishes just the right "sting" for this uncanny new beat. Native orchestras in Cuba, from whence the Rumba was imported, use the dried Maraca gourd for this effect, but drummers who have tried the gourds in this country find them unsuitable. Moisture and temperature changes have a detrimental effect on the gourds, and in addition, their shells are light and delicate which means, of course, that they break easily. Leedy developed the bakelite Maraca to meet the needs of modern drummers. It is durable and cannot be harmed by changes in moisture and temperature. It has just the right "sting."

Emergency Tom-Tom Holder

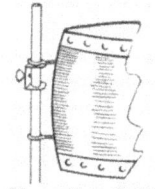

Obtain two screw eyes with the eyes large enough to fit over upright posts on Leedy Hoop adapters (page 70 of catalog "S") or posts of Trap Rail, Trap Table or Trap Console, or Handy Cymbal Stand. Screw eyes into tom-tom shell as shown in drawing. To keep Tom-Tom from slipping on post use cow bell holder clip No. 7220 (page 60 of catalog "S").

$2.00 award to Ray Larson, 57 Ryder Avenue, Melrose, Mass.

World's Finest Drummers' Instruments

Leedy Drum Topics

Endorsed by the Green Brothers

GEO. HAMILTON GREEN

"We consider this to be the finest all-around Xylophone ever made. We use it on all engagements and recommend it to every professional and school player."

Geo. Hamilton Green
Joe Green.

Famous Radio and Phonograph Stars.

JOE GREEN

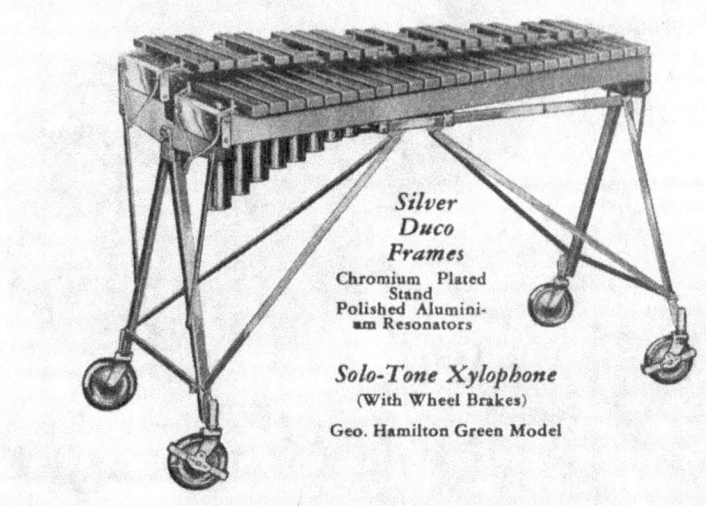

Silver Duco Frames
Chromium Plated Stand
Polished Aluminium Resonators

Solo-Tone Xylophone
(With Wheel Brakes)
Geo. Hamilton Green Model

Ted Whitney
A well-known Canadian drummer who has also played prominent spots in this country and in England, Ted Whitney has been in the biz for about 15 years and during that time has played everything from burlesque to grand opera. In England, Ted worked under Jackson Hylton who has made a name for himself as the Paul Whiteman of those parts.

Whitney is an ambitious fellow continually trying to improve his technique and his outfit.

Over three thousand professional, school and home xylophone players have adopted the Geo. Hamilton Green Solo-Tone model as the best instrument for all around use. Its marvelously rich, brilliant and powerful tone combined with the ease with which it can be knocked-down and carried from place to place, are the chief reasons for its popularity. It was constructed exactly to specifications laid down by the famous radio and phonograph xylo stars, Geo. Hamilton and Joe Green. The bars are of genuine Honduras Rosewood. Can be set up or packed away in three minutes. A wonderful instrument for dance and radio work as it is lighter than most models.

New Beauty Finish—Standard On All Geo. Hamilton Green Model Solo-Tone Xylophones. Silver Duco Wood Frames and Chromium Plated Resonators, Stand, etc.

Prices Include Split Frames and Resonators—Wheels—Resonator Adjuster Chromium Plating and 4 Pair Assorted Mallets.

No. 5620—3½ octaves, F to C, 44 Bars, 1½" Wide by ⅞" Thick, Length 52", Width Lower End 28", Height 33½", Weight 72 pounds.... $175.00

No. 5621—4 octaves, C to C, 49 Bars, 1½" Wide by ⅞" Thick, Length 59", Width Lower End 31", Height 33½", Weight 83 pounds...... $190.00

Either Black or White Duco on Wood Frames—No Extra Charge.

Hand Carrying Cases for Geo. Hamilton Green Model

Made of hard black vulcanized fibre with two leather straps all the way around. Each part of instrument fits snugly into inside fittings, assuring protection at all times.

†No. 6965—Two cases for 3½ Oct. Size $30.00
Weights Packed: Large Case 52 lbs. Small Case 47 Lbs.

†No. 6966—Two Cases for 4 Oct. Size $35.00
Weights Packed: Large Case 58 Lbs. Small Case 53 lbs.

‡No. 6970—One Trunk for 3½ Oct. Size $65.00

‡No. 6971—One Trunk for 4 Oct. Size $70.00

Leedy   World's Finest Drummers' Instruments   Leedy

The Exclusive Drummers' Paper

Ben Takes A Lesson

Ben Lyon, noted RKO star, is shown taking a lesson in drumming from Jack Wills, well-known drummer of Hartford, Conn. Mr. Wills reports that Lyon is an apt pupil, learning well and rapidly.

True, Brother, True

"All work and no play makes Jack a dull boy" says the old adage. On the other hand all play and no work makes no jack.

TELL YOUR FRIENDS ABOUT LEEDY. WE'LL APPRECIATE IT AND IN THE LONG RUN THEY WILL TOO!

Geo. H. Way, sales manager, and Jack Roop, ass't. sales manager, are shown looking over the new Leedy Tunable Tom-Toms and some of the other new merchandise.

The Xylophonist Who Became A Shoemaker—contributed by Martin Schneider, Holland.

Fibre Drum Case for Various Effects

Drum Topics Idea Dept. has received three letters from well known drummers, explaining how they use their Leedy fibre trap cases for various effects. A. Edw. Vigneault, of Passumpsic, Vermont, writes — "I place my round telescope fibre snare drum case against a chair to keep it from moving. Sometimes I use Leedy jazz felt stick No. 1600 (P. 66, Catalog "S") in regular tom-tom beat fashion. The hollow sound the case makes is a little different from a tom-tom and fits very well in certain numbers. Other times I use two wire brushes in one hand. Either of these goes on hot piano solos or soft trumpet strains."

Harold von Linden, of Central Bridge, New York, writes—"I lay my Elite fibre trap case on its side on the floor. For loud sock choruses where a distinct cutting sock effect is needed I slap one drum stick along its entire length with considerable force on the side of the case, grasping the stick at the small end. This will cut through everything and make them sit up and take notice."

Earl Peronto, of Manitowoc, Wisconsin, writes—"I take my square fibre telescope case apart, lay the large half flat on the floor and insert the small half into the large half on an angle. On the top side of the small half I obtain a very fine tom-tom effect by using felt end sticks. Also great when wire brushes are used."

$2.00 Awards to A. Edw. Vigneault, Box 64, Passumpsic, Vermont.

Harold von Linden, c/o Yo-Sko-Haro Orchestra, Central Bridge, N. Y.

Earl Peronto, 411 Park Ave., Manitowoc, Wis.

On The Air

June Collier and his O. N. G. orchestra were on the air sure enough recently. They covered the entire state of Oklahoma in the plane shown in the picture advertising a carnival which was put on by the Ladies Oriental Shrine at Tulsa. The plane was equipped with amplifying horns and transmitting apparatus by means of which the orchestra showered the natives of Oklahoma with their red hot harmonies. Charles Mead Tooker plays drums for the outfit.

Leedy   World's Finest Drummers' Instruments   Leedy

Leedy Drum Topics

Brooklyn Drummer Suggests Education Through Rhythm

By Frieda Wyandt
(From The New York Evening Graphic)

Rhythm usually isn't associated with morals.

Ordinarily one thinks of rhythm as something inseparable from jazz and black bottoming and Charlestoning. Moralists have been shaking their heads, lamenting the downfall of the youth of the nation, all because the younger generation has gone rhythm-mad.

That this same instinct which prompted the flapper and cake eater to master the intricate beats and muscular control which made the Charleston and the black bottom so popular could be used to develop a moral sense has never occurred to any one.

But along comes Charles Kritzler of Brooklyn, a veteran drummer—not the traveling salesman kind, but the kind who can do wonders with two sticks and a drum—and Charles Kritzler conceives the idea of teaching morals with drumsticks.

HIS NEW SYSTEM

And he doesn't mean "drumming morals into the younger generation," but LETTING THE MORALS SINK IN, ALONG WITH THE RHYTHM.

He has devised a system of exercises in rhythm which will teach children that muscular control, which makes trap drumming or the Charleston possible, and at the same time is putting into the heads of the youngsters a lot of useful ideas.

His idea is that youngsters should be taught drumming as soon as they are taught their A B C's, and his system of setting maxims to drumbeats has won favor with the New York public schools and may be adopted as part of the curriculum.

His maxims are usually double headers, two lines with different rhythms which the child pounds out on his desk or his practice board, and later taps off with his drumsticks.

The simpler drum strokes are taught with simple maxims, and when he comes to the complicated series of taps that make up a drum roll, the

You Ought to Hear Them Play

Under the capable direction of their manager, F. A. Urice, this Boy Scout Drum Corps of Sheboygan, Wis., has developed to a point of unusual proficiency. The corps is sponsored by the American Legion Post of Sheboygan.

As an illustration of the drumming ability of the corps, Mr. Urice writes, "I put those boys at the head of the Legion men for a night parade over a two-mile stretch at 128 steps to the minute without the loss of a beat by any drummer." That's drumming!

philosophy is supposed to become all the more complicated.

TEACHES FILIAL LOVE

For instance, the child of 5 or 6 in kindergarten is taught to tap out with his hands:—

"I love ma-ma. I love dad-dy."

The exercise runs like this: The left hand goes down on "I," the right on "love," the left on "ma" and the right on the second "ma." Then the process can be reversed for the second sentence, starting with the right hand instead of the left on "I," the left on "love," etc.

Sounds very simple, but just try it.

See if you are sure that your left hand will obey you when you tell it to. See if you can make the shift from left to right.

Too few children know their left hands from their right.

"These drumming exercises will develop co-ordination between the child's brain and its muscles," Mr. Kritzler explained. "To execute even a simple drum motif, the child will have to use all of its powers of concentration. Eye and hand and brain will all have to be functioning together, with the vocal chords helping to keep them all together."

And the idea of a nation of potential drummers, with a drummer's control of his hands and his muscles and his mind, is a very interesting one.

World's Finest Drummers' Instruments

The Exclusive Drummers' Paper

THE NEW ERA

Everything You Ever Wanted In A Cymbal Holder

In the NEW ERA, you'll find everything you ever wanted in a cymbal holder. It is sturdier, freer from "wobble" and has more adjusting features than any other cymbal holder on the market. Adjusts to any height or distance and gives a full clear cymbal tone because of the self-aligning cymbal rests. The Vise-Grip hoop clamp is the heaviest and strongest clamp of its kind that can be bought. The NEW ERA is the king of cymbal holders—there isn't a better at any price. Try one and you'll agree that this is an absolute fact.

No. 7540—Complete, N.P.		$4.00
No. 7541—Complete, N.G.		6.00
No. 7542—Complete, C.P.		6.00
No. 7545—With 1 arm, N.P.		2.50
No. 7546—With 1 arm, N.G.		3.75
No. 7547—With 1 arm, C.P.		3.75
No. 7550—1 Arm and Block, N.P.		1.50
No. 7551—1 Arm and Block, N.G.		2.25
No. 7552—1 Arm and Block, C.P.		2.25

Harold A. Edens

Harold A. Edens of Manistee, Mich., is now playing with "Swede" Christianson and his nine-piece orchestra playing northern Michigan resorts and country clubs. Mr. Edens is 24 years old and has been playing drums for more than seven years. Besides playing dance work he is snare drummer in the Manistee Iron Works band. He has also had three years experience in theatre and vaudeville drumming.

Leedy equipment is the world's finest. When you buy Leedy, you get the best there is.

THE SCOTCH VIBRAPHONIST

Tom Webster, Cartoonist

Tom Webster, who drew "The Scotch Vibraphonist," cartoon shown on this page is a good friend of Al. "Rags" Anderson and drew the cartoon especially for Drum Topics at "Rags'" request. Tom is not a musician—no, though, as he confesses, all his life he has had a longing to be one.

Instead of sticks and mallets Tom works with pen and pencils but judging from the amount of cartoons he turns out, one would almost imagine that his hands are kept as busy as those of a xylophonist playing a four hammer solo.

Dog Bark Effect

This is a very novel effect for which you will need the Leedy dog bark No. 7840 P. 76 catalog "S". It can be used in the last ensemble chorus of hot numbers, especially those choruses in which everyone is bearing down. It will fit better into the rhythm if the brass or the sax sections are accenting the first and third count.

The dog bark, of course, is played in the regular manner, pulling the rosined canvas clip over the string. The drummer is to work the dog bark on the accented count, only first and third.

This is a real novelty—try it!

$2.00 award to Donald Patterson, c/o Leon Knapp's Drum Shop, 211 Monroe St. N. W., Grand Rapids, Mich.

Bill Gilcher

Drummer Gilcher is these days by way of being something of a movie magnate. He is the big musical power behind the scenes at the Warner Brothers Studio in Hollywood. That is to say Bill is contractor of all the musicians used on the Warner lot. In addition to that he personally plays for all the big feature pictures made on the coast by Warner Brothers.

Bill was formerly at the California Theatre, San Francisco, and before that the St. Louis Symphony.

World's Finest Drummers' Instruments

Leedy Drum Topics

Above—Legion Post No. 23, Auburn, Neb., 1930 state champions, Mr. Charles A. Grovenburg, Drum Major.—Photo Courtesy Geo. A. Smith, Omaha, Neb.

Left—Leland M. Barnett Post, No. 123, Norwood, Ohio, E. J. Ertel, Captain.

"Zenjian" Turkish type cymbals, specially strong and thick selected for Drum Corps. No. 7313—13", Each $9.00. No. 7314—14", Each $10.00. No. 7315—15", Each $12.00.

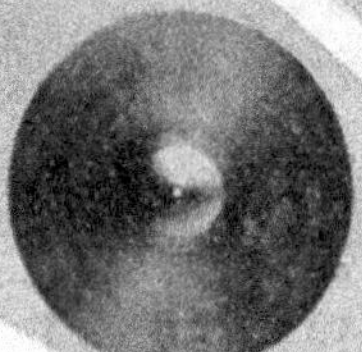

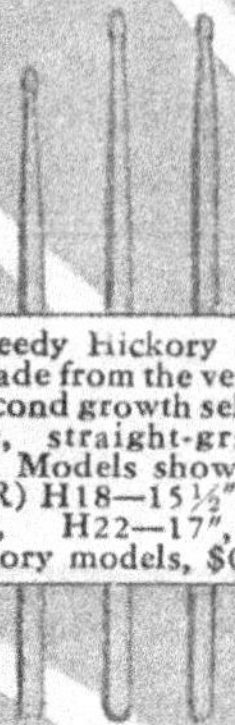

All Leedy hickory sticks are made from the very finest second growth selected white, straight-grained stock. Models shown are (L to R) H18—15½", H20—17", H22—17". All Hickory models, $0.45.

Military Model Street Drum—This drum has 3-ply Spartan Laminated Shell and is extremely light. Furnished in separate tension as shown at $32.50, also in single tension at $27.50. Sticks and sling included.

Tenor Drum—The importance of the tenor drum is recognized by all prize-winning corps. No. 3155, 18"x12", separate tension, $37.50, No. 3156, single tension, $32.50. Sticks and sling included.

Tenor Drum Sticks—The correct sticks for tenor drum playing. Balls are of right texture, solid felt, will not beat flat or come loose. Sticks, polished white hickory. No. 1610, $2.50.

Below—The prize-winning Elyria, O., corps, one of the largest outfits of its kind in the country, runners-up in the 1930 national contest at Boston. All Leedy equipped. Photo Courtesy Day's Music Shop, Elyria.

COMPLETE DRUM Le

Page Twelve

The Exclusive Drummers' Paper

Above—American Legion Post No. 61, Revere, Mass., J. A. DiPesa, Commander.—Photo Courtesy Conn Boston Co.

Right—Peninsula Post, No. 41, Monterey, Calif., Dick Hilbun, Drum Major, Ken Lyman, Commander.

Doughboy Street Drum—A high grade separate tension, low, metal hoop drum at a lower price than the floating head model. $32.50, sticks and sling included. All regular sizes.

Lite-Wate Twirling Baton—Here's a new twirling model especially designed for those who want a light weight baton. Weight 16 oz., length 34". Nickel finish. Aluminum ball. No. 1924, $10.00.

"Two Way" Practice Pad—Has two playing surfaces, rubber side for soft practice, fibre side for loud practice. Both sides inclined at proper angle. No. 2755, $2.75.

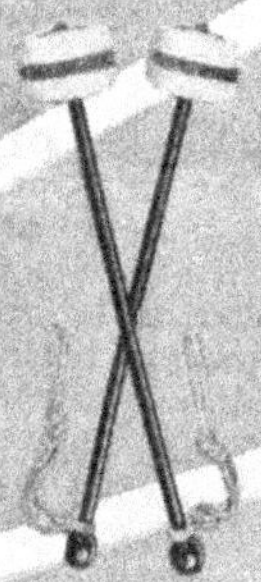

Scotch Bass Drum Sticks—These new design sticks have three layers of the right texture solid felt. Special metal collars and washers insure against balls flying off. No. 1635, 15", per pair, $5.00.

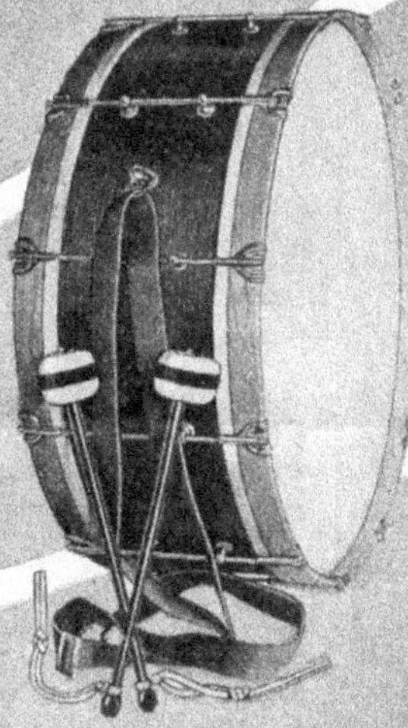

Scotch Type Bass Drum—Especially designed for Scotch two-stick playing, also practical for straight work on parade. In three sizes. Separate tension, $47.00 and up. Single tension, $39.50 and up.

Page Thirteen

Leedy Drum Topics

Meet The "Kaiser"

Just where and how Joe Marshall acquired the title of "Kaiser", is a story that we have yet to hear, but be that as it may, Marshall is, if not the "Kaiser" of all dance drummers, at least one of the grand high potentates of the order. He is now leading his own orchestra, known as Joe "Kaiser" Marshall and His Czars of Harmony, filling vaudeville and ballroom dates. The "Kaiser's" former engagements include such famous spots as Fletcher Henderson's Original Roseland Orchestra, which kept the corner of 51st and B'way all hot and bothered for so many seasons, and he has also served time with the celebrated McKinney's Cotton Pickers of Detroit.

The "Kaiser" claims as his teachers those master drummers, George Stone and Wm. Maloney, and adds the fact that if all his experience as a professional drummer were laid end-to-end it would make at least 12 and one-half years.

Jimmy Garcia

When last heard from Jimmy Garcia was playing dance dates in California with his own orchestra, "The Dixie Demons." He is well-known to dance enthusiasts in and around Los Angeles. Jimmy has a complete Leedy Sparkling Gold outfit.

Orchestra Leader: Wot's the idea—what have you got in the carriage?
Trap Drummer: My kid sister—I'm gonna start her crying during our Baby Number.
—Life.

Bennie Washington

Bennie Washington is a very fine modern drummer and one of the best in Chicago where he is now playing with Earl Hines Orchestra at the Grand Terrace Cafe. He formerly had his own outfit in St. Louis and has also played with the well-known Fate Marible and Charley Creath orchestras.

Bennie has a lot of stuff on the sticks and his fine work is undoubtedly one of the things responsible for the large and enthusiastic crowds that chase the flying hours with dancing feet nightly at the Grand Terrace.

New Hot Wash Board

Procure a small metal wash board at the Five & Ten Cent Store, also a small wire sink brush. Hold board against bass drum head (or lay flat on tympani head) and "scrub out" hot rhythm beats with the sink brush on the corrugations of the wash board. Fine for novelty accompaniments in both loud and soft hot choruses.

$2.00 award to "Muddy" Waters, 1069 S. Lafayette Ave., Grand Rapids, Mich.

"Do you think jazz is dying?"
"I don't know, but it always sounds to me as if it were suffering horribly."
—Slices.

Here's to the drummer with nice, quiet rhythm—
The rest of the orchestra's got to go with him.
The man who keeps cool, but, if needed, gets hot
On wood blocks, and cymbal, and tymp—plays the lot.
The man who's expected to stick to the rhythm
And can't have a drink but what the rest all go with him.

Likes It

Just received your Leedy Drum Topics No. 21 and was tickled to death to get it. I can never wait 'til I receive the Drum Topics because I think it's the finest little book on the market.

Vincent "Pete" Meier,
Germantown, Ill.

Busy Days For Mamma's Tots.

Teacher: Horatio, where is your sister today?
Horatio: Gettin' measured for a new dress; she's flower girl in a divorce case.

World's Finest Drummers' Instruments

The Exclusive Drummers' Paper

Al Wentzell

Al hails from Biloxi, Miss., and has attained an enviable reputation around that big winter resort. He is now playing with his own orchestra at the Crystal Ballroom in Biloxi, and during his eight years as a drummer he has played some of the most fashionable spots in the gulf coast playground. He and his orchestra were for two years at exclusive Hotel Markham.

Shambah Revelers

This splendid drum and bugle corps is the pride of Shambah Temple, Dramatic Order of the Knights of Khorassan, Indianapolis, Ind. They won first place at the state convention of their order held at Springfield, O., Sept., 1930, and expect to be on hand for the big international conclave at Cincinnati, week of Aug. 9, this year.

Dave Price is president of the corps, Joseph H. Foley, secretary-treasurer, John A. Walker, Sr., drum instructor, and Arthur E. Krebs, bugle instructor.

Johnny Ulch

Johnny is a popular California drummer now playing with Ray West at El Cortez Hotel, San Diego. He learned his drumming from Harry Bower and is a very capable performer in all kinds of drum work.

A "Gum Leaf" Band

This photograph of a "Gum Leaf" band of Australian aboriginals was sent in by Ray Perkins, an Australian drummer whose photograph appears in another part of this issue. The three drummers are members of an aboriginal Australian tribe of New South Wales. The drums, which were made by the old fellow shown in the centre, are a work of art the wood in them being taken from old tea chests.

In addition to the drums the bandsmen use the leaf of a certain gum tree to play upon, and for this reason the outfit is called a "Gum Leaf" band. Drummer Perkins reports that their music is completely different.

A Drum Stick Holder

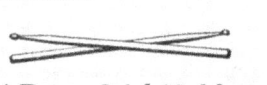

Obtain a cardboard shoe box. Glue the cover on same. Cut out one end of the box. Cover entire box with any kind of material such as denim or felt by carefully and neatly gluing same all over the surface. Punch four holes about 2 inches apart on one side of the box. Through these holes insert shoe lacing or like cord and tie box to leg or rung of drummer's chair. Have the open end of the box up. This device will make a handy container for an assortment of sticks and place them where they will be easily reached throughout the job.

$2.00 award to Johnny Snarski, 37 Old Terrace St., Bellows Falls, Vt.

"Just think! The island of Manhattan was bought from the Indians for a bottle of pre-war whisky and $24."

"What! Twenty-four dollars besides?"—*Chicago Phoenix*.

On The Cover

The Van Gelder twins, Leon and Rudy, have been big hits at Warner Brothers' Stanley Theatre, Jersey City, N. J., for a long time back. Leon is the house conductor at the Stanley, and Rudy is, of course, the drummer. They are shown on the cover of this issue together with Eddie Peabody, popular banjo comic. The trio are posed on the stage at the Stanley which is the third largest and most beautiful theatre in the state of New Jersey.

Rudy recently purchased a set of Leedy chimes in gold. These together with his Leedy Pedal Tympani, which are also in gold, make a wonderful flash on the stage and have done a lot to increase Rudy's popularity with the audiences. He is wonderfully pleased with the chimes and has received all kinds of compliments on them as well as the rest of his superfine outfit from directors and other members of the show.

For almost 20 years Rudy has been playing in the leading vaudeville theatres in and around New York City. He was a former pupil of the celebrated Karl Glassman and is considered one of the best all-around theatre and concert drummers in the East. Rudy was born in Amsterdam, Holland.

World's Finest Drummers' Instruments

Page Fifteen

Leedy Drum Topics

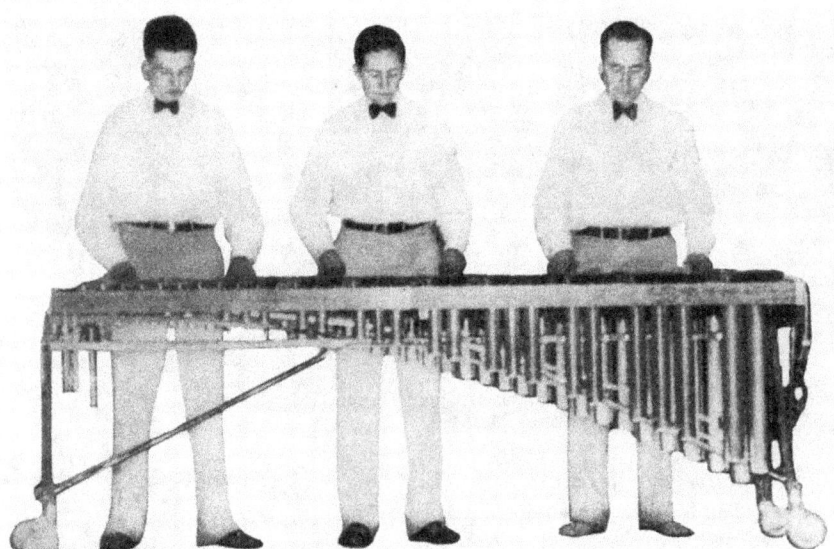

The Drum Shop Marimba Band
—under that title the trio above consisting of (L to R) Dean Pullins, Fred E. Cooley, Jr., and John B. Quick have won the enthusiastic approval of many audiences in their home city, Phoenix, Ariz.

Both Pullins and Cooley are pupils of Quick, who is the owner of the Phoenix Drum Shop and a drummer of many years experience. He is glowing in his praise of both Pullins and Cooley, and says they are drummers and xylophonists of unusual talent.

Of Cooley, says Quick, "His work on the Monarch xylophone is very much in demand and he is usually the feature attraction on the bill wherever he appears."

This is the big hand he gives to Pullins, "This lad is one of those boys you often hear about but seldom meet. He came to me some 11 months ago, and said he wanted to take up drums—didn't know a note from a box car. Today he can play everything in 401-G1 perfectly and up to tempo—that's saying a lot, but I mean just what I say—He has the most beautiful Leedy outfit in Arizona, including Rollaway Console and complete line of traps with everything in Nobby Gold. He is very likeable, has a fine personality and a good voice."

One for the Bull's Side

Charles J. Kramer, Tacoma, Wash., Drummer, Cops The Sawbuck for the Prize Story This Issue.

A few years back, in the days of the silent thrillers, "Blood and Sand" was playing the Main Street Theatre. The house drummer, who was viewing the lithographs which adorned the front of the theatre, remarked to his friend that it reminded him of his trouping days in Mexico. "Having nothing to do one afternoon in Juarez", he said, "I decided to see a bull fight. My idea of a bull fight was nothing more or less than a guy on horseback stabbing a he-cow with a spear. Passing in to the arena, I saw about 20,000 spigs, all pepped up, waiting for the show to start. When the guy that was going to fight the bull came out, they gave him a cheer that you could have heard in Yucatan. He was on horseback, and after the gent had taken a couple of bows, they led in the bull. Everybody rooted for the guy on the horse but myself. The bull made one dash at the bold toreador, and tossed him higher than a rooky pitcher in a Spring training camp. There wasn't a sound from the mob until I uncorked one yelp, "HOOK 'IM COW!" I was the only friend the bull had. When the Mexican police fished me out of the riot, all that I had left was my membership in the A. F. of M. and a set of Leedy drums on the show-lot. While doing 30 days in the village bastile, I thought of a good motto: "Never come between a bull-fighter and his audience."

Our idea of an optimist is the guy who sits in the last row of the gallery and winks at the chorus girls.—*Sour Owl.*

Flash Spoon Clappers

It has been noticed that drummers are taking up the old gag of using tablespoons for "bones" or clappers. They certainly do sound good in hot novelty numbers. By holding two tablespoons loosely in the right hand with the fingers separating the ends and slapping the bowls of the spoons on the palm of the left hand or the knee, etc., an excellent rhythm effect is produced. The bottoms, or outside of the bowls of the spoons coming together create a different metallic tone than any other trap or instrument. Short rolls are possible by slapping the ends of the spoons across the fingers and thumb of the left hand.

$2.00 Award to Chester Tamillo, Box 23, Milwaukee Ave., Niles, Ill.

Mary Eileen Kinyon

Pretty Miss Kinyon plays her Leedy marimba in the Gothenburg, Neb., high school band and orchestra, and she is a feature attraction at every performance. More and more high school musical organizations are featuring this beautiful instrument in their presentations every year.

$10.00 Reward

Drum Topics pays a reward of $10.00 each issue for a favorite drummer story. Send yours in. It may be the winning story and if so the sawbuck will be yours. The story need not be long and it need not be true—but it must be good. Don't pass up this chance to make 10 bucks easy.

Leedy World's Finest Drummers' Instruments **Leedy**

The Exclusive Drummers' Paper

The Solo-Tone MARIMBA

- Equipped with wheel brakes.
- Split frame and resonator device.
- Three and a half or four octaves.

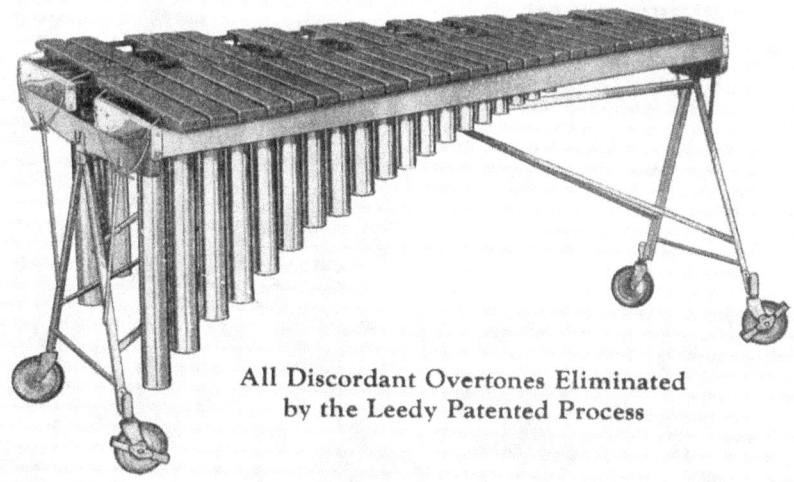

All Discordant Overtones Eliminated by the Leedy Patented Process

Your Choice of Elevated or Level Mounting of the Sharps and Flats

Fred Paine, 1st percussionist Detroit Symphony Orchestra, and his Leedy Marimba.

"For beautiful, resonant, organ-like tones the Leedy Solo-Tone Marimba has no equal in the world. It is a perfect instrument from the lowest to the highest note in its scale—an instrument worthy of the finest artist."

This is the unstinted praise given to the Leedy Solo-Tone Marimba by Fred Paine, celebrated percussionist and marimba soloist of the Detroit Symphony Orchestra. Mr. Paine is known from coast to coast as one of the truly great marimba artists of this country. He, of course, uses the Leedy marimba exclusively as do the great majority of the other well-known players of this instrument. Photo courtesy Conn Detroit Co., Irv Wilkie, Mgr. Drum Dept.

THE above photograph shows the Solo-Tone Marimba with the bars level mounted; however, you may order them with the elevated sharps and flats without extra charge. Most Marimba players prefer level mounting, as it is claimed to be easier for four-hammer playing. This Marimba is mellow and the sustained tone qualities are similar to the organ, especially in the lower range, and it has exceptional carrying power. The special brake wheels and split frame and resonator device are included with each instrument. All models are equipped with our resonator adjusting feature. Genuine Honduras Rosewood bars. The metal crotchets, over which the cord supporting the bars is drawn, are rubber insulated and also act as separators. The cord, after being tightly drawn up, supports the bars in mid-air and they are securely held by a unique spring clamping device. Tuned to low pitch (A-440) unless otherwise specified.

The NEW BEAUTY FINISH—Standard On All Solo-Tone Marimbas
Silver Duco Wood Frames and Chromium Plated Resonators, Stand, etc.

Prices Include Split Frames and Resonators—Wheels—Resonator Adjuster Chromium Plating and 5 Pair Assorted Mallets

No. 5610—3½ octaves, F to C, 44 Bars, 2½" to 1¾" Widths by ⅞" Thick, Length 62", Width Lower End 32", Height 34", Weight 100 lbs. $210.00

No. 5611—4 octaves, C to C, 49 Bars, 2½" to 1¾" Widths by ⅞" Thick, Length 71", Width Lower End 35", Height 34", Weight 115 lbs. 260.00

Either Black or White Duco on Wood Frames—NO EXTRA CHARGE

Nobby Gold on Resonators, Stand and All Metal Parts .... $25.00 Extra
Marine Pearl on Front, Back and Ends of Wood Frames .... 10.00 Extra

‡No. 6855—One Trunk for 3½ Oct. Marimba $80.00
‡No. 6956—One Trunk for 4 Oct. Marimba 85.00

World's Finest Drummers' Instruments

Leedy Drum Topics

A Fair Question

"I can't marry you," said the justice of the peace to the nervous bridegroom. "If this girl is only seventeen, you will have to get her father's consent."

"Consent!" yelled the groom. "Say, who do you think this old guy with the rifle is, Daniel Boone?"—*Ionic Club News.*

In a live cow the head is the noisy end.

Tell Us About It

Drum Topics is not an advertisement. It is a newspaper for drummers and news is its first consideration. If you know of some news that will be interesting to drummers, send it along. We'll be glad to publish it.

Two heads are better than one. Two "Hardwhites" are better than four of some others.

From "Old Kaintuck"

There is some difference of opinion as to just exactly what kind of an animal the one shown on the drumhead above is, but we maintain that if it isn't a Bearcat it should be for the drummers of the University of Kentucky Band certainly deserve that title. They are Bearcat drummers and no mistake. It's from college band drum sections like the one shown here that more and more young men are graduating to well-paid jobs as professional drummers.

Cymbal Clamp

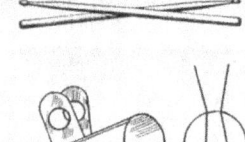

Here is one that will stop pedal cymbal ring. Buy a 2" heavy spring type paper clip at a stationery store. Glue two strips of felt on the inside edges of the clip. Snap this on your foot cymbal and it will eliminate that annoying ring.

$2.00 award to George Bennett, 3236 Ormond Rd., Cleveland Heights, Ohio.

Faking By Instinct

Vicar (to rustic in village orchestra): "I didn't know you were a drummer, John."

John: "Nor be I, zur. An I knows nowt 'bout drum music, neither; but I deals it one when I think it wants it."—Contributed by Cyril Kitchener, Liverpool, England.

Marimba Marvel

Down in Peoria, Ill., eight-year-old Harry Detmer is hailed as a marimba marvel. He played with orchestra accompaniment at the annual Peoria food show, and according to report, brought the house down. Harry is the official mascot and xylophone soloist of the Peoria American Legion Band and the Abbas Grotto Band. He has also played in Publix and independent theatres in Illinois, Iowa, Indiana, Missouri. (*Photo courtesy Conn-Peoria Co.*)

Chief Many Drums

Here's William J. Johnson all dolled up for an Indiana war dance using a Leedy Chee Foo tom-tom. The picture was taken while Johnson was touring the western states with the Haskell Indian orchestra of Lawrence, Kan. Bill is really and truly an Indian—a full-blooded Ute.

Violin For Sale Cheap

"Down with the fiddles and up with the drums," says Vincent L. Mott, Jr., of Paterson, N. J., as he grabs the sticks to beat upon his trusty Leedy. Vincent's father runs The Drummer's Service Station at Paterson.

Leedy World's Finest Drummers' Instruments *Leedy*

The Exclusive Drummers' Paper

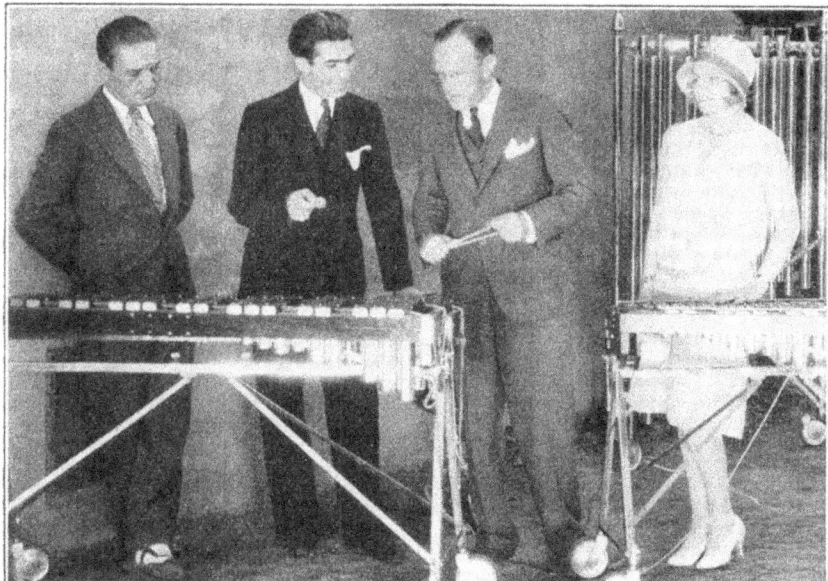

"It Works This Way"

—says Murray Spivack, (second from left) drummer and sound effects expert for Radio Pictures, as he explains all about the Leedy mallet-played instruments to Luther Reed, Radio Pictures director, while Victor Baravalle, musical director for the outfit, and Helen Kaiser, one of the featured players in "Rio Rita," stand by in rapt attention. In producing sound effects only the finest percussion instruments can be used to advantage, that's why Leedy equipment is so popular in the "talkies."

How He Got Ahead
(Hartford City News)

A Texas newspaper publisher who recently retired with $50,000 in the bank was asked how he did it, and replied as follows: "I attribute my ability to retire with a $50,000 bank account, after thirty years in the country newspaper field, to close application to duty, always hewing to the mark and letting the chips fall where they may, the most rigorous rule of economy, never spending a cent foolishly, everlastingly keeping at my job with a whole heart — and the death of an uncle who left me $49,999.50."

Ham: "Why is a girl like a drum?"
Hammer: "Slip us the news."
Ham: "It takes a roll to play both of them."

The Cheese Song

"Cheese the kind of a girl that men forget."—*Enarco News*.

"That's just two bad," murmured the doorman as the college boy and his date got into the roadster.—*Pennsylvania Punch Bowl*.

To Liven Up Your Felt Sticks

Special felt sticks such as Leedy's Nos. 1600, 1601, 1602 and 1603 on page 66 of Catalog "S" and 1721 to 1726 inclusive on page 99 oftentimes become hard with age caused by imbedded dust packed in with usage. To soften the felt, slash the surface lightly with a razor blade all around the ball. Be sure to go easy and draw the blade evenly and carefully horizontal with the hickory stick. Finish off with sandpaper or a coarse file. You will find the tone of the stick greatly improved when treated in this manner.

$2.00 award to Richard Jacobson, Plentywood, Montana.

FAMOUS LAST WORDS: "It can't be played that way."
Billy Cleve, Portland, Ore.

A Safe Risk

Glee Club Leader: "What'll we sing for an encore."
Sarcastic Guy: "Sing the same song—they'll never recognize it."—*Yale Record*.

Another Cow Bell Effect

Cut the proper size piece from an old inner tube and stretch same over your cow bell. If small bells are used, bicycle inner tubes are just the thing. Many effects can be had in this way. All metallic tones are taken out of the cow bell and very deep temple block-like tones are the result. The metal edge of the cow bell should be left protruding slightly beyond the rubber and this edge can be played upon with thick part of drum sticks or felt sticks such as Leedy's Hard Felt Xylophone Mallets No. 1721, page 99 of Catalog "S".

$2.00 award to Robert Totman, Sheridan, Wyoming.

Asking Papa

"Sir," began the bashful young man, "I—er—well, your daughter—"
"I see," interrupted her father. "You want to marry her, then, is that it?"
"Oh, we've been married five months. What I am after now is a divorce."—*Bramwords*.

Special Notice To Teachers

Leedy has thousands of drummer names on the mailing list but we do not know which of these drummers is making a specialty of teaching.

We would like to compile a separate list classifying all those who come under the head of instructors. Drop us a postal giving name and latest address and telling us how many pupils you have at present. We will then place you in the teacher classification. Who knows but what we might be able to assist you in one way or another some time in the future? We have a couple of good ideas on this subject if you will cooperate.

Do You Like It or Not?

If you like Drum Topics, give the editor a little hand by telling him about it in a little letter. If you don't like it, you've got a kick coming so don't hesitate to tell us just where we head in. This is your paper and we want to make it just as you like it. Oke?

The New Austin Song

"The little things in Life."

Quarter notes are as hard to play as whole ones.

Leedy — World's Finest Drummers' Instruments — Leedy

Leedy Drum Topics

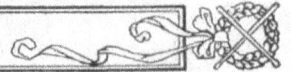

Martin Snitzer

Mr. Snitzer is a theatre, band and orchestra drummer of many years experience. He has held down some of the best jobs in the business in his line of work and is now playing with Snedeker's Band and also Maurer's Band both of which organizations have their headquarters in Philadelphia.

He has played with such famous outfits as the 101 Ranch, the Sells-Floto Circus, Hummel's Band and the Fox Theatre orchestra. Mr. Snitzer is constantly experimenting with drums and drummers' traps and has developed many interesting and useful effects of his own.

Champ Twirler

Here is Frank J. Bosman of Aberdeen, S. D., with the cup he captured as winner of second place in the competition for twirling drum majors at the 1930 Boston Convention of the American Legion. Frank is drum major of Sydney L. Smith post of the American Legion.

Hopeless

In Washington they tell the story of a golfing clergyman who had been badly beaten on the links by a parishioner thirty years his senior and had returned to the clubhouse rather disgruntled.

"Cheer up," his opponent said. "Remember, you win at the finish—you'll probably be burying me some day."

"Even then," said the preacher, "it will be your hole."—*Drexerd*.

Decoration for Bass Drum Head

It has become quite the vogue to glue cut-out paper figures and designs on the inside surface of bass drum heads. Of course, interior lights are a necessary part of this idea. When the lights are on, the design or figure forms a silhouette on the head, and when the lights are out the decoration is invisible. Some drummers have used cut-out letters spelling the name of their band. Either design or lettering can be removed by moistening the glue. (Thin LePage's glue is best). Be sure to smooth out all wrinkles, especially at the edges of the design. If the edges are not flat to the head they will look fuzzy. Many attractive designs can be found at wall paper and art shops that sell novelty crepe paper for Halloween and other interior party decorations.

$2.00 Award to V. C. Willet, Oelwein, Iowa.

Those Green Boys Again

Reading from left to right the famous Green brothers, George and Joe, are with us again. This time they are introducing a set of plate glass bells, made especially for them by Leedy, for use in broadcasting from New York City over the nationwide radio hook-ups. The bars of these bells are of thick, high grade plate glass, and while the tone which they produce does not sustain so long as that produced by steel bars, it is very pleasing for certain effects and especially adapted for radio work inasmuch as the tone carries very distinctly over the air.

The bells were designed for George and Joe by Herman Winterhoff, the world's foremost designer of mallet played instruments and a member of the Leedy organization. Mr. Winterhoff is the inventor of the Vibraphone.

Return of Stage Shows Next Fall Is Seen in East

Indications of the return of stage shows next fall is seen in reports from eastern centers.

Word from Rochester, N. Y. is that prospects are for stage shows in four and possibly five theatres next fall, against two at present. The Eastman one of the largest theatres in Rochester, is expected to open in September with orchestra and local stage number or else with unit shows.

From Buffalo comes word that overtures have been made by the Publix theatres to stage hands and motion picture operators regarding reductions in wage scales, elimination of overtime and other concessions. Publix hopes to lop off enough in union overhead to make it more practical to play stage attractions, needed in many places, but up to now too costly.

"Publix and other picture chains have realized something besides the screen is desired as a drawing card," says Variety, theatrical publication. "High operating overhead and apparent unwillingness of unions to budge until conditions became as bad as they now have, in the main held back the spread of live stage entertainment * * * If the chain can make the right deals in the right situations throughout the country during the summer it will be expected to take the big vaudeville leap in the fall."

Synco-Jazz Brush Stunt

Synco-Jazz brushes are often used as in the drawing above, but it is difficult to hold the wires in this position while playing. To insure the wires remaining at this point, insert two or three pieces of a match stick and tap the ends of the aluminum tubes down with a hammer. Of course, this means that the brushes will be good only for this type of playing as the wires will have to remain in this position once to top of the tube is tapped down. For the usual manner of playing an additional pair of sticks will have to be added to your kit.

$2.00 award to Bruce P. Cambies, 164 Lexington Ave., Rochester, N. Y.

Leedy — World's Finest Drummers' Instruments — **Leedy**

The Exclusive Drummers' Paper

A Dutch Drummer

Martin Schneider, Jr., is one of the finest drummers in Europe. He is now playing with Frigge's Symphonie and Jazz Orchestra at Groningen, Holland, but in spite of the fact that he is only 26 years old, he has filled some of the most important drumming jobs in his country and in other parts of Europe. His list of drumming accomplishments includes theatre, dance, military, concert and recording work.

Mr. Schneider is the author of the first drum instruction book ever to be published in the Dutch language, and is also an artist of ability as a cartoon from his pen which appears in another part of this issue of Drum Topics will attest. His outfit is almost completely Leedy, and he is very enthusiastic about its many fine qualities.

Say what you will about drummers, but you've got to admit that they're smart, look at all the head work they do.

Slap Drum Sticks

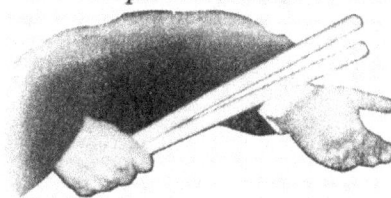

By holding your sticks in the position shown in the accompanying photograph you can obtain fast light slap effects with a minimum of ease. Speed is a big factor in favor of this stunt. When the tips of the sticks are held in this manner the taper of the body of each stick causes a slight opening at the butt end. It is the butt ends coming together that causes the slap. It can be played on the knee or left hand. When played on the knee, the left hand is free for other action.

$2.00 Award to Elvin Schulenburg, 3840 Lobadie Avenue, St. Louis, Missouri.

Rubber Tipped Drum Sticks

A simple, cheap and handy way of making a pair of drum sticks with rubber tips for soft playing is as follows:

Buy the large size red rubber pencil erasers (the kind that slip over the ordinary lead pencils) at the Five & Ten Cent Store. These can be slipped on and off over drum stick tips. Very good for soft playing on "Sizzle" cymbals, tom-toms, temple blocks, wood blocks, etc.

$2.00 award to Forbes Satre, Courtenay, North Dakota.

Jobbing in Switzerland

The jobbing drummer who curses his luck because he has to transport his equipment around in taxis or street cars would hardly like to change places with this Swiss drummer. He's packed his equipment on his back and is skiing his way up the side of a mountain to play a job at one of the famous Switzerland winter resorts. We hope he hasn't forgotten anything.

Broad: "What is the most important roll?"

Way: "Why the five, the seven, the nine—"

Broad: "Wrong, it's the bank roll."

H. Martin Snitzer,
Philadelphia, Pa.

Opal Hall

Although she has never taken a lesson in her life and has obtained all of her instruction from the Green Brothers Method, nevertheless, Miss Hall is an unusually accomplished marimba player. She plays with the high school orchestra and is much in demand for entertainments in her home town of Creston, Iowa.

Leedy — World's Finest Drummers' Instruments — **Leedy**

Leedy Drum Topics

A Master and His Pupil

This is Bill Spedick (left), famous drummer, with his pupil, William Black of Baldwin, Long Island, N. Y. Bill says that the youngster is a great performer on drums and has one of the finest rolls he has ever heard. This is, indeed, high praise from a drummer of such long experience and big reputation.

Spedick, if you don't happen to remember, is the drummer who travelled with Gertrude Hoffmann for so many years. It was Bill, in fact, who taught Miss Hoffmann the drum number which she does.

Synco-Jazz Brush Stunt

Don Landers, a top notch drummer who has his own orchestra playing throughout Arkansas, Tennessee, and several other southern states, writes—
"I play piano strains in several numbers throughout an evening program, using Synco-Jazz brushes on the bell of the bass player's horn. His horn has a light down in the bell which reflects on the shiny surface of the bell in a most effective manner. Naturally, I have to stand up to perform this idea, and this adds to the flash. No, the brushes do not scratch the bell, as I only use them gently in piano choruses. The effect is most pleasing."

$2.00 Award to Don Landers, Lander's Orchestra, Harrisburg, Arkansas.

Going Back

As far as we know, the first instruction book on rudimental drumming produced in this country appeared in 1862. It was called "The Drummers' and Fifers' Guide" and was written by George B. Bruce and Dan D. Emmett at the time when the former was instructor of drumming for the U. S. army at Governors and Bedloes Islands, N. Y.

In this book Bruce gives credit to a former drum method called "Ashworth's Rudimental School". We do not know whether Ashworth's book was written and printed in England or in the United States, but we are inclined to believe it to be of English origin.

There are only a very few—in fact, only three or four in number—of the old Bruce and Emmett books in existence and, of course, they are highly prized by the owners. We know of no one who owns the Ashworth book and neither have we met any drummers who have ever seen it.

Dan Emmett, who edited that portion of the Bruce and Emmett book devoted to the fife, was a famous minstrel man who, by the way, was the author of that world renowned Southern song, "Dixie".

A few years later Drum Major Gardner A. Strube of the 12th Infantry New York State National Guard, formerly drummer in Company "A", 5th Regiment, New York, and Duryeas Zouaves wrote another drum method entitled "Strube Drum and Fife Instructor". This book was adopted as official by the United States government in 1869. In it Strube refers to "Upton's Tactics" now out of print many years past and, like the Ashworth book mentioned above, it is not known to the writer whether "Upton's Tactics" is of English or American origin.

We would certainly like to know more about both the Ashworth and the Upton books, and if any drummer reading this can tell us about them the information would certainly be welcome and we know that the readers of "Drum Topics" would like to know the details.

In the Strube book there were twenty-five plus one rudiments set down. Of course, there could have been many more "formations" or groups of notes which could well be called by some name and practiced by the drummer who wants to become more proficient. However, these twenty-six (as listed in the No. 20 issue of Drum Topics) form the backbone of the military drummers' technique. Any military drummer who can play them all in smooth fashion is indeed proficient. However, the expert should familiarize himself with all other possible groups.

Throughout the country the old timers and the old old-timers accept Strube as the authority. The Strube book contains the complete "Tatoo" and the Bruce and Emmett book contains some wonderful fife and drum quick steps. Of course, these are not obtainable unless you happen to have a friend who owns one of these books and who will jot them down for you.

(Editor's Note—Notes for the above article kindly supplied by George L. Stone of Boston, Mass.)

When it comes to "hitting things right on the head," you've got to hand it to drummers. They do it more often than anybody else.

Complete --- Simple

Easy To Understand

JUST off the press Leedy's new 72 page illustrated Elementary Instructor for Vibraphone is a complete and thorough course by means of which beginners can learn to play the instrument unaided and advance to great proficiency. Experienced players, too, will find the scales, chords, ear training, exercises and harmony which it contains of great benefit.

Printed in large, easy-to-read type on good grade paper and bound in a handsome two-color cover, this instruction book fills a long felt need of students and teachers of Vibraphone playing. It is clearly and authoritatively written by one of the master players of the instrument. If your dealer cannot supply you, order direct from the factory. Every player of the Vibraphone should have a copy of the Elementary Instructor. Order yours now.

No. 1785 .... $2.50

 **World's Finest Drummers' Instruments**

The Exclusive Drummers' Paper

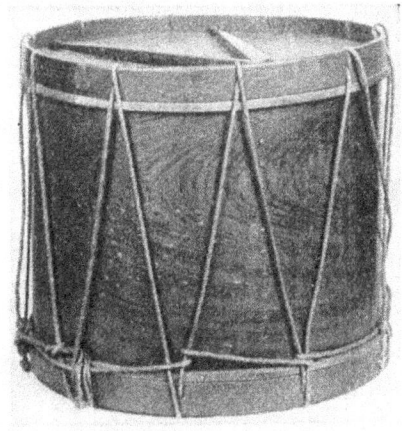

Field Army Drum

Property of Julian R. Howe, Advertising Manager, The Bourbon News, Paris, Ky.

This drum is now 69 years old and it was made in an old tan yard in the hills back of Cincinnati in the summer of 1862.

The Tan Yard, at that time, was owned by Mr. Robert Thornton and was located on the Lebanon Road near Montgomery Pike not far from what is known as Walnut Hills. A. M. Dolph, a young man about 17 years old, at that time, lived in Cincinnati in this neighborhood and like all young men was anxious to get in the war and being of a mechanical turn of mind he conveived the idea of making his own drum and enlisting as a drummer boy. The shell and hoops were cut out and steamed in a large wooden trough at the tan yard and the heads were from sheep skins also obtained there. In September, 1862, when Kirby Smith threatened Cincinnati two regiments called "The Cincinnati Reserves" were formed and started drilling. A. M. Dolph joined one of these regiments as a drummer boy and took part in a few skirmishes against General John Morgan and Kirby Smith. Some time after the war was over Dolph turned his attention to machinery and invented several laundry machines. In later years he became interested in gas and electric properties and from 1900 to 1915 he owned the gas and electric properties at Paris, Ky., where J. R. Howe was in his employ. When he sold his home in Cincinnati and moved into an apartment hotel he brought the old drum to Paris and gave it into the keeping of Howe saying that at his death it would become the property of Howe. Mr. Dolph died in Cincinnati in 1917.

The Leedy name on any drummers' equipment is your guarantee of its quality.

Save Your Bass Drum Hoops

A drum worth buying is worth protecting. The clamps of metal trap holders are undoubtedly severe on bass drum hoops. In time they scar and dent the best hoops made. To avoid this why not place a few short pieces of inch wide adhesive tape of three or four layers thickness on both sides of the counter hoop where you attach the various clamps such as spurs, pedal cymbal holders, trap rail, etc. These pieces of tape need not be any longer than the width of the clamp and therefore will not prove unsightly. They protect your hoops to the full extent and are easily removed, leaving the hoops as good as new. You will find this stunt worth while when you sell or trade in your drum on a new model.

$2.00 award to Joseph M. Zuban, Box 157, Gilberton, Pa.

John Schell Cartin

John Cartin is a Leedy booster from the City of Brotherly Love. He plays with concert bands, dance and theatre orchestras and over the radio in his native city. John was born and raised in Philadelphia and learned his drumming from Oliver H. Bundick.

(Photo courtesy Henton-Knecht, Philadelphia, Pa.)

Leedy's reputation has been built on sound policies of quality and service, we never knowingly slight a customer in any way, but sometimes we make mistakes. If we ever make one in our dealings with you, tell us about it and we'll correct it.

The cartoon above was contributed to Drum Topics by Mr. Roman Bates, drummer and Leedy enthusiast of Sleepy Eye, Minn.

 **World's Finest Drummers' Instruments**

Leedy DRUM TOPICS
The Exclusive Drummers' Paper

July 1931

22nd Edition

Illustration Courtesy of the New Yorker

POSTMASTER—Return Postage Guaranteed

LEEDY MANUFACTURING CO.
Elkhart, Indiana

Sec. 435½ P. L. & R.
U. S. POSTAGE
PAID
ELKHART, IND.
Permit No. 6

Joseph G. Benoit,
165 Hildreth,
Lowell, Mass.

Al. 'Rags' Anderson and 'Rusty' Parker

"Rags" Anderson, at left in the picture, is just as well known to the drum fraternity as the Leedy equipment which he uses and swears by. He is one of the real top-notch drummers of this country—an artist and one of the finest fellows you ever met. "Rags" is now playing with "Rusty" Parker's orchestra at the State Restaurant, Columbus, O., and doing a lot of broadcasting as well. In fact, "Rags" is kept so busy hopping from the restaurant to the broadcasting studios that he gets darn little time out for sleeping. "Rusty" Parker, director of the State Restaurant orchestra is a well-known and versatile musician. He plays banjo, doubles on trumpet, sings ballads and directs. He was formerly banjo player, vocal soloist and trio singer with Ted Weems' orchestra.

PRINTED IN U.S.A.

Leedy Drum Topics Issue 23

Leedy Drum Topics

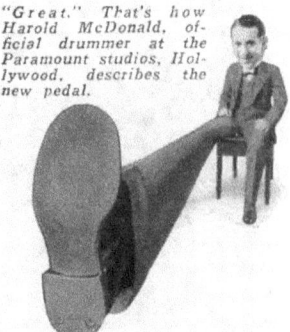

"Great." That's how Harold McDonald, official drummer at the Paramount studios, Hollywood, describes the new pedal.

"The X-L Pedal is another proof that Leedy makes the world's finest drummers' instruments," says George Marsh, now playing with Ferde Grofe's orchestra in New York City.

"The world's best." That's how "Rags" Anderson, famous Columbus, O., drummer, rates the new pedal.

Poley McKlintock, drummer with Waring's Pennsylvanians, says, "The X-L is a wonderful improvement."

These Famous Drummers' Feet Are Now Working *Leedy's* New X-L Pedal

Get your right foot on one of these new Leedy X-L pedals and you'll say, with the famous drummers shown on this page, that it's the greatest professional pedal ever made! It's easy on the foot and easy on the pocketbook too, as the price is the lowest at which a high quality pedal has ever been offered.

Clean Response

Hunt up the nearest Leedy dealer and ask him to show you the new X-L. Try it out and you'll agree that it's the greatest relief ever invented for "that tired feeling" in the old right leg, which drummers usually experience after playing a long program. That's because there is not the slightest resistance or unevenness in the action—no wavering ... no slipping ... no friction, no side strain or lost motion—just clean, instantaneous response. From start to finish of the stroke, there is the same even, easy flow of action—no stiffness as the ball nears the head.

Right "Feel"

What's more, the X-L pedal has the right "foot-feel" which gives you "tempo confidence" under all conditions. You can play the longest "gallops" without fatigue and without fear of "losing the beat."

Ask to See It

The ball sockets on each end of the beater shaft and the finely balanced mechanism give a light, feathery action with a minimum of effort. The tension spring can be adjusted to fit your own particular "feel". Beater rod and cymbal striker are also adjustable. Try this new high quality, low-priced pedal. It will give you that clean, "right on time" technique which makes all the difference in the world in a drummer's playing. Ask the nearest Leedy dealer to show you the new X-L pedal or write 2300 Leedy Bldg., Elkhart, Ind., for full details.

7010	Pedal only in Black Duco and Polished Aluminum	$10.00
7012	Pedal only in Gold Duco and Nobby Gold	12.00
7014	Pedal with Ideal Spurs and Cymbal Holder in Black Duco and Polished Aluminum	11.50
7016	Pedal with Ideal Spurs and Cymbal Holder in Gold Duco and Nobby Gold	13.50

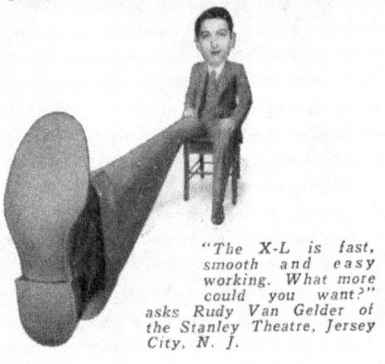

"The X-L is fast, smooth and easy working. What more could you want?" asks Rudy Van Gelder of the Stanley Theatre, Jersey City, N. J.

Paul McKnight, of Jack Crawford's orchestra, is an X-L enthusiast, plus. "It's smooth as silk and fast as lightning," says he.

"The X-L solves all pedal problems," says Art Layfield, celebrated drummer now playing at the Chicago Theatre, Chicago.

Leedy **World's Finest Drummers' Instruments** *Leedy*

Copyright March, 1932 by Leedy Mfg. Co., Inc.

The Exclusive Drummers' Paper

How The Bass Drummer Got His "Spots"

Many of our readers having seen bass drummers clad in Leopard skins have written in wanting to know "what causes that?" We are glad to be able to present below the interesting explanation of this custom as given in the London, Eng., magazine "Fighting Forces," and relayed to us by Harry Angell, drummer on the staff of the Northwest Conn. Co., Seattle, Wash.

This is the Dalzell Highland Pipe Band of Motherwell, Scotland, world's champion outfit of its kind. As you will note, the bass drummer continues the ancient British custom of wearing a leopard skin. The photo was sent in by Mr. James Cartherwood, (Who appears in the front row left), old friend of Geo. H. Way, sales mananger of the Leedy co.

In the 17th and early 18th centuries the drummers in the British service were practically always negroes. Many of the British regiments acquired these fellows while serving in the West Indies and North America.

The playing of drums, clashpans, cymbals and similar instruments was admirably suited to these negroes because of their great size and their strong, innate sense of rhythm. To add to the picturesqueness of the negro drummers, the British regiments adopted the custom of clothing them in as much of their barbaric splendor as possible. Thus, the black drummers wore leopard skins, turbans and brilliantly tinselled uniforms of one kind or another.

Gradually the practice of employing negro drummers in the British army was discontinued. The last of them disappeared about 1840.

Although the modern British drummers have not copied all the antics of the former "sable musicians", nevertheless, these latter are still directly responsible for at least two of the customs which are observed by drummers in the British army today. These customs are the full armed figurations of the tenor drummers and the Scotch bass drummers and the wearing of leopard skins by bass drummers and sometimes tenor drummers as well.

Arthur A. Prokesch

Mr. Prokesch is now living at Ridgewood, L. I., and leading his own orchestra which is engaged at Kee's Restaurant, Woodside, L. I. He has only been in professional drumming for about four years but during that time has had such varied experience as vaudeville, dance and theatre work. Mr. Prokesch is a pupil of Karl Glassman and Alvin Broemmel.

Flapper: "I'd like to see the captain of the ship."
Rookie: "He's forward, miss."
Flapper: "I don't care, this is a pleasure trip."

Machine Gun and Anvil Imitations

A fair machine gun imitation can be obtained by drumming on the back of an ordinary wooden ukulele with xylophone mallets. Leedy hard rubber mallets, No. 1700, page 99 catalog "S", work fine in this stunt.

A good anvil imitation can be made by filling two one quart gingerale bottles, one-half full, the other three-fourths full of water. Hang them up with a piece of string and use a Leedy solid brass xylophone mallet, No. 1701 catalog "S", on them.

$2.00 award to W. C. Hall, 69 Maplewood, N. J.

A FAIR QUESTION
Ad: "Are you still playing drums?"
Noids: "Aw who the H— could be still playing drums?"

"Dick" Martin

"Dick" hails from Roanoke Rapids, N. C., and is now playing at the Cinderella Ballroom, Miami, Fla. He reports that he has a Leedy snare drum which has been in constant use for more than four years and is still in perfect condition.

"I might add," says "Dick", "that I've always wanted to act a lady among durms. That's why I'm 'Leedy Like'." And you can take that or leave it.

Employment Officer: "A floor walker, eh? Any experience?"
Dick: "Sure, three children."
—Calumet Vacuum Cleaner

Leedy — World's Finest Drummers' Instruments — **Leedy**

Leedy Drum Topics

A Brand New *Leedy* Idea
SPARKLING TWO-TONE DIAMONDS

"A Knock-out", Say "Duke and Sonny"

Here's the famous "Duke" Ellington and his equally famous drummer "Sonny" Greer. "Sonny" just purchased the set of Leedy Sparkling Two-Tone Diamond decorated drums with which he is shown in the picture and both the "Duke" and "Sonny" agree that they are "knockouts." "Sonny's" drums are finished in Marine Pearl and the diamonds are of Sparkling Gold with Sparkling Green borders—a real flash, and what a drummer! The Ellington orchestra is now on Publix Circuit.

●

SPARKLING TWO-TONE DIAMONDS are the newest and finest decorations for "Full Dress" drum shells ever devised, and if you act quick, you can be the first in your community to have them, for this is the first time that they have ever been advertised anywhere! The black and white illustration above gives only a faint idea of the dazzling beauty of SPARKLING TWO-TONE DIAMONDS. When you see them in their sparkling, resplendent colors, you'll agree that they are a real sensation!

Custom Made

When you order a set of Leedy "Full Dress" drums with SPARKLING TWO-TONE DIAMONDS, you get something absolutely individual, absolutely your own—for the diamonds are available in 12 different color combinations and are custom made to your order. The diamonds can be made up in any one of the 12 different combinations which it is possible to obtain from the following beautiful colors: Sparkling Gold, Green Diamond, Red Diamond, Sparkling Silver.

60 COLOR COMBINATIONS

As the diamonds are overlaid on the finishes named above plus the other two Leedy "Full Dress" finishes (Marine Pearl and Black Pearl), it is now possible to obtain Leedy "Full Dress" drums with SPARKLING TWO-TONE DIAMONDS in 60 different combinations! Think of the thrill of owning a drum set made up in your own exclusive color combintion.

Street and Band Drums Too

Orchestra drummers are not the only ones who can take advantage of this sensational new idea. Street and band drums are also available in the new, beautiful color combinations. For drum corps, SPARKLING TWO-TONE DIAMONDS offer an unequalled opportunity to step out and be different. Think of the flash your corps would make if equipped with SPARKLING TWO-TONE DIAMOND decorated drums!

See the Leedy Dealer

SPARKLING TWO-TONE DIAMONDS are so new that even many of the Leedy dealers have not yet had time to obtain samples of drums with this great new decoration. If you will go to the nearest Leedy dealer, however, and tell him your needs, he will be able within a very short time to show you samples of SPARKLING TWO-TONE DIAMONDS. Remember in ordering the diamond decorations it is best to select contrasting colors.

Diamonds For Your Present Outfit

The prices quoted below cover the cost of diamonds either for new drums or for your present outfit. If you have "Full Dress" drums at the present time, SPARKLING TWO-TONE DIAMONDS can be added at the prices shown below plus the cost of transporting your drums to and from the factory. Remember that SPARKLING TWO-TONE DIAMONDS will not come off. They are guaranteed to stay on for the life of the drum shell.

Orchestra (Snare) drums, each $4.50
Street Drums, each 6.50
Bass Drums (regular sizes) each 10.00

World's Finest Drummers' Instruments

The Exclusive Drummers' Paper

Ralph Hansel

Mr. Hansel is staff artist on xylophone and Vibraphone at radio station KOA which is the Denver, Colorado, unit of the National Broadcasting Co.

Ralph is one of the finest performers on mallet played instruments in the country today. His stuff is new and absolutely different as he, himself, writes most of the numbers which he plays in his radio programs. At the radio station, Ralph is working under the direction of A. B. DeLa Vergne and musical director Scheuerman of KOA, with whom he has been associated for a number of years. Mr. Scheuerman is well-known in Denver musical circles having had charge of orchestras at a number of the leading theatres for years. It was he who gave Ralph Hansel his start in the music business.

Subdued Cymbal

A rubber suction cup, of the type used to hold ash trays and other articles on automobile windshields, placed on the under side of a cymbal produces a good subdued cymbal effect. $2.00 award to R. F. Colburn, 118 W. Oak St., Watseka, Ill.

Ghandi and The Drummer Boys

"Be good little boys, practice hard on your open rolls and don't buy anything from England." That, or something very much like it, is what we suspect Mahatma Ghandi said to these drummer boy members of the Italian Balilla, on a recent visit to Rome. This, we admit, is a pretty flimsy excuse for the use of this picture in *Drum Topics*, but what, after all, is a magazine these days without a picture of Mahatma Ghandi?

Four Leedy-Equipped Juvenile Corps

Organized in June, 1931, this Junior Order of Moose corps of Philadelphia copped first prize at the 1931 Moose convention in Atlantic City. The outfit is under the command of Capt. Rob't. W. Winthrup with John Hartnett as drum major. 100% Leedy.
(Photo Courtesy Henton-Knecht, Phila.)

90 strong is this great Battle Creek, Mich., Council Boy Scout drum and bugle corps. Mr. L. Flanders has charge of the drum section and Mr. Claude Hardwick takes care of the bugles. The Scouts are very enthusiastic about the corps and make a fine appearance.
(Photo Courtesy Flanders Music Co., Battle Creek, Mich.)

This Junior American Legion corps of Utica, N. Y., has attained a high degree of playing skill under the direction of Legion Post members. In a recent competition with 10 senior corps, the boys took second place and a special award.
(Photo Courtesy Al. Sittig's Music Shop, Utica, N. Y.)

This fine looking Cadet drum and bugle corps is the pride of Lawrence E. Delaney Post, Philadelphia, Pa., of the American Legion. Under the direction of Capt. Geo. Hoffman, these boys won the Pennsylvania state title in 1930. All Leedy.

Leedy — *World's Finest Drummers' Instruments* — **Leedy**

Leedy Drum Topics

Special Notice to Teachers

Leedy has thousands of drummer names on the mailing list but we do not know which of these drummers is making a specialty of teaching.

We would like to compile a separate list classifying all those who come under the head of instructors. Drop us a postal giving name and latest address and telling us how many pupils you have at present. We will then place you in the teacher classification. Who knows but what we might be able to assist you in one way or another some time in the future? We have a couple of good ideas on this subject if you will cooperate.

Harry Marshad

Mr. Marshad is one of the East's most competent drummers. He is now playing with Jacques Renard's Orchestra at the Club Mayfair, Boston, and has played many other prominent "Bean City" spots in the seven years of his professional career. Harry is a pupil of Meyer Sternberg, well-known eastern drummer. He is now living at 147 Columbia Rd., Dorchester, Mass., and still boosting Leedy as strong as ever.

PROMOTION

"What did the boss say when you told him it was triplets?"

"He promoted me to head of my department."

"What department are you in?"

"Production."

The Imperial Xylophonists

Under the capable direction and management of their Director—Mr. Ira R. Anthony, this fine looking group has played in fourteen theatres, this past winter.

The Personnel of this act includes; Xylophone—Jack Haskell, Phillip Abbott, Director, Ira R. Anthony, Cramer Adams, Don Ferrara, M. Hough, Harold Sanderson and Bobbie Haskell.

Piano—Charles J. Loeffler, Bass—Charles Rockwell, Drums and Tympani—Herbert Canfield. They are all pupils of Mr. Anthony.

Mr. Anthony is Teacher of xylophone and percussion instruments. Having played them for seventeen years, he no doubt knows his drums.

Last but not least—the Instruments are all Leedy.

Tuneable Tom-Tom Muffler

A very effective muffler for the new Leedy Tuneable Tom-Toms can be made from two ordinary snare drum tone controls, No. 7635, page 68 catalog "S".

Remove the clamps from the tone controls. File the rivet holes a little larger to accommodate the rods, then remove two tension rods from opposite sides of the tom-tom, and run them thru the tone control spring arms. Replace tension rods and the muffler arm will be between the tension screw and the hoop hook.

$2.00 award to D. L. Ulrey, Elkhart, Indiana.

One shudders to think what it will take to constitute disorderly conduct ninety years from now.

Believe It Or Not

A man in Ft. Smith, Ark., admitted under oath in the office of Justice of the Peace Aron Barnstable that he enjoyed listening to a soprano singer over the radio. He is apparently normal in other respects.

The man who aims at nothing in particular, usually hits his mark.

Sterling R. Rennoll

"I've tried all the other makes during the past four years and now I use Leedy drums, sound devices and traps. They give me the best results and stand up under hard usage," says Sterling R. Rennoll of Spring Grove, Pa. Mr. Rennoll has had a great deal of jobbing experience in and around his home town and is now playing with the Papermakers' Band, an organization which represents a big local paper mill.

The xylophonist had just finished playing for a large delegation of club women and was packing up to leave. A very dignified woman, who was the mother of a famous violinist, came up to him.

"Pardon me," she said, "but I just wanted to tell you how much I enjoyed your playing. I am so fond of the harp."

Contributed by Harry G. Hamilton, Benton, Illinois.

World's Finest Drummers' Instruments

The Exclusive Drummers' Paper

NEW INDIVIDUALITY

The "Floating Head"

The "Battalion"

The "Standard"

FOR LEEDY DRUM CORPS MODELS

Now Leedy offers new beauty, new individuality and new finer performance in all drum corps models. All drum corps models are now obtainable with the famous Leedy self-aligning rods and the beautiful, modernistic Leedy, twice-as-strong center supports. This means that in appearance, performance and ability to "take it on the chin", the new Leedy drum corps models are unequalled by any drums on the market today. And more than that, the new Leedys are absolutely individual in appearance. No other drums can approach their handsome good looks, just as no other drums have ever been able to equal their sparkling tone and matchless playing qualities. Now more than ever the new Leedy drum corps models are worthy of the Leedy slogan, "The World's Finest Drummers' Instruments!"

The "Floating Head"

What Stradivarius means to the violinist, Leedy "Floating Head", means to the drum corps drummer. Champion drum corps and champion individual drummers acknowledge this to be the finest outdoor drum in the world today. The new type laminated shell makes this drum lighter in weight than former models without sacrificing any of its rugged, wearing qualities. It is unexcelled for volume and easy playing qualities. Heads tension separately.

No. 3135— 9" x 15" ⎫
No. 3136—12" x 15" ⎬ $35.00
No. 3137—12" x 16" ⎭

The "Battalion"

This is the drum that takes the place of the former "Military" model. It has the same light weight and big, snappy tone of the old model and now, in addition, it has the big advantages of Leedy self-aligning

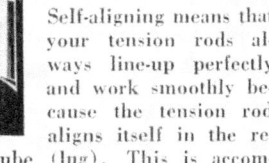

What Self-Aligning Means and How It Works

Self-aligning means that your tension rods always line-up perfectly and work smoothly because the tension rod aligns itself in the receiving tube (lug). This is accomplished by placing the receiving tube on a modified universal joint so that it is free to move in all directions.

rods and new, modernistic center supports. Best of all these big improvements have been included on the drum at no advance in price. Choice of Duco colors on shell and wood hoops if desired—no extra charge. It is illustrated above in separate tension and is also available in single tension.

Separate Tension

No. 3200— 9" x 15" ⎫
No. 3201—12" x 15" ⎬ $32.50
No. 3202—12" x 16" ⎪
No. 3203—12" x 17" ⎭

Single Tension

No. 3205— 9" x 15" ⎫
No. 3206—12" x 15" ⎬ $27.50
No. 3207—12" x 16" ⎪
No. 3208—12" x 17" ⎭

The "Standard"

Here's the successor to the old "Doughboy" model. With its beautiful new center supports and self-aligning rods, this drum is now the world's finest plain metal hoop drum. It's better looking, better playing and has a better, snappier tone.

Separate Tension

No. 3230— 9" x 15" ⎫
No. 3231—12" x 15" ⎬ $35.00
No. 3232—12" x 16" ⎪
No. 3233—12" x 17" ⎭

Leedy — World's Finest Drummers' Instruments — *Leedy*

Page Seven

Leedy Drum Topics

The Oldest Drum In America

For Many Years Drum Topics Has Been On The Trail of The Oldest American Drum and, Herewith, We Present The History and Photograph of What We Believe To Be The Grandaddy of 'em All. This Material Has Been Obtained for Us, After Much Painstaking Research, by Theodore A. Kurtz of Corporal Coyle Post, American Legion, Waterbury, Conn.

THIS drum was owned and carried by Capt. John Gallup in the Great Swamp Fight during King Philip's War at South Kingston, R. I., on the 19th day of December, 1675.

According to Fiske's History Canonchet, the leader of the Narragansett Indians had gathered some 3,000 Indians in a palisaded fortress in the middle of the Great Swamp in South Kingston, R. I., preparatory to an attack on the whites. But a force of 1,000 white men from all over New England took the place by storm, destroyed it and killed more than 1,000 of the Indians. This was in December, 1675.

This is the drum as it appears today, reposing on the shelves of The Monument House, Groton, Conn.

The drum is at present located in the museum of the Monument House, Groton, Conn. The Monument House is on the site of Fort Griswold of Revolutionary fame. It is owned by the State of Conn. and is in the keeping of the Anna Warner Bailey Chapter of the Daughters of the American Revolution.

The Drum measures 18½" across by 13¼", and is constructed of chestnut wood. The ropes and heads are missing but the counter and flesh hoops are in wonderful condition, considering their age.

During the Great Swamp Fight according to George M. Bodges "the Soldiers of King Philip's War," Captains Gallup, Marshall and Selley, were killed and Capt. Mason was mortally wounded. Barber, in his "History of Connecticut and its Antiquity" refers to Capt. John Gallup as the "Bold Gallup".

In Savage's book, Capt. John Gallup was from Boston, Mass., in 1637. He served in the Pequot War for which Connecticut made him a grant of one hundred acres of land. He removed to New London in 1651.

The donor of the drum to the museum is Miss Alice Satterlee of Gales Ferry, Conn., a descendant of Capt. John Gallup.

The First 3 National Champion V.F.W. Corps Are All Leedy Equipped

The 1931 convention of the Veterans of Foreign Wars held at Kansas City, Mo., witnessed another great triumph for Leedy drums. The three fine corps shown here carried off first, second and third prizes respectively—and they turned the trick with Leedy drums. All three of these remarkable drum corps use Leedy equipment exclusively — proof that Leedys are "Choice of Champions."

Right — Wayne County Council, Detroit, Mich., won first prize.

Second place went to Earl E. Aurand Post, Harrisburg, Pa.

Freemond Madson Post, Albert Lea, Minn., copped "show" money.

Leedy — *World's Finest Drummers' Instruments* — **Leedy**

The Exclusive Drummers' Paper

RUMBLE TIPS » » » » »

A Brand New 50c Accessory That's Worth $$$s To Any Drummer!

DRUMMERS all over the country have tested this great new Leedy accessory and they all say it's a real knockout—you'll certainly want to have a pair or two. Roll, rumble or roar these are only a few of the effects which can be obtained with the new rubber "Rumble Tips".

By dragging them across the snare drum, bass drum or tom-tom head a roar-like rasp is produced which can be used with startling effect in such pieces as "Tiger Rag", etc. They bounce as you drag, making either open or closed rolls depending on the pressure applied.

Make Good Two-Way Sticks

They are also excellent for rapid passages in modern music where a quick change to felt sticks for soft symbal and tom-tom effects is not convenient. Your Leedy dealer has them now. Try a pair of "Rumble Tips" and you'll find that the longer you use them the more effects you will be able to produce. See your dealer or write 2300 Leedy Bldg., Elkhart, Ind.

No. 1604 per pair $0.50

A Big Time Britisher

Len W. Hunt has won the title of "England's greatest show business drummer and snare drum technician." He is now playing with Percival Mackey's Band at the London Hippodrome in Jack Buchanan's production, "Stand Up and Sing". During his long career Hunt has played nearly all of the important spots in London including Ciro's, the British National Opera Co., and his Majesty's Theatre. Len uses Leedy equipment.

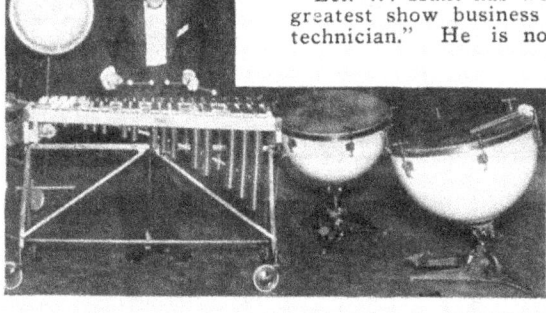

Do You Like It or Not?

If you like Drum Topics, give the editor a little hand by telling him about it in a little letter. If you don't like it, you've got a kick coming so don't hesitate to tell us just where we head in. This is your paper and we want to make it just as you like it. Oke?

BILLY SUNDAY WAS NOT ORIGINAL IN THE IDEA OF HAVING HIS HIDE TANNED FOR A DRUM HEAD.

Many of us certainly are great enthusiasts about drumming but we doubt that there is anybody among us whose enthusiasm about drumming goes as far as to giving order that after his death his skin should be used for a drum head. History reports that Ziska, the wild, one eyed Bohemian, chief of the Hussits, asked his followers to use his skin for a drum which should be carried in front of the troops. His idea was that thus he would, even after his death, be able to encourage and lead his men to victory by the sound of his skin on a drum.

Rowland G. Ritte

"I am the proud owner of a set of Leedy drums, tympani, xylophones, bells and traps", so says Mr. Rowland G. Ritte, of Baltimore, Md.

Mr. Ritte studies under Mr. J. W. Soistman, also of Baltimore. He is at present playing with the 104th Medical Regiment Band, M. N. G. Has had quite a wide experience, having played in the Evening Sun Band, Fifth Reg. Band, Hendrick Essers Symphonic Orchestra, and also played Xylophone Solos over WCAO, WFBR, and WCBM.

A drummer who has been playing musical comedy, burlesque and vaudeville for 10 years has just been married; which shows how impossible it is to escape.

To Protect Your Song Whistle To Clean Your Cymbals

To protect your Leedy Song Whistle when packed in a case with other traps, wrap it in a soft cloth and keep it in a cardboard mailing tube. Cut the tube to a length that will just fit in the trap case. The whistle cannot fall out of the tube, packing is quicker and the instrument is positively protected. This stunt can also be used with other wind traps.

For cleaning cymbals, pumice stone is hard to beat. It will polish the dirtiest brass cymbal with less effort than ordinary prepared polishes. Buy the powdered pumice. It can be obtained at any paint or drug store, and five or ten cents worth will clean many cymbals.

2.00 award to Richard Jacobsen, P. O. Box 473, Plentywood, Mont.

That's Different

Minister: "Is your father at home my boy?"

Little Boy: "No sir, he's just gone over to the golf club."

Minister: "What, on Sunday!"

Little Boy: "Oh, don't take it wrong sir. He's not going to play golf, he just dropped in for a couple of highballs and a few hands of poker."

World's Finest Drummers' Instruments

 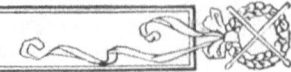

Leedy Drum Topics

Leedy Mfg. Co.,
Elkhart, Ind.
Dear Mr. Way:

I have done business with many individuals and firms, but the treatment I have received from Leedy surpasses anything I have ever experienced. I could not ask for better tone than my Vibraphone possesses. It is mellow and holds out better than anything I have ever tried.

I wish to express my sincere thanks for all you have done for me and will always be a loyal Leedy booster.

Sincerely,
Oscar M. Haney,
E. Akron, Ohio

Handy Good Looking Stick Holder

Here's an easy way to make a handy, durable and good looking stick holder. Procure a strong cardboard box about 9" x 5" x 5", open at one end and securely closed at the other. The most likely place to obtain a box like this is at a jewelers or a high class gift shop where they are used for packing candlesticks and other novelties. With two short, but fairly heavy screws, bolt the box, a little above the center of one side, to a Leedy Pedal Cymbal Holder, No. 7130, page 55 catalog "S". Be sure to use washers both between the head of the bolt and the cymbal holder and the nut and the side of the box. The box will look better if covered with bright colored paper and varnished.

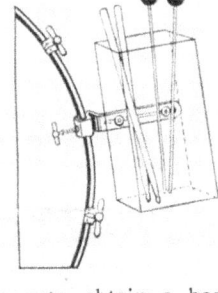

$2.00 award to Walter Boyd, 479 Manor Rd., Rockcliffe Pk., Ottawa, Ontario.

"John," snapped the drummer's wife, "I wish you would begin to study the faces of the women you know!"

"What's the big idea?" he asked in surprise.

"So you will be able to recognize them when they quit wearing short skirts," she retorted.

(Photo courtesy Henton-Knecht, Philadelphia)

C. Marsden Smith

Known far and wide as "Smilin' Smitty," C. Marsden is one of the best "hot" men in the state of New Jersey. At present he is playing with Charlie Kerr's Pioneer Radio Orchestra in Philadelphia, Pa., and is also on the staff of radio station WCAU. In addition to this work, he is doing a good deal of teaching in connection with Henton-Knecht, Philadelphia music store. "Smilin' Smitty" is not only a first class "hot" man on drums, but is also A No. 1 at this style of playing on Vibraphone, chimes, tymps and etc.

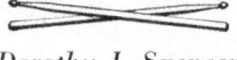

Dorothy J. Spencer

After having her Xylophone only three months, Miss Dorothy J. Spencer, of New London, Conn., played a three day program in Warner Bros. Garde theater. That is plenty good.

Miss Spencer plays at church, school and social functions continually. She has also broadcast on her Xylophone over station WTIC of Hartford, Conn.

The Silent Side of Drumming

As is the case with almost every other form of endeavor, there are two sides to drumming. The first side, of course, is that which is heard—the various sounds, noises, etc., which a drummer produces. Then there is the equally important but generally neglected, "Silent Side of Drumming."

To change from one instrument to another, to be able to pick up mallets, tympani sticks, tambourine, castanets, etc., without noise or awkwardness requires considerable skill. The drummer should adapt himself to a system of changes that will enable him to be familiar with all obstructions which are liable to place blemishes on the finished product. This finished product is, of course, smooth, accurate playing without meaningless noises that have no part in the rhythm. Thus, it should at once be apparent to the drummer that the silent side of his work is just as important as the side which is heard. Indeed, it is doubtful if any drummer can ever become a real, first class artist until he has thoroughly mastered the silent side of drumming.

Orchestra bells that click as perceptibly as they ring, cymbals that are allowed to sound long after the desired effect has been produced, these are two common faults. There are many others, for instance drummers too often produce an obtrusive "skin" sound in parallel with their tympani playing, and there are innumerable thuds, thumps and clicks produced by awkwardness in handling sticks, mallets and various other traps. All these uncalled for noises are blemishes on the art of drumming and those who strive to reach the top must eliminate them from their playing.

This, of course, takes care and practice but it also takes something else—the right equipment. Without the proper holders in which to keep your sticks and traps arranged in an orderly manner, it is almost impossible to do a good, clean-cut job of drumming.

If your nose is close to the grindstone rough,

And you keep it down there long enough,

For you there'll be no birds that sing,

No babbling brook, no flow'rs in Spring;

These three will all your world compose—

Just you and the stone and your darned old nose!

 **World's Finest Drummers' Instruments**

Page Ten

The Exclusive Drummers' Paper

Simple As Turning A Corner

To Tune These New Low-Price Leedy Machine Tympani

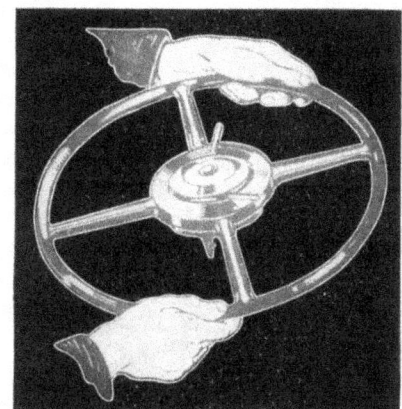

THE new Leedy "Turn-Tune" Tympani are the answer to the long-felt need for low-priced machine kettles. Professional drummers as well as school bands and orchestras will appreciate the quick, accurate tuning of these new machine tympani. As the name implies, you simply "turn to tune"—right for higher notes, left for the lower ones. The action is rapid, easy and definite—simple as turning a corner in an automobile.

The tension is always even throughout the surface of the head. You will never be troubled with "dead" spots caused by uneven tensioning as is often the case with hand type tympani. That's because all of the tension rods are attached to a central control inside the kettle which is operated simply by turning the kettle on its base.

Ask the nearest Leedy dealer to show you the new "Turn-Tune" Tympani. Let him give you a demonstration of the simple, sturdy mechanism that is designed to last a life time. There is nothing to get out of order. The kettles simply screw up or unscrew a strong, threaded post attached to a "spider" which pulls or loosens the tension rods.

The kettles, themselves, can be adjusted to height and tilted to meet the player's requirements. The tympani are played with equal ease from both sitting and standing positions. For packing and transporting, the kettles can be removed from their bases quickly and easily—and just as readily replaced.

The kettles are made in one piece of best quality copper and finished with a lustrous, satin sheen. Tensioning rods and handles are heavily nickeled. Heads are the famous Leedy Kafette brand. Base is sturdy and folds conveniently. One pair of sticks and fibre head protectors are included with each pair of tympani. Tympani are 25" and 27" diameters.

No. 5504—Leedy "Turn-Tune" Tympani, per pair $250.00

How They Work

The kettle is attached to an aluminum "nest" which rolls on ball bearings. The nest is fixed to the screw, which controls the tension rods, by means of a key which is free to work up and down in a slot in the "nest" casting. The screw threads in a nut which is held in place by three set screws and as the screw moves up and down it pulls or loosens the tension rods. A small screw, inside the larger one, prevents the kettle from being screwed out of its base.

27" "Turn-Tune" Tympanum

TURN·TUNE Tympani Patent Pending

25" "Turn-Tune" Tympanum

Leedy **World's Finest Drummers' Instruments** *Leedy*

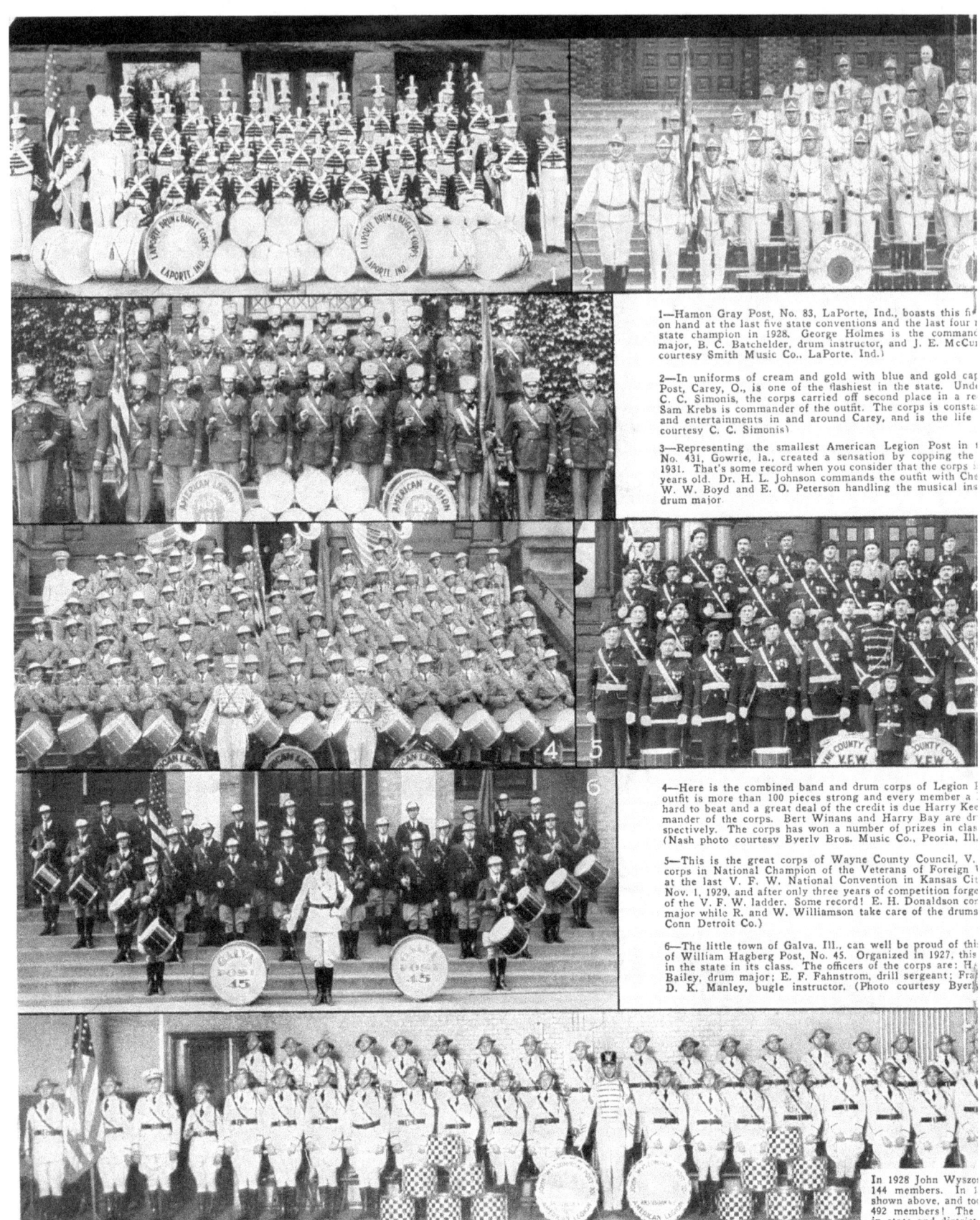

Famous Drum Corps

Lodi, N. J., is the home of the great corps of the Joseph M. Lane Post of the American Legion, shown above. Fred Colden is the name of the tall, handsome drum major in the white uniform. The corps is, of course, all Leedy equipped. (Photo courtesy Selmer-Conn, Newark, N. J.)

Organized in April, 1930, this Rockland, Mass., Legion corps already has 48 members. And here's a record that is a record—this corps has won first prize in every competition it ever entered! M. L. Walls, commands. (Photo courtesy Conn Boston Co.)

"Sweethearts of the convention"—that's the title this American Legion Auxiliary corps of Crookston, Minn., won when they attended the recent state convention at Rochester. The corps raised all the money for its equipment by its own activities. (Photo courtesy Munn's Music Store, Crookston, Minn.)

The splendid corps of Leland M. Barnett Post, Norwood, O., was judged the best marching organization at the 1930 Ohio convention. The corps has recently purchased a new set of Leedy Marine Pearl floating head street drums and new uniforms. E. J. Ertel is the commander. (Photo courtesy Wulitzer's, Cincinnati.)

Leedy Drum Topics Issue 23

The Exclusive Drummers' Paper

A Siberian Drummer

The thing this fellow is playing looks more than anything else like an oversize tambourine without jingles. Authorities tell us, however, that, believe it or not, it's a drum. The old fellow is a priest of the Oyrotes, those strange inhabitants of the Altai Mts. in Siberia. The drum is no doubt used for calling the faithful to worship and they continue to respond in spite of the fact that Mr. Stalin and his buddies in Moscow sent around an order for them to cease sometime ago.

Fair For A Cow

Here's the $10.00 prize winning story for this issue, sent in by George B. Burnwood, well-known drummer of Philadelphia. George says it's true, so help him, but true or not, it's a darn good story.

I was recently in Henton-Knecht's music store in Philadelphia, which, as all know who have visited the City of Brotherly Love, is the Leedy headquarters. The place, of course, abounds with things drumistic. There are whistles, bass drums, baby crys, cymbals, sleigh bells and xylophones; in fact, anything and everything that even a drummer might ask for.

I noticed another customer deeply engrossed in a perusal of the latest copy of the Leedy catalog, while a clerk waited patiently for him to decide what he wanted. Just at this moment I heard a loud rumbling noise, and looking up saw a truck loaded with cattle on its way to the stock yards. At the moment when the truck was in front of the store one of the animals let out a loud, "Moo."

Without lifting his eyes from the Leedy catalog, the customer, out of the corner of his mouth, exclaimed to the clerk, "Swell cow effect, I'll take it!"

Test Your Short Rolls

Lay a piece of carbon paper on a hard surface, carbon side up. On top of this lay a clean piece of white paper. Then play a five stroke roll on the white paper. Now lift it up and examine the impressions the carbon paper has left on the under side. Count them—there should be exactly five. You will be surprised. Now try it with the rest of the short rolls, viz.; seven, nine, fifteen, etc.

$2.00 award to George Burnwood, 992 Wakeling St., Philadelphia, Pa.

Glenn Rogers

This is Glenn Rogers, organizer and manager of the Wichita marimba band, using Leedy instruments exclusively. Mr. Rogers is soloist at the mid-week services of the Central Christian church regularly, and plays for his young men's Sunday school class. He plays for many lodge and club meetings. "A marimba solo, soft and reverent, makes inspiring church special music," he says.

Two other xylophonists, in this popular, all Leedy, marimba band, are Earnest Enders and Tom Sutherland. This trio is making marimba music much in demand around Wichita, Kansas.

$10.00 Reward

Drum Topics pays a reward of $10.00 each issue for a favorite drummer story. Send yours in. It may be the winning story and if so the sawbuck will be yours. The story need not be long and it need not be true—but it must be good. Don't pass up this chance to make 10 bucks easy.

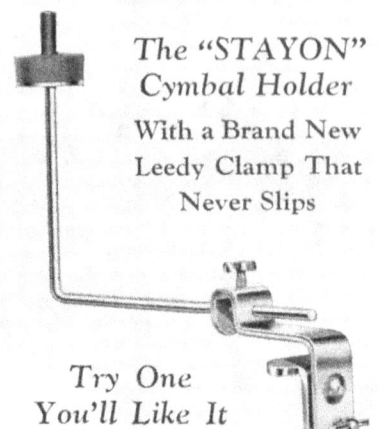

The "STAYON" Cymbal Holder

With a Brand New Leedy Clamp That Never Slips

Try One You'll Like It

There's no longer any need to worry about your cymbals and other equipment holding fast to the hoop of your bass drum while you're playing a job. The new Leedy "Stayon" clamp has solved that problem completely, absolutely. The "Stayon" introduces a new principal of leverage into hoop clamp construction which gives more than 100% more gripping power than any old type clamp. What's more, the "Stayon" is made fast with just about half as many turns of the tensioning screw. You don't have to twist and twist to make it stick. Just a couple of turns and the "Stayon" stays on! No need to break your thumb and ruin your hoops with hard-to-fasten clamps, see your Leedy dealer and ask him to show you the new "Stayon", or order one from 2300 Leedy Bldg., Elkhart, Ind. Try it, you'll like it.

No. 7518—N.P.—For Single Cymbals $2.00
No. 7519—N.G.—For Single Cymbals 3.00
No. 7520—C.P.—For Single Cymbals 3.00

Rumble Tips on Fibre Case

When used on the top or side of a fibre snare drum case, the new Leedy Rumble Tips (see page 9) give a fine and very different effect, something like a bass fiddle but of a new quality of sound. This is especially useful when an effect that will cut through the rest of the band is desired. Place the drum case against your chair to keep it from slipping and drag the Rumble Tips across the top.

$2.00 award to "Rags" Anderson, Columbus, Ohio.

Leedy — **World's Finest Drummers' Instruments** — **Leedy**

The Exclusive Drummers' Paper

$2.00 Apiece for "Ideas"

Drum Topics will pay $2.00 apiece for each drummer suggestion or "Idea" that is published in the next issue No. 24. If you have a new trap of your own invention or a new way to use a standard trap or collection of traps, send a description of your "Idea" to the Editor of Drum Topics. If your suggestion is published, you will receive a $2.00 cash award and full credit when the article concerning your suggestion appears. No "Idea" or stunt is too large or too small, too important or too insignificant to find a place in this magazine so long as it has to do with drums and drummers. Think it over; haven't you some pet trick or stunt of your own that other drummers would like to know about? If so, send it along and earn yourself two bucks.

A New Tambo Effect

A fine Tambo effect may be obtained with a Leedy 10 inch tambourine, No. 7761, page 74 catalog "S", and a pair of Synco-Jazz Brushes. Hold the tambourine firmly against the leg with the left hand, in the manner illustrated, and beat out the rhythm with the wire jazz brush on the tambo head. A soft "swish" effect may be obtained by using the brush very lightly.

"On hot choruses the tambo effect makes 'em sit up and take notice," says the contributor of this stunt.

$2.00 award to Garnett "Red" Stewart, 51 E. Woodbury Ave., Dayton, Ohio.

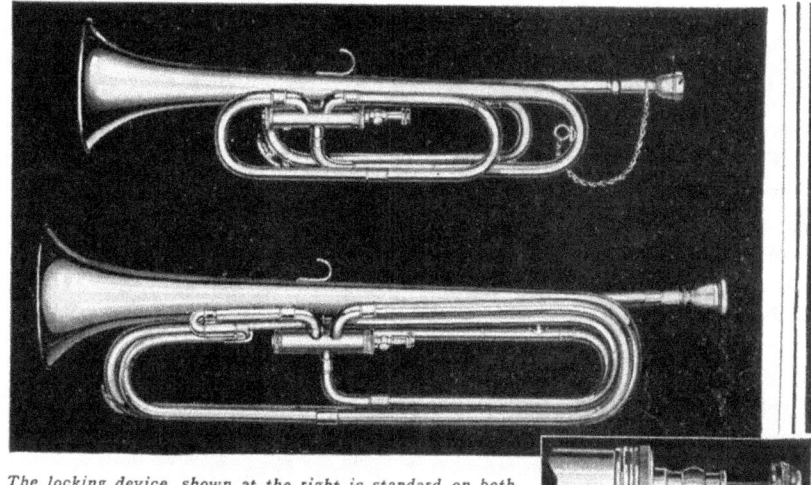

The locking device, shown at the right is standard on both Soprano and Baritone Piston Bugles. By means of the thumb screw, the piston is locked so it cannot be used, thus making the bugle acceptable for all competition purposes.

New Possibilities For Your Corps!

Leedy's two new Piston Bugles open up a whole new field of musical possibilities for your corps. With the adoption of these two new bugles, your corps can play real musical numbers—marches, melodies, etc.—with beautiful four part harmony. An almost unlimited musical repertoire will be placed at your command, and the best part of it all is that your buglers will be able to use these new instruments after receiving only a few simple instructions and with very little practice.

Don't pass up this opportunity to put new life, new vigor and new music into your corps. You can be among the first to have this great improvement and be one of the outstanding corps at the next competitions. Write 2300 Leedy Bldg., Elkhart, Ind., for complete details of the new Piston Bugles.

Above In Illustration Soprano Piston Bugle

The Soprano Piston Bugle is built in "G" with piston change to "D" and slide to "F". It is 21 inches long and can be supplied in the following finishes:

No. 5577, Polished Brass	$21.50
No. 5578, Satin Silver	26.00
No. 5579, Silver, Gold Bell	27.50
No. 5580, Polished Chrome	29.00
No. 5581, Polished Chrome, Gold Bell	30.50

Below In Illustration Baritone Piston Bugle

The Baritone Piston Bugle is built in "G" with piston change to "D". The tone of the Baritone is one octave lower than that of the Soprano. It is 24 inches long and can be supplied in the following finishes:

No. 5583, Polished Brass	$30.00
No. 5584, Satin Silver	36.00
No. 5585, Silver, Gold Bell	37.50
No. 5586, Polished Chrome	39.50
No. 5587, Polished Chrome, Gold Bell	41.00

Chick Webb

"Have used all makes of drums, I find Leedy the best", that is the tribute to Leedy by Chick Webb of Baltimore, Md. He has played drums for a period of ten years, having great success, using Leedy Instruments. Without a doubt he will continue successfully.

Mr. Webb has had his own orchestra for five years. In the past he has played at the Roseland Ballroom in N. Y., Cotton Club, N. Y., Savoy Ballroom, N. Y., and "Nuttings on the Charles", Boston.

Farmer: "An' 'ow be Lawyer Barnes doin', doctor?"
Doctor: "Poor fellow! He's lying at death's door."
Farmer: "There's grit for 'ee—at death's door an' still lyin'!"

Leedy — World's Finest Drummers' Instruments — Leedy

Leedy Drum Topics

An Anti-Slip Idea

Use a rubber stair step tread (obtainable at the 10c store) under your Low Sock Cymbal Pedal. It will keep it from slipping. These rubber pads can be obtained at any 5 & 10c store and for keeping the pedal from slipping, they can't be beat.

$2.00 award to Woodbury Bailey, 23 Pratt St., Bath, Maine.

John H. Diaz

Mr. Diaz hails from San Antonio, Texas, and is an ardent booster of Leedy Instruments.

The experience of Mr. Diaz includes playing in theaters, inns, hotels, and Broadcasting.

At present Mr. Diaz is with the K. T. S. A. Radio Orchestra in San Antonio.

Having played Percussion and Mallet Played Instruments for all of twenty-five years, his opinion verifies the statement that Leedy Instruments are "World's Finest Drummers' Instruments."

Fishing

Ever fish for Silver Tarpon?

He's a gentle little playmate. He tips the beam all the way from 150 to 500 pounds and when hooked, frequently becomes friendly and hops right into the boat with you.

But he's great sport. Big hook and line men from Europe even, come to Florida to match their skill with him: and they must use the right equipment or they are S. O. L.

The Bamboo-rod and the cork bobber are all right for landing the little fish, but it takes heavy equipment, knowledge and experience to put a Silver Tarpon where you want him.

And isn't that just like it is in the drumming game? If you use old style, shabby looking equipment, you may land the small-fry jobs, but to get the really worth-while big money spots you must have the latest and best outfit that money can buy.

Marsh Joins Grofe In New Orchestra

George Marsh

Here is George Marsh, until recently drummer with the Whiteman orchestra (for 10 years), posed on the Beach Walk at the Edgewater Beach Hotel, Chicago, last summer just before he went East to do things in a big way.

At the present time George is doing considerable radio work in New York City, playing the Listerine Hour, the Blue Coal Hour and several other radio spots. As this issue goes to press Marsh is reported to have joined forces with Ferde Grofe, in a new orchestral venture. With Grofe, who is famous as the arranger of most of Whiteman's hits, and Marsh at the helm, there can be little doubt that the new outfit will go over in a big way. Rumor has it that Grofe has already been offered several big radio contracts and no doubt by the time this issue is in your hands the new orchestra will already be going strong. *Drum Topics* and the entire Leedy organization join in wishing George and Ferde the best of luck in their new venture. And more than that, we predict that when these two boys hit their stride radio fans will be in for some brand new thrills.

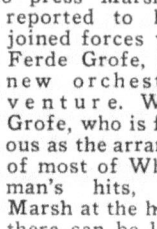
Ferde Grofe

Clothes Brush Gives New Effect

Beating on the snare drum with a clothes brush of the type shown above produces a different effect than is obtained with ordinary wire Jazz Brushes. The best type of brush to use with this stunt is one with very stiff bristles. Either one or two brushes may be used according to the type of rhythm desired. A good locomotive effect can also be obtained in this way.

$2.00 award to Edward M. Ruhlig, Concordia College, Ft. Wayne, Ind.

Synco Jazz Brush Stunt

By drawing a Synco Jazz Brush across the bass drum head in an upward circular motion striking underneath the bottom cymbal on the "High Hat" sock cymbal stand at the end of the stroke a very effective stunt can be performed. The effect can be varied by allowing the cymbals to remain open or closing them at the same time that it is struck by the wire brush. This stunt can be used either on accents in breaks or at the end of a strain or number.

$2.00 award to Harold E. Schulze, 2015 Arlington Ave., Middletown, O.

Howard J. MacDonald

Mr. MacDonald hails from Bayonne, N. J. He has 17 years of professional drumming to his credit and deserves a rating with some of the best boys in the business.

He has played with such big time dance outfits as George Olson's orchestra, Charles Dorenberger and Al. Mitchell. For a time he dished up the rhythm with Carr's band at New York's famous Silver Slipper night club. When last heard from, Howard was about to join up with the musical show, "Everybody's Welcome," under the direction of Thomas L. Jones.

"I can't Give You Anything but Love, Baby," sang father, as he rocked the infant back to sleep.

Fond Mother—"How much do you charge for taking children's photographs?"

Photographer—"Five dollars a dozen."

Fond Mother—"You'll have to give me more time, I have only ten now."

Is This Service?

Lady—"Can you give me a room and bath?"

Clerk—"I can give you a room, madam, but you will have to take your own bath."

Friend—"Whom does your little son look like?"

Happy Father—"His eyes are mine, the nose is my wife's, and his voice, I think, he got from our auto horn."

World's Finest Drummers' Instruments

 **The Exclusive Drummers' Paper**

New Possibilities For The Jobbing Drummer
with the New Solo-Tone
ZYRIMBA

New effects, new flash, greater popularity are waiting for the jobbing drummer who equips himself with the new Leedy Solo-Tone Zyrimba! It's the smallest and lightest marimba-xylophone in the Leedy line and it combines in one instrument the resonance of the marimba and the sparkling tones of the xylophone. The exceptional tone and volume of this instrument combined with its ready portability make it well adapted to a variety of uses. Bars are selected Honduras Rosewood accurately tuned. Frame is finished in Silver Duco. The aluminum resonators are highly polished and the plated stand is of the rigid, fast-folding type. Ask your Leedy dealer to show you this great new instrument or write 2300 Leedy Bldg., for complete details.

Three octaves C to C. Bars are 1¾″ to 1¼″ wide by ¾″ thick. Length 44″. Width at lower end 28″. Height 25″. Weight 40 lbs. Instrument with case, 62 lbs.

No. 5612—Leedy Solo-Tone Zyrimba	$125.00
No. 8148—Four Rubber Tired Wheels (two with brakes)	25.00 Extra
No. 8145—Extension Legs for above	3.50 Extra
Nobby Gold on Resonators, Stand, etc.	25.00 Extra
Marine Pearl on Wood Frame Front, Ends, etc.	10.00 Extra
†No. 6973—Case for Solo-Tone Zyrimba	20.00
‡No. 6958—Trunk for Solo-Tone Zyrimba	60.00

Robt. K. Shuey

Here is a young booster of Leedy Instruments. He is only sixteen years old and has played with orchestras and bands for over four years. His name is Robert Kenneth Shuey, and his present address is Marshalltown, Iowa.

Robert is the proud owner of a set of Leedy Drums and many Leedy Traps. He says he certainly likes Leedy Instruments and hopes to be able to add to his outfit just as soon as possible a pair of tympani chimes and a few others.

Friend: "Just been lunching with your husband, darling."
Mrs. Griffin: "So good of you, angel, but I do hope it won't come to his secretary's ears; she's so jealous."

Novel Tom-Tom Stunt
FOR PRESENTATION DRUMMERS

Jack Turner, drummer with a presentation band in Minneapolis, gets credit for the novel tom-tom stunt mechanical details of which are explained in the illustration at right. Jack claims that he got a big hand from the audience with this novelty, and here's the way he explains it: "I used two 16″ x 16″ Leedy white enamel tom-toms, No. 8011. These I had nickle plated and mounted on pipe work frames as shown in the accompanying illustration. The pipes also were nickle plated. Small pulley wheels were attached to the ends of the pipes which passed through the tom-toms, and these were connected to two electric fan motors by means of leather belts. The motors were so arranged that they turned the tom-toms slowly in opposite directions.

"I used this stunt on a special arrangement of 'Moonlight On The Ganges', which had an eight bar tom-tom introduction. Blue and red spots were thrown on me, and I used two tympani sticks with a cross arm ad lib motion, playing the Congo rhythm much like a Scotch drummer. As I was mounted high in the back, above the rest of the band, the effect was great."

$2.00 award to Jack Turner, 1517 2nd Ave. So., Minneapolis, Minnesota.

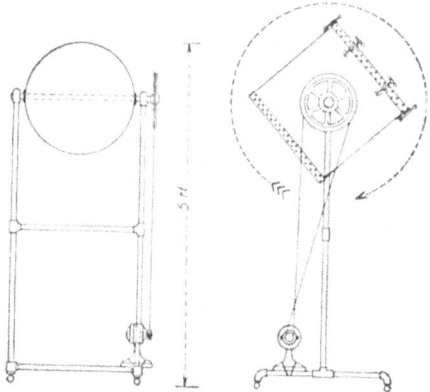

 **World's Finest Drummers' Instruments** *Leedy*

Page Seventeen

Leedy Drum Topics

Bud Struck and John L. Wakefield

Here are Bud Struck, popular Minneapolis orchestra leader and his drummer, John Lewis Wakefield. Struck and his band are rated the No. 1 dance outfit of the Twin Cities. They are now playing at the exclusive Minneapolis Athletic Club. The outfit broadcasts regularly over WCCO and before coming to the M. A. C. were at the Terrace Cafe of the Lowry Hotel in St. Paul, which is considered the best spot in the Twin Cities. Wakefield recently purchased a brand new Leedy Sparkling Green Pearl. outfit. He uses nothing but Leedy equipment and tells us that he is not bashful in letting other drummers know about it. Thanks for the boost, John, say we.
(Photo courtesy Hausner Music Co., Minneapolis, Minn.)

Man Behind the Drum

Many writers pay great tribute to all kinds of soloists, pointing to their ability and singing praise of their work, but "the man behind the drum" is almost entirely ignored, just as though his position was one of minor importance.

As a matter of fact, the bass drum is really the most important instrument in the band. The drummer is sometimes spoken of as "the conductor in the rear," and indeed his work has a very great controlling influence.

In order to handle the drum efficiently, one must be a thoroughly schooled musician. On no one of the other instrumentalists rests so much responsibility for the perfect performance of any composition. The drummer's work must be so performed that it will not cover the work of the other members of the band. His readings must be correct at all times—there dare not be any guess. An erratic drummer can easily upset the best intentions of both composer and conductor. Being sure is what gives one the impetus to go ahead and produce 100 per cent efficiency.

Judging from the style of work of some of the drummers, it would seem as though they regard the drum merely as an instrument for athletic purposes, something on which to develop the muscles of the right wing. In some instances that's about all they get out of it, but the drummers in our many excellent orchestras and artistic concert bands have got to be musicians of the highest type. In many of the standard and classical selections, the bass drum and cymbals are called on to produce special effects. But unless this descriptive work is taken care of with a nicety, it will not produce the realistic effects desired by the composer—it will mar, rather than improve the result.
—From the "Interborough Bulletin"

Some Leedy Movie Stars

Here is Murray Spivack, sound effects expert of the RKO studios, Los Angeles, posed with a group of Leedy drums which have recently starred in the movies. The street drums were used in the Radio Pictures comedy success, "Half Shot at Sunrise," with Wheeler and Woolsey. The big bass drum has been used in a number of RKO productions. Leedy instruments are used almost exclusively by RKO studios.

A Temple Block Beat

Temple blocks are very effective when used in piano waltz passages and played in the following manner:
Play three beats to the bar striking both sticks at once on two different blocks, but always using blocks next to each other.

$2.00 award to—Arthur A. Prokesch, 2029 Himrod St., Ridgewood, L. I., N. Y.

New "Sock" Cymbal Effects

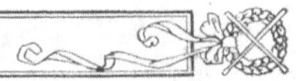

Several different effects may be obtained by sandwiching various kinds of material between your sock cymbals. If you use either the low or the high hat sock cymbal pedals (such as shown in the Leedy catalog on page 65) it is a very simple matter to cut a circle of paper about 1" larger than the largest cymbal, and cut it as shown in the accompanying drawing. Cutting in this fashion allows the drummer to quickly slip the paper between the cymbals for certain numbers and eliminates the necessity of having to remove the top cymbal to put the paper in place. If the drummer wishes to leave the paper between the cymbals permanently he should not cut as shown in design, but simply slip it down over the rod. Materials other than paper produce different tones: some drummers are using cloth of various kinds—flannel, cotton, silk, etc. Others are using chamois. Experiment until you find the material that best suits your taste. Any one of these materials wholly eliminates the ring in the cymbal and lends more "hollowness" to the tone, but we believe that most drummers will prefer the paper effect.

$2.00 award to—Joe Smole, 5806 Bonna Ave., Cleveland, Ohio.

Also to—Bob Zika, 2600 First Ave., Cedar Rapids, Iowa.

When You Move

When you change your address, be sure to notify *Drum Topics* immediately. Otherwise you will miss your copy of the next issue. Every year more than 300 drummers fail to get their copy of this magazine for just that reason. This is inconvenient for them and it means a loss of postage to us, a bad deal all around. So don't forget, when you change your address, notify us immediately. It only takes a minute and saves all kinds of time and trouble for everyone concerned.

World's Finest Drummers' Instruments

The Exclusive Drummers' Paper

A Great Solution

Well, as luck would have it, I was talking to Mr. Dudley Diggs, the actor, a few days ago and he told me about a family he knowed back in Ireland who the wife's maiden name was a Miss Kettle and the husband was Mr. Drum. Came several kiddies to curse the home. The first, a girl, was christened Beta Drum. The second, a boy, was baptized Fife N. Drum. The third, a girl was named Clarinet N. Drum, and goes under the nickname of Clara and Nettie. The fourth, another girl (not the same girl), is Snare. And finally what should arrive but a pair of twins and the parents was puzzled for quite a wile, but at last, then they discovered that the 2 kiddies was always together when you wanted them, hit on the idear of naming them each Tom and always calling both of them at once—Tom-Tom.

—*Contributed*

Harold C. Hine

This is Mr. Harold C. Hine, of Battle Creek, Michigan, who is considered one of the best drummers in that part of the state. He's just plenty "Hot" at the present moment, as the accompanying picture shows.

Mr. Hine has had seven years experience playing drums, and has used Leedy five of those seven years. In fact, his present equipment is completely Leedy.

Edward Homand

Here we have a young man, by name, Edward Homand, who hails from Ontario, Calif. A Leedy xylophone is one of his prize possessions.

This young man entertains at many social affairs. A party is not complete without Edward and his xylophone. He has played over many of the leading Radio Stations and for several Vaudeville bookers. This year will finish his schooling after which he intends to "hit the boards". Edward has turned "professional" now, and from a standpoint of his former appearances, we know he will be a success, especially since he is going to add a New Leedy Vibraphone to his act.

Freddie Crump

Speaking of going places and doing things, here is Freddie Crump who really does just that when it comes to drumming. It's rumored around that he can make a sizzle cymbal speak right up and say "Uncle", and the appearance of his photograph is almost convincing enough to make us believe that this is no foolin'. Freddie is hot and no mistake, but he's A-No. 1 on the straight stuff too.

At present he is playing with the Norman Thomas Quintette, a Fanchon and Marco act now booked on the Fox circuit. The photograph of Freddie was taken while he was playing with the Hotel Rhythm Boys, a band which appeared with great success recently in connection with one of the units on the Publix circuit. Altogether Crump has more than 12 years professional playing experience to his credit. He uses Leedy equipment exclusively.

Two Good Tom-Tom Stunts

Place Leedy 10" x 4" "Full Dress" tom-tom, page 72 catalog "S", on your snare drum and beat out rhythm with felt ball tenor drum sticks, No. 1610, page 40, catalog "S". This stunt can be worked either with the snares on or off. With the snares on, the tone is a combination of snare drum and tom-tom. With the snares off, play alternately on the tom-tom head and the drum head. This gives a very peculiar two-tone tom-tom effect. Both of these effects are especially fine for "sweet" choruses or hot "push" choruses.

$2.00 award to Tip Tipton, 1000 No. Axtelle St., Clovis, N. M.

A variation of the "idea" given above has been suggested by Russel S. Lee. He says that an effect slightly different from one above can be obtained by holding the tom-tom in the left hand just barely above, not touching, the snare drum head.

$2.00 award to Russel S. Lee, R. F. D 5, So. Akron, Ohio.

A Genuine Leedy Drum in 2232 AD.

First Drummer—I've got something I want to show you fellows that I bought today. A real genuine Leedy Snare, made in the eighteen hundreds. I guess from the model, about the time that chap Abraham Lincoln lived. What do you think of it. Listen to that snap. And look at the shape it is in, that surely shows that they made stuff to last in those days.

Second Drummer—Say Jack, I've been wanting to get hold of one of those famous old drums for years. I heard of one in New York but when I tried to get it, the fellow had sold it. It had been in a "hockshop" and the old fellow hadn't any idea what it was and sold it for twenty-five dollars. I understand that the one who bought it is holding it for $5,000.00. I'd surely like to get in touch with him.

First Drummer—Well my boy don't look any further, I'm the boy who bought that drum in N. Y. but the amount you heard is all wrong. Why I'd never think of selling a REAL GENUINE LEEDY SNARE for a cent less than $10,000.00. I'll not sell it for a cent less.

Second Drummer—Well I'll tell you what you do, I will take it at that figure but I can't pay cash. If you will take half down and the balance in two months I'll take it.

First Drummer—That will be all right, SOLD. A real genuine Leedy Snare for $10,000.00. I know I could have gotten half again as much for that drum if I'd have held on to it. The only reason I'm selling it at all is that I'm a little short on cash and need some quick money. My aeroplane has a broken propeller, and I have to get it fixed or I'll not get to the theatre on time. Thanks for the check, I hope you don't feel I've stung you old man, for I believe it's worth it.

Second Drummer—Sure it's worth it, for I have a friend who is a curio seeker, and he has offered me $20,000.00 for a Real Genuine Leedy Snare, any time I could get one.

First Drummer—My Gosh.

—Contributed by Herman Rinne, Indianapolis, Ind.

After using his drum for nearly two years, a certain drummer wrote to the company from whom the drum had been purchased, saying, "After using your drum for two years, I find it cannot be beat." Wonder what he'd been doing with the darn thing all that time.

Contributed by Earl Schniztler, Hamilton, Ohio.

 **World's Finest Drummers' Instruments**

Leedy Drum Topics

Yes Sir! He's Carrying The New Leedy Case Vibraphone

> » » and It's Complete in One Case, Ready To Play, Resonators and all. Remove the lid and You're Ready to Go. No Bars or Resonators to mount

PICK it up and carry it away, set it down and it's ready to play! That's what you do with the new Leedy Case Vibraphone, Mr. Drummer. It's the most amazing thing you ever saw—a genuine Leedy Vibraphone built complete, resonators and all, right in its own convenient hand-carrying case. It weighs little more than some sets of orchestra bells, and the secret of the compactness is in the ingenious arrangement of the resonators. They are laid flat in the bottom of the case. In spite of its many big features, however, the Case Vibraphone is the lowest priced Leedy instrument of its kind. In every respect, price, tone and portability, this instrument fits the needs of the Jobbing Drummer. You owe it to yourself to investigate the possibilities of this great new Vibraphone. See your Leedy dealer or write 2300 Leedy Bldg., Elkhart, Ind., for full details of this great new instrument.

Pick it up and carry it away, set it down and it's ready to play! That's the slogan of the drummer who is equipped with the new Leedy Case Vibraphone. He's always ready to get on the job with this beautiful instrument which so increases the flash, playing ability and earning power of any drummer who owns one. Ask the nearest Leedy dealer to show you the Case Vibraphone or write 2300 Leedy Bldg., Elkhart, Ind., for full details.

No. 5658—2½ octaves, F to C, 32 bars 1¼" wide by ⅜" thick. Case measures 35" long by 20" wide by 5" deep. Total weight, 42 lbs. $180.00
Instructor, four pair mallets and detachable music rack included.

No. 1750—Folding stand as illustrated $6.00

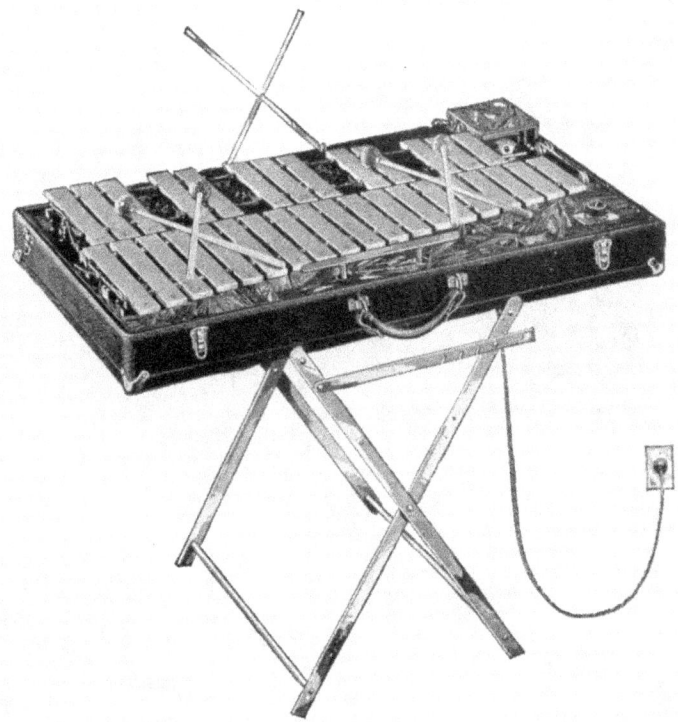

Six Big Features

Complete In Case—The Leedy Case Vibraphone is built right in its own strong carrying case. This makes it ideal for the jobbing drummer.

Rheostat Speed Control—A reliable rheostat controls the rate at which the fans revolve. Five pulsations per second produces normal vibrato but speed can be increased or decreased at will.

Efficient Damper Device—The duration of tone is easily controlled by an efficient damper similar in action to a typewriter spacing bar.

Tempered Aluminum Bars—Tempered aluminum alloy bars insure a sweeter and more sustained tone than steel bars can produce.

Resonator Vibrating Fans—The revolving fans in the tops of the resonators give the Vibraphone its distinctive vibrato which has made it so popular.

Sturdy Universal Motor—The motor which drives the resonator fans is a small, sturdy Universal (110 volt AC or DC) which operates from any light socket.

Leedy   **World's Finest Drummers' Instruments**   *Leedy*

The Exclusive Drummers' Paper

Hold Your Horses, Folks Here Come the Elephants

(In which "Ollie" Payne, himself, an old time circus drummer, now in show business at South Bend, Indiana, tells you all about three Big Shots of the Big Tops, who, as "Ollie" says, are just about the last of their kind.)

by "Ollie" Payne

Here are the "Old Timers", themselves; left to right, Evans, Thompson and Paulsen.

Listen, "You Wire Brush Artists", and you shall hear of two drummers who have trouped both far and near.

It's all too true, they're the last of their kind, so all you "Hot Lickers" bear this in mind.

If you want to improve, and get into the dough, get a load of these boys with the Barnum Show.

You'll hear more new beats in less than two hours than those ever dreamt of by Stone, Straight or Bowers.

When the show plays your town you be inside of that top, and you'll hear two drummers that are even hotter than hot.

Thompson and Paulsen are these kids' names if you care, and when Leedy invented his drum these two eggs were there.

They've made them all, Musical Comedy, Grand Opera and Burlesque, and trouped years ago with Buffalo Bill Cody's Wild West.

But come all you "chislers", and listen to their old familiar strain, it's their swan song children, they sang it to me, "Never Again".

NO, don't let the above depicted trio mislead you, it's not John Law and a couple of culprits. It's my old congenial friend, and highly proficient musical director, Merle Evans, of the Barnum & Bailey Ringling Bros. Circus in company with his drum section, namely, Amos Thompson back of the snare drum, and Henry Paulsen with the big skin.

The Ringling Shows have always maintained high class musical organizations, and their circus band this season is upholding the reputations of the past. Bandmaster Evans should be congratulated upon his selection of a battery section. These boys keep the entire band on their toes, and drive them on at a tempo most incredible.

A circus drummer must be not only versatile, but able to read and execute all modern and rudimentary beats at lightning speed. Furthermore, he must be possessed with the stamina, and durability of an iron man. The circus performance proper embraces one hundred and forty musical numbers, *forty of which are gallops, played at a record breaking speed.*

Thompson and Paulsen gave me a real thrill when I saw the circus recently. In fact I can truthfully say that they are one of the finest drum teams I have ever listened to, and I have heard them all. Little Thompson on snare drum, weight about a hundred and fifteen, slugging away at that big band model Leedy, equipped with rhinoceros skin heads, and zebra gut snares, using a couple of Louisville Sluggers, originally intended for Babe Ruth, as sticks, catching all the feature tricks in the arena, and rolling almost continually. That guy can't be human. Then big Henry Paulsen at the bull drum, What-A-Man! He plays bass drum like a harpist, and with the steady precision of a metronome, juggling that heavy cymbal like a feather.

The Ringling Bros. should surely have a sixteen sheet stand of special lithographs made of these boys, for they are about the last of a fast disappearing race. Come on all you bums, lets give Amos and Henry a great big hand.

Sousa's Battery

This is the most recent photo of the battery section of the famous Sousa Band as they appeared during an engagement at Atlantic City, N. J. From left to right the members are: J. J. Heney, Frank Holt, and "Gus" Helmecke. These boys are the nation's premier band drummers and it is significant that all of the equipment which they use is Leedy. Heney now makes his home at St. Augustine, Fla., Hol

at Haverhill, Mass., and Helmecke in New York City.

Leedy — World's Finest Drummers' Instruments — **Leedy**

Page Twenty-one

Leedy Drum Topics

Eloise E. Redfield

Although still a student in high school Miss Eloise Redfield of Shenandoah, Ia., is already an artist on the Leedy Solo-Tone Marimba. Last year in contests for high school students she won firsts in city, district and sub-district contests, second in the state contest and third in the national at Tulsa, Okla. She says that in all the contests which she has entered, the judges have complimented her on the beautiful tone of her Leedy Marimba. In addition to school and church playing, Miss Redfield also plays with the Elks Municipal Band of Shenandoah.

FFF Pedal Cymbal Effect

The following stunt will be found very effective on last choruses where a rather loud (fff) four beats to the bar is used. Use two 7" American Brass Cymbals, No. 7437, page 62 Leedy catalog "S", and several jingles from an old tambourine. Bolt the two cymbals together face to face (sock fashion) with the tambo jingles inside. Fasten to bass drum with regular pedal cymbal holder (No. 7135 catalog "S") and play with pedal cymbal striker.

$2.00 award to Donald Gardner, Box 55, Wellsville, New York.

Hats Off to the Old Timers

I cannot agree that the legitimate drummer should scorn the dance man as a painful intruder, or regard him as a nine days' wonder, since orchestral and dance drumming are two entirely different branches of the percussionists' art, and the one requires just as much skill and dexterity as the other.

But when we hear a "straight" band, and see a venerable old man with white hair playing an old-fashioned drum at a rakish angle—a veteran to whom the pedal is an unknown quantity—holding his wrists well down and proudly lifting the acorns high, let us not laugh in superiority, let us not regard him as an antiquity with his open beats. Rather let us uncover in reverence, for he is the veteran on whose skilled technique our new art is based; he is the pioneer who showed us our handicraft, and devoted a lifetime to make the percussion what it is today!

Julien Vedey, London, Eng.

PP

"Gus" Helmecke, famous bass drummer of the Sousa Band tells this one.

Gus had been listening to an orchestra playing very softly when suddenly the bass drummer whacked his instrument as loud as he could. After the concert Helmecke met the man and indignant over the way he had played the bass drum part, said to him, "Do you know that you ruined that number by the way you played your part?"

"I played it just as it was marked," replied the erring bass drummer.

"And how was it marked?" demanded "Gus".

"Pp," was the reply, "and everyone knows—"

"You jackanapes," said Helmecke, "pp means very softly."

"Oh," said the crestfallen drummer, "I thought that pp meant 'pretty powerful'."

It's good to have money and the things that money can buy, but it's good, too, to check up once in awhile and make sure you haven't lost the things that money can't buy.
—George Horace Lorimer

"That brother of mine is sure smart. He's only 16 but he's been clear through Reform School."

Fred Whyte

Fred Whyte, of Los Angeles, has been in the business of precussion and mallet playing for over twenty-five years. He chooses Leedy.

Mr. Whyte has played with many Theater orchestras including, the Rialto, California and Kinema theaters. Besides these, he has played with the Catalina Island Band and the Long Beach Band. At present the Figueroa Playhouse Orchestra has the honor of his services.

"Rumble Tip" Tambo Stunt

A new and different effect may be had by pulling one of the new Leedy "Rumble Tips" across a tambourine. Any size tambo will do, and, of course, as the "Rumble Tip" is pulled across the head, it causes the tambourine to jingle. This is a fine effect which can be used in a variety of numbers.

$2.00 award to Charles Manning, 730 Carew St., Springfield, Mass.

Owing to the fact that length, thickness and density govern the pitch of a steel or wood bar, it is impossible to make bells, xylophones, etc., without carefully tuning each individual bar.

Leedy — World's Finest Drummers' Instruments — **Leedy**

The Exclusive Drummers' Paper

Easy Sure Way To Make Tambourine Thumb Roll

Many drummers have trouble making a good tambourine thumb roll and here's an easy efficient way to solve the difficulty. Smear a thin semicirclar layer of LePage's glue around the upper edge of the tambo head. Make this layer of glue about 2½ inches wide in the shape shown in the illustration above. While the glue is still wet scrape two pieces of sandpaper (No. 2) together allowing the sand grits to fall on the wet glue. Allow the glue to dry, and you will find that enough of the sand has stuck to the tambourine head so that you now have a surface just rough enough to give you the right action for a good roll when the tambo is dragged across your thumb.

$2.00 award to "Sonny" Greer, Duke Ellington's Band, N. Y. C.

Ned Cleveland

"I am using the Leedy drums and I think they are the best made. The workmanship is A-1. They stand the test, what more can you ask? You can't go wrong in buying a Leedy."

That is the testimonial as Mr. Ned Cleveland of Fitchburg, Mass., puts it. He has used Leedy instruments for a good many years, therefore he certainly knows what he is talking about. Mr. Cleveland has played drums for thirty-five years. Some of the organizations with which he has played are:—Mt. Roulslone Orchestra, Leominster Concert Band, and Empire Theater Motion Pictures in Brattleboro, Vermont. Mr. Cleveland is one of the few remaining old time stars with the bone clappers.

Earl MacLane

When last heard from, Earl was in Berlin playing with "Kapelle B. Ette," the Paul Whiteman orchetra of Germany. He hails originally from Boston, Mass., but has been in Europe for about a year now, and from all reports is going over in a big way.

In a recent letter to the Leedy Co., "Mac" explained that he was not only playing a night club, broadcasting and recording, but was also preparing to make a "talkie", all of which made him about as busy, say we, as a cat on a tin roof. In the photograph Earl is shown with just a little more than half of his outfit. Altogether he has just about everything and anything that was ever invented for drummers. He claims to have the largest outfit in Europe—and what's more, it's all Leedy.

"Mac" is a composer and arranger and a good all-around musician as well as a first class drummer. He has been in almost every type of musical work imaginable, including concert orchestras, burlesque shows, vaudeville acts, dance bands and picture houses.

More "Zip" for The Sock Cymbal Pedal

Use a regular 12" "Sizzle" cymbal, No. 7452, page 63 catalog "S", for the top cymbal on the sock cymbal pedal, and a 10" deep cup Zenjian, No. 7320, catalog "S", for the bottom cymbal. Using these cymbals gives more of a "zip" effect than is obtained from the regular combination. This arrangement, moreover, seems to record and broadcast better.

$2.00 award to Nick Henderson, 447 Miami St., Piqua, Ohio.

YOU CAN'T WIN

"Did you ever go to that telephone girl's house?"
"Oh, yes, after I'd called at the three wrong addresses she gave me."

Eddie—I'm writing a song.
Vera—What's the subject matter?
Eddie—It doesn't.

DEEP STUFF

Men and women
  chasing around
    after each other
      is what makes
        the human race.

J. F. Sullivan

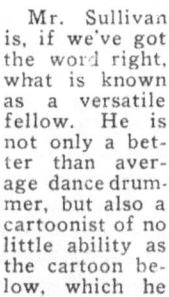

Mr. Sullivan is, if we've got the word right, what is known as a versatile fellow. He is not only a better than average dance drummer, but also a cartoonist of no little ability as the cartoon below, which he contributed to *Drum Topics*, will attest. Sullivan is at present living in Indianapolis playing dance jobs and improving his technique by taking lessons from Herman Rinne. He has also done considerable playing in Florida and throughout the Southwest with several very popular dance bands.

World's Finest Drummers' Instruments

Leedy DRUM TOPICS
The Exclusive Drummers' Paper

March 1932 » » 23rd Edition

See Page 4

POSTMASTER—Return Postage Guaranteed

LEEDY MANUFACTURING CO.
2300 Leedy Bldg., Elkhart, Indiana

Mr. Joseph G. Benoit,
165 Hildreth,
Lowell, Mass.

Under the direction of Prof. Paul S. Emrick, who has worked untiringly with the organization for more than 20 years, Purdue University, Lafayette, Ind., has developed one of the finest college bands in the United States. The percussion section of the Purdue Band, whose photograph appears above, is equipped with Leedy instruments. From left to right, back row, the players are: Lieut. L. M. Condrey, concert bass drummer and parade drum major; F. C. Brunka, cymbals; Corp. L. McClary, xylophone; H. B. Swain, chimes; Sgt. H. E. Firestone, tympanist and principal musician, (Mr. Firestone is now a member of the Leedy staff); the players seated are (L. to R.): E. B. Smith, Lieut. R. W. Cline, Corp. L. W. Trueblood and Lieut. A. W. Ginther.

Leedy Drum Topics Issue 24

THE GREATLY IMPROVED
LEEDY UNIVERSAL PEDAL TYMPANI

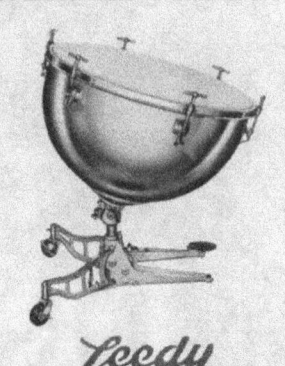

Leedy PRESENTS

—its famous Universal Pedal Tympani on NEW "easy wheeling" bases so you can move your kettles wherever you want them more easily than you can move your Vibraphone or xylophone around—another Leedy improvement that all drummers will appreciate.

The two front legs of the base have been redesigned and reinforced to accommodate solid rubber wheels of the same type as used on the Leedy Vibraphones and xylophones. Now, by slightly raising the tympani by the tension handles nearest you, you can move the kettles quickly and without effort, wherever you want them.

The locking brakes on the wheels, operated by the toe of the foot, will prevent the instruments from "creeping" away from you even in the hardest of playing.

Leedy Universal Pedal Tympani have long been recognized by leading professional drummers and tympanists as the finest machine tympani on the market because of their superior tone, accurate tuning, easy operation, correct design and mechanical construction. Now we have added improvements which will give them even greater favor. The tension system has been improved and strengthened, the pedal ratchet action has been made more positive, and the bases are now provided with two solid rubber wheels as illustrated and described to the right. This permits easier moving of the instruments when set up. Locking brakes on the wheels prevent "creeping" of the tympani when being played—even under terrific beating. Bowls are finest copper machine drawn to perfect roundness and highly polished, bases are buffed aluminum castings, and other metal parts are heavily nickel plated. Finest "Kafette" heads.

Sticks and Fibre Head Protectors Included

*No. 5500—Standard Size, 25" and 28", (Without Special Legs and Wheels) Bright copper bowls, other metal parts nickel plated and polished aluminum. Per pair $350.00

Two Legs With Wheels and Brakes, $15.00 Extra

*No. 5501—Symphony-Opera Size, 26" and 29", (Without Special Legs and Wheels) Bright copper bowls, other metal parts nickel plated and polished aluminum. Per pair $385.00

Two Legs With Wheels and Brakes, $15.00 Extra

Bowls in Glossy Black or Gleaming White Duco .... No Extra Charge
*Hoops, Handles, Brackets, Etc., in Nobby Gold .... $30.00 Extra
*Hoops, Handles, Brackets, Etc., in Chromium .... 30.00 Extra

---

THE NEW LEEDY "ROLL-OFF" No. 3
For The Band and Drum Corps Drummer

A bigger, better and more complete "Roll-Off" than Leedy has ever produced before! Its 72 pages are brimming full of just the kind of information the band and drum corps drummer needs and wants. Helpful information on organizing and conducting drum corps, formations and instrumentations, definitions of military and contest terms, the technique of Tenor and Scotch Bass Drumming explained, new "Full Dress" finishes, new and improved instrument models and a number of other new or improved items and pictures of 40 outstandingly fine drum corps in all parts of the country. The third edition of this valuable text, the Leedy "Roll-Off" No. 3, which has become known as the "Outdoor Drummers' Encyclopedia of Information and Equipment", will be sent free and without obligation to those interested in band and drum corps.

Address Your Request to Dept. 2108

LEEDY BLDG.   *Leedy Mfg. Co., Inc.*   ELKHART, IND.

The Cover On This Drum Topics Issue

The names of Fred Waring, Waring's Pennsylvanians and Poley McClintock are so well known throughout the nation that they certainly need no introduction to Drum Topics readers. Fred's versatile showmanship, the inimitable presentations of the band and Poley's foghorn-like voice effect have enjoyed an almost unprecedented radio, stage, dance and record popularity among the young and old alike. Their many achievements are their greatest praise.

Untiring consistent hard work, a few lucky "breaks", and undeniably good leadership that has brought the band's talent to the front to the best possible advantage are the reasons for the band's success. Our drummer readers may be interested, for instance, in the fact that Poley has not missed a rehearsal, or a radio or stage appearance in more than 15 years.

Stuart Churchill, whose picture we show on these pages for the first time, has been with the band for five years, plays sax and banjo, and takes a turn on the Vibraphone and tymps when Poley is busy on the drums or taking a vocal. Churchill's home was originally St. Francis, Kans., and is now New York City.

Righto! The equipment is 100% Leedy.

Rudy Vallee and Frank Frisselle

With Rudy Vallee, who has played and sung himself to world fame and directed his orchestra to enviable radio, stage and screen success, is Frank Frisselle who furnishes that necessary rhythm for this wonderful organization. Frisselle studied the drums under the late George B. Stone of Boston, and has played them for 15 years—the last two with Vallee. He played the Inaugural Ball in 1933 with his present organization, and was with Mal Hallett prior to being with Vallee. Thinks his Leedy drums, tympani and Vibraphone can be described in just one word, "Marvelous." (May 31, 1934). Frisselle's home is Methuen (near Lawrence), Mass.

Glen Gray and Anthony Briglia

Glen Gray and His Casa Loma Orchestra have won a well deserved niche in music's hall of fame for their excellent work on the "Camel Hour" and other radio programs as well as at New York's smart Glen Island Casino so—we are glad to present Glen Gray, director of this splendid organization, and Anthony Briglia, his drummer, with his "Broadway" Dual Floating Head drum. Of his Leedy snare drum, bass drum and pedal Briglia wrote on August 1, 1934: ". . . I personally think they are the best."

Charm Galore —and Talent Aplenty

This lovely, versatile mistress of the marimba, Billy Hammond, featured radio, vaudeville and supper club artist, was in the factory recently and chose another Leedy for her exacting work—a 4-octave Solo-Tone Marimba in Chromium with Sparkling Silver frame and Two-Tone Sparkling Diamond Decorations this time. Here she is with her new instrument on which she did a few numbers for us — and then posed for the picture you see here. Her home is Detroit — her address we won't give!

Page Three

Leedy Drum Topics

Tommy Whalen

Tommy Whalen, New York City, top-notch rhythmist with Don Bestor's deservedly famous radio and dance band for the last four years, is now displaying his wares at the exclusive "Pennsylvania Hotel Roof" in New York where Don Bestor and his boys are the feature attraction. Prior to his present berth, Whalen furnished the rhythm for the renowned "Husk" O'Hara Orchestra. Of his Leedy snare and bass drum Whalen wrote August 13, 1934: "... 'The Last Word' in service and dependability."

To Prevent "Creeping" Pedals

If your low or high hat sock cymbal pedal creeps while playing on either a wood or cement floor, obtain a rubber stair tread from your nearest 5 and 10c store. Place it under the footboard and your troubles will be over. One of these stair treads also works well underneath your pedal or bass drum spurs.

$2.00 award to Thomas C. Bishop, 9020 169th St., Jamaica, L. I., N. Y.

●

Drummers may stand for a ring in the tub but never in their drums.

●

She was so dumb that she thought a "scratch drummer" was one who had the hives. No, Annie doesn't live here anymore!

To Drummers Who Tuck Their Own Heads

Many drummers who put on their own heads (and also repairmen in music stores) do not realize the necessity of being very careful about the water used for soaking the heads. Not long ago we saw a fellow crush a drum head down into a small wash basin, wrinkling it and thereby damaging the fibres. Heads should never be crushed while soaking—they should lay perfectly flat in a container plenty large enough to permit this. The wash basin mentioned above was dirty and soapy, which also helped ruin this particular head. The water should be clean and cool—not hot and not cold. Hot or even warm water will ruin a head immediately it is submerged. Such water makes a head shrink. Heads must dry very slowly if the original appearance is to be preserved.

Phil H. Chenault

A fine all-around drummer and vibra-cussionist, Phil Chenault, Oklahoma City, Okla., has played many of the more important engagements in his part of the country. He has had wide experience in stage presentation and dance work, and has been featured over radio stations KGFG, KFXR, KFJF and KOMA. Now playing with Ward Fowler and His Nebraskans under Director Ward Fowler. Of his Leedy drums, Chimes, Tympani and Vibraphone he wrote August 13, 1934: "For performance from percussion instruments, nothing in the drum world compares with Leedy."

For the Social Entertainer

How to give a girl a surprise party: Place arms around her, draw her close and start to kiss her. When she says, "Stop, how dare you!" release her unkissed. Note surprise on her face. . . . . !

A New One

Place a wide tooth comb flat on the head of your snare drum, holding same lightly with fingers of left hand. Hold heavy banjo pick in right hand and rasp on comb at will. Different tones may be obtained on different parts of the comb and by varying the pressure of the left hand fingers on the comb and the pick. Something different and very effective.

$2.00 award to C. J. Cant, Athabasca, Alberta, Canada.

●

Puzzle

Why do girls tap their cigarettes on both ends before lighting up?

Figure This One Out

It has been estimated that if an elephant could jump in proportion as far as a flea, he would make it across the Atlantic from Africa to the Ringling Bros. headquarters in Sarasota, Florida, in two jumps.

Leedy — WORLD'S FINEST DRUMMERS' INSTRUMENTS — Leedy

The Exclusive Drummers' Paper

Louder Sand Block Effect

While the old sand blocks are not used much nowadays they are still a good effect. In the past the ordinary blocks have not produced enough volume, but here is a stunt that gives plenty: Lay a sheet of No. 2 sandpaper flat on the head of your snare drum. Tack a smaller piece of No. 0 sand paper around a block of wood in the ordinary manner. You will find this a really improved sand block effect that has greater volume because of the fact that the drum acts as a resonator. Highly effective in playing modern rhythm phrases, especially in "stop" time as, for instance, in "Tea for Two," by playing in groups of four stroke ruffs on the beat with the accent on the first note.

$2.00 award to Dow Helmers, 211 N. Union St., Pueblo, Colo.

"Frankie" Davis, Parkersburg, W. Va.

Davis, formerly with the S. S. Leviathan Orchestra under Meyer Davis, with whom he played on that ship's Maiden Voyage, is now "doin' the time" with the Marie Purl Revue of 25 people on the RKO and Loew vaudeville circuits presenting a hot band, a bevy of beautiful dancers and singers and other attractions in a clever, modern musical revue act. Davis is a featured singer, dancer and drummer in the company and uses Leedy drums, chimes, bells, Vibraphone and tympani which he says are "THE BEST MADE," in his letter of April 20, 1934.

Frank Gariepy ·· Montreal ··

Frank Gariepy, now playing at the "Cascades" of the Windsor Hotel, Montreal, under the leadership of Adolf Ginsburg, is one of Leedy's many Canadian friends with whom we became acquainted through the courtesy of the Archambault Music Co., Montreal, and through whom we received the above photograph. The genial looking leader is Bill Munro under whose baton Gariepy played at Montreal's *Chez Maurice*, Canada's finest cabaret.

Gariepy has played drums since the age of six, and was drum instructor to St. Peter's Cadets, Montreal, when only 14. His experience since then includes six years in Montreal theatres, and numerous of the finest Montreal engagements under Hal White, Al. Gerson and Charley Dornberger in addition to those already mentioned.

On the usual form which we ask drummers to give us information about themselves, Gariepy states that he is now using Leedy snare drum, bass drum, pedal, orchestra bells, Vibraphone, tympani and Tunable Tom Toms, and that he has used all makes of drums but finds Leedy the best (dated July 30, 1934). Thank you, Frank, we believe you mean it.

And may we take this opportunity to suggest that other of our Maple Leaf drummer friends and Leedy users let us know of their activities so we can include a few more Dominion "briefs" in our next issue?

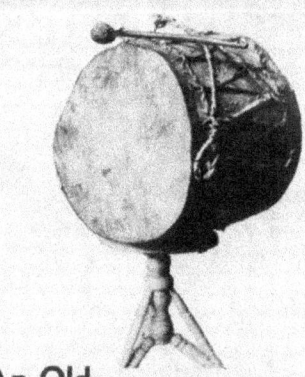

An Old Sioux Indian Drum

C. H. Stephens of Fairmount, Indiana, sent us the photograph of the interesting drum reproduced above. It is obviously a signal and ceremonial drum, and is 17"x22" in size. The shell is a hollowed log and the heads and "ropes" are of buffalo hide—the beater ball being covered with the same skin. The drum is known to be of Sioux Indian origin and is credited with being from 200 to 300 years old. This primitive instrument is in a perfect state of preservation, is owned by Mr. Stephens and in his possession at this time—a valued and interesting specimen of North American Indian percussion when this country was yet unexplored by our pioneer ancestors.

Leedy — WORLD'S FINEST DRUMMERS' INSTRUMENTS — Leedy

Leedy Drum Topics

Allen J. Schwartz

Schwartz is one of the foremost drummers in Albany, N. Y., and has been with the Manhattan Club Band, directed by Albert DeLucia, for the past seven years, playing dance and radio engagements. Was with Chick Roberts and His Orchestra playing dance jobs prior to his present connection. Uses Leedy snare drum, bass drum, pedal, bells and tympani of which he wrote July 28, 1934: "I've never played on any finer equipment than Leedy."

●

A Radiokick

"Your announcer is Graham Crackers" — who gives a hoot — but we *would* like to know the names of those xylphone soloists and a little about them.

Walter G. Howe

Walter Howe, Boston, Mass., is a graduate of the New England Conservatory of Music and played with the Conservatory Orchestra there. Later at the McDowell Club under Arthur Fiedler. Also two summers at the Fabyian Hotel in New Hampshire, and was recently with the WBZ Studio Band in Hotel Bradford under Director Oscar Elgart. Is now playing with the E. R. A. Orchestra under William Dodge. Shown with Howe in the picture at the right are his Leedy snare and bass drums, xylophone, chimes and tympani of which he wrote on July 30, 1934: "Made well, sound well and wear well".

A New Deep Cup Choke Cymbal Set-up

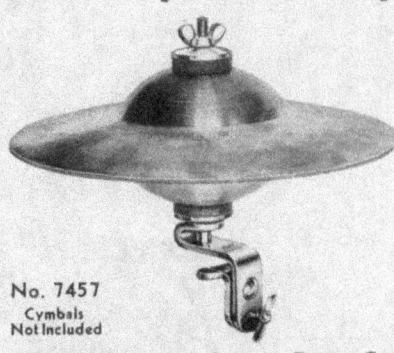

No. 7457
Cymbals Not Included

Here is a brand new Deep Cup Choke Cymbal set-up for the bass drum hoop that is a peach. Two Deep Cup American Brass Cymbals 10" in diameter (Leedy No. 7450 at $1.25 each) are used with the holder. Use the cymbals loose for hollow, deep-toned "sizzle" effects — or screw them tight for a deeper "washboiler" effect that can not be gotten with any other choke cymbal set-up. Either way, this new cymbal tone effect will come in mighty handy often enough to make it well worth while adding to your outfit.

No. 7457—In Nickel		$0.90
No. 7458—In Chrome		1.35
No. 7459—In Nobby Gold		1.35

●

Question

Has anyone ever found out why the minute the waiter takes your order he grabs the menu as though he were afraid you would steal it?

Another Sock Cymbal Effect

Many materials have been used between sock cymbals to obtain various effects. Paper has been the most popular but, of course, does not last very long. Here is one that lasts indefinitely: Take an old snare head of the thin transparent type and first cut it round the exact size of the lower cymbal. Next mark off a 2" circle in the center. Then divide the head into 12 sections, like a pie or the spokes of a wheel. Next cut out every other section down to the center 2" circle. Of course, you have to cut a hole for the rod going through the center. The accompanying illustration gives the correct idea.

$2.00 award to Len Johnson, 827 Rutland St., Houston, Texas.

Do you know that when a drum head of medium thickness and of 14 inches diameter is pulled up to average playing tension, the strain is 200 lbs. to the square inch?

●

Ever Have A - - -

Bathing beauty peel her sunburn and show it to you when you were biting into a cold frankfurter?

Leedy — WORLD'S FINEST DRUMMERS' INSTRUMENTS — Leedy

The Exclusive Drummers' Paper

SOUSA'S DRUMMERS DURING THE "MARCH KING'S" REIGN

Mr. Geo. H. Way,
Leedy Mfg. Co., Inc.,
Elkhart, Ind.

Dear Friend George:

Have your recent, welcome letter .... and answering that portion about the various Drum Sections of Sousa's Band from the time it was organized to the time of the famous "March King's" last concert, I am only too glad to give you the following information which is accurate from the year 1910, when I became a member of Sousa's band. The data prior to 1910 has been gathered from various sources and while I do not guarantee every detail, I believe it to be fairly accurate.

The band, as nearly as I can remember, made its first tour in the fall of 1892. The engagement was for nine weeks or longer. The Drummers were: Tympani—Gericke; Small Drum—Lewis Ingalls; Bass Drum—Gericke. The Tympanist and Bass Drummer were brothers. During the first tour Patrick Gilmore died and

FRANK A. SNOW

A nationally famous Tympanist and Drummer with a background of 50 years in the profession, and an Author, Composer, Arranger and Teacher of note, Mr. Snow formerly played with Sousa and is now playing with the famous Long Beach Municipal Band under the renowned Herbert Clarke. Uses a Leedy snare drum, bass drum, pedal and tympani.

the Sousa Band closed its season and reorganized, taking on several of the Gilmore players.

In 1893, which was the year of Chicago's first World's Fair, the Drum Section was: Tympani—Chas. P. Lowe; Snare Drum—William Lowe; Bass Drum—Herman Foster. Before the Band opened at the Chicago World's Fair, William Lowe was displaced by Harry Stone, brother of Fred Stone, the popular comedian. From that time until 1900 is uncertain, except that Herman Foster's record as Bass Drummer was unbroken up until 1910.

In 1900 the Band played at the Paris Exposition, and Herbert Clarke says that was the time Mills joined the Band. The Snare Drummer was Chris Chapman, and Herman Foster was, of course, Bass Drummer. Later, Chapman played Tympani and Dan Kenn the Snare Drum, but I have no knowledge of the dates these Drummers served until 1910, as I said before.

At that time the Section was: Tympani—William Lowe; Snare Drum—M. Francis Haynes; Bass Drum—F. A. Snow. The Season was fourteen months, opening at the Metropolitan Opera House in New York and closing at the New York Hippodrome. In the intervening time we played England, Ireland, Scotland and Wales, then a three weeks ocean trip to Capetown, S. A., playing one month on that continent. Then another three weeks trip found us in Hobart, Tasmania. From there we went to Australia for a twelve weeks tour and continued to New Zealand for a five week engagement. From there we proceded to British Colombia stopping en route at Suva, Fiji and Honolulu. After completing a tour of the United States we again played in New York after covering 60,000 miles and spending 10 weeks on the oceans.

The next change in the Drum Section was in 1913 when we had: Tympani—Frank A. Snow; Snare Drum—M. Francis Haynes; Bass Drum—Herman Foster.

In 1914 it was Snow, Haynes and James M. Harrington.

In 1915 at the Panama Exposition, the Drum Section was Snow, Haynes and Geo. Maurer. When the Band returned to New York for the 35 weeks engagement with "Hip Hip Hurray," August Helmecke displaced Maurer and remained in that position.

The next change was 1917-18-19. It was then Snow, Joe Green, and Helmecke.

In 1920 the Section was made up of Carey, Goulden and Helmecke and there was no change for several years until Goulden went to Tympani, and a pupil of mine, Frank Holt, Haverhill, Mass., went on Small Drum. During 1931, also, J. J. Heney of St. Augustine, Fla., served with the Band for several months as Xylophone Soloist and Snare Drummer.

That, George, concludes the chronicle except for the fact that during the earlier years of the Band there were several drummers who served for short periods of time: Jos. Zettelman—Tympani; Max Nichol—Snare Drum; and a Mr. Reitz. Also Paul Dierkes, Palisade Park, N. J.

Hoping that this is the information you want, I am, with kindest regards,

Yours very truly,
(Signed) Frank A. Snow.

A Cymbal Stunt

By holding an ordinary derby hat on top of a Zenjian cymbal many effects may be obtained inasmuch as the hat acts as a resonator. A little practice will enable you to manipulate the hat, holding it by the rim and a cymbal at the same time and tipping the hat closer to and away from the cymbal at will. Beating the cymbal with a rumble tip on a drum stick is fine in hot choruses.

$2.00 award to Lyndon S. Warren, Kennebunk, Maine.

Marie Edson

An attractive and talented little lady is Marie Edson, Decatur, Ill., drummeress with the Isa Foster Ohio Girls, a girls' orchestra playing theatre, dance and cafe engagements. The band just concluded 10 months at Decatur's Peacock Inn and are now at the Harbor Inn, Decatur, for an unlimited engagement. Marie was formerly with the "Gypsy Sweethearts" and "Eloise Wismer's Playgirls" doing 10 weeks in the Cincinnati theatres and an engagement at the Whitcombe Hotel, St. Joseph, Mich. Taught drums by Ray Mann, Rockford, Ill., and uses Leedy snare drum, bass drum and bells. She wrote August 2, 1934, "The finest I have ever used."

Leedy Drum Topics

A SENSATIONAL "HIT" THAT HAS BROKEN ALL PEDAL RECORDS

Some splendid pedals have been put on the market, but none has enjoyed the popularity and praise that the famous Leedy "X-L" Pedal met with immediately upon its introduction to the drum world. It is the sensational "hit" of all times, and was adopted by more high-class professionals during its first year on the market than any other new model ever made because it has everything that Drummers demand in a pedal . . . the utmost in speed—feather ease in action—no faltering—no friction—no side strain—and no "stiff spots" anywhere in the travel of the beater rod. Just clean-cut, smooth response without any extra effort whatever. It is scientifically designed and precision built of only the finest materials. The uprights and footboard are of cast aluminum. This facilitates speed of action, and makes it light in weight. The ball and socket principle in the beater shaft is a new departure in pedal mechanism giving that easy "foot flow" and perfect balance that has made this the greatest of all pedals. There are no delicate working parts to get out of order—everything is sturdily constructed so as to give long and satisfactory service. The tension spring can be adjusted to satisfy the particular "feel" that you like best. All the usual adjustable features, such as beater rod, cymbal striker and spring tension, are also incorporated. Finished in baked Black Duco, highly polished aluminum footboard and nickel metal parts.

No. 7010—Pedal in Black Duco and Polished Aluminum, Without Spurs and Cymbal Holder $10.00

No. 7014—Pedal in Black Duco and Polished Aluminum, With Spurs and Cymbal Holder 11.50

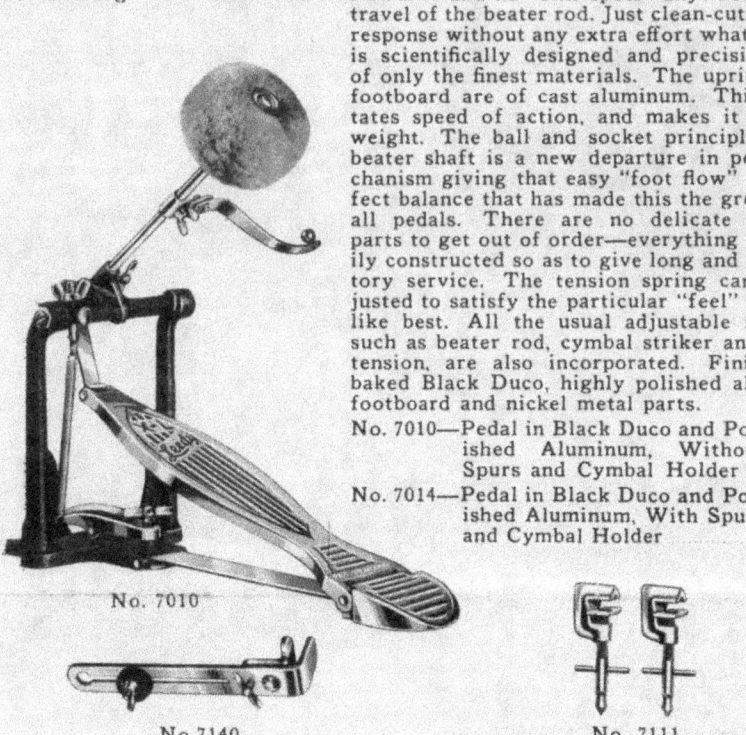

No. 7010

No. 7140

No. 7111

Stayon Cymbal Holder is strongly made of pressed steel. Clamps to the bass drum hoop with a non-marring Stayon clamp.

No. 7140—Nickel $ .75
No. 7142—Chromium 1.10
No. 7141—Nobby Gold 1.10

Grip-Tite Spurs are sturdy and serviceable. Cast steel with sharp-pointed tips and non-marring swivel clamp.

No. 7111—Nickel $ .75
No. 7113—Chromium 1.10
No. 7112—Nobby Gold 1.10

A Different Tom Tom Tone Effect

A different and somewhat deeper tom tom tone may be obtained by glueing a circular disc of wood about ¾" thickness on the bottom head of the tom tom. Most any kind of wood can be used. The disc should come practically to the edge of the circle of the head. This gives an effect similar to that of the genuine Indian drums as used among the various American tribes.

$2.00 award to Stan Macios, 3213 Central Ave., N. S. Pittsburgh, Pa.

"It Happened One Night"

Lights down . . . a famous band begins its stage presentation . . . drums down front near the leader . . . a grand opening that about blows 'em off their seats . . . lights come up . . . curtain rises AND the fringe along the batten catches in a bass drum rod . . . up goes the drum, pedal, trap console and all, leaving poor Mr. Drummer sitting alone with a snare drum and stand . . . when the mess broke loose and hit the stage . . . imagine the rest for yourself.

(It happened to Bob Perry when he was with Gus Arnheim.)

It Ends That Way

Young percussionists who roll their eyes in dance halls instead of rolling their drums soon find themselves rolling baby carriages.

Richard "Dick" Brucato

Dick Brucato of Brooklyn, N. Y., is a cracker-jack rhythm artist who has played some of the finest vaudeville, radio, recording and dance engagements to be had with such famous orchestras as Rudy Vallee, Red Nichols, Anthony Trini, Neil Golden, Herbert Diamond Entertainers and Benny Meroff. At present is jobbing with his own organization, and is a staff contributor of drum articles for the "Orchestra World" monthly, and the "Rhythm" magazine of London, Eng., is N. Y. correspondent for Vivian M. Gardner, and Radio Editor for a well-known mid-western newspaper which operates its own radio station. The accompanying photo-drawing was sent us by the New York Band Instrument Co., Inc., of Brooklyn, inscribed by Brucato as follows, "Best wishes to Leedy—Sincerely, Dick Brucato." Brucato's equipment is exclusively Leedy, as shown,—Vibraphone, tympani and chimes included.

Leedy — WORLD'S FINEST DRUMMERS' INSTRUMENTS — *Leedy*

The Exclusive Drummers' Paper

Ted Tillman With The Jovial Henry Busse

Ted Tillmann, Chicago, is the versatile drummer with the inimitable Henry Busse and his popularly famous radio, presentation and dance orchestra now delighting the radio audiences on national hook-ups and all-comers at Chicago's distinguished Chez Paree club featuring fine food, music-as-the-public-likes-it, and brilliant entertainment. Tillmann is a flashy "stickster" with plenty of showmanship, whose splendidly complete equipment is exclusively Leedy.

Improved Bass Drum Tone Controls

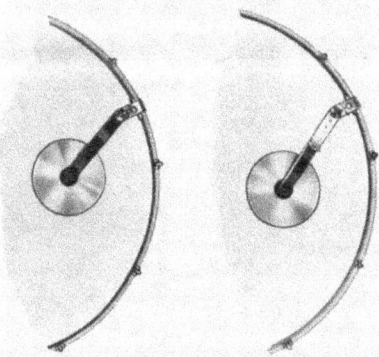

No. 7871   No. 7874

Newly improved and the best on the market. Both have 6 inch discs heavily plated with thicker felt muffler—pads and the non-marring Stay-on hoop clamps. New stiffer springs prevent disc "jumping" away from head. Discs move in an arc for position adjustments, and the No. 7874 has a new "pressure adjustment" feature which permits any desired amount of pressure on the drum head for the desired drum tone.

No. 7871—Nickel	$1.75
No. 7872—Chromium	2.40
No. 7873—Nobby Gold	2.40

With "Pressure Adjustment"

No. 7874—Nickel	$2.25
No. 7875—Chromium	3.25
No. 7876—Nobby Gold	3.25

Drummer's Auxiliary Seat

It has become quite the vogue in late years for a drummer to sit a little higher than the ordinary chair provides. The accompanying drawing shows how an auxiliary seat may be built so that the drummer can raise himself a few inches higher and be very comfortable and solid. This seat is collapsible and will fit in the end of a Carry-All and other style drum cases. The material may be either ½" or ¾" lumber. The seat and base do not need to be any wider than 6". When folded it is only 14½" long. Very simple to make and will set solid in the average chair. A rubber sponge mat glued to the top makes it quite comfortable. These mats may be bought at any 25c store. Note how hinges are attached in the corners. The metal strips can be made from an old music rack, or if same is not available any small machine shop can make them up special. Really a very fine idea.

$2.00 award to Ralph Thomas, 1103 Stone St., Great Bend, Kansas.

Speaking Figuratively

One must know something about figures and their influence upon both sexes, as will be observed from what follows:

Figures that have attracted men—
  Venus de Milo
  Cleopatra
  Helen of Troy
  Salome
  Carmen
  Ruth St. Denis
  Annette Kellerman
  and Mae West

Figures that have attracted women—
  $3.98
  $5.97

The difference between one man and another is not always mere ability: it is 90% energy.

Martin Snitzer

Martin Snitzer, Philadelphia, an A-1 drummer with a world of concert, radio, theatre, recording, dance and circus experience, is now playing with the Philadelphia City Concert Band under the baton of Frank B. Maurer. Played the Chesterfield hour with the Philadelphia Orchestra and trouped with Miller Bros. 101 Ranch Wild West Show. Uses Leedy equipment exclusively including tympani and two xylophones of which he wrote July 30, 1934: "For my work I must have the best, and Leedy suits me and my Leaders."

Professor: "Name the three principal reasons why men go crazy."
Stude: "Powder, rouge and silk hose."

WORLD'S FINEST DRUMMERS' INSTRUMENTS

Leedy Drum Topics

The Improved Leedy Trap Table

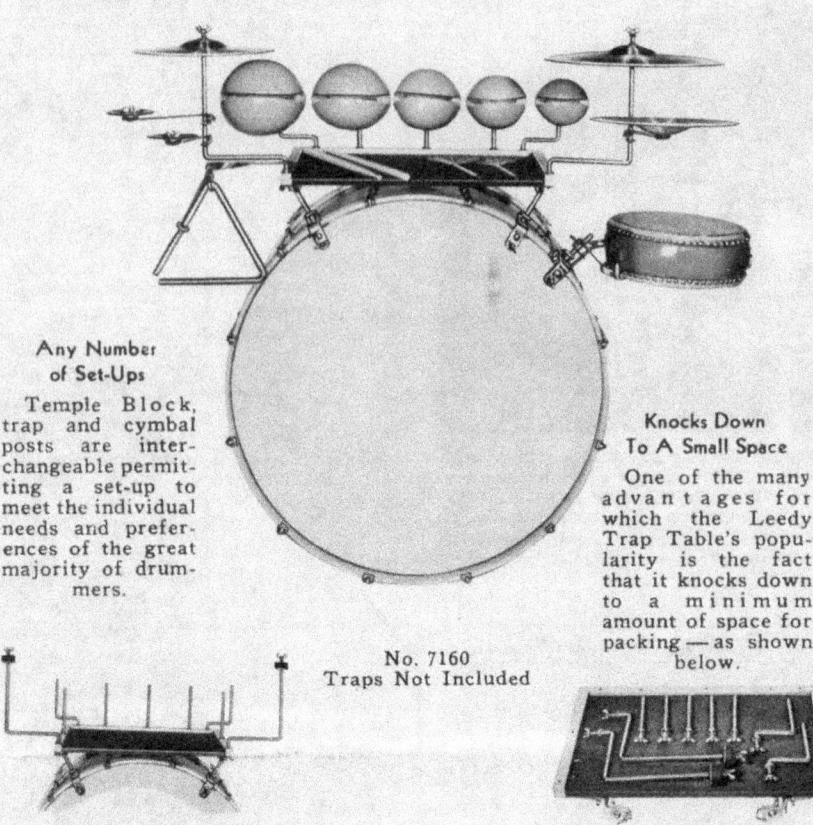

Any Number of Set-Ups

Temple Block, trap and cymbal posts are interchangeable permitting a set-up to meet the individual needs and preferences of the great majority of drummers.

Knocks Down To A Small Space

One of the many advantages for which the Leedy Trap Table's popularity is the fact that it knocks down to a minimum amount of space for packing — as shown below.

No. 7160
Traps Not Included

Five, instead of four, Temple Blocks are now provided for on the improved Leedy Trap Table. The size of the table remains 20"x14" as before so it is as easy and compact to carry as ever. Made of 3-ply basswood with three sides guarded by wooden strips to prevent sticks, etc., from falling off. Top surface of table is covered with good quality, heavy felt, and the entire table weighs only a trifle more than seven pounds. Fastens to the bass drum hoop with Stay-on non-marring clamps while felt covered wood block rests on drum shell giving greater solidity to the table. Strong, sturdy and rigid, this table also presents an impressive appearance which will give you greater prestige with your audiences and add to your playing ability by having everything within easy reach when you need what you need in a hurry.

No. 7160—With Cymbal Holders and Posts (No Trap Holders) Nickel	$ 9.00
No. 7162—With Cymbal Holders and Posts (No Trap Holders) Chromium	13.00
No. 7161—With Cymbal Holders and Posts (No Trap Holders) Nobby Gold	13.00

TRAP HOLDERS FOR THE LEEDY TRAP TABLE

(Finishes Indicated: N—Nickel; C—Chromium; N. G.—Nobby Gold)

Temple Block Holders	No. 7200—N $ .75;	No. 7202—C $1.25;	No. 7201—N.G. $1.25
Wood Block Holders	No. 7205—N .60;	No. 7207—C .90;	No. 7206—N.G. .90
Small Tom Tom Holders	No. 7210—N .60;	No. 7212—C .90;	No. 7211—N.G. .90
Adjustable Tom Tom Holders	No. 7230—N 1.10;	No. 7232—C 1.65;	No. 7231—N.G. 1.65
Non-Swing Cymbal Holders	No. 7225—N 1.50;	No. 7227—C 2.25;	No. 7226—N.G. 2.25
Afterbeat Cymbal Holders	No. 7215—N .60;	No. 7217—C .90;	No. 7216—N.G. .90
Triangle Holders	No. 7240—N .60;	No. 7242—C .90;	No. 7241—N.G. .90
Tambourine Holders	No. 7235—N .60;	No. 7237—C .90;	No. 7236—N.G. .90
Cow Bell Holders	No. 7220—N .15;	No. 7222—C .25;	No. 7221—N.G. .25

Above Trap Holders Also For Leedy Trap Console, Trap Rail And Hoop Adapter

Welcome, Visitors!

Following are the names of a few of the prominent drummers who have stopped in to see us recently.

RALPH HANSELL of Denver, one of the West's best known xylophone soloists on the air. The Leedy Company publishes three of Ralph's compositions, which are listed in our general catalog. Ralph spent a whole day with us on his way to New York.

FRED PAINE of the Detroit Symphony spent a day with us getting odds and ends ready for the season at the World's Fair.

HAROLD McDONALD, xylophone soloist at the Paramount Studios in Hollywood, stopped off while on his way to Flint, Michigan, to pick up a new Buick. Had his dad with him for a little vacation trip. He drove the Buick back to Hollywood without mishap.

BILL HAMMOND, proprietor of Hammond & Gerlach's Drum Shop, Pittsburgh, and a drummer of national prominence, was here for a couple of days digging into the whys and wherefores of how Leedy puts them together.

ART LAYFIELD of the Chicago Theatre orchestra comes down to see us quite often to visit the boys he knows personally in our office.

GEORGE NEWNHAN, who runs a drum shop in Toronto, Ontario, Canada, was with us a couple of days a few weeks ago and kindly consented to play our new Octarimba (as described on pps. 12 and 13) at Elkhart's Annual Music Fiesta. George did a wonderful job and his act went over in a really big way.

VINCE MOTT, former professional drummer and now proprietor of Vincent Mott's Music Shop, Paterson, N. J., came west and spent four days with us.

SCHUYLER ALWARD, St. Louis xylophone radio star and one of the proprietors of the St. Louis Band Instrument Company, spent a few days here last month. He played a couple of Octarimba solos for a group of dealers who were in town at the time. It went over with a bang and Schuyler says there will be several Octarimbas in St. Louis before long.

The above is handled as news and without inference as to the equipment used.

Leedy — WORLD'S FINEST DRUMMERS' INSTRUMENTS — Leedy

The Exclusive Drummers' Paper

Edwin W. Bereman

Edwin W. Bereman, Wichita, Kans., now playing public and private dance engagements in and around Wichita with Morris Martin and his well known orchestra, and formerly with Guy Greenamyer's Orchestra which played similar engagements, is a former pupil of another well known midwest drummer—Ernest Storey. Bereman, whose equipment is 100% Leedy, wrote August 1, 1934, "My outfit is 100% Leedy now, and I like it fine."

There Are Lots of 'Em

Girls who tell you that you look like John Barrymore but go out with guys who resemble "Bull" Montana.

Ray Vaughn

Ray Vaughn, internationally known vaudeville and radio xylophone artist, visited the Leedy factory a short time ago just prior to leaving on an extended tour of Ireland, the British Isles and Europe on his third such trip, and from there will proceed to the Orient, South Africa, Australia and New Zealand on what will constitute his second round-the-world playing tour.

Vaughn's versatile ability as a performer and producer of novelties on the vaudeville stage rank with the highest, and his 4 octave Leedy Solo-Tone Monarch Xylophone-Marimba finished in gleaming "Full Dress" white duco presents a most attractive appearance under the many-hued, modern stage lighting effects. Both Vaughn and Leedy instruments have many friends on the itinerary described above and their return engagements by popular demand are sure to be even more triumphant than those of the past. Bon voyage, Vaughn!

"Knock Wood"

One ta-ta-ta, two ta-ta-ta,
Gradually select it;
Slowly, slowly, faster, faster,
Now you can perfect it.

Strike the center of the bar,
Keep the mind unladen,
Do not wander near or far
In quest of some fair maiden.

Run a scale in nothing flat,
Memorize your chord work,
Be as nimble as a cat—
And then, just do some more work.

Practice thru the night and day,
Make "blue ones" sound still bluer,
Until you've hit "The Great White Way"
A Green or a Breuer.

By Ben Halprin
1745 Davidson Ave.
Bronx, N. Y.

Dead Bell Effect

Lay your bell bars on a piece of felt resting on a perfectly flat hard surface, such as a table, and play with hard mallets in hot choruses. Of course, this produces a dead metallic effect with no ring, which is quite pleasing as a novelty in certain numbers.

$2.00 award to "Bink" Gustat, St. Louis Band Instrument Co., 1113 Olive St., St. Louis, Mo.

Famous Last Words

"It can't be played that way, Mr. Leader."

Flash Effect For Wire Brush Work

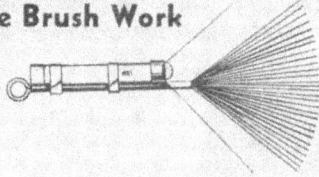

You have all seen the little "fountain pen" electric flash lights. They are inexpensive and can be obtained in any electric and many drug stores. Hold one of these in each hand parallel with your wire brushes. Different colored bulbs can be used. Makes a marvelous flash when the lights are low in waltz numbers, especially in criss-cross cymbal work. After a little experimenting it will be found that you can throw the lights on and off while playing. It is a good idea to tape the flash light to the handle of the brush. A special set of brushes can be kept for this stunt alone.

$2.00 award to Chas. Carrel, 420 W. Tiffin St., Fostoria, Ohio.

And Then He Walked Away

Fresh "Hoofer" (after first show): "Say, Drummer, what's the matter with ya—cantcha get with it? What's your regular trade—boilermaker?"

Pit Drummer: "No, Bud, but I used to be the middleweight champion of this town."

By Charlie Wilcoxon
Palace Theatre,
Cleveland, Ohio.

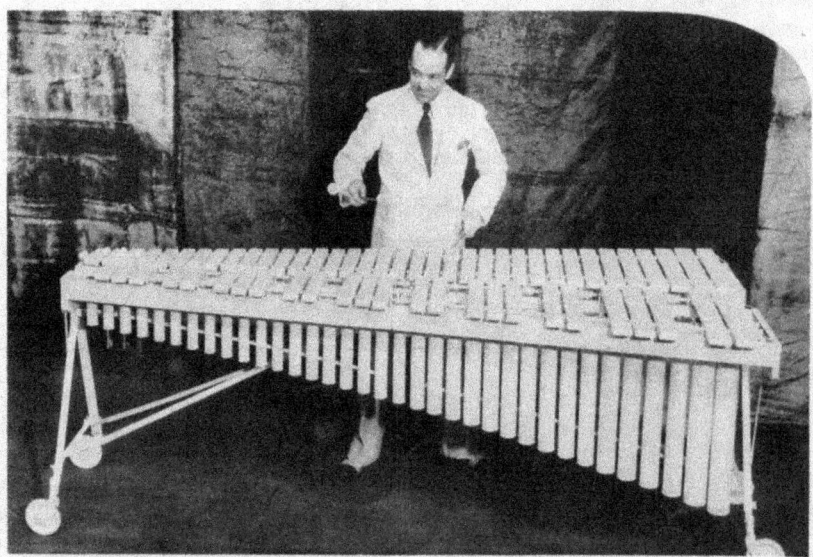

Leedy — WORLD'S FINEST DRUMMERS' INSTRUMENTS — **Leedy**

IT'S NEITHER XYLOPHONE BUT A BRAND NEW and ORIGINAL *Leedy* CREATION—the

"ALWAYS SOMETHING NEW UNDER THE SUN"

The Only Real Departure In Wood-Bar Instruments Since The First Resonator Instrument of This Type Was Conceived By The Earliest Savage Centuries Ago

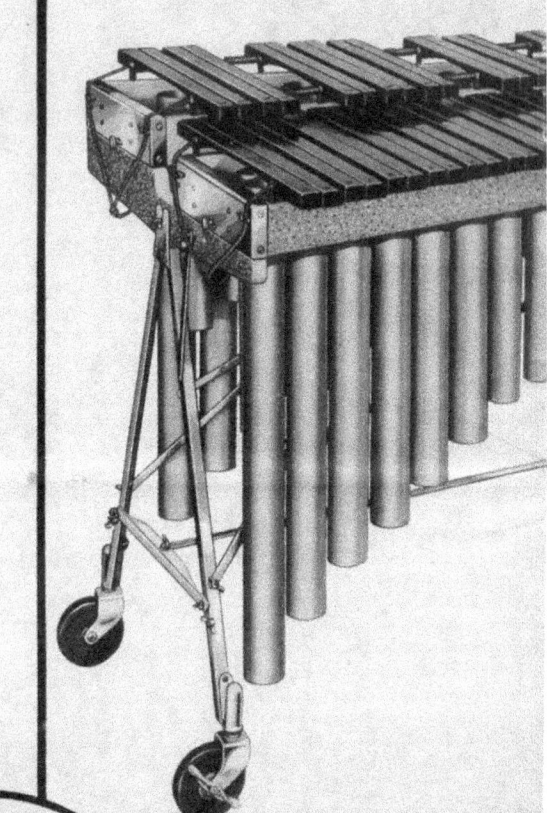

LEEDY originated and developed the Vibraphone which is so universally used and imitated today! Now Leedy has again originated and developed another sensational new instrument for the drummer—a new wood-bar instrument that is the only musically correct Marimba-Xylophone ever made, and which we present here for the first time as the Leedy OCTARIMBA.

The Octarimba offers you a fascinatingly beautiful, new and wider spectrum of tone with which to color your music, and gives you a richness of musical expression that has never before been approximated in wood-bar instruments because the full resonant speaking voice of the marimba is now *actually combined* with the higher and more brilliant timbre of the xylophone *in the same playing octave.* Never has there been a wood-bar instrument to equal the Octarimba's versatile eloquence, sympathetic response, or latitude of expression.

The essential difference between the Octarimba and other wood-bar instruments, as well as the basic reason for its remarkable new qualities, lies in the fact that each playing note of the Octarimba is really composed of two bars of the same size, tuned an octave apart, which are struck simultaneously with specially designed double-headed forked mallets. Thus, the lowest double bar of the Octarimba is a combination of C-28 and C-40 tones on the piano keyboard, the C-28 being the lowest note of our largest 5-octave marimba. (See chart in Leedy catalog.) In other words, two bars act as one as far as playing is concerned, giving a 1-octave tonal range when only one note is struck. With this bar set-up the lower three octaves of the 5-octave marimba and the lower three octaves of the 4-octave xylophone are

BARS of genuine Hondu ented process which eli suspension cord to permit frames; split aluminum re atmospheric conditions. S polished, and two of the fo No. 5602—3 Octaves, comb C-76, 74 Bars 1 Width at Lower F
5 Pair A
Following Finishes o
Choice of Other
Finishes
Nobby Gold on Res
†No. 6974—3 Vulcanized F
Octarim

NOR MARIMBA
Octarimba

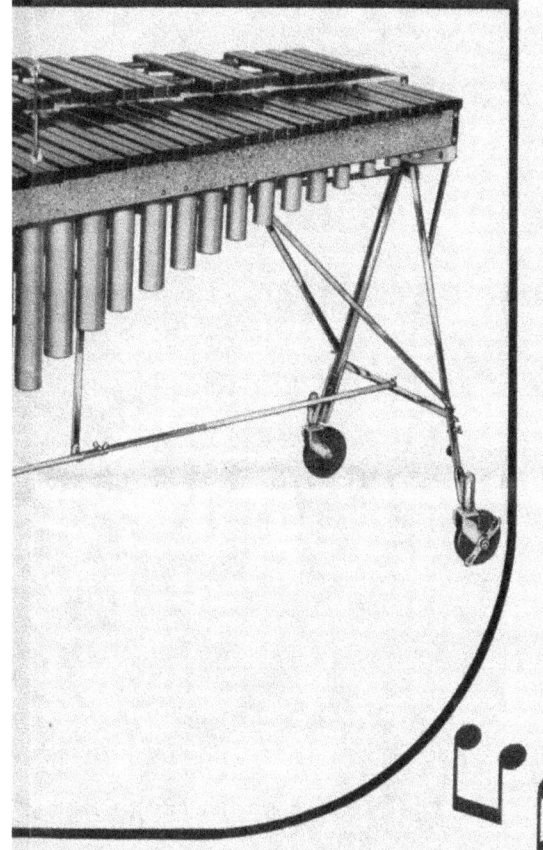

combined into one instrument with a 3-octave playing range and sounding as a 4-octave tonal range. The ordinary 3-octave xylophone or marimba has 37 bars, while the Octarimba boasts 74 bars, with an individual resonator under each bar properly designed to give the best tone and maximum volume.

The Octarimba is a legitimate musical instrument in every way and should not be considered as a novelty. Outstandingly prominent xylophonists and drummers from various parts of this country and Canada have performed on it over important radio stations and before large audiences with results that have been overwhelmingly gratifying. "Sounds like double marimbas," was one remark overheard in an audience of 15,000 persons before which it was played as a feature at a charity music festival. "Tops any wood-bar instrument I've ever heard for tonal excellence and color," was the enthusiastic endorsement made by one who had asked if he might "try it."

Only two mallets are used on this instrument to get the effect ordinarily requiring four hammers, with the result that it can be mastered even by a novice in a very short time, and anyone now playing xylophone or vibraphone with multiple hammers will find it a "snap" by comparison. Played with the mallets shown below, and packs into the carrying cases illustrated.

...duras Rosewood tuned by the exclusive Leedy pat-
...liminates all discordant overtones, and mounted on
...t free, full tone. Sparkling Silver pyralin on split
...esonators in satin finish and adjustable to meet all
...Strong, rigid stand chromium plated and highly
...four solid rubber wheels are equipped with brakes.
...bined C-28 and C-40 to combined C-64 and
...1 3/32" Wide by ¾" Thick. Length 61".
...End 31". Height 34". Weight 82 Lbs.____$240.00
Assorted Octarimba Mallets Included
on Special Order—10 Days Required for Delivery
"Full Dress" Pearl, Sparkling Pyralin or Duco
s on Wood Frames—No Extra Charge
sonators, Stands, Etc., ... $25.00 Extra
Fibre Hand Carrying Cases for Octarimba___$60.00
mba Trunk Made Specially To Order

MALLETS of flat strip, flexible rattan forked at one end and strongly reinforced. Beveled, flat-end cylindrical heads of graded rubber and combinations of graded rubbers:

No. 1735 — Soft Rubber, per pair _____$2.00

No. 1736—Comb. Soft and ½ Hard Rub. Pr. _$2.00

No. 1737—Half-Hard Rubber, per pair_____$2.00

No. 1738 — Comb. ½ and ¾ Hard Rub. Pr._$2.00

No. 1739 — ¾ Hard Rubber, per pair_____$2.00

Leedy Drum Topics

EAST SURREY REGIMENTAL DRUMS OPEN MUSEUM TO PUBLIC

The East Surrey Regimental Drums played for the public in true King's fashion on January twenty-seventh of this year to honor the occasion of the opening of the Regimental Museum in the barracks at Kingston to the public. Prior to the public opening, visitors had not been admitted to the Museum. Note the ornate trappings which the drummers wear, and the emblazoned, traditional rope tension drums. Careful scrutiny of the photo also indicates that each drummer has a bugle slung at the back by a silk cord.

Tape Your Silk Wire Wound Snares

Silk wire wound snares can be prevented from cutting the head where they pass over the edge of the flesh hoop by placing a small strip of adhesive tape underneath the snares at this point. This tape will not interfere with the snare action or tone.

(Editor's Note — Many drummers know about this, it not being a new idea. However, we believe that all drummers who use silk wire wound snares should use this tape as instructed above. Drum factories would include this on all drums with silk wire wound snares but it has not been customary because of the fact that purchasers of new drums might think it was in some way a patched job.)

$2.00 award to L. Douglas Snackenbery, Annandale, Minn.)

Some Information About Gut Snares

Of course, it is necessary to submerge gut snares in water before putting on the drum; however, be careful not to soak them too long as it will make small "hairs" rise from the otherwise smooth surface. Also be careful when pulling the strands through the holes in the snare strainer. If the snares are too wet and soft, more "hairs" will come up. These "hairs" dry hard and prevent the snares from laying snug to the head, which, of course, robs the drum of much of its sensitiveness.

Beauty at Any Cost

He: "Where did you get those sweet little dimples?"
She: "By sleeping on collar buttons all night."

He lost control of his roll when the judge ordered alimony.

To Save Yourself Work

If a Drummer will carry a pair of 5 and 10c store cotton gloves in his chime case and wear them when setting up and taking down the instrument, he will find that they will retain their brightness and be void of finger marks and will, therefore, look much nicer on the job. This is also true in setting up xylophones, marimbas and vibraphones. In other words, handling the chromium, nobby gold or nickel metal parts with gloves will save a lot of cleaning work.

$2.00 award to Bill White, 181 Remsen St., Cohoes, N. Y.

Ralph C. Specia

Ralph Specia, New York City, drummer with Joe Cappi and his Million-Airs Orchestra of radio station WABC on the CBS hook-ups, studied drums under Karl Glassman and is well known for his unusual ability to play almost any of the trickiest ultra-modern and imported rhythms.

Specia's past engagements include three consecutive years with John Marinaro's Orchestra at the exclusive New York "Cafe Des Beaux Arts," five years with Hazel Green on the Keith Vaudeville Circuit, a year with Anthony Trini and his Broadcasting Staff Orchestra with radio stations WMCA, WABC and WOR and other splendid bookings too numerous to enumerate here.

Of his present equipment which includes snare drum, bass drum, pedal, Tunable Tom Toms, Vibraphone, and tympani, all of Leedy make, Specia wrote on July 30, this year: "Have used Leedy for the past 14 years and have found them the World's Finest for appearance and service."

Leedy — WORLD'S FINEST DRUMMERS' INSTRUMENTS — Leedy

 ## The Exclusive Drummers' Paper

$10.00 Prize Winning Drummer's Story

Here is the $10.00 prize-winning story of this issue sent in by Bobby Haynes, 86 Riley St., Buffalo, N. Y.

We were playing in one of those cross-road, old-time dance halls that was sadly in need of repairs. Of course, a storm had to come up in the middle of the program. It rained buckets full and did not stop at the roof but came right through all over my outfit while we were down in the basement during intermission.

The batter head of my snare drum became soaking wet and ripped around the edge. I thought that by raving a bit I might get the price of a new head out of the old duffer who ran the hall. Our leader agreed to support me, so he hunted up the little rube, who was smarter than he looked.

After listening to the leader's story he drawled out, "Well, tell yer drummer I'm durned sorry, but y'know, conditions are all wet everywhere."

Tympani Muffler

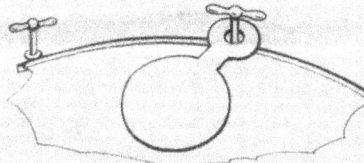

Cut a piece of ¼" thick felt as per the accompanying drawing. This is 11" over all. The large circle is 6½" in diameter and the small circle is 3¼" in diameter. The "handle" between the two circles is 1¼" long by 1½" wide. The hole in the small circle, which is cut out to accommodate the tympani handle, is 1" in diameter. The idea is to hang this over one tympani handle and allow the large felt disc to rest on the head of the kettle opposite the player. This muffles the kettle for certain effects. This idea was born while playing Gilda Gray's dancing act, the drummer having been requested to have staccato muffled tympani. It will be seen that when the muffler is not needed it is a simple matter to throw it to one side without its dropping to the floor. This is a dandy stunt.

$2.00 award to George B. Burnwood, 992 Godfrey Ave., Philadelphia, Pa.

●

She's only a drummer's daughter but she snares 'em right and left.

The New Leedy STANOPLE Cymbals

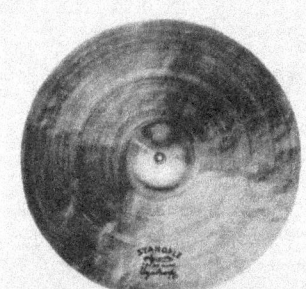

The New Leedy STANOPLE cymbals are 100% true Turkish type cymbals with all the desired "ring" and vibratory qualities for large or small orchestra, band and drum corps use. These are carefully selected imported cymbals which are very popular with the drummers because of their fine quality and moderate price. All drum corps cymbals should be heavy for best tone results.

Specify Thin, Medium or Heavy

No. 7299—10". Deep cup		$ 7.00
No. 7300—10". Thin only		5.50
No. 7301—11". Thin only		6.00
No. 7302—12". Thin, md. or hy.		7.00
No. 7303—13". Thin, md. or hy.		9.00
No. 7304—14". Thin, md. or hy.		11.00
No. 7305—15". Thin, md. or hy.		13.50
No. 7306—16". Thin, md. or hy.		15.00

$2.00 Apiece For New "Ideas"

"Drum Topics" will pay $2.00 for each drummer suggestion published under the "New Idea" heading in issue No. 25. If you have a new trap of your own invention, or a new way to use a standard trap, write us about it in detail and including a rough sketch if a sketch will help to explain the idea. If your idea is published, you will receive a $2.00 cash award, and full credit for having sent in the suggestion when the item appears.

Think it over! Haven't you some pet idea, trick, or stunt of your own that other drummers would like to know about? If so, send it along and earn yourself a couple of bucks.

●

When is a good Drummer like a Cop? When he "sticks" on the "beat".
(By Sidney L. Simon, Paterson, N. J.)

●

The Charming Burvedell Sisters

These two personality-plus girls, Harriette and Lorraine, billed as the Burvedell Sisters and featured in revues and stage presentations here and in Canada, put on as clever a xylophone act as you are ever likely to witness. The girls were instructed in xylophone by Schuyler Alward, St. Louis Band Instrument Co., St. Louis, Mo., and are thoroughly pleased with their 4-octave Leedy, of which Harriette wrote on July 30, 1934: "None Better," and Lorraine added, "The best at any price."

Leedy — WORLD'S FINEST DRUMMERS' INSTRUMENTS — **Leedy**

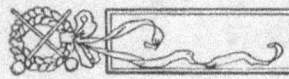 # Leedy Drum Topics

THE LIGHTWEIGHT VIBRAPHONE—
ORIGINAL INSTRUMENT ON THIS TYPE

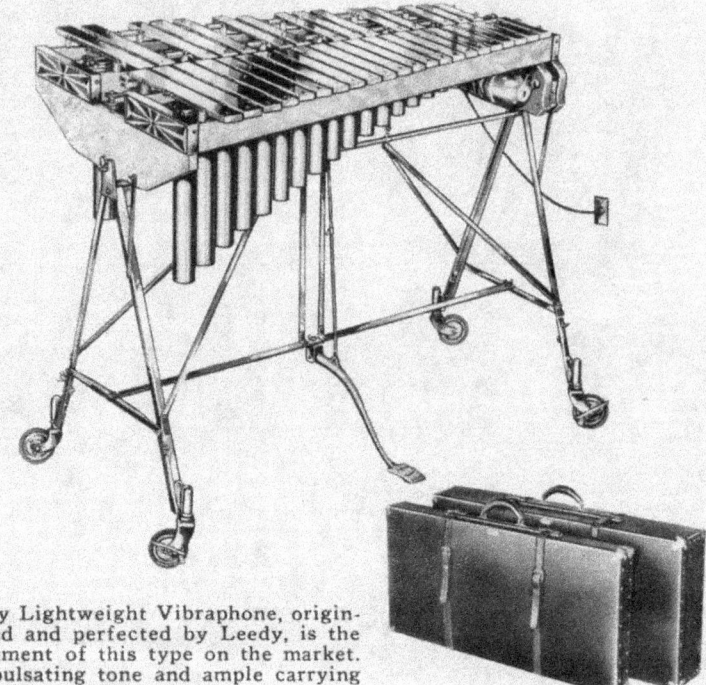

The Leedy Lightweight Vibraphone, originally invented and perfected by Leedy, is the finest instrument of this type on the market. Its sweet, pulsating tone and ample carrying power in even the largest halls has made it so well known that little description is needed here. Materials, construction and workmanship are the very finest. Made in a choice of 2½ or 3 octaves, sturdy and rigid, the instrument is easily and quickly set up or knocked down, and packs in two convenient fibre hand carrying cases.

No. 5655—3 Octaves, C-40 to C-76, 37 Bars, 1½" to 1¼" Wide, by ½" Thick. Length 44". Height With Wheels for Standing Position 35"; Without Wheels for Sitting Position 27". Weight 67 lbs. Finished with "Full Dress" Black Pearl on Wood Frames, Chromium Plated Stand and Polished Aluminum Bars and Resonators $295.00

No. 5656—2½ Octaves, C-40 to F-69, 30 Bars, 1½" to 1¼" Wide, by ½" Thick. Length 38". Height with Wheels for Standing Position 35"; without Wheels for Sitting Position 27". Weight 62 lbs. Finished with "Full Dress" Black Pearl on Wood Frames, Chromium Plated Stand and Polished Aluminum Bars and Resonators $270.00

Instructor and Four Pair Choice Mallets Included.
Following Finishes on Special Order---10 Days Required.
Choice of Other "Full Dress" Pearls, Sparkling or Duco Finishes on Wood Frames---No Extra Charge
Nobby Gold on Resonators, Stands and End Boxes---No Extra Charge

†No. 6925—2 Hand Carrying Cases for 3 Oct. 103 lbs. packed $45.00
†No. 6926—2 Hand Carrying Cases for 2½ Oct. 87 lbs. packed   40.00

Frankie Carr and His Bell Hops

Frankie Carr, Drummer-Director of his own Frankie Carr Bell Hops Orchestra, Freeland, Pa., for the past twelve years, enjoys the distinction of heading one of Pennsylvania's and New Jersey's most popular dance bands. Has played virtually all the leading ballrooms in Pennsylvania and for nine consecutive years has been in demand for Penn State College dances. Much of the orchestra's success is due to Carr's versatile work on the drums on which he has a background covering fifteen years. His present outfit is 100% Leedy and includes snare drum, bass drum, pedal, bells, chimes, xylophone and tunable tom toms. When asked for his honest and sincere opinion of his Leedy equipment, he said heartily, as thousands of others say, "WONDERFUL." (Aug. 1, 1934).

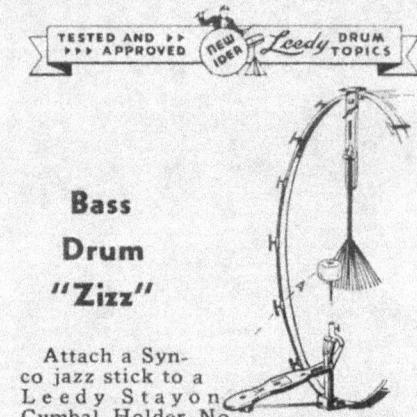

Bass Drum "Zizz"

Attach a Synco jazz stick to a Leedy Stayon Cymbal Holder No. 7140. Clamp the cymbal holder in the center at the top of the bass drum hoop and let the brush hang straight down so that the wires will come directly behind the beater ball of your pedal. Adjust so that wires are about 1" away from drum head. The beater ball first striking the wires and then pushing them on to the bass drum head produces a very pleasing effect suitable in certain types of numbers in both "piano" and "forte" passages.

$2.00 award to Chas. V. Jones, 827 E. Broadway, Centralia, Ill.

•

A single piece of canvas never carried a ship very far. A single beat behind the drums seldom brings in the "bacon," either. When the sailing vessel wants to make way she crowds on all her canvas. And the drummer who would make way must add many ideas, stunts, beats and much originality, to say nothing of fine equipment, if he is to ride the top of the waves in his chosen profession.

Leedy ════ WORLD'S FINEST DRUMMERS' INSTRUMENTS ════ *Leedy*

The Exclusive Drummers' Paper

WITH THE DRUMMERS OF THE U. S. MARINE BAND SINCE 1850

Frank S. Lusby
Wm. Giacchetti
Samuel Johnson

Because drums and drumming and everything in the least drumistic is so vitally a part of us, and believing that the same is true of many drummers who read "Drum Topics," we pass on to you the following interesting brief thumb-nail histories of the drummers who have helped make history while serving in the gallant and colorful U. S. Marine Band which was originally founded by an Act of Congress on July 11, 1798, which authorized a Drum Major, a Fife Major and thirty-two "drums and fifes."

The names and data of the Marine Band drummers prior to 1850 were not procurable even with the intensive effort that was made toward that end, and even the following briefs may contain an inaccuracy or two despite every effort that was made to secure the correct information. "Drum Topics" will appreciate receiving further authentic data or corrections for future use and reference.

Joseph A. Arth—born Washington, D. C., 1840, enlisted in 1850, served in the band 35 years and was retired in 1885 as Musician 1st Class. Active in Washington musical affairs until 1893 when he entered the U. S. Naval Academy Band, where he served until 1903. Resigned, returned to Washington and was active in music there until just prior to his death August 22, 1923. Buried in Congressional Cemetery in Washington. Played inaugurations of Presidents Fillmore, Pierce, Buchanan, Lincoln, Johnson, Grant, Hayes, Garfield, Arthur and Cleveland; played funerals of all Presidents from Fillmore up to and including Grant's; and was a member of the orchestra in Ford's Theatre playing under Director Wm. Withers the night Abraham Lincoln was shot. Played under Marine Band Directors Triay, Scala, Fries, Schneider and Sousa. In Arth's day all military calls were played on drum and fife, and Arth was a strict disciplinarian in rudimental drumming. His instructor was "Daddy" McFarlan, an old Marine Corps drummer.

Frank S. Lusby—born Washington, D. C., 1851, enlisted 1861, served in the band for 28 years and was discharged in 1889 because of illness which caused his death a short time later. Buried in Congressional Cemetery, Washington, D. C., December 1889. Played inaugurations of all Presidents from Lincoln up to and including Harrison's, and the funerals of all Presidents from Fillmore to Arthur, under the same leaders as Arth. Lusby and John Philip Sousa, born and raised in the same neighborhood, were close friends for years and together wrote a number of drum corps tunes as well as a manual called a "Book of Instructions for the Field Trumpet and Drum, Together with the Trumpet and Drum Signals Now in Use in the U. S. Army, Navy, and Marine Corps."

Samuel Johnson—born Washington, D. C., enlisted as apprentice drummer in the Marine Corps in 1863. Served 22 months, given a special discharge, re-enlisted six months later and served 8 years during which time he finished his apprenticeship, made several trips to sea, and saw service in Northern Africa and South America as a drummer abroad ship. At that time all ship's calls were beat on a drum. Studied drums under Lusby, and on Arth's retirement joined the Marine Band in 1885 and was retired in 1911 as Musician 1st Class. Played all Presidential inaugurations from Pres. Cleveland up to and including Taft. Served under Band Leaders Sousa, Fanciulli and Santelmann. Active and alert today, Johnson praises the ability of his instructor, Lusby, and that of Mr. Arth.

Wm. Giacchetti—born Brooklyn, N. Y., in 1856, enlisted in Brooklyn Navy Yard Band in 1866, served until 1868 when he was discharged. Re-enlisted at Ft. Monroe and served in the band there from 1868 until 1889. On retirement of Lusby from the Marine Band, Giacchetti obtained his discharge at Ft. Monroe to enlist in the Marine Band in 1889 where he served until his retirement in 1898, after 32 years' service. While in the Marine Band he played the inaugurations of Presidents Harrison, Cleveland and McKinley. From 1898 to 1914, played in a local theatre orchestra and from 1914 until 1930 played in the band at Soldiers' Home in Washington when he again retired. Was taught drums by an old sailor who had been aboard ship for many years, and who knew the rudiments

(Continued on Page Twenty-three)

The U. S. Marine Band as it appeared under Leader John Philip Sousa, "The March King," in 1890 when copious whiskers and abundant gold braid were in vogue.

Leedy ——— WORLD'S FINEST DRUMMERS' INSTRUMENTS ——— *Leedy*

Leedy Drum Topics

NEW AND BETTER BELLS FOR RADIO AND DANCE WORK

Leedy Solo-Tone Aluminum Bells, with bars of specially tempered aluminum alloy such as is used in all Leedy Vibraphones, were specially designed to meet the need for modern radio, dance and general orchestra and band work of today. Especially desirable in radio work because overtones are practically eliminated and "hammer impact" is reduced to the minimum without the sacrifice of volume. Thoroughly practical and technically correct for all types of orchestra and band work. Bars accurately tuned to A-440 pitch and mounted on finest felt assuring maximum volume from each bar. Case is made of 3-ply wood covered finest quality Fabrikoid, strongly reinforced and equipped with best grade, heavily nickeled hardware and stout, serviceable leather carrying handle. Detachable music rack and two pair choice mallets included.

The demand for these bells has been so overwhelming since they were first introduced a little more than a year ago that we now feature them as the finest in the Leedy line and have discontinued those bells which previously sold for several dollars more than these. You can make no mistake in choosing this set. If you need a set of orchestra bells now, or will need a set in the near future, we suggest that you visit your nearest Leedy dealer's store and try this set. You will find these bells ideally suited to your every need.

No. 5664—2½ Octaves, G-59 to C-88, 30 Bars 1¼" Wide by ⅜" Thick. Case 28" Long by 11" Wide by 3" Deep. A-440 Pitch Unless Ordered Otherwise. Weight only 15 lbs. Fabrikoid Case. Complete with Detachable Music Rack and 2 Pair Selected Mallets $50.00

When Packing the Traps

Many drummers throw all their traps and snare drum indiscriminately into their trap case, then eventually complain because the plating on the instrument doesn't stand up. I find it pays to protect the finish on my entire outfit just as zealously as the other instruments are cared for. Horns are carefully placed in plush cases. I use a Leedy mackintosh cover for my snare drum, which protects it from traps, and I have separate pieces of good cloth in which to individually wrap each trap, stand, pedal, tom-tom and holders. It takes a little longer to pack up, but I find those few minutes well spent in the preservation of my instrument and do not find it necessary to knock the manufacturer's plating which probably was perfect in the first place.

$2.00 award—Harold von Linden, Central Bridge, N. Y.

About Mackintosh Covers

It has been discovered that the rubber (which contains sulphur) in any make of mackintosh drum cover has a disastrous effect on chromium plating. The sulphur in the rubber in some way blisters the chromium, causing it to peel. It is a chemical action which cannot be overcome. Therefore, do not use rubberized mackintosh covers for any drum with chromium plated parts.

James Crawford

James Crawford, New York, featured "hot" drummer and vibracussionist with Jimmie Lunceford and his famed colored orchestra famous hit of New York's celebrated Cotton Club, where white-hot rhythm, "blues" songs and high-jinx entertainment is the nightly attraction, is an entertainer in his own right by virtue of his superb dexterity with the sticks, his radiant personality and his inherent showmanship. Has been with the Lunceford Artists for the past seven years, his entire professional career behind the drums. His outfit is 100% Leedy, including chimes, Vibraphone and machine tympani. Crawford wrote to us on May 29, 1934, of his equipment as follows: "The smoothest, fastest and most reliable outfit I've ever used"—and he should know whereof he writes.

Jimmie Lunceford's Orchestra, directed by the versatile and popular Jimmie Lunceford himself, has been featured nine times weekly over the major radio networks and is a sensational box office attraction wherever, and whenever, it appears. Only recently back in New York after a very extensive engagement tour that took it as far west as Des Moines, Iowa.

Ancient Pictures of Drums

On the monuments and walls of ancient temples in Egypt, Assyria, India, Greece and Persia—hundreds of years before the time of Christ—drums in a variety of shapes and sizes are included in the scenes which have recorded the histories of those countries.

Leedy — WORLD'S FINEST DRUMMERS' INSTRUMENTS — *Leedy*

The Exclusive Drummers' Paper

Ceylonese Temple Drummers at the Posen Festival

On June tenth of every year the Buddhists celebrate the Posen Festival of the fifth month by making a pilgrimage to the temple at Anaradhabura in northern Ceylon. To this temple come more than two hundred thousand pilgrims from many miles in every direction with their offerings. Shown above are some of the temple drummers with their primitive drums which are variously played with rude beaters and carried in what appears to be a very uncomfortable manner. Note that the two "double-drums" shown in the picture to the left are quite similar in everything but size to the Cuban *Bongos*.

Miles Henslow on Xylophones

I have been plagued with queries from all over the world about the playing of the xylophone. I must confess that the xylophone is not exactly the strongest of my many strong points: nevertheless, I am always ready to oblige, and I should like to settle this business once and for all.

Aching (Acton) writes: "Sir, I have a xylophone. I use six hammers. Is this a record?"

No, Aching. It isn't.

Sambo writes from the Sudan:—"Suh!—Ah hab a xylophone. Ah play her pretty-dam-good, yes. Twelve hammers, yes, suh! Ah guess no one can play dat xylophone lak me with twelve hammers, no suh!—Yours respectably, Sambo."

Sambo is right!

The truth is that xylophones were originally intended to be played with two hammers. Some idiot tried to be clever, and used four. It was certainly an idea, but, of course, somebody else had to use six. And that started it. I suppose it *is* possible to hit one or two right notes with six. But eight? And *ten*?

And now competition is so intense anyone who attempts to play with less than twelve is booed down. Therefore the problem is—How can anyone get a job xylophoning if he can't use twelve hammers? And is it better to hammer out a tune with six, or to look clever with ten?

The answer is, "Heaven knows." I think, after all, that, as progress must not be retarded, the more the merrier. Let us set a new standard. Let us say twenty hammers, ten in each hand. That will leave very few idle notes and, if a certain amount of speed is used, there is no reason why all the notes should not be struck together.

This system would wash out all need for tricky runs, and would give the beginner a chance of mastering this now very complicated instrument. And I think it should be possible, by use of pedals, to silence the unwanted notes.

Therefore, in all probability, the xylophone of the future will consist of a foot manual and one large hammer, capable of hitting all notes at once.

All correspondence on this subject is now closed.—Courtesy *The Melody Maker*, London, Eng., July 22, 1933.

Wood Block Stunt

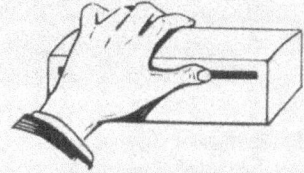

By holding the left-hand cupped over a Chee Foo Chinese wood block of any size and sliding the hand back and forth along the block with the thumb over the slot, different effects may be obtained that are similar to temple block tones. Of course, this hasn't the volume of the temple block but it is especially effective on soft, sweet choruses. Use a hard felt or a soft rubber mallet. Resting the block on the knee while doing this stunt is better than leaving it on a holder as the knee acts as a cushion and does not absorb the tone.

$2.00 award to Jack Schiffour, 650 Maplewood Ave., Ambridge, Pa.

Write now to reserve your copy of the new Leedy Catalog "U" — it's more complete than any drum catalog ever published!

Leedy — WORLD'S FINEST DRUMMERS' INSTRUMENTS — Leedy

Leedy Drum Topics

THERE'S A LEEDY STICK MODEL FOR YOUR PARTICULAR REQUIREMENTS

A Nifty, New Cymbal Carrying Idea

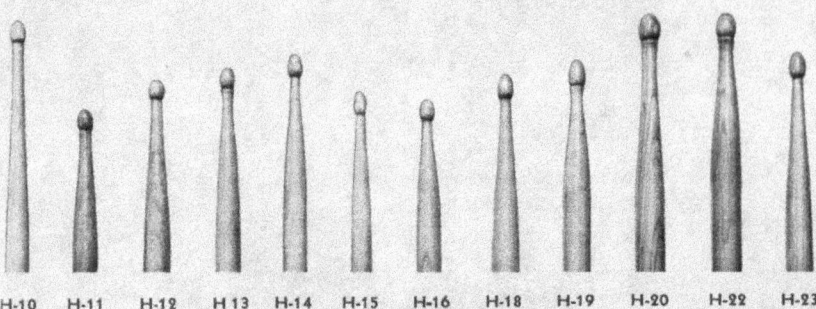

H-10 H-11 H-12 H-13 H-14 H-15 H-16 H-18 H-19 H-20 H-22 H-23

All Leedy drum stick models are obtainable in either Hickory or Rosewood, and are made from the finest stock obtainable. Hickory models are made from selected, straight-grained, second-growth white hickory, and Rosewood models are made from the choicest British Honduras Rosewood selected from our xylophone bar stock. All models are carefully finished, have a smooth "feel" and appearance, and are guaranteed to please you in every way.

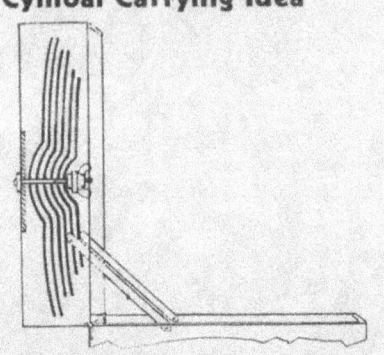

H-10—17" long, weight about 4¼ oz., per pair
H-11—14¾" long, weight about 3¾ oz., per pair
H-12—15½" long, weight about 3¼ oz., per pair
H-13—15¾" long, weight about 3½ oz., per pair
H-14—16" long, weight about 3¾ oz., per pair
H-15—15¼" long, weight about 3 oz., per pair
H-16—15" long, weight about 3¾ oz., per pair
H-18—15½" long, weight about 5 oz., per pair
H-19—16" long, weight about 4¼ oz., per pair
H-20—17" long, weight about 5½ oz., per pair
H-22—17" long, weight about 5¾ oz., per pair
H-23—16" long, weight about 3½ oz., per pair

45c PER PAIR (In Hickory)

Please Order by Both Letter and Number

"H" Denotes Hickory Models   "R" Denotes Rosewood Models
"R" Models (ROSEWOOD), per pair .... $ .80
RED END Selected Models, per pair .... .75
Hickory Models Ducoed in any Color (or choice of 2 Colors) to match Drum Corps Drums *(providing they are ordered with drums)*, per pair 1.00

Cymbals have always been more or less of a problem for the jobbing drummer. They rattle around in drum cases and very often do damage to heads and traps, to say nothing of breaking themselves. This drawing shows how they can be carried on the inside of the lid of any drum case of the lid type. Be sure to use good sized washers on the bolt, both inside and outside. In fact, a block of wood 2" or 3" square on the inside would also help. The wing nut with plenty of thread on the bolt will give ample adjustment according to the number of cymbals carried. It is possible to carry as many as six in this manner. No more broken cymbals or damaged traps when this idea is used.

$2.00 award to Francis H. Smith, 23 The Grove, Palmers Green, London, N. 13, ENGLAND.

A Veteran Leedy Drummer

Verne Kalt wrote on July 28, 1934, of his Leedy equipment: "None better in the World" and evidently means it because he got his first set of Leedys at the age of eight and he is using Leedys today after twenty-five years in the profession. He also has the distinction of having had the first Vibraphone in Toledo, where he now has his own orchestra, which has played at Ruggles Beach for 18 seasons, the Green Mill for five seasons and a like period on the Steamer Greyhound. Has played almost every type of musical engagement during his career since studying under Harold Foster, Sandusky, O.

His present equipment includes a Leedy snare drum, bass drum, pedal, orchestra bells and Vibraphone, all of which he swears by, not at, as he'll tell you in all sincerity. (July 28, 1934)

Leedy — WORLD'S FINEST DRUMMERS' INSTRUMENTS — Leedy

The Exclusive Drummers' Paper

A Good Megaphone Stunt

Hold the large end of a megaphone over the batter head of your snare drum. Roar into megaphone, loud or soft as desired. Tone may be varied by holding megaphone either flat on the head or slightly away, or by tipping with one edge resting on the head. Fine for tiger roars and other animal growls. Also good for soft rhythm beats used in conjunction with stick work on cymbals. In other words, a voice effect thru a megaphone onto a snare drum that has many possibilities.

$2.00 award to John Carbone, 232 N. 7th St., Brooklyn, N. Y.

•

Did you ever hear about the Scotch drummer who loosened his heads and played everything on the wood block?

•

Richard C. Duryea

Young Richard Duryea, Binghampton, N. Y., 12 years old, is studying drums under S. C. Sunness, who operates the Drum Shop in Binghamton, and is really "going places," according to his teacher, who advises us that Richard has "—the smoothest roll I have heard in years, and an uncanny faculty of dividing and reading." Richard is using a Leedy professional trap drum outfit.

An English Limerick

Old Mother Hubbard
Went to the cupboard—
Her lodger was out for a bit;
So she looked thru his chattels,
Found squeaks, squawks and rattles—
Her lodger—a drummer—his kit.

James D. Salmon

Honored for his ability on drums and xylophone in National, District and State school contests, and awarded the Waukegan, Ill., Lion's medal for outstanding worth to his high school band and orchestra, James Salmon, Waukegan, Ill., is now conducting his own dance orchestra as well as playing in the Waukegan Symphony Orchestra under Director Sandor Kish. Salmon is shown above with his Leedy Broadway Dual drum.

Protection for Temple Blocks

They will last much longer if you will stick a small square of chamois over the playing spot on the block. This chamios does not interfere with the tone in the least. Chamois skin may be obtained at any drug store. Here is a real money-saver.

$2.00 award to Al. "Rags" Anderson, 815 Seymour Ave., Columbus, Ohio.

•

We Think You'll Agree

More persons would be better satisfied if they learned to believe that quality is a greater attraction than price. There are few of us who haven't found, at some time or other, that something not truly good is actually the most expensive in the last analysis.

This applies to drums and drummers' equipment just as it does to clothes, furniture and everything.

Effect for Sock Choruses

As simple as it looks in this picture. Beat out you rhythm with a stick on a Leedy Bass Drum Tone Control No. 668. Sort of a slap bass effect and fine in "ride" choruses. And, of course, the left stick can be used on snare drum, tom-tom or temple blocks at the same time.

$2.00 award to Bob Cook, 7049 Prairie Ave., Chicago, Ill.

Editor's Note: See the two new larger Leedy Bass Drum Tone Controls illustrated and described on page 9 of this "Drum Topics"— the new pressure adjustment is a pip.

Carl F. Pratt

Carl F. Pratt, a fine concert, theatre, and dance drummer of Norwich, N. Y., studied drums under the famous late Geo. B. Stone of Boston, is teaching about a dozen pupils in addition to playing with Wm. K. Johnson's Orchestra at Smalley's Theatre, Norwich, and doing local dance work. Carl has been playing drums for the past 27 years and wrote on July 28, 1934, "—am so satisfied with Leedy equipment that I have always used it and when I buy now it is Leedy for myself and my pupils." His equipment is 100% Leedy.

Band drummers and Drum Corps members are invited to write for the new Leedy "Roll-Off" No. 3—a complete catalog of Drum Corps and Band Drummers' equipment.

Leedy — WORLD'S FINEST DRUMMERS' INSTRUMENTS — Leedy

Leedy Drum Topics

THE FINEST DRUM HEADS EVER KNOWN

SUPERIOR "HARDWHITE" HEADS

The finest and smoothest white, hard tight-fibred head procurable anywhere, and at any price.

Snare Drum—Batter Side Only

No. 5717—17" for 13" Shell	$3.20
No. 5718—18" for 14" Shell	3.50
No. 5719—19" for 15" Shell	3.80
No. 5720—20" for 16" Shell	4.10
No. 5721—21" for 17" Shell	4.40
No. 5722—22" for 18" Shell	4.70

Bass Drum

No. 5728—28" for 24" Shell	$ 7.20
No. 5730—30" for 26" Shell	7.90
No. 5732—32" for 28" Shell	8.60
No. 5734—34" for 30" Shell	9.30
No. 5736—36" for 32" Shell	10.20
No. 5738—38" for 34" Shell	11.20
No. 5740—40" for 36" Shell	13.20

REGULAR "HARDWHITE" HEADS

Tight-fibred hard, white heads of even thickness with plenty of stick response, and unusual durability.

Snare Drum—Batter Side Only

No. 5817—17" for 13" Shell	$2.70
No. 5818—18" for 14" Shell	3.00
No. 5819—19" for 15" Shell	3.30
No. 5820—20" for 16" Shell	3.60
No. 5821—21" for 17" Shell	3.90
No. 5822—22" for 18" Shell	4.20

Bass Drum

No. 5828—28" for 24" Shell	$ 6.00
No. 5830—30" for 26" Shell	6.70
No. 5832—32" for 28" Shell	7.40
No. 5834—34" for 30" Shell	8.10
No. 5836—36" for 32" Shell	9.00
No. 5838—38" for 34" Shell	10.00
No. 5840—40" for 36" Shell	12.00

TRANSPARENT "UKA" HEADS

The finest resilient transparent heads that have stood the "gaff" for 25 years and are the favorites of thousands of drummers. These heads are finished in the hide's natural state, meaning that the fibres are alive and flexible, which assures finer and more resonant tone and the utmost in service from heads of the transparent type. You'll like these.

Snare Side Only

No. 5917—17" for 13" Shell	$2.30
No. 5918—18" for 14" Shell	2.45
No. 5919—19" for 15" Shell	2.60
No. 5920—20" for 16" Shell	2.70
No. 5921—21" for 17" Shell	2.80
No. 5922—22" for 18" Shell	2.90

Batter Side Only

No. 6017—17" for 13" Shell	$2.30
No. 6018—18" for 14" Shell	2.45
No. 6019—19" for 15" Shell	2.60
No. 6020—20" for 16" Shell	2.70
No. 6021—21" for 17" Shell	2.80
No. 6022—22" for 18" Shell	2.90

"KAFETTE" TYMPANI HEADS

The finest tympani heads known. Transparent and assure fine tone.

For Tympani Only

No. 6430—30" for 24" Kettle	$ 7.90
No. 6431—31" for 25" Kettle	8.25
No. 6432—32" for 26" Kettle	8.60
No. 6433—33" for 27" Kettle	8.90
No. 6434—34" for 28" Kettle	9.30
No. 6435—35" for 29" Kettle	9.75
No. 6436—36" for 30" Kettle	10.20

DRUM HEAD FORM

Will keep 2 heads on wood flesh hoops from warping and immediately available for replacements.

Specify Shell Diameter on Order

No. 1967—(Without Heads)	$2.00

TUCKING AND FLESH HOOP PRICES

No. 1973—Tucking Snare Drum Head (any size)	$ .50
No. 1974—Tucking Bass Drum Head (any size up to 40")	.75
No. 1975—Tucking Tympani Head (any size)	1.00
No. 1950—Metal Flesh Hoop for Snare Drum— (State whether Batter or Snare, and Shell Size)	.75
No. 1951—Wood Flesh Hoop for Snare Drum— (State whether Batter or Snare, and Shell Size)	.40
No. 1952—Wood Flesh Hoop for Bass Drum (State Shell Size)	.80
No. 1953—Metal Flesh Hoop for Tympani (State Shell Size)	2.00

When You Move

When you change your address, be sure to notify *Drum Topics* immediately. Otherwise you will miss your copy of the next issue. Every year more than 300 drummers fail to get their copy of this magazine for just that reason. This is inconvenient for them and it means a loss of postage to us, a bad deal all around. So don't forget, when you change your address, notify us immediately. It only takes a minute and saves time and trouble for everyone concerned.

Charles J. Danese

More than twelve years behind Leedy drums playing theatre and dance jobs in the New England states qualifies Charles Danese, Haverhill, Mass., to say with some authority that his "- - Leedy outfit has pleased the manager in every theatre I have worked and it cannot be excelled for tone, easy playing qualities or appearance." His letter of July 30, 1934 also stated that he studied drums under the direction of Adolph Blaser.

Sock Cymbal Swish Effect

Here is a cymbal combination that produces a sort of a cymbal slur or swish effect instead of the solid staccato sock effect. Use a 12" Zenjian cymbal on the bottom and a 10" Zenjian on the top. These positively must be thin cymbals so they will "give" when struck together. For those who want the swish instead of the sock—there it is.

$2.00 award to Ray Michael, 2015 E. 90th St., Cleveland, Ohio.

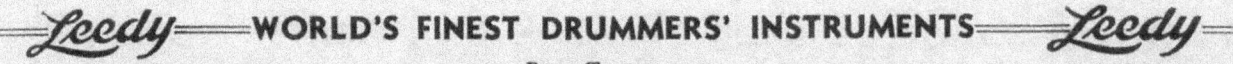

WORLD'S FINEST DRUMMERS' INSTRUMENTS

The Exclusive Drummers' Paper

With the Drummers of the U. S. Marine Band Since 1850
(Continued from Page Seventeen)

Richard E. Guthier

and the many ship's calls that a drummer of that day had to beat in the daily routine. Mr. Giacchetti cannot recall the sailor's name but says that he was a cracker-jack with a pair of sticks. Mr. Giacchetti is in tip-top physical shape today at the age of seventy-eight years.

Harry G. Sims—born Washington, D. C., 1869, enlisted in the Marine Band in 1897 and was retired from service on March 15, 1926, after thirty years in the band. Played inaugurations of Presidents McKinley, Roosevelt, Taft, Wilson, Harding and Coolidge, and the funerals of McKinley, Wilson and Harding. Mr. Sims was taught by Samuel Johnson and started as a drummer in the old Kit Carson G. A. R. Drum Corps in Washington before joining the Marine Band. Nearly 65 years old now, Mr. Sims is physically fit and feeling fine.

W. D. Kieffer — born Lancaster, Pa., in 1888, enlisted in the Marine Band in 1915 and is now serving his twentieth year. Played the inaugurations of all the Presidents from Wilson to and including F. D. Roosevelt's. Was taught by W. H. Potts, Lancaster, Pa., and by Dan Clemmens, both old-time Civil War drummers. Later became an apprentice in the Old Vets' Drum Corps in Lancaster, and then played in the High School Orchestra. During the early days played many funerals for Civil War veterans when the music was generally a fife and a drum. Frank S. Haines was the fifer on these occasions, but on more than one occasion he stopped the procession to show Kieffer how a certain beat should have been played since he was a drummer of no mean ability as well as a fifer, sometimes accompany the lesson with a cuff on the ear—and then the procession would proceed. All three of Mr. Kieffer's instructors played the old school of rudiments, and all had faith in the old rule of "Spare the Rod and Spoil the Child."

John Auer plays snare drum, bells and traps beside Kieffer in the band today. He has been there for several years — just how many we do not know at this writing. Neither have we the detailed data on Johnny's birthplace, past history, etc. However, he is one of the finest of fellows and a marvelous drummer in every respect. He also doubles on violin way up near the first chair on the orchestral engagements which the members of the band are so often called upon to play.

Chas. L. Viner, of the present-day drum section, has also been with the band for more than twenty years. He is the fellow they all talk about, for he is known as one of the finest bass drummers in the country. Charlie hails from Massachusetts and is one of the most popular boys in the organization. Drum Topics hopes to run special stories on Johnny Auer and Charlie Viner at a later date.

Captain Taylor Branson, present Leader of the Marine Band since April 27, 1927, is a composer of merit as well as a director for he has written a number of fine marches which he has dedicated to the Marine Corps. Among these marches are: "Tell It to the Marines," "Marines of Belleau Woods," "The President's Own," and the "Eagle, Globe and Anchor."

Editor's note: In the above article, no inference is intended as to the kind of instrument used.

First Division winner as drum soloist in District and National High School Contests, playing professionally and in school, radio xylophone soloist on several stations, recommended for a Bandmaster's scholarship at Interlochen, teaching drums and xylophone while he is studying tympani, and entering Illinois U. this fall where he will play in the band, Richard Guthier of Huntington, Ind., is well on his way to prominence in the profession. Uses Leedy military and orchestra snare drums, pedal, orchestra bells and tympani.

Anyone can cut prices, but it takes brains to make a better article.
—*Philip D. Armour.*

Write Today For
THE NEW LEEDY CAT. "U"

Always the first with the newest and finest, and maintaining its reputation for always issuing the most complete drum and drummers' equipment catalog available—Leedy upholds its reputation in its new 1934-35 Catalog "U" that is just about to come from the printers. Its 112 pages are crammed full of everything that the modern drummer needs. Improved drum models! New outfits! New "Full Dress" finishes, Tympani on wheels! The amazing NEW Octarimba! The NEW Leedy Damper Chimes! Scores of NEW or IMPROVED holders and accessories and a dozen or more other vitally interesting things for the drummer are contained between its beautiful new covers which includes pictures of the Drummers and Directors of four of the country's most famous orchestras which use Leedy drums and equipment! Seventy-three photos of famous drummers in the catalog itself! You just CANNOT afford to miss the new Leedy Catalog "U". Sent free, postpaid and without obligation on receipt of your request.

Simply Address Desk 24,

LEEDY BLDG.   *Leedy Mfg. Co., Inc.*   **ELKHART, IND.**

Leedy DRUM TOPICS

AUGUST, 1934 NUMBER 24

Sec.
U. S.
ELKHART
IND.

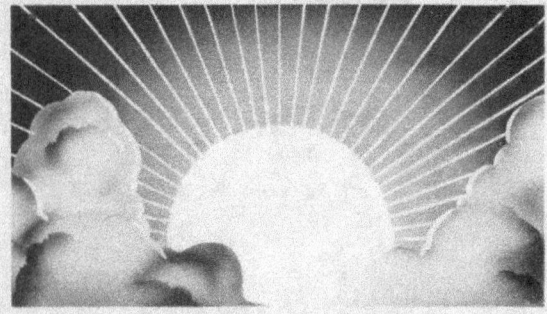

"ALWAYS SOMETHING NEW UNDER THE SUN"

(See pages 2, 9, 12-13 and 23)

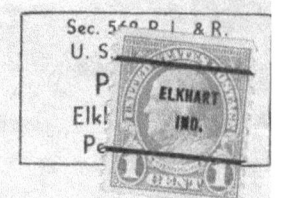

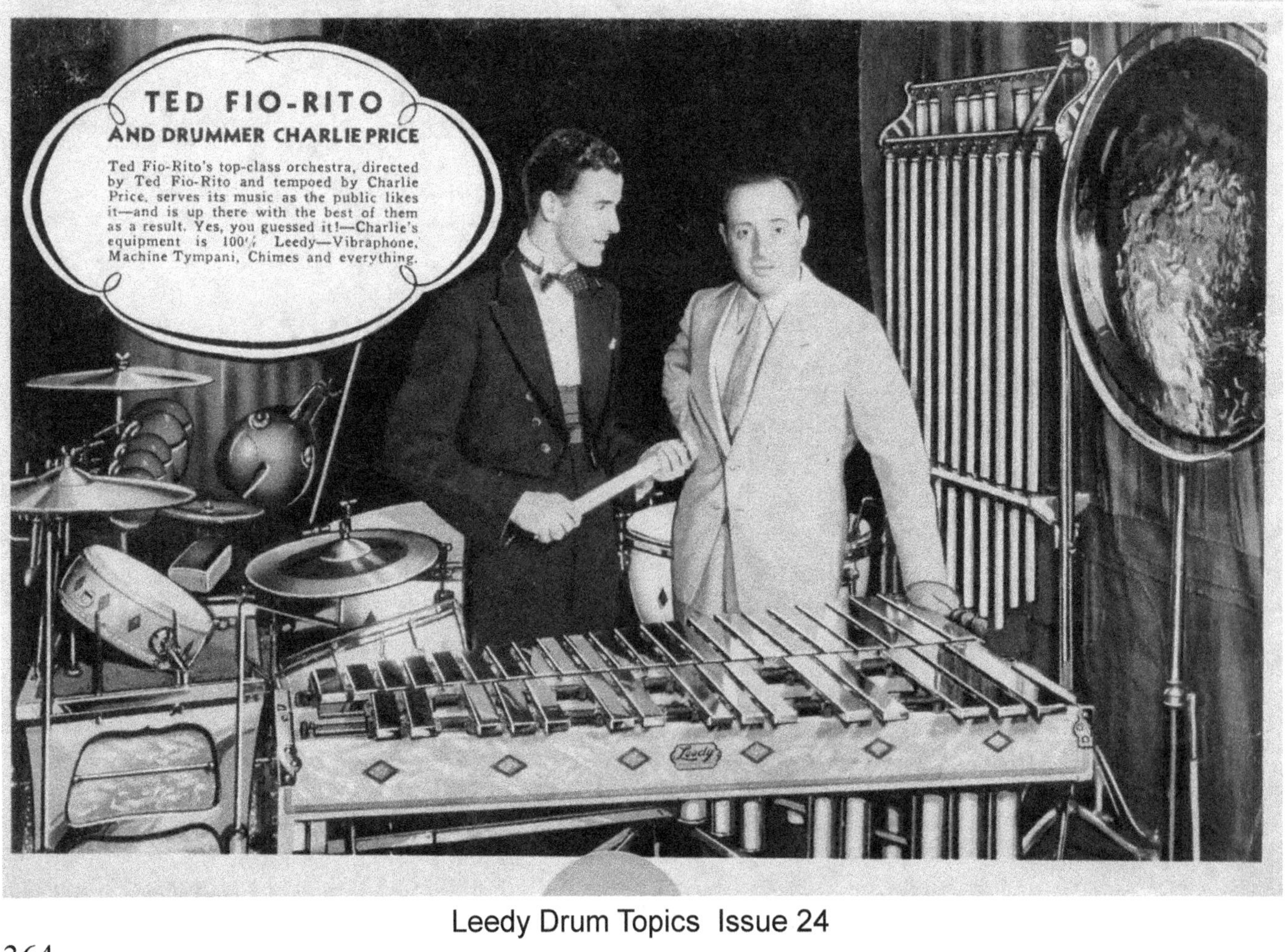

Mr. Joseph G. Benoit,
165 Hildreth,
Lowell, Mass.

POSTMASTER—Return Postage Guaranteed

Leedy Mfg. Co., Inc.

LEEDY BUILDING, ELKHART, INDIANA

TED FIO-RITO
AND DRUMMER CHARLIE PRICE
Ted Fio-Rito's top-class orchestra, directed by Ted Fio-Rito and tempoed by Charlie Price, serves its music as the public likes it—and is up there with the best of them as a result. Yes, you guessed it!—Charlie's equipment is 100% Leedy—Vibraphone, Machine Tympani, Chimes and everything.
Leedy

Leedy Drum Topics Issue 25

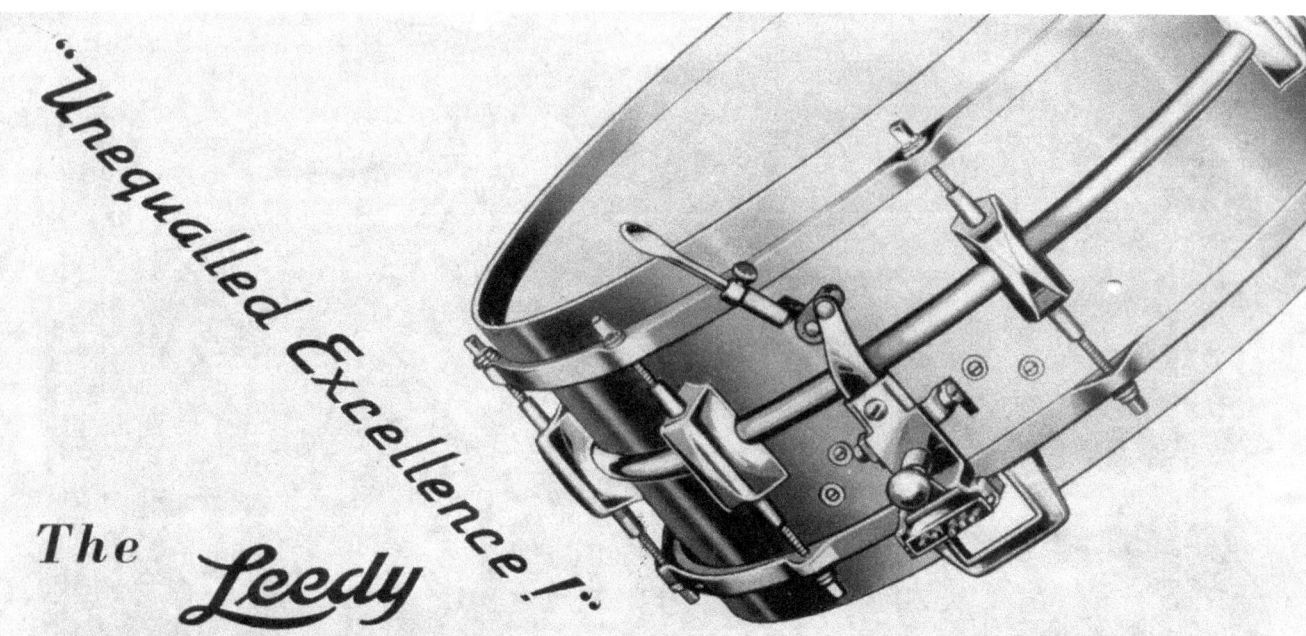

"Unequalled Excellence!"

The Leedy "BROADWAY" Parallel Floating Head Snare Drum

Double Flanged Hoops

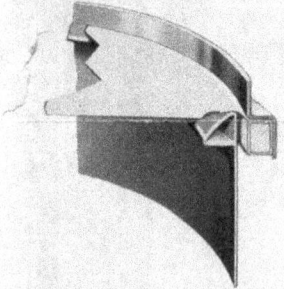

Leedy double flanged counter hoops serve six distinct purposes on BROADWAY drums: they are (1) stronger, (2) more rigid, and (3) better looking than ordinary flanged counter hoops. (4) with the Self-Aligning rods they hold the flesh hoops away from the shell at all points in a perfect circle which is the Floating Head feature, (5) they eliminate unsightly collar hooks and (6) fully conceal the flesh hoops.

Automatic Tension Snares

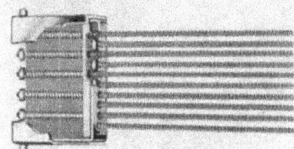

This wonderful Leedy invention is now a part of the Parallel snare strainers on both Parallel and Dual model "Broadway" Drums. One end of each snare "floats" within a short coiled wire spring arranged alternately in two metal housings, one at each end. This spaces the snares so they cannot touch each other at any point and keeps them always at exactly the same tension. They align themselves on the springs.

Designed to meet every playing requirement of the present day professional drummer, the Leedy Broadway Floating Head Snare Drum is the finest on the market today. Tone, playing ease, sensitive snare response, durability and reliability are built into this drum of unsurpassed beauty and efficiency. Everything on it, and in it, is there for a definite purpose as explained elsewhere on this page. NO drum without ALL of these important features can give Leedy BROADWAY *Floating Head* drum performance or playing satisfaction as hundreds of the finest drummers with the leading bands and orchestras in every phase of music work will testify from actual experience—and that is why there are more BROADWAYS used in the strictly professional field today than any other make of drum on the markets of the world.

If you have never tried a BROADWAY, by all means play one before you buy another snare drum. Its splendid qualities under actual playing conditions will convince you of its superiority far more than anything that can be said in its behalf.

Your local Leedy dealer will be glad to show you the three BROADWAY models which are supplied in a choice of wood or all-metal shells in a wide variety of plain and "Full Dress" finishes—at prices no higher than those of ordinary makes.

The All-Metal BROADWAY PARALLEL

Nickel Plated

No. 2030—Size 5"x14"		$45.00
No. 3032—Size 6½"x14"		45.00

Chromium Plated

No. 2036—Size 5"x14"		$60.00
No. 2038—Size 6½"x14"		60.00

Floating Heads

» WITH THE FLOATING HEAD

Floating Head Slopes Away From Edge of Shell Eliminating all Head and Flesh Hoop Binding. This Assures Even Head Tension

Flesh Hoop Fits Counter Hoop and Remains Away from Shell at all Points

» WITHOUT THE FLOATING HEAD

Head Turns Sharp Angle in Passing Over Edge of Shell on Other Style Drums. This Jams the Head and Prevents Even Head Tension

Flesh Hoop Hugs Shell and Causes Binding

Floating Heads mean that the flesh hoops do not and cannot touch the shell at any point of the circle. They fit snugly in the flanges of the counter hoops instead of hugging the shell as on other models. This eliminates all possibility of binding flesh hoops, reduces head breakage and guarantees even head tension, which results in an easier playing, better sounding instrument.

Self-Aligning Rods

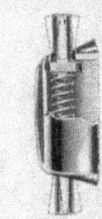

All Broadway Floating Head Drums are equipped with SELF-ALIGNING rods—an exclusive Leedy feature found on no other drum made. The receiving tubes (lugs) swing within the center supports (casings) on modified universal joints which are free to move in every direction. This assures a perfect alignment of threads which eliminates binding and stripping, and permits uniform head tension.

*6½" x 15" sizes supplied on special order at an additional cost of $5.00. Week to 10 days required for delivery.
**All Drums Supplied with Silk Wire Wound Snares unless ordered otherwise. Gut or James Snares Supplied at No Extra Cost.
***Black or White Duco on Shells supplied on special order at no extra cost.

Page Two

Ray Michaels with Archie Bleyer

When you hear Archie Bleyer's orchestra on the NBC or CBS networks, electrical transcriptions or Brunswick recordings now, you'll know that Ray Michaels is doing the percussion honors. Michaels will soon complete his second year with this popular MCA attraction during which time it has held down such spots as the Commodore Hotel and the Hollywood Restaurant in NYC. Prior to being with Bleyer, Ray played with Kay Kyser during four of his eight years in the profesh. Says West Lafayette, Ohio, is his birthplace, and that he studied under Ray Dean of Cleveland. Director Bleyer, and Michaels with his 100% Leedy outfit, are shown above—a couple of really swell fellows who deserve the success that is theirs—all of it.

Albert Grimes
With Dick Jurgens' Versatile West Coast Orchestra

Dick Jurgens' orchestra's triumphant engagements at the Palomar Ballroom, Los Angeles, the St. Francis Hotel in San Francisco and the Lake Tahoe resorts definitely place his name among the big ones on the west coast. The orchestra has the youthful versatility and zip that seems to satisfy with the result that it is in high demand and really going places. Shown here with Jurgens is Al Grimes who has contributed the rhythms from the drums during the past two years and who recently purchased his third consecutive set of Leedys. Here he's telling Jurgens that ". . . Leedy drums are the best money can buy." His home town is Redding (Cal.) and he's been playing drums seven years—started in the public schools with little idea that he would ever play professionally.

•

The late Mr. U. G. Leedy, founder of the Leedy Mfg. Co., made his first drum at Fostoria, Ohio, in 1892—just forty-three years ago. It was this drum that inspired the forming of the present Leedy Mfg. Co. which was founded in 1895.

•

Chinese Cymbal Markings

The markings on Chinese cymbals that we associate with "Sam Lees's" laundry tickets are not, as some believe the name or trademark of the maker. Cymbals of exactly the same sizes and shapes as we now find them were used in China for religious ceremonies before the Christian era. Undoubtedly the "crashes" were intended to scare away "evil demons." etc.

Benjamin Podemski, Philadelphia Symphony

Without a doubt one of the finest and foremost drummers in the profession today is Benjamin Podemski who is playing his fourteenth year with the Philadelphia Symphony Orchestra and whose eventful professional career extends back over the past three decades. Born in Riga, Latvia, and studied drums under Peter Lewin. In addition to playing under Leopold Stokowski in Philadelphia's famed Academy of Music, Podemski has played under that illustrious maestro for Victor recordings, on the Chesterfield Hour over the air, operas and in the Robin Hood Dell Summer Concerts. The names of other directors under whom he played includes a majority of the most renowned leaders of his time—Arturo Toscanini, Fritz Reiner, Victor Herbert, Richard Strauss, Jose Iturbi, Alex. Smallens, Ossip Gabrilowitch, Victor Kolar, Clemens Crauss, Ormandi, Issay Do-

browen, Hans Kindler, Sir Walter Beacham, Bernardino Molinari, Eugene Goosens, Rodsinski, Sokoloff, Frederic Stock, Igor Strawinsky, Albert Coates and Bodansky to mention some of them.

Mr. Podemski has used Leedy instruments during twenty-five of his thirty years in the profession. Shown with him above is his Leedy Broadway drum.

•

Therefore, as the cymbals represented the good spirits, they were given titles and even to this day the custom prevails to name and write on them. The writing on each cymbal varies from the next and translated means: *Moon, Clouds, Stars, Sun, Water, Snow, Rain*, etc., etc. The names of the flowers and of the gods are often used also.

—*From DRUM TOPICS No. 14.*

Leedy Drum Topics

Rudy Van Gelder with the Inimitable Ted Lewis

EVERYBODY knows the inimitable Ted Lewis for his superb showmanship and his splendid picture, radio, theatre and dance work, and most of Drum Topics readers know Rudy Van Gelder who presides over the drums in the Lewis band which recently completed "Here Comes the Band" for MGM pictures in Hollywood. Two noted film comedians, Bert Roach and Fred Santley, appear with Gelder on the snare drums in that picture; Geo. Beebe (used to be with Paul Whiteman) plays the bass drum; Otto Fries (of "Chocolate Soldier" fame) plays cymbals and Freddy Sanborn of vaudeville note does the xylophone honors in the picture, by the way. Thought you MIGHT be interested. Gelder has played drums for twenty years and they've ALWAYS been Leedy. Formerly played with Paul Ash, Charlie Davis, Ed Lowry, Eddie Peabody and Jules Silver.

DRUM TOPICS is Leedy's contribution to the Drumming Fraternity in appreciation for the support of thousands of drummers who play and boost Leedy instruments.

DRUM TOPICS is a magazine for drummers exclusively. Its aim is to let drummers know what other drummers are doing.

DRUM TOPICS is NOT strictly an advertising medium. NEWS is its first consideration.

DRUM TOPICS is made up chiefly of the news, photographs, ideas, stories and articles received from its readers.

Material received by DRUM TOPICS Editor will be judged on its merits and be used in the order that it is received. May we hear from YOU?

Johnny Minton with the "Crown Prince of Rhythm"

Almost half of Minton's six year professional career has been spent under the baton of Ted Jennings, the "Crown Prince of Rhythm", playing the choice hotels, ballrooms, theatres and a number of radio stations in the southern middle states. Also made a highly successful tour of old Mexico with the band, and when last heard from was with Jennings at The Palms in Nashville, Tenn. Minton has played 100% Leedy for the past two and one-half years and says: "I consider Leedy instruments the finest manufactured. Tone quality, snap and ease of playing cannot be equalled. They are truly 'job insurance!'" Prior to playing with Jennings, Minton had his own band and played hotels and ballrooms. Paris, Texas, is his OHT (old home town) but he now receives his mail at Fort Worth.

Edward Breazeale of the Tucson Symphony and the U. of Arizona Band

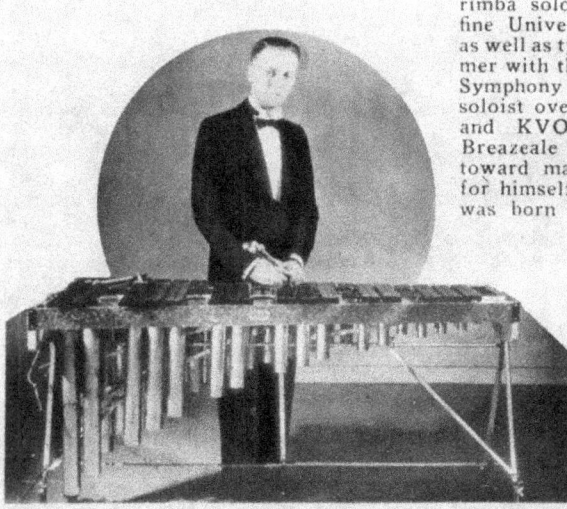

Featured xylophone and Octarimba soloist with the unusually fine University of Arizona Band, as well as tympanist and first drummer with that band and the Tucson Symphony Orchestra, and featured soloist over radio stations KGAR and KVOA in between times, Breazeale is well on his way toward making a fine reputation for himself in the profession. He was born in Manassas, Va., and has played drums for the past 14 years which is more than half of his life thus far. Has played with the U. of A. band for six years and with the Tucson Symphony for eight. Says of his Leedy instruments: "The finest I have ever played, and I have played all the popular makes on the market today."

Leedy — WORLD'S FINEST DRUMMERS' INSTRUMENTS SINCE 1895 — *Leedy*

The Exclusive Drummers' Paper

1895 — Forty Years — 1935

Because we think that our readers will be interested, we mention it here that—

This year, 1935, marks Leedy's fortieth anniversary in the drum business—forty years of friendly service to the drummer and to the profession which we all love and which many of us consider the most interesting and one of the most colorful on earth.

To the thousands of Leedy users who have helped to build the house which is today famous for "The World's Finest Drummers' Instruments," we say here, where our many friends are most sure to see it, a very, very sincere "thank you", and we pledge ourselves anew to continue and strengthen the policies which have merited your confidence in us during the past four decades so that we may deserve and continue to enjoy your friendship and patronage in the future.

•

Fred E. Albright
with B. A. Rolfe Orchestra

Six years with that famous radio orchestra under the skillful baton of the great B. A. Rolfe during which time he has played the Lucky Strike radio commercial for three years, the Terraplane Hour for one and one-half years and more recently the Goodrich Hour, entitles Fred E. Albright to a bit more than ordinary recognition in professional circles. Prior to his present berth he was Staff Musician with the CBS in New York City and played in the N. Y. Symphony Orchestra. Albright studied under Alfred Freise and has been

in the game for the past twenty-five years, and Leedys have been his choice of drums during that entire period. Albright, by the way, is a native Indianan having been born in Kokomo which is only a hundred miles or so from the present Leedy factory. Says: "Leedy drums are my personal choice." The above photo shows him with his present Leedy BROADWAY snare drum finished in Marine Pearl with Sparkling Two-Tone Diamonds.

"Muddy" Berry
with Kay Kyser's Ever-Popular Orchestra

Berry has been with the Kay Kyser band for the past three years during which time it has played a number of the better hotels and cafes in New York, Chicago and the west coast, and been featured over one or the other of the national radio chains. Played the world premier of Eddie Canter's "Roman Scandals" at Sid Grauman's Chinese Theatre in Hollywood, did a capacity business at Chicago's Blackhawk Cafe, has been an unusual drawing card at university 'proms' and is, at this time, holding down

the Hotel Wm. Penn job in Pittsburgh and has the situation well in hand in that city.

Berry has seen this country from the middle to all its edges as well as a good part of South America and the Orient with his Leedys during the past fifteen years. Of them he says, "They're the 'nuts'!" Have tried all makes but still stick to Leedy. 'Nuf Sed." His home—Chicago; his birthplace Elizabeth City, N. C. Yessiree—he's a down souther.

A champion is a fellow who gets licked two or three times a week, and keeps right on calling himself a champion.—*William Muldoon.*

Leedy's best advertising is the praise of its products by the thousands of satisfied users. It is to them that Leedy owes its present success!

•

The Lovely Emily Gage

Charming, lovely and talented Emily Gage, shown here with her recently acquired Leedy Octarimba, is a featured soloist and member of both the Roberts & Duffy Ensemble and of the Pasco Marimba Band which are constantly in demand in and around Jacksonville, Fla., for theatre, club, dance and other engagements in addition to playing weekly over radio station WMBR. Her teacher was Mr. Pasco Roberts, who is also director of the Roberts & Duffy Ensemble with which organization she has been for the past two years. She is delighted with the Octarimba's colorful tone and splendid volume and says, in part: "- - well satisfied with the new Octarimba. . and think ALL Leedy instruments are the finest." Her husband is her business manager.

WORLD'S FINEST DRUMMERS' INSTRUMENTS SINCE 1895

Leedy Drum Topics

Bill Harty and Director Ray Noble

Ray Noble came from across the pond, and assembled a nifty band here to tickle the music palates of the American public with a brand of rhythmic melody that found instant favor with his listeners. Featured on the Coty hour over the NBC network and at the Rainbow Room in NYC, he has won wide acclaim for his splendid work. Shown with Noble above is W. G. (Bill) Harty, Noble's business manager and rhythm-disher-outer with the band. Harty's birthplace is Waterford, Ireland, and he has played drums for twelve years—six of them with Noble and the last four on nothing but Leedy. And Harty certainly knows how to use them!

Temple Block Clamp

No. 7200 — FOR TRAP CONSOLE, TRAP TABLE, TRAP RAIL AND HOOP ADAPTER

Strong, light and durable, and ideally suited for the job. Fits any size temple block up to 8" diameter.
No. 7200—Nickel $0.75
No. 7202—Chromium 1.25

Bass Drum Temple Block Holder

For use on bass drum hoop when only one or two blocks are needed. Strong, rigid and adjustable for position. Strong STAY ON clamp.

No. 7660—Nickel $1.25
No. 7662—Chromium 1.90

No. 7660

NOW! Finer CHEE FOO Temple Blocks Than You've Ever Seen or Heard Before!

Only the best blocks of the finest unlacquered Korean importations are accepted by us so faulty materials and workmanship can be detected and rejected. Blocks are then filled, sealed, tuned to correct tone intervals and lacquered with the finest American lacquers in our own factory. Only in this way can we assure you of the finest and most perfect Temple Blocks on the market today.

Chee Foo Temple Blocks have that weird, deep and mysterious tone that is so desirable in many of the modern rhythmic numbers. In glossy black, bright red and rich gold lacquer, they present a splendid appearance, too. Played with half-hard rubber mallets (Leedy No. 1704), these blocks will give you complete satisfaction in every respect. The Leedy trademark on temple blocks is your definite guarantee of superior temple block quality.

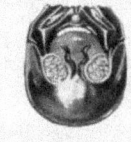
No. 7640
4½"
$2.50

No. 7641
5"
$3.50

No. 7642
5½"
$4.00

No. 7650
Complete set of 5 blocks
$18.00

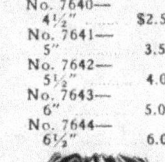

No. 7643
6"
$5.00

No. 7640— 4½" $2.50
No. 7641— 5" 3.50
No. 7642— 5½" 4.00
No. 7643— 6" 5.00
No. 7644— 6½" 6.00

Temple Blocks finished in a combination of any three lacquer colors of your choice per set .... $4.00 EXTRA

No. 7644
6½"
$6.00

In 1892, Leedy introduced the first thumb screw rods for snare and bass drums—a vast improvement over the old type cast claw hook rods and rope tension type, and a forerunner of the present key tension rod.

George G. "Red" Jackson with Ace Brigode and his Virginians

George G. (better known as "Red") Jackson is now playing his third year with Ace Brigode's popular MCA aggregation which has "wowed" the customers wherever it has appeared. First saw the light of day at Venice, (Calif.) and has been caressing the calfskins for the past twenty-two years, having started his career at an early age. Played with Freddie Rich for one year; with Lloyd Huntley three years and with Ernie Caldwell at the Granada Cafe in Chicago for three years. Vaudeville and musical comedy work claimed his attention for five of the twenty-two years too. Shown with Ace Brigode and Jackson above is Red's 100% Leedy outfit which includes *everything*. Of his outfit he says: "Twelve years using Leedy speaks for itself." Yes, it does, Red.

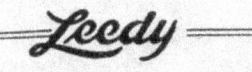 WORLD'S FINEST DRUMMERS' INSTRUMENTS SINCE 1895

The Exclusive Drummers' Paper

The Relation of the Rudiments To Modern Drumming

A "straight-from-the-shoulder" article on the WHYS of the rudiments in drumming by a well known professional drummer, instructor and author, Leon Knapp of the Knapp-Poole Music Company, Leedy's exclusive dealer in Grand Rapids, Michigan.

New Cow Bell and Cymbal Set-Up

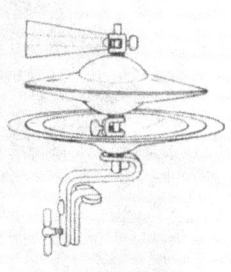

LEON KNAPP

First, in writing this article, I have but one desire in mind and that is that I might bring to a closer understanding, the rudimental drummer and the so-called jazz or modern drummer. Each, in his own field has much to be desired. It is furtherest from my thoughts to belittle in any way the clowning and jazz antics of the exponents of modern drumming.

The ability to hold a tempo must always be the drummer's first consideration. To accomplish this, the left hand must be trained as well as the right. To be explicit, to play a drum properly, one must acquire a balance of speed and power in the hands. A sluggish left hand is very often the cause of many other ills in Modern Drumming. The action of one's foot on the drum pedal depends largely on the speedy analysis of a given figure and trained hands to properly execute it. A fast right hand will invariably cause "rushing the tempo" in the simple passages and a sluggish left hand, a tendency to drag in the more intricate figures. Having produced a great number of students, now playing professionally, and many of whom are now nationally known, I speak with experiences of a great many years in stating that the commonest fault with drummers, at least in the United States, is their inability to play anything from hand to hand. The first thing a student must dispel from his mind, is the erroneous idea that there is more than one correct way to play a drum. The rudiments are as fundamental to drumming as the alphabet is to the study of language. The natural rhythm of the body compels the left arm to swing in unison with the right foot, as in the most natural of all exercise, that of walking. Is it then sensible to expect perfect co-ordination of the left hand and right foot without that balance of speed and power, which only the perfected execution of rudiments can give?

Let's for a moment, consider style in drumming. This surely is the drummer's greatest asset as the drummer always has and always will be in the spotlight, due to the necessity of physical action in drumming. Here again the rudiments play an important part. The execution of the short rolls from hand to hand throw the body and arms in a graceful movement of rhythm.

Surely no drummer can afford to overlook this one angle alone. Due to the very nature of a drum and the fact that a student will, with a natural bent for rhythm, do much without the aid of a teacher, causes him to overlook the rudiments without the knowledge of which he can never play with the freedom and grace and true artistry of the schooled drummer. The execution of the single paradiddle on tom toms of different pitch serve as an excellent example of the adaptability of the rudiments to modern music.

The writer having trained many Drum and Bugle Corps and drum sections of the major High School Bands in Michigan, has had many an amusing experience with the Jazz Drummer who occasionally substitutes for the rudimental drummer. On the street, the "any way to get it Drummer" is a pitiful sight to behold, with rolls running overboard, no style and very little co-ordination of the feet. Here again is the result of the sluggish left hand. Let me repeat here that the Jazz Drummer is the man of the hour and no amount of belittling of his many gifts will deter his popularity one iota. It is my contention only, that the employment of the rudiments must necessarily facilitate style and ease of playing, to say nothing of originality, which is of great importance.

Thirty minutes practice a day on a practice pad will prove all my statements. The short rolls practiced slowly and open is a sure fire remedy for too much pressure which one must eliminate to acquire ease of playing which is so closely related to style that is only present in the thoroughly relaxed body. Hand to hand practice of the better known rudiments will give the student undreamed of technique.

To my many friends in the United States, and I hope in England, I wish to state in conclusion that my hat goes off to the modern drummer and may he find his rightful place in the sun, as he well deserves. To this end, I have been prompted to write this article, that I might inspire those in their first years of experience, to combine the qualities of the old school drummer with those of the new and be of greater service to the profession in general.

Here's a novel idea for a set-up of choke cymbal, sizzle cymbal and cow bell: Use a Leedy Stay-On hoop adapter No. 7670. Use a 12" or 14" Chinese cymbal on the bottom, cup down, with a 10" American Brass cymbal on top, cup down. Press the cymbals together and hold them in place with the Leedy cow bell clamp No. 7220. Use two regular Leedy 10" American brass cymbals facing them cups opposite just above this. Hold them together at the desired pressure with the Leedy cow bell clamp No. 7220, and fasten into the clamp cow bell No. 7797. This is an ideal set-up for different cymbal effects where space is limited.

$2.00 award to L. B. Anderson, 1742 Parker Ave., Indianapolis, Indiana.

Little Miss Ruth Richards

Only nine years old but an accomplished xylophonist, little Miss Richards is a prominent member of the Kansas City Toy Symphony and has appeared as xylophone soloist at the Rockhill Theatre and radio station WLBF in Kansas City, as well as at other theatres and radio stations, during the past two years. She studied xylophone under Wm. Drew, tympanist with the Kansas City Philharmonic. Her instrument is a 4½ octave Leedy Solo-Tone Marimba-Xylophone.

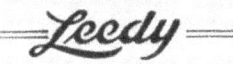 WORLD'S FINEST DRUMMERS' INSTRUMENTS SINCE 1895

Leedy Drum Topics

John F. Williams — CBS Staff Artist

One of the most interesting, as well as one of the most difficult, drumming jobs in existence is that of staff drummer with one of the major radio networks because it calls for a most thorough knowledge of the business, a broad all-inclusive background of experience, adaptability and a maximum of versatility. Williams, shown here with his Leedy Broadway, has been a CBS Staff Artist in the New York studios for the past three years playing programs under such conductors as Mark Warnow, Freddie Rich, Leith Stevens and others. Prior to his present berth played with such leaders as Leo Reisman, Vincent Lopez, Jacques Renard, Arnold Johnson, Meyer Davis and other equally well known top-notchers.

A New Rhythm Stunt for Orchestra Bells

Take four of your bells, the largest possible, that will comprise the tonic chord of the key in which the particular number is written. Lay these bells on the felt covering of your trap table beating out your rhythm as on temple blocks, using a Leedy No. 1712 three-quarter hard Green rubber mallet.

$2.00 award to Jack Morrissey, 4 Wyman St., Worcester, Mass.

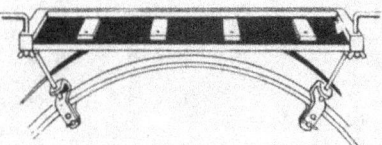

New "Lick" for "Jam" Numbers

Secure an ordinary rubber fly swatter, that may be purchased at a 5 & 10c store. Using just one swatter, strike the head of the bass drum with the swatter so that the part of the rubber that is least flexible, which will be the butt end, will strike the head first causing the flexible end of the swatter to fall with a sharp slap. This can be used in conjunction with a straight four-beat with the wire brush or drum stick on tom tom or snare drum. It may require a little practice, but, as explained above, it will be found ideal for "rides."

$2.00 award to Craig M. Westlake, 817 Oby Place, N. W., Canton, O.

•

Did you know that the late Mr. U. G. Leedy, founder of the Leedy Mfg. Co., designed and placed the first Muffler Snare Strainer on the market?

•

All-Adjustable Bass Drum Tone Control

"It's a Wow!"
Fully Adjustable for PRESSURE and for POSITION on the head!

No. 7874
$2.25
in Nickel

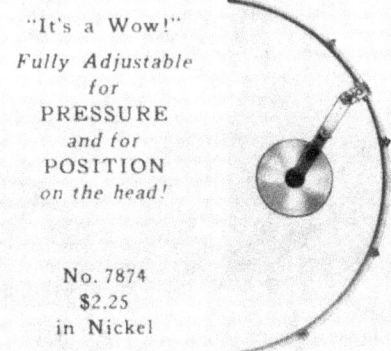

The best on the market. Has 6-inch disc with thicker muffler-pad and non-marring Stayon hoop clamp. New stiffer spring prevents disc from "jumping" away from head. Disc moves in an arc for desired position on head and the "pressure adjustment" feature permits any desired amount of pressure on the drum head for just the desired drum tone.

No. 7874—In Nickel $2.25
No. 7875—In Chromium 3.25

Johnnie Werner, Casino Guild Orchestra

Werner has been with the Casino Guild Orchestra for the past three years during which time he has played such well known Detroit spots as the Cascades, the Everglades, Fair Star Inn and La Plaza Cafe—the latter place an eighteen month engagement. Before tempoing his present band, Werner rhythmed bands under Bert Milan, Johnny Vidor, Leonard Seel and Freddie Zierer. Born in Detroit, studied under Selwyn Alvey and Dave Bach, and has been in the profession for seven years. His equipment is 1,000 percent Leedy and says of it: "Since appearance and performance are essential to the modern drummer (as well as durability), count on me to use Leedy's."

New Bass Drum Pedal Cymbal Effect

While most of the dance drummers are not using pedal cymbals, take our tip and dig out that old pedal cymbal and holder and try this one: Take an ordinary wire brush, fasten it to the cymbal striker on the pedal, adjusting the cymbal so that nothing but the wire part of the brush will strike. This is more effective if a 10" thin, high pitch Zenjian cymbal is used in place of the ordinary 10" American brass.

$2.00 award to C. R. Albea, 2434 S. Main St., Winston-Salem, N. C.

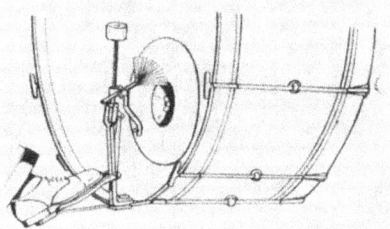

WORLD'S FINEST DRUMMERS' INSTRUMENTS SINCE 1895

Leedy Octarimba

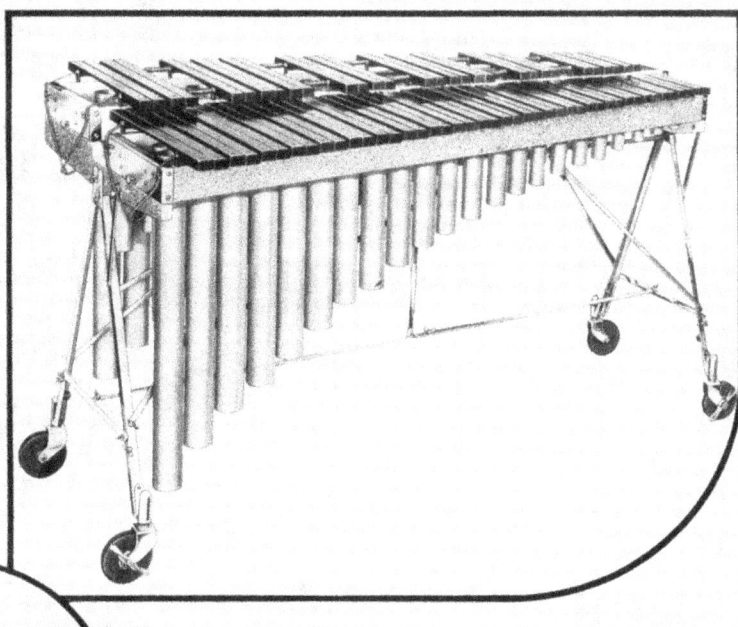

WHY the Octarimba Is Essentially Different!

The essential difference between the Octarimba and other wood-bar instruments lies in the fact that each playing note of the Octarimba is really composed of two bars of the same size, tuned an octave apart, which are struck simultaneously with specially designed double-headed forked mallets. Thus, the lowest double bar on the Octarimba is a combination of C-28 and C-40 tones on the piano keyboard, the C-28 being the lowest note of our largest 5-octave marimba. (See chart in Leedy catalog.) In other words, two bars act as one as far as playing is concerned, giving a 1-octave tonal range when only one note is struck. With this bar set-up the lower three octaves of the 5-octave marimba and the lower three octaves of the 4-octave xylophone are combined into one instrument with a 3-octave playing range and sounding as a 4-octave tonal range. The ordinary 3-octave xylophone or marimba has 37 bars, while the Octarimba boasts 74 bars, with an individual resonator under each bar properly designed to give the best tone and maximum volume.

Only two mallets are used on this instrument to get the effect ordinarily requiring four hammers, with the result that it can be mastered even by a novice in a very short time. Anyone now playing Xylophone or Vibraphone with multiple hammers will find this a "snap" by comparison.

The Octarimba Offers a Fascinatingly Beautiful, New and Wider Spectrum of Tone With Which to Color Your Music, and Gives You a Richness of Expression That Has Never Before Been Possible With a Wood Bar Instrument . . .

This recently introduced amazing, new and exclusive Leedy instrument is the only musically correct Marimba-Xylophone ever made because the full, resonant speaking voice of the marimba is *actually combined* with the higher and more brilliant playing timbre of the xylophone *in the same playing octave on one instrument*.

Never before has there been a wood-bar instrument to equal the Octarimba's eloquence, sympathetic response or latitude of expression!

The Octarimba is a legitimate musical instrument in every respect and can not in any way be considered as a novelty for, while it is still comparatively new, there are already a number of these instruments being used by prominent drummers and xylophonists both as accompanying and solo instruments in their regular concert, radio, stage and dance work. Few instruments have enjoyed the immediate, widespread and enthusiastic reception in a short time as has the Octarimba.

Bars of genuine Honduras Rosewood tuned by the exclusive Leedy patented process which eliminates all discordant overtones, and mounted on suspension cord to permit free, full tone. Sparkling Silver pyralin on split frames; split aluminum resonators in satin finish and adjustable to meet all atmospheric conditions. Strong, rigid stand chromium plated and highly polished, and two of the four solid rubber wheels are equipped with brakes.

No. 5602—3 Octaves, combined C-28 and C-40 to combined C-64 and C-76, 74 Bars 1 3 32" Wide by $3/4$" Thick. Length 61". Width at Lower End 31". Height 34". Weight 82 lbs. $240.00

5 Pair Assorted Octarimba Mallets Included.
Choice of Other "Full Dress" Pearl, Sparkling Pyralin or Duco Finishes on Wood Frames No Extra Charge. 10 Days Required for Delivery.

No. 6974—3 Fibre Hand Carrying Cases or Octarimba $60.00
Octarimba Trunk Made Specially To Order

Leedy Drum Topics

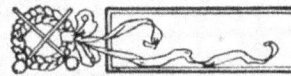

String Bass Effect

Place a sheet of music or any fairly heavy paper over the head of your large tom tom, beating out your licks on the paper and tom tom with wire brushes. This is much more effective if the paper is placed directly on the tom tom heads and not on cloth. Paper can be held in place with 2 strips of adhesive tape.

$2.00 award to Billie Edwards, 621 N. 9th St., Walla Walla, Wash.

Wm. Stirzaker of Preston, England

It has been our pleasure to have had some very interesting correspondence with Mr. Stirzaker during the past several years and we are happy to introduce him to Drum Topics readers at this time.

Mr. Stirzaker learned drums under Drum Major Jos. Taylor, 4th Loyal North Lancaster Regiment, and has been a drummer for twenty years. He has had wide experience in cinema orchestra pits and is now playing with Bert Flintoff's Prize Dance Band, and with the British Legion Military Band which is called upon to play at all the important local functions. Among other great musical directors, he has played under Mr. Fraser and Mr. Donner during his career. Of his Leedy drums and tympani Mr. Stirzaker says: "Great!", and adds that he has found perfect satisfaction with them in every respect.

To Match Your Broken Drum Head

The next time you break a head on a drum that thoroughly suits you—snare or batter, bass drum or tympani—cut the remaining parts up into sample pieces that will fit in your pocket. Use the sample when choosing a new head. By doing this you will stand a better chance of getting the drum back to where it was before in respect to tone and "feel" under the sticks. *From DRUM TOPICS No. 14.*

Gilbert Webster, Drummer with Jack Hylton's Famed English Orchestra Is 100% Leedy Equipped

Jack Hylton's orchestra, top notch on the British Isles and famous on several continents, has as its drummer none other than Gilbert Webster who has been with that organization for the past six years during which time he has played two Royal Command performances and every type of radio, concert and vaudeville playing. For ten years prior to playing with Hylton, Webster played with concert and military bands and with symphonies. Was born in Bradford (Eng.), studied drums under Freddie Power, and has been in the profession fifteen years. Has used Leedy instruments for six years and says of his present Leedy outfit which is EXCLUSIVELY Leedy: "Have tried every make of instrument in Europe's finest band, but find Leedy is the only make that can stand the playing strain and excessive travel."

The "X-L" Pedal Beats the Tempos For America's Foremost Big-Name Orchestras

Some splendid pedals have been put on the market, but none has enjoyed the popularity and praise that the famous Leedy "X-L" Pedal met with immediately upon its introduction to the drum world. It is the sensational "hit" of all times, and was adopted by more high-class professionals during its first year on the market than any other new model ever made because it has everything that Drummers demand in a pedal ... the utmost in speed—feather ease in action—no faltering—no friction—no side strain—and no "stiff spots" anywhere in the travel of the beater rod. Just clean-cut, smooth response without any extra effort whatever. It is scientifically designed and precision built of only the finest materials. The uprights and footboard are of cast aluminum. This facilitates speed of action, and makes it light in weight. The ball and socket principle in the beater shaft is a new departure in pedal mechanism giving that easy "foot flow" and perfect balance that has made this the greatest of all pedals. There are no delicate working parts to get out of order—everything is sturdily constructed so as to give long and satisfactory service. The tension spring can be adjusted to satisfy the particular "feel" that you like best. All the usual adjustable features, such as beater rod, cymbal striker and spring tension, are also incorporated. Finished in baked Black Duco, highly polished aluminum footboard and nickel metal parts.

No. 7010

No. 7010—
Pedal in Black Duco and Polished Aluminum, Without Spurs and Cymbal Holder $10.00

No. 7014—
Pedal in Black Duco and Polished Aluminum, With Spurs and Cymbal Holder 11.50

Leedy — WORLD'S FINEST DRUMMERS' INSTRUMENTS SINCE 1895 — **Leedy**

The Exclusive Drummers' Paper

To Protect Temple Blocks When Packing Them

Obtain three pairs of extra heavy woolen socks. These may be secured from the average 5 & 10c store. Put each block in a sock and pack in your trap case as usual. The socks will prevent your traps and holders packed with the blocks from marring and nicking them during transportation.

$2.00 award to T. Rutkowski, 6712 Fleet Ave., Cleveland, O.

Jack Ledingham—Popular Detroit Radio Artist

One of Detroit's finest and most popular drummers is Jack Ledingham shown in the accompanying photo. Staff artist with radio station WJR of that city for the past seven years under the stick of Benny Kyte. Ledingham has made a splendid name for himself in his present capacity and attained wide prominence for his excellent xylophone work and solos on the air. Formerly played with Leon Barzin and tickled the calfskins in several theaters in the Canadian Paramount circuit. Also served several enlistments in various Canadian Army bands. Born in Sunderland, England, at the opening of the present century, and studied drums under Sergeant Poole—evidently while in the army. Ledingham's present outfit includes Leedy drums, tympani, chimes and xylophone of which he says: "The very best." The above photo was taken in Detroit's WJR studios.

Al Derrick, Paterson, N. J.

Tympanist with the Paterson, (N. J.) Symphony Orchestra under the baton of Victor Durbin and featured drummer with Johnny Russo's aristocratic Alps Castle Dance Orchestra for the past three years, and previous to that time with Warner Bros. RKO Pictures, playing vaudeville the length and breadth of these U.S.A., and head of his own Xylophone with the stock company of Wm. Tilden II, the tennis star, Derrick has a wide and varied background which places him in the ranks with the finest. Started his career 24 years ago as Drum Sergeant over 30 drummers in his school's Fife and Drum Corps of 105 pieces, studied drums and tympani under the famous Carl Glassman, and xylophone under Geo. Hamilton Green and Wm. Dorn, and now has his own studio in Paterson which is his birthplace. Uses a 1,000 percent Leedy outfit.

Geo. Lawrence Stone, famous Boston drummer who conducts the country's largest drum school at 61 Hanover St., Boston, Mass., is now offering a new book of drum technique (not rudiments) which will definitely improve one's drumming by a series of exercises for the sticks. Any drummer, regardless of what type of work he does, will benefit by using this book. It is called "Stick Control" and has the endorsement of many leading drummers as being unique in the field and a very wonderful means for improving a drummer's ability. Those interested in this new text may secure it by writing to Mr. Stone direct at the address mentioned above. The cost of the book is $1.50.

White Pyralin Mallets

The finest bell and xylophone mallets made. As nearly "clickless" as it is possible to make mallets and guaranteed not to break. Seven-eighths hard White Pyralin balls with stiff cane handles — the genuine Friscoe models that are the favorites of the nation's finest professionals.

No. 1707—1" Balls, per pair $1.25
No. 1706—1⅛" Balls, per pair   1.50

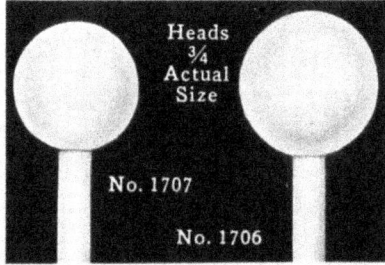

Did you know that Leedy originated the first drum stand, making the first ones for the market in 1898? Drummers used chairs for drum stands prior to that time.

When the going gets tough . . . that's when we like it.
—Knute Rockne.

Achille D'Amico

Though only eighteen years of age, Achille D'Amico has played tympani for the Newark Civic Opera Company for the past four years, and also is a very capable drum instructor in the Newark Public School System. He was born in Newark and studied drums under Edward Rubsam, Sr. Has been in the drumming fraternity for the past seven years and has used Leedy equipment all that time and says: "Leedy's is the finest drum equipment obtainable." His Leedy tympani, he says pridefully, are at least twenty-five years old, and still going strong.

Leedy — WORLD'S FINEST DRUMMERS' INSTRUMENTS SINCE 1895 — **Leedy**

17th NATIONAL AMERICA[N]

ST. LOUIS, MO., SEPTEM[BER]

FINALISTS IN THE AMERICAN LEGION NA[TIONAL]

1st Place — NATIONA[L]

San Gabriel, Calif., Post N[o.]

2nd Place

Germantown (Phila.), Pa., Post No. 3. Score—96.31.

3rd P[lace]

Commonwealth Edison Post No. 1[1]

5th Place

Herbert F. Ackroyd Post No. 132, Marlboro, Mass. Score—94.84.

7th Place

"Les Combatants" Post No. 69, Malden, Mass. Score—94.41.

9th Place

East Orange, N. J., Post No. 73. Score—93.92.

10th Place

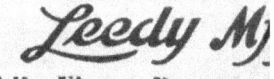

Harvey W. Seeds Post No. 29, Miami, Fla. Score—93.38.

FREE — Leedy Drum Corps Service — FREE

The Leedy Drum Corps Service Department—made up of men who merit your confidence through their many years of actual experience as professional drummers in every field of music—is at your service at all times in any problem or question that may arise in Drum Corps procedure or work from time to time. Whether it is a question of the proper size drum or cymbal, a technical question in the use of an instrument, Corps instrumentation, contests or judging—these men are always ready and glad to serve you promptly, efficiently and without charge or obligation. Their knowledge and experience is yours to command. Write as freely and as often as you wish—it is their desire to help you in all matters pertaining to Drum Corps and Drum Corps work, procedure and routine.

Leedy Building

Leedy M[fg.]

"The World's Finest Drummer[s]"

AN LEGION CONVENTION
EMBER 23rd to 26th, 1935

NATIONAL DRUM CORPS CONTESTS

CHAMPIONS—1935

Post No. 442. Score—96.39.

4th Place

Morristown, N.J., Post No. 59. Score—94.96.

d Place

No. 118, Chicago, Ill. Score—95.91.

6th Place

Hamon Gray Post No. 83, LaPorte, Ind. Score—94.53.

8th Place

Anderson-Dunn Kochis Post No. 42, Stratford, Conn. Score 94.03.

12th Place

Elyria, Ohio, Post No. 12. Score—92.95.

11th Place

Bonnie Sloan Post No. 28, New Albany, Ind. Score—93.18.

Mfg. Co., Inc.   Elkhart, Indiana

"mers' Instruments Since 1895"

FREE — Leedy "Roll-Off" No. 3 — FREE

The Outdoor Drummers'
Encyclopedia of Information and Equipment

The finest and most valuable text of its kind ever published—tells how to start your own Drum Corps, suggests instrumentation and ways and means of raising funds for equipment, gives valuable pointers in every phase of Drum Corps work, explains military and contest terms, contains splendid inspirational matter and shows pictures of many of the country's leading Corps. Also shows the most complete line of the finest Drum Corps equipment made. 72 pages. Profusely illustrated. Mailed free to your Post on request, without obligation. Also, if you are interested in organizing a Junior Drum Corps, request the new free Leedy Junior Drum Corps brochure just published.

Leedy Drum Topics

New Era Cymbal Holder

No. 1862

An improved wood handle cymbal holder that will not permit the cymbal to work itself loose and yet permits maximum vibration of the cymbal for the fullest, finest cymbal tone. Cymbal is fully cushioned between two thick felt washer pads and held most securely by a newly developed slotted post bolt which is drawn tight to the wood handle by a long screw which passes through both the wood handle and the cast aluminum handle post. Post will not turn or loosen. Adjustable strap for secure hand hold on handle. Sold in pairs.

No. 1862—Per pair $2.50

Lambs Wool Covered Cymbal Straps and Pads

Pads No. 1856
Straps No. 1857

The oldest, but still the finest and most practical, cymbal holding device made is the strap and pad combination. Here it is vastly improved for greater comfort. Both horsehide straps and pads have a generous, soft padding around them and are then covered with a fine quality lambs wool which prevents knuckle bruises, gives a firm, soft grip for the hands and yet permits the fullest, finest tone from the cymbals. Ideal!

No. 1856—Pads, per pair $2.50
No. 1857—Straps, per pair 1.50

2-Way Drum Practice Pad

Ideal for practice purposes. Has two playing sides—a rubber side for silent practice and a fibre side for loud practice. Both are inclined at the proper playing angle. Will not creep under strong beating, and is sturdily built of best materials.

No. 1755—Practice Pad $2.75

No. 1755

Fibre Side   Rubber Side

Preliminary Drum Corps Contest
17th National American Legion Convention, St. Louis

Following is a complete list of drum corps that competed in the Preliminary Drum Corps Contest at Walsh Stadium, St. Louis, on Wednesday, September 25, 1935. How they placed in the preliminaries, the corps' names, their scores and the order of their appearance on the field is indicated below.

PLACE	CORPS AND CITY	SCORES	Order of Appearance
**	Marlboro, Mass., No. 132	1934 Champions	23
1	San Gabriel, Calif., No. 442	93.83	35
2	East Orange, N. J., No. 73	93.75	43
3	Stratford, Conn., No. 42	92.87	48
4	Morristown, N. J., No. 59	92.81	38
5	LaPorte, Ind., No. 83	92.75	55
6	Commonwealth Edison No. 118, Chicago	92.50	14
7	Philadelphia, Pa., No. 3	91.72	3
8	New Albany, Ind., No. 28	91.35	47
9	Malden, Mass., No. 69	91.27	21
10	Elyria, Ohio, No. 12	91.02	36
11	Miami, Fla., No. 29	90.54	5
12	Board of Trade, Chicago, No. 304	90.46	32
13	Aberdeen, S. Dak., No. 24	90.35	18
14	Lima, Ohio, No. 96	90.07	53
15	Evanston, Ill., No. 42	90.07	27
16	Massillon, Ohio, No. 221	89.95	6
17	Victory Post No. 7, Chicago	89.80	20
18	Racine, Wisc., No. 76	89.67	24
19	Cape Girardeau, Mo.,	89.55	31
20	Square Post No. 232, Chicago	89.40	50
21	Joplin, Mo., No. 13	88.82	34
22	Park Ridge, Ill., No. 247	88.78	13
23	Chicago Police Post, Chicago, No. 207	88.75	46
24	Logan, W. Va., No. 19	88.35	22
25	Galva, Ill., No. 45	88.10	39
26	Danville, Ill., No. 210	87.92	9
27	Dorchester, Mass., No. 65	87.90	16
28	Spokane, Wash., No. 9	87.82	26
29	Biddeford, Me., No. 26	87.80	17
30	Emporia, Kans.	87.62	51
31	Wilmington, Dela., No. 1	87.52	8
32	Oak Park, Ill.	87.00	54
33	Dubuque, Ia., No. 6	86.95	41
34	Jefferson City, Mo., No. 5	86.55	52
35	Brookville, Ind.	86.47	28
36	Louisville, Ky., No. 15	86.15	49
37	Peoria, Ill., No. 2	86.01	37
38	Port Arthur, Texas, No. 7	85.67	44
39	Cheyenne, Wyo., No. 6	85.35	42
40	Indianapolis, Ind.	85.25	40
41	Jackson, Miss., No. 1	84.87	25
42	Waterloo, Ia., No. 138	84.85	19
43	Lincoln, Nebr., No. 3	84.32	29
44	Bartlesville, Okla., No. 105	84.15	15
45	Auburn, Nebr., No. 23	83.52	1
46	Cincinnati, Ohio	83.47	4
47	Greensboro, N. Car.	83.42	45
48	Okmulgee, Okla., No. 10	83.37	7
49	Memphis, Tenn., No. 1	83.32	11
50	Cleveland Heights, Ohio, No. 104	83.12	12
51	Ashville, N. Carolina, No. 2	82.32	30
52	Fargo, N. Dak., No. 2	81.80	10
53	Rhinelander, Wisc., No. 7	81.67	2
54	Jacksonville, Fla.	80.82	33

**By virtue of the fact that the preceding year's National Championship Drum and Bugle Corps automatically is eligible for the Finals, the Marlboro, Mass., Corps was not scored in the preliminaries but appeared on the field for the required five minute preliminary drill.

WORLD'S FINEST DRUMMERS' INSTRUMENTS SINCE 1895

The Exclusive Drummers' Paper

A Crown and Laurels for Individual Drummers at Legion Convention in St. Louis

Left to right: Jas. S. Whitelaw, Miami, Fla., Post No. 29, who annexed the 1935 National American Legion Individual Drumming Championship with a score of 93.13; Emile Cote, Old Orchard, Me., Post No. 57, who was second with a rating of 93; and H. R. Todd, Chicago, Ill., Post No. 118, whose 92.7 score earned third place for him.

The Show Boat, beautiful St. Louis ballroom, rang with the thunder of the drums as eighteen of the nation's finest exponents of the drum rudiments competed for the National American Legion Individual Drumming Championship during the 17th National American Legion Convention. When the final contestant unslung his drum and the final tabulation of the scores was announced, Jas. S. Whitelaw, Miami, Fla., Post No. 29, was declared the new National Champ with a score of 93.13; with Emile Cote, Old Orchard, Me. Post No. 57 runner-up with a score of 93, and H. R. Todd, Chicago, Ill. Post No. 118, third with a rating of 92.7. The contest took place on Monday, Sept. 23, 1935.

Legion Band Contest Results

Winners of the American Legion Band Contest held on Wednesday, September 25, 1935, during the 17th National American Legion Convention in St. Louis were, with their scores:

1st—Chicago Board of Trade	90.80
2nd—Columbus, Ohio	87.80
3rd—Omaha, Neb.	85.48
4th—Mineral Wells, Texas	69.06

A Bit About the Big Parade

A huge throng, variously estimated at from 225,000 to 275,000 persons, witnessed the 17th National American Legion Convention parade held in St. Louis on Tuesday, September 24, 1935. There were, by actual count, exactly 224 musical units in the parade of which 169 were drum and bugle corps and the balance bands. This does not include drill teams or comedy units of which there was the usual run. The parade lasted from 9:15 a.m. until 6:05 p.m.

It's an extraordinary man who hits the bases whether the umpire is looking or not.—*Elbert Hubbard*

Individual Bugle Contest

The individual Bugle Contest held during the 17th National American Legion Convention in St. Louis was run off simultaneously with the Individual Drum Contest but in another part of the city. Due to the fact that there were two contestants tied for second place with identical scores and the final official decision was not publicly announced either at the close of the contest or during the convention itself, Drum Topics cannot publish their pictures at the time this edition goes to press. However, according to the information just received from the Official Contest Committee as this publication goes to press, Jas. A. Mason, Instructor of the Evanston, Ill. Post No. 42 Drum & Bugle Corps is the 1935 National Bugle Champion. His score was 97.23. Ray Rausch, Evansville, Ind., and Col. W. R. Buehler, Norwood, O., were tied for second place with scores of 96.73 and E. Goudeg, Hamtramck, Mich., annexed third place with a score of 96.4.

Drum Rain Slicker of Finest Oiled Silk

You can see the drum through this new rain slicker and it is considerably more durable than the rubber type cover. For wood hoop drums, an adjustable metal band that extends around inside of counter hoop to hold cover tight against batter head is used. Metal retaining band may be left on drum inside of wood counter hoop when not in use. Metal retaining band is not used on metal counter hoop drums. Thoroughly waterproof and practical in every respect. Will save its cost in broken drum heads many times over. Light and can be folded without injury and carried in pocket when not needed. Please mention both shell and overall size of drum when ordering.

No. 1838—Rain Cover (with metal adjustable head band) $4.00
No. 1839—Rain Cover (without metal band) 3.00

Music Lyre For Street Drum

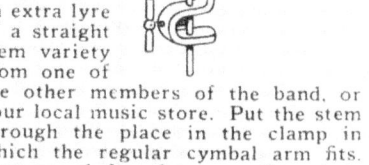

Take the clamp part of a Leedy No. 7518 Stay-On Non-Swing cymbal holder. Fasten this to the batter side counter hoop of your street drum. Secure an extra lyre of a straight stem variety from one of the other members of the band, or your local music store. Put the stem through the place in the clamp in which the regular cymbal arm fits. Very good for those wanting their music fastened to their instrument.

$2.00 award to Jacob Schwenot, Jr., 14 Jersey St., Trenton, N. J.

 WORLD'S FINEST DRUMMERS' INSTRUMENTS SINCE 1895

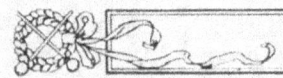
Leedy Drum Topics

Roxanne, "Radio's Foremost Lady Orchestra Leader" and Samuel Brief

Brief, one of NY's finest drummers, is now playing with the swanky Joe Moss orchestra under the direction of Alex Drasein in NYC's classy Vanderbilt Hotel and adding one more attraction to that famed hostelry's drawing powers—a swell band doing a swell job in a swell way with an A-1 calfskin artist supplying the rhythms!

Previous to his current engagement, Brief supplied the swing for the music of Raxanne and her Broadcasting Orchestra under the personal direction of that lovely lady of the air lanes on such outstanding radio commercials as the "Woodbury Hour," United Cigar Stores Program, Herbert's Diamonds, I. Miller Shoes, Five-Boro Taxis and the Ybry Perfume program.

Brief was born in Brooklyn about thirty years ago, and has been in the profesh for nearly seventeen years. His equipment is 100% Leedy and doing alright for him in his important, outstanding engagements.

Why "Matched" Cymbals Should NOT Match in Tone

Many drummers who request a "matched" pair of cymbals do not understand the true meaning of that phrase. They believe that a "matched" pair should consist of two cymbals with approximately the same pitch and tone. This is exactly what they should NOT be. Matched (or mated) pairs of cymbals should consist of one cymbal HIGHER in pitch and tone than the other so that when the two cymbals are struck together there is an even greater multiplicity of tones than could possibly be obtained from any one cymbal alone. This is the result that is DESIRED in cymbals.

While the above may be confusing on the surface, it is readily understood by those who have studied musical history because they know that from the time of the most primitive savage the tom toms, wood blocks, castanets, tambourines and (later) gongs and bells have been used in pairs to represent the male and female voices—the larger, lower toned instruments representing the male voice and the smaller, higher pitched instrument the female voice. It is on this principle that music was founded.

New Cymbal Set-Up

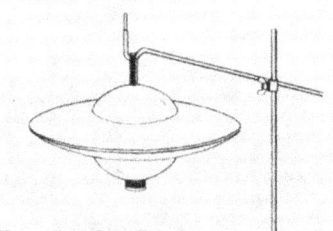

Use the Leedy No 7585 arm cymbal holder with two Leedy deep cup 10" cymbals (Cat. No. 7450) suspended face to face, or cups opposite, with the regular cymbal strap No. 7600. It will be necessary to lengthen the strap to accommodate the extra cymbal. This gives you a real hollow plop cymbal tone if choked with the left hand when struck or can be used as a sizzle cymbal if hit without choking. Very good for "ride" choruses.

$2.00 award to Harold Firestone, 921 Prairie St., Elkhart, Ind.

Vic Berton

According to our last information from him, Berton has started out with his own band under the management of Irving Mills—and with him goes our heartiest best wishes for success in all his undertakings.

Berton, though still a young fellow, has nearly thirty-five years of excellent experience to his credit in the profession with such well-known leaders and organizations as Whiteman, Vorrhees, Lanin, Lyman, the Chicago Symphony, Arnold Johnson, Earl Carroll, Roger W. Kahn, Nichols, CBS, Paramount Studios and pictures, RKO Music Hall Center, Roxy, and all the major Hollywood studios, and 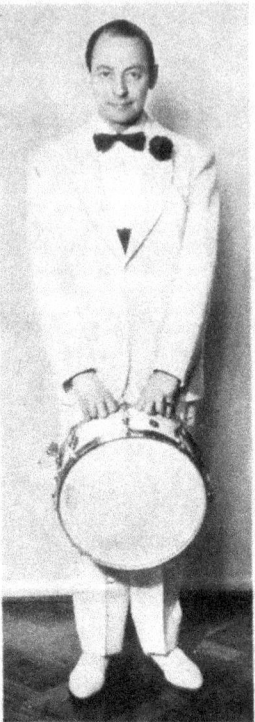 many more too numerous to mention —his last show engagement being with Dowling's "Thumbs Up." With Berton now is his 100% Leedy outfit. Has used Leedy for 34 years.

●

Interesting Bits About Fellows You Know

George Marsh, of many famous radio broadcasts and former drummer with Paul Whiteman, does a strenuous three times a week gym routine that keeps him in first class physical trim . . . Master Sgt. Wm. D. (Bill to most of you) Kieffer of U. S. Marine Band fame has retired from active service with a pension after twenty years service with that splendid outfit . . . Dick Brucato is doing a column of real merit in the *Orchestra World* . . . Rudy Van Gelder doing ditto in the same magazine under the heading "Our Rambling Reporter" . . . the famous Green Brothers, George Hamilton and Joe, to demonstrate the Leedy mallet played line in the east, *but more of that on page 21 of this issue of DRUM TOPICS.*

 WORLD'S FINEST DRUMMERS' INSTRUMENTS SINCE 1895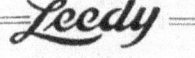

The Exclusive Drummers' Paper

To Pack Your Trap Table

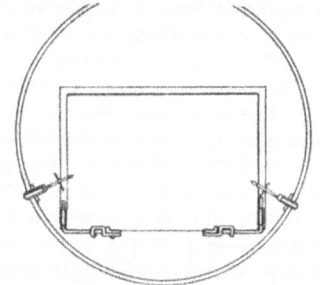

Nearly every drummer in the past has experienced difficulty in finding a convenient place in which to carry his trap table. Here is an idea that will solve this problem: Place your trap table against your bass drum head, top side in. Secure it at each end by reversing your spurs so that the ends point in to the center of the bass drum locking the trap table in place. The bass drum can then be put in your Mackintosh bag or fibre case, insuring protection for both table and drum. This is a good stunt, particularly if your snare drum case is not large enough to accommodate your trap table, and on the other hand, you will have more room in your snare drum case for other items.

$2.00 award to W. A. (Mike) Chumbler, New Holland, Georgia.

Guillermo Galilea, One of Spain's Outstandingly Fine Drummers

In that ancient land which has had such a definite influence on the present music of the entire western world is an outstandingly fine drummer whom we are glad to introduce to our Drum Topics readers as one of our 100% Leedy users. He is Guillermo Galilea of San Sebastian, Spain, playing with the Good Star Orchestra under the direction of Juan P. Heredero which recently finished a nine month engagement at the Casino de la Playa, and which is the popular orchestra of the finest clubs, hotels and casinos in that section, and over EAJ-8-Union Radio station. Senor Galilea was born in San Sebastian, studied under D. Vega, and has also played in the band of the Infantry Regiment No. 7, and in the San Sebastian Municipal Band. Notice his up-to-the-minute Leedy outfit!

May Fluhmann, Montreal Philharmonic Orchestra Tympanist

This is May Fluhmann who for the past eighteen months has done an enviable job as tympanist for the Montreal Philharmonic Orchestra which gives year around concerts in the Salle Doree concert hall of the Mount Royal Hotel under the direction of Mr. Eugene Chartier, and which are broadcast over radio station CKAC in Montreal. She was formerly assistant tympanist for the St. James Orchestral Society, was born in Roberval, Quebec, Canada, and received her training from Mr. Louis Decair.

Jim Davidson and his own A. B. C. Dance Orchestra

Jim Davidson and his A.B.C Dance Orchestra, for which Davidson does both the directing and the honors at the drums, hold an envied top position in excellence and popularity among Australia's theater, radio, recording and dance bands. Davidson has been drummer-director of this band for the past eight years which is at this time staff band in the Australian Broadcasting Commission studio in Melbourne and has, in the past, presented its music via the air from radio stations 2UE and 2UW, on the Union Theatres Circuit, at the Palais Royal, Oriental Cafe, Palais-de-danse, Ambassadors Cabaret and on Columbia records. Davidson's unusually complete equipment is 1,000 percent Leedy and was supplied through W. H. Paling & Co., Ltd., Sydney, New South Wales, Australia, by Mr. W. Dibley. Davidson has used Leedy equipment for the past twelve years!

For Tambourine Trills

Secure an ordinary rubber thumb cap as used by bank clerks, etc. Use the rubber cap on the thumb with which to trill the tambourine. It may be advisable in some cases to put a little packing in the bottom of the cap, such as gauze or cotton. You will find this much more satisfactory than wetting your thumb, which is necessary sometimes in obtaining the desired results.

$2.00 award to Geo. Burnwood, 922 E. Godfrey Ave., Philadelphia, Pa.

Let us be thankful for fools. But for them the rest of us could not succeed.—*Mark Twain*.

Leedy — WORLD'S FINEST DRUMMERS' INSTRUMENTS SINCE 1895 — **Leedy**

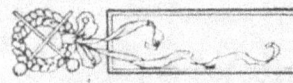 # Leedy Drum Topics

"DIRECT ACTION" Wood Sock Cymbal Pedal

Fast, smooth, sturdy and reliable, here, at last, is a low-priced Sock Cymbal Pedal that will give more service and greater satisfaction than any other cymbal pedal in its price class.

The outstanding features that will recommend this pedal to value-conscious drummers are: footboard works on a sturdy bearing rod and pivot yoke arrangement that will far outlast the spring-hinge type pedal; lower cymbal attaches to a pivot yoke which assures perfect self-alignment of the two cymbals at all times; direct-action for effortless operation; cast aluminum heel-plate to which is anchored the adjustable tension spring which controls the action of the pedal —tighten it for stiff action and loosen it for easy action to your own liking.

Standard and footboard are of seasoned hardwood finished in black lacquer, and "creeping" and slipping of the pedal is prevented by non-skid rubber "feet." Heel-plate is cast aluminum and spring adjustment nut is nickel plated. Pivot yokes supporting the lower cymbal and footboard are lacquered black.

This pedal has been approved and acclaimed by discriminating drummers after long use, and abuse, on the job. Ask your dealer to let you see it and to try it—you'll like it and the price will suit you, too!

No. 7568
(less cymbals)
$4.50

FEATURES
"Direct-Action" Foot Stroke
Adjustable Spring Tension
Self-Aligning Cymbals Mate Perfectly—Always
Footboard Works on Sturdy Bearing Rod
Will Not "Creep" or Slide
Solid, Sturdy, Rigid and Fool-proof
Maple Footboard and Standard
Aluminum Alloy Heel-plate

No. 7568—Wood Sock Cymbal Pedal (does not include cymbals) $4.50

CYMBAL RECOMMENDATION
Two Leedy 10" Deep Cup American Brass Cymbals (Cat. No. 7450 at $1.25 each) are recommended for deep, hollow squash effects, or two Leedy regular 10" American Brass Cymbals (Cat. No. 7440 at $1.15 each) for a higher, less hollow cymbal tone.

About the "DIN PILE" and the Producer of "DIN"

Written by Serge S. Fockler, Lima, O., a Leedy Drummer, for "Tune Times," a modern musical magazine published in London, England, and printed here with Mr. Fockler's and "Tune Times" permission.

SERGE S. FOCKLER

"Four in a bar, with a heavy accent on two and four." This demand, while a bit humorous, seems to be the hue and cry of the modern dance orchestra leader. While there is no doubt that this is the "fullest" way to play drums, if this style is used over a prolonged period it does become quite irksome.

On jam choruses it appeals to me as being quite all right, especially so when the number is being "flashed up" with *all* the possible fullness of the ensemble. However, there is a great deal more to artistic percussion than "four in a bar" work.

The real artist drummer of to-day must possess both physical and mental personality, and naturally the possession of these qualities makes him a highly developed piece of sensitive mechanism. He cannot have a single track mind; he must develop himself to the highest degree in flexibility; he must be an expert "salesman." The co-ordination of all his faculties, as well as his muscles must be instantaneous.

Every musical organization has a peculiar style of its own, and the "artist drummer" must be able to blend and fit into these various styles, enhancing and embellishing their tonal pictures to a nicety, contributing finesse for the ensemble as a whole.

Since drums are basically rhythmic and dominant, I think it would behoove *all* rhythm sections to rather "lean" or lay stress, on the percussion section, as all the percussion work should be "solid" and "positive." By being this way, it becomes individualistic.

After it's all said and done, it takes years of concentration and conscientious effort to become an individualistic artist drummer, and I might add that real ones are as scarce as the proverbial hen's teeth. I trust the above statement will not seem too pessimistic or discouraging, but it is true. The sooner the young drummers coming on realize that plenty of effort and study is required in order to become proficient, the sooner all leaders and musicians will look up to the percussionist and will recognize that he is the greatest asset in the entire ensemble.

According to my idea, there are three men in the modern dance combinations that the artist drummer subconsciously "feels," "senses," or listens to, as it were. These three are the piano, chordist (guitar or banjo) and first trumpet. The artistic drumming of to-day is composed of "licks," and syncopation that must be felt or sensed through the melody or lead. Naturally, the artist drummer must originate these "licks" and "flourishes," thus adding finesse and fire to the numbers. The so-called "hot numbers" to-day couldn't be what they are without modern artistic interpretation, employing a liberal quantity of technical embellishing.

Modern bands demand modern instruments, evolution has taken place in this field as surely as it has in all others. There was a time when everyone "in the know" thought the 3" by 14" wood shell orchestra drum, equipped with wire snares, was the last word in fine instruments. This drum had snap galore, and was very easy to "roll" upon, but it gave way to the 5" by 14" size. The sales for this style of drum were tremendous. Now it's an accepted fact that the ideal size for general orchestra work is the 6½" by 14". This size drum is sensitive enough, as it seems to be a general certainty that the best leaders to-day do not want a small drum to cut through the ensemble too much. The 6½" by 14" has a more professional appearance.

As a whole, the present day fine artistic drumming is very much subdued, representing the perfect background for the tonal setting. For the roundness of tone needed for this background effecting the necessary solidity desired in small orchestra drums, my preference is the 6½" by 14".

Then there are times when one wants a tom-tom or a dead drum effect, and this is entirely lost on a narrow-shelled drum. When giving a 6½" by 14" everything you have, in other words, for tremendous roll, you will find that this drum will take it without choking, which cannot be truly said of the smaller instruments.

Relative to drum finishes, I believe the American drummer was the first to realize the importance of fancy pearl and gold outfits, because he realized that the eye plays a big part in the modern dance orchestra. Appear-
(Continued on Page Twenty-three)

 WORLD'S FINEST DRUMMERS' INSTRUMENTS SINCE 1895

The Exclusive Drummers' Paper

Frank M. Hood Pursued By the Law

It was funny the way it happened. Frank M. Hood was returning home late one night after a concert of the North Carolina Symphony orchestra in a nearby city. He carried two tympani—drums—in the back of his car. As he rolled leisurely along, the lights from a car behind shown in upon the bright copper bowl of one of the drums, the cover of which had blown off.

After a while it occurred to him that the car behind had been trailing his for miles. With a little feeling of alarm, he wondered why. To test the correctness of his surmise, he stepped on the gas and sprinted for a mile. Just as he thought, the other car stayed close, and, finally, overtook and pulled in front of his, forcing it to a halt.

Two deputy sheriffs stepped out and ordered him out of his car. He complied, looking more than a little out of place out there on a country road in his Tuxedo. Flashing their badges, the officers demanded, "What's that you've got on the back seat there?" Gladly he showed them, even explaining how the drums are used in a large orchestra. They seemed satisfied, and said goodbye.

But—Mr. Hood had gone almost a mile before he realized that those officers had thought they were trailing a moonshiner moving his blockade outfit to a new location. — *From the Greensboro (N.C.) Record dated June 24th, 1935.*

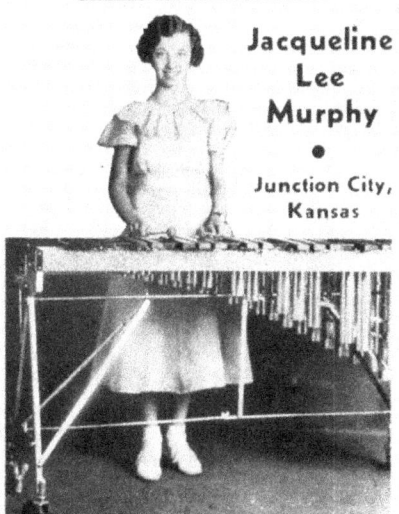

Jacqueline Lee Murphy

Junction City, Kansas

Although only thirteen years old, Miss Murphy has played with the Junction City H. S. Orchestra for the past year, has played for civic clubs and organizations and has appeared as guest artist with the Municipal Band a number of times. Studied under Chas. Moorman, and is very, very pleased with her Leedy Mellorimba.

Merle Evens, Director, with Paulson and Thompson

The next time you see the world famous Ringling Bros. and Barnum Bailey Circus band you'll know, after reading this, and seeing the photo above, that it's Merle Evans who's directing, and that Henry Paulson and Amos Thompson are at the bass and snare drums respectively—that is, unless you see a third drummer who is likely to be genial George Way, Leedy Sales Manager, who has, no doubt, bribed Merle and Amos to let him "set in" for the performance which he *has done on occasion (and Ye Ed has seen him)*. Anyway, the circus is a swell show, the band is a great outfit and the boys pictured here are regular fellows, and you can take it from the writer that watching these boys work on the drums with Director Evans leading and hitting them higher and with more power than any cornetist in the business, is worth the price of admission to the big-top even without the three ring features.

About Striking Cymbals

(Reprinted from Issue No. 17 Drum Topics)

On straight crashes, it is the type of blow rather than the force that breaks a cymbal. The "whip" blow is severe and dangerous because the contact of the stick is too sudden to allow the cymbal to give. The "push" blow is less likely to cause harm but it does not bring out the proper tone. The safest and best is the "glance" blow. A "glancing" blow not only brings out the best cymbal tone, but can be used with more force than either of the two blows mentioned in the first part of this item.

●

When you call upon a thoroughbred, he gives you all the speed, strength of heart, and sinew in him. When you call on a jackass, he kicks.—*Selected.*

Paul DeDroit

When last heard from, DeDroit was playing with Walderman Guterson's Orchestra in the Orpheum Theatre, Los Angeles where that organization had been playing for one year. Has played with Rubinoff's Orchestra on the Chase & Sanborn Coffee Hour from the Hollywood NBC Studios, in the Fox Studios, the Paramount Theatre in Los Angeles, Grauman's Chinese Theatre, Hollywood, done sound for "Flip The Frog" cartoons, played with Scott Bradley's Hollywood Orchestra, and made recordings with Johnny DeDroit's Okeh Recording Orchestra. Was

born in New Orleans, studied drums under George Peterson, and has been in the profession fifteen years. Has played Leedy's for fifteen years and is 100% Leedy equipped now—ample proof of what he thinks of the "World's Finest Drummers' Instruments."

A New Set-Up for Low or High Sock Pedals

The regular Leedy American brass 10" deep cup cymbal, No. 7450, is used on the bottom of Hi-Hat sock cymbal pedal. On the top use either a 10" and 11" fairly thin Zenjian, or two 10" Zenjian cymbals inverted, or cups opposite. Use the regular top supporting clamp for the support of one cymbal, or the Leedy No. 7220 cow bell clamp. Different effects can be obtained by adjusting the two top cymbals with the wing nut on top.

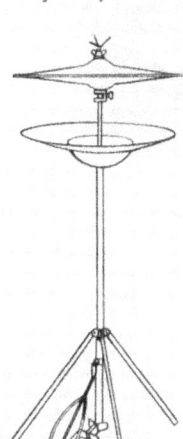

$2.00 award to Geo. A. Eastwood, 82 Exeter Ave., Pawtucket, R. I.

The next time you play a job, look at your outfit as critically as an audience does!—then take steps to do something about it.

 WORLD'S FINEST DRUMMERS' INSTRUMENTS SINCE 1895

Leedy Drum Topics

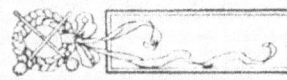

Everett Dunbar

Although only eighteen years old, Everett Dunbar, St. Joseph, Mo., has played marimba for eleven years. At eight, was hailed as a musical prodigy after several theatrical performances. Has filled many theatre, concert, radio and dance engagements, and is at present Staff Artist with radio station KGBX, plays with the Collegians, school orchestra and is teaching his own pupils. His equipment is 100% Leedy and includes a Leedy Solo-Tone Marimba with which he is shown in the above photograph. The photo and information about Everett were supplied through the courtesy of Mr. E. C. Miller, Eshelman Music House, St Joseph, Mo., our dealer in that city.

Put Handles on Your Large Chinese Tom Toms

How many of you have picked up a regular Chinese tom tom of the large variety by the carrying ring only to have the carrying ring let loose and the tom tom go rolling down the street? Here's a way to get around that and at the same time make the tom tom more convenient to carry: Go to your local hardware or dime store and purchase one or two regular screen door handles (not the knob type). With the screws supplied, fasten these to your tom toms.

$2.00 award to Chas. H. Acton, 4815 Winthrop St., Indianapolis, Ind.

The Last Word In The Instrument Originated by Leedy

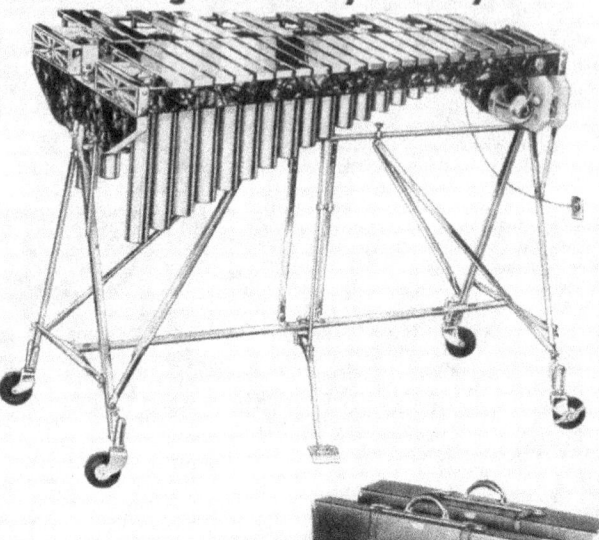

NEW IMPROVED STRONGER STAND Than on former models

The Leedy Lightweight Vibraphone, originally invented and perfected by Leedy, is the finest instrument of this type on the market. Its sweet, pulsating tone and ample carrying power in even the largest halls has made it so well known that little description is needed here. Materials, construction and workmanship are the very finest. Made in a choice of 2½ or 3 octaves, sturdy and rigid, the instrument is easily and quickly set up or knocked down, and packs in two convenient fibre hand carrying cases.

No. 5655—3 Octaves, C-40 to C-76, 37 Bars, 1½" to 1¼" Wide, by ½" Thick. Length 44". Height 35". Weight 67 lbs. Finished with "Full Dress" Black Pearl on Wood Frames, Chromium Plated Stand and Polished Aluminum Bars and Resonators $295.00

No. 5656—2½ Octaves, C-40 to F-69, 30 Bars, 1½" to 1¼" Wide, by ½" Thick. Length 38". Height with Wheels 35". Weight 62 lbs. Finished with "Full Dress" Black Pearl on Wood Frames, Chromium Plated Stand and Polished Aluminum Bars and Resonators $270.00

Instructor and Four Pair Mallets Included.
Following Finishes on Special Order---10 Days Required.
Choice of "Full Dress" Pearls, Sparkling or Duco Finishes on Wood Frames---No Extra Charge.

No. 6925—2 Hand Carrying Cases for 3 Oct. 103 lbs. packed $45.00
No. 6926—2 Hand Carrying Cases for 2½ Oct. 87 lbs. packed 40.00

Clean Cymbals

And about cymbals! Every drummer uses them but few ever take the time to keep them clean and bright-looking—and bright cymbals DO add flash and beauty to an outfit in much the same way as the finish and plating on your drums do. A little Bon Ami and a soft dampened cloth with a bit of work will do wonders. Don't use more than a minimum of water as it is the fine abrasive quality of the Bon Ami under friction that polishes.

To Clean Nickel

Ordinary whiting rubbed over nickel plated metal parts with a soft, dry cloth will bring out its full brilliance and not harm the plating in the process. Do NOT wet the powder or the cloth, but use absolutely dry. If the nickel shows rust specks, you may need a harsher abrasive nickel polish, but for nickel in good condition, whiting will turn the trick. Whiting can be bought from any drug store and is very inexpensive.

Leedy — WORLD'S FINEST DRUMMERS' INSTRUMENTS SINCE 1895 — **Leedy**

 *The Exclusive Drummers' Paper*

Special Music Arrangements by George Hamilton Green

DRUM TOPICS takes pleasure in announcing that George Hamilton Green will make special arrangements of any and all types of musical selections for two, three or four hammer playing for xylophone and piano accompaniment and that he will make special full orchestration arrangements of any modern or standard music numbers for band or orchestra use in radio, dance or concert rendition. His fees will be reasonable and based on the type of work required. Full information and estimates will be cheerfully and promptly supplied by George Hamilton Green himself by addressing him at 44 West 77th St., New York City, N. Y.

The Famous Green Brothers— World's Greatest Xylophone Artists

(See photograph on Front Page)

The first DRUM TOPICS back in 1923 (yes, this is DRUM TOPICS' twelfth birthday) featured the renowned Green Brothers as the "World's Greatest Xylophone Artists," and almost every issue between that and the present No. 25 DRUM TOPICS has carried accounts of each succeeding triumph that has been theirs during these years. While others rise to stardom only to fall back to obscurity again, these two lads continue to rise in fame and to remain supreme. Today, more than ever before, they ARE among the world's finest in the field.

Featured artists on too many of the finest and most popular radio commercial hours on the major national chains to mention here, headliners in all their stage appearances wherever they may be, their recordings always among the best sellers, authors of several of the most widely used xylophone instructors ever published, and constantly in demand for private instruction, the Green boys are probably the hardest working fellows in the profession. In addition to this George Hamilton Green has an outstanding reputation as an arranger of all types of music for use as xylophone and piano accompaniment and for full orchestrations for band and orchestra use in radio, dance, theatre and concert work. Work? They eat, sleep, dream and live it, because they LIKE it and that, after all, is one of the basically necessary ingredients for success in any field.

The Green Brothers' Opinion of Leedy Instruments Holds True Today In Even Greater Degree Than Then!

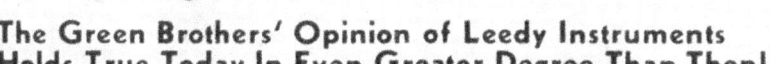

DRUM TOPICS No. 1, way back in 1823, featured the Green Brothers in its pages and quoted their opinions of Leedy instruments as reprinted below. The Green Brothers and Leedy instruments have risen to greater heights of leadership than any of us could possibly foresee at that time, but what the Green Brothers said of Leedy instruments at that time holds even truer today than it did twelve years ago!

Geo. Hamilton Green said:
"My many years as a professional xylophonist have naturally given me a chance not only to try different makes but I have owned many different brands and played extensively on them all. At present I have three of the Leedy manufacture, and there is not one point on any of these instruments that is not far superior to any other make, even including the hammers and cases. I am through experimenting and shall use Leedy exclusively in the future. My brother and self fully believe that the Geo. Hamilton Green Special is going to be the biggest selling xylophone the market has ever known." (This is the Leedy model (now called "Broadcaster") Nos. 5620 and 5621 on page 105 in the present Leedy Catalog "U.")

Joe Green said:
"My brother and I have been using Leedy xylophones and marimbas built by Leedy, for eight months, and I have given it very severe usage jobbing around New York and at all the phonograph studios. The instrument is making a bigger hit with me every day and I consider it far in advance of any xylophone I have ever used. The tonal qualities are exquisite and the appearance, general make-up, workmanship and detail are wonderful leaving absolutely nothing to be desired—the proverbial last word in xylophone construction. The Leedy Mfg. Co. is to be congratulated on its ability to manufacture an instrument that at last meets every exacting requirement." (This instrument is shown on page 105 of Catalog "U").

George Hamilton Green To Demonstrate Leedy Instruments Shortly

Without a doubt many DRUM TOPICS readers have heard the famous Green Brothers on the radio, bought their recordings or seen them in their stage presentations, but now you may have the opportunity to see and speak to George Hamilton Green in person in the near future.

Through recently made arrangements, George Hamilton Green will appear in person in the stores of some of the Leedy dealers to meet DRUM TOPICS readers, to give them pointers in xylophone playing and execution and to demonstrate the Leedy line of mallet played instruments including the Vibraphone and the recently introduced Octarimba which has received such an instantaneous and favorable reception wherever it has been shown and heard.

Detailed information concerning dates, dealers and cities cannot be given at this particular time inasmuch as Mr. Green's appearance in the various stores will begin shortly after the first of January, 1936, and be arranged in such a manner so as not to conflict with his 1936 professional playing engagements.

DRUM TOPICS readers in the vicinities of the stores in which Mr. Green will make his appearances will be advised by postcard or letter direct from the Leedy factory, of definite dates and places of his appearances. Look for these announcements and plan to see and visit with Mr. Green when he comes to your city. He'll be expecting you and you may be assured that your visit will be well repaid.

LOOK FOR ANNOUNCEMENTS!

Leedy — WORLD'S FINEST DRUMMERS' INSTRUMENTS SINCE 1895 —

Leedy Drum Topics

To Stop Cymbal Swing on Suspension Holders

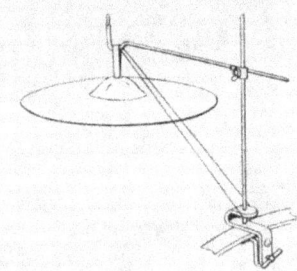

For those who prefer to use the suspended cymbal we dedicate this hint: Fasten a long, heavy rubber band between the bottom of the cymbal holder clamp and the crook part of the cymbal arm itself, and when the cymbal is struck for an open crash the rubber band will keep it from swinging up and hitting the metal arm. This will enable you to reduce the swing of the cymbal by permitting you to use a shorter thong for suspending the cymbal.

$2.00 award to Merle S. Burdick, of 213 Scranton Ave., Lake Bluff, Ill.

Under the Big Top with the Seils-Sterling Circus

Here's Director Art Hellar of the Seils-Sterling Circus Band with Ed Shampeau, bass drummer and Billy Todd holding the deep snare drum. Todd has been in the game twenty years playing circus, minstrel show, dramatic stock, vaudeville and dances. Has always used Leedy and says of the white drum he is holding: "... is 9 years old and still has the original batter head and it can still take it on hour and forty-five minute programs without a squawk. NUFF SAID." Todd's home town is Cedar Rapids, Neb. It IS Nebraska—that's no mistake!

Ornately Carved Giant African War Drums

Of never failing interest are these war drums of Africa. This one stands in the Trocadero Museum, Paris, a gift of General Dodds, and is an unusually fine specimen of fine carving. Of fine hardwood, this one is about eight feet tall and has large wood pegs near the top to which the head is fastened with leather thongs.

Ideal Auxiliary Tom Tom Stand

Use the Leedy No. 7265 Marvel Drum Stand. Fasten the arms that hold the snare drum in a horizontal position, adjusting the adjustable arm so that it is just a trifle smaller in size than the tom tom to be put in the stand. The Marvel Stand is made to grip the snare drum and if properly adjusted, as explained above, will hold the tom tom snugly in place.

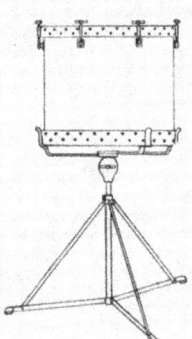

$2.00 award to Everett Conway. En Route—

New Tone Control For Bass Drum

Secure one or two bunion plasters in the large size. Stick these to the bass drum head just at the spot where the pedal ball strikes. You will have to experiment with one or two plasters, one on top of the other, until the desired results are obtained. You will find this to be particularly effective and fine for soft playing over radio if the felt type ball (Leedy Cat. No. 7066) is used on the pedal.

$2.00 award to Wm. Alexander, 308 Lenox Ave., Oneida, N. Y.

Robert R. Perry

Playing with Columbia and Pathe Studio orchestras in Hollywood under Lou Silvers and C. Bakaleinikoff respectively during which time he worked on the sets with Grace Moore. Perry now makes his home in the Golden State. Previously was with Earl Burtnett, Gus Arnheim and Jimmie Grier and played 27 weeks on the Franco Hi-Jinks program which was piped nationally by CBS from station KHJ. Was born in Algoma, Wisc., and saw America from a bus window for MCA. Has played Leedy for 10 years and is 100% Leedy now. Says: "There is a reason for the added, patented features on Leedy drums—they make them the world's best."

IDEAS! IDEAS! IDEAS!

DRUM TOPICS pays $2.00 for each idea printed under the "New Idea" heading of which there are three on this page. If YOU are making good use of a novel idea, stunt or trick, are using some standard trap for a different effect or have devised some little gadget that is useful in your playing—why not submit it to DRUM TOPICS Editor so it can be passed along to the rest of the fraternity? In this way you will not only be helping your brother drummers, but will profit $2.00 cash for each idea that is printed.

WORLD'S FINEST DRUMMERS' INSTRUMENTS SINCE 1895

The Exclusive Drummers' Paper

The "Din Pile"—

(Continued from Page Eighteen)
ance of the instruments used is not overlooked in this country. Americans are particularly fond of display, and "flash" seems to be one of the basic demands in the blood-stream of all our showmen, and surely the artistic drummer is one of America's greatest showmen.

I rather surmise that the general impression afloat among English drummers is that the American drummers are millionaires. This idea, I assure you, is quite an incorrect one. Our problems over here are quite similar to those encountered by the general run of English drummers. Possibly the only slight advantage we may have is in the great number of automobiles available. Naturally, this tends to simplify our transportation problem. As for the automobiles, you know most of them are not paid for in full until they are almost worn out, so don't let their presence mislead you.

Bands here have been known to jump from three to four hundred miles between engagements. Here the automobile does play an important part. Orchestras here have travelled all night from the close of one engagement to the next, affording but a few hours' sleep in between rehearsal and another performance at the new location. These jumps are exceptional, for which we are thankful. But when even a two hundred-mile jaunt tires the musicians considerably—it's grim humor to watch these bands pile out of the autos in a worn-out condition and then go immediately to the various hotels, "catch" two or three hours' rest, bathe, and then come on the job, seemingly in pink of condition, and play a marvelous job.

A "trouper" must be physically fit at all times, it's certainly no job for a weakling.

I believe the American drummers, as a whole, are not as fine musicians as the English drummers. Neither is the American drumming much better than the English drumming, collectively speaking. This, I believe, is due to the natural tendency of Americans to hurry up and rush. In doing so, they slip up on some of the fine points and rudiments which mark the difference between schooled artistry and self-made proficiency.

A point not to be overlooked is figuring the remuneration of artist drummers. One of the things to be considered is the fact that they have a bigger investment in their musical equipment, and that they are constantly forced to add to their outfits from time to time. In view of this fact, I sincerely believe they are entitled to more money. Do you agree with me?

Edwin Franko Goldman Made "Chief Bugle" of Pawnees

The occasion of this picture was the adoption of Dr. Edwin Franko Goldman, Director of the Goldman Band, by the Pawnee Indian tribe at Pawnee, Okla., last spring during the Third Annual Tri-State Band Festival which was held at Enid, about sixty miles away. Here he is shown being welcomed into the tribe by Chief "Bacon Rind" after the title of Chief Bugle had been bestowed upon him together with the headdress denoting his rank. The pale faces shown in this group at Pawnee Bill's Hut, Old Town, Pawnee Okla., are, left to right: Wm. McClarin, Frank Lewis, of Paul Bennett Music Co., Tulsa., A. A. Harding, Director, University of Illinois, Herb Gutstein, C. G. Conn Ltd., Geo. H. Way, Sales Manager, Leedy Mfg. Co., Chief Bugle, Chief Bacon Rind, Pawnee Bill (Maj. Gordon W. Lillie), Dick White, H. N. White Co., and Paul Bennett, Paul Bennett Music Co. Mr. Harding and Dr. Goldman were among the band judges at the Band Festival.

Sidney Hambro

One of the well known jobbing drummers in and aroung Boston is Sidney Hambro whose professional career includes playing with Jacques Renard, Meyer Davis, Dok Eisenbourg, Sammy Liner, Roy Lamson, Ruby Newman and many others. Hambro has played drums for the past thirteen years, was born in Roxbury, Mass., studied under Meyer Sternburg, and now lives in Brookline, Mass., which is just outside of Boston. Has played Leedy drums during the past eight years.

New Rubber Grip For Wire Brushes

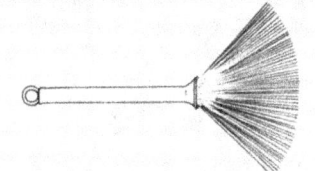

Secure a piece of rubber tubing at any drug store long enough to cover the entire handle of the regular Leedy wire brushes No. 1645 and 1646. Cut the rubber tubing so that it will be approximately ¼", or so, longer than the metal handle on your brush. Slip the tubing over the handle letting the additional length extend down over the handle and on to the wires of the brush. This makes the handle a little thicker and gives it a firm grip, and by letting the edge extend down over the end of the handle protects the head of the drum from the sharp edge of the wire brush handle.

$2.00 award to Danny Sansom, Box 653, Prince Albert, Sask., Canada.

Edward Andre

If you were to attend the Metropolitan Theatre in Boston tonight, you would see Edward Andre hard at work behind the drums under the direction of Fabian Sevitzky, and doing a swell job of it. Has had a wealth of experience in theatre and dance work, and is considered one of Boston's foremost drummers. Was born in New Bedford, Mass., studied drums under Arthur W. Geldard, and has been playing them for the past sixteen years or so. His equipment is predominantly Leedy and he writes that ". . . when better drums are made Leedy will make them." That's the way we feel about it, too!

Leedy — WORLD'S FINEST DRUMMERS' INSTRUMENTS SINCE 1895 — *Leedy*

Leedy
DRUM TOPICS

December, 1935   Number 25

Sec. 562 P. L. & R.
U. S. POSTAGE
PAID
Elkhart, Indiana
Permit No. 6

Leader: "What—no bird whistle? You're Fired!"

Leverette Owens,
Crawfordsville, Ind.

Postmaster: Return Postage Guaranteed.

Leedy Mfg. Co., Inc.
2311 Leedy Bldg.   Elkhart, Indiana

THE ROYAL COLLEGIANS MARIMBA BAND
Damon H. Shook, Director

That the marimba band is one of the most popular musical ensembles today, both because it is a deviation from the conventional and because of its all-embracing appeal, is proved by the sensation that the Royal Collegians Marimba Band creates wherever it plays. Made up of high school and college students who were taught and are directed by Damon H. Shook, every member plays saxophone and at least one other instrument with the result that the organization besides being a marimba band is a saxophone band and a dance band as well, and plays concert, radio, theatre and dance engagements the year around. Band is made up of twelve instrumentalists who live in Milwaukee and vicinity and uses four solo xylophones, three accompanying mellorimbas, three obligato marimbas, one Monarch bass marimba and one Grand marimba—all Leedys. Organized five years ago and is steadily gaining in popularity with ever-increasing demands for its services.

Leedy Drum Topics Issue 26

Leedy Drum Topics
JULY Issue No. 26 1937

Charlie Agnew and E. L. "Sock" Sockwell

A top-class drummer with a top-class band is "Sock" Sockwell who sets the tempo for Charlie Agnew and his ever-popular dance aggregation. Agnew, who has done time behind the drums himself, is shown here tickling out a tune on a miniature xylophone. "Sock" has played drums for the late Earl Burtnett, Joe Reichman, Ray Teal and others in some of the country's best spots during his fourteen years in the game. His home town is Greenville, Texas, way down south.

Frank R. Kutak

Below is a picture of Frank R. Kutak taken late last summer at Reading, Pa., during an engagement there of the famous Goldman Band under the able direction of the renowned Dr. Edwin Franko Goldman. Kutak has served with this splendid organization for the past seven years as snare drummer and is a past master in his profession as Dr. Goldman's drummers must be to hold their chairs. He's a loyal Leedy-ite.

Dave Monahan

Perched on a 6-foot stool and using both his hands and his feet to play "hot" six-hammer xylophone numbers, Monahan "wows" the customers in leading vaudeville houses on the RKO and other big time circuits with his highly entertaining, spectacular novelty act. Once a theatre pit drummer and xylophonist, Monahan got the idea for his act one day while he was sitting on the apron of the stage and tapping the toes of his shoes on his xylophone in the pit. Yes, it's the new Leedy Geo. Hamilton Green model xylophone he uses—with special display resonators. It's a "nifty."

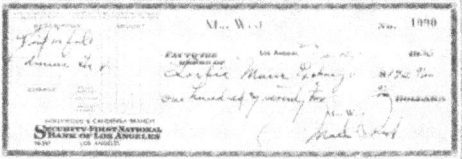

Leedy Drums Go West!

Mae West, buxom blonde siren of the cinema who has injected more "this-a and-a that-a" into films than any other actress, recently purchased a Leedy trap drum outfit from Bob Perry of the Lockie Music Exchange, Los Angeles. The use to which she will put the drums is not known definitely, but there's a story goin' 'round—well, skip it for the time, but anyway here's the check that proved she chose Leedys—and anything Mae chooses has to have what it takes, you know! Lucky Leedy drums!

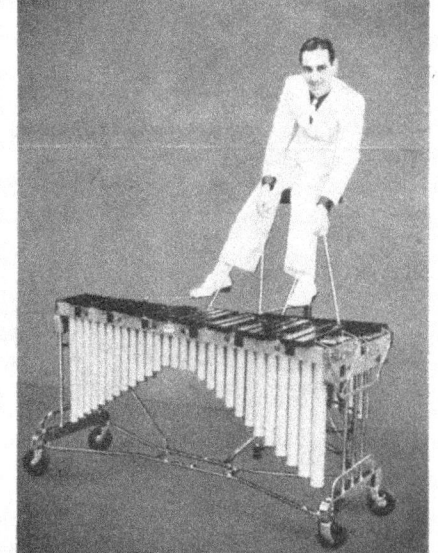

Charles Calkins and Leo Forbstein

You've heard this drummer and these Leedy instruments in many Warner Bros. First National Pictures even though you may not have seen them before. Leo Forbstein, Studio Musical Director for Warner Bros. First National, Los Angeles, is shown on the left looking at the snare drum held by Charles Calkins, who is a Warner Bros. Studio drummer, as he explains some of the reasons for the Leedy Broadway's superiority. The photograph was sent to us through the courtesy of Bob Perry who is in charge of the drum department of Lockie Music Exchange, Los Angeles.

George Beebe—Fred Astaire Johnny Green—Bob Perry

When Fred Astaire, star of R.K.O's "SWING TIME", does his world famous tap dancing on the famous PACKARD HOUR radio program, he is doing his stuff to music of the popular Johnny Green orchestra which is tempoed by George Beebe and his all-Leedy equipment. Included in Beebe's outfit are the new BROADWAY "SWINGSTER" snare drum shown above, bass drum, pedal, xylophone, Vibraphone, chimes and tympani. Beebe also plays with Victor Young on the Shell Oil Co. radio hour and with Jacques Renard on the Texaco Program, and has played with such outstanding bands as those of Meyer Davis, Roger Wolfe Kahn, Red Nichols, Paul Whiteman and others. Shown above (left to right) are George Beebe, Fred Astaire, Johnny Green and Bob Perry of Lockie Music Exchange.

Page 3

Johnny Johnson and Bob Treaster

Twelve of the twenty-one years that Bob Treaster has put in behind his Leedy drums and equipment have been spent with Johnny Johnson and his increasingly popular orchestra which recently finished a two year engagement in New York City's Commodore Hotel. Also made a year tour of Europe with Paul Specht's band. That's Johnson on the left.

Charlie Blake

Charlie Blake took over the drummer's chair with Mal Hallett's orchestra in '33 and has played most of the important theatres and every college and large ballroom in the east since going with that fine band. Blake was born in Patton, Pa., has played drums for 14 years (Leedys for the past two) and says his Leedys are the finest he has ever worked on. The band is now playing college dates.

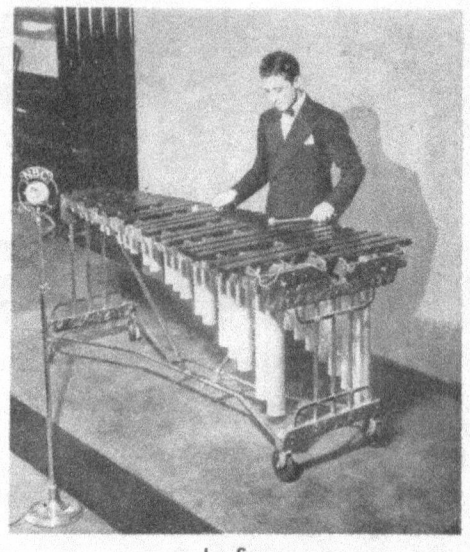

Joe Sorace

Nine of Sorace's sixteen years behind drums have been with Leedy equipment which now includes marimba, xylophone and chimes. He's now playing with Jess Hawkin's orchestra which is on tour playing popular ballrooms east of the Mississippi. Formerly played with Sammy Watkins and Ed Day. Was born in Morgantown, W. Va., studied under Fred E. Albright, another Leedyite and now calls Bedford, Ohio, his home. Says of Leedy equipment: "Wouldn't consider any other make."

Chas. E. Watts

Has played drums with the the Denver Symphony Orchestra for the past 8 years under the baton of Horace E. Tureman, appeared on radio stations' KOA and KLZ programs, and with the El Jebel Shrine Band. Is a native of Denver, and manages the drum department of Chas. E. Wells Co., Denver. Uses 100% Leedy.

Geo. Hamilton Green and a pupil, Miss Dorothy Spencer

The above picture was taken of Geo. Hamilton Green and Miss Spencer at the Music Supervisors' National Convention in New York last year. Geo. Hamilton Green, accepted as the world's finest xylophonist, and Miss Spencer, herself a top-notcher through study under Mr. Green's capable instruction, demonstrated the new Leedy mallet played line which was just being introduced and with which he and Miss Spencer are surrounded in the photo. In the background are shown other Leedy instruments in the display.

Paul De Droit and Leon Leonardi

A Leedy drummer since he started in the business twenty years ago, De Droit is now playing with the Warner Bros. Radio Station KFWB Staff Orchestra in Los Angeles, Cal., which played the Chase & Sanborn Coffee Program for 26 weeks over the NBC chain under the baton of Director Leo Leonardi with Rubinoff and his famous violin. Has played the best theatres in the south and southwest, done his stuff for the Fox and M. G. M. Studios and made sound effects for Scott Bradley "Flip the Frog" animated cartoons. Birthplace, New Orleans; 100% Leedy.

Harry Lindeman

Now playing a third indefinite engagement with Larry Becker and his band at the Hollywood Inn, Madison's (Wisc.) most popular night spot; toured entire west with Freddie Wilson's Golden Bears and the south and east with Paul Graham and his Crackers. Present band formerly with Fritz Miller at WBBM, Chicago. Born in Farmer City, Ill., played drums 15 years. Has been 100% Leedy for 14 years.

Jimmie Whitelaw and Dave Wallison

Whitelaw, a key drummer of Miami, Fla., doing theatre, radio and dance work, was American Legion National Champion Drummer in 1936 and is a mainstay in the famous Harvey Seeds A. L. Post Drum and Bugle Corps which was several times National Champion. Dave Wallison, at right, owner of Dave's Music Shop in Miami's Arcade, sold Whitelaw the Leedy outfit shown above. He plays trombone and was with Honey Boy Evans Minstrels at the same time that Geo. H. Way, Leedy Sales Manager was with that famous show when it was at its height in 1910-11.

THE FAMOUS DRUMMERS OF THE UNITED STATES MARINE BAND

Chas. Owen

Born Youngstown, O., started drumming at 12, played trombone and bassoon in Rayen High School and was 1st Bassoonist with the 1930 National High School Orchestra in Chicago. Joined Marine Band in 1934 and studied drums under Bill Kieffer, retired.

Oliver Zinsmeister

Born Rochester, N. Y., studied 8 years under Wm. G. Street, was 1st percussionist with Eastman School of Music and member of Rochester Philharmonic for 4 years. Also did xylophone solo and studio work at WHAM (NBC). Joined Marine Band in 1935.

John Auer

Has been with the band for about eighteen years and plays snare drum, bells and traps. Doubles on the violin in concert engagements which the band is called upon to play. A small drummer and a dandy fellow. Used to play alongside Kieffer.

Chas. Viner

Hails from Massachusetts, has been with the band for more than twenty-five years and is one of the most popular fellows in it. Known as one of the finest bass drummers in the business and is a valued mainstay in Capt. Taylor Branson's organization.

Frank Holt and Sousa Equipment

Frank Holt, Haverhill, Mass., one of the country's finest drummers, playing the finest jobs in eastern New England and owner of a drum shop in Haverhill, played with Sousa for many years and is shown here with some of the drums, traps and effects given to him by Sousa's family after the death of the March King.

Paul Hart

An all-Leedy drummer who has played the finest jobs in the southwest with Eddie Fitzpatrick's Jr. orchestra since 1931, says of his Leedy equipment: "... the finest precision in percussion instruments I've ever known."

Emil Farnlund—Marion Talley
Jos. Koestner—Wm. Gilcher

Emil Farnlund, Leedy drummer in the Hollywood (Cal.) NBC Studios, plays the national chain NBC RYE-KRISP program which features the lovely operatic Marion Talley. Jos. Koestner directs the orchestra. Wm. H. Gilcher, shown on the extreme right, a veteran Leedy drummer, is now Orchestra Manager of the Hollywood NBC Studios.

Warren Luce

According to word received with this photo of Warren Luce from Sherman, Clay & Co., San Francisco, Luce, a first-water, all-Leedy drummer, is playing with the popular Griff Williams and his versatile orchestra in San Francisco's hospitable Mark Hopkins Hotel. Luce played with Paul Whiteman for several months during one of the noted leader's famous N. Y. runs.

Percussion Section of the Fine U. of Iowa Band

This fine drum section of the capable and colorful 100-piece University of Iowa band directed by Dr. O. E. Van Doren is 100% equipped with Leedy instruments as shown in the above photograph. The band is a big attraction at all college games and is the pride of the Hawkeye state as well as of the school itself. In addition to this splendid marching band, the school boasts of an equally fine 75-piece concert band also under the direction of Dr. O. E. Van Doren.

Gus Helmecke

Gus Helmecke's photograph needs no introduction to old-time DRUM TOPICS readers for he is well known to them, but some of the younger generation drummers should know that he is truly the Dean of the country's bass drummers being both a veteran and an artist in the profession. He has played with most of the finest bands in the country and John Philip Sousa's death terminated a twenty-year berth which he had held with that splendid organization. Now he plays with Dr. Edwin Franko Goldman's famous concert band in the summer and with the Metropolitan Opera in the winter where he wields the beater with a style that is all his own and a beauty to behold. It is to Martin Snitzer of Philadelphia that we are indebted for this recent photo of Gus.

Dick Powell—Ray Paige—Earl Hatch

Again to Bob Perry of Lockie Music Exchange, Los Angeles, we are indebted for this intimate group picture taken in Hollywood. On the left is Dick Powell, the popular movie and radio star, whose voice and personality have made him a favorite with the whole nation, looking at Earl Hatch's new Leedy BROADWAY "SWINGSTER" snare drum. Hatch (holding the drum) is Swing Master with Ray Paige's orchestra which plays CBS programs originating in the Hollywood studios including the Hollywood Hotel and Standard Symphony Hour programs under the direction of Ray Paige who is shown in the center. Hatch's birthplace is Greeley, Colo., and he has played drums for the past twenty years—the last three of them with his present organization which is "tops" out on the coast.

F. J. Race

Old drums are always interesting. Below is one that was used in the War of 1812, on the Constitution and all during the Civil War. It is 17"x17", is made of ash, now has two Leedy heads, and a label on the inside states "Pittsfield Drum Shop, Est. 1794, A. D. Stevens, No. 103 North St., Pittsfield." F. J. Race, who sent us the photo, is shown playing a drum that was played at U. S. Grant's funeral by P. J. Race in 1885. The drum has been in the Race family since 1880. Race, a drummer since the age of six, played with the Co. F, Tenth Reg. Drum Corps from 1910 to 1933 and has played with the V.F.W. Post No. 1314 Drum Corps since 1934. His home is Hudson, N. Y.

University of Arizona

The splendid U. of Arizona band boasts one of the finest school percussion sections in the country. Shown above with its all-Leedy equipment (left to right) are: Edw. L. Breazeale, tympani, snare drum and all mallet instruments; Bacil B. Warren, tympani and snare drum; Sherrill Smith, bass and snare drum; Elsworth Fiscel, cymbals, snare drum and bass drum, and on the extreme right is Maurice F. Anderson, Ass't Professor of Music and Band Director at the University which is at Tucson.

Gilbert Webster and George Marsh

Webster, the all-Leedy drummer with Jack Hylton's famous English band struck up an acquaintance with another famous all-Leedy drummer, Geo. Marsh, when he was in New York a while back. Marsh is now on the west coast and Webster is back in London playing with the Hylton band. Marsh, we understand, is doing booking in Los Angeles and vicinity.

Phyllis Brownell

An all-Leedy drummer with Babe Egan and her Hollywood Red Heads with whom she has played vaudeville, radio and several pictures. Studied xylophone under Geo. Hamilton Green, was born in Allen, Neb., and now calls Los Angeles her home. Of her Leedys, she says: "Very fond of them—won't use anything else."

Walter P. Meyen

A topnotch drummer who has used Leedys for twenty years. Born in Omaha, Neb., studied under Geo. A. Smith, the Leedy dealer in that city, and is now playing under Waldemar Guterson in the Orpheum Theatre in Los Angeles. Played six years with the West Coast Theatres, with M.G.M. and Fox film studios and many other big jobs, with other fine orchestras.

Charlie Russ

Russ has supplied the rhythm for such well-known bands as those of Johnny Matzers, Stanley Hall, Eddie Minnich and Nelson Maple's S. S. Leviathan Orchestra. Above photo shows Russ (left) and Bill Kenworthy with whose orchestra he was on tour when heard from last. Russ's birthplace and home is Wilkes-Barre, Pa.

THE DRUMMERS' EASY ROCKIN' CHAIR

(Reprinted from the August, 1936, "DOWNBEAT" by permission of its publishers.)

Dean Stevenson, versatile all-Leedy drummer with Joe Sander's "Ducky-Wuckies," offers you drummers a simple symbol system for marking your tempos which will prove a great help to many of you. Below is the system and its full explanation.

Disproving the fact that drummers aren't musicians — Dean Stevenson, one of Joe Sanders' "Ducky-Wuckies", comes along with a symbol system that rightfully deserves international recognition and, to our mind, general adoption. If we had had some such system in our early vaudeville days and later on for musical comedy work, our biggest problem would have been easily solved. The actual headaches of leaders, pianists, trumpet players and drummers have never been estimated, but those aches which arise from the source of indefinite tempos alone constitute one of the biggest problems of the musician. In the old days of vaudeville, a half dozen or more acts were given inadequate rehearsal periods—a few bars were played here and there—a conception of tempo was nebulously understood for the moment, and perhaps some musician's hieroglyphic was placed on an already unmarked part of the score. The orchestra then proceeded to trust in God when the show opened, and it usually became the drummers' job to get in the groove on the first beat and set the tempo.

Popular numbers in the past, as they are at the present, were obviously murdered and every tempo under the sun was requested except that which the composer originally intended. After weeks of trouping the scores would be marked with characters understood by only the musicians who made them. To add to the general ambiguity of tempo symbols there were always numerous cues for the drummer written hurriedly (in every language but English)—"When man falls downstairs—gliss on xylo and drop c. b. or "In Love Scene—play very tacet." To all this confusion, acts in the old days, like those of the present, not only required the drummer, leader, etc., to hit the tempo on the nose but to actually sell the act.

And now, Dean Stevenson, talented drummer and arranger for the 'Ole' Left-Hander, presents a practically infallible system for marking these show tempos. Here it is—simplicity itself:

See Illustration

This symbol system, while applicable particularly to show-band work, can be used in many other ways. The idea is not new but up to the moment there has never been standardization. We grant that it is even improbable that these markings will become universally accepted because of the difference of opinion on tempos; however, if once used the system should be immeasurably helpful due to its simplicity and idea of "tune association." If arrangements are marked with the symbols or just the arrangements used by the leader, the pianist, first trumpet, and drummer, accidents and embarrassments are practically impossible. It has been used successfully not only by Joe Sanders but by many other bands who have played the same show arrangements marked by Stevenson.

Explanation of Symbols

There are four major tempos (from very slow to very fast) marked herein as Triangle 4, Circle 4, Square 4, and Diamond 2. The numeral inclosed in the symbol designates the leader's beat. Suppose we take our first illustration—Triangle 4. This is interpreted to mean very, very slow. However, if the tempo, designated by Triangle 4, is a little too slow and a slightly faster beat is required, another Triangle is added inside the original Triangle. By the same token, when a circle is drawn inside of the Circle 4, the tempo is slightly faster than the ordinary Circle 4, and so on down the line.

There is one more modification of these symbols. If you want the tempo a little slower than Circle 4, of any group into another group (like Circle modified by Triangle) you place the Triangle outside the Circle which gives you that shade difference of slowness. The point is that tempo identification consists of both a numeral and a symbol. These remain unchanged in each of the four Divisions and modification retains its identity by simply placing the added modification on the outside of the group symbol.

Here's another example: Suppose a little slower tempo than Jig-4 (Square 4) is desired. (Jig-4 is represented by a few bars of "Dinah.") Merely superimpose a Circle around the Square 4 and the tempo becomes a Lazy Swing, using its tune association—"Sweet Sue." Examples of well known tunes have been used for purposes of quick identification and every musician is familiar with not only these names but the tempo in which these selections should be played.

The idea of marking show-music with signs and hieroglyphics to designate certain tempos is certainly not new.

There are several ways of marking, and all are good. For a certain sign or figure immediately identifies itself with a certain tempo.

In the following system there are four major tempos: "Triangle Four" . . . . (a numeral four enclosed in a triangle) . . . very, very slow, *"Blue Four"* . . . (a numeral four enclosed in a circle) Ex: "Old Rockin' Chair," *"Jig-Four"* . . . (a numeral four enclosed in a square) Ex: "Dinah," and *"Kick Two"* (a numeral two enclosed in a diamond) Ex: "Who" . . . so called because it suggests a chorus-routine and is directed; "in two."

If you will notice now that from *slow* to *fast* the order runs Triangle, Circle, Square and Diamond you will readily see the way of indicating the many "in-between" tempos.

Well-known dance tunes have been deliberately picked for quick recognition and association of tempo-symbols.

Now the original four tempos: Triangle, Circle, Square and Diamond have grown to three modifying "Triangle" tempos, three modifying "Circle" tempos, three modifying "Square" tempos, and two modifying "Diamond" tempos.

A plus or minus sign after any of the symbols, makes it a shade faster or slower.

Universal acceptance of any system of this kind is highly improbable due to the naturally human difference of opinion about various tempos . . . but it will be a great help to many, I know . . . and if tried out once will be used always.

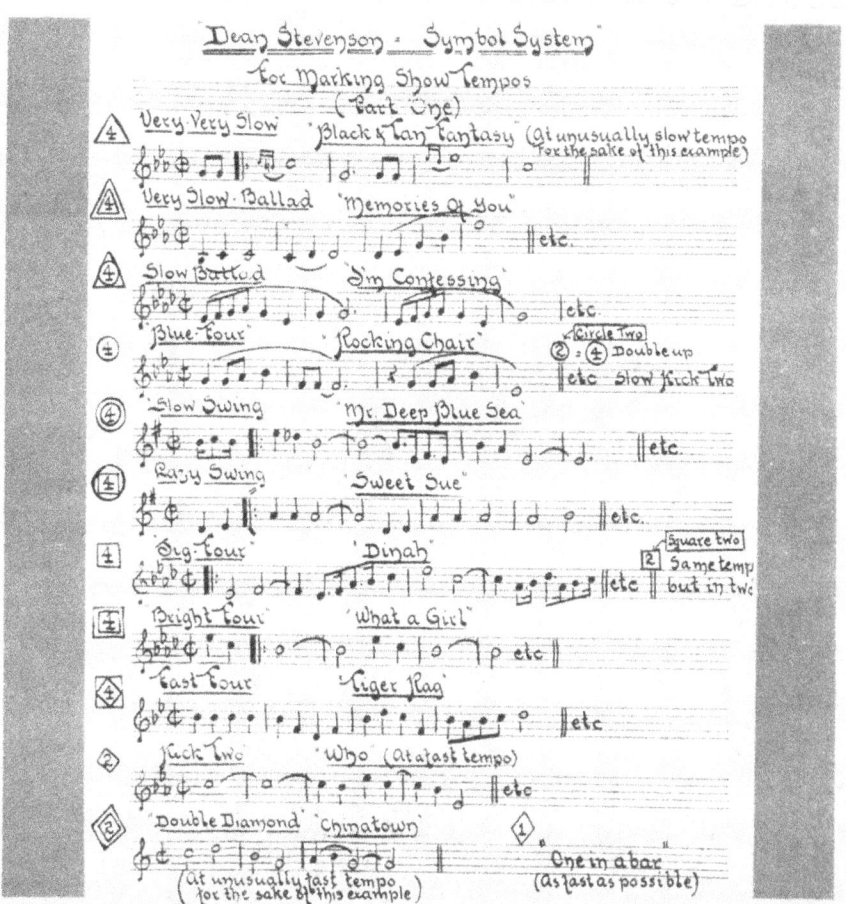

A "Set-up"....
TO SATISFY EVERY DRUMMER NEED

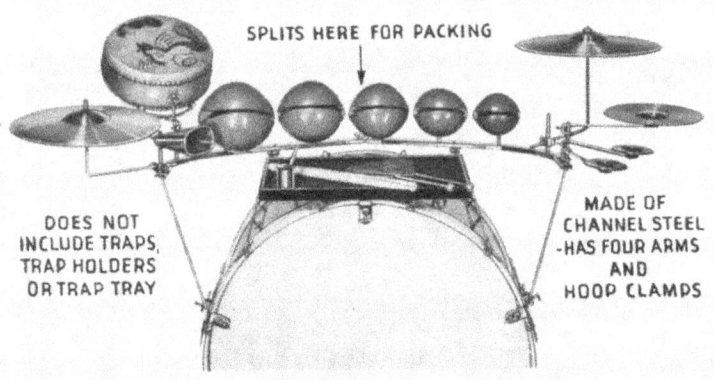

SPLITS HERE FOR PACKING

DOES NOT INCLUDE TRAPS, TRAP HOLDERS OR TRAP TRAY

MADE OF CHANNEL STEEL —HAS FOUR ARMS AND HOOP CLAMPS

Holders Shown on Page 17

No. 7172—Circular Trap Rail (less traps, holder and tray). Nickel.............$10.00
No. 7173—Circular Trap Rail (less traps, holder and tray). Chromium......... 15.00

• • • • • CIRCULAR TRAP RAIL

A new wrinkle in set-ups! This semi-circular trap rail of angle steel holds a full set of five temple blocks and has TWO extra trap posts at each end for other traps. EVERYTHING is EASILY within REACH for maximum ease and convenience in playing and permits freer, more rapid execution. Nothing quite equal to it has ever been offered to the profession before. Turns the average outfit into a display set-up. Held firmly and securely to the bass drum by four arms equipped with Stayon hoop clamps and splits in the middle for compact, convenient packing. Light, practical, convenient, good-looking and moderate in price. The "Handy" Trap Tray shown above and listed below allows ample room for sticks, brushes, etc., and clamps to the bass drum hoop as an independent unit. Holders for the rail are illustrated and listed on page 17.

ALL-IN-ONE TEMPLE BLOCK RAIL • • • • •

This is the simplest, neatest, most practical and economical temple block set-up on the market for the drummer who must have temple blocks but must get along with a minimum of bulk, weight and expense. No individual holders are needed with this rail—temple blocks are merely placed on the threaded posts (over the felt pads), a metal piece placed on the posts over the blocks and the whole assembly held in place by a winged thumb nut. The rail is made of channel steel and fastens to the bass drum hoop by two arms equipped with the famous Leedy Stayon clamps. Rail splits in the middle for packing with the blocks on or off, and is strong and durable. Cymbals and other traps may be fastened to the drum hoops by Leedy holders. Price does not include blocks, cymbal set-ups or Handy Trap Tray.

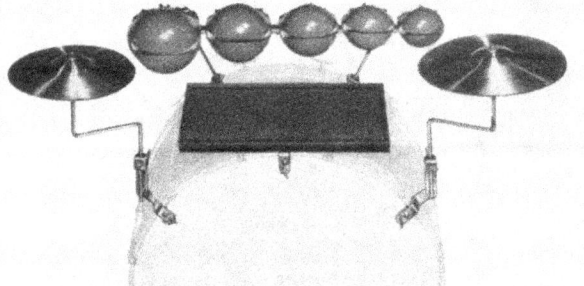

No. 7147—All-In-One Temple Block Rail Only. Nickel $5.50
No. 7148—All-In-One Temple Block Rail Only. Chromium...... 7.50

• • • • "HANDY" TRAP TRAY

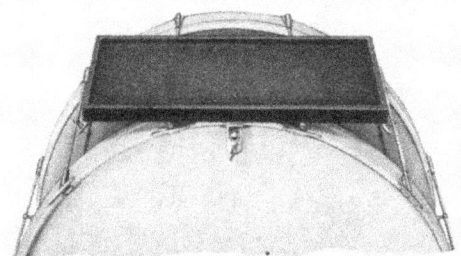

A mighty handy trap tray for use with the Circular Trap Rail, the All-In-One Temple Block Rail or in conjunction with bass drum hoop trap holders. It is well made, strong, rigid and convenient. Clamps to the near bass drum hoop with a Stayon hoop clamp. Tray surface is covered with fine quality green felt and raised edge prevents traps, sticks, etc., from rolling off. Light in weight, compact and easy to pack and carry, you will find plenty of use for this item. Supplied in nickel only. See it at your nearest Leedy dealer.

No. 7170—"Handy" Trap Tray with Stayon Bass Drum Hoop Clamp in Nickel...$3.50

The Sensational "BEST-ALL" Cymbal Holder

"The Best Cymbal Holder Ever Made"

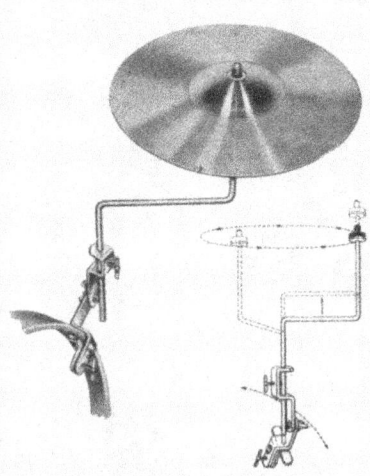

Clamps anywhere on the bass drum hoop with the famous Stayon clamp. Ratchet device permits cymbal to be used in an upright position regardless of where holder is placed on drum hoop. Double angle cymbal post permits cymbal to swing in a full circle—to the right, to the left, away from you or closer to you with a generous height adjustment. Cymbal vibrates freely.

No. 9000—Nickel. Complete.........................$2.00
No. 9001—Chromium. Complete......................... 3.00

Joseph Torreano

A Leedy drummer since 1902 with such famous bands as those of Herbert L. Clarke, the leading circuses and others. Torreano is now playing with the splendid Shredded Wheat and Carborundum bands at Niagara Falls, N. Y., with which he has been for the past 11 years. He has been a drummer for 45 years and is now living in Niagara Falls. His birthplace was Calumet, Michigan.

Allen Kimmey and Carlton Kelsey

Kimmey (left), staff drummer with Carlton Kelsey (right) at the CBS—WBBM Air Theatre, Chicago, has played the Rainbo Casino, Chicago, with the Savoy Opera Co. on tour and the Sears "Then and Now" radio program under the same leader. His past experience includes 4 years theatre work, 3 seasons with the Chicago Civic Opera Co. under Directors E. DeLamater and Hans Lange and engagements with Louis Panico, Jos. Cherniavsky and Jos. Gallicchio. Born in Erie, Kans., studied drums under Geo. A. Smith of Omaha and Art Layfield and Roy Knapp of Chicago. Has been in the business fifteen years and has used Leedys during that entire time. Note the completeness of his outfit!

Frank Horscroft

During his 35 years of drumming has played with Paul Whiteman, Philadelphia Symphony, Sousa, Pryor and the New York Philharmonic and for the past 6 years has played for the United Artists and Selznick picture studios in Hollywood under Alfred Neuman and Max Steiner. Has played Leedys 15 years. Birthplace was Philadelphia.

HOW TO STRAIGHTEN RATTAN OR REED MALLET HANDLES

Bend handle held in the hands under a hot iron as shown in illustration. This will straighten warped handles. Hold with a little pressure until it does not spring back into former warped position. If care is used handle will remain straight for a long time and give extra service for but little effort and time.

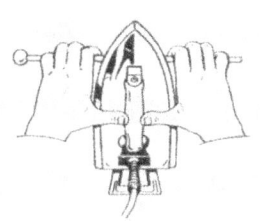

$2.00 award to — Irvin J. Steltz, 1029 Tatum St., Woodbury, N. J.

SIMPLE, BUT EFFECTIVE

Robert S. Kenney of Wollaston, Mass., objected to the "ugly black heads" of Chinese Tom Tom tacks. Therefore he finished each head carefully with gold paint and says it improved their appearance a great deal. Kenney states that several drummer friends have followed suit, but some have used silver. Seems like a fine stunt.

$2.00 award to—Robert S. Kenney, 11 Albion Road, Wallaston, Mass.

Harold Wasson

Playing with Bob Black's band at the Hotel Pere Marquette, Peoria, Ill., with which band he has been for two years. Formerly played with Jack Wedell, Fritz Miller, Miller Welch and others. Born in Clinton, Ill., studied drums under Frank Fanscher and Ed. Straight, has been in the game 16 years and is using a complete Leedy "Full Dress" outfit finished in Black Pearl and chromium which makes a snappy combination.

Billy Markas—Maxine Doyle—Jimmy Grier

Markas has played the Jack Benny, Hall of Fame, Bing Crosby and Lucky Strike radio programs under Grier's baton; also Brunswick records and Ambassador and Biltmore Hotels, Los Angeles. Also played with Lennie Hayton and Leo Forbstein at 1st Nat. Warner Bros. Studios. Born N. Y. C., in profession 15 years, played Leedys 10 years. Miss Doyle is a featured Warner Bros. actress.

Evelyn Kenyon

The sweet and smiling young miss standing behind her 4 octave Geo. Hamilton Green model Leedy xylophone is Evelyn Kenyon of Hawthorne, N. J., who mastered her instrument under the expert training of the famous Geo. Hamilton Green who designed the model which carries his name. We believe that DRUM TOPICS readers will hear more about this young lady in forthcoming issues of this magazine.

Dave Burnside and Ray Mozley

At Mozley's last writing he was playing at the Cataract Hotel, Niagara Falls, N. Y., under the baton of Dave Burnside with whom he has been for the past three years playing hotel and radio engagements in the east and south. Has played with Frank McSherry, Sunny Clapp, Jack Kerr and others, too. Born in Atlanta, has drummed for 10 years, bought this new Leedy outfit last year. His home address is Lakeland, Fla.

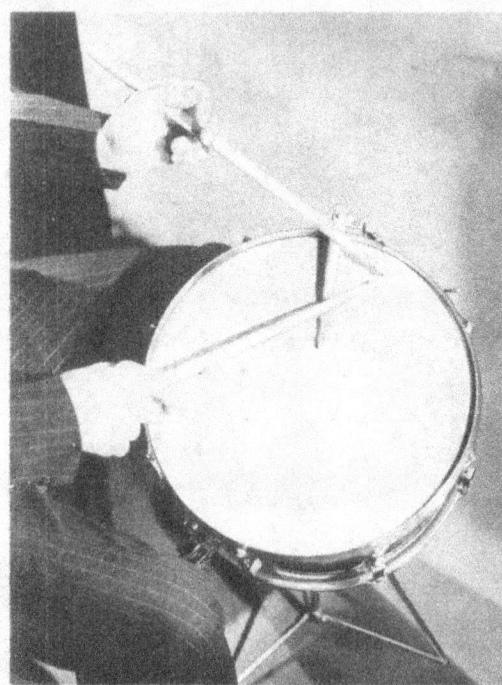

"Calling All Rim-Shots"

with the NEW Leedy "RIM-SHOT" GADGET
(Patent Pending)

• The Stick Rests on the Counter Hoop •

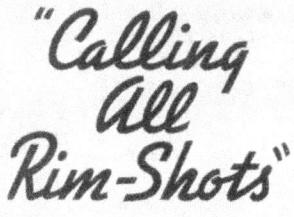

It's NEW! It's HOT! It's DIFFERENT! Produces a wood hoop rim-shot effect with a snare undertone when struck with the sticks. Just the thing for fast rim-shot effects, snappy "swing" stuff, rhythm after-beats and accents. Designed for use on Leedy BROADWAY Floating Head drums. Drum rod holds "Rim-Shot" Gadget in place and wood post rests both on drum hoop and drum head.

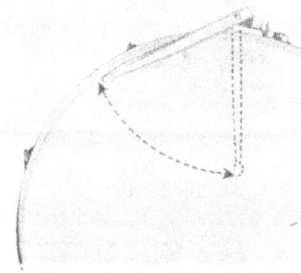

WITHOUT a doubt the hottest, handiest, snappiest little trick in the up-to-the-minute drummer's trap case today. Worth $100 in effects, but costs only six-bits to own and takes only a minute to attach.

Now you can get wood hoop rim-shot effects on your metal hoop BROADWAY drum with the natural depth of drum tone thrown in for good measure! Ideal for hot "swing", rhythm after-beats and accents with the snares on. With the snares off, it produces an entirely different tom-tom tone that's deep down and dirty for rhumba numbers. And when you don't want it, just swing it around to the hoop where it is out of the way and doesn't affect the drum tone at all!

This new, never-miss rim-shot gadget is the nuts; it's sturdy, fool-proof and effective—and the price is right "down your alley." Get one for yourself today!

No. 1615   "RIM-SHOT" GADGET . . . . $ .75 Each

"Salvy" Ferraro and George Claesgens

Owner of a music store in Utica, N. Y., and drummer with Salvy Ferraro's "Club Moderne" band with which he has played for several years, Claesgens is a busy fellow. Has played the Gaiety, Majestic and Stanley theatres in Utica, with the 147th Inf. Band during the war, and played tympani with the Utica Symphony Orchestra now under the baton of Edgar Alderwick. If you live in, or visit, Utica, look up Claesgens—he'll be glad to see and talk drums and drumming with you. You'll find he's a "regular" fellow.

Albert J. Kottmann, Seymour, Conn.

Born in Seymour, plays drums at the Rainbow Inn, West Haven, with Angelo Morasco with whom he has also played in the Catskill's Shandelee Lake Hotel, the Actors' Colony Inn on the Hausatonic and for many studio radio programs. Formerly with "Doc" Hellar and had his own 6-piece swing combination for a time. Studied under the famed J. Burns Moore, has played Leedys for nearly seven of his ten years in the game. Says of his Leedys: "Have always found them to be 'tops'".

Good Idea For Patching Base Drum Head

Apply patch as per directions that come in the small ordinary inner tube repair kits, obtainable at any auto supply store. Be sure to sandpaper head as directed. It is a good idea to apply to both sides of head, but not absolutely necessary as a patch on one side will hold indefinitely.

$2.00 award to—Stanley Hindman, 1318 Wheeler St., Covington, Ky.

Davidson College Band Percussion Section

This is the all-Leedy equipped percussion section of the Davidson College Band, Davidson, N. C., which is celebrating its centennial this year. James Christian Pfohl, Director of Music, directs the band which he says is now the finest he has ever had. Director Pfohl is on the extreme right in the photograph; Thane McDonald, Ass't Conductor is fourth from the right.

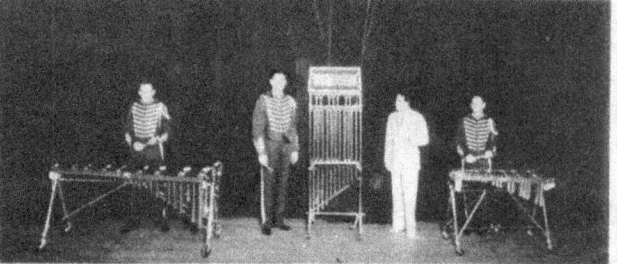

Northeastern Teachers College Band Percussion Section

Shown here with Director Henri Minsky of the Northeastern Teachers College Band are the members of the band's percussion section posed with a few of the Leedy instruments they use. The school is located at Tahlequah, Okla., and its band is one of the finest in the state. Left to right, the members are Houston Davis, Gaines West, Dir. Minsky and Orlan Lemler. The photo was sent through the courtesy of Paul Bennett, Leedy dealer at Tulsa.

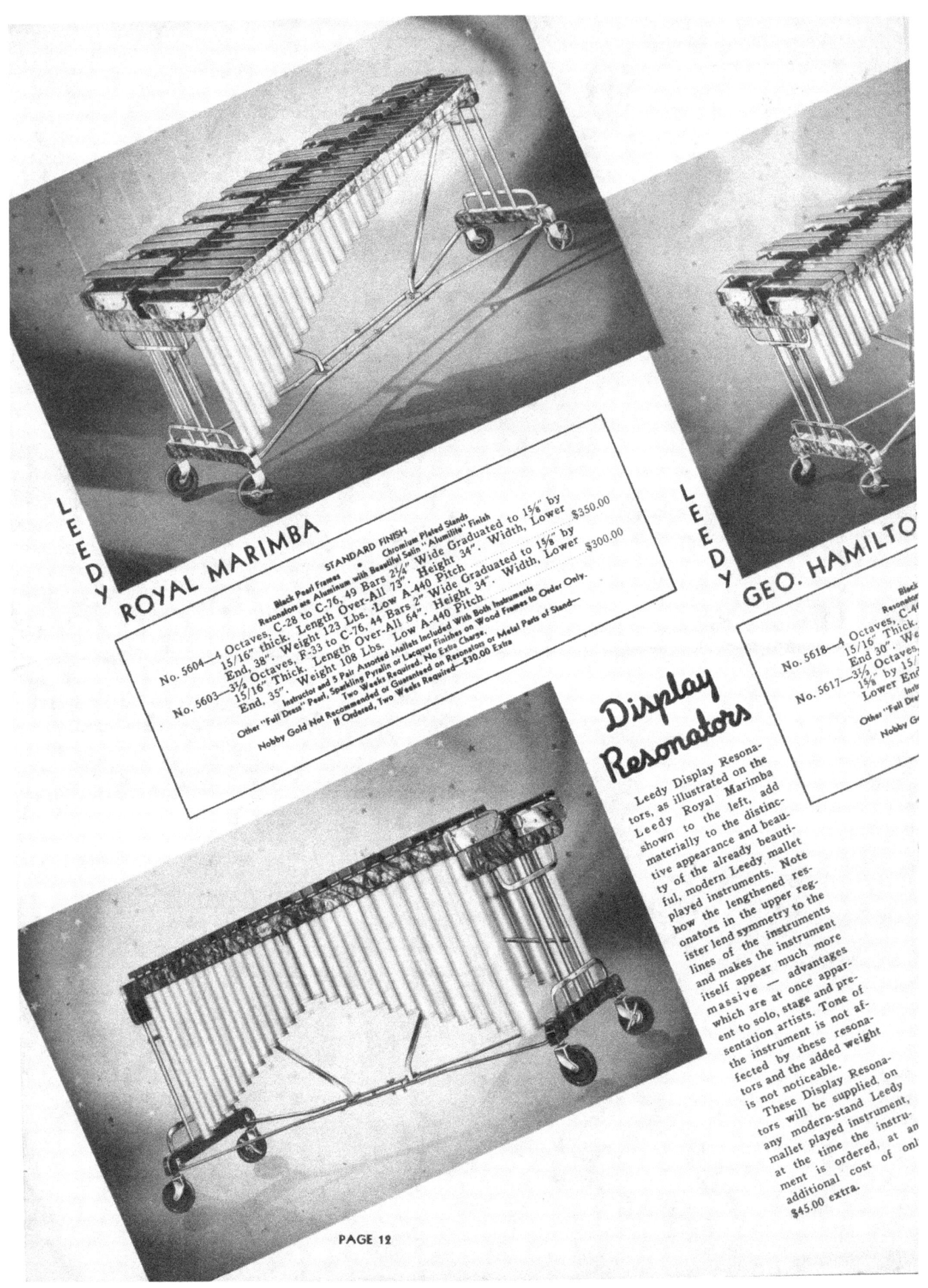

LEEDY ROYAL MARIMBA

STANDARD FINISH
Black Pearl Frames • Chromium Plated Stands
Resonators are Aluminum with Beautiful Satin "Alumilite" Finish

No. 5604—4 Octaves, C-28 to C-76, 49 Bars 2¼" Wide Graduated to 1⅝" by 15/16" thick. Length Over-All 73". Height 34". Width, Lower End, 38". Weight 123 Lbs. Low A-440 Pitch $350.00

No. 5603—3⅓ Octaves, F-33 to C-76, 44 Bars 2" Wide Graduated to 1⅝" by 15/16" Thick. Length Over-All 64". Height 34". Width, Lower End, 35". Weight 108 Lbs. Low A-440 Pitch $300.00

Instructor and 5 Pair Assorted Mallets Included With Both Instruments
Other "Full Dress" Pearl, Sparkling Pyralin or Lacquer Finishes to Order Only.
Nobby Gold Not Recommended or Guaranteed on Resonators or Metal Parts of Stand—
Two Weeks Required. No Extra Charge.
If Ordered, Two Weeks Required on Wood Frames to Order Only.—$30.00 Extra

Display Resonators

Leedy Display Resonators, as illustrated on the Leedy Royal Marimba shown to the left, add materially to the distinctive appearance and beauty of the already beautiful, modern Leedy mallet played instruments. Note how the lengthened resonators in the upper register lend symmetry to the lines of the instrument and makes the instrument itself appear much more massive — advantages which are at once apparent to solo, stage and presentation artists. Tone of the instrument is not affected by these resonators and the added weight is not noticeable.

These Display Resonators will be supplied on any modern-stand Leedy mallet played instrument, at the time the instrument is ordered, at an additional cost of only $45.00 extra.

PAGE 12

THE LINE OF THE Stars

LEEDY presents new quality of tone, new perfection in mechanical construction and new beauty in Xylophone and Marimba design.

Portrayed on these pages is the culmination of more than forty years of intensive study, research, designing and building the world's finest percussion musical instruments. Never have instruments of these types possessed finer, richer, more resonant tone or greater reserve volume and carrying power than these; never have they been more perfect from a mechanical standpoint or more beautiful in appearance!

The first thing you will notice as you look at these photographs will be the distinctive beauty of the new modern stands. They are stronger than any others on the market, and they can be set up or taken down and packed with greater ease and in less time, too.

These instruments are positively guaranteed to possess greatly improved tone, volume and carrying power as the result of the new, scientifically correct bar and resonator sizes. Playing just a few bars of music on these instruments will convince you at once that here, at last, are instruments that will fill your every need.

You'll be proud to own one of the new Leedy instruments because — mechanically, musically and in appearance — they "top" all others and are truly the "Line of the Stars"!

LEEDY
Mallet Played Instrument Features:

All Leedy Mallet Played Instruments are designed and constructed for flawless musical performance, and embody only the finest materials and workmanship throughout. . . . . . .

All stands have been improved to combine maximum strength, rigidity, durability and beauty with minimum weight and bulk.

All instruments feature scientifically correct bar and resonator proportions which assure the artist of the utmost in tonal quality combined with rich resonance and maximum volume and carrying power. The Leedy method of full bar suspension, the patented method of tuning and the resonator adjustment for temperature are important factors in attaining these superior standards. . .

All of the larger models feature split frames and resonators—built on the sturdy cantilever principal—for ease and convenience in packing, carrying, setting-up and taking down. . . . . .

Bars are genuine Honduras Rosewood of finest quality thoroughly seasoned, accurately tuned and beautifully finished. . . . .

Resonators are of aluminum alloy with double beads at the bottom to afford protection against damage by bumps, knocks, falls, etc. They are riveted to metal strips for rigidity and to prevent rattling and touching each other. Finished in the beautiful satin "Alumilite" which is so popular finish. . . . . . .

"JUMBO" BASS DRUM SPURS

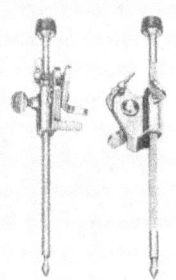

Reversible Pointed Steel and Rubber Tips

These are new, extra length spurs equipped with the famous Leedy Stayon clamp and are specially designed to prevent bass drums from overbalancing, tipping and tottering when they are heavily loaded with a lot of traps such as temple blocks, tom toms, cymbals, etc., either on individual holders or on a trap table, rail, tray or temple block rail. Fasten high on the bass drum hoop without marring. Spurs have reversible rubber and steel pointed tips and can be slid up out of the way for packing without removing the spurs from the drum hoop. Strong, substantial and nicely finished. Spurs measure 9" long.

No. 7098—Nickel. Per pair $2.50
No. 7099—Chromium. Per pair 3.75

Geo. Hamilton Green "The World's Outstanding Xylophonist" is at YOUR SERVICE

Recognized as the world's finest xylophonist and famed for his flawless technique and brilliant artistry in his stage, screen, radio, recording and concert performances, noted also as a composer, arranger, author and teacher, and designer of the famous Geo. Hamilton Green model xylophone made by Leedy, Geo. Hamilton Green is well known to DRUM TOPICS readers among whom he has countless personal friends, pupils and acquaintances.

In answer to countless requests from xylophone and marimba players and students throughout the country who have expressed a desire to develop their ability to improvise and render their own variations in any known style of playing, Mr. Green is now offering to ADVANCED players and students a new, complete "Geo. Hamilton Green MODERN IMPROVISING COURSE" of THIRTY-FIVE INDIVIDUAL THREE-PAGE LESSONS through which this entire subject can be mastered easily.

This new course being offered by Geo. Hamilton Green is undoubtedly the finest thing that has ever been offered to the advanced player and student by ANY instructor or school. It shows how all different types of variations and arpeggios are formed in their relation to fundamental chords, tells how variations are applied to all types of modern melody, shows the proper application of arpeggios, double-stops, scale-forms, etc. A thorough routine covering the invention of ideas, the writing of original variations, and adapting from printed piano parts is given and "swing", rhythm effects and "sock" style are clearly analyzed.

In addition to the above, this course will greatly improve general technique and develop speed and precision in playing.

RESULTS ARE GUARANTEED IF INSTRUCTIONS ARE FOLLOWED, ACCORDING TO MR. GREEN.

The purpose of this course is to help the student who, due to location, cannot come personally to Geo. Hamilton Green's studio for lessons. These same lessons are given to pupils visiting Mr. Green's studios. Regardless of where you live, you can now study marimba and xylophone with Geo. Hamilton Green and receive and adapt yourself to the same training and routine that you would receive if you were to go to his studio in person. COMPLETE instruction, advice and suggestions of WHAT to do, HOW to practice and HOW to play are clearly printed in every lesson.

Those who subscribe for the course receive ONE lesson per week until the COMPLETE course of THIRTY-FIVE lessons has been received. Under no circumstances will ALL the lessons be mailed at one time.

The fee for the course is $1.00 per lesson which can be paid by the week. Substantial savings are available to those wishing to pay for five, ten, twenty, or the full thirty-five lesson course in advance. You can choose your own method of payment.

Here is the EASY, SURE, GUARANTEED way to learn to improvise and adapt chords from the piano part so YOU can match the style of leading dance and radio band music which is "tops" today.

You can start the course by sending a dollar bill to Geo. Hamilton Green, 44 West 77th Street, New York, New York, or you can write him at the same address for further and more complete information which he will mail to you gladly, promptly and without obligation.

Earl Mac Lane

Born in Holyoke, Mass., studied drums under Larry Stone and Bob Persons and is now playing the finest jobs in Europe—in Europe's finest concert and dance band under Bernhard Ette. Until six years ago played in America on every conceivable kind of job from burlesque to opera including radio, records and pictures. Has used 100% Leedy equipment for 15 years of the twenty he has played drums. Credits his Leedy outfit for getting him his present splendid job.

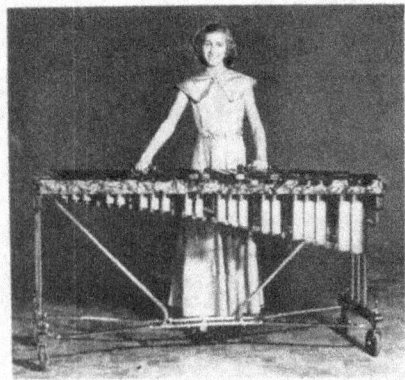

G. Eleanor Keim

Though only 12 years of age now, Eleanor made her first public appearance on the xylophone three years ago and has since played school band, stage, dance, banquet and radio engagements. Does a novelty tap dance act while playing 3-hammer xylophone, too. Lives in Easton, Pa., studies now under Geo. Hamilton Green and is mighty proud of her 4 oct. Geo. Hamilton Green model xylophone with which she is shown above.

Vincent L. Mott

Won the 1936 American Legion National Rudimental Drumming Championship at Cleveland. Vince is one of the "key" drummers in the Eastern States and has for many years operated a fine music store at Paterson, New Jersey. In addition to his Paterson activities he is also Manager of the Drum Department of C. G. Conn, Ltd., Rockefeller Center, New York City. Vince is known to Drum Topic readers all over the country and he has a host of personal friends in every state as well. Drummers are invited to meet him in the New York store or at Paterson where they will find him one of the real fellows and always at the service of fellow drummers.

John J. Heney

Drummer and Xylophonist for several years with the world famous John Phillip Sousa and his band. Also several seasons with McDonald's famed Royal Scotch Highlanders Band. Heney is now Director of Bands at The John B. Stetson University, Deland, Florida. In addition he is Director of Bands and Teacher of Instrumental Music in the Deland Public Schools. During the summer season John plays drums with the Daytona Beach Professional Band, Ray Eberling, director. Heney was born in San Francisco and studied with Wm. H. Noltings. Has been in the business 25 years and used Leedys for 17.

DRUM TOPICS pays $2.00 each for ideas printed under the "NEW IDEAS" heading shown at the top of this page. If you have an idea that will be valuable to other drummers in their playing—send it in. YOU may find yourself $2.00 richer! Send in as many ideas as you wish.

Weird, Deep Tone Tom Tom Effect, plus Lion Roar and Deep Rumbles.

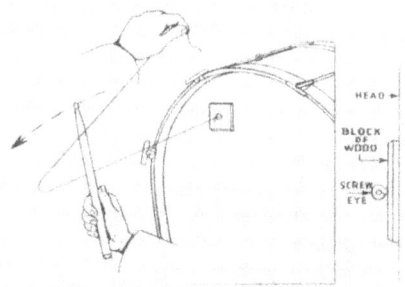

Obtain piece of soft pine wood and cut to 2"x2"x¼" thick. Bevel edges. Remove head from bass drum and use LePage's glue to attach block about four inches from counter hoop near top at either side. Use weight on block and allow to dry over night. Then screw ⅜" eye into center of block. Next obtain piece of hard linen cord about one yard long. Work powdered rosin (obtainable in any drug store) into cord thoroughly. (Use old rolling pin and literally grind in the rosin.) Wear cheap canvas glove with rosin on fingers for roars and rumbles. A wonderful deep-toned Tom Tom effect is obtained with this "gadget" by holding string loose and tapping in loop with drum stick as illustrated.

$2.00 award to—Clinton Boseker, Rye Star Route, Box 23, Pueblo, Colo.

New High Hat Sock Cymbal Effect

Max A. Lauterbach of Lawrence, Mass., writes that he has used the following set-up with fine results. First, remove the "sizzle washers" from the regular 10" (No. 7452) Leedy Brass Sizzle Cymbal. Leave the rivets in place by peening over the ends so they will not fall out. Place this cymbal (cup down) as the under cymbal on the High Hat pedal. Then place a 10" (No. 7450) Brass Deep Cup Cymbal (cup up) on top. The light sizzle tone of the rivets with good stick work makes it possible to produce many novel effects. Also fine for loud, hot ride choruses.

$2.00 award to—Max A. Lauterback, 40 Mann St., Lawrence, Mass.

To Hold Small Tunable Tom Tom

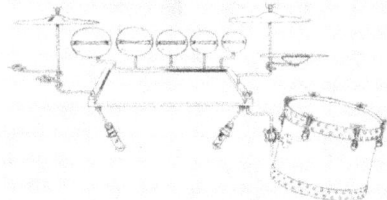

Drill an extra hole in the right hand side ridge of your trap table. Place angle temple block post No. 7258 in this hole upside down, as shown in illustration. Next, use adjustable Tom Tom holder No. 7230, screwing plate to Tom Tom and of course using adjustment on the angle post. (See page 35 of Leedy catalog No. 41 for these parts.) This attachment will hold a 9x13" or 12x14" Tunable Tom Tom very nicely. Looks nice, too. You will find this is adjustable to heights and angles.

$2.00 award to—Lou W. Gordon, 275 Central Park West, New York City.

A Novel Bass Drum Scenic Effect

Frank G. Forgione of Haverhill, Mass., writes that the following lighting effect has created a great deal of favorable comment from the dancers where he plays. The idea is quite simple but, at the same time, brand new as far as we know.

By painting a silhouette of a girl (such as in the Moonlight Silhouette Scene No. 6704) on the outside of the drum head, and the figure of the man on the inside of the drum head, a most startling effect is produced when intermittent lights flash on and off. It can readily be understood that the girl shows up nicely when the lights are off and no figure of the man is visible; then when the lights are on they are both visible. Most any artist can frame a different scene than the one described and there is no limit to possible variations. For instance, a silhouette of a girl could be painted with outstretched arms, as if waiting for someone, then when the lights go on the man appears in a close embrace.

$2.00 award to—Frank G. Forgione, Naples St., Haverhill, Mass.

Practical Method of Transporting Trap Table

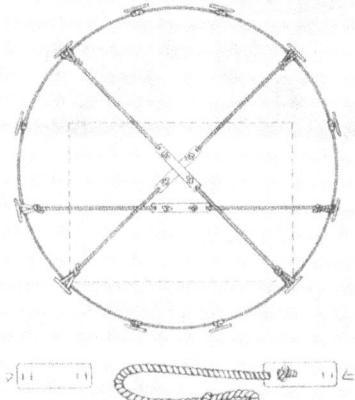

Willis S. Serfass shows us a very clever and practical method of transporting a trap table safely and at the same time eliminating a piece to carry. The table is held close to the bass drum head by means of cord and inner tubing arranged as follows. First, obtain three pieces of old inner tubing: cut them 3" long by 1" wide. Next, cut two ¼" long "slots" at each end of each piece, like in Fig. A, then insert ends of ⅜" diameter cord and tie knot in ends as shown in Fig. B. Tie loops at ends of cord, these loops to "hook over" bass drum rod tension handles as shown in drawing below. It is an easy matter to determine the proper lengths so that there will be enough tension caused by the stretching of the rubber pieces to hold the table flat and firmly against the head.

$2.00 award to—Willis S. Serfass, 633 Berwick St., Easton, Pa.

To Muffle Tom Tom Tone

This is particularly good for Tunable Tom Toms. Place a round disc of muslin under the batter head, having the muslin large enough to drape down a short distance under the counter hoop. You will find that when you place a strain on the head the muslin will also tighten up. This gives the Tom Tom a full, deep tone, without any ring whatever, regardless of where struck. Also makes the use of wire brushes sound a bit different.

$2.00 award to—Edwin Bereman, 415 S. Poplar St., Wichita, Kansas.

Good Bass Drum Effect

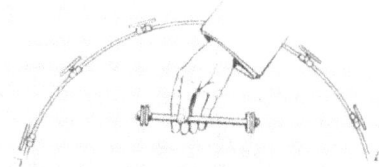

Cut off old drum stick to 9 or 10 inches in length. Place a Leedy Rumble Tip (No. 1604) on each end and use for deep tone rumble effect on bass drum head.

$2.00 award to—Kenneth Farrar, 625 Walnut St., Freeland, Pa.

Good Anvil Effect

If you are short an anvil try the following when one is needed. By laying a Low G bell bar on the head of the large tympani, and a C bell bar on the head of the small tympani, a very good anvil effect may be obtained by playing on these bars with a metal mallet. A little experimenting will show just where these bars should be placed on the heads and at just what tension the heads should be strained to produce the maximum tone.

$2.00 award to—John Gelder, 214 E. Washington Ave., Bath, N. Y.

Appearance Means Much

Eugene Caucci of Bristol, Pa., says that he uses Simonize on his Temple Blocks, the shells of both his snare and bass drums (mahogany) and even on cymbals. On investigation we find this a fine idea inasmuch as it makes it easier to keep these items clean. When they become dirty a light wiping with a clean soft cloth makes them look like new. Simonize helps to retain a bright shine on cymbals for a long time.

$2.00 award to—Eugene Caucci, 1100 Wood and Lincoln Aves., Bristol, Pa.

Another Way to Mount Your "Lick" Cymbal

Set up your pedal cymbals on High Hat sock cymbal pedal in the regular way. Then secure a Leedy No. 7220 cow bell clamp, putting it down over the threaded part of the rod on your High Hat pedal that extends above the regular upper cymbal. This is to support a third or "lick" cymbal which is fastened down on the clamp with an additional wing nut on top. Very good for flash work.

$2.00 award to—R. Keith Syre, 24 Home St. S. E., Grand Rapids, Mich.

(Continued on page 19)

Andy Daugherty
When last heard from was on tour with Henry Bagini's orchestra playing ballroom engagements. Formerly with Austin Wylie and others and has been drummer-director of his own bands. Has been an all-Leedy drummer for 14 years. His home is Clinton, Indiana.

E. W. Montgomery 2nd
Mississippi State Xylophone Champion in the 1935 and 1936 School Band contests and 2nd Division winner in the 1935 Dixie Contest, this lad is a "comer". Uses a Leedy Solo-Tone Grand Marimba-Xylophone. Also plays Leedy drums and tympani. Home is Yazoo City.

Earl P. Cotter
At his last writing was doing radio and dance work in Detroit's best night spots with Arthur Weaver and his band. Also played with Al Fortune, Bill Shelbe and Jack McKay. Born in Wapakonita, O., played drums for 9 years and on Leedys for 8. His home is now Detroit.

Ralph Hawkins
One of Boston's best. has played Loew's Orpheum Theatre there for many years under Director Jim Lindner. Has been in the game more than twenty years and is a staunch Leedy booster and user. Has played the old Howard Theatre and Fleck Opera Co. Home is Everett, Mass.

Tommy Hawkins
One of Boston's finest. Taught his brother Ralph (left), plays Keith's Boston Theatre under Eddie Rosenfield, and has played every theatre there and directed the old Howard Theatre orchestra for 4 years. Also played for Boston Opera Co. Born in Boston. A Leedy booster and user.

Geo. Hamilton
Top rank drummer playing in Detroit's leading Fox Theatre. Has played all the best jobs in and around the automobile city with the best bands, and has held berths with practically every musical organization in that city. Is Leedy equipped throughout which he endorses.

Pierce Knox
Though blinded at an early age, Knox today is one of the finest juvenile xylophonists in the country. Won 1st Division honors at the National High School Band Contest held in Cleveland last year, has toured throughout Iowa and many states under the auspices of the Rotary Club to play at their meetings. Recently played for Geo. Hamilton Green in New York who pronounced him an exceptionally talented and brilliant performer. Uses a 4 oct. Leedy Broadcaster model. Pierce now lives in Oakland, Calif.

Jack Denny and "Whitie" Palmer
Palmer, a really fine drummer, has just finished a long engagement in New York's French Casino with Jack Denny and his truly swell orchestra, and is now on tour. He has been with Denny for fourteen years. Previous engagements the orchestra has played include: Mt. Royal Hotel, Montreal, 5½ years; Waldorf-Astoria Hotel, N. Y. C., 2 years; Pierre Hotel, N. Y. C., 1 year; Biltmore and Pennsylvania Hotels. Radio commercials include: Hudnut Powder, Gem Razor, Conoco Oil and Lucky Strike. Born in Mansfield, O., studied under Henry Brofay, has played drums 25 years, has used Leedys all during that time and is 100% satisfied.

Opal L. Petters
Talented xylophone and vibraphone soloist and performer with Virginia Davis and her "Ladies of Note" playing jobbing engagements in and around Philadelphia and Harrisburg. Was Drum Major and Ass't Drum Instructor in High School, has played xylophone for 7 years and studied music since she was six. Says of her Leedy Vibraphone wih which she is shown here: "The most wonderful instrument I have ever played." Her home is Lancaster, Pa.

Robert Dryden, London, England
This famous all-Leedy English drummer is one of London's most talented veterans. Our most recent correspondence stated that he was doing stage work and recordings with Nat Gonella's Georgians and also playing with Mantovani's Hollywood Restaurant Orchestra. During his 18 years behind the drums he has played many of England's finest hotel, ballroom and radio engagements, and several in other parts of the Empire. His birthplace was Leeds, York.

Bruce Parkinson
Drummer with Leo Remilland's orchestra playing night spot and dance engagements out of Kankakee, Ill., which is Parkinson's home town. When last heard from had played 3 months at Club Roma in that city and was scheduled there indefinitely. Just prior, had finished 13 weeks in a leading Hammond, Ind., ballroom. Parkinson learned drums under Ed. Straight of Chicago and has played for six years. His equipment is exclusively Leedy.

Wm. F. and Wm. C. Flanagan
Wm. C. Flanagan (standing) learned drums from his father (seated) who is a veteran in the business and handles Leedys in his Brockton, Mass., music shop. Has played with Bunny Berigan, Irving Aronson, Mal Hallett, Red Norvo and other famed leaders. Was born in Brockton, Mass. Has played Leedys for 15 years and is known as a top-notcher. When last heard from he was with Charles Barnett playing Glen Island Casino at New Rochelle, N. Y.

Holders for Carry-All Rollaway Trap Console

Gooseneck Cymbal Holder

Made of ⅜" steel. Suspends cymbal up to 16" diameter. Fine for "ringing" crashes. See Console set-up to right.
No. 7233—N. P. $5.00
No. 7234—C. P.   7.50

Snare Drum Holder

Fastens to Console upright. Use post and arms of your present stand. Cast of alloyed aluminum. Makes a fully adjustable holder.
No. 7248 $6.00

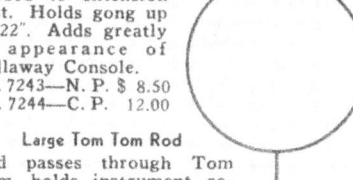

Gong Ring

Ring of ⅜" steel welded to extension post. Holds gong up to 22". Adds greatly to appearance of Rollaway Console.
No. 7243—N. P. $ 8.50
No. 7244—C. P.   12.00

Large Tom Tom Rod

Rod passes through Tom Tom, holds instrument securely with thumb nut. Cast aluminum alloy.
No. 7245—N. P. $2.50
No. 7247—C. P.   3.75

Post Trap Holders

For use on Leedy Carry-All Rollaway Trap Console, Trap Rail, Trap Table and Hoop Adapters

N.P.—Nickel Plate   C.P.—Chromium Plate

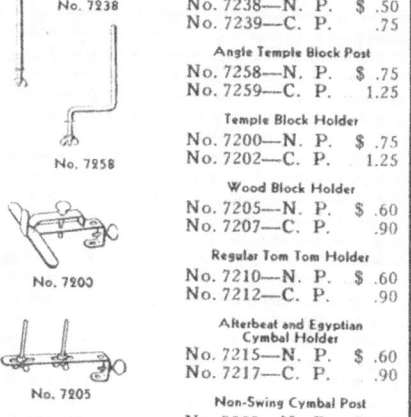

Straight Temple Block Post
No. 7238—N. P. $ .50
No. 7239—C. P.   .75

Angle Temple Block Post
No. 7258—N. P. $ .75
No. 7259—C. P.   1.25

Temple Block Holder
No. 7200—N. P. $ .75
No. 7202—C. P.   1.25

Wood Block Holder
No. 7205—N. P. $ .60
No. 7207—C. P.   .90

Regular Tom Tom Holder
No. 7210—N. P. $ .60
No. 7212—C. P.   .90

Afterbeat and Egyptian Cymbal Holder
No. 7215—N. P. $ .60
No. 7217—C. P.   .90

Non-Swing Cymbal Post
No. 7268—N. P. $1.00
No. 7269—C. P.   1.50

Triangle Holder
No. 7240—N. P. $ .60
No. 7242—C. P.   .90

Cow Bell Holder
No. 7220—N. P. $ .15
No. 7222—C. P.   .25

Imagine yourself
WITH A CARRY-ALL ROLLAWAY TRAP CONSOLE

Does NOT Include
Gong Ring, Goose Neck Cymbal Holder, Drum Holder, Tom Tom Rods, Trap Holders or Traps

This is the most thoroughly modern, up-to-the-minute trap console ever made. It will meet every requirement of the most exacting drummer in the profession because it will hold all the traps that will be needed on any job—more even than are shown in the illustration—and there is no end to the number of different ways they can be arranged and adjusted. The entire set-up—including the bass and snare drums—can be pushed a few inches, or several hundred feet, as easily, as quickly and as conveniently as a xylophone. In playing position, the wheel brakes can be set and the entire outfit is as firmly locked in place as though it were nailed there.

The Carry-All Rollaway Trap Console is thoroughly practical, beautiful in appearance, strong, rigid and solidly built to give long, faithful service. It is scientifically designed and constructed of finest tubular steel for maximum strength, efficiency and beauty and minimum weight. The trap board is covered with high quality felt and the wheels are rubber composition—two of them equipped with strong, reliable brakes. The entire console is carefully finished and, when set up on job, presents a fine display appearance. Note the new drum holder which fastens to the left front upright, and the new goose-neck cymbal holder in the left rear—both of these are described at the left on this page.

No. 7144—Carry-All Rollaway Trap Console as illustrated below. Nickel Plated $57.50

No. 7145—Carry-All Rollaway Trap Console as illustrated below. Chromium $80.00

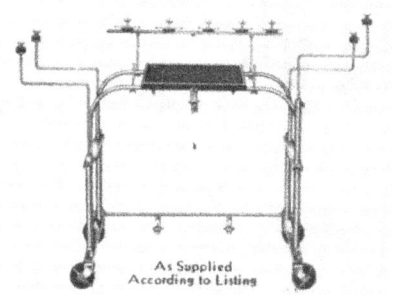

As Supplied According to Listing

Page 17

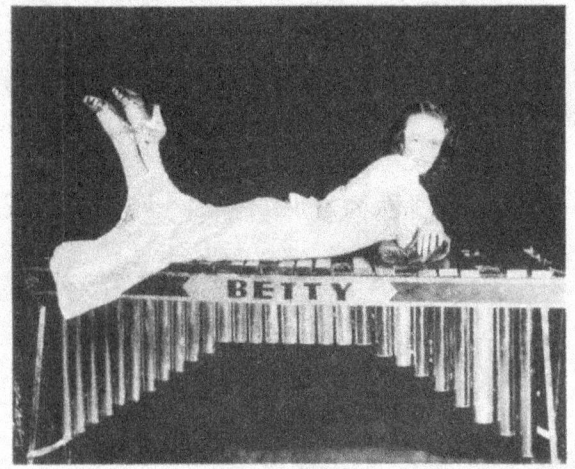

Betty Reed

A truly fine drummer and marimba artist is Betty Reed of Kansas City, Mo., shown here with her Leedy marimba on which her name is displayed in sparkling pyralin. She has played marimba in a vaudeville act during the past three years and before that was featured behind the drums in stage presentations and dance work. All of her equipment is Leedy of which she says: "It's the very finest." Cute pose, what?

Godfrey Hirsch

Hirsch, a "way-down-south-in-Dixie" drummer whose home is hospitable New Orleans, La., is rated as one of the best below the Mason and Dixon line. Has played with Joseph Cherniavsky, Van Forbes and the Saenger Theatre Orchestra to mention only a few. At the last writing, was playing under the direction of Gordon Kirst in the splendid orchestra which was doing the rhythm for the Roosevelt Hotel dances in the Crescent City. His outfit is all-Leedy as shown.

Jungle Drum

The centuries bring but little change to the jungle fastness of the Congo District of Africa and drums remain the same crude, primitive instruments today that they were centuries ago. Shown in the photograph is a group of Bako gathered around a hollowed-out, slotted cylindrical drum, made from the trunk of a jungle tree, being beaten with wood "hammers" by the native drummer. Note that the drum is nothing but a giant replica of the wood block used by modern drummers. Children here, as all over the world, are fascinated by drums and drummers' technique!

Jules Mendelsen

Now on tour with Ted Lewis and his Rhythm Rhapsody Review. One of the finest, Mendelsen has played with the best — with the Shubert Shows, "Artists and Models" with Phil Baker, "Gay Paree" with Chick Sales and Sophie Tucker, with Blue Steele, Tal Henry, Leon "Snooks" Freidman, Jerry Friedman, Ted Mack, Charles Barnett and numerous others. Born in New York City but Memphis has been his home for nearly thirty years. Has played big-time drums since before he was able to vote and is now only in his early thirties. With him in the above photo is the 100% Leedy outfit which is featured in the Ted Lewis show.

When Leedy Was Host at a Detroit Drum Show

Many of the finest drummers of Detroit and vicinity attended the recent drum show sponsored by Leedy at the C. G. Conn Ltd. Detroit branch store. In the above group assembled in the store are (left to right): Fred Paine, Detroit Symphony; Jack Ledingham, Star Xylophonist of WJR, Detroit; Geo. H. Way, Leedy Sales Manager; Art Cooper, Detroit Symphony; Milt Holman, Studio Drummer, Station WXYZ, Detroit; Frank Huzzey, former Ringling Bros. Circus Drummer; Adolph Wohl, Drummer and Librarian, Station WJR, Detroit; Chas. Cooper, Detroit Symphony and Irv Wilke, Conn Store Manager.

Raul G. Garza

Drummer with Ramon Jimenez and his International Orchestra, when last heard from was playing radio station X. E. P. N. and XX Gardens, Mexico. Played Jardines Terpsicore and stations X. E. X. and X. E. T. at Monterrey., N. L. Mexico under the same leader. Prior to present berth played symphony, shows, vaudeville and dance work. Jimenez' home is Piedras Negras, Coah. Mexico, has played drums for 24 years and Leedys exclusively since 1917 which is 20 years. We're certainly glad to hear from drummers outside of our own country!

Florence N. Olmstead

This winsome little lady, who lives in Hawthorne, N. J., studied marimba under Miss Evelyn Kenyon whose photograph you undoubtedly saw on a previous page and who received her training from Geo. Hamilton Green. Miss Olmstead uses a Leedy Marimba in her school, club, church, benefit and other engagements which she fills in and around her home city. Has been playing for three years now and is a splendid artist with a promising future. Writes of her Leedy after switching from another: "Leedy instruments are best—that's why I bought a Leedy" for which words we thank Miss Olmstead.

The Exclusive Drummers' Paper

Frank M. Hood Pursued By the Law

It was funny the way it happened. Frank M. Hood was returning home late one night after a concert of the North Carolina Symphony orchestra in a nearby city. He carried two tympani—drums—in the back of his car. As he rolled leisurely along, the lights from a car behind shown in upon the bright copper bowl of one of the drums, the cover of which had blown off.

After a while it occurred to him that the car behind had been trailing his for miles. With a little feeling of alarm, he wondered why. To test the correctness of his surmise, he stepped on the gas and sprinted for a mile. Just as he thought, the other car stayed close, and, finally, overtook and pulled in front of his, forcing it to a halt.

Two deputy sheriffs stepped out and ordered him out of his car. He complied, looking more than a little out of place out there on a country road in his Tuxedo. Flashing their badges, the officers demanded, "What's that you've got on the back seat there?" Gladly he showed them, even explaining how the drums are used in a large orchestra. They seemed satisfied, and said goodbye.

But—Mr. Hood had gone almost a mile before he realized that those officers had thought they were trailing a moonshiner moving his blockade outfit to a new location. — *From the Greensboro (N.C.) Record dated June 24th, 1935.*

Merle Evans, Director, with Paulson and Thompson

The next time you see the world famous Ringling Bros. and Barnum Bailey Circus band you'll know, after reading this, and seeing the photo above, that it's Merle Evans who's directing, and that Henry Paulson and Amos Thompson are at the bass and snare drums respectively—that is, unless you see a third drummer who is likely to be genial George Way, Leedy Sales Manager, who has, no doubt, bribed Merle and Amos to let him "set in" for the performance which he *has* done on occasion *(and Ye Ed has seen him)*. Anyway, the circus is a swell show, the band is a great outfit and the boys pictured here are regular fellows, and you can take it from the writer that watching these boys work on the drums with Director Evans leading and hitting them higher and with more power than any cornetist in the business, is worth the price of admission to the big-top even without the three ring features.

About Striking Cymbals
(Reprinted from Issue No. 17 Drum Topics)

On straight crashes, it is the type of blow rather than the force that breaks a cymbal. The "whip" blow is severe and dangerous because the contact of the stick is too sudden to allow the cymbal to give. The "push" blow is less likely to cause harm but it does not bring out the proper tone. The safest and best is the "glance" blow. A "glancing" blow not only brings out the best cymbal tone, but can be used with more force than either of the two blows mentioned in the first part of this item.

●

When you call upon a thoroughbred, he gives you all the speed, strength of heart, and sinew in him. When you call on a jackass, he kicks.—*Selected.*

Paul DeDroit

When last heard from, DeDroit was playing with Walderman Guterson's Orchestra in the Orpheum Theatre, Los Angeles where that organization had been playing for one year. Has played with Rubinoff's Orchestra on the Chase & Sanborn Coffee Hour from the Hollywood NBC Studios, in the Fox Studios, the Paramount Theatre in Los Angeles, Grauman's Chinese Theatre, Hollywood, done sound for "Flip The Frog" cartoons, played with Scott Bradley's Hollywood Orchestra, and made recordings with Johnny DeDroit's Okeh Recording Orchestra. Was born in New Orleans, studied drums under George Peterson, and has been in the profession fifteen years. Has played Leedy's for fifteen years and is 100% Leedy equipped now—ample proof of what he thinks of the "World's Finest Drummers' Instruments."

A New Set-Up for Low or High Sock Pedals

The regular Leedy American brass 10" deep cup cymbal, No. 7450, is used on the bottom of Hi-Hat sock cymbal pedal. On the top use either a 10" and 11" fairly thin Zenjian, or two 10" Zenjian cymbals inverted, or cups opposite. Use the regular top supporting clamp for the support of one cymbal, or the Leedy No. 7220 cow bell clamp. Different effects can be obtained by adjusting the two top cymbals with the wing nut on top.

$2.00 award to Geo. A. Eastwood, 82 Exeter Ave., Pawtucket, R. I.

The next time you play a job, look at your outfit as critically as an audience does!—then take steps to do something about it.

Jacqueline Lee Murphy
●
Junction City, Kansas

Although only thirteen years old, Miss Murphy has played with the Junction City H. S. Orchestra for the past year, has played for civic clubs and organizations and has appeared as guest artist with the Municipal Band a number of times. Studied under Chas. Moorman, and is very, very pleased with her Leedy Mellorimba.

WORLD'S FINEST DRUMMERS' INSTRUMENTS SINCE 1895

She Twirled Her Way to Stardom

Leading the Famous Hagenbeck-Wallace Circus Band Directed by Henry Kyes

A Circus Star at Eighteen!

That, briefly, is the reward that pretty Catherine Clarke, Elkhart, Ind., high school student, has earned for herself as a result of her baton-twirling activities during the past five years.

Interest in the art of twirling developed at age twelve when her father, Ed Clarke, Elkhart's stalwart "smoke-eating" Assistant Fire Chief, was "doing his stuff" in front of the Thomas McCoy American Legion Post No. 74 Drum and Bugle Corps. Hours on end of training by him, more endless hours of practice by her, won her a place at the head of the fine Elkhart High School Band which has won laurel after laurel under the baton of Director David W. Hughes.

At fourteen, while still in Junior High, she competed for individual twirling honors at the National High School Band Contests held in Madison, Wisc., and won a rating of "Excellent"; a few weeks later she took an undisputed Junior Championship at the Chicago Tribune's Chicagoland Music Festival held in Chicago's mammoth Soldiers' Field.

Today, with flawless routine, with grace, beauty, ease and timing that is marvelous to behold and worthy of a seasoned veteran, Miss Clarke, with her baton, heads Director Henry Kye's famous Hagenbeck-Wallace Circus Band doing a sensational routine in the "spec" and climaxing it with a two-baton specialty in the center ring that starts the show with speed and pep setting a fast pace for every performance.

Lee Hickle

A 100% Leedy drummer for 16 years; playing ballroom engagements with Jimmy and Bill Richard's Victor Recording Orchestra. Born in Uniontown, Pa., now living in Pittsburgh. Studied under Amos Thompson, Ringling Circus drummer and Byron (Sunny Jim) Galbraith. Has played with Vastines Westinghouse Band, Geo. Mathews, Art Giles, Marty Gregor, Gene Green, Joe Falvo, Ed Perrigo and others. Says of his Leedys: "... think they are the finest money can buy."

Twelve things to remember—

1. The value of time.
2. The success of perseverence.
3. The pleasure of working.
4. The dignity of simplicity.
5. The worth of character.
6. The power of kindness.
7. The influence of example.
8. The obligation of duty.
9. The wisdom of economy.
10. The virtue of patience.
11. The improvement of talent.
12. The joy of originating.

—Marshall Field.

Leslie G. Card

Another 100% Leedy drummer. Plays with Irving Rose's Orchestra out of University City, Mo.; last heard from was at Chase Lawn Club, Chase Hotel, St. Louis, Mo. Has played with numerous well known bands in and around St. Louis. Studied under Schuyler Alward of that city and has been in the profession for 12 years. University City, Mo., is his home. Outfit includes Leedy xylophone, chimes and tymps.

Jack Stearns, San Diego, Cal.

Talented little xylophone soloist with the "Greater San Diego Boys Band", nationally known musical organization sponsored by Bonham Bros., undertakers, San Diego. The band is 7 years old, is directed by Jules Jacques, and admits boys only between the ages of 11 and 12 years. Has 140 pieces and all percussion equipment is Leedy. Photo supplied by Thearle Music Co., San Diego Leedy dealer.

Miss Clark uses a Leedy

Lightweight TWIRL-MASTER Baton

Unexcelled for twirling ease and speed. Perfectly balanced, flashy and has a nice "heft". Undentable aluminum ball, spiral center shaft with reinforcing hickory dowel core, half-round tip—the most popular model of today. Correct weight, length and shaft diameter for fastest twirling, throws, finger spins, around-the-neck, under-arm and leg passes. Shaft ¾" diameter, length 32", weight 22 ounces. Heavily nickel plated over-all. Sturdy, durable and good-looking in every way, and is the choice of the finest twirlers.

No. 1929—Lightweight TWIRL-MASTER Baton $10.00

★

The TWIRL-MASTER Baton

Same as the above with ⅞" diameter shaft, 34" length and 28 ounce weight. Recommended for adult, or adult-size juveniles with sufficient strength to manipulate, where heavier, longer, thicker model is wanted.

No. 1904—TWIRL-MASTER Baton $12.00

Geo. W. Marsh   **Ferde Grofe**   **Joe Green**

New York again had the opportunity early this year to listen and thrill to another of Ferde Grofe's recently instituted annual concerts which featured his latest compositions and arrangements for which he is celebrated. This concert, as the several prior to it were, was rendered with an augmented orchestra and was held in the famous Metropolitan Opera House. Geo. W. Marsh, well known veteran Leedy drummer formerly with Paul Whiteman, and until recently with Grofe, manned the drums and Joe Green, famous brother of the famous Geo. Hamilton Green, featured radio xylophonist on numerous radio commercials and director of his own well known orchestra, presided behind an impressive array of Leedy mallet played instruments.

Vivian Penner

A brilliant and versatile student of Rob't. Baxter, Miss Penner, recently eighteen, is featured marimba-ist with Raymond Dehnbostle's Trumbull County Fadettes Girl Band of Warren, O. Was soloist in two concerts played at the recent Cleveland Exposition and at a Buhl Park, Sharon, concert under Dehnbostle. Also played with the Warren High School Band and Orchestra. Her instrument is a Leedy, of course!

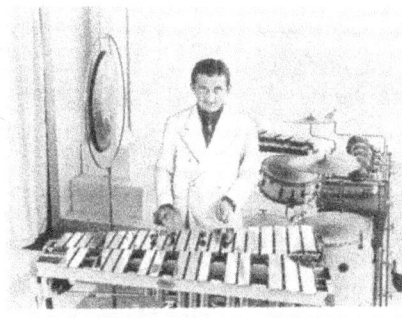

Stanley Fraszczynski, Lodz, Poland

An all-Leedy drummer, one of Poland's finest playing with the Kataszek-Karasinshi dance, radio, recording and motion picture band. Last heard from was at Kit-Kat Casino, Beirut, Syria, for a 10-month engagement, during a tour of Palestine, Syria, Egypt and India. He also played with the finest bands on the best jobs throughout Poland and other European countries during the past ten years. Has used Leedys for 7 years.

Swinging's Easy
with a LEEDY "X-L" PEDAL

For That "Certain Bass Drum Tone"

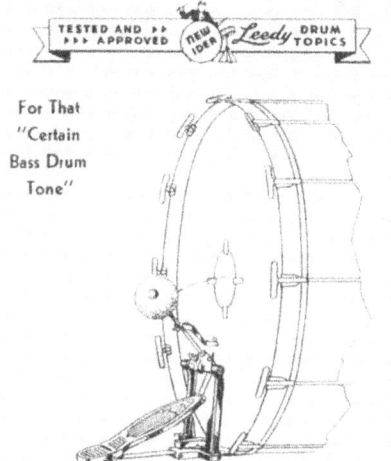

Go to the 5 and 10c store and purchase one piece of medium thickness chamois skin. Cut out a 4" circle; attach this to the bass drum head so that the center comes directly behind the pedal ball, doing this by means of four strips of adhesive tape as shown in drawing. This produces a little different tone than can be obtained in any other way . . . it may be that "certain tone" you will like and what your leader has been asking for.

$2.00 award to—Bob Ladd, 3320 Jennings Ave., Fort Worth, Texas.

The Leedy "X-L" Pedal has proven a real "hit" in the drum world. It was adopted by more high-class professionals during its first year on the market than any other new model ever made because it has everything that Drummers demand in a pedal . . . the utmost in speed — feather ease in action—no faltering—no friction—no side strain—and no "stiff spots" anywhere in the travel of the beater rod. Just clean-cut, smooth response without any extra effort whatever. It is scientifically designed and precision-built of only the finest materials. The uprights and footboard are of cast aluminum. This facilitates speed of action, and makes it light in weight.

The ball and socket principle in the beater shaft is a new departure in pedal mechanism giving that easy "foot flow" and perfect balance that has made this the greatest of all pedals. There are no delicate working parts to get out of order—everything is sturdily constructed so as to give long and satisfactory service. The tension spring can be adjusted to satisfy the particular "feel" that you like best. All the usual adjustable features, such as beater rod, cymbal striker and spring tension, are also incorporated. Finished in baked Black Lacquer with highly polished aluminum footboard and heel plate. All other parts are high quality steel heavily nickel plated.

• Feather Action
• Extremely Fast
• Perfect Balance—Strong
• Foolproof—Durable—Low in Price

No. 7010—Pedal Only (without Spurs and Cymbal Holder) in Black Lacquer and Polished Aluminum $10.00

No. 7014—Pedal As Above But Complete With Nickel Grip-Tite Spurs and Stayon Cymbal Holder $11.50

Percussion Section—University of Kentucky Band

This is the snappy, all-Leedy equipped percussion section of the fine, colorful marching band of the University of Kentucky located at Lexington and founded in 1866. Known as "The Best Band in Dixie", it is a drawing card at all school athletic events which it attends. The university's concert band, composed mainly of marching band members, is one of the "Bluegrass" state's finest and most popular concert organizations.

Drum Sticks for the World's Finest Drummers

Above is a frequently enacted scene on the railroad siding at the Leedy factory—the unloading of a carload of finest, seasoned, second-growth white hickory dowels from which will be made thousands of pairs of the world-famous quality hickory drum sticks which are used by the finest drummers throughout the world. Geo. H. Way, Leedy Sales Manager, is shown at the extreme right of a group of Leedy factory men.

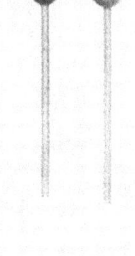

NEW PROCESS FELT XYLOPHONE MALLETS

Balls of finest felt impregnated with a special chemical by a new process to give better tone. Will not beat flat and guaranteed against wear.

No. 1742—1¼" Balls. Per Pair $1.60
No. 1743—1⅜" Balls. Per Pair 1.80
No. 1744—1½" Balls. Per Pair 2.00

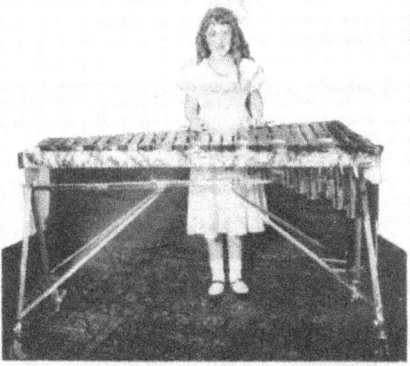

Virginia Edwards

One of the younger Leedy users is Virginia Edwards, ten years old, of New London, Conn., shown in the above photo which was sent to DRUM TOPICS by Walter Damas, Leedy dealer and xylophone teacher of that city. Virginia plays at schools, clubs, socials, church, and other engagements. Charming little Miss!

Leedy
SEPARATE TENSION TOM TOMS

Now, more than ever before, you can get that true, weird, throaty jungle tom tom tone whenever you need it without a thought of Old Man Weather! These Leedy Separate Tension Tom Toms have what it takes and produce it at will. Constructed with finest laminated shells, sturdy key tension double claw hook rods, finest selected pigskin heads and an internal tone control for each head. Guaranteed to give you the utmost in appearance, all-around satisfaction and long service!

16" x 16" With Nickel Plated Rods and Internal Tone Controls
No. 8034—With Choice of "Full Dress" Finishes.............................$45.00
No. 8035—With Choice of Lacquer colors.. 36.50
　　　With Chromium Plated Rods...$3.00 Extra
　　　With Diamond Decorations... 6.50 Extra

14" x 12" With Nickel Plated Rods and Internal Tone Controls
No. 8036—With Choice of "Full Dress" Finishes.............................$39.00
No. 8037—With Choice of Lacquer colors.. 31.00
　　　With Chromium Plated Rods...$3.00 Extra
　　　With Diamond Decorations... 6.50 Extra

13" x 9" With Nickel Plated Rods and Internal Tone Controls
No. 8038—With Choice of "Full Dress" Finishes.............................$30.00
No. 8039—With Choice of Lacquer colors.. 24.50
　　　With Chromium Plated Rods...$3.00 Extra
　　　With Diamond Decorations... 6.50 Extra

Not Illustrated　　10" x 4"—Regulation Size　　Not Tunable
No. 8067—With Choice of "Full Dress" Finishes.............................$9.00
No. 8068—With Choice of Lacquer colors.. 7.00
　　　With Diamond Decorations... $2.00 Extra

FOLDING ADJUSTABLE TOM TOM STANDS
As Shown In Above Photo
No. 7750—Nickel, Each.............$4.00　　　No. 7752—Chromium, Each..........$6.00

Al Anderson

Played tympani and drums with the San Antonio, Tex., Vocational and High School Orchestra which won the Texas District and State Championships in 1935; now playing with Johnnie Fielder's Orchestra at the Randolph Field Officers' Club, the Fort Sam Houston Officer's Club, and the San Antonio Country Club, San Antonio. Uses all Leedys.

Hillsdale (Mich.) City Band Percussion Section

Left to right: Wm. E. Lint, Director; Carl Schultz, snare drum and bells; Mark Taylor, snare, bass drum and xylophone, graduate U. S. Army School of Music, Washington, D. C. and with 2nd Inf. Band for 3 years; John K. Murray, bass drum and bells, also plays Moslem (Detroit) Shrine Band and is an ex-vaudeville drummer of Flint, Mich. This is an unusually fine percussion section of a really fine band.

Dorothy Goetsch

Marimba soloist with the Odebolt, Iowa, High School Band, Dorothy Goetsch last year was First Division Winner in the xylophone contests held in Cleveland, Ohio, during the National High School Band Contest there. Director of the band is Dan Jensen who, with Kermit Chase, taught Miss Goetsch. She had played marimba only three years at the time of winning championship honors. In addition to playing in the school band, she plays various solo engagements in and around Odebolt.

Joseph B. Herman

An exceptionally fine musician and drummer of Dorchester, Mass., has played many of the finest jobs in New England under famous directors and has played tympani with the New England Coke Orchestra for many years under the baton of Hy Fine. Born in Russia, has played drums for 25 years. Has been a Leedy user for the past fifteen years or so.

Esther Taylor, Washington, D. C.

Talented marimba artist playing exclusive professional jobs in and around Washington, D. C., which is her home. Studied under Geo. Hamilton Green and has made quite a name for herself in her work. Uses a Leedy Royal Marimba of the latest model finished in Marine Pearl with which she is 100% satisfied and if you don't think she's satisfied, just notice her big smile!

Joe MacMartin

Drummer with the West Lafayette, (Ind.) High School band and orchestra, young MacMartin won a rating of "Excellent" in the individual drumming contests held in connection with the National High School Band Contests in Cleveland last year. Because of Joe's sincerity and earnestness, we believe that DRUM TOPICS readers will have occasion to hear more of this young Leedy drummer.

Louisiana U.

The mammoth 208-piece band of the Louisiana State University located in New Orleans is directed by Colonel Castro Carazo and its rhythm is supplied by this exceptionally fine and large percussion section using all Leedy equipment. The band is famed throughout the south for its splendid concert work as well as for its sparkling march music and excellent parade ability.

High School Band

This is the percussion section of the McKinley High School 2nd Regiment Band, Washington, D. C., which is directed by Capt. L. E. Manley shown second from the right in the above photo. The band has played several theatre, radio and concert engagements in and around Washington, etc. Most of these young drummers also do professional and semi-professional playing in addition to their school band work.

Harvey C. Class, Cleveland, O.

A former theatre drummer, xylophonist and tympanist, Class (extreme right) today devotes all his time to teaching and is known as one of Cleveland's finest. Conducts the Class Studio of Drumming and is Supervisor of Percussion at the Glenville College of Music and other music schools in that city. Shown with Class and the Leedy Octarimba in the above picture are Rob't Dell, Cleveland Heights, John Postransky, Cleveland and Norman Mundy, Lakewood (reading from right to left) all of whom have won xylophone distinction and championships under the able instruction of their teacher, Mr. Class who has long used Leedys.

THE END

LEEDY DRUM TOPICS

JULY, 1937   **No. 26**

Boola Bango

SAYS:

"They call me the best drummer in Africa but think what I could do if I had a LEEDY!"

Mr. Joseph G. Benoit,
165 Hildreth,
Lowell, Mass.

POSTMASTER: RETURN POSTAGE GUARANTEED

Leedy Mfg. Co., Inc.

2307 Leedy Bldg.   Elkhart, Indiana

PERCUSSION SECTION
THE CHICAGO SYMPHONY ORCHESTRA
Lionel Sayers ★ Ed. Kopp ★ Bohumir Vesely ★ Ed. M. Metzenger

The splendid percussion section of the world-noted Chicago Symphony Orchestra, one of the very finest, directed by the eminent Dr. Fredrick Stock, uses 100% Leedy equipment as shown above. Its members are (left to right): Lionel Sayers, snare drum, cymbals, traps and effects; Ed Kopp, bass drum; Bohumir Vesely, snare drum, bells, chimes, xylophone, traps and effects, and Ed. M. Metzenger, tympani—and each is an outstanding artist.

Leedy Drum Topics Issue 27

Every Drummer Knows It!
(But Nobody Else Seems to Care)

For fifty years or more, Drummers of all nations have been raising the cry "We should get more money than other musicians except the leader." This is a lament that falls on deaf ears in 999 cases out of 1000. This one, like all others before it, will probably fade into nothingness and avail the profession naught. There is, however, no law to prevent us "hide pounders" from weeping on each others' shoulders once again. Hope springs eternal so here goes another bombardment on the same old, old subject. Let's state some of the facts again if for no other reason than to D. C. what we all know.

We know—that the Drummer who owns even the barest necessities for the ordinary band or orchestra job has invested more money in instruments and equipment than most other players in the organization.

We know—that one trunk for a xylophone, marimba or vibraphone costs more than the average priced trombone.

We know—that a set of pedal tympani, complete with the trunks, costs more than the average bass horn or Sousaphone and as much, or more, than the next TWO highest priced instruments in the organization.

We know—that a first class snare drum and bass drum, such as are demanded by most leaders, means more money out of the Drummer's pocket than the price of the finest cornet or trumpet made.

We know—that a Drummer spends more money per year for replacements of drum heads, sticks, wire brushes, mallets and trap holders than the combined cost of all the reeds, strings and oil bought by the entire band.

We know—that cymbals and renewals (because of breakage) add up to more money than most fiddlers pay for their "saw box."

We know—(and here's the punch) that the completely equipped Drummer on the "name" jobs of today often has more money tied up in instruments and accessories than the price of the best grand piano on the market.

Do we have a legitimate argument in favor of more dough? We'll say we do! How to get it? Some might say "A Drummer's union or association." That would require an organizer and a leader. Who is he? Where can he be found? We don't know, but the idea is there.

We've all heard the old crack "Why be a Drummer?" The answer is that most of us love the business for itself. We love drums and everything pertaining to drums. Then, too, somebody has to be a drummer in order to keep the rest of the musicians on the beat.

ORIGINAL INVESTMENT

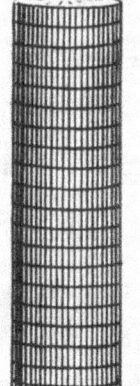

ANNUAL UPKEEP, ETC.

WEEKLY SALARIES

Leedy Drum Topics

JANUARY   Issue No. 27   1939

Walter G. Howe, National Symphony

Howe has been tympanist with the National Symphony, Washington, D. C., Hans Kindler, Conductor, for the past 3 years and played concerts in more than 30 cities with that organization. Home is Washington; Birth place, Stoneham, Mass. Studied at New England Conservatory and under Francis Mont and Lawrence Stone. An exceptionally fine tympanist. Formerly played radio, dance and hotel jobs under Meyer Davis. Uses Leedys.

Berlioz Grand Requiem Mass with Sixteen Tympani

This is probably the largest concert drum section ever assembled in Canada. It was the occasion of the first performance in Canada (and only the second on the continent) of Berlioz Grand Requiem Mass by the Mendelssohn Choir and full Symphony Orchestra rendered in Varsity Arena, Toronto, Canada, last April. The original score, calling for sixteen tympani, was played. Players (front row, left to right) are Duncan Reid, Thomas Burry, Earl Norton, Ivan Specht and (rear row left to right) Jack Breach, Harold Slater, Ernest Ainley, Archibald Cooper and George H. Newnham. Newnham is the Leedy dealer-distributor for Ontario Province. All tympani, except two pair, are Leedy.

Marshall Baker

When last heard from, was playing with Art Paulson and his orchestra with whom he has played the Larchmont Shore Club, and New York theatre and hotel engagements. Baker uses Leedys.

Geo. S. Tillinghast

Pit drummer in the Earle Theatre, Washington, D. C., for the past 6 years now under director Joe Lombardi. Formerly with U. S. Navy Band, National Symphony, Washington and at Loews Palace Theatre in Washington. Born in Providence, R. I., studied under Geo. B. Stone in Boston.

Ralph Hansell

Last word was that Hansell was playing the Paramount Theatre, Los Angeles, under Director Rube Wolff. A very fine drummer and one of the nation's best xylophonists, Hansell has been featured over N. B. C., played the Elitch Symphony and leading theatres in Denver which is his birthplace.

Fair Park High School Drum Section

The Fair Park High School Band, Shreveport, La., under the leadership of H. Hines Sims, is one of the finest in its state and may well be proud of this fine percussion section. Equipment is Leedy.

Rudy Van Gelder

Drum editor of "Orchestra World" magazine. Formerly featured drummer with Ted Lewis and many of the biggest "name" bands in the dance, theatre, radio and record fields, this Leedy drummer is well known to our readers as one of the "tops" in the profession.

Bill Kaiser with Jack Marshard's Orchestra

Favorite band for New England debutante's coming-out parties and other society balls and dances for several years has been Jack Marshard's orchestra. Drummer with this fine aggregation for the past five years has been Bill Kaiser who is shown with Marshard above. Kaiser's home is Roxbury, Mass., he is a former pupil of Simon Sternberg and uses nothing but Leedy.

Sam Bass with George Hall's Orchestra

Bass is a truly fine drummer who at his last writing was playing with the popular George Hall and his orchestra with which organization he has been for several years. Hall's band recently closed at Loew's State in N. Y. and is now playing a successful road tour. Was formerly located at Hotel Taft, N. Y. C. for several seasons where they were featured over 2 C.B.S. network 5 times per week. Bass uses Leedy.

Neal de Luca with Henry King

A drawing card wherever it plays, Henry King's orchestra, with Neal de Luca at the drums, is now playing the Fairmont Hotel, San Francisco. Drums used by de Luca are all Leedy as shown.

Dorothy Barneck

This pretty little miss "steals the show" when she appears on parade leading the band of which she is guest. Popular throughout North Dakota, she has also appeared in Chicago at the Chicagoland Music Festival. Her home is Bismark, N. D.

Percussion Section North Fulton H. S. Band

Atlanta, Ga.'s finest. Left to right—W. T. Jackson, (Leader) Edwin Lunsford, Hollis Hope, Leckie Mattox, Erle Cocke, Arthur Burdett, Elbert Tuttle. Equipment is 100% Leedy and the youths play like professionals.

Carrol Consitt

Formerly with Ken Moyer with whom he is shown to the left. Consitt is now with Henry Waldeman's orchestra playing theatre and hotel engagements. Also played with Blue Steele and Jack Morgan doing theatre, radio, hotel and ballroom work. He was born in Montreal but now calls Detroit his home. His equipment is all Leedy.

James Ghiglietti

This 100% Leedy drummer does duty at the drums for "Len" Perry and his orchestra doing radio, night club and dance work out of Jeannette, Pa., which is Ghiglietti's home address. Has been with Perry for two years. Formerly with Jack Gregory, studied under Ira Miller. He uses Leedy.

"Sonny" Greer's Complete New Leedy Outfit

DUKE ELLINGTON
Personable, congenial, fine musician, showman and director, Duke Ellington continues as one of the most popular leaders of the day. Famed for his many compositions and arrangements as well as his batoneering, the Duke has not only thrilled the entire United States with his "swing" music, but also many European countries as well.

"SONNY" GREER
Staunch standby of Ellington's rhythm department is none other than the versatile, dynamic, hot "Swingster" "Sonny" Greer who literally was born with drum sticks in his hands and who can "rap-'em-out" with the best in the field—and who does so seemingly for the sheer love of just doin' it.

This is the brand new outfit with which "Sonny" is making 'em sit up and take notice—one of the finest and most complete of any used in the profession. Of all his Leedy outfits, Greer says that this one "tops 'em all" for good looks, completeness, convenience and quality. And "Sonny" should know because he gives everything shown above a pretty thorough going over during the course of an evening or during a show. A fine showman himself, Greer places great value on a flashy outfit and credits a portion of his success with Duke Ellington to his Leedys. The above photograph was taken at the Leedy factory before the outfit was shipped to "Sonny" and does not show the trunks into which the outfit packs —and there were six of them!

Jos. W. Soistman

Native of Baltimore and veteran key drummer of that city where he still resides. Soistman is one of the best known, all-around, fine drummers in that section. Has played opera, theatre, dance, circus and military work in Baltimore and surrounding territory, has organized and taught numerous drum corps and always has a large studio class. Is now instructor of the Shrine Band and drum corps and teaches drum and all percussion instruments in all the Baltimore public schools including high school and colleges and is identified with the drum department of C. G. Conn, Ltd., in that city. He has always used Leedy.

On This DRUM TOPIC'S Cover

Greatest single swing sensation of the day is Larry Clinton whose picture appears on this DRUM TOPIC'S cover. Larry's cornet and trombone work is outstanding as he fronts his famous "Swing" band. He is one of the most popular composers, arrangers, and directors in public favor today. He and his boys played to capacity crowds at Glen Island Casino all last summer and records have been shattered and re-shattered during his present engagement at New York's International Casino. The recordings of this organization are becoming more popular than ever and the Quaker Oats-Clinton NBC commercial is one of the best on the air. Drummer with this sensational swing band under this swing-sational leader is—you guessed it—none other than Charlie Blake whose reputation as a truly fine swing drummer is known to the entire profession. Prior to being with Clinton, he was with Mal Hallett for many years, playing the finest jobs from the Mississippi to the eastern seaboard. Blake's birthplace is Patton, Pa., and his present address is Long Island City, N. Y. He studied drums under Wm. Simpson and uses Leedy equipment exclusively, of which he says: "The finest I've ever worked with and their appearance is 100%."

Nebraska Farm Boy Makes Good in the Big City

The time and locale indicated in the above picture apparently have little in common with one of the world's most renowned mallet played instrument artist, composer, author, arranger and teacher of today but—s'help us—it's true that the 11-year-old lad with the two-fisted grip on his Winchester who is modeling the latest '05 corduroy pants, et al, is none other than the famous Geo. Hamilton Green of 33 years ago back on the old homestead in Fort Calhoun, Nebraska

Frank Vesely (left)
One of Pittsburgh's up-and-coming, versatile young drummers, Frank Vesely, is playing Leedys in competent manner for Joe Ravell's orchestra currently holding sway in Pittsburgh's Arlington Lodge.

Arthur A. Prokesch (right)
Has played many fine European and American spots with some of the finest shows and dance bands and is now heading his own aggregation as well as playing in two other bands in and around Brooklyn, N. Y., which is his birthplace and home. Uses Leedy exclusively.

ABILITY TO IMPROVISE IS SURE WAY TO GOOD JOB and GOOD PAY

★ The Vibraphone, more popular in the modern dance band and on the air than ever before, and increasing in favor all the time,
★ offers unprecedented opportunities to work into a better job with really worthwhile pay.

Tony Lombardo, Pittsburgh, Pa.

Staff artist with all radio stations and featured soloist with almost every band, and principal of several small combinations in Pittsburgh, Lombardo is undoubtedly one of Pittsburgh's busiest and most popular musicians. His OHT is Florence, Pa.

Ralph Kempf with Louisiana Kings

On last information was with Louisiana Kings playing radio, dance and hotel engagements in Baton Rouge, La., territory. Kempf was born in

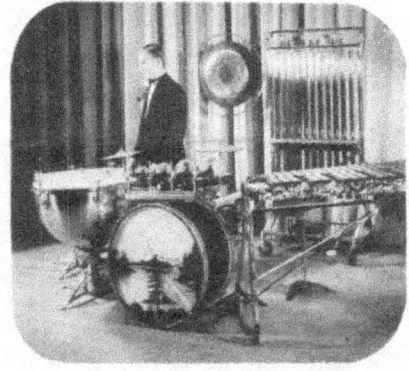

Coshocton, O., studied under Charlie Wilcoxson and has been with several very fine bands. Has used Leedys all during his 12 years playing.

Anyone who "scouts" the travelling bands that play his town or takes the time via the radio to get a line on what the country's leading dance orchestras are offering to rate their popularity and the choicest jobs cannot fail to have noticed that almost EVERY one of them features a Vibraphone with variations, hot rhythm effects, fast melodies and other specialties. And the public loves it—goes for it in a large way!

In the majority of instances the performers that we've heard play the Vibs pretty much like a xylophone, with medium-hard mallets and with very little pedal.

We learned from George Hamilton Green, during our last trip East, that this is the newest feature in all the best dance bands and that the majority of fellows playing Vibs with these bands are IMPROVISING — and panning heavy pay-dirt for their ability and effort.

Right now, according to Green, there are more jobs waiting for good Vibraphone players than there are fellows to fill them and the player of mallet instruments can look forward to plenty of work providing he can improvise.

There was an article in the last, No. 26, issue of DRUM TOPICS which announced the fact that Mr. Green was offering a new, complete "Geo. Hamilton Green Modern IMPROVISING COURSE" of thirty-five individual three-page lessons.

We learned from Mr. Green that the large majority of the fellows that we have heard playing Vibraphone with the big-name bands on the air are those who have completed this course of study which he offers.

If the "plug" that we gave Green's improvising course in last DRUM TOPICS induced any DRUM TOPICS readers to study this method and they have profited thereby, we are happy to have helped them.

For the benefit of those who may not have received the last DT issue, and those who may have lost or loaned their copy to a brother drummer, we reprint the following in the belief that more DT readers may want to subscribe to the Green Improvising Course to which we have referred:

This course being offered by Geo. Hamilton Green is undoubtedly the finest thing that has ever been offered to the advanced player and student by ANY instructor or school. It shows how all different types of variations and arpeggios are formed in their relation to fundamental chords, tells how variations are applied to all types of modern melody, shows the proper application of arpeggios, double-stops, scale-forms, etc. A thorough routine covering the invention of ideas, the writing of original variations, and adapting from printed piano parts is given and "swing", rhythm effects and "sock" style are clearly analyzed.

In addition to the above, this course will greatly improve general technique and develop speed and precision in playing.

The purpose of this course is to help the student who, due to location, cannot come personally to Geo. Hamilton Green's studio for lessons. These same lessons are given to pupils visiting Mr. Green's studios. Regardless of where you live, you can now study marimba and xylophone with Geo. Hamilton Green and receive and adapt yourself to the same training and routine that you would receive if you were to go to his studio in person. COMPLETE instruction, advice and suggestions of WHAT to do, HOW to practice and HOW to play are clearly printed in every lesson.

Write to Geo. Hamilton Green, Box 143, South Station, Yonkers, New York, for complete information which he will mail to you gladly, promptly and without obligation.

Kurkowski's Xylophone Band

This splendid Marimba-Xylophone Band, made up of 11 to 18 year old boys and girls each of whom doubles on other instruments or does some specialty act, is taught and directed by Jack Kurkowski, Richmond, Ind. Organized six years ago, it plays vaudeville, Chautauquas, state fair, radio and convention engagements and is constantly gaining in popularity and demand. Kurkowski has played dance, theatre and radio drums, was with the 32nd Division's 127th Inf. Band overseas, studied under Green, Ainsworth, Zettleman, Lange and others. Was born in Berlin, Wis.

Orlen O. Hungerford, Terre Haute, Indiana

Drummer and xylophonist with the Terre Haute, Ind., H. S. Band and the Indiana State Teachers College Band. He has played numerous radio and other engagements. Orlen, though only in his middle 'teens, might be considered a veteran. He studied under Jack O'Grady and Joe Beasley. Born in Clinton, Ind. Has used Leedy instruments four years.

Sindle with Marvin Frederick

Drummer doing a splendid job with Frederick's band which has played many fine dance spot and hotel jobs in Chicago, including the Stevens Hotel, is Hal Sindle shown left above. He's an all-Leedy user and booster.

James M. Elliott

Directs and tempoes his own dance band in Miami, Fla., where he has been playing the American Legion Gardens. Was with Smith's Scotch Highlanders 5 years. In the biz 18 years, born in Nokomis, Ill., and studied under Rusick, Straight and Zettleman. A very fine drummer.

Bobby Waters, Auburn Heights, Mich.

Leedy drums have won State Championships for Bobby who is a member of the Northwest Sons of the American Legion, Detroit, and for his father, C. A. Waters, member of the Cook-Nelson A. L. Post, Detroit.

Splendid Junior Corps

Organized, equipped and trained by the American Legion and Auxiliary Posts of College Hill, Pa., this exceptionally fine Junior corps is a consistent prize winner in competition and was American Legion Junior Champion of Pennsylvania in 1936. This is a genuine accomplishment in a state where corps are as numerous and competition as keen as it is in Pennsylvania. Equipment is Leedy, of course.

Carl Dengler and His Rainbow Rhythm Orchestra

Director and featured Vibraphonist of his own orchestra which offers "Music in the Moderne Mode", Dengler's is considered the leading society orchestra in Rochester, N. Y., and surrounding New York territory playing leading colleges, hotels and country clubs there. Dengler's home is Rochester; his teacher was Floyd "Tommy" Thomas.

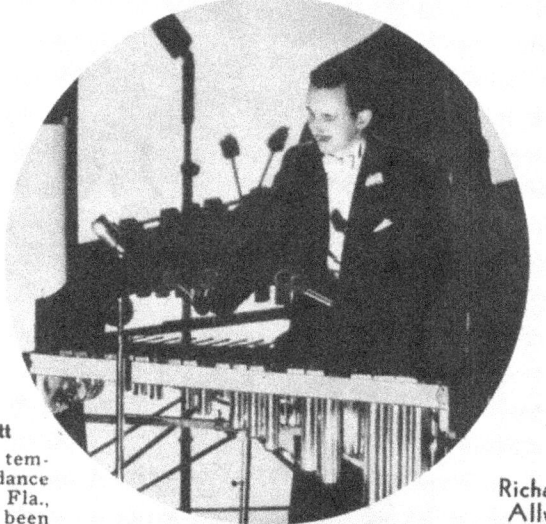

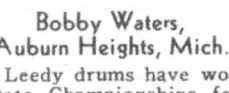

Maurer with Leighton Noble

Johnny Maurer recently closed at the Edgewater Beach Hotel, Chicago, and opened at the Statler in Boston with Leighton Noble and his splendid outfit. Previously played Palace Hotel, San Francisco, and the Arcadia, Philadelphia. Formerly played with Bob Sperling at British Colonial Hotel, Nassau. Home and birthplace is Somerville, N. J.

Ted Tillman with Henry Busse

Tillman rates among the best in the profession and is a veteran with the Busse band now playing in first class hotel jobs. Skillful, versatile and personable, Ted is valued by Busse and is popular with all who know him.

Richard W. Allwright

Is drummer with the Greyhound Hotel Dance Orchestra, which has played 4 years in the Greyhound Hotel, Chadwell Heath, Essex, England. Born in Clapham, Eng., and studied under Len Wood. Says Leedys are the finest he's ever used.

XYLOPHONE MUSIC RACK HOLDER

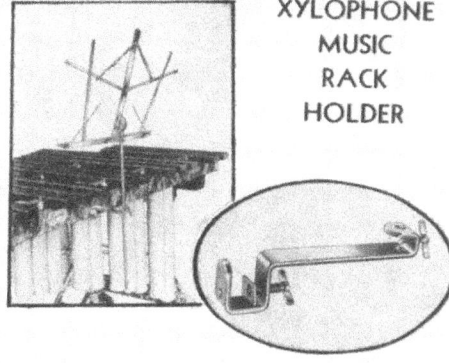

Fills a long felt need! Use your own music rack with this holder which clamps securely to the under edge of the xylophone or marimba frame. Music rack post inserts into the holder, is adjustable to the desired height and is held firmly in place by the wing screw bolt. Makes your music rack a part of your instrument and holds your music right in front of you within reading distance. Strong, serviceable, inexpensive.

No. 7867—Nickel $1.00
No. 7868—Chromium 1.50

Mel Obsen

Drummer with Ted Nering and his Orchestra for four years, studied under Harold Firestone who is employed by Leedy, and lives in Gary, Indiana, his birthplace. Played Iroquois Gardens, Louisville, Station WHAS, Colonial Club, Evansville, Ind., and numerous Big 10 Colleges.

John J. Yock

Born in Chicago, studied drums under Joe Rusick and has played for six years with Bill Kuelb (at left) playing various ballrooms and dances in Chicago. Has been a Leedy user and booster for seven years.

Daniel A. Tyler

A versatile dance, theatre and radio drummer and xylophonist and teacher of Tampa, Fla., who uses all Leedy. Has played professionally for eleven years. Studied under Professors Godding, Geisser and Spaine and is recognized as one of the finest drummers in his part of the state.

NEW! LEEDY RUBBER "ROCKING CYMBAL" SEAT

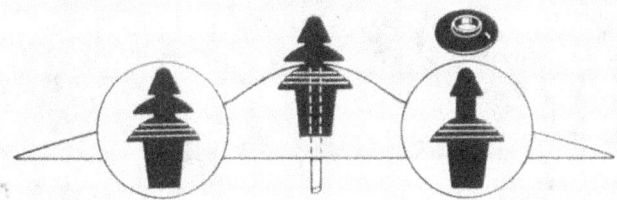

Above: Cymbal on Seat.
Right: Cymbal Seat Assembly.
Left: Units before Assembling.

Here is a brand new, all-rubber "ROCKING CYMBAL" Seat that gives maximum, unhampered cymbal vibration and tone and which permits the easiest and fastest means of setting up and knocking down your cymbals ever devised. Consists of two parts—the seat and removable "collar"—as shown above at the left. To assemble, remove collar, place cymbal on the seat. Next slightly moisten the Tip of seat, then place collar on top of cymbal, and mount the set-up on the cymbal post. Set-up permits finest, fullest cymbal tone. To pack, remove cymbal and seat from post together as a unit and pack. Do not take off collar. When setting up again, cymbal is on seat ready to be placed on your cymbal holder.

No. 9010—Leedy Rubber "ROCKING CYMBAL" Seat. Each $0.40

AND NOW—
IT'S SWING THAT'S KING

To the drummers who have come into the business in the past ten years, we will try to draw a little picture of the changes in styles of playing and explain why they are now occupying the place "in the sun" that they really deserve.

In the so-called "old days" when a musician had to study and practice many months before being able to hold a job, the drummer was able to take his place in an orchestra, and, therefore, earn money sooner than the cornet player or the other musicians. The brass and string players studied long and hard along what was called legitimate lines and when they were finally accepted as professionals, they continued to strive for tonal quality and execution as per accepted musical laws. The more proficient they became, the closer they stuck to their past teachings. "Noodling" and "hot stuff" both or "straying from the lead" was unheard of. Those playing brass, string, and other "lead" instruments, were required to stick to their arrangements. The only thing acceptable was that they stick to the notes as laid down by the arranger. Playing arpeggios and accented notes to bring out the rhythm was not required. The drummer and the piano player supplied all the rhythm necessary. They were supposed to put in beats and fill up spots to the best of their ability, first because the arrangements for drummers in those days were all written out in straight time and not much thought to these drum parts was given by the arranger. No matter how far the drummer strayed from the orthodox, there were no complaints. He was merely complimented for his dexterity and originality. This was called "Rag-time".

Then came the "bomb-shell" . . . .

It started with the original Dixieland Jazz Band and other history-making organizations such as "Jelly Roll" Morton, W. C. Handy, and many others. According to statistics, this style originated in New Orleans territory, spread to the Pacific Coast, and up came Paul Whiteman, Earl Fuller, Art Hickman, Ted Lewis and others as exponents of the new type jazz band. Most of these bands used no arrangements whatsoever; the idea of the entire group was to produce a rhythmic improvisation around a hot solo. Of course, each man would take the lead, and at times these numbers would be presented in a way that would give each lead instrument in the band, such as the saxophone, clarinet, trumpet, trombone, and piano a chorus and the remainder of the band, including the drummer, would form a rhythmic background. This rhythm had to change to fit the type of solo being played in front. Paul Whiteman was one of the first to change all this. Whiteman was a school musician and could not fake as was required, so assembled around himself some of the finest swing artists in the business at that time and had arrangements made so that each and every member of the organization had a specific part, of course, in keeping with the type of music in vogue at that time. In a great many cases the drummer was still allowed to do his stuff. Back in 1920 everything from frying pans to cow bells were used in a complete kit and the drummer that could cover the most of this was considered the best. Of course, it was only natural that Whiteman with his special arrangements should forge to the front, and as is always the case, other leaders followed as best they could. New ideas in arrangements were developed and we had at that time what was called "JAZZ".

Another "bomb-shell" was broken . . . .

Isham Jones, and a few years later Guy Lombardo, Wayne King, and Rudy Vallee's style of music came to the front. This type of music pushed the drummer in the background. All that was required was that he keep up a solid rhythm of four-to-a-bar, and very little originality was required. As a matter of fact, some of these bands did not use drummers on their broadcasts or recordings except for cymbal crashes, gongs, etc. That type of music was sweet and flowing with very little pronounced rhythm. As is always the case, the type of music written in that period was of the sweet style without much rhythm. Almost any drummer could handle this type of job, for it was just a question of his being routine to what was required of him and he was considered good if he could play soft enough so that he was felt by the band, but really not heard. In a great many cases, he was hired for his ability to put on a "hokum" act, sing a song, or for his good looks and personality more than for his ability as a drummer.

Another "bomb-shell" was broken and what an explosion!

After many years of the drummer being the necessary "evil" in an orchestra, he is at last coming into his own. A number of bands such as Benny Goodman, Casa Loma, Bob Crosby, Jimmy and Tommy Dorsey, Duke Ellington, Fletcher Henderson, Artie Shaw and Larry Clinton have started the swing craze which has given birth to the "Jitter Bugs". The drummer is again getting his chance to "go to town". This is particularly true of bands from coast to coast and the public has accepted it as the greatest musical entertainment in the past decade. The drummer not only has an opportunity to show off his ability but has proven that he is very often the "cog" on which the band revolves. This style of music is protecting the drummer that really has the ability and is doing more to give the all-around drummer the break that he so richly deserves. Never in the history of the United States has such enthusiasm been shown towards music and its rendition as has been shown in the past two years. The swing concerts at Carnegie Music Hall in New York City alone have proven this beyond a doubt, and the famous so-called "Jam Sessions" held throughout different parts of the country have really given the drummer his just dues and they tell us that King Swing is here to rule indefinitely.

Are we anticipating too much? We believe not. It is in the atmosphere and the wise drummer who has come into the business in the past few years will go into the wood-shed and obtain the musical fundamentals that he has neglected for so long. Those who have creative ability and who will study up on what they lack will not only earn more money in the future but will once more sit in the "spot light" and "reap the harvest".

Esther Taylor with the "Dixie Debs"

Esther Taylor is the talented, versatile and charming marimba player with the popular "Dixie Debs" combination which is playing engagements in Washington, D. C., and doubling at the George Mason Hotel, Alexandria, W. Va. The marimba naturally is a Leedy!

Phil Patton with Orrin Tucker

Born in Rockford, Ill., studied under Walter Van Dugn, of that city and under Ray Mann, Chicago. Played Rockford territory, later joined Tom Temple's band out of Appleton, Wis. Joined Orrin Tucker's fine band at Lowry Hotel, St. Paul, three years ago and has since played many of the finest hotels in the country, including Edgewater Beach Hotel and Palmer House, Chicago. Orrin Tucker (shown at left) is now one of the country's most versatile and popular leaders. Phil is established as one of the finest modern Drummers in the business. He uses all Leedy.

Robert J. Fuelgraff

Fuelgraff has been with Jimmy Green (standing) for five years playing Chicago's finest ballroom and cafe jobs and doing out-of-town hotel work with this fine band. Bob is a native Chicagoan, studied under Harry Kelow and has been all Leedy for the past ten years.

Frank E. Laughead

A fine drummer with the Smith Superba Band which has just finished a season playing fairs. Director Smith is shown on left in photo. Frank played in the "FOUR HORSEMEN" picture, has played circus and numerous shows. His OHT is Zanesville, O. He studied under Henry Stemm and has played Leedys for twenty years.

Arlene Stouder and Her Marimba Band

This fine marimba aggregation has played numerous radio, dance and club engagements in northern Indiana and is popularly received wherever it appears. Bob Widmar is the drummer, and also has his own dance orchestra. All the marimbas and drums are Leedy. The band's home is Bremen which is just south of South Bend.

THE NEW LEEDY ARCH·TRAP·RAIL

The ONLY Trap Rail That Fits Down CLOSE TO THE BASS DRUM SHELL!

★

NOTE "STAYON" CLAMP — HOLDS HOLDER TO RAIL IN A VISE-LIKE GRIP. TRAP HELD FIRM AND RIGID UNDER ANY AND ALL CONDITIONS! Heavy Duty Ratchet Tom-Tom Holder illustrated. Universally adjustable — upward, downward, forward, back and for all angles. For all size tom-toms except 10" x 4".

No. 9026—Nickel. Each......$4.25

No. 9027—Chrome. Each...... 6.25

(Lightweight tom-tom holder listed below)

Stronger, more rigid, more practical and more convenient in every respect, this NEW Leedy Arch Trap Rail has EVERYTHING! An unusually wide selection of traps can be mounted on the rail with full assurance of convenient location and rigid, vibrationless support—nothing need be fastened to the bass drum hoops! Flat rail, made of high grade steel, conforms exactly to the radius of the drum and is anchored securely to the shell just above the rods by four metal spools placed at equidistant points. Rail remains on drum at all times, is compact, inconspicuous and out of the way, saves time in setting up, knocking down and packing. Your fibre bass drum case or Mackintosh cover will accommodate drum with the rail attached. Because trap rail fits close to drum shell, special trap holders are required. STAYON type clamps are used assuring strength, durability and long life. Holders will not "twist" or "turn" after being set. Holders afford the maximum degree of flexibility in mounting the traps and traps are fully adjustable for height, angle and distance from you. Holders available for use on Arch Trap Rail are illustrated below to the right and are listed at the right. Illustration above at right shows clamp for attaching to rail. Rail and all holders available in Nickel or Chromium at prices indicated. See this set-up at your nearest Leedy Dealer's store—today!

No. 9020—ARCH Rail, complete Nickel .... $ 4.00
No. 9021—ARCH Rail, complete Chromium 6.00
No. 9026—Heavy Duty Ratchet Tom-Tom Holder, Nickel 4.25
No. 9027—Heavy Duty Ratchet Tom-Tom Holder, Chromium... 6.25
No. 9032—Lightweight Ratchet Tom-Tom Holder, Nickel...... 1.50
No. 9033—Lightweight Ratchet Tom-Tom Holder, Chromium... 2.25
No. 9028—Wood Block and Cow Bell Holder—Nickel 1.75
No. 9029—Wood Block and Cow Bell Holder—Chromium 2.60
No. 9030—Temple Block Rail, complete—Nickel 7.00
No. 9031—Temple Block Rail, complete—Chromium 10.50
No. 9022—Bestall Cymbal Holder—Nickel. Each 2.00
No. 9023—Bestall Cymbal Holder—Chromium. Each 3.00
No. 9024—Offset Cymbal Holder—Nickel. Each 2.25
No. 9025—Offset Cymbal Holder—Chromium. Each 3.25
No. 9018—Complete ARCH Rail and all holders as shown in illustration below including: two HEAVY DUTY Tom-Tom Holders; two BESTALL Cymbal Holders; two OFFSET Cymbal Holders; one Combination Wood Block-Cow Bell Holder; and one Temple Block Rail—Nickel, only.................... 27.50
No. 9019—Same as 9018—Chromium 41.25

ARCH TRAP RAIL No. 9020
No. 9020—Nickel $4.00
No. 9021—Chromium 6.00

NEW and HOT!

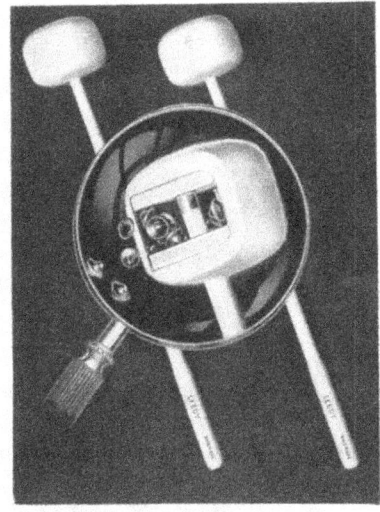

LEEDY "BONGO-RACA" STICKS

A real novelty effect that has proven to be a "hit" with drummers, leaders and the public, from coast to coast. Has unlimited uses in the present-day "ride" band on tom-toms, and cymbals and is "torrid stuff" for "hot" marimba work. Too, they add pepper to tango, bolero and rhumba numbers.

As shown in the cutaway illustration to the left, each stick has a miniature maraca built into the felt covered ball. The small metal pellets bounce around inside a vulcanized fibre chamber producing loud or soft realistic effects at will. They are the size of the average tympani sticks. Sturdily built of best quality felt-fibre and hickory materials. Correct weight and nicely balanced, these sticks will give you perfect playing satisfaction and add ZIP to your numbers.

Try a pair of these sticks and you'll want 'em; use them on your next job and you'll feel that their cost was worth the effect that they will have on your fellow musicians, on the director and on the paying public. See them at your local Leedy Dealer's store!

No. 1616—Leedy Bongo-Raca Sticks. Per pair.............. $3.00

Ray Mitchell, Pittsburgh, Pa.

Was 1931 New England States Champion Pocket Billiard Player and is still in the champion class on both drums and billiards. While playing exhibition games in Pittsburgh, Ray bought the Kenyon bowling and billiard establishment there. Still plays exhibition billiards and does jobbing on drums. Formerly with the Joe Schaffer and Art Farrar orchestras. Is a close friend of the famous Bill Hammond.

Sally Martin

Miss Martin, while attending school, annexed 1st Division honors in District four times, one 2nd and three 1st's in State Contests and 1st Division honors in National competition at Columbus, O., in 1937. Has played dances in her mother's orchestra for five years, now attending the Conservatory of Music at James Milliken U., Decatur, Ill., where she directs her own all-girl concert and swing band. Studied drums with Harry E. Hart, P. Z. Green, Art Layfield and Allen Henny. Birthplace is Robinson, Ill. Her Ambition? To have her own symphony.

George Howard of the "King's Jesters"

With Howard and his Leedy BROADWAY are Fritz Bastow (left) and John Ravencroft, the Original King's Jesters who were an attraction feature with Paul Whiteman. Now have their own outfit which has played long engagements at the LaSalle Hotel, Chicago, has made transcriptions for Sterling Ale and National Biscuit, appeared on the Magic Key Hour for RCA and was featured for two years from NBC, Chicago.

Art Crippen —Phil Ohman Orchestra

A native of Los Angeles and a pupil of Ed Straight, Crippen joined Phil Ohman's Trocadero Orchestra when it was organized. Played a 3-year contract at the Cafe Trocadero in L. A., on Eddie Cantor program and Brunswick recordings with that band. Previous to that had his own band at Santa Barbara's Biltmore Hotel and was with Fox Studios for four years. His equipment is all Leedy which he bought from Bob Perry of Lockies Music Exchange, Los Angeles.

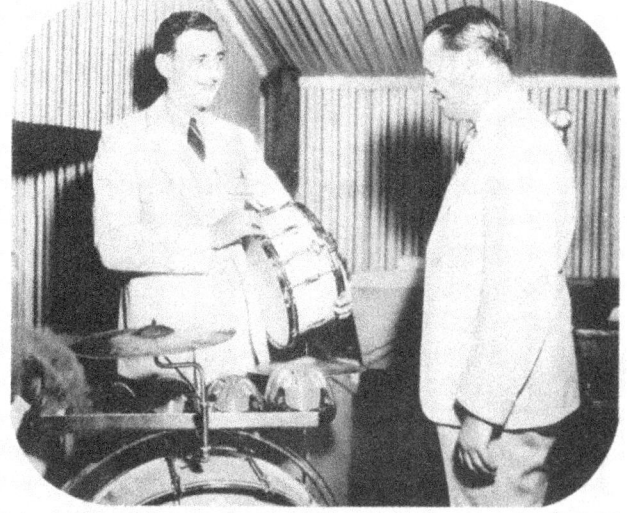

THE LEEDY "HIGHBOY"
SOCK CYMBAL PEDAL

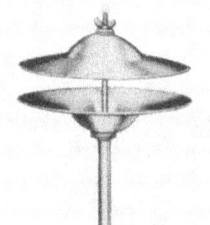

Does Not Include Cymbals

FEATURES:

1. 20-inch leg spread assures absolute playing solidity—no wobble, weave or danger of tipping.
2. Has a slip-proof, cast aluminum, type footboard and heelplate.
3. Cymbals and attachments come off together as a unit for quick, easy packing and assembling on the job.
4. Each cymbal held by top and bottom adjusting nuts—permitting loose or tight adjustments for full range of cymbal tone and sock effects.
5. Accurately machined and assembled—quiet, smooth, easy operating with no chatter or rattle.
6. Knocks down in three parts for convenient packing.
7. Sturdy—yet weighs only 4 lbs. 12 oz.

This is the recently introduced, greatly improved, smoother, easier working, sturdier Leedy "HIGHBOY" Sock Cymbal Pedal which has proved to be a sensation with the discriminating drummers in the profession. Completely redesigned with a number of noteworthy features added which have "made" this sock pedal. Thoroughly proven both in our own engineering department and in actual use on the job under actual playing conditions. See, try and use this pedal once and you'll be convinced of its superiority. Your local Leedy Dealer stocks the new model—see him at your earliest convenience.

No. 7563—Leedy HIGHBOY Sock Cymbal Pedal. Nickel $10.00
No. 7564—Leedy HIGHBOY Sock Cymbal Pedal. Chromium   15.00

Bill Geiss with Leon Mojica

Bill Geiss, dexterous drummer with Leon Mojica's popular west coast band currently playing San Francisco's El Patio Ballroom, shows plenty of the real McCoy in his work with that outfit which is also featured on the leading radio networks. Geiss uses Leedy.

William Long

Shown in the photo reproduced at the right is William Long, Akron, Ohio, who is playing his fourth year with the Akron University Symphony under the direction of Mr. J. M. Campbell. Though only seventeen, Long has played drums and xylophone for 11 years—always using Leedys in his work. Was a member of the National High School Orchestra and with the North Eastern Ohio Teachers Band. Long studied under the able Geo. O. Moody.

American Virtuoso

Drummer, Vibracussionist with the Boston Symphony Orchestra, composer and director, self-taught Lawrence White, born in Salmon, Idaho, again proves that America is the Land of Opportunity for those who have the will to succeed. Has played marimba for Paderewski, directed several outstanding eastern orchestras as guest conductor and is headed for even greater fame. Is now only twenty-one years old.

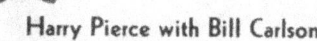

Irvin Daege

With Joe Martin and his orchestra playing beach, hotel and ballroom jobs with radio outlets over leading Wisconsin stations. Has played Wisconsin, Futuristic and Eagles Ballrooms in Milwaukee, which is his home.

Harry Pierce with Bill Carlson

With Bill Carlson's Orchestra for 11 years playing Chicago theatre, hotel, night club and ballroom jobs including the famous Trianon Ballroom. Pierce (right) was born in Pensacola, Fla. He studied under Burt Winas, is a fine drummer and uses all Leedy. Bill Carlson, Director, is shown on the left.

George Schaber, Chicago

Well known drummer and Vibra-cussionist in Chicago and surrounding territory is George Schaber shown (left) above with Charlie Gaylord with whom he has played for some years. Gaylord's band was regular relief band for Wayne King during that band's Palmer House engagement, is a popular ballroom, theatre and supper dance outfit and is "aired" over the leading Chicago radio stations. Lyons Band Instrument Co., Inc., one of Leedy's Chicago dealers, efficiently serve Schaber in all his percussion requirements.

Thomas M. Knox

A Chicagoan by birth, Knox has sought gentler climate and now lives in St. Petersburg, Fla., where he plays drums with Ray Williams and his Orchestra at the Million Dollar Pier where that band has held sway for the past eight years. Studied drums with O'Neil Spencer of New York's Onyx Club. Of his Leedys, Knox says: "I've tried them all and I'm convinced Leedys are 'tops'."

Russ Isaacs with Buddy Rogers

Born in Boston which might be called the "Cradle of American Drumming", Russ Isaacs has played drums for the past eight years or so during all of which time his choice has been Leedy equipment. Formerly with the renowned Bobby Hackett and with Boston's Theatrical Club and the Frank Daily Club jobs to his credit, Isaacs now plays with Buddy Rogers and his orchestra which recently finished playing Chicago's College Inn.

Drexel Lamb

Drummer-director of his own band which is now playing its fourth season (ending 6-15-'39) at Club Ledo, Jackson, Mich., also played Cape Fear Hotel, Wilmington, Del., "Wonder Bar", Grand Rapids, Mich., and Ye Olde Tavern, Ft. Wayne, Ind. Also numerous radio stations. Formerly with Ray Sliker, "Doc" Lewis and Ralph Miller Bands. Born in Chicago, taught by Harold Firestone and uses all Leedy equipment.

Don Baird

Has played with Larry Kent, Russ Plummer and Eddie Oliver orchestras at following spots: Del Mar Club, Santa Monica, Cal., Sir Francis Drake Hotel, San Francisco, Cal., Alexander Young Hotel, Honolulu, T. H., Rendevous Ballroom, Balboa Beach, Cal., etc. Born Herington, Kans., studied drums under John DeSoto and has been in the business 8 years. Of his Leedys he says: "They are the best." When last heard from was playing with Eddie Oliver at Victor Hugo Cafe.

THE NEW LEEDY "S-N-E-E-Z-E" CYMBAL

Here it is—the cymbal for that PERFECT "s-n-e-e-z-e" effect that is being demanded by many professionals in the business. Light taps give a refined, hissing "s-n-e-e-z-e" effect; a sharp stroke gives a dandy, pronounced "buzz" "s-n-e-e-z-e" comparable to the sound of a giant bumble bee that is ripping mad and preparing for a strong attack. Consists of a 15-inch Chinese cymbal especially selected for fine tonal qualities and carrying power into which are riveted a number of small, loose "rocking rivets" which produce the highly unusual, desired effect. Special care and precision are required in fastening the rivets to the cymbals as cymbals have a tendency to split in the operation. After the rivets are attached, however, the cymbal is as durable as ever and will give usual service. Try this innovation—you'll like it and it'll create a sensation on the job!

No. 7363—Leedy "S-n-e-e-z-e" Cymbal. Each $6.00

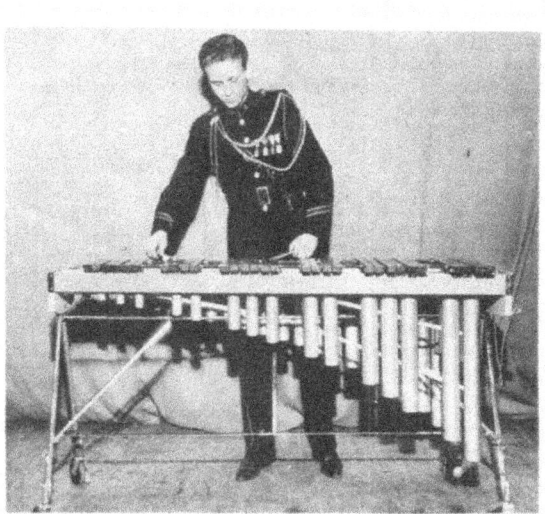

Geo. E. Gates

This lad is a member of the Kankakee High School Band of Kankakee, Ill., which is his birthplace. Has played with that organization for seven years under Director Geo. Piersol. Studied drums under his present director and has used Leedys for 6 of the 10 years he has played. His equipment includes Leedy drums, tympani, Vibraphone, Marimba.

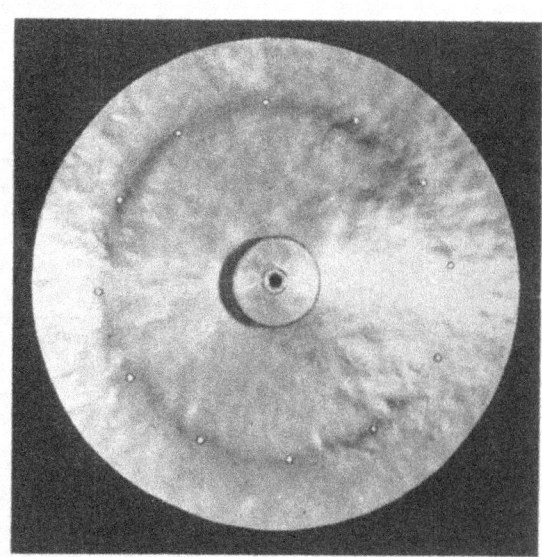

LEEDY-MADE P-I-G-S-K-I-N CHINA-TYPE TOM-TOMS

TRUE CHINESE TONE
GENUINE PIGSKIN HEADS ● TWO NEW LARGER SIZES
5-PLY SHELLS ● FINER APPEARANCE ● GREATER DURABILITY
(Note Chrome Inlay Head Tucking Strip on Larger Sizes)

You cannot buy finer Chinese-type tom-toms than these at any price. They EXCEL the Chinese products in the very qualities for which they are famous—depth and richness of tone, beauty and ornateness—and are at the same time structurally stronger and more durable. Shells are strong, damp-resisting, 3-ply wood, heads are genuine pigskin colorfully decorated and securely fastened (smallest size by sturdy tacks; two larger sizes by chrome inlay strip and tacks). Shells are durably finished in beautiful red lacquer. Once you've used these new toms, you'll never be satisfied with the crude importations.

(Standard with Red Lacquer Shells and Decorated Heads)

No. 7734—10" x 4"	$ 4.00	No. 7739—11" x 7"	$10.00
No. 7737—13" x 9"	13.00	No. 7738—14" x 12"	15.00

RATCHET 10" x 4" TOM-TOM HOLDER
(Patents Pending)

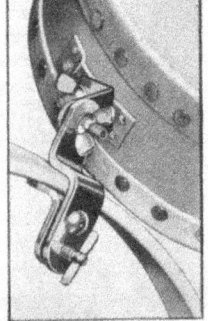

The tom-tom holder that the whole drum world has been waiting for—the one that permits the tom-tom to be placed in the EXACT desired position for every playing need. You can tilt the tom head to just the right playing angle, raise it, lower it, move it left, right, up or down, and place it where it meets your convenience! Identical to Tunable Tom holder in principal but made of formed steel. Two ratchet adjustments and Stayon hoop clamp. Screws solidly to tom-tom shell.

For Bass Drum Hoop
No. 7718—Nickel ... $1.50
No. 7719—Chromium ... 2.25

For ARCH Trap Rail
No. 9032—Nickel ... $1.50
No. 9033—Chromium ... 2.25

HEAVY DUTY RATCHET TOM-TOM HOLDER
(Patents Pending)

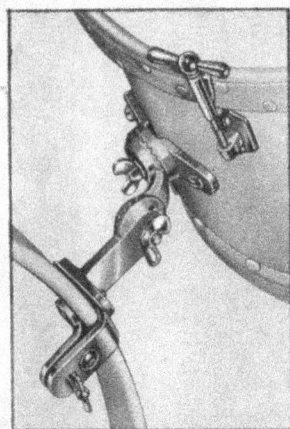

Universally adjustable! Tilts forward, backward, upward and downward by means of two ratchet adjustments thus giving you the desired playing angle at all times. Holds tom-tom securely even under heavy beating. Made of finest cast brass and features the Stayon clamp, which has been improved recently. Fastens to the tom-tom shell by two strong bolts. You'll like this remarkable new tom-tom holder which is without a doubt the most serviceable on the market.

For Bass Drum Hoop
No. 7723—Nickel. Each ... $3.50
No. 7724—Chromium. Each ... 5.25

For ARCH Trap Rail
No. 9026—Nickel ... $4.25
No. 9027—Chromium ... 6.25

Has Six Xylophone Arrangements Published

Joe Green, co-owner of the famous Green Brothers name and fame, busy as he is with his teaching and playing, still finds time to do a bit of arranging for xylophone which is his favorite instrument and on which he shares honors with George Hamilton. Most recent fruits of his efforts are six numbers for xylophone, with piano accompaniment, which have been published by Mills Publishing Co., Inc., 619 Broadway, N. Y. City. Numbers are "Farewell Blues", "Havana", "Lonesome and Sorry", "Dardanella", "Yaaka Hula Hickey Dula", and "Star Dust" (priced at 50c each with full orchestrations are available on special order). And here's another tip! Tune in on WJZ next, or any, Sunday morning (8:15 to 8:30 E. S. T.) if you get up that early and listen to Cloister Bells program on the NBC blue network. That'll be the Green Brothers performing. Then on Monday, any Monday, tune in the same station and hear Joe rip off some choice xylophone solos from 2:30 to 3:00 P.M. (also the blue network).

James Morris with Dick Hall

When last heard from, Morris was playing with the Dick Hall band out of Fargo, N. D., booking theatres, ballrooms and hotels. Jim is shown above with pianist Arvil Erfert, since replaced by Bob Olson. Morris studied under Dr. C. S. Putnam and uses Leedy equipment. He was born in Fargo.

FACTS ...
About TUNABLE Tom Tom Heads

> Whether you choose the non-tunable type tom-toms or the more recently introduced tunable tom-toms which are available in either single or separate tension, you will do well to choose Leedy-made instruments. (Leedy China-Types are the finest in their field—they excel the imported toms in strength, tone, workmanship and all-around satisfaction.) The NEW Leedy Tunable Toms shown on page 18 surpass any you have yet seen or played. See them, as well as the non-tunables at your nearest Leedy Dealer's store without delay!

When the Tunable Tom-Tom craze entered the drum world by way of the "Swing" route, it was only natural that the drum manufacturers should strive to imitate as closely as possible the tone of the conventional and long-used Chinese types.

It was not recognized at the beginning of the craze that the rhythms of swing would eventually demand short "boardy" tones from these instruments. The manufacturers generally knew that in order to obtain the conventional resonant and sustaining tone like the Chinese Tom-Toms, it would be necessary to employ pigskin heads. The hide of pigs in this country is of about the same texture and quality as those in China. Pigskin heads are not as plentiful in this country as is generally supposed. Leedy was the first drum company to locate a permanent source of supply—the makers agreeing to lay aside enough skins for our requirements from their activities comprised of the making of leather as supplied to manufacturers of gloves, sports jackets, footballs, bags, etc.

Pigskin hides cannot be tucked on wood flesh hoops in the same manner as calfskin heads because they contain an excess of natural fat or grease which is almost impossible to eliminate without completely removing the life and flexibility of the head. Therefore, inasmuch as we were all striving for the Chinese tone at the beginning, there was nothing left to do but to tack the head either to the shell as per the Chinese system or to tack the head to the counter hoop. The Leedy Company used both methods and was the first to introduce the pigskin head on these instruments. Leedy was also the first to devise a way to make pigskin heads hold on wood flesh hoops. We are employing this method at present on pigskin models.

As time went on and swing became the vogue of the day with vast improvements from a musical standpoint, it was inevitable that the character of swing music called for the shorter or "butter tub" tone. There is no question but what this quality can best be obtained by using medium thickness calf heads pulled fairly tight. They are naturally not as flexible as the pigskin. In other words, the trend has switched from pigskin to calf heads for swing drummers. Concert drummers still prefer the pigskin heads.

Please note that the Leedy Company can supply either type as outlined on page 18 of this Drum Topics issue. It is stated at the bottom of the page enclosed within ruled lines that pigskin heads and wood counter hoops can be supplied on both single and separate tension models at the same price as the calf heads. So, boys take your choice! They each have their place in "this here" drumming business.

Keith Rosenthal

One of South Australia's most popular and best equipped dance, radio and concert drummers is Keith Rosenthal of Adelaide who is shown in the above photo with his very complete Leedy outfit. South Australian drummers find Allan & Co., Leedy distributors with stores in Adelaide and Melbourne, ready, willing and able to serve them in all their drum requirements.

Roy Lebens with Jerry Gibeau

Lebens mans the drums for Jerry Gibeau's jobbing dance band which plays out of Minneapolis, Minn. Roy studied drums under Howard McElroy; lives in Shakopee, Minn.

Dick Perry

The "hit" of a Major Bowe's program and a veteran performer in radio, theatre and "flickers" on his drums at age 11 forecasts a brilliant future for Dick. He is the son of the Ralph Perrys, Herkimer, N. Y., and the student of Charles Allen, New Hartford, N. Y.

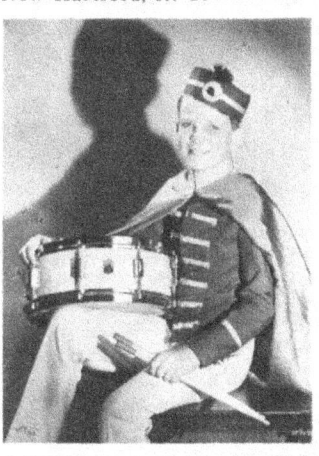

June Boyd, Jersey City, N. J.

This winsome and clever miss plays her Leedy Xylophone throughout N. J. and N. Y. City at leading hotels, radio stations, theatres and conventions and has appeared with Fanchon & Marco and for Coco Cola.

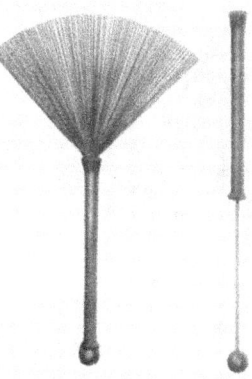

NEW!

MOLDED RUBBER COVERED HANDLE WIRE BRUSHES

$1.00 Per Pair

These wire brushes with the NEW molded rubber cover on the handles will make a world of difference in your brush rhythms. In the first place the molded rubber jackets add a desirable "heft" to the brushes which eliminates much of the necessity of "pushing" them while playing. Then they offer a "non-slip" grip even when the hands perspire freely. Jackets are flared for rim-shot and sock effects. Ball-ends are handy for hot-licks on cymbals, temple blocks, tom-toms, cow bells and wood blocks. Rubber will NOT soil the hands, is alive and resilient and will give long, satisfactory service. You'll like this new number once you try a pair. And we honestly believe that a pair of these brushes will outlast those which do not have the rubber jackets on the handles. Ask your local Leedy Dealer to show you a pair the next time you are in his store.

No. 1644—Per Pair $1.00

Elkhart, Ind., H. S. Band Drum Section

Much of the 1st Division Elkhart H. S. Band's success is due to its well trained, fully equipped percussion section shown above. Director David W. Hughes (extreme right in photo) stresses the important relation of thoroughly trained percussionists to good band music with the result that all his bands have enjoyed unusual success. All equipment is Leedy.

NEW! LEEDY TUNABLE TOM-TOMS NEW!
(With Self-Aligning Casings)

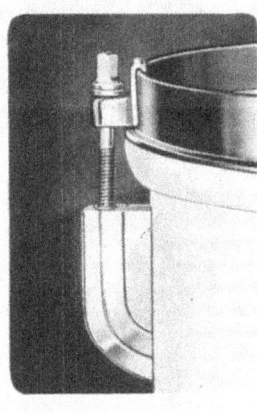

Now, "The World's Finest" tunable tom-toms have been improved so that they are more beautiful, more practical and better suited to the professionals' needs than ever before. The TUNING makes the difference—possible by use of the new, beautiful, streamlined casings which make the rods "SELF-ALIGNING" exactly like the rods on the famous Leedy Broadway Snare Drums which are the choice of the professionals the world over. This feature practically eliminates binding of the flesh hoops against the shell and permits more even tensioning of the heads, better, more uniform tone over the entire head surface and reduces head breakage. The spring and the rod receiving tube which works on the modified universal joint principle INSIDE the casing does the trick. The moderne, streamlined casings, beautifully plated and polished, add 100% to the appearance of the instruments, too! Tom-toms are available in separate or single tension as listed below and with choice of calfskin or pigskin heads. Tone controls identical to those used on Leedy Broadway drums are included. Shells are highest grade laminated wood noted for its strength and are beautifully finished. Note that a new size—11" x 7"—tom has been added which makes possible a wider tonal range and greater tone effects.

	SINGLE TENSION	SEPARATE TENSION
16" x 14" With Nickel Plated Rods		
With Choice of "Full Dress" Finishes	No. 8014—$38.50	No. 8018—$45.00
With Choice of Lacquer Colors	No. 8015— 30.00	No. 8019— 36.50
With Chromium Plated Parts	$4.25 Extra	$8.50 Extra
14" x 12" With Nickel Plated Rods		
With Choice of "Full Dress" Finishes	No. 8027—$33.00	No. 8036—$39.00
With Choice of Lacquer Colors	No. 8028— 25.00	No. 8037— 31.00
With Chromium Plated Parts	$4.25 Extra	$8.50 Extra
13" x 9" With Nickel Plated Rods		
With Choice of "Full Dress" Finishes	No. 8047—$22.00	No. 8038—$30.00
With Choice of Lacquer Colors	No. 8048— 16.50	No. 8039— 24.50
With Chromium Plated Parts	$4.25 Extra	$8.50 Extra
11" x 7" With Nickel Plated Rods		
With Choice of "Full Dress" Finishes	No. 8075—$20.50	No. 8076—$28.00
With Choice of Lacquer Colors	No. 8077— 15.00	No. 8078— 22.50
With Chromium Plated Parts	$4.25 Extra	$8.50 Extra

FOLDING ADJUSTABLE TOM-TOM STANDS (As shown above)
Fits all tom-toms above 10" x 4" size including Chinese. Folding and adjustable.
No. 7750—Nickel. Each..........$4.00   No. 7752—Chromium. Each..........$6.00

★ PIGSKIN HEADS AND WOOD COUNTER HOOPS SUPPLIED ON SINGLE AND SEPARATE TENSION MODELS AT SAME PRICES AS FOR CALFSKIN HEADS ★

Lee Hickle, Former Pittsburgh Drummer, Now on Leedy Service Staff

Hundreds of drummers and the great majority of dealers the country over are now acquainted both via personal contact and correspondence with Lee Hickle who joined the Leedy sales and service staff last April. Lee is a former professional drummer with twenty years professional experience with the best of them in all branches of drumming, xylophone playing and as a tympanist and teacher. This, of course, means he "speaks the language" which, in turn, means that you will get the best of service at all times. A real fellow in the bargain and Leedy is proud to have him on the job.

HEAVY DUTY RATCHET TOM-TOM HOLDERS

Recommended for use with ALL tunable tom toms and for all but the 10"x 4" Chinese or China-type non-tunable models. Adjustable forward, backward, up and down by means of two ratchet adjustments. Gives you ANY desired playing angle. Made of finest cast brass, perfectly machined and fitted and carefully assembled. Features the STAYON clamp. Tom tom shell fastens to holder by two strong bolts.

FOR BASS DRUM HOOP

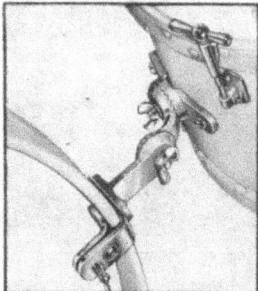

No. 7723 Nickel $3.50 Each

No. 7724 Chrome $5.25 Each

FOR ARCH TRAP RAIL

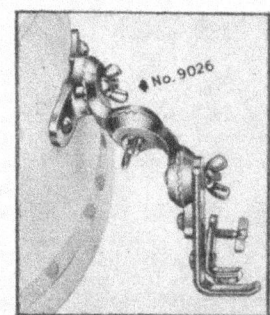

No. 9026 Nickel $4.25 Each

No. 9027 Chrome $6.25 Each

Geo. G. (Red) Jackson with Charlie Agnew

The drummer with Charlie Agnew has GOT to be good because Agnew himself is a former drummer and knows just what he wants in the line of tempo. George (Red to everybody who knows him) fills the bill perfectly for Agnew and his band which at latest information was on tour playing ballroom, radio and hotel engagements. Red was formerly with Ace Brigode, Freddie Rich and Ernie Caldwell and played vaudeville and musical comedy for five years prior to that. He was born in Venice, Cal.

Arthur G. Longhorst

This talented young musician is chief percussionist with the Carthage College Band, Carthage, Ill., which is under the able direction of Lyle Atkins. The equipment used by the band is entirely Leedy.

Bob Kallsen, Chicago

Has played with Louis Panico, Morrie Sherman, Jimmy Garrigan and other splendid bands. Now with Stan Morris and his orchestra which recently completed a successful engagement at Merry Garden Ballroom, Chicago. Bob studied under Straight and Graham.

Charming Trio of Drummers

Very attractive, and proficient, too, are these three snare drummers of the Mason City (Ia.) H. S. Band which is directed by Carlton Stewart. They are Lauretta and Dorothy O'Hearn (left and right), sisters and Connie Clark (center). The drums are Leedy Concert Kings.

THEY'RE ALL SWINGING TO THE LEEDY "X-L" PEDAL

The Leedy "X-L" Pedal has proven a real "hit" in the drum world. It was adopted by more high-class professionals during its first year on the market than any other new model ever made because it has everything that Drummers demand in a pedal . . . the utmost in speed—feather ease in action—no faltering—no friction—no side strain—and no "stiff spots" anywhere in the travel of the beater rod. It is scientifically designed and precision-built of only the finest materials. There are no delicate working parts to get out of order—everything is sturdily constructed so as to give long and satisfactory service. The tension spring can be adjusted to satisfy the particular "feel" that you like best. All the usual adjustable features, such as beater rod, cymbal striker and spring tension, are also incorporated. Finished in baked Black Lacquer with highly polished aluminum footboard and heel plate. All other parts are high quality steel heavily nickel plated.

No. 7010—Pedal Only (without Spurs and Cymbal Holder) in Black Lacquer and Polished Aluminum $10.00

No. 7014—Pedal As Above But Complete with Nickel Grip-Tite Spurs and Stayon Cymbal Holder $11.50

Chas. Kegley with Paul Sabin's Orchestra
Visits
C. G. Conn, Ltd.
at
Syracuse, N. Y.

THE "JAM SPECIAL" OUTFIT
No. 5375 (In White Lacquer and Nickel) $150.50

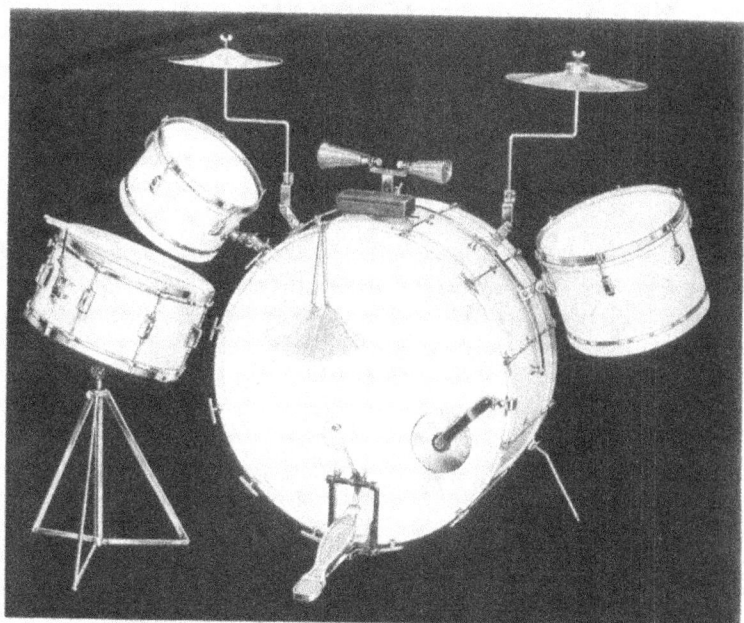

When Paul Sabin and his orchestra played the Syracuse Hotel, Syracuse, N. Y., recently, Charles Kegley, Sabin's drummer, found the drum department of the C. G. Conn, Ltd., store of that city able and ready to serve him in his several drum needs. Ralph Kurkowski, drummer with the Syracuse Symphony, is in charge of the Conn store's drum department, is a very fine drummer and an A-1 xylophone player. In the top photo are (L. to R.) Paul Sabin, Chas. Kegley and Ralph Kurkowski; in the lower photograph are Ralph Kurkowski and Joe Achilles, Manager of the Syracuse Conn store. Traveling drummers and those in the Syracuse territory are invited to make fullest use of the store's facilities.

Fine Drummers and Fine Fellows All Three

Below, shown in front of the Wm. F. Hammond Music Store at 630 Penn Ave., Pittsburgh, Pa., is the capable drum staff of that store. Center is Wm. F. (Bill) Hammond, owner of the store and very fine rudimental and theatre drummer and drum corps organizer and instructor; left, Geo. Behr, drummer with the Pittsburgh Symphony Orchestra, who is the drum instructor in the Hammond store; right, Davey Jones, assistant drum instructor and dance drummer. Hammond's is the leading drum shop in Pittsburgh and you are invited to stop in and meet these men when you are in the vicinity.

This new outfit is a "100 Percenter" in every respect. Its makeup includes several of Leedy's newest offerings—the new Leedy ARCH Trap Rail, ARCH Trap Rail trap holders, TWO of the new style casing-tunable tom-toms—one of them the new 7" x 11" size—and the new Leedy "S-n-e-e-z-e" Cymbal which is described elsewhere in this magazine. The "JAM SPECIAL" is complete enough for the great, great majority of jobs, is light enough for "one nighters" and is "showy" and good looking. All items are first quality merchandise and have been assembled into an outfit with your needs uppermost in our minds.

"JAM SPECIAL" OUTFIT SET UP AS FOLLOWS:

Qty	No.	Description	Price
1	No. 2829	6½" x 14" Broadway Floating Head Metal Hoop Snare Drum—Separate Tension Self-aligning Rods, White Lacquer and Nickel	$ 38.00
1	No. 5132	14" x 28" Spartan Bass Drum—White Lacquer, 12 Single Tension Tympani Model Rods with center supports—Nickel Plated	40.00
1	No. 8048	9" x 13" Tunable Tom-Tom—Single Tension with new Leedy Streamline Self-aligning Rods—nickel plated, metal counter hoops and calf heads	16.50
1	No. 8077	7" x 11" Tunable Tom-Tom—Single Tension with new Leedy Streamline Self-aligning Rods—nickel plated, metal counter hoops and calf heads	15.00
1	No. 9020	Arch Trap Rail	4.00
2	No. 9026	Heavy Duty Ratchet Tom-Tom Holders for Arch Trap Rail (with extra arm) @ $4.25	8.50
2	No. 9022	Bestall Cymbal Holders for Arch Trap Rail @ $2.00	4.00
1	No. 9028	Wood Block and Cow Bell Holder for Arch Trap Rail	1.75
1	No. 7361	13" Sneeze Cymbal	4.50
1	No. 7301	11" Stanople Cymbal	5.00
1	No. 7010	"X-L" Pedal	10.00
1	No. 7103	Pair Economy Giant Spurs	1.50
1	No. 7255	Standard (heavy) Drum Stand	5.00
1	No. 7871	Bass Drum Tone Control	1.75
1	No. 7680	7" Wood Block	1.00
1	No. 7795	3½" Cow Bell	.90
1	No. 7796	4½" Cow Bell	1.00
1	Pair H-14	Hickory Drum Sticks	.45
1	No. 1645	Pair Aluminum Handle Wire Brushes	.60
		Value	$159.45

Drums and Tom-Toms in Sparkling Silver
      Sparkling Gold
      Marine Pearl
      Black Pearl . . . . $43.50 Extra

Drums and Tom-Toms in Tri-Tone Black and Gold
      Tri-Tone Blue and Silver
      Black Lacquer . . . . 4.50 Extra
      (With Inlaid Hoops on Bass Drum)

NEW! ECONOMY GIANT BASS DRUM SPURS

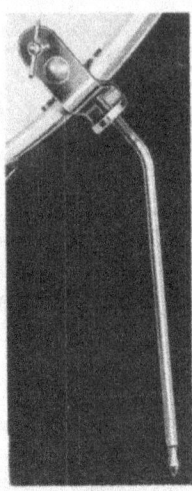

A new, longer, stronger GIANT bass drum spur of a different design! Gives the drum plenty of support to hold the present top-heavy set-ups of temple blocks, tunable toms, cymbals and other traps and accessories. STAYON hoop clamp assures positive grip on the bass drum hoop without marring. Sturdily constructed to stand the "gaff" of hard use. Carefully finished in choice of nickel or chrome plating at the economy prices shown below.

No. 7103—Nickel. Pair $1.50
No. 7104—Chrome. Pair 2.25

Torrington, Conn., Post 38 Drum and Bugle Corps

A fine playing and appearing corps. Organized in 1932, entered competition nine months later and won 1st prize. Drums taught by Otto Jacob; bugle by John Winzler.

Drum Section, Bonham Bros. Boys' Band, San Diego, Cal.

One of America's most famous boys' bands. Has 250 members and a waiting list. Instruction is free to boys selected. Jules F. Jacques is director. Percussion is 100% Leedy.

CONTEST
20TH NATIONAL AMER-
LOS ANGELES, CALIFORNIA

PRELIMINARY DRUM AND BUGLE CORPS CONTEST

1. Henry H. Houston Post No. 3
   Philadelphia, Pa. 96.60
2. Harvey Seeds Post No. 29
   Miami, Fla. 96.10
3. East Orange Post No. 73
   East Orange, New Jersey 96.00
4. Commonwealth Edison Post No. 118
   Chicago, Illinois 95.85
5. Morristown Post No. 59
   Morristown, New Jersey 95.70
6. Herbert F. Akroyd Post No. 132
   Marlboro, Mass. *95.25
7. Massillon Post No. 221
   Massillon, Ohio *95.25
8. Anderson-Dunn-Kotchhiss Post No. 42
   Stratford, Conn. **94.55
9. Manhattanville Post No. 1057
   New York City, New York **94.55
10. Riverside Post No. 79
    Riverside, California ***93.85
11. Chicago Police Post No. 207
    Chicago, Illinois ***93.85
12. Philip Tighe Post No. 26
    Biddeford, Maine 93.80
13. Racine Post No. 76
    Racine, Wisc. 92.90
14. San Jose Post No. 89
    San Jose, California 92.70
15. Hamon Gray Post No. 83
    LaPorte, Indiana 92.65
16. Square Post No. 232
    Chicago, Illinois 92.05
17. Press-Lloyd Post No. 247
    Chisholm, Minnesota 91.70
18. Delaware Post No. 1
    Wilmington, Delaware 91.50
19. Sidney L. Smith Post No. 24
    Aberdeen, South Dakota 91.50
20. Tirey J. Ford Post No. 21
    Independence, Missouri 90.80
21. Cook Nelson Post No. 20
    Pontiac, Michigan 90.50
22. Old Dorchester Post No. 65
    Boston, Massachusetts 90.25
23. Fresno Post No. 4
    Fresno, California 90.15
24. Valley Post No. 620
    West Des Moines, Iowa 89.70
25. Santa Ana Post No. 131
    Santa Ana, California 89.60
26. David A. Solari Post No. 151
    Pittsburg, California 88.95
27. Hastings Post No. 11
    Hastings, Nebraska 88.85
28. Spokane Post No. 9
    Spokane, Washington 88.05
29. Memphis Post No. 1
    Memphis, Tennessee 87.10
30. Henry J. Sweeney Post No. 2
    Manchester, New Hampshire ...... (2 points penalty) 86.80

Saint Peter's Drum Corps, Torrington, Conn.

Steady 1st Prize winners since organized in 1930. New England State Champions in 1932. Drum instructor, Daniel Santore; bugle instructor, Salvatore Scarfo. Has attended corps events in five states and sponsored two successful competitive meets. Is self-financed. Drums are Leedy.

Qualifications necessary for a really good drummer are:

Rudiments
Reading
Musicianship
Versatility
Good Sense.

Lack of ONE of the above qualities is a serious drawback to professional success.

SCORES

AMERICAN LEGION CONVENTION
SEPTEMBER 19 to 22, 1938

31. Edwin K. White Post No. 10
    Okmulgee, Oklahoma 85.70
32. Klamath Post No. 8
    Klamath Falls, Oregon 84.45
33. Santa Barbara Post No. 49
    Santa Barbara, California 83.80
34. Merced Post No. 83
    Merced, California 82.70
35. Victor Candlin Post No. 18
    Greeley, Colorado   (2 point penalty) 82.30
36. Austin Post No. 76
    Austin, Texas 78.70
* Tied Scores; ** Tied Scores; *** Tied Scores.

FINAL DRUM AND BUGLE CORPS CONTEST
1. Herbert F. Akroyd Post No. 132
   Marlboro, Massachusetts 96.25
2. Commonwealth Edison Post No. 118
   Chicago, Illinois 95.65
3. Morristown Post No. 59
   Morristown, New Jersey 95.55
4. East Orange Post No. 73
   East Orange, New Jersey 95.45
5. Henry H. Houston Post No. 3
   Germantown, Philadelphia, Pennsylvania *95.35
6. Anderson-Dunn-Kochiss Post No. 42
   Stratford, Connecticut *95.35
7. Harvey W. Seeds Post No. 29
   Miami, Florida 95.25
8. Manhattanville Post No. 1057
   New York, New York 95.15
9. Chicago Police Post No. 207
   Chicago, Illinois 94.30
10. Massillon Post No. 221
    Massillon, Ohio 93.80
11. Philip Tighe Post No. 26
    Biddeford, Maine 93.40
12. Riverside Post No. 79
    Riverside, California 91.55
* Tied Scores.

SONS OF AMERICAN LEGION DRUM AND BUGLE CORPS CONTEST
1. Baldwin-Patterson Squadron No. 274
   Des Moines, Iowa 89.00
2. William E. Sheridan Police Squadron No. 1059
   Brooklyn, New York 88.60
3. Allein Squadron No. 3
   Vicksburg, Mississippi 86.70
4. Lindsay Squadron No. 128
   Lindsay, California 85.00
5. Morgan McDermott Squadron No. 7
   Tucson, Arizona 84.80

BAND CONTEST
1. Zane-Irwin Post No. 93
   San Francisco, California 96.667
2. Canton Post No. 44
   Canton, Ohio 94.934
3. Crescent City Post No. 125
   New Orleans, Louisiana 93.667
4. Alameda Post No. 9
   Alameda, California 88.334

Many enthusiastic drummers try hard to imitate the work of their "idols" with the result that they ruin their own individual style and fall far short of the ideal that they have set for themselves. The finest drummers develop the necessary foundation first; individual style comes with time and experience.

Downers Grove, Ill., H. S. Band's Percussion Section

Fine musicians, well trained and fully equipped is the percussion section of the Downers Grove H. S. Band of Downers Grove, Ill., directed by Bandmaster J. C. Shoemaker who is shown second from the left in the photo at the right. Equipment is 100% Leedy.

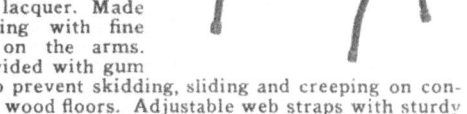

TUBULAR STEEL BASS DRUM RACK

Here, at last, is a really substantial bass drum stand that will hold a bass drum securely in place without rattling or "creeping" even under heavy beating in fff gallops. It is adjustable to height and folds compactly, is light in weight, easy to carry, durably constructed and attractively finished in black crackle lacquer. Made of steel tubing with fine quality felt on the arms. Feet are provided with gum rubber caps to prevent skidding, sliding and creeping on concrete, tile and wood floors. Adjustable web straps with sturdy buckles hold drum securely in place.

No. 1749—Includes Web Straps $11.00

V. F. W. National Champion Drum Corps
The Royal Oak, Mich., Veterans of Foreign War Post No. 1669 annexed the 1938 National V. F. W. Championship at the competition held in connection with the V. F. W. National Convention staged at Columbus, O. Holder of the State Championship in 1933, '36, '37 and '38. Drums are 100% Leedy.

Fine High School Band Percussion Section
The fine percussion section of the splendid Lincoln H. S. Band, Wisconsin Rapids, Wisc., is equipped with Leedy instruments throughout. Note completeness of the equipment. Directed by Bernard T. Ziegler shown on the extreme right. The band is one of Wisconsin's finest.

LEEDY DRUM TOPICS

JANUARY, 1939   No. 27

OUR OWN MINIATURE MOVIES

POSTMASTER: RETURN POSTAGE GUARANTEED

Leedy Mfg. Co., Inc.

2301 Leedy Bldg.   Elkhart, Indiana

Sec. 562 P. L. & R.
U. S. POSTAGE
PAID
Elkhart, Ind.
Permit No. 6

Mr. Joseph G. Benoit,
165 Hildreth,
Lowell, Mass.

LEEDY DRUM TOPICS

On the Air with Johnny Williams!

1. Johnny Williams, ace drummer on a dozen nationally acclaimed CBS radio programs, with his complete NEW Leedy outfit.
2. Johnny Williams and Raymond Scott who is director of the famous Raymond Scott Quintette, Lucky Strike program feature.
3. Johnny Williams and Mark Warnow, CBS house leader and director of the very popular Lucky Strike Hit Parade program.
4. The educated, tap dancing feet of the famous Bill "Bojangles" Robinson set a gruelling pace for even Johnny Williams' dynamic drumsticks and his new Leedys.
5. Johnny Williams, his band and his Leedys are an important part of the Kate Smith program. Photo shows: (l. to r.) "Kate," Johnny, Jack Miller, director, and Ted Collins, manager.

See Story on Page 8.

OCTOBER, 1939 ★ ★ ★ ★ ★ NUMBER 28

Leedy Drum Topics Issue 28

WHETHER IT'S "Swing or Sweet or Sweet-Swing"
THE NEW LEEDYS are "TOPS"

BROADWAY STANDARD "SWINGSTER"
WITH THE NEW, IMPROVED STANDARD EXTENSION SNARE STRAINER AND THE NEW STREAMLINED SELF-ALIGNING "BEAVER TAIL" RODS

7"x14" SHELL SIZE				8"x14" SHELL SIZE			
NICKEL		CHROMIUM			NICKEL		CHROMIUM	
No.	Price	No.	Price	SHELL FINISH	No.	Price	No.	Price
600	$40.00	601	$47.50	Mahogany	650	$40.00	651	$47.50
602	40.00	603	47.50	White Lacquer	652	40.00	653	47.50
604	40.00	605	47.50	Black Lacquer	654	40.00	655	47.50
606	40.00	607	47.50	Tri-Tone Blue	656	40.00	657	47.50
608	40.00	609	47.50	Black and Gold Lacquer	658	40.00	659	47.50
620	47.50	621	55.00	Sparkling Gold	670	47.50	671	55.00
622	47.50	623	55.00	Sparkling Silver	672	47.50	673	55.00
624	47.50	625	55.00	Marine (White) Pearl	674	47.50	675	55.00
626	47.50	627	55.00	Black Pearl	676	47.50	677	55.00

Choice of JAMES or SILK WIRE WOUND or GUT SNARES
Wood Counter Hoops Supplied on Special Order.................No Extra Charge

BROADWAY PARALLEL "SWINGSTER"
WITH THE IMPROVED INDIVIDUAL TENSION PARALLEL SNARE STRAINER AND NEW STREAMLINED SELF-ALIGNING "BEAVER TAIL" RODS

7"x14" SHELL SIZE				8"x14" SHELL SIZE			
NICKEL		CHROMIUM			NICKEL		CHROMIUM	
No.	Price	No.	Price	SHELL FINISH	No.	Price	No.	Price
700	$51.50	701	$64.00	Mahogany	750	$51.50	751	$64.00
702	51.50	703	64.00	White Lacquer	752	51.50	753	64.00
704	51.50	705	64.00	Black Lacquer	754	51.50	755	64.00
706	51.50	707	64.00	Tri-Tone Blue	756	51.50	757	64.00
708	51.50	709	64.00	Black and Gold Lacquer	758	51.50	759	64.00
720	59.00	721	71.50	Sparkling Gold	770	59.00	771	71.50
722	59.00	723	71.50	Sparkling Silver	772	59.00	773	71.50
724	59.00	725	71.50	Marine (White) Pearl	774	59.00	775	71.50
726	59.00	727	71.50	Black Pearl	776	59.00	777	71.50

Choice of JAMES or SILK WIRE WOUND or GUT SNARES
Wood Counter Hoops Supplied on Special Order.................No Extra Charge
PRICES SUBJECT TO CHANGE WITHOUT NOTICE DUE TO PREVAILING UNCERTAINTIES

Features:

IMPROVED "PARALLEL" STRAINER

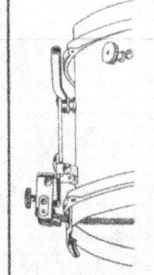

The new Leedy Parallel Snare Strainer has several outstanding features found on NO other drum. Of particular note is the elimination of all side play and lost motion in the mechanical parts. Also, the "direct" pull of the strainer tension-knob does away with the former "loose" track. Individual snare tension has also been incorporated, and an improved throw-off lever and links have been provided.

STANDARD "EXTENSION" STRAINER

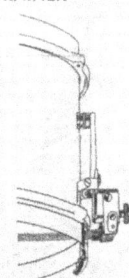

Named "Extension" because the strainer permits the snares to extend beyond the head of the drum and thereby does away with the necessity of bending the snares, or snare cords, over the flesh hoop and shell. This prevents head breakage caused by "chafing" snares at those points. Longer snares can be used with this strainer, thereby assuring easier playing and more brilliant tonal qualities. Note that base is designed in one strong unit.

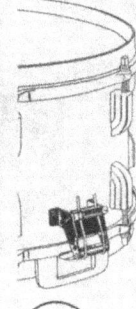

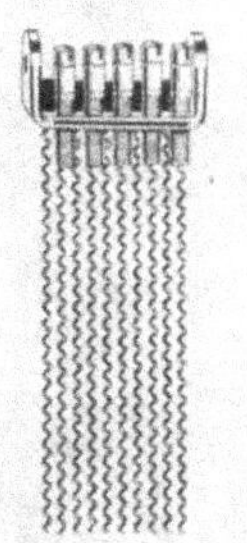

"Hairline" adjustment of each individual snare is now possible with the new individual snare tension mechanism now used on all Leedy Parallel model drums. Mechanism accommodates coiled wire, silk wire wound or gut snares.
At right is shown the detail of the internal working parts of the stream-lined, self-aligning "Beaver Tail" rods used on new Leedy model snare drums

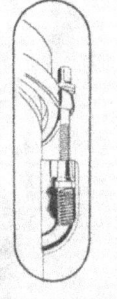

Leedy Drum Topics Issue 28

Leedy Drum Topics

OCTOBER — Issue No. 28 — **1939**

Charlie Green and Ray "Red" Floyd
If you've ever attended the Ringling Bros. Barnum and Bailey Circus and purposely taken a seat near the bandstand so you could watch the drummers as we do, you'll certainly recognize Charlie Green and "Red" Floyd, whose photo appears below. You'll know, too, then that they're topnotch drummers and that the drums they use are Leedy.

Dody Jeshke
Miss Jeshke is the lovely, talented mistress of the drums with the Anne Wallace (all girl) Orchestra playing at the 230 Club, Long Beach, Cal. She's been with that band for three years; has played NBC and CBS radio, theatre pit and vaudeville, concert and symphony. Studied under Edw. Millard; plays Leedy drums and mallet instruments. Thanks to Bob Perry, Lockie Music Exchange, Los Angeles, for this photo.

O. E. S. Drum Corps
Denver, Colorado, boasts the first and only ladies' drum and bugle corps in the state of Colorado. It is the fine appearing, well trained Order of Eastern Star Drum and Bugle Corps shown above which was organized in the Spring of 1938. By the first of the following year, 1939, it had already made fourteen public appearances at Eastern Star and Masonic activities and social functions. Officers are: Fred Everhart, Commander and Drum Instructor; Edith Fretz, Secretary; Kathryn Zimmerman, Treasurer; Ralph Keenan, Business Manager and Drill Sergeant; Phil Palmer, Bugle Instructor. Although our information doesn't state, we believe the gentleman on the left is Fred Everhart, organizer of this splendid corps. All drum and bugle equipment is Leedy, of course!

Geo. J. Carey
One of the nation's finest percussionists. For the past fourteen years has been 1st percussionist and assistant tympanist with the Cincinnati Symphony which is directed by Eugene Goosens and featured on the NBC network. Has played under Innes, Goldman, Sousa and Simon as well as with the Victor Herbert Orchestra and the Metropolitan Opera Co. Was born in Boston, Mass., studied drums under Harry Waterhouse and has been in the business for 33 years. Has played Leedys for the past 26 years and writes that they "have always led the field in new improvements."

Al Pearce—Bob Conzelmann and Carl Hoff
Bob Conzelmann is the drummer with Carl Hoff's fine orchestra which provides the music for the popular Al Pearce program which is making GRAPE NUTS famous over the NBC hook-ups. Bob is a very fine drummer. Has played with Biederbecke, Biese, Jones, Kemp, Arnhein, Goodman and Teagarden and the Chicago Civic Orchestra. He was born in Chicago but is now on the west coast—Beverly Hills, Cal., to be exact—with the Hoff band. His new Leedys shown here came from the Southland Music Co., Van Nuys, Cal.

Raymond Paige—Wm. T. Paulson—Milt Schlesinger—Howard Goulden—Edw. Rubsam

When you listen to the very popular CBS radio program "99 Men and a Girl," sponsored by the U. S. Rubber Company, it's the well-known Raymond Paige Orchestra that you hear providing that very swell music. Shown above is the percussion section of the orchestra. Shown with Raymond Paige, director (left), are (l. to r.) Wm. T. Paulson, tympani; Milt Schlesinger, at the outfit; Howard N. Goulden, snare drum, xylophone and vibraphone, and Edward C. Rubsam, xylophone, vibraphone and bells. All of these men are outstanding percussionists who have been presented on these pages before. The equipment shown in the photo is exclusively Leedy!

Emil Flindt—Roy F. Winters

Emil Flindt's Orchestra, playing a year's contract at the Paradise Ballroom, Chicago, is tempoed by Roy F. Winters, who is shown behind his Leedy outfit below. Winters has been with Flindt for nine years. Played the O'Henry Ballroom for four years, and engagements at the Palmer House, Stevens, Sherman and Drake Hotels, Chicago. Winters' birthplace is Rock Island, Illinois; his present residence is Berwyn, Illinois. His equipment, including a vibraphone which is not shown, is 100% Leedy of whose beauty and durability he writes high praise.

James "Jerome" Rosenberg

Rosenberg is one of Cincinnati's finest—and busiest—percussionists. In addition to playing drums with the Cincinnati Symphony under Eugene Goosens, he plays with the Armco band under Frank Simon, teaches forty-five pupils, directs the "Woodpeckers" xylophone band and is xylophone soloist at WLW radio station. Was born in Boston and studied drums under Geo. Stone. Has played drums 21 years. Was with the original "Yerkes Flotilla Band" of N.Y. and played solo xylophone with Roxy's Gang at the Roxy Theatre. Uses Leedy equipment throughout.

Robert D. Pfaltzgraff, Dumont, Iowa

The two biggest events in Bob's life were the winning of High Superior rating in drumming at the school band Regional Contest at Minneapolis and playing as guest xylophone soloist with Frank Simon and his Armco Band on its April 9th, 1939, program heard through WLW, Cincinnati. Bob has been playing drums in his school bands for seven years and is student director of the junior school band. Studied under Helen McClellan of Mason City, Ia. Merlin Seippe is director of the Dumont school bands.

Charles Fitch

Fitch plays with the Jack Spratt Orchestra, which is a featured Cincinnati night club and mid-west college dance band. Charlie was born in Evansville, Ind., studied drums under Geo. Carey of the Cincinnati Symphony and has played professionally for 16 years. His equipment (all of it not in photo) is all Leedy.

Redd French
with Happy Felton's Orchestra

Redd French and his Leedy drums set the tempo for Happy Felton's Orchestra which, according to our information, is playing a long engagement at the Hotel Sherman's famous College Inn, Chicago. Redd is a mighty fine drummer who studied under none other than our friend Bill Hammond who operates the Wm. F. Hammond Music Store in Pittsburgh, Pa., which is Redd's home town. Redd's residence is now N. Y. C. Shown in the photo below with Redd is Director Happy Felton and the Leedy outfit which was purchased through Bill Hammond.

Sons of the American Legion Drum Corps, Knoxville, Tenn.

Squadron No. 2's drum corps was organized in 1936 and has made an enviable showing for itself in competition. In 1936 it won second honors in the state convention at Nashville and in 1938 took the state championship in junior corps competition. C. C. (Pat) Cottrell, veteran top ranking drummer, is the corps' drum and bugle instructor and Sgt. W. A. Pratt, member of Knoxville American Legion Post No. 2, is Drill Sergeant. All members of the corps are sons of vets of the World War—except, of course, the charming little Drum Major-ess! Captain of the Squadron is Robert L. Lyle. Drums and bugles are 100% Leedy and they have, according to Cottrell who also supplied us with this fine photograph, given 100% satisfaction in every respect. Send us photos of YOUR drum corps!

Juan Diaz, San Antonio, Texas

This versatile Leedy drummer plays with Emilio Cacares, who is known as the "Mexican King of the Swing Violin" and whose band plays dance, radio, theatre and hotel engagements throughout the southwest. Diaz formerly played with Don Francisco and his Charros and with Angell J. Mercado and his Tipicia Orchestra. His birthplace and home are San Antonio, his father was his drum teacher and he has played Leedys for twenty years. Says: ". . . find Leedy 100%."

Melvin "Monte" Mountjoy
with "Tiny" Hill's Orchestra, Chicago

"Tiny" Hill's "Music with The Mood" is known to thousands of dance lovers in and around Chicago. When last heard from, the band was playing an 8-month contract at the Melody Mill Ballroom. "Monte" is a native of Montana, has been in the profession for 10 years and uses Leedy equipment exclusively, of which he says: "It's a great outfit that always produces clearer and more resonant tones."

Chas. Bailey, Huntington, W. Va.

Has played drums for five years. Teachers were Joe Lusk and W. R. Wiant. Now appearing with Barney Theiss' orchestra under the direction of Bill Tweel playing hotel, ballroom and college dances. Now playing the Hotel Frederick in Huntington, which is Bailey's birthplace and home. Bailey's outfit is exclusively Leedy which he says: ". . . are 'TOPS' in my opinion."

Be sure to notify us of any change in address so you'll be sure to receive your DRUM TOPICS regularly!

THE IMPROVED LEEDY TUNABLE TOM TOMS

- NOW MADE IN FOUR NEEDED SIZES
- MADE IN SINGLE OR SEPARATE TENSION
- CHOICE OF CALF OR PIGSKIN HEADS

CLOSE-UP VIEW OF THE BEAUTIFUL, NEW, STREAMLINED "BEAVER TAIL" SELF-ALIGNING RODS

Now, "The World's Finest" tunable tom toms have been improved so that they are more beautiful, more practical and better suited to the professional's needs than ever before. The TUNING makes the difference—possible by use of the new, beautiful, streamlined casings which make the rods "SELF-ALIGNING" exactly like the rods on the famous Leedy Broadway Snare Drums. This feature permits more even tensioning of the heads, better, more uniform tone over the entire head surface and reduces head breakage. The spring and the rod receiving tube which works on the modified universal joint principle INSIDE the casing does the trick. The modern, streamlined casings add 100% to the appearance of the instruments, too! Tom toms are available in separate or single tension as listed below and with choice of calfskin or pigskin heads. Tone controls identical to those used on Leedy Broadway drums are included. Shells are highest grade laminated wood noted for its strength and are beautifully finished.

The new streamlined "Beaver Tail" rods used on the improved Leedy Tunable Tom Toms shown here have everything—advance modern design, beauty, strength and—above all—the INTERNAL self-aligning feature which is shown in detail on page two. The self-aligning feature is IMPORTANT to you. All drum rods with casings are NOT self-aligning. INVESTIGATE!

	SINGLE TENSION		SEPARATE TENSION	
14"x16" IN NICKEL	Cat. No.	Price	Cat. No.	Price
In Pearl Finishes	8014	$38.50	8018	$45.00
In Lacquer Finish	8015	30.00	8019	36.50
With Chrome Parts	$4.25 Extra		$8.50 Extra	
12"x14" IN NICKEL				
In Pearl Finishes	8027	$33.00	8036	$39.00
In Lacquer Finish	8028	25.00	8037	31.00
With Chrome Parts	$4.25 Extra		$8.50 Extra	

	SINGLE TENSION		SEPARATE TENSION	
9"x13" IN NICKEL	Cat. No.	Price	Cat. No.	Price
In Pearl Finishes	8047	$22.00	8038	$30.00
In Lacquer Finish	8048	16.50	8039	24.50
With Chrome Parts	$4.25 Extra		$8.50 Extra	
7"x11" IN NICKEL				
In Pearl Finishes	8075	$20.50	8076	$28.00
In Lacquer Finish	8077	15.00	8078	22.50
With Chrome Parts	$4.25 Extra		$8.50 Extra	

CALFSKIN HEADS AND METAL HOOPS SUPPLIED UNLESS ORDER SPECIFIES PIGSKIN HEADS WHICH REQUIRE WOOD FLESH AND COUNTER HOOPS.

LEEDY HEAVY DUTY RATCHET TOM TOM HOLDERS

WITH SINGLE ARM FOR BASS DRUM HOOP (NOT SUITABLE FOR USE ON TRAP RAILS)	WITH DOUBLE ARM FOR BASS DRUM HOOP (MORE ADJUSTABLE THAN SINGLE ARM MODEL)	WITH DOUBLE ARM FOR ARCH TRAP RAIL AND ARCH ROLLAWAY TRAP CONSOLE RAIL	WITH DOUBLE ARM FOR ARCH ROLLAWAY TRAP CONSOLE (WITH CASTING FOR POSTS)
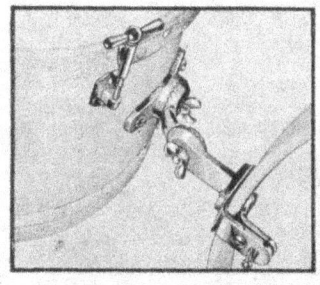	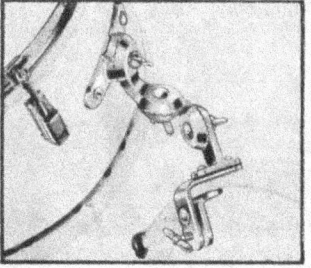	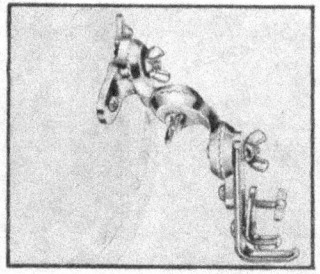	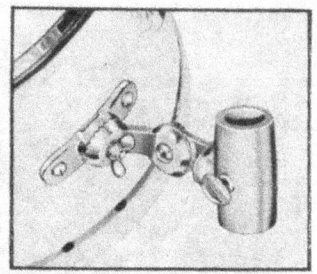
No. 7723—Nickel ... $3.50	No. 7728—Nickel ... $4.25	No. 9026—Nickel ... $4.25	No. 7253—Nickel ... $4.25
No. 7724—Chromium ... 5.25	No. 7729—Chromium ... 6.25	No. 9027—Chromium ... 6.25	No. 7254—Chromium ... 6.25

ADJUSTABLE TOM TOM STANDS

Fits all tom toms larger than 10"x4" size including the imported Chinese type. Simply turn thumb screw for height adjustment. Are sturdily made of quality materials, accurately fitted and assembled, and carefully finished. Rubber bumpers on arms protect tom tom finish. Rigid and dependable. Fold compactly.

No. 7750—Nickel. Each ... $4.00
No. 7752—Chromium. Each ... 6.00

LIGHTWEIGHT RATCHET TOM TOM HOLDERS

Identical in principle to the holders shown above but made of formed steel. Features the double arm adjustment. Clamps securely to bass drum hoop. For China-type and Chinese tom toms sizes 4"x10", 7"x11", and 9"x13"; also for 7"x11" Tunable Tom Tom. Well made of quality materials, accurately tooled and assembled and carefully finished.

No. 7718—Nickel. Each ... $1.50
No. 7719—Chromium. Each ... 2.25

PRICES SUBJECT TO CHANGE WITHOUT NOTICE DUE TO PREVAILING UNCERTAINTIES

**Booth Bertram
with Larry Kent's Orchestra**

Larry Kent's band, with Bertram at the Leedys, is now playing in the U. S. Grant Hotel, San Diego, Cal. Bertram, formerly with Gus Arnheim, Carol Lofner and Gene W. Quaw, was born in New Britain, Conn., but now calls Los Angeles his home. He has played drums for 12 years and says of his Leedys: "It is my opinion that other makes of drums do not compare with my Leedys." Thanks to Bob Perry of Lockie Music Exchange, L. A., for the photo.

**Harry Lindeman
with Freddie Fisher's Schnickelfritz Band**

From earnings of $19.50 per man per week for playing at the Sugar Loaf Tavern in Winona, Minn., to a high of $6,225.85 gross for the six man band in Hollywood is the success story of this outfit that has been described as ". . . the corniest outfit that ever massacred a tune for the delectation of an American audience." You've heard the band on the air! And the man behind the drums is none other than our friend, Harry Lindeman, who is well known to Drum Topics readers. Yes, believe it or not, that's Harry behind the drums. The other maniacal looking gentleman is Freddie Fisher. Naturally, the drums are all Leedys!

Fred Everhart

Everhart is the director of the OES all girl drum and bugle corps shown on page 3, and has played with the El Jebel Shrine Band of Denver, directed by John Leick, for the past eight years. He is an outstandingly fine drummer of more than 30 years standing and is well known throughout the Rocky Mountain states. Has used Leedy drums during his entire drumming career. Says: "Girls' corps uses 20 Leedy drums and not one head broken in 18 months. How's that?" Good going, we'd say!

Ralph Kester, Jr., Mishawaka, Ind.

Has his own band which he directs on dance jobs in northern Indiana. Played with the Mishawaka High School band and orchestra for four years. Studied drums under Harold Firestone, who is one of our staff here at the factory in Elkhart.

Hamilton Witter

This Evans City, Pa., chap won 1st Division rating in the state and national school band contests this year with the Leedy drum shown in the photo. Studied under Bill Hammond of Pittsburgh, Pa., and says he believes him to be one of the finest instructors in the country —in which belief he is 100% right. Witter's band leader is I. B. Weinstein.

Eddie Beanblossom

This Leedy drummer has had a wealth of experience in all phases of drum work—hotel, ballroom, radio, theatre pit and stage, and military—during his ten years in the profession. Now playing with Jimmy Richard's popular dance orchestra throughout the central U. S. in leading hotels and ballrooms. Eddie was born in Youngstown, O., attended Ohio State U. and now names Columbus, O., as his home. The factory recently had the pleasure of a visit from him and shortly thereafter he bought a complete new Leedy outfit from Wurlitzer's of Columbus.

James H. Howard

A professional drummer of 25 years standing, directs the Port Arthur, Tex., VFW and American Legion Drum and Bugle Corps—the latter a six-time State Champion in as many years until it withdrew from competition last year. Operates Howard Music Company in Port Arthur. Born in South Bend., Ind., and played professionally in the middle west until moving to Texas. Has always used Leedy and now features them in his music store because ". . . they are unequalled."

LEEDY SOLORIMBA

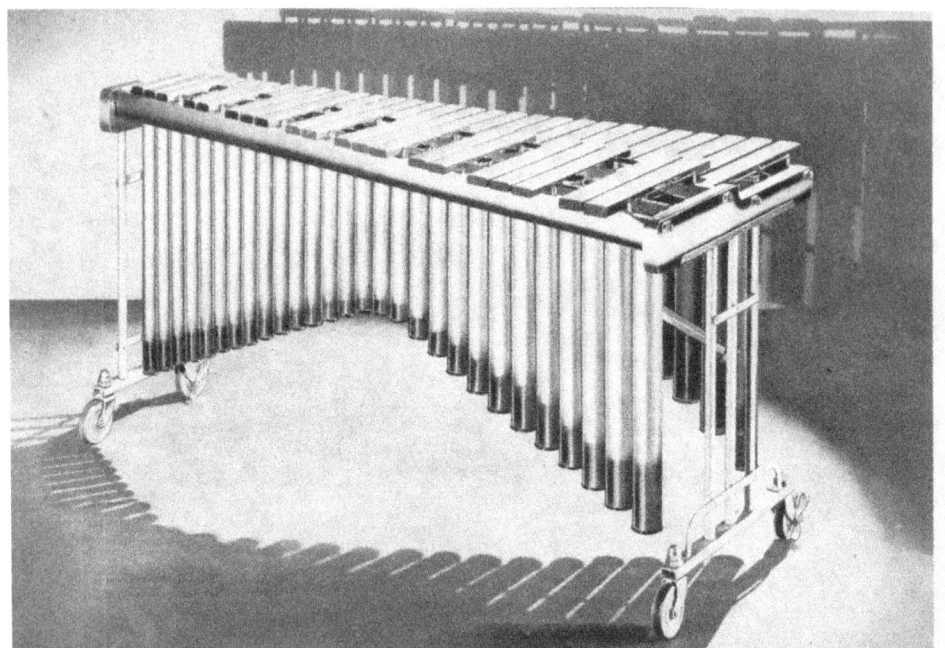

Here is the finest marimba that can be made and offered at the very modest price that is asked. It is first and foremost an outstandingly fine musical instrument of highest professional quality in every respect with fine, rich, pure, resonant tone, accurate intonation and volume to meet the most discriminating demands. It is beautiful in appearance and sturdy in construction so that it is ideal for every type of work. The price is far lower than you would normally expect to pay for an instrument of the Solorimba's quality and character. Never before has Leedy been able to incorporate its finest, most worthwhile EXCLUSIVE features in ANY model at this low price. By all means, see this remarkable instrument at your nearest Leedy dealer's store if you want the biggest marimba value that has ever been offered!

STANDARD FINISH
Display Resonators, Stands and Frames in Rich Grecian Gold and Black Lacquer

No. 5614—4 Octaves, C-28 to C-76, 49 Bars 2⅛" to 1½" Wide by ¾" Thick. Length Over-All 66". Height 33". Width Lower End 33". Weight 92 Lbs. Low A-440 Pitch ... $205.00

Instructor and Mallets Included

For Any Other Two-Color Lacquer Finish (On Special Order Only) ... $15.00 Extra
For Choice of Two-Color Lacquer Finish on Stands and Resonators and Choice of "Full Dress" Pearl or Sparkling Pyralin on Frames ... $25.00 Extra
†No. 6964—Two Fibre Hand Carrying Cases for No. 5614 ... $45.00

Trunk Price on Application

GEO. HAMILTON GREENE XYLOPHONE

STANDARD FINISH
Display Resonators, Stands and Frames in Rich Grecian Gold and Black Lacquer

No. 5632—4 Octaves, C-40 to C-88, 49 bars 2" Wide Graduated to 1⅝" by 15/16" Thick. Length Over-All 63". Height 33". Width Lower End 30". Weight 90 Lbs. Low A-440 Pitch ... $240.00
No. 5633—3½ Octaves, F-45 to C-88, 44 Bars 1-13/16" Wide Graduated to 1⅝" by 15/16" Thick. Length Over-All 56". Height 33". Width Lower End 28". Weight 80 Lbs. Low A-440 Pitch ... $220.00

Instructor and Mallets Included

For Any Other Two-Color Lacquer Finish (On Special Order Only) ... $15.00 Extra
For Choice of Two-Color Lacquer Finish on Stands and Resonators and Choice of "Full Dress" Pearl or Sparkling Pyralin on Frames ... $25.00 Extra
†No. 6943—4 Cases Required for 4 Octave ... $60.00
†No. 6944—3 Cases Required for 3½ Octave ... $50.00

Trunk Prices on Application
PRICES SUBJECT TO CHANGE WITHOUT NOTICE DUE TO PREVAILING UNCERTAINTIES

Designed to meet the exacting needs of the artist whose name it bears, and acclaimed by leading artists and directors in every branch of music as being the ONE xylophone that possesses EVERYTHING that a truly fine professional instrument SHOULD have, the Geo. Hamilton Green model is the ultimate in xylophone value at very moderate cost. Easy speaking, with brilliant, rich tone, perfect scale, ample volume and carrying power, and classic beauty that is skillfully combined with sturdy construction and great strength, are outstanding features which distinguish this model. Bars are thoroughly seasoned, genuine Honduras rosewood accurately tuned by the Leedy patented tuning process and mounted in full suspension for fullest, freest, finest tone. Stand is easily set up and can be knocked down and packed in a jiffy. New, beautiful finish on stands, resonators and frames will not tarnish or rust.

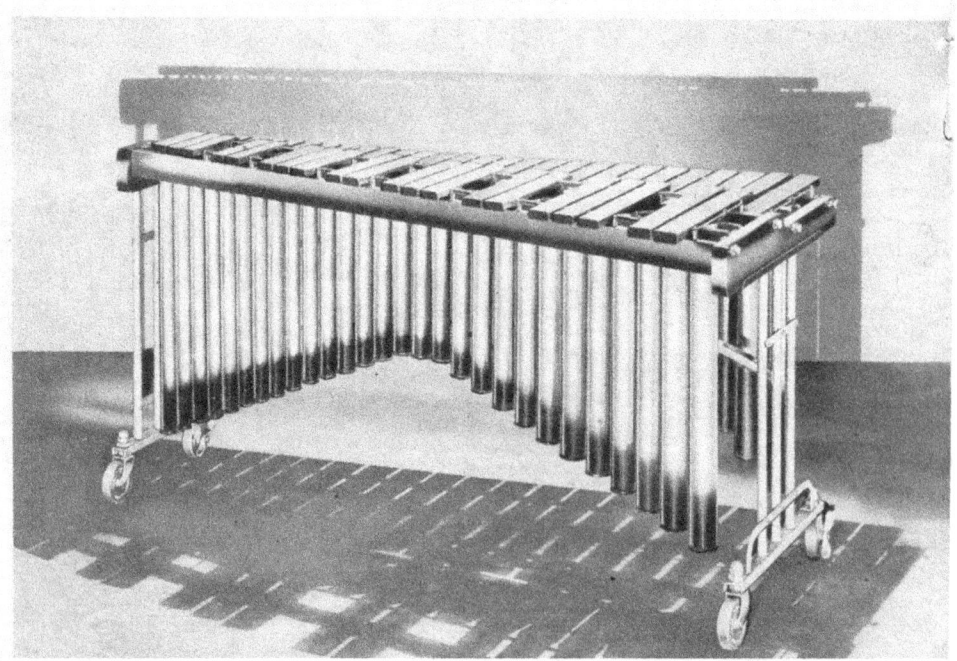

Leedy Drum Topics Issue 28

Ray Herbeck and "Whitie" Boyd

Ray Herbeck's orchestra is known throughout the nation as a result of its radio, theatre, and hotel appearances and its fine recordings. Drummer with the band is "Whitie" Boyd shown above (right) with Herbeck. The band recently closed at the Edgewater Beach Hotel, Chicago, and is, at this writing, at Elitch's Gardens, Denver. Boyd formerly was with Ralph Bennett and Artie Simmonds. Leedy equipped, of course!

Nick Pelico

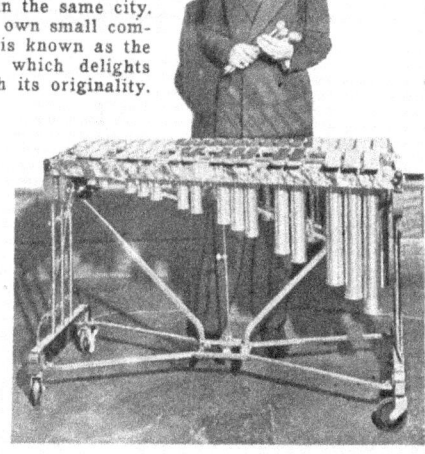

Pelico's swing technique on vibraphone was one of the feature attractions at Nick's Cafe, New York's Greenwich Village brightest swing spot where he played in conjunction with Bobby Hackett's orchestra until just recently when they moved to the Trocadero in the same city. Nick heads his own small combination which is known as the "Pelicans" and which delights the crowds with its originality. Pelico studied under Geo. Geer, has played Leedys for 8 years and thinks them tops in every respect. His birthplace is Providence, R.I.; his home now is N.Y.C. Formerly played with Ed Drew, Ray Belair, Carl Tatz and other bands.

Sydney C. Ball
Dumfriesshire, Scotland

Brother Ball is a self-taught drummer who does a fine job on the drums with Jim McKendrick's Red Aces which plays all the large Legion, Tennis, Choir and Staff dances in Dumfriesshire, and is contracted to play weekly at the Coloseum there. Ball was born in London. His drums are Leedy which—using our own slang—he says are "Wows." Formerly played with Richardson's Dance Orchestra and at one time headed his own band which was known as "Syd Ball and his Boys."

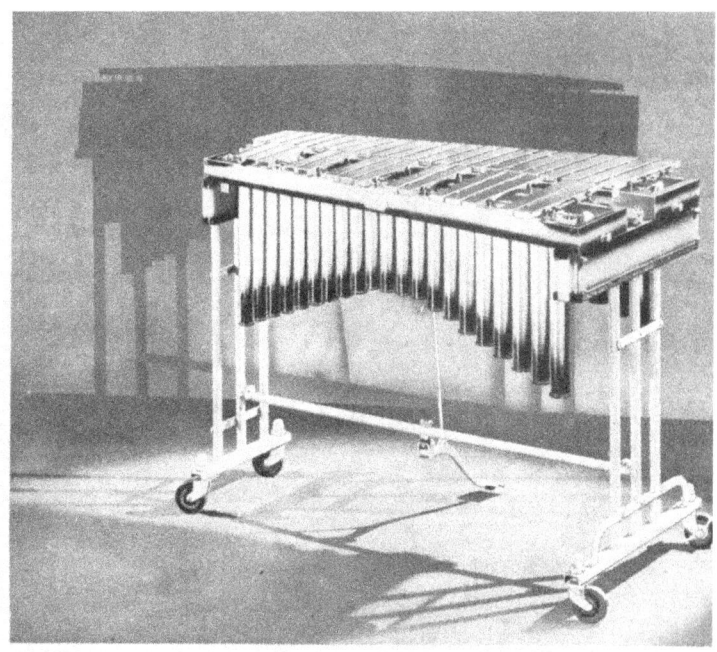

THE NEW LEEDY LIGHT WEIGHT VIBRAPHONE

Styled—and PRICED—to meet the needs and demands of today without sacrificing any of the outstanding musical qualities for which this instrument has long been famous, this new Vibraphone is certain to meet with even greater popular favor than former models.

It is more beautiful than ever before. Its graceful display resonators add distinction to its lines and the handsome Grecian Gold and black lacquer finish—appropriate in any setting—gives it new richness and dignity. The stands are tarnish and rust proof and will not show finger prints.

The instrument is lighter in weight than before and can be set up or knocked down and packed in two minutes. Fixed suspension mounting of the bars on the frames speeds setting up, knocking down and packing and eliminates all danger of damage. The stand is made up of fewer parts and the number of wing nuts has been reduced to an absolute minimum.

Bars are of finest specially alloyed aluminum for full, rich tone and resonance. The motor is a sturdy, smooth-working, dependable, universal type. The damper control is rigid, adjustable and positive in action.

Instrument is equipped with four solid rubber composition wheels—two with brakes.

STANDARD FINISH
Display Resonators, Stands and Frames in Grecian Gold and Black Lacquer

No. 5662—3 Octaves, C-40 to C-76, 37 Bars 1½" to 1¼" Wide by ½" Thick. Length Over-All 45". Height 33". Width Lower End 25". Weight 73 Lbs. Low A-440 Pitch.................................$275.00

Instructor and Mallets Included

For Any Other Two-Color Lacquer Finish (On Special Order Only) ..$15.00 Extra
For Any Other Two-Color Lacquer Finish on Stands, Frames and Resonators and Your Choice of "Full Dress" Pearl or Sparkling Pyralin on Frames ....$25.00 Extra
†No. 6927—Two Fibre Hand Carrying Cases for No. 5662 Vibraphone......$37.50

Trunk Prices on Application

PRICES SUBJECT TO CHANGE WITHOUT NOTICE DUE TO PREVAILING UNCERTAINTIES

NEW! "FULL-TONE" Vibraphone Mallets

Definitely the finest mallets ever made for vibraphone and other vibrato instrument playing. Ideal for ANY metal bar instrument. Mallets bring out the finest, fullest tone of the instrument. Heads are yarn wound felt covered rubber core. 1¼" diameter. Sturdy, flexible handles of 5/16" selected rattan. Mallets are perfectly balanced, and of correct length and weight. Like ALL Leedy mallets, this model can "take it," too!

No. 1733—Per Pair...$2.25

ABOUT HICKORY DRUM STICKS

Hickory sticks will warp, some more and some less. It is not the fault of poor material or workmanship; it simply is the "nature of the beast," and no manufacturer has yet been able to overcome this action. Hickory is a light, pliable fibre wood, and the fact that it will warp is one of the reasons we see so little of it used in furniture and other articles.

Hickory drum sticks are made carefully enough and they leave the factory perfectly straight, but they will "go" even in shipment over night.

This wood varies considerably in its natural growth as to grain and some sticks will warp quicker than others. Hickory sticks will also become crooked in use, such as beating them on Cow Bells, Cymbals, Wood Blocks, etc.

Not many drummers know that the life of a hickory stick can be greatly prolonged by a simple straightening process which consists of bending the stick with the hands over a solid edge, such as a table top, as shown in the illustration above.

However, with all their faults, they are the best kind of sticks for all-around use.

Don Ahrens, Tacoma, Wash.

This young Leedy drummer, before graduation from the Stadium H. S. Band, Tacoma, Wash., played with that school's 148th F. A. Band and won Superior rating at the annual music contest held at the U. of Washington, Seattle. His band director was R. C. Fussell and his drum teacher was Chas. Kramer. Ahrens also plays trap drums in a jobbing orchestra. Ahrens' equipment is all Leedy.

Harry Campbell
with Eddie Duchin Orchestra

Eddie Duchin's MCA orchestra at this writing is on tour playing theatre, hotel and radio engagements with Harry F. Campbell doing a swell job on the Leedys. Campbell has been with the band for the past 8 years prior to which he played with Leo Reisman, Al Donahue, Meyer Davis and others for fifteen years. He has been in the business for 23 years. His birthplace is Chelsea, Mass., and he studied under the famous Lawrence Stone of Boston whose reputation as a drummer and teacher is second to none. Campbell's home is now Revere, Mass. Of his Leedys, Campbell says: "They're fine—the best there are." In the photo with Campbell is leader Eddie Duchin.

Four Talented Bell Lyra Players

The four charming Bell Lyra players with the St. Rita Cadets of Lowell, Mass., are (l. to r.) Ruth Lefevbre, Mildred Woolfall, Bernice St. Hilaire and Dorothy Callahan who are all talented pianists as well. Mildred plays Alto Lyra—the others soprano.

LEEDY "3-SECTION" CYMBAL STAND

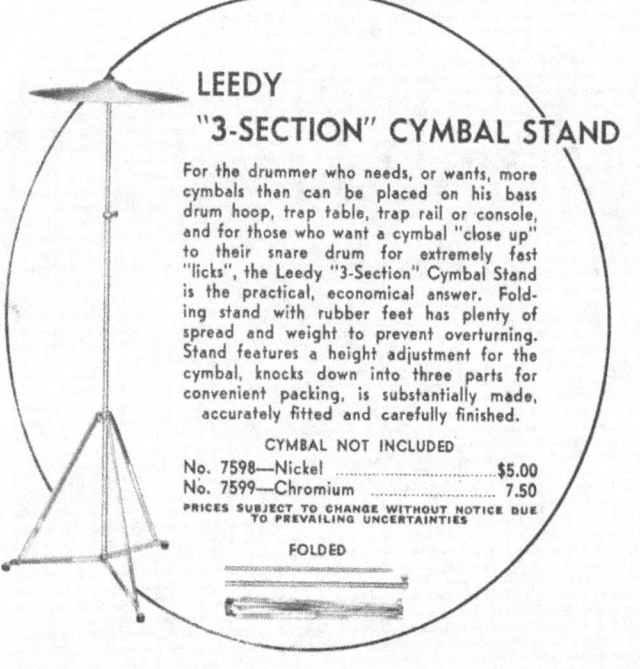

For the drummer who needs, or wants, more cymbals than can be placed on his bass drum hoop, trap table, trap rail or console, and for those who want a cymbal "close up" to their snare drum for extremely fast "licks", the Leedy "3-Section" Cymbal Stand is the practical, economical answer. Folding stand with rubber feet has plenty of spread and weight to prevent overturning. Stand features a height adjustment for the cymbal, knocks down into three parts for convenient packing, is substantially made, accurately fitted and carefully finished.

CYMBAL NOT INCLUDED

No. 7598—Nickel $5.00
No. 7599—Chromium 7.50

PRICES SUBJECT TO CHANGE WITHOUT NOTICE DUE TO PREVAILING UNCERTAINTIES

FOLDED

LEEDY "BESTALL" CYMBAL HOLDER FOR BASS DRUM HOOP

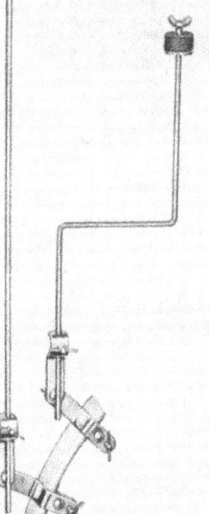

This is the cymbal holder that is absolute "tops" with the professional drummer today. It is the BEST non-swing type cymbal holder made. Clamps anywhere on the bass drum hoop with the famous Stayon clamp. Ratchet device permits cymbal to be used in an upright position regardless of where holder is placed on drum hoop. Cymbal vibrates freely without swinging.

WITH ANGLE ROD

No. 9000—Nickel $2.00
No. 9001—Chromium 3.00

WITH 32" STRAIGHT ROD

No. 9012—Nickel $2.25
No. 9013—Chromium 3.25

EXTRA ANGLE ROD ONLY

No. 9016—Nickel. Each $1.00
No. 9017—Chromium. Each 1.50

EXTRA 32" STRAIGHT ROD ONLY

No. 9014—Nickel. Each $1.00
No. 9015—Chromium. Each 1.50

New London, Conn., A. L. Drum & Bugle Corps

Sponsored by the J. Coleman Prince American Legion Post No. 9, New London, Conn., this corps which carries the same name, is a consistent prize winner in contest and parade work. It was state champ in 1937 and is one of the finest corps in a state that is famous for fine corps. It was organized in 1931. Its drum and bugle instructor is Walter Damas, a veteran drummer of the first water. Leedy drums and bugles shown are original equipment still doing 100% satisfactory service in every way.

Joe H. Sorace with Tommy Hopton

Joe Sorace, who has played hotel, ballroom, radio, theatre and night club engagements under the batons of Jess Hawkins, Sammy Watkins, Harry Shannon and other popular leaders, has been with Tommy Hopton for the past 3 years. Recently finished a 10 month contract at Cleveland's popular Bedford Glens after playing 36 weeks at the Southern Tavern Nite Club with radio outlets through WTAM, WHK and WGAR. Joe was born in Morgantown, W. Va., studied under Fred Albright and now lives in Bedford, O. He has used Leedys for 12 years.

Burton Flurkey, Elkhart, Ind.

Though only 13, young Flurkey plays drums with his school's Regimental and concert bands and with a dance band. He is a pupil, and a very good one, of Harold Firestone of the Leedy staff. He uses Leedys and says: "They're Tops."

Knox Pugh with Jack Russell

Pugh (left), a former Detroit drummer, now mans the Leedys for Jack Russell's popular orchestra which recently finished a 12 week contract at Chicago's palatial Pershing Ballroom. The band is well known around Chicago. Pugh has played Leedys for more than 10 years. Russell, the leader, is shown on the right in the photo.

With Ringling Bros. Famous Side Show Band

Bass drummer Edw. W. Warren (left) and snare drummer J. W. Wright (right) have been with Arthur Wright (center) and his Ringling Side Show Band and Minstrels for 5 and 8 years respectively. Both are veteran drummers with a wealth of experience in the field. Warren's home is Dayton, O.; Wright's home is Sandusky, O. Both use Leedy.

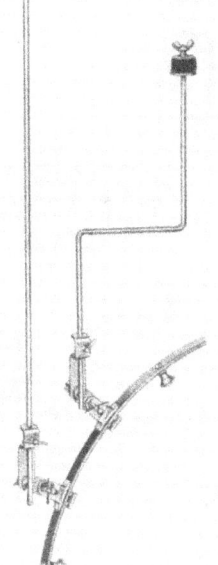

LEEDY "BESTALL" CYMBAL HOLDER FOR LEEDY TRAP RAILS

This is the famous Leedy "Bestall" Cymbal Holder (shown on the left) adapted for use on the Leedy Arch Rollaway Trap Console and the Leedy Arch Trap Rail shown on page 15 of this DRUM TOPICS. In features and adjustments, the two type of holders are the same, but the clamps are necessarily different for bass drum hoop and rail use. Choice of angle or 32" straight rod. Use the same holder for either type rod.

WITH ANGLE ROD
No. 9022—Nickel $2.00
No. 9023—Chromium 3.00

WITH 32" STRAIGHT ROD
No. 9034—Nickel $2.25
No. 9035—Chromium 3.25

EXTRA ANGLE ROD ONLY
No. 9016—Nickel. Each $1.00
No. 9017—Chromium. Each 1.50

EXTRA 32" STRAIGHT ROD ONLY
No. 9014—Nickel. Each $1.00
No. 9015—Chromium. Each 1.50

LEEDY "HIGHBOY" SOCK PEDAL

The finest sock pedal on the market—by far the smoothest, fastest, most quiet and sturdiest pedal made. Has a 20-inch leg spread and a slip-proof, cast aluminum footboard with a stationary heelplate. Cymbals can be adjusted for "squashy" or "solid" efforts and for short, fast action or great "sock" and volume. Cymbals 36" from floor. Easy to set up and knocks down in three pieces for convenient packing. Weighs only 4 lbs. 12 oz. Carefully designed, made of finest materials, accurately machined, perfectly assembled and durably finished—the finest pedal EVER made.

CYMBALS NOT INCLUDED
No. 7563—Nickel $10.00
No. 7564—Chromium 15.00

PRICES SUBJECT TO CHANGE WITHOUT NOTICE DUE TO PREVAILING UNCERTAINTIES

THE NEWLY IMPROVED "SWINGSTER" OUTFIT

No. 5385   IN BI-COLOR BLACK AND GOLD LACQUER AND NICKEL PARTS   **$168.00**

Here is America's "No. 1" outfit! Designed especially for the modern swing band drummer's needs, it has met—and satisfied—a popular demand as no other outfit has. Sales have skyrocketed and the setup has been imitated by other drum manufacturers but the "Swingster" still leads them all. In beauty, completeness, convenience, compactness and high quality, it has no equal at its very moderate price, so we offer it to you again—with the beautiful new and finer snare drum and TUNABLE TOM TOMS—as America's leading outfit.

THE "IMPROVED SWINGSTER" OUTFIT CONSISTS OF:
No Substitutions or Omissions

1—No. 428	6½"x14" Broadway Floating Head Snare Drum, Standard Extension Strainer, Beaver-Tail Streamlined Self-Aligning Rods. Bi-Color Black and Gold Lacquer. Nickel	$38.00
1—No. 5092	14"x28" Broadway Bass Drum, Inlaid Hoops, Single Tension "Half-Moon" Rods, Bi-Color Black and Gold Lacquer. Nickel	43.00
1—No. 8028	12"x14" Tunable Tom Tom, Single Tension Beaver-Tail Streamlined Self-Aligning Rods, Metal Hoop, Calf Head, Bi-Color Black and Gold Lacquer and Nickel	25.00
1—No. 8048	9"x13" Tunable Tom Tom, Single Tension Beaver-Tail Streamlined Self-Aligning Rods, Metal Hoop, Calf Head, Bi-Color Black and Gold Lacquer and Nickel	16.50
1—No. 7723	Heavy Duty Ratchet Tom Tom Holder, Single Arm for Bass Drum Hoop	3.50
1—No. 7718	Lightweight Ratchet Tom Tom Holder	1.50
1—No. 7010	"X-L" Pedal	10.00
1—No. 7103	Pair Standard Giant Spurs	1.50
1—No. 7260	Ideal Drum Stand	3.50
1—No. 7871	Bass Drum Tone Control	1.75
1—No. 7563	Highboy Sock Cymbal Pedal	10.00
2—No. 9000	Bestall Cymbal Holders for Bass Drum Hoop	4.00
1—No. 7302	12" Stanople Cymbal for Bestall Holder	5.75
1—No. 7300	10" Stanople Cymbal for Bestall Holder	4.50
1—No. 7450	10" Brass Deep Cup Cymbal for Sock Pedal	1.25
1—No. 7440	10" Brass Cymbal for Sock Pedal	1.15
1—No. 7607	Wood Block and Cow Bell Holder	1.75
1—No. 7680	7" Chinese Wood Block	1.00
1—No. 7797	5" Cow Bell	1.20
1—No. 7796	4¼" Cow Bell	1.00
1—No. 1645	Pair Aluminum Handle Wire Brushes	.60
1—No. H-14	Pair Hickory Drum Sticks	.45
1—	Beginners' Drum Method	.50

                  TOTAL VALUE........$177.40
                  SPECIAL PRICE......168.00

The "Improved Swingster" Outfit in:

Tri-Tone Blue and Silver Lacquer and Nickel	NO EXTRA CHARGE
White Lacquer and Nickel	
Black Lacquer and Nickel	
Choice of "Full Dress" Pearl or Sparkling Pyralin Finishes and Nickel	$42.00 EXTRA
Chromium Plated Metal Parts	37.50 EXTRA

PRICES SUBJECT TO CHANGE WITHOUT NOTICE DUE TO PREVAILING UNCERTAINTIES

Harold Popper, Radio Station WRVA

Popper is studio drummer of radio station WRVA, Virginia's only 50,000 watt station, located in Richmond from which several prominent CBS and MBS programs originate. Burt Repine shown with Popper in the photo below is director of the studio orchestra. Harold is a former pupil of Bob Steele, was born in Staten Island, N.Y., and has lived in Richmond for several years. Has been with Ken Moyer, played the Keith vaudeville circuit and has played college dances in the past. Has played drums for twelve years—ten of them with Leedys of which he says: "Meet every requirement. Have tried 'em all and find Leedys are always tops for any job."

Martha Jean Oberlin

This little miss of Canton, O., though only 14, is making a real name for herself. She plays with her school band, with a girls' orchestra and has played solo vibraphone on numerous radio programs. Orrie Smith, a Leedy drummer for 20 years, is her teacher. A. W. Silverstein, Edfred's Music Co., Akron, O., supplied her Leedy equipment and is interested in her work.

Eldon J. D'Orio

D'Orio is an exceptionally fine drummer and fine musician. Now on a coast-to-coast tour playing xylophone in hotels, night spots, vaudeville and radio. Has studied under the finest teachers, played the best spots all over the country and is "tops" in his field. He uses Leedy exclusively.

When You're On The Road . . . . .

When you are in a strange town and have that lonesome feeling, step into the Leedy dealer's store and get acquainted. More than likely you will find an experienced drummer in charge who will be more than glad to meet you. More than likely you'll both learn something from a technical standpoint and you'll both benefit from a friendly chat. And if he can serve you in any way, you can bet that he'll be more than glad to do so!

Even if you're not lonesome, it will be worth your while to look up the Leedy dealer in whatever town you happen to be. Try it in the next town you're in!

Natrona County (Wyo.) H. S. Cadet Band Drum Section

This is the splendid drum section of the splendid Natrona County High School Band of Casper, Wyoming, which has won Superior rating for the last two years in the annual Wyoming State Music Festival. The band is directed by Blaine D. Coalbaugh to whom much credit for the band's success is due. Director Coalbaugh advises us that Sgt. Drummer Junior Jones of this group is now lead drummer with the Nebraska U. Band but failed to state which lad is Jones. Drum equipment of the band is now all Leedy according to the information which we have

Ervin Oakes

Oakes is drummer-director of the dance band that is billed as Ervin Oakes and his Acorns which plays hotel, cafe and ballroom engagements in the middle west. The band recently finished a long contract at the Trianon Ballroom, Detroit. Oakes was born in St. Cloud, Minn., and studied drums under Harold Larson. His home is now Detroit and it is in that vicinity that he plays most of his jobs. He has used Leedy equipment for the past eight years.

Did you know that it requires 18 separate operations to make a transparent snare drum head and 27 operations to make a Leedy "Hardwhite" head?

Sonny Greer, Leedy drummer with Duke Ellington, is one of the most completely equipped drummers in the world!

Look at your sticks when practicing the rudiments. Don't look off into the distance and depend on your ear for the "right sound." Watch the movement of the sticks carefully. Make sure that they travel straight up and down—NOT in circles or half circles.

Do you own a practice pad? If not, get one. It will be one of the best investments you can make. Try the Leedy TWO-WAY pad (No. 1755; price $2.75). It is "tops."

LEEDY "ARCH • TRAP • RAIL"

The Only Trap Rail That Fits Down Close to the Bass Drum Shell

Stronger, more rigid, more practical and more convenient in every respect, this NEW Leedy Arch Trap Rail has EVERYTHING! An unusually wide selection of traps can be mounted on the rail with full assurance of convenient location and rigid, vibrationless support—nothing need be fastened to the bass drum hoops! Flat rail, made of high grade steel, conforms exactly to the radius of the drum and is anchored securely to the shell just above the rods by four metal spools placed at equidistant points. Rail remains on drum at all times, is compact, inconspicuous and out of the way, saves time in setting up, knocking down and packing. Your fibre bass drum case or Mackintosh cover will accommodate drum with the rail attached. Because trap rail fits close to drum shell, special trap holders are required. STAYON type clamps are used assuring strength, durability and long life. Holders will not "twist" or "turn" after being set. Holders afford the maximum degree of flexibility in mounting the traps and traps are fully adjustable for height, angle and distance from you.

9020	ARCH Trap Rail Only. Nickel	$ 4.00
9021	ARCH Trap Rail Only. Chromium	6.00
9026	Heavy Duty Ratchet Tom-Tom Holder, Nickel	4.25
9027	Heavy Duty Ratchet Tom-Tom Holder, Chromium	6.25
9032	Lightweight Ratchet Tom-Tom Holder, Nickel	1.50
9033	Lightweight Ratchet Tom-Tom Holder, Chromium	2.25
9028	Wood Block and Cow Bell Holder—Nickel	1.75
9029	Wood Block and Cow Bell Holder—Chromium	2.60
9030	Temple Block Rail, complete—Nickel	7.00
9031	Temple Block Rail, complete—Chromium	10.50
9022	Bestall Cymbal Holder—Nickel. Each	2.00
9023	Bestall Cymbal Holder—Chromium. Each	3.00
9024	Offset Cymbal Holder—Nickel. Each	2.25
9025	Offset Cymbal Holder—Chromium. Each	3.25

No. 9018—Complete ARCH Rail and all holders as shown in illustration below including: two HEAVY DUTY Tom-Tom Holders; two BESTALL Cymbal Holders; two OFFSET Cymbal Holders; one Combination Wood Block-Cow Bell Holder; and one Temple Block Rail—Nickel, only................ 27.50
No. 9019—Same as 9018—Chromium................ 41.25

PRICES SUBJECT TO CHANGE WITHOUT NOTICE DUE TO PREVAILING UNCERTAINTIES

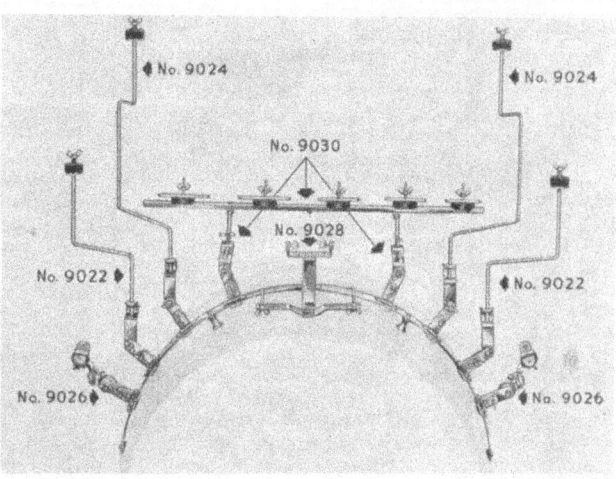

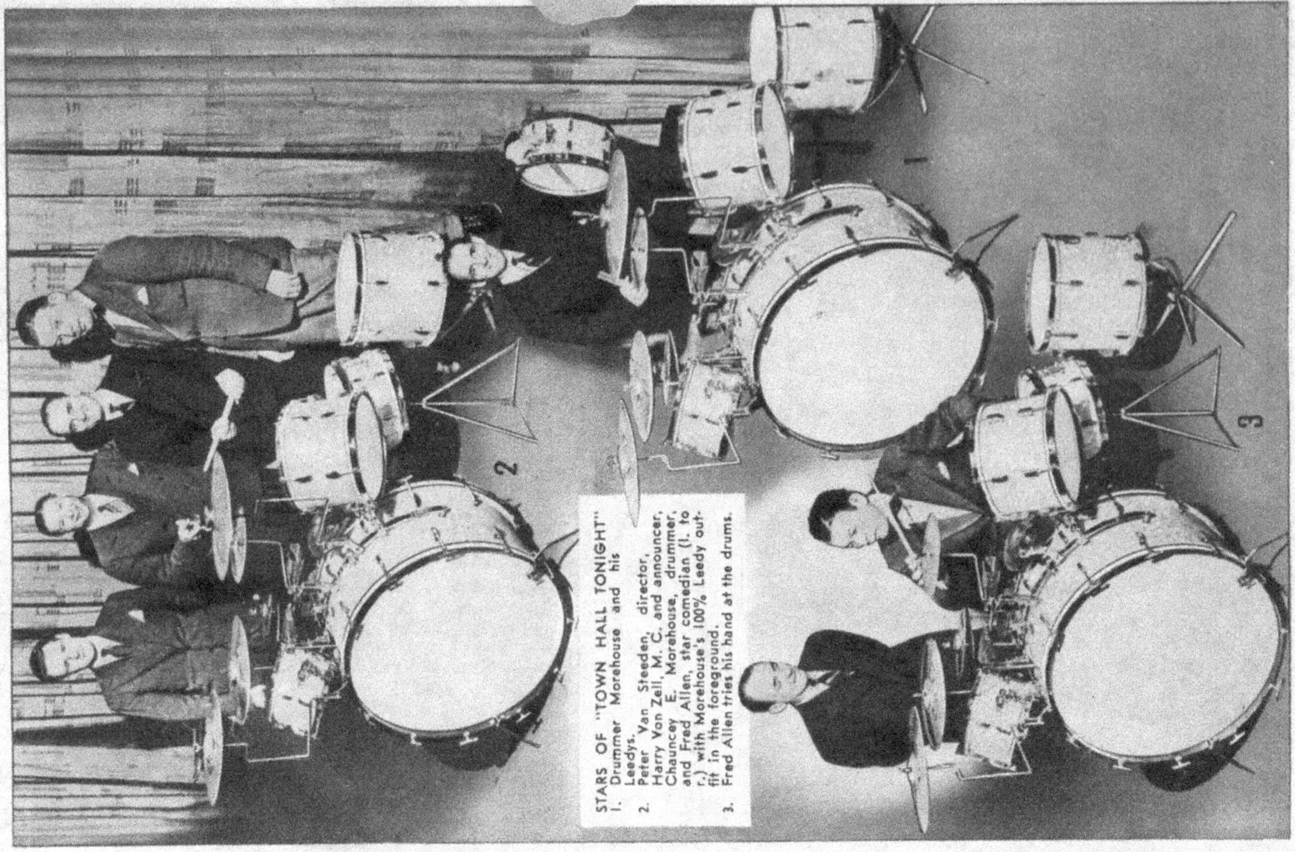

Did Someone Mention "THE GOOD OLD DAYS" . . . . ?

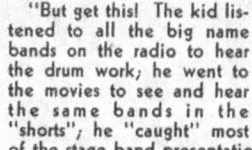

"Hello, Joe, how's tricks?"

"Well, Well, if it ain't the ol' Harry himself. Sure glad to see you. Where've you been keeping yourself all these years? How ya doin'?"

"Oh, fair enough. Makin' a livin' sellin' insurance. Int'resting game. What you doin'?"

"Been with a gents furnishing store for the last three years and doin' pretty fair. Playin' any these days?"

"Not much. Oh, I sit in with the Legion band once in a while just to keep up on my paradiddles. Pretty good band and a swell bunch o' fellows but I sure get lonesome for the sound of the overture buzzer down at the old show shop every once in a while."

"Boy, so do I! Many's the time I wish I could bang out a bunch of good old vaudeville acts and catch a few kicks . . . but, on the other hand, it's nice to be able to knock off at six an' go home to the wife and kids. No night work except Saturdays, and Sundays are my own. I can't kick but it ain't like the good old days. Could be a lot worse off. There's still a lot of the old theatre men having a tough time of it. Guess the vaudeville game is just about washed up . . . and the young fellows are getting all the dance work."

"Yep, you're right. Times have changed. These days belong to the new generation, I guess. But we aren't exactly "has beens" as far as ability is concerned. We could still knock 'em out with the best of 'em if we had the chance but there's just not enough of our kind of work to go around, I suppose. What do you think of the new crop of drummers?"

"Well, there's one thing that's certain. . . . Mr. and Mrs. John Q. Public like them plenty and the good ones are reaping a harvest. I know they're making a lot more dough than we ever did."

There was a pause in the conversation as Joe offered a cigarette to Harry, took one himself and both men lit up.

"You know, Harry, you and I came up the hard way compared to the young fellows of today," continued Joe.

"How do you mean, Joe?"

"Well, you know the old routine. First, we got hold of a pair of sticks, a book and a practice pad and our teacher kept us on the "Daddy-Mammy" and the other rudiments for months. Most of us in those days never even owned a drum until we could play about half the book and some teachers even insisted that their pupils master all the rudiments before they'd start teaching 'em to read music. It took two or three years of the hardest kind of study before we could play even the easiest dance job and another two or three years before we even dared to try to play vaudeville or a musical show.

"And what opportunity did we have to hear and see other drummers do their stuff? Only when we went to the theatre or when some travelling concert band came to town! Sure, we had phonograph records but in those days you could hardly distinguish the drum work. We just didn't have the opportunities to observe and hear other drummers in our day like the youngsters can—and do—now, and the result was we didn't get along as fast as they do today.

"My own kid is a good example of what I mean! He's only sixteen and right now he's playing more drums than either of us could at twenty-five or thirty.

"About a year ago Bill decided he wanted to play in the high school band and he asked me if I'd help him get started on drums. I taught him the rudiments and the fundamentals of reading and I'm not saying this because he's my kid, but he sure caught on in a hurry.

"But get this! The kid listened to all the big name bands on the radio to hear the drum work; he went to the movies to see and hear the same bands in the "shorts"; he "caught" most of the stage band presentations and most of the dance bands that hit the dance spots and hotels in this neck of the woods while he was studying and I'll say that he learned something worthwhile from every one of the drummers.

"So, in one short year this kid, like hundreds of others, becomes a real drummer—in less time than it took us to get up speed with a decent roll.

"Do you get the comparison between the way we learned and the way the young drummers of today are learning the business?"

Joe tossed his cigarette away before he answered.

"Yea, I get it but I never thought of it just that way before. I've noticed how fast these school kids learn and the thought has struck me at times that I must have been pretty dumb when I was learning to play. But, as you say, things are different today. There's no doubt about it—the boy or girl who takes up drums today can learn faster, get a lot more kick out of it while he's studying, become a finer drummer in every way and has more chances of really cashing in on it than we ever did. More power to 'em. I'm for them, myself.

"But you left out a few things, Harry. One is that they can listen to modern records played by high-fidelity phonographs with the result that they really can hear what the drums are doing. Another is that they can record their own playing and pick out their mistakes and imperfections when they listen to the play-backs. Still another is that they get actual playing experience in their school bands almost every day. Finally, I've noticed, these same kids also get together in small swing groups OUTSIDE of school and continually play at home or at parties of one kind or another for the experience and fun of it. Some of these little jitterbug groups soon develop into real organizations and many of our big name professionals today started just that way. In other words, the youngsters of today are playing while they learn and learning while they play which is something we COULDN'T do."

Both men were silent with their thoughts for a few moments before Harry spoke up.

"I wonder if the kids of today really realize how lucky they are. A lot of 'em don't, I know. Some of 'em let their success go to their heads. Hope Bill doesn't let that happen to him because he's got the makin's of a real musician. Right now he's studying xylophone and tymps and doing a better than average job of it. Say . . . why don't you and the Mrs. go to the school concert next Friday night and get a load of the kid in action?"

"Gee, Harry, I'd like to. Let's go together, shall we?"

"SWELL! And listen! Bring the wife over to the house for dinner that night and we'll all go from there. Helen just finished her house-cleaning and she'll be tickled to death to see you both again. Okeh?"

"Suits me fine, Harry. Glad to have seen you again and we'll be seein' you next Friday. About six, I suppose?"

"Right! Until Friday night then, Joe. And maybe we can knock out a few rudiments ourselves that night, huh, just for the fun of it?"

"Sure, that'll be fun. Well, so long, then, Harry."

"So long, Joe."

Leedy DRUM TOPICS
ISSUE NO. 29

Ernie Rudisill with Sammy Kaye's Orchestra

Ernie Rudisill and his 100% Leedy outfit play an important part in the success of Sammy Kaye's ace orchestra which delights all who listen to it whether via the radio or from the dance floor. Shown with Ernie here is Sammy Kaye himself whose band is currently packing 'em in at the Essex House in New York City.

They Are the "King's Jesters"

Now playing the Brown Derby, Chicago, and several radio commercials, the "King's Jesters" are "tops" in their field. At one time a feature attraction of Paul Whiteman's. Left to right below are: Johnny Ravencroft, George Howard with his new Leedys, and Fritz Bastow. George has played Leedys for 15 years.

Val Eddy

Billed as "Val Eddy and his Symphony in Wood" in leading theatres and night clubs, Eddy has built an enviable reputation for himself through his fine performances on his Leedy Xylophone and drums. Studied under R. C. Light of Akron, and lives in Cuyahoga Falls, Ohio.

Dean Stevenson — Drummer   Adrian — Vocalist

Dean Stevenson, percussion-master with Joe Sanders' long-famous orchestra, needs no introduction to DRUM TOPICS readers as he is an all-Leedy user and booster of many years standing. Here he is shown with vocalist Adrian who, it goes without saying, lends a lot of that well known "oomph" to the Sanders aggregation. The band, at this writing, is on tour of the first class big city theatres from coast to coast.

Tops for Fourth Consecutive Year In Louisiana State Competition!

This is all-Leedy equipped percussion section of the Fair Park High School Band, Shreveport, La., which for four consecutive years has won "Superior" rating in Class "A" state competition. Director W. Hines Sims, the school and the city have every right to be proud of their band and its splendid playing record. Thanks to J & S Music Co., Shreveport, for equipping this wonderful band with Leedys.

W. F. Ehrlich — St. Louis Symphony

Ehrlich, eminently fine tympanist and xylophonist with the St. Louis Symphony under the baton of Vladimir Golschmann, has been a member of that splendid organization for 15 years. Born in Mainz, Germany, he studied under Walter Pelzner, tympanist of the Hanover Symphony, and has used Leedys exclusively since coming to America in 1927.

Miguel A. Gandia

Since this photo was taken, Gandia, who is shown here with Nano Rodrigo, has joined Enri Madriguero as his featured drummer and is at this writing playing the St. Francis Hotel, San Francisco. Gandia was born in Puerto Rico, studied drums under the capable tutorship of his father and has played Leedys for 8 years.

E. E. (Joe) Stokes—Philmore Gilbert—Vladimir Nikiforoff

Ernst H. Hoffmann, director of the Houston (Tex.) Symphony Orchestra has an outstandingly fine percussion section made up of this trio who (l. to r.) play snare drum, tympani and bass drum respectively. Between them, these men have played professionally for more than 78 years, have played Leedys for more than 68, and have played with the Houston Symphony for 43 years. "Joe" is Secretary of the A. F. of M. Local No. 65. All are staunch Leedy boosters.

Mary Barnett—Elmhurst, N. Y.

Pretty, talented and only seventeen, Mary and her Leedy Xylophone already have been featured in M-G-M pictures and in leading New York dinner and show spots. She is the daughter of Roy Barnett who was featured xylophonist and saxophonist on the "Roemers Homer's" program, one of WMCA's top programs in pioneer radio days.

Jeanne Schaefer

When the Muskingum College Band, New Concord, O., goes on parade, gives a concert or appears on the football field, it is headed by the gracefully high-stepping, highly proficient and VERY winsome twirling Drum Major-ess whose picture graces this page immediately to the left. Of course it's a Leedy Baton she twirls.

Joe Taylor, Gas City, Ind.

Joe, though only 13, has played drums for 4 years, plays in his high school band and orchestra and has a little orchestra of his own on the side. He is shown here with his Leedy "New Yorker" outfit of which he is mighty proud as he well may be.

James Fraser

Fraser has played with the Norfolk & Western Railway Company's Band, Roanoke, Va., for 14 years. During the 1st World War was Band Sergeant, 209th Engineers Band, has played vaudeville and pictures and is member of the Rajah Temple Band, No. 195, D. O. K. K. He has used Leedy equipment for more than 30 years in all his work.

Dick Maxfield

Winner of a "1st Division" rating in the National School band contests last year on snare drum and marimba, Maxfield, Coldwater, Mich., High School bandsman, was declared by the judge to be one of the best snare drummers in the U. S.

Oscar M. Haney with Al Marsico

Haney is the "man behind the Leedys" in Al Marsico's Orchestra which provides dinner and dance music for the patrons of Pittsburgh's Nixon Restaurant. Haney, born in Pittsburgh, studied under Fred Zender, and has played for 20 years. Equipment and photo supplied by Wm. F. Hammond's store.

U. of Arizona Concert Band Percussion Section

The University of Arizona's Concert Band is a top-ranking musical organization and boasts an exceptionally fine percussion section that is 100% Leedy equipped. Members of this section, shown above, are (l. to r.) Robert Garing, Sherrill Smith, Harvey Webb, Edw. Breazeale, Allen Dittman, James Coffey, Homer Williams and Geo. C. Wilson who is Director of Band and Orchestra. Smith, Williams and Breazeale are also members of the Tucson Symphony Orchestra, and Smith, in addition, is also one of Tucson's professional drummers.

George Gaber

Tympanist with the Pittsburgh Symphony Orchestra which was reorganized a few years ago and is now under the direction of Fritz Reiner, Gaber is one of the top-ranking tympanists in the business. A user of Leedy equipment for many years, this photo of Gaber and his Leedy Tympani was taken in New York during an engagement there.

Cole Bros. Circus Band Drum Section

Who sets the tempo for Vic Robbins' swell, rapid-fire Cole Bros. Circus Band? None other than Amos Thompson—2nd from left—(Uniontown, Pa.) and Al Yoder (Kulpmont, Pa.) topnotch drummers who play snare and bass drum respectively—Leedy, of course. In the photo is shown Vic Robbins (right), Bangor, Me., one of the nation's Ace bandmasters, Geo. H. Way (left) of the Leedy company who "sits in" with the band as guest drummer a few times each season.

Louis Goucher

Goucher, a veteran of outstanding ability in the profession for many years, has been with the U. S. Navy Band, Lt. Chas. Benter, Leader, for the past twenty years or so as Xylophone Soloist and snare drummer. Goucher's equipment, like that of the entire percussion section, is 100% Leedy.

Dick Tagliabue with Larry Wade

Dick is doing a nice job of "sending" for Larry Wade and his Blue and Gold Orchestra doing club and radio work in N. J. He is a pupil of the late Joe Green and of Vince Mott, American Legion National Champion Rudimental Drummer and owner of the Mott Music House, Paterson, N. J., with whom he is pictured here. His equipment is Leedy throughout.

Bridget O'Flynn

Via Bob Perry of Lockie Music Exchange, Los Angeles, comes this fetching picture of Miss O'Flynn who wields wicked sticks with Sally Banning's Orchestra which is a well known and popular all-girl's band in southern California. Teacher was Lee Young, home is Gardena, Cal., and drums are all Leedy.

A Fine Drum Section

Any high school band would be glad to have a drum section as fine as that of the Daytona Beach (Fla.) High School Band which is shown here. Left to right, the drummers are: Ted Stevens, Nora Lee Stanley, Bill Richardson, Jno. Hinton, James Bain, Dick Gardiner, Jean Nickerson and Gordon Hall. The section is 100% Leedy equipped. W. P. Heney is director of the band. Thanks to The Music Studio, Daytona Beach, for the excellent photo.

Samuel I. Latimer, Jr.

Latimer has been playing drums with Dean Hudson and his Florida Clubmen for the past 7 years doing hotel, dance and a lot of radio work. At present this swell band is holding forth at the Cavalier Beach Club, Virginia Beach, Va. Sam uses Leedys, of course.

Spencer Prinz with Richard Himber

Prinz, a Leedy drummer for more than 15 years, is now with Richard Himber's standout orchestra. Has played with Rube Wolf, Artie Shaw, done Victor recording, played all major radio networks, in all major and mutual picture studios, with "Burns and Allen" show and in the picture "Rhythm on the River."

Leedy Drum Topics Issue 29

Rudy Van Gelder

Ace drummer with a number of the nation's ace name bands doing theaters, records, radio and cafe work, Rudy was with the inimitable Ted Lewis for 5 years, was Associate Editor and Drum Editor of the "Orchestra World" magazine, and is considered one of the finest show drummers in the country. Van Gelder is at this writing playing the better theater engagements in N. Y. C. Has used Leedys for 27 years.

Charlie Owen

Without exception every prominent drummer who knows Charlie states there is no finer percussion artist. Such compliments from brother drummers are the ultimate in praise. He hails from Youngstown, O. Joined the U. S. Marine Band in 1934. His wonderful xylophone solos and exceptional technique on tympani and snare drum are indeed a treat to all ears.

Ralph Tilkin with Johnny McGee

Ralph and his Leedys are featured with Johnny McGee's popular GAC orchestra which plays the better hotels and dance spots in New York. Has played with Jack Marshard, Frank Weingar, Teagarden and others, too. Says his Leedys are the best equipment he's ever had.

The Williams Sisters

Dorothy (left) and Jeannette Williams are as talented as they are pretty. They were members of the prize-winning Deering High School Orchestra in 1939 and now are playing sustaining and commercial programs on WGAN and WCSH, Portland, Me., which city is their home.

They're Peacock Military Academy Drummers

This fine photo is of the drummers of the splendid drum and bugle corps of the Peacock Military Academy, San Antonio, Tex., which is the "West Point of the South." Cadets are (l. to r.) Harold Pool, J. Salum, J. Koerth, J. Leopard, S. Peckham, T. Lamkin, S. Salum, C. Garrison and H. Todd—a talented and fine looking group. Drums, of course, are all Leedy.

Irv Rothman with Henry Jerome's Orchestra

Irv was born in Norwich, Conn., studied under Dick Kyle and has played drums and Vibraphone under the baton of Henry Jerome since that orchestra was organized about ten years ago. "The Stepping Tones of Henry Jerome", as the band is called, has played for the past several years at Child's Paramount Rendezvous in N.Y.C., and is doing four coast-to-coast air shots on WOR and the MBC network. Irv uses a Leedy Vibraphone as shown here.

LEEDY "HIGHBOY" SOCK CYMBAL PEDAL
POINTS OF SUPERIORITY
SMOOTH, QUIET, NON-FATIGUING ACTION
SUBSTANTIAL, FULLY BRACED, 20-INCH LEG SPREAD
CAST ALUMINUM, SLIP-PROOF FOOTBOARD
WITH STATIONARY HEELPLATE
CYMBALS STAND 36-INCHES HIGH
EASY TO SET UP—KNOCKS DOWN INTO FOUR PARTS
WEIGHS ONLY 4 LBS. 12 OZ.

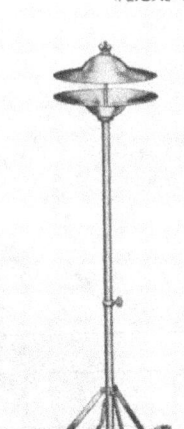

This is a greatly improved, smoother, quieter and easier working, sturdier sock cymbal pedal than any that has been offered to the profession up to this time. It has a 20-inch, fully braced leg spread which makes it practically topple-proof. Non-slip cast aluminum footboard with stationary heelplate is designed to eliminate muscle strain and fatigue. Cymbals are held at exactly the right height to permit using them for stick work if desired. Fully adjustable for solid "sock" or "washy" cymbal effects, for short, fast pedal strokes or for greater sock and more volume. Cymbal assembly packs and sets up as a unit for convenience. Entire pedal locks into one unit when assembled—can be lifted and moved without coming apart; made in four pieces for easy packing; easy to set up and knock down. Weight only 4 lbs. 12 oz. Made of finest materials, accurately machined, perfectly assembled and durably finished.
DOES NOT INCLUDE CYMBALS
No. 7563
$10.00
IN HEAVY NICKEL PLATE

Bob Wear

Bob played hotel, ballroom, college and country club dates with Gene Hileman's orchestra for 5 years and now has his own orchestra playing the same kind of jobs in northern Indiana and southern Michigan. He has played Leedys for the past seven years and says: "They are best by far." Bob's home is Elkhart, Ind., where Leedys are made.

Prices Subject to Change Without Notice. Because Defense Production has Created Uncertainty of Supply of Most Raw Materials Used in Leedy Instruments, Construction Specifications are Subject to Change Without Notice.

Byrd High School Band Drum Section

This splendid all-Leedy equipped drum section of the Byrd High School Band, Shreveport, La., is one reason why that band has won "Superior" ratings in Class "A" school band competition. The band boasts 90 pieces and is directed by Dwight G. Davis who "took over" in 1936. Mr. Davis is a Past President of the Ark.-La.-Tex. Directors' Association. Thanks to J&S Music Co., Shreveport, for the photo.

James Welch with Paul Moorhead

Prior to joining Paul Moorhead's Orchestra about seven years ago, Welch played drums and headed his own band which played hotel and night club engagements in and around Minneapolis and St. Paul. The Moorhead orchestra headquarters in Omaha, Neb., and has played jobs in seven states. Welch plays Leedys, likes them 100% and says, "— most of the drummers out here have Leedy drums."

Jere Evans' Rhythm Masters

These young professionals play theater engagements and private functions throughout the state of Pennsylvania. Jere Evans (third from left) and his Leedy Marimba head the ensemble. He's eight. Walter H. Pogue, Jr. (right) is eleven and does a swell job on the drums. He was taught by his father who is Small Goods Manager of J. H. Troup Music Co., Lancaster, Pa. Miss Opal Petters, Leedy xylophonist and supervisor of the trio, is shown on the left. Oscar Petters, 2nd from left, Miss Petters' brother, plays piano and accordion and is 14.

Prices Subject to Change Without Notice. Because Defense Production has Created Uncertainty of Supply of Most Raw Materials Used in Leedy Instruments, Construction Specifications are Subject to Change Without Notice.

The Ultimate in Outfits

THE NEW "NITE CLUB" OUTFIT

No. 5325

$358.00

WITH LEEDY "AUTOGRAPHS OF THE STARS" PYRALIN AND NICKEL METAL PARTS

The new "Nite Club" Outfit is distinctively different in appearance, drumistically correct in every detail and complete in makeup. Finished in the exclusive new Leedy "Autographs of the Stars" pyralin—top-time Leedy drummers' authentic autographs indelibly and permanently processed in a star-studded blue background—this outfit packs more drum personality, punch, character and pride of ownership than any outfit ever before offered to the profession! Names of 212 Leedy STANDOUT drummers appear on this outfit! SEE the "Nite Club" at your dealer's store for a thrill!

THE "NITE CLUB" OUTFIT
In Leedy "Autographs of the Stars" Pyralin and Nickel Metal Parts

1—No. 780 8" x 14" Broadway Parallel Swingster Snare Drum	$ 59.00
1—No. 5101 14" x 28" Broadway Separate Tension Bass Drum	81.50
1—No. 8018 14" x 16" Separate Tension Tunable Tom-Tom	47.00
1—No. 8036 12" x 14" Separate Tension Tunable Tom-Tom	42.00
1—No. 8038 9" x 13" Separate Tension Tunable Tom-Tom	33.00
1—No. 7010 "X-L" Pedal	10.00
1—No. 8800 New Leedy Arch Trap Rail attached to Bass Drum	5.75
1—No. 7118 Pair Bass Drum Wheel Spurs	5.00
1—No. 7255 Standard (Heavy) Snare Drum Stand	5.00
1—No. 7871 Brass Drum Tone Control	1.75
2—No. 9026 Heavy Duty Ratchet Tom-Tom Holders at $4.25 each	8.50
1—No. 7753 Set Tunable Tom-Tom Legs (Brackets bolted to 14" x 16" Tom-Tom)	3.00
2—No. 9045 Heavy Duty Angle Extension Cymbal Holders at $1.50 each	3.00
1—No. 9042 15½" Arm Heavy Duty Non-Swing Cymbal Holder	1.75
1—No. 9040 22½" Arm Heavy Duty Non-Swing Cymbal Holder	2.00
1—No. 7310 10" Zenjian Cymbal — Thin	7.90
1—No. 7311 11" Zenjian Cymbal	9.00
1—No. 7312 12" Zenjian Cymbal	10.00
1—No. 7364 16" Chinese Sneeze Cymbal	7.25
1—No. 7563 Leedy Highboy Sock Cymbal Pedal	9.00
2—No. 7311 11" Zenjian Cymbals for Highboy Sock Cymbal Pedal at $9.00 each	18.00
1—No. 9028 Combination Cow Bell and Wood Block Holder	1.75
1—No. 7796 4¼" Cow Bell	1.00
1—No. 7797 5" Cow Bell	1.20
1—No. 7680 7" Chee Foo Chinese Wood Block	1.00
1—No. 1642 Pair Rubber Covered Wire Brushes	1.15
1—No. 25 Pair Swing Stix	.60
(No Substitutions or Omissions) TOTAL VALUE	$377.10
SPECIAL PRICE	358.00

No. 5330—Same in Bi-Color Cream and Gold Lacquer (without Autographs). $310.00

THE NEW "PALOMAR" OUTFIT
No. 5335
$216.25

IN BI-COLOR CREAM AND GOLD LACQUER, SPARKLING GOLD PYRALIN INLAID COUNTER HOOPS ON BASS DRUM AND NICKEL PARTS

For eye-arresting beauty, richness, dignity, completeness and 100% drumability at VERY moderate price, the "Palomar" is a HEADLINER! The new Bi-Color Cream and Gold lacquer finish—newly styled by Leedy and introduced here for the first time—makes it distinctively different from any on the market. Featured in the set-up are THREE tunable tom toms, plenty of cymbals, the NEW Leedy Arch Trap Rail and Arch Trap Rail holders.

THE "PALOMAR" OUTFIT
In Bi-Color Cream and Gold Lacquer and Nickel Parts

1—No. 660	8" x 14" Broadway Standard Swingster Snare Drum		$40.00
1—No. 5092	14" x 28" Broadway Single Tension Bass Drum		48.00
1—No. 8800	Arch Trap Rail (attached to bass drum)		5.75
1—No. 8028	12" x 14" Tunable Tom-Tom, Single Tension		25.50
1—No. 8077	7" x 11" Tunable Tom-Tom, Single Tension		17.50
1—No. 8015	14" x 16" Tunable Tom-Tom, Single Tension		30.00
1—No. 9026	Heavy Duty Ratchet Tom-Tom Holder		4.25
1—No. 9032	Lightweight Ratchet Tom-Tom Holder		1.25
1—No. 7753	Tunable Tom-Tom Adjustable Legs		3.00
1—No. 7010	"X-L" Pedal		10.00
1—No. 7108	Standard Giant Bass Drum Spurs, Rubber Tip		1.50
1—No. 7260	Ideal Drum Stand		3.50
1—No. 7871	Bass Drum Tone Control		1.75
1—No. 7310	10" Zenjian Cymbal		7.90
1—No. 7312	12" Zenjian Cymbal		10.00
1—No. 7364	16" Chinese Sneeze Cymbal		7.25
2—No. 9045	Heavy Duty Angle Extension Cymbal Arms for Arch Trap Rail @ $1.50		3.00
1—No. 9042	Heavy Duty Non-Swing Cymbal Holder, 15½" Arm		1.75
1—No. 9028	Wood Block and Cow Bell Holder		1.75
1—No. 7680	7" Chinese Wood Block		1.00
1—No. 7797	5" Cow Bell		1.20
1—No. 7796	4¼" Cow Bell		1.00
1—No. 1641	Pair Wire Brushes		.65
1—No. 3	Pair Hickory Drum Sticks		.45

(No Substitutions or Omissions)

TOTAL VALUE......$227.95
SPECIAL PRICE.....$216.25

Prices Subject to Change Without Notice. Because Defense Production has Created Uncertainty of Supply of Most Raw Materials Used in Leedy Instruments, Construction Specifications are Subject to Change Without Notice.

Wm. (Bill) Weber with Howard Becker

Bill Weber is the "man behind the drums" with Howard Becker's band which now is on an extended tour playing hotel, nightery, radio and ballroom jobs. Bill was born, and lives, in Altoona, Pa., studied drums under Foster Johnson, and is 100% satisfied with his drums which are Leedy throughout. Ford's Music Store, Altoona, sent us the very fine photo and supplied Bill with his Leedys.

Berkeley Marimba Quartet

Members of this talented quartet which was taught and is directed by Herbert Sanford are (l. to r.) Emma Kasch, Betty Kasch, Frank Wheeler and Mrs. Bayless Wheeler, all residents of Berkeley, Cal., and all very fine musicians. They play all types of music from classic to sweltering swing on their Leedy instruments. Their engagements throughout Texas and California include radio, concert, vaudeville and club jobs as well as summer engagements at Yosemite National Park.

DeLand (Fla.) Senior H. S. Band Drum Section

John J. Heney, former Sousa Band xylophone soloist and drummer and now Director of the DeLand High School Band personally has instructed his drum section and has done a first class job of it as the many First Division State and Regional Contest medals worn by its members clearly testify. The members (l. to r.) are Clifton Loveland, Marshall Lane, Tom Pattillo, Ruth Hunter, Don McEmber, Jack Smith, Donna Smith, Director Heney and Rolland Cazer. Equipment is Leedy.

Stan Meyers and Tommy Romersa

Bob Perry, Lockie Music Exchange, Los Angeles, sent us this swell photo of Stan Meyers (left) and Tommy Romersa who does the vitally necessary behind the Leedys in a truly outstanding manner for the Stan Meyers band. Romersa was born in Red Lodge, Mont., studied drums under his own father, H. T. Romersa, who is a fine drummer and teacher. The band plays theaters, clubs, ballrooms, radio and RCA records.

Olive Johnson, Ashtabula, O.

This winsome miss and her Leedy drum help to make the Ashtabula Harbor (O.) High School Band the fine musical organization it is. Olive studied drums under Leedy dealer-drummer Charlie Wilcoxon of Cleveland and has played with her school band for the past 4 years under the direction of Uro Seppelen. She says, "Leedys surpass all others in workmanship and fine tone quality."

Donald   Barnhart

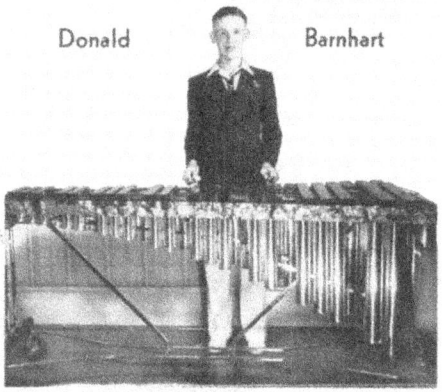

This Constantine (Mich.) lad plays fine marimba and snare drum with his city high school band and is reported to be a "comer" in the music profession. His instrument is a Leedy Royal Marimba. Harold Firestone, Elkhart, Ind., his teacher, says that Don is an unusually apt pupil and already shows talent far in advance of his years.

The "Tone" and "Feel" of a Snare Drum Are Two Entirely Different Things

Geo. H. Way, Manager of the Leedy company and a former professional drummer of many years standing himself, clarifies the difference and offers some pertinent and very worthwhile suggestions that should help you to make ANY drum a better sounding and easier playing instrument. You'll find this article helpful.

The TONE of a snare drum is one thing and the "FEEL" is quite another. A drum may sound exactly as you would have it but due to the matching of the heads and the type of snares, plus the tension of the heads (relative degree and evenness) it may play hard and "feel" terrible. On the other hand, it may "feel" fine under the sticks and be wholly lacking in snap and brilliance.

Drummers do not always define the difference between tone and "feel". It is quite natural to condemn a fine tone snare drum if it plays hard because no drummer can be satisfied if he has to put forth an unreasonable amount of effort in playing, regardless of how the drum sounds. He should not be called upon to do so. Hard playing drums can be made easy once the cause is well understood.

Let us consider the batter head. There are two things to keep in mind in order to obtain the best tone and the best "feel". First is the degree to which the heads should be tensioned; second, the evenness of that degree over the entire surface of the head.

Drummers differ in opinion on the degree to which the head should be tensioned due to the various styles of playing ("fingering") and the different weights of sticks used but there can be no difference of opinion when it comes to even head tension. Uneven head tension is the cause of more playing dissatisfaction than any other factor. Drummers in their necessarily hurried way of doing things often are careless on this point. It takes time to even up the tension of a batter head but it can be done systematically and is well worth the effort. First, tension the head to the degree best suited to your style of playing. That is easy. Then, think of the head areas that are governed by each rod. Next, sound the head with a drum stick about 2" in from the hoop exactly opposite each rod. Strike softly at the points shown by X's in the accompanying diagram. Note the difference in the tone. The trick is to get them all the same just as the tympanist does in "ironing out"

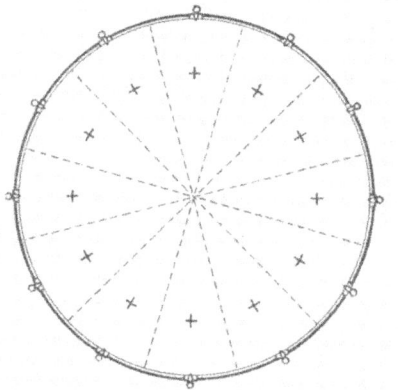

the head to a given note. They must sound that exact note at every point. If the drummer's ear is not keen enough to accomplish this, he can obtain the help of a violin player or one of the other musicians. Once the head is evened up in tone, it is easy to keep it that way if one carefully tightens or loosens all the rods exactly the same amount each time they are changed.

Some may ask, "Why should the head have to sound the same at all points?" Simply because all points or areas being the same means that the "fibres" or "grains" of the heads are pulling at the same strain and this condition automatically evens up the elasticity (or vibrations) of the head making it "feel" much better when playing. Explaining this another way . . . . If the fibres in the head are tighter in some areas than others, they do not all move or vibrate in unison. One "fights" the other in the upward and downward movement of the head. This condition is responsible for more hard playing drums than any other factor.

Next, let us consider the snare head. It is not possible to tension the snare head so that each point will sound exactly alike because of the two snare beds which place more tension at those areas than at others. The evenness, however, can be brought into approximately the same tone by the same method as described above. This will assure a more even head movement than by the usual "guess" method. Of course, the snares have to be released during this "ironing out" process.

All agree that the batter head should be tighter than the snare. How much tighter is a matter of personal preference based on the style of playing and weight of sticks. This can only be decided upon by the individual player who must learn by experiments until he has found the relative tensions that suit him best. Some like tight combinations; others, medium; others, fairly loose. It will be noticed that the drummer who plays close to the head prefers less tension than the one who plays away from the head, so to speak.

The EVENNESS of tension of both heads is the secret of an easy playing drum and should be carefully watched by every drummer.

Next, the question of snares . . . . This, too, is a matter of preference based on the kind of work the drummer may be engaged in. "Mushy snares" (partly loose) are preferred by some leaders of modern dance orchestras. This effect can best be obtained by using coiled wire snares called "James" or "Snappy". Others prefer a heavier tone with more volume. This can also be obtained by using "James" or "Snappy" snares but they must be pulled tighter.

Silk wire wound snares can also be used for this type of playing. For the drummer who plays in large orchestras or concert bands and who demands the true drumistic tone from his instrument, either silk wire wound or gut snares are best. These, too, must be used fairly tight but not so tight that they "choke" or interfere with the movement of the snare head. All snares must be adjusted evenly so that each one will vibrate the same under either light or heavy blows of the stick.

There are hundreds of drummers who can tighten a drum quickly and, by experience combined with a "sixth" sense, arrive at an easy playing, fine sounding drum. There are others who have difficulty in doing this. It is for the latter that we have tried to outline a remedy and we hope that this article will be of some help to them.

THE STORY BEHIND THE MODERN TYMPANI "BOWL"

The drum's origin is always a subject of interest among those to whom drums are a part of life itself. This article touches on that subject and delves into the "whys" and "wherefores" of the materials from which tympani are made, their sizes and their shape.

While practically all writers of books on musical history agree that the drum in one form or another was the first rhythm instrument invented by man, they seem to disagree considerably as to the country of origin.

It is written in some histories that the Chinese were the first to introduce tom tom drums. One book states that they were constructed of stone slabs of various sizes which, of course, gave forth different notes, even though there is nothing to substantiate that they were definitely tuned; therefore, these slabs could not have been considered as musical instruments. They were undoubtedly rhythm instruments.

Another history gives India as the birthplace of the drum, and still another assures us that Egypt was its birthplace. Perhaps the Black Races of Africa were the first, using hollow logs for shells. No one knows; however, we are inclined to favor the Egyptian theory simply because drums have appeared in their ancient art dating back further than that of any other country . . . . at least the oldest pictures of drums—consisting of a cylindrical or bowl shape shell—came from there.

Some of these pictures portray a bowl or shell of the same shape as our present-day tympani. No one could claim that the Egyptians used copper because that metal was best for tonal quality. They used it principally because of the scarcity of wood and other metals. They also used copper for cooking utensils, building material, weapons of war, etc.; therefore, it was only natural that they employ the same metal to produce the drum or tom tom.

The continual use of copper for tympani down through the years has not been because it produced a superior tone as many drummers and leaders believe. It has been used only because it is the one metal that is easy and most economical to work into the required bowl shape. Providing the bowl is not too small or too large for the range of tone required from a certain diameter head, it could be manufactured from any one of several kinds of materials.

Many years ago in Europe, successful tympani were manufactured of wood and built very much like the bodies of old-fashioned mandolins—meaning in shaped strips or segments. The tone was excellent.

Some manufacturers years ago used to spin the bowls out of sheet metal. Some used copper; others steel and even aluminum. This process did not permit even thickness, however, as the bowl continued to become thinner as it was spun from the bottom toward the edges. Other manufacturers made bowls of cast aluminum. These were unsatisfactory because the metal was even softer than copper and easily dented.

Brass is not practical as it is too hard to form into the required shape. If brass soft enough is used, it, too, is subject to easy denting.

Copper is by far the best but it does not contribute to superior tonal quality in the least. If copper did assist in improving the tone, it would be used in the manufacture of other musical instruments such as the delicate French Horn.

Hand hammering was looked upon in the past as the superior method of construction. Hammering played no part whatever in tonal quality or even the strength of the bowl. Hammering was simply a method of stretching the metal to the required shape. Hand hammered bowls were not made in one piece and, therefore, required seaming the sheets by the brazing method. This was always unsatisfactory because no two bowls were exactly the same size and each bowl had to have a specially fitted counter and flesh hoop.

Contrary to the belief of many prominent players, tympani bowls do not act as resonators. If such were the case, they would have to be of a different size for every note the head was tuned to in order to be in unison with a given note, just as resonators have to be of a different size under each xylophone or marimba bar. The tympani bowl acts as a reflector or sounding board which throws back the various tones of the head just as the sounding board of the piano reflects each individual note and just as a band shell reflects all the notes of each instrument. It should be remembered that the head gives off the tone, not the shell or kettle. Also that the small internal rods of machine tympani have not the slightest detrimental effect on either the intonation or tone.

Each size tympani bowl must be built within certain limits as to cubic air content. To go beyond these limits with freak shapes and extra depths does not in any way improve the tone. LEEDY tympani bowls are formed over dies by the hydraulic drawing method. A separate set of three precision-made steel dies is employed for each size. The sizes and shapes have been scientifically worked out so that all of the notes within the required range of each size bowl are reflected to a maximum degree of volume.

The method of drawing bowls was perfected by LEEDY after four years (1916 to 1921) of experiments at a cost of over eighteen thousand dollars. There is nothing anywhere near the size of a tympani bowl in the metal industry involving such a deep draw. The process is quite complicated and consists of both expanding and contracting the metal as it is formed. This method assures the same cubic air content in every bowl of the same size and that uniformity insures true reflection of the tones. The metal is even in thickness over every square inch of surface and this contributes greatly to their strength and wearing qualities. Careful workmanship and the finest quality of copper are also contributing factors which make LEEDY tympani bowls the best obtainable.

Serious Drummers—Look Into This

Charley Wilcoxon, famous Cleveland drummer, has recently composed and published a book of Drum Solos that has proven to be an outstanding achievement in the Drum World. Geo. H. Way, Mgr. of the Leedy Co., says, "Every serious Drummer should own a copy of this book. Every page is a sensation of creative drumming, chuck full of new structures in phrasing. I heard Charlie Owen (U. S. Marine Band in Cleveland on vacation) and Charley Wilcoxon play every note in the book together and boys, it was a thrill of a lifetime. Wow! What skill! Get the book and become a better technician. It sells for $1.50 and is worth $5.00." Note Wilcoxon's address accompanying his picture on page 17.

Laddie Timko Has Own Orchestra

Timko has played drums for the past ten years and has had his own band for the past five playing major college, night club and country club engagements throughout Pennsylvania. For two summers played on trans-Atlantic steamers. His home is Winber, Pa. Teacher was George Slater, Johnstown, Pa. He's used Leedys all during his career and says they've given "complete satisfaction."

Denise Henneger

That Denise is a proficient drummer is attested by the fact that she was one of three in a field of thirty-nine to win a "Highly Superior" First Division rating in National High School competition held in Minneapolis last year. In addition to playing drums, she plays Vibraphone, chimes and tympani—all Leedy! Ferdinand Di Tella, the director of the Dubuque Senior High School Band, Dubuque, Ia., of which she is a member, is her drum instructor—and a very fine one, too.

Victor F. Bolley

Vic plays in the Bronson (Mich.) High School Band and is a member of the "Bolley Family Ensemble" consisting of father, mother and the five Bolley children of whom Vic is the eldest. The group plays and sings all types of music and is in popular demand throughout the Bronson territory. Vic was born in Howe, Ind., studied music under Roy Lockwood, and uses Leedy equipment.

Angel R. Pagan and Juanito Sanabria

Pagan has played with Juanito Sanabria and his orchestra at the Havana Madrid, N. Y. C., for the past 3 years and recorded Decca discs with him during that time. Formerly with Hugo Mariani and Carlos Molinas on A-1 hotel, night club and cafe jobs. Was born in Porto Rico and has played Leedys during 9 of 15 years.

Eddie Camden and Fred Sisk

Sisk is the Leedy drummer with Eddie Camden's orchestra which is playing the finer ballrooms and hotels out of Detroit. Last heard from at Averill Park, N. Y. Fred studied under Al "Rags" Anderson, another Leedyite, calls Columbus (O.) home, and plays a solid Leedy setup.

Rodney W. Pierce

Pierce is a student at Ithaca College, Ithaca, N. Y., and plays drums in the Ithaca College Symphonic Band which is directed by Walter Beeler and in the Ithaca College Symphonic Orchestra under the baton of Pierre Hennrotte. Rodney was born in Canandaigua, N. Y., has his home there now, studied drums under William Gaboury, and has played Leedys for the past nine years.

FOR *More Power* ... CHOOSE THE LEEDY BROADWAY "SWINGSTER"

WITH THE IMPROVED STANDARD EXTENSION SNARE STRAINER AND THE BEAUTIFUL STREAMLINED SELF-ALIGNING "BEAVER TAIL" RODS

Features:

FLOATING HEADS
STREAMLINED "BEAVER TAIL" RODS
DOUBLE FLANGED COUNTER HOOPS
METAL NON-WARPING FLESH HOOPS
100% SELF-ALIGNING RODS
STANDARD SNARE STRAINER
MAHOGANY WOOD SHELL

If you haven't tried a Leedy Broadway "Swingster" Snare Drum yet, you don't know what a truly snappy, really sensitive, easy playing and fine sounding drum is. This model features the Standard Extension Snare Strainer which permits the use of longer snares which extend *beyond* the head giving freer snare action and results in a more sensitive, easier playing, better sounding and more brilliant toned drum. You'll like its many outstandingly fine qualities.

7" x 14" SHELL SIZE				8" x 14" SHELL SIZE	
NICKEL	CHROMIUM	SHELL FINISH		NICKEL	CHROMIUM
No. Price	No. Price			No. Price	No. Price
600...$40.00	601...$47.50	Mahogany		650...$40.00	651...$47.50
606... 40.00	607... 47.50	Tri-Tone Blue Lacquer		656... 40.00	657... 47.50
608... 40.00	609... 47.50	Black and Gold Lacquer		658... 40.00	659... 47.50
610... 40.00	611... 47.50	Cream and Gold Lacquer		660... 40.00	661... 47.50
624... 47.50	625... 55.00	Marine (White) Pearl		674... 47.50	675... 55.00
626... 47.50	627... 55.00	Black Pearl Pyralin		676... 47.50	677... 55.00
630... 47.50	631... 55.00	Autographed Pyralin		680... 47.50	681... 55.00

Equipped with JAMES Snares

"FLOATING HEADS" ASSURE EVEN HEAD TENSION AT ALL TIMES

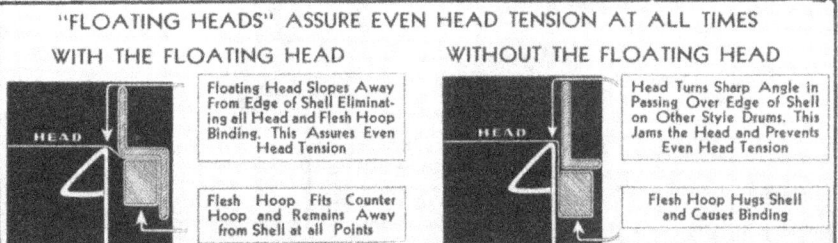

Prices Subject to Change Without Notice. Because Defense Production has Created Uncertainty of Supply of Most Raw Materials Used in Leedy Instruments, Construction Specifications are Subject to Change Without Notice.

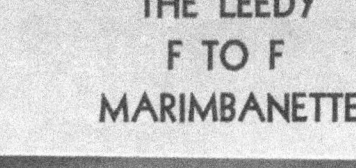

TOP-[TIME] Le[edy] DRUM[MERS]

1. Sharing the spotlight with Edgar Bergen and provi[ding...] NBC program every Sunday evening is Robert A[...] (left) setting the pace and supplying the rhythm on [...]

2. Gerald D. (Gary) Gillis, standout drummer who has [...] Abe Lyman and other top-flight leaders, now is p[...] Holden (left) and his much-in-demand orchestra.

3. Seventeen years behind Leedy drums have convinc[ed...] really swell orchestra, that there aren't any finer d[...] under Charlie Seibert in Springfield, Ill., which is [...]

4. Orrin Tucker (right) and his top-time orchestra are [...] Leedys in the photo is Phil Patton who has "beat [...] the past six years. Phil is a product of Rockford ([...]

5. Benny Meroff's stage presentation band and fast mo[ving...] can take it and a drummer that can "give it out." A[...] fine job for Meroff (left) as is plainly indicated by [...]

6. Eddie Lopez, versatile young Porto Rican drumme[r...] mighty pleased with his new Leedy outfit. The ba[...] after packing 'em in at New York's Copacabana and [...]

7. Much of the sparkle of Lawrence Welk's Champagne [...] on Leedy drums being tested by Director Welk [...] hotel and ballroom following. Reese hails from G[...]

8. America's most successful nonsensical band is Ste[n...] drummer Howard McElroy (right) one of the fine[st...] a highly competent job of dishing out his share of [...]

CHOOSE — USE and ENDORSE [LEEDY]

STANDARD FINISH
Stand in Taupe Lacquer; Frames and Display Resonators in Shaded Gold Lacquer

No. 5623—3 Octaves, F-33 to F-69, 37 Bars 1¾" to 1⅜" Wide by ⅞" to ⅝" Thick. Length Over-All 47".
Height 33". Width, Lower End, 29". Weight 52 Lbs. Low A-440 Pitch..................$175.00

Instructor and Mallets Included

For Any Other Two-Color Lacquer Finish (On Special Order Only)..................$15.00 Extra
For Choice of Two-Color Lacquer Finish on Stands and Resonators and Choice of
"Full Dress" Pearl or Sparkling Pyralin on Frames..................$25.00 Extra
†No. 6954—Two Fibre Hand Carrying Cases for No. 5623..................$37.50

Trunk Price on Application

THE LEEDY F TO F MARIMBANETTE

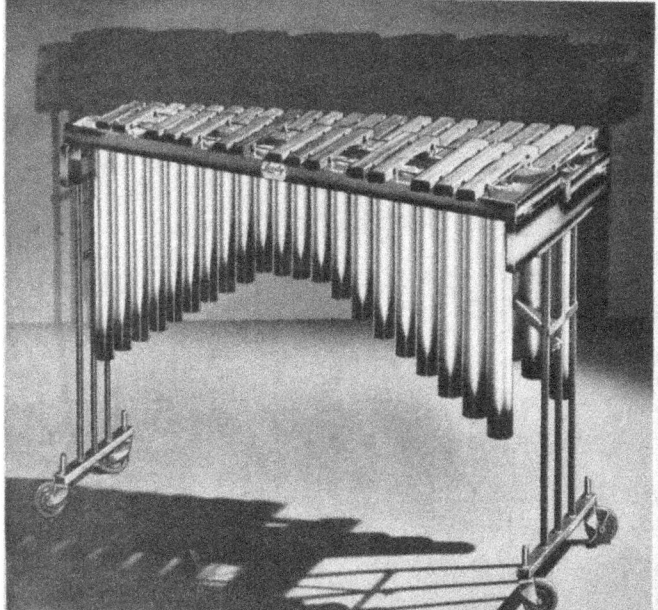

Leedy here presents an innovation in Marimba design. It was a "hit" with all those who saw and tried the original model. And here are some of the reasons: The range is 3 octaves starting at F-33, below middle C, on up to F-69. Never before has Leedy been able to offer this low register at anywhere near such a low price. Yes, it is guaranteed to have maximum qualities in full rich tones and to be "easy speaking" with volume and carrying power consistent with the sizes of the bars and resonators. Here is a small, genuine Marimba that unquestionably leads all others in the field with both professional and school players where such an instrument is desired. It is the finest instrument ever designed for the beginner and at a price that almost all can afford.

Note its fine appearance. The stand is the new type lightweight welded tubular steel taupe finish. Can be set up or taken apart in two minutes. The "fixed" suspension "eye post" method of mounting keeps the bars in place at all times.

See it—try it at the nearest store that handles the Leedy line. They will be glad to get one if they do not have it in stock.

Prices Subject to Change Without Notice. Because Defense Production has Created
Specifications are Subject [...]

TIME

edy

MERS

...cative Charlie McCarthy on the popular Chase & Sanborn
...Armbruster (right) and his orchestra with Clinton Wardrop
... a solid setup of Leedy drums which is shown in the photo.

...s been featured by Russ Morgan, Fred Rich, B. A. Rolf,
...performing on another brand new set of Leedys with Lou
... Gary started on Leedys; says he'll finish on 'em.

...ced Dan M. Hall (left), drummer with George Hamilton's
...drums made—and he's tried 'em all. Hall studied drums
...s his birthplace and his present home.

...e a stellar attraction wherever they appear. Behind the
... out the tempo" in grand fashion for Tucker's orchestra for
...(Ill.) where he studied under Walter Van Dugn.

...ying specialty numbers always have required drums that
...Al DeVito (right) and his solid Leedy setup do an all-out
...y the famous smile of that great showman.

...er with Fausto Curbelo's smooth performing orchestra, is
...and recently finished a long stay at Detroit's Statler Hotel
...d the Gay White Way. Curbelo is shown here with Lopez.

...e music is due to John A. Reese (left) and his high artistry
... in our photo here. The band has a wide radio, theater,
...Green Bay, Wis., has played Leedys 12 years.

... Fritts' "Korn Kobblers" band. With Stan in the photo is
...st fellows and best drummers in the business, who does
...f the crazy corn by punishing his setup of Leedy drums.

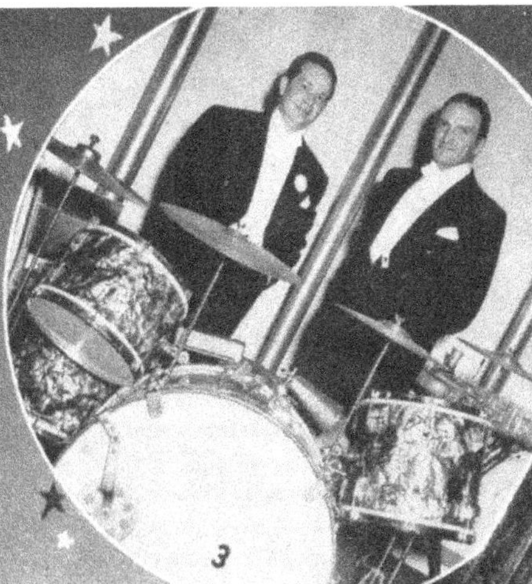

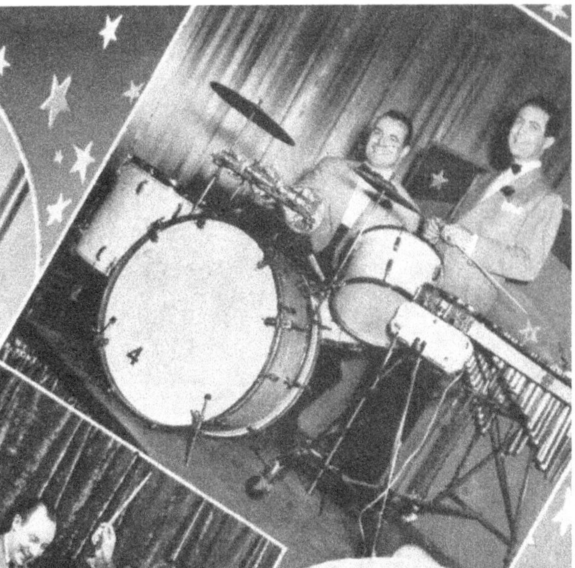

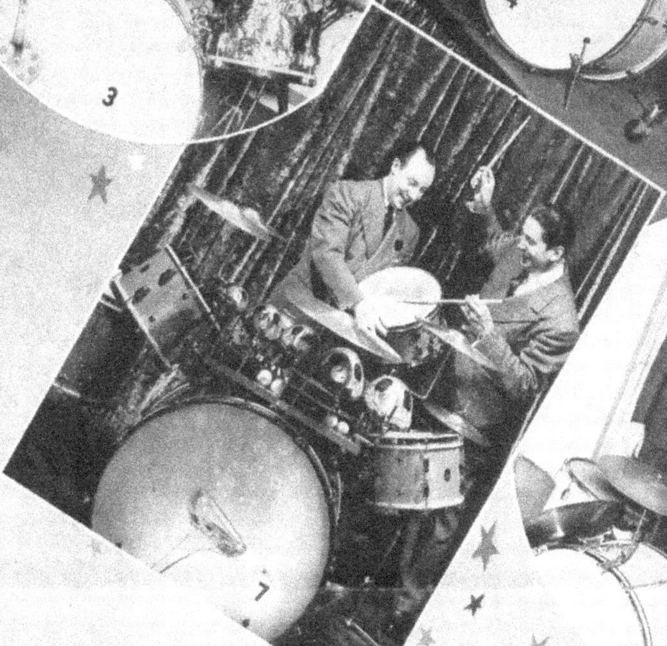

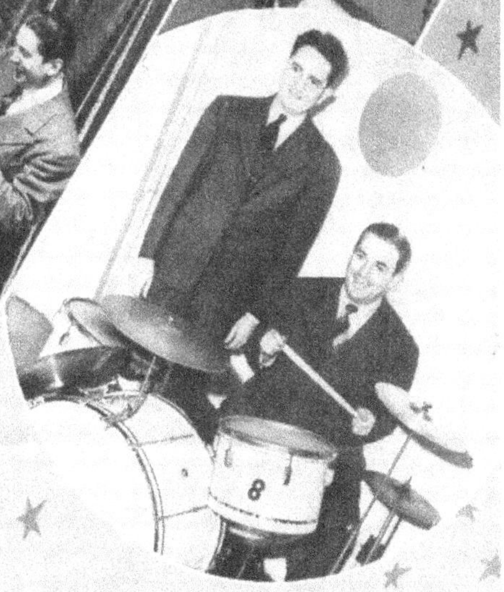

LEEDY DRUMS and EQUIPMENT

LIGHTWEIGHT F TO F CONCERT VIBRAPHONE

STANDARD FINISH

Stand in Taupe Lacquer; Frames and Display Resonators in Shaded Gold Lacquer

No. 5657—3 Octaves, F-33 to F-69, 37 Bars 1¾" Wide Throughout by ½" Thick. Length Over-All 45". Height 33". Width Lower End 29". Weight 82 Lbs. Low A-440 Pitch........................$300.00

Instructor and Mallets Included

For Any Other Two-Color Lacquer Finish (On Special Order Only)..............................$15.00 Extra

For Any Other Two-Color Lacquer Finish on Stands and Resonators and Your Choice of "Full Dress" Pearl or Sparkling Pyralin on Frames..............................$25.00 Extra

†No. 6929—Two Fibre Hand Carrying Cases for No. 5657 Vibraphone..............................$37.50

Trunk Prices on Application

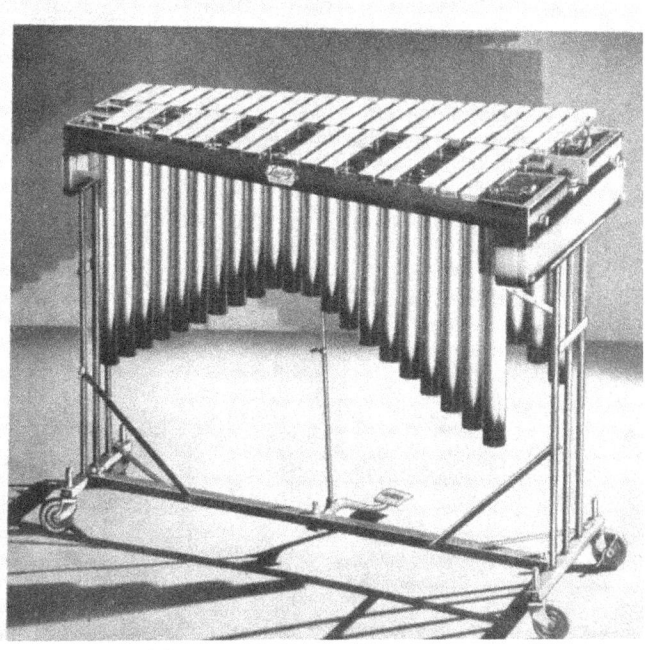

This is the new, and lower priced Leedy Concert Vibraphone which has become so popular. While slightly smaller than the famous Concert Grand model, it has the same "proven to be the best" three octave F to F range.

The new and 100% practical combination of bar and resonator sizes was chosen from many scientific tests. You are assured of ample volume and carrying power for the great majority of playing needs, and of the same rich, mellow vibrato tones for which all Leedy Vibraphones are famous.

Another new idea embodied in this instrument is the lightweight, welded, tubular steel stand which we guarantee for reasonable strength, rigidity and service. Two minutes is all that is required to set up and take down.

The finish on the wood frames is Black and Gold Lacquer and the finish on the stand is Taupe Lacquer.

All Leedy Vibraphones are now equipped with a new AC brushless, and therefore practically silent, motor. It will not operate on DC current without the use of a converter. We can supply converters.

...Uncertainty of Supply of Most Raw Materials Used in Leedy Instruments, Construction
...o Change Without Notice.

Morris Seltzer

Seltzer is the drummer with Marty Kalan and his Happy Hoosier Orchestra that raps 'em out in keen fashion on an all-Leedy outfit. Morris has been with Kalan for the past 5 years, lives in Cincinnati and was a pupil of Lyle Faulkner. Band does jobbing in the middle west.

Leslie Hines with Dannecker

Hines, drummer with Paul Dannecker's (Fort Wayne, Ind.) Orchestra, last year switched to a complete new Leedy outfit and as a result writes: "I am convinced now that there are no finer drums made." Drums were bought from Tom Berry, Ft. Wayne. Hines was born in Everett, Wash., has played drums 8 years. The Dannecker band is a smooth outfit.

George Marsh with Ray Kinney's Orchestra

George Marsh (right), former drummer with Ferde Grofe, Paul Whiteman and other big name bands, is now manning the Leedys for Ray Kinney (left) whose band at this writing is playing in the Hotel Lexington, N. Y. C. Marsh, a veteran Leedy-ite, is ranked as one of the nation's finest drummers, a talented musician and versatile showman.

Carl F. Bigler

Bigler, an Elkhart, Ind., lad, was 1st drummer with the Elkhart H. S. Band and now is doing dance work in and around his home town with Jack Bowman's orchestra with which he has played for the past 5 years.

Did You See the "BIG ONE" This Year?

We hope you didn't pass up the Ringling Bros. and Barnum & Bailey Circus when it came to town this year. There were 12 Leedy Street Drums played by 12 pretty girls in gay costumes heading the "spec" in connection with Merle Evans' (right in the photo) and his great band.

Circus band drummers are Ray Brownell (of Providence, R. I.) and Rollin Sherbondy (of Elkhorn, Wisc.), widely recognized as one of the finest concert and program "teams" on drums that ever trouped with the "Big One". They play Leedy drums, chimes, etc. There's a reason. Leedy instruments stand up under the hard usage, weather and difficult playing conditions encountered in the circus business. Merle Evans, most famous of all circus band directors, conductor of the Ringling-Barnum band for 24 years, says: "I've had drummers try every make but they all eventually get back on the Leedy bandwagon and stay there. Fact is, I now insist on Leedy." Third from left in the photo is Geo. H. Way of the Leedy company, "sitter-inner" with the band from time to time during the season.

Ray Brownell — Rollin Sherbondy — Geo. H. Way — Merle Evans

THE NEW LEEDY BASS DRUM WHEEL SPURS

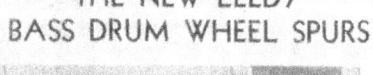

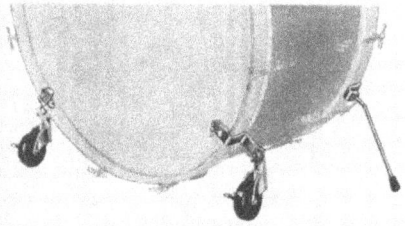

BRAND NEW! PRACTICAL!

Convert Your Bass Drum Setup into a Convenient Roll-away Unit!

Now—with these new Leedy Bass Drum Wheel Spurs—you can ROLL your entire bass drum setup wherever you want it almost as easily as you can push your Vibraphone and xylophone around. Simply lift the bass drum by the counter hoop until the spurs clear the floor and pull the bass drum with its entire setup of traps wherever you want it—safely, easily and quickly—without danger of upsetting the outfit. Move it a few inches or a dozen feet.

Wheels are the same brake equipped rubber disc type which we use on our finest mallet instrument stands. They are attached to adjustable, pressed steel holders which fasten to the bass drum hoop with the famous Leedy STAY-ON clamps. Wheels are used on pedal-side of the drum while the regular giant type spurs are used as usual on the opposite counter hoop.

No. 7118—Set of Two Wheels. Nickel. $5.00

Vivian (La.) H. S. Band Drum Section

The Vivian H. S. Band of 60-pieces, directed by Richard McCluggage, is tempoed by the fine appearing, talented young drummers and the Leedy drums shown in this photo. Few bands in cities the size of Vivian (pop. about 3,000) have a finer, better equipped or trained drum section.

Hildegarde Volkmann

Plays in the Dedham (Mass.) H. S. band and orchestra and was chosen State Championship Girl Scout Drummer in '37. Studied under Geo. H. Carter who says she is one of the finest girl drummers he's ever heard.

Have We Your CORRECT Address?

If you haven't received YOUR copy of this issue of DRUM TOPICS, it may be due to the fact that we don't have your correct, full address. We'll be glad to send YOU a copy if you'll write and tell us where to send it—free, postpaid and without obligation to you.

Prices Subject to Change Without Notice. Because Defense Production has Created Uncertainty of Supply of Most Raw Materials Used in Leedy Instruments, Construction Specifications are Subject to Change Without Notice.

LEEDY ARCH TRAP RAIL AND HOLDERS

THE FINEST, MOST CONVENIENT, MOST PRACTICAL AND MOST IMPRESSIVE SETUP EVER DEVISED FOR THE DRUMMER

Rail and Holders are Original Leedy Creations

You can mount an unusually wide selection of traps on the Leedy Arch Trap Rail with full assurance of convenient location and rigid, vibrationless support. Nothing need be fastened to the bass drum hoops! The Arch Trap Rail is now made with two built-in holders, one at each end, for heavy duty extension cymbal holders No. 9045. The rail is made of flat, high grade steel and conforms exactly to the shape of the drum. It is anchored securely to the shell by four steel posts. Rail remains on the drum at all times, is inconspicuous and saves time in setting up, knocking down and packing. Your fibre bass drum case or Mackintosh cover will accommodate drum with hoop attached. The special holders with Stayon type clamps will not "twist", "turn" or become loose after being set. Holders afford maximum flexibility in adjusting traps for height, angle and distance.

THE NEWLY IMPROVED LEEDY ARCH TRAP RAIL

This detailed photo of the newly improved Leedy Arch Trap Rail shows the flat steel construction of the rail itself, how the rail is fastened to the drum shell on solid steel spools and how it clears the drum rods so that holders can be placed exactly where you want them. Notice the newly added, integral holder at the bottom of the rail for the Heavy Duty Extension Cymbal Holder arm. There is one of these at each end of the rail. Note illustration (below at left) showing detailed construction of Stayon holder and how it grips the rail.

No. 8800—Arch Trap Rail. Nickel for 28" drum $5.75
No. 8802—Arch Trap Rail. Nickel for 26" drum 5.75

LEEDY ARCH TRAP RAIL HOLDERS

HOW TRAP HOLDERS FASTEN TO ARCH TRAP RAIL

TOM TOM HOLDERS FOR ARCH TRAP RAIL SHOWN ON PAGE 23

WOOD BLOCK AND COW BELL HOLDER
No. 8815—Nickel ... $1.75

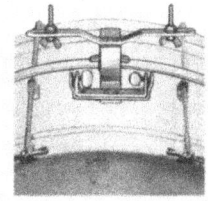

TRAY FOR STICKS AND TRAPS
Handy for holding brushes, sticks and miscellaneous traps.
No. 7154—Nickel $2.50

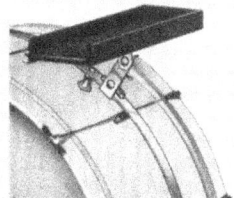

COMPLETE TEMPLE BLOCK RAIL
No. 9030—Complete, Nickel $7.00

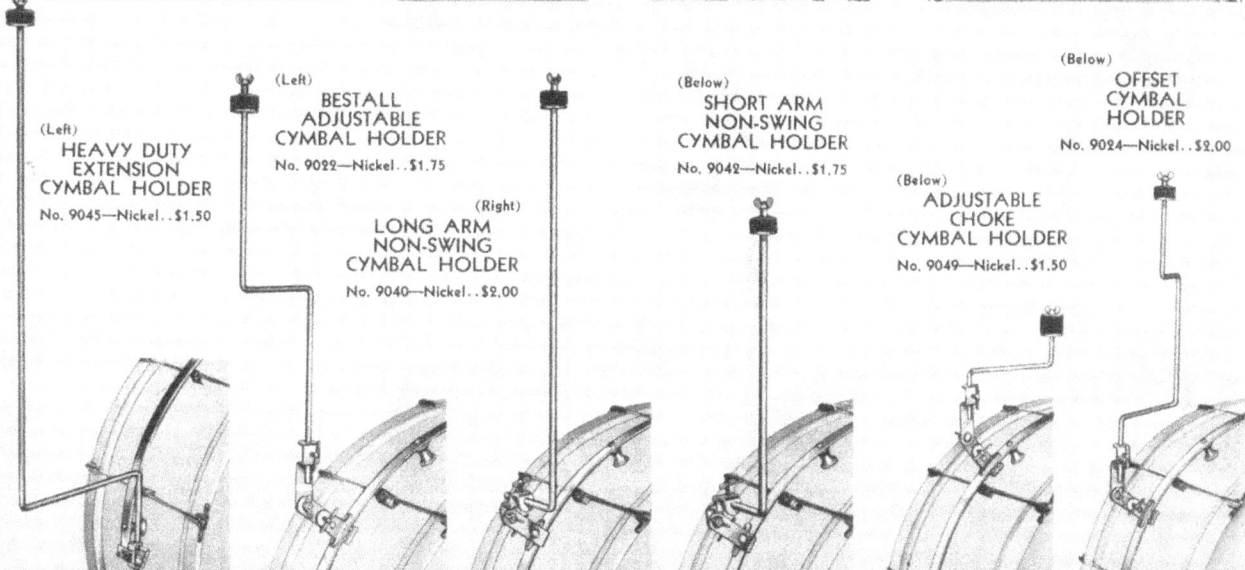

(Left) **HEAVY DUTY EXTENSION CYMBAL HOLDER** No. 9045—Nickel..$1.50

(Left) **BESTALL ADJUSTABLE CYMBAL HOLDER** No. 9022—Nickel..$1.75

(Right) **LONG ARM NON-SWING CYMBAL HOLDER** No. 9040—Nickel..$2.00

(Below) **SHORT ARM NON-SWING CYMBAL HOLDER** No. 9042—Nickel..$1.75

(Below) **OFFSET CYMBAL HOLDER** No. 9024—Nickel..$2.00

(Below) **ADJUSTABLE CHOKE CYMBAL HOLDER** No. 9049—Nickel..$1.50

Jess Altmiller with Albert A. Knecht

For seventeen years with the Fox Theater Grand Orchestra in Philadelphia, and with such outstanding musical organizations as those directed by Leopold Stokowski, Erno Rapee, Georges Enesco, Sousa and many others, Jess Altmiller (right) during his 35 years in the profession as a drummer, musician and teacher has enjoyed a career that is surpassed by few drummers. His fine musicianship, high artistry and splendid showmanship have earned for him a reputation that is extraordinary. Mr. Altmiller recently retired from active playing to take complete charge of the drum department of the Albert A. Knecht music store, 24 S. 18th St., Philadelphia, and to devote more time to teaching. He is shown here with Albert A. Knecht, owner of the store. Mr. Altmiller invites drummers to call on him at the store, to visit with him, discuss their drum problems and needs with him, to become acquainted with, and use, the store's fine facilities and to make the greatest possible use of its many services.

H. J. Wills

A former Ringling Bros. Circus, theatre and concert drummer who has used Leedys for 24 years. Now is teacher of Machine Shop Practice and Auto Mechanics at Jefferson High School, LaFayette, Ind., and plays only semiprofessionally. Note effects of heavy circus "rim shot" playing on batter counter hoop of drum in photo.

Arthur P. Seyler

Charley Wilcoxon, drummer, teacher and Leedy dealer in Cleveland, O., tells us that we're going to hear more about this lad who has been studying rudimental and swing drumming under him for the past several years. Seyler was born in Pittsburgh, now lives in Cleveland Heights, O., uses Leedy equipment and is doing some semi-professional dance work.

Ernest F. Ulmer

Ulmer, drummer and director of his own "Esquires" band which plays ballroom, hotel and night club jobs in and around San Antonio, Texas, studied drums under George Peterson in New Orleans, La., has used Leedy drums exclusively for 12 years. Has been with Marshall Van Pool, Leslie George, Harry Mendelson and others. Was born in New Orleans.

PEDALS with a Pedigree!

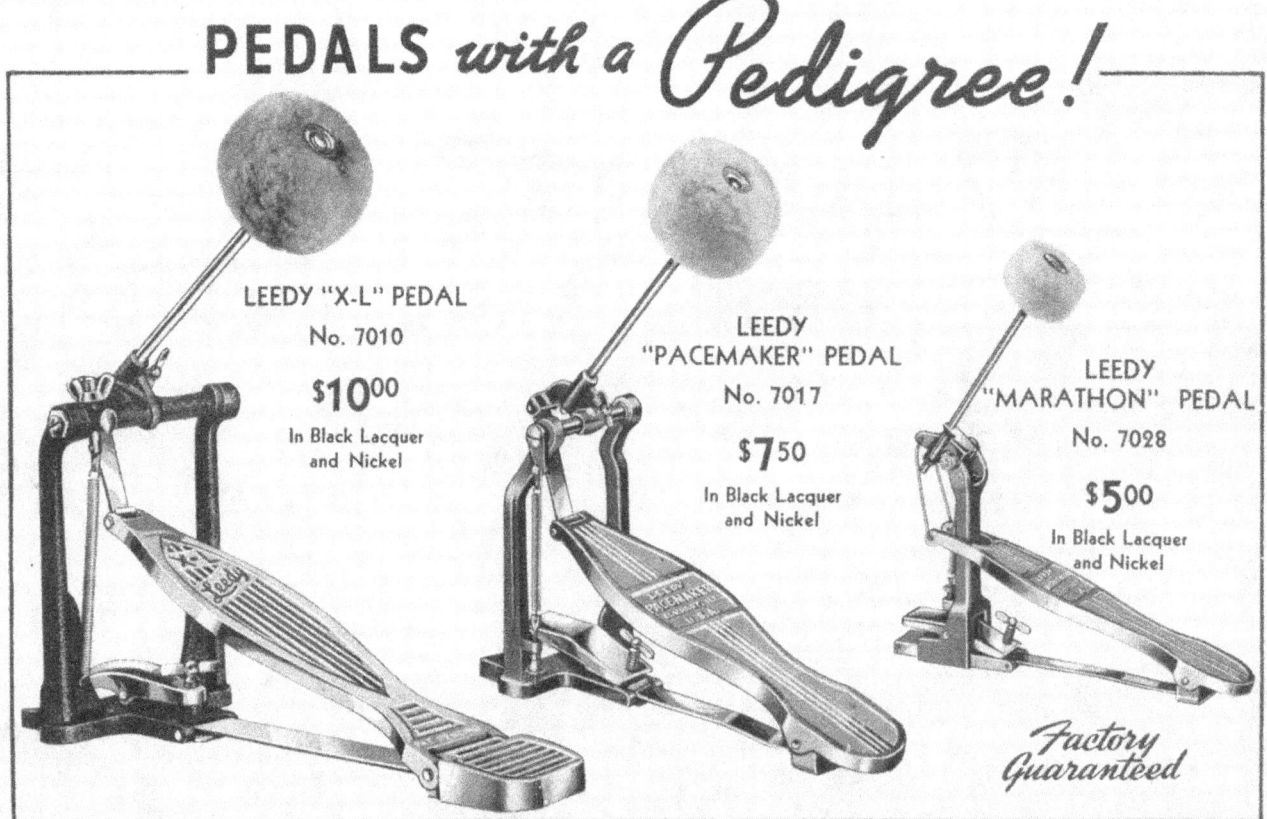

LEEDY "X-L" PEDAL
No. 7010
$10.00
In Black Lacquer and Nickel

LEEDY "PACEMAKER" PEDAL
No. 7017
$7.50
In Black Lacquer and Nickel

LEEDY "MARATHON" PEDAL
No. 7028
$5.00
In Black Lacquer and Nickel

Factory Guaranteed

Prices Subject to Change Without Notice. Because Defense Production has Created Uncertainty of Supply of Most Raw Materials Used in Leedy Instruments, Construction Specifications are Subject to Change Without Notice.

Lawrence White with Boston Symphony

Lawrence White is drum, xylophone, Vibraphone and marimba artist with the Boston Symphony under the direction of Dr. Serge Koussevitzky and is widely known for his fine artistry on these instruments. Has played percussion for 24 years —the past 14 with the Boston orchestra. He is shown here with Arthur Fiedler, Ass't Director of the Boston Symphony who directs the popular summer concerts played on the Charles River Esplanade.

Warren Shelley

Consistent medal winner on drum and xylophone in competition while a member of the champion Elkhart H. S. Band, Warren now is a member of the U. of Michigan Concert Band.

"Bob and the Twins"

That's the way Bob L. Ryan and twins Doris Stauffer (left) and Daphne Ryan are billed when their trio plays hotel engagements in and around N. Y. C. Bob is director. He was born in Huntington, Ind., is self-taught, has played 12 years. The trio played at the Schlitz Palm Gardens during the N. Y. World's Fair in 1939-40. Home is Forest Hills, N. Y.

Sons of V.F.W., Canton, O.

Jerry Sileo

Sileo, Leedy drummer with Tony Gerace's orchestra playing at the Mayfair Club, Buffalo, N. Y., has been in the game for 17 years, studied under Henry Baker and has always played Leedys. He is an A-1 performer and his playing is responsible for much of the success of the Gerace band.

This 100% Leedy equipped junior drum corps of the Floyd Hughes Post, Canton, O., has been State Champion since 1936. Buddy Jones is instructor and director and the success of the corps reflects his splendid ability. The corps now is equipped with Solo-Tone G-D Piston bugles which adds immeasurably to its musical expression. This photo was sent to us by Green's Music Store of Canton.

Charley Wilcoxon—Leedy Dealer—Cleveland, O.

He's "Charley" to everyone who knows him and, in addition to being a swell fellow, is an ace in the business. During his many years in the pit of RKO Keith's Palace Theater in Cleveland he built a rep as the "drummer who never misses a cue." Our photo of Charley shows him as the owner of the Wilcoxon Drum Shop, one flight up in the Erie Bldg., East 9th and Prospect, Cleveland, where, because of his splendid knowledge of drums and drumming, his complete stock of drummers' equipment and his splendid teaching ability, he is serving the drummers of Cleveland and outlying areas in a 100% manner. You will like Charley when you know him—look him up SOON! "Mrs. Charley" is always on the job in the shop to help the drummer, too, and she knows drums plenty.

Ray Hodous

Ray has been drummer with Bob Pettay's orchestra in Cleveland, his home, for the past several years. The band plays college, prom and hotel dates. Ray studied under Charley Wilcoxon, has played drums 8 years, has played with several other Cleveland orchestras prior to joining Pettay, and is considered a "solid" drummer with a fine flair for showmanship.

LEEDY NEW POSITION Wood Block and Cow Bell Holder

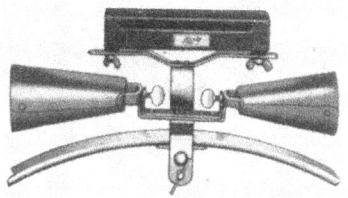

For use on the bass drum hoop. Holds Chinese wood block and two cow bells as shown in the illustration. Holds any size wood block because post holders are adjustable. Wood Block held horizontally above and in back of cow bells. Holder features the improved STAYON hoop clamp. An improved arrangement for this combination of rhythm traps.

No. 7607—Nickel. Each..................$1.75

(Does NOT Include Block or Bells)

Scranton, Pa., S.O.T.A.L.

Squadron No. 121, Sons of the American Legion Drum Corps is part of the Koch-Conley Post No. 121, American Legion, Scranton, Pa. Has been organized since 1935, been State Champion in '35, '36 and '40. Drums are Leedy throughout. Charles Emmell, Jr., is Drum Instructor and reports state that the corps is one of the finest junior organizations of its kind in the country.

Boyertown, Pa., Corps

This was the official corps at the 1940 Legion Convention in Reading and is always in demand for parade purposes. Robert Hare is Director. E.W. Frankhouser, Business Manager of the corps, is Band Instrument Manager of Wittich's, Inc., Leedy dealer, Reading, Pa., and is a veteran drummer.

Woodrow Wilson H. S. Band Drummers

The Woodrow Wilson H. S., Beckley, W. Va., has 4 bands, composed of more than 400 members, which are directed by Glenn Sallack. Drummers and Leedy equipment shown here "double" in the First Band and in this drum corps which provides special effects at all football games.

New Haven (Ind.) H. S. Band Drum Section

This is the percussion section of the New Haven, Ind., H. S. Band which is directed by Richard Guthier. It uses all Leedy equipment which was supplied by Tom Berry Music Co., Inc., Fort Wayne.

Murray Hose Co. No. 4 Drum Corps, Dunkirk, N. Y.

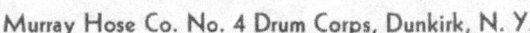

This Volunteer Firemen's drum corps is as fine a musical and marching corps as it is handsome in appearance and is a consistent prize winner in competitive parades throughout the state of N. Y. Anthony Strychalski, Chairman of the Corps, writes that its 100% Leedy equipment is 100% satisfactory and is a real factor in the success of the corps.

Hialeah Jr. Legion Drum Corps, Hialeah, Fla.

Six months after it was organized, this corps, composed entirely of beginning drummers and buglers, won 2nd Prize in Florida State Competition and has continued to win honors for itself wherever it has appeared. Drum equipment, which is 100% Leedy, was bought through Amidon's, Miami, Fla., to whom DRUM TOPICS is indebted for this photo.

THE LEEDY MODERN DRUM METHOD
By Haskell W. Harr

Drummers, teachers and students everywhere have welcomed this new, more thorough, more complete, concise and authoritative drum method which surpasses in every respect any that has been offered on the market up to this time. The author is Haskell W. Harr, widely known and outstandingly fine concert and military drummer in every branch of the playing field. Many leading bandmasters and drum teachers have placed their seal of approval on this book, declaring it to be the correct answer to their percussion instruction problem. Its 96 pages are crammed full of studies, exercises and illustrations to clarify the text. Page size is 9" x 12". The cover is stiff laminated and cellophane covered board and the book features a plastic binding which permits pages to lie absolutely flat when open. A wonderful book in every respect.

No. 1779............$2.00

Junior Police Band

The Denver, Colo., Police Department sponsors a fine Junior Police Band which is tempoed by the drum section shown in this photo. At the left is Sgt. L. F. Nevin of the department; at extreme right is Geo. V. Roy, Director and drum instructor.

This Lathe "Shapes" Leedy Hickory Drum Sticks

This is one of the precision lathes that shapes Leedy hickory drum sticks from hickory dowels at the rate of about 200 per hour. A separate "shaping knife" is required for each drum stick model. Sticks shaped by each "knife" are of uniform length, shape and weight making it possible for you at all times to obtain exact duplicates of the model best suited to your needs. Shaping is the first of 12 operations necessary to make one finished stick.

Girls' H. S. Drum Corps

The Fort Wayne, Ind., Central High School and Director Leo Madden are mighty proud of this all-girl drum corps which was organized early in 1940 and supplied with Leedy equipment throughout. The corps presents a fine appearance and musical repertoire and always is heartily received by the crowds at athletic events and parades.

"Talking Drums" of Ashanti

These ancient and renowned "talking drums" today are still the telephone and telegraph of the Gold Coast of Africa. Shown behind the drums are the musicians who beat them in exactly the same manner, and with the same meaning, that they have been beaten for countless generations.

The Sensational NEW Leedy "SUPER-BALANCED" HICKORY DRUM STICKS

THE DIFFERENCE IS HERE

The main difference is in the new, tapered butt ends and in the improved contour of the shoulders. A trial will convince you that they are the finest sticks ever made!

The new tapered butt ends plus the improved contour of the shoulders eliminate excess, or dead, stick weight and redistribute the remaining weight to make these the ONLY perfectly balanced drum sticks on the market. This in turn gives these "super-balanced" sticks a rebound that is as strong as the stroke itself and does away with the necessity of "lifting" the sticks which is "lost motion" in drumming.

Leedy "SUPER-BALANCED" Hickory Drum Sticks are the easiest "travelling" sticks made.

These models are made from finest, specially selected, thoroughly seasoned, second-growth white hickory. Each stick is "filled" and finished to a fine, rubbed lustre and clear lacquered for fine, smooth feel and appearance.

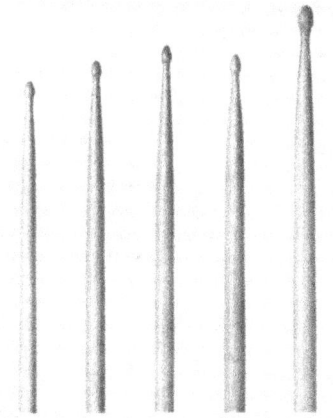

No. 1   No. 2   No. 3   No. 5   No. 21

Please Order by Number

No. 1—14⅜" long, weight about 3 oz. per pair
No. 2—15⅝" long, weight about 4 oz. per pair
No. 3—15¾" long, weight about 3½ oz. per pair
No. 5—15½" long, weight about 4 oz. per pair
No. 21—17" long, weight about 6 oz. per pair

Only 45¢ PER PAIR

V.F.W. Post 1524 Junior Drum Corps

The Witch City (Salem, Mass.) V.F.W. Junior Drum and Bugle Corps is Massachusetts State and New England Champion and proves that it is a topnotch playing and marching unit as well as a fine appearing outfit. Equipment is 100% Leedy.

Leedy would like to have a photo of YOUR corps or band percussion section with the view of using it in future "DRUM TOPICS" issues. Address it to the Leedy Mfg. Co., Elkhart, Ind.

Taylor (Pa.) Junior Drum and Bugle Corps

This corps, part of American Legion Post No. 306, Taylor, Pa., is one of the crack junior outfits of its state and has won prizes galore. Geo. H. Summerson and Guy Hall, both of Wilkes-Barre, supervise the music. Percussion, including 4 tenor drums, is 100% Leedy.

LEEDY STAYON CYMBAL HOLDERS
(FOR USE ON BASS DRUM HOOP)

Good cymbal holders are just as important to the modern drummer as the cymbals themselves. The Leedy Stayon Cymbal Holders shown here are, from every standpoint, the finest on the market. Each is specially designed to do a specific job in a 100% efficient manner and offers the drummer the utmost in setup adaptability and playing convenience. All holders feature the famous non-marring, dependable Stayon hoop clamp made of pressed steel which, when set, will stay firmly in place under any and all kinds of playing. All holders are universally adaptable for use on the top, right or left sides of the hoop except the Student (No. 7594) which is intended for use only on the top of the drum. The Heavy Duty Extension Cymbal Holder is the most practical model yet devised for use with tom toms. This new holder is completely adjustable. It can be turned in a full half circle under the tom tom, thereby placing the cymbal in the most convenient position. The Heavy Duty Non-Swing Holders are companion models. Holders permit cymbals to be used in an upright position regardless of where they are placed on the bass drum hoop. Horizontal arms can be moved forward or backward for best cymbal placement.

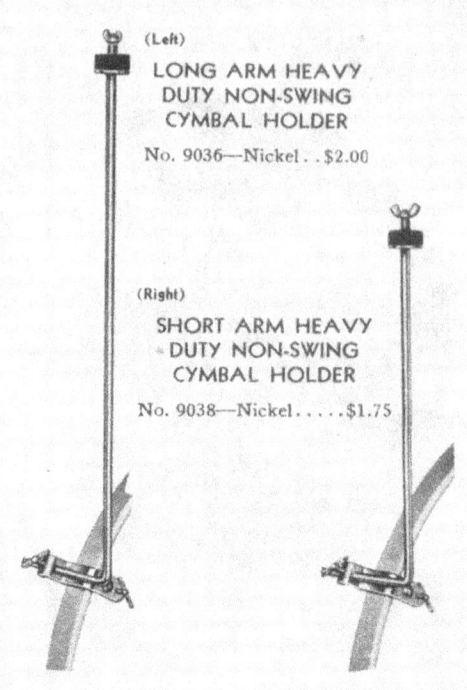

(Left)
LONG ARM HEAVY DUTY NON-SWING CYMBAL HOLDER
No. 9036—Nickel..$2.00

(Right)
SHORT ARM HEAVY DUTY NON-SWING CYMBAL HOLDER
No. 9038—Nickel.....$1.75

(Below, Center)
BESTALL CYMBAL HOLDER
No. 9000—Nickel.....$1.75

(Below)
STRAIGHT ARM BESTALL CYMBAL HOLDER
No. 9012—Nickel.....$1.75

STANDARD NON-SWING CYMBAL HOLDER
No. 7518—Nickel.....$1.50

EXTRA CYMBAL ATTACHMENTS
For use with No. 7518 Holder
No. 9003 Nickel Only $ .40

ADJUSTABLE CHOKE CYMBAL HOLDER
No. 7470—Nickel.....$1.50

STUDENT CYMBAL HOLDER
No. 7594—Nickel.....$ .85

STAYON CHOKE CYMBAL HOLDER
Cymbals NOT included with the holder.
No. 7460—Nickel.....$1.10

CORRECT CYMBALS FOR CHOKE EFFECT
One No. 7352—12" Chinese Cymbal..........$3.50
One No. 7438—8" American Brass Cymbal........ .75

AFTERBEAT and EGYPTIAN CYMBAL HOLDER
Price does NOT include cymbal.
No. 7218—Nickel.....$1.25

DEEP CUP CHOKE CYMBAL HOLDER
Cymbals NOT included with the holder
No. 7457—Nickel.....$1.25

CORRECT CYMBALS FOR ABOVE HOLDER
Two No. 7450—10" Deep Cup American Brass Cymbals at, each........$1.25

(Above)
HEAVY DUTY EXTENSION CYMBAL HOLDER
No. 9047—Nickel.....$2.00

George W. Howe with Glenn Garr

The distinctive music of Glenn Garr, heard by all America over the major radio networks, and by thousands in the nation's leading ballrooms and hotels, is tempoed by George Howe and his all-Leedy outfit. George was born in Trenton, N. J., studied under Wm. Groom and has played Leedys for more than 16 years. Shown below is Glenn Garr (left) with Howe at the drums.

Martha Jackson

This pretty lass of Pittsburgh, Pa., is a student at West View H. S. and a pupil of Bill Hammond of that city. A champion.

Dorothy Yancey

Another winsome, high-stepping baton twirler is Miss Yancey, Memphis, Tenn., whose photo was sent in by the Melody Music Shop, Memphis.

Drum Major Eddie Sacks

This Westmont-Upper Yoder H. S. lad, Johnstown, Pa., has won many twirling honors for himself and his school in both state and national competition.

Bright Cymbals Mean More Flash at No Extra Cost

Bright cymbals are attention getters and help build up the flash of your outfit. Take your cymbals to the nearest electroplating shop (look up in classified section of phone book—there are several in every town) and have them buffed, NOT polished. Buffing is done on a soft cloth wheel with an applied soft rouge compound. Polishing is done on a felt wheel with applied hard cutting rouge compound. The former shines the cymbal, the latter takes away some of the metal and is likely to change the tone if not actually ruin it. After buffing, have the plater apply a coat of *clear* metal lacquer which forms a very thin film over the entire surface and greatly prolongs the life of the high lustre. The cost is only a few cents per cymbal. Looks swell! Wrap your cymbals in cloth or light flannel (purchased at any dime store) for packing.

This also applies to Chinese Gongs.

LEEDY "CYCLONE" BATONS

These are the world's MOST POPULAR, all-around twirling batons on the market today. Their weight, length, shaft diameter and perfect balance make them ideal for class work, school use, and practice purposes by adults and juniors alike. Perfect for one or two-baton twirling, high throws, leg, back and neck passes, bounces, spins and flips. Shafts are strong, 3/4", seamless, specially alloyed, non-rusting metal tubing heavily chromium plated for "feel" and fine, flashy appearance. Solid white sponge rubber ball and tip are appreciated features because they permit unusual "bounce" routines, are noiseless and protect the floor and furniture from damage when the baton is dropped. White (not painted) rubber ball and tip are easily cleaned with soap and water. Shafts will stay bright and shiny with an occasional wiping with a soft cloth. Made in 28" length with smooth shaft for twirlers up to age about 12 years; in 30" length with choice of smooth or spiral shaft for adults' use and for juniors over 12 years of age. All models are extremely durable.

THE "CYCLONE 28"

Length 28". Weight about 13 oz. Smooth 3/4" shaft. Chromium.

No. 1617

$2.50

THE "CYCLONE 30"

Length 30". Weight about 14 oz. Smooth 3/4" shaft. Chromium.

No. 1618

$2.50

SPIRAL "CYCLONE"

A NEW "Cyclone" model made with a 3/4" spiral shaft which is preferred by many twirlers who believe that the spiral feature affords a better grip and more twirling "flash". Features chromium plated shaft of same alloy as described above and washable white rubber ball and tip. Made only in 30" length; weight approximately 15 ounces. Practically unbreakable and the finest baton value for the money on the market to date!

No. 1619

$3.00

No. 1617	No. 1618		No. 1619
$2.50	$2.50		$3.00

Prices Subject to Change Without Notice. Because Defense Production has Created Uncertainty of Supply of Most Raw Materials Used in Leedy Instruments, Construction Specifications are Subject to Change Without Notice.

LEEDY
BROADWAY TUNABLE TOM TOMS

Made with "Self-Aligning" Beaver Tail Casings,
Reinforced Plywood Shells, Flanged Metal Counter Hoops and Calfskin Heads.

For up-to-the-minute appearance, design, mechanical perfection and best tonal qualities, choose Leedy Broadway Tunable Tom Toms. The SELF-ALIGNING rods are exactly like those used on the famous Leedy BROADWAY snare drums and permit uniformly even tension over the entire head surface which results in better, more uniform tone. Now made in five sizes for wider tonal range and greater tone effects.

Single Tension	14" x 16" With Nickel Plated Rods	Separate Tension
No. 8014....$38.50	Choice of Pyralin Finishes	No. 8018....$47.00
No. 8015.... 30.00	Choice of Lacquer Colors	No. 8019.... 38.50

12" x 14" With Nickel Plated Rods
No. 8027....$33.50.....Choice of Pyralin Finishes.....No. 8036....$42.00
No. 8028.... 25.50.....Choice of Lacquer Colors.....No. 8037.... 34.00

9" x 13" With Nickel Plated Rods
No. 8047....$26.50.....Choice of Pyralin Finishes.....No. 8038....$33.00
No. 8048.... 21.00.....Choice of Lacquer Colors.....No. 8039.... 27.50

8" x 12" With Nickel Plated Parts
No. 8054....$24.50.....Choice of Pyralin Finishes.....No. 8056....$32.50
No. 8055.... 19.00.....Choice of Lacquer Colors.....No. 8057.... 27.00

7" x 11" With Nickel Plated Rods
No. 8075....$23.00.....Choice of Pyralin Finishes.....No. 8076....$30.50
No. 8077.... 17.50.....Choice of Lacquer Colors.....No. 8078.... 25.00

FOR CHROMIUM PLATED PARTS
$3.50 Extra....On Any Size Tom Tom, Add to Above Prices....$7.00 Extra

Size 16" x 16" Tunable Tom Toms Supplied on Special Order in Same Finishes and at Same Prices as for 14" x 16" Size Listed Above.

LEEDY TUNABLE TOM TOM LEGS

 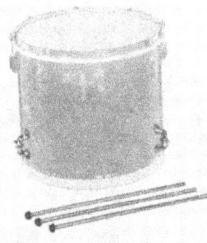

The most practical means ever devised for holding tunable tom toms. Setup consists of three steel brackets bolted near the bottoms of the tom tom shells at equidistant points from each other, and three steel legs which are adjustable in the brackets for height and playing angle. Legs have non-skid rubber feet which hold the instrument firmly wherever set. Legs can be slid up alongside the shell, or quickly removed, for easy packing.

Outstanding advantages are the ease and speed with which tom toms can be set up at just the desired height and playing angle and that the instrument STAYS at the proper adjustment under the heaviest beating.

No. 7753—Legs complete with brackets. Nickel..............$3.00
No. 7754—Legs complete with brackets. Chromium.......... 4.50

Prices Subject to Change Without Notice. Because Defense Production has Created Uncertainty of Supply of Most Raw Materials Used in Leedy Instruments, Construction Specifications are Subject to Change Without Notice.

Ken Baker and Louis Paino
Lou Paino has manned the drums for Ken Baker's orchestra for the past 5 years. He was born in Union City, N. J., has played drums 8 years and switched to Leedys 4 years ago. Formerly played with Garwood Van and Spud Murphy orchestras. Now lives in L. A., Cal.

John Greenwood
Greenwood, Canadian drummer with Canadian orchestra leader Bob Lyon is shown in this photo taking over a Leedy outfit in the Allan & Co. Music Store, Melbourne, Australia, while touring that continent.

Jimmy Hennessy
Leedy drummer Hennessy is kept busy in Elizabeth, N. J., his home, playing club dates with the various bands and is doing all right for himself. Studied under Joe Lucas, Leedy drummer with the old Ted Lewis band, and says he played his first Leedy setup when only 7 years old.

Harold "Swish" Swearingen
"Swish" has been playing jobbing dates in Wisc., Iowa and Illinois with Joey Tantillo and his orchestra for the past 3 years. Ramsey Eversoll was his teacher and Madison (Wisc.) is his home. "Swish" has played drums for 15 years and changed to a complete Leedy setup 3 years ago.

J. E. "Lad" Haverty

"Lad" has been playing with "Hack" Proper and his band in Tucson, Ariz., for 5 years. Band had a long stay in the Pioneer Hotel there and is on KVOA twice weekly. Haverty has played drums 8 years and always used Leedys with which he is 100% satisfied.

Gil Lokey

Gil has been playing drums with Fess Jackson and his orchestra in the Bee Hive Cafe, Tucson, Ariz., for the past 6 years. He was born in Brooklyn, has played drums 11 years.

Fritz R. Evers

The "Musical Steelmakers," directed by Earl Summers, Sr., and heard via WWVA, Wheeling, W. Va., over the MBC every Sunday, play to tempos set by Fritz Evers and his Leedy drums. Fritz was born in Napoleon, O., studied under "Rags" Anderson and M. Lombardi, has a broad and varied musical background, and has played Leedys for 12 years.

HEAVY DUTY DOUBLE LINK TOM TOM HOLDER FOR ARCH TRAP RAIL

For use on the Leedy Arch Trap Rail shown on page 15. Universally adjustable, it permits forward, backward, upward, downward, right and left adjustments of the tom tom thus giving you the exact playing angle under any and all conditions. Made of cast brass, fastens to tom tom shell with two bolts and holds instrument securely under the heaviest beating.

No. 9026—Nickel..........................$4.25

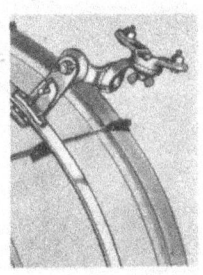

Carolyn "Red" Beyer

"Red" does a man-sized job of drumming behind her Leedys for Herb Cook (right) and his "Swinghearts". That popular middle-west girl band is a sure-fire attraction wherever it appears. The band plays the better hotel and club jobs. Carolyn has played Leedys for 4 years.

LIGHTWEIGHT DOUBLE LINK TOM TOM HOLDER FOR ARCH TRAP RAIL

Made for use on the Leedy Arch Trap Rail shown on page 15. It has all the adjustment features of the Heavy Duty model shown above but is made of pressed steel and is intended for use with only the smaller size tunable tom toms or the Chinatype (non-tunable) models up to and including size 9" x 13".

No. 9032—Nickel..........................$1.25

George Caruso

This Akron, O., lad finds perfect satisfaction with his new Leedy outfit in his jobbing dance work that keeps him busy in and around Akron. This photo was sent to us by Edfred's, Leedy dealer in that city.

HEAVY DUTY RATCHET TOM TOM HOLDER FOR BASS DRUM HOOP
(WITH DOUBLE LINK)

This tom tom holder for use on the bass drum hoop permits every angle adjustment of the tom tom to be made that is necessary to place it in the exact playing position that may be wanted under any and all conditions. Made of cast brass, fastens to tom tom shell with two bolts and will hold the instrument firmly in the desired position under all kinds of playing.

No. 7728—Nickel..........................$4.25

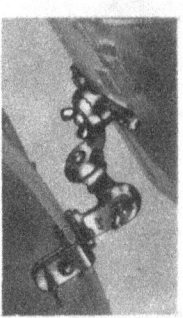

Seth L. Cochrane

Cochrane, whose home is Brooklyn, N. Y., has played with the Imperial Elks Band for 15 years and also is playing local dance jobs. Seth has played Leedys for 20 years. Elks Band leader is Ralph Redmond.

HEAVY DUTY RATCHET TOM TOM HOLDER FOR BASS DRUM HOOP
(WITH SINGLE LINK)

This heavy duty, cast brass tom tom holder for use on the bass drum hoop is similar to the No. 7728 holder shown above but, because it hasn't the extra link featured in that model, it hasn't quite the maximum adjustability for which that holder is famous. Adjustments for the majority of playing needs can be made with this holder and thousands of drummers find perfect satisfaction with it.

No. 7723—Nickel..........................$3.50

A "Wiz" at Seventeen

Lee Rosenberg, Atlanta, Ga., at 17 is featured drummer of Harry Hearn's orchestra and has "jammed" with Benny Goodman who says Lee is good enough for anybody's orchestra.

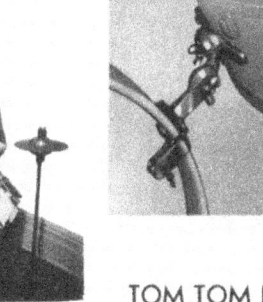

DETACHABLE TOM TOM HOLDER FOR BASS DRUM HOOP

A fully adjustable, lightweight tom tom holder for use on the bass drum hoop. Features a tongue and socket device whereby the tom tom can be removed from the drum or the holder without removing wing nuts, or bolts and therefore permits easier and quicker packing and setting up. Suitable for use with all tom toms up to and including size 9" x 13".

No. 7708—Nickel..........................$1.75

Sherrill Smith

Smith has played drums with the U. of Arizona Concert Band, Tucson Symphony, V. F. W. Drum Corps and several dance bands. Now playing with Billy Knighton's orchestra in Tucson. Yes, his home is Tucson, Ariz. and his drums are Leedys.

STANDARD DOUBLE LINK TOM TOM HOLDER FOR BASS DRUM HOOP

This tom tom holder, for use on the bass drum hoop with tom toms up to and including 9" x 13" sizes, features three ratchet adjustments for maximum adjustability of the instrument for every playing need. Made of pressed steel, it is strong, serviceable, dependable and economical. Will hold tom toms of sizes mentioned wherever placed on the bass drum hoop under normal playing conditions.

No. 7718—Nickel..........................$1.25

Prices Subject to Change Without Notice. Because Defense Production has Created Uncertainty of Supply of Most Raw Materials Used in Leedy Instruments, Construction Specifications are Subject to Change Without Notice.

Leedy Drum Topics Issue 29

REBEATS PUBLICATIONS
visit the Rebeats website or contact us for details

THE GRETSCH DRUM BOOK
by Rob Cook
with John Sheridan
Business history,
dating guide

THE SLINGERLAND BOOK
by Rob Cook
Business history,
dating guide

THE ROGERS BOOK
by Rob Cook
Business history,
dating guide

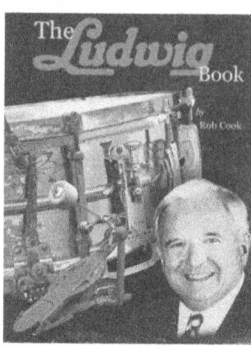

THE LUDWIG BOOK
by Rob Cook
Business history,
dating guide

THE MAKING OF A DRUM COMPANY
The autobiography of Wm. F. Ludwig II,
with Rob Cook

BEST SEAT IN THE HOUSE
Memoir of Humble Pie's
Jerry Shirley

THE LEEDY WAY
Biography of George Way,
History of Leedy, Camco,
Conn, L&S

MY LIFE IN PERCUSSION
Five Decades In The Music
Products Industry
Karl Dustman memoir

HAL BLAINE & THE WRECKING CREW
Memoir of Hal Blaine,
with Mr. Bonzai

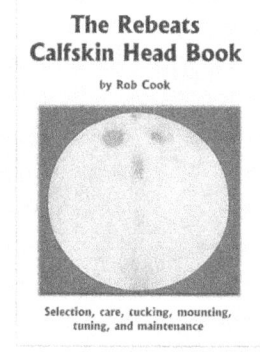

THE REBEATS CALFSKIN HEAD BOOK

George Way
mini-biography,
vendor directory

GENE KRUPA, HIS LIFE AND TIMES
biography of
Gene Krupa,
by Bruce Crowther

THE BABY DODDS STORY
Memoir of
Baby Dodds,
as told to
Larry Gara

Gretsch 1941
Catalog Reprint

P.O. Box 6, Alma, Michigan 48801
989 463 4757
www.Rebeats.com   rob@rebeats.com

www.ingramcontent.com/pod-product-compliance
Lightning Source LLC
Chambersburg PA
CBHW081613100526
44590CB00021B/3420